SOVIET FOREIGN POLICY

SOVIET FOREIGN POLICY

Classic and Contemporary Issues

Frederic J. Fleron, Jr.
Erik P. Hoffmann
Robbin F. Laird

EDITORS

ALDINE DE GRUYTER

New York

About the Editors

Frederic J. Fleron, Jr. is Professor of Political Science, State University of New York at Buffalo. He is coauthor of *Comparative Communist Political Leadership* and editor of *Communist Studies and the Social Sciences: Essays on Methodology and Empirical Theory* and *Technology and Communist Culture: The Socio-Cultural Impact of Technology under Socialism.*

Erik P. Hoffmann is Professor of Political Science, The Nelson A. Rockefeller College of Public Affairs and Policy, State University of New York at Albany. He is coauthor with Robbin F. Laird of *Technocratic Socialism: The Soviet Union in the Advanced Industrial Era, The Politics of Economic Modernization in the Soviet Union,* and *"The Scientific-Technological Revolution" and Soviet Foreign Policy,* as well as editor of *The Soviet Union in the 1980s.*

Robbin F. Laird is Senior Researcher, Strategy, Forces, and Resources Division, Institute for Defense Analyses, Alexandria, Virginia. His most recent books are *The USSR and the Western Alliance* (co-author with Susan Clark), *The Soviet Union, West Germany and European Security,* and *The Europeanization of the Alliance.*

ALDINE DE GRUYTER
A division of Walter de Gruyter, Inc.
200 Saw Mill River Road
Hawthorne, New York 10532

The paper used in this publication meets the minimum requirements of American National Standard for Information Sciences—Permanence of Paper for Printed Library Materials, ANSI Z39.48-1984. ∞

Library of Congress Cataloging-in-Publication Data

Soviet foreign policy : classic and contemporary issues / edited by
    Frederic J. Fleron, Jr., Erik P. Hoffmann, Robbin F. Laird.
        p. cm.
    Includes bibliographical references and index.
    ISBN 0-202-24170-X (cloth) : —ISBN 0-202-24171-8 (paper)
    1. Soviet Union—Foreign relations—1917-   . I. Fleron, Frederic J.,
Jr., 1937–   . II. Hoffmann, Erik P., 1939-   . III. Laird, Robbin
F. (Robbin Frederick),   1946-
DK266.S573   1991
327.47—dc20   91-17674
                                                                         CIP
Manufactured in the United States of America

10 9 8 7 6 5 4 3 2 1

Contents

III.   IDEOLOGY AND BEHAVIOR

IV.   PROSPECT AND RETROSPECT

Contemporary Issues in Soviet Foreign Policy

V.   PERSPECTIVES AND POLICYMAKING

VI. POLICY AND PERFORMANCE

VII. RETROSPECT AND PROSPECT

List of Contributors

Hannes Adomeit — Fletcher School of Law and Diplomacy, Tufts University

David E. Albright — Air War College

Vernon V. Aspaturian — Pennsylvania State University

James A. Baker, III — U.S. Secretary of State

Susan L. Clark — Institute for Defense Analysis

John W. Coffey — U.S. Department of Commerce

Charles H. Fairbanks, Jr. — Paul H. Nitze School of Advanced International Studies

Frederic J. Fleron, Jr. — State University of New York at Buffalo

Raymond L. Garthoff — The Brookings Institution

Colin Gray — National Institute for Public Policy

Pierre Hassner — Centre d'Etudes et de Recherches Internationales, Paris

Richard Herrmann — Ohio State University

Erik P. Hoffmann — State University of New York at Albany

Arnold Horelick — RAND/UCLA Center for the Study of Soviet International Behavior

R. N. Carew Hunt — deceased

William G. Hyland	*Foreign Affairs*
Akio Kawato	Former Director of the East European Division—Ministry of Foreign Affairs of Japan
George F. Kennan	Institute for Advanced Study
Meryl A. Kessler	Harvard University
Amy W. Knight	U.S. Library of Congress
Stanley Kober	The Cato Institute
Mark Kramer	Center for Foreign Policy Development Brown University
Robbin F. Laird	Institute for Defense Analyses
F. Stephen Larrabee	The RAND Corporation
Robert Legvold	The Harriman Institute for Advanced Study of the Soviet Union Columbia University
Richard Lowenthal	Freie Universität Berlin
Allen Lynch	The Harriman Institute for Advanced Study of the Soviet Union Columbia University
William E. Odom	Hudson Institute
Alex Pravda	St. Anthony's College Oxford University
Condoleezza Rice	Stanford University
Alvin Z. Rubinstein	University of Pennsylvania
Stephen R. Sestanovich	Center for Strategic & International Studies Georgetown University

Samuel L. Sharp   deceased

Raymond Smith   U.S. Department of State

Jack Snyder   Columbia University

Helmut Sonnenfeldt   The Brookings Institute

William Taubman   Amherst College

Adam B. Ulam   Harvard University

Thomas S. Weiss   Institute of International Studies
                  Brown University

Donald S. Zagoria   Hunter College
                  City University of New York

William Zimmerman   University of Michigan

Classic Issues in Soviet Foreign Policy

Introduction

Frederic J. Fleron, Jr., and Erik P. Hoffmann

The purpose of this anthology is to deepen Western understanding of the sources, substance, and significance of Soviet foreign policy from 1917 to the mid-1980s. Our book is designed primarily for students of Soviet politics, comparative foreign policies, and international relations. Also, it is structured to help government, business, legal, and media professionals and other citizens assess the USSR's international aims, activities, and accomplishments. The present work complements our anthologies *Contemporary Issues in Soviet Foreign Policy* (1991), *Classic Issues in Soviet Domestic Politics* (1992), and *Contemporary Issues in Soviet Domestic Politics* (1992) (all published by Aldine de Gruyter, Hawthorne, NY). Together, these volumes provide a comprehensive survey of notable Western writings about Soviet external and internal behavior and their interrelationships. They are successors to our previous lengthy anthologies (also published by Aldine de Gruyter): *The Conduct of Soviet Foreign Policy*, 2nd ed. (1980), *Soviet Foreign Policy in a Changing World* (1986), and *The Soviet Polity in the Modern Era* (1984).

Contributions to this collection come from American and West European academic specialists on Soviet foreign policy, present and past government officials, and full-time researchers in organizations that counsel government leaders. These contributions address many key topics and are among the most insightful and knowledgeable in the field. By juxtaposing different viewpoints, we hope to raise the level of debate and to stimulate informed and independent-minded analysis of Soviet foreign policy and its implications for the West. This anthology has both policy and practical relevance as well as general and academic interest. It is written by and for Western policymakers and their advisors as well as the university community and the international professions.

We intend to supplement, not supplant, the preeminent histories of Soviet international behavior: Adam B. Ulam's *Expansion and Coexistence: The History of Soviet Foreign Policy, 1917–73*, 2nd ed. (New York: Praeger, 1974) and *Dangerous Relations: The Soviet Union in World Politics, 1970–1982* (New York: Oxford University Press, 1983). Likewise, our volume complements succinct texts such as Jonathan R. Adelman and Deborah Anne Palmieri, *The Dynamics of Soviet Foreign Policy* (New York: Harper & Row, 1989), Joseph L.

Nogee and Robert H. Donaldson, *Soviet Foreign Policy since World War II*, 3rd ed. (Elmsford, NY: Pergamon Press, 1988), Alvin Z. Rubinstein, *Soviet Foreign Policy since World War II: Imperial and Global*, 3rd ed. (Glenview, IL: Scott, Foresman, 1989), and Richard F. Staar, *Foreign Policies of the Soviet Union* (Stanford, CA: Hoover Institution Press, 1991). In addition, our anthology complements collections of carefully selected and translated Soviet writings such as Fred Schulze, ed., *Soviet Foreign Policy Today: Reports and Commentaries from the Soviet Press*, 4th ed. (Columbus, OH: Current Digest of the Soviet Press, 1990).

OVERVIEW

This first half of the book is divided into four broad parts: history, methodology, ideology and behavior, and prospect and retrospect. Part I begins with Erik P. Hoffmann's survey of Soviet foreign policy aims and accomplishments from Lenin to Brezhnev. Hoffmann's central theme is that Soviet foreign policy has been characterized by a shifting mix of revolutionary and great-power goals in different time periods and in different geographical and issue areas. He develops the argument that the overall trend in Soviet foreign policy since 1917 has been toward increased differentiation and concludes that "Soviet leaders since Lenin have stressed that the goals and priorities of the USSR must be tailored to the distinctive characteristics of each period because of changing political-administrative, socioeconomic, and scientific-technological conditions at home and abroad." Helmut Sonnenfeldt and William G. Hyland examine "how successive Soviet leaderships have sought to define the security requirements of the Soviet Union, how they have gone about satisfying these requirements, and how successful they have been." Not surprisingly, they observe that the quest for security "has been among the most basic and persistent Soviet concerns since the Revolution." But they affirm that Soviet definitions of security have undergone substantial transformation over the years in response to changing internal and external conditions. Sonnenfeldt and Hyland conclude that the past offers little help in assessing Soviet security requirements in the future. Raymond L. Garthoff examines the Soviet conception of détente in relationship to peaceful coexistence, the meaning and role of strategic parity, the correlation of forces, and how détente fits into Soviet ideological views of the world and history. He stresses, as does Hoffmann, the divergence between declared and actual Soviet goals: "Declared Soviet policy has been very consistent," although "veiled reflections of real policy differences do appear in the Soviet media." Garthoff concludes that the failure of détente in the 1970s can be attributed primarily to the fact that leaders of both sides failed to understand or pursue the principal task of détente: "to clarify and enlarge the areas of common interest on which cooperation can be built, and to identify and seek to manage the continuing competition in the large areas of diverging and conflicting interest which remain."

Part II contains four essays that examine a variety of methodological issues in the study of Soviet foreign policy. William Zimmerman examines the linkages between theory construction in international relations and the study of Soviet foreign policy in four major areas of inquiry: "the comparison of various approaches to world politics, the comparison of international systems, mass and elite foreign policy attitudes, and civil-military relations including the societal determinants of military performance." The evolution of theory, he argues, is the result of change both in our own thinking and in the object of our study as the Soviet Union moves "in the direction of becoming a more or less 'normal' state." Jack Snyder's methodological critique of Western studies of Soviet foreign policy employs two distinct methodological cultures (positivism and holism) and assesses their strengths and weaknesses. He argues that, while there are some irreducible disagreements between practitioners, the two approaches are compatible and can enhance each other. Snyder feels that recent developments in international relations theory provide scholars with the opportunity to bridge the methods gap between these two methodological cultures in the study of Soviet foreign policy. Vernon V. Aspaturian provides us with a comprehensive framework for analyzing Soviet foreign policy based on five groups of gross variables: motivations/purposes/intentions, capabilities/power, risks, costs/benefits, and opportunities. He suggests that the variables within each of these five categories can be divided into two distinct types: voluntaristic and deterministic. Aspaturian presents checklists of relevant variables within each of the five groups and cautions that these variables "must be viewed in dynamic interaction with each other, as not always explicitly deliberated upon by the Soviet leaders but nevertheless constantly scanned, screened, and related to each other in their minds." Richard K. Herrmann identifies three American images of the causes of Soviet international behavior: communist expansionism, realpolitik expansionism, and realpolitik self-defense. After analyzing these images in terms of general theories of motivation and foreign policy and locating them at different points on the spectrum between hard-line and soft-line approaches, he then evaluates the validity of each image based on an empirical investigation of Soviet leaders' pronouncements and behavior.

Part III contains a symposium plus three essays that examine the relationship between Communist ideology and Soviet international behavior. This part begins with the now classic 1958 debate among R. N. Carew Hunt, Samuel L. Sharp, and Richard Lowenthal concerning the motivational role of Communist ideology for Soviet foreign policy. Carew Hunt stresses the importance of ideology, Sharp stresses the importance of national interest, and Lowenthal—rejecting Sharp's dichotomy between ideology and national interest more forcefully than does Carew Hunt—stresses that Soviet leaders determine the national interest through an ideological orientation that always seeks to enhance the power of the Communist Party. Adam B. Ulam argues that "we have little reason to expect basic changes in the Soviet philosophy of foreign relations" because (1) the process of making foreign policy decisions is elitist, secretive, and based on hard-boiled pragmatism, and (2) "very little in their own experience or in the international picture, as it has evolved during the past 20 years or so, could have persuaded the Kremlin that its basic guidelines for dealing with the outside world needed revision.'' Contrary to the conventional wisdom of much American scholarship, Hannes Adomeit argues that ideology does continue to play an important role in the explanation of ''operational principles and recurring patterns of behavior which are specifically Soviet.'' His argument, like Lowenthal's, is built on the distinction among various parts of Soviet ideology (dialectical materialism, historical materialism, political economy, and political thought) and the functions performed by each part: the analytical or cognitive function; the operational or tactical function; the utopian, revolutionary, or missionary function; the legitimizing function; and the socializing function. In Adomeit's view, it is fallacious to argue that ''ideology is 'nothing but *ex post facto* rationalization' . . . and has nothing to do with motivation'' since rationalization and motivation ''can be *mutually reinforcing* mechanisms.'' Raymond F. Smith views the dialectical nature of reality and the correlation of forces as two concepts central to an understanding of Soviet negotiating behavior. Dialectics is a ''back of the mind'' concept (''an analytic tool used routinely for interpreting the world, but rarely itself examined analytically''), whereas the correlation of forces is a decidedly ''front of the mind'' concept. (''A correct analysis of the correlation of forces in any situation is essential if the Party is to act correctly.'') Smith examines the impact of Marxist-Leninist ideology on four basic traits of Russian political culture (authoritarian political traditions, ambivalence toward the West, preference for tradition over novelty, and aversion to risk-taking) and their combined impact on Soviet negotiating behavior.

Part IV, the final one, contains two essays: one prospective on Soviet foreign policy from the vantage point of 1947, the other a retrospective from 1986. George F. Kennan's essay (the famous Mr. ''X'' article) is probably the single most influential interpretation of the nature and prospects of Soviet foreign policy. Based on his assessment of the sources of Soviet conduct, Kennan outlined a theory of containment as the most appropriate American response to Soviet expansion in Eastern Europe and possible expansion in Western Europe in the late 1940s. However, a much broader theory about the containment of Communism around the world became the cornerstone of American foreign policy in successive administrations from Harry Truman to Ronald Reagan. William Taubman's essay reviews five American books from the mid-1980s that examine the sources of Soviet foreign conduct in the post–World War II era. Taubman takes as his point of departure what Seweryn Bialer calls ''the Soviet paradox''—namely, ''the ironic combination of external expansion and internal decline [that] has been the most striking feature of Soviet politics in recent years.'' Taubman concludes with his own ironic perspective of a ''Soviet-American paradox''—namely, that ''ambitious grand strategies designed to 'prevail' over the USSR may end up delivering less than may more modest attempts to coexist with the Soviets.'' He suggests that containment has outlived its utility as the cornerstone of American foreign policy.

THE STUDY OF SOVIET FOREIGN POLICY

Soviet foreign policy is a field in which "theories" abound. A survey of the literature in 1956 identified at least eight prevalent theories, each purporting to have found the main factor that influences and "explains" Soviet foreign policy behavior (for example, Marxist political philosophy, great Russian imperialism, bureaucratic tyranny, Byzantine traditions, national defense, Eurasian environmental characteristics, the urge to the sea, Russian national character).[1] Another review of the literature conducted a decade later again revealed many diverse theories that focus on four major themes: the impact of ideology, "Soviet nationhood," history, and geography on the foreign policy of the USSR.[2]

Most of these theories contend that one or more factors are especially important determinants of Soviet behavior in all or most situations. Implicit are generalizations to the effect that certain factors consistently influence Soviet actions more than others. Reference to these factors, it is claimed, will always or usually provide the best possible explanation of Soviet policies and performance. Critics replied that there was little empirical evidence to support the sweeping generalizations contained in most existing theories, that certain Soviet political, economic, and environmental characteristics may or may not influence Soviet behavior generally or in specific cases, and that factors may vary in relative importance in different situations.

The several decades that separate such classic studies from contemporary works have seen dramatic changes on a number of fronts. Soviet foreign policy has undergone several spectacular twists and turns. The amount and quality of information about the Soviet Union has increased substantially, and, as a result, Western studies of Soviet internal and external behavior have increased considerably. Nevertheless, broad generalizations—verified, unverified, and unverifiable—remain integral parts of past and present theories of Soviet foreign policy. The essays in this volume contribute to an assessment of those theories.

Different theories not only affect one's perception of the facts, but also one's assumptions about which facts are factors (i.e., relevant variables). One's theoretical orientation, whether consciously or unconsciously held, significantly affects the form, nature, and quality of one's explanations. Indeed, some philosophers argue that

> One theory cannot be understood literally as fitting the facts better than any other because each, in a significant sense, carries with it its own facts and observation reports. . . . To adopt a theory is ultimately to change one's observational framework, and this means more than one's perspective on a basically unchanging reality; it means, in one degree or another, to accept a new reality.[3]

Graham Allison's landmark discussion of conceptual models and the study of foreign policy illuminates these ideas. He outlines a "rational actor" model, an "organizational process" model, and a "bureaucratic politics" model.[4] Each has its own basic unit of analysis, organizing concepts, dominant inference patterns, and general and specific propositions.

The "rational actor" model is the most widely used by students of international relations and Soviet foreign policy.[5] It assumes that national governments act purposefully and respond in a calculating manner to perceived problems. However, if one accepts the view that conceptual models do not order "reality" but create it, one must seriously consider alternative paradigms. Students of Soviet foreign policy may find the "organizational process" and "bureaucratic politics" models particularly appealing, because they directly challenge the view that the USSR is a "totalitarian" or "monolithic" state.[6] They also focus attention on the implementation of policy, not merely on the decisions made by Soviet leaders. In short, alternative modes of analysis contain different assumptions and often produce very different explanations (for example, of the Cuban missile crisis).

Which theories and models best help one explain and understand what one wants to know about Soviet foreign policy behavior? One's approach to the subject will shape both the questions one asks and the answers one finds. The "rational actor" model, for example, relies heavily on the "motive-belief" pattern of explanation. Explanation of this kind "consists of showing what goal the government was pursuing in committing the act and how this action was a reasonable choice, given the nation's objectives."[7] However, it is very difficult to ascertain the motives and beliefs of the Soviet decision-makers in general and in specific instances. Perhaps the easiest task is to document the views of an individual Party leader on a single issue at a given moment in time. But even this may require considerable "Sovietological" insight and skillful use of content analysis.[8] Furthermore, the relationships between beliefs and behavior pose formidable research problems in all of the social sciences. They present especially great problems in the study of international relations, where much available data is contained in highly manipulative communications and reliable and significant information is often lacking.

Knowledge of many factors that may influence Soviet behavior is important to the student of Soviet foreign policy. The conceptual framework depicted in Figure 1 suggests numerous possible influences. "All foreign policy systems," it is argued, "comprise a set of components which can be classified in three general categories, inputs, process, and outputs. The notion of flow and dynamic movement in a system which is constantly absorbing demands and channeling them into a policy machine which transforms these inputs into decisions and outputs is portrayed [below]."[9]

We continue to find the diagram in Figure 1 useful and wish to call it to the attention of all readers. Some of the terms in the diagram are not self-evident and require further definition. For the authors of this diagram, the *global system* is "the total web of relationships among all actors within the international system (states, blocs, organizations)."[10] On the other hand, a *subordinate system*

INPUTS

OPERATIONAL ENVIRONMENT

External:	Global	(G)
	Subordinate	(S)
	Subordinate Other	(SO)
	Bilateral	(B)
	Dominant Bilateral	(DB)
Internal:	Military Capability	(M)
	Economic Capability	(E)
	Political Structure	(PS)
	Interest Groups	(IG)
	Competing Elites	(CE)

COMMUNICATION — The transmission of data about the operational environment by mass media and face-to-face contacts

PSYCHOLOGICAL ENVIRONMENT

Attitudinal Prism: Ideology, historical legacy, personality predispositions

Elite Images: of the operational environment, including competing elites' advocacy and pressure potential

PROCESS

FORMULATION of strategic and tactical decisions in four issue areas:

Military-Security	(M-S)
Political-Diplomatic	(P-D)
Economic-Developm'l	(E-D)
Cultural-Status	(C-S)

IMPLEMENTATION of decisions by various structures: head of state, head of government, foreign office, etc.

OUTPUTS — the substance of acts or decisions

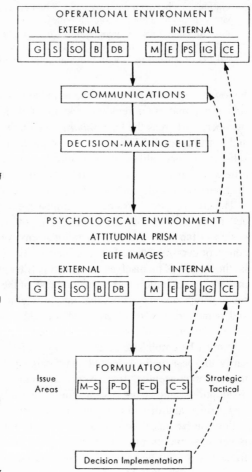

Figure 1.   Conceptual framework for a foreign policy system. Reprinted from Michael Brecher, Blema Steinberg, and Janice Stein, "A Framework for Research on Foreign Policy Behavior," *The Journal of Conflict Resolution*, XIII, 1 (March, 1969), p. 80. Copyright 1969 by The University of Michigan, reprinted by permission.

represents an intermediate level of interaction between the global system and the relationships between any two states. Theoretically there may be as many subordinate systems as there are foreign policy issues, but logically they can be grouped into four categories: (1) geographic, with contiguous membership; (2) geographic, with noncontiguous members; (3) organizational, with contiguous membership; and (4) organizational, with noncontiguous members.[11]

Following the authors' usage, the term *subordinate system* "refers mainly to the first type, that is, a regional system of which the state under analysis is a member," whereas the term *subordinate other* "encompasses the second, third, and fourth types."[12] The remainder of the terms in the diagram are more or less self-explanatory, although the reader may wish to consult the authors' original article and Brecher's later work[13] (based on the relationships outlined in the diagram) for a fuller discussion of these factors.

The creators of this framework emphasize that foreign policy decision-makers act in accordance with their perceptions of reality: "Underlying this research design is the view that the operational environment affects the results or outcomes of decisions directly but influences the choices among policy options, that is, the decisions themselves, only as it is filtered through the images of decision-makers."[14] An important but difficult task of the analyst is to identify and suggest relationships among factors that may link elite images with decisions, policies, and behavior. Whether certain factors do indeed influence Soviet actions in general or in specific cases are, of course, empirical questions.

It must be emphasized that this "systems" model is not the only nor necessarily the best method of studying foreign policy behavior.[15] Like any theory, model, or conceptual framework, it contains numerous explicit and implicit assumptions and is not "value-free." Recalling our earlier discussions, one might reject out of hand the authors' assertions that "all data regarding foreign policy can be classified in one of these categories" and that "all foreign policy issues may be allocated to four issue areas."[16] To be sure, other conceptual frameworks may generate different data and produce better explanations. But this framework does identify numerous potentially relevant sets of factors that may influence the external behavior of the Soviet Union, and it also suggests some general possible relationships among these factors. For both these reasons the framework merits careful study.

Considering the difficulties involved in using the "motive-belief" pattern of explanation and in studying the "psychological environment" of foreign policy-makers, it is perhaps unfortunate that many analysts assume that certain factors significantly influence Soviet behavior in all or most situations. It is probably more fruitful simply to look at certain situations and ask, Why were these decisions reached and why were these actions taken? (Why did the USSR sign the Nazi-Soviet pact? Why were satellite regimes created in Eastern Europe after World War II? And why did the Soviet Union permit, or perhaps even encourage, them to self-destruct in 1989? Why does the Soviet Union pursue its present policies in Eastern Europe, the Middle East, Southeast Asia, Latin America,

Africa? Why do Soviet leaders compete and cooperate with the United States in various fields?) Careful study of individual events, policies, and policy changes has made it possible and will continue to make it possible to evaluate the relevant importance of factors—external and internal—that influence individual Soviet decisions and types of activities. From this less shaky empirical base, with its emphasis on discovering and describing the actual behavior of Soviet officials at home and abroad, one can gradually verify, refine, or reformulate one's generalizations so that, employed with creativity and caution, they may help to explain Soviet behavior in other contexts.

Two of the classic textbooks in the field of Soviet foreign policy employ strikingly different methodological approaches. Adam Ulam's *Expansion and Coexistence* is a "traditional history"; Jan Triska and David Finley's *Soviet Foreign Policy* is primarily "social science" research. Each seeks to provide different kinds of insights into Soviet international behavior. Indeed, these two books reflect the ongoing state of flux in Soviet studies. Both are important efforts to explain Soviet foreign policy behavior. But they are based on fundamentally different concepts of explanation. Ulam's analysis is essentially eliminative—that is, he seeks to demonstrate that other possible explanations of events do not logically and empirically "fit" as well as his. Triska and Finley, employing various deductive and inductive research strategies, seek to generate and verify probabilistic generalizations to be used in explaining different aspects of Soviet behavior. The strength of the former approach is that it helps us to understand complex nonrecurring events about which information is difficult to obtain; the strength of the latter is that it helps to uncover trends and behavioral patterns through more rigorous analysis of available data.

The chapters in Part II of this volume address these methodological issues in ways that both relate to and go beyond the conceptual framework presented in Figure 1. Vernon Aspaturian (Chapter 6) elaborates on the "inputs" part of that conceptual framework by identifying five groups of gross variables as "inputs or factors, whether domestic or external, that condition, shape, or animate Soviet foreign policy": (1) motivations/purposes/intentions, (2) capabilities/power, (3) risks, (4) costs/benefits, and (5) opportunities. He then suggests a qualitative distinction among the individual variables within each of the five categories: voluntaristic and deterministic. "Voluntaristic variables are those whose weight and effect can be directly varied by the action of human will, whether individual or aggregate, whether conscious, inadvertent, or fortuitous." On the other hand, "deterministic variables are those whose effects and weight are independent of direct human will, but whose relative impact may vary because of conscious changes in the dimensions and value of the voluntaristic variables." He then reviews the strengths and weaknesses of each set of variables that may contribute to our understanding of Soviet foreign policy and international behavior. While Aspaturian's checklists of variables in each category may boggle the mind of the new student of Soviet foreign policy, the very length of these lists underscores the complexity of the subject and the need for multifaceted explanations. Students should not expect to apply these checklists of variables in any mechanical fashion and then think they can somehow magically arrive at an explanation of Soviet international behavior, for Aspaturian warns us that "the relevant variables from these five sets must be viewed in dynamic interaction with each other. . . . Serious changes in one gross variable can result in fundamentally reconstructing the relative relevance of the others, which may then recombine to feed back and again alter the initial variable." His several illustrations prove the point.

Shifting from the identification of relevant variables to a discussion of theory, William Zimmerman (Chapter 4) retraces his own intellectual odyssey over three decades of studying Soviet foreign policy. Twenty-five years ago the prevailing intellectual climate in the West was founded on two major assumptions concerning Soviet foreign policy. First, the foreign policy of the Soviet Union was distinctive because party leaders shared a common Marxist-Leninist outlook that motivated them to try to supplant the existing international order rather than accept the status quo and react accordingly. Second, as a result, Soviet foreign policy was essentially active in nature, not merely reactive to external influences. In his early work, however, Zimmerman found considerable evidence "that changes in the international environment . . . and Soviet perceptions of these changes had major consequences for Soviet goals and the Soviet assessment of the international system." In turn, "these changes in perception had profound implications for Soviet interactions with the other actors in the international system." Zimmerman's research, as well as that of Marshall Shulman, Jan Triska, David Finley, and others challenged the basic presumption of the time by demonstrating that Soviet foreign policy was in large measure reactive to the international environment. This was an important step in linking the study of world politics and Soviet foreign policy. Zimmerman describes "the evolution of theory building at the intersection of world politics and Soviet foreign policy" during the last quarter century. He argues that this "evolution has been in keeping with the movement of the Soviet Union in the direction of becoming a more or less 'normal' state. It has been partly a process of ruling out some long-standing concepts about the Soviet Union. In several instances this has been as much a function of change in the Soviet Union as it has of change in our thinking." This is but one illustration of our earlier suggestion that different theories affect one's perception of the facts and, therefore, the form, nature, and quality of one's explanations.

Jack Snyder (Chapter 5) illustrates the impact of one's assumptions on one's conclusions in his comparison of the strengths and weaknesses of two methodological cultures—positivism and holism—as they have been employed by Western scholars in the study of Soviet foreign policy. The positivists, more than the holists, have borrowed from general theories of international relations. As a result, they have contributed more to the linkage of Soviet foreign policy studies to international relations theory (along the lines suggested by Zimmerman) and are less prone to view the foreign policy of the Soviet Union as qualitatively different from that of other countries. The holists, on the other hand, have tended toward an understanding of "behavior in terms of the actor's own frame of reference, and explaining it by placing it in a rich context." In other words, argues Snyder, "empathy and context-dependent nuances of meaning are the watchwords of this approach." The result of this holistic orientation is a view of Soviet foreign policy as qualitatively different from that of other countries since it is based on peculiarly Soviet perspectives and calculations. The identification of a positivist-holist methods gap in the study of Soviet foreign policy is a variation on an issue that has haunted Soviet studies for decades: the bifurcation of the subdiscipline into two distinct worldviews: one idiographic, the other nomothetic. The methodological issues of each approach were brought to the forefront of scholarly debate in the late 1960s only to retreat into the background when no consensus was reached. Only recently have these issues again begun to receive the serious attention they deserve.[17]

Richard Herrmann (Chapter 7) demonstrates the possibility of "bridging the methods gap" (as Jack Snyder put it) by examining the relationships between Soviet perceptions and Soviet international behavior as well as by using both empirical evidence about Soviet perceptions and general theories of international relations. "Although estimating Soviet perceptions and aims is difficult," he argues, "it is done quite frequently." Indeed, "claims about motives are usually the core ideas in competing theories about Soviet international behavior." Herrmann's study gives life to Aspaturian's framework for analyzing Soviet foreign policy by focusing explicitly on motivations, capabilities, costs, and opportunities (four of Aspaturian's five major groups of gross variables). Herrmann warns us, as does Aspaturian, that applying these variables to the analysis of real-life situations is no mere mechanical process.

Drawing on the work of Ole Holsti and James Rosenau, Herrmann focuses on three distinct and mutually exclusive images of the Soviet Union commonly held by American elites: communist expansionism ("the Soviet Union is motivated by a determination to spread communism and dominate the world"), realpolitik expansionism ("Moscow seeks to expand its influence by exploiting opportunities while protecting its security"), and realpolitik self-defense ("the USSR is primarily committed to self-defense"). The aim of Herrmann's empirically based approach to the study of foreign policy motivation was not so much to settle the political debate among these three theories, "but rather to press the academic debate into areas where assumptions about motivation must be defended explicitly and empirically." The assessment of these three dominant American images and the results of his study lead Herrmann to "cast doubt on the accuracy of current theories of Soviet foreign policy that assume that the USSR's primary motive is to expand its domination over others." This important conclusion is of more than academic interest because it suggests "that U.S. efforts to reinforce the containment of Soviet influence may be counterproductive: they are not likely to reduce undesirable Soviet behavior or to enhance American security or prospects for peace. These are disturbing possibilities."

Since the late 1960s the pendulum of Western opinion has apparently swung away from the view that Soviet foreign policy is distinct from that of all other countries. This is, no doubt, the result of both another quarter-century of Soviet behavior and another quarter-century of experience in evaluating and assessing that behavior. The result is a view that sees the Soviet Union as a more or less "normal" actor on the international scene. Alexander Dallin, a respected student of Soviet foreign policy, put the case this way when writing about the domestic sources of Soviet foreign policy at the end of the Brezhnev era:

> We are thus led to conclude that, despite all caveats and reservations, certain universals and concepts must apply to the Soviet experience as they do anywhere else. This would be true, for example, of the role of belief systems, cognitive processes, and mind-sets, and of processes like learning or small-group dynamics. At the same time, it is important especially in the Soviet case to distinguish between the formal, ritual, explicit, and overt public images of states and systems, friends and foes—and the actual, often unstated, and at times unwitting or un-acknowledged operational assumptions and beliefs of particular actors.[18]

With this in mind, we can now proceed to a more detailed consideration of the relative importance of internal and external factors on Soviet foreign policy and international behavior.

INTERNAL FACTORS: DOMESTIC POLITICS

At the outset, it must be emphasized that one cannot discuss the impact of "domestic politics" on "Soviet foreign policy" without first stipulating which internal factors and which aspects of Soviet international behavior one is talking about. Some domestic influences have greatly affected major Soviet foreign policy decisions, while other domestic factors have had little or no discernible effect on the same decisions. *Which* factors have *what kind of* influence under *what* conditions during *which* time periods are empirical questions, albeit difficult ones. Informed observers, in efforts to identify and confirm these relationships, can and do differ. But one cannot meaningfully analyze "the" influence of domestic politics on international behavior.

In an important anthology, *Domestic Sources of Foreign Policy*, a central premise and basic dilemma are clearly stated. "The premise is that domestic sources of foreign policy are no less crucial to its content and conduct than are the international situations toward which it is directed. The dilemma is that the links between the domestic sources and the resulting behavior—foreign policy—are not easily observed and are thus especially resistant to coherent analysis."[19] In the Soviet context, this dilemma is particularly acute. One has no a priori reason to reject the central premise, but verification of the presumed relationships has relied heavily on informed speculation and generalization from a few cases. The conceptualization and measurement of "influence" are particularly intractable problems. For example, it is exceedingly difficult to ascertain the calculations of Soviet leaders and the information they have at their disposal when they make their decisions. We should not assume that all of the input variables identified by Aspaturian are of equal weight in determining outcomes in policy and behavior, but it is difficult to ascertain what factors are decisive in Soviet leaders' final selections (or compromises) among perceived alternatives. Prior to the era of *glasnost* (openness, or public candor), the analyst's sources of information were almost always limited to a handful of written documents, from which inferences had to be made with utmost care and sophistication.[20] The outpouring of public discussion and information since the mid-1980s has presented Western scholars and analysts with a different set of problems: the difficulty of separating authoritative statements from policy options under consideration and from personal opinions.

In the course of the past seventy years, the structure and functions of the Communist party have undergone significant transitions. This suggests that domestic sources of foreign policy—and their relative importance in different situations—have also undergone major changes.[21] For example, since 1956 there has been a dramatic increase in the quantity and quality of Soviet research on international affairs. This was perhaps especially true of research on the United States and Western Europe and on selected developing countries during the 1960s and 1970s. In the late 1980s there was another dramatic increase in the quantity and quality of Soviet research on international relations and the outside world. Moreover, Gorbachev has sought to give civilian analysts much greater access to classified information traditionally guarded by the Soviet military, in an effort to foster multiple sources of policy-relevant advice.[22] Whether this fresh information is being used in the formulation and implementation of policy is a very difficult empirical question. Writing in 1983, Adam Ulam (Chapter 9) expressed pessimism in this regard owing to the closed and centralized nature of Soviet decision-making: "The only participants in the decision-making process in the USSR, outside the 20-odd members of the inner circle, are those whom it chooses to consult, and only while it does so." But the fact remains that large quantities of accurate information are now available to Soviet decision-makers—information of the kind that was simply not generated or communicated prior to 1956. Good scientific and social science research institutes are not automatically major "domestic" influences on Soviet foreign policy, but they are surely important potential factors in most policy areas, especially when the directors of those institutes are close advisors to the General Secretary.

The identification of potentially significant influences on Soviet foreign policy does not constitute verification of their actual impact under different conditions. Nor does identification of variables that may be related to one another warrant undocumented assertions about the nature of these relationships. The formulation and testing of unconfirmed empirical generalizations (hypotheses) are highly desirable, but one must carefully distinguish among generalizations that are well confirmed, partially confirmed, or not at all confirmed by the data available.

While there appears to be general (but no universal) agreement among Western scholars that domestic factors *do* influence Soviet foreign policy and behavior, there is considerable disagreement over *which* factors are important and the *nature* of their impact. Writing in 1967 about the relationships between domestic and foreign policy in the post-Stalin era, Sidney Ploss hypothesized that Soviet international behavior is significantly influenced by "domestic politics in the form of bureaucratic group struggle over functions and funds."[23] In another context, a respected student of American politics concluded that "interest group influence on foreign policy is slight."[24] John Armstrong and Richard Pipes would perhaps agree that this is also true in the Soviet Union.[25] Alexander Dallin and Carl Linden, on the other hand, would probably argue that certain institutional and nonassociational groups in Soviet society have vested interests in different foreign policies, and that some of these groups significantly influence the formulation of policy alternatives and actual decisions.[26] Vernon Aspaturian has emphasized that Soviet behavior in this respect is very similar to that of all nations: "Foreign policy, including external defense, is more a function of preserving the social order and the interests of its dominant groups than of the state or the national interests in the abstract . . . [and] functions more to serve tangible internal interests than intangible or abstract ideological interests abroad."[27] For example, the Soviet military heavy-industrial "complex" in fact and/or in rhetoric favors an aggressive foreign policy. Other coalitions of interest clearly favor a less militant posture and less defense spending.[28]

The analysis of "interest group" and "political structure" influences (see Figure 1) on Soviet foreign policy is hazardous for both empirical and conceptual reasons. Not only is "influence" exceedingly difficult to measure, but Sovietologists simply do not agree on what constitutes an "interest group"[29] Therefore, one must very carefully examine the way that this concept is used before evaluating the descriptive accuracy or explanatory power of propositions employing the concept.

John Armstrong has suggested that one aspect of domestic politics—the competition for power among political leaders—is generally the most important factor influencing Soviet international behavior, and that foreign policy issues tend to be manipulated not in the interests of the USSR as a whole, or even of congeries of interest, but primarily to the personal benefit of individual Politburo members and cliques.[30] Grant Pendill has challenged this view.[31] On at least one major issue (Soviet policy toward the Third World) resolved during an intense power struggle (1953–1956), Pendill found far-reaching decisions that may have been "truly collective" or "bipartisan." Careful investigation revealed little evidence that this issue was used as a "pawn" in personal rivalry for power and positions.

There is probably more agreement among scholars that group influence on foreign policy varies with the issue.[32] Ploss and Linden have emphasized that genuine policy choices are always present, and that since Stalin's death the power and prestige of Soviet leaders are dependent on the success of their domestic and foreign policies. This was more true of Khrushchev than Brezhnev, and it is clearly true of Gorbachev. However, high party officials, individually and collectively, often appeal to bureaucratic institutions and groups for political support and technical expertise in the constant competition over policy alternatives and resource allocation. Thus, institutional and nonassociational interests can and do exert considerable influence on *some* policy issues—generally and in single instances.

Furthermore, political leaders who hold certain views on foreign policy often hold distinct views on domestic policy. There may not be any apparent logical connection between the two, but political attitudes do tend to cluster. As Linden has persuasively argued, competing Soviet views on domestic and foreign policy also tend to cluster:

> The antagonism in the post-Stalin period between those leaning toward orthodoxy and conservatism, on the one hand, and those disposed to reform and innovation, on the other, can be roughly defined in terms of an internal versus an external orientation in policy. The more orthodox emphasize the necessities of the world struggle and the dangers from the outside enemy. Those inclined toward reform stress internal problems, the prospects for a relatively stable international environment, and the possibilities of developing less dangerous forms of struggle with the adversary abroad. In domestic policy the orthodox stress the ideological function of the party, doctrinal continuity, the need for limits on de-Stalinization, maintenance of centralized control of the economy, close supervision of the intelligentsia, and a heavy industry-defense weighted resource allocation policy. The reformers, by comparison, lean toward innovation in theory and practice, pragmatic solution to economic problems, greater reliance on material rewards than on ideologic stimuli, more local initiative and less centralization, and concessions to the consumer.[33]

How these attitudes and interests affect Soviet policy in different "issue areas" is the key question. James Rosenau hypothesizes that "the more an issue encompasses a society's resources and relationships, the more will it be drawn into the society's domestic political system and the less will it be processed through the society's foreign political system."[34] But this hypothesis and others have not been and perhaps cannot be rigorously tested in the Soviet context. Even in the Gorbachev period, Westerners' conceptual confusion and inadequate evidence place a premium on creative speculation and on cautious inferences from limited data. To be sure, there is little general theory about the relationships between domestic and foreign policies, and data on American and West European policymakers can also be difficult to muster.[35] But in the study of Soviet foreign policy, these problems are compounded. This is well illustrated by contemporary Soviet and Western debates on the relationships between *perestroika* and "new thinking" and between the USSR's domestic and international priorities (see *Contemporary Issues in Soviet Foreign Policy*, Part I).

INTERNAL FACTORS: IDEOLOGY AND BELIEF SYSTEMS

Observers of Soviet behavior have long been vexed by the question of the motivational role of Communist ideology. Many writers on this subject can be located on a spectrum running between two extreme positions based on certain assumptions about the motives of Soviet leaders: (1) that Communist ideology is a post facto rationalization of actions motivated by other considerations (personal power, national interest, imperialism, etc.) and (2) that ideology motivates Soviet leaders to take particular kinds of actions, or at least serves as "a guide to action."[36] Some of the chapters in Part III represent positions that approach one or the other extreme, while others implicitly or explicitly reject this dichotomy and approach the question of the motivational role of Communist ideology from quite different perspectives.

Samuel Sharp (Chapter 8) comes down clearly on the side of national interest as the key to Soviet politics, including foreign policy. Sharp rejects the view that "the *ultimate* aims of the Communist creed are operative in policy determinations" and function as "a guide to action." He would probably concur with the findings of two major studies, which conclude that "at no point does it appear that Leninist theory excludes a significant range of policy choices from being considered by the Soviet leadership,"[37] and that Soviet political leaders and analysts, "rather than let Lenin do their thinking for them, found they could utilize Lenin to legitimate their thinking no matter how un-Leninist those thoughts might be. . . . [For] the ideological high priests under Khrushchev created the doctrinal legitimation for regarding *Leninism* as irrelevant to atomic age international politics by declaring that the period when the nature of imperialism determined the style of international politics had been historically transcended."[38]

While admitting that Communist ideology may be significant for the internal working of the regime, Robert Daniels concluded in 1965 that "foreign policy is one of the least ideological aspects of Soviet politics, in reality if not in words. Rather than foreign policy being governed in any substantial way by ideological requirements, the chief connection of the two lies in the decision and situations which foreign policy considerations bring about and require the ideology to justify or explain away."[39] For both Sharp and Daniels, ideology serves mainly as a post facto rationalization for policy.

However, R. N. Carew Hunt (Chapter 8) contends that both ideology and "power politics" have a significant impact on Soviet foreign policy. He emphasizes that Soviet ideology affects the thinking and perceptions of Soviet leaders, whose actions are often influenced by the concepts and principles "to which all Communists subscribe." Indeed, Carew Hunt maintains that certain Marxist beliefs have "led the Soviet rulers to take so distorted a view of the world as to make it harder to deal with them than any government in the annals of diplomacy; and this . . . is just what may be expected from an 'ideology' in the sense in which Marx originally used the term." Carew Hunt concludes that "There is no yardstick which permits a measure of the exact relation between power politics and ideology in the politics which result; but surely neither factor can be ignored.'' Hannes Adomeit (Chapter 10) seems to concur with this view, arguing that "it is difficult to uphold the distinction between 'Marxist–Leninist ideology' and 'the Soviet national interest.' ''

In support of Carew Hunt's position, David Forte believes that "Soviet ideology bears an intimate relationship to Soviet foreign policy . . . and is not a mere philosophical rationalization for basically nationalist designs.''[40] In support of these views, Forte presented a detailed study of the Soviet response to the early development of the European Economic Community (the Common Market) Significantly, he found that shifts in ideological premises nearly always *preceded* changes in policy; ideological change thus "set the stage for new practical policies.''[41] Far from rationalizing or legitimizing policies already initiated, Soviet leaders and ideologists—at least on this crucial issue and during this period—played important parts in assessing the situation, planning new courses of action, and reformulating ideological principles in anticipation of policy changes.

In his contribution to the debate with Sharp and Carew Hunt, Richard Lowenthal (Chapter 8) emphasizes three very important ideas: (1) that some parts of an ideology have a much greater influence on elite perceptions, beliefs, and behavior than others; (2) that a crucial question to ask about any ideological statement or belief is, What *functions* does it perform? and (3) that the "operative'' parts of Soviet ideology are those that maintain and justify the predominant role of the Communist Party in the Soviet political system.

Lowenthal is by no means the only scholar to distinguish among the component elements of Soviet ideology and to suggest that certain parts perform different functions under various circumstances.[42] Zbigniew K. Brzezinski, in his monumental 1960 study *The Soviet Bloc: Unity and Conflict*, carefully distinguished among the "philosophical component,'' the "doctrinal component,'' and the "action program'' of Soviet ideology. Brzezinski noted that these three elements "cannot always be neatly compartmentalized and will often overlap,'' but he stressed that their susceptibility to change and their impact on policy vary considerably.[43] J. M. Bochenski also identified three basic aspects of Marxism-Leninism: "the basic dogma,'' "the systematic superstructure,'' and "the declassified doctrines.''[44] Other scholars distinguish among "ideology,'' "dogma,'' and "doctrine''; "operational ideology'' (the way Soviet leaders think), "official ideology'' (what the people are told), and "national ideology'' (what the people believe); and even "popular ideology,'' "cadre ideology,'' and "ideologists' ideology.''[45] These distinctions have been applied not only to ideology, but to other aspects of belief systems as well. Raymond Smith (Chapter 11) suggests that "those who study political culture find it useful to distinguish between official, dominant, and elite political cultures.''

Assessing the impact of Soviet ideology on foreign policy, Adam Ulam identified three potential uses of Marxism: (1) "implied prescriptions (implied, because Marx and Engels never devoted much attention to the problem of foreign policy of a socialist state)''; (2) ''an analytical discipline for viewing international as well as domestic politics''; and (3) ''a symbol and quasi-religion giving its practitioners the sense that they are moving forward with the forces of history and that the success of their state is predicated upon the truth of the doctrine.'' The first of these, Ulam argued, no longer plays a significant part in the conduct of Soviet foreign policy, ''while the analytical and symbolical uses of Marxism remain important and necessary to the understanding of Soviet policy.''[46] Ulam would perhaps agree that even the realpolitik pursuit of ''national interest'' is ''totally conditioned by the way in which the policy-makers apprehend reality.''[47]

Ulam also anticipated Alfred G. Meyer's important arguments on the ''legitimizing'' and ''self-legitimizing'' functions of Soviet ideology—that is, the use of ideological statements ''to convince the citizenry that the party and its leaders have a legitimate claim to rule them,'' and as ''a continual attempt on the part of the rulers to convince *themselves* of their legitimacy.''[48] Ulam's views, published over three decades ago, retain a special significance in that they were written by the author of *Expansion and Coexistence*, by far the most comprehensive and influential history of Soviet foreign policy by any Western scholar.

Drawing on the works of Meyer, Marshall Shulman, and William Zimmerman, Hannes Adomeit (Chapter 10) argues that Soviet ideology is so broad in scope that study of its impact on foreign policy must recognize that it consists of four distinct parts: (1) dialectical materialism, (2) historical materialism, (3) political economy, and (4) scientific communism. Since a variety of functions may be formed by each of these parts of ideology, it is also necessary to specify those functions: (1) the analytic or cognitive function, (2) the operational or tactical function, (3) the utopian, revolutionary, or missionary function, (4) the legitimizing function, and (5) the socializing function. The importance of these distinctions for Adomeit is that they permit us ''to make allowance for the possibility that the manifold activities in politics and society may be influenced by ideology to differing degrees, and to be aware of the problem that the relative importance of various aspects of ideology may change over time.'' Adomeit takes a stand against Sharp and Daniels when he states that ''it is still a fallacy to argue that ideology is 'nothing but *ex post facto* rationalization' . . . and has nothing to [do] with motivation,'' and he affirms that rationalization and motivation ''can be *mutually reinforcing* mechanisms.'' Viewed in this light, ideology does continue to matter in Soviet foreign policy and international behavior.

Careful readers have undoubtedly noted that we have yet to present a precise, lucid, and succinct definition of the concept of ''ideology.'' David Joravsky, in a stimulating and insightful 1966 article, offered just such a definition: ''When we call a belief ideological, we are saying at least three things about it: although it is unverified or unverifiable, it is accepted as verified by a particular group, because it performs social functions for that group.'' Joravsky explained that '' 'group' is used loosely to indicate such aggregations as parties, professions, classes, or nations,'' and '' 'because' is also used loosely, to indicate a functional correlation rather than a strict causal connection between acceptance of a belief and other social processes."[49]

Joravsky's distinction between unverified beliefs ("grand ideology") and verifiable but unverified beliefs ("petty ideology") is important. Beliefs of the former kind include powerful emotional appeals such as "All men are created equal," whereas more specific and perhaps verifiable derivatives of this precept include propositions such as "Universal suffrage would allow the poor to control or even take the property of the rich."[50] Fundamental Soviet beliefs at the level of grand ideology include: "Matter is all that exists, reality is essentially dialectical, the triumph of communism is inevitable, the aims of communism coincide with the aims of working mankind, and the Party is the vanguard of mankind and will lead it to communism."[51] Beliefs at the level of petty ideology include, for example, many of Khrushchev's doctrinal innovations: "Wars are not inevitable," "violent revolutions are not inevitable," "peaceful coexistence with the West is possible and desirable," and "countries of the Third World 'peace zone' are unaligned and uncommitted to either socialist or capitalist 'camps.' " In short, petty ideology consists of the more "specific, verifiable beliefs that cluster about the grand ideologies," and both the content and the social functions of petty ideology are more susceptible to change than those of grand ideology.

It has long been our experience as teachers of Soviet foreign policy that both undergraduate and graduate students find it difficult to grasp how the seemingly abstract concepts of theoretical Marxism-Leninism can influence actual Soviet behavior. Raymond Smith (Chapter 11) helps us with our understanding of this important issue when he suggests that "Dialectical materialism performs for educated Soviets what Meyer sees as one of the fundamental functions of an ideology: it provides their set of concepts for perceiving the world and its problems, their means of orienting themselves in the universe. The foundation for this understanding is dialectical materialism's theory of knowledge." Smith then elaborates on the three core elements of this theory of knowledge and shows how they enable the believer to perceive reality in particular ways.

Theoretical ideology, in both its grand and petty forms, must be sharply distinguished from "political realism," which Joravsky defines as "a constantly shifting jumble of commitments to particular judgments and persons":

> Perhaps the most basic, the golden rule of the "realist" politician, is his practical way of recognizing that politics is the business of arranging people in hierarchies of power. . . . His basic principle, though rarely stated, is evident in his behaviour: If a belief reduces one's influence in one's group, it is wrong; if it increases one's influence, it is right. This is an ideological principle.[52]

Joravsky goes on to observe that "it is clear to most Western students of Soviet affairs that grand and petty ideology have been giving way to political 'realism' in the thinking of the Soviet elite. This is the process that Meyer calls 'the routinization of indoctrination'; others have called it the erosion, exhaustion, or even the end of ideology.''[53] The latter phrases are very misleading, Joravsky argues, because they suggest that "political realism" is devoid of ideology merely because it does not contain serious philosophical or theoretical statements. Hannes Adomeit also criticizes proponents of the "erosion of ideology" view, because "they juxtapose as antitheses 'ideology,' on the one hand, and 'opportunism' or 'pragmatism,' on the other, thereby overlooking the fact that rigidity in doctrine does not by any means imply rigidity in tactics."

The gradual transformation of Soviet thinking from Lenin to Brezhnev has created difficult problems for analysts of Soviet ideology and political behavior. "Political realism" consists of the "basic rules of thought" that shape the motives, beliefs, judgments, and actions of Soviet leaders. But the lack of data on the belief systems of Soviet officials, the nature of the Soviet policymaking process, and the organizational, social, and psychological constraints on party leaders make it exceedingly difficult to study the "operative" political beliefs of Soviet elites individually or collectively.

Addressing these problems, Alexander George has attempted to reconcile both the philosophical and instrumental beliefs that comprise "the operational code" of Soviet leaders, especially in the Lenin and Stalin eras. In far greater detail than Lowenthal and others, George has described the maxims or "approaches to political calculation" that seem to have shaped Soviet decisions and behavior: "Knowledge of the actor's beliefs helps the investigator to clarify the general criteria, requirements, and norms the subject attempts to meet in assessing opportunities that arise to make desirable gains, in estimating the costs and risk associated with them, and in making utility calculations.''[54] These considerations greatly influence foreign policy decisions, and are almost certainly what Joravsky had in mind when he referred to "political realism," as distinct from theoretical ideology.

George's reformulation of Soviet "optimizing strategy" is particularly interesting in light of past and present Soviet performance, for example, the "dual policy" of the 1920s and "peaceful coexistence" of the 1950s and 1960s. George argued that knowledge of belief systems and the ways in which they change provides

> one of the important inputs needed for behavioural analyses of political decision-making and leadership styles. The "operational code" construct does this insofar as it encompasses that aspect of the political actor's perception and structuring of the political world to which he relates, and within which he attempts to operate to advance the interests with which he is identified. This approach should be useful for studying an actor's decision-making "style," and its application in specific situations.[55]

Unfortunately, few students of Soviet foreign policy have followed George's lead in this area of inquiry.

When the question of the motivational role of communist ideology for communist behavior is placed in the broader context of the relationship between belief systems and behavior, one finds a huge set of potentially relevant variables and important questions, which have been infrequently applied in the Soviet context. For example, a distinction must be made between ideologies and belief systems. Milton Rokeach has suggested that the term *belief-disbelief system* (as applied to both individuals and to groups) includes "*all* of a person's beliefs and therefore is meant to be more inclusive than what is normally meant by ideology."[56] Ideology, on the other hand, "refers to a more or less institutionalized set of beliefs—'the beliefs someone picks up.' Belief-disbelief systems contain these too but, in addition, they contain highly personalized pre-ideological beliefs."[57] In Rokeach's view, pre-ideological beliefs are unstated but basic primitive beliefs out of which the individual's "total belief-disbelief system grows": "Every person may be assumed to have formed early in life some set of beliefs about the world he lives in, the validity of which he does not question and, in the ordinary course of events, is not prepared to question."[58] Ideologies are more or less formalized, institutionalized sets of beliefs that are "out there" in society, embodied in the programs of political parties, religious orders, voluntary associations, or even in the culture of a society. These ideologies may or may not be incorporated into the belief-disbelief systems of particular individuals in that society.

What we are accustomed to calling "communist ideology" or "Marxism-Leninism" is an example of ideology in the above sense and, as such, constitutes only part of an individual's total belief-disbelief system. What are the other parts? And what are the interconnections among beliefs, attitudes, and values? These are matters for empirical determination. The extent to which Marxism-Leninism as an institutionalized set of beliefs has been internalized into the total belief-disbelief system of individual Soviet citizens (whether rank-and-file or elite) is also a matter for empirical determination.

Raymond Smith (Chapter 11) assists us in this effort by pointing to both similarities and differences between Marxism-Leninism (as ideology and hence as one part of belief-disbelief systems) and Russian political culture (as another part of belief-disbelief systems) to form a distinctive Soviet political culture. These are important questions, because "Areas in which contemporary ideology reinforces traditional institutional patterns and outlooks of political culture should be particularly important drivers of Soviet negotiating style and behavior. Conversely, in areas where the traditions are in conflict, we should expect far greater ambivalence, uncertainty, and mixed signals in how the Soviets negotiate." While Russian political culture manifests itself in Soviet negotiating behavior in a number of ways, Smith argues, "the impact of ideology on these traits is mixed." This suggests that certain aspects of traditional Russian political culture have been incorporated into the belief-disbelief systems of Soviet negotiators to a greater extent than have elements of Marxism-Leninism as ideology (in Rokeach's sense).

The purpose of the foregoing discussion is to suggest to students that the question of the motivational role of communist ideology on Soviet international behavior is much more complex than was indicated by the 1958 Carew Hunt–Sharp–Lowenthal debate (Chapter 8) and many subsequent discussions by Sovietologists. The conceptual apparatus and theory needed to resolve this debate require the inclusion of many more variables than hitherto acknowledged, including the psychological variables just mentioned and many others.[59]

That there still remain practical barriers to the conceptualization and measurement of these phenomena and then the formulation and testing of theories about them in the Soviet context is no excuse for pretending that they are not relevant variables or that empirically grounded theories connecting images, beliefs, and actions have no place in the study of *Soviet* international behavior. Although psychological theories are not the only source of such variables and questions, it does seem that there is more systematic evidence for psychological theory than there is for many others. Our insistence on such "evidence" may prolong debate on these issues for the indefinite future, but it is epistemologically sound and remains the main standard of usefulness and proof currently employed in the social and policy sciences.

In the study of international relations, the key issue "is not *whether* psychological processes are relevant, but *how* they are relevant."[60] Fundamental questions concerning the psychological environment of Soviet foreign policymakers (see Figure 1) include: How do Soviet leaders perceive the interests, capabilities, and intentions of other nations? To what extent does Soviet ideology shape these perceptions? Which parts of the ideology shape values, attitudes, and beliefs more than others? What effects do these values, attitudes, and beliefs have on Soviet behavior? Why do they have these effects? When do they do so? In short, "whose images count, under what conditions, and at what points in the future in the international policy-making process"?[61]

Thus, if ideology is "a broad system of concepts with educational and integrative functions,"[62] and if "the chief function of ideology—whether theoretical, 'realistic', or a mixture of the two—is to rationalize a group's readiness to act, or refuse to act,"[63] then some parts of Soviet ideology may significantly influence the social-psychological processes of Soviet leaders (e.g., "those relating to motivations, perception, trust, and suspicion, definition of the situation, stress, communication, leadership, influence, norm formation, role prescription, group cohesiveness, loyalty").[64] For foreign policymakers, particularly important general processes include defining the nature of a situation, formulating possible initiatives and responses, assessing threats, risks, and likely consequences of different policies, and developing criteria for choosing among alternative courses of action. Hence, Zimmerman concluded more than twenty years ago that the serious researcher finds himself returning to the study of the "cognitive and affective maps of particular decision-makers—but at a greater level of specificity . . . and within a general framework which stresses the impact of external factors on Soviet behavior."

Herbert C. Kelman, a distinguished social psychologist, adds an important caveat. He warns that the study of foreign policymaking should not be based entirely on psychological variables. Such an analysis would be inadequate, because "it ignores the role of situational constraints (i.e., constraints deriving from the specific context in which national decision-makers arrive at their decision and in which they interact with their counterparts in other nations) and/ or structural constraints (i.e., constraints deriving from the structure of national and international political systems)."[65] But Kelman also argues that certain social-psychological processes can and should "enter importantly into various general conceptualizations of the interaction between nations and foreign policymaking"—particularly those internal constraints and personality dispositions of important decision-makers. Situational and psychological constraints both

> may operate to varying degrees, depending on the occasion for the decision and on numerous other factors, and they may interact with one another in various ways. Structural factors may create dispositional constraints, and dispositional factors, in turn, may create structural constraints. We are dealing here with societal and inter-societal processes and with the complex functioning of national and international systems. These processes, however, can be in part illuminated by a microanalysis of the cognitive and social processes that occur at the locus of decision-making, as long as we recognize that these merely represent the culmination of a large array of prior events and interactions. Most important, by studying the perceptions and action tendencies of the decision-maker and the interactions within the decision-making unit, we can learn a great deal about the nature of the constraints that operate in different situations and the way in which they affect each other and the final decision outcome.[66]

For the researcher, then, it is very difficult to ascertain what Soviet leaders from Stalin to Brezhnev believed and which perceived factors and beliefs actually shape policies and behavior under certain circumstances. Joravsky notes that after the first five or ten years of Soviet rule, party leaders ceased to make serious efforts to state their operative political beliefs in explicit theoretical form and, as a result, a significant portion of the political process ceased to be publicly documented: "After that brief period, the increasing replacement of theoretical ideology by closemouthed 'realism', and the growing passion for closed politics, limited the Western student to very gross inferences about the interaction of political beliefs and political processes."[67] Adam Ulam (Chapter 9) seems to concur with this characterization when he argues that the Soviet process of decision-making is both elitist and secretive.

Joravsky argues that

> The Western student of Soviet ideology faces a choice. He can limit himself to areas of thought where Soviet ideology can be identified from the vantage point of genuine knowledge and its social functions discovered by rigorous empirical scholarship. Or he can turn boldly to the political process, where ideology is most important—and nearly impossible to study in a rigorous empirical scholarly fashion. He can aspire to a scientific analysis of Soviet ideology or to an ideological critique of it. The choice can hardly be thoroughly rational; it is unavoidably

influenced by one's ideological hopes and fears concerning the relationship between politics and scholarship.[68]

For the most part, students of Soviet ideology have chosen the latter approach—they have engaged in ideological critiques of communist ideology rather than in scientific analysis. In some cases these ideological critiques (or "counterideologies") have masqueraded as "scientific" analysis, especially by some Western academics who marketed their views to policymakers. As Rita Kelly and Fleron pointed out more than twenty years ago, every "expert" on communist affairs is expected to have some answer to the question of the motivational link between communist ideology and communist behavior. Prior to Gorbachev, however, the locked door of the archive and the paucity of candid interviews ruled out rigorous scientific analysis of the social functions performed by Soviet ideology. Hence it was impossible for the more objective scholar or political analyst to refute the theories (and rantings and ravings) of anticommunist counterideologists.[69] But now, thanks to increasing *glasnost* about current and past Soviet foreign policy, efforts in these directions can be more fruitful. Such efforts are of enormous importance in the study and practice of international relations, because, as a respected social psychologist reminds us, "situations defined as real are real in their consequences."[70]

EXTERNAL FACTORS: THE ORIGINS OF THE COLD WAR

There is much disagreement about whether external factors significantly shape Soviet behavior, which factors exert influence under various circumstances, and in what manner they do so. Western, especially American, debates on the origins of the Cold War illustrate these disagreements. "Traditional" historians contend that external factors had little effect on Soviet policies and actions during and immediately after World War II. "Revisionist" historians assert that external influences—especially American diplomacy—had a significant impact on Soviet behavior. The former emphasized the aggressive, inflexible, inexorable, inevitable nature of Soviet policies, especially in Eastern Europe; the latter stressed the adaptive, responsive, reactive, flexible nature of Soviet policy, particularly Stalin's willingness to consider alternative courses of action and to negotiate certain crucial issues with his American and British allies. The chief implication of the former interpretation is that Soviet "expansionism" was the primary cause of the breakdown of Allied cooperation and the onset of the Cold War; the latter view concludes that unrealistic and sometimes truculent Western diplomacy (especially between 1945 and 1947) was a major cause of the Cold War in that it reduced policy alternatives open to Stalin and thus induced him to choose "hardline" policies (for example, the satellization of *all* of Eastern Europe) he might not have chosen otherwise.

A definitive analysis of Cold War origins is impossible without more information from Soviet sources, but evidence concerning Western intentions and behavior is more accessible, albeit subject to varying interpretations. In his famous "X" article (Chapter 12), George F. Kennan unwittingly provided the rationale for more than four decades of American foreign policy. His language suggested that military "containment" of Soviet "expansive tendencies" should be the cornerstone of American policy. But Kennan and fellow members of the State Department's Policy Planning Staff in 1947 did not see any danger of Soviet military expansion into Western Europe. What they did consider a serious threat was that large West European countries and major industrial centers might come under Soviet control by internal political changes—that is, by local communist parties seizing power.

The military implications of the "containment" doctrine had a vastly greater impact on American foreign policy than did its political or ideological implications. As Kennan ruefully observed in his memoirs, a "serious deficiency of the X-Article—perhaps the most serious of all—was the failure to make clear that what I was talking about when I mentioned the containment of Soviet power was not the containment by military means of a military threat, but the political containment of a political threat.''[71]

In a "traditional" or "orthodox" interpretation of the origins of the cold war, Arthur Schlesinger stressed three factors often de-emphasized or omitted in other assessments—"the intransigence of Leninist ideology, the sinister dynamics of a totalitarian society, and the madness of Stalin"—and concluded that "the Cold War could have been avoided only if the Soviet Union had not been possessed by convictions both of the infallibility of the communist word and of the inevitability of a communist world.''[72]

Directly addressing himself to Schlesinger, William Appleman Williams sharply criticized the view that Stalin's paranoia was "a primary operational factor" in the genesis of the Cold War.[73] Even if Stalin had been paranoid, Williams contended, other factors would be equally crucial to an accurate historical explanation of the Cold War's origins. For example, he observes that no major American policymaker in the mid-1940s seems to have perceived Stalin's paranoia and acted on this belief: in other words, the United States' policies and counterresponses were not adapted accordingly. Had flexible American initiatives failed because of Stalin's intransigence, this might well constitute indirect evidence of Stalin's "madness." But Williams concluded that Stalin was not intransigent and, considering American policies, Soviet actions cannot be accurately described as paranoid.

Christopher Lasch was particularly critical of the view that misunderstandings, misperceptions, and "communication problems" were major factors contributing to the inception and escalation of the Cold War.[74] Soviet leaders probably understood Western policies very well and had good reason to consider them hostile, Lasch implied. Indeed, revisionists argue that the primary goal of

American policy in 1945 was "to force the Soviet Union out of Eastern Europe," and Lasch would quite likely contend that this view gains considerable credence in light of Allied decisions at Teheran (November–December 1943), the Moscow "percentages" agreement (October 1944), the Allied armistice agreements with Rumania, Bulgaria, and Hungary (September 1944–January 1945), and the decisions, "nondecisions," and unresolved issues at Yalta (February 1945) and Potsdam (July–August 1945).

To the orthodox observer, the famous Yalta "Declaration on Liberated Europe" was a major Allied policy agreement that the Soviet Union repeatedly violated in subsequent months and years; to the "revisionist," this document was merely rhetoric intended for domestic consumption in the democracies, a statement whose real purpose was to mask previous explicit and implicit agreements regarding separate Allied "spheres of influence" in Western and Eastern Europe. Revisionist historians dare suggest that the American decision to drop atomic bombs on Japan may have been a show of force primarily intended to dislodge the Red Army from Eastern Europe and to renege on previous Allied agreements. Orthodox historians retort that this argument stands or falls on the crucial assumption that there was in fact "atomic diplomacy," and that no convincing evidence has been produced to confirm this because no such bargaining or threats took place.[75]

Most explanations of Cold War origins ignore the role of international Communism. Joseph Starobin has helped fill this gap by describing the real and "incipient" diversity in the nonruling Communist parties, "among whom the changes produced by the war had outmoded earlier ideological and political premises."[76] He noted, too, the apparent indecisiveness of Soviet policy toward this "nascent polycentrism" as late as 1947. Starobin argued that probably the most important single factor shaping Soviet foreign policy was Stalin's wish to unify and control the international Communist movement. To do this, the Soviet leader could hardly create close economic and political ties with the major "imperialist" and "colonial" states or accept greater ideological and institutional diversity within the USSR. All of these considerations were interrelated, and in many ways the policies chosen were logically consistent with one another. Each of these factors may well have contributed to Stalin's eventual decision to reconstruct the shattered Soviet economy in the time-tested autarkic manner, with assistance from the new satellite regimes in Eastern Europe, rather than await possible (but improbable) large-scale American assistance or German reparations.

In short, the implications of the Starobin argument are that American "hard-line" policies under President Truman may have made Stalin's basic decision somewhat easier, but that Western diplomacy and actions were probably not the decisive factor in shaping Soviet policy. Cooperation with the United States, "different roads to socialism" in the world Communist movement and in Eastern Europe, greater internal diversity at home were all new and untried paths. In time of war, these paths were worth exploring, and some had to be explored. In time of peace, old policies were less risky and probably more in line with Stalin's personal goals and those of other Soviet leaders. Above all, the Red Army remained in Eastern Europe, which it had occupied before the end of the war by virtue of its military victories over Nazi Germany and by explicit agreements with the other Allied powers. James F. Byrnes touched on a crucial issue when he said of Yalta, "It was not a question of what we would let the Russians do, but what we could get the Russians to do."[77]

EXTERNAL FACTORS: PEACEFUL COEXISTENCE AND DÉTENTE

Under Khrushchev and Brezhnev, Soviet analysts identified two epochs in the history of the USSR's foreign policy. In the first period, from 1917 to 1945, the USSR struggled alone to build a socialist society. Capitalist systems were dominant, Soviet Russia weak and vulnerable. In the second period, beginning with the defeat of German and Japanese fascism in World War II and the establishment of "people's democracies" in Eastern Europe, socialism became a regional and then a global system: "The cardinal feature of the second stage is that the world socialist community has firmly grasped the historical initiative."[78]

The essence of the second period, according to Soviet theorists, was "the shift of the correlation of forces in favor of socialism." A chief factor producing this shift was the disintegration of the capitalist colonial system. The weakening of direct Western political control over Asian and African countries meant that the Third World no longer played the role of a reserve and supply base for imperialism. Soviet writers concluded: "The formation of the socialist community and the appearance of new countries on the international political scene have fundamentally changed the balance of strength in the world. The possibilities of imperialists for pursuing an aggressive policy have narrowed substantially."[79]

"Peaceful coexistence" with the West was perceived to have passed through two phases, which paralleled the rise of the power of socialism. The first phase (1917–1953) was a *defensive* form of coexistence. Socialism had to be built and consolidated in the face of extreme hostility from the capitalist world. Soviet Russia, the first socialist state, was militarily and economically vulnerable and had to make the most of its very limited political and diplomatic resources. By contrast, the second phase was an *active* form of peaceful coexistence in which socialism was allegedly becoming the ascendant historical force. Under Stalin's successor, Nikita Khrushchev, peaceful coexistence became the cornerstone or "general line" of Soviet foreign policy. Under Leonid Brezhnev peaceful coexistence was temporarily reduced to equal status with other goals and principles, as it had been under Stalin and Lenin before him.

However, throughout the 1970s, peaceful coexistence—now more often referred to as "détente"—was returned to a central place in the theory and practice of Soviet foreign policy. With the winding down of the Vietnam War, Soviet leaders again viewed the expansion of East-West cooperation as possible and desirable, for the USSR's military power had protected—and would continue to protect—the socialist world from capitalist aggression: "Soviet foreign policy paralyzes the aggressive actions of the imperialists. The Soviet Union's immense military and economic potential serve the cause of peace."[80] In short, the newer active phase of peaceful coexistence was characterized by a growing Soviet capability (real and perceived) to influence the course of historical development in favor of socialism.

Soviet domestic and foreign policy initiatives, which were taking place in an increasingly complex international system, were becoming, by choice or circumstance, increasingly sensitive and responsive to external trends and conditions. The international behavior of the USSR was more and more shaped by an important objective force, which Soviet political leaders and social theorists termed "the scientific-technological revolution" (STR). Remarkable scientific, technical, and socioeconomic changes had indeed transformed capitalist and socialist societies and the relations between them since World War II. These changes have had both positive and negative consequences. On the one hand, the STR created pressures for a more efficient division of labor in the global economy and for international cooperation in a broad range of scientific and technological fields. On the other hand, the STR had produced the danger of thermonuclear warfare, not only among the superpowers but among lesser powers as well. For the first time in world history, nations had the power to annihilate one another and permanently to damage the earth and its environment. But the very destructiveness of modern weapons technology reduced the possible benefits of initiating an all-out war and thereby restraining potential aggressors. Civil defense programs notwithstanding, there were not likely to be "winners" after a nuclear exchange.

It was to Khrushchev's and Brezhnev's credit that they not only recognized this fact, but adjusted the Soviet concept and policy of peaceful coexistence accordingly. As a Soviet writer declared in 1975: "In the nuclear age, peaceful coexistence of the socialist and capitalist countries is dictated by the objective necessity of social development. Wars of plunder and conquest cannot be a method of settling international disputes. History poses the problem thusly: either peaceful coexistence or a catastrophic thermonuclear world war."[81]

Soviet analysts did not maintain that the avoidance of nuclear war through a policy of peaceful coexistence signified the reconciliation of capitalism and socialism. Peaceful coexistence and détente, in Soviet theory and practice, consisted of both competition (conflict) *and* cooperation with major Western nations: "The contradiction between socialism and capitalism has been and remains the principal contradiction of our epoch. A political, economic, and ideological struggle has been and will continue to be waged between them."[82]

Throughout the Khrushchev and Brezhnev periods differing views of détente in the East and West, and differing views of détente within and among the major Western powers, seriously undermined Soviet-American cooperation. Relations between the United States and USSR deteriorated to the point where two

American presidents rejected the very term "détente," and Soviet leaders felt they had little to lose by American displeasure over the forceful occupation of Afghanistan in 1979, the first overt use of Soviet military power outside the Soviet bloc since World War II. One important consequence of this Soviet action was an immediate stepping-up of the Soviet-American arms race. Both sides then placed renewed emphasis on developing new military technologies that would offset the other's offensive and defensive capabilities. And both sides more vigorously pursued geopolitical advantages (e.g., in the Persian Gulf and the Horn of Africa) to preserve or enhance their perceived security and economic interests.

But the Brezhnev collective leadership did not abandon peaceful coexistence. In the Soviet view, active coexistence consisted of various combinations of competition and cooperation. Depending on the circumstances, Soviet policy-makers placed greater or less emphasis on *expanding* the areas of East-West cooperation, and on the *extent* of cooperation with *various* Western partners, especially the United States, Western Europe, and Japan. As a Soviet analyst, buttressing his authoritative interpretation with quotes from Brezhnev, asserted shortly after the Soviet occupation of Afghanistan:

> Detente . . . has demonstrated its viability and stability. It advances thanks to its profoundly objective, historical basis, thanks to the political forces of our time, *including the policies of certain Western countries*, which realistically see the mainstream of history and work for the triumph of detente, for peace and securi-ty. . . . *There is no reasonable alternative to detente in present-day international relations.* It is noteworthy that in the complex situation of the beginning of 1980 the Soviet Union found it necessary to reaffirm its confidence in the vitality of detente. . . . Detente is an absolutely necessary and indispensable prerequisite for any constructive approach to the solution of crucial world issues."[83]

Briefly stated, Soviet writers usually emphasized the following three basic principles of peaceful coexistence and détente: (1) the repudiation of nuclear war as a means of resolving political disputes between industrialized capitalist and socialist countries; (2) the expansion of mutually advantageous cooperation between capitalism and socialism; and (3) the recognition of national sovereignty and noninterference in the internal affairs of other nations.[84] Unlike most West-erners, Soviet officials do not find this third principle incompatible with Soviet military and economic support for promising "national liberation movements" in Third World countries. Raymond Garthoff (Chapter 3) more fully examines the official Soviet view of détente.

In the closing years of the Brezhnev period, did the active phase of Soviet foreign policy revolve primarily around the inevitability of confrontation be-tween capitalism and socialism, while avoiding nuclear war, or did it give considerable emphasis to the expansion and deepening of cooperation with the West? Serious disagreements existed in the United States and Western Europe concerning which element—competition or cooperation—was and should be predominant in the current phase of East-West relations. Those arguments of the 1970s and early 1980s are worth examining in some detail, because they are quite relevant to present Western debates over the significance of *perestroika* and new political thinking for Soviet international behavior. The current debate is examined in detail by several contributors to our companion volume, *Contemporary Issues in Soviet Foreign Policy*.

One school of thought in the Richard Nixon, Jimmy Carter, and Ronald Reagan administrations emphasized that Soviet concepts of détente and peaceful coexistence were merely tactical in nature. The Soviet Union, it was argued, wanted to cooperate with Western nations only in areas to its advantage and to the disadvantage of capitalism. The inevitability of military competition, Soviet territorial expansion, and violent conflict between East and West—occasionally direct, but more often by proxy forces—were underscored.

Another Western school of thought emphasized that the current stage of détente represented a strategic shift in soviet thinking. These American and West European analysts contended that the USSR seriously sought to avoid nuclear war, had accepted the need to channel historical conflict into nonmilitary forms of competition, and was striving to broaden and deepen East-West cooperation in various fields. American receptivity to these initiatives, it was argued, would in due course mitigate the "siege mentality" of Soviet leaders and restrain the USSR from using its newly developed military might throughout the world. U.S.-Soviet collaboration on global and bilateral issues, together with regularized competition in economic, military, and political spheres, could increasingly supersede confrontation and defuse international tensions.

Influential advocates of the first position were Zbigniew Brzezinski, President Carter's national security advisor, and Richard Pipes, President Reagan's first senior Sovietologist in the National Security Council. In their writings, Brzezinski and especially Pipes stressed the historical continuity in the Soviet policy of peaceful coexistence.[85] Whereas in earlier periods peaceful coexistence was a tactic to protect the Soviet Union from outside invasion, peaceful coexistence was now a tactic to promote Soviet ascendancy in the international arena.

The 1970s Soviet policy of détente, in this view, had several dimensions. Economically, détente was designed to compensate for Soviet weaknesses in technology, organization, manpower, and labor incentives, without risking potentially destabilizing reforms of existing party and state institutions and institutional relationships. While modernizing the USSR's economic system and increasing industrial and agricultural productivity, the Brezhnev administration allegedly sought to maximize the dependence of the West on Soviet raw materials, especially in the energy area.

Politically and militarily, the goals of détente were to gain international recognition of the USSR's superpower status, to extend Soviet influence throughout the world, to consolidate the domestic political order, and to sustain the weapons and troop buildup in the USSR. In addition to efforts to upset the balance of strategic and conventional forces in Western Europe, the highest Party officials were thought to have placed a premium on the capacity to mount flexible military interventions in Third world countries. Also, détente was designed to enable the Soviet Union to become directly involved in influencing Western policy. This influence was to be achieved by promoting the image of the USSR as a peace-loving power and a responsible business partner, thereby validating the arguments of Western (e.g., Eurocommunist) opponents of capitalist military-industrial complexes, and reducing the West European nations' political, economic, and military dependence upon the United States.

In contrast, Marshall Shulman, chief advisor on Soviet affairs to Carter's Secretary of State Cyrus Vance, and Princeton University professor Robert C. Tucker were major proponents of a second orientation.[86] Shulman and especially Tucker argued that the then current phase of peaceful coexistence represented a historic shift in the foreign policy of the Soviet Union toward cooperation with the West. While recognizing the continued presence of competitive elements in East-West relations, Shulman and Tucker stressed considerably more than did Brzezinski and Pipes the possibility and desirability of broadening and deepening the cooperative aspects of détente.

Shulman, in particular, was sensitive to the ongoing political debates within the Soviet elite regarding the nature and effectiveness of détente. Conservatives feared the abandonment of self-sufficiency; centrists sought to strengthen authoritarian planning and management through greater involvement in the global economy; and reformers hoped that economic decentralization would promote domestic productivity and growth and a broad range of interdependent relations with the capitalist and developing nations. For Shulman, the expansion of East-West ties could help both the Soviet and American economies. The ability to compete economically in the developed world and to penetrate global markets was an important dimension of power that the USSR and the United States could no longer minimize. Also, better trade relations could provide incentives for improved political relations, including the possibility of Soviet restraint, and even of cooperative efforts to reduce tensions, in selected Third World trouble spots.

The nuclear weapons race provided an important source of Soviet-American conflict and cooperation. Brzezinski and Shulman, as members of the Carter administration, both supported the Strategic Arms Limitation Treaty (SALT). Arms control negotiations, and SALT in particular, were founded on the recognition of the increasing interdependence of American and Soviet security interests. For example, the United States and the USSR were seen to have a common interest in preventing nuclear war and the proliferation of nuclear weapons among middle-sized and Third World countries. But Shulman, more than Brzezinski, stressed the complementarity of American and Soviet security needs, and the mutual benefits of diverting scarce resources to the nonmilitary sectors of their respective economies. Finally, the broadening of scientific and technical cooperation, such as in the environmental, energy-related, and medical areas, provided other possible channels for mutually beneficial accords between the

Soviet Union and the West. In short, while competition remained central to East-West relations, pressures for cooperation were becoming a significant reality as well. Agreed-upon modes of competition and active collaboration in key fields were deemed a necessity, if wars were to be avoided and peaceful change was to be ensured.

The strength of Pipes's position rested upon three basic aspects of Soviet behavior during the period of détente launched in the early 1970s. First, the Soviet Union had conducted a strategic and conventional arms buildup since the mid 1960s. Second, Soviet leaders had excluded from the détente relationship conflict between the USSR and the West in the developing world. Third, repression of dissidents and "loyal oppositionists" in the Soviet Union had accompanied détente in the international arena.

But the weakness of Pipes's position and the concomitant strength of Shulman's was that, the vestiges of the cold war conflict notwithstanding, Soviet officials and theorists were well aware that the relationship between domestic and foreign policies and the very nature of international politics were undergoing major transformations. That is, Soviet analysts understood that socioeconomic conditions within the USSR and the national interests of capitalist and communist nations were dramatically changing under the impact of the forces of advanced modernization—a worldwide process the Soviets referred to as "the scientific-technological revolution." Hence, détente in the 1970s was shaped by evolving Soviet perspectives on the STR and "developed socialism," on the changing international political and economic systems, and on the interrelationships among these complex and dynamic clusters of variables.

Significantly, Soviet reformers linked domestic modernization—especially economic growth and productivity—with improved East-West and North-South relations in the era of the STR. A new Soviet approach to international politics was emerging—an approach that was rooted in a better understanding of advanced modernization, and that was oriented toward much broader and deeper interaction with the West (the United States *and/or* Western Europe and Japan) than had been legitimate in earlier periods of Soviet history. Soviet analysts were arguing that a new era had just begun in which the USSR must substantially increase cooperation with the highly industrialized capitalist nations in order to develop the capabilities of the Soviet economy and polity in rapidly changing conditions, and to compete more effectively for economic and political advantage over those very same nations. In short, a strategic shift in Soviet thinking about détente had begun, and it had progressed even farther in the policy and academic communities than Shulman himself suggested.

Although this gradual reorientation was portentous, the Soviet approach to international politics still emphasized East-West competition much more than cooperation. For example, the aging Brezhnev administration made the highly unfortunate decision to prop up a faltering Marxist regime in Afghanistan by sending in the Red Army, thereby abandoning détente with the United States for the immediate future, risking the deterioration of political and commercial relations with Western Europe and Japan, and eliciting the condemnation of the entire Islamic world. Also, Brezhnev and his Politburo colleagues threatened to quash the Solidarity trade union movement in Poland with Soviet troops, if the Polish party-government did not do so itself by imposing martial law.

However, what Soviet reformers perceived to be changing were the sources, ground rules, and geographical and substantive areas of competition and cooperation needed to promote the modernization of the USSR and its allies in Eastern Europe and elsewhere. As Georgii Shakhnazarov, then head of the Soviet Political Sciences Association and more recently a top advisor to Mikhail Gorbachev, asserted in 1977:

> It is a distinctive feature of the present historical moment that the interests of survival, the scientific and technological revolution, and all the other objective trends of social development operate in such a way as to draw peoples and countries closer together and prompt them to solve the problems of mankind through common efforts, while at the same time the struggle between the two social systems continues to unfold.[87]

These competing pressures and trends were the subject of greatly increased debate among Soviet policymakers and analysts after Brezhnev's death in 1982.

PROSPECT AND RETROSPECT: CONTINUITY AND CHANGE IN THE NATURE AND USES OF SOVIET POWER

Predicting the future course of Soviet foreign policy has been a concern of statespersons, scholars, and media analysts for many decades. While some pundits have been correct in their prognostications, many more have been wrong. In the preceding discussion, we have seen that various authors have presented arguments emphasizing the importance of one or more sets of factors—for example, internal factors such as Soviet ideology and external factors such as American foreign policy—that may explain events, phases, or trends in Soviet international behavior—for example, Soviet negotiating behavior, the origins of the Cold War, and the nature of "peaceful coexistence" and détente.

We turn now to a discussion of two major sets of issues: (1) the extent of continuity and change between Stalinist and post-Stalinist Soviet foreign policy, and (2) the relative impact of internal and external factors on Soviet international behavior. A careful analysis of these issues will provide the reader with a fuller understanding of what we know and do not know about Soviet activities abroad, and why they may have been undertaken. This analysis may also help scholars and policymakers discern underlying patterns in Soviet thinking and behavior, and thereby anticipate and influence Soviet actions. But we do not claim to possess any secret formula that will enable one to predict Soviet initiatives and responses in the international arena in the months and years ahead. If anything, wisdom lies in a deeper appreciation of what we do not and cannot know about complex and ever-changing psychological and operational environments at home and abroad (see Figure 1).

Following the dictum that those who ignore the errors of the past are doomed to repeat them, many students of Soviet society have attempted to identify elements of continuity and change in the foreign policy of the USSR. As illustrated by a 1980 debate between Charles Gati and William Zimmerman, there are great differences of opinion on this question. Gati, comparing the Stalinist and post-Stalinist periods, concluded that the elements of continuity are much more significant than the elements of change. In Gati's view, Soviet Russia is a pragmatic and cautious power that has, since its inception in 1917, pursued both the competitive and cooperative aspects of peaceful coexistence and détente. Gati affirmed:

> If there has been a basic pattern in Soviet foreign policy from Lenin to Brezhnev, it is characterized by the persistent, though cautious, pursuit of opportunities abroad—"persistent" because the overall objective of advancing Soviet influence has not changed and "cautious" because the Soviet leaders have sought to promote Soviet influence so gradually as to make strong and concerted Western counter-measures unjustifiable. [88]

Zimmerman directly challenged this view. [89] He contended that since the death of Stalin there have been important changes in the *substance* of Soviet foreign policy, as well as in the *processes* by which it has been made and carried out. While Gati affirmed that Soviet international behavior was a "mix of assertiveness and accommodation," Zimmerman found this characterization to be of little use in analyzing continuity and change. Zimmerman maintained that Gati's argument was so general that it failed to recognize the shifts in emphasis between competition and cooperation, and that it obscured some fundamental changes in Soviet motivations, perspectives, and behavior during the Khrushchev and Brezhnev periods. Hence, Zimmerman concluded that change rather than continuity was the hallmark of post-Stalin foreign policy.

Identifying and assessing the importance of various internal and external influences on Soviet foreign policy was of great importance in this debate. Gati examined three *internal* factors that shape Soviet policy and behavior: (1) "the substantially increased relative power of the Soviet Union since Stalin's reign," (2) "the apparent decline of ideological rigidity," and (3) "the broadening of the decisionmaking process since Stalin, including the rise of elite factions and competing interests."

Analyzing the first factor, Gati argued that neither domestic weakness nor strength could be correlated with an assertive or an accommodative foreign policy. Assessing the second factor, he seriously questioned whether a dogmatic ideological environment would necessarily lead to foreign policy assertiveness, and whether a decline in ideological zeal would lead to foreign policy accommodation. As for the third factor, Gati maintained that we simply cannot assume that a narrowing of the decision-making process and its informational base will produce an assertive foreign policy. Nor can we infer that a broadening of the decision-making process and its informational base will produce an accommodative policy. Hence, Gati concluded that there was insufficient evidence to support broad generalizations about the domestic influences on the foreign policy of the USSR.

In contrast, Zimmerman found at least one major area in which there was probably a clear-cut linkage between the Soviet policymaking process and Soviet international behavior. Zimmerman emphasized that there had been a dramatic increase in both the quantity and quality of Soviet research on foreign affairs since 1956. Newly established organizations, the most prominent of which were the Institute of the World Economy and International Relations and the Institute of the United States and Canada, had conducted many policy-relevant studies of international politics and economics. Zimmerman viewed this increased Soviet research capacity as a major "structural adaptation," which was based on the recognition by both Khrushchev and Brezhnev that "Stalin's policies were inadequate partly because they were uninformed," and that "low-information systems are low-performance systems."[90] Indeed, the Khrushchev and Brezhnev administrations gathered vastly greater information about the outside world than did Stalin's, and some of this information was utilized in the formulation and implementation of foreign policy.

But for what *purposes* was this information being used, and what *effects* was it having on the thinking and behavior of the Soviet leadership? These were the key questions. Zimmerman believed that the greater knowledge and sophistication of Soviet officials were reshaping their "psychological environment" (see Figure 1), and that these evolving elite images and beliefs, in turn, were apparently having a moderating influence on Soviet policy and behavior. For example, Zimmerman would probably maintain that Khrushchev and Brezhnev placed much greater emphasis on East-West cooperation and interdependence than did Stalin, and that Khrushchev's and especially Brezhnev's informed and differentiated perspectives on the Third World helped to produce many diplomatic and economic ties where none existed previously.[91]

Gati, Alexander Dallin,[92] and others would agree that Soviet foreign policy was increasingly based on significantly more and better information about international relations and about the polities, economies, and societies of other nations. Gati would be likely to argue, however, that institutional changes in a political system do not necessarily produce changes in the attitudes and behavior of its leaders, let alone attitudinal and behavioral changes of a conciliatory or cooperative nature in foreign policy. And Gati would conclude that increased information had sometimes led to the irresponsible use of this greater power, as in Hungary in 1956, Cuba in 1962, Czechoslovakia in 1968, and various Third World countries in the 1970s.

The role of information in Soviet policymaking is important because it can shed some light on the Western debate about the extent to which the foreign policy of the USSR was, is, and can be influenced by *external* factors. The Khrushchev and particularly the Brezhnev administrations valued more timely and accurate information about the USSR's complex and changing international and domestic environments. But Gati criticized Zimmerman's hypothesis that more sophisticated Soviet perspectives on world events would help to restrain the USSR's assertiveness, and that accommodative Soviet international behavior could be encouraged by the diplomatic activities of Western nations, especially a "strong and reassuring," rather than a "weak and threatening," American posture toward the USSR. Gati argued that, while the West could alter Soviet policies in marginal ways, "there is good reason to be skeptical about the possibility of achieving 'a lasting adaptation' in Soviet foreign policy as a consequence of external influences."[93] In his view, a more knowledgeable and experienced Soviet elite was likely to utilize these capabilities to seize low-risk and low-cost geopolitical opportunities in the international system and to strengthen rather than reform the centralized domestic political and economic systems.

Helmut Sonnenfeldt, a top Soviet specialist in the Nixon-Kissinger administration, would probably agree with at least part of Gati's conclusion. Sonnenfeldt argued in 1978 that "experience does not bear out the hope that acts of American self-restraint induce reciprocal acts by the Soviets; on the contrary, they tend to make negotiations more difficult."[94] For example, Sonnenfeldt maintained that "external powers, notably the United States, have had little ability to influence the growth of Soviet military power."[95] Sonnenfeldt concluded that the drive to amass military power was a major element of continuity in the foreign policy of the USSR and "seems pervasive among the Soviet ruling elite regardless of generation."[96]

At the same time, Sonnenfeldt was convinced that the United States could and must try to influence the role the USSR plays in the world. One thing American policies can do is to "maximize the restraints upon the uses of Soviet power."[97] Sonnenfeldt believed that the "gradual emergence of the USSR from isolation" was an important precondition for the greater impact of external factors on Soviet policy and actions. An important example would be the formulation and implementation of an American and West European "economic strategy that uses Soviet needs to draw the USSR into the disciplines of international economic life."[98] Sonnenfeldt affirmed that "it would be both desirable and feasible for Western nations to evolve harmonized concepts in [many] respects, with the goal of reducing the autarkic nature of Soviet economic decisionmaking and complicating Soviet resource choices."[99]

Sonnenfeldt suggested that there were at least seven specific issue areas in which the external environment could have some effect on Soviet policy. All of these areas transcend territorial boundaries and must be reckoned with in Soviet policy calculations: (1) currency fluctuations and inflationary trends beyond Soviet borders, (2) global energy shortages and price rises, (3) the spread of nuclear weapons and nuclear manufacturing capabilities around the world, (4) the industrial and agricultural development of the oceans, (5) the exploration and commercial use of outer space, (6) the need to curb environmental pollution, and (7) international civil aviation.

Since the USSR is a major part of an increasingly interdependent world, all seven of these factors are bound to have an impact on Soviet foreign policy *and* on Soviet domestic development. Indeed, Sonnenfeldt concluded that "in these and other ways, the Soviet Union has slowly and often grudgingly accepted foreign constraints on its freedom of action."[100]

Opportunity as well as adversity, and choice as well as circumstance, are increasingly compelling all industrialized nations to participate more actively in the international community. Robert Keohane and Joseph Nye, two American political scientists, argued that a nation's *sensitivity* and *vulnerability* to external influences are very important dimensions of power and interdependence:

> Sensitivity means liability to costly effects imposed from outside before policies are altered to try to change the situation. Vulnerability can be defined as an actor's liability to suffer costs imposed by external events even after policies have been altered. . . . Sensitivity interdependence can be social or political as well as economic. . . . The vulnerability dimension of interdependence rests on the relative availability and costliness of the alternatives that various actors face.[101]

In other words, a nation's openness to external influences may be a strength or a weakness, and permeability does not necessarily produce malleability. Much depends on a country's capacity to respond purposefully and effectively to the constructive opportunities and problems posed by the international environment. Conversely, external forces may penetrate a closed society with great difficulty, but have a considerable impact when they do. In any case, criteria and standards for assessing the sensitivity and vulnerability of a nation are essential to understanding the influence of external factors on its domestic and foreign policies.

Writing in 1977, Robert Legvold developed these insights and suggested that a nation's power was "increasingly a matter of managing interdependence and, therefore, increasingly a matter of the structure and range of one's dependencies. To be positioned at the intersection of numerous and different forms of interdependence is power—unless too many of them are seriously unequal."[102] He went on to argue that the international setting had changed so much in the past three decades that the United States found itself in "a world in which fewer and fewer of our problems are caused by the Soviet Union or can be solved by it, save for the ultimate matter of nuclear war."[103] Legvold identified five major elements of change in the international system: (1) the transformation of alliances, (2) the exponential growth of interdependence, (3) the collapse of the old economic order and the challenges confronting a new one, (4) the regionalization of international politics, and (5) the changing strategic and conventional military balance between the two superpowers.

Of particular relevance to our present discussion are the second and third

elements of change. By emphasizing the economic as well as the military
dimensions of power, Legvold affirmed that the increasingly interdependent
world and the changing international economic order "have made the issue of
national security far more complex than defending the integrity of one's territory
and political values. Increasingly, the stake is also in the security of foreign
markets and key resources, in the freedom from economically dislocating external price increases, and even in the success of other governments' domestic
programs."[104]

Legvold suggested that in the existing international system "the Soviet-
American rivalry has now evolved into something less intensive and something
more extensive."[105] Because of the USSR's greatly increased military capabilities and its growing economic needs, party leaders in the 1970s and 1980s
were shifting from a "preoccupation [with] the struggle to secure Soviet power
against the external world to a quest for a larger place in it."[106] Also, "the
elusiveness of opportunity in U.S.-USSR relations" and "the distractions of
multiple international challenges" had induced the Soviet leadership to focus its
hopes and fears less on the United States and more on Western and Eastern
Europe, China, and the Third World.

Writing in the same year (1977) as Sonnenfeldt and Legvold, Vernon Aspaturian saw the USSR "increasingly drawn into the intersection vortex of the
various international environments in which it acts,"[107] and projected that Soviet
policy would be more and more affected by external influences. But Aspaturian
disagreed somewhat with Sonnenfeldt, Legvold, and others about the primary
reasons for those developments and about the relative importance of specific
external factors that shape Soviet behavior. Aspaturian viewed the mounting
Soviet assertiveness in the Third World (especially in the 1970s) as largely the
result of diminishing American power and the will to use that power. While
Soviet military capabilities increased greatly in the 1960s and 1970s, the "withering" of American "global reflexes" made it possible for the USSR to use
those capabilities to support pro-Russian elements in selected Third World
countries.

Yet, Aspaturian argued, the current low costs and risks of an assertive Soviet
foreign policy did not make such a policy inevitable. Indeed, he thought these
costs and risks would become much greater in the coming decades, increasing
the possibility of moderation in Soviet foreign policy. He observed that the
changing international environment and internal economic difficulties presented
the USSR with a very important choice. Should the party leadership "step up its
militancy in foreign policy," or should it "reallocate priorities and pay greater
attention to chronic and serious domestic problems, now that such a shift would
not be at the expense of either lessened defense or a reduction of diplomatic
gains"?[108] On these and other key issues, top Soviet leaders had differing views,
and their disagreements greatly intensified after Brezhnev's demise.

Sonnenfeldt stressed the importance of the domestic and international pressures on the USSR to participate responsibly in mutually advantageous econom-

ic, political, and arms limitation ties with the major Western industrialized states, including cooperative efforts to solve the global problems described above. But while contending that American policies and diplomacy can have only marginal effects on Soviet behavior, Sonnenfeldt implied that the USSR's sensitivity to external factors was greater than its vulnerability. The diminishing ability of the United States to influence Soviet policies was seen largely as the result of the growing economic and political power of Western Europe and Japan, of the multipolar nature of the emerging international system, and of the USSR's increasing military might. In contrast, Aspaturian emphasized the centrality of the Soviet-American relationship and the continuing ability of the two superpowers to influence each other and other nations by action and inaction. Aspaturian placed particular stress on the strategic balance between the United States and the Soviet Union, which he viewed as "the single most important equation in the international community today." He also observed that

One of the unnoticed by-products of Soviet-American global rivalry has been the increasingly interpenetrative character of Soviet-American relations, which could no longer be characterized as simply the intersection of foreign policy outputs. Both powers are intimately concerned and have become progressively implicated in the domestic affairs of one another and seek in diverse yet unevenly effective ways to influence domestic events and conditions."[109]

Aspaturian concluded that "The American domestic condition emerges as one of the most significant changes in the external environment and appears to be having a fundamental impact on the perception of Soviet leaders with respect to future Soviet behavior."[110]

In 1947, George Kennan (Chapter 12) forcefully argued that external factors—namely, containment of Soviet expansion—would have a profound impact on the Soviet Union. This impact would be twofold: in the short run, it would lead to a change in Soviet foreign policy because the Soviet leadership would not risk armed conflict with the United States in order to further its expansionist plans; in the long run, this would result in a mellowing of the Soviet regime internally. Kennan was a member of the realist school (what Herrmann in Chapter 7 calls Theory 2: Realpolitik Expansionism) in that he viewed Soviet foreign policy as driven by "normal" great power considerations of influence and security, rather than by peculiarly Soviet ideological goals of world domination.

From the perspective of mid-1990, it appeared that Kennan was correct. From the perspective of early 1991, the picture was much less clear. For the first five years of Gorbachev's leadership, there was a dramatic mellowing of both Soviet foreign and domestic policies. *Perestroika* was accompanied by *glasnost* and *demokratizatsiia* (the deepening of democracy through a multiparty system and open elections). Innovative political thinking in foreign policy brought the destruction of the Berlin Wall, the collapse of East European communist regimes, and the reduction of nuclear and conventional weapons systems. But eventually Gorbachev tightened domestic controls, including a military crack-down in several republics, and conservative elements called for a more assertive foreign policy, including retention of Soviet forces in Eastern Europe. Briefly stated, the Soviet liberation of its East European empire was not immediately followed by the liberation of its internal empire. To Western eyes, these develop-ments were logically inconsistent. To more and more Soviet eyes (including Gorbachev's), they were logically consistent, for the virtually simultaneous liberation of both empires was deemed neither feasible nor desirable.

These reforms and initial reversals apparently resulted from growing contra-dictions in the Soviet position that was characterized a decade ago by Seweryn Bialer as "the Soviet paradox": external expansion combined with internal decline. While many leading Sovietologists acknowledged the existence of these trends, William Taubman (Chapter 13) points out that there was in the mid-1980s "still plenty of disagreement about the meaning of the two trends, and especially about the connection between them." Taubman's review of five major works published between 1983 and 1986 indicates the state of our knowledge on these questions through the first year of *perestroika*. Now, after more than a half decade of experience with *perestroika*—probably the most dynamic period of Soviet history since 1917—analysts continue to debate the nature of Soviet foreign policy and the relative impact of internal and external factors on Soviet foreign policy and international behavior. Those diverse assessments are pre-sented in our companion volume, *Contemporary Issues in Soviet Foreign Policy*.

NOTES

1. William Glaser, "Theories of Soviet Foreign Policy: A Classification of the Literature," *World Affairs Quarterly*, XXVII, 2 (July 1956), pp. 127–152. See also Daniel Bell, "Ten Theories in Search of Reality," *World Politics*, X, 3 (April 1958), pp. 327–65.

2. Richard Brody and John Vesecky, "Soviet Openness to Changing Situations: A Critical Evaluation of Certain Hypotheses about Soviet Foreign Policy Behavior," in Jan Triska (ed.), *Communist Party-States: Comparative and International Studies* (Indi-anapolis: Bobbs-Merrill, 1969), pp. 353–85. See also William Welch, *American Images of Soviet Foreign Policy* (New Haven, CT: Yale University Press, 1970).

3. John G. Gunnell, "The Idea of the Conceptual Framework: A Philosophical Critique," *Journal of Comparative Administration*, I, 2 (August 1969), p. 165. On the controversial subject of the nature and functions of theories and models, see, for example, Abraham Kaplan, *The Conduct of Inquiry* (San Francisco: Chandler, 1964).

4. Graham Allison, "Conceptual Models and the Cuban Missile Crisis," *American Political Science Review*, LXIII, 3 (September, 1969), pp. 689–718. See also James Rosenau, "Foreign Policy as Adaptive Behavior: Some Preliminary Notes for a Theoreti-cal Model," *Comparative Politics*, II, 3 (April 1970), pp. 365–87; K. J. Holsti, "Nation-al Role Conceptions in the Study of Foreign Policy," *International Studies Quarterly*, XIV, 3 (September 1970), pp. 233–309; and Roger Hilsman, *The Politics of Policy Making in Defense and Foreign Affairs* (Englewood Cliffs, NJ: Prentice-Hall, 1987).

5.   For example, see Hans Morgenthau, *Politics among Nations*, 6th ed. (New York: Knopf, 1985); Joseph Frankel, *The Making of Foreign Policy* (London: Oxford University Press, 1963); and Arnold Horelick and Myron Rush, *Strategic Power and Soviet Foreign Policy* (Chicago: University of Chicago Press, 1966).

6.   Carl Linden, *Khrushchev and the Soviet Leadership, 1957–1964* (Baltimore: The Johns Hopkins Press, 1966); and Michel Tatu, *Power in the Kremlin from Khrushchev to Kosygin* (New York: Viking, 1969).

7.   Allison, "Conceptual Models, and the Cuban Missile Crisis," p. 693.

8.   See Frederic J. Fleron, Jr., "Introduction," and Erik P. Hoffmann, "Methodological Problems of Kremlinology," in Frederic J. Fleron, Jr. (ed.), *Communist Studies and the Social Sciences: Essays on Methodology and Empirical Theory* (Chicago: Rand McNally, 1969), pp. 1–33, 129–49. Also see Alexander George, *Propaganda Analysis* (Evanston, IL: Row, Peterson, 1959).

9.   For elaboration of this research design and statement with some preliminary findings supported by quantitative data, see Michael Brecher, Blema Steinberg, and Janice Stein, "A Framework for Research on Foreign Policy Behavior," *The Journal of Conflict Resolution*, XIII, 1 (March 1969), p. 80. On the nature of "issue areas," see James Rosenau, "Foreign Policy as an Issue-Area," in James Rosenau (ed.), *Domestic Sources of Foreign Policy* (New York: Free Press, 1967), pp. 11–50; and James Rosenau, "Pre-theories and Theories of Foreign Policy," in R. Barry Farrell (ed.), *Approaches to Comparative and International Politics* (Evanston, IL: Northwestern University Press, 1966), pp. 27–92.

10.   Brecher et al., "A Framework for Research on Foreign Policy Behavior," p. 82.

11.   Ibid., p. 83.

12.   Ibid.

13.   Michael Brecher, *The Foreign Policy System of Israel: Setting, Images, Process* (New Haven, CT: Yale University Press, 1972), Chapter 1; *Decisions in Israel's Foreign Policy* (London: Oxford University Press, 1974), Introduction; and *Israel, the Korean War and China: Images, Decisions and Consequences* (Jerusalem: Jerusalem Academic Press, 1974).

14.   Brecher et al., "Framework for Research on Foreign Policy Behavior," p. 81.

15.   For an analysis of many of these same questions that does not utilize systems theory, see Harold and Margaret Sprout, *The Ecological Perspective on Human Affairs with Special Reference to International Politics* (Princeton, NJ: Princeton University Press, 1965).

16.   Brecher et al., "A Framework for Research on Foreign Policy Behavior," pp. 80, 87.

17.   See, for example, Frederic J. Fleron, Jr. (ed.), *Communist Studies and the Social Sciences: Essays on Methodology and Empirical Theory*, especially the editor's introduction; and Roger E. Kanet (ed.), *The Behavioral Revolution and Communist Studies: Applications of Behaviorally Oriented Political Research on the Soviet Union and Eastern Europe* (New York: Free Press, 1971). For a recent reexamination of these issues, see Alexander Motyl, *Sovietology, Rationality, Nationality: Coming to Grips with Nationalism in the USSR* (New York: Columbia University Press, 1990), especially the Introduction ("The Dilemmas of Sovietology") and Chapter 1 ("The Labyrinth of Theory").

18.   Alexander Dallin, "The Domestic Sources of Soviet Foreign Policy," in Seweryn Bialer (ed.), *The Domestic Context of Soviet Foreign Policy* (Boulder, CO: Westview Press, 1981), p. 343.

19.   James Rosenau, "Introduction," in Rosenau (ed.), *Domestic Sources of Foreign Policy*, p. 2. See also Henry Kissinger, "Domestic Structure and Foreign Policy," in James Rosenau (ed.), *International Relations and Foreign Policy* (New York: Free Press, 1969), pp. 261–75.

20.   The essays included in Bialer, *The Domestic Context of Soviet Foreign Policy*, constitute the most comprehensive analysis of the subject published by Western scholars up to that time.

21.   See Edward Morse, "The Transformation of Foreign Policies: Modernization, Interdependence, and Externalization," *World Politics*, XXII, 3 (April 1970), pp. 371–92.

22.   This issue is explored by Condoleezza Rice in Chapter 7 of our *Contemporary Issues in Soviet Foreign Policy*. For other recent commentaries on this trend under Gorbachev, see Walter C. Clemens, Jr., "Inside Gorbachev's Think Tank," *World Monitor* (August 1989), pp. 28–36; Scott R. Atkinson, *Soviet Defense Policy Under Gorbachev: The Growing Civilian Influence* (Alexandria, VA: Center for Naval Analyses, 1990); Eberhard Schneider, "Soviet Foreign-Policy Think Tanks," *The Washington Quarterly* 11, 2 (Spring 1988), pp. 145–55; and Bruce Parrott, "Soviet National Security Policy Under Gorbachev," *Problems of Communism*, XXXVII, 6 (1988), p. 35. For a discussion of this general trend prior to the Gorbachev era, see Alexander Dallin, "The Domestic Sources of Soviet Foreign Policy," in Bialer (ed.), *The Domestic Context of Soviet Foreign Policy*, esp. pp. 348–50.

23.   Sidney I. Ploss, "Studying the Domestic Determinants of Soviet Foreign Policy," *Canadian Slavic Studies*, I, 1 (Spring 1967), pp. 44–59. Reprinted in Hoffmann and Fleron (eds.), *The Conduct of Soviet Foreign Policy*, pp. 76–90.

24.   Lester Milbrath, "Interest Groups and Foreign Policy," in Rosenau (ed.), *Domestic Sources of Foreign Policy*, p. 251.

25.   See John A. Armstrong, "The Domestic Roots of Soviet Foreign Policy," *International Affairs*, XLI, 1 (January 1965), pp. 37–47. This article was reprinted in Hoffmann and Fleron (eds.), *The Conduct of Soviet Foreign Policy*, pp. 50–60. Also see Richard Pipes, "Domestic Politics and Foreign Affairs," in Ivo Lederer (ed.), *Russian Foreign Policy: Essays in Historical Perspective* (New Haven, CT: Yale University Press, 1962), pp. 145–69.

26.   Alexander Dallin, "Soviet Foreign Policy and Domestic Politics: A Framework for Analysis," *Journal of International Affairs*, XXIII, 2 (1969), pp. 250–65; and Linden, *Khrushchev and the Soviet Leadership*. See also Dallin, "The Domestic Sources of Soviet Foreign Policy," pp. 335–408.

27.   Vernon V. Aspaturian, "Internal Politics and Foreign Policy in the Soviet System," in Farrell (ed.), *Approaches to Comparative and International Politics*, p. 230. Also see Linden, *Khrushchev and the Soviet Leadership*. The most recent statement by Aspaturian on this and other related issues can be found in Vernon V. Aspaturian, "Soviet Foreign Policy," in Roy C. Macridis (ed.), *Foreign Policy in World Politics: States and Regions*, 7th ed. (Englewood Cliffs, NJ: Prentice-Hall, 1989), pp. 181–250.

28.   See Linden, *Khrushchev and the Soviet Leadership*, and Aspaturian, "Internal Politics and Foreign Policy in the Soviet System" and "Soviet Foreign Policy." especially Vernon V. Aspaturian, "The Soviet Military-Industrial Complex—Does It Exist?" *Journal of International Affairs*, 26, 1 (1972), pp. 1–28; and William T. Lee, "The 'Politico-Military-Industrial Complex' of the U.S.S.R.," *Journal of International Affairs*, 26, 1 (1972), pp. 73–86.

29.   See Philip Stewart, "Soviet Interest Groups and the Policy Press," *World Politics*, XXII, 1 (October 1969), pp. 29–50.

30.   John A. Armstrong, "The Domestic Roots of Soviet Foreign Policy."

31.   C. Grant Pendill, Jr., " 'Bipartisanship' in Soviet Foreign Policy-Making," in Hoffmann and Fleron (eds.), *The Conduct of Soviet Foreign Policy*, pp. 61–75.

32.   See Milbrath in Rosenau (ed.), *Domestic Sources*, p. 248.

33.   Linden, *Khrushchev and the Soviet Leadership*, pp. 18–19.

34.   James Rosenau, "Foreign Policy," p. 49.

35. For an important study of pressure groups, public opinion, and foreign policymaking in the United States, see Raymond Bauer, Ithiel Pool, and Lewis Dexter, *American Business and Public Policy: The Politics of Foreign Trade* (New York: Atherton, 1963).

36. Several articles have appeared over the years that classify the literature on Soviet ideology and foreign policy, and the student should consult them for a more detailed categorization. For example, the articles cited in note 1 by Glaser and Bell, also Adam Bromke, "Ideology and National Interest in Soviet Foreign Policy," *International Journal*, XXII, 4 (Autumn 1967), pp. 547–62.

37. Michael Gehlen, *The Politics of Coexistence* (Bloomington, IN: Indiana University Press, 1967), p. 294.

38. William Zimmerman, *Soviet Perspectives on International Relations, 1956–1967* (Princeton, NJ: Princeton University Press, 1969), pp. 287, 290.

39. Robert V. Daniels, "Doctrine and Foreign Policy," in Hoffmann and Fleron (eds.), *The Conduct of Soviet Foreign Policy*, p. 157. Daniels's article originally appeared in *Survey: A Journal of Soviet and East European Studies* 57 (October 1965), pp. 3–13.

40. David Forte, "The Response of Soviet Foreign Policy to the Common Market, 1957–63," *Soviet Studies*, XIX, 3 (January 1969), p. 373. Cf. Barrington Moore, Jr., "The Relations of Ideology and Foreign Policy," in Barrington Moore, Jr., *Soviet Politics—The Dilemma of Power* (Cambridge, MA: Harvard University Press, 1951), pp. 384–401; and Bertram D. Wolfe, "Communist Ideology and Soviet Foreign Policy," *Foreign Affairs*, XLI, 1 (October 1962), pp. 152–70.

41. Forte, "The Response of Soviet Foreign Policy To The Common Market," pp. 373, 386ff.

42. Alfred G. Meyer, "The Functions of Ideology in the Soviet Political System," *Soviet Studies*, XVII, 3 (January 1966), pp. 273–85. For general discussions of the functions performed by attitudes, opinions, values, and beliefs, see M. Brewster Smith, Jerome Bruner, and Robert White, *Opinions and Personality* (New York: J. Wiley, 1964); and Daniel Katz, "The Functional Approach to the Study of Attitudes," *Public Opinion Quarterly*, XXIV, 2 (Summer 1960), pp. 163–204.

43. Zbigniew K. Brzezinski, *The Soviet Bloc: Unity and Conflict*, rev. and enlarged ed. (Cambridge, MA: Harvard University Press, 1967), p. 489, from the important chapter "Ideology and Power in Relations among Communist States," pp. 485–512. See also Brzezinski's *Ideology and Power in Soviet Politics* (New York: Praeger, 1967), especially Chapter 5. On the important subject of *change* in the content and functions of Marxist theory and ideology, see Robert C. Tucker, *The Marxian Revolutionary Idea* (New York: Norton, 1969), especially "The Deradicalization of Marxist Movements," pp. 172–214.

44. J. M. Bochenski, "The Three Components of Communist Ideology," *Studies in Soviet Thought* 2, no. 1 (March 1962), pp. 7–11.

45. For example, Kurt Marko, "Soviet Ideology and Sovietology," *Soviet Studies*, XIX, 4 (April 1968), pp. 465–81.

46. Adam B. Ulam, "Soviet Ideology and Soviet Foreign Policy," in Hoffmann and Fleron (eds.), *The Conduct of Soviet Foreign Policy*, p. 141.

47. Forte, "The Response of Soviet Foreign Policy to the Common Market," p. 373.

48. Meyer, "The Functions of Ideology," especially pp. 279–81.

49. David Joravsky, "Soviet Ideology," *Soviet Studies*, XVIII, 1 (July 1966), p. 3.

50. Ibid., pp. 3–8.

51. Richard DeGeorge, *Patterns of Soviet Thought* (Ann Arbor, MI: University of Michigan Press, 1966), pp. 234ff.

52. Joravsky, "Soviet Ideology," p. 9.

53. Ibid., p. 10.

54.   Alexander L. George, "The 'Operational Code': A Neglected Approach to the Study of Political Leaders and Decision-Making," in Hoffmann and Fleron (eds.), *The Conduct of Soviet Foreign Policy*, pp. 172–173. George's article originally appeared in *International Studies Quarterly*, XIII, 2 (June 1969), pp. 190–222.

55.   George, "The 'Operational Code,' " p. 189.

56.   Milton Rokeach, *The Open and Closed Mind* (New York: Basic Books, 1960), p. 35. For another discussion of the relationship between ideology and belief systems, see Samuel H. Barnes, "Ideology and the Organization of Conflict: On the Relationship between Political Thought and Behavior," *Journal of Politics*, XXVIII, 3 (August 1966), pp. 513–30.

57.   Rokeach, *The Open and Closed Mind*, p. 35.

58.   Ibid., p. 40. Rokeach gives examples of pre-ideological beliefs on pp. 75–77.

59.   For a more detailed discussion of these variables as they related to the analysis of Soviet foreign policy, see Rita M. Kelly and Frederic J. Fleron, Jr., "Personality, Behavior, and Communist Ideology," *Soviet Studies*, XXI, 3 (January 1970), pp. 297–313. Reprinted in Hoffmann and Fleron (eds.), *The Conduct of Soviet Foreign Policy*, pp. 191–211. An expanded version of this article appeared under the title "Motivation, Methodology, and Communist Ideology" in Roger E. Kanet (ed.), *The Behavioral Revolution in Communist Studies*, pp. 53–77. See also the voluminous subsequent literature on the psychology of international relations by scholars such as Robert Jervis, John Steinbruner, and Robert Axelrod.

60.   Herbert C. Kelman, "The Role of the Individual in International Relations: Some Conceptual and Methodological Considerations," *Journal of International Affairs*, XXIV, 1 (1970), p. 4. See also John G. Gunnell, "The Idea of a Conceptual Framework: A Philosophical Critique," *Journal of Comparative Administration*, I, 2 (August 1969), pp. 140–76; Philip E. Tetlock and Charles B. McGurre, Jr., "Cognitive Perspectives on Foreign Policy," in Samuel Long (ed.), *Political Behavior Annual* (Boulder, CO: Westview, 1985); and Robert Mandel, "Psychological Approaches to International Relations," in Margaret G. Hermann (ed.), *Political Psychology: Contemporary Problems and Issues* (San Francisco and London: Jossey-Bass, 1986), and the literature cited therein.

61.   Herbert C. Kelman, "Social-Psychological Approaches: The Question of Relevance," in Herbert C. Kelman (ed.), *International Behavior: A Social-Psychological Analyses* (New York: Holt, Rinehart & Winston, 1965) p. 456.

62.   Rudolf Schlesinger, "More Observations on Ideology," *Soviet Studies*, XIX, 1 (July 1968), p. 87.

63.   Joravsky, "Soviet Ideology," p. 15.

64.   Herbert C. Kelman, "Social-Psychological Approaches to the Study of International Relations: Definition of Scope," in Kelman (ed.), *International Behavior*, p. 17.

65.   Kelman, "The Role of the Individual in International Behavior," p. 9.

66.   Ibid., pp. 9–10.

67.   Joravsky, "Soviet Ideology," pp. 12–13.

68.   Ibid., p. 15.

69.   Not surprisingly, this latter form of ideology may also perform important social functions. See Herbert J. Spiro and Benjamin R. Barber, "Counter-Ideological Uses of 'Totalitarianism,' " *Politics and Society*, I, 1 (November 1970).

70.   W. I. Thomas, quoted in Urie Bronfenbrenner, "Allowing for Soviet Perceptions," in Roger Fisher (ed.), *International Conflict and Behavioral Science* (New York: Basic Books, 1964), p. 166. For evidence that at least in some respects Soviet international perspectives were becoming increasingly similar to Western perceptions, see Zimmerman, *Soviet Perspectives on International Relations*. A recent study indicates that this process accelerated in subsequent years and sewed the seeds of Gorbachev's "new thinking" in Soviet foreign policy. See Allen Lynch, *The Soviet Study of international*

Relations (Cambridge: Cambridge University Press, 1987). This latter interpretation is developed in Allen Lynch, "Changing Soviet Views on the International System and Soviet Foreign Policy," which appears as Chapter 3 in our companion volume, *Contemporary Issues in Soviet Foreign Policy*.

71. George F. Kennan, *Memoirs: 1925–1950* (Boston, MA: Atlantic–Little, Brown, 1967), p. 358.

72. Arthur M. Schlesinger, Jr., "Origins of the Cold War," in Hoffmann and Fleron (eds.), *The Conduct of Soviet Foreign Policy*, p. 253. This article originally appeared in *Foreign Affairs*, XLVI, 1 (October 1967), pp. 22–52.

73. William Appleman Williams, "The Cold War Revisionists," *The Nation*, CCV, 16 (November 13, 1967), pp. 492–95. Reprinted in Hoffmann and Fleron (eds.), *The Conduct of Soviet Foreign Policy*, pp. 255–61.

74. Christopher Lasch, "The Cold War, Revisited and Re-Visioned," *The New York Times Magazine* (January 14, 1968). Reprinted in Hoffmann and Fleron (eds.), *The Conduct of Soviet Foreign Policy*, pp. 262–74.

75. Adam Ulam, "Re-reading the Cold War," *Interplay*, II, 8 (March 1969), pp. 51–53. Cf. Gabriel Kolko, *The Politics of War: The World and United States Foreign Policy, 1943–1945* (New York: Random House, 1968); Barton Bernstein and Allen Matusow (eds.), *The Truman Administration: A Documentary History* (New York: Harper & Row, 1966); and the references listed by Norman A. Graebner, "Cold War Origins and the Continuing Debate: A Review of the Literature," *The Journal of Conflict Resolution*, XIII, 1 (March 1969), pp. 123–32.

76. Joseph R. Starobin, "Origins of the Cold War," in Hoffmann and Fleron (eds.), *The Conduct of Soviet Foreign Policy*, p. 287. This article originally appeared in *Foreign Affairs*, XLVII, 4 (July 1969), pp. 681–96.

77. Quoted in John Bagguly, "The World War and the Cold War," in David Horowitz (ed.), *Containment and Revolution* (Boston, MA: Beacon, 1967), p. 110. For an important study of Yalta, see Diane S. Clemens, *Yalta* (New York: Oxford University Press, 1970).

78. *A Study of Soviet Foreign Policy* (Moscow: Progress, 1975), p. 18.

79. Ibid., p. 24.

80. Ibid., p. 30.

81. Vitalii Korionov, *The Policy of Peaceful Coexistence in Action* (Moscow: Progress, 1975), p. 28.

82. *A Study of Soviet Foreign Policy*, p. 29.

83. Vladimir Gantman, "Detente and the System of International Relations," *Social Sciences* (Moscow) 2 (1980), pp. 177, 180–181 (emphases added). See also Georgii Arbatov, "Vnechnaia politika SShA na poroge 80-kh godov," *SShA* 4 (1980), especially pp. 51–52.

84. Vitalii Korionov, *The Policy of Peaceful Coexistence in Action* (Moscow: Progress, 1975), pp. 28–29.

85. Zbigniew K. Brzezinski, "U.S.-Soviet Relations," in Henry Owen (ed.), *The Next Phase in Foreign Policy* (Washington, DC: The Brookings Institution, 1973), and Richard Pipes, "Detente: Moscow's View," in Richard Pipes, *Soviet Strategy in Europe* (New York: Crane, Ruzzak, 1976), pp. 3–42. Both articles are reprinted in Hoffmann and Fleron (eds.), *Conduct of Soviet Foreign Policy*.

86. Robert C. Tucker, "United States-Soviet Cooperation: Incentives and Obstacles," *The Annals of the American Academy of Political and Social Science* 372 (July 1967), pp. 2–13; and Marshall D. Shulman, "Toward a Western Philosophy of Coexistence," *Foreign Affairs*, LII, 4 (October 1973). Both articles are reprinted in Hoffmann and Fleron (eds.), *The Conduct of Soviet Foreign Policy*.

87. Georgii Shakhnazarov, "New Factors in Politics at the Present Stage," *Social Sciences* (Moscow) 1 (1977), p. 49.

88. Charles Gati, "The Stalinist Legacy in Soviet Foreign Policy," in Hoffmann and Fleron (eds.), *The Conduct of Soviet Foreign Policy*, p. 646. See also Charles Gati, "The Stalinist Legacy: A Reply to Zimmerman," ibid., pp. 671–72.

89. William Zimmerman, "The Soviet Union and the West: A Critique of Gati," in Hoffmann and Fleron (eds.), *The Conduct of Soviet Foreign Policy*, pp. 664–70.

90. Zimmerman, "The Soviet Union and the West," p. 668.

91. For evidence supporting this interpretation, see the two chapters by Robbin F. Laird and Erik P. Hoffmann, " 'The Scientific-Technological Revolution,' 'Developed Socialism,' and Soviet International Behavior," and "Soviet Perspectives on North-South Relations in the Era of 'The Scientific-Technological Revolution,' " pp. 388–405, 479–494, respectively. For a much fuller and later analysis of issues raised in these essays, see Erik P. Hoffmann and Robbin F. Laird, *The Politics of Economic Modernization in the Soviet Union* (Ithaca, NY: Cornell University Press, 1982); and Erik P. Hoffmann and Robbin F. Laird, *"The Scientific-Technological Revolution" and Soviet Foreign Policy* (New York: Pergamon, 1982).

92. note 13, Dallin, "The Domestic Sources of Soviet Foreign Policy."

93. Gati, "The Stalinist Legacy in Soviet," p. 659.

94. Helmut Sonnenfeldt, "Russia, America and Detente," in Hoffmann and Fleron (eds.), *The Conduct of Soviet Foreign Policy*, p. 726. This article originally appeared in *Foreign Affairs* (January 1978).

95. Ibid., p. 727.

96. Ibid.

97. Ibid.

98. Ibid., p. 729. An outstanding analysis of the economics and politics of East-West relations as of the mid-1970s is contained in Franklyn Holzman and Robert Legvold, "The Economics and Politics of East-West Relations," *International Organization*, 29, 1 (Winter 1975), pp. 275–320. This article was reprinted in Hoffmann and Fleron (eds.), *The Conduct of Soviet Foreign Policy*, pp. 428–78.

99. Sonnenfeldt, "Russia, America and Détente, p. 730.

100. Ibid., p. 731.

101. Robert Keohane and Joseph Nye, *Power and Interdependence: World Politics in Transition*, 2nd ed. (Boston: Little, Brown, 1989), p. 13 ff.

102. Robert Legvold, "The Nature of Soviet Power," in Hoffmann and Fleron (eds.), *The Conduct of Soviet Foreign Policy*, p. 679. This article originally appeared in *Foreign Affairs* (October 1977).

103. Ibid., p. 674.

104. Ibid., p. 676.

105. Ibid., p. 690.

106. Ibid., pp. 690–91.

107. Vernon V. Aspaturian, "Vulnerabilities and Strengths of the Soviet Union in a Changing International Environment: The Internal Dimension," in Hoffmann and Fleron (eds.), *The Conduct of Soviet Foreign Policy*, p. 697 ff. This article originally appeared in *Soviet Union*, 4, 1 (1977), pp. 17–39.

108. Ibid., p. 704.

109. Ibid., pp. 705–6.

110. Ibid., p. 704.

I
History

1

Soviet Foreign Policy Aims and Accomplishments from Lenin to Brezhnev*

Erik P. Hoffmann

Probably the most important characteristic of Soviet foreign policy is its *differentiation*. The USSR is an enormous multinational country whose ruling party's ideology commits it to revolutionary goals at home and abroad as well as to great-power goals, such as national security and international political and economic influence. The Soviet Politburo must balance the incompatibilities and tensions between these revolutionary and great-power goals under changing internal and external conditions. Soviet leaders' aims and especially their instruments vary considerably over different geographic areas, issue areas, and periods. Vladimir I. Lenin's "dual task," Joseph V. Stalin's "socialism in one country," Nikita S. Khrushchev's reinterpretation of "peaceful coexistence," Leonid I. Brezhnev's "détente," and Mikhail S. Gorbachev's "new political thinking" all contain strategic and tactical flexibility in conceptualizing and pursuing Soviet interests throughout the world. Soviet international behavior became less differentiated between 1917 and 1939, but it became more differentiated between 1939 and 1941 with territorial acquisitions and much more differentiated since World War II with the creation of socialist regimes in Eastern Europe and China, the USSR's increasing prominence in global politics, and the advent of the nuclear age. These trends from Lenin to Brezhnev will be analyzed in this essay.

ASSESSING SOVIET AIMS

Soviet leaders, individually and collectively, have often identified the chief aims of Soviet foreign policy. For example, the USSR Constitution of 1924 expressed the hope "that the new federal state will be the worthy crowning of the principles

*Reprinted by permission of the author and publisher from *Soviet Foreign Policy*, ed. Robbin F. Laird (New York: The Academy of Political Science, 1987), 10–31.

laid down as early as October 1917, of the pacific co-existence and fraternal collaboration of peoples, that it will serve as a bulwark against the capitalistic world and mark a new decisive step towards the union of workers of all countries in one World-Wide Socialist Soviet Republic.''[1] And the USSR Constitution of 1977 declared: ''The USSR's foreign policy is aimed at ensuring favorable international conditions for building communism in the USSR, protecting the Soviet Union's state interests, strengthening the position of world socialism, supporting the peoples' struggle for national liberation and social progress, preventing wars of aggression, achieving general and complete disarmament, and consistently implementing the principle of peaceful coexistence of states with different social systems.''[2]

But are these declaratory or actual goals? What is the relative importance of diverse, even contradictory, Soviet goals? Does the top leader always have the support of other leaders for his short- and long-term priorities? If not, how do coalitions compete or bargain for all or some of their preferences? Are some policies ineffectively and inefficiently implemented? Do policy outcomes often differ from policy outputs because of unanticipated circumstances at home or abroad? How are goals and priorities reassessed and altered? What impact can the foreign policies of other nations have on Soviet policies, institutions, and society?

To answer such questions, Westerners have put forward many different interpretations of Soviet intentions and capabilities. Soviet international activities have been characterized as Communist expansionist, realpolitik expansionist, and real-politik self-defensive;[3] fundamentalist, opportunistic, and insecure;[4] and essentialist, mechanist, and interactionist.[5] Western conservatives tend to favor the Communist expansionist, fundamentalist, and essentialist approaches; centrists the realpolitik expansionist, opportunistic, and mechanist approaches; and liberals the realpolitik self-defensive, insecure, and interactionist approaches.

Which of these interpretations is correct? Each interpretation accurately characterizes and explains Soviet international behavior in some important context. It is possible to cite examples of Communist expansionism, realpolitik expansionism, and self-defense in different geographic and issue areas under Lenin, Stalin, Khrushchev, and Brezhnev. While universal generalizations produce misleading explanations of Soviet foreign policy, probabilistic generalizations can help explain diverse Soviet aims, activities, and accomplishments. Moreover, some events, issues, and patterns in Soviet foreign relations cannot be explained by any of the interpretations noted above. Hence, different analytical approaches and combinations of approaches may help explain ''Soviet international behavior under various conditions.

The Soviet leadership has always sought national security, economic growth, and political stability at home; dissemination of its ideology and social institutions abroad; territorial expansion; and increased influence over non-Communist governments and parties, ruling and nonruling Communist parties, and revolutionary movements. But some of these basic goals are contradictory. An important example is that the pursuit of world communism has often made the defense of the USSR much more difficult. Also, different Soviet leaders and policy groupings favor different foreign-policy goals. For instance, Soviet officials have frequently debated the risks and costs of trading with the West.

It is prudent to expect complexity, contingency, and change in the internal and external influences on Soviet foreign policy. As Franklyn Griffiths has observed, Soviet international activities, especially in the Lenin and post-Stalin eras, "are not likely to be well understood when they are viewed in terms of a unilinear, internally consistent policy whose direction is deliberately changed by the leadership as circumstance requires. . . . Soviet conduct is better regarded as internally contradictory, consisting of a series of persistent tendencies whose relative strength alters in response to international and domestic variables." In other words, top Soviet officials continuously debate domestic and foreign-policy priorities, and other countries often respond to the USSR's actions in erratic or unexpected ways. Hence, Soviet international behavior simultaneously displays "dominant tendencies . . . and a propensity to oscillate as tendencies are combined and recombined to produce an array of responses."[6]

Soviet foreign policy aims have changed considerably in different contexts. Changes in foreign policy have often been tailored to changes in the domestic policies and policy-making processes of distinctive periods, such as "war communism" (1917–21), the New Economic Policy (1921–29), "The third revolution" (1929–37), Stalinist autocracy (1937–41), World War II (1941–45), Stalinist autocracy reimposed (1945–53), Khrushchev's revitalization and fragmentation of the Communist party (1953–64), and Brezhnev's consolidation and enervation of the Communist party (1964–82). Also, Soviet foreign policy has been adjusted to major international trends and the changing policies of other countries, such as the diminishing appeal of revolutionary regimes in Europe after the Treaty of Versailles, the eagerness of Weimar Germany to cooperate with its fellow "pariah," the rise of German, Japanese, and Italian fascism, the imperatives of collaborating with the United States and Great Britain during World War II, the American efforts to "contain" Soviet expansion with the Marshall Plan and Truman Doctrine, the decline of Western colonial empires, the failure of emerging Third World countries to embrace communism, and the impact of the worldwide "scientific-technological revolution" on military and economic relations between the superpowers.

It is not surprising, then, that Western analysts have been unable to document the universal applicability of hypotheses about external and internal influences on Soviet international behavior. For example, "it is not at all clear whether the outside world should be or should appear to be weak or strong, reassuring or threatening, in order to generate 'moderation' in Soviet foreign policy." Similarly, none of the following hypotheses can be confirmed under all circumstances.

1. Domestic weakness leads to foreign-policy accommodation.
2. Domestic weakness leads to foreign-policy assertiveness.
3. Domestic strength leads to foreign-policy accommodation.
4. Domestic strength leads to foreign-policy assertiveness. . . .[7]

Rather, it is important to identify when, where, and to what extent such generalizations can help to describe and explain different aspects of Soviet foreign
policy. There are patterns in Soviet international behavior, but most of them hold
only for particular periods and for geographic and issue areas. One of the few
consistent patterns is that the Soviet leadership considers its principal adversary
to be the dominant country in Europe (France until 1924, Great Britain until
1930, Germany until 1944, and the United States since 1945). Adversaries,
however, can produce varying kinds and degrees of threat, and occasionally a
lesser adversary (such as China from the mid-1960s to the mid-1970s) can be
more threatening to the USSR than its major adversary.

LENIN

The Bolshevik leaders, while sharing some images and assumptions about
international politics, did not come to power with clear-cut or unified views on
foreign policy, especially on the key issue of the day—war and peace. Significantly, they did not agree on the relative importance of domestic and international goals or on the interconnections between them. There were sharp disputes
among Lenin and his colleagues in 1917 and early 1918, more agreement during
the height of the civil war (1918–20), and intense, wide-ranging, public disputes
until the late 1920s. For example, in the heated Central Committee debate
leading up to the Brest-Litovsk treaty of 1918, Nikolai Bukharin called for
"revolutionary war," Leon Trotsky for "no war, no peace," and Lenin for
"immediate peace." Lenin's views prevailed by the slimmest of margins,
effectively taking Russia out of World War I and enabling Germany and its allies
to launch a major offensive on the Western front shortly thereafter. The Bolsheviks did not want to assist any capitalist nation by signing a treaty with their
former enemies, but in effect Russia changed sides in the war.

The portentous decision at Brest-Litovsk spurred American, British, French,
and Japanese intervention in the bloody Russian civil war, not only to reopen the
Eastern front but also—especially in the view of Marshal Ferdinand Foch and
Winston Churchill—to destroy Bolshevism. Moreover, withdrawal from the war
paved the way for what Bolshevik leaders termed their "dual task" and Western
analysts their "dual policy." On the one hand, the Bolsheviks—especially Lenin
and Stalin—began to shed their "contempt for traditional foreign policy and
ingrained internationalism" and inclined toward "a policy directed to meet
national interests and national requirements."[8] On the other hand, the traditional
elements of the "dual policy"—first to stop the world war, then to expel foreign

troops from Russia, and thereafter to cooperate with capitalist governments on selected political, military, and especially economic issues—were pursued simultaneously with its revolutionary elements, to help the working class of all countries seize state power and accelerate the socialist transformation of Europe and of the entire world.

As John M. Thompson has observed, the traditional and revolutionary elements of Soviet foreign policy occasionally "complemented each other, as when revolutionary agitation and propaganda undermined the morale of Allied soldiers in Russia and provoked protests against intervention from labor and liberal circles in the West." But much more frequently the two elements of the Soviet policy "contradicted each other, as when the Soviet drive for revolution and the inflammatory appeals of the Bolsheviks spurred Allied efforts to defeat Bolshevism and caused Western leaders to doubt the sincerity of the peace [and economic] proposals made by the Soviet government."[9]

Both elements of the "dual policy" were institutionalized during the war communism period. Narkomindel, a precursor of the Ministry of Foreign Affairs, pursued traditional state-to-state relations, while the Comintern and the Central Committee's Foreign Office, a precursor of its International Department, pursued revolutionary party-to-party relations.

Because the survival of Bolshevism was in jeopardy during the civil war, the Soviet leadership was unable to provide substantial assistance to promising revolutionary regimes and movements in Europe, and Lenin was especially eager to mollify his foreign adversaries to obtain a "breathing space." Because most Soviet leaders eagerly sought trade, aid, and credits from the West in the 1920s, they pursued good relations with capitalist governments rather than with local Communist parties trying to overthrow these governments. The promise of world revolution has always been part of Soviet declaratory policy, but, as the new socialist state demonstrated that it could survive without help from the working classes of other nations, the utopian idea of a "World-Wide Socialist Soviet Republic" became an increasingly less important component of actual policy.

Soviet Russia implemented both sides of the "dual policy" in Germany in the early 1920s. When the Treaty of Rapallo was signed in 1922, the Soviet leaders reduced and redirected Comintern activities there. But when popular discontent and German Communist Party support increased dramatically in the summer of 1923, the Soviet Politburo began a lengthy and heated debate about how to respond. It belatedly decided to encourage the German Communists to seize power and gave them generous financial assistance, some of which had been received from the Weimar government for secret military deals circumventing the Treaty of Versailles. Nonetheless, the German Communist Party's popularity waned, the new Weimar leadership gained the support of the army, and Stalin—who had been much more cautious about aiding and abetting the German Communists than Trotsky—came away with another victory in the bitter struggle to succeed Lenin and to discard the concept of "permanent revolution" in favor of "socialism in one country."

STALIN

Stalin transformed the Comintern from an instrument seeking world revolution into one serving his domestic policy preferences and his drive to create a personal dictatorship. However, a year after Soviet Russia had openly incited a revolutionary uprising in Germany, nine European countries had extended diplomatic recognition to the new socialist country, and political, military, and especially economic ties between the USSR and Germany expanded until the early 1930s. Stalin, even more than Lenin, understood that it was counterproductive to try to overthrow another government whose cooperation was useful to economic development and security in a hostile world.

Stalin's reemphasis on domestic concerns, however, did not prevent the USSR from supporting "progressive" movements in Great Britain in 1926, China in 1927, and Spain in 1936. As Adam Ulam has written: "In China . . . at one brief moment the Soviet regime followed four separate yet integrated lines of activity: it maintained diplomatic relations with the official government in Peking; it advised and helped the national movement (Chiang Kai-shek), which was conducting a military campaign that sought to overthrow that regime; it helped and abetted the coalition (Left Kuomintang) that sought to overthrow Chiang Kai-shek; finally, it controlled the Chinese Communists who sought to take over the Left Kuomintang!"[10] But the hallmarks of Stalin's foreign policy were its lack of involvement in anticolonial revolutionary movements and its efforts to mollify the more aggressive capitalist powers, either through direct negotiations with them or through "collective security" pacts with the less aggressive capitalist powers.

Soviet domestic goals were most important in the years 1928–39. The decisions to use as much coercion as necessary to centralize economic management and launch Five-Year Plans (1928), to abolish private ownership of land and establish collective farms (1929), and to transform a one-party dictatorship into a one-man dictatorship (1934) were truly revolutionary and called for a quiescent foreign policy. Stalin stifled any inclination to spur revolutions abroad, but he mounted a propagandistic war-scare to legitimize terror at home and compelled the foreign Communist parties to oppose their governments and other left-wing parties. Soviet foreign trade increased considerably under the First Five-Year Plan and dropped precipitously only with the deepening of the world depression in 1932.

In February 1931 Stalin underscored the urgency of rapid industrialization and national defense and their interconnections. "We are fifty or a hundred years behind the advanced countries. We must make good this distance in ten years. Either we do it, or we shall be crushed."[11] Correspondingly, during 1931 the USSR down-graded its special relationship with Germany and sought and eventually signed nonaggression treaties with France, Poland, Italy, and many smaller countries bordering the USSR. These diplomatic initiatives seemed all the wiser when Japan occupied Manchuria in September 1931, threatening the Soviet Far

East and raising the terrifying prospect of Soviet involvement in a two-front war. When Adolf Hitler became chancellor of Germany in January 1933, he proceeded to liquidate the German Communist Party. Throughout the year, Stalin made clear his willingness to cooperate with Hitler while trying to create a French-Polish-Soviet security system. Only when Germany and Poland signed a nonaggression pact in January 1934 did Stalin reduce or relinquish his hopes for a political agreement with Germany and turn to the major Western democracies to try to safeguard his momentous domestic initiatives. Western scholars debate whether Stalin and Foreign Minister Maxim Litvinov sought to preserve or strengthen links with Germany between 1934 and mid-1936, and there is limited but growing evidence that they did both.[12]

In a classic essay, Henry Roberts affirmed:

> There were at least two contending lines of foreign policy within the Politburo, and perhaps within Stalin's own mind, in the 1930s: one, the "Litvinov policy," of which Litvinov himself was not only the agent but probably also the advocate and possibly even the formulator (even in a monolithic state ideas cannot all originate at the apex of the pyramid); the other, the policy which emerged with the pact of August 23, 1939, and acquired explicit characteristics in the two years following. Stalin, while perhaps inclined toward the second, was willing to give the first a trial, especially since no other alternative appeared profitable after 1933: the revolutionary line had brought few results and did not fit well with domestic developments, and the Rapallo connection seemed impossible with Hitler's Germany behaving in an exceedingly unfriendly fashion. On the other hand, "the Litvinov policy" depended upon achieving results. When these failed to come about, the balance—whether between persons in the Politburo or between ideas in Stalin's own mind—would swing away from it. Thus, Litvinov's warnings after 1936 that "collective security" could be wrecked if the Western Powers did not change their ways may be regarded as a reflection of a decision still in suspension in the Politburo, a forewarning of a course which he himself may not have favored but which was in the cards if collective security failed.[13]

The USSR's chief foreign-policy goals between 1931 and 1939, in order of priority, probably were: (1) noninvolvement in the impending war; (2) alliance with the winning side if war erupted; (3) avoidance of simultaneous invasions by Germany in Europe and by Japan in Asia; (4) avoidance of any battles fought on Soviet territory; (5) territorial expansion; and (6) support of Communist takeovers in other countries. For the USSR an alliance with Great Britain, France, and the United States held out the faint hope of preventing a world war altogether but, more realistically, promised the postponement of Soviet involvement in a two-front war and of emerging victorious with limited damage. Because the major Western powers were more interested in appeasing fascism than in creating an antifascist coalition with the USSR, Stalin pursued his alternative well-planned policy and quite possibly his only viable option. By signing a nonaggression treaty with Germany in 1939, Stalin immediately ended over a year's heavy fighting with Japan on the Manchurian border. Even more important, Stalin expected to delay the inevitable German and renewed Japanese attacks, better to prepare the Soviet armed forces (whose general staff had just been decimated by the bloody purges), to take more precautions that the Ukrainian population (which had suffered millions of deaths in the forced collectivization and artificially created famine of 1932 and 1933) would not collaborate with the invading Nazis, to join a winning alliance with several Western democracies, and to gain territories lost in the interwar period and probably additional territories.

If Germany had not attacked the USSR in June 1941, Stalin's decade-long efforts to keep his country out of World War II or to limit its ravages on Soviet soil might well have succeeded. The implications for postwar Europe are truly extraordinary. Would Eastern Europe be Communist today if the Red Army had not repelled the Wehrmacht from the USSR and virtually all of East-Central Europe as agreed by Stalin, Franklin Roosevelt, and (reluctantly) Churchill at Teheran, Iran, in November 1943? Furthermore, Stalin took advantage of the Nazi-Soviet pact (annexing territory from Poland, the Baltic States, Finland, and Romania) and obtained the power to mold the postwar political order in the occupied Eastern European countries.

The high priority the USSR gave to these goals was revealed clearly in the major wartime conferences of the Allied leaders, in the successful Soviet efforts to create common borders with Czechoslovakia and Hungary, and in the decisive Soviet actions to assist their supporters in Bulgaria and Romania. The low priority the USSR gave to potentially independent incipient Communist regimes was demonstrated by Stalin's refusal to recognize Tito as the leader of the Yugoslav resistance or to assist the partisans until well after the West had done so. Stalin was extremely cautious toward the Yugoslav Communists, in large part because he did not want to give the United States and Britain any pretext for further delays in establishing an effective second front against Germany.

American, British, and Soviet priorities differed greatly as the war drew to a close. In probable order of importance, the United States was concerned with (1) removal of procedural obstacles to the creation of the United Nations; (2) war strategy in the Far East and Allied assistance in subduing Japan; and (3) the political and territorial status of postwar Europe, especially Germany and Poland. Great Britain was concerned with (1) its colonial empire; (2) the political ramifications of the fighting in Europe, especially the final location of Allied troops and the future of Germany, France, Poland, and the Balkans; (3) the Far East military situation; and (4) the United Nations. The USSR was concerned with (1) ensuring national security against Germany, other European powers, and the United States; (2) strengthening Stalin's control over the Soviet polity and the international Communist movement, which now included potentially powerful parties in Eastern Europe; (3) reconstructing the devastated Soviet economy, preferably with reparations from a united but permanently weakened Germany; (4) preserving the territories gained under the Nazi-Soviet pact; and (5) reacquiring territories lost to Japan in 1905 and acquiring new territories in Norway, Germany (East Prussia), Poland, Czechoslovakia, Turkey, Iran, and Japan.

The Soviet priorities did not include military expansion into Western Europe. Western fears notwithstanding, Stalin sought only to assist the French, Italian, and other Communist parties to gain greater influence in their countries and thereby to expand Soviet political influence in Western Europe.

The Soviet priorities also did not include the immediate satellitization of all of Eastern Europe. Here again are carefully differentiated Soviet aims. According to Charles Gati, Stalin perceived three distinct regions in Europe and pursued distinctive policies in each:

> 1. a non-Communist, relatively stable region in Western Europe, one that would also include Greece;
> 2. a Communist region under Soviet control in Eastern Europe—along the vital routes to Germany and the Balkans—that would range from Poland and the eastern part of Germany to the Black Sea states of Rumania and Bulgaria; and
> 3. an intermediate region in East Central Europe of coalitional political systems under only gradually increasing Communist influence, extending from Yugoslavia in the south through Austria, Hungary, and Czechoslovakia to Finland in the north.[14]

In the first region, Stalin sought limited but growing influence over national policies; in the second region, extensive and immediate political, military, and economic influence over policies, policy-making institutions, and societies; and in the third region, selective but cautiously increasing political, military, and economic influence together with a willingness to forgo or delay Sovietization in exchange for concessions in other geographic and issue areas.

Zbigniew Brzezinski has stressed that "during the years immediately following its entrance into Eastern Europe in the mid-1940s, the Soviet Union sponsored quite literally the physical liquidation of the region's political elite." Gati agreed, but—recalling the postwar experience of France, Italy, Austria, Finland, and other Western European countries—underscored that Communist participation in coalition governments did not automatically lead to Communist takeovers and that satellitization was not inevitable even where the Red Army occupied all or most of the country, as had happened in Hungary and Czechoslovakia. Also, Gati argued that Stalin sought "a measure of stability in Western Europe to divert attention from the Sovietization of Eastern Europe," by Brzezinski contended that the Soviets "were prepared . . . to camouflage [the creation of] . . . politically acquiescent regimes in east-central Europe . . . if it served to promote attainment of . . . a preponderant voice regarding the political organization of the rest of Europe."[15]

Were Soviet postwar aims largely defensive and opportunistic or aggressive and carefully planned years in advance? Neither seems to have been the case. Because security and control were intertwined in Stalin's thinking and behavior, it is impossible to distinguish between the Soviet leadership's perceived security needs and its overtly expansionist activities. The Soviet concept of security is much broader than Western concepts, and Stalin viewed Eastern Europe not only as a "military buffer [but] also as constituting the outer lines of defense against various forms of ideological and psychological challenge that emanated from the 'capitalist' world.''[16] Stalin saw the Marshall Plan as an aggressive move and strove to prevent the formation of the North Atlantic Treaty Organization (NATO) and then to dissolve or emasculate it.

The effects of Stalin's policies were easy to discern. The rapid deterioration of East-West relations and the accelerated satellitization of all of Eastern Europe created from late 1947 to mid-1949 a period of maximum militancy and minimum differentiation in Soviet foreign policy. But "cold war" and insularity quickly produced negative consequences for the USSR: greater allied unity spurred the formation of NATO; staunch Western defense of the division of Germany resulted in the dangerous but ineffective Berlin blockade; Stalin-ordered stridency of the European Communist parties diminished their influence over government policies and their electoral appeal; and efforts to control and exploit Yugoslavia culminated in the expulsion of an avowedly Communist government from the newly established Cominform (successor to the Comintern, formally but not in fact disbanded in 1943). In a word, the Marshall Plan was a huge success in limiting and countering Soviet aspirations in Western Europe, and the Truman Doctrine and the withdrawal of Soviet troops from northern Iran under Western pressure were similarly successful in the Mediterranean, Dardanelles, and Persian Gulf regions.

Stalin continued to impede or to give merely token support to incipient Communist regimes not under Soviet control. He pressed for geostrategic advantages vis-à-vis China (in Mongolia, Dairen, and Port Arthur) and urged the Chinese Communist Party *not* to try to seize power from the Kuomintang—advice the Chinese Communists ignored to their benefit in 1949. The Soviet leaders then, with surprising but short-lived cooperation from China, proceeded to Stalinize political, military, and economic relations between the USSR and China as well as Chinese domestic policies, institutions, and social relations.

However, the USSR provided sustained military support to a Communist satellite, North Korea, when it attempted forcibly to annex South Korea and prompted United Nations troops and eventually Chinese forces to intervene. The USSR did not supply North Korea with infantry. But Stalin viewed the dispatch of abundant matériel and combat aircraft as a low-risk and low-cost program to assist an aggressive and anti-Western ally, to revive the revolutionary image of the USSR in China and in the former colonies, and to strengthen the USSR's geostrategic position vis-à-vis China and United States–occupied Japan. These perceptions were inaccurate, as events quickly proved and Khrushchev later acknowledged.

The involvement of the USSR in the Korean War notwithstanding, Soviet foreign policy was more cautious, experimental, and flexible from mid-1949 to Stalin's death in 1953. Soviet leaders tried to respond to the failures of previous policies, the rapidly changing military technologies, and the new bipolar relationship with the United States. Reducing East-West confrontation and dividing the Western alliance became higher priorities.[17] What is novel about Soviet international behavior in this period is the USSR's much greater power in world politics coupled with the guarded but increasingly open competition between modernizing and conservative top party officials (such as Georgii Malenkov versus Viacheslav Molotov). At issue were the USSR's role in a dramatically changing international political order and alternative courses of soviet political and economic development.

KHRUSHCHEV

Stalin's death was of enormous political significance, because it marked the end of a personal dictatorship and the beginning of the revitalization of a party dictatorship. Georgi Malenkov, Stalin's much less powerful successor, initiated major foreign-policy changes, but greater support for these and other changes came in 1955 and 1956. The years 1949–55 were a transition period, because Stalin's old age and death accelerated competition among political leaders and groups over policy alternatives, policy-making procedures, and power.

Malenkov helped to end the Korean War, played the role of peacemaker in Indochina, launched the "new course" program of reduced controls in Eastern Europe, tried to improve relations with China and Yugoslavia, renewed diplomatic negotiations concerning the future of Berlin and Austria, and argued that nuclear war could destroy "world civilization." Malenkov also used the Red Army to suppress popular uprisings in East Germany, waged an unsuccessful campaign to weaken the Western alliance despite a rapprochement with France, and made no major initiatives in the Third World. This mixture of change and continuity in Soviet foreign policy reflected the intense and well-balanced competition among political ideas and alliances in top leadership bodies more than indecision or imprecision in the thinking of individual leaders, especially conservatives such as Molotov and Mikhail Suslov. Most oscillation and vacillation stemmed from the unpredictable interplay between policy preferences and the internal power struggle and from a heightened awareness (especially among modernizers like Malenkov and Khrushchev) of the dramatic political, economic, and scientific-technological shifts and uncertainties in the international arena. Soviet conservatives and modernizers have struggled over policy and power throughout the post-Stalin era.

Western observers often overlook or minimize the diversity in Soviet interpretations of "peaceful coexistence" and "détente." Soviet leaders and analysts perceive East-West relations as a dynamic mix of conflict and collaboration and of centrifugal and centripetal tendencies. But conservatives emphasize East-West conflict and West-West collaboration; modernizers emphasize East-West collaboration and West-West conflict. There are numerous centrist positions as well.

Soviet conservatives have a strong vested interest in the argument that military power is the primary component of political influence in the generally hostile international environment. But modernizers contend that economic and military power are vitally important in the increasingly interconnected world. Conservatives tend to view East-West relations as a "zero-sum game" and nuclear war as winnable or survivable. Modernizers tend to view East-West relations as a "positive-sum game" and nuclear war as disastrous and preventable. Although both conservatives and modernizers advocate the use of conventional forces in the Third World, modernizers favor more selective military actions and more sustained efforts to develop diplomatic and commercial ties with non-Communist Third World governments.

Khrushchev, briefly a centrist but then a major modernizer, initiated a new phase in Soviet foreign policy in the mid-1950s. He laid the ideological, institutional, and policy foundations for Soviet international behavior up to and including the Gorbachev period. Virtually all of Gorbachev's "new political thinking" and Brezhnev's perspectives on "détente" built on Khrushchev's conceptualization and implementation of "peaceful coexistence," which discarded or revised much of the Leninist and Stalinist approaches to world politics. Khrushchev formulated innovative policies toward the United States and Western Europe, the Soviet bloc, and the Third World, and made many important ideological changes.

Khrushchev thought that the East and the West had a mutual interest and responsibility to avert a nuclear exchange and to end the cold war. His initial policies toward the Western alliance were highlighted by the acceptance of a unified and neutral Austria, a willingness to establish diplomatic ties with West Germany, and an eagerness for more East-West trade and technology transfer. At the 1955 Geneva summit conference, Khrushchev and Premier Nikolai Bulganin tried unsuccessfully to negotiate a European security pact, a reunification of Germany, and a phased nuclear disarmament, which abandoned earlier Soviet demands for complete disarmament before NATO and Warsaw Pact troop withdrawals. The insistence of the United States on verifiable arms control agreements and Soviet refusal of on-site, or "open-skies," inspection launched three decades of stalemate on this key issue. But the serious content and the businesslike, even amicable, style of these peacetime negotiations contributed to improved Soviet-American relations on a range of issues until 1960 and periodically thereafter. The Geneva Surprise Attack Conference in 1958, for instance, paved the way for agreements on military "confidence-building measures" at Helsinki (1975) and Stockholm (1984–85).

Khrushchev envisioned a "socialist commonwealth" that would include Yugoslavia and China. This alliance was to be based on a common foreign policy and ideology, an integrated defense system, a more equitable division of economic labor, and more independence for Eastern European countries to develop national forms of communism, especially in socioeconomic and cultural policies and in the selection of political leaders. Particularly important were Khrushchev's trips to Belgrade, Yugoslavia, to pledge respect for common interests throughout Eastern Europe and to Peking, China, to negotiate payment for economic and scientific-technological assistance, abolish exploitative joint stock companies, and withdraw Soviet troops from the Port Arthur military base.

Khrushchev greatly expanded ties with neutral or potentially neutral third World countries, especially in Asia and the Middle East. The 1955 Asia-Africa Conference in Bandung, Indonesia, successfully portrayed the USSR as a principled opponent of both colonialism and American pressure to join regional security pacts. Khrushchev and Bulganin traveled to India to extend long-term credits for a steel mill, which were enthusiastically accepted, and to sell low-cost arms, which were politely rejected. They also journeyed to Burma and Afghanistan to dispense economic and technical assistance and (ironically) to sell arms to Afghanistan. Weapons were sold to Egypt and Syria, too, despite the legal ban of the Egyptian Communist Party. In all, Khrushchev created diverse ties and good will with the established governments and peoples of Third World countries that had had little or no contact with Soviet officials or were hostile toward or wary of the USSR because of Soviet-controlled local Communist parties.

Khrushchev's ideological innovations, which shaped and legitimized his policies, were far-reaching and portentous. Rejecting Stalin's "two-camp" theory of international politics and his view of the former colonies as "bourgeois" countries still obeying their former masters, Khrushchev distinguished among five types of nations ranging from the most to the least "progressive": the USSR, other socialist countries, neutral or uncommitted countries, members of regional security pacts with the United States and American allies, and the United States itself. Also, five key maxims (the first three of which were generated by Lenin, Stalin, and Malenkov respectively) acquired new content and prominence: "peaceful coexistence" is the cornerstone of a Soviet global strategy to expand the USSR's influence, not merely a tactical expedient to respond to pressing problems or fleeting opportunities; there are "different roads to socialism" for the Soviet-bloc countries; East-West wars are not "inevitable"; the Communist and Socialist parties of capitalist countries should "cooperate" with one another for a lengthy period, in order to spur social and economic progress at home and abroad; and revolutionary changes in the Third World can be achieved through "parliamentary" or violent means.

Khrushchev's comprehensive foreign policy quickly met with unexpected and undesired results, however. His denunciation of Stalin's "crimes" in February 1956 unleashed Eastern European demands and hopes for even greater desatellitization and de-Stalinization. These aspirations induced a divided Soviet leadership to use diplomacy and intimidation to avert a rebellion by the united Polish party, church, and masses and to try to suppress a revolutionary impulse in Hungary that had created divisions within the party and security forces while enjoying the support of the people. But the deployment of Soviet tanks in Hungary radicalized the situation and emboldened Hungarian leaders to call for a multiparty system. Then additional Soviet troops entered Hungary, inducing Imre Nagy to proclaim his country's neutrality.

Sino-Soviet relations declined markedly as a consequence of Khrushchev's integrated international strategy. China initially insisted that the USSR play the "leading role" in a disciplined global Communist movement. But when the USSR failed to pursue Chinese interests in key geographic and issue areas, China began to compete for influence in the Third World and to prod the USSR into taking more aggressive and risky policies against the United States and its allies. Particularly annoying to Chinese leaders were the disinterest of Soviet leaders in regaining Taiwan, their friendliness toward China's archrival India, their reluctance to brandish their new intercontinental ballistic missiles to help dislodge Taiwan from the Quemoy and Matsu islands, and the withdrawal in June 1959 of Soviet nuclear-weapons components provided to repay China for helping to legitimize—especially to Eastern European leaders—the suppression of the Hungarian revolt. Unlike Khrushchev, Mao Tse-tung held to Stalinist views about the inevitability of nuclear war and the importance of stockpiling nuclear arms.

The widening Sino-Soviet rift loosened Soviet control over Eastern Europe. Desatellitization proceeded in all bilateral relationships at different rates (speedily in Soviet-Romanian relations and slowly in Soviet-East German relations, for example), and de-Stalinization proceeded in most countries and at different rates (steadily in Hungary, slowly in Bulgaria, and not at all in Romania). Khrushchev failed to unify world communism, but he transformed Stalin's feudalistic control over Eastern Europe into hegemonic influence.

Since the rule of Stalin, the Warsaw Pact has controlled the military and security policies and personnel of Eastern Europe. Although Khrushchev gave local parties greater leeway from the USSR in international and especially domestic politics, this independence in crisis situations depends heavily on the independence of their military and civil-defense capabilities. As Christopher Jones has written: "Soviet influence in East Europe depends on Soviet control over appointments to the upper echelons of the East European party leaderships and on the preservation of a Soviet capacity for military intervention to prevent either the capture of the local party hierarchy by Communists with domestic bases of support or the destruction of the party control system by local anti-Communist forces."[18]

In his determined pursuit of better relations with the United States, Khrushchev risked severing the USSR and Eastern Europe from the world Communist movement and seriously alienated China, thereby creating a potentially powerful *Communist* adversary bordering the USSR. He understood intellectually and intuitively that it was crucial to cooperate with the United States to avert nuclear war. Khrushchev welcomed competition with the United States throughout the world, because he truly believed in the moral and eventual material superiority of his socioeconomic system. But he also acknowledged the USSR's temporary economic and scientific-technological backwardness and recognized that expanded ties with the United States could help to remedy these deficiencies.

For Khrushchev, "peaceful coexistence" was a dynamic set of cooperative and confrontational relationships, with emphasis on extending East-West cooperation to new issue areas, establishing agreed-upon rules of competition, and projecting Soviet ideology and power worldwide. "Peaceful coexistence" was a form of intense political, economic, and ideological struggle between socialist and capitalist systems, which included selective support of "national liberation movements" and virtually excluded Soviet-American collaboration to defuse Third World trouble spots (the agreement to establish a neutralist government in Laos in 1961 was an exception). But Khrushchev underscored the benefits of diplomatic, military, economic, and scientific-technological cooperation with the West to accelerate the construction of communism in the USSR.

Khrushchev's powers, though always circumscribed, expanded after a majority of conservative and modernizing Politburo members failed to oust him in 1957 and after a triumphant trip to the United States in 1959 gave promise of reduced East-West tensions and greater commercial and cultural ties. But these hopes evaporated when a U-2 spy plane was shot down over the USSR on 1 May—May Day—1960. This event, more than any other before the Vietnam War, stunted Soviet-American cooperation. Frustrated by the apparent deceitfulness of President Dwight D. Eisenhower and embarrassed by the demonstrable weakness of the Soviet strategic defense forces, Khrushchev looked for new ways to counter the choruses of criticism from Soviet and Chinese conservatives. Also, he sought both to complete the West to resolve outstanding conflicts in Europe and Asia on Soviet terms and to seize mutually beneficial bilateral opportunities.

The Soviet leadership's breathtakingly comprehensive, risky, and "quick-fix" solution was to implant missiles in Cuba. Twenty or more nuclear warheads probably reached Cuba before the United States blockade and were subsequently removed, according to Raymond Garthoff.[19] Adam Ulam has affirmed: "Once in Cuba, the missiles would become negotiable, their removal conditional upon the United States' meeting Soviet conditions on the German peace treaty and other pressing international issues. Appearing in New York in November, Khrushchev would present to the world a dramatic package deal resolving the world's most momentous problems: the German peace treaty, containing an absolute prohibition against nuclear weapons for Bonn; and a similar proposal in reference to the Far East, where the Soviets would demand a nuclear-free zone in the Pacific and, under this guise, extract a pledge from China not to manufacture atomic weapons."[20] If indeed these were Soviet intentions, and the evidence is necessarily sketchy, they produced very different consequences than intended—for Khrushchev, the USSR, and the world. This grand scheme nearly resulted in a nuclear exchange, hastened Khrushchev's ouster in 1964, and spurred his successors to achieve nuclear parity as soon as possible. The USSR and the United States, surprisingly but far-sightedly, signed a limited nuclear test-ban treaty in 1963. However, the Cuban missile crisis was a major catalyst to the USSR's unprecedented strategic and conventional weapons buildup for two decades. This massive buildup did not prevent Brezhnev and President Richard M. Nixon from launching "détente" but retarded its development and hastened its decline.

BREZHNEV

Brezhnev's view of "peaceful coexistence" was similar to Khrushchev's, but Brezhnev saw "détente" (a relaxation of tensions) as the chief means of inducing the West to strive for or acquiesce in "peaceful coexistence." The key difference in the two leaders' global strategies was that Brezhnev's was implemented in a much more favorable international environment. A remarkable and propitious set of circumstances made possible the initiation of East-West détente in the early 1970s.

Between 1964 and 1969, the most portentous Soviet decision was to expand the strategic and conventional arms buildup. The modernization and amassing of weapons was largely a reaction to the Soviet vulnerability underscored by Khrushchev's capitulation to United States military pressure over Cuba. At that time, the strategic weapons of the USSR were not powerful enough to deter the United States from using the explicit or implicit threat of nuclear attack to achieve political objectives. But the new Soviet leadership was determined to eliminate this strategic imbalance and did so around 1970.

Between 1964 and 1969, the most difficult Soviet decision was the military intervention in Czechoslovakia in 1968. The use of Warsaw Pact might against one of its own members was largely a Soviet reaction to the prospects of disintegrating party control and of radical political, economic, and cultural demands, fanned by anti-Sovietism, throughout Eastern Europe. The successful use of coercion in Czechoslovakia energized and unified the Soviet leadership. It then enunciated the "Brezhnev doctrine," which promised similar "assistance" in future bloc crises, removed the increasingly unpopular old-guard leaders in East Germany and Poland to facilitate negotiations for major Soviet-bloc treaties with West Germany, and constructed an integrated, comprehensive, and long-term strategy of domestic and foreign initiatives promulgated at the Twenty-fourth Party Congress in 1971.

Crucial to Brezhnev's concept of détente were improved relations with the United States and Western Europe. In the middle and late 1960s, the intensification of United States military activities in Vietnam, a Soviet client state of mounting importance because of its traditional enmity toward China, precluded any Soviet-American cooperation. But as the Vietnam War drew to a close and as Soviet and American attitudes evolved, arms-control agreements, greatly expanded trade, and scientific-technological, cultural, and even citizen exchanges became possible and mutually beneficial. The Soviet military buildup was in part intended to spur strategic-arms limitation, primarily to further the USSR's interests but also those of a weakened United States, now a ready partner for détente. Nuclear parity and the antiballistic missile treaty (SALT I) were viewed as great accomplishments in Moscow and still are.

The Brezhnev leadership recognized that nuclear parity might accelerate the arms race. This was especially unappealing for two reasons: worsening relations with China had twice erupted into major clashes along the shared border in 1969, and a nuclear-armed China, hostile to the USSR and friendly to the United States, would pose a formidable long-term threat. Indeed, the USSR may have seriously considered preemptive nuclear strikes against China at this time, and a USSR/United States/China "triangle" emerged in Soviet strategic thinking. Also, Premier Aleksei Kosygin's economic reforms of 1965 were sputtering. Soviet economic difficulties were sufficiently serious to warrant a top-level decision in 1969 to buy, copy, or expropriate a wide range of advanced western technologies. Fortunately, the new Social Democratic government in West Germany not only sought to create long-term and mutually beneficial commercial ties with the Soviet-bloc countries but also expeditiously settled territorial, political, and financial disputes lingering since World War II on terms highly favorable to the USSR. These multifaceted accords, because of their durable impact on Soviet-Western European relations, are probably the major achievement of Brezhnev's diplomacy.

Soviet-American relations never fulfilled their promise and became increasingly acrimonious through the 1970s. Improving Chinese-American relations made it much more important to the Soviet leadership to expand ties with the United States. SALT II was signed but not ratified by the United States Senate, and the Helsinki accords on human rights and international communication were approved by the East and West. However, the root causes of deteriorating superpower interaction were the sizable disparities between the Soviet and the American conceptions of détente, as well as the smaller disparities between the American and Western European conceptions and between the Soviet, Western European, and Eastern European conceptions. Soviet leaders misinterpreted the increasing resistance of the United States leaders to East-West cooperation and their mounting anger at Soviet-bloc assistance to "national liberation movements" in Angola, Ethiopia, Afghanistan, and South Yemen, at Vietnamese aggression in Laos and Cambodia, and at the subsequent Soviet occupation of Afghanistan. Brezhnev and his colleagues had never forsworn such assistance; it was part of their understanding of détente. Again, the incompatibilities and tensions in Soviet foreign policy, which are produced by the highly differentiated nature of Soviet aims, came to the fore.

During the 1970s, the top Soviet leadership thought that the USSR could simultaneously support "national liberation movements," develop and stockpile strategic and conventional weapons, and participate more fully in the East-West and North-South division of economic labor. On the one hand, "most-favored-nation" trade status was actively pursued and seemed within reach until 1975, Watergate and United States executive-legislative branch disputes about Soviet emigration policy notwithstanding. On the other hand, North Vietnam's victory over South Vietnam and takeover of Laos in 1975 and the Angolan civil war in 1975 and 1976 were the first in a series of successful Soviet and Soviet-supported military activities in the Third World. Many Soviet leaders emphasized the importance of commercial and political ties with Western Europe and Japan as well as the pitfalls of Soviet-American trade and arms-control talks after the mid-1970s. Indeed, some Soviet commentators concluded that vigorous pursuit of the two chief elements of détente—selective East-West *cooperation* in economic relations and strategic arms limitation and selective East-West *confrontation* in the Third World—had the added advantage of weakening the Western alliance.

The USSR called for collaboration and mutual restraint in East-West relations within Europe in order to continue—even accelerate—the rivalry with the West in the Third World. The United States advocated East-West cooperation and restraint within Europe as a means of reducing international tensions and of stabilizing the multifaceted Soviet-American competition. With the United States gradually recovering from the "Vietnam syndrome," the responses of Jimmy Carter and Ronald Reagan to the war in Afghanistan made it very clear that the United States government rejected the Soviet interpretation of détente. However, United States political, military, and economic power were unable to deter the Soviet leadership from acting on its own conception of détente, especially vis-à-vis selected African and Asian countries in the 1970s and major Western European democracies in the 1970s and 1980s.

Unlike the United States, Western Europe has maintained a détente relationship with the USSR throughout the 1970s and 1980s. This relationship is based on political, economic, and scientific-technological ties that the countries of Europe perceive to be mutually advantageous. Had the Soviet-Western European bonds created in the early 1970s failed to constrain the USSR from dispatching additional troops into Poland in the early 1980s, Western European governments and citizens would have been much more inclined to accept President Reagan's sharp criticism of Soviet motivations and behavior. But, because the USSR did not directly intervene in Poland, the Western Europeans' support for commercial and diplomatic collaboration continued.

During the Brezhnev administration Soviet modernizers underscored the opportunities for improving the USSR's economic growth and productivity through selective transactions with the formidable industrialized Western powers. Soviet conservatives saw opportunities to exacerbate "the general crisis of capitalism" and to promote the independence of socialist countries from the "degenerating" capitalist systems. The first outlook stressed the cooperative elements of détente and the vulnerabilities generated by East-West confrontation. The second outlook stressed the adversarial elements of détente and the vulnerabilities generated by East-West cooperation. Some centrists favored closer East-West ties to avoid domestic economic reforms, while others favored closer East-West ties to spur domestic economic reforms. And some centrists preferred ties with the United States, while others preferred ties with Western Europe, Japan, or both.[21]

Furthermore, Soviet conservatives and modernizers disagreed about the merits of pursuing strategic superiority. Conservatives emphasized the risks and costs of failing to confront the global military, political, ideological, and economic challenges posed by the common interests of the innately aggressive capitalist states. Modernizers emphasized the economic challenges presented by contemporary capitalism and the diverging interests of Western countries, whose policies are shaped by both "belligerent" and "realistic" elements. Conservatives did not belittle nuclear parity, but, unlike modernizers, they perceived strategic superiority to be a feasible and desirable means of enhancing national security. In order to achieve strategic superiority, conservatives affirmed, the Soviet military and heavy industrial sectors must continue to receive a disproportionate share of scarce resources. Modernizers, however, advocated more equitable allocation of science-based high technology to military and civilian industries.

The Soviet conservative and modernizing tendencies competed, and their relative power varied throughout the Brezhnev period. For example, the Soviet leadership did not achieve a durable consensus on technology imports and exports. In the early 1970s, despite differences among top party leaders, the technological preeminence of the United States was emphasized. But by the mid-1970s opinion was divided over whether the USSR should pursue a United States- or a Europe-oriented strategy or a more balanced program of technology trade with the United States, Western Europe, and Japan. The United States rejection of "most-favored-nation" terms and especially its economic boycott of the USSR after the occupation of Afghanistan strengthened the hand of Soviet conservatives and modernizers who favored economic ties primarily with Western Europe, regardless of the possible advantages of trade with the United States.

As the 1970s progressed, Soviet leaders paid greater attention to the instability of the world economy. Because the USSR was hurt by the recession in the mid-1970s, Soviet officials and analysts became much more cognizant of the advantages of insulating the USSR's economy from oil embargoes and other international economic disturbances. True, the USSR benefited considerably from the inflated prices of oil and gold in the late 1970s, but the disadvantages of fluctuating world prices and markets, as well as the political vagaries of East-West trade, were of increasing concern to the Brezhnev administration. Also, the USSR and its allies, especially Poland, were finding it difficult to use expensive and imported technologies and to manufacture higher-quality products of their own. Hence, Soviet modernizers' optimism about technology trade was tempered by a more conservative assessment of the costs and benefits of extensive participation in an unpredictable global economic system.

Soviet conservatives favor trade within the Soviet bloc rather than East-West trade. But some of the modernizers who are the most vocal advocates of East-West trade also strongly support Soviet-Eastern European trade. Eastern Europe has had mixed results from its commercial dealings with the West (such as Poland's disastrous debt and East Germany's beneficial de facto inclusion in the European Economic Community). This experience has prompted cautious Soviet modernizers to call for the diversification of foreign economic ties, thereby maintaining the economic leverage of the USSR over its allies, cushioning the USSR from abrupt changes in world prices and markets, and enhancing Soviet participation in the global division of labor. In all, Eastern European trade with Western Europe reinforces the proclivities of Soviet modernizers toward economic interdependence between East and West.

The disruptions associated with the United States economic boycott of the USSR and Poland in the early 1980s strengthened the position of Soviet conservatives who opposed East-West cooperation in general and trade with the United States in particular. But the boycotts—and perhaps especially the inability of the United States to induce other Western powers to impose sanctions on the USSR and Poland—also fortified the position of Soviet modernizers who advocated close ties with Western Europe as the chief component of USSR technology trade policy.

Soviet conservatives prevailed in more geographic and issue areas than modernizers in the Brezhnev years, but neither tendency predominated. Some of the chief reasons behind the enduring support for both conservative and modernizing orientations were the freer debate over policy alternatives and administrative methods; the complexity and fluidity of domestic and international conditions; the need for many kinds of information and skills in policy making and implementation; and the importance of *differentiated* initiatives and responses to tensions generated by incompatible Soviet aims and to interrelated problems and opportunities in a period characterized by increasing scarcities and difficult choices.

CONCLUSION

Soviet leaders since Lenin have stressed that the goals and priorities of the USSR must be tailored to the distinctive characteristics of each period because of changing political-administrative, socioeconomic, and scientific-technological conditions at home and abroad. The official ideology of the Soviet polity charges the USSR to support "progressive" changes throughout the world, but both the polity and its ideology have adapted to external and internal circumstances that the Communist party does not control and over which it has limited influence. Soviet foreign policy has been adjusted to the aspirations and accomplishments of competing "socialist" and "capitalist" governments and to the "correlation of forces" among countries. Also, it has been adjusted to many shifts in domestic priorities and to diverse phases in the development of the Soviet political system—from "war communism" to Brezhnev's "develop*ed* socialism" to Gorbachev's "develop*ing* socialism."

Lenin and Stalin used meager diplomatic resources effectively and efficiently in the interwar years. The treaties of Brest-Litovsk, Rapallo, and (arguably) the Nazi-Soviet pact are good examples. But foreign intervention in the Russian civil war and the threat of attack by a fascist coalition hardened the coercive internal policies and authoritarian policy-making procedures of Soviet leaders. In addition, the fabricated claims about imminent British and French attacks during the late 1920s and early 1930s and the show-trial accusations of Western, German, and Japanese spying during the mid-1930s helped legitimize forced collectivization and the purges, respectively. The real and imagined challenges from abroad, especially the extraordinary human and material losses the USSR suffered in World War II, strengthened Stalin's resolve to create a monolithic, secure, and self-sufficient country that could dominate all Soviet society, satellite states, and societies throughout Eastern Europe.

Stalin transformed the USSR into a great regional power, but Khrushchev began to transform it into a global power. Stalin's successors had a wide range of foreign-policy choices, which were often intensely debated because of factional rivalries within the party leadership. Also, Soviet choices were neither simple nor self-evident because of the rapidly changing international system and the USSR's enhanced though untested political, ideological, military, and economic capabilities, especially in the new bipolar relationship with the United States and in the Third World. "Peaceful coexistence" became an active and offensive, rather than a reactive and defensive, strategy. But Khrushchev was highly sensitive to the destructiveness of nuclear weapons and to the nonmilitary components of national power. Khrushchev's influence over his colleagues, like that of Litvinov in the 1930s, depended heavily on expeditious and appropriate Western responses to ensure the success of his initiatives.

The Brezhnev years brought still more options and opportunities. Soviet officials disputed the policy implications of the shift from a bipolar to a multipolar world, of the evolving United States role in the Western alliance, and of the complex and perplexing developments in the Third world. Progress toward political and economic "détente" was achieved through stronger ties with Western Europe and with many established Third World governments. But despite or because of setbacks in the Third World, Soviet support for indigenous and exported revolutions was revived in the 1970s. Only in neighboring Afghanistan did a Communist government take power and quickly falter, prompting a prolonged Soviet military occupation. Other new Communist regimes consolidated power in regions of geostrategic importance to the USSR or to its ally Vietnam. These revolutionary initiatives, together with the Soviet decision to deploy SS-20 intermediate-range missiles in Eastern Europe, European Russian, and the Far East, were probably the chief reasons Brezhnev could not make substantial progress toward détente on military issues with the West. Brezhnev's failing health and policy mistakes notwithstanding, he never lost much power because of the oligarchical nature of national decision making.

At the outset of the Brezhnev period, as Vernon Aspaturian has observed, Soviet leaders may have perceived "not only that an aggressive ideological orientation in foreign policy tends to mobilize the capitalist world against them but also that it serves to drain scarce resources required to enhance the material prosperity of the Soviet population, ideologically described as 'building Communism.' "[22] However, Soviet international behavior in the 1970s was not grounded on this perception. The reasons probably included the collapse of executive authority in the United States as well as the mistaken belief of the Brezhnev Politburo that the American government and people had accepted the Soviet interpretation of détente. The Soviet leaders accordingly concluded that the risks and costs of military ventures in the Third World would not be so high under conditions of nuclear parity and enhanced East-West diplomatic and commercial cooperation. Also, Brezhnev and his colleagues overestimated the capacity of the USSR to produce weapons and consumer goods while subsidizing Eastern Europe and supporting selected national liberation movements. Furthermore, the Soviet leadership probably thought that the economic competition among the United States, Western Europe, and Japan would ensure a steady supply of advanced technology and markets for Soviet semiprocessed goods and raw materials.

In summary, the Brezhnev administration failed to acknowledge or agree on the trade-offs that would have to be made among its chief foreign-policy aims and between domestic- and foreign-policy aims. Vernon Aspaturian was right in stating: "While the contradiction between Soviet security interests and ideological goals in foreign policy has long been recognized by observers of the Soviet scene, a new variable in Soviet policy is the contradiction between enhancing economic prosperity at home and fulfilling international obligations.[23] Both contradictions intensified under Brezhnev. His successor, Mikhail Gorbachev, clearly understands the seriousness of these contradictions and is energetically trying to mediate and resolve them.

NOTES

1. Robert Daniels (ed.), *A Documentary History of Communism*, vol. 1, *Communism in Russia* (Hanover, NH: University Press of New England, 1984), 167.
2. Robert Sharlet (ed.), *The New Soviet Constitution of 1977: Analysis and Text* (Brunswick, OH: King's Court Communications, 1978), p. 85.
3. Richard Herrmann, *Perceptions and Behavior in Soviet Foreign Policy* (Pittsburgh: University of Pittsburgh Press, 1985), especially chapters 1 and 6.
4. Seweryn Bialer, *The Soviet Paradox: External Expansion, Internal Decline* (New York: Alfred A. Knopf, 1986), p. 260 ff.
5. Franklyn Griffiths, "The Sources of American Conduct: Soviet Perspectives and Their Policy Implications," in *Soviet Foreign Policy in a Changing World*, ed. by Robbin F. Laird and Erik P. Hoffmann (Hawthorne, NY: Aldine 1986), p. 349 ff.
6. Griffiths, pp. 364–65.
7. Charles Gati, "The Stalinist Legacy in Soviet Foreign Policy," in *The Soviet Union in the 1980s*, ed. by Erik P. Hoffmann (New York: The Academy of Political Science, 1984). pp. 218, 222; and Laird and Hoffmann, pp. 20, 24.
8. E. H. Carr, *The Bolshevik Revolution, 1917–1923*, vol. 3 (New York: W. W. Norton, 1981), pp. 17, 20 ff.
9. John M. Thompson, *Russian Bolshevism, and the Versailles Peace* (Princeton, NJ: Princeton University Press, 1965), p. 384.
10. Adam Ulam, *Expansion and Coexistence: Soviet Foreign Policy, 1917–73*, 2d ed. (New York: Praeger, 1974), p. 669.
11. Daniels, p. 230.

12. For an analysis of the recent literature, see Peter B. Kaufman, "Soviet Attitudes toward Collective Security in Europe, 1936–1938," *Russian History* (forthcoming).

13. Henry Roberts, "Maxim Litvinov: Soviet Diplomacy, 1930–1939," in *Power and Process in Soviet Foreign Policy*, ed. by Vernon Aspaturian (Boston: Little, Brown, 1971), p. 180.

14. Charles Gati, *Hungary and the Soviet Bloc* (Durham, NC: Duke University Press, 1986), p. 15.

15. Ibid., pp. 15, 98–99; Zbigniew Brzezinski, *Game Plan: How to Conduct the U.S.-Soviet Contest* (Boston: Atlantic Monthly Press, 1986), pp. 80–81; and "The Future of Yalta," *Foreign Affairs* 62 (Winter 1984–85), p. 286.

16. Helmut Sonnenfeldt and William Hyland, "Soviet Perspectives on Security," in Laird and Hoffmann, p. 228.

17. See, e.g., Marshall Shulman, *Stalin's Foreign Policy Reappraised* (New York: Atheneum, 1965).

18. Christopher Jones, *Soviet Influence in Eastern Europe: Political Autonomy and the Warsaw Pact* (New York: Praeger, 1981), p. 1.

19. Raymond Garthoff, *Reflections on the Cuban Missile Crisis*, rev. ed. (Washington, DC: Brookings Institution, 1989), p. 42 ff.

20. Ulam, p. 669.

21. See, e.g., Erik P. Hoffmann and Robbin F. Laird, *The Politics of Economic Modernization in the Soviet Union* (Ithaca, NY: Cornell University Press, 1982), and *"The Scientific-Technological Revolution" and Soviet Foreign Policy* (Elmsford, NY: Pergamon Press, 1982); and Allen Lynch, *The Soviet Study of International Relations* (Cambridge: Cambridge University Press, 1987).

22. Vernon Aspaturian, "Internal Politics and Foreign Policy in the Soviet System," in Aspaturian, p. 499.

23. Ibid.

2

Soviet Perspectives on Security*

Helmut Sonnenfeldt and William G. Hyland

INTRODUCTION

The purpose of this essay is to explore Soviet conceptions of security. More particularly, we are concerned with determining how successive Soviet leaderships have sought to define the security requirements of the Soviet Union, how they have gone about satisfying these requirements, and how successful they have been.

To examine the security conceptions of any nation, or those of its leaders, is at best fraught with difficulties. Security is not a fixed or quantifiable condition, although some of its elements are concrete enough. But it is in many respects a state of mind, which is affected by many stimuli, some going far back into historic experience.

The Soviet case is beset by particular problems because so much of the USSR's own discussion of security issues is either shrouded in secrecy or obscured by ritualistic and convoluted terminology. Soviet conduct is, of course, visible and constitutes a major and important body of evidence. But the motivations behind the conduct, and the debates and judgments associated with it, are rarely elucidated in the documentary material that is only sporadically available. It hardly needs to be noted that there is no investigative reporting in Moscow, nor a Freedom of Information Act, nor any wholesale opening of archives. Thus, even at this late date, we must still rely on speculation about the Soviet role in the invasion of Korea in 1950 or, to take a more recent example, about the calculations, expectations, and objectives that led Khrushchev to deploy missiles to Cuba in 1962. For written material, we have to rely almost entirely on the public record such as official releases, speeches, articles, and diplomatic communications.

Publicly available pronouncements, of course, cannot be discounted. They serve, among other things, as one form of communication between the Soviet

*Reprinted by permission of the authors and publisher from Adelphi Papers, no. 150 (Spring, 1979), pp. 1–19, 24. Copyright ©1979 by The International Institute for Strategic Studies.

leadership, the subordinate elites, and the population at large. They are also used in some measure to communicate with foreign Communist parties and with the outside world generally. Careful scrutiny of these materials over time can and does provide some insight into Soviet concerns and goals.

Analysis of official or officially inspired Soviet materials has been intensively conducted in the West for more than 30 years now. It has produced a methodology which involves in the main a search for shifts in emphasis or phrasing, frequently minute, which are interpreted to reflect policy changes or differences among the leadership elite. At the same time, most Western analysts believe that the Soviet Union usually means what she says on policy matters and should be taken at her word; that is to say, the reiteration of statements should be accorded substantial weight. We tend to agree with these approaches to the analysis of the contents of public Soviet materials.

But it needs to be remembered constantly that in sifting these materials one is still dealing only with very partial evidence, and that what is withheld almost certainly greatly outweighs in importance what is accessible. Among other things, we are denied the kind of "feel" that we might gain from an occasional sampling of the papers used by top leaders in their deliberations. It is a lack of which one is particularly conscious when dealing with an issue like security, which involves intangibles.

The absence of what would normally be considered historical evidence has been somewhat offset in recent years by the intensification of contact between Soviet and foreign representatives at summit level and below. Most of these occur in a bargaining context. They lack the candor and, generally speaking, the informality and the broad range of topics which characterize meetings among Western leaders, for example. They do offer a hint, but only a hint, about the preoccupations of Soviet leaders. In addition, Soviet representatives (below decision-making levels on the whole, but members of the governing elite) participate in increasing numbers in exchanges with foreign counterparts. Over the past few years they have adapted their discourse to a terminology and a style more compatible with those of Western debates about the issues that concern us here.

But even the greater intensity and variety of contacts and the decline of jargon leave considerable room for doubt about whether the USSR thinks about security issues in the terms to which we are accustomed in our own deliberations over these issues. In any event, anyone who has participated in discussions with Soviet representatives will be aware that, even if the terms of discussion have become more compatible, differences in substance and perception remain wide and deep.

Thus, the problem of inadequate and defective evidence is compounded by the problem of perspective. Any attempt by foreigners to comprehend and represent the conceptions of other nations and their leaders is always beset by pitfalls; these dangers are almost certainly more pronounced when dealing with the USSR.

Relations with the USSR have been a matter of enormous concern for Americans and many others for more than a generation. Issues are involved which have the gravest and most far-reaching implications. Almost inevitably in such circumstances, the line between analysis and policy preferences becomes quite fine. Indeed, experience has demonstrated that certain analytical conclusions are not merely a contribution to scholarship or theory; they may well become the basis for action. To call on an example from the past, one needs only to read some of the official American documents now available for the 1949–1950 period to see the close connection between conclusions reached about the nature of the Soviet Union and her objectives, on the one hand, and the policy options considered and advocated, on the other.

We recognize, therefore, that we cannot be fully objective in the pages that follow. Inevitably, we will be presenting something of our own view of Soviet perspectives, based on evidence with the imperfections we have noted.

Our discussion focuses on Soviet security perspectives. But security is, in part, a function of power, although the correlation is far from a simple one. Many nation lacking some of the principal prerequisites of power nevertheless feels relatively secure against external attack or pressure. Other more powerful nations may be troubled, and often are, by anxieties concerning their survival or freedom of action. Some states seek to curb their fears by accumulating military power; others rely on alliances as well, on skillful diplomacy, on the manipulation of their putative adversaries, and on many other devices and courses. For the USSR, power—especially its military component—has long been considered the principal means of assuring survival and the creation of conditions in which the regime can pursue its domestic and other aims. Consequently, in undertaking this examination of the Soviet view and pursuit of security, we will constantly encounter the question of Soviet power and its role and purposes. But we will also encounter the complexities of the interaction between security and power, particularly as, for the USSR, concepts like alliances, interdependence, and international institution-building until now have played a far less significant role in the search for security than has been true for most Western nations.

The approach we have used in our discussion is basically chronological. That is, viewing Soviet conduct as a whole, we will trace the evolution of Soviet security conceptions through various stages from the Revolution to the present. The essay is organized roughly around the leadership periods of Lenin, Stalin, Khrushchev, and Brezhnev. We recognize, of course, that changes in Soviet leadership are not necessarily coterminous with historical periods, especially when the problem under study is partly affected by developments and events that are either not at all, or only very indirectly, under Soviet control. Still, we have found this rough division of the period under consideration useful for our purposes, acknowledging that the stages in the evolution we are seeking to trace are not wholly congruent with the tenures of the four men who have ruled the USSR since 1917.

THE REVOLUTIONARY PERSPECTIVE

There has been a tendency in Western analysis to regard Soviet "goals" as immutable and to interpret changes in policy and fluctuations in the tone and climate of East–West relations as essentially "tactical" shifts. This is far from a unanimous Western view, but it is widely and tenaciously held. It is encouraged by the USSR herself because of her constant insistence that she is operating on the basis of "scientific" doctrines or even laws (which the USSR herself "discovers" and interprets); that she is the agent of history, which is said to be on her side; and that, while policies are adapted to new and changing conditions, the commitment of Soviet policy to "Leninist" prescriptions remains unwavering. There is a large body of Soviet pronouncements that holds strategy to be broadly unchanging while allowing for—indeed, urging—shifts in tactics as required by prevailing circumstances.

One consequence is that analysts speculate endlessly about where tactics end and strategy begins. Similarly, the somewhat contrary point is often made that when "tactics" are infinitely flexible, they are bound sooner or later to affect even the most devoutly held goals; resolution of these conflicting views is unlikely to be accomplished by abstract argument.

Turning to the problem of security, then, it can readily be seen that the quest for it has been among the most basic and persistent Soviet concerns since the Revolution. Survival is the most fundamental task of any state, and hence of the governments of all states. It is also the most basic element in any concept of security. Very soon after the Revolution the Bolshevik state began to manifest a degree of concern about its survival not dissimilar to that of other states or of its Tsarist predecessor.

Indeed, at the outset the new Soviet government could not ignore this most elementary aspect of security: A large part of the Soviet Union was occupied by the German army. Bolshevik authority was tenuous, and war or peace was an urgent political question in 1917. What constituted the most effective means of securing Soviet power was an urgent, practical problem and no longer a theoretical proposition to be debated by exiles in the coffee houses of Zurich. Soviet pronouncements insist that Lenin set the fundamental course even then, and that Soviet policy has simply been elaborated in the light of modern conditions.

Yet it seems obvious that the question of what constitutes security has been answered differently at various times in the history of the Soviet Union. And, despite the generally high degree of uniformity of Soviet pronouncements on matters of high policy, it has been answered differently by different Soviet leaders.

In the early days of the Revolution, and for many years before it occurred, most Bolsheviks appeared to be genuinely convinced that after the Revolution had taken place in Russia, similar upheavals in adjacent countries would quickly follow. Communist theory, in fact, had assumed that more advanced "capital-

would have their revolutions well before backward Russia. In the
believed that Russia and her ruling proletariat would soon find
rrounded by class allies who had wrested power from the bour-
iers and state sovereignty would lose their meaning, and class
uld override national differences as old political entities became
caught up in revolutionary change. The security problem would thus no longer
present itself in its traditional form.

These early notions constituted perhaps the most radical departure from the
conventional conception of security which had evolved historically in the system
of states and nations that had developed since the Middle Ages. The Bolsheviks
did not see themselves at first as governing a state but as leading a revolutionary
detachment, part of a movement which, if not world-wide, would be widespread,
at least in Europe. Security to them meant the physical survival and the further
development of the regime that had been established in a part of Russia; it was an
important but nevertheless temporary problem. It also meant safeguarding the
regime's ability to institute the societal and other changes it planned—but still in
the context of a broader, revolutionary environment. The content of these notions
of survival and development did not in themselves differ significantly from those
entertained by rulers of traditional states. What was new was the conception that
survival and the fulfillment of revolutionary goals depended on similar events
occurring in adjacent and other countries, and the conviction that these events
would then merge into a single universal movement.

Since the survival of the Russian Revolution and the implementation of its
goals were seen as depending on revolutions elsewhere, it was only natural that
the Russian revolutionary vanguard should seek to trigger such revolutions and
help to sustain them. Thus, security clearly was not confined within the old
frontiers of Russia, nor within the areas where the Russian revolutionaries held
sway (which were far smaller than the territory of Russia, however defined at
that fluid moment); it became consciously and deliberately contingent on events
well beyond those territorial confines. Yet the capacity of the Russian revolutionaries to affect events beyond the borders of the Soviet Union, and even within
their own area of more or less tenuous control, was highly circumscribed. They
did have certain ties with revolutionaries elsewhere, but their principal instruments were the presumed force of their ideas and doctrines, and the illusion that
history had ordained a revolutionary tide in the capitalist world at that particular
moment. These notions, however, proved to be false, and the more clearly their
falsity was demonstrated, the more the Bolsheviks, lacking at that time other,
traditional manifestations of power, resorted to conspiratorial, clandestine, and
other means of encouraging revolutionary movements.

Events unfolded quite differently from expectations. Soviet-style revolutions
were confined to a very few countries and proved to be short-lived. Circumstances in the Soviet Union, and the manner in which Lenin's Bolsheviks staged
the take-over of the country's government and other institutions, proved to be
virtually unique. The USSR soon found herself confronting problems typical of

those encountered by states functioning within a system of states. Having challenged the outside world with revolutionary upheaval, she now had to cope with numerous threats to her own territorial integrity and to the survival of the new regime. While in many countries, adjacent as well as more distant, there sprang up Communist parties and other groups sympathetic to the Soviet state, these turned out to have only a limited capacity to support the Soviet rulers' quest to secure themselves against external threats. Their capacity to buttress the new regime in its struggles against internal enemies was even more limited. The novel notions of security and how to promote it entertained by the Russian Bolsheviks thus had only a very brief life, although they continued to color the security conceptions that subsequently evolved.

The Communist rulers of the USSR had to adjust to the fact that their earlier definitions of the conditions for survival and of how to ensure it were no longer pertinent and may indeed have been no more than hopes in the first place. But they were convinced that if the country and the hope of eventual widespread revolution were to survive, the regime itself had to be preserved. To Soviet leaders, and to the evolving elite with which they surrounded themselves, national security (to use a Western term) became synonymous with regime security.

These redefinitions of security, which began in Lenin's lifetime, did not come easily. Many of the early disputes and schisms in the regime revolved precisely around the ability of the new revolutionary state to survive. Even before Lenin's death important sections of the revolutionary leadership remained persuaded that the Soviet Union and her regime could not long survive as an island in a capitalist sea. They were dubious about, and opposed to, Lenin's domestic concessions, as in the case of the New Economic Plan, by which he sought to safeguard the economic viability of the Soviet Union. Some also doubted the wisdom and propriety of Lenin's willingness to deal with capitalist powers in the early 1920s in an effort to prevent the formation of hostile coalitions against the Soviet state. Hence the alternative policy associated broadly with Trotsky, that of permanent revolution and active support for revolutionary movements and enterprises in other countries, continued to enjoy support.

Stalin's victory established an enduring conception of security that in its fundamental elements was essentially traditional. The Soviet Union was a state which had to stand guard over her frontiers and territorial integrity. To do so, she needed military forces to deter or ward off potential invaders; she could utilize—and even to an extent rely upon—the admittedly fragile but still not insignificant protection of the "bourgeois" international order and its legal norms; she could seek alliances or other forms of association, including economic ones, with others members of the traditional state system; and she could and would try to manipulate the external balance of power. Before turning to this new period and the evolution of more traditional security policy, it is worth noting some of the effects of this early period on both the Soviet Union and her adversaries.

First, the Communist International absorbed much of the energy of the Soviet regime and in a sense supplanted more normal forms of diplomacy. Since the Soviet Union was excluded from the European councils, her reliance on foreign Communists was in part a natural reaction, but it may be that the alliance gave the Soviet regime a false impression of the ability of foreign Communists to influence events. In any case, the maintenance of party links with Moscow was a constant source of suspicion abroad and continued to play a role in the exclusion of the Soviet regime from European affairs.

Second, the question of the "legitimacy" of the Soviet regime lingered on for a considerable period. The Soviet Union herself contributed to the notion that what was happening in the USSR was transitory and bound to be replaced by some new revolutionary order in Europe. The regime's opponents abroad also continued to hope and believe (though for different reasons) that it would not last. There was widespread expectation that some upheaval would take place or, if not, that the regime's character would evolve in a more benign and traditional direction.

Thus, in the post-Lenin period the regime found itself having to define its own interests, and being forced to do so in a climate still essentially hostile, if not overtly threatening.

CONSOLIDATION AND NEW DANGER

Traditional conceptions of security—and far from revolutionary methods of safeguarding it—continued to be accompanied by other elements that gave Soviet views of security a special character. Even as Stalin established the most rigid and repressive internal order and created the first modern totalitarian state, he believed in and practiced a form of forward defense deriving from the Bolshevik notion that class solidarity extended beyond national frontiers. Particularly when the external dangers to her security mounted in the mid-1930s, through the consolidation of the Nazi regime in Germany, the Soviet Union sought to build "reserves" among Communist parties and sympathizers abroad to consolidate her own strength. She gradually ended the sectarian phase of the external Communist parties, ordering and pressing them to seek allies among non-Communist parties and other groups so as to form united fronts against the Fascist threat.

It is quite possible that Stalin saw these alliances as temporary arrangements dictated by the Nazi threat and that, in some instances at least, he envisaged subsequent stages when Communist takeovers could be staged (for example, in Spain). In other words, the Soviet conception of security, while heavily conditioned by anxieties about external dangers (as well as internal threats from residual "capitalist" elements), retained offensive aspects harking back to earlier notions of spreading Communist revolutions and class alliances transcending national borders. Pretensions to the leadership of the international working class were muted but not renounced. This was the united-front tactic, in fact, built on the mechanisms of the Comintern which had its origins in the early revolutionary optimism that had prevailed immediately after the Revolution. And, under Soviet orders, Communists sought to retain their separate identity to avoid contamination by other groups and theories.

Still, for the time being at least, such offensive aspects were subordinated to more immediate concerns: the search for allies wherever they could be found, including alliances formed through a "collective security" system; and the effort to deter and delay external aggression and prevent the isolation of the USSR in the event of such aggression.

In the end, these concerns led to an alliance with the enemy himself, when it appeared that neither united fronts nor alliance arrangements could be worked out with the Western democracies and with Germany's potential victims in Eastern and Southeastern Europe. (The Western democracies and their Polish and Romanian associates may have been short-sighted in their failure to enter into defense arrangements with the USSR—most historians believe this to be the case. But it is worth reflecting that it was not the first time, and certainly not the last, that the Soviet Union's own conduct and the legacy of her revolutionary pretensions served to heighten the dangers to her own security and prevent cooperative measures that might have reduced them.)

The Nazi–Soviet alliance quintessentially represented the use of a traditional means of seeking safety or of delaying danger—the manipulation of external forces. But, cynicism (or realism) apart, it was another instance, and perhaps the most dramatic up to that time, of a recognition that the imperatives of security required certain entanglements with the external world of class enemies. Moreover, as the period between 1939 and 1941 was to show, in Soviet eyes the interests of security even required the propitiation of the potential enemy with economic and military support while class allies were left to their own devices— and in consequence deserted the socialist motherland in droves. In addition, as had been evident on earlier occasions after the Revolution, security considerations were seen as ample justification for the acquisition of territory and demands for spheres of influence and control (as advanced in Soviet–Nazi diplomatic haggling in 1940), with no regard for "revolutionary" conditions or the interests and concerns of indigenous Communist parties.

Thus, in the 20 years after the consolidation of Soviet power, the regime's security conception had evolved from considerations determined largely by the expectations of Communist revolutionary doctrines to ones quite similar to those that had traditionally assured the physical survival of nation-states in times of peril. Since they had not envisaged a single Communist state, Communist doctrines appeared to have little to offer to meet these concerns in practical terms, although they were used to consolidate further Stalin's domestic power. Externally, the Soviet Union was concerned with her essential territorial integrity and physical security; she sought to extend her frontiers as far as possible against the incursions of the potential enemy; she sought allies, regardless of political orientation; she tried to buy time with economic and other concessions; and she set aside revolutionary goals abroad both because they obstructed the palliation of more fundamental anxieties about survival and because, if pursued, they might even have heightened the threat.

It may be said that at this moment of grave danger and considerable weakness the Soviet definition of security involved the most elementary imperative of survival and little else. When the dangers confronting the regime became even graver after the Nazi invasion, it did not, in seeking to assure its survival, shrink from moderating certain of the internal essentials of Communist rule by invoking, *inter alia*, nationalism, patriotism, military discipline and prestige, faith and religion to motivate and mobilize the population against the external threat. The survival of the country and the survival of the leadership were still essentially synonymous, but a certain dilution of the character of the regime occurred which, in conjunction with but quite separately from the external threat, might in fact have placed its survival in question, had the Soviet Union not succeeded in reversing her military fortunes.

The point here is not just that Stalin proved extremely flexible and cynical in pursuing his goals; it is somewhat simpler but no less important: Soviet conceptions of fundamental interests and of how to protect and advance them have not been immutable. The means chosen by, or forced upon, the regime in the pursuit of its interests have involved not only choices normally described as tactical or expedient, but also some that could not have been readily derived from the basic Marxist–Leninist texts or even from the statements of the very practitioners of the policies outlined above. The Soviet conception of security, and the actions designed to safeguard it, must then be seen in the light as much of Soviet operational conduct as of Soviet pronouncements and the Marxist–Leninist classics. Predispositions stemming from the Bolshevik heritage of the leadership can be and have been significantly affected by other factors.

World War II and After

World War II—still referred to, characteristically, as the Great Patriotic War—was plainly a deeply traumatic experience for the Soviet Union. Not only did it cause enormous destruction and human suffering, but it shook the regime to its foundations. Had German occupation policy been less brutal and stupid, large portions of the population (especially, but not exclusively, non-Russians) might well have defected from the Soviet state. As it was, hundreds of thousands—if not millions—of soldiers and civilians surrendered or were captured. A large number agreed to serve against the Soviet Union, and many others refused to return there. In the end capitalist allies were needed to help sustain the USSR's military efforts and defeat the enemy.

It is hardly surprising that, even in the exhilaration of victory, Stalin should have had uppermost in his mind not abstract questions about a just and lasting peace settlement, but the fundamental issue of how to prevent such catastrophes from recurring. The territorial buffers he had hurriedly erected in the short period before disaster struck had been of little use. The military preparations he had undertaken had been flawed and inadequate. The "socialist transformations" implemented in the years between the Revolution and the war had done little, if anything, to inspire in the population loyalty to the regime; the opposite was closer to the truth, and traditional Russian values and symbols had had to be reintroduced to inspire the populace to sacrifice and heroism.

Throughout the wartime conferences Stalin was determined to assure for the USSR territorial gains that would provide a more effective buffer against attack. Where he did not or could not subsume territory, he operated on the premise that mere hegemony over adjacent land was insufficient and that the political order of such territories itself had to be transformed to fit the Soviet pattern. Either Soviet military occupation or the proximity of Soviet military power facilitated the process—and certainly justified it in Stalin's eyes, whatever the preferences, traditions, and other circumstances of the populations involved.

It is not clear whether the establishment of a satellite empire in the form in which it emerged in the late 1940s in Eastern and Southeastern Europe was already clearly part of Stalin's wartime design. The wartime and immediate postwar arguments about Poland indicate that the essentials were clear to Stalin, and he then adapted the pace, intensity, and particular methods of the satellization process to the circumstances obtaining in the individual countries concerned. To some degree, he also considered potential foreign reaction. The security concerns of the USSR were thus transformed and expanded to include the security of the new empire and the maintenance of the regimes imposed on the populations with the aid of Moscow-trained Communists. (Czechoslovakia was only marginally exceptional, in the sense that her Communist party, though still a minority, was larger than those of other East European countries. Yugoslavia was a separate case, since the Tito regime had established itself essentially by its own efforts, although Tito and many of his associates also had extensive connections with Moscow.)

Stalin's conception of security in the postwar world, of course, was not confined to the physical protection of the Soviet Union against renewed military threats. Since the safety of the regime, and the political order over which it presided, were of equally crucial concern, especially in the light of wartime events and the dilution of party orthodoxy, Stalin saw the East European satellite empire as more than a military buffer. He regarded it also as constituting the outer lines of defense against various forms of ideological and psychological challenge that emanated from the "capitalist" world, a wall from behind which conformity could be reimposed only with great difficulty on the peoples of the USSR. This concern with external subversion was almost certainly reinforced by the recognition that the Soviet population would be called upon to make extraordinary sacrifices in terms of their living standards and well-being as the regime pressed forward with reconstructing the industrial base of the country and the maintenance of large military forces. If the East European buffer states were to play this role, it became as essential to identify the survival of their regimes with the physical security of the countries themselves as was the case with the Soviet Union herself. It was, moreover, not sufficient that these regimes should carry the Communist label. (Actually, of course, according to the Soviet ritual, they were not yet Communist regimes but regimes run by Communists, engaged in building socialism as a preliminary to the eventual construction of Communist societies. The Soviet Union herself was said to be still only building socialism.) It was vital that the regimes should be intensely loyal and subservient to the Stalinist regime in Moscow. The designation "People's Democracy" was attached to each of them, and they were instructed to follow the model "pioneered" by the USSR in the era of socialism in one country. This course carried the seeds of later difficulties.

There had thus emerged an extended concept of security which involved the territorial integrity of both the Soviet Union and the newly acquired empire as well as the ideological and structural conformity of all the parts of the empire and its subordination in all major respects to the needs and concerns of the USSR.

Although the establishment of this empire was portrayed as resulting from a renewal of the revolutionary tide which had subsided after the 1917 Revolution, it had in fact occurred as a result of the use and refinement of largely traditional means of power. Stalin had wielded force, directly and indirectly, to create the empire. But he had not done so indiscriminately; that is, he acted where he judged the risks of doing so to be acceptable in terms of possible Western responses. Later, in 1948–1949, when Yugoslavia failed in several respects to conform to Soviet prescriptions, he was prepared (in his view, perhaps, only temporarily) to overlook one defection because the risks and costs of preventing it seemed to him excessive. This decision probably did not stem so much from fear of Western intervention as from the realization that Tito commanded sufficient support to enable him to put up vigorous resistance to the application of Soviet force.

The question of why Stalin chose to establish buffers in the form of satellites only in Eastern Europe is still open. He had, of course, made demands upon Turkey and Iran, which were designed to provide the USSR with territorial and other advantages associated with security. He had also laid claim to former Italian colonies in the Mediterranean area. But when they were rejected, he refrained from pressing these ambitions, presumably because he considered that resistance might embroil the USSR in complications which he was not then prepared to countenance. In the case of Finland he preferred a form of neutrality and indirect hegemony to satellization, perhaps because he recognized that the establishment of a subservient and conformist pro-Soviet Communist regime would be far more difficult than in Eastern and Southeastern Europe and because he was less certain of Western passivity. He did, of course, impose territorial concessions and other constraints on Finland. In the case of the Far East he held on to territories seized from Japan or Japanese control at the end of the war, but he was not ready to challenge the United States' dominant postwar position on Japan's main islands.

In general, Stalin displayed considerable caution in pressing or undertaking actions which he judged would halt or reverse American withdrawal from the

Soviet periphery. The wartime meetings had evidently persuaded him that this was the American intention. Indeed, it was one of the ironies of the split with Yugoslavia that Stalin viewed the latter's intervention in the Greek civil war as potentially detrimental to Soviet security because of possible British and American reactions. Stalin's instinct was right: It was the fragility of the Greek situation, along with fears about the integrity of Turkey, which triggered the first major American decisions leading to the permanent involvement of the United States in Europe.

Stalin displayed similar caution with regard to Communist prospects in France and Italy. He was concerned more with consolidating what he had than with expansion, and he was probably doubtful about whether he could maintain over Communist activities in these more distant areas the kind of control he considered essential in countries adjacent to the USSR. In general, although it was not fully apparent at the time, Stalin had serious doubts about the contribution that would be made to Soviet security by Communist regimes that came to power largely on their own strength. Although Communist theory held that Communist revolutions would be essentially compatible with the Soviet regime, Stalin seems to have been unconvinced. Yugoslavia was already an object lesson; China and Albania were also to defect soon after Stalin died.

Stalin had increased substantially the sphere of dominant Soviet power and had thereby seemingly strengthened the physical security of the USSR. Yet he never lost the siege mentality that had marked Soviet evolution in the 1920s and 1930s. "Capitalist encirclement" remained for him a reality, both in terms of the military threat to the Soviet Union that he envisaged and in terms of potential connections between internal opposition to the regime and external enemies. Internal repression was therefore as necessary an expedient for him as defense against external aggression.

These very attitudes and the policies they produced resulted in developments which left the position of the USSR considerably less secure than Stalin had hoped. For among the consequences of his policies were the creation of a new Western alliance system, including, after 1950, the permanent stationing of large numbers of American combat forces on the European continent, the gradual incorporation of West Germany in the alliance system, and the development of a potent American nuclear arsenal, together with systems capable of delivering these new weapons onto Soviet soil.

From the late 1940s onward Stalin, facing these developments, had to raise his sights above the consolidation of his homeland and empire to ways of impeding the formation of a potent, new, hostile coalition. This gave rise to the peace movement and its campaigns against the nuclear weaponry that was being acquired by the United States and the alliance system in process of construction in the West. Some of the united-front tactics employed in the 1930s against Hitler were revived, and a certain diplomatic flexibility began to manifest itself (e.g., in the resolution of the Berlin blockade).

Meanwhile, Stalin laid the economic and technological foundation for expanded Soviet military power which looked beyond the defense of the Soviet perimeter and incorporated nuclear weapons in the USSR's military forces. Stalin died as these developments were under way; his successors were left to cope with and build upon them.

Observers of the Stalinist era have pointed out that Stalin's vision was a limited one, coinciding with Soviet artillery range. Within these limits he was, in fact, relatively successful; a dominant position in Eastern Europe, diminished German strength, a weak China, and some voice in Japan's future made the USSR relatively more secure than before the war.

Stalin had assumed that the postwar settlement was to be a "spheres of influence" arrangement. What actually happened, however, was that the USSR's inferior nuclear position inevitably limited her power. At the time, of course, few understood that Stalin was a rather conservative statesman. Western opinion attributed to him and to the USSR the most grandiose aspirations and ambitions. In 1950, in the famous American policy paper, NCS-68, the Soviet Union emerged as a towering giant, casting her shadow over almost all of the world and bent on total conquest. This view was corroborated, shortly after the document was promulgated, by the invasion of Korea. But if Khrushchev is to be believed, this was initially a rather casual affair, with Stalin approving an adventure by Kim Il Sung, which Western statements could have led Stalin to believe was a relatively safe probe. On January 12, 1950 Secretary Acheson had, after all, said the defensive perimeter excluded South Korea.

In short, the immediate postwar period saw the extension of the USSR's security perimeter, but by 1953 the process had about run its course. The limits had been determined first in Iran, then in Greece and Turkey, then in Germany, and finally in the Far East.

Few observers would claim that the position of the Soviet Union was "secure" in 1953. Indeed, Stalin's heirs apparently regarded it as unsatisfactory. In his memoirs Khrushchev gives a summary of this moment: "We had doubts of our own about Stalin's foreign policy. He overemphasized the importance of military might for one thing, and consequently put too much faith in our armed forces." Khrushchev goes on to describe Soviet nervousness over dealing with the Western powers and the Soviet delegation's sense of inferiority in meeting the Western leaders at the Geneva summit in 1955. Yet, freed from Stalin's restraint, his successors began to broaden their horizons and to grope for definitions of security more suited to the emerging situation. For this was no longer simply the post–World War II era, but a time of dramatic changes in military technology and the world political map.

THE UNCERTAIN SUPERPOWER: KHRUSHCHEV

It is a commonplace but nevertheless valid contention that the transition from Stalin to Khrushchev reflected the shift from a regional conception of security to a global one, from a basically defensive orientation to an offensive one, and from the era of World War II to the nuclear-rocket age.

In the simplest terms, what happened was that Stalin's successors found that it was not only feasible to project Soviet influence beyond the more traditional range of her neighboring areas, but that this might well pay dividends in terms of the security of the Soviet state. The Soviet Union, however, was quite slow to discover the political consequences of the colonial era's end, having originally regarded newly independent nations like India as likely to remain in the capitalist camp. The process of "liberation" was already well advanced when Khrushchev and his colleagues began to make their first tentative forays into the Third World.

What did they expect to achieve? The advantages were obvious. If some of the Soviet Union's principal adversaries were caught up in the agonies of relinquishing their colonial holdings, this process might not only be encouraged but could also reinvigorate the broader revolution the older generation had expected, albeit in advanced capitalist countries, 30 years earlier.

Involvement in this process of "liberation" also had the attraction that in the various struggles the USSR, not the West, was the "legitimate" power; indeed, it was the USSR that provided a model for transforming relatively weak and backward countries into modern industrial powers, for organizing an economy and forcing its development, and even for reconstructing the social and political order.

Although she was still facing capitalist encirclement in Eurasia, it was thought, the Soviet Union might in turn be able to leapfrog the containment barriers and to encircle the capitalists. A simple calculation revealed that Soviet security—that is, the security of the heartland—would be reinforced if the positions held by the enemy were weakened over a broad front in areas where the Western world still saw its essential reserves.

The story of the USSR's involvement with Nasser, Nehru, Sukarno, etc., need not be rehashed. But it is worth noting that doctrinal rationalization was elaborated *ex post facto* and piecemeal; the policy was well launched before the Twentieth Party Congress and the international Communist meetings of the late 1950s.

The very process of elaborating theories concerning "national democracies" and the like probably reinforced the belief that the policy was, in fact, advantageous. Nevertheless, the fact remains that the Soviet Union's reading of historical development was erroneous. The Soviet model was not widely adopted; local Communists were only marginally effective and sometimes a burden; the West accommodated itself slowly to neutrality; its losses in Asia and Africa were to some extent compensated for by the reawakening of Western Europe: NATO expanded; Germany began to rearm; and the treaty of Rome envisaged European unity.

There was also the problem that, as time passed, newly won Soviet advantages and positions had to be reinforced. Stalin had made the complete control of the Eastern European parties synonymous with Soviet security, permitting no deviations and underwriting his position with the physical presence of the Red Army. This approach was both impracticable and inappropriate to the new era and the regions to which Soviet attention turned. Most of the political forces in these regions were unsuited to the imposition of old-style Comintern discipline and were far from the Soviet homeland. Thus, the Soviet Union was forced to commit herself increasingly to the defense—at least in political and economic terms—of a highly disparate aggregation of states, political parties, and movements. And in so doing, she was obliged to accept new obligations and risks in areas where her control was far from complete.

In short, the arena of Soviet security concern expanded and the policy instruments multiplied, but the gains were tenuous and had to be consolidated periodically. In the course of adopting a global policy, the USSR was gradually transforming her techniques in ways that drew on the expertise of her only true global competitor, the United States.

Indeed, the process of expansion was accompanied inexorably by a growing confrontation with the one power capable of countering the USSR. Where Stalin might have envisaged various political combinations with the capitalists in 1938–1939, the range of options available to Khrushchev was more constricted. Soviet security was, above all, defined in terms of competition with the United States. Moreover, that competition was at the highest level a military one. The United States had the longest strategic reach. For the first time the USSR could be threatened directly and devastated by a power that was not bordering on or near her own territory. The nuclear competition could not be affected by "national liberation" as such; nor was there any firm ideological basis for examining the relationship between the destructiveness of nuclear war and the USSR's political aims.

The problem of adjusting to the nuclear age was obviously a cardinal security issue in the 1950s. It was debated in the military literature and, presumably, in other forums. It had to be confronted during a period of internal tensions and power struggles. What evidence there is suggests that it was one of the issues debated among the various political contenders. Malenkov's deviation, emphasizing the dangers and even the inutility of nuclear war, is well known. It is doubtful that it was an accidental misstatement. Probably it represented a cautious viewpoint that took account of the possibility, even the necessity, of accommodations with the West. The position that prevailed must have argued for political maneuvering but involved doctrinal adjustments that avoided the fundamental conflict with Marxist–Leninist prescriptions on war.

The major decisions proclaimed at the Twentieth Party Congress in 1956 reflected a rather clever compromise. The inevitability of war was qualified: it was no longer "fatal"; war could be prevented. The means by which it would be circumvented were associated with the new "social and political forces" that would combine to deter the capitalists. It is worth pausing to note the confusion surrounding the doctrine of the inevitability of war. It stemmed from prerevolutionary notions concerning relations among capitalist states. The wars that were said to be inevitable were those generated by the inherent antagonisms and conflicts between capitalist states fighting for markets, resources, etc. It was in the era of socialism in one country that the notion was transformed into one applying to relations between socialist and capitalist states. Capitalism, that is, would delay its own demise by resisting forcibly the onward march of socialism. In its original version, the inevitability-of-war doctrine served to benefit the advance of revolution, since the "peoples" would rebel against the recurrent bloodshed engendered by capitalism and would find their salvation in socialism. As the prospect of intracapitalist wars seemed to dim after World War II, the emphasis shifted to the inevitability of capitalist–socialist war. Even then, well into the Khrushchev period, the greatest gains of socialism were said to have been the results of the two intracapitalist world wars (World War II having become a modified socialist–capitalist one only after 1941). The advent of nuclear weapons complicated adherence to the doctrine of inevitable socialist–capitalist war, since it seemed to make the USSR an implicit advocate of such a war. Moreover, if a catastrophic war were inevitable, there was a danger that the Soviet populace would become apathetic and resigned; the "preventability" of war both allowed for active policies and gave the population hope for prolonged peace.

Meanwhile, Soviet diplomacy would attempt to neutralize the nuclear issue. In effect, what emerged was a more vigorous and diversified version of Stalin's tentative return, in the late 1940s and early 1950s, to some of the popular front approaches of the 1930s. To some extent, Soviet security again became dependent on the manipulation of political forces—Communists, nationalists, neutralists—outside the immediate areas of Soviet control. It was in this context that the principle of "peaceful coexistence" was revived. It was no doubt viewed as a soporific; it permitted the Soviet leaders to avoid more fundamental choices, and it was useful in rationalizing of policies that had already been adopted out of necessity.

But was it wholly tactical? One can only speculate, but it seems plausible that, having resurrected a doctrinal expression to suit their purposes, the Soviet leaders, in continually defining and defending the "preventability" and coexistence doctrines, found them increasingly comfortable and convenient. Almost certainly, Mao's insistence on the likelihood, and even the desirability, of a cataclysmic showdown found no support in Moscow. In short, tactics blended with strategy. Despite changing external conditions and the growth of Soviet power, the general line of peaceful coexistence has been maintained, and at no point since 1956 has any Soviet leader challenged the contention that a world war was no longer inevitable—nor has there been any real effort to define the limits of the period of coexistence.

To be sure, the Soviet Union recognized that there were fatalistic, passive, and defeatist connotations to peaceful coexistence (as well as to the "inevitability of war''). Enormous energy has been expended on defining what peaceful coexistence is *not* (it does not, for example, exclude "struggle" or the support of national liberation). Some basic ambiguities have been permitted, and it is this grey area between devastating war and placid peace that has provided Western analysts with endless scope for speculation about real Soviet "intentions."

But it is also reasonable to conclude that Khrushchev introduced a period of considerable confusion in Soviet security policy. For one thing, he was entranced by nuclear rockets. The political potential he saw in them emerges clearly from his memoirs, in which he belittles "rifles and bayonets" and claims that the USSR's defense depends on the "quality and quantity of our nuclear missile arsenal." The Soviet warning to Britain and France in the Suez crisis of 1956 foreshadowed the more aggressive conduct of the USSR after 1957. Not only could the Soviet Union compensate for intercontinental inferiority by holding Europe hostage, but the threat of a "missile gap" offered a chance to achieve some of the recurrent Soviet aims in a period of offensive pressures. Thus Khrushchev's demands in 1958–1960 were strikingly reminiscent of earlier Soviet demands: the exclusion of the West from Berlin and final settlement of the German problem.

The events of the period cannot be recounted here. Khrushchev ran a gigantic bluff that became increasingly complicated and dangerous. In some desperation, he sought a breakthrough by means of a bold stroke in Cuba. He failed and thereby brought the optimistic and most assertive phase of his policy to a close.

Any assessment of Soviet security in the Khrushchev period must note some major internal developments and the state of international Communism. First, the initial "thaw," the subsequent de-Stalinization, and the disappearance of mass terror had a bearing on security problems. Stalin's successors were less paranoid, though still concerned about internal enemies. Having lived through the various plots and counterplots concocted by Stalin, they must have concluded that the internal threat was exaggerated. In the light of what happened in Poland and Hungary, however, one must ask why Khrushchev launched his internal repudiation of Stalin. Moreover, why did he promote the reconciliation with Tito, going so far as to revise the doctrine of a single road to socialism?

It is important to remember that de-Stalinization and internal liberalization were by no means unanimously supported policies; they were resisted at very high levels and were thus instruments in Politburo struggles. Most important, de-Stalinization was not a process which the Soviet Union had foreseen in all its consequences once it had spread outside her borders. Far from operating on a master plan, it seems probable that the Soviet Union became engaged in a series of *ad hoc* decisions and struggles. De-Stalinization was a weapon against Malenkov and Molotov. The reconciliations with Tito accorded with the same strategy.

In retrospect, the various cross-currents of domestic and foreign policy were much stronger throughout Khrushchev's period than was generally recognized.

Much as Stalin feared that his "enemies" had never accepted the legitimacy of his own rule, Khrushchev continued to see "Stalinists," or at least professed to see them, as his principal opponents. Thus his policies, which might otherwise have seemed reasonable, were often justified and defended in strident and dogmatic terms. His obsession with Stalin, which comes through in his memoirs, had the effect of driving him to extremes; his own apprehensions compounded his tendency to overreact and overachieve.

Indeed, it may be that Khrushchev felt driven to prove that his anti-Stalinism would be crowned with success: Where Stalin ignored the Third World, Khrushchev courted it; where Stalin insisted on iron rule, Khrushchev proclaimed relaxations; where Stalin ruled Eastern Europe through the army and the KGB, Khrushchev hoped for loyalty to principles; where Stalin sought security in the Red Army, Khrushchev sought it in the strategic rocket forces (though he bluffed about their strength). The result was that Khrushchev defined Soviet interests so broadly that he became overcommitted, and some breakdown or retrenchment was probably inevitable.

One can only speculate about the extent to which Khrushchev was also driven by his resentment or fear of China. Khrushchev claims in his memoirs that he told his comrades as early as 1954 that conflict with China was "inevitable." Whether or not this is true, his policies hastened the conflict. It is likely that by 1959, when China claims Khrushchev halted Soviet assistance for her nuclear weapons program, China had acquired the status of an adversary, if not an outright enemy. This was not fully appreciated at the time; until 1964 it was believed in the West that there was a continuing prospect of a Soviet–Chinese reconciliation. Since the split was fully confirmed after Khrushchev's fall, it is probable that his antipathy toward or apprehensions about China were not personal predilections but reflected a new dimension of Soviet security concerns.

A review of the Khrushchev period proffers certain conclusions. First, the Soviet Union began to view her security in much broader geographical and functional terms, and in doing so she accepted commitments and risks that made the management of national security policy more complex. Second, the nuclear issue assumed more urgency and the competition with the United States came to be judged more and more in terms of the strategic nuclear balance. Third, the relaxation of tension inside the USSR accelerated centrifugal tendencies in the Communist orbit, leading to a partial reconciliation with, but also concessions to, Yugoslavia and a deepening split with China—in effect stimulating pluralism. Fourth, the shift from regionalism to globalism cost the Soviet Union a good deal: It imposed new military–economic burdens but yielded only a marginal weakening of the regime's main adversaries abroad. By 1964 national security for the USSR was a complex equation. It involved calculations concerning the internal repercussion of foreign policies, the cost of sustaining large economic and political commitments in Eastern Europe as well as in much more remote areas, the burden of armaments to offset Western build-ups, and the ideological and doctrinal consequences of the era of disintegrating Communist ranks. In this light, it is not surprising that more elements of the Soviet bureaucracy, particularly the military, were drawn into policy deliberations.

THE ACCUMULATION OF POWER: BREZHNEV

We do not have access to any systematic, internal Soviet definition of the security status of the USSR in the mid-1960s. Nor can we say precisely how the Soviet Union defined the notion of security at that point in her history.

If security is to be regarded chiefly as a function of military power, the Soviet sense of security must have been substantially greater then than at any other time in the country's history. Security (defined as safety from imminent attack) was certainly greater than in the past. It should be observed, however, that even in the mid- and late 1920s, as well as in the 1940s, when the USSR's military power was much less formidable, her security concerns revolved chiefly around a generally hostile environment which might, over a longer or shorter period of time, evolve toward active aggression—or, more accurately, toward active resistance to Soviet incursion. Soviet fears of imminent, active aggression were justifiably greatest in the late 1930s, as intensive German rearmament proceeded amidst violent hostility against Bolshevism, thinly disguised claims to "living space" adjacent to or even within the USSR, and in the context of the anti-Comintern pact. In the postwar world there may have been intermittent fears of imminent strategic attack, but they were associated with crises often caused by the USSR's own actions.

By any measure Soviet power had vastly increased between 1945 and 1965. Ground and air forces had been modernized and were deployed in substantial numbers in all areas where attacks might conceivably occur (with some exceptions in the Far East). Large reserves were maintained. The navy was in the process of evolving from a coastal defense force designed to support a land battle to one that could be used, at least for purposes of showing the flag, in more remote places. A squadron was permanently deployed in the Mediterranean, and some facilities were available in Cuba. Plans were under way to increase and diversify the navy and to enlarge the merchant marine. Long-range intervention forces, in the form of air transports, airborne divisions, and amphibious forces, were making their appearance. Strategic forces, though numerically and technically inferior to those of the United States, were growing with sustained momentum and were losing their initial vulnerability to preemptive or preventive strikes by the United States. Industry and technology were harnessed to a permanent effort to maintain and improve these forces.

These developments in their totality had begun to place a serious question mark over Western strategy for the defense of Europe. The West could no longer place unqualified reliance on the first use of nuclear weapons to compensate for disadvantages in conventional theater forces and for extended overwater lines of communication. In addition, at this stage the United States was increasingly preoccupied with the war in Vietnam, which deflected forces and energies from the power competition with the USSR. The Soviet Union almost certainly considered it in her interest to see the United States thus diverted, although that judgment came gradually to be qualified. Along with this preoccupation in Asia, the United States found her presence and influence in the Middle East seriously impaired after the 1967 war, largely—but not wholly—to the benefit of the USSR.

But if these trends in the power equation were a necessary condition, they still did not turn out to be a sufficient condition for security. For one thing, despite her enormous gains in power, the Soviet Union remained obsessed by the notion of inequality. She still saw the United States as an established world power and herself merely as an aspiring one. American influence, although less imposing than before and despite declining relative military power, remained widespread and deep-seated. Soviet influence, meanwhile, was increasing generally but continued to fluctuate, and it seemed much less secure than that of the United States and, indeed, of other physically much weaker Western powers. Economic and cultural ties between the West and the Third World, although often challenged by the latter, still seemed more durable than similar ties between the USSR and the Third World. The appeals of Soviet ideology were more superficial than real; political ties were vulnerable to changes in Third World regimes and nationalist resistance. Soviet efforts at transforming positions of influence into outposts of power (and hence security) frequently met only temporary success and at times outright failure.

Closer to home, Soviet power and a quarter of a century of Communist rule had failed to eradicate strivings for national identity in Eastern Europe. Beneath the crust of Stalinism—and probably encouraged by it—popular hostility toward the Soviet Union and resistance to imposed uniformity grew. The regional economic, military, and political structures which Khrushchev had sought to substitute for crude and direct domination had not produced the commonwealth of which he had dreamt. If anything, centrifugal forces revived with renewed force. If, as the Soviet Union argued, her power was forcing the West to accept a form of peaceful coexistence, this very evolution also increased the pressures in Eastern Europe to renew earlier ties with the Western world and to reduce dependence on the USSR. The Prague Spring in 1968 demonstrated that popular resistance to incorporation in the Soviet order remained a strong, latent force, ready to erupt in defiance of virtually certain Soviet military action calculated to crush it.

These trends, and the diverse expression they found in the several East European countries, showed that continued Soviet dominance did not necessarily spell control of events. Interestingly enough, it was in the face of these realities that Khrushchev's successors set out in the late 1960s to seek Western confirmation of Soviet hegemony in Eastern Europe. (The renewed pressures for a European security conference and for confirmation of the "results of World War

II'' clearly had this intent.) Ironically, the Soviet Union thus sought legitimacy for her position from her putative enemies. The Soviet Union no doubt believed that her power entitled her to this. Ironically, her allies in the West, the Communist parties, found it difficult to offer help unreservedly to the Soviet Union. By this time, these parties were seeking increasing voter acceptance by demonstrating, in form if not in substance, that the era of total subservience to the USSR had ended in the international Communist movement.

In many ways, the persistent and mounting challenge from Peking was an even more serious threat to the sense of security which great and growing power might have conferred upon the Soviet Union. Here was not only a separate and competing pole of attraction and orthodoxy in the Communist world; Peking also challenged the Soviet quest for influence and recognition in the Third World. More than that: Although she was backward in terms of modern military capacity, China voiced claims to Soviet territory and did not shrink from frontier altercations. If the Soviet Union approached the rest of the world with a sense of grievance over real and imagined wrongs perpetrated on her and her Tsarist predecessors, China managed to place the Soviet Union on the defensive by identifying her with "unequal" treaties of the past. Whatever the turmoil of the "Great Leap Forward" and the "Cultural Revolution," the Soviet Union could not shake off the nightmare of nearly a thousand million determined people eventually gaining the power to seek to redress the wrongs of the distant and recent past. The dream of nonantagonistic contradictions had long since evaporated, and there was scant comfort in the claim that the Chinese leaders had left the path of Marxism–Leninism. The USSR could retain intact the illusion that there can be no basic conflict between genuine revolutionaries, but she could not ignore the fact that here was a hostile power abutting on millions of square kilometers of rich but sparsely populated Soviet land, which was linked with European Russia by fragile communications and peopled at the rim by non-Russians whose affinity with Muscovite rule had its own historic uncertainties.

The accumulation of military force and the extension of its reach beyond the Eurasian landmass thus had not overcome some of the inherent flaws in the polity that the Soviet rulers had constructed over half a century. At the same time, the sense of power conferred on the Soviet Union by the steady shift in the military balance increased the Soviet appetite for tangible and intangible pay-offs. As in the past, this appetite had its defensive as well as offensive elements. But, for the first time since the Revolution, aspiration was being buttressed by great and growing power. In this respect, the late 1960s (and the period since then) differed from the optimistic phase of Khrushchev's term of office. While he was fascinated by modern weaponry, he had, like others before him, seen as the most potent sources of growing Soviet influence the nature of the Soviet system and the supposed confluence of revolutionary currents. His successors seemed less sanguine on these counts and relied more on the (by then) cumulative impact of raw power. It was not so much that they intended to use this power directly, although they plainly did not exclude that possibility; they believed, rather, that power would pay political dividends. Indeed, they believed that the USSR was entitled to these dividends; that she was entitled to be treated and respected as a superpower; and that this role should be given formal recognition through treaties and understandings, above all with the United States.

The Soviet concept of security thus became closely associated with the concept of equality and with the determination that the USSR should have her rights of access, presence, and influence acknowledged on a world-wide basis in form as well as substance. As power grew, so did the definition of security. The safety of the homeland was the principal consideration; the inviolability of Soviet predominance in Eastern Europe was a close second; "friendly" powers elsewhere on the Soviet periphery were next; and entitlement to a role at least equal to that of the United States elsewhere came last.

Yet the implementation of such plans was problematic. The homeland was safe from land attack, but it could not be protected either from vast destruction if nuclear war should break out or from infection by alien ideas. Eastern Europe was in the Soviet camp but full of cross-currents which diluted Soviet control. While Soviet power based in the area aimed an arrow at the West, the region was also an avenue for Western influence. Other countries on the periphery, while not actively hostile toward the Soviet Union, were far from friendly and were not deterred from maintaining and building military forces and alliances that enabled them to resist Soviet pressures. China was hostile, an active rival, and, in Soviet eyes, potentially a long-term physical threat. Japan was moderately friendly but hardly supine. Further afield the Soviet presence was growing but remained contested and uneven.

Security had thus become a goal whose attainment would require ever-increasing measures of military power and unceasing effort. As Soviet security was being defined in terms of the security situation of the United States—the Soviet Union was now demanding "equal security"—commitment to it was increasingly open-ended. Even if Soviet missile forces reached rough numerical parity with those of the United States, as they did in the late 1960s, that still did not spell a condition of equality. For American missile technology was more advanced than that of the Soviet Union; the USSR faced not only the United States but Britain and France as well, who represented the "forward-based" systems of the United States; and the USSR needed strategic forces to act as a threat (or deterrent) to China. If Soviet ground forces were substantially more extensive than those of the United States, the USSR was still not in a position of parity *vis-a-vis* the United States, because the latter had no land enemy comparable with China. Indeed, wherever the Soviet Union looked she seemed to feel herself in need of "compensation," either for discriminations and disadvantages suffered in the past or for contemporary or future ones. A natural consequence of this outlook was that as "compensation" was piled on "compensation," the United States and others against whom the Soviet Union measured her security considered their own interests to be in jeopardy and undertook a variety of counteractions which in turn established new military requirements for the

USSR. [It should be noted that during the Vietnam war particularly, but at other times too, the United States and her allies did not, in fact, respond to all accretions in Soviet power. Indeed, real defense outlays, apart from Vietnam-related expenses, declined steadily during the 1960s and 1970s. Moreover, with increasing personnel costs, outlays on military hardware declined even more sharply. Individual programs, such as the introduction of multiple independently targetable reentry vehicles (MIRV) in American land- and sea-based missile forces, did proceed, however.]

Brezhnev and his colleagues had thus inherited from Khrushchev the conviction that the Soviet Union could not and should not be satisfied with securing the borders of the homeland and its Western outposts but should strive for a status resembling that of the United States. Khrushchev had had the notion that the Soviet Union could match and overtake the economic strength of the United States and that this would render the Soviet example irresistible elsewhere in the world. Military power, which Khrushchev did not neglect but which he had tried to channel into particular areas, would be the concomitant of economic power and the power of example. Brezhnev was realistic enough to see the failings of this conception. Once he had consolidated his political position at home, he muted the themes of economic and ideological competition and generally sought to avoid head-on collisions with the USSR's principal antagonists, the United States and China. He proceeded methodically to build Soviet military power in all its dimensions and, having failed in his overtures to China and then in efforts to contain and surround her with Soviet allies, shifted to an "opening to the West." It was this strategy that was shaped in the period leading up the Twenty-fourth Communist Party Congress in 1971 and proclaimed in programmatic terms on that occasion.

Defense and Security

The unveiling of the "peace program" of the Twenty-fourth Party Congress marked the start of the present period. It has been characterized by a continuation of older political–security concerns, especially in Europe, by some new elements, especially in relations with the United States, and by some enduring uncertainties over China and Asia and over the question of leadership succession. Above all, it has been a period in which commitment to the growth of the Soviet Union's military power has become an increasingly predominant characteristic of the regime. This has raised persistent questions abroad about Soviet intentions–about how the USSR will conduct her policies in an era of military parity, if not superiority.

By the time of the Twenty-fourth Party Congress, the "détente" with the Federal Republic of Germany was well advanced. The Eastern treaties were a culmination of postwar aims to ratify the *status quo*, although they were by no means entirely the product of skillful Soviet policy; changes in West Germany played a considerable role in the conclusion of the treaties and the Soviet Union prudently worked with the new forces. But the consolidation of a European détente, as defined by the USSR, proved elusive. The West introduced new demands involving respect for human rights and increased contacts at the very time when the older issues of territorial integrity, recognition of borders, etc., were being settled. And at the same time, the willingness of the Soviet Union to temper or resist these new trends was inhibited by her growing economic interest in securing trade and credits from Western Europe. Reversion to harsher Soviet alternatives in Europe would thus entail economic losses that might not seem justified by any political advantages to be gained from taking a harder line. On the other hand, the Soviet Union faced the dilemma of whether or not she should risk the further military relaxation in Europe which the West was demanding ever more insistently.

Soviet superiority in conventional military forces, of course, has been an essential support for Soviet policy since 1945. But this advantage clearly raises for the Western partners the question of the terms for continuing the European détente, especially as each cycle of force modernization seems to create new advances. A persistent Western search for some means to eliminate some, if not all, of the USSR's conventional military advantages could pose problems which Soviet regimes in the past have managed to evade. The basic security issue is whether the Soviet Union could afford to compete and coexist in Europe under conditions of near parity of conventional forces in Central Europe. Could she, in fact, withdraw large numbers of her forces as a result of a negotiated settlement or agree to stabilize a regional balance of nuclear forces? How would this affect her security interests in Eastern Europe?

How these questions are eventually answered will depend in part on the Soviet perception of the China problem. A prominent analytical line is that the Soviet Union has sought a period of relaxation in the West in order to consolidate her buildup in the East. This is plausible and consistent with the evidence provided by the share of Soviet military resources devoted to China. But it is an explanation more of tactics than of a well-defined strategy. What does the Soviet Union do in the post-Mao period?

It seems likely that at one time the USSR harbored hopes that after Mao a *modus vivendi* could be agreed with China; while this is still possible, especially given the propensity for internal turmoil in the Chinese leadership, the entire relationship seems to be shifting to a new level of geopolitical competition ushered in by the Chinese economic modernization program, the Sino–Japanese treaty, the conflict in Indochina, and normalization with the U.S.

We can only note that the Soviet treaty with North Vietnam is a new element in Soviet security policy; it has antecedents in friendship treaties with several Third World countries, but the Soviet Union could not have been oblivious to the risk that this particular treaty might become a blank check. At present all that can be hazarded is that the odds on a confrontation with China are now shorter. The prospect of Western willingness to underwrite Chinese economic and military modernization must raise the old specter of encirclement. It also raises the question of whether and which Soviet policies will be adopted to break up a hostile coalition. "Encirclement" clearly does not accord with the regime's appreciation of Soviet power and its consequent demand for "equal security." Soviet leaders must be asking themselves whether they can accept a policy of détente with the West which could lead to an underwriting of Chinese armament efforts by the USSR's European détente partners.

The question of how to manage a European détente and a Chinese confrontation inevitably involves a consideration of Soviet policy toward the United States. The decision taken in the early 1970s to enter into a period of relaxation with Washington was not a sudden one. The factors which appear to have prompted the decision are: (1) the conclusion of the Eastern treaties, which required a further payment in the Berlin negotiations that involved the United States; (2) the American opening to China in 1971, which helped to produce the American–Soviet summit of 1972; (3) the prospect of an antiballistic missile (ABM) race; (4) economic needs; and (5) the ascendency of Brezhnev. All (except perhaps the last factor) necessitated an active policy of maneuver.

Of course, the Soviet Union expected dividends, primarily in the form of economic assistance, which she needed in a period of intensive economic development requiring major inputs of capital and technology, but also in the form of the curtailment of certain areas of strategic competition. Having embarked on the détente policy, the Soviet Union found that, as it evolved, she could not disengage herself from it, even though it yielded smaller dividends than expected and elicited new challenges.

The point is that the Soviet Union became to some extent the prisoner of her own commitments. Having proclaimed the irreversibility of détente, she could not easily dismiss it as a temporary aberration without calling into question the judgment of her own leadership. Having entered into the Strategic Arms Limitation Talks (SALT) negotiations and signed one treaty of indefinite duration, she could not easily jettison the process, even though it had become more complex. Having committed herself to multibillion dollar programs, she could not run political risks that could jeopardize them.

This is not to say that the Soviet Union has been straining to abandon the line of the Twenty-fourth Party Congress. Brezhnev's personal identification with it is a powerful impediment to such a course. Moreover, new gains have been achieved, and others may be looming. In Africa, in particular, the Soviet Union has found a novel approach to the projection of her power—through proxy military forces. This was foreshadowed to some extent in the Middle East, when Soviet forces were in combat along the Suez line during the tensions of 1970–1971. But the stationing abroad of sizable forces of a Soviet ally is new; it provides new leverage in an area of major Western concerns. The impressive fact is that the Soviet Union has accepted the concomitant risks with apparent equanimity. The two incursions—in Angola and in Ethiopia—thus suggest that the Soviet Union has already reappraised the opportunities and inhibitions of a more forward policy. The most intriguing question is whether this reappraisal reflects only an assessment of local conditions or a broader evaluation of a change in the overall balance of power.

In any case, the more traditional notion of security relating to the periphery of the USSR has probably received a new impetus by events along her southern periphery, particularly in Afghanistan, but also in Turkey and Iran. At present, the situation in Iran is uncertain. The Soviet Union has played a cautious hand— in part because of her interest in a continuous flow of natural gas, in part because the religiously motivated opponents of the Shah could have undesired effects on the USSR's own Muslim population, and in part because the Soviet Union has probably not yet seen an effective indigenous Iranian force with which to ally herself. Nevertheless, she has issued solemn warnings against foreign intervention, asserting her own state security interests because of the proximity of her borders. Moscow is probably as uncertain about the future course of events as anyone, but it must at least be harboring hopes of, and possibly taking some action to encourage, a more congenial regime in an area which Russians have historically viewed with a mixture of fear and ambition.

At the same time, the peace program of the Twenty-fourth Party Congress has suffered the effects of a number of events, some well beyond Soviet control: the resignations of Brandt and Nixon; Soviet expulsion from the Middle East and the revival of American presence and influence there; the modest economic benefits of relations with the United States; and the reappearance of human rights as an international political issue.

The Soviet Union has thus encountered some serious contradictions. On the one hand, her military power has grown both absolutely and relatively. Her reach has made itself felt in distant places, and favorable tides may be running on the USSR's southern rim. On the other hand, there is a budding relationship among the Soviet Union's principal adversaries—Western Europe, Japan, China, and the United States. The Soviet Union seems to recognize this, but how she will handle it is far from clear. At present she appears to be still at the stage of issuing "serious" warnings.

Yet it must be clear to the Soviet regime that the USSR neither has been able to translate her military preponderance into lasting favorable political alignments nor to neutralize alignments she considers inimical. Thus the curious paradox of strategic nuclear power seems to have affected the Soviet Union perhaps even more than it has affected the United States.

Finally, it is obvious that for more than a decade Soviet security has been defined and presided over by a group of leaders who will not survive more than a few more years. One can only speculate about the turmoil that the change of leaders will provoke. The most fascinating aspect is that a new leadership will inherit a position of far greater power than any of its predecessors; but it will also inherit a new set of problems, particularly in the management of economic resources, which in part is the price to be paid for the massive increases in Soviet power.

CONCLUSION

The emerging situation for Soviet security policy in the next decade could resemble that of 1958–1962, when Khrushchev attempted to turn a military advantage into lasting geopolitical gains. But there would be a significant difference: Soviet military power would meanwhile have gone through some 20 years of modernization and enlargement. Strategic forces would be massive and diverse rather than rudimentary. Close to a generation of momentum in military growth would be behind the Soviet leadership of the day, and by all indications this momentum would not be arrested, even if anticipated economic slowdown increased its relative cost.

Yet when all of this is added up, would Soviet leaders in the end dismiss the forces that would be arrayed against them in any open and direct challenge to the international geopolitical balance? Would political leaders, including those principally charged with the development and modernization of the Soviet economy and with managing far-flung ties with the outside world, accept without serious reservation estimates that the gains to be derived from pressure, threats, and, ultimately, the use of force, are inevitably destined to outweigh the costs? Would Soviet leaders, even assuming they believed themselves to have gained substantial military advantages, be certain of their ability to control the course of crises or war? How certain would Soviet leaders be that the gains they made through pressure or force would, in fact, enhance the security of the Soviet state and the progress of its political system?

None of these questions can be answered conclusively by drawing on the experience of the past. Nothing in that portion of Soviet discourse available to us sheds clear light on the answers. The Soviet attacks on Finland, Poland, and Bessarabia in 1939–1940 took place in the anticipation of fairly imminent attack, but with a green or amber light from the enemy-to-be who was then still an ally. The moves into Angola and Ethiopia seem to have been based on the calculation that the risks were modest, and therefore they do not give us much guidance for gauging Soviet reaction in situations in which risks may be judged to be more serious. On the other hand, Soviet actions in successive crises over Berlin, the Middle East, and Cuba, in which assertiveness was followed by caution when risks became higher than apparently anticipated, do not provide clear answers either. All these crises occurred before the military balance had reached the state prevailing now or that which is expected to prevail in the next 5 to 10 years.

We thus reach a point where speculation about Soviet behavior must inevitably merge with expectations of American behavior and that of other powers in the world. We do not see a Soviet leadership brimming with optimism about the prospects of the USSR in relation to the United States, the Western world generally, China, and others. But nor do we see that leadership overcome with pessimism. Its economic and other plans project effort and sacrifice for years to come. Its external economic and other commitments are also essentially long-term. Its military plans seem to envisage further cycles of modernization and improvement.

How a new leadership will handle this inheritance we cannot say. But whatever departures from Lenin it adds to those sanctioned already by its predecessors, we tend to believe that it will continue to adhere to Lenin's adaptation of Clausewitz: "War is the continuation of the policies of peace; and peace, the continuation of the policies of war." If we are right in that judgment, then the West has it in its power to help the soviet Union remain true to the scripture in this one fateful instance, by making certain that no meaningful political gain and no security advantage can be obtained from resort to the threat or use of force.

NOTE

1. V. I. Lenin, *Bourgeois Pacifism and Socialist Pacifism* (March 1919).

3
The Soviet Conception of Détente*

Raymond L. Garthoff

What is détente? What do we mean by that term? Détente above all means overcoming the "cold war" and transition to normal, equal relations among states. Détente means a readiness to resolve differences and disputes not by force not by threats and sabre-rattling, but by peaceful means, at a conference table. Détente means a certain trust and ability to take into account the legitimate interest of one another.[1]

Such was General Secretary Leonid I. Brezhnev's characterization of détente in a speech keyed to the change in American administrations in 1977. Détente, or the relaxation of international tensions, is also frequently characterized in Soviet discourse as a companion, if not an equivalent, to peaceful coexistence between states with differing social systems. Again to cite Brezhnev, who addressed the subject frequently, the connection between peaceful coexistence, détente, and the renunciation of force in the Soviet conception is clear in this passage from a speech in 1975:

Over recent years conviction in the possibility and, indeed, in the necessity of peaceful coexistence has been confirmed in the thinking of both the peoples and the leaders of most countries. Détente became possible because a new correlation of forces in the world arena has been established. Now the leaders of the bourgeois world can no longer seriously count on resolving the historic conflict between capitalism and socialism by force of arms. The senselessness and extreme danger of further increasing tension under conditions when both sides have at their disposal weapons of colossal destructive power are becoming ever more obvious.

The norms of peaceful coexistence between states are already fixed in many official bilateral and multilateral written commitments. Of course, that did not just happen by itself. In order to do away with the "cold war" and reduce the danger of a new world war tremendous political work was needed. And we can say that the decisive role in achieving détente was due to the combined efforts of the Soviet Union and the other countries of the socialist commonwealth, their consistent struggle against the forces of aggression and war.

Now the world is entering on a period when the task of embodying the principles of peaceful coexistence and mutually advantageous cooperation in daily practice has come to the fore.[2]

*Reprinted by permission of the author and publisher from Raymond L. Garthoff, *Détente and Confrontation*, pp. 36–53. Copyright © 1985. By The Brookings Institution, Washington, DC.

While the Soviet adoption and pursuit of a policy of détente was linked to Brezhnev's name and period of rule, it has been a policy of the leadership as a whole, and has continued to be reaffirmed by General Secretaries Yury V. Andropov, Konstantin U. Chernenko, and Mikhail S. Gorbachev, and other Soviet leaders. There have naturally been differences within the Soviet leadership over various aspects and applications of the policy of détente, as the discussion in this study makes clear. It is also relevant that the gradual adoption of a policy and strategy of détente in the late 1960s and early 1970s coincided with Brezhnev's rise and the consolidation of his leading role. Nonetheless, it also has represented a consensus of the collective Soviet leadership under Brezhnev, Andropov, and Chernenko. Thus Andropov, from his first speech as the new leader at Brezhnev's funeral, stressed: "We shall always be loyal to the cause of the struggle for peace, for détente."[3] And Chernenko (who in 1982 had also stressed that "détente is unquestionably the path to peace and cooperation"),[4] after succeeding Andropov, in 1984 continued to state that "the development of events can be turned from confrontation to détente."[5] Restoration of détente has continued to be held as the aim of Soviet policy.

In the Soviet view détente was made possible by the Soviet attainment of a nuclear retaliatory capability in the early 1960s and a rough strategic parity by the 1970s. The Soviet leaders had felt keenly their inferiority in overall and strategic military power, and greatly welcomed this development, which they had long sought. The ebullient Nikita A. Khrushchev had tried, prematurely and unsuccessfully, to bluff his way past Soviet inferiority, but this approach resulted only in setbacks, most notably in the Cuban missile crisis. By the end of the 1960s, however, his more cautious successors believed that the power of the Soviet Union, and in particular its nuclear deterrent, had contributed to establishing a general correlation of forces between the Soviet Union and the United States, and the Soviet and Western camps overall, sufficient to permit dealing with the West on a basis of equality.

In the Soviet perception, the United States had used its military superiority to build "positions of (superior) strength" and, more directly, to threaten and on occasion to use military power to advance its own interests. It had also sought to prevent comparable Soviet global political presence and influence. This perception accorded with their ideological beliefs as well as their experience, and it was only by strenuous efforts to improve their relative power position that the Soviets had achieved a posture of rough parity. (In fact, as the Soviets well appreciated, in the early 1970s they were still well short of full equality in military power in many respects.)

Accordingly, in the Soviet view, as stated in a key Central Committee resolution in mid-1980, "Détente is the natural result of the correlation of forces in the world arena that has formed in recent decades. The military strategic balance between the world of socialism and the world of capitalism is an achievement of truly historic significance."[6]

The meaning and role of strategic parity are addressed presently, but in the context of the present discussion it is necessary to recognize the key importance of the changed balance of power (including, but not limited to, strategic nuclear military power) from the standpoint of the Soviet conception of détente. The Soviets saw the achievement of general military parity between the two super-powers (and their camps or alliances) as having important political implications.

Détente, as conceived by *Soviet* leaders, would help manage the transition of *the United States* into a changing world, one no longer marked by American predominance but by a political parity of the Soviet Union with the United States that matched their military parity. While in many ways logically parallel to the purposes of détente in the American conception (in a reverse mirror reflection), the Soviet view in practice carried quite different implications. Some of these are fairly obvious, but others are not, as will be seen.

How does détente, as conceived by the Soviet leaders, fit into their ideological view of the world and history?

Marxism-Leninism is based on historical determinism, a belief that socio-economic forces, through a struggle of *classes,* are the driving dynamic of history. The advent of the Soviet Union as a socialist state raised the issue of war between *states* as a possible form of class struggle. Indeed, to the early Bol-shevik leaders, it was the central fact of life. Successive Soviet leaders have seen the greatest danger to the socialist cause (identified with the Soviet Union) as coming from the imperialist (capitalist) military threat. And the one mortal danger faced during the first half-century of Soviet rule after the victorious conclusion of the Civil War (and defeat of coincident foreign military interven-tions) was the attack by Germany in World War II. In Soviet eyes, the greatest threat since that war has been the unparalleled destructive power of the American nuclear arsenal.

The primary role of military power is therefore defense of the achievements of world socialism—preeminent of which is the Soviet Union. In addition, Marxist-Leninist ideology sanctions the use of military power (and any other means) available to socialist (Soviet) leaders whenever, but only if, expedient in advanc-ing the socialist cause and not jeopardizing the security of what has already been gained, above all in terms of the security of the Soviet Union. Military power is *not,* on the other hand, seen as the decisive element in advancing the historical process. The progressive revolutionary process will advance through indigenous actions by the rising working class in each society when conditions are ripe.

When a "world revolution" failed to occur after the successful conclusion of the Civil War, the new Soviet state turned to recovery and then to achievement of "socialism in one country." Priority was given to economic development and to assurance of political control. The key role of military power on behalf of world socialism was to guarantee the survival of the first socialist state. Although the term was not then in vogue, *deterrence* of renewed military intervention by the capitalist powers was the underlying strategic concept. Later, when attacked, the role of the armed forces was of course defense and defeat of the attacker. The same concept of deterrence has governed the period since World War II, except that now there is a socialist camp or commonwealth, and military power in the nuclear age is recognized as enormously more dangerous and important.

The principal role of Soviet military power has consistently been to dissuade imperialist powers from resorting to *their* military power against the Soviet Union (and, later, against the other countries of the socialist camp) in an effort to thwart the progressive course of history driven by revolutionary socioeconomic dynamics—not by military conquest. While the Soviets see other important and ideologically sanctioned uses of military force, including support for an active Soviet foreign policy, the basic Marxist-Leninist ideological framework predicates a fundamentally deterrent role for Soviet military power.[7]

To cite again the 1980 Central Committee resolution, détente was further characterized as "a factor deterring the aggressive aspirations of the imperialists." By this time, the Soviet view was that the United States had "taken the course of upsetting the military balance that has developed in the world in its favor and to the detriment of the Soviet Union" and, of course, also to the detriment of "international détente." The imperialist hopes of upsetting parity were said to be "doomed to failure," but only because the party leadership recognized under these conditions the requirement for "the comprehensive strengthening of the defense capability of our state in order to frustrate the plans of imperialism aimed at attaining superiority and establishing a world *diktat*."[8]

This preview of one aspect of the Soviet perception of the reasons for the decline of détente at the end of the decade helps to place in perspective their conception and their expectations at the outset.

Peaceful coexistence has been a central feature of the Soviet conception of détente. The conception has a long history, originating with the early recognition by the Bolsheviks that the expected world revolution was not going to occur as a single process and therefore that the new Soviet Socialist Republic would have to coexist with the capitalist states for an indefinite period. Peaceful coexistence among states with differing social systems meant no more than that—recognition of the fact of coexisting with an absence of war.

Peaceful coexistence acquired a new emphasis in 1956, when the Twentieth Party Congress rejected the Marxist tenet of the inevitability of war, and declared that the foreign policy of the Soviet Union was based on peaceful coexistence.[9] Again at the Twenty-fourth Congress in 1971 (reaffirmed at the Twenty-fifth in 1976 and the Twenty-sixth in 1981), Soviet policy was said to be based on peaceful coexistence. Indeed, the new Constitution of the USSR adopted in 1977 states that the foreign policy of the USSR is directed "to consistently implementing the principle of peaceful coexistence of states with different social systems."[10]

Skeptics in the West are inclined to regard such pronouncements as propaganda, or even dark deception, while apologists invest them with an undeserved aura of benign and unselfish goodness. Both err by reading into the Soviet pronouncements their own perceptions of Soviet motivation. In fact, while stating their position in the way most favorable to their image (as do all states), the Soviet leaders have tended to lay out their general line of policy forthrightly. They *do* desire to avert war though peaceful coexistence among states. They also believe that a progressive revolutionary movement of history is unfolding inexorably and that the Soviet Union is on the side of history. History is not dependent on the actions of the Soviet Union; the Soviet Union should support and assist the historical process, but without attempting to force its pace. Nor should its support involve actions that could put at risk the historic achievement of the Soviet state. In the nuclear age, war would mean an incalculable disaster for the Soviet Union and setback for world socialism.

The Soviet leaders believe that the imperialists (leaders of capitalist states) have a proclivity to resort to military force and war to extend (and, still more, to preserve) their strategic, political, and economic interests. Hence, as stated in 1969 at the International Conference of Communist and Workers' Parties in Moscow, the Soviet view is that a "struggle to *compel*" the imperialists to accept peaceful coexistence is required.[11] Again, it is not necessary to ascribe sinister motives to a Soviet statement meaning that they see a tough uphill effort to get Western leaders to agree, both in principle and still more in practice, to letting history take its course without resorting to force to try to stop it (as in Vietnam, the Dominican Republic, Guatemala, and many other cases in the 1950s and 1960s). Nor is it necessary to accept the Soviet view of "history." Rather, it is important to understand how *they* perceive history, and therefore world politics.

While aiming to end war and, indeed, imperialist resort to military force anywhere, the Soviets have not only "disclosed" but have insisted loudly that peaceful coexistence among states does *not* mean an end to "the class struggle" or the "national liberation movement" in colonial or neocolonial situations. On the contrary, it is avowed authoritatively and frequently that peaceful coexistence and détente will aid national liberation, progressive, and socialist revolutionary class struggle. This theme was not a new element under détente in the 1970s. In Brezhnev's first major address as party leader, made on the forty-seventh anniversary of the October Revolution in 1964, he had stated that "a situation of peaceful coexistence will enable the success of the liberation struggle and the achievement of the revolutionary tasks of peoples."[12] Brezhnev again made the point clearly in his speech on the fiftieth anniversary of the founding of the USSR seven months after the first summit meeting.[13] This position was held consistently and reiterated frequently as détente developed. For example, Politburo member Fyodor D. Kulakov declared, on the eve of the first Brezhnev-Nixon summit meeting, "Peaceful coexistence is the best foundation for practical solidarity with the revolutionaries of the whole world."[14] Moreover, "peaceful coexistence does not mean the end of the struggle between the two world social systems," but represents a struggle which will continue "right up to the complete and final victory of communism on a world scale."[15]

At the key Twenty-fourth Party Congress in March 1971, Brezhnev stated that peaceful coexistence provided the basis for relations with the United States.[16] The decision to seek to improve relations with the United States, which Brezhnev successfully advanced at that congress, had been reached only after overcoming the opposition of many skeptical members of the Central Committee and the Politburo.[17]

Following the first Soviet-American summit meeting in May 1972, many discussions explained to Soviet readers the political and ideological meaning of the new course of détente. It meant that the overall correlation of forces in the world, including the "social, economic and military power of the Soviet Union and other socialist countries," was compelling the United States to undergo an agonizing reappraisal and to change course from pursuing a hegemonic "Pax Americana" that relied on a policy of "positions of strength" to accepting peaceful coexistence.[18]

For the Soviet leaders, the most significant aspect of this changed correlation of forces and the necessity for peaceful coexistence was that the United States and the imperialist powers could no longer count on being able to destroy the Soviet Union and world socialism by military means because of the state of mutual deterrence in the nuclear age. Brezhnev stated this clearly in 1975:

> Détente became possible because a new correlation of forces in the world arena has been established. Now the leaders of the bourgeois world can no longer seriously count on resolving the historic conflict between capitalism and socialism by force of arms. The senselessness and extreme danger of further increasing tension under conditions when both sides have at their disposal weapons of colossal destructive power are becoming ever more obvious.[19]

Soviet ideology, positing a continuing conflict between communism (socialism) and capitalism (imperialism), provides a natural basis for Soviet acceptance of competition along with cooperation as a part of détente and peaceful coexistence. "Détente took shape as a result of the dialectical interaction of two foreign policy courses of opposite class nature and ultimate class direction—the socialist and the bourgeois."[20] Accordingly, "cooperation and confrontation are most important facets of peaceful coexistence, as components of a single process. Their unity is of a dialectical character: they cannot be isolated from one another, nor can one of them be discarded and the other retained."[21] Acceptance of continuing conflict does not, however, include war between states. "It is vitally important to preserve peace in order to build the new society, socialism, and communism."[22] In addition, "world peace is determined to a decisive degree by the reality of peaceful coexistence between socialism and capitalism."[23] At the same time, in light of the military hostilities between nonaligned countries (for example, Iraq and Iran) and even between socialist countries (for example, China and Vietnam) in recent years, Soviet theoreticians have now come to advocate "extending the principle of peaceful coexistence to cover not only relations between socialist and capitalist countries, but also its operation on a wider scale."[24]

In short, détente, and peaceful coexistence, "does not and cannot mean forgoing the objective processes of historical development. It is not a safe conduct for corrupt regimes. . . . It does not eliminate the need for social transformations. But the people themselves in each country resolve this question."[25] There should be neither attempts to "export revolutions" nor "to export counterrevolution."[26]

After the signing of the détente agreements of 1972 and 1973 with the United States, at a time when Soviet leaders were especially sensitive to charges from the left, Brezhnev took the occasion of a global communist-led World Congress of Peace-Loving Forces to reaffirm that "revolution, the class struggle, and liberation movements cannot be abolished by agreements. No power on earth is capable of reversing the inexorable process of the renovation of the life of society."[27]

In the mid-1970s, and especially in the period leading up to and following the Twenty-fifth Party Congress in 1976, Soviet theoreticians began to develop a concept of a "fundamental restructuring of international relations" to exclude war. In June 1974 Brezhnev commented in his Supreme Soviet election speech: "Evaluating the general correlation of forces in the world, we already several years ago reached the conclusion that there exists a real possibility to achieve a fundamental change in the international situation."[28] A year later, in 1975, on the eve of the Helsinki Conference on European security and the Vladivostok SALT accord with President Gerald R. Ford, Brezhnev went further. He declared:

> In the past few years, conviction in the possibility, and moreover in the necessity, of peaceful coexistence was confirmed in the consciousness both of the broad popular masses and also in the ruling circles of the majority of countries. International détente has become possible because a new correlation of forces has been established in the world arena. . . . Norms of peaceful coexistence between states have already been consolidated in many binding official bilateral and multilateral documents, as well as in political declarations.[29]

Foreign Minister and Politburo member Andrei A. Gromyko stressed in 1981 that when the program of détente had been launched at the Twenty-fourth Party Congress ten years earlier, the party had first "perspicaciously" evaluated the international situation as providing "favorable opportunities for the restructuring of the entire system of international relations that had evolved in the postwar period as a result of the change in the correlation of forces in the world in favor of socialism."[30] And in 1973, Brezhnev and Gromyko had been saying that " 'détente is not a temporary phenomenon but the beginning of a fundamental restructuring of international relations.' "[31]

Soviet theoreticians and commentators have further elaborated on this point, stressing the role of détente, growing Western acceptance of peaceful coexistence, the attainment of strategic parity, and general world political developments; in sum, "the changing correlation of forces between the two social systems in favor of socialism has been the decisive factor determining the acceleration of the fundamental restructuring of international relations."[32]

Soviet commentators have stressed the dynamic nature and role of détente, which has been central to this process of "restructuring." In Vladimir Petrovsky's words, "Détente is regarded by the Soviet Union not as a static condition, but as a dynamic process, in the course of which the restructuring of international relations on the principles of peaceful coexistence will be completed."[33]

Brezhnev and other Soviet leaders, as well as Soviet theoreticians, have stressed that the accomplishments of détente by the mid-1970s had not been easy and that they had not yet been made "irreversible." Indeed, "the dialectics of the breakup of the old structure of international relations and the creation of a new one is not simple, because it is a process involving efforts to overcome contradictions and resistance from opponents of détente and peaceful coexistence."[34]

An interesting elaboration of the Soviet conception of détente in the mid-1970s was the coining of the term "military détente," with reference to the application of détente to military affairs, principally in agreed "confidence-building" measures, crisis management, and arms control and arms limitation agreements. The expression was apparently first used by Brezhnev in his speech to the Twenty-fourth Party Congress in 1971.[35] It began to be used widely after the Helsinki Conference in 1975 to refer to measures aimed at reducing military confrontation in Europe. Both applications of the term, to European security and to broader arms control, are discussed in later chapter.[36] Here, however, it is important to note the relation of military détente to the Soviet conception of restructuring international relations. As one Soviet academic analyst put it, within détente as a whole, "Military détente is an indispensable condition and one of the most important means for restructuring international relations on the principles of peaceful coexistence."[37] While political détente was seen as primary and "decisive" and the first step, military détente was also said to be necessary.

Military détente, as political détente, rests on the new correlation of forces and, above all, on strategic parity between the United States and the Soviet Union: "From the standpoint of the possibilities and prospects for military détente, it is extremely important that imperialism has already been forced to take seriously into account the realities of the contemporary world, above all the fact of Soviet-American 'nuclear parity'—the condition which has developed of a dynamic equilibrium of the strategic nuclear missile power of the two states."[38] And on the basis of this military parity, political parity can lead to the consolidation of military as well as political détente in formally regulated relations, all in the framework of the restructuring of international relations. "New and important in principle is the fact that under the contemporary world correlation of forces a real possibility has appeared to use the traditional treaty form for gradual alterations of interstate military-political relations, bringing them into correspondence with the tasks of restructuring the whole system of international relations on a new basis."[39]

Following the Twenty-fifth Party Congress in 1976, Soviet political—and military—theoreticians began to elaborate a theory of states and types of peace (as well as war). Thus, in addition to distinguishing various categories of local wars and other forms of warfare, several categories of "levels of peace" with different characteristics began to be developed. Peace was identified as a dialectical combination of cooperation and conflict. The lowest level was the cold war, defined as the mere absence of military hostilities, a "negative peace." This level might include not only harsh political, ideological, and economic warfare, but also tensions that could erupt into armed conflict. Détente was the second level of peace, a "positive peace." Within détente, which includes many gradations and forms, were two sublevels: political détente and military détente. The former included the development of political, economic, scientific, and cultural ties and cooperation; the latter extended into arms control, especially disarmament. "Thus 'cold war,' or negative peace, is merely an absence of war not buttressed with positive social content. Political and military détente are stages of positive peace, based on the principles of peaceful coexistence, which are realized in the peaceful cooperation of states and in arms reduction."[40]

In the Soviet conception, peace is not the only or ultimate objective. Soviet theoreticians have made clear that "unlike pacifists," Marxist-Leninists do not regard peace as an absolute goal and do not regard "any peace as progress." Lenin's adaptation of Clausewitz' thesis is reflected in the shrewd observation that "like war, peace is a continuation of policy."[41] The distinction is in the means: "The essence of peace presupposes the achievement of political objectives by non-armed means, that is, by economic, scientific, technical, diplomatic, cultural, and ideological means . . . by nonviolent means of conducting policy."[42] Foreign Minister Gromyko, in a major article on Soviet foreign policy in the authoritative theoretical journal of the Communist party, has laid out the ideological position for the Soviet political elite. He stated that "the fundamental underlying principles" of Soviet policy are: "proletarian internationalism and peaceful coexistence of states with differing social systems." As he explained further, "Proletarian internationalism as a fundamental principle of Soviet foreign policy means that this policy consistently upholds the basic interests of world socialism, the forces of the international communist and workers movement, and of the national-liberation movement. As for peaceful coexistence, it represents a specific form of the class struggle—peaceful competition, ruling out the use of military force, between the two counter-posed social-economicsystems—socialism and capitalism."[43] In short, it was clearly recognized that peace is "waged" under peaceful coexistence, notwithstanding a theoretical construct of an ascending structure of levels of peace with growing components of cooperation and disarmament.

In concluding this overview of the Soviet conception of détente it is instructive to note what the Soviets have indicated détente does *not* mean. The most clear and strong statements have been articulated in recent years as part of a critical retrospective analysis of the American interpretation of détente in the 1970s, or, as one important member of the party Central Committee staff calls it, "détente American-style"[44] Imperialists put "at the center of their conception of détente and peaceful coexistence the idea of the preservation of the status quo. One cannot agree with such an interpretation. The policy of peaceful coexistence has clearly drawn boundaries. Its sphere is relations among states."[45] Only in one crucially significant respect do the Soviets accept this approach: the absolute necessity of averting world nuclear war. "The policy of peaceful coexistence is designed to find a solution to the most acute political problem of our time—to avert a total nuclear missile clash. . . . It is possible and necessary to ban war as a means of 'clarifying relations' among states. And in this sense peaceful coexistence includes the requirement of the status quo. But it is impossible to 'ban' a civil war or national liberation war, to 'ban' revolution as a means of changing social and political systems."[46]

While Western observers have usually seen Soviet statements in support of national liberation and progressive revolutionary movements as reflecting an offensive thrust in Soviet foreign policy, Soviet leaders have in fact usually made such statements in a defensive context that related to internal controversies within the world communist movement and domestic Soviet politics. Controversy on this point became especially clear after the first major steps in détente with the United States in 1972.[47] Nor did the issue die. A consultant to the International Department of the Central Committee commented in *Pravda* in 1976 that the question of the impact of détente on the class struggle "often crops up in the international workers movement," including among anti-Soviet radicals whom he accused of "leftist fabrications to the effect that détente strengthens the positions of capitalism." Acknowledging that détente had "complicated" the global ideological struggle and given some new opportunities to opponents of socialism, he argued that on balance détente had been more favorable to the class and national liberation struggles.[48] In addition, it has been constantly stressed that peaceful coexistence and the prevention of war are of the highest priority for world socialism, benefiting the peoples of the world.

The Soviets have, especially in retrospect since the late 1970s, noted that capitalist leaders sometimes justified détente on the basis of its achievement of expanded relations "as a means of bringing about the gradual internal 'erosion' of socialism, as a means to 'dull vigilance' and for the ideological penetration of the socialist countries." And "the overall normalization of relations with the USSR was portrayed as a means of compelling our country to reduce or even to cease active assistance to the national liberation, anti-imperialist and socialist movements in other countries." These views were depicted as inconsistencies in the *Western* approach to détente.[49]

The Soviet also object strongly to the concept of linkage, contending that steps in détente should not be tied to other matters. In particular, the Soviets are sensitive to any implication that they need détente more than the United States does, and they constantly affirm that the United States and the Soviet Union have an "equal interest" in détente and arms control. (American and Soviet use of linkage in practice is discussed later.)

The Soviet conception of détente relies heavily on negotiation of specific issues, especially security matters. Thus at the Twenty-third Party Congress in 1966, the Soviet leaders stressed their aim "to resolve disputed international questions by means of negotiations and not by means of war."[50]

Finally, the Soviets claim to have initiated the policy of détente and to have been its champions against reluctant and opposing Western imperialist circles.[51] The Soviets place great weight on their relations with Western Europe and the European détente in East-West relations. But they also recognize (and during the 1970s came to stress) the special importance of Soviet relations with the United States. Not only are these relations "an important factor on which to a great extent the situation in the world as a whole depends," but they are also uniquely important with respect to "the degree of danger that a global conflict will arise,"[52] and the incalculable destruction that a world nuclear war would entail for everyone. Hence, "the creation of the optimal conditions for the contest between the two systems within the framework of peaceful coexistence and cooperation in order to prevent a global catastrophe and to end the arms race is inseparably linked with the nature of relations between the USSR and the USA."[53] While Soviet-American détente prevailed, the Soviets were at pains to assure others that the special significance of Soviet-American relations "does not signify, by any means, that the USSR and the USA have any special rights or advantages relative to other peoples." At the same time, however, they asserted that the two countries, "as the most powerful and influential powers of our times . . . bear a special responsibility for the preservation and consolidation of international peace and security."[54]

In the Soviet conception, détente and peaceful coexistence would serve "to make the world safe for historical change," so to speak, by depriving the imperialist powers, above all the United States, to resort to military force to curb the revolutionary social-economic-political transformations that would ultimately lead to world socialism and communism. The Soviet Union itself would serve the cause of revolutionary change not by military action, but by balancing and serving to counter and deter America's use of its military power, and by pursuing its own economic and political development at home and the expansion of its political influence abroad. Peaceful coexistence among states would provide stability to the international system and to the historical process, but *not* to the status quo. As Brezhnev put it, the historically inevitable class struggle between the capitalist and socialist systems would be directed into ideological, economic, and political "channels that do not threaten wars, dangerous confrontations, or as uncontrolled arms race."[55]

Soviet belief that there is an underlying historical process and that the Soviet Union is riding the wave of the future does not mean they see their own role as passive. Soviet leaders are active and experienced political and diplomatic practitioners, and Soviet policy is geared to seize opportunities to advance Soviet interests and influence. Détente in no way superseded active competition in the world political arena, but it was based on a recognition of the need to limit competition to actions short of war with the imperialist powers in the nuclear age.

Declared Soviet policy has been very consistent. The Soviet Union has steadfastly supported détente and peaceful coexistence among states. It has also supported the progressive movement of history and revolutionary transformation of society. If relations between the Soviet Union and the United States became more tense, it was because the United States was attempting to interfere with the course of history in the third world and even in the socialist world. Soviet advocacy of peaceful coexistence is real and not a mere rationalization, much less a deception of the West. But it is also not a prescriptive constraint on Soviet policy action, which continues to be guided by calculations of relative cost, risk, and gain in any initiative or response. Moreover, *actual* Soviet policy has always contained a strong competitive element, along with the cooperative elements. That competitive element may increase, and even become confrontational, *if* required to meet competitive or confrontational challenges.

As noted in the discussion of American policy pronouncements, it is necessary to bear in mind the limits of public (and even internal) statements of policy as a guide to understanding actual patterns of action. Clearly, for anyone outside the Soviet milieu there are special problems in weighing Soviet pronouncements. Most Soviet statements cited here have been directed to the Soviet elite and establishment. They represent authoritative statements of what the Soviet leaders at least want their own constituents to believe is Soviet policy. But they are also a reflection of the mindset and framework of cognition and perception of the policymakers themselves. Those in the leadership may differ in internal deliberations about whether to accept a given agreement under negotiation, or whether and what kind of assistance to provide to a revolutionary movement abroad, but the terms of their private debates are set in the same mold as reports to the Central Committee or lead articles in *Pravda*.

Veiled reflections of real policy differences do appear in the Soviet media. Moreover, contrary to a widespread impression, there are sometimes significant differences in the weight to be given to various Soviet authors and publications. Some reflect specific institutional interests; others reflect political constituencies. Differences in viewpoint and schools of thought exist in the Soviet academic institutions and press. Analysts must familiarize themselves with these considerations, and must take into account the standing of the author, intended audience, and purposes of any Soviet statement. While this process enlarges opportunities for analysis, it also requires caution in using sources. For example, many commentators from various institutes of the Academy of Sciences dealing with international relations and Soviet-American relations are naturally among those contributing most to discussions relevant to the present study. The relationship of these institutes, of individual leading scholars, and of published academic analyses to the Soviet official and policymaking establishment is complex. As sources of publicly articulated Soviet policy, they are usually informed and authoritative. In presenting interpretations they may or may not be consonant with (or, indeed, may influence) official thinking. But such problems are part of the challenge for those of us who professionally study Soviet affairs. In this study Soviet sources have been extensively researched and used to illustrate in their own words the Soviet view (or in some cases diverging views). Statements about policy are, of course, only one source for analysis. But particularly for examining Soviet policy conceptions, they are a valuable source.[56]

In concluding this summary analysis of the Soviet conception of détente, it should be recalled that while the Soviet leaders have accepted a policy of détente throughout the 1970s and 1980s, various members of the Soviet leadership and various constituencies of the Soviet political system have not always agreed on some of the political issues relating to détente. A number of such disagreements arose during the period under review and are examined in this study. Moreover, the Soviet leaders have had to adapt to the change in American policy from the mid-1970s to the mid-1980s.

It should also be observed that the Soviet approach to détente has had both strengths and weaknesses, even apart from those aspects of the policy and strategy that have been more or less effective from the Soviet standpoint and more or less objectionable from an American standpoint. First, the Soviet view of the existing world order includes recognition that the world is in a state of flux, and they have therefore been prepared for change to a greater extent than the United States has, given the more static American vision of the status quo. The Marxist-Leninist view of history may (as I believe) be basically flawed, and its projection of a particular pattern of world revolutionary change in error. But it does provide a flexible framework for accepting ebb and flow in the correlation of forces in the world. In many other respects, however, the Soviet leaders display little flexibility.

In retrospect, the Soviets were wrong in their evaluation that the United States was ready to accept the changed correlation of forces as they appeared to *Soviet* leaders in the early 1970s. While the Soviets have not directly acknowledged that error, they have had to recognize the fact of a changed American outlook and policy, a change that they ascribe to a victory for unreconciled foes of détente in the United States.

The Soviets have been reluctant to see that their own erroneous expectations about other aspects of détente also contributed to the deterioration of relations from the mid-1970s to the close of the decade. In particular, the Soviet leaders harbored illusions not only that the United States was ready to accept changes in the third world but, even more, that it would regard active Soviet support for ''progressive'' changes in the third world as compatible with Soviet-American détente.

The Soviet approach has also been based on an implicit double standard with respect to waging the ideological struggle under peaceful coexistence. That approach assumes that it is all right and consistent with détente for the Soviet Union to carry on such a struggle in the capitalist and third worlds, but that the same does not apply to the United States or others within the socialist world. The Soviet distinction between state and other activities is too contrived and too biased to Soviet advantage, given the disparities in the extent of state control in communist countries as compared with that in many others. The Soviet effort to distinguish the impact of such activities on *state relations* is more valid. But in the West state relations cannot be insulated from other activities. Moreover, waging a political and ideological struggle tends to undermine, if it does not contradict, declared desires for increasing trust and confidence, and ultimately even the ability to conduct a policy of détente. This observation is not meant to suggest that the Soviet Union alone has been engaging in political and ideological competition, only that there was an internal contradiction in the Soviet conception and expectation as to what could be done under détente.

In general, the Soviet leaders expected in the 1970s to achieve more clout in international affairs as a result of their increased relative power than they were able to obtain. As a result, they pursued policies that contributed to undercutting support for détente in the United States and that antagonized elements of world opinion not only in the West but in the third world. The Soviet intervention in Afghanistan is the clearest example, and one that also illustrates an inability to control events not only in terms of reactions elsewhere, but within Afghanistan itself.[57]

The Soviet belief that the United States had accepted military parity, and that the two sides could agree on what constituted parity and could succeed in controlling the arms race, also proved too optimistic, a subject addressed shortly.

Finally, while it is possible to take issue with the premises and aims of Soviet policy, as I do, it is harder to argue either that the Soviet policy has been inconsistent with *their* conception of détente, or that they have deluded the West about their understanding of the meaning of détente, or to speak of Soviet violation of détente—in the context of an interpretation that they never accepted and have openly and consistently rejected.

The real task is both to clarify and enlarge the areas of common interest on which cooperation can be built, and to identify and seek to manage the continuing competition in the large areas of diverging and conflicting interest which remain. This task was *not* sufficiently understood or pursued in the 1970s by the leaders on either side.

NOTES

1. L. I. Brezhnev, *Pravda,* January 19, 1977.
2. L. I. Brezhnev, *Pravda,* June 14, 1975.
3. Speech of Comrade Yury V. Andropov,'' *Pravda,* November 16, 1982.
4. K. U. Chernenko, *Izbrannye reci i stat' i* [Selected Speeches and Articles], 2d ed. (Moscow: Politizdat, 1984), p. 551.
5. Speech of Comrade K. U. Chernenko,'' *Pravda,* April 30, 1984.
6. On the International Situation and Foreign Policy of the Soviet Union: Resolution of the Plenum of the Central Committee of the CPSU, June 23, 1980,'' *Kommunist* [The Communist], no. 10 (July 1980), p. 9.
7. In addition to the very summary discussion in these paragraphs, see Raymond L. Garthoff, *Soviet Military Policy: A Historical Analysis* (New York: Praeger, 1966), pp. 3–28, 65–97, 191–206, 220–38.
8. *Kommunist,* no. 10 (1980), pp. 8, 9, 10.
9. There are indications that even before the death of Stalin, some of his lieutenants—and later successors—had begun to recognize that in the nuclear age war could no longer be countenanced as inevitable. See Raymond L. Garthoff, ''The Death of Stalin and the Birth of Mutual Deterrence,'' *Survey* 25 (Spring 1980), pp. 10–16.

10. "The Constitution of the USSR," adopted by the Supreme Soviet on October 7, 1977, *Pravda,* October 8, 1977. The foreign policy of the USSR is also said to be directed at six other objectives, including "supporting the struggle of peoples for national liberation and social progress" and "securing the state interests of the Soviet Union"; these are all consistent in terms of the *Soviet* conception of détente.

11. "Tasks of the Struggle against Imperialism at the Present Stage and the Unity of Action of the Communist and Workers' Parties and All Anti-Imperialist Forces," *Pravda,* June 18, 1969. Emphasis added.

12. L. I. Brezhnev, *Izbrannye proizvedeniya* [Selected Works] (Moscow: Politizdat, 1981), vol. 1, p. 21.

13. L. I. Brezhnev, "On the Fiftieth Anniversary of the USSR," *Pravda,* December 22, 1972.

14. F. D. Kulakov, "Leninism Is the Great Creative Force in Communist Construction," *Pravda,* April 22, 1972. For other discussions in the 1970s, see Yu. Molchanov, "Peaceful Coexistence and Social Progress," *International Affairs (Moscow),* no. 12 (December 1976), especially p. 11; and A. Bovin, *Izvestiya,* September 11, 1973.

15. F. Ryzhenko, "Peaceful Coexistence and the Class Struggle," *Pravda,* August 22, 1973.

16. Brezhnev, "Report of the Central Committee of the CPSU to the XXIV Congress of the Communist party of the Soviet Union, March 30, 1971, *O vneshnei politike KPSS i Sovetskogo gosudarstva: Rechi i stat'i* [On the Foreign Policy of the CPSU and the Soviet State: Speeches and Articles], 3rd ed. (Moscow: Politizdat, 1978), p. 179.

17. Interviews with members of the Central Committee of the CPSU.

18. See A. Pumpyansky, "A Triumph of Realism," *Komsomol'skaya pravda* [Komsomol Truth], June 4, 1972; and many other Soviet articles at that time and subsequently.

19. Brezhnev, *Pravda,* June 14, 1975.

20. N. Lebedev, "The Dialectics of the Development of International Relations," *International Affairs,* no. 9 (September 1980), p. 109.

21. Ibid.

22. Ibid., p. 111.

23. [Maj. Gen.] A. S. Milovidov and Ye. A. Zhdanov, "Social-Philosophical Problems of War and Peace," *Voprosy filosofii* [Questions of Philosophy], no. 10 (October 1980), p. 43.

24. Ibid., p. 43. The first indications that peaceful coexistence should extend to relations among states that do not have different social systems came in the early 1970s. The first instance I have noted was an article by Aleksandr Bovin, *Izvestiya,* September 11, 1973.

25. "Statement of the Soviet Government," *Pravda,* May 22, 1976.

26. Brezhnev, Speech of January 29, 1974, *O vneshnei politike,* p. 382. This long-standing Soviet view had been restated many times since the 1960s.

27. Brezhnev, Speech of October 26, 1973, ibid., p. 349. The speech was given just a few weeks after the overthrow and murder of President Salvador Allende in Chile; Brezhnev referred to that event just before the statement cited here.

28. Brezhnev, Speech of June 14, 1974, ibid., p. 397.

29. Brezhnev, Speech of June 13, 1975, ibid., p. 473.

30. A. Gromyko, "Leninist Foreign Policy in the Contemporary World," *Kommunist,* no. 1 (January 1981), p. 14.

31. See A. A. Gromyko, Speech to the UN General Assembly, *Pravda,* September 26, 1973, in which he cited Brezhnev as having stated that in a recent speech.

32. N. Lebedev, "The Struggle of the USSR for the Restructuring of International Relations," *Mezhdunarodnaya zhizn'* [International Life], no. 12 (December 1975) p. 7. Lebedev is head of the Moscow State Institute of International Relations.

33.   V. F. Petrovsky, "The Struggle of the USSR for Détente in the Seventies," *Novaya i noveiy-shaya istoriya* [Modern and Contemporary History], no. 1 (January–February 1981), p. 3. Petrovsky is both an experienced diplomat and a leading scholar in the field of diplomatic history.
In addition to the sources cited above on this discussion, see V. V. Kortunov, "The Relaxation of Tensions and the Struggle of Ideas in Contemporary International Relations," *Voprosy istorii KPSS* [Questions of History of the CPSU], no. 10 (October 1975), p. 16; and see D. Tomashevsky, "Toward a Radical Restructuring of International Relations," *Mirovaya ekonomika i mezhdunarodnye otnosheniya* [The World Economy and international Relations], no. 1 (January 1975), pp. 3–13 (hereafter MEiMO); and V. V. Kortunov, *Perestroika mezhdunarodnykh otnoshenii i ideologicheskaya bor'ba* [The Restructuring of International Relations and the Ideological Struggle] (Moscow: Znaniye, 1977). Kortunov is an official of the Central Committee.

34.   Lebedev, *Mezhdunarodnaya zhizn'*, p. 10.

35.   Brezhnev, *O vneshnei politike*, p. 175.

36.   See chapters 14 and 22 of Raymond L. Garthoff, *Détente and Confrontation*.

37.   A. Nikonov, "Military Détente and the Restructuring of International Relations," *MEiMO*, no. 6 (June 1977), p. 28.

38.   Ibid., p. 31.

39.   Ibid., p. 33.

40.   Milovidov and Zhdanov, *Voprosy filosofii*, no. 10 (1980), p. 46. This interesting article includes many useful bibliographic references to the burgeoning Soviet literature on the philosophical anatomy of war and peace.

41.   Ibid., p. 38.

42.   Ibid., p. 44.

43.   Gromyko, *Kommunist*, no. 1 (1981) p. 14.

44.   V. Kortunov, "Disastrous Relapses into a Policy of Strength," *Kommunist*, no. 10 (July 1980), p. 102.

45.   A. Bovin, "The Permanent Significance of Lenin's Ideas," *Kommunist*, no. 10 (July 1980), p. 79.

46.   Ibid. See also Kortunov, *Kommunist*, no. 10 (1980), p. 102.

47.   See the discussion in chapter 9 of Raymond L. Garthoff, *Détente and Confrontation*.

48.   Yu. Krasin, *Pravda*, September 24, 1976.

49.   Yu. A. Zamoshkin, "Ideology in the United States: For and Against Détente," *SShA: Ekonomika, politika, ideologiya* [USA: Economics, Politics, Ideology], no. 4 (April 1982), p. 7.

50.   "Resolution of the Twenty-third Congress of the CPSU on the Report of the Central Committee of the CPSU," April 8, 1966, *Materialy XXIII s'yezda KPSS* [Materials of the Twenty-third Congress of the CPSU] (Moscow: Politizdat, 1966), p. 157.

51.   For example, see V. Zagladin, Radio Moscow, TV Studio 9, May 26, in Foreign Broadcast Information Service, *Daily Report: Soviet Union*, June 11, 1979, p. CC1. (Hereafter FBIS, *Soviet Union*.) He attributed the origination of détente to Brezhnev at the Twenty-third Party Congress in 1966. For Brezhnev's speech at the Congress, see *O vneshnei politike*, p. 40. See also A. Sovetov, "Leninist Foreign Policy in the World Today," *International Affairs*, no. 3 (March 1980), p. 6, typical of many other Soviet commentaries. Zagladin is first deputy chief of the International Department of the Central Committee.

52.   V. F. Petrovsky, "The Role and Place of Soviet-American Relations in the Contemporary World," *Voprosy istorii* [Questions of History], no. 10 (October 1978), p. 91.

53.   Ibid., p. 80. He also cites Brezhnev in this regard.

54. Ibid., p. 91.
55. L. I. Brezhnev, *Leninskom kursom* [On Lenin's Course[(Moscow: Politizdat, 1974), vol. 4, p. 81.
56. In many cases, either in the text or in brief footnote notations, I have provided information on the standing or position of Soviet authors cited. It may be appropriate also to note that I have been using Soviet source materials in analyzing Soviet political and military affairs for thirty-five years.
57. See chapter 26 of *Détente and Confrontation* for a detailed analysis of Soviet involvement and intervention in Afghanistan.

II
Methodology

II

4

Soviet Foreign Policy and World Politics*

William Zimmerman

This essay examines the links between the study of Soviet foreign policy and theory building in world politics. It is intentionally an idiosyncratic and indeed almost autobiographical account. I hope to accomplish three things in the process. The first is to impart some sense of how one research practitioner has worked at the interface between world politics and Soviet foreign policy. The second is to provide some indication of the evolution of Soviet studies over the last quarter century. Third, I seek to persuade the reader that trafficking at the inter-section of world politics and Soviet foreign policy is advantageous to each area of inquiry. An attention to the literature on world politics enhances the likelihood that the study of Soviet foreign policy will produce results of interest to persons not especially interested in the Soviet Union *per se*. Moreover, Soviet foreign policy constitutes an important testing ground for hypotheses pertaining to the behavior of states.

To accomplish these tasks I focus on four areas of inquiry of interest to students of world politics, drawing upon Soviet materials. The areas are: the comparison of various approaches to world politics, the comparison on interna-tional systems, mass and elite foreign policy attitudes and civil-military relations including the social determinants of military performance.

Each of these represents an area where William T. R. Fox either worked or encouraged the work of others. Thus, with respect to the comparison of ap-proaches to world politics, Fox chaired Kenneth Waltz's thesis that became *Man, the State and War*, a classic study of the alternative explanations by political philosophers for the causes of war in the international system. In the case of the comparison of actual and putative international systems, he was similarly sup-portive of Morton Kaplan's *System and Process in International Politics*. Like-wise, he sponsored Gabriel Almond's seminal study of the foreign policy attitudes of elites and attentive mass publics, *The American People and Foreign Policy* (as well as, it should be noted, Robert Dahl's *Congress and Foreign*

*Reprinted by permission of the author and publisher from the *Journal of International Affairs*, 44, 1 (Spring/Summer 1990). Copyright © 1990 by the Trustees of Columbia University in the City of New York.

Policy). Finally, Fox himself had an enduring research interest in civil-military relations and, as director of Columbia University's Institute of War and Peace Studies, encouraged a host of studies by others within the broad domain of civil-military relations.

Each of the four domains also represent instances in which I have devoted considerable effort to utilizing Soviet materials to illuminate theoretically interesting propositions. The four also illustrate a progression in Western Soviet studies that reflects the evolution of our perceptions of the Soviet Union. To put too simple a gloss on that evolution, I would characterize it as a movement away from the attempt to ascertain whether and in what ways the Soviet Union is unique, and toward a view of the Soviet Union as a more or less ordinary state both in its international behavior and in domestic relations between state and society. That evolution in Western thinking, moreover, has been both a product of and a guide to research on the Soviet Union. It has moved our research agenda increasingly in the direction of middle-range theorizing comparable to the research questions asked in world politics or in the study of American foreign policy.

SOVIET PERSPECTIVES ON INTERNATIONAL RELATIONS

Thus, in the mid-1960s, I began the research that ultimately resulted in *Soviet Perspectives on International Relations*[1] in an intellectual climate in which there was a strong and well-founded presumption of the distinctiveness of Soviet foreign policy. The radical transformation of Russian society brought about by the Bolshevik seizure of power in 1917 and Stalin's subsequent "revolution from above" resulted in a novel political system which in turn gave a unique cast to Soviet foreign policy goals and to the outlook of the Soviet leadership. Unlike most great powers, the Soviet Union was perceived to be seeking to transform and supplant the contemporary international system. It was, moreover, thought to be ruled by leaders sharing a novel outlook an international events that the label "Bolshevik" aptly described.

Beginning with Marshall Shulman's *Stalin's Foreign Policy Reappraised,*[2] and Jan Triska and David Finley's "multiple symmetry model" of Soviet-American relations,[3] however, a more reactive interpretation of Soviet foreign policy began to evolve.

I, in turn, found that changes in the international environment—most notably the advent of the atomic era and the onset of the Sino-Soviet dispute—and Soviet perceptions of these changes had major consequences for Soviet goals and the Soviet assessment of the international system. These changes in Soviet perception extend over a decade beginning with Malenkov's statement in 1954 that nuclear war would be a catastrophe for all civilization and culminating in the Soviet statement to the Chinese in 1963 that the atomic bomb does not observe the class principle.

These changes in perception had profound implications for Soviet interactions with the other actors in the international system. Persons thinking in the Marxist-Leninist tradition took as axiomatic the inevitability of the revolution and the desirability of the transformation of the existing international order. Those thinking in the Leninist-Stalinist tradition assumed that world war was functional for global revolutionary advance—that World War I had resulted in the Bolshevik seizure of power in Russia and that World War II had resulted in the formation of the Soviet bloc.

But the possibility of nuclear war called these core assumptions into question. Most important, Soviet international-relations commentary, both among scholars and among the leadership, came increasingly to recognize that nuclear war might put an end to history. If it was an open question as to whether there would be a future, so too was it an open matter as to the direction global events might take. If the future was not inevitable, then neither was particular future, even a communist one.

In addition, coming to grips with the possibility of nuclear war placed Soviet decision makers in what I have characterized as the "revisionists' dilemma." In other words, how does one accomplish the radical transformation of an existing order in which one has a stake? There were two reasons in Marxist thought as to why the proletariat would lead the revolution. First, Marx believed that with modernization and the development of capitalism's general crisis, the proletariat were capable of revolutionary consciousness because, lacking any stake in society, they had no ideology and thus could see capitalism for what it was. In the well-known phrase from *The Communist Manifesto,* the workers of the world would unite because they had "nothing to lose but their chains." Late nineteenth-century German socialists encountered this dilemma when they found that they had a stake in the preservation of the German social and economic order which they were committed to overthrow. Under Eduard Bernstein, they ultimately opted for instrumental goals and democracy rather than retaining an increasingly costly revolutionary purity.

The potential consequences of nuclear war posed the same dilemma for Soviet aspirations to transform the existing international order. As *World Marxist Review* editorialized in the aftermath of the Cuban missile crisis, "Gone are the days when the working men rising in struggle against capitalism had indeed nothing to lose but their chains. Through selfless, heroic struggle, the masses have won immense material, political and cultural gains, gains that are embodied in the socialist world system."[4] When it comes to revolutionary transformation, nothing fails like success.

The perception of the consequences of nuclear war challenged the inevitability of the desirable transformation of the international system. Whatever else Soviet elites may or may not have believed traditionally, they held the view that relations among socialist states would be better than those among capitalist states or between capitalist and socialist states. The Sino-Soviet dispute challenged the desirability of what had been thought to be inevitable: In a socialist international order, conflict might be even greater than among capitalist states or between capitalist and socialist states in the existing international order.

The ability of Soviet observers of the international scene to absorb the implications of the development of thermonuclear weapons and long-range delivery vehicle systems, the inferences they drew as a consequence of the Sino-Soviet split, as well as changes in the nature of the Soviet political system led me to several conclusions about how we should theorize about the links between world politics and Soviet foreign policy. These conclusions subsequently influenced my approach to the study of Soviet foreign policy after the publication of *Soviet Perspectives*.

COMPARING REGIONAL SYSTEMS

First, it no longer made sense to think seriously about the emergence of a world system dominated by the Soviet Union and composed primarily of communist states, which had seemed at least a plausible alternative to the contemporary international system as recently as the early 1960s.[5] By the beginning of the 1970s it had become clear that a communist alternative to the contemporary international order could no longer be seen as a shot on the board. Communist states in general revealed neither the boundary-maintaining nor conflict-containing qualities that would have been necessary for the emergence of an "international relations of a new type," an alternative communist system that would supplant the current international system. What did seem appropriate, however, was to treat the Soviet Union and its East European allies (i.e., those communist states whose interactions were separable behaviorally from relations with both noncommunist and other communist states) as constituting a regional system that might be compared with other regional systems.

This approach permitted the systematic comparison of Soviet and American foreign policy behavior in relatively similar settings and with a minimum of extraneous confounding variables.[6] Moreover, it made it possible to explore some interesting propositions about the behavior of great powers and small powers in a hierarchical regional system, that is, a system composed of a single great power—the regional hegemon—and a number of relatively small states.

One set of questions pertained to the behavior of the regional hegemon with respect to the maintenance of the "boundaries" of the regional system. (System boundaries here may be defined geographically, by marked discontinuities in international transactions or by identifying norms, especially those pertaining to conflict management and resolution, specific to a group of states.) In this important domain of superpower international behavior, it turned out that long before the Gorbachev era with its putative new thinking, one could get rather considerable purchase on Soviet behavior by focusing on general patterns of regional hegemon behavior rather than by emphasizing that which was distinctively novel about Soviet foreign policy. Thus, an initial proposition that had some *prima facie* attractiveness in describing the behavior of both regional hegemons was that they pursue policies intended to maintain or increase the barriers which separate the regional system from the outside world. This proposition seemed to account for behavior such as the colorful Soviet utterances concerning the involvement of the United Nations in Eastern Europe in the aftermath of the Soviet occupation of Czechoslovakia (Western "pigs were told to keep their snouts out of the socialist garden") and the long-time Soviet position that relations among members of the East European system should be based on proletarian internationalism (i.e., should include the unilateral Soviet right to intervene to preserve socialism) and not peaceful coexistence, which was a norm governing relations between states with different social systems.

Some reflection, however, reveals that the proposition failed to account for several important considerations that affect hegemonic behavior. Regional hegemons are not merely great powers; following the distinction made by William T. R. Fox in 1944, they are world powers. As such, they are engaged in multiple games, only one of which is the regional system game. The zeal, therefore, with which they pursue boundary-maintaining policies in a region may be tempered by an awareness that their influence outside the region depends somewhat on the perceptions of relations within the regional system held by actors outside that system. Likewise, superpower decision makers may conclude that the achievement of any influence in a region dominated by another great power is purchased in part by tolerating the erosion of the superpower's own regional system boundaries. Beyond that, the regional hegemon's decision makers are often disposed to view the regional system as a potential resource to be mobilized against an extra-regional rival with the result that the lesser states in the regional system will emphasize the limited domain of that system. The United States sought to involve Latin American states in the Korean war and was generally rebuffed. So too Soviet efforts to include the Mongolian People's Republic in the Warsaw Treaty Organization (WTO) and to station East European military units along the Ussuri against the People's Republic of China (PRC) during the nadir of Soviet-Chinese relations were rebuffed by the Romanians who stressed that the WTO was a *European* organization.

When in 1972 I first examined Soviet and U.S. behavior *vis-à-vis* the East European and U.S. regional systems, it was important to emphasize that there were differences between the behaviors of the regional hegemons that stemmed primarily from the nature of the Soviet system. There was compelling evidence that Soviet decision makers had been and remained more intense in their determination to maintain system boundaries than were U.S. leaders.

At the onset of the 1980s, however, it had already become evident from Soviet behavior that "in some instances the Soviet Union might at the margin trade off reduced intra-regional system cohesion for gains elsewhere."[7] Therefore, by the early 1980s, one could already generate plausible hypotheses about possible Soviet attitudes toward Eastern Europe that were driven by assumptions about the cross pressure a superpower experiences in its roles as a world and regional power. These differed from those that emphasized the distinctiveness of Soviet behavior *vis-à-vis* its regional allies as a consequence of the nature of the Soviet political system. At this writing they also appear to have anticipated Soviet behavior better than did the latter.

Indeed, while in some domains the claim of novelty in the putatively "new thinking" of Gorbachev's early tenure as General Secretary was tenuous or dubious, there can be no mistaking the novelty of Gorbachev's assertion in his speech on the 70th anniversary of the October Revolution in 1987 that peaceful coexistence, with its implied commitment to military non-intervention, should be the basis of Soviet relations with its East European allies. Such a statement by no means precluded the possibility that in practice the Soviet Union would under certain circumstances resort to military force to prevent changes from transpiring in Eastern Europe. It does suggest that the worries small European communist states have about Soviet behavior in the 1990s are more characteristic of any acutely asymmetrical power relationship than of one that stems from specific attributes of the Soviet Union as a regional hegemon. Being located between Germany and Russia is a lousy place for a state whose elites seek to behave independently in the international system, but that is a proposition whose validity does not depend on the nature of the Soviet political system.

IMPLICATIONS FOR DEPENDENCY THEORY

The Soviet-East Europe hierarchical regional system can be used to assess the explanatory power of dependency theory as well. Dependency theory shares with much of the traditional literature on Soviet foreign policy the assumption that the nature of the domestic system of the hegemonic state explains that state's relations with other, lesser states. Where the two differ is that one sees in the American socioeconomic system—capitalism—the explanation for the observed dependency relationships, whereas the other focuses on the Soviet political system—socialism—for an explanation.

The only way, after all, that hypotheses linking the nature of the socio-economic and/or political systems of states and the character of relations between those states can be verified or falsified is by comparing relations between states that have capitalist socioeconomic systems and those that do not. Consider the proposition that "everyone dies under capitalism." It turns out, of course, that everyone dies under feudalism and socialism as well. This being the case, there might well still be a sense in which capitalism is a cause of death but most persons would find searching for other, more proximate, causes a more fruitful pastime.[8]

What I did, therefore, was to compare international systems by applying four concepts central to dependency theory that have been used in analyzing U.S.–Latin American relations—inequality, penetration, dependency and exploitation—in the Soviet–East European context. Doing so did not lend credence to the dependency theorists' focus on the causal role of capitalism. To the extent that conditions dependency theorists have ascribed to relationships between developed and less-developed capitalist states are actually observed, preliminary findings indicated they were found at least as often in the Soviet–East European regional system as in asymmetrically configured systems of capitalist states. At the same time, my findings also constituted evidence that the credibility of the argument that there was something distinctive and distinctively opprobrious about interstate relations among asymmetrically powerful socialist states had diminished substantially since Stalin's time.

There was, to be sure, some evidence to suggest that (between 1957 and 1972 in any event) interstate inequality as measured by GNP among the WTO members had actually increased—thus indicating, ironically, that it might be that under socialism the rich states get richer and the poor, poorer. The East European states are also more dependent on trade with the Soviet Union than the larger Latin American states are with the United States, exacerbating the level of inequality.

On the other hand, it is noteworthy how trade-oriented the East European states remain, despite the strong traditional Soviet impetus to autarky, and how much the Soviet Union has found itself encouraging East European states to decrease their trade dependence on the Soviet Union. Moreover, however one operationalizes the notion of political, socioeconomic and cultural penetration, it is clear that Soviet penetration of East European states has diminished substantially since the late 1940s.

Finally, it is important to appreciate how complicated and controversial is the issue as to whether the Soviet Union has exploited Eastern Europe economically since Stalin's time. The answer may be said to be one of the following: Either Eastern Europe has exploited the Soviet Union economically, an action the Soviet Union has tolerated for the political peace it buys within the WTO, or after 1956 the Soviet Union has marginally exploited Eastern Europe.

Neither answer serves as evidence for the proposition that there is something distinctive about the level of exploitation in Soviet–East European relations, a claim that could have been advanced about the years prior to 1956. As Paul Marer has shown, after World War II the Soviet Union took out of Eastern Europe about what the United States put into rebuilding Western Europe.[9]

ELITE AND MASS ATTITUDES TOWARD FOREIGN POLICY

The second conclusion linking world politics and Soviet foreign policy to which I came was that given the perceived implications of the thermonuclear era, further efforts to assess Soviet perspectives on the international system would require a much greater level of specificity. This was partly because it was clear that using the terms ''Bolshevik'' and ''Soviet'' interchangeably to depict Soviet thinking about contemporary international relations was just plain wrong. One was not likely to improve analytical clarity by invoking hypotheses about the "Bolshevik" thinking of persons who, long before "new thinking" became *de rigueur*, had explicitly rejected the proposition that the workers had nothing to lose but their chains. There were other vividly un-Bolshevik utterances in the early 1960s as well, including the dramatic declaration by the Communist Party of the Soviet Union (CPSU) in its polemics with the Chinese and that the atomic bomb did not observe the class principle, authoritative charges that another putatively socialist state was pursuing a Cold War policy against the Soviet Union and open questioning of Clausewitz's dictum that war is a continuation of politics.

In addition, the open-ended quality of the Soviet reading of international relations combined with the general political decompression epitomized by the 20th Congress of the CPSU to produce a noticeably more diverse political dialogue within the political leadership, and even more so among analysts specializing in international relations. Documenting that diversity and taking steps to develop criteria for predicting which elements among elites and either the attentive or mass public would be more disposed to particular attitudes became an important task.

An example of the documentation of elite diversity was the paper assessing the Soviet lessons of Vietnam that I published with Robert Axelrod in 1981.[10] It came at a time when there had been a resurgence in the West of views emphasizing the homogeneity of Soviet elite perspectives and the unchanging, purposive nature of Soviet goals. We concluded that the notion of monolithic Soviet preferences was unsustainable. Rather, we found—as had others in the early and mid-1970s—that in speaking of Soviet goals, it was necessary to specify the particular individual, institutional or media source as well as the context.

There was clear tension in Soviet commentary among those who ranked peace as priority and who showed only token obeisance to the support of the national liberation movements, and those who attached great weight to supporting national liberation movements but were considerably more cavalier in their protestations in favor of peace.

The Soviet commentary we examined was also divided as to whether increasing U.S. weakness was a favorable or unfavorable development. In several instances, the proposition was advanced that the weaker the United States became, the more prone it would be to lash out violently and to engage in aggressive acts. Other statements reached the opposite conclusion that as the United States became weaker, it would become more reasonable and pliant.

Similarly, it turned out that one could not speak about *the* Soviet view of the role of force in world politics. We encountered utterances that were quite in keeping with conventional Soviet and with indeed Bolshevik utterances. We found, for instance, claims that superior military force for (their) good guys was conducive to peace and that the imperialists were rethinking the role of force in international politics in light of the changed global distribution of power.

However, we also encountered assertions, prefiguring observations that have become commonplace in the Gorbachev period, that one lesson of Vietnam was that the role of force had lost some of its value for everyone including, by implication, Moscow.

A criterion that has proved an important discriminator of mass and attentive public attitudes in the Soviet Union is that of age. This is certainly important for developing broad notions about the evolution of the Soviet system and probably for Soviet foreign policy in particular. We now have data from three major surveys which bear on Soviet foreign policy attitudes. The results are mixed with respect to the relevance of inter-generational differences for foreign policy attitudes. The data from the Soviet Interview Project (SIP), which in 1983 interviewed almost 3000 Soviet emigres to the United States, most of whom arrived in 1979–80, are unambiguous about the link between age and foreign policy attitudes.[11] Deborah Yarsike and I found, for example, a negative and almost straight-line relation between the age of former Soviet citizens and their assessment of the relative power of the United States and the Soviet Union. The younger the Soviets, the less likely they were to say that the United States was more powerful than the Soviet Union. They were also more likely to assert that the Soviet Union was more likely to win a war between the two. Two Moscow telephone surveys, in May 1988 and January 1989, were considerably less clear-cut in identifying inter-generational differences that bear directly on foreign policy.[12]

All three, however, are unambiguous in showing that support for traditional Soviet institutions decreases with the age of the Soviet citizen, and conversely that the younger Soviets are, the more likely they are to support attitudes one would associate with *perestroika* and *demokratizatsiia*.

Another major potential dimension differentiating Soviet society with respect to foreign policy attitudes involves the supporters and opponents of political and economic reform. It turns out that those who support the decentralization and marketization of industrial and agricultural strategies are less likely to support an activist foreign policy in the Third World and more likely to support reductions in military expenditures, a key element in the Soviet Union's overall disposable surplus for foreign policy.

By comparison, the answer to the question as to whether there is an important attitudinal link between support for political democratization and support for a more benign foreign policy turns substantially on each respondent's notion of democracy. It is, of course, another matter—but should be stressed—that attitudes notwithstanding, increased political participation increases the number and intensity of domestic claims on Soviet resources and thus likely will result in a decrease in the disposable surplus available for foreign policy. If one interprets support for democratization as support for authentic political participation, then support for democratization and for a more benign foreign policy are linked at both the level of mass and of attentive publics.

If, however, one's concept of democracy is grounded in liberal notions such as the marketplace for ideas or the legal priority of individual rights over those of society, then the answer is different. With such a definition in mind, one would conclude that in the Soviet Union, support for political democratization has practically no implications for foreign-policy attitudes. Those who support political democratization in this sense are no less or more likely to support an activist foreign policy than others, and they are at most only marginally more likely to differ from others in attitudes toward military expenditures.[13] Consequently, there are no easy and automatic answers to questions about the links between domestic cleavages and foreign policy attitudes. We will make, however, little headway in anticipating Soviet behavior unless we treat these links as matters to be discovered empirically rather than assumed *a priori*.

CIVIL-MILITARY RELATIONS

A fourth area of research that encourages a view of the Soviet Union as an increasingly normal state with performance attributes relevant for foreign policy comparable to other states is civil-military relations. Data from the Soviet Interview Project along with interviews of more than a thousand male former Soviet citizens, almost all of whom were of military service age in the early or mid-1970s, testify to a trend extending from World War II at least through 1980 (the last year for which we have data), and, in all probability, continuing today, judging by Soviet news accounts in 1988–90. The more recent the birth date of those interviewed, and hence the year in which they would have been called to service, the higher the proportion of those reporting that they attempted to avoid military service. As the years when terror was used as an instrument of social control recede into the past, it has become less and less plausible to regard the Soviet Union as a political system distinctive in its capacity to mobilize its citizenry for foreign and security policy goals.

Instead, service avoidance has become a major problem in a state where virtually universal military service was long thought to be the norm. As one Soviet military commentator observed wryly in 1988, in place of the old Soviet adage that "the army is a school for life," young people today assert that "the army . . . is, of course, a school, but it is better to graduate from it as an external [correspondent] student."[14] Small wonder Gorbachev has sought to achieve a new and more truly authentic political participation.

Data from the same surveys, moreover, reveal that the notion that the Soviet Union is uniquely advantaged in its competition with Western states is suspect in another important respect. There has been a widespread tendency to view the Soviet military as performing better than the civilian economy. Certainly, the military sector is relatively advantaged in the allocation of high-quality materiel and resources that are a critical component of military performance. Moreover, it has often been maintained that the Soviet Union has a comparative advantage over Western political systems in the use of military power and in providing states with arms and other military aid. By extension, a plausible hypothesis would be that performance levels in the military were higher than in the notoriously inefficient Soviet civilian sector.

However plausible *a priori*, this was not what we were told by our informants. Michael Berbaum and I found that our respondents in the aggregate saw no difference in the level of performance in the civilian and military domains, though the mix of variables affecting performance differed between them.[15] What this serves to do for the broader study of Soviet foreign policy is to intensify our doubts about the validity of thinking about the Soviet Union as a political system able to perform at a distinctive level at least in the military security domain. For while we do not have comparable data for American military performance, a finding that peacetime Soviet military performance levels are the same as performance levels in the Soviet civilian sector runs counter to the image of a distinctive Soviet political system with a comparative advantage in a competitive East-West relationship.

CONCLUSION

This has been an account of the evolution of theory building at the intersection of world politics and Soviet foreign policy. That evolution has been in keeping with the movement of the Soviet Union in the direction of becoming a more or less "normal" state. It has been partly a process of ruling out some long-standing concepts about the Soviet Union. In several instances this has been as much a function of change in the Soviet Union as it has of change in our thinking. The results of research presented in this paper testify that considerable demobilization has occurred in the Soviet Union rather than disproving hypotheses about mobilization systems and their behavior in world politics. Similarly, the evolution of Soviet perspectives on international politics in the late 1950s and early 1960s constituted fundamental departures from traditional Bolshevik-Stalinist modes of thinking.

This evolution of theory has altered our research agendas. Increasingly, the research questions we will want to address in the study of Soviet foreign policy are those asked in the general study of foreign policy rather than in the specific study of the Soviet Union. As if to emphasize this point, Gorbachev and his advisors—many of whom (Gennadi Gerasimov, Boris Piadishev, Fedor Burlatskii, Evgeny Primakov *et al.*) were the young turks of international relations in the early 1960s—are fond of speaking of common global problems. A truly comparative foreign policy, in which all states are involved and may be constructively discussed as members of a truly international political system, may be on the horizon. We can see the prospect of asking parallel questions about Soviet and American foreign policy and of joint collaboration by, for instance, Soviet and American students of the foreign policies of the two states. Not only is Soviet foreign policy becoming more akin to the foreign policy of a "normal" state, it is now seriously possible to imagine "normal" social science being done about an increasingly normal, while militarily very powerful, Soviet Union. In such a pursuit, it will inevitably be profitable to compare Soviet foreign policy and that of other "normal" states, both for the light such comparisons shed on the behavior of the Soviet Union and the other states in question and for the broader insights into world politics theory that may result.

NOTES

1. William Zimmerman, *Soviet Perspectives on International Relations* (Princeton, NJ: Princeton University Press, 1969).

2. Marshall Shulman, *Stalin's Foreign Policy Reappraised* (Cambridge, MA: Harvard University Press, 1963).

3. Triska and Finley argued that both the United States and the Soviet Union respond *in kind* to the foreign policy innovations of the other. "Soviet-American Relations: A Multiple Symmetry Model," *The Journal of Conflict Resolution* IX (March 1965), pp. 37–53.

4. "The Policy of Peaceful Coexistence Proves Its Worth," *World Marxist Review* (December 1962), p. 6.

5. George Modelski, *The Communist International System* (Princeton, NJ: Princeton University Press for the Center of International National Studies, Woodrow Wilson School of Public and International Affairs, Research Monograph No. 9, 1960).

6. For a recent extensive effort in this respect, see the articles in Jan Triska, ed., *Dominant Powers and Subordinate States* (Durham, NC: Duke University Press, 1986).

7. William Zimmerman, "Soviet-East European Relations and the Changing International System," in Morris Bernstein, Zvi Gitelman, and William Zimmerman, eds., *East-West Relations and the Future of Eastern Europe* (London: Allen and Unwin, 1981), p. 96.

8. I am indebted to David Abernathy for this example.

9. "Soviet Economic Policy in Eastern Europe," in *Reorientation and Commercial Relations of the Economies of Eastern Europe,* Joint Economic Commission, U.S. Congress, 2d. session (Washington, DC: U.S. Government Printing Office, 1974), p. 144.

10. William Zimmerman and Robert Axelrod, "The 'Lessons' of Vietnam and Soviet Foreign Policy," *World Politics* 34 (October 1981), pp. 1–24.

11. On SIP generally, see James Millar, ed., *Politics, Work and Daily Life in the USSR* (Cambridge: Cambridge University Press, 1987).

12. Both Moscow surveys were done by the Institute for Sociological Research, the first for the *New York Times*/CBS news poll and the second in conjunction with a Martilla and Kiley Study of four cities in the United States. William Zimmerman and Deborah Yarsike, "Intergenerational Change in Soviet Foreign Policy," unpublished paper, 1987, and "Mass Publics and Soviet Foreign Policy in William Zimmerman, ed., *The Changing Soviet Union and Western Security Policy,* in draft.

13. These findings are based on the Soviet Interview Project data. The 1988 Moscow survey responses support the findings drawn from the SIP data regarding the link between attitudes favoring political participation and foreign policy attitudes. Unfortunately, no questions were asked that addressed economic decentralization or the liberal notions of democracy. William Zimmerman, "Economic Reform, Democratization and Foreign Policy Attitudes in the Soviet Union," in Seweryn Bialer and Robert Jervis, eds., *East-West Relations in the 1990s* (Durham, NC: Duke University Press, 1990).

14. *Krasnaia Zvezda,* 9 April 1988, translated in *FBIS-SOV-88-077,* p. 68.

15. William Zimmerman and Michael Berbaum, "Equal But Not Separate: A Comparison of Soviet Military and Civilian Performance," paper presented at the 1987 annual meeting of the American Political Science Association. We achieved this result by asking them to "think about the *best* possible way [the unit] could have performed. That would be 100 percent. Overall, during your stay with that unit, what percentage would you give it for the performance of its mission?" Our informants were all former Soviet citizens living in the United States. Almost all of those served in the 1970s.

5

Science and Sovietology: Bridging the Methods Gap in Soviet Foreign Policy Studies*

Jack Snyder†

Everyone is in favor of greater scholarly rigor, but people define rigor in seemingly antithetical ways. Two methodological cultures, positivism and holism, coexist uneasily in the social sciences. For "logical positivists," rigor means deducing an "if, then" hypothesis from a general theory, and testing whether the predicted relationship holds true over a set of cases in which the influence of extraneous factors is held constant. Holism is more eclectic in its methods; for most holists, rigor means reconstructing the meaning of an action in the subject's own terms, and interpreting it in light of a richly detailed cultural, social, and historical context. Thus, positivists usually seek objective causes; holists typically explain behavior through the prism of the actor's subjective understanding. Positivists trace patterns across many cases, setting context aside by holding it constant; holists trace patterns within cases, exploring connections between context and action.[1]

Underlying these different approaches to scholarly method are different assumptions about the nature of reality. Holists see a world of great complexity and interrelatedness. In any situation, many independent elements interact in complex ways to shape the ideas and actions of actors. Artificial attempts to focus on some small number of factors and relationships, which could be compared across cases, only hinder understanding. Emphasis is placed on the unique aspects of each situation, not on superficial or partial similarities across situations. Consequently, theories designed to illuminate more than one case must be rich, open-

*Reprinted by permission of the author and publisher from *World Politics* XL, No. 2 (1988):169–193. Copyright © 1988 by The Trustees of Princeton University. Reprinted by permission of The Johns Hopkins University Press.

†The present article is based on a report prepared for the Subcommittee on Soviet Foreign Policy of the Joint Committee on Soviet Studies of the Social Science Research Council and the American Council of Learned Societies; the views expressed do not necessarily reflect the views of the subcommittee of its members. Douglas Blum, Richard Herrmann, Theodore Hopf, Robert Jervis, Friedrich Kratochwil, Robert Legvold, Cynthia Roberts, and Marshall Shulman have offered helpful suggestions and criticisms.

ended checklists, not deductive, narrow-beam searchlights. Some holists even take the position that objective reality is so complex, diverse, and unknowable that only subjective (or "intersubjective") dialogues about reality can be profitably studied.

Positivists, on the other hand, believe that the analytical convenience of simplification is legitimate because it can be shown empirically that some factors are more important than others. Complex interactions between some important variables may occur, but everything is not inextricably related to everything else. Even "unique" situations are not considered to be *sui generis,* but rare types whose differences from other cases can be described in general terms. Moreover, when positivists look at whole systems, they assume that relationships among the parts can be explained in terms of some relatively simple and regular structural effects.

The relationship between positivism and holism is especially important for Soviet foreign policy studies. In that field, as in area studies more generally, a scholar's regionalist culture pulls him toward holism, while his disciplinary culture of political science pulls him toward positivism. In this conflict of cultural and institutional cross-pressures, it is important to find some firm intellectual ground on which methodological choices can be based.

The distance between positivism and holism is not as great as it appears. Each captures a valuable truth, and the two work best in conjunction. Positivism—and in particular its driving engine, deductive theory—poses questions in a way that clarifies arguments, facilitates testing, and directs research to ripe, important questions. Holism, on the other hand, reminds us that in the Soviet field causal generalizations that hold true 60 percent of the time are not the ultimate goal of research. Rather, such generalizations must contribute to understanding in full contextual detail the one particular case that we care most about—the present. Moreover, reconstructing the Soviets' thinking may sometimes be easier than understanding the underlying causes of their behavior, and just as valuable in guiding policy choices.

The benefits of positivism and holism can often be captured simultaneously by recasting holist interpretations in deductive, causal terms. A holist's "context" can in most cases be translated into the positivist's "causal variables." Even when holist explanations deal with ends and means rather than with causes, they can often be sharpened by expressing them in deductive terms.

Most Sovietologists are already using a method that combines the reconstruction of Soviet thinking with a complex causal explanation of behavior. In executing this method, however, positivist rules for stating and testing causal arguments are often ignored. As a result, debates go in circles and irrelevant evidence piles up. The most urgent need in the field of Soviet foreign policy today is to reformulate research questions in terms of deductive arguments, but without sacrificing the sound holist traditions of the discipline.

In an earlier article on a similar theme, I laid out the logic of positivist testing procedures, paying only brief attention to the central role of deductive theory in the positivist approach; I was similarly brief on the compatibility of positivism and holism.[2] The present essay will focus on these more basic questions as they relate to Soviet foreign policy studies. Its sections will focus on (1) what positivism is, and the role of deductive theory in it; (2) what holism is, and its relation to positivism; (3) the shortcomings of holism; (4) the use of deductive theory to repair holism's shortcomings and, more generally, to set a research agenda for the field; (5) the shortcomings of positivism; and (6) the use of hybrid methods to repair the shortcomings of positivism. Illustrations will show the value of deductive theory in addressing some of the major questions of the field, including Soviet views on the political implications of military imbalances and the domestic sources of Soviet expansionism. These and other illustrations will be drawn from some of the best secondary works in the field.

POSITIVISM

Explanation and testing in the positivist framework can be summarized in terms of five elements, the most central one being deductive theory.[3]

Causal Generalization

Positivists state their hypotheses in the form of "if, then" generalizations. They seek to explain individual events by identifying "if, then" generalizations, or covering laws, that match the patterns of those events. For example, a hypothesis in the literature of international politics posits that, if offense becomes easier, then international conflict will increase.[4] Thus, one explanation for the origins of the cold war could be that the fluid political situation in Europe after Germany's defeat made offensive tactics advantageous, both for opportunistic and security purposes. The converse suggests that if offense becomes more difficult, then conflict will diminish. Thus, one explanation for the rise of detente in Europe is that the Berlin crisis of 1958–1961 showed it was easier to defend the status quo than to change it.

Operational Definitions of Variables

The terms of the hypothesis, including causes and consequences, must be clearly defined to minimize disagreements about the classification of particular cases. For example, definitions of offensive advantage and defensive advantage must be clear enough so that a researcher can decide into which category his case falls.[5]

Covariation

Testing must show that offensive advantage correlates with increased conflict, and that defensive advantage correlates with decreased conflict.

Controlled Comparison

Testing focuses on cases in which competing hypotheses make opposite predictions. For example, it might be argued that international conflict is caused not by offensive advantage but by domestic political pathologies that promote expansionism. If so, offensive advantage might be spuriously related to increased conflict, because domestically motivated expansionists work to create offensive capabilities. In order to disentangle the effects of the two putative causes, the researcher looks for cases where there is an offensive advantage but no domestic motivation to expand, and for cases where there is a defensive advantage but high domestic motivation to expand.[6]

Deductive Theory

Just as "if, then" generalizations at a low level of abstraction act as covering laws that explain individual events, so too generalizations at higher levels of abstraction explain the covering laws. For example, the hypothesis that offensive advantage causes conflict even among status quo powers is just one application of the more general Prisoners' Dilemma theorem in game theory.[7] According to a strictly mathematical proof, rational players in a single-play Prisoners' Dilemma, by the logic of their situation, are constrained to compete even though they end up worse off than if they had cooperated. Offensive advantage increases the incentive for competitive play by magnifying the gains that arise from exploiting one sided cooperation in a single play of the game, and by magnifying the losses that arise from being exploited. If international politics is like a Prisoners' Dilemma, and if offensive advantage makes it resemble a single-play contest, then, by logical deduction, offensive advantage should promote conflict.

Deductive theory is the predictive engine that drives the positivist method as a whole. It generates "if, then" hypotheses, which in turn generate testable predictions in specific cases. As a result, the implications of arguments are made clearer when they are expressed as theoretical deductions, and tests for them are easier to think up.

HOLISM

In a study of Soviet views on the role of military power in international politics, Robert Legvold has reiterated the main tenets of the holistic position: understanding behavior in terms of the actor's own frame of reference, and explaining it by placing it in a rich context. Thus, "the student of politics who looks only at patterns of behavior but leaves out the meanings that actors give to their own and to each other's conduct turns into a specialist of shadows."[8] Analyzing another culture's approach to strategic thought in terms of one's own theories (in this case, Thomas Schelling's ideas about the "diplomacy of violence") introduces an ethnocentric bias that hinders understanding. Moreover, "Soviet thoughts about semiabstractions, like the functioning of force in contemporary international politics, are but a fragment of the larger issue."[9] They must be understood in the larger context of Soviet goals and fears, the broader Soviet worldview, and the international environment in which the Soviets calculate. Understanding also requires distinguishing among different contexts in which the question arises:

using force, deterring the use of force, indirectly influencing diplomatic trends, and so forth.[9] Empathy and context-dependent nuances of meaning are the watchwords of this approach.

Though the general epistemological stance of holism is quite clearly articulated, its methodological prescriptions rarely are. In part, this reflects a conscious choice to avoid imposing *a priori* concepts and approaches, and a preference to be guided *ad hoc* by the data of the particular case. Still, Sovietologists, like anthropologists setting out to do fieldwork, like to bring along a checklist of questions to think about. These initial concepts of theories are usually designed to be flexible and nondeductive so that they adjust to fit the case rather than force it into a Procrustean bed.[10]

In the Soviet field, the clearest exposition of this method is the framework that Marshall Shulman used in his study of Stalin's foreign policy and his attempt to think through contemporary Soviet arms-control policy while he served in the Carter administration.[11] The method is roughly as follows: prepare a chart arraying the major domestic and international developments impinging on Soviet calculations; track these developments over the period to be studied, along with the development of Soviet statements and actions; and reconstruct a plausible line of Soviet reasoning that could have led to those actions, using a background knowledge of Soviet history and politics for guidance. The objective international setting and the peculiarly Soviet way of looking at it are both included.

In this style of analysis, positivist and holist elements are mixed. At one level, situational constraints and deep structural effects of history and the social system are treated like *causes*, in a basically positivist fashion. Thus, the Soviets behave a certain way "because of" the effects of these variables. However, these causal inputs are integrated through an analysis of the Soviets' *reasons* for pursuing certain ends with certain means, in a holist fashion. Thus, the Soviets' subjective perspective leads them to behave in a particular way "in order to" achieve certain goals.

There is nothing in this method that bars the development of a general thesis from which testable hypotheses can be derived. When this occurs, it comes close to replicating the positivist method. In *Stalin's Foreign Policy Reappraised,* for example, Shulman adopted what amounts to a rational-choice theory of Soviet international behavior, arguing for "the largely rational responsiveness of Soviet policy to changes in the world environment, and particularly to changes in power relationships." According to this case study, the Soviet leadership by 1949 began to recognize the counterproductive effects of its confrontational policies, decided that adverse trends in both the socialist and capitalist camp dictated the need for a breathing spell, and consequently moved toward a policy of peaceful coexistence in order to demobilize the opposing bloc.[12]

From this rational-choice theory, Shulman deduced testable "if, then" hypotheses—some explicit and some implicit. One is that the Soviets are less confrontational when the balance of power is against them in the short run and favors them in the long run. Another is that the Soviets are more confrontational in situations of offensive advantage (e.g., when the status quo is fluid) than in situations of defensive advantage (e.g., when militancy is seen to unify opponents, when peace propaganda sells better than revolutionary appeals).[13]

Because of the emphasis on the interaction of multiple factors in chronological context, however, effects of the individual variables, such as the balance of power, are not fully tested as separate hypotheses.[14] From a positivist standpoint, this leads to some puzzles in the course of the narrative. Weakness and fear sometimes appear as motives for restraint; at other times they serve as rationalizations for militancy—as in Zhdanov's response to the Marshall Plan and in Molotov's reasons for retaining the confrontational line even after the Berlin crisis.[15] Likewise, the strength of socialism sometimes appears as an argument for militancy, sometimes as an argument for the feasibility of peaceful coexistence.[16] These apparent anomalies do not stand out in the chronological narrative because they are plausibly integrated into reconstructions of how a whole range of incentives came together to shape Soviet thinking.

This might lead a positivist to question whether the balance of power really was the key factor in Soviet policy—or indeed, whether it had any systematic effect at all. Perhaps the relative advantages of offense and defense determined Soviet policy, and not the current or prospective balance of power. Or perhaps the effect of these two factors varies, depending on the aggressiveness of the opponent. To test this, the positivist might want to set up a chart with eight boxes, think through the logic of all the permutations, and look for cases to test each one.

To the holist, such testing might seem beside the point, since the main thing is to demonstrate the validity of the general thesis about the rational responsiveness of Soviet policy, not to produce law-like statements about the effects of separate variables. Once he knows that the Soviets are rationally responsive to their environment, he can interpret their moves in specific contexts *ad hoc*. In this view, to be valid, laws would have to be so complex, qualified, and cumbersome that they would offer no advantage over *ad hoc* reconstruction.

To the positivist, the basis for the larger generalization is shaky without the separate testing of the effects of individual variables. Unless a close connection between specific incentives and specific policies is shown, there is a possibility that Soviet policy is not based on rational calculations, but on a rote response to the failure of the previous policy. It makes a great deal of difference whether the Soviets are rationally reacting to specific geopolitical incentives or whether they are cybernetically alternating between stereotyped policies of militancy and lulling.[17] Indeed, Shulman identifies two patterns of Soviet learning: a cyclical alternation between confrontational "left" and nonconfrontational "right" tactics, which seems to be cybernetic, and a secular shift to the right which may be a rational response to a secular decline in revolutionary opportunities.[18] It might also be caused, however, by factors such as the evolution of the Soviet political system. A recasting of these questions in terms of explicitly competing theories and deducing testable "if, then" hypotheses from them could open up a fresh line of research, building on Shulman's ideas and leading to practical conclusions about how the Soviets learn in response to U.S. behavior.

In short, some forms of holism are not far from positivism in their implicit use of deductive theory and "if, then" hypotheses. In such cases, it may be quite easy to recast the holist argument in terms of explicit, deductive theory. Holism may be farther from positivism, however, in its reluctance to test the effects of individual variables in controlled contexts. Problems arise when the deductive links in a theory are left implicit and when multiple causes are examined all at once.

SOME SHORTCOMINGS OF HOLISM

The lax attitude of holism toward deductive logic leads to two errors. The first is that its predictions tend to be logically underdetermined. Causal assertions are made without showing why the same stimulus could not just as easily have led to the opposite consequences. The second error is that holistic explanations after the fact tend to be logically over-determined. Several independent factors are indiscriminately listed as the joint causes of an action, even though any one of them might have been sufficient to cause it. This shortcoming is serious in cases where different causes might have different policy implications for the West. Closer attention to the deductive logic of arguments can help to avoid these problems.

Predictive Underdetermination

Harry Gelman's argument about the role of Soviet leadership politics in promoting an opportunistic, expansionist approach to detente illustrates the problem of logical underdetermination.[19] Gelman's book is a good example of eclectic holism, integrating causal explanations with the reconstruction of Soviet ends/means calculations. Despite some logical loose strands, it offers the best available account of the domestic politics of foreign policy in the Brezhnev period, if reinterpreted in the light of rational-choice theories of logrolling, it constitutes a significant theoretical advance as well.

Gelman offers three kinds of causal factors to account for the Soviet Union's tendency toward opportunistic expansion and for variations in its intensity. The first—not an argument that is distinctive to Gelman—focuses on the balance of costs, risks, and opportunities present in the international environment. The second is an endemic "attacking compulsion" rooted in the deep structure of the Leninist political culture and operational code. Gelman does not advance direct evidence for this proposition aside from its general plausibility in light of the obvious facts of Soviet expansionism. As such, it functions as a kind of residual, explaining what cannot be explained in any other way.

The third line of explanation rests on consensus building and leadership politics. Though the narrative sounds persuasive, Gelman never makes clear why consensus building produces an expansionist result rather than the opposite. His historical reconstruction holds that,

> since Brezhnev was confronted simultaneously with temptation (Podgornyy's assumption of a vulnerable political stance [in favor of restraint on defense spending]), positive incentives (the political rewards waiting in the form of support from the military and Suslov), and competition (the extreme rhetoric Shelepin offered the military and the ideologues), his reaction was a foregone conclusion.[20]

But why was it a foregone conclusion? Couldn't this whole formulation be turned on its head: temptation in the form of the vulnerability of Shelepin and the military, due to their reckless rhetoric and opposition to obviously beneficial arms restraint; positive incentives in the form of Podgornyy's support; competition in the form of Kosygin's budgetary alliance with Podgornyy—leading to international entrenchment? It didn't work out this way, but why?

The simplest explanation would be that elite groups and institutions with an interest in expansion (Gelman cites the military and the Central Committee's International Department) became disproportionately powerful in the Brezhnev years. That, however, begs the questions of where their power came from, and why it increased in this period. Moreover, Gelman's own account emphasizes that the rising power of these groups was as much a result or a concomitant of the expansionist consensus as a cause of it. The basic levers of power, Gelman argues, remained in the hands of the Politburo, above the level of institutional interests.[21]

Another explanation (which Gelman does not explicitly advance) would argue, along with George Berslauer, that the process of logrolling and consensus building in itself tends to produce "taut," overcommitted policies.[22] Gelman's evidence, reinterpreted in light of this theory, suggests that Brezhnev succeeded politically because he devised a policy of expansionist detente that promised to reconcile an arms build-up for the military, expansion into the third world for the ideologues, and increased technology transfer to co-opt Kosygin's domestic economic issue. For this line of argument, it need not be true that expansionist interests were more powerful than anti-expansionist interests. Rather, in a system where each interest gets what it wants most, expansion will result as long as *any* veto groups have an interest in it. That is a straighforward deduction from rational-choice theories of logrolling.[23]

Lacking this theoretical element, however, Gelman is unable to explain the expansionist character of the coalition in terms of domestic political dynamics alone. Consequently, he resorts to the notion of an "attacking compulsion": for reasons rooted in the deep cognitive structures of Leninists, it is political death to be considered, as Podgornyy was, "unacceptably 'soft.' "[24] If that is true, an entirely different research design is indicated. Domestic politics, the area in which Gelman carried out most of his original research, "becomes all product and is not at all productive."[25] If the "attacking compulsion" is really the key to the explanation, then it would have been better to look for propositions and tests focusing on the origin, structure, and evolution of belief systems. Alternatively, Gelman could have stayed with the domestic focus while recasting and sharpening his hypothesis with the help of rational-choice logrolling theory.

Explanatory Overdetermination

As if to compensate for arguments that are loose enough to predict any outcome and its opposite, holists tend toward explanatory overkill, piling up any number of logically unrelated or logically contradictory reasons for an occurrence. It is true that a variety of unrelated factors may sometimes come together to produce an outcome or a decision, but psychologists tell us that decisions are often taken on the basis of one salient consideration, and that multiple rationales are invented later.[26] When each of several candidate explanations implies a different policy prescription, it is especially important to distinguish which of them are really operating and which are spurious.

An example is provided by explanations that consider aggressiveness in Soviet foreign policy to be rooted in the totalitarian origins of the political system. This argument is often invoked without supplying any logical connection at all, relying on the analogy to Nazi German for persuasiveness. At other times, a whole list of reasons is supplied: (1) totalitarians take their ideology seriously; (2) their political style requires either total control or total conflict; (3) they manufacture foreign threats and successes abroad to shore up their tenuous legitimacy; and, more subtly, (4) real pressures of international competition force the leader of a backward state to use domestic repression and militant appeals to mobilize his inefficient society.[27]

Each of these explanations is logically distinct. There is no reason to believe that if one of them is true, the rest are true also. Moreover, each of them seems to imply a different strategy for the opponent: (1) firm deterrence while waiting for the totalitarians' ideology to atrophy; (2) subversion to change their political system; (3) symbolic international agreements to replace symbolic conflict as the basis for their domestic legitimacy; and (4) an easing of external pressure to reduce the need for internal repression. Since some of these policies are opposites, lumping these explanations together indiscriminately, in typical holist fashion, would destroy their practical value. Logically independent explanations need to be disentangled and tested separately, in positivist fashion.

In short, holist studies of Soviet foreign policy often include causal arguments as part of their interpretation. Typically, these arguments suffer from the errors of predictive underdetermination and explanatory overdetermination. Such problems can be corrected by recasting the arguments in terms of deductive theory and by adopting positivist testing procedures. In the examples cited above, this could be accomplished through relatively small adjustments to the original holist argument. The intervention of deductive theory can also transform a holist debate in a more fundamental way, refocusing its arguments and establishing an entirely new research agenda.

TRANSFORMING A RESEARCH AGENDA
BY MEANS OF DEDUCTIVE THEORY

Deductive theory can do much more than just clean up the loose ends of holist arguments. At its best, it can reformulate the questions asked in academic and policy debates, clarify the branchpoints where contending arguments diverge, and reorient research toward more decisive tests. Beyond this, a deductive theory can turn diverse, narrowly focused studies into contributions toward a unified research program. Historians of science have found that the take-off point for most disciplines comes when work is focused on a stable core of explanatory goals that are expressed as a set of deductively interrelated puzzles.[28] One of the main barriers to progress in the field of Soviet foreign policy is the absence of this kind of research program that would provide direction to its work.

In recent years, the discipline of international politics has been making considerable progress toward defining a coherent, productive, yet flexible and relatively pluralistic research program. Though this field is hardly a perfect model for emulation, it is normal in science for the more applied fields to borrow ideas and approaches from the more basic, more theoretical field that is most closely related to it. Thus, it is natural for Soviet foreign policy studies to look to the discipline of international politics for guidance in setting an agenda for research.

One of the core aspirations of the field of international politics is to explain outcomes on the two game-theory dimensions of cooperation/conflict and win/ lose—especially counterintuitive outcomes produced by the perverse effects of international anarchy. From this core explanatory goal and rational-choice base, puzzle-solving activity radiates outward in a variety of directions toward systems theory, deterrence theory, bargaining theory, regime theory, theories about the effects of anarchical competition on domestic structure, and theories about adjustments needed in rational-choice models to take into account systematic psychological biases.[29] This is a rich and diverse agenda, which unites the security and political economy subfields and even accommodates nonpositivist offshoots.[30] Despite this diversity, the research program hangs together because of its core puzzles and common intellectual style, much of which can be traced back to Thomas Schelling.

If this research agenda is applied to the Soviet field, it offers some advantages and some potential disadvantages. To demonstrate the advantages, an extended example will show how Schelling's theoretical insights can be used to restructure the Garthoff-Pipes debate on Soviet attitudes regarding nuclear deterrence by clarifying the opposing arguments, proposing new empirical tests, and pointing toward a broad agenda for further research. In a subsequent section, I will discuss the potential disadvantages of importing a deductive research program of this kind into the Soviet field: its ethnocentrism, its monolithic character, and the questionable applicability of the special skills of Sovietologists to the research program it proposes.

The disagreement between Raymond Garthoff and Richard Pipes over Soviet attitudes on the nature of nuclear deterrence has been one of the most lively and consequential debates in research on Soviet military strategy.[31] In essence, Garthoff contends that the Soviets accept the inexorability of a deterrent relationship based on mutual assured destruction, though they retain the vestiges of a war-fighting doctrine and force posture in case deterrence fails. Pipes avers that the Soviets seek a war-winning capability, though they are resigned temporarily to its infeasibility. When the debate is formulated in this way, it is unclear what evidence might constitute a test of the two views. Garthoff could explain the war-fighting capability of the SS-18 as a hedge against the failure of deterrence, while Pipes could explain the ABM Treaty as a temporary expedient. War-fighting statements in the military press could be explained as reflecting only the military-technical level of doctrine, while politicians' renunciation of nuclear first-use and the possibility of victory in nuclear war could be explained as eyewash for the West.

As a result of this impasse, empirical research has moved on to narrower, more concrete questions such as Soviet force posture and doctrine for a major conventional war in Europe. The Garthoff-Pipes debate is hard to escape, however, because the question of what deters nuclear escalation is central to interpreting Soviet conventional strategy. Do the Soviets believe that mutual vulnerability will deter both sides from nuclear use regardless of the nuclear balance, or do they believe that superiority in nuclear war–fighting capability is needed to prevent NATO from escalating? The answer to this question has profound implications for the choice of forces to deter a Soviet conventional offensive, the strength of Soviet inclinations to preempt, and the interpretation of Soviet diplomatic and arms-control motivations.

Because the Garthoff-Pipes debate, in one guise or another, cannot be avoided, perhaps it can be reformulated in ways that make it more amenable to testing. To produce findings that cannot be easily explained away, the testing strategy should focus on evidence that is unambiguously at the political level of doctrine, and on behavior that is too important to be used for the purposes of disinformation. Only Soviet crisis diplomacy and coercive bargaining meet these criteria. But exactly what predictions should follow from the views of Garthoff and Pipes in such circumstances? Here is where Schelling's help is essential in clarifying arguments and deducing empirical hypotheses.

Schelling and other game theorists have argued that, under conditions of mutual assured destruction, the outcome of coercive diplomacy depends not on who is stronger (since the ability to punish is absolute), but on who is more willing to run risks and who bears the onus of the last clear chance to avoid disastrous escalation.[32] From this logic of the game of Chicken, Robert Jervis has deduced the corollary that, in most situations, nuclear weapons give a double advantage to the defender of the status quo.[33] First, defenders will be more willing to run risks, since people usually value what they have more than what they covet. Second, the onus of the last clear chance to avoid the risk of uncontrolled escalation normally weights more heavily on the side trying to change the status quo. That is why Schelling found deterrence to be easier than compellence. He added, however, that this is less true when there is uncertainty about who has the last clear chance, or when clever tactics can shift it to the opponent.

These deductions help to clarify the Garthoff-Pipes dispute and to devise tests that would determine which side is right. If the view that the Soviets accept the implications of the mutual deterrent relationship means anything, it should mean that Soviet coercive bargaining behavior fits Schelling's pattern. That is, the Soviets are predicted to stand firm when the balance of motivation favors them (in particular when defending the status quo), and to be extremely cautious in trying to change the status quo by force. Nonetheless, we would expect them to try to manipulate the last clear chance and to take advantage of ambiguities in the status quo in order to make limited gains. Assuming that both sides have at least minimum assured destruction capabilities, the balance of nuclear capabilities should *not* correlate strongly with Soviet behavior. Moreover, the more strongly the Soviets share Schelling's view that the function of conventional combat is to generate the risk of escalation,[34] the less strongly Soviet behavior will be shaped by the local balance of conventional forces.

Pipes should make the opposite predictions. He believes that Soviet strategic calculation "always involves matters of relative not absolute advantage."[35] Even if both players are Chicken, to use Schelling's categories, relative war-fighting disparities make some players more Chicken than others. Following this logic, Soviet coercive diplomacy should not be decisively driven by the balance of motivations in a particular case, nor should it distinguish strongly between defending the status quo and changing it, or between deterrence and compellence. Rather, the Soviets are predicted to stand firm when they enjoy dominance in nuclear war–fighting capabilities and/or a local conventional preponderance, and to give in when their war-fighting capabilities are weaker than those of their opponents. Rather than manipulating the last clear chance, the Soviets' coercive bargaining tactics are predicted to focus on demonstrating their ability to deploy or alert a superior war-fighting force.

With these deductions in hand, tests bearing on the Garthoff-Pipes debate are easy to devise and to carry out. In fact, an existing analysis of Soviet naval diplomacy by James McConnell comes close to being a test of Schelling's theory, and thus of the Garthoff-Pipes debate, though he did not conceive of it as such.[36] McConnell's tests illustrate many of the procedures used in positivist comparative methods, but they also reveal some of positivism's pitfalls.

Covariation

McConnell tests for covariation between the defense of the status quo and the achievement of one's aims in coercive diplomacy. He finds that the two correlate in the vast majority of his cases; but this result is marred by his *ad hoc* approach to determining what the status quo is and who is defending it. In a few cases, the judgment of who was the defender in a showdown seems to be influenced by who was the winner.[37]

Alternative Explanations

McConnell also tests for covariation between the military balance and success in coercive diplomacy—a relationship that Pipes would predict to be a strong one. McConnell does not explicitly discuss the nuclear balance; if he had, he would have found no correlation over the 1967–1976 period that he examined.[38] Instead, he focused on the local naval balance, finding little correlation between it and the outcome. In most cases of naval confrontation on the high seas, the superpowers simply matched each other's deployment, each carrier task force calling forth a comparable anti-carrier force.[39] Regardless of the ships available for further reinforcement, deployment races to achieve local superiority failed to occur, implying that the superpowers viewed the purpose of the forces not as war-fighting, but as a token of commitment and risk-taking.

Crucial Cases

McConnell looks for crucial cases that stack up all other alleged explanations against the status quo explanation. Enclaves within the opponent's sphere of interest, such as Berlin and Cuba, are cases of this type, in which the balance of local capability and the balance of strategic interests (apart from the reputational interest in defending the status quo) work against the survival of such enclaves.[40] The fact that they do survive against challenges means that McConnell and Schelling pass a hard test.

Process Tracing

Schelling's predictions concern not only outcomes, but also tactics and process; so these too can be the basis for corroborative tests. Schelling expects that players will try to manipulate the status quo and the "last clear chance" to their advantage. McConnell offers some illustrations of the Soviet's use of such tactics. For example, during the Angolan civil war, there was no stable status quo, so outsiders were relatively free to jockey for advantage. In doing so, the Soviets counted on using the freedom of the seas (a kind of normative status quo or, for Schelling, an escalation threshold) to protect the movement of Cuban troops through seas dominated by the U.S. Navy.[41]

Deviant Cases

McConnell seeks out deviant cases in order to refine his hypothesis. The Middle East wars, for example, show that the bargaining advantage of the defender extends only to the protection of a client's core areas and not to peripheral aspects of the status quo, such as desert frontiers.[42] This raises the question of how to distinguish progressive refinements of a theory from *ad hoc* rationalizations to excuse its degeneration. The general rule is that refinements are progressive if they help explain many cases rather than just one, and if they suggest ways to apply the theory to new questions.

To sum up, the Schelling/McConnell example shows that recasting holist debates in positivist terms can help to clarify arguments and make them more amenable to testing. It also sets in motion a self-sustaining program of research, involving the analysis of deviant cases, the refinement of the original hypothesis, and the tracing of the implications of the theory into new areas. In this case, for example, an important extension of the theory might examine what happens under conditions in which conflict is predicted to be greatest—in cases where the status quo is ambiguous or where both sides believe they are defending it.[43] Research might address the causes and consequences of such situations, how the Soviets behave in them, and what tactics have proved safe and effective in confronting such dilemmas.

This theory-driven research program can also suggest questions for holist scholars engaged in the detailed reconstruction of Soviet perceptions and calculations in individual cases. Direct evidence of Soviet thinking could be important for corroborating or refuting McConnell's interpretation of his cases, for example. Schelling himself uses a number of Khrushchev quotations to illustrate his tactical theories. In one partially apocryphal example, Khrushchev is said to have remarked that Berlin was not worth a war, but his Western interlocutor reminded him that this shared risk was a two-edged sword. Khrushchev, as if coached by Schelling, replied that "you are the ones that have to cross a frontier"—thereby showing that he did think in terms of the manipulation of shared risk as well as the manipulation of the status quo as a means to pass the onus of the last clear chance to the opponent.[44] Sovietological scholarship producing this kind of evidence would nicely complement multi-case analyses of overt behavior by specialists in international relations.

More generally, the game-theoretic perspective opens up a variety of questions for the area-studies scholar. Though simplified versions of game theory assume a generic rational player, the character and tactical style of the player can be treated as a variable in the theory. In Chicken games, for example, Schelling argued for surrendering the initiative by means of irrevocable preemptive defection, but Nathan Leites's Bolshevik chooses to probe cautiously and to retain the last clear chance to avoid disaster.[45] The work of Sovietologists on such questions is likely to be better focused and more helpful if they use game theory to shape the questions they ask.

In short, deductive theory can undoubtedly be used to reformulate holist debates and direct the work of holist scholars. Certain obvious benefits would result, but at what cost? Because of some of the shortcomings and limitations of positivism, caution must be exercised against completely subsuming holist research under a monistic program of positivist research.

SHORTCOMINGS AND LIMITATIONS OF POSITIVISM

Three objections may be raised to the use of positivist international relations theory to reformulate the research agenda of the field of Soviet foreign policy: the question of ethnocentrism, inherent problems of implementing the positivist method in the social sphere, and the danger of adopting any single approach.

Ethnocentrism

In order to minimize the danger of ethnocentrism, holists suggest analyzing the Soviets' behavior in terms of the Soviets' own categories and concepts. Certainly one way of testing an interpretation of Soviet behavior is to find out whether the Soviets share it. That has its limits, however. Robert Legvold, in his study of Soviet attitudes toward military power, starts with the Soviet literature, but then adds distinctions and concepts that are entirely his own. The question, then, is not whether Western ideas are admissible, but when and with what safeguards they are introduced.

In view of these criteria, does the imposition of Schelling's categories on Soviet behavior constitute unchecked, unvarnished ethnocentrism? Schelling's ideas, like those of Clausewitz, were produced by particular historical experiences in a particular social setting. Both transcend that setting, however, by virtue of their high degree of abstraction, their deductive clarity, and their susceptibility to empirical refutation. Using Western concepts like "escalation dominance" in an *ad hoc* manner to describe Soviet thinking is surely ethnocentrism, but using Schelling's theory self-consciously as a guide for careful testing is not. How could a science make any headway if it were forbidden to use ideas that it had thought up itself?

Inherent Flaws in Positivist Testing Procedures

A more fundamental objection is that positivism, at least in the social sciences, is unable to fulfill its promise to carry out conclusive tests. McConnell's tests, for example, are not fully satisfying because he does not offer a reliable definition of the status quo, such that any two researchers would always agree on who was defending it and who was challenging it in a given case. As a consequence, deciding whether a case supports or contradicts his hypothesis involves partly subjective, *ad hoc* judgment.

Though it is possible that more precise measures could have reduced arbitrariness, nonpositivist philosophers of science contend that the underlying problem is inherent: in their view, the variables in social theories do not closely correspond to hard observables in nature. The variables exist only as conventions, either as a linguistic custom of the people under study or as a category imposed by the scientist. Several consequences thus undermine the positivist method. First, most of the phenomena that social scientists find interesting will be difficult to measure. Second, measurements must either be subjective or rely on highly artificial protocols that measure a variable only indirectly. Third, the scientist is allowed a degree of arbitrariness in deciding whether cases fit his theory and, if they do not, whether the theory or the measurement procedures are at fault. Under these conditions, "objectivity" can at best mean agreement among subjective observers, each of whom brings biases and preconceptions to the task of observation.[46]

William Zimmerman and Robert Axelrod's quantitative study of the lessons that Soviet commentators drew from the Vietnam War illustrates some of these difficulties.[47] In testing the hypothesis that different Soviet press organs serve as forums for the articulation of "left" and "right" opinions in foreign policy debates, these authors first classify press statements on the lessons of Vietnam as either left or right, using well-articulated criteria and requiring agreement among multiple coders. They then show that press organs vary on the left/right spectrum, with differences across various newspapers and journals that were, for the most part, just barely significant by conventional statistical standards. Despite the extreme case taken in measuring left and right lessons, residual ambiguities in the research design make it difficult to judge whether the results support or contradict the hypothesis.

One view might be that these results impressively confirm the existence of pluralistic press debates, on the grounds that the findings would have been even stronger if sharper concepts and better measures had been used. Because the operational definitions of left and right failed to capture logically coherent and mutually exclusive belief systems, correlations were watered down by extraneous, random data. On some of the dimensions measured, the left/right dichotomy is clear: for example, the sharp contrast between the left assertion that "the aggressive essence of imperialism is unchanged" with the right view that "realistically thinking circles of the capitalist states have become increasingly conscious of the necessity for peaceful coexistence." But the connection between this and dichotomies that are less stark seems problematic. Compare, for example, the allegedly left statement that "the patriots of South Vietnam will surmount all the obstacles in the path to the complete triumph of their just cause" with the allegedly right statement that "there is no force that could turn back developments in South Vietnam."[48] In short, debate on the general left/right dimension surfaces in the data even though some murky conceptual distinctions and operational measures tend to blur it.

In an opposite view, the findings tend to refute the hypothesis, since the small variations across different press organs could easily have been caused by differences in propaganda strategy or institutional function. For example, Zimmerman and Axelrod note,

> We treated as leftist those statements that emphasized the role of military aid to Vietnam and the significance of military and political doctrine in the North Vietnamese victory; as rightist those statements that stressed economic and material support.[49]

By this coding rule, a military newspaper could be expected to wind up on "the left" simply by devoting disproportionate space to issues within its own functional purview or by targeting "lessons" considered appropriate for its distinctive readership.

In short, all the inherent difficulties of positivism seem to show up in this example. In order to test a hypothesis whose variables do not closely correspond to hard facts in nature, cases must be classified either by partially subjective judgments or by indirect, artificial measures. When subjectivity is permitted, researchers tend to see what they want to see; when indirect measures are concocted, there is a tendency to get weak correlations. And when that happens, it is unclear whether the fault lies with the measures or with the theory.

Defenders of positivism, however, could argue that the solution lies in tightening up the sources of ambiguity: control for alternative explanations, develop logically tighter ideal types for the left and right syndromes, and throw out ambiguous dimensions that water down the findings. Only then—if the hypothesis continued to produce weak correlations across a shrinking range of successful applications—would we know that the research program based on that theory was degenerating. Although an evaluation of the results of any particular test may involve subjective judgments, objective criteria can be applied to appraising the long-run outcome of a whole research program.[50]

Though positivism can answer its critics in principle, in practice there are limitations to what can be expected from the use of positivist methods in the social sciences. Positivism is like democracy—the worst system except for all the rest. Because of its limitations, however, it makes sense to use other methods to cross-check its findings and to provide alternative guides when it falters.

The Danger of Monolithic Dogmatism

Academic strategy, like military strategy, must avoid the equal dangers of dogmatic attachment to a single doctrine and of aimless activity in the absence of any doctrine at all. Though the game-theoretic, rational-choice traditions of the field of international politics are flexible enough to encompass a variety of opinions and approaches, the exclusive adoption of any theoretical stance will tend to focus attention on some new ideas and blinker it toward others. For this reason, it is healthy for some proportion of the research to be conducted outside the dominant paradigm. In the Soviet field, research driven by international relations theory should be supplemented by research on ideas that emerge more directly from the data. Even in the latter case, however, positivism can play a role in increasing the payoff from the work.

HYBRID METHODS

Some holist arguments are causal, staying close to the Soviets' categories and tending toward complex, case-specific explanations. Other holist arguments are reconstructions of Soviet ends/means calculations, interpreting Soviet behavior in terms of what it was trying to achieve. In arguments of both types, positivist methods and deductive thinking can be usefully applied without undercutting the distinctive character of the holistic approach.

Recasting Causal Arguments

In the study cited earlier, Robert Legvold argues that the Soviets evaluate the utility of military power according to different criteria in different contexts. He quotes Vasilii Kulish as saying that the effectiveness of military power is "determined not only by the forces themselves," but "depends upon the specific international-political situation." Kulish then goes on to muse about the "complicated interlacing" of national interests, political constraints on the use of force, the strength of the national liberation movement, and so forth.[51] In testing whether the Soviets actually behave in accordance with these notions, however, the "complicated interlacing" of putative causes can only be the final step in a systematic process. The first step is to make a list of "contexts" or characteristics of "international-political situations." Such a list might include Legvold's own distinction among peace, crisis, and war situations, as well as items from Kulish's list. These are the independent variables. The next step is to offer a hypothesis about how the Soviets view the utility of military superiority in each of these contexts. For example, one hypothesis might be that superiority is useful in preventing NATO escalation in the context of an ongoing war, but that it has no value for supporting progressive change in peacetime. What counts in that context is whether strong national liberation movements can achieve gains on their own initiative—which strategic parity will suffice to defend. Subsequent steps would carry out the usual kinds of positivist testing across a varied range of behavioral and verbal evidence. Only at the final stage could there be complicated interlacing of the hypotheses—for example, by specifying which conditions were necessary or sufficient conditions for certain outcomes, how the interaction of two variables might change their effects, and so forth.

If a large number of variables must be considered simultaneously, this procedure will become too cumbersome. In that event, it may be necessary to step back and look for a few "taproot" causes, like bipolarity or nuclear weapons technology, which exert their effects simultaneously and systematically on a lot of seemingly independent variables.

Deductive Reconstruction of Soviet Ends/Means Calculations

Michael MccGwire's analysis of Soviet military policy in terms of a changing set of military objectives shows how a Sovietologist can use deductive logic and positivist testing procedures to reconstruct Soviet aims and strategies.[52] Mcc-Gwire argues that around December 1966, a decision was taken to change the objective of Soviet military strategy in a world war from "do not lose the war" to "avoid the nuclear devastation of Russia"—a shift that reflected the new belief that a war might be kept limited. He proceeds to deduce a set of specific missions, doctrines, force structures, and organizational structures that would logically follow from those general objectives.

At this point, MccGwire is ready to carry out a number of tests based on the predictions that flow from his deductive model and his tentative identification of a decision period in late 1966. In the jargon of social science, he is carrying out cross-sectional and lagged time-series tests of covariation. The cross-sectional tests involve checking whether his predictions are borne out—not only, say, in the area of doctrinal writings, but also in the areas of force posture and arms control. The time-series test is a before-and-after check to show that the hypothesized changes in higher-level objectives correspond to observed changes in doctrine and force posture, with adjustment for necessary lead times. In carrying out these before-and-after tests, MccGwire tries to hold constant as many perturbing factors as he can. Therefore, in reading the Soviet press to establish the data of the decision to pursue a conventional option in Europe, he compares relevant passages in back-to-back editions of the same authoritative book, one signed to press just before the presumed decision, the other after.

In short, MccGwire's theory is holistic in the sense that it explains various parts of Soviet policy in terms of their relation to a larger whole that gives them meaning. It is also holistic in paying more attention to reconstructing Soviet perspectives and calculations than to discovering their underlying causes. Nonetheless, he constructs and tests his deductive argument according to standard positivist procedures.

CONCLUSION

Both positivism and holism can make valuable contributions to the study of Soviet foreign policy. Positivist theories, borrowed in part from the field of international politics, can provide sharp, testable arguments and a fertile research agenda. Holism can provide the means to harness positivist generalizations in a detailed understanding of particular cases, including the present.

Far from being incompatible, holism and positivism can often work synergistically. Holists, while taking up questions appropriate to their particular skills, can use positivist theories to shape their research agenda. Even when they pursue research questions suggested mainly by their own data, holists can use deductive logic and positivist methods to help structure their work.

Despite this complementarity, some irreducible disagreements between the practitioners of holist and positivist methods are likely to persist. Differing attitudes about such issues as simplification, generalization, and empathy are rooted in different views of the nature of reality and of the purposes that knowledge is meant to serve. However, because the implicit stance of most Sovietologists lies not at the extremes of this dichotomy but in the middle, the complementary use of both approaches will be compatible with these scholar's assumptions about the natural order of social life.

In the past, the positivist side of Soviet foreign policy studies has remained underdeveloped. In the present, therefore, the most pressing task is to use the opportunity presented by recent developments in international-relations theory to correct that weakness, and to do this in a way that leaves the old virtues of the field's nonpositivist traditions intact. Together, these complementary research strategies can sharpen old debates, spark new ones, and generally put scholarly discourse in the Soviet field on a livelier, sounder footing.

NOTES

1. These are ideal types. Real scholars often use both approaches in varying combinations or proportions. For example, some positivist scholars, like Kenneth Waltz, look at whole systems or, like Robert Jervis, try to explain the subjective understandings of actors. Despite these qualifications, I would contend that the above distinctions capture the most important lines of epistemological cleavage. The term "holism" is unsatisfactory, but alternatives like "traditionalism" or "non-positivism" are even more problematic. For further discussion, see Paul Diesing, *Patterns of Discovery in the Social Sciences* (New York: Aldine, 1971), and Donald Polkinghorne, *Methodology for the Human Sciences* (Albany: State University of New York Press, 1983).

2. Jack Snyder, "Richness, Rigor, and Relevance in the Study of Soviet Foreign Policy," *International Security* 9 (Winter 1984–85), pp. 89–108.

3. For elaboration and qualifications, see Snyder and Diesing.

4. Robert Jervis, "Cooperation under the Security Dilemma," *World Politics* 30 (January 1978), pp. 167–214.

5. Jack S. Levy, "The Offensive/Defensive Balance of Military Technology: A Theoretical and Historical Analysis," *International Studies Quarterly* 28 (Summer 1984), pp. 219–38.

6. Robert Jervis, *Perception and Misperception in International Politics* (Princeton, NJ: Princeton University Press, 1976), chap. 6, illustrates how to detect spurious causal inferences.

7. See Jervis, "Cooperation under the Security Dilemma."

8. Robert Legvold, "Military Power in International Politics: Soviet Doctrine on Its Centrality and Instrumentality," in Uwe Nerlich, ed., *Soviet Power and Western Negotiating Strategies* (Cambridge, MA: Ballinger, 1983), p. 124, quoting Stanley Hoffmann, "Perception, Reality, and the Franco-American Conflict," *Journal of International Affairs* 21, no. 1 (1967), p. 57.

9. See Legvold pp. 125, 123, and passim. I will return to Legvold's study in order to suggest how it might be recast in positivist terms.

10. See Diesing.

11. Marshall Shulman, *Stalin's Foreign Policy Reappraised* (New York: Atheneum, 1969); Strobe Talbott, *Endgame* (New York: Harper Colophon, 1980), p. 80.

12. See Shulman pp. 3, 50, 259, and passim.

13. Ibid., pp. 8, 14, 123, and passim.

14. Ibid., pp. 8, comes close to doing this, citing a few instances of Soviet attempts to buy time during periods of weakness.

15. On Zhdanov and Molotov, see ibid., pp. 14–15, 117–18. Suslov's militancy, however, is linked to the argument that the correlation of forces was turning in favor of socialism; see ibid., p. 119.

16. See especially the discussion of Malenkov, ibid., pp. 111–17.

17. On cybernetic decision making and how it differs from analytic rationality, see John Steinbruner, *The Cybernetic Theory of Decision* (Princeton, NJ: Princeton University Press, 1974).

18. Shulman, pp. 3–9, 263–71.

19. Harry Gelman, *The Brezhnev Politburo and the Decline of Detente* (Ithaca, NY: Cornell University Press, 1984). On the problem of *a priori* underdetermination and *a posteriori* overdetermination, see James Kurth, "United States Foreign Policy and Latin American Military Rule," in Phillippe Schmitter, ed., *Military Rule in Latin America* (Beverly Hills, CA: Sage, 1973), pp. 244–322.

20. Ibid., p. 83.

21. Ibid., pp. 46, 52–58.

22. George Breslauer, *Khrushchev and Brezhnev as Leaders* (London: Allen & Unwin, 1982), conclusion, esp. pp. 280, 284–90.

23. William H. Riker and Steven J. Brams, "The Paradox of Vote Trading," *American Political Science Review* 67 (December 1973), pp. 1235–47.

24. See Gelman, p. 73; also pp. 79, 90, 114.

25. Kenneth Waltz, *Theory of International Politics* (Reading, MA: Addison-Wesley, 1979), p. 50, used this phrase to characterize earlier systems theories.

26. See Jervis, *Perception and Misperception in International Politics,* pp. 128–42.

27. The last hypothesis, omitted in most accounts of the links between totalitarianism and foreign policy, is based on Alexander Gerschenkron, *Economic Backwardness in Historical Perspective* (Cambridge, MA: Belknap, 1962). For other arguments, see Carl Friedrich and Zbigniew Brzezinski, *Totalitarian Dictatorship and Autocracy* (Cambridge, MA: Harvard University Press, 1956), and Zbigniew Brzezinski, *Ideology and Power in Soviet Politics* (New York: Praeger, 1962).

28. See Stephen Toulmin, *Human Understanding* (Princeton, NJ: Princeton University Press, 1972).

29. A recent example of work done in this tradition is the special issue of *World Politics* 38 (October 1985), also published as *Cooperation under Anarchy,* Kenneth A. Oye, ed. (Princeton, NJ: Princeton University Press, 1985).

30. See, for example, Friedrich Kratochwil and John Ruggie, "International Organization: A State of the Art on an Art of the State," *International Organization* 40 (Fall, 1986).

31. "A Garthoff-Pipes Debate on Soviet Strategic Doctrine," *Strategic Review* 10 (Fall 1982), pp. 36–63.

32. Thomas C. Schelling, *Arms and Influence* (New Haven, CT: Yale University Press, 1966), chaps. 2 and 3; Schelling, *The Strategy of Conflict* (London: Oxford University Press, 1960), chap. 2.

33. Robert Jervis, "Why Nuclear Superiority Doesn't Matter," *Political Science Quarterly* 94 (Winter 1979–80), pp. 617–33.

34. Schelling, *Arms and Influence,* p. 106.

35. *Strategic Review* p. 57.

36. James M. McConnell, "The 'Rules of the Game': A Theory on the Practice of Superpower Naval Diplomacy," in Bradford Dismukes and James McConnell, eds., *Soviet Naval Diplomacy* (New York: Pergamon, 1979).

37. For example, the argument (*ibid.*, pp. 265–66) that the United States was the defender in the mining of Haiphong Harbor, though not unreasonable, makes use of *ad hoc* criteria that place more weight on American statements linking the action to the defense of South Vietnam than on the *prima facie* offensive character of U.S. behavior.

38. See also Barry Blechman and Stephan Kaplan, *Force without War* (Washington, DC: The Brookings Institution, 1978), pp. 127–29.

39. For this point, and qualifications to it, see McConnell, p. 244.

40. Ibid., pp. 247–48.

41. Ibid., p. 265.

42. McConnell's own conclusions from these cases are somewhat more complex. See ibid., pp. 246, 267–76.

43. Richard K. Betts, "Elusive Equivalence: The Political and Military Meaning of the Nuclear Balance," in Samuel P. Huntington, *The Strategic Imperative* (Cambridge, MA: Ballinger, 1982), p. 108, draws attention to this question. See also Richard K. Betts, *Nuclear Blackmail and Nuclear Balance* (Washington, DC: The Brookings Institution, 1987), which carries out detailed, sophisticated tests similar to those described above.

44. See Schelling, *Arms and Influence*, pp. 46–47. This vignette seems to be a conflation of several Khrushchev remarks. For an example of the invocation of uncontrollable risk, see Robert Slusser, *The Berlin Crisis of 1961* (Baltimore: The Johns Hopkins University Press, 1973), pp. 98–99; for asymmetry in motivation, Hannes Adomeit, *Soviet Risk-Taking and Crisis Behavior* (London: Allen & Unwin, 1982), p. 207, and Jack Schick, *The Berlin Crisis, 1958–1962* (Philadelphia: University of Pennsylvania Press, 1971), p. 178; for the onus of the last clear chance, Strobe Talbott ed., *Khrushchev Remembers: The Last Testament* (New York: Bantam, 1974), p. 575. For more examples and for some qualifications to this view, see Hope Harrison, "Was Khrushchev a Student of Thomas Schelling?: Khrushchev's Coercive Diplomacy in the 1958–1961 Berlin Crisis," unpub. (Harriman Institute, Columbia University, 1987).

45. Nathan Leites, *A Study of Bolshevism* (Glencoe, IL: Free Press, 1953); Alexander George. "The 'Operational Code': A Neglected Approach to the Study of Political Leaders and Decision-Making," in Erik Hoffmann and Frederic Fleron, eds., *The Conduct of the Soviet Foreign Policy*, 2d ed. (New York: Aldine, 1980), pp. 191–212.

46. See Polkinghorne, p. 107 and passim.

47. William Zimmerman and Robert Axelrod, "The 'Lessons' of Vietnam and Soviet Foreign Policy," *World Politics* 34 (October 1981), pp. 1–24.

48. Ibid., pp. 10–11.

49. Ibid., p. 8.

50. See Polkinghorne, pp. 117–18; Imre Lakatos, "Falsification and the Methodology of Scientific Research Programmes," in Imre Lakatos and Alan Musgrave, *Criticism and the Growth of Knowledge: Proceedings of the International Colloquium in the Philosophy of Science, London, 1965*. Vol. IV (Cambridge: Cambridge University Press, 1970).

51. See Legvold, p. 131.

52. Michael MccGwire, *Military Objectives in Soviet Foreign Policy* (Washington, DC: The Brookings Institution, 1987).

6

A Framework for Analyzing Soviet Foreign Policy*

Vernon V. Aspaturian

A comprehensive and usable framework for the analysis of Soviet foreign policy, at this point in the state of the art or science, should be sufficiently elastic and plastic not only that it might offer insights into current and future behavior, but also so that it can be quickly and appropriately reshaped to adjust and accommodate to new realities, data, fortuities, and situations, which themselves are unpredictable, such as sudden deaths of key leaders through accident, illness, and assassination. Such a framework would seek to intelligently utilize all avenues of knowledge, all methods of measurements, and all theories, selectively and with imagination and skill. The variables, constants, factors, and inputs that contribute to Soviet behavior are enormous, and their significance, relatively as well as absolutely, has varied so considerably over time and space (and will continue to do so) that it would be more hazardous to rely upon a rigid, closed, and tightly integrated model or theory than one that remains opened-ended and subject to continuous modification, as distinct from the necessity of "patching up" or "rectifying errors" in closed models or theories. The variables, defined as inputs or factors, whether domestic or external, that condition, shape, or animate Soviet foreign policy can be classified into five groups of gross variables, as follows:

1. *Motivations/Purposes/Intentions*: These variables are subjective preferences defined in terms of purposes, goals, values, norms, and interests, organized into a dynamically related scheme of priorities and formulated in terms of demands upon the outside world.

2. *Capabilities/Power*: These variables, some of which are subject to precise measurement if access to the data and information is possible, include the means, instruments, institutions, structures, and resources whereby demands upon the outside world are asserted, activated, or realized.

*Reprinted by permission of the author from *Process and Power in the Soviet Foreign Policy*, pp. 56–83. Copyright © 1971 by Vernon V. Aspaturian.

3. *Risks*: The risk variables are defined in terms of three interrelated perceived calculations of chance involved in the initiation of a voluntary action (demand, threat, lack of response), whose outcome is uncertain, but whose consequences can be harmful: (a) chance of success, (b) chance of harm, and (c) chance in the magnitude or level of harm.

4. *Costs/Benefits*: These variables represent perceptions of calculated anticipated or certain costs measured against perceptions of anticipated or certain benefits under three sets of circumstances: (a) if voluntary action is initiated to press or realize demands, (b) if responses are made to events or conditions taking place in the external environment, and (c) no action or response is taken.

5. *Opportunities*: These variables are perceived situations where optimal intersection of demands, capabilities, risk, and cost variables occur.

These groups of variables are in constant dynamic interaction with each other over space and time, their absolute and relative significance varying accordingly. As will be seen below, when broken down into more discrete categories and individual factors, most of them are qualitative and judgmental in character, rather than quantifiable and measurable. The variables themselves may not be quantifiable, although information about them is susceptible to quantification in various forms. Thus, although ideology as a variable cannot be objectively measured, content analysis can be employed to gain an insight as to its relative weight as an input into policy, depending upon time and circumstance. Similarly, the personality variable cannot be quantified, but aggregate biographical data may be subjected to quantitative analysis as aids in arriving at judgments concerning their relative significance as an input. Applying quantitative methods to information variables should not, however, be confused with the measurement of the variable itself.[1] The only variables subject to objective measurement are those involving material and human resources, economic, technological, and military hardware, etc., provided the data are available.

The individual variables within the five categories of variables can be characterized qualitatively into two types, voluntaristic (*i.e.*, normative, volitional, subjective) and deterministic (*i.e.*, nonvolitional, objective). Voluntaristic variables are those whose weight and effect can be directly varied by the action of human will, whether individual or aggregate, whether conscious, inadvertent, or fortuitous. Deterministic variables are those whose effects and weight are independent of direct human will, but whose relative impact may vary because of conscious changes in the dimensions and value of the voluntaristic variables. For example, geographical location is not subject to significant change through human action (except in cases where territorial expansion significantly alters the geographical character and dimensions of the state), but the relative value of geography in contributing to Soviet behavior in foreign policy has been fundamentally altered by the advent of nuclear-missile capabilities developed by human technology. Similarly, a state's natural resources may be fixed and finite, but its weight as a factor varies with the human ingenuity, effort, and will invested in their development.

Some variables betray both voluntaristic and deterministic characteristics in mixed proportions. Political culture, including national character, for example, is the aggregate, cumulative product of human volition and changes slowly over time. Nevertheless it is essentially deterministic in its effects, since decision-makers cannot readily alter national character nor easily shed both the conscious and unconscious (especially the latter) conditioning effects it has had upon the shaping of their individual personalities. In many instances, the deterministic or voluntaristic quality is a dominant rather than exclusive characteristic, but the transformational direction of change is generally for voluntaristic variables to assume deterministic characteristics. This has been the case, for example, of religion and ideology, whose impact may initially have been almost entirely voluntaristic in their effects, but which tend to take on deterministic attributes as they are progressively assimilated into the political culture.

MOTIVATIONS/PURPOSES/INTENTIONS

Although this tripartite label for a group of variables suggests the intricate interrelationships among motives, intent, and purposes, they can be distinguished. *Motivations* are those underlying forces that activate a state in its political behavior; they are the driving power that energizes the will to action. Examples in the case of the Soviet Union would be the messianic urge to liberate mankind from capitalism or imperialism that originates in ideology. (Party-oriented motivation) or the urge to enhance and advance the greater glory of the Soviet Union and/or Russia (state and Russian nation-oriented motive).

Purposes are the objects or goals toward which the motivational energy is directed, for example, the impulse to liberate mankind from capitalism will find its ultimate fulfillment in achieving the goals of world revolution and world Communism, and the passion to advance the greater glory of Russia could be achieved by the goal of territorial expansion.

Intentions are closely related to purposes and are often used interchangeably. As used in this framework, intentions (or intent) characterize a psychological or mental readiness to act as opposed to the urge or impulse to act. It is possible to be both motivated and purposive in orientation, but without the readiness to act in order to realize purposes prompted by motives, a crucial ingredient in the formulation of foreign policy is absent.

As noted earlier in another connection, Soviet motives, purposes, and intentions have often been misrepresented as the total of foreign policy in the past; although they combine to constitute attitudes and desires at the most, one must resist the temptation to readily equate motives, purposes, and intentions with foreign policy.[2] The general predisposition of scholars to be fascinated with the prospect of constructing a framework that can predict Soviet foreign policy stems largely from the fact that basic Soviet motives, purposes, and intentions, *i.e.*, attitudes and desires, are constantly articulated and expressed in speeches, documents, pronouncements, resolutions, books, laws, and articles. By now, everybody knows that the "ultimate aim" of Soviet policy is something called "World Communism," and that it possesses a "blueprint" (strategy and tactics) for action. According to some, even a "timetable" or "schedule" for its realization can be distilled out of Soviet speeches and writings. Although all this may constitute inputs into Soviet foreign policy, it is not policy itself. There is little doubt that, if the Soviet leaders had their way, they would indeed establish something called "World Communism," although this idea has undergone a multiple transmutation in perception and meaning for the Soviet leaders over the past fifty years. Thus, Khrushchev somewhat petulantly noted in 1964:

> If it depended only on our desire to make revolution, I can guarantee you that the Central Committee would have done everything so that there would be no bourgeois world and the Red Flag would wave over the entire world. But comrades, let's not indulge in fantasies, let's be people who think realistically. Just to want something is not enough, even if the Party wants it.[3]

Words and Intent in Soviet Foreign Policy

Since a principal, but by no means exclusive, source for divining Soviet motives, purposes, and intentions, has been Soviet verbal output, the relationship between Soviet words and intent should be clarified. The assumption that Soviet speeches, resolutions, and other published output are significant sources for clues to current or future intent is, of course, true in a limited sense. But just as Soviet verbal output is not the exclusive repository of Soviet intent, Soviet speeches and writings are not exclusively concerned with intent, since they perform multiple functions and serve many purposes, only one of which is to communicate or reveal (deliberately or inadvertently) Soviet intent in foreign and strategic policy. Aside from the multiform purposes served by Soviet words, the important time dimension should be considered as well: The relationship between *words* and *policy* varies with the nature of the factional balance or conflict within the Soviet leadership itself. Thus the relationship between verbal output and policy during the Stalinist years was substantially different than it had been since his death. Stalin was an all-powerful and unchallenged dictator, the sole fount of ideological wisdom and orthodoxy and the ultimate arbiter of policy. Everything stated or published during the Stalinist era was essentially an elaboration of the dictator's output, and a systematic examination of Soviet publications and speeches could plausibly provide guidelines to Soviet policy.[4] Soviet-published output was relatively limited and hence manageable as well; furthermore, it was predictably uniform in content at any particular time, enabling the observer to detect with relative ease changes and variations in content.

Since Stalin's death, the Soviet leadership has been in a state of chronic factional conflict, with the eruption of acute crisis in the leadership making themselves manifest during periodic intervals, resulting in shifts, realignments, dismissals, promotion, and rotation of various personalities in accordance with the given factional balance or consensus. On the basis of nearly twenty years of post-Stalinist behavior, a basic assumption of Soviet politics, in contrast to the Stalinist era, is that factional conflict (and even institutional conflict) is a continuing characteristic of the Soviet leadership. This means that the relationship between words and policy has become considerably more complicated as compared to the Stalinist years, since statements contain not only possible intent, but conflicting possible policies. In other words, Soviet-published output now communicates (deliberately, esoterically, exoterically, or inadvertently) not only intent but controversy about future policy.

All statements, writings, and speeches by Soviet civilian and military leaders can be viewed as possible sources of information concerning current and future intentions. But the question of whose intentions becomes the supreme conundrum in the post-Stalinist period. Under Stalin, policy formulation and decision-making were tightly centralized in his person. Under his successor, however, the inconclusive struggle for power has resulted in the fragmentation of the decision-making structure, distributing power among various individuals and factions, each in command of parallel institutional power structures. Ideological orthodoxy has been divorced from personalities and policy formulation, which in turn has been frequently out of phase with the administration and execution of policy as rival factions assumed control over policy-making bodies. The fragmentation of the decision-making structure meant that factional politics replaced one-man decisions in the Soviet leadership. Personalities, factions, and eventually socio-functional and socio-institutional groupings assumed a more variable role in the shaping of Soviet behavior, and a new fluid relationship was established among Soviet capabilities, ideology, personalities, and institutions in the decision-making process. Although this made it even more difficult to judge Soviet intentions and predict Soviet behavior, it was compensated for by the corresponding inability of the Soviet Union to pursue the single-minded and precisely calibrated type of foreign policy that was characteristic of the Stalin era, since Soviet leaders are apparently as uncertain as western Kremlinologists in charting the course and outcome of internal factional conflict.[5]

It is thus no simple matter to elicit future intentions from Soviet words, uttered or printed. Three general observations should be stated at the outset: (1) long-range intentions have always been and continue to be more clearly discernible than short-range, although even in this realm, as the Sino-Soviet conflict illustrates, long-range Soviet intentions are by no means clearly charted and, as noted earlier, are constantly subjected to erosive and corrosive internal and external influences; (2) the more distant and remote in time a statement of policy intent, the more unified the outlook of the Soviet leadership is likely to be; and (3) debate, controversy, and differences over long-range strategy and goals are most likely to be explicitly echoed by contrasting statements and pronouncements issued by foreign Communist leaders and parties, most notably those of Communist China.[6]

Thus, although Soviet words are not always statements of intention, they are vehicles of communication, for both external and internal audiences, often serving different and even contradictory purposes. Soviet words may represent: (1) propaganda (for various internal or external audiences); (2) deception: (3) concealment and camouflage of actual intent; and (4) rationalization, legitimization, or justification of various actions and policies.

Intent and Factions

The appearance of factional groupings and conflict in the Soviet leadership has thus added yet another dimension to the relationship between words and intent, as various individuals and factions articulate their views through newspapers, periodicals, and other media subject to their control or influence, and sometimes even implement their views as policies through Party and state institutions and organs under their direct administrative control, thus conveying the impression of contradictory, inconsistent, and ambivalent behavior in Soviet policy. Although this is the net effect for the Soviet system as a whole, it is not necessarily true of individual groups, factions, or personalities whose own views may be consistent and firm but are unable to prevail over equally consistent and obdurate views held by other groups and individuals. The possibility of factional vacillation and ambivalence is, or course, not ruled out.

Collective leadership, therefore, may not necessarily contribute to more rational or controlled action but may, under certain conditions, be even more unpredictable, dangerous, and difficult to contend with than one-man rule. Under some circumstances collective leadership may turn out to be collective irresponsibility as decisions are made and unmade by shifting conditions or autonomous action is taken by powerful socio-institutional bodies in the face of factional paralysis or bureaucratic inertia. The deliberations of a divided oligarchy are not only secret but anonymous as well and can yield many surprises. More than ever Soviet decisions in foreign policy may reflect the anxieties, fears, insecurities and ambitions of individual factions and personalities involved in secret and faceless intrigue and maneuver. In the absence of crisis situations, whether acute or chronic, the assumption of Soviet rationality will continue to be valid. As personalities and as individual factions, the Soviet leaders appear to be a sober and calculatingly rational group and in their separate capacities are determined, forceful, and animated by purpose. But in the absence of a stable majority or durable consensus and with the fluidity of the decision-making process characterized by rapidly dissolving and reconstituted majorities on various issues, the behavior of the Soviet leadership as a collectivity is likely to be fluctuating and inconsistent. The multiplication of divergent rational inputs can thus produce a collective, irrational output. In this restricted sense institutionalized irrationality may come to characterize Soviet behavior. Under these conditions, Soviet verbal output can thus represent debate, controversy and conflict, making it even more difficult to determine intent, since the Soviet leaders themselves may not know the outcome of the controversy. As a consequence, Soviet verbal output may reflect a bewildering variety of possibilities, as even the correspondence between statements of formal office-holders and those actually wielding power becomes disjointed. Thus, for brief periods of time Malenkov and Bulganin, successively, retained their formal positions as head of the government and hence were official spokesmen, although they articulated views to which they did not presumably subscribe personally. As clues to whose intent Soviet verbal output actually reflects, Soviet words must be examined within the various possible contexts from which they issue, and in particular, the status and role of the leader making them. Thus, for purposes of convenience and clarification, the possible implications of statements issued by the formal spokesmen of the Party (Secretary-General) and state (Chairman, Council of Ministers) will be listed separately from those made by other leaders.

Thus, whenever a statement is made by the Secretary-General of the Party and/ or the Chairman of the Council of Ministers, the formal spokesmen of the Party and state, it can reflect one or more of the following:

1. the unanimous view of the leadership;
2. the dominant (majority) view in the leadership, including his own personal view;
3. the view of a plurality faction, including his own view;
4. his personal view;
5. the dominant view in the leadership, but with which he personally may disagree; and
6. the consensus or compromise view of the leadership.

On the other hand, when other Soviet leaders make statements, they can reflect one or more of the following:

1. the unanimous view of the leadership;
2. the dominant (majority) view in the leadership, including his own view;
3. view of a plurality faction, of which he is a member;
4. view of a minority faction, of which he is a member;
5. his personal view;
6. the consensus or compromise view of the leadership; and
7. the view of the socio-functional or socio-institutional group or sub-faction (Armed Forces, Party Apparatus, Heavy Industry, etc.) that may or may not accord with other factional views, dominant, plurality or minority.

The most nettlesome and yet fascinating situations are those reflected by statements made by a formal spokesman who must articulate positions with which he is in disagreement, but which represent those of the dominant faction. This can occur when the formal spokesman is on his way out (Malenkov, late 1954) or when he has temporarily lost his majority and represents perhaps only a plurality or fluctuating majority (Khrushchev between May, 1960, and May, 1963).

Factions and Policy

Under conditions of factional differences and cleavages in the Soviet leadership, distinctions must be drawn between verbal statements that correspond with actual policy and behavior and those that are in contradiction. Three possible relationships can exist: (1) correspondence or compatibility between actual policy and behavior and all verbal statements of intent and views; (2) correspondence or compatibility between actual policy and behavior and some statements of verbal intent and substantial divergence or incompatibility with other statements and views; and (3) no correspondence or compatibility between actual policy and behavior and any of two or more mutually divergent or incompatible statements of intent and policy (Khrushchev during the period May, 1960–May, 1963). The relationships among verbal output, factions, capabilities, and policies are further discussed below.

Soviet verbal output is thus only one possible source for clues or information concerning intentions. Information concerning Soviet motives and intentions is derived from four principal sources: (1) words, (2) conduct, (3) personal contact with the Soviet leadership, and (4) intelligence and espionage technological and otherwise. And since Soviet intentions, individually or collectively, ultimately reflect the intentions of individuals, Soviet behavior cannot be analyzed in separation from the character and personality traits of the principal decision-makers in the Kremlin, who constitute a well-defined, if not always united, oligarchy.

Verbal statements that correspond with actual policy and behavior can be defined as "output policy," and statements that diverge or are incompatible with existing policy can be characterized as "factional intent." Policy or actual behavior that continues in the absence of positive correspondence or compatibility with any of two or more mutually divergent statements of intent reflects "continuity policy," that is, "muddling through." The implications of these relationships are as follows:

1. *Output Policy:* Our policy refers to the official intent of the Soviet state as articulated by its designated spokesman, together with supplemental and support positions by various spokesmen and media representing various socio-institutional and socio–functional entities. Normally, output policy is articulated by the Secretary-General of the Party and/or the Chairman of the Council of Ministers (Premier). Whenever the two positions are occupied by a single individual (Stalin, 1941–1953; Khrushchev, 1958–1964), the authoritative character of the output is maximized. Whenever the two positions are occupied by two different individuals (1953–1955: Malenkov, Premier; Khrushchev, First Secretary; 1955–1958: Bulganin, Premier; Khrushchev, First Secretary; 1964–present; Brezhnev, Secretary-General; Kosygin, Premier), the situation is more complicated and may represent one of the following:
   a. Rivalry between the two leaders as individuals and/or as leaders of two chief factions in uneasy equilibrium or consensus.
   b. Factional instability or acute conflict, involving more than three contending personalities or factions, coexisting in uneasy and unstable accommodation, usually temporary or provisional. Under these conditions, other individuals assume a prominence and ex-

plicit influence approximating that of the two official spokesmen, whereupon the situation can be characterized as a triumvirate, quadrumvirate, etc.

c. A stable coalition between two or more factions operating on a consensus or majority basis.

d. The existence of a dominant faction with a continuing majority. Under these conditions the Party leader enjoys definite primacy, with the Premier as a definite number two man in the hierarchy. This condition in the past has usually been a prelude to a struggle between the two, with the Party Secretary usually assuming the position of Premier as well in order to eliminate any ambiguity in ultimate authority.

   Note: Sometimes, there is a time lag of varying duration between the time a factional power conflict has been decided and resolved and the time that legal-constitutional adjustments are made. Under these conditions, the Premier is a "Lame Duck" for several months and is no longer the authoritative spokesman for official policy (Malenkov between September, 1954 and February, 1955; Bulganin between July, 1957 and March, 1958; no time-lag was permitted following the decision to dethrone Khruschev as Party and government spokesman).

2. *Factional Intent:* Factional intent represents statements, etc. that significantly deviate from output policy. These may vary in number and intensity depending upon the number of factions, the intensity of the conflict, and the relative role and power position of the contending groups. Factional views may constitute alternatives to output policy, in which case they constitute potential output policy. If the faction wins out, its factional views become output policy, in total or in part. Under conditions of chronic conflict, a faction may be sufficiently powerful to actually modify, change, or reshape the direction of output policy. It operates, in effect, as a pressure group: powerful enough to influence policy and force a compromise output but not sufficiently powerful to reverse or displace existing policy.

3. *Continuity Policy:* Continuity policy is not an intent, but a condition. It represents continuing policy in the absence of any explicit accompanying statements of intent. Continuity occurs because of the following:

   a. Factional standoff or paralysis, in which case existing policy continues by default or inertia because of inability to make decisions to arrest, modify, or reverse existing policy. It represents essentially a condition of drift.

   b. Bureaucratic or institutional momentum, inertia, or sabotage. Policy continues because administrative or executive agencies are under the control of individuals who are out of sympathy with changes in policy, in which case continuity represents a form of factional policy. (Beria, Molotov, and Marshal Zhukov, among others, have been charged with refusing to execute changes in policy in their respective administrative jurisdictions.) In the absence of agreement at the top, continuity sometimes represents simply the functional and role momentum of lower-level bureaucrats and officials.

c. Policies carried over from the preceding period because they are noncontroversial, uncontested, or represent the ongoing, spontaneous, and natural output of technical and scientific research and development. In the latter case, continuity is essentially deterministic rather than the product of explicit intent.

Note: It should be emphasized that in large, complex, and unwieldy bureaucracies, policies are often deterministically influenced by the role, structure, ingrained habits, competence, and normal functioning of the organization. Thus, with specific reference to a possible relationship between strategic arms development and continuity as the result of bureaucratic momentum: Assume that at a given time, the Soviet leadership was united in achieving strategic superiority and that the necessary development, production, and deployment decisions were made. Now assume that, for various reasons, the majority on this issue broke down, but no majority could be formed to reverse of arrest earlier decisions. That is, the Soviet leadership was divided three or more ways. Development, production, and deployment of weapons in accordance with previous decisions continues. Consequence: development and production may result in a de facto policy of seeking strategic superiority, although the policy does not enjoy an explicit endorsement by the leadership. Bureaucratic momentum continues and results in a policy without conscious intent. Needless to say, the Soviet bureaucracy is also not immune from the maddening and bizarre concatenation of phenomena subsumed under the rubrics of "Parkinson's Law" and the "Peter Principle."

Analyzing Soviet intentions purely on the basis of documents, speeches, and ideological statements gives undue weight to "rational" factors since the irrational, non-rational, accidental, and fortuitous factors can hardly be divined from verbal sources. On the other hand, calculating Soviet motives on the basis of capabilities or past responses and patterns of behavior can also result in faulty projections, since significant acts can depart from past behavioral patterns. Two historical illustrations are pertinent in this connection. During the final years of the Eisenhower Administration, extrapolations of future Soviet missile strength were based upon existing productive capabilities, resulting in the famous "missile gap'' controversy. The Soviet leaders, however, for various reasons did not produce the missiles they were capable of producing, and the ''missile gap'' turned out to be an illusion.[7] Similarly, in 1962, it was the general consensus of Soviet specialists (inside and outside the government) that the Soviet Union would not attempt to establish nuclear-tipped missiles in Cuba, a judgment that also turned out to be erroneous. In both cases, judgments were based upon past Soviet behavior. In the past, Soviet leaders usually employed their productive capacities to the limit, and Soviet leaders had scrupulously avoided establishing nuclear-based missiles on non-Soviet territory.

As a general rule, the more dominant the role of a single personality in Soviet foreign policy, the more voluntaristic the behavior of the Soviet Union in the choice of values and purposes, in the latitude for fulfilling personal ambitions, drives, and aspirations of the leader, and the more apparent the idiosyncratic characteristics (neuroses, psychoses, anxieties, suspicions, maturity, emotional balance, volatility, temperament, and style) of the personality in the behavior of the Soviet state.

On the other hand, if the regime is governed by an oligarchy, Soviet policy is more likely to allow wider latitude for the influence of deterministic factors such as history, force of tradition, pattern maintenance, bureaucratic routine, inertia, or momentum. This is likely to condition Soviet behavior to be more prudent and less innovating. The sober and pedestrian nature of Soviet behavior under Brezhnev and Kosygin thus reflects not only their own personalities but also the absence of a dominating charismatic leader, whereas the cautious character of Soviet behavior under Stalin, as well as the mercurial flamboyance under Khrushchev, were reflections of two dominant personalities.

Estimates of the ''human equation'' in Soviet behavior, whether derived from personal observation or biographical or psychoanalytical studies of the Soviet leadership are themselves essentially subjective in character. They originate with observers and scholars who are free from neither ignorance, prejudice (cultural or individual), nor gullibility, and their estimates are apt to vary accordingly. Any attempt to distill the essence of Soviet intentions solely from personality considerations is thus also likely to be seriously deficient. A sound analysis of Soviet intentions must take into consideration words, conduct, and personalities, not as separate and independent articles, but as basic variables whose relative and relational significance is in a constant state of flux. Furthermore, they should be examined within the fivefold framework of variables and factors mentioned above and outlined in detail below.

The following table is a simple partial checklist of the variables that should be considered when assessing Soviet motivations, purposes, and intentions:

Group I Checklist

A. *Ideological* (Teleological and normative components only)
    1. Beliefs, assumptions, perceptions (dialectical laws, class struggle, economic determinism, theories of human nature and behavior, scientific inevitability, etc.)

2. Definitions of normative and purposive goals (world revolution; world Communism; stateless, classless, conflictless society; proletarian internationalism, etc.)

3. Definitions of strategy and action (revolutions: proletarian, national, colonial, anti-imperialist; just wars: class, popular, anti-imperialist, national liberation, etc.)

B. *Self-Interest*
   1. Self-preservation (maintenance, survival)
      a. Leader, oligarchy
      b. State
      c. Party
      d. Social system
      e. Russian nation
      f. Non-Russian nation (variable)
      g. Multinational Commonwealth
   2. Development (material well-being, growth, wealth)
      a. State
      b. Social system (according to structured hierarchy)
      c. Party
      d. Russian nation
      e. Non-Russian nation (variable)
      f. Multinational Commonwealth
   3. Self-image (self-esteem, pride, prestige)
      a. State
      b. Social System
      c. Leaders
      d. Party
      e. Russian nation
      f. Non-Russian nation (variable)
   4. Self-extension (territorial, ideological, system)
      a. Social system
      b. State
      c. Party
      d. Russian nation
      e. Non-Russian nation (variable)
      f. Multinational Commonwealth

C. *Power* (As a goal or purpose)
   1. Leader, oligarchy
   2. State
   3. Party
   4. Social system (various institutions, Armed Forces, Secret Police, etc.)
   5. Russian nation

D. *Personalities*
   1. Drives

a. Conscious (ambitions, goals, purposes, values, self-fulfillment)
b. Unconscious (resentments, frustrations, sublimations, displace-
    ments, personal idiosyncrasies)

2. Character (moral, amoral, deceitful, trustworthy, etc.)
3. State of mind (sanity, rationality, emotional balance)
4. Style or mode of behavior
5. Biographic variables (national origin, social origins, age, education,
    etc.)

E. *Political Culture/National Character* (The cumulative, aggregate, and
    generationally transmitted psychocultural patterns of reaction, response,
    and behavior to various internal and external circumstances, conditions,
    and events that condition the attitudes and actions of both leaders and
    various groups and strata of the population, both Russian and non-
    Russian)

1. Behavior under conditions of stress (privation, deprivation, war,
    destruction, occupation, surprise, oppression, suppression, etc.)
    a. Toward leaders, socio-political system, and institutions
    b. Toward outsiders (enemies, allies, neutrals)
    c. Toward each other (social groups; Russians *vis-a-vis* non-
        Russians and *vice versa*)

2. Behavior under conditions of success, victory, and/or prosperity
    (victory in war, occupation of foreign territory and population,
    economic prosperity, relaxation of tensions, domestic reforms, etc.).
    a. Toward leaders, socio-political system, and institutions
    b. Toward outsiders (the defeated and occupied, allies, neutrals)
    c. Toward each other (social groups, nationalities)

F. *Historical Traditions and Legacy*

1. Unconscious
    a. Russian
    b. Non-Russian (variable)

2. Conscious (*i.e.*, assimilated to "Soviet" values and norms)
    a. Russian
    b. Non-Russian (variable)

CAPABILITIES/POWER

Past experience has shown that predicting Soviet foreign policy on the basis of
Soviet capabilities can be as unreliable as predicting Soviet behavior purely on
the basis of stated intentions and purposes. Even a marriage between intentions
and capabilities, *i.e.*, raising capabilities to match desires, does not always
produce policy either. Actually, there can be an intimate dynamic interaction
between capabilities and intentions, whereby although the latter originally may

inspire the development of capabilities, as these grow, they feed back to influence and reshape intentions and purposes. As Soviet capabilities have expanded, the Soviet leaders have reevaluated original goals and intentions (particularly those inspired by Marxism-Leninism) in the light of the risks involved in relation to the possible returns. Factional differences not only result from changing and conflicting perceptions of risks, but they also represent changing configurations of purpose and interests, both domestic and external. Furthermore, growing capabilities in a context of factional differences create new choices and options, giving rise to new perceptions of priorities and the consequent erosion of commitment to earlier purposes and goals.

In recent years, the growth of Soviet capabilities, instead of reinforcing or intensifying commitment to ideological goals like "World Communism," has actually contributed to the erosion of commitment in that direction and its partial redirection toward other purposes and goals, more restrictive and traditional in character. Soviet commitment to ideological goals thus has been attenuated, not only because of factional conflict, but also because the commitment is now more widely diffused among the goals and purposes generated by its five identities. It becomes increasingly more difficult for the Soviet leaders to sacrifice the interests of one Soviet identity for another, and since intense commitment to ideological interests (Party identity) seriously undercuts and even endangers the interests of other identities and their constituencies, they become increasingly reluctant to pursue it.

As noted earlier, statements of intent are far from sufficient to explain Soviet foreign policy. Statements of intent must therefore be correlated with capabilities and when there is a correspondence between the two, it suggests very strongly that statements of intent should be taken seriously. Thus, another clue to predicting future Soviet behavior is the relationship between statements of intent ("intent observables") and the observed developments of capabilities ("capabilities observables"), particularly, but not exclusively so, in the field of weapons development and deployment. Because of the fragmented character of the Soviet decision-making system, among other reasons, the relationship can assume a number of forms, depending upon the given factional balance internally or the balance of power externally. These relationships, together with their possible explanations, are as follows:

1. *Intent observables correlate with compatible capabilities observables,* i.e., statement of intent is accompanied or followed by compatible capabilities development. *Hypothetical illustration:* Statement that Soviet Union possesses inter-continental ballistic missile (ICBM) correlates with information that ICBMs are being produced: This suggests that the intent observables represent official policy, which in turn can mean the existence of (a) a dominant faction; (b) majority coalition; (c) a consensus, compromise, or accommodation; (d) a unified position.

2. *Intent observables fail to correlate with compatible capabilities observables*, i.e., statement of intent is not accompanied or followed by any compatible capabilities development. *Hypothetical illustration*: Statement that conventional Armed Forces are to be reduced is not accompanied or followed by any actual reduction in forces: This suggests a wide range of possibilities: (a) inability to form a stable majority or to arrive at a consensus, compromise, or accommodation; (b) sabotage by executing or administering agency controlled by dissident leaders; (c) change of policy due to change in factional balance; (d) change in policy, due to external reactions, responses, or situations; (e) technical, resource, or research difficulties or failures; (f) desire to deceive or conceal.

3. *Intent observables correlate with incompatible or contradictory capabilities observables*, i.e., statement of intent is accompanied or followed by capabilities development or deployment that contradicts statement of intent. *Hypothetical illustration*: Statement by Soviet leader that Soviet Union will not establish nuclear missile bases on foreign territory is accompanied or followed by establishment of such bases: This also suggests a wide range of possibilities: (a) desire to mislead, misinform, or deceive; (b) change in the factional balance, particularly if the capabilities observable is compatible with an earlier statement of an alternative intent; (c) cleavage between official Party and state spokesmen and the dominant factional or consensus policy; (d) ongoing fluctuational factional conflict, resulting in modifications and changes of policy; (e) changes in the external situation; (f) perception of new opportunities stimulated by the development of the weapons systems themselves.

The relationships between intent and capabilities observables become even more complicated and fascinating when two or more incompatible or contradictory statements of intent correlate with capabilities developments as outlined above. Aside from the fact that the coexistence of contradictory statements of intent confirms sharp factional or institutional conflict, the possible explanations of these relationships can be extrapolated from the three basic relationships between intent observables and capabilities observables outlined above.

In the instance of situations outlined in number three above, the relationship between intent observables and capabilities observables would be reversed: *The appearance of capabilities observables would probably be followed by the expression of new intent observables* to correspond with the capabilities achieved or being developed—whether or not these intent observables had earlier appeared as the view of the minority or dissident faction.

In the following partial checklist of capabilities/power variables, it will be noted that certain variables reappear from the first checklist. This is because variables such as ideology and personality possess different dimensions and are simultaneously factors of both intent and capabilities. Thus, the analytical, epistemological, communication, and legitimization components of ideology are capabilities, rather than purposive, factors, as are the intelligence, skill, and abilities of Soviet leaders.

Group II Checklist

A. *Military* [Immediate and potential]
1. Strategic
2. Tactical
3. State of readiness
4. Alliances

B. *Economic* [Immediate and potential]
1. Industrial
2. Agricultural (food supply)
3. Transportation and communication
4. Trade and aid
5. Autarchical (self-sufficiency)
6. Technological and scientific

C. *Ideological*
1. Cognitive, epistemological, and analytical
2. Mobilizational and inspirational (internal and external)
3. Legitimizational (internal and external)
4. Communicational

D. *Political/Institutional*
1. Decision-making (effectiveness, rapidity of response, etc.)
2. Conflict-resolving and conflict-containing
3. Mobilizational and communicational
4. Crisis management
5. Self-correcting
6. Legitimizational
7. Diplomatic

E. *Personalities* (Leadership)
1. Abilities, skills, competence, intelligence
2. Education
3. Character (imagination, courage, audacity, nerves, etc.)

F. *Systemic* (Socio-political)
1. Legitimizational and socializational
2. Mobilizational and inspirational
3. Integrative
4. Functional and structural

G. *Demographic*
1. Size, diversity, distribution, and density of population
2. Skills, education, industriousness
3. Loyalty, morale, endurance

H. *Geographical*
1. Size, location, and distribution of territory
2. Topographical, physical, and climatic
3. Natural resources

   a. Sufficiency
   b. Availability (immediate and potential)
   c. Location and distribution

RISKS

The risks variables are highly subjective, involving almost pure perception, judgment, and chance, rather than something that can be objectively measured. Judgments about Soviet risk-taking propensities can, of course, be quantified, as can other forms of opinion or attitudes, but the quantification of opinion about Soviet risk-taking is not the same as objectively measuring it. The degree of risk (whether high or low) should not be confused with anticipated or actualized level of gain or loss.[8] The risk variable, as defined here, involves the perception of the Soviet leaders as to the probable chance of: (1) success or failure, (2) harm, and (3) high level of harm. For example, when Khrushchev decided to establish nuclear missile bases in Cuba, he had to assess simultaneously its chances of success, estimate the chances of harm in the process, and finally to chance the level or magnitude of harm that might be inflicted. Although all three risk components are organic links in a single decision, each chance factor is independent of the other and may be unevenly distributed among the three risk components. Thus, not only is the calculation of the risks on the part of the Soviet leaders essentially subjective in character, varying with individual decision-makers, but the analyst's judgment of the decision-maker's risk judgments is equally subjective and varies with the individual observer. Thus, the analysis of Soviet risk-taking carries within it a built-in futility, because the only concrete reference points are the decision itself and its success or failure. The outcome of a particular action cannot be used to retrospectively validate or invalidate the risk calculation, since, by definition, the consequence of a risk is uncertain and any of various outcomes are possible, although the degree of probability for various outcomes can be calculated differently. A successful outcome cannot serve to validate a low-risk assessment any more than failure can invalidate it, since either result is possible, irrespective of the risk calculated. *Ex post facto* quantitative analyses of Soviet risk-taking, as measured in terms of success or failure, thus cannot yield results of any higher certitude, because the success or failure of an action can total 100 per cent, although the probabilities of success may have been calculated at 99 per cent before the event. Similarly a 1 per cent chance of success may result in a 100 per cent actual success. As an illustration, it has been said by one of the participants in the decision that the Bay of Pigs action was rated as a 95 per cent probability of success, but that it resulted in a 100 per cent failure. A similar relationship between the calculation of risk and the outcome was probably the case eighteen months later when Khrushchev attempted to establish nuclear-missile bases in Cuba. Anticipating gains and losses of the risk operation, although crucial in determining whether a risk action should be taken, is not causally related to the probabilities of success or failure and is a separate and distinct variable, which, however, can be employed retrospectively to judge whether the risk was worthwhile.

Measuring the risk level of a particular action thus involves simultaneous assessment of the perceptions of three risk components, which, however, cannot be "averaged" out. The three risks are not additive in character. How then can we distinguish between a high-risk action and one that is low risk? The simple Risk Matrix Chart below might be helpful in this connection by clarifying the various combinations that are possible among the three risk components in a decision. It should be emphasized that the matrix is extremely simplified; it characterizes risk levels only in terms of high or low, although it is obvious that the chance element can be more precisely calibrated in terms of perception, if not objective measurement. The matrix is for illustrative purposes only and is not meant to be analytical. The suggested historical illustrations reflecting various combinations of risk are based on the author's judgment, as are the expected gain level and the designation of the action as a success or failure. Furthermore, the matrix does not pretend to account for risks whose effects may be protracted or delayed, since this would involve intricate calculations of the impact of interstitial decisions taken between action and effect.

The column labeled "Gain expectations" refers to the decision-maker's anticipation of the level of gain from the risk, again described simply in terms of high or low. Gain is defined not only in positive terms but also as a prevention of loss. The Soviet occupation of Czechoslovakia in 1968, for example, is given as an illustration of a risk in which the gain expectation is rated high, although in actuality the action was taken to prevent possible serious losses that would be risked by inaction.

The confusing and frequently contradictory comparisons and contrasts often made between Stalin's foreign policy behavior and that of Khrushchev results not only from an inability to distinguish between risk and cost estimates as two distinct variables (this is discussed below), but also because the risk among the three components in their decisions were different combinations of high and low. Khrushchev is sometimes characterized as being a higher risk-taker than Stalin, whose foreign policies, in retrospect, appear cautious by comparison. The reasons for the contradictory perceptions are several, a significant one being the accelerated and unprecedented technological revolution in weaponry after Stalin's death. Under these conditions, any high or low risk policy, involving a confrontation between the U.S. and the U.S.S.R., risks a high level of harm.

Khrushchev's political career was that of a man who favored combining high risk of failure with low risk in the level of harm. He was by nature a shrewd and calculating gambler who played long shots but bet small stakes and shied away when the ante was raised. In the domestic political realm, Khrushchev could exercise some control over the stakes involved, but once he appeared on the world stage, his penchant for gambling and bluffing, plus his instinctive survival impulse to quickly retreat if the stakes were raised, made him vulnerable to a counter-strategy of "brinksmanship" or "eyeball to eyeball" confrontation.[9] For this reason, Khrushchev sedulously sought to redefine Soviet-American relations so that he could indulge his penchant for flamboyant and extravagant risk-taking without losing control over the magnitude of the stakes. His détente policy, for example, sought to remove the vital interests of both parties from the arena of confrontation, leaving only peripheral interests to be contended over, which would thus enable him to bluff, bluster, and gamble at high levels of risks, secure in the knowledge that in the event of failure, the costs would be acceptable.[10]

His hope to gain agreement with Eisenhower after the Camp David preliminaries however, was undercut by the U-2 affair and led him to seriously underestimate Kennedy's will and resolution (based upon his perception of the Bay of Pigs fiasco) at their meeting in Vienna, and he carelessly embarked upon a risky venture over Berlin and was forced to retreat when Kennedy unexpectedly raised the ante. The Berlin failure impelled him to embark upon an even more perilous adventure that resulted in the Cuban missile crisis and another Soviet retreat after the president raised the stakes.[11] Finally, the partial Test Ban Treaty provided Khrushchev with the kind of arrangement he was seeking, but events were to overtake both Kennedy and Khrushchev, as the former was assassinated four months after the treaty was signed, and Khrushchev was toppled less than a year later.

In contrast to Khrushchev, Stalin was a more calculating personality, who combined low risk-taking with high stakes.[12] Unlike Khrushchev, he did not find it necessary to virtually disown the goal of "World Communism," since he pursued it pragmatically, cautiously, and without excitement, at a level likely to arouse serious counteraction only from the ideologues of Fascism and the right. Stalin constantly warned against the revolutionary penchant for inadvertently "showing one's true colors" or prematurely "raising the Red Flag" (warnings, incidentally, that were disregarded by both Tito and Mao, who gambled instead and won). Whereas Khrushchev's preferred risk behavior was typically combinations three and four in the Risk Matrix, which allowed him to project a flamboyant and risky image, Stalin preferred risks approximating combination six, *i.e.*, actions that were low risk in terms of failure and harm, but high risk in possible level of harm combined with high-gain expectations. Since scholars as a general class are low-risk-taking personality types, their perceptions of the level of risk may vary widely from that of the decision-makers whose risk they are examining. What may appear risky to the scholar may not be perceived as risky to the individual statesman. This wide divergence in perceptions of the level of risk between scholars and decision-makers raises a formidable barrier to rendering meaningful conclusions about risk-taking. And when the observers are part of a larger socio-cultural milieu in which risk-taking is frowned upon, it becomes even more difficult to render judgments about perceptions of risks taken by decision-makers who are products of a political system that catapults risk-taking personalities to positions of power.

The risk variable thus involves an intricate and complex judgment about personalities, both on the part of the decision-maker contemplating the risk and the scholar who attempts to make judgments about the risk-taking propensities of the decision-maker. All other factors are essentially peripheral to the personality factor, although the institutional matrix within which he functions serves to create some restraint and conditioning mechanism. But statesmen in both authoritarian and democratic countries appear to be able to evade these restraints if their commitments are sufficiently intense, their self-confidence high, and their temperament appropriate. Not only the Bay of Pigs, but the Franco-British assault on Suez, the two Israeli Bluitz attacks on Egypt, and the escalation of the Vietnamese war by President Johnson are all examples of substantial risk-taking by democratic decision-makers.

On the surface it would appear that decision-makers in authoritarian states have greater latitude in taking risks than statesmen in democratic countries, if they are so inclined. This is probably true, but an authoritarian regime does not, *per se*, induce high risk-taking. Politics as a vocation is a risky enterprise, and in authoritarian regimes probably riskier than most, which thus results in a higher proportion of successful risk-taking personalities occupying decision-making positions. Newly formed revolutionary regimes probably contain the highest proportion of risk-taking personalities, since revolution is an extremely risky business to begin with.

Aside from personality considerations, which are dominant in the risk variables, some objective conditions may facilitate high risk-taking. These are:

1. *Flexibility of the decision-making system*, i.e., the relative freedom of decision-makers to act and react quickly without institutional restraints;

2. *Command control*, i.e., the ability of the decision-maker to communicate, execute, and implement high-risk decisions through the chain of command;

3. *Image projection*, i.e., the ability to project a false image of strength, determination, or boldness and to sustain a bluff for a considerable period of time;

4. *Information security*, i.e., the ability to control and manipulate all internal items of information concerning the risk operation; and

5. *Recovery capability*, i.e., the ability to retreat, fall back, or recover with minimum loss in the event the operation is exposed before it is launched.

In the final analysis, risk, like beauty, is in the eye of the beholder, and what may appear risky to one individual may not to another.

COST/BENEFITS

The risk variables are obviously closely related with the costs/benefits variables and at points the two tend to merge and become blurred. Both are highly subjective and vary widely in accordance with the personalities and capabilities of the decision-makers. Costs and benefits are usually assessed in terms of advanced estimates and calculations, but no matter how carefully calibrated in terms of assessing relative capabilities, or as Soviet leaders themselves say, "calculating the correlation of the world forces," the estimates remain highly subjective and uncertain. What Soviet leaders can do is to carefully estimate the anticipated costs of certain decisions and policies and decide whether the benefits are sufficiently compensating to absorb them if necessary. Analysts of Soviet foreign policy also develop frameworks that attempt to assess the kinds and dimensions of costs that Soviet leaders may find acceptable ("acceptable damage" in the event of nuclear war, for example) in order to arrive at judgments as to when and where the Soviet leaders may risk as acceptable certain precalculated levels of damage and cost in the event of action.[13] The decision to invade Czechoslovakia in 1968, for example, involved intensive debate concerning the relative levels of cost in the event of action as opposed to inaction.[14] Indications are that the Soviet leaders were prepared to accept a higher level of cost than they actually had to endure. Similarly, with respect to the Soviet presence in Egypt, costs of the Soviet decision to arm Egypt and support her diplomatically involved a calculation not only of the risks involved in such a venture, but also the costs.

There is still another intricate relationship between risks and potential costs that requires exploration, particularly where Soviet foreign policy is concerned. Sometimes a high-risk policy is confused with a high-cost policy, and conversely a low-cost policy is confused with a low-risk policy. Although there is obviously some correspondence between the level of potential cost and the level of risk involved, the two can nevertheless be discretely separated for analysis. If risk is defined in terms of the estimated chance of success or failure, it can stand independently of the level of costs that are perceived as acceptable or must be endured, since the cost level can be calculated in advance often more accurately than the risk variables. Thus, it becomes possible to devise a high-risk, potentially high-cost policy, as well as a high-risk policy, whose potential cost level is calculated to be relatively low. Similarly, it is possible to combine a low-risk policy with a potentially high-cost or low-cost factor.

A prudent and cautious foreign policy would be one that combined low-risk with low potential costs; an adventurous one would be a combination of high-risks, and high potential costs. The confusing and frequently contradictory comparisons and contrasts often made between Stalin's foreign policy and that of Khrushchev result from an inability to distinguish between the risk and cost estimates as two distinct variables, as well as the failure to appreciate the uneven combination of risk components.

In summary, it can be said that Stalin ran low risks in pursuit of high stakes, whereas Khrushchev preferred high risks for low stakes but was impelled to run high risks for high stakes instead.

Costs variables (benefits variables are in most cases simply the mirror-image of the costs variables), generally speaking, are of two types: limited and unlimited. Unlimited costs are by their very nature intrinsically unacceptable, but such costs may result through miscalculation of both risks and costs.

Group IV Checklist

A. *Limited Costs*
1. Material/physical loss
   a. Territorial loss
      (1) Annexation
      (2) Occupation (temporary or permanent)
      (3) Demilitarization, depopulation of territories
   b. Demographic/population loss
      (1) Diminished size
         (a) Deaths
         (b) Loss through annexations
         (c) Loss through deportations, emigration, defections
      (2) Diminished capabilities
         (a) Loss of skilled populations
         (b) Loss of ethnic and national groups
         (c) Casualties (cripples)
         (d) Altered sex ratio and structure
         (e) Altered age structure and ratios
         (f) Altered fertility rates, birthrates, deathrates
         (g) Altered capacity for livelihood because of economic dislocation, etc.
   c. Economic loss
      (1) Physical destruction (partial or total) of cities, economic structures, buildings, transportation and communications facilities, food supply, natural resources, etc.
      (2) Loss of same through annexation of territory
      (3) Reparations and compensations
      (4) Other financial loss
   d. Military loss and diminished security
      (1) Loss of strategic territory
      (2) Reduction of forces
      (3) Destruction or surrender of equipment
      (4) Loss of trained manpower
2. Intangible loss (psychological and social)
   a. Diminished confidence in political, social, and economic system
   b. Diminished motivation, energy, enthusiasm, and industry on the part of the leadership and/or sectors of the population
   c. Psychological feelings of inferiority and incapacity on the part of the population
   d. Lowered civilian and military morale and self-confidence
   e. Diminished national pride, self-esteem, and prestige
   f. Increased social and ethnic instability

    g. Loss of allies, client states; dissolution of alliances
    h. Increased vulnerability to pressures, threats, and demands
    i. Diminished diplomatic capabilities and influence
B. *Unlimited Costs*
    1. Material/physical
        a. Total physical destruction of structures
        b. Total annihilation of population
    2. Social/political loss
        a. Annihilation of political and social elites
        b. Dissolution and disestablishment of the socio-political system
        c. Dissolution of state (or national) sovereignty and existence
        d. Total territorial dismemberment
        e. Total military occupation or political subjugation

The defeat of Nazi Germany is a recent concrete illustration of a state suffering a type of unlimited costs as a consequence of its policies. The Nazi socio-political order was disestablished, its elites annihilated or imprisoned, and the country dismembered territorially and politically and subjected to total military occupation. Soviet leaders have traditionally viewed the outcome of a war between the U.S. and the U.S.S.R. as one that will involve various forms of unlimited costs for the loser, although the traditional expectation of system annihilation has been conjoined since about 1953 with various versions of physical and demographic annihilation as well. Thus, Stalin, in 1952, before the advent of perceptions of mutual annihilation, provided the orthodox Marxist-Leninist vision of an unlimited type of cost: "War with the U.S.S.R., as a socialist land, is more dangerous to capitalism than war between capitalist countries. . . . War with the U.S.S.R. must certainly put in question the existence of capitalism itself."[15] This apocalyptic consequence of a war between the U.S. and the U.S.S.R. perceived as a war between social systems rather than states, *per se*, is still adhered to in various degrees by Stalin's successors, but unlike Stalin they reject the inevitability of such a war.[16] For a brief period during Khrushchev's incumbency, various notions of perceived mutual physical annihilation in the event of nuclear war were directly and indirectly formulated. This view was vigorously rejected by Mao in 1957 and by some in the Soviet leadership. Currently, the Soviet leadership appears divided over the *inevitability of mutual annihilation* in the event of nuclear war as distinct from the inevitability of war, and some factions appear to believe that one side can emerge relatively victorious under certain conditions and circumstances.[17]

OPPORTUNITIES

Opportunity variables are extremely difficult to conceptualize, but they constitute nevertheless an essential ingredient in the calculation of Soviet foreign policy. Opportunities are by definition perceived situations and hence are essentially subjective. Like beauty and risk, opportunity is in the eye of the beholder and outside observers can do little more than catalogue past opportunity situations and how they were apprehended by the Soviet leaders. Somewhat akin to the risk variable, in that it is related to chance, the opportunity variable is different in that it is frequently a perceived stroke of fortune or a fortuitous concatenation of favorable events not directly assembled or brought about by conscious action. The opportunity variable is particularly significant as an input in Soviet behavior, because Leninist strategy and tactics have explicitly conditioned the Soviet leaders to be in a state of constant search for opportunities and readiness to quickly perceive and exploit favorable combinations of events that may materialize and dissipate quickly or that may appear unexpectedly and evaporate just as suddenly.[18]

The opportunity variable can be defined in terms of both timing and chance and often involves both. Unlike the risk variable, which is a conscious initiative based upon a subjective calculation and voluntary acceptance of blind chance (a gamble), the opportunity variable is the manifestation of an unambiguously favorable combination of circumstances determined externally and objectively by good fortune (a windfall). Thus, the risk variable involves a situation in which, if action is taken, the outcome is doubtful or uncertain, whereas the opportunity variable is a perceived situation where the outcome will be favorable if action is initiated.

The opportunity presents itself when intentions, capabilities, risks, and costs fortuitously intersect to maximize the possibility of realizing goals or objectives. It is thus a kind of dialectical astrology, whereby the Soviet Union is the beneficiary of objectively determined dialectal forces intersecting to provide the occasion for successful behavior. The opportunity situation in foreign policy is the external counterpart to what Lenin described as a "revolutionary situation" in the domestic realm.

Thus an opportunity may differ little from a low-risk situation in terms of consequences, but the geneses of the two situations are different, and the psychological attitudes required for behavior are distinguishable from one another. Risk, even low risk-taking, requires positive action to create situations, whereas opportunity spontaneously develops. Sharp distinctions between the two, however, cannot always be drawn.

SUMMARY

In analyzing Soviet foreign policy, the relevant variables from these five sets must be viewed in dynamic interaction with each other, as not always explicitly deliberated upon by the Soviet leaders but nevertheless constantly scanned, screened, and related to each other in their minds. Serious changes in one gross variable can result in fundamentally restructuring the relative relevance of the others, which may then recombine to feed back and again alter the initial variable. Thus, originally, it was envisaged by the Soviet leadership that since the normative goals and purposes of its ideology were constant and absolute truths, their realization would be maximized by the development of Soviet resources and capabilities. In other words, once capabilities developed to the point that they could implement purposes, policy behavior would result. Theoretically, as Soviet capabilities grew, ideological goals would be progressively transformed into policy goals. World Communism would thus exfoliate more or less in accordance with the expansion of Soviet power and capabilities, until they were sufficiently developed to universalize Communism.[19]

But as capabilities developed, other variables were seriously affected. The risks of converting ideological purposes into policy goals, however, appeared to grow even faster than Soviet capabilities, since, as Soviet power grew, while ideological goals remained constant, other powers revised their estimates of Soviet intent, assigned greater seriousness to ideological purposes, and reacted in a defensive or hostile manner to Soviet behavior. The rise of Hitler in Germany was largely attributable to the growing capabilities of the Soviet Union, which served to impart greater credibility to Soviet ideological intentions and to the "Bolshevik danger."

With the advent of nuclear weapons in 1946, the risks of a forward ideological policy were sharply increased and qualitatively assumed a perceptibly different character, since Stalin would now have to calculate the costs/benefits variables not simply in terms of limited material/physical and unlimited social costs, but in terms of unlimited material/population costs. With the development of thermonuclear weapons and the advent of missile delivery systems, the risk and costs variables were actually qualitatively transformed as a consequence. The more powerful the Soviet Union became in terms of advanced weaponry, the riskier and potentially more costly became a militant commitment to a policy of advancing World Communism.

As a consequence, the commitment to ideological goals and purposes was seriously eroded and the Soviet leaders searched for new surrogate objectives that could be consummated with their new capabilities without running grave risks or involving potentially suicidal costs. New options and avenues proliferated as a result of enhanced capabilities, and a new equilibrium was established among the five sets of variables in Soviet calculations.

Because of the multiple identities of the Soviet Union, Soviet leaders possess a wide range of constituencies they can serve and cultivate to more than compensate for those that they would lose as a consequence of their attenuating commitment to World Communism. In concrete terms, this meant shifting away from serving the interests of external constituencies (ruling and non-ruling Communist Parties, particularly China), as the Soviet leadership under Khrushchev directed greater attention to serving domestic Soviet constituencies.[20] This also involved a subtle but fundamental redefinition of ideological priorities. "Building Communism" (internal development) replaced "world revolution" (condemned as "export of revolution" by Khrushchev), as the highest ideological priority of Soviet policy.

Technological advances in weapons systems or other factors that might seriously alter the existing strategic balance between the United States and the Soviet Union can also feed back to fundamentally alter the equilibrium among the variables determining Soviet foreign policy. Just as the relative weight of ideology as a motivating factor diminished as risks multiplied and increased, a substantial reduction in the risk variable and/or potential costs could trigger a rise in the relative weight of the ideological factor. For example, the strategic balance could shift radically in favor of the Soviet Union because of one or more of the following developments: (1) failure, through inability or unwillingness, to match Soviet technological and scientific developments in weapons technology; (2) failure, through inability or unwillingness, to match the production and deployment of weapons systems sufficient to preserve the existing strategic balance; (3) paralysis of political will develops in the United States because of domestic racial conflict, student disorders, economic disturbances, war weariness, and mass demoralization because of the Vietnam war, etc.; and (4) failure to freeze the existing strategic balance through mutually agreed upon controls over weapons stockpiles, deployment, and development via the SALT Talks.

If any of the above happens, individually or in combination, the stage would be set, for a rearrangement of the variables mix in the calculation of Soviet foreign policy and alter the relative attractiveness of various options.[21] But as noted earlier, the relationship between intent and capabilities is not a simple one-to-one factor, since the other three gross variables, like intent, are largely functions of leadership perceptions. The character of the leadership and the goals it selects from the array of purposes and objectives will largely determine which options the Soviet Union will exploit, whether it be to enhance the Soviet role as a Global Power, as a revolutionary Party, a Russian state, or as a multinational commonwealth, individually or in combination.

NOTES

1. On this point, *cf.* the perceptive and penetrating critique by Giovanni Sartori, "Concept Misinformation in Comparative Politics," *The American Political Science Review*, (December 1970).

2. *Cf.* the excellent study of William Zimmerman, *Soviet Perspectives on International Relations* (Princeton, NJ: Princeton University Press, 1969), which examines the Soviet outlook on international politics, which is distinguishable from Soviet foreign policy, *per se*.

3. *Pravda*, April 6, 1964.

4. *Cf.* George Morgan ("Historicus"), "Stalin on Revoluttion," *Foreign Affairs* (January 1949); *Soviet Political Mind* (New York, Praeger, 1963); and the two works by Nathan Leites, cited earlier. In an effort to do for the Khrushchev period what he did for the Stalin period but with less successful results, *cf.* Nathan Leites, *Kremlin Moods* (Santa Monica, CA: The RAND Corporation, 1964). No sooner was the study completed than Khrushchev was toppled, just as two decades earlier, Stalin mysteriously died soon after the appearance of *A Study of Bolshevism* (Glencoe, IL: The Free Press).

5.   See Selections 15, 17, 23, 24, and 30 in Vernon V. Aspaturian, *Process and Power in Soviet Foreign Policy* (Boston: Little, Brown, 1971); see also Herbert Dinerstein, *War and the Soviet Union*, 2nd ed. (New York, Praeger, 1959); Carl Linden, *Khrushchev and the Soviet Leadership: 1957–1964* (Baltimore: The Johns Hopkins Press, 1966); Sidney Ploss, ed., *The Soviet Political Process (Waltham, Ma: Ginn, 1971);* Roman Kolkowicz, *The Soviet Military and the Community Party* (Princeton, NJ: Princeton University Press, 1967); Thomas Wolfe, *Soviet Strategy at the Crossroads* (Cambridge, MA; Harvard University Press, 1964); and Raymond Garthoff, *Soviet Strategy in the Nuclear Age* (New York: Praeger, 1958).

6.   See Selection 20 in Aspaturian, *Process and Power in Soviet Foreign Policy.*

7.   See Arnold Horelik and Myron Rush, *Strategic Power and Soviet Foreign Policy* (Chicago: University of Chicago Press, 1966).

8.   *Cf.* Jan F. Triska, *Pattern and Level of Risk-Taking in Soviet Foreign Policy Making: 1945–1963* (Stanford, CA: Stanford Studies of the Communist System, 1964); and Robert Jervis, *The Logic of Images in International Relations* (Princeton, NJ: Princeton University Press, 1970), p. 237 ff.

9.   *Cf.* Horelick and Rush, *Strategic Power and Foreign Policy.*

10.   See Selections 23 and 30 in Aspaturian, *Process and Power in Soviet Foreign Policy.*

11.   *Cf.* Arnold Horelick, *The Cuban Missile Crisis: An Analysis of Soviet Calculations and Behavior* (Santa Monica, CA: The RAND Corporation, 1965); and Ole R. Holsti, Richard Brady, and Robert C. North, ''Measuring Effect and Action in International Reaction Models: Empirical Materials from the 1962 Cuban Missile Crisis,'' in Louis Kriesburg, ed., *Social Processes in International Relations* (New York: Wiley, 1968).

12.   *Cf.* Marshall Shulman, *Stalin's Foreign Policy Reappraised* (Cambridge, MA: Harvard University Press, 1963).

13.   *Cf.* Herman Kahn, *On Thermonuclear War* (Princeton, NJ: Princeton University Press, 1960); J. David Singer, *Deterrence, Arms Control and Disarmament* (Columbus: Ohio State University, 1962).

14.   See Selection 25 in Aspaturian, *Process and Power in Soviet Foreign Policy.*

15.   J. V. Stalin, *Economic Problems of Socialism* (New York: International Publishers, 1952), p. 29.

16.   See Selections 10 and 12 in Aspaturian, *Process and Power in Soviet Foreign Policy.*

17.   *Cf.* Roman Kolkowicz, *The Red ''Hawks'' on the Rationality of War* (Santa Monica, CA: The RAND Corporation, 1966), and *The Dilemma of Superpower: Soviet Policy and Strategy in Transition* (Washington, DC: Institute for Defense Analyses, 1967); and Thomas Wolfe, *Soviet Military Policy Trends under the Brezhnev-Kosygin Regime* (Santa Monica, CA: The RAND Corporation, 1967).

18.   The image that politicians may have of the Soviet predilection for opportunity situations is sometimes very graphic. ''I regard the Soviet Union,'' Senator Henry Jackson has been quoted as saying, ''as an opportunistic hotel burglar who walks down corridors trying all the door handles to see which door is open.'' *The Washington Post,* March 7, 1971.

19.   See Selection 4 in Aspaturian, *Process and Power in Soviet Foreign Policy.*

20.   See Selection 15 in Aspaturian, *Process and Power in Soviet Foreign Policy.*

21.   See Selections 27, 29, and 30 in Aspaturian, *Process and Power in Soviet Foreign Policy.*

7

Perceptions and Behavior in Soviet Foreign Policy*

Richard K. Herrmann

Although estimating Soviet perceptions and aims is difficult, it is done quite frequently. Claims about motives are usually the core ideas in competing theories about Soviet international behavior. In the United States, three dominant theories assume the following: (1) that the Soviet Union is motivated by a determination to spread communism and dominate the world, (2) that Moscow seeks to expand its influence by exploiting opportunities while protecting its security, and (3) that the USSR is primarily committed to self-defense. Each theory requires a brief review.

THREE PERSPECTIVES ON SOVIET MOTIVES

American images of the Soviet Union are aligned along a spectrum running between the "hard-line" and the "soft-line" approaches.[1] Such variation in interpretation is related to estimates of the relative importance to Soviet foreign policy of expansionist aims versus self-defense. Any number of views might be identified along this continuum; I will focus on only three typical examples. Quite naturally, this will make a complex debate seem artificially simple. My purpose is not to examine each argument in detail but rather to identify the propositions that lie at the center of the dispute.

These three viewpoints about Soviet motives are popular among the American elite. Ole Holsti and James Rosenau have found that among Americans who are highly attentive to foreign policy three distinct and mutually exclusive "belief systems" are common.[2] Integral to each is an image of the USSR. I have labeled them *communist expansionism*, *realpolitik expansionism*, and *realpolitik self-defense*.[3]

*Reprinted by permission of the author and publisher from Richard K. Herrmann, *Perceptions and Behavior in Soviet Foreign Policy*. Copyright © 1985 by the University of Pittsburgh Press.

To provide a richer picture of these arguments, I have drawn on the work of authors whose descriptions of Soviet motives resemble the three distinct "beliefs" found by Holsti and Rosenau. My intention is not to critique any particular scholar's work but rather to develop the main lines of argument in each perspective. I have examined only part of these analysts' works, and then not as representative of their personal perspectives but rather as examples of the claims about the USSR that Holsti and Rosenau found to be typical. Each presentation by necessity simplifies a complicated viewpoint and focuses only on how it describes Soviet aims and motives. My intent is merely to capture the central architecture or key foundations of alternative interpretations with no pretense that these sketches reproduce all the complexity and subtleties of differing perspectives.

By focusing only on motivation I may exaggerate the differences among these perspectives. On a number of important points they are in agreement. All three, for example, recognize that the USSR is a powerful country that can threaten the interests of the United States. All agree that it has extended a repressive imperial control upon peoples and nations living near its frontiers and has employed its military might in brutal fashion in various parts of the world. Moreover, they all regard these military and imperial actions as "bad."

While the perspectives agree on the undesirability of various Soviet actions, they disagree profoundly over what causes the USSR to engage in these activities. Consequently, analysts differ sharply over what strategic prescriptions the United States ought to follow in response to them. They disagree on how to prevent potential threats from materializing and on how to remedy existing unacceptable situations.

The reviews that follow treat each perspective as an argument that leads to a prescription for dealing with the Soviet Union. I examine these arguments to see what possible propositions might be derived from them. Then I will test these propositions against a body of empirical evidence and use them to compare the relative accuracy and utility of the differing theories. At this point, however, the issue is not whether a view is the most accurate or useful description of Soviet behavior but whether it can be translated into a meaningful proposition. Can it be tested against empirical evidence? Is it even theoretically possible to disconfirm its accuracy?

I treat each motivational claim as a simple model. In evaluating a model, one must answer two important questions. First, it is internally logical and clearly stated? Second, is it relevant when describing Soviet foreign policy? To address the second question, one must have some way of comparing the model to empirical evidence. If the model does not generate expectations that can be compared to historical evidence, then its relevance cannot be evaluated and the model is thus questionable. The appearance of consequences predicted by a model, while enhancing its relative merit, of course does not prove its importance. Even though it may be logically impossible to prove the accuracy of a model, if it is going to be evaluated and compared to others, it must at least yield predictions that in theory could be falsified.

THEORY 1: COMMUNIST EXPANSIONISM

In this view the Soviet Union is described as bent on achieving global hegemony and establishing worldwide communism.[4] Moscow's "imperial adventurism" and "quest for supremacy" are attributed not to unfortunate policy choices in the Kremlin but rather to the unavoidable product of its political system. This assessment claims that Soviet leaders rule over a totalitarian system and seek to impose on the world a universal ideology. It assumes that Soviet leaders need foreign expansion and victory over other political systems in order to preserve their domestic dominance. The mainspring of communist expansion is said to be the totalitarian system. At its core are the self-interested rulers who are described as using foreign conquests both to demonstrate the legitimacy of their vanguard role, and to distract the public's attention from their domestic failures.

Proponents of this assessment sometimes depict Soviet behavior as that of a "paper tiger." They see a constant probing for easy prey and a quick retreat in the face of solid resolution and resistance. The more sophisticated describe Soviet policy as guided by the "art of operation" and relate the USSR's instrumental behavior to a set of tactical rules of bargaining.[5] With only military power to rely on, and facing serious internal vulnerabilities, the Communist leadership, according to this view, seeks every opportunity to expand Soviet influence and to undermine American positions. Picturing the USSR as inherently weak, proponents of this theory argue that American power can be used to contain Soviet expansion. They suggest that if the United States denies the USSR foreign policy successes, the Communists will be compelled to turn inward, effecting changes in the system.

The central claims of the communist expansionism diagnosis are difficult to evaluate because they are nonfalsifiable. By arguing that the expansion-minded Communists are at the same time very unwilling to run risks, and instead seek easy victories, one can discount the lack of observable Soviet efforts toward expansion. In the same vein, by picturing the USSR as a "paper tiger," proponents of this theory can interpret evidence inconsistent with the expansionist proposition as evidence of Soviet restraint in the face of U.S. strength; the USSR was simply "compelled to behave." Testing the causal claims is made more difficult by the complementary disclaimer that much of Soviet behavior is designed to lull the West into a false sense of complacency and thus failure to act cannot be counted as disconfirming evidence.[6]

At times advocates of this perspective back up their claims with evidence drawn from the history of Russian expansion over the centuries and the backgrounds and personalities of members of the Soviet elite. The chronicle of Russian and Soviet history, which certainly includes a drive for expansion, does not prove that expansionism is at present the motive for Soviet behavior. The dangers of historical determinism are well known. The fact that Russian leaders a century ago aspired to have warm-water ports is no assurance that current leaders are so inclined. To assert without evidence drawn from the contemporary scene that expansionist aspirations transcend generations and motivate current leaders badly distorts the nation-state concept. It introduces a determinism that not only is without foundation but also violates the logic of empirical investigation.[7]

The claims about the Russian character or the legacy of the muzhik, or peasant, personality run the risk of stereotyping and provoke angry rejections by proud Russian nationalists.[8] From a social scientist's perspective, these general claims—even if they could be proven accurate, which seems highly dubious—cannot serve as evidence for describing particular members of the elite. Some of these arguments claim that an individual's background such as peasant birth predicts or even determines his or her contemporary political orientation. This claim is difficult to defend and minimizes the importance of education and training. Even if it were a useful general rule, it still would not substantiate the description of a particular individual. Specialists on the Soviet leadership have found it difficult to associate personal background with political attitudes.[9] Moreover, given the closed nature of the Soviet system, even the most diligent analysts have found it hard to determine the political attitudes of specific leaders.[10]

THEORY 2: REALPOLITIK EXPANSIONISM

A second set of analysts argue that the USSR may optimally desire world domination, but that the Soviet Union is not actively driven by this aim; instead, it is simply opportunistic.[11] The advocates of this second view tend to minimize the importance of communist ideology in determining Soviet foreign policy, concluding instead that the USSR is a "great power" and as such will compete for influence and security as all major states do. At times some advocates of this diagnosis minimize the importance of intentions and suggest that power politics or Realism guides their examination. They make clear, however, that in their judgment the USSR is expansionist whereas the United States favors the status quo. While emphasizing the expansionist impulse as dominant, this perspective argues that the Soviet leadership is averse to taking risks. Rather than being adventurous, the USSR is better described as opportunistic. The advocates of this view claim that the Soviet leadership will take a "long view of history" and will await opportunities for expansion if they can predict low costs for exploiting them.

While suggesting that the USSR is thoroughly committed to revising the international status quo, proponents of this theory also describe the Soviet Union as a profoundly insecure and defensive state. They argue that it is striving to protect its empire and its security relations in Europe by trying to regulate the central, direct, bilateral aspects of the relationship with the United States. Simultaneously, it is said to be promoting political change and Soviet expansion in the Third World. According to this view, the Soviet Union is attempting to weaken U.S. strategic power in peripheral contests so as to allow Soviet exploitation of aspirations for social, political, and economic change in Third World countries. Moscow is said to take advantage of regional conflicts to expand its power. This diagnosis attributes Soviet actions in the Third World not only to revisionist aspirations but also to defensive concerns. It describes the Soviet Union as plagued by internal weaknesses and vulnerabilities such as ideological exhaustion, agricultural crises, energy shortages, demographic and labor dilemmas, ethnic conflicts, bureaucratic inefficiency, and the inability to shift comfortably to intensive economic development. Consequently, the diagnosis tends to attribute Soviet actions and perceived successes in Third World affairs to military intervention and a failure in U.S. policy. Soviet military ventures, it says, succeed primarily because the United States fails to use its strength either to raise adequate costs to deter Soviet action, or to teach the USSR that military intervention will not pay. In the long run, however, it sees Soviet success in the Third World as very limited, constrained not so much by U.S. counteraction as by the Soviet Union's own inability to facilitate economic development.

Proponents of theory 2 prescribe a strategy of containment that firmly denies Soviet expansion but simultaneously offers a second track of possible cooperation. Combining expansionist and defensive concerns, this dual-track strategy is not suggested as a means to produce change in Soviet system, since according to this theory externally compelled or influenced system change is beyond the capacity of the United States. Instead, they insist that the United States must prepare a long-term, probably permanent, policy of deterrence toward the USSR.

The realpolitik-expansionist theory depicts the USSR as opportunistic, exploiting opportunities for extending its influence that promise reasonable benefit and entail minimum risk or cost. This notion, like the "paper tiger" image of theory 1, is hard to evaluate because it does not lead to clear predictions about Soviet behavior. In most formulations it remains nonfalsifiable. It cannot be subjected to empirical tests without a working definition of "opportunity," and analysts promoting this diagnosis have not defined it adequately. They tend to argue that when the USSR acts, this is evidence of the Soviets taking advantage of an opportunity, and failure to act proves lack of opportunity. Such a tautological definition makes it impossible to test whether the USSR seizes opportunities when they appear, whether it exercises restraint, or whether it is likely to do one or the other in different times and places.

One major problem in ascertaining what constitutes an opportunity for the Soviets is related to the additional claim that leaders in Moscow are averse to taking risks. "Risk" is a subjective concept intricately tied to varying perceptions, and is thus hard to identify. The degree of fear of violence or retaliation said to be inherent in Soviet action will depend not only on one's analysis of Soviet behavior but also on judgments about the probable reaction of the United States or other nations. Analysts disagree on these questions and argue over the likelihood of reactions and escalation of conflict.[12] Since even Western analysts disagree among themselves as to whether the USSR may have taken a risk, no doubt Soviet analysts also have varying estimates of the risks involved in their contemplated behavior, and different ones from those of outsiders. One must either create an operational framework that can decipher the risk as it is perceived in Moscow, or combine the notion of taking a risk with the concept of seizing an opportunity and its related conditions.

The operational testing of what represents an opportunity for Soviet leaders is further complicated by the complementary notion that they are especially sensitive to what any action will cost them. This suggests that in cases where an expected payoff far exceeds expected costs (assuming these could be known), the Soviets may still not see an opportunity because of the significant expected costs entailed in taking action. Someone, for example, might recognize opportunities for Soviet action in the Persian Gulf, but would explain the USSR's inaction as the result of a decision by Soviet leaders to wait for another opportunity with still lower costs and greater hopes of success. The argument makes good sense, but creates difficulties for the analyst trying to infer a nation's aims. The claim is essentially teleological in that it explains current evidence with a speculation about future intentions.[13]

The argument that Soviet leaders are averse to taking risks and incurring costs makes it difficult to identify what they see as an opportunity. More important, it raises fundamental questions about measuring the aims of Soviet foreign policy. If the USSR is unwilling to risk significant resources to expand its territory, why should expansion be treated as a major motive of Soviet behavior? Economists interested in measuring what particular individuals perceive as valuable or useful in any given action have introduced the notion of sacrificial scales attached to choices.[14] The amount an actor is willing to risk and what he is willing to pay are presented as precisely the measures of what he values. Preferences that an actor reveals through behavior are then better indicators of values and aims than declared or assumed preferences. This logic seems equally appropriate in the analysis of Soviet foreign policy. If the USSR is seen to be unwilling to risk resources or to make significant sacrifices for expansion, then one cannot conclude that Soviet leaders are primarily motivated by a desire for expansion. Likewise, to argue that the Soviets will take unilateral action to their own advantage if an opportunity offers itself, but only if little or nothing is required of them, is to cast doubt on the importance of a desire for expansion as a cause of their behavior. The refinement of this diagnosis and its test will require that we not only define and measure ''opportunity'' but also locate the point at which the Soviets' willingness to take risks and to pay for expansion is so low that a given action is no longer an expansionist matter.

Without a clear and explicit definition of opportunity, it is also difficult to consider whether theory 2 takes nonoccurrences into account. Most Soviet restraint will be attributed to lack of opportunity, by definition. Without an independent definition of opportunity, it becomes impossible to test whether this theory ignores important cases when the Soviets failed to act in the face of opportunity. The perspective in general is likely to include symptomatic expectations quite similar to those of theory 1.

THEORY 3: REALPOLITIK DEFENSE

A third diagnosis of the Soviet Union's foreign policy is attentive to the issues raised in power politics but concludes that the USSR is better described as defensive.[15] The Soviet Union is presented as a profoundly conservative state primarily motivated by security concerns; its leaders seek to stabilize their international relations so as to allow for greater concentration on internal problems of development. The USSR's domination of Eastern Europe is not attributed to "any conscious desire to mistreat or oppress the peoples involved." This claim is in fact explicitly rejected. Instead, such "imperial" control of nations in its orbit, while not condoned, is attributed to security interests.

The proponents of theory 3 generally ascribe to Soviet leaders a geostrategic approach that identifies other nations as important elements in the superpower contest. Soviet involvement in the Third World is described as analogous to U.S. interference there. It is attributed to "cold war" bipolar perceptions of political contests. The USSR is also described as having less global political leverage than the United States and as disadvantaged in the alliance systems it can mobilize. In addition, it is said to face many serious domestic problems such as paralysis and backwardness in industrial and technological development, low labor productivity, strains caused by ethnic and nationalist loyalties among its member republics, a deficient agricultural system, and a multitude of inefficiencies related to the centralized bureaucratic system, public apathy, and a disaffected intellectual class. While proponents of theory 3 acknowledge these problems to be serious, they do not think that the system is in danger of imminent crisis. They conclude that the Soviet bureaucracy is "highly stable" and very unlikely to crack or capitulate to Western pressure.

Describing security as the primary motive driving Soviet behavior, advocates of theory 3 argue for a disengagement strategy that would reduce perceptions of mutual threat in both Moscow and Washington. The prescription is intended to reduce fears in Moscow rather than to manipulate these diagnosed Soviet anxieties as in a deterrence strategy. It is also designed to lend support to reformist elements in the Kremlin who, by prevailing over "conservatives" and "neo-Stalinists," my lead to modifications in the Soviet system.

Those who argue that Soviet leaders are primarily motivated by a concern for self-defense face the conceptual problem of identifying what actions constitute self-defense. The proponents of theory 3 recognize that an expanded notion of defense can be used to describe actions that could just as easily be called cases of expansion. As Robert Jervis has noted, "In extreme cases, states that seek security may believe that the best, if not the only, route to that goal is to attack and expand."[16] Clearly, a maximum conception of what is necessary for Soviet security could sanction an almost unlimited expansion of Soviet influence. Some actions like an unprovoked assault on France or a demand that West Germany must accept a Communist government, most Western analysts would agree, go beyond what could be considered actions taken in self-defense. These hypothetical cases, however, are not of great interest because they do not help to clarify less extreme behavior in specific regional settings. Moscow's minor moves that may be preliminary indicators of some change in foreign policy are far more interesting. In these situations the scene is more complicated, the actions more likely, and there is less consensus about whether to interpret a given action as motivated by security concerns. Although the task is one of definition, it nevertheless is essential and is too often neglected. Without a definition, the general claim cannot be empirically tested.

This definitional problem is complicated by the notion of what constitutes provocation. Behavior that is defined as ''reactive'' is treated as confirming the self-defense theory, while other actions that might disprove the proposition are attributed to perceived provocations. The problem for the analyst is to determine which actions should be treated as responses to provocations and at what point they can be attributed to motives other than a concern for self-defense.

Soviet support for Vietnam's invasion of Cambodia raised this fundamental problem. The act could be attributed to a defensive impulse vis-à-vis China and described in Realist terms as simply a shift in the balance of power. The shift in power represented by Chinese-Japanese and Sino-American rapprochement, the Realist could argue, led to an adjustment in Soviet influence in Southeast Asia represented by Vietnam's control of Cambodia. The act, however, called into question the limits of the self-defense explanation. The act after all forced a revision in Cambodia through military occupation and dismembered China's alliance in Southeast Asia. The fact that Pol Pot was a hideous leader or that the United States failed to raise equal objections to the ouster of Idi Amin by foreign intervention, arguments often made by the Soviets, does not change the facts of their behavior.

Recognizing that issues are often linked, as in the above example, is common in theories of American foreign policy.[17] When Americans think about containment, they often explain U.S. behavior in one region as a reaction to Soviet behavior. The American involvement in Vietnam is often seen as a defensive move responding to a broader threat of communist expansion. An American leader might reason that if the Soviets gain in one area, then the United States must counter this challenge, sometimes in a different area.[18] Understanding containment as a strategy allows the leader to link a number of actions across different arenas into an interrelated set of policies. However, integrating the issues in the Soviet case above, while just as necessary, will be not only controversial but also hard to substantiate because of the closed nature of the Soviet system.[19]

As a general rule, it seems that when tensions among great powers rise, so does the value their leaders place on allies and clients. When Britain and France were great competitors, British interests in Egypt fluctuated according to the intensity of the perceived threat from France.[20] The same pattern in Soviet-American relations is central to theory 3. To argue that security is a primary motive behind the USSR's policy toward Cambodia, one must show that Soviet leaders perceived threats from the United States or China, and that these concerns were related to specific actions. Because of the closed nature of Soviet decision making, the argument will often depend on plausibility and conjecture.

The self-defense theory is generally based on evidence parallel to that used to bolster the other two arguments. For example, it is often based on a reading of Soviet history that emphasizes periodic invasions of Russia and domestic hardships rather than a desire for expansion; or it may cite statements coming from Moscow that stress security concerns. In cases that the realpolitik-expansionist argument defines as opportunistic and mischievous, the logic of theory 3 makes different assumptions about actions in different areas and contrary estimates of available Soviet options, drawing a picture of restraint and patience. The lack of definition and failure to clarify auxiliary assumptions, problems that plague the other two arguments, also trouble this one. One lesson from attribution theory that seems clear is that in order to test propositions about internal motivations, one must explicitly define the environmental situation in which actions take place.[21]

THEORIES ABOUT MOTIVATION AND FOREIGN POLICY ANALYSIS

Because the interpretation of Soviet policy is at the center of U.S. strategy, the above three theories about the causes of Soviet behavior are at the core of intense political debate. Those who borrow from the various theories and operate with fundamentally different assumptions about the aims of Soviet policy describe the strategic suggestions of the competing interpretations as incomprehensible or worse. Proponents of the first (expansionist) theory, for example, are inclined to see the strategy following from the self-defense view as appeasement. Those favoring theory 2 at times describe the advice of the first group as romantic and unrealistic while depicting the advocates of military disengagement as naive. On the other hand, advocates of theory 3 can conclude that proponents of the hardline containment strategy of the first theory are insensitive to the dangers of military escalation and war. They also decide that adherents to the second theory are unwilling to pursue real compromises instead of looking for what is advantageous to the United States. Advocates of the third theory claim that the prescriptions for containment in theories 1 and 2 overextend U.S. power and the rightful exercise of its influence. They doubt that the USSR can be changed for the better with outside pressure and find advocates of the second theory overconfident about the United States' ability to control the international environment (especially in the Third World) outside the USSR. Proponents of the two expansionist interpretations describe advocates of the third theory as defeatists or isolationists.[22]

Alexander George has recently argued that "crisis prevention may well be considered the orphan of strategic studies."[23] Despite the charged polemics and ideological convictions, however, all three perspectives offer strategies for pursuing peace and preventing crises. The wisdom of these prescriptions of course is heavily dependent on the accuracy of their assumptions about Soviet motives. Scholars interested in peace research and conflict resolution, consequently, have few more important tasks than evaluating competing theories about Soviet motives.

Basic research designed to test these interpretive theories is necessary. Philosophers of science have argued that the key contribution that social scientists can make is the understanding of causes. In the study of Soviet international behavior, it is often theories about aims that define competing paradigms.[24] How to test the usefulness of the different theories should be an aim of academic research. It is not enough to accept one interpretive paradigm a priori and then merely chronicle behavior in the light of that theory.

Inferring motivation is essential not only for research on comparative foreign policy, and Soviet behavior in particular, but also for the study of human conflict in general. Analytical models such as game theories should be assessed not for their "truth" but rather for their relevance as simplified representations.[25] In the more sophisticated models, this requires the identification of an actor's perceptions, motives, and subjective analysis of the utility of a given action.[26] Naturally, if these models are to be used to represent Soviet behavior, judgments on motives are necessary. As should be clear from the intense dispute among advocates of the three theories, judgments about motives will not be resolved by reference to area experts.[27] A similar dilemma remains in deterrence studies where the primary starting point is identifying an "initiator" and a "defender" rather than why the action was initiated. The value of a prescription for deterrence must be based on knowledge of motives.[28]

The social psychologist Fritz Heider has argued that an observer explains social and political actions as a function of the motives and capabilities attributed to the actor.[29] Attribution theory can help identify the basic differences among the three perspectives, but has no ready method for gauging the relative accuracy of the competing descriptions. Yet accuracy and usefulness are the criteria used to judge which paradigm to adopt. This is the most important decision a scholar studying Soviet foreign policy makes. Only by attributing a motive can one interpret a pattern of behavior and understand a chronicle of events or a set of data. For politicians, it serves as an absolutely necessary foundation for the logical formulation of strategy.[30]

It is disturbing that all three competing theories remain essentially nonfalsifiable and thus immune from empirical evaluation. Each remains too largely dependent on an assertion, ideological commitment, or "enlightened" assumption. Proceeding from one viewpoint or another, a scholar can muster illustrations to support any original claim. The enterprise in the political arena can resemble a lawyer's advocacy more than a searching inquiry.

Although an apparent political victory for one theory or another may define the limits of a debate, scholars must continue to recognize the central premises on which the entire strategic paradigm rests and insist that these be defended not by acts of faith or political power but by empirical evidence logically reviewed. If it is true that "shared images" define the limits of any debate about strategy within government bureaucracies, then independent scholars must continue to examine the basic theoretical assumptions.[31] The central diagnostic question should not be closed in order to protect the integrity of the strategy a government has chosen. In an era when the implementation of strategy often develops a bureaucratic momentum of its own, it is vital that independent analysts continue to test and question the basic political diagnosis that justifies it.

Describing the diagnostic function of theory, Alexander George presents the scholar's challenge in this way:

> Disagreements on what is the correct basic view of the opponent tend to become linked somewhat prematurely and rigidly with competing policy preferences. The ensuing struggle over policy choices then tends to squeeze out the possibility of a more systematic and objective analysis of the fundamental disagreement over the nature of the opponent. One of the most challenging tasks for those interested in the further development of policy-relevant theory, therefore, is to find ways of reexamining dominant images and of adjudicating in a scholarly way disputes over the correct image of adversaries.[32]

The following study is driven by a recognition of the importance of the question of motives, yet I have few illusions about the prospects for "solving the problem" in any definitive sense. Any new effort to tackle the old problem can only be humbled by Robert Jervis's observation: "Although mountains of governmental memoranda and scholarly books have been written about the Soviet Union, I suspect that few people have been convinced by anyone else's arguments. Similarly, the past thirty-five years have seen all sorts of Soviet and American actions, but the basic debate has not been resolved."[33]

If Jervis is correct, there are many explanations for why analyses of Soviet behavior and aims have not been able to convince people who did not already agree with the conclusions. Psychological and political factors may be partially responsible, for surely if scholars do not approach the issues with an open mind and a commitment to detachment, the prospects for a productive dialogue are limited. The difficulty of the task, however, is also certainly to blame. Any analysis will depend on definitions of key concepts like what constitutes expansion or self-defense and on complex inferences from complicated data. Moreover, to test empirically these concepts and others, such as what represents an opportunity, we must have detailed pictures of situations, pictures that are themselves controversial and often necessarily include speculations about the credibility of deterrent threats and degrees of risk. These issues cannot be avoided and should be debated. They will not necessarily be resolved by more data and are usually not only more important than a particular fact about Soviet behavior, but are the real issue of controversy.

Debate that rests only on assumptions, however, will not be very productive if the central concepts remain undefined. The arguments will simply concern semantics and eschew the real questions. More critically, if the formulations of the central arguments remain nonfalsifiable and immune from empirical consideration, then the debate will be largely theoretical and increasingly divorced from Soviet foreign policy. Perhaps the interpretive debate can be advanced by making the definitional and logical issues explicit.

Although many scholars have analyzed Soviet foreign policy, relatively few studies have tried to test the rival theories regarding motivation.

IMPLICATIONS OF THE THREE THEORIES

Because these theories are usually presented in a nonfalsifiable form, this study has adopted a method that translates the core claims about motivation into more testable propositions. The hypotheses derived this way represent only a part of each competing theory, but my hope is to capture the central differences in the interpretation of Soviet motives. Let us consider the implications for each of these perspectives that may be derived from the preceding study.

Theory 1: Communist Expansionism

The first theory attributes Soviet behavior to a drive to enlarge the area of the world controlled by the USSR. This theory is difficult to test because it simultaneously argues that the USSR will not be willing to pay a high price for this expansion. Advancing a "paper tiger" image, the theory suggests that the Soviets will constantly be searching for easy conquests but will retreat in the face of resistance and rising costs. The Communists are described as desirous of world domination, but not war, and as waiting for the unilateral surrender of their foes. Their objective is said to be global hegemony without great cost. The expansionist hypothesis consequently does not rest upon observable commitment and is impossible to test or to disprove.

This study considers only the claim about motivation. I have connected the expansionist proposition theoretically to an "enemy" image and a revisionist strategy. Soviet commitment to revisionist actions, in terms of sacrifice and investment, has been defined as a critical indicator of expansionist motives; thus, it differentiates the test from the "paper tiger" assumption and the comprehensive theory. In this examination, the expansionist hypothesis is not supported by either the verbal behavior of Communist spokesmen or the foreign policy choices of the USSR.

In none of the three periods did the image of the United States prevailing in the Soviet media resemble a "degenerate" stereotype or indicate that Soviet leaders regarded the United States as presenting an opportunity. In 1967 the imagery on all major dimensions indicated an "enemy" stereotype and, according to the theory advanced in chapter 2, *Perceptions and Behavior in Soviet Foreign*

Policy, reflected intense perceived threat on the part of the prevailing leaders in Moscow. The shift in 1972 reflected less of a sense of threat, as would be predicted in an era of detente. It did not reveal an ascendance of perceived opportunity as a result of seeing the United States as relatively weak.

The changes in imagery between 1972 and 1979 suggest that the comparative security of detente gave way to heightened anxiety in Moscow and greater fear of the United States. This finding is contrary to assertions that Soviet leaders were increasingly willing to take bold risks in the later half of the 1970s. The analysis of imagery suggests that Soviet activity in the Third World during this period was not correlated with a declining respect for American will; quite the opposite, it indicates a growing concern about an escalating American threat. In other words, the opportunities Soviet leaders perceived in third countries were not correlated with perceptions of American weakness, or opportunities vis-à-vis the United States, as they would regarding a "degenerate" state, but to the contrary were related to intensified fear of a still powerful adversary. Additionally, the "enemy" imagery indicates that in the prevailing Soviet view the United States was still regarded as either comparable in capabilities and power or stronger than the USSR and as striving for continued superiority.

The imagery suggests that prevailing Soviet perceptions between 1967 and 1979 are better described as defensive rather than expansionist or imperialist. The case studies of foreign policy behavior complement this finding, lending little support to the expansionist theory. In most of the arenas considered, Soviet behavior could be more plausibly seen as indicating a containment strategy rather than revisionism. Although in a number of arenas the evidence was inconclusive, the USSR's commitment to revisionist actions was never strong, and the revisionist proposition was rarely compelling. This of course is not inconsistent with the expansionist theory which predicts a low commitment to expansion. It does, however, suggest the Soviet Union, in functional terms, does not value expansion very highly.

Because the expansionist theory is nonfalsifiable, the evidence from concrete foreign policy behavior cannot disconfirm its accuracy. However, we can evaluate the evidence often used to defend the expansionist hypothesis. This study suggests a number of important lessons on this point.

First, the Soviet military buildup is not incontrovertible evidence of a drive for superiority and does not substantiate charges of revisionist or expansionist aims. The analysis of strategic weaponry demands exceptional technical and psychological complexity and does not lend itself to such simple and clear-cut interpretations. Evaluating a nation's capability to deter aggression and compel other nations, the core issue, is too often surrendered to the comparison of weapon systems in the abstract without considering their assigned missions and political purpose. Meaningful measures are difficult to construct, and many comparisons do more to obfuscate the fundamental assumptions about the defense requirements than to clarify the net evaluations. Estimates of "superiority" and "equivalence" are based on assumptions about the psychological effect of various weapon systems on both sides. They inherently include critical political assumptions about the "will" of the adversaries and their tolerance for risk and damage. Consequently, such simplistic comparisons are inadequate for understanding motivation and lead quickly to circular arguments and a technical emphasis that overlooks the fundamental assumptions.

Second, the USSR's involvement in a region and its support for various regimes is not equivalent to revisionism or a drive for expansion. To regard the development of influence as necessarily indicative of expansionism is to commit a cardinal error of political analysis. This mistake treats power as an absolute rather than a relative phenomenon. The exercise of Soviet influence in Syria, Libya, Ethiopia, and South Yemen, for example, does not of itself indicate a nation committed to enforcing political change in those countries. Instead, it must be analyzed in the context of international competition in the Middle East. Too often Soviet activities are seized upon as the exclusive focus of study and not integrated into a political context that includes other events unfavorable to the USSR or Soviet options not taken.

When Soviet activity and influence in the Middle East is placed in a regional and relative perspective, the expansionist hypothesis is not convincing. The lack of Soviet involvement in Egypt and Iraq in 1972 is starkly obvious. Likewise, the Soviet Union's potential friends in Tripoli, Damascus, and Aden appear rather unimpressive in comparison to those lost in Cairo and Baghdad or those aligned with the United States in Tel Aviv and Riyadh. Moreover, Soviet support for the Steadfastness Front seems less of an effort to court "Arab radicalism" when the important differences between the Soviet and Arab positions on peace terms and the USSR's reluctance to back Arab concerns in Lebanon are considered. Soviet intervention in Ethiopia and Afghanistan, likewise, reflect a disregard for Arab allies and represent rather mixed payoffs in terms of regional influence.

Third, movements and events in third countries that may reduce U.S. influence are not necessarily evidence of Soviet revisionism even if the USSR endorses their aims and refuses to prevent their success. Soviet applause and even encouragement for forces seen as "anti-imperialist" is not necessarily inconsistent with containment any more than is the United States' enthusiasm for Poland's Solidarity movement. Welcoming an indigenous movement is not the same as causing it. It is imperative that domestic movements and revolutions that run counter to U.S. policy be analyzed carefully and not inappropriately attributed to Soviet instigation. For example, this study regards Bengali grievances as so immense that the independence of Bangladesh was considered a change induced more by regional forces than by Soviet orchestration. The importance of indigenous grievances also makes it unwise to attribute to the Soviet Union the struggles of the NLF and the PLO. In these cases Soviet support was obvious, but with a rather marginal commitment to change. The USSR was willing to compromise the cause of either to preserve detente with the United States.

The communist expansionism theory logically leads to a policy of active containment and even rollback of Soviet influence. If the United States were to deny the "totalitarians" international success, the weakness of the "paper tiger" would be revealed and in turn internal change would occur in the USSR. The logic of this theory derives from George Kennan's analysis of nearly forty years ago: "The United States has it in its power to increase enormously the strains under which the Soviet policy must operate, to force upon the Kremlin a far greater degree of moderation and circumspection than it has had to observe in recent years, and in this way to promote tendencies which must eventually find their outlet in either the breakup or the gradual mellowing of Soviet power."[34] The results of this study, which do not support the expansionist diagnosis, have at least three general implications for such a strategy.

First, the USSR's commitment to unilaterally assured nuclear deterrence is supreme. U.S. efforts to compel the Soviets to accept U.S. domination or "margins of security" are likely to fail. The USSR has demonstrated little confidence in arms control agreements and no willingness to trade its forces for "bargaining chips." This study's analysis of Soviet perceptions and foreign policy strategy suggests that Soviet leaders perceive a basic parity between the superpowers' strategic military power and not a Soviet advantage. Consequently, they are likely to perceive U.S. "bargaining chips" as efforts to achieve superiority and as evidence of bad faith vis-à-vis detente. In this atmosphere, one-sided proposals or associated weapons procurements meant as bargaining ploys are likely to reinforce the Soviets' skepticism both about the value of arms control and the prospects of protecting their security through negotiations with the United States.

To the extent that Soviet weapons development is a symptom of security calculations and bureaucratic momentum, the strategy of reinforced containment will stimulate further growth in the arms race. Although the Soviets demonstrated some interest in stabilizing the deterrent relationship, they remained throughout the 1970s first and foremost committed to unilateral strength. It is unlikely they will reduce the heart of their strategic force (that is, ICBMs) to achieve more stability until they achieve the technical capacity to match U.S. forces in other systems. This is particularly likely as the U.S. deploys cruise missiles in Europe and attempts to extend its deterrent power from its strategic forces into the Persian Gulf. Concerned about credibility, Soviet leaders are likely to preserve the limited and accurate options that ICBMs represent and refuse agreements that reduce the range of options and hence the credibility of their nuclear responses. Because in submarine-based missiles, long-range aircraft, and cruise missile programs the Soviet Union lags behind the United States in terms of quantity, quality, and accuracy, it is not likely the Soviets will surrender their advantage in ICBMs. Their interest in stability has not superseded a commitment to credible deterrence both bilaterally and in an extended case.

Second, the USSR has demonstrated its capacity to enforce its imperial control over other socialist countries and to project its influence. Notions of rolling back Soviet involvement or compelling its expulsion from third countries are romantic. Although the USSR reduced its participation in the Middle East and Southeast Asia in 1972, it demonstrated later in the decade that it retained the capability to interfere in those regions. The proposition that detente could be used to exclude the USSR from contests in the Third World and thereby secure American alliances for containment seems to be disconfirmed by Soviet actions in Ethiopia, Afghanistan, and Vietnam.

The cases in this study suggest that the "paper tiger" theme underpinning the logic of reinforced containment leads to both an overestimation of the relative Soviet military capabilities and a dangerous underestimation of Soviet power. While not recognizing the range of possible options available to the USSR to counter American pressure, the diagnosis assumes too much latitude for Soviet retreat.[35] As demonstrated, in strategic arms development, Ethiopia, and the Middle East (for example, Syria in 1967, Egypt in 1970 and 1973), the USSR can compete with the United States and use its might to set limits on retreat. Its logistic and military advantages in the Persian Gulf present contemporary opportunities to counter U.S. containment efforts. Before surrendering to American pressure and accepting the disintegration of its regime and empire, the USSR could be expected to exploit all of its options in the Persian Gulf. At the same time, given the predominance of the "enemy" image among Soviet leaders, it is likely to be reluctant to show weakness or retreat, especially in the face of U.S. pressure. Prevailing Soviet leaders perceive the United States as contained by Soviet might and seem to express a "paper tiger" theme of their own. They probably reason that Soviet power is all that American leaders understand and respect, and they will respond accordingly. Because of the importance of credibility in nuclear deterrence and the priority of strategic deterrence in Soviet behavior, it is most unlikely that Soviet leaders will perceive much latitude for retreat under pressure without jeopardizing Soviet security.

Third, American intervention in third countries, which is designed to reinforce a containment strategy by suppressing internal disaffection, may be counterproductive if deep-seated grievances in those countries are not alleviated. Associated with the inclination to attribute too much importance to the USSR as a cause of political change in other nations is a tendency to minimize the power generated by internal grievances and resentment of U.S. interference. While advocates of reinforced containment understand instantly the USSR's problem with indigenous nationalism in East bloc countries and resistance to repression in Poland and Afghanistan, they often fail to recognize similar limits on U.S. policy in Vietnam, Bangladesh, or Iran. Rising mass participation and ascendant aspirations for self-determination make intervention by outsiders exceedingly complex and difficult to effect successfully. Abstract generalities about the utility of force cannot be substituted for concrete political diagnoses in specific cases. If the citizenry of a country reject the ruling regime as a foreign creation, then forceful intervention by another nation to protect that regime is unlikely to enhance its legitimacy or stability. Long-term suppression, as the USSR has demonstrated, may be one option, but the maintenance of imperial control will probably fail to secure an independently reliable ally necessary for containment. An excessive commitment to containment may produce not only Soviet aggression and repression that otherwise could have been avoided, but also an unwise American reliance on deterrence in third countries where such coercive tactics are both inappropriate and counterproductive.[36]

Theory 2: Realpolitik Expansionism

According to a second theory, the Soviet Union is driven by a fundamental commitment to self-defense, and once securing this, it will opportunistically seek to expand its area of domination. The commitment to defense can be tested, but the expansionist claim is not so easily proved. Because according to this theory the USSR will seize low-risk, low-cost opportunities, theory 2, like the Communist expansionism theory, does not predict a high commitment to revisionist acts. This study finds that Soviet behavior in all three time periods did reveal a major commitment to defense and rather marginal sacrifices for expansion; however, we cannot conclusively determine whether this indicates a lack of expansionist ambition or the lack of opportunity. Because of the difficulty of measuring the extent to which opportunities exist in concrete situations, I was forced simply to assess whether or not the lack of revisionist behavior can be plausibly explained by lack of opportunity. For the most part, I was not persuaded by the proposition that the Soviet Union, no matter how opportunistic, is dedicated to forcing revisionism in other nations.

Theory 2 suggests that the USSR is both defensive and expansionist. The Soviet Union's recognition of the nuclear stalemate and the status quo in Europe is described as a holding action complementing its expansionist activities in the Third World. To capture this complexity I focused on a set of arenas including strategic arms and Europe as well as critical regions in the Third World. I sought to make independent judgments regarding Soviet strategy in each arena and in each period to allow for possible inconsistencies, mixed motives, or trends across regions and time. I concluded my discussion of each period with a net assessment. This aggregate picture obviously ignores lower-level complexity, but is useful in analyzing general strategy. Such a broad picture is necessary in strategy formation and seems appropriate to the global nature of Soviet-American competition.

While the USSR's commitment to nuclear deterrence and the status quo in Europe was found to be high, its inclination to exploit opportunities in the Middle East and South Asia was less clear. In 1967, and especially in 1972, the USSR's commitment to its allies in Egypt, Iraq, and North Vietnam failed to resemble even a containment strategy, much less a revisionist one. In 1979, opportunities for strategic involvement in Lebanon and Iran also provoked little Soviet action. At the same time, the USSR's behavior in Syria in 1967, Egypt in 1970 and 1973, Iraq in 1974, Ethiopia in 1977, and Afghanistan in 1979 indicated that it was neither unable nor unwilling to threaten and use force in the region, despite the risks of potential U.S.-Soviet confrontation.

The failure of the USSR to seize plausible opportunities, coupled with its willingness to act vigorously in Third World areas, casts doubt on the accuracy of the "opportunistic" explanation for Soviet policy. A more convincing hypothesis would be that tough Soviet action in the Middle East and southern Asia is stimulated not by perceptions of opportunity for expansionist gain but by perceived threats of imminent loss.[37] The concern about possible setbacks and U.S. advantage also cast doubt on the notion that the USSR has a proclivity to fuel local conflicts.

The realpolitik expansionist perspective claims that the USSR encourages regional turmoil in the Third World. Regional conflict, however, has been found in this study not only to present opportunities for Soviet penetration but also to create expensive tests of Soviet reliability; in turn, such conflicts threaten or actually undermine Soviet alliances such as in Egypt, Iraq, and Somalia. The Soviet interest in fueling turmoil, consequently, is not always great. Moreover, the definition of what constitutes encouraging turmoil is impossible to determine without invoking assumptions about the causes of regional conflicts. For U.S. government officials it may be reasonable to argue that any aid to forces resisting American interests abroad is abetting conflict. For independent scholars, however, the task is exceedingly more difficult. The ethnocentric assumption that the capability of parties to resist the will of the United States or its allies is the "cause" of conflict is unacceptable. To assume that the successful suppression of regional opposition to U.S. interests and exclusion of the USSR from an area will produce stability is to take a very narrow and short-sighted approach to peace.

All parties to a conflict want peace, but on their terms. For world powers, peace is one of many objectives and is not generally the highest in priority. Protecting territory, maintaining independence, defending certain conceptions of justice, and gaining strategic advantage often supersede an interest in peace. Take, for example, the United States' aid to the Kurds. Both superpowers provide weapons and support to regional combatants, allowing them to defend their terms and usually to resist defeat. Whether or not this constitutes fanning the flames of turmoil depends on a number of controversial assumptions, not the least of which relate to the "legitimacy" of the competing terms and the "fairness" of the proposed settlements. Many would consider the Soviet Union's effort to compel the Afghan resistance forces to surrender, and the severe repression in Afghanistan, as more important "causes" of the ongoing turmoil than the aid given by the United States and others to the rebel groups. Likewise, in the Ogaden region the Ethiopian policy toward ethnic Somalis contributed to conflict, along with Somalia's irredentist ambitions and armed invasion. Determining the cause of violence requires the examination of both the outstanding grievances and the relative balance of power in any region. It is extraordinarily difficult to determine how various acts such as the U.S. support for Somali aspirations or the USSR's aid to the Ethiopian government will affect the prospects for resolution of the conflict. Fighting can be ended in many ways, including total victory by either side. At the same time, the infusion of foreign aid may create a more equitable balance between the contenders, forcing mutual compromise and possibly a more secure settlement.

The USSR has often rejected peace terms endorsed by the United States, but this is not the same as aggravating instability. In some cases the USSR has advocated terms of settlement no more one-sided than those advanced by the United States and at least equally likely, or no more unlikely, to produce possible compromise. For example, in Vietnam the Soviets, like many in the United States and around the world, attributed the turmoil as much to Thieu and the U.S. presence there as to the NLF's resistance. While rejecting Thieu, they did advocate negotiations and a process of reform to ameliorate the intense internal sources of discord. The process failed, but not only because of the USSR's involvement. U.S. encouragement of Thieu's efforts to press his advantage in 1973–1974, and Thieu's own refusal to accept change, contributed to the impasse as did North Vietnam's refusal to accept a cease-fire without real political change.

In East Pakistan, the U.S. efforts to protect Pakistani control were not likely to resolve conflict there. The turmoil was not a product of Soviet mischief but Pakistani repression. For months the USSR pressed for compromise and none was imminent. To attribute the turmoil to Bengali resistance, one must adopt a bias that is unwarranted. The Soviets did little to encourage the Bengalis and endorsed what was perhaps the most credible formula for stability.

The Soviet Union has refused to accept Israeli occupation of the West Bank, Gaza, and the Golan Heights, and has spurned any peace plans that fail to deal directly with these issues. It has also provided the Arab Steadfastness Front with the capability to resist Israeli terms for peace that do not surrender the West Bank to Palestinian self-determination. It will also not legitimate any Israeli efforts to settle the issues unilaterally through Lebanon and the elimination of the PLO. However, it has not refused to negotiate for peace. George Breslauer has concluded: "It is not that the Soviets do not want a settlement that will defuse the constant threat of war in the region; it is rather that the Soviets have been consistently committed to the realization of *a particular kind of settlement*, one that is based on the four terms outlined above."[38] The four terms Breslauer outlines are: (1) U.S.-Soviet comediation of the settlement process, (2) Israeli withdrawal from territories occupied in 1967, (3) establishment of a Palestinian homeland, and (4) U.S. and Soviet guarantees of the security of all states in the region, including Israel. It has consistently supported Israel's right to exist in peace with secure boundaries along roughly the 1967 frontiers. Its proposals, while unacceptable in Israel, are not radically different from formulas advocated by the United States, although they include Soviet participation and PLO representation.[39]

The causes of turmoil in Arab-Israeli relations are many and are not exclusively the product of Arab intransigence. Israeli reluctance to accommodate Palestinian nationalism is significant. The USSR has not allowed its allies to be forced into surrender (although it did little to help them in Lebanon), but it has not backed their efforts to impose unilateral terms to the extent that the United States has supported Israel. U.S. preoccupation with excluding the Soviet Union has not led to a more compromising attitude in Israel. Moreover, it is not clear whether or not Israeli efforts to retain the West Bank and decide the issue by force in Lebanon, or Palestinian and Syrian efforts to resist the Israeli terms, are fueling the persistent turmoil more.

To conclude that the USSR encourages regional turmoil, one must accept a number of contentious and politically loaded assumptions. That it vigorously and deliberately fuels anti-Americanism, on the other hand, is clear. As in Iran, the Soviet Union may have nothing to do with the origins of anti-American sentiments, but it will encourage those that exist. This interest in "anti-imperialist" forces and reducing U.S. influence, however, is not necessarily evidence of expansionist motives. The United States is likewise energetically committed to anti-Soviet propaganda and minimizing Soviet involvement in third countries. The interest in relative power, as all Realists agree, is a universal concern integral to self-defense and expansion. By itself it is indicative of neither.

The logic of the realpolitik expansionist theory leads to a dual-track strategy of containment that mixes deterrence and detente. Proponents of theory 2 prescribe a complex integration of firmness and cooperation as a response to both defensive and expansionist Soviet motives. Granting first priority to deterrence, the dual-track strategy aims to modify Soviet behavior by punishing it for resisting U.S. terms and offering incentives for cooperative behavior. The intent of the strategy is to eliminate Soviet perceptions of opportunity for expansion while not provoking intensified perceptions of threat. The results of this study present three implications for this strategy.

First, it is likely that Soviet leaders will perceive the dual strategy just outlined as a uniform strategy of containment and interpret offers of cooperation as either dangerous ploys or attempts at subversion. The predominance of the "enemy" image in Soviet statements and their obvious fear of an American threat suggests that Soviet leaders could translate the U.S. plan into a consistent plot.[40] For the strategy to succeed, a tremendously efficient mode of communication between the superpowers would be necessary, which is rare in international relations, especially between adversaries. Soviet leaders with an "enemy" image of the United States are likely to seize upon evidence of U.S. firmness and deterrence and dismiss offers of cooperation as insincere.[41] Their attitudes are likely to resemble the reactions of American conservatives when confronted with Soviet offers of good will simultaneously with larger Soviet programs of arms development, regional power projection, and firm deterrence. Not even brilliant implementation and excellent communication would be likely to persuade prevailing Soviet leaders that a relaxation of vigilance was safe and that U.S. gestures of cooperation were sincere if the United States is simultaneously deploying B-1 bombers, and new Trident, MX, and cruise missiles, excluding the USSR from Middle East negotiations, developing facilities in Egypt, Oman, Kenya, and

Somalia, enlarging and strengthening NATO, and playing the "China card."

Second, U.S. efforts to raise the cost of action and thereby deter Soviet behavior in third areas may, in Soviet calculations, simply raise the risks of not moving. In this study I found that aggressive Soviet behavior is often associated with fear of loss, not perceived opportunities for gain. This was probably the case in Czechoslovakia (1968), Egypt (1970, 1973), Ethiopia (1977–1978), Afghanistan (1979), and Poland (1981). The risks associated with losing a position in these areas, as it is perceived in Moscow, are greater than the costs the United States can credibly threaten should the USSR act to prevent the setback. U.S. efforts to deter a given Soviet act, therefore, are likely to be ineffective and probably counterproductive. First, U.S. warnings and diplomatic efforts to deter the Soviet Union are likely to heighten perceived threats in Moscow and raise the apparent security value of the endangered position. Second, escalating U.S. deterrent efforts force Soviet leaders to calculate that "inevitable" and "necessary" moves to protect their influence are better taken sooner rather than later. Third, U.S. efforts at deterrence are likely to convince Soviet policymakers with an "enemy" image of the United States that not moving decisively would signal weakness and invite further U.S. pressure for rollback. They would be reluctant to risk setbacks in any case. In the face of American threats or in a situation where U.S. leaders may claim credit for having compelled Soviet restraint, the incentive to move would probably be irresistible. U.S. deterrent attempts, while incapable of raising costs any higher than those already at stake, may have the effect of destroying U.S. credibility and ensuring the very outcome that the United States sought to deter.

U.S. deterrence and coercive diplomacy in circumstances where Soviet leaders perceive threats from pending setbacks and exclusion from certain areas, such as in Poland, the Middle East, and Afghanistan, may expose Soviet imperialism and reflect American outrage, but are unlikely to have a positive effect on the situation. The USSR would most likely answer the perceived challenge with tougher policy of its own. It might, for example, bolster its own commitments and enforce greater solidarity and obedience from its allies. Rather than enhancing containment, American pressure is likely to narrow the latitude vis-à-vis Moscow that regional parties such as Poland have in which to maneuver. The prospects for independent movements like Solidarity in those countries will be dimmed, not brightened.

Furthermore, in efforts to deter Soviet involvement in the Middle East and Southwest Asia, the United States may engage in counterproductive interference. Based on a Pavlovian analogy, the strategy assumes that the United States can "teach" the USSR to accommodate American concerns. This, however, requires a substantial degree of control over the political environment. In areas like Southwest Asia this is increasingly beyond the reach of either superpower. The advocates of this strategy generally recognize the importance of local nationalism and indigenous grievances and argue that the Soviet Union fosters rather than causes turmoil. Ironically, the strategic prescription, which emphasizes excluding the Soviet Union from Southwest Asia, leads to a projection of U.S. power there that, rather than fostering regional resolution and stability, is likely to fuel "anti-imperialist" sentiment. Such a strategy would further associate the United States with repressive and inherently unstable regimes and deepens its dependence on projected force such as with the Rapid Deployment Force now in the Central Command. The net result may be to diminish U.S. leverage and enhance the USSR's ability to encourage anti-Americanism.

Third, the assumption that the Soviet Union seizes available opportunities can lead to an underestimation of Soviet power and overextension of American commitment. "Opportunity" is often tautologically defined: if the USSR takes action, this is proof that is saw the opportunity; when it does not, this proves that no opportunity existed. Naturally, this type of definition leaves no room for evidence of Soviet self-restraint. This reasoning is dangerous because it allows an assumption about motives to interfere with the analysis of the exercise of power. I have tried to measure the concept of opportunity independently of Soviet behavior and evaluate the plausibility of attributing inaction to lack of opportunity. In a number of critical cases such as the Persian Gulf I found the deterrent caveat less than compelling. This suggests that the realpolitik diagnosis might underestimate both Soviet leverage and the expected costs of U.S. actions. Moreover, it may lead to misplaced confidence in the United States' ability to deter Soviet acts and unfounded expectations of success when defeat is probable.

Theory 3: Realpolitik Defense

Imperialist and aggressive Soviet behavior toward many third countries is, according to a third theory, attributed to an increased sense of threat from the United States, China, or both. The USSR is described as defensive and driven by paramount security concerns, even if they are exaggerated. This study has tested the defensive theory by means of two hypotheses regarding behavior: first, that the prevailing Soviet image of the United States resembles the "enemy" stereotype; and second, that the USSR's behavior in many world arenas indicates a strategy of containment. In 1967 and 1979 the verbal and behavioral evidence weighed most heavily in favor of these hypotheses. In 1972 Soviet defensiveness seemed to have relaxed somewhat, as was appropriate during an era of detente. Although this study has not disproved the defensive hypotheses, it obviously cannot prove their accuracy either. It does argue that, of the general theories considered, the defensive explanation of Soviet international behavior is more plausible than the other two interpretations, at least in the arenas examined.

The defensive interpretation is certain to be controversial. In a survey of American leaders conducted in 1976 and 1980 by Ole Holsti and James Rosenau, the issue on which they found the greatest consensus was the belief that the Soviet Union is generally expansionist rather than defensive in its foreign policy goals. In 1976, 83 percent either agreed strongly or agreed somewhat that the USSR was expansionist. In 1980, 85 percent agreed.[42] The results of this study, as with Gamson's and Modigliani's earlier test of rival theories, do not support this widely shared perspective. These results may, however, be more consistent with other research than might appear from this conclusion alone.

In my study of Soviet motives I have assumed a hierarchy of inclusiveness, beginning with self-defense. Consequently, all three theories agree that the USSR is driven by defensive aims and security concerns. The two expansionist perspectives, however, claim that Soviet behavior goes beyond mere self-protection and is also driven by expansionist motives. Quite often the argument is nonfalsifiable because its proponents do not expect the USSR to run great risks or sacrifice very much in order to achieve these aims. Sometimes a teleological qualification is introduced, suggesting that Soviet leaders take a long view of history and therefore one cannot trust current behavior that shows patience and restraint: they are bent on expansion. As mentioned in the case of Southwest Asia, these concerns are important precautions and underlie sound reservations in policy planning, but can make contemporary analysis impossible. Without rejecting these future possibilities, I tested a part of the expansionist argument by seeking evidence of the "degenerate" stereotype and revisionist strategy. I evaluated actual Soviet behavior in terms of commitment to the policies a revisionist model might predict. This is essential to empirically based research, but does not provide a direct test of the competing perspectives. After all, they are driven as much by theory as evidence and are nonfalsifiable. The expansionist theories can account for the lack of observable commitment to revisionism. In fact, in the short run they predict it.

While Soviet leaders verbally described the U.S. threat as global, their behavioral commitments in different regions indicated substantial variation in their sense of threat. As might be expected, the USSR granted highest priority, in terms of relative commitment, to maintaining a nuclear deterrent and dominating Eastern Europe. In these arenas it demonstrated little faith in diplomacy and no willingness to relax its security systems. In the Middle East, on the other hand, the Soviets exhibited less concern than might be expected if they saw the United States as a serious threat. Their behavior in Egypt, Kurdistan, and Lebanon was less vigorous than a containment model would predict. They exhibited, for example, a substantial willingness to sacrifice Soviet credibility in the Middle East and Southeast Asia in order to pursue detente. As demonstrated in Ethiopia in 1977–1978, in South Yemen in 1979, and in Syria in 1980, however, there remained a basic commitment to preserving regional influence that caused the Soviets to resist exclusion, particularly as talk of detente disappeared.

The three periods chosen for this study were selected to span the development of Sino-American relations. One reason for this choice was to consider whether the United States' playing the "China card" would correlate with more accommodating Soviet behavior. The results suggest that the answer is no. Increased U.S.-Chinese cooperation coincided with intensified perceptions of threat in Moscow and led not to capitulation but to reinforced Soviet commitments in Afghanistan, India, and Vietnam. U.S. efforts to join with China in common cause against the USSR were seen in Moscow as incompatible with detente. While the Sino-American rapprochement coincided with an increasing Soviet interest in detente with Bonn, the USSR linked the prospects for improved Soviet–West German relations to the West Germans' reluctance to endorse the United States' reinforcement of containment efforts. By 1979 the Soviet interest in detente with West Germany was perceived by many Americans as an effort to undermine NATO and hardly the kind of "accommodation" they had hoped the pressure of Chinese-American cooperation would produce.

A strategy of disengagement or detente is associated with the logic of realpolitik self-defense. Although the results of this study support the general thrust of such a strategy, they also point out obstacles to its success. First, Soviet leaders have been very conservative with respect to the USSR's security and inclined to trust only unilateral military power. To persuade such conservatives to accept a relaxation in vigilance would be no mean task. No confidence in arms control can be expected. With the deployment of weapons like the cruise missile that complicate if not defy verification, arms control as a device for building confidence may no longer be viable.

Confidence-building measures and economic interdependence could foster relaxation in Europe and reduce the likelihood of confrontation. While this would be no small achievement, the long-term success of any military detente will be limited by the persisting Soviet domination of Eastern Europe. Western public opinion will insist that the process of detente include the relaxation of domestic repression in Eastern Europe and this in turn will threaten the survival both of the Communist regimes and of the Warsaw Pact. Soviet leaders may never accept this and will certainly not tolerate such change if no comparable dissolution is occurring in NATO. It would require strong positive incentives such as economic cooperation and a forthright Western commitment to reducing Soviet perceptions of threat to convince enough leaders in Moscow that the risks of change are worthwhile.

Second, U.S. efforts to allay Soviet fears may be read in Moscow as evidence of weakness. The paradox of the "enemy" stereotype is that the "paper tiger" image interprets accommodating behavior as capitulation. Because the prevailing Soviet elite accept the "enemy" image of the United States, they are likely to interpret U.S. efforts to revive detente as reflecting the successful application of Soviet might. Rather than understanding an American gesture toward detente as indicative of peaceful intent, Soviet "hawks" are likely to attribute the move to fear of Soviet strength and advocate pressing still harder. An initiative intended to persuade Soviet leaders who hold a moderate "enemy" picture of the United States that detente is possible, may instead convince the hawks in Moscow that a hard-line policy is working. At the same time, a strong signal of American resolve may discourage the enthusiasm of Soviet hawks, yet only convince them as well as those with less intense fears that their worst estimates of American intentions were correct.

Designing diplomatic strategies to reduce enemy images is a perplexing task. Neither accommodation nor strength will be effective independently. At the same time, a dual-track strategy that reinforces containment and aims to compel

Soviet acceptance of American terms is likely only to intensify Soviet resistance. Detente, which by definition means relaxation, will not be easily combined with efforts to reinforce Western containment either through NATO, China, or Soviet exclusion from Third World events. The results of this study suggest that the USSR will not relax its vigilance in return for trade or negotiated arms control if the primary focus of U.S. policy is the strengthening of containment. For a dual-track strategy to work effectively, the United States will need to demonstrate a commitment to change in its own security arrangements commensurate with those expected from the USSR. As seen in the case studies, reciprocal trust and mutual relaxation are very difficult to manage. Well-established suspicions in both Washington and Moscow will incline analysts to perceive an asymmetrical pace of change. Each side is likely to be more sensitive to the potential alterations in its own systems and will see only the "enemy's" persisting strength, not its restraint.

The "enemy" stereotype inherently assumes bad faith. The perceptions of those holding this image are independent of the behavior of the observed country. Its restraint is not perceived, nor are its accommodating overtures taken seriously. Challenges are seen irrespective of the country's efforts to reassure and even these efforts are likely to be interpreted as disingenuous and manipulative. The "enemy" stereotype sets up self-fulfilling predictions and interprets whatever is going on in light of prior expectations. Regardless of the actual pattern of events, the enemy will be seen as probing and retreating, as responsive to the carrot only if the stick is ever present. Definitions of the situation will be derived from the general stereotypes and will reaffirm its predictions. A psychological theory may argue that the stereotype reflects great fear of an enemy, but this does not tell how to transcend stereotypical thinking. Because the stereotype cannot be empirically disconfirmed, it greatly complicates any attempts at conflict management, much less peacemaking.

Given the "enemy" images that leaders in Washington and Moscow have of each other, neither nation is likely to respond appropriately to the behavior of the other. Both may be motivated by security concerns, but the dynamics of competition will probably not follow a neatly spiraling stimulus-response pattern. Neither side will see the restraint of the other. Both will interpret the actions in the worst possible light, assuming bad faith. Initiatives intended as signals of flexibility will be missed, dismissed, or misinterpreted. Actions seen as benign and ordinary by the initiator will be read by the other as threatening and probably malevolent. Efforts to stimulate relaxation are, therefore, not likely to produce quick and clear counteroffers. Communication is likely to be so imperfect that behavior may not even appear to be related to the adversary's previous actions except to the initiator or each act. The clear processes of escalation and deescalation expected in an action-reaction model may never appear.

In the 1970s Soviet perceptions of the United States resembled the "enemy" stereotype but did not fit the ideal case, as assumed in the argument above. Nevertheless, the "enemy" image, as expected, made communication and signaling very difficult and the action-reaction model quite inadequate. These results create problems not only for deterrence advocates but also for those who promote a strategy of "graduated and reciprocated initiatives in tension reduction." Several critiques of deterrence policy have demonstrated that the degree of rationality and level of effective communication it assumes is not compatible with international reality. The tension-reducing strategy is also dependent on accurate communication. In fact, it assumes that not only threats will be understood but also flexibility and gestures of compromise will be perceived and correctly deciphered. Unfortunately, in an atmosphere dominated by "enemy" images, this is not likely to be the case.

My results suggest that communicating with the Soviet Union is certain to be complicated. Ironically, they suggest that the task the United States has put the most energy into, signaling resolve and credibility, is likely to be the easiest. Soviet leaders are predisposed to see American threats. The much more difficult task of signaling flexibility and relaxing Soviet fears has received less attention. Soviet insecurity has led to a number of imperialist and brutal policies. The United States, therefore, must act to reduce Soviet perceptions of threat while simultaneously registering strong opposition to authoritarianism. Because communication with the USSR is likely to be distorted, there will probably be a significant lag between flexible initiatives and positive responses. Moreover, in many cases perceptions of the situation are so different that completely incompatible definitions of reciprocity are certain to exist. Any search for greater detente will be a very imperfect process for a long time. Powerful leaders on both sides who operate with stereotypical images will never be convinced that their relaxation of military vigilance is reciprocated. The fits and starts and inconsistent behavior that are to be expected will certainly complicate the strategy and provoke domestic and bureaucratic pressures that may undermine its viability at home. The problems derived from the predominance of "enemy" images may not be insurmountable, but they surely reduce the prospects for a mutual disengagement strategy.

Monitoring the effects and appropriateness of any strategy is an ongoing endeavor that is particularly difficult in foreign policy. In a dual strategy that emphasizes detente and a willingness to allay rather than exacerbate or manipulate Soviet fears, positive change will be long in coming and is not likely to be achieved smoothly. The process, for example, is likely to facilitate change in third regions such as the Middle East that may appear threatening to different groups in the United States, regardless of their concern about the Soviet Union. The multiple effects of such a strategy on many relationships will make it hard to assess the strategy's effect on the USSR. It may produce intense lobbying from regimes dependent on American aid and in danger of domestic or regional challenges if U.S. support should wane, as U.S. commitment to containment relaxes. This will only heighten concerns about the costs of detente and fuel concerns about Soviet involvement in those nations.

This book was stimulated by a concern that U.S. policy prescriptions toward the USSR are often based on rigidly accepted yet largely unexamined theories of Soviet international behavior. Its main aim has been to explicate such unquestioned assumptions about motivation and treat them as propositions. Therefore, although my results support the interpretation that the Soviets are primarily concerned with self-defense, I will not conclude by outlining and advocating a disengagement policy. A greater emphasis on detente may be called for, but no strategy is likely to be a panacea that quickly and effectively reduces undesirable Soviet behavior. More important, my purpose in this book is not prescriptive but diagnostic.

Political analysis, like medical analysis, is time-bound, uncertain, and limited by imperfect information. Political actors can change. A single diagnosis of Soviet policy is not wisely translated into a general theory assumed to have permanent utility. An analysis can yield a temporary logic for treatment, but it must be continually revised and questioned as the effects of the preliminary probes are evaluated. Analysis of motivation is both an essential and ongoing process that should never be assumed to render definitive final interpretations. Although this study has offered substantive findings, its more fundamental purpose has been to draw attention to unexamined assumptions about motivation. While certain assumptions about motives and perceptions are unavoidable in intelligent strategy formulation, their analysis needs both theoretical and methodological refinement. The essential role of theory in strategic diagnosis ensures that heated debate will continue even if our access to evidence improves.

ANALYSIS OF MOTIVATION AND FOREIGN POLICY THEORY

I have focused on Soviet leaders' verbal images of the United States found both in public statements and in foreign policy commitments. I organized my search for evidence and its analysis on two theoretical conceptions: first, a theory of perceptions and images, and second, a theory of strategic models applied to specific arenas of competition. In my application of the conceptual framework, I found that the two streams of evidence led to similar conclusions. Both suggested that prevailing Soviet perceptions of the United States are dominated by a sense of threat and that it is plausible to attribute Soviet foreign policy behavior primarily to a concern for self-defense. This does not suggest that the Soviets always express their views in the public media. However, perceptions might be determined in a less direct way. This study finds that verbal imagery indicates an "enemy" stereotype of the United States and that this image can be usefully integrated with a theory of perception.

Because I have stressed behavior at the state level and international behavior of the USSR, I have sought to describe only prevailing Soviet perceptions of the United States. Much internal complexity has been missed, and it might prove very informative to compare various patterns of perception to different voices within the USSR. This task would require more rigorous coding definitions for each stereotype and substantial access to Soviet propaganda. If coupled with an analysis of the prevailing view, such a study might offer insight into probable influence patterns and possible associations between various roles and perceptions of the United States.[43]

Policy debates surely go on in Moscow, but I did not design this study to examine the policy formulation process. Instead I sought to address fundamental motivational theories at the strategic level of Soviet international behavior. As with the understanding of motives, interpretation of strategy also needs theoretical refinement. The discipline has accepted concepts about motives such as expansion and self-defense that are not easy to define or measure. It is as if diseases central in medical diagnoses were not connected to identifiable symptoms. Analysts grasp the concepts in the abstract, but understand less about the consequences they might be associated with in concrete arenas. Testing the usefulness or appropriateness of these concepts is not simple. It requires a set of assumptions about each situation and theoretical deductions that translate the general conception into context specific options.

Deriving concrete hypotheses to represent general theories of motivation requires an assessment of the USSR's capabilities and opportunities. This is a project burdened with probable attributional biases and contextual complexity.[18] The probable leverage and expected costs are impossible to calculate except in terms of probability and plausibility. The task of estimation is made still more difficult because of the cross-cutting biases of governments that have vested interests in both overselling the likely retaliation for deterrent purposes and understating their ability to retaliate for reasons of budget politics. Moreover, the analysis must be tailored to each region under examination; it must be sensitive to the concerns of third countries and the USSR's ability to court and intimidate them.

Defining what could be expected of a world power following various strategies in particular arenas is not a mechanical process. It demands the development of a thoughtful logic that explicitly reveals its assumptions regarding each situation and argument. This situational theorizing will define the "meaning" of whatever evidence is collected in both actions and nonoccurrences and must be at the center of scholarly dispute. In this study the logic in each arena is made explicit. My intention is not to win the polemic of the day, but rather to identify where intellectual and situational definitions may differ and where further evidence might alter existing evaluations.

Nothing in this study suggests that analyzing motivation is a simple task or one likely to avoid controversy. Arguments will rage over definitions, theories, and evidence. It is easy to understand why scholars such as Hans Morgenthau sought to circumvent the endeavor, and others like J. David Singer decided to concentrate at a different level of analysis.[44] The retreat to Realism, however, will not suffice. Strategic prescription must be based on a political diagnosis that provides a logic explaining why the prescription is likely to have a desired effect.

This will require an assessment of not only the relative capabilities but also the motivating factors producing the USSR's undesirable behavior. Attribution of motives will, consequently, remain at the center of prescriptions for strategy and will be a necessary target for research.

Concepts about motivation and perception serve as core variables in many foreign policy models. Efforts to avoid them have not been successful in producing important and convincing explanations for international behavior. Often these attempts have not circumvented claims about motivation but simply incorporated them as either implicit assumptions or explicit, yet undefined, assertions. Moreover, frequently employed concepts such as defense, expansion, perception of threat, and perception of opportunity imply certain judgments about motives. The careful consideration of the relevance and accuracy of these concepts in specific cases, however, has not received the necessary attention. Deduced logic and explicit theories are required to connect these powerful analytical concepts to empirical evidence drawn both from what leaders say and what they do. Broader-level theories of international relations cannot be empirically tested and thus will remain premature if the root assumptions on which they are based are not examined. Unless we tackle the basic problems inherent in generating the data about aims, values, motives, or perceptions, a good deal of research in international relations will suffer from a lack of meaningful evidence.

I have attempted to devise an empirically based approach to the study of foreign policy motivation. While the scheme was applied in the case of only one country, the framework should also be useful in comparative research. The complexity of defining the situation and the difficulty of inferring the perceptions of national leaders in a single case, however, highlight the magnitude of the challenge for cross-national comparison and theory-building in international relations.

The results of this study cast doubt on the accuracy of current theories of Soviet foreign policy that assume that the USSR's primary motive is to expand its domination over others. Moreover, they suggest that U.S. efforts to reinforce the containment of Soviet influence may be counterproductive: they are not likely to reduce undesirable Soviet behavior or to enhance American security or prospects of peace. These are disturbing possibilities.

My aim in this study, however, is not to settle a political debate but rather to press the academic debate into areas where assumptions about motivation must be defended explicitly and empirically. Such assumptions must be treated as hypotheses and not as matters of faith, ideology, or national patriotism. This fundamental question in foreign policy analysis should not be surrendered to untested assumptions, shared images, bureaucratic vested interests, or—worse still—government doctrine. Attributions about motives provide a logic for the prescriptions of strategy. If they are in error, then they can doom the prospect for policies derived from them, however well applied. The study of foreign policy motivation, therefore, is essential not only for academic understanding but also for national defense and effective peacemaking.

NOTES

1. See, for example, William Welch, *American Images of Soviet Foreign Policy: An Inquiry into Recent Appraisals from the Academic Community* (New Haven, CT: Yale University Press, 1970).

2. Ole Holsti and James Rosenau, *American Leadership in World Affairs: Vietnam and the Breakdown of Consensus* (Boston: Allen and Unwin, 1984), pp. 108–39.

3. These labels correspond to what William Gamson and Andre Modigliani called "destructionist," "expansionist," and "consolidationist," in *Untangling the Cold War: A Strategy for Testing Rival Theories* (Boston: Little, Brown, 1971).

4. This summary is meant to describe an abstract or ideal version of the theory, but is based on the following works: Richard Pipes, *U.S.-Soviet Relations in the Era of Detente: A Tragedy of Errors* (Boulder, CO: Westview Press, 1981), and Richard Pipes, ed., *Soviet Strategy in Europe* (New York: Crane, Russak, 1976); Walter Laqueur, "Containment for the 80s," *Commentary* 70 (Oct. 1980), pp. 33–42, and "Pity the Poor Russians?" *Commentary* 71 (Feb. 1981), pp. 32–41; Colin Gray, "Nuclear Strategy: The Case for a Theory of Victory," *International Security* 4 (Summer 1979), pp. 54–87; and Robert Conquest, *Present Danger: Towards a Foreign Policy* (Stanford, CA: Hoover Institution Press, 1979).

5. The core logic of the "operational art" or probe and retreat is spelled out by Nathan Leites in *The Operational Code of the Politburo* (New York: McGraw-Hill, 1951). For a recent study that concludes that such "operational principles" usefully describe Soviet behavior, see Hannes Adomeit, *Soviet Risk-Taking and Crisis Behavior: A Theoretical and Empirical Analysis* (London: Allen and Unwin, 1982), pp. 51–62, 315–25.

6. For a discussion of the independence of this theory from observable data see Ole R. Holsti, "Cognitive Dynamics and Images of the Enemy," in David J. Finlay, Ole R. Holsti, and Richard R. Fagen, eds., *Enemies in Politics* (Chicago: Rand McNally, 1967), pp. 25–96. Also see Douglas Stuart and Harvey Starr, "Inherent Bad Faith Reconsidered: Dulles, Kennedy, and Kissinger," *Political Psychology* 3 (1982), pp. 1–33.

7. The notion of contemporaneity argued for by Kurt Lewin is applicable in foreign policy analysis. Lewin argued that causal claims about human behavior in a particular period require an empirical defense drawn on evidence from that same period. Lewin's rigor does not minimize historical data, but guards against the substitution of historical determinism for contemporary diagnosis. For a review of Lewin's notion see Morton Deutsch, "Field Theory in Social Psychology," in *The Handbook of Social Psychology*, 2d ed., ed. by Gardner Lindzey and Elliot Aronson (Reading, MA: Addison-Wesley, 1968), pp. 412–87, 418–19.

8. See Richard Pipes, "Why the Soviet Union Thinks It Could Fight and Win a Nuclear War," *Commentary* 64 (July 1977), pp. 26–29. Also see Richard Pipes, "Militarism and the Soviet State," *Daedalus* 109 (Fall 1980), pp. 1–12; and "A Reply," *Encounter* 54 (April 1980), pp. 72–75. For the response of a Russian nationalist, see Alexander Solzhenitsyn, "Misconceptions about Russia Are a Threat to America," *Foreign Affairs* 58 (Spring 1980), pp. 797–834. Also see Wladislaw Krasnow, "Richard Pipes' Foreign Strategy: Anti-Soviet or Anti-Russian?" and Pipes's response in the *Russian Review* 38 (April 1979), pp. 180–97.

9. See, for example, Jerry Hough, *Soviet Leadership in Transition* (Washington, DC: Brookings, 1980).

10. One excellent study that illustrates how difficult this is even for the first secretary is George W. Breslauer, *Khrushchev and Brezhnev as Leaders: Building Authority in Soviet Politics* (London: Allen and Unwin, 1982).

11. This summary is an ideal type, but is based on the following works: Seweryn Bialer, *Stalin's Successors: Leadership, Stability, and Change in the Soviet Union*

(Cambridge: Cambridge University Press, 1980); "Poland and the Soviet Imperium," *Foreign Affairs* 59 (1980) pp. 522–39; "The International and Internal Contexts of the 26th Party Congress," in *Russia at the Crossroads: The 26th Congress of the C.P.S.U.*, ed. by Seweryn Bialer and Thane Gustafson (London: Allen and Unwin, 1982), pp. 7–38; and Seweryn Bialer and Joan Afferica, "Reagan and Russia," *Foreign Affairs* 61 (Winter 1982/83), pp. 249–71. The notion of "opportunistic expansion" is a theme running throughout the articles in *The Soviet Union in the Third World: Successes and Failures*, ed. by Robert Donaldson (Boulder, CO: Westview, 1981). Also see Robert Legvold, "The 26th Party Congress and Soviet Foreign Policy," in Bialer and Gustafson, *Russia, at the Crossroads*, pp. 156–77; and "Containment without Confrontation," *Foreign Policy* 40 (Fall 1980), pp. 74–98; William Hyland, "U.S.-Soviet Relations: The Long Road Back," *Foreign Affairs* 60 (1981), pp. 525–50; Dimitri Simes, "The Death of Detente," *International Security* 5 (Summer 1980), pp. 4–25; "Disciplining Soviet Power," *Foreign Policy* 43 (Summer 1981), pp. 33–52; "Deterrence and Coercion in Soviet Policy," *International Security* 5 (Winter 1980/81), pp. 80–103; and "The Clash over Poland," *Foreign Policy* 46 (Spring 1982), pp. 49–66.

12. There have been very few efforts to study Soviet risk-taking. In their study, Jan Triska and David Finley asked five experts to estimate risk and accepted their subjective estimates [*Soviet Foreign Policy* (New York: Macmillan, 1968), pp. 310–49]. Hannes Adomeit takes exception to the judgments of the Triska and Finley panel and argues for a different ordering of high-risk situations (*Soviet Risk-Taking*, pp. 51–55). The problem of identifying the environmental circumstances and probable reactions of other states in any objective fashion has not been adequately addressed. Because the task often requires speculation, it may be impossible to defend with tools other than logic and argument and thus never be reduced to an "objective" category.

13. For one effort to deal with this case, see Hyland, "U.S.-Soviet Relations," pp. 538–39.

14. See, for example, Kenneth Arrow, *Social Choice and Individual Values* (New Haven, CT: Yale University Press, 1963). Robert Jervis develops a similar argument linking the concept of "basic intentions" to demonstrated risk taking and sacrifice [*Perception and Misperception in International Politics* (Princeton, NJ: Princeton University Press, 1976), pp. 48–52].

15. This summary is an ideal type, but is based on the following works: George Kennan, *The Cloud of Danger: Current Realities of American Foreign Policy* (Boston: Atlantic Monthly Press, and Little, Brown, 1977), and *The Nuclear Delusion: Soviet-American Relations in the Atomic Age* (New York: Pantheon, 1982); Stephen Cohen, "Common and Uncommon Sense about the Soviet Union and American Policy," in House Committee on International Relations, *The Soviet Union Internal Dynamics of Foreign Policy: Present and Future*, 95th Cong., 2d sess. (Washington, DC: USGPO, 1978); Fred Warner Neal, ed., *Detente or Debacle: Common Sense in U.S.-Soviet Relations* (New York: Norton, 1979). Also see Richard Barnet, "U.S.-Soviet Relations: The need for a Comprehensive Approach," *Foreign Affairs* 57 (Spring 1979), pp. 779–95; and Richard Barnet, *The Giants: Russia and America* (New York: Simon and Schuster, 1977).

16. Jervis, *Perception and Misperception*, p. 63.

17. See, for example, Ernst Haas, "Why Collaborate? Issue Linkage and International Regimes," *World Politics* 32 (1980), pp. 357–405.

18. Richard Cottam, *Foreign Policy Motivation: A General Theory and A Case Study* (Pittsburgh, PA: University of Pittsburgh Press, 1977), pp. 157–257.

19. See E. J. Phares, *Locus of Control in Personality* (Morristown, NJ: General Learning Press, 1976); also see . . . etc.

20. Cottam, *Foreign Policy Motivation*, pp. 157–257.

21. See Phares, *Locus of Control in Personality*; also see Kelley G. Shaver, *An Introduction to Attribution Processes* (Cambridge, MA: Winthrop, 1975).

22.   Glen Snyder and Paul Diesing, *Conflict Among Nations: Bargaining, Decision Making, and System Structure in International Crises* (Princeton, NJ: Princeton University Press, 1977), p. 254.

23.   Alexander George, *Managing U.S.-Soviet Rivalry: Problems of Crisis Prevention* (Boulder, CO: Westview, 1983), p. 4.

24.   In theories concerning foreign policy, attributions of motivation often define the essential "understanding," and at a lower level of abstraction, are analogous to what Thomas Kuhn might identify as the central theory defining a analogous to what Thomas Kuhn might identify as the central theory defining a scientific paradigm [*The Structure of Scientific Revolutions*, 2d ed. (Chicago: University of Chicago Press, 1970)].

25.   See Snyder and Diesing, *Conflict Among Nations*, pp. 66–68.

26.   Ibid., pp. 24, 44, 85, 156–57.

27.   Snyder and Diesing discuss this problem but offer no method for inferring motives or perceptions (ibid., pp. 6–21). In their case studies they refer to an area expert (pp. 103, 105, 115). Richard Ned Lebow also recognized the problem in *Between Peace and War: The Nature of International Crisis* (Baltimore: Johns Hopkins University Press, 1981), pp. 224–25, 30–37, 206–11, 243–45, 278.

28.   See Alexander George and Richard Smoke, *Deterrence in American Foreign Policy: Theory and Practice* (New York: Columbia University Press, 1974). In the case studies presented by George and Smoke, the key judgments about motivation are offered on pp. 397–403, 418–21, 459–66. In *The Limits of Coercive Diplomacy: Laos, Cuba, Vietnam*, ed. by Alexander George, D. Hall, and W. Simons (Boston: Little, Brown, 1971), p. 216, George concludes that there are eight conditions required for the success of deterrence. The first three are (1) strength of U.S. motivation, (2) asymmetry of motivation favoring the United States, and (3) clarity of American objectives.

29.   Fritz Heider, *The Psychology of Interpersonal Relations* (New York: Wiley, 1958), pp. 79–124. Also see Jones et al., *Attribution: Perceiving the Causes of Behavior* (Morristown, NJ: General Learning Press, 1971).

30.   The inescapable need for motivational and political diagnosis in strategy formulation is a central theme developed by Ken Booth in *Strategy and Ethnocentrism* (New York: Holmes and Meier, 1979). George and Smoke conclude that what is necessary in policy science is the development of "empirical theory" concerning "how things work" in order to derive policy-related predictions on the probable effects of various prescriptions (*Deterrence in American Foreign Policy*, p. 618).

31.   On the issue of shared images, see John Steinbruner, *The Cybernetic Theory of Decision: New Dimensions of Political Analysis*, (Princeton, NJ: Princeton University Press, 1974), pp. 88–139; and Morton Halperin, *Bureaucratic Politics and Foreign Policy* (Washington, D.C.: Brookings Institution, 1974), pp. 11–16.

32.   Alexander George, *Presidential Decisionmaking in Foreign Policy: The Effective Use of Information and Advice* (Boulder, CO: Westview Press, 1982), p. 242.

33.   Robert Jervis, "Beliefs About Soviet Behavior," in *Containment, Soviet Behavior, and Grand Strategy*, ed. by Robert Osgood (Berkeley, CA: University of California Institute of International Studies, 1981), pp. 56–59.

34.   See Thomas Etzold and John Gaddis, eds., *Containment: Documents on American Policy and Strategy, 1945–1950* (New York: Oxford University Press, 1982), p. 89.

35.   This is a common perceptual impairment. See Alexander George, *Presidential Decision-Making in Foreign Policy: The Effective Use of Information and Advice* (Boulder, CO: Westview Press, 1980), pp. 48–49.

36.   See Alexander George and Richard Smoke, *Deterrence in American Foreign Policy: Theory and Practice* (New York: Columbia University Press, 1974); Alexander George, David Hall, and William Simons, *The Limits of Coercive Diplomacy: Laos, Cuba, Vietnam* (Boston: Little, Brown, 1971). Also see Leslie Gelb and Richard Betts, *The Irony of Vietnam: The System Worked* (Washington, D.C.: Brookings Institution, 1979), pp. 363–69.

37. This argument is also made by Dennis Ross (deputy director of the Office of Net Assessment, Department of Defense). See "Considering Soviet Threats to the Persian Gulf," Woodrow Wilson Center for International Security Studies, paper no. 29, September 1981, pp. 7–8.

38. George Breslauer, "The Dynamics of Soviet Policy toward the Arab-Israeli Conflict: Lessons of the Brezhnev Era," working paper #8 (Providence, RI: Brown University Center for Foreign Policy Development, Oct. 1983), p. 19, emphasis in original.

39. Seth Tillman, *The United States in the Middle East: Interests and Obstacles* (Bloomington: Indiana University Press, 1982), pp. 230–89.

40. Robert Jervis, *Perception and Misperception in International Politics* (Princeton, NJ: Princeton University Press, 1976), pp. 319–80; and John Steinbruner, *The Cybernetic Theory of Decision: New Dimensions of Political Analysis* (Princeton, NJ: Princeton University Press, 1974), pp. 88–139.

41. Davis Bobrow's study of Soviet perceptions, 1966–1980, found this to be the case ["Uncoordinated Giants," in *Foreign Policy USA/USSR*, ed. by Charles Kegley, Jr., and Pat McGowan (Beverly Hills, CA: Sage, 1982), p. 42].

42. See Ole Holsti and James Rosenau, *American Leadership in World Affairs: Vietnam and the Breakdown of Consensus* (Boston: Allen & Unwin, 1984), pp. 188, 229, 231, 233, 271, 282.

43. Franklyn Griffiths has completed one very interesting study of Soviet academic journals that finds four views of the sources of American foreign policy. The images he finds all share something in common with the "enemy" pattern but range from the very simple indicating intense threat to the quite complex indicating a more relaxed posture. He concludes as I do that in the late 1970s the simpler and more stereotypical views have prevailed over the more complex images and have led to more aggressive and competitive Soviet international behavior ["The Sources of American Conduct: Soviet Perspectives and Their Policy Implications," *International Security* 9 (Fall 1984), pp. 3–50].

44. Edward Jones and Richard Nisbett find that subjects tend to attribute their own actions to situational requirements and the actions of others to predispositional factors. Balance theory would predict that praiseworthy acts of an "enemy" would be attributed to situational requirements, and blameworthy acts to predisposition. It would predict the opposite interpretation of similar acts taken by the observer's country. See "The Actor and Observer: Divergent Perceptions of the Causes of Behavior," in *Attribution: Perceiving the Causes of Behavior*, ed. by Edward Jones et al. (Morristown, NJ: General Learning Press, 1971), pp. 79–94. Also see E. J. Phares, *Locus of Control in Personality* (Morristown, NJ: General Learning Press, 1976).

45. See Hans Morgenthau, *Politics among Nations: The Struggle for Power and Peace*, 5th ed. (New York: Knopf, 1973), pp. 4–7; and J. D. Singer, "The Levels of Analysis Problem in International Relations," in *The International System: Theoretical Essays*, ed. by Klaus Knorr and Sidney Verba (Princeton, NJ: Princeton University Press, 1961), pp. 77–92.

III
Ideology and Behavior

8

Ideology and Power Politics: A Symposium*

THE IMPORTANCE OF DOCTRINE

R. N. Carew Hunt

The term "ideology" is one which is more often used than defined. As the present study will be concerned with what the Russian Communists, and Communists in general, mean by it, a definition taken from a Soviet source is in order. The *Filosoficheskii Slovar* (Philosophical Dictionary, 1954 ed.), calls ideology "a system of definite views, ideas, conceptions, and notions adhered to by some class or political party," and goes on to say that it is always "a reflection of the economic system predominant at any given time." In a class-divided society the ideology will be that of one or another of the struggling classes, but under socialism, when there is no longer any class division, it will be that of society as a whole. A quotation from Lenin is added to the effect that there can be no "middle way" between the ideology of the bourgeoisie and that of the proletariat. The one is false and the other true.

Such a summation, albeit neat, is not altogether satisfactory. Broadly speaking, Marx was right in contending that the ideology of a society—the complex of ideas which determine its "way of life"—will be that of its dominant class, that is, of those whose abilities (whether used rightly or wrongly is irrelevant in this context) have raised them above the common herd. But this sociological fact applies equally to the Soviet Union, where the party certainly constitutes such a class and indeed is assigned the duty of fertilizing the masses with its ideas. Undoubtedly the current Soviet ideology is intended to strengthen the party and reinforce its claim to rule. But one must probe further to explain why the party should have adopted the particular body of doctrine that it has. The fact is that the ideology has been largely determined by the type of collective society which has been established in the Soviet Union.

The authors of the October Revolution were Marxists, and were thus committed to abolishing the capitalist system and replacing it by a nationwide planned

*Reprinted by permission of the authors from *Problems of Communism* VII, 2, (March-April 1953) and VII, 3 (May-June 1958).

economy. For a brief period the experiment of allowing the workers to take charge was tried out, but, when this led to chaos, the party assumed control and has ever since retained it.

If a Communist regime, is to be set up in a backward country, the first prerequisite, as Lenin saw, is industrialization; this is likely to be carried out as rapidly as possible, since the quicker the country is developed, and particularly its war potential, the stronger will be the position of its rulers. The execution of such a program of necessity demands the centralization of power in the hands of a small group of leaders, along with the adoption of such unpopular measures as the fixing of wages, the direction of labor, and the prohibition of strikes. And as large-scale planning geared to an expanding economy is impracticable if the plan is liable to be upset at any moment by a vote in a popular assembly, it is not to be expected that the planners will long tolerate any opposition. Furthermore, they will be tempted to interfere in one branch of human activity after another, seeing that all can be so manipulated as to assist the execution of their grand design.

All this has happened in the Soviet Union, and the outcome has been an ideology which derives from the logic of collectivism. Its basic principles are to be found in Marx's revolutionary doctrine, the implications of which were spelled out by Lenin and Stalin when confronted with the practical problem of setting up the type of social order Marx had advocated. Communist literature and propaganda have made us familiar with the doctrine, and there is no need to analyze it here even if space permitted. The issue to be decided is what role ideology plays today, and how far it influences Soviet policy.

Myths and the Masses

Virtually all analysts would agree that in the years of struggle before the October Revolution the Bolsheviks took the theory which lay behind their movement in deadly earnest; there is also general agreement that in the 1920's the doctrine acted as a stimulus to the workers, who took pride in building up their country. In the 1930's, however, the situation changed. Stalin assumed absolute power. The machinery of the state and of the secret police was greatly strengthened, and all prospect of establishing a genuine classless society disappeared. With the Stalin-Hitler Pact, if not before, the Soviet Union entered an era which can plausibly be represented as one of naked power politics, perpetuated after World War II in the aggressive and obstructive policies pursued by the regime. Hence it is sometimes argued that Communist ideology has now ceased to possess any importance; that it is simply a top-dressing of sophistries designed to rationalize measures inspired solely by Soviet interests; and that apart from a few fanatics, such as may be found in any society, no one believes in the doctrine any longer, least of all the leaders themselves.

Yet such unqualified assertions are erroneous. Consider, first, the outlook of the ordinary Soviet citizen vis-à-vis the ideology. Day in, day out, he is subjected to intensive and skillfully devised propaganda through every known medium, designed to demonstrate that the ideology on which the Soviet Union is based makes it the best of all possible worlds, and that on this account it is encircled with jealous enemies bent on its destruction. The Soviet leadership has always considered it essential that every citizen possess as deep an understanding of Communist principles as his mind is capable of assimilating, and those holding positions of consequence are obliged recurrently to pass through carefully graded schools of political instruction.

It is significant that whenever the leaders feel themselves in a tight corner—as in the recent aftermath of de-Stalinization and the intervention in Hungary—their invariable reaction is to intensify indoctrination in an attempt to refocus public attention on "first principles." As hard-headed men they would certainly not attach such importance to indoctrination if they did not know that it paid dividends—and experience has provided that the persistent repetition of a body of ideas which are never challenged is bound to influence the minds of their recipients. Of course, the present generation does not react to the formal ideology with the same fervor as did its forebears who made the revolution, and there are doubtless those who view official apologetics with a large degree of cynicism. But between total commitment and total disillusionment there are many intermediate positions; it is quite possible for a man to regard much of what he is told as nonsense while still believing that there is something of value behind it, especially if he identifies that "something" with the greatness of his country as "the first socialist state" and believes in its historic mission.

Leadership Credence—A Hope or a Habit?

More significant, in the present context, than the attitude of the ordinary citizen is that of the ruling elite which is responsible for policy. What its top-ranking members believe is a question which no one, of course, can answer positively. But before surmising, as do some analysts, that the Soviet leadership cannot possibly believe in the myths it propounds, we should remind ourselves that no class or party ever finds it difficult to persuade itself of the soundness of the principles on which it bases its claim to rule.

The Soviet leaders are fortified in this conviction by the very nature of their creed. They have been nurtured in it from birth, and it would be strange indeed if they had remained unaffected. It has become second nature to these men to regard history as a dialectical process—one of incessant conflict between progressive and reactionary forces which can only be resolved by the victory of the former. The division of the world into antagonistic camps, which is an article of faith, is simply the projection onto the international stage of the struggle within capitalistic society between the bourgeoisie, which history has condemned, and the proletariat, whose ultimate triumph it has decreed. The leaders seem to be confident that history is on their side, that all roads lead to communism, and that the contradictions of capitalism must create the type of situation, which they can turn to their advantage.

Democratic governments desirous of recommending a certain policy normally dwell upon its practical advantages. But in the Soviet Union this is not so. Any important change of line will be heralded by an article in *Pravda* often of many columns, purporting to show that the new policy is ideologically correct because it accords with some recent decision of a party congress, or with Lenin's teaching, or with whatever other criterion may be adopted. How far the policy in question will have been inspired by considerations of ideology as opposed to others of a more mundane nature can never be precisely determined. This, however, is not an exclusive feature of the Communist system; in politics, as for that matter in personal relations, it is seldom possible to disentangle all the motives which determine conduct. The policies of any party or government are likely to reflect its political principles even if they are so framed as to strengthen its position, and there is no reason why the policies adopted by the Soviet leaders should constitute an exception.

Analysts of the "power politics" school of thought hold that the Kremlin leaders are concerned solely with Soviet national interest, and merely use the Communist movement to promote it. Yet here again the difficulty is to disengage factors which are closely associated. The future of the Communist movement cannot be disassociated from the fortunes of the Soviet Union. If the Soviet regime were to collapse, that movement would count for little, and whether it would long survive even in China is doubtful. Recognizing this, non-Russian Communist parties generally have remained subservient to Moscow even when threatened with large-scale defections of rank-and-file members in the fact of particularly odious shifts in the Moscow line.

The "Separate Paths" Issue

The quarrel between the Soviet and the Yugoslav Communists parties—which an intergovernmental agreement of June 1956 has failed to resolve—is a good example of the interpenetration of ideological and non-ideological factors in policy determinations. The immediate occasion of the quarrel was Tito's unwillingness to allow the spread of Soviet influence through the presence of Soviet military officers and technological experts on Yugoslav soil. As a result Stalin determined to crush Tito, and resorted to various political and economic measures in an unsuccessful attempt to do so. It was at least a year before the struggle was extended to the ideological plane. But that it should have been was inevitable. One may well sympathize with Tito's desire for independence and hope that other national leaders will follow his example. Yet from the Communist point of view, if the movement is to be an international one, it must have an international center, and upon historical grounds alone Moscow has a strong claim to the mantle. Ever since Communist parties were formed, it was in fact to Moscow that their internal disputes were referred for settlement, just as it was Moscow which directed their general policy. Whether this role was performed well or ill is beside the point.

Hence the principle of "separate paths to socialism," approved by the Twentieth CPSU Congress for tactical reasons, is one which Moscow can accept only with reservations. If it merely means that in establishing communism in a given country consideration must be given to local conditions, and that every country's experience adds to the common store, then it is not only unobjectionable but is a salutary corrective to the earlier dogmatism which insisted on the universal applicability of the Russian experience. Such is the attitude nowadays expressed by Soviet theoreticians, though they insistently stress the dangers of exaggerating the importance of national characteristics, denying "the common laws of socialist development," or playing down the October Revolution. The official Soviet position is best expressed in an article in *New Times,* March 1956, which states that "while *serving as an example* to other working-class parties, the CPSU *draws upon their experience and formulates it in general theoretical principles* for the benefit of all working-class parties."

Clearly the Soviet leaders are on the defensive in this matter. They recognize that concessions must be made, but will make no more than they can help. The desire to perpetuate their own power doubtless influences their stand, but considering the fact that communism professes to be a world movement, it would be unreasonable to conclude that either national or personal interests are the sole factors motivating them.

Inefficiency—An Index of Ideology

Indeed, if the analysis given earlier in this article of the genesis of the Communist ideology is correct, the attitude of the Soviet leaders *must* be attributed at least in part, to the theoretical principles which distinguish Communist regimes from other forms of dictatorship. Certainly the leaders shape and phrase their domestic and foreign policies to fit the general framework established by these principles, and the latter often do not allow much room for maneuver. In fact, their application may sometimes weaken rather than strengthen the country.

To take a simple example, much waste would be avoided if small traders were permitted to operate on a profit basis; the fishmonger, for instance, would have an incentive to put his fish on ice, which he frequently fails to do to the discomfort of the public. Allowance of profits, however, would constitute a return to private enterprise, which cannot be tolerated.

Similarly, in the Communist view it has long been regarded as indefensible to subordinate a higher to lower form of socialized enterprise. Thus, while it has been apparent for years that Soviet agriculture would be more efficient if the Machine Tractor Stations (MTS) were handed over to the collective farms, the issue has been consistently dodged, because the MTS are fully state-owned organs and therefore "higher" than the farms, which still belong in part to the peasants. When the economist Venzher advocated this measure some years ago, he was slapped down at once by Stalin, the fact that it had already been adopted in Yugoslavia only making his suggestion the more objectionable. Just two years ago Khrushchev launched an extensive program to strengthen the organization and power of the MTS. Very recently, however, he indicated that the regime was—at long last—prepared to yield to practical necessity on this point; in a speech on farm policy, he advocated the transfer of farm machinery to the collectives, and although his proposals are not yet legalized, it would appear that a number of MTS have already been dissolved.

The principle of hierarchy has not been repudiated, however, and still governs other aspects of agricultural organization—for example, the relative status of the two forms of agricultural enterprise. From the standpoint of productive efficiency the collective farms are bad, but the state farms are worse. Nonetheless, the latter represent a "higher type" of organization, and thus the present virgin lands campaign has been based upon them.

Dogmatism in Foreign Policy

The same point can be scored by examining the Soviet Union's treatment of its satellites. Poland affords a good example. With the country at its mercy after World War II, the Soviet regime decided, among other measures, to integrate the Polish economy with its own. Now had Poland been regarded merely as a colony to be exploited, the operation would have been viewed primarily as a business proposition, and due attention would have been paid to such questions as the nature of the country's resources and the aptitudes of its people. The need to proceed with caution was very evident. The traditional hostility of the Poles to everything Russian should have been taken into account, as well as the fact that the Polish Communist Party had no public support (due in part to the liquidation of its established leaders during the Great Purges). Yet it was decided that the country must pass through, in shorter time intervals, precisely those stages of development which the Soviet Union had traversed. The result was a serious disruption of the economy through the erection of a top-heavy industrial structure on the basis of a depressed agriculture. This policy cannot be attributed to Stalin alone as it was continued after his death. It proved disastrous, and is only intelligible on the assumption that it was primarily motivated by ideological considerations.

The argument can be carried further. By its behavior throughout its history, the Soviet Union has incurred the hostility, or at least the suspicion, of the entire free world. Yet there was no practical reason why it should have done so. After the October Revolution the Bolshevik regime was faced with appalling domestic problems, and it had nothing to gain by courting the animosity of the West. The Soviet leaders might well have built up their country in accordance with the principles to which they were committed without exciting such widespread hostility. What governments do at home is commonly regarded as their own affair. Fundamentally, the regime in Yugoslavia is as Communist as that of the Soviet Union, and was established with an equal ruthlessness. But Tito, having asserted his independence from Moscow, has muffed his attacks on the West, and in turn the Western governments have demonstrated their desire—albeit tempered with caution—to believe in his good faith.

What no country will tolerate is the attempt, deliberately engineered by a foreign power, to overthrow its form of government; this has been the persistent aim and effort of the Soviet regime in defiance of its express diplomatic guarantees of noninterference. It is hard to see how this strategy has assisted the development of Soviet Russia, and that it has never been abandoned cannot be dissociated from those messianic and catastrophic elements in the Communist creed which influence, perhaps impel, the Soviet drive for world power.

In conclusion, it is frequently stated that communism has created an ideological cleavage between the West and the Soviet bloc. Yet his statement would be meaningless if the issue today were, as some believe, simply one of power politics. An ideology is significant only if it makes those who profess it act in a away they would not otherwise do. The fact that large numbers of persons accept communism would not constitute a danger if it did not lead them to support policies which threaten the existence of those who do not accept it. It is true that many people, especially in backward countries, call themselves Communists without having any clear idea so what it means. Yet the movement would not be the force it has become were there not in every country men and women who sincerely believe in the ideas behind it which form collectively what we call its ideology.

To represent this ideology as a species of opium with which the Soviet leaders contrive to lull the people while taking care never to indulge in it themselves is to attribute to them an ability to dissociate themselves from the logic of their system—an ability which it is unlikely they possess. For the concepts which make up that system, fantastic as many of them appear to be, will be found on examination to be interrelated, and to be logical extensions of the basic principles to which all Communists subscribe.

To turn it the other way around, Communists claim a theoretical justification for the basic principles in which they believe. But these principles must be translated into appropriate action; and action, if directed by the rulers of a powerful country like the Soviet Union, will take the form of *Realpolitik*. There is no yardstick which permits a measure of the exact relationship between power politics and ideology in the policies which result; but surely neither factor can be ignored.

NATIONAL INTEREST: KEY TO SOVIET POLITICS

Samuel L. Sharp

An enormous body of Western research and analysis focuses on Marxist-Leninist ideology as a clue to understanding Kremlin policy. This extensive and intensive preoccupation with matters doctrinal is, at least in part, the result of a rather widely circulated belief that the democratic world was guilty of neglect when it refused to take seriously the "theoretical" writings and pronouncements of Adolf Hitler. It has been alleged that these writings later guided Hitler's actions and that a ready key to his conduct was thus overlooked.

When, at the end of World War II, the Soviet Union appeared on the international scene as a power—and a menace—of the first order, led by a group consistently claiming its adherence to a body of doctrine as a guide to action, legions of experts began to dissect that body in a search for a key to Soviet behavior, current and future. The material at hand was certainly more promising than the intellectually scrawny homunculus of Nazi or Fascist "ideology." After all, Marxism has its not entirely disreputable roots in legitimate Western thought. Even in terms of sheer bulk there was more to operate on, what with Lenin's and Stalin's additions and modifications of the original scriptures and the voluminous exegetic output of a generation of Soviet propagandists.

The massive study of Communist ideology has had one happy result in that some serious scholarly output has been provided to counterbalance party-line apologias, thereby destroying a number of primitive notions concerning the Soviet system and what makes it tick. At the same time, this writer's view, preoccupation with the search for a formula of interpretative and predictive value has produced its own distortions. These distortions seem to be the composite result of cold-war anxieties, faulty logic, and disregard of some of the elementary principles and practices of international relations. To these causes must be added the human tendency to look beyond the simple and obvious for the complicated and mysterious in attempting to explain any condition which is exasperating and which is therefore perceived as strange and unique. Baffled by the Soviet phenomenon, millions in the Western world have found a negative consolation of sorts in the famous statement by Winston Churchill that Russian policy is "a riddle wrapped in a mystery inside an enigma." But how many have bothered to read the qualifying words which followed? Having disclaimed ability to forecast Soviet actions, Churchill added: *But perhaps there is a key. That key is Russian national interest.*[1]

Clearly implied in this observation was the logical supposition that the policy-makers of the Soviet Union act in what they believe to be the best interest of the state over whose destinies they are presiding. In this sense the Soviet Union is to be looked upon as an actor, a protagonist, on the stage of international politics; and in this writer's view, its actions can be interpreted most fruitfully in terms of behavior *germane* to the practice of international politics. Without denying the possible pitfalls of this approach, the writer proposes to argue its usefulness as a key to understanding a phenomenon which the non-Communist world can ill afford to envelop in a fog of self-generated misinterpretation.

The Doubtful Art of Quotation

Whenever the suggestion is made that the concept of national interest be applied as an explanation of Soviet behavior on the international scene, objections are raised in many quarters. The most vigorous protests come, of course, from Soviet sources. It is a standard claim of Soviet spokesmen that their state is by definition something "different" (or "higher") and that the foreign policy of this entity is different in principle (*printsipialno otlichna*) from that of other states because the latter are capitalist and the former is socialist.[2] It would seem that only uncritical adherents of communism could take such statements seriously. Yet non-Communists very often cite them as a convenient *ipse dixit* in support of their own claim that the Soviet Union is indeed "different," though not in the way Soviet propaganda wants one to believe. The claim is that the Soviet Union is, at best, "a conspiracy disguised as a state" and cannot be viewed as a "normal" member of the world community of nations. There is no attempt to explain on what basis some Soviet statements are to be taken as reliable indices of regime motivations, while other statements, no less abundantly scattered throughout the Marxist-Leninist scriptures, are rejected as lie and deception.

It is surely dubious scholarship to collect quotations (sometimes reduced to half a sentence) from Lenin and Stalin without regard to the time, place, circumstances, composition of the audience, and, whenever ascertainable, immediate purposes of such utterances. What results from such compilations, no matter how laboriously and ingeniously put together, is, as a thoughtful critic has pointed out, "a collection of such loose generalizations and so many exceptions and contradictions that few readers can find much guidance in it."[3] Stalin, for example, can be quoted as once having said that "with a diplomat words must diverge from facts" and that "a sincere diplomat would equal dry water, wooden iron"; yet this not too astute observation was made in 1913 in an article dealing with bourgeois diplomacy written by an obscure Georgian revolutionary who probably had never met a diplomat. His view in this instance is identifiable as a variant of the classic image of the diplomat as "an honorable gentleman sent abroad to lie for his country." This image may very well have stayed with the congenitally suspicious and pessimistic Stalin in later life, and thus might indeed afford us a clue to his "real" nature. However, sound scholarship would seek to reconstruct the attitudes of the Kremlin ruler out of words and deeds of a more relevant period of his life rather than from this loose piece of Djugashvili prose torn out of context.

The Vital Factor of Feasibility

Some objections to the interpretation of Soviet policies in terms of national interest are rooted in the aforementioned line of analysis which conjures up the ghost of Adolf Hitler. The democracies erred, did they not, in initially looking upon Hitler's aims as an expression of "legitimate" (we will return to this phrase in a moment)—however distasteful—national aspirations, only to discover later that they were dealing with a maniac whose appetites were unlimited. Since it is generally agreed that Soviet policy, like Hitler's, belongs to the totalitarian species, would it not be impardonable to repeat the same mistake by looking upon the aims of the Soviet leaders as the expression of the aspirations of a "normal" nation-state?

Two points should be made here. First, Hitler bears comparison with no one;

there is no other leader in history who has combined his precise mental makeup with his enormous concentration of power. He was, as his biographer Allan Bullock pointed out, a man "without aims," that is, without *limited* and therefore tractable aims.[4] At one point in his career Hitler began to disregard the cardinal rule of politics—the necessity of aligning ambitions with capacity to translate them into reality. He broke the barrier of the *feasible,* motivated by what could most likely be diagnosed as the death-wish. Whatever else may be said about the Soviet leaders, no one, including people who suspect them of ideological self-deception, has denied them the quality of caution. Far from seeking self-destruction, they are lustily bent on survival. This in itself, even in the complete absence of scruples, makes their aims *limited.*

Mr. Carew Hunt argues elsewhere in these pages that there are "messianic and catastrophic elements in the Communist creed which influence . . . the Soviet drive for world power." While there may indeed be a degree of messianism in the Soviet leadership's view of its mission, the "catastrophic" tendency seems to be held carefully in check. Hitler was propelled by the absurd notion that he had to accomplish certain aims before he reached the age of sixty—an arrogant and, from the point of view of German national interest, totally irrelevant assumption. Granted that the Soviet leaders aim at "world power" (a concept which in itself should be defined more explicitly than it usually is), they have long since decided not to fix any specific time limit for the achievement of this ultimate aim. Certainly the present generation of leaders has acted to modify (perhaps "refine" is a better word) the aggressive drive for power abroad at least to an extent which will allow some enjoyment at home of the tangible fruits of the revolution this side of the Communist heaven. Even back in the early days of Bolshevik rule, Lenin, though at times carried away by expectations of spreading revolution, never sacrificed practical caution to missionary zeal; repeatedly he warned his followers to look after the "bouncing baby" (the Soviet state), since Europe was only "pregnant with revolution" (which it wasn't).

An Applicable Concept of Interest

The second point to be made is a crucial one. Reluctance to analyze Soviet aims in terms of national interest is due, in part, to the aura of legitimacy which surrounds the "normal" run of claims of nation-states, giving rise to the notion that the term itself infers something legitimate. However, suggesting that Kremlin moves can best be understood in terms of what the leaders consider advantageous to the Soviet state by no means implies subscribing to their aims or sympathizing with them. In international relations the maxim *tout comprendre c'est tout pardonner* does not apply. The concept of national interest, by focusing attention on the *objective sources of conflict*—that is, those which *can* be explained rationally as issues between nations—permits us to view the international scene in terms of a global problem of power relations rather than a cops-and-robbers melodrama. We can then perceive which are the *tractable* elements in the total equation of conflict, and devote our energies to reducing or altering these factors.

This approach seems to the writer to be indispensable both to the scholar and to the statesman. The scholar who accepts the "natural" (in terms of the nature of international politics) explanation for Kremlin behavior is not likely to violate the "law of parsimony" by unnecessarily piling up hypotheses which are unprovable and which in any case simply confuse the issue, insofar as dealing practically with the Soviet Union is concerned. The statesman finds that he is coping with a phenomenon which he knows how to approach both in accommodation and in opposition, rather than with some occult and other-worldly force.

Those who object to the framework of analysis where proposed would say, as does Mr. Hunt, that there are many cases on record when the Soviet leaders have acted in a way clearly inconsistent with the Russian national interest and intelligible only in terms of ideological dogmatism. The answer to this argument is simple: it does not matter what Mr. Hunt—or anybody else—considers to be the Russian national interest; as the term is defined here, the only view which matters is that held by the Soviet leaders. By the same token it is a rather fruitless thing to speak of "legitimate" vs. "illegitimate" Soviet interests. One of the essential attributes of sovereignty (and the Soviet leaders are certainly jealous where their own is involved!) is that it is up to the sovereign to determine what serves him best.

Yet doesn't this reasoning render pointless the entire conceptual approach proposed? If Soviet national interest is what the Soviet leaders take it to be, and if one agrees—as one must—that their view of the world is derived largely from their adherence to Marxism—Leninism, isn't this another way of saying that Soviet behavior is the result of ideological conditioning? Not quite. The point at issue is whether the "pure" Soviet view of the world is important *as a guide to action,* whether the *ultimate* aims of the Communist creed are operative in policy determinations. In the present writer's view they are not; the fault of the opposing line of analysis is that in dwelling on the supposed impact of ideology on the leadership, it tends to ignore the degree to which the pursuit of ultimate goals has been circumscribed in time and scope by considerations of *the feasible.* In simple arithmetic, doctrine minus those aspects which are not empirically operative equals empirically determined policy. If a policy action is called "revolutionary expediency," it is still expediency. Why then introduce into the equation an element which does not affect the result?

A supporting view in this respect is W. W. Rostow's characterization of Soviet foreign policy as a series of responses to the outside world which, especially before 1939, "took the form of such actions as were judged most likely, *on a short-range basis,* to maintain or expand the national power of the Soviet regime." Despite the Soviet Union's vastly greater ability to influence the world environment in the postwar era, says Rostow, "there is no evidence that the foreign policy criteria of the regime have changed."[5] If some instances of

Soviet behavior appear to have produced results actually detrimental to the Soviet interest, we must not only refrain from applying our view of Soviet interest but also—as Rostow's viewpoint suggests—judge the policy decisions involved in terms of their validity at the time they were made and not in the light of what happened later (remembering, too, that mistakes and miscalculations are common to all policy-makers, not just those who wear "ideological blinders").

The words "on a short-range basis" have been underscored above to stress that the term "policy," if properly applied, excludes aims, ambitions, or dreams not accompanied by action visibly and within a reasonable time capable of producing the results aimed at or dreamed of. In the case of the Soviet leaders, concentration on short-range objectives and adjustment to political realities has, in the brilliant phrase suggested by Barrington Moore, Jr., *caused the means to eat up the ends.*[6]

The objection will still be raised that the Soviet leaders mouth every policy decision in terms of ideological aims. Enough should have been said on this score to obviate a discussion here; as able students of the problem have pointed out, the Soviet leaders' claim to rule rests on their perpetuation of the ideology and their insistence on orthodoxy; they have no choice but to continue paying lip-service to the doctrine, even if it is no longer operative. The liberal mind somehow balks at this image of total manipulation, of an exoteric doctrine for public consumption which has no connection with its esoteric counterpart—that is, the principles or considerations which really govern Kremlin behavior. Yet allowance must be made for this possibility.

Moscow and International Communism

One serious argument of those who reject the image of the Soviet Union as a "legitimate" participant in the balance-of-power game played in the arena of international politics is that the Soviet leaders consistently violate the rules of the game by enlisting out-of-bounds help from foreign Communist parties. This point invites the following brief observations:

1. Early in its history the Communist International was transformed into a tool of Soviet foreign policy, at a time when few other tools were available to Moscow.

2. As soon as the Soviet state felt at all sure of its survival (after the period of civil war, foreign intervention, and economic chaos), it reactivated the apparatus of foreign policy along more traditional lines.

3. Under Stalin, the Third International was reduced to a minor auxiliary operation. An index of his attitude toward it is the fact that he never once addressed a Comintern congress. Probably the International was kept up in the interwar period because it seemed to produce marginal dividends in terms of nuisance value. Moreover, Stalin could hardly have divorced himself from it officially at a time when he was jockeying for total power inside Russia, since this would have helped to confirm his opponents' accusations that he was

"betraying the revolution." But he certainly did everything to show his belief in the ineffectiveness of the organization and its foreign components as against the growing power of the Soviet state.

4. When the entire record of Soviet success and failure is summed up, the achievements are clearly attributable to Soviet power and diplomacy with no credit due to the international Communist movement. Furthermore, the ties between the Soviet Union and foreign parties have never deterred Moscow from useful alliances or cooperation with other governments—including, from one time to another, the astutely anti-Communist Turkish government of Ataturk; the more brutally anti-Communist regime of Adolf Hitler; and, during World War II, the Western powers. That the Soviet leaders, by virtue of their doctrine, entertained mental reservations about the durability of friendly relations with these governments can hardly be doubted. But it is equally clear that the cessation of cooperation was due in each case to the workings of power politics rather than Soviet ideological dictate—that is, to the historical tendency of alliances to disintegrate when what binds them (usually a common enemy) disappears.

5. Finally, it might be argued that the Soviet appeal to foreign Communist parties is not dissimilar to the practice of various governments of different periods and persuasions to appeal for support abroad on the basis of some sort of affinity—be it Hispanidad, Slav solidarity, Deustschtum, or Pan-Arabism. The Soviet appeal is admittedly broader and the "organizational weapon" seems formidable, but their importance should not be exaggerated. Actually, there is no way at all to measure the effectiveness of the appeal *per se* since Communist "success" or "failure" in any situation always involves a host of other variables—including military, geographical, social, political, or economic factors. In the last analysis, virtually every instance where Moscow has claimed a victory for communism has depended on Soviet manipulation of traditional levers of national influence.

An Exception to Prove the Rule

There remains one area of Soviet "foreign policy" where the Soviet leaders have supplemented power politics—or more accurately in this instance naked force—with an attempt to derive special advantage, a sort of "surplus value," from claiming ideological obeisance to the Soviet Union as the seat of the secular church of communism. This area is the so-called Soviet orbit in Eastern Europe.

The term "foreign policy" is enclosed in quotation marks here because Stalin obviously did not consider areas under the physical control of Soviet power as nations or governments to be dealt with in their own right. He was clearly impatient with the claim of at least some Communist parties that their advent to power had changed the nature of their relationship to Moscow, and that the party-to-party level of relations must be separated from the government-to-government level (as Gomulka argued in 1948). In Stalin's thinking, especially after 1947, the East European regimes were not eligible for more real sovereignty than the "sovereign" republics of the Soviet Union. He attempted to extend the principle of *democratic centralism* (a euphemism for Kremlin control) to these countries, allowing them only as much of a facade of sovereignty as was useful for show toward the outside world.

One need not necessarily dig into doctrine to explain this attitude; in fact, doctrine until recently said nothing at all about relations between sovereign Communist states. The explanation lies to a large extent in Stalin's personal predilection for total control, plus the need to tighten Moscow's bonds to the limit, by whatever means or arguments possible, in the face of the bipolarization of global power after World War II.

Stalin's successors began by pressing the same claims of ideological obeisance from the satellites. But rather striking—in the same period that their foreign policy has scored substantial successes in other areas in traditional terms of diplomatic advances and manipulation of the economic weapon[7]—they have failed in the one area where they attempted to substitute the ties of ideology for the give-and-take of politics. Communist parties in power, it turned out (first in the case of Yugoslavia, while Stalin still reigned, and later in Poland, not to mention the very special case of China), claimed the right to be sovereign—or at least semi-sovereign—actors on the international scene. Whether or not this makes sense ideologically to the Soviet leaders is unimportant; they have recognized the claim.

It is not necessary to review here the post-Stalin history of fluctuating Soviet relations with Eastern Europe which began with the B. & K. pilgrimage to Belgrade. Let us take only the most recent attempt to reformulate the nature of relations between the USSR and other Communist countries—the inter-party declaration issued on the occasion of the fortieth anniversary of the Bolshevik revolution. On the surface, the declaration, published in the name of twelve ruling Communist parties, seems to reimpose a pattern of ideological uniformity as well as to recognize the special leadership position of the Soviet Union.[8] However, the circumstances of the gathering and the internal evidence of the declaration, together with the reports of some of the participants, show a far more complex situation.

The following aspects of the conference deserve attention: First, the very fact that the parties representing governments of sovereign countries were singled out for a special meeting and declaration instead of being lumped together with the mass of parties (many of them illegal, some leading no more than a paper existence) is a significant departure from past practice. Second, the Yugoslav party, though represented at the festivities, refused to sign the declaration, apparently after long negotiations. Third, attempts to revive in any form an international, Moscow-based organization resembling the Comintern were unsuccessful. Gomulka's report on the meeting made it clear that the Polish party opposed both a new Comintern (for which it nevertheless had a few good words) and a new Cominform (for which it had nothing but scorn).[9]

A point of particular significance was the revelation that future international gatherings of Communist parties, especially those in power, are to be based on previous agreements concerning the agenda. According to Gomulka, problems which each party thinks it can best solve *for itself and its country* will not be decided by interparty conferences.[10]

Perhaps most significant for the purposes of the present discussion was a statement by Mao Tse-tung, who next to Khrushchev and Suslov was the main speaker at the meeting of the "ruling" parties and was billed as co-sponsor of the declaration. Mao bolstered his argument for the recognition of the leading position of the Soviet Union in the "socialist camp" with the remark that "China has not even one-fourth of a sputnik while the Soviet Union has two."[11] Now, the possession of a sputnik is a symbol of achievement and a source of prestige for the Soviet Union, but certainly not in terms of ideology. It was Soviet national power to which Mao paid deference.

In sum, the entire circumstances of the gathering indicate a disposition on the part of the Soviet Union to substitute—wherever it has to—the give-and-take of politics for its former relationship with the orbit countries, which relied on naked power to enforce demands of ideological subservience.

From all the foregoing, it should be clear that the task of the non-Communist world is not to worry itself sick over the ultimate goals of the Soviet leadership or the degree of its sincerity, but to concentrate on multiplying situations in which the Soviet Union either will be forced or will choose to play the game of international politics in an essentially traditional setting. How the Kremlin leaders will square this with their Marxist conscience is not really our problem.

THE LOGIC OF ONE-PARTY RULE

Richard Lowenthal

To what extent are the political decisions of the Soviet leadership influenced by its belief in an official ideology—and to what extent are they empirical responses to specific conflicts of interest, expressed in ideological terms merely for purposes of justification? The phrasing of the question at issue suggests the two extreme answers which are *prima facie* conceivable—on the one hand, that ideology provides the Kremlin with a ready-made book of rules to be looked up in any situation; on the other, that its response to reality takes place without any reference to ideology. Yet any clear formulation of this vital issue will show that both extremes are meaningless nonsense.

A ready-made book of rules for any and every situation—an unvarying roadmap to the goal of communism which the Soviet leaders must predictably follow—cannot possibly exist, both because the situations to be met by them are not sufficiently predictable, and because no government which behaved in so calculable a manner could conceivably retain power. On the other hand, empirical *Realpolitik* without ideological preconceptions can exist as little as can "empirical science" without categories and hypotheses based on theoretical speculation. Confronted with the same constellation of interests and pressures,

the liberal statesman will in many cases choose a different course of action from
the conservative—and the totalitarian Communist's choice will often be different
from that of either.

It seems surprising, therefore, that at this late stage of discussion Professor
Sharp is apparently in earnest in defending the extreme of the *Realpolitik*
interpretation and in denying completely the relevance of Communist ideology
for the formation, and hence the understanding, of Soviet foreign policy. The
latter, he assures us, can be adequately understood in terms of national interest,
just as with any other state. When reminded by Mr. Carew Hunt of certain
irrational features of Soviet foreign policy, he replies that what matters is not any
outsider's concept of Soviet interests, but the Soviet leaders' own. Yet this
reduces his thesis to a tautology: he "proves" that national interest motivates
Soviet foreign policy by the simple device of labeling whatever motivates it
"national interest."

Surely Professor Sharp cannot have it both ways. Either there are objective
criteria of national interest, recognizable by the scholar—and then the view that
these interests explain Soviet actions is capable of proof or refutation; or else it is
admitted that different statesmen may interpret national interest in different but
equally "legitimate" ways—and then the concept of a self-continued study of
international relations collapses, because a consideration of the internal structures of different national communities and of the "ideologies" reflecting them
becomes indispensable for an understanding of their foreign policies.

The latter observation does not, of course, apply to Communist states alone,
although it is only reasonable to expect the influence of the monopolistic
ideology of a single-party state to be specially pervasive. Mr. George Kennan, in
his 1950 lectures on American diplomacy, has convincingly shown the relevance
of ideological factors to an understanding of modern United States foreign policy
as well. To deny this influence *a priori* and to admit, as Professor Sharp
apparently would, only the *Ding an sich* of national interest on one side, and the
accidental element of human error or pathology (such as Hitler's "death-wish")
on the other, seems to this writer to be an unjustifiable renunciation of one of the
limited roads to understanding which are available to present-day political
science.

The Function of Doctrine

Assuming, then, that the Soviet leaders' ideology is relevant to their conduct,
the real problem remains to discover which are the actual operative elements in
it, and in what way they affect policy decisions. Clearly it would be folly to
expect that Soviet policy could be predicted solely from an exegetic study of the
Marxist-Leninist canon. Not only is it impossible for any group of practical
politicians to base their decisions on an unvarying book of rules; there is any
amount of historical evidence to show that the rules have been altered again and
again to fit the practical decisions *ex post facto*. Moreover, there are vast parts of
the Communist ideological structure, such as the scholastic refinements of

"dialectical materialism" or the labor theory of value, which in their nature are so remote from the practical matters to be decided that their interpretation cannot possibly affect policy decisions. They may be used in inner-party arguments to *justify* what has been decided on other grounds, but that is all.

How, then, are we to distinguish those elements of Soviet ideology which are truly operative politically from those which are merely traditional scholastic ballast, linked to the operative elements by the historical accident of the founding fathers' authorship? The answer is to be found by going back to the original Marxian meaning of the term "ideology"—conceived as a distorted reflection of social reality in the consciousness of men, used as an instrument of struggle. The fundamental, distinctive social reality in the Soviet Union is the rule of the bureaucracy of a single, centralized, and disciplined party, which wields a monopoly of political, economic, and spiritual power and permits no independent groupings of any kind. The writer proposes as a hypothesis that the operative parts of the ideology are those which are indispensable for maintaining and justifying this state of affairs: "Marxism-Leninism" matters inasmuch as it expresses, in an ideologically distorted form, the logic of one-party rule.[12]

Totalitarian Parallels

There are a few interconnected ideological features which are common to all the totalitarian regimes of our century—whether of the nationalist-fascist or of the Communist variety. We may designate them as the elements of chiliasm, of collective paranoia, and of the representative fiction. Each totalitarian regime justifies its power and its crimes by the avowed conviction, first, that its final victory will bring about the Millennium—whether defined as the final triumph of communism or of the master race—and second, that this state of grace can only be achieved by an irreconcilable struggle against a single, omnipresent, and multiform enemy—whether Monopoly Capitalism or World Jewry—whose forms include every particular opponent of the totalitarian power. Each also claims to represent the true will of the people—the *volonté générale*—independent of whether the people actually support it, and argues that any sacrifice may be demanded from the individual and the group for the good of the people and the defeat of its devilish enemies.

The Communist version of these basic beliefs is superior to the Nazi version in one vital respect. Because the appeal of racialism is in its nature restricted to a small minority of mankind, the Nazis' goal of world domination could not possibly have been attained without a series of wars, preferably surprise attacks launched against isolated opponents. Because the appeal of communism is directed to all mankind, it can be linked with the further doctrine of the inevitable victory of the rising forces of socialism over the imperialist enemy, which is disintegrating under the impact of its own internal contradictions. This central ideological difference, and not merely the psychological difference between Hitler and the Soviet leaders, explains why the latter are convinced that history is no their side and that they need not risk the survival of their own regime in any attempt to hasten its final triumph: they believe in violence, revolutionary and military, as one of the weapons of policy, but they do not believe in the inevitability of world war.

Awkward Aims and Claims

Yet the Communist version of totalitarian ideology also suffers from some weaknesses and contradictions from which the Nazi and Fascist versions are free. In the first place, its vision of the Millennium has more markedly utopian features—the classless society, the end of exploitation of man by man, the withering away of the state—which make awkward yardsticks for the real achievements of Communist states. Second, in a world where nationalism remains a force of tremendous strength, an internationalist doctrine is bound to come into conflict with the interests of any major Communist power, or with the desire of smaller Communist states for autonomy.

Third, by rejecting the "Fuehrer principle" and claiming to be "democratic," Communist ideology makes the realities of party dictatorship and centralistic discipline more difficult to justify; yet because appeal to blind faith is not officially permitted, justification is needed in "rational" terms. It is precisely this continuous need for the pretense of rational argument—the awkward heritage of communism's origin from revolutionary Western democracy—which has led to the far greater elaboration of its ideology compared to that of "irrationalist" right-wing totalitarianism, and which gives it constant interpretation so much greater importance in preserving the cohesion of the party regime. Due to the fictions of democracy and rationality, the morale of party cadres has been made dependent on the appearance of ideological consistency.

The result of these inherent weaknesses of Communist ideology is that the component doctrines—dealing with the "dictatorship of the proletariat," the party's role as a "vanguard" embodying the "true" class consciousness, "democratic centralism," "proletarian internationalism," and the "leading role of the Soviet Union"—become focal points of ideological crises and targets of "revisionist" attacks whenever events reveal the underlying contradictions in a particularly striking way. Yet these are the very doctrines which the regime cannot renounce because they are the basic rationalizations of its own desire for self-preservation.

We can expect, then, that Communist ideology will have an effective influence on the policy decisions of Soviet leaders when, and only when, it expresses the needs of self-preservation of the party regime. We can further expect that ideological changes and disputes within the Communist "camp" will offer clues to the conflicts and crises—the "contradictions"—which are inseparable from the evolution of this, as of any other, type of society. The fruitful approach, in this writer's view, consists neither in ignoring Communist ideology as an irrelevant disguise, nor in accepting it at its face value and treating it as a subject for exegesis, but in using it as an indicator of those specific drives and problems which spring from the specific structure of Soviet society—in regarding it as an enciphered, continuous self-disclosure, whose cipher can be broken by sociological analysis.

Two Camps—One Enemy

Let us now apply this approach to the doctrine of the "two camps" in world affairs. The "two-camp " concept was not, of course, a Stalinist invention, although this is sometimes supposed. The postwar situation with its alignment of the Communist and Western powers in two openly hostile politico-military blocs merely gave plausibility to a world image which was inherent in Leninism from the beginning, but which attracted little attention in the period when the Communist "camp" was just an isolated fortress with several outposts. Nor has the doctrine disappeared with the post-Stalin recognition of the importance of the uncommitted, ex-colonial nations and of the tactical value of incorporating them in a "peace zone;" it remains one of the basic ideas of the Moscow twelve-party declaration of last November and one of the fundamental subjects of the ideological disagreement between the Soviets and the Yugoslav Communists.

The Yugoslavs can reject the "two-camp" doctrine because they admit the possibility of "roads to socialism" other than Communist party dictatorship—"reformist" roads for advanced industrial countries with parliamentary traditions, "national revolutionary" roads for ex-colonial countries. It follows from this view that Communist states have no monopoly on progress, and that alliances have no ultimate ideological meaning.

The Soviets still assert that while there can be different roads to Communist power, and minor differences in the use of power once gained, there is no way of achieving socialism except by the "dictatorship of the proletariat exercised by its vanguard." It follows that tactical agreements with semi-socialist neutrals are not different in kind from the wartime alliance with the Western "imperialists," or the prewar pact with Hitler—maneuvers which are useful in dividing the forces of the "class enemy" but which remain subordinate to the fundamental division of the world into the Communists versus the Rest.

In other words, the "two-camp" doctrine is the Communist version of what we have called the element of "collective paranoia" in totalitarian ideology—its need for a single, all-embracing enemy which is assumed to pull the wires of every resistance to the party's power. The term "paranoia" is used here not to infer that the phenomenon in question is due to psychotic processes in either the leaders or the mass following of totalitarian parties, but merely to describe, through a convenient psychological analogy, the ideological mechanism of projection which ascribes the regime's drive for unlimited power to an imagined all-enemy. The essential point is that in the nature of totalitarianism, any independent force—either inside or outside the state—is regarded as ultimately hostile; the concept of "two camps" and that of "unlimited aims" are two sides of the same phenomenon.

Moscow's Double-Indemnity Tactics

Now Professor Sharp is, of course, entirely right in asking where this doctrine impinges on actual Soviet foreign policy—given the undoubled facts that actual Soviet aims, and the risks incurred in their pursuit, are limited at any given moment; that the Soviets are perfectly capable of concluding "temporary" alliances with "bourgeois," "imperialist," or even "fascist" states; and that most other alliances in this impermanent world are proving to be "temporary" as well, for quite nonideological reasons. The present writer would suggest to him that the difference has manifested itself in the peculiar suspicion with which the Soviets treated their "imperialist" allies even at the height of the war, seeking in particular to isolate their own population from contact; in the manner in which they sought to create additional "guarantees" for the reliability of those allies by the use of local Communist parties wherever this was possible, and above all, in the difference between the traditional and the Communist concepts of "spheres of influence" as illuminated by the different interpretations of Yalta agreements.

The peculiar forms taken by Moscow's suspicion of its wartime allies are too well known to need elaboration here; but it is less generally realized that such behavior was merely the reverse side of Soviet efforts to "strengthen" such temporary alliances where possible, by the use of party ties. Existence of the party channel has not, of course, been a *sine qua non* fro Moscow's intragovernmental deals, as is shown by the examples of Russo-Turkish cooperation after World War I, the Stalin-Hitler pact, and perhaps also present Soviet cooperation with Egypt. But wherever Communist parties were tolerated by the partner, Soviet foreign policy has assigned to them a vital role. Indeed, the implication that Stalin never used the foreign Communists for any important purposes is perhaps the most astonishing aspect of Professor Sharp's article.

In the 1920's, Stalin's Chinese policy was openly run in double harness; diplomatic support for the Nationalist advance to the North was supplemented by an agreement of affiliation between the Chinese Communist Party and the Kuomintang, enabling the Communist to occupy influential political and military positions—an attempt no less serious for its ultimate total failure in 1927. In the 1930's, a variant of the same "dual policy" was evident when Moscow supported the League and "collective security," while Communist parties in France and Spain pursued "popular front" policies which soft-pedalled economic and social demands for the sake of influencing governmental foreign policy. In the Spanish case the Communists, aided by the Republicans' dependence on Soviet supplies, ended up in virtual control of the republic on the eve of its final collapse.

Again during World War II, Communists in the resistance movements and in the free Western countries were ordered to pursue the same tactics of social moderation and occupation of key positions as were practiced in China in the 1920's and Spain in the 1930's. Wartime military and political cooperation between "Soviet China" and Chiang Kai-shek was urged in the same spirit, with considerable success. All these are the foreign policy methods of a state *sui generis*—a one-party state enabled by its ideology to make use of a disciplined international movement organized for the struggle for power. To compare them—and the secondary opportunities for infiltration and espionage which they offer in addition to their main political objectives—to the use of vague cultural influences like "Hispanidad" is to show a notable degree of innocence.

Yalta—A Historic "Misunderstanding"

The crucial example to illustrate the role of ideology in Soviet foreign policy, however, remains the history of the postwar division of Europe. The writer is not concerned here with the political controversy over whether this division, as first laid down in the wartime agreements at Teheran and Yalta, was inevitable in the light of the military situation as seen at the time, or whether the Western statesmen committed an avoidable mistake of disastrous dimensions. What matters in the present context is the different meaning attached by the Western and Communist leaders, in concluding these agreements, to the concept of "spheres of influence," and the consequences of this "misunderstanding."

That Great Powers are in a position to exert a measure of influence over their smaller neighbors, and that they use this influence in one way or another to increase as far as possible their security against attack by other Great Powers, is an experience general in the politics of sovereign states and unlikely to be superseded by any amount of declamation without "equality of rights"; hence, the fact that the wartime allies, in drawing a military line of demarcation from north to south across the center of Europe, should have tried to agree about their postwar spheres of influence is, by itself, proof of realistic foresight rather than of morally reprehensible cynicism.

To Mr. Roosevelt and Mr. Churchill, however, these spheres of influence meant what they had traditionally meant in the relations of sovereign states—a gradual shading over from the influence of one power or group of powers to that of the other, a shifting relationship which might be loosely described in terms of "percentages of influence," ranging from 50/50 to 90/10. To the Soviets, "spheres of influence" meant something completely different in the framework of their ideology—the ideology of the single-party state. To them there could be no securely "friendly" government except a government run by a Communist party under their discipline; no sphere of influence but a sphere of Communist rule; no satisfactory percentage short of 100. Hence the consistent Soviet efforts, which began even before the end of the European war, to impose total control by Communist parties in every country on their side of the demarcation line—an effort that was finally successful everywhere but in Finland and Eastern Austria; hence also the indignant protests of the Western powers that the Soviets had broken the agreements on free elections and democratic development, and the equally indignant Soviet retort that they were only installing "friendly governments" as agreed, that theirs was the truly "democratic" system, and that they had kept scrupulously to the essential agreement on the military demarcation line.

A large section of Western opinion has concluded from this experience that agreements with the Soviets are useless in principle, because "you cannot trust them"; and Professor Sharp's insistence on national interest as the sole key to Soviet policy is probably at least in part a reaction against this emotional and moralizing approach. In fact, any interpretation of the postwar experience over-looking the fact that the Soviets have for reasons of national self-interest, kept to the "self-enforcing" agreement on the demarcation line, would be as seriously one-sided as one overlooking the fact that they have, for reasons of ideology or party interest, broken every agreement on "percentages" and free elections.

There is no need, however, to base future policy on either of two one-sided views equally refuted by experience. Nobody in the Western world has argued more powerfully against the "moralizing" approach to foreign policy, and for a return to the give-and-take of diplomacy based on real interests, than George Kennan; yet in his recent Reith lectures as before, he insists that the specific ideological distortion in the Soviet leaders' image of the world, far from being magically cured by a return to diplomacy, has to be taken into account continu-ously in judging which kind of agreements are possible and which are not. After all, the peoples of Eastern Europe are still paying for the illusion of the West that the Soviet Union was a state like any other, pursuing its power interests without regard to ideology.

The Soviet Dilemma in Eastern Europe

If we now turn to interstate and interparty relations within the Communist camp, we seem at first sight to have entered an area where ideology is adapted quite unceremoniously to the changing requirements of practical politics. Lenin, having barely seized power in Russia and looking forward to an early spreading of Communist revolution, could talk airily enough about the sovereign equality and fraternal solidarity of sovereign "socialist" states. Stalin, having determined after the failure of short-term revolutionary hope to concentrate on "socialism in a single country," came to regard international communism as a mere tool of Soviet power, and to believe that revolutionary victories without the backing of Soviet arms were neither possible nor desirable; he wanted no sovereign Com-munist allies, only satellites, and he got them in postwar Eastern Europe.

The independent victories of the Yugoslav Communists at the end of the war and of the Chinese Communists in 1949 nevertheless posed the problem he had sought to avoid, and thus required a revision of policy and ideology. But, so one argument goes, the stubborn old man had lost the flexibility to accept the situation; he precipitated a needless quarrel with the Yugoslavs and generally prevented the necessary adjustment while he lived. His heirs, however, hastened to correct his mistakes and to put inter-Communist relations back on a basis of sovereign equality and diplomatic give-and-take, not only with China and Yugoslavia but, after some trial and error, with all Communist states. Or did they?

In the above "common-sense" account, not only the facts of the final phase are wrong; by deliberately neglecting the ideological aspect, it loses sight of all the real difficulties and contradictions which remain inherent in the situation. Because the Soviet Union is both a great power and a single-party state tied to an international ideology, it cannot be content either to oppress and exploit other Communist states or to come to terms with them on a basis of expediency; it must act in a way that will ensure the ideological unity of the Communist "camp" and its own authority at the center.

Stalin's insistence on making the "leading role of the Soviet Union" an article of the international creed expressed not just the idiosyncrasies of a power-mad tyrant, but his perception of one side of the dilemma—the risk that a recognition of the sovereign equality of other Communist states might loosen the solidarity of the "camp" in its dealings with the non-Communist world, and weaken the ideological authority of the Soviet party leaders, with ultimate repercussions on their position in the Soviet Union itself. His successors disavowed him because his Yugoslav policy had failed, and because they perceived the other side of the dilemma—that rigid insistence on Soviet hegemony might break up the unity of the "camp" even more quickly, and might in particular lead to open conflict with China. But by going to Peiping and Belgrade and admitting the "mistakes" of Stalin's "Great Russian chauvinism" (as well as the "mistakes" of his internal terrorist regime), they precipitated the very crisis of authority which he had feared.

The Reassertion of Soviet Primacy

Even Khrushchev and his associates, however, never intended to grant effective sovereign equality to the other Communist satellite regimes of Eastern Europe, which in contrast to Yugoslavia and China had come into being exclusively through the pressure of Soviet power; they merely had planned to make the satellite regimes more viable by reducing Soviet economic exploitation and administrative interference, while maintaining full policy control. In the one case in which not full sovereignty, but at least effective internal autonomy, was in fact granted—the case of Poland—the Soviet leaders were forced to act against their will as a result of open local defiance in a critical international situation. To say that the other East European participants in the Moscow twelve-party meeting of last November, or for that matter the participants from Outer Mongolia and North Korea, represented "governments of sovereign countries" is to mistake the fancies of Communist propaganda for political facts. Nor do the facts bear out Professor Sharp's interpretation that the outcome of the conference showed the Soviet leaders' willingness to rely in their future relations with these "sovereign governments" on the give-and-take of diplomacy. Rather, they confirm Mr. Carew Hunt's view that the need for a single center of international authority is inherent in the Soviet Communist Party's conception of its own role and in its ideology.

The real purpose of that conference was to exploit the recent successes of the Soviet Union as a military and economic power in order to restore the indispensable but lately damaged ideological authority of its leaders in the international Communist movement. The principle of "proletarian internationalism"—that is, unity in foreign policy—had been recognized by all participants, including for the first time in many years the Yugoslavs, before the conference started. Now Moscow was aiming at the further recognition both of its own leadership role and of the need for doctrinal unity, a joint struggle against "revisionism" on the basis of common principles, abolishing once and for all the heresy of "polycentrism" (that is, the concept of a plurality of truly autonomous Communist movements).

As it turned out, the Yugoslavs refused both propositions, while the Polish Communists and the non-ruling but important Italian Communist Party accepted them only with mental reservations, insisting in practice on their right to decide for themselves how the "common principles" would be applied in their own countries. As opposed to this partial failure, however, Moscow was successful in winning full acceptance of the new dispensations by the Chinese Communists and the satellites, as well as in getting agreement on a new, elaborate international liaison machinery within the secretariat of the Soviet Communist Central Committee, in implementation of its renewed claim to international authority.

Moscow's partial failure, therefore, does not indicate that the Soviets will be content with less than they demanded, but that conflict continues. The Soviet press has already reactivated its campaign against Polish "revisionist" ideologies, insisting to Mr. Gomulka that revisionism is the chief internal danger in *all* Communist movements, including that of Poland. Moreover, the proposition defending a Communist party's autonomy in deciding its policy—conceded in principle at the time of Khrushchev's Belgrade visit and at the Twentieth CPSU Congress—is now singled out as a "revisionist" heresy; increasingly the example of Imre Nagy is invoked to show how a demand for autonomy led him down a "road" of "betrayal" and finally "counterrevolution." While the methods of Khrushchev remain conspicuously different from those of Stalin, the logic of the one-party regime, which requires insistence on Soviet authority as a precondition for unity both in foreign policy and in ideological principles, has forced the present first secretary to reassert some of the very doctrines he rashly threw overboard in 1955–56.

Ideology on the Home Front

Ultimately, the need to fight "revisionism" in Eastern Europe, even at the price of renewed difficulties with both Yugoslavia and Poland, arises from the need to strengthen the ideological defenses of the party regime in Russia itself. To admit that in Hungary the workers rose against a Communist government would call into question the basic identification of the ruling party with the working class—the fiction of the "dictatorship of the proletariat." To let Yugoslav propaganda for "workers' management" pass unchallenged would confirm the implication that Soviet factories, having no workers' councils with similar rights, are managed in the interest not of the workers but of the privileged bureaucracy. To keep silent when the Poles proudly report the improvement of their agricultural yields since the dissolution of most of their collective farms would encourage Soviet peasants to dream of similar reforms. To condone the increased, if still limited, freedom of artistic, literary, and philosophical discussion now permitted in Poland and Yugoslavia would strengthen the demands of Soviet writers and scholars for similar freedom.

The obvious and intended implication here is that Soviet reconciliation with Yugoslavia and the near-revolutionary changes in Poland merely aggravated pressures for change which *already* existed in Russia itself. Thus the present account would be incomplete without some attempt to indicate, however sketchily, how ideological changes can be used as aids in interpreting the Soviet domestic sense as well as Kremlin foreign policy and bloc relations.

Earlier in the paper, reference was made to some of the basic tenets which seem inseparably bound up with the preservation and justification of a Communist one-party regime. But within this unchanging framework, considerable variations in detail have taken place in the history of the Soviet Union. The appearance or disappearance of one of these "ideological variables" may be a valuable indicator of the kind of pressures which are exerted on the regime by the growing society and of the manner in which the leaders try to maintain control, sometimes by partly ceding to such pressures and seeking to canalize them, other times by a sharp frontal counterattack.

The "Permanent" Revolution

Among the most revealing of these variables are Soviet doctrines dealing with the economic role of the state and with the "class struggle" within Soviet society. The underlying reality is that a revolutionary party dictatorship, once it has carried out its original program and by this contributed to the emergence of a new privileged class, is bound to disappear sooner or later—to fall victim to a "Thermidor"—unless it prevents the new upper class from consolidating its position by periodically shaking up the social structure in a "permanent revolution from above." The ideological expression of this problem is the classical doctrine that the dictatorship of the proletariat should gradually "wither away" after it has succeeded in destroying the old ruling classes; thus, if continued dictatorship is to be justified, new goals of social transformation must be set and new "enemies" discovered.

In the early period of Stalin's rule, the new "goal" was the forced collectivization of the Russian countryside; the prosperous peasants—the *kulaks*—took the place of the former landowners and capitalists as the "enemy class" which had to be liquidated. Summing up the achievement in 1937, Stalin wrote in his "Short Course" on party history that collectivization had been a second revolution, but a revolution carried out from above, by state power "with the help of the masses," not just by the masses from below. The ideological groundwork was thus laid for assigning the state a function of continuous economic transformation from above, in addition to its terminable revolutionary task.

The second step, also taken by Stalin in 1937, at the height of the Great Blood Purge, consisted in proclaiming the doctrine that the "class struggle" in the Soviet Union was getting more acute as the "construction of socialism" advanced, because the "enemies" were getting more desperate. This was the ideological justification of the purge itself; at the same time, it was a veiled indication that another revolution from above was in effect taking place, though Stalin refrained this time from trying to define the "enemies" in social terms. In fact, what Stalin accomplished was a mass liquidation of both the bearers of the party's older revolutionary tradition—considered unsuited to the tasks of a bureaucratic state party—and of the most confident and independent-minded elements of the new privileged bureaucracy; the end result was a transformation of the party's social and ideological composition through the mass incorporation of the surviving frightened bureaucrats.

Stalin's final ideological pronouncement was contained in his political testament, "Economic Problems of Socialism," published in 1952. In this work, he mapped out a program for the further revolutionary transformation of Soviet society, with the taking over of *kolkhoz* property by the state as its central element.

Khrushchev's Formula for Perpetual Rule

The first major renunciation of these Stalinist ideological innovations was made by Khrushchev in his "secret speech" at the Twentieth Congress. Apart from his factual disclosures concerning Stalin's crimes, he denounced Stalin's doctrine of the sharpening class struggle with societal progress as dangerous nonsense, calculated to lead to the mutual slaughter of loyal Communists after the real class enemy had long been liquidated. This statement affords the master clue to the puzzle of why Khrushchev made the speech: it was a "peace offering" to the leading strata of the regime in the party machine, army, and managerial bureaucracy alike—a response to their pressure for greater personal security. But by his concession, Khrushchev reopened the problem which Stalin's doctrine and practice had been intended to solve—that of preserving and justifying the party dictatorship by periodic major shakeups of society.

By the spring and summer of 1957, Khrushchev showed his awareness of the practical side of the problem: his dismantling of the economic ministries, breaking up the central economic bureaucracy, and strengthening the power of the regional party secretaries, was another such revolutionary shakeup. By November, he responded to the ideological side of the problem. First he repeated, in his solemn speech on the fortieth anniversary of the Bolshevik seizure of power, his rejection of Stalin's doctrine of ever-sharpening class struggle and ever-present enemies, thus indicating his wish to avoid a return to Stalin's terroristic methods even while following his social recipe of permanent revolution. Then he proceeded to develop his own alternative justification for maintaining the party dictatorship—a unique argument which identified the strengthening of party control with the "withering away of the state" predicted by Lenin.

Reviving this formula for the first time since it was buried by Stalin, Khrushchev explained that the military and police apparatus of the state would have to be maintained as long as a hostile capitalist world existed outside; but he added that the economic and administrative functions of the state bureaucracy would henceforth be steadily reduced by decentralization and devolution, thus strengthening the organs of regional self-government and of national autonomy within the various republics. At the same time, he quietly took steps to strengthen the control of the central party secretariat—his own seat of power—over the republican and regional party organs, thus following the old Leninist principle that the fiction of national autonomy must be balanced by the fact of centralized discipline within the ruling party.

In short, the same aim of maintaining the social dynamism of the party dictatorship and justifying its necessity, which Stalin achieved by exalting the economic role of the state, is pursued by Khrushchev by means of the reverse device of claiming that the state's economic functions have begun to "wither away." On the face of it, this doctrinal manipulation seems to reduce the role of ideology to that of ingenious trickery, obscuring rather than reflecting the underlying social realities. Yet in fact, the very need for a change in the ideological argument reflects the change that is taking place in the underlying social situation—the resistance against a return to naked terrorism, the growing desire for a lessening of state pressure and a greater scope for local activity. Whether in industry or agriculture, in the control of literature, or in relations with the satellite states, the basic conditions which the regime needs for its self-perpetuation have remained the same—but they can no longer be assured in the same way. That, too, is reflected in the variables of the official ideology.

FORM AND FUNCTION

R. N. Carew Hunt

It seems to me important to distinguish between the *function* of the Soviet ideology and the peculiar *form* it has assumed. In the last analysis, its *function* is to provide a rationalization of the one-party system of government and of the policies to which the Soviet rulers are committed. The doctrine of the party is thus its central theme, and to this are related in all its other elements, "proletarian democracy," "proletarian internationalism," "capitalist encirclement," "socialist realism," *etc.* On the other hand, the *form* it has taken derives primarily from Marxism with its insistence upon conflict as the main-spring of history and the force behind all progress within society—a conflict which is teleological and can only end in one way. The division of the world into two antagonistic camps, the one "progressive" and the other "reactionary," and the belief that the victory of the former, as represented by the Soviet Union, is predestined by the logic of history, is simply the Marxist class struggle between the bourgeoisie and the proletariat projected onto the international plane, and it constitutes the basis of all Soviet political thinking. It has led the Soviet rulers to take so distorted a view of the world as to make it harder to deal with them than with any government in the annals of diplomacy; and this, as Mr. Lowenthal says, is just what may be expected from an "ideology" in the sense in which Marx originally used the term.

Professor Sharp argues that Soviet national interests alone count, though his definition of these interests is tautological, as Mr. Lowenthal rightly points out. Yet to take a single example: if the Soviet rulers had consulted their national interests only, how are we to explain their strenuous efforts to promote revolution in China during the 1920's, that is, at a time when their country was weak, and was seeking to strengthen its position by entering into trade agreements and diplomatic relations with the Western powers? Such zeal for the welfare of the Chinese masses in intelligible only on the assumption that the rulers believed that they had a mission to spread the revolution wherever there was a chance of doing so effectively. Lenin had repeatedly declared this to be a primary obligation before he seized power—that is, before there was any question of promoting national interests—while after the revolution he never said a word to suggest that there was any connection between the two.

Naturally, the concepts of an ideology have to be translated into action, and when this action is undertaken by a powerful country such as Russia has now become, it can be plausibly represented as *Realpolitik*. Yet it does not follow that it belongs solely, or even primarily, to this category, or that we can afford to ignore the principles of which it claims to be the expression. The objection to such agreements as that of Yalta is precisely that they failed to take this into account, and assumed that any conflicts which might later arise with the Russians would be of a political nature only.

Further, it is not easy to see what process of logic entitles us to assume that while the leaders of the West believe in their standard of values and seek to formulate their policies in accordance with them, the Soviet rulers neither believe in theirs nor seek to apply them. Doubtless Professor Sharp is right in saying that they proceed with caution. But this has no bearing upon the matter as there is nothing in their ideology which requires them to act otherwise.

Finally, I would join issue with Mr. Lowenthal on one point where we disagree. Certainly Marx, who had no interest in social technology, did not develop a concept of total planning. Yet he and Engels consistently advocated the replacement of "the anarchy of social production" under capitalism by production to be carried out upon a "common plan," though who was to do the planning was not explained. Yet this was sufficient to excite the suspicion of his Anarchist opponents. Both Anarchists and the Marxists agreed that the state must be abolished; but whereas the Anarchists held that the whole object of the revolution was to destroy it, Marx held that its object was to set up a new form of society in which the means of production would be developed in the interests of all, though once it was established, the state would "wither away." The

Anarchists reasoned, however, that in any such society it would be necessary to retain some form of coercive authority, and whether it was called the state or something else was immaterial. Subsequent events were to prove how right they were.

From the early days of the revolution Lenin made clear that his objective was a nationwide planned economy, though it was left to his successor to introduce it. My contention is that if such an economy is to be introduced and made effective, the state (or the party) will have to do many unpopular things. The reason why the Soviet Union has become so powerful in so short a time is precisely because its rulers were able to enforce measures which would never have been tolerated under a democracy, and one of the functions of the ideology is to justify their right to act in this manner. Naturally, such a policy has led to the emergence of a bureaucracy which is the virtual owner of the means of production. My criticism of Djilas is that he approves the economic objectives of communism, but objects to the state of affairs to which the attempt to realize them inevitably gives rise. He wants a "democratic communism." It is a contradiction in terms.

THE POLICY PIE

Samuel L. Sharp

The differences of opinion expressed by the participants in the symposium on the roles of ideology and of power politics in Soviet policy decisions bring to mind the story about a product labeled "rabbit pie" which, on closer scrutiny, turns out to be not quite pure rabbit but a mixture of rabbit and horse meat, in the proportion of one horse to one rabbit. Although Mr. Lowenthal insists that I deny "completely" the relevance of Communists ideology to the formation of Soviet policies, or that I overlook "completely" the use made of foreign Communist parties by the Soviet Union, this is not so. The controversy is actually one about the proportions in which the ingredients of ideology and power politics appear in the final product, Soviet policy (especially within the area to which my original arguments were directed, namely foreign policy).

I find it difficult to pick a quarrel with Mr. Hunt since, while seeming to argue that the product is pure rabbit (ideology), he is careful at all times to leave open a gate wide enough for the horse (power politics) to be brought in. At his most specific, Mr. Hunt argues that the significance of ideology lies in that "it makes those who profess it act in a way that they would not otherwise do," presumably with a frequent sacrifice of efficiency for the sake of principle. The burden of proof, of course, rests on him, and in his comments appearing in the current issue he refers to Soviet support of the nationalist revolution in China in the 1920's as obviously the result of "zeal for the welfare of the Chinese masses" (Mr. Hunt is ironical, I hope) or of a sense of "mission" to spread revolution *whenever there was a chance of doing so effectively*. This, he maintains, was a mistake from the standpoint of Soviet state interests because Russia was then seeking trade agreements and diplomatic recognition from the West. His argument, however, is debatable. The establishment of Communist regimes outside Russia, if it could be "effectively" achieved, would have been definitely to the advantage of the weak Soviet state under the circumstances of the time. The case of Soviet "support" for the Chinese revolution ("encouragement" would be more accurate) is, of course, notorious because there was nothing "effective" about it: it was a case of miscalculation to be sure, but not necessarily a miscalculation caused by ideological zeal or a sense of mission. As to the effect of the policy on relations with the West, Stalin apparently was following in the footsteps of nineteenth-century Tsarist foreign ministers who attempted to "bring in the East in order to redress an unfavorable balance in the West" (as suggested, with respect to Lenin's policies, by E. H. Carr).

Since Mr. Lowenthal agrees that ideology will effectively influence policy decisions of the Soviet leaders "when, and only when, it expresses the needs of self-preservation of the party regime" (and I need not remind him that those in charge of a going concern tend to identify the interests of the concern with their own continued tenure), there would be little for me to object to were it not for his previously mentioned distortions of my views, his introduction of the gratuitous compliment of "innocence" (hereby acknowledged as an undeserved but charming relief from the much stronger epithets collected by this writer on other occasions), and for his own excursion into the theory of international relations and recent diplomatic history which—to return the compliment—is not only innocent but presumptuous.

Mr. Lowenthal states that the doctrine of "two camps" was not invented by Stalin, but was "inherent in Leninism." This is unhistorical. The temptation to present the world as divided into "good" and "bad" camps is as old as international conflict itself. And certainly in recent times the "two-camps" image has been used on both sides of the dividing line; it fits admirably into a bipolarized world situation. "At the present moment in world history nearly every nation must choose between alternative ways of life," declared President Truman in his message to Congress in March 1947, several months before the late Andrei Zhdanov came out with the first vigorous postwar reformulation of the old cliche on the Soviet side. Politics operates this side of the ultimate. The persistence of the enemy image and the drive for "unlimited power" may well be present in the minds of the Soviet leaders, but the history of future years will be shaped, not by this admittedly unfriendly view of the outside world, but by what the Soviet leaders are *persuaded or compelled* to do; not by their "collective paranoia" (a term given a completely arbitrary definition by Mr. Lowenthal), but rather by their desire for survival and appraisal of the limits of the feasible. I do not doubt that they will grasp every opportunity to press any advantages to the utmost. This makes them unpleasant and tough opponents, but not totally intractable ones. To posit a world that would be animated by general harmony were it not for a single disturber of the peace is to sacrifice all history on the altar of deceptive imagery.

Mr. Lowenthal points out the difference between the "traditional" and Soviet concepts of spheres of influence, ascribing the controversy over the Yalta agreements to this difference. However, there is a built-in and often deliberate vagueness in the concept of spheres of influence, and differences of interpretation are not necessarily rooted in differences of *Weltanschauung*. Examining the historical record, one will find that conflicts of interpretation have usually occurred between those who acquired a sphere of influence and those who conceded one. This is not the time and, Mr. Lowenthal will admit, not exactly the place to enter into a debate over what Yalta meant and whether the representatives of the West were on that occasion laboring under an illusion about the real nature of the Soviet Union, or rather were trying to salvage what could be salvaged in a situation determined by the division of military theaters. Nor is it correct to say that complete Communist control was immediately imposed throughout the Soviet sphere of influence. In at least some countries (especially Czechoslovakia, but also, to some extent, Poland and Hungary until 1947) there was the kind of fuzzy situation characteristic of an in-between area. The Soviet Union, for a variety of practical considerations, on some occasions actually seems to have curbed the enthusiasm of local Communists for a speedy transition to full control. The present writer certainly did not err on the side of optimism about the lasting nature of this halfway arrangement. It was obvious that the fuzziness could not survive the onset of the cold war; yet it is wrong to mistake one of the symptoms of the cold war for its cause.

There is no serious controversy between Mr. Lowenthal and myself with regard to recent developments in Eastern Europe, except that I offer a guess while he professes to know for certain what the meaning of these developments is. Of course, the Soviet Union would like to derive advantages in its dealings with "ruling" Communist parties from the magic of ideological control. However, in this case as in others, the intentions of the Soviet leaders, or their views about what would be the optimum situation, do not exclusively determine the outcome. When they saw the need to shift relations with at least some of the countries in the Soviet sphere to a more "traditional" basis, this was done whether graciously or not. If the Soviet Union appears currently to be reassuring its ideological domination over Eastern Europe, this reflects an acknowledgment by the leaders of these countries of Russia's strengthened international power position. Obviously, the Soviet Union, like any big power in a position of leadership, will try to hold together by various means the grouping over which it presides. To the extent that its leaders disregard the general rules of international relations from which on one is exempt, they will be inviting trouble and failure. There are no cut-rate worlds to be had.

A DIFFERENCE IN KIND

Richard Lowenthal

I am sorry that Professor Sharp should feel that I have distorted his position. He, in turn, has certainly mistaken my meaning if he attributes to me the view that our world would be animated by general harmony were it not for a single disturber of the peace. That view is nothing but a reflection of the Leninist dogma of the two camps, which consists precisely in the delusion of seeing all conflicts, and ultimately all independent forces, as manifestations of a single enemy. It is not unhistorical to regard this outlook as characteristic of the totalitarian movements of our time; on the contrary, it is unhistorical to confuse it with the age-old tendency to regard one's own side in a given conflict as good and the enemy as bad.

I agree with Professor Sharp on one point of great practical importance—that the Soviets are not intractable in his sense, that is, that they are tough politicians liable to be influenced by the hard facts of power and the processes for negotiation, rather than madmen pursuing a preordained plan of world conquest regardless of risk. But while Soviet policy differs from Hitler's in this vital respect, I hold that it is also different in kind from that of nontotalitarian great powers. Professor Sharp persists in seeking to blur this difference, while I wish to show that it is not confined to motives and ultimate aims, but constantly affects the Soviets' *modus operandi*.

For instance, Professor Sharp accepts my formula that Soviet ideology influences policy decisions only when it expresses the needs of self-preservation of the party regime, but adds that it is normal for any government to identify the interests of its country with its own. But my point is that the interests of a one-party government which uses an international movement as a weapon are highly peculiar, and I gave examples to show just how they affect its foreign relations. Since we wrote, the new Soviet quarrel with Yugoslavia—a quarrel which both Khrushchev and Tito would have liked to avoid for realistic reasons, but which was forced on them by Tito's need to justify ideologically his position outside the Warsaw pact, and Khrushchev's need to restore ideological unity and discipline within the bloc—has further illustrated by thesis.

Again, Professor Sharp claimed in his article that taking the entire Soviet record to date, the achievements are clearly attributable to Soviet power and diplomacy with no credit due to the international Communist movement. I find it impossible to fit into this formula the victory of communism in China, which has been to an overwhelming extent the outcome of the struggle of indigenous forces under indigenous leadership, but has resulted in a major shift in the balance of world power in favor of the Soviets. Some rabbit!

But we remain farthest apart on the Soviet conquest of Eastern Europe. In referring to Yalta, I explicitly disclaimed any intention to pass judgment on whether the Western statesmen committed an avoidable mistake of disastrous dimensions. I was concerned to show that, whether the concessions were avoidable or not, the later fate of the Soviet sphere of influence was implicit in the nature of Soviet power. Professor Sharp denies this on the ground that the "peoples' democracies" were somewhat fuzzy coalition regimes until 1947, and concludes that their later total sovietization was a symptom and not a cause of the cold war. Yet readers of this journal are familiar with the overwhelming evidence that preparations for total sovietization, such as the occupation of all key positions of power (armed forces, police, press, *etc.*), by Communists and the systematic undermining of the independence of the other parties were begun throughout the area almost from the moment of the first entry of Soviet forces. I can find no evidence to back the hypothesis that these preparations would not have been pursued to their logical conclusions if the West had acquiesced in the first steps instead of reacting to the challenge of the forcible expansion of the Soviet system, nor can I accept the implication that the cold war began only when the West took up the challenge.

NOTES

1. Radio broadcast of October 1, 1939, reprinted in W. Churchill, *The Gathering Storm* (Boston: Houghton-Mifflin, 1948), p. 449. Author's italics.

2. To quote just one recent source, cf. V. I. Lissovskii, *Mezhdunarodnoe Pravo* [International Law] (Kiev, 1955), p. 397.

3. Marshall Knappen, *An Introduction to American Foreign Policy* (New York: Harper & Bros., 1956). The quote is from the chapter entitled "Capabilities, appeal and, intentions of the Soviet Union" and refers specifically to the well-known effort by Nathan Leites in *A Study of Bolshevism* (Glencoe, IL: Free Press, 1953) to construct out of thousands of quotes from Lenin and Stalin bolstered with excerpts from nineteenth-century Russian literature, an "image of Bolshevism" and an "operational code" of the Politburo. See also the remarks on "Difficulties of content analysis" and "The problem of context" in John S. Reshetar, Jr., *Problems of Analyzing and Predicting Soviet Behavior* (New York: Doubleday & Co., 1955). In all fairness to Leites and his prodigious undertaking it must be pointed out that he was aware of a "spurious air of certainty" in his formulations, which were intended to be only "guesses about the mind of the Soviet Politburo" (*op. cit*, p. 27).

4. Allan Bullock, *Hitler—A Study in Tyranny* (New York: Harper & Bros., 1953).

5. W. W. Rostow *et. al., The Dynamics of Soviet Society* (New York: W. W. Norton & Co., 1952), p. 136. Authors's italics.

6. Barrington Moore, Jr., *Soviet Politics—The Dilemma of Power* (Cambridge, MA: Harvard University Press, 1950).

7. Samuel L. Sharp, "The Soviet Position in the Middle East," *Social Science* (National Academy of Economics and Political Sciences) 32, no. 4 (October 1957).

8. The text of the declaration, adopted at a meeting held on November 14–16, 1957, was published in *Pravda* on November 22. A separate "peace manifesto" issued in the name of all of the Communist parties present at the congregation appeared in *Pravda* a day later.

9. Gomulka's report was published in *Trybuna Ludu,* Warsaw, November 29, 1957.

10. Gormulka, *ibid.* See also an analysis of the conference entitled, "Gescheiterte Komintern-Renaissance" [Failure of Comintern Revival], *Ost-Probleme* (Bad Godesberg) X, no. 1 (January 3, 1958).

11. Cited in Friedrich Ebert's report to the East German party (SED), published in *Neues Deutschland,* East Berlin, November 30, 1957, p. 4.

12. While this comes close to the position outlined in Mr. Carew Hunt's paper, I cannot follow him in his assumption that the totalitarian party monopoly is a by-product of the attempt to establish collectivist economic planning or to achieve the speedy industrial-

ization of a backward country. This neo-Marxist view, held by such otherwise divergent authors as Professor Hayek and Milovan Djilas, is contradicted by the fact that the Bolshevik party monopoly, including the ban on inner-party factions, was fully established by Lenin at the time of the transition to the "New Economic Policy (1921), when economic planning was reduced to a minimum and forced industrialization not yet envisaged. Independent of the concrete economic program, totalitarianism was implicit in the centralized, undemocratic structure of a party consciously created as an instrument for the conquest of power, and in the ideological characteristics resulting (to be discussed further in this article). Of course, totalitarian power, once established, favors total economic planning and the undertaking of revolutionary economic tasks by the state, but this is a consequence, not a cause. Marx never developed a concept of total planning, and even Lenin never imagined anything of the kind before 1918. But Marx in his youth at least equated the "dictatorship of the proletariat" with the Jacobin model, and Lenin followed this model throughout.

9

*Anatomy of Policymaking**

Adam B. Ulam

Contemplating the vast volume of Kremlinology produced in this country since World War II, a layman might well paraphrase Karl Marx's famous thesis on Feuerbach and complain that various experts have only interpreted the Soviet Union in different ways, while the urgent need is to find out how its policies can be changed. There have been many prescriptions as to how the United States, through its own policies, might influence the USSR to alter a disquieting pattern of Soviet behavior on the world scene. But before trying to formulate such prescriptions, we must first of all try to understand the process of Soviet policymaking.

To repeat what this author wrote in another study, "The student of Soviet affairs has as his first task to be neither hopeful nor pessimistic, but simply to state the facts and tendencies of Russian politics. It is when he begins to see in certain political trends the inevitabilities of the future and when he superimposes upon them his own conclusions about the desirable policies of America towards the USSR that he is courting trouble."[1] American policymaking ought to profit by a dispassionate analysis of the Soviets' motivations and actions, but it cannot be a substitute for such analysis.

The fulcrum of the Soviet political system is the 20-odd full and alternate members of the Politburo and those Central Committee Secretaries who are outside it. Yet we still need to know more about how this group operates and its relationship to the wider Soviet political elite and to the Soviet people at large. For our purposes, it is especially important to establish some analytical guidelines about how the inner ruling group arrives at its decisions on foreign policy and to what extent it is susceptible to influences form the larger international environment.

Elitist and secretive as the process of Soviet decision making is in general, it is especially so when it comes to foreign policy. One may find occasionally in the

*Reprinted by permission of the author and The MIT Press, Cambridge, Massachusetts, from *The Washington Quarterly*, 6, no. 2 (Spring 1983), pp. 71–82. Copyright © 1983 by the President and Fellows of Harvard College and of the Massachusetts Institute of Technology.

Soviet press and in the utterances of lower officials fairly far-reaching criticisms, particularly of the country's economic systems and performance. It is almost inconceivable for such public discussion to take place in connection with any major Soviet position on international affairs. This taboo is observed also when it comes to Moscow's past foreign policy.

Those who see the Soviet system moving toward pluralism or who hypothesize about the growing influence of the military in decision making disregard the exclusive prerogative of decision making to which the inner ruling group, especially in the Brezhnev era, has held with such tenacity. Even Nikita Khrushchev, who intermittently attempted to enlarge his political base by using the Central Committee to curb his fellow oligarchs, guarded jealously the party's monopoly of power. He could speak slightingly in the presence of foreigners about Andrei Gromyko, then "only" minister of foreign affairs, but not yet a member of the charmed circle; and he dismissed Zhukov largely because the marshal had helped him in his 1957 scrap with the Vyacheslav Molotov faction, and it was intolerable that a professional soldier should be allowed to interfere in settling future disputes on the Soviet Olympus.

In their turn, Leonid Brezhnev and his colleagues were especially insistent not only on preserving the party's role as the only source of political power, but also on recouping the narrower oligarchy's prerogative as final arbiter in policymaking. There is a Soviet equivalent of the U.S. National Security Council, but it is presided over ex officio by the general secretary, and nothing indicates that it is more than an advisory body to the Politburo. Since 1964 the Central Committee has been relegated again to being a forum where decision of the top leadership are announced and perhaps explained in greater detail than they are to the public at large, but not debated. Emperor Paul I once told a foreign ambassador that the only important public figures in Russia were those to whom he talked, and even their influence disappeared once they were no longer in actual conversation with the sovereign. The only participants in the decision-making process in the USSR, outside the 20-odd members of the inner circle, are those whom it chooses to consult, and only while it does so. Unless he is simultaneously a member of the Politburo, the status of the head of an important branch of the government—the armed forces, security, foreign ministry, or economic planning—is similar to that of a high civil servant in the West rather than that of a minister and policymaker.

Because of its very rigidity, and in view of the average age of the ruling oligarchy, the pattern we just sketched is likely to become exposed in the future to increasing strains and might well break down, at least temporarily, during a succession struggle or a situation similar to that of 1956–1957 and the early 1960s. Then the inner group splits into hostile factions and, especially on the latter occasion, the leader found himself increasingly out of tune with his senior colleagues.

For the present and immediate future we must assume, however, that the USSR will continue to be governed under a system where policy options and moves are freely discussed by and fully known only to some 25 people, and the ultimate decisions are made by an even smaller group—the 13 or 15 full members of the Politburo.

This being so, we have little reason to expect basic changes in the Soviet philosophy of foreign relations. The present leaders and their prospective successors have seen the Soviet Union develop from the backward, militarily and industrially weak state of the early 1920s to one of the two superpowers of the post-1945 world. They have been brought up in the belief that the Soviet Union's connection with the worldwide communist movement has been a source of strength to their country, and it is only recently that they have had occasion for doubt on that score. Their formative years witnessed the Soviet system surviving the ravages of terror and the tremendous human and material losses of World War II. As rising bureaucrats in the immediate postwar period, the people of the Politburo generation could observe how Soviet diplomacy managed to offset the Soviet Union's industrial and military inferiority vis-à-vis the principal capitalist state, and even when the country's resources had to be devoted mainly to the task of recovery from the war, the USSR still managed to advance its power and influence in the world at large.

In brief, very little in their own experience or in the international picture, as it has evolved during he past 20 years or so, could have persuaded the Kremlin that its basic guidelines for dealing with the outside world needed revision. The external power and influence of the USSR has been used in propaganda at home to demonstrate the viability and dynamism of the Soviet system and its historical legitimacy. Granted the essentially conservative approach of the present leadership of the Soviet Union toward international affairs, one could hardly imagine it responding to a specific internal emergency by contriving a dangerous international crisis. But the Kremlin still persists in seeking to impress upon its people the paradoxical dichotomy of world politics: The imperialist threat remains as great as ever, and yet the USSR is steadily growing more powerful. Both beliefs are seen as essential to preserving the cohesion of Soviet society. The average Soviet citizen is never to be dissuaded from seeing the capitalist world as a source of potential danger to his country and its allies. By the same token, he must not lose faith in the ability of his government and its armed forces to repel this threat and to ensure even in this nuclear age the security and greatness of the USSR and of the entire socialist camp. It would take an extraordinary combination of domestic political, social, and economic pressures to form a critical mass capable of impelling the regime to change its outlook on world politics.

It is virtually impossible to conceive of the Soviet system surviving in its present form were its rulers to abandon explicitly, or even implicitly, the main premises behind their foreign policy. Practically every feature of Russian authoritarianism is ultimately rationalized in terms of the alleged foreign danger inherent in the existence of the "two struggling camps," one headed by the USSR and the other, the capitalist one, by the United States. Writing at the most hopeful period of détente, and painting a very rosy picture of the future of

Soviet–American relations. Georgi Arbatov still had to add the caveat, "There can be no question as to whether the struggle between the two systems would or would not continue. That struggle is historically unavoidable."[2] If the struggle continues, the Soviet citizen must be made to believe that his side is steadily forging ahead on the world stage. Otherwise, what can compensate him psychologically for his perception—increasingly unsuppressible—that life is freer and materially more abundant in the West?

To be sure, this official rationale of Soviet foreign policy becomes vulnerable in cases where its ideological premises cannot be readily reconciled with the nationalist ones, and it is mainly on that count that one can foresee the possibility of popular reactions at home affecting the course of foreign policy. Tito's apostasy could be dismissed by the Kremlin as being in itself not of great significance. The burdens inherent in standing armed guard over Eastern Europe or in suppressing the Afghan insurgency have been explained in the official media by the necessity of warding off the class enemy and, less explicitly, in terms of Russia's historical mission and interests antedating the Revolution. All these developments could be interpreted as still not in conflict with the thesis that communism is a natural ally and an obedient servant of the Soviet national interest.

However, the Sino–Soviet conflict has struck at the very heart of the ideology/ national interest *Weltanschauung* of Soviet foreign policy. In his *Letter to the Soviet Leaders,* Aleksandr Solzhenitsyn formulated very cogently the essential dilemma that has confronted the Kremlin in public since the eruption of the dispute, in fact since Mao's forces conquered the mainland. It is another communist state, and precisely because it is communist, writes Solzhenitsyn, it has posed the greatest threat to Russia's future. Thus, even when it comes to the outside world, he charges, one can readily see how this false ideology has had disastrous consequences for the true interests and security of the Russian people and threatens it eventually with having to fight for survival. This is not the isolated opinion of a writer and dissident who abhors every aspect of communism. Fear of China because of its enormous size, vast industrial–military potential, and the nature of its regime and ruling philosophy is probably the most visceral reaction of the average Soviet, insofar as his outlook on world affairs is concerned. No other aspect of the regime's policy has had so wide approval among the Soviet population as its efforts to contain and isolate the other great communist state.

It is important to note that even this problem has not been allowed to affect the official rationale of Soviet foreign policy. This rationale is still couched in terms inherited from the era when the world communist movement was monolithic in its subservience to Moscow. When it first erupted in public, the Sino–Soviet dispute might well have prompted a foreign observer to prophesy that its implications were bound to change not only the Kremlin's actual policies, but its whole approach to international situations. The confrontation between ideology and reality inherent in the clash ought to have led to a thorough reevaluation of the former, not merely as a justification but also as an operating principle for foreign policies. The USSR should have abandoned even the pretense that what it was doing in Africa, the Near East, and other areas was in the furtherance of socialism.

Yet, in fact, such secularization of Soviet foreign policy has not taken place. One might object that the USSR has tried to cope with the Chinese problem without any ideological inhibitions. It has attempted to enlist the United States in a joint effort to stop or delay China's nuclear development. It has encouraged India to attack and fragment China's only major ally in Asia. The Kremlin viewed with equanimity the massacre of the pro-Beijing Indonesian Communist party, and it encouraged and helped Vietnam in its open defiance of its huge neighbor. Ideological kinship has not restrained the Soviet Union from hinting at times that it might have to resort to a preemptive strike against China.

Yet, for all such unsentimental measures and attitudes, the Soviet leadership has refused to draw what to an outsider would be the logical deductions of its predicament with China. The doctrine of the two camps is still being maintained as stoutly as when the two great communist powers were linked "by unshakeable friendship" and alliance against a potential capitalist aggressor. China's departure from the straight and narrow path of "proletarian internationalism" has been explained in the official Soviet rhetoric as a temporary lapse, while even at the most hopeful periods of peaceful coexistence, the conflict with the capitalist world has been presented as an unavoidable and permanent feature of world politics. There have been fairly serious armed clashes along the Sino–Soviet border, and a sizable proportion of the Soviet armed forces is deployed along the frontier. Those Russian military manuals, however, that are accessible to the public discuss at length the dangers and various scenarios of conventional and nuclear warfare between the USSR and the capitalist powers, while not even alluding to the possibility of a war with another communist power.

This bizarre pattern of behavior cannot be ascribed solely to the Soviet leaders' cynicism and ability to divorce their actions entirely from their words. Nor can it be attributed to some lingering ideological scruples. Given a truth serum, a Soviet statesman would readily confess that barring something very unexpected, the danger of unprovoked capitalist aggression against the USSR is virtually nil, while the possibility of China someday advancing territorial and other claims on his country is very real indeed. The immobilism of the Soviet foreign policy doctrine finds its roots in the nature of the political system as a whole. The 13 or so men at the apex of the Soviet power structure have to think of themselves not only as rulers of a national state, but also as high priests of a world cult, which in turn is the source of legitimacy for the system as a whole and for their own power in particular. Could that legitimacy (and with it, the present political structure of the Soviet Union) endure, were its rulers to renounce one of the most basic operating tenets of communist political philosophy?

To a Westerner it might appear that the regime could greatly strengthen itself by curtailing its expansionist policies abroad and by conconcentrating on raising the living standards of the Soviet people. It would gain in popularity, the argument would continue, by being more explicit about the real dimension of the problem the USSR faces in relation to China and by putting the alleged threat from the West into proper perspective. But it is most unlikely that the present generation of leaders would, or feels it could, afford to heed such arguments. They remember how even Nikita Khrushchev's modest and clumsy attempts at domestic liberalization and at relieving the siege mentality of his countrymen had, in their view, most unsettling effects on the party and society. Without a continuing sense of danger from abroad, economic improvement at home, far from being an effective remedy for political dissent, is in fact likely to make it more widespread. For the die-hards within the elite, even some of the side effects of détente, such as increased contacts with and knowledge of the West, must have appeared potentially harmful, because they brought in their wake ideological pollution and threatened the stability and cohesion of Soviet society.

History has played an unkind trick on the masters of the USSR. Probably no other ruling oligarchy in modern times has been so pragmatically minded and power-oriented as the current Soviet one. Compared to them, even Nikita Khrushchev, who joined the party in 1918 during the Civil War, showed some characteristics of a true believer. Ironically, it is precisely because of power considerations that the rulers cannot disregard ideological constraints on their policies.

A superficial view of Soviet politics would lead us to believe that a Soviet statesman enjoys much greater freedom of action, especially in foreign affairs, than his Western counterpart. He can order and direct rather than having to plead or campaign for his program. If he has to persuade others, it is a small group rather than an unruly electorate or a partisan legislature. The Politburo's decisions are not hammered out in the full glare of publicity or subjected to immediate public debate and criticisms. Whatever the fears, hesitations, and divisions among the rulers, they seldom become known outside the precincts of the Kremlin. Hence, how can a democracy avoid finding itself at a disadvantage when negotiating with the Kremlin? Neither budgetary constraints nor fear of public opinion can deflect Brezhnev and company from a weapons policy or an action abroad that they believe to be necessary for their purposes and for the prestige and power of the USSR.

This picture, while correct in several details, is greatly misleading overall. The structure of the decision-making process in the USSR enables the Kremlin to be free from many of the constraints under which nonauthoritarian governments must operate. Yet, the nature of the Soviet political system creates its own imperatives, which the leaders must heed and which may make the leaders' choice among foreign policy options more difficult and cumbersome than is the case in a democracy. Superbly equipped as it is for moving rapidly and effectively on several fronts, the Soviet political mechanism has not shown equal capacity during the last 20 years for effectively braking the momentum of its policies once launched. Whether the Soviet political mechanism can develop such braking devices must be of special interest to any student or practitioner of international affairs.

The immediate background of Soviet policies in the 1980s lies in the series of agreements and understandings reached between the USSR and the United States, as well as other states of the Western bloc, which set up the foundations of what has come to be known as détente. It would be a gross oversimplification on our part to view détente as simply an attempt by the Kremlin to deceive the West or, conversely, as a definitive change in Moscow's philosophy of international affairs. Soviet leaders sought a temporary accommodation with the West and a consequent lowering of international tension for reasons inherent in their interpretation of the world scene as of 1970.

Even if undertaken solely as a tactical maneuver, détente was not cost-free for the Soviets. Domestically it gave more resonance to the voices of dissent and placed the government under the obligation of relaxing restrictions on Jewish emigration, a concession that would have been unthinkable a few years earlier. Abroad, it was bound to raise doubts and suspicions in the minds of the Soviet Union's clients and friends. Only a few weeks after the Nixon–Brezhnev summit, Anwar Sadat ordered some 20,000 Soviet military personnel out of Egypt, a step very largely motivated by his conviction that his country's foreign policy now had to be more balanced between the two superpowers.

The Soviet policymakers' usual skill at having their cake and eating it too was thus put to a severe test. The 1972–1973 period offers a convincing example of the Soviet Union's sensitivity to its antagonists' actual policies and of the importance it places on its perception of the overall condition of the noncommunist world. In 1972 the economy of the West as a whole was still flourishing and expanding. Political stability appeared to be returning in the United States. With his successes in the international field, Nixon was virtually assured a second term. This political and economic strength of the West, as well as several other international developments, added up to compelling reasons for the Soviets to pull in their horns.

How long this restraint would have prevailed in the councils of the Kremlin and whether there was any possibility of more fundamental alternation in Soviet foreign policy remains unknown. Within a year and a half of the inauguration of détente, the premises on which the Soviets' restraints had been based began to crumble. By the end of 1974 Moscow was bound to conclude that the West was not nearly as stable and strong politically or economically as it had appeared to be in 1972.

Beginning in 1974, the USSR became much less concerned about U.S. reactions to its policies abroad, even the ones that were openly directed at undermining the influence and interests of the United States and its friends. Unlike the case of the 1973 Middle Eastern conflict, Soviet actions in Angola, Ethiopia, and South Yemen betrayed little hesitation or fear that they might bring effective U.S. countermeasures or even seriously damage overall Soviet–U.S. relations, thus diminishing the benefits the USSR was reaping from détente. To be sure, the Soviets have always been aware of how sensitive the United States is to what happens in the Middle East, and in comparison the average American knows little and cares less about Angola or South Yemen. However, what should have been cause for alarm to U.S. policymakers was not so much the targets but the character of Soviet activities in Africa. It was not merely another example of the Soviet skill at scavenging amidst the debris of Western colonialism and wresting yet another country from its nonaligned or pro-Western position through ideological appeal or an alliance with the local dictator or oligarchy. Angola was the testing ground for a new technique of Soviet imperial expansion.

The experiment was allowed to succeed and thus became a precedent for further employment of this technique. Nonnative, up to now Cuban, troops would be used to establish Soviet presence in the country and to maintain the pro-Soviet regime in power. Thus, wars of "national liberation" could be carried out and won by the pro-Soviet faction, because it was helped not only by Soviet arms and advisers, but also by massive infusion of communist bloc troops. Had the general international situation remained similar to that of 1972–1973, it is unlikely that the conservative-minded Brezhnev regime would have attempted such a daring innovation as projecting Soviet power into areas thousands of miles away from the USSR.

The reasons for the Kremlin's confidence that this innovative form of international mischief-making was not unduly risky were probably very similar to those that persuaded North Vietnam about the same time to launch a massive invasion and to occupy the south. A North Vietnamese general spelled out candidly the rationale of his government's actions and why it was certain the United States would not interfere. "The internal contradictions within the U.S. administration and among U.S. political parties had intensified. The Watergate scandal had seriously affected the entire United States. . . . It had faced economic recession, mounting inflation, serious unemployment and an oil crisis."[3]

This revealing statement illustrates well the hard-boiled pragmatism of the Soviets and their disciples and how free they can be of the dogmas of their own ideology in their socioeconomic evaluations of a given situation. According to classical Marxist–Leninist doctrine, an internal crisis impels the capitalists to act more aggressively and to seek a remedy for economic troubles, as well as to distract the attention of the masses through imperialist adventures. Here we had quite a realistic analysis of the reasons for this country's acquiescence in North Vietnam's flagrant violation of the agreement it had signed only 2 years before, and of the debilitating effects of domestic crisis on a democratic country's foreign policies. The statement demonstrates once again how in their calculus of potential risks and gains in world politics, the Soviet tend to go beyond the arithmetic of nuclear missiles, tanks, and ships and pay even closer attention to the psychopolitical ingredients of the given situation. It did require a degree of sensitivity to U.S. politics to perceive how seriously American foreign policy was harmed by reopening the wounds of Vietnam and by pitting Congress against the executive branch. The Watergate affair had crippled America's capacity to act effectively abroad, especially when it came to meeting the Soviet and/or communist challenge in the Third World.

It was less remarkable for the Kremlin to draw the proper lesson from the energy crisis that now grips the West's economy. If the world's leading industrial nations were incapable of synchronizing their policies to counteract or soften the blow from the Organization of Petroleum Exporting Countries, a blow more serious in its implications to the West than anything done by the Soviet Union since World War II, how could they be expected to mount concerted action to deal with the Soviets' expansion in Africa or outright invasion of a neighboring country?

The effect of the Soviets' redefinition of détente in light of the economic crisis in the West weakened American leadership, and the fissiparous tendencies within the Atlantic alliance could be observed at the 1979 Vienna Brezhnev–Carter summit. Anxious as the Russians were to seal SALT II and to prevent relations between the two countries from deteriorating, there was little at Vienna of that studied courting of the Americans that had characterized the 1972 Moscow conference. This time there were no grandiloquent declarations about both countries scrupulously respecting each other's broad policy interests throughout the world. Instead, Brezhnev chose to lecture Carter and his entourage in public on the impermissibility and uselessness of trying to link the fate of SALT II and détente to Soviet restraint in foreign policy. "Attempts also continue to portray social processes taking place in one or another country or the struggles of the peoples for liberation as ''Moscow's plots or intrigues.' Naturally, the Soviet people are in sympathy with the liberation struggle of various nations. . . . We believe that every people has the right to determine its own destiny. Why then pin on the Soviet Union the responsibility for the objective course of history, or what is more, use this as a pretext for worsening our relations?''[4] With the worldwide configuration of forces now much more in their favor than it had been in 1972, it was probably genuinely incomprehensible to the Soviet leaders how anyone could expect them to abide by the same obligations and cautions they had pledged to observe on the earlier occasion.

CHOICES AND PROJECTIONS

Their actions in the recent past and present offer a suggestive guide to Soviet leaders' choices and decisions in the future. While it is of little use to try to divide the Kremlin decision makers into hawks and doves or to try to define who might represent the hard or soft factions, there is within the Politburo and its affiliates a considerable division of opinion when it comes to foreign policy. These differences, however, are not found in any permanent groupings or factions, but in the fluctuation between two main tendencies present in the mind of the leadership as a whole.

One such approach might be likened to that of the rentier. This view holds that the USSR can afford to be patient and circumspect in its foreign policies, eschew risky ventures abroad, and continue to collect the dividends of its past successes and the inherent and worsening afflictions of the capitalist world. The rentier's attitude is based not so much on the preachings and certitudes of Marxism as on the deductions from the historical experiences of the Soviet state, especially since World War II, when the United States has been its only real rival for worldwide power and influence. The Americans have been unable to oppose effectively the Soviets' advance, and they are unlikely to do so in the future. The cumbersome procedure of American foreign policymaking and the unruly democratic setting in which it operates will always place the United States at a disadvantage vis-à-vis the flexible and unconstrained apparatus of Soviet diplomacy. Hence, it is unwise to provoke the Americans and risk a confrontation, when the U.S. position is bound to grow weaker and that of the USSR stronger in the natural course of events.

The rentier puts the "imperialist danger" in a pragmatic perspective. It does exist as a general tendency within the capitalist world, but with proper caution on Moscow's part, it will not assume the form of a concrete menace. The United States was not able to threaten the USSR at the time of greatest American superiority. It is not likely to do so now, when there is general awareness in the West of what a nuclear war might mean. The Reagan administration's early rhetoric has already been blunted by the realization that the Soviet Union cannot be intimidated and that both the economic realities and the realities of European politics will not permit the United States to regain superiority in strategic weapons or to match quantitatively those of the USSR.

The rentier would urge the Soviets to moderate the pace of their nuclear arms buildup and to be prepared to offer timely concessions in the course of negotiations. The USSR has already gained great political advantages from having surpassed the United States in several categories of these weapons and would compound the gains by making what the world at large (if not the Pentagon) would hail as a magnanimous gesture—say, stopping the production of the Backfire bomber. Piling up arms eventually becomes politically counterproductive. The goal is to disarm the West psychologically and prevent it from recouping the momentum toward political integration; and Soviet military intimidation, if kept up for too long, is bound to have the opposite effect.

The same reasoning would apply to the general guidelines of Soviet policies throughout the world. Having established bridgeheads in Africa and the Caribbean, the Soviet Union would be making an error by trying to expand them too blatantly. The problems facing the United States in those areas are essentially intractable, and it is much better for Moscow to wait upon events in the Third World than to attempt to give history a push, fro example in South Africa. The USSR must refrain from any action likely to touch on a raw nerve of American politics, such as identifying itself with the extreme Arab position on Israel or reaching too obviously for control of the oil routes. In most of these areas of contention, time is essentially working for the Soviet Union, and precipitate actions by the Soviets might tend to reverse the trend.

The rentier's case on this last point becomes most debatable when the Politburo discussions turn to Eastern Europe and China. But even there, the rentier instinct would plead for a conservative approach. Soviet bloc countries can always be handled, though preferably not by military means. In China, it is true, time does not seem to work in the Soviets' favor. But for the balance of the 1980s and probably considerably beyond that, China can be contained, provided that the West and Japan do not launch a massive effort to help Beijing modernize its economy and become a major industrial (and hence military) power. Therefore, the need to contain China makes it all the more important to exercise restraint and blend firmness with conciliatory gestures in their approach toward the West.

The other side of the Soviet leadership's split personality might be called that of the speculator. For him the imperialist danger is not merely a doctrinal or propaganda phrase. It is not that he believes any more than the rentier that the United States is about to attack the USSR or engineer a revolution in East Germany or Poland. But only the constant growth in power by the Soviet Union and its avowed readiness to contemplate nuclear war have kept the West off balance and have prevented it from more explicit attempts to undermine the socialist camp. The USSR, therefore, must not desist from active and aggressive exploitation of the weaknesses and vulnerabilities of the world capitalist system, even where it involves a possibility of a major clash with the United States. Such brinkmanship becomes especially important for the immediate future, because any lessening in the Soviets' militancy would be read by Washington as a vindication of tough U.S. rhetoric, would encourage the United States to play to the hilt the China card, and could embolden the West Europeans to follow Washington's pleas to join in applying economic pressures upon the Soviet Union.

The speculator would not desist from trying to enhance and exploit whatever military advantages the USSR has already secured over the United States. To give up any of those advantages would be a grave mistake politically, even more so than militarily. It is awe of Soviet military might that has kept the United States from interfering in the Czechoslovak and Polish crises, has made the Europeans fearful about offending Moscow by imposing effective economic sanctions, and in fact makes then ever more eager to propitiate the Soviet colossus with trade and credits. Any slackening in the arms buildup would be taken in the West as confirmation of the thesis that internal economic and other problems have made the USSR more malleable to defense and international issues and that consequently one can pressure the Soviets to alter not only their military and foreign polices but also their domestic ones. One has to negotiate with the United States and NATO on tactical and strategic nuclear arms, but to offer any one-sided concessions, even if not substantive, would be most damaging for the USSR's image and bargaining position.

The speculator would stress the necessity of militancy, and not only from the angle of relations with the West. In the years ahead some Third World leaders might well be tempted to imitate Sadat's gambit and exploit the USSR for their own purposes, only to switch to the other side once the Soviet connection had been fully exploited. In retrospect it may have been a mistake to make Egypt the fulcrum of Soviet policies in the Middle East and to pour so much money and effort into buttressing its regime without obtaining a firmer grasp on its internal politics. Future Soviet ventures in the Third World must not only lead to a temporary discomfiture for the West, but also result in firm Soviet ideological and military control over the new client.

Analysts in the West and even some figures within the Soviet establishment keep pointing to Afghanistan as an illustration of the dangers of overt and precipitate Russian aggression. In fact Afghanistan, for all its troublesome aspects, has served as a salutary lesson to those of Moscow's protégés who might contemplate following Egypt's example and try to get the benefits of Soviet political and economic support while maneuvering between the two camps. For all the initial indignation, the Afghanistan coup served to strengthen the Muslim world's respect or fear of the USSR. When a mob tried to attack the Soviet embassy in Teheran, it was protected (unlike the embassy of another power) by the forces of that very fundamentalist Muslim regime. Direct Soviet military intervention is not something to be used too often, but once in a long while it serves as a useful reminder that the USSR is not to be trifled with.

Similar considerations indicate that the Soviet Union cannot afford to be a passive observer or just assist occasionally and indirectly in the erosion of U.S. influence in Latin America or that of the West in general in Africa. In fact it is doubtful whether this process can continue to benefit the Soviet Union's interests, unless the latter promotes it energetically with more than just rhetoric and military supplies. All radical and liberation movements are inherently unstable and volatile in their political allegiance. If rebuffed in their pleas for more active Soviet help, they may turn to others or tend to disintegrate. It would thus be a mistake for Moscow to stand aside if and when armed struggle erupts in South Africa or in the case of a violent confrontation between the forces of Left and Right in a major Latin American country.

Our speculator tends to question, not explicitly of course, the thesis that "the objective course of history" must favor the Soviet cause. Where would the USSR be today if it had allowed "objective factors" to determine the fate of Eastern Europe? In Latin American, Africa, and Asia one ought not be confuse the emotional residue of anticolonialism and local radicalism with a secular tendency toward communism or with automatic gravitation of the new and developing societies toward the Soviet model. Anticapitalism and perhaps anti-Western sentiments may be the common denominator of most radical and liberation movements in the non-Western world. But once in power, if they feel they can afford it, such movements tend to seek freedom from any foreign tutelage. Their leaders have brown sophisticated enough to understand the complexities of the international scene and, if left to themselves, they would prefer to be genuinely nonaligned and able to play one side against the other. It is not by patiently waiting upon events but by bold coups that Soviet power and influence have been projected into all areas of the globe, and it is not the "inherent logic of economic and social development" but the greatly expanded naval and airlift capabilities that have maintained and enlarged those enclaves of influence. And so for the balance of the 1980s the objective course of history must continue to be carved out by strenuous Soviet efforts including, when necessary, the use of military force.

Political and economic stability is a natural ally of the capitalist world. The USSR, therefore, can have no interest except in special cases in a general U.S.– Soviet understanding that would lessen the intensity of political ferment in the troubled areas of the world or reduce appreciably the present level of international tension. The speculator rejects the practicality or desirability of any long-term accommodation between the USSR and the United States. Even if it pursues the most peaceful policies, the United States will always represent a standing danger to the Soviet system and the socialist camp, simply by virtue of what it is. Close relations with the democracies lead inevitably to ideological pollution at home and to the weakening of political vigilance and social discipline that is *sine qua non* of a communist regime.

The rentier and the speculator would disagree most violently concerning the degree of urgency of the Chinese problem. The activist rejects emphatically the notion that the USSR can afford to sit and watch while China's economy is being modernized and its stockpile of nuclear weapons keeps growing. Some efficacious solution to the problem must be found during the next few years. Perhaps the intrafaction struggle that has been going on in China since the Cultural Revolution might assume the proportions of a civil war. Barring that rather slim hope, the USSR would have to take some measures beyond simply trying to contain China. Perhaps Beijing could still be enticed to paper over its dispute with the Soviets and be pushed again onto a collision course with the United States. Conversely, a moment might come when the Soviets will have sufficiently intimidated the West to compel it to leave them a free hand for even the most drastic resolution of their Chinese dilemma. Since the Sino–Soviet dispute heated up, and even when relations between Washington and Beijing were at their worst, it has in fact been America's nuclear power that has been a key factor in restraining the Soviets from trying to resolve the conflict by force.

Neither of the two impulses currently coexisting in the minds of the Politburo is likely to achieve complete mastery during the balance of the decade. Ascendancy of the rentier mentality would clearly make the Soviet Union much less of a destabilizing force in the world arena and in the long run could open up prospects of a major change in the Soviets' philosophy of international relations. The speculator motif, if dominant, would greatly increase the danger of an all-out war. For the immediate future the Soviet leaders can be expected to seek a middle course between the two approaches, the benefits and risks of either determined by their perceptions of the strengths and weaknesses of the noncommunist world.

NOTES

1. Henry L. Stimson and McGeorge Bundy, *On Active Service in War and Peace* (New York: Octagon, 1947), p. 644.
2. Georgi Arbatov, "Soviet-American Relations," in *The Communist* (Moscow: February, 1973), p. 110.
3. Fox Butterfield, "Hanoi General Was Surprised at Speed of Saigon's Collapse," *New York Times,* April 26, 1976.
4. Quoted in *State Department Bulletin,* no. 2028 (Washington, DC: U.S. Government Printing Office, July 1979), p. 51.

10
Soviet Ideology, Risk-Taking, and Crisis Behavior*

Hannes Adomeit

If it is correct that there are operational principles and recurring patterns of behavior which are specifically Soviet, what accounts for them? "Soviet ideology" must be an important part of the answer—a conclusion that is likely to contradict conventional wisdoms in American scholarship.[1] It may be useful, therefore, to look more closely at the arguments put forward in support of the thesis that Soviet ideology need not be taken all too seriously in the analysis of post–World War II Soviet foreign policy and to state in more detail why, in the argument of this study, ideology continues to matter.

One reason for the reluctance in American scholarship to attribute a significant role to Soviet ideology in shaping Soviet behavior very likely has something to do with the image in the mind of the analyst associating "ideological" with "irrational," "reckless," "adventurist," and the like, but contrasting it with "pragmatic," "opportunist," or "realistic."[2] Ideology as a factor shaping Soviet behavior is as a consequence being eroded in the mind of the analyst when he is faced with instances where Soviet representatives display diplomatic skill, act as shrewd and calculating businessmen, or pay much attention to military power as an instrument of furthering state interests.

Another possible explanation for the Western diagnosis of the erosion of ideology in Soviet foreign policy is to be found in a very narrow—and hence inadequate and misleading—definition. "Ideology" is often conceived of as nothing but the equivalent of the degree of Soviet support for world revolution, and sometimes even this is measured by the degree to which the Soviet Union is willing to employ military force on behalf of local communists in various areas of the world. As a consequence, the importance of ideology in Soviet foreign policy is being reduced for the Western analyst when the Soviet leaders apparently close their eyes to the oppression of local communists while engaging in

*Reprinted by permission of the author from *Soviet Risk-Taking and Crisis Behavior: A Theoretical and Empirical Analysis* (London: George Allen & Unwin, 1982), pp. 317, 320, 322, 324, 328–35, 345–46. Copyright 1982 by Hannes Adomeit.

cooperation with the oppressors at the state level (as in many countries of the Arab world), stand by with folded arms as Marxist regimes are being crushed (as in Chile), or fail to exploit alleged or real advantages for deepening the "crisis of capitalism" (as in the wake of the oil crisis after 1973).

Other explanations have much to do with the philosophical preconditioning of the Western analyst. To scholars reared in the Anglo–Saxon tradition of empiricism and pragmatism, the very thought that leaders in the practical realm of politics in the twentieth century should be guided in their actions by a rigid belief system appears incredible or inconceivable.[3] They find the Hegelian form of Soviet ideology difficult to grasp, and "the pronouncements of Soviet ideologists appear to them similar to the chants and litanies of some esoteric religious cult."[4]

These basic tendencies of analysis have been much reinforced recently. On the one hand, there are many scholars now who have had some form of contact with their Soviet counterparts, and an increasing number of them are able to read the Soviet scholarly output of the various institutes of the Academy of Sciences of the USSR in the original. Many of their Russian counterparts appear to be (and often are) men of reason, and many of the scholarly analyses, give or take some of the obligatory references to Lenin, resemble Western modes of analysis. Hence the conclusion that Western and Soviet perspectives on the international system are essentially similar.[5] On the other hand, the basic tradition of empiricism and pragmatism has found specific expression recently in the behavioral revolution in the social sciences with the generation of pressures, often justified, for more stringent measurement and higher standards of verification. These pressures have been extended to Soviet studies. But there are tremendous problems of "operationalizing" a research problem such as the influence of ideology in Soviet foreign policy. As a result it often appears more appropriate to delete a factor such as ideology altogether than to lay open a research plan to the charge of being unscientific because an immeasurable factor has been introduced. Ideology, therefore, has often been eroded by default rather than design.

In order to arrive at a realistic assessment of ideology as a factor of Soviet behavior it is necessary to abandon some faulty distinctions altogether, to recognize that the term has a broad scope, and to acknowledge that what matters most are not so much the perceptions and products of the *institutchiki,* or the thin apologias and rationalizations of lower- and middle-level *apparatchiki* one is allowed to meet, but the probable belief system and actual, observable behavior of the political leadership.

The broad *scope* encompassed by Soviet ideology needs to be considered first. As summarized by Alfred Meyer, Soviet ideology can be said to include, among other parts, a philosophy called dialectical materialism; generalizations about man and society, past and present, called historical materialism; an economic doctrine called political economy, which seeks to explain the economics of capitalism and imperialism, on the one hand, and of socialist construction, on the other; and a body of political thought, or guidelines, now called scientific communism, which deals, first, with the strategy and tactics of communist revolutions and, second, with political problems of socialist states.[6]

The next stage in the examination of the problem of ideology is to assume that there may be a variety of *functions* played by each individual part of Soviet ideology, to make allowance for the possibility that the manifold activities in politics and society may be influenced by ideology to differing degrees, and to be aware of the problem and that the relative importance of various aspects of ideology may change over time. The precise delimitation of functions of ideology may be a matter of preference (there will always be overlaps to a certain extent), but their existence itself has not been in dispute. They could be called as follows: (1) analytical or cognitive function; (2) operational or tactical function; (3) utopian, revolutionary, or missionary function; (4) legitimizing functions (5) socializing function.[7]

Briefly, the analytical function refers to a conscious process and asks questions such as "How do the Soviet leaders see the world?" and "What, in the view of the Soviet leadership, are the basic structural elements of the international system, the sources of conflict, the factors accounting for stability or change, and so on?" The second function is more difficult to define. It can be taken as meaning (a) that the Soviet leadership is acting on the basis of the results of analysis (the impact of perception on behavior); (b) that the Soviet leadership codifies and formalizes the main line of a particular era in world affairs, defines the scope of peaceful coexistence, sets forth its view on the correlation of forces and the like, and arrives from there at the main tasks to be pursued (that is, the impact of doctrine on behavior); or (c) that there exist deeply engrained operational principles formed by ideology (the impact of socialization and experience on behavior). It is within this function of ideology that the left/right dichotomy finds its proper place of discussion.

The third function of ideology—the utopian, revolutionary, or missionary function—is often (but incorrectly) taken to be the only one that matters. It is also the one that is at the basis of the dichotomy of ideology versus "the national interest." By referring to it the analyst asks questions such as "To what extent is world revolution still a goal of Soviet foreign policy?," "To want extent is the Soviet leadership committed to supporting local communists and their bids for power?," and "What is the role of the USSR within the international communist movement?"

The fourth function has two important dimensions—one domestic, the other international. Legitimacy of power in the USSR is based on Marxism–Leninism; although other forms of legitimacy may eventually emerge, at the present state of development it would appear that any Soviet leader, or leadership, attempting to deviate from that basis would be destroying the very ground on which he or it is operating. By extension this applies to the legitimacy of Soviet rule in Eastern Europe, where the Soviet system has been transplanted and where it is being protected by the various means of control available to the Soviet Union.

The last function rests in the dialectical interplay between ideology and the education, upbringing, experience, and career patterns of the top leadership. This must lead an open-minded analyst to ask: "What kind of psychological makeup of the leadership results from socialization processes in the Soviet Union?" Behind such a question would lie the assumption that the experiences in the control and organization of society, and the criteria of success or failure in the domestic *kto-kogo* struggle, are apt to be transplanted by the successful leaders to the international arena.

As regards Soviet behavior in the Berlin crises of 1948 and 1961, nothing could be further from the truth, therefore, than the statement, "ideology had nothing to do with it."Combined operational, legitimizing, and socializing aspects of soviet ideology (functions 2, 4, and 5 of the above categorization) have much to do with the shaping of Soviet interests affected in the crises and with the existence (and persistence) of the following operational principles:

1. Do not embark on forward operations against an opponent which are not carefully calculated in advance and move forward only after careful preparation.
2. "Push to the limit," "engage in pursuit" of an opponent who begins to retreat or make concessions, but "know when to stop" (in conditions of challenging an adversary); "resist from the start" any encroachment by the opponent, no matter how slight it appears to be, but "don't yield to enemy provocations" and "retreat before superior force" (in conditions of responding to a challenge by an adversary).[8]
3. Before engaging in forward operations "carefully construct a fallback position" so as to meet unexpectedly high resistance by the adversary.
4. Never lose sight of the political objectives to be achieved, and in pursuing them do not let yourself be diverted by false notions of bourgeois morality.

Concerning the operational aspect, some of the axions summarized above could have been taken straight form Lenin's *"Left Wing" Communism, an Infantile Disorder,* for instance, the admonition that "To tie one's hand before-hand, openly to tell the enemy, who is at present better armed than we are, whether we shall fight him, and when, is stupidity and not revolutionariness"[9] or the advice that

> The more powerful enemy can be conquered only by exerting the utmost effort, and by necessarily, thoroughly, carefully, attentively and skillfully taking advantage of every, even the smallest "rift" among enemies.[10]

When Lenin adds in characteristic polemical fashion that those who did not understand this "do not understand even a particle of Marxism" he makes a charge that to some degree also applies to adherents of the "erosion of ideology" view when they juxtapose as antithesis "ideology," on the one hand, and "opportunism" or "pragmatism," on the other, thereby overlooking the fact that rigidity in doctrine does not by any means imply rigidity in tactics.[11] Attention must be paid to the Leninist distinction between short-term considerations and long-range ideological goals. In a certain sense, as Leo Labedz has argued, all politics, ideological or not, tend to be concerned first of all with short-term considerations.

> But there is a difference between policies which appertain to nothing else, and those which take long-term considerations, ideological or other, as their frame of reference. To confuse the two as "pragmatic" in the same sense is to misunderstand the character of Soviet policies in the past, and . . . at present.[12]

The view that the education, upbringing, experience, and career patterns ("socialization") of the Soviet leaders account for specific behavioral patterns in domestic and international politics impinges on the argument that the Soviet leaders are cynical with regard to ideology, in particular to the aspect of a universal classless society. Well they might be. Revolutionary idealism and romanticism may very well be regarded as a thing of the past, and "ideological evolution during six decades of Soviet history can be summarized as a reluctant retreat from the utopian and universalistic claims of Marxist doctrine *without, however, their abandonment.*"[13] In addition to that, other aspects of ideology have become more pronounced (legitimacy, for instance, which will be dealt with presently), and still others have been retained. To be counted among them are the ideas that life, including "international life," is an unending struggle, that this struggle can only end with the victory of one socioeconomic system over the other, and that to stand still, and not to plan for advances and gains, means falling behind and to be thrown on the rubbish heap of history. In Western societies, by analogy, processes of secularization have progressed far, but the influence of Protestantism and Catholicism will tend to affect even the cynic's behavior (as does the influence of ideology in the USSR) because he will not be able to rid himself of unquestioned assumptions and ideas which he takes as given or erroneously holds to be self-evident.

Even if the credibility of Soviet ideology is wearing thin and, in international politics, is becoming more of a liability than an asset, it is still a fallacy to argue that ideology is "nothing but *ex post facto* rationalization" (*Rechtfertigung*) and has nothing to do with motivation (*Antrieb*). Rationalization and motivation, for an individual, a political leadership, or a state (and particularly when it comes to a state conforming to the notion of "an ideology in power"), can be *mutually reinforcing* mechanisms.[14] This leads directly to the problem of legitimacy.

No matter whether it is the power of the Soviet leadership, the power of institutions (the party, the armed forces, the police, the courts, and so on), relations among the countries of the socialist community (that is, the exercise of Soviet control and influence in the ruling communist states), or Soviet claims— open or tacit—to preeminence in the international communist movement, all of this is justified in terms of ideology. Criteria of achievement and well-being, too, are used by the Soviet leadership to elicit cooperation and compliance. Such criteria, however, belong to the realms of practical politics and expediency. They are only subsidiary to and derivative of the basic ideological principles.

Marxism, as Robert Wesson has argued, would probably have been "effectively if not overtly left behind as the new state settled down after the revolution, to be replaced by a straightforward faith of patriotism, Russianism and loyalty to the new rulership," but it was "indispensable because the new Soviet state undertook to govern a multinational domain."[15] Marxist internationalism was practically dropped during the war, but it became important again as the Russian armies recovered the Ukraine and other minority areas. "As Soviet forces asserted hegemony over nations of Eastern Europe, the role of ideology became still more vital."[16] This much, at least, seems to be granted also by adherents to the "erosion of ideology" school. Although, in their view, ideology has come to play a much lesser role in Soviet foreign policy in general, Eastern Europe is nevertheless being regarded as an exception.[17]

The fallacy of this view can be shown quite simply, and quite legitimately, by substituting "Soviet sphere of influence" or "socialist community" for "Eastern Europe." As Cuba, Mongolia, and Vietnam belong to it, as Angola, Ethiopia, and South Yemen are allied with it, and as strenuous efforts are made to integrate Afghanistan in it the (as they perceive it) "limited" and "regional" importance of ideology is immediately transformed into a phenomenon of global significance. For all these reasons, to say that the USSR is only a "new name for old Russia" would be to convey the wrong idea; to assume that Soviet foreign policy is merely Russian imperialism in a new garb would be, as Vernon Asparturian put it, "a catastrophic mistake."[18]

Certainly these considerations are valid with regard to East Germany and the Berlin crises. To assert that the GDR was but a new name for old East Germany would not only have been anathema to the SED leadership in 1961, but it would have been an idea extremely alien to *all* Germans, no matter what their political orientation, because in their conception old East Germany (*Ostdeutschland*) used to begin east of "East Germany"—odd as this may sound in English.[19] But the legitimizing function of Soviet ideology enters forcefully into both crises because the type of system in the making on German soil in 1948, and the system as it existed in 1961, derived their tenuous claim to legitimacy neither from German history nor from achievement but exclusively from ideology. The problems for the Soviet Union were complicated by the fact that ideology had not only to swim against *currents of nationalism* in Germany and cope with a singular *lack of socialist achievement* there but also to contend with strong rival variants of *German Marxism* as opposed to Russian Bolshevism.

This threefold challenged to ideological legitimacy of the Soviet zone of occupation, and later the GDR, took different forms in the two crises, but in both cases the challenge is inseparable from important or (if one prefers) vital Soviet interests as defined by the respective leaderships. In 1948 options other than confrontation were still open to the Soviet Union. In recognition of nationalism as a strong political force some form of neutralized Germany might have been preferable to an irredentist, hostile West Germany as a spearhead of "American imperialism"; in recognition of Marxism and independent socialism as a strong current in Germany some form of third road for that country could have prevented its inclusion in schemes of "capitalist encirclement" such as NATO. With such a Germany, neutralized and democratic-socialist, some form of friendship and cooperation was possible. But all this could have happened only *if* there had been dramatic change in Soviet ideology toward the genuine acceptance of "many roads to socialism" externally and the opening up of the Soviet system to a kind of "socialism with a human face" internally. It is in large measure because of the rigidity and the unacceptable face of Stalinist ideology that these theoretical alternatives had no chance of being tried out in practice.

In 1961 the threefold challenge to ideological legitimacy had by no means disappeared. The challenge was evident in the form of an economically successful West Germany and its claim of sole representation, in West Berlin as a center of attraction for East Germans and East Europeans, and in the rising attractiveness of social democracy as a political force. It was evident also in the fact that the Soviet-type system on German soil had been thoroughly discredited and was suffering a worsening political and economic crisis. But by then the GDR had become so much bound up with the USSR, and economically and politically had become so much part and parcel of the Soviet bloc, that alternatives other than physical action to remedy this state of affairs no longer seemed to exist.

In sum, Marxist-Leninist ideology furnished important portions of the analytical and perceptual framework, operational principles, and legitimation of Soviet behavior in both crises. These are the constant features. However, when comparing the role of ideology in the two Berlin crises there is also one feature of change. In 1948 a broad congruence of elements of the left still existed, both in doctrine and in actual policy. But in 1961 such congruence was absent, as demonstrated by the fact that the predominant elements of the right coexisted with confrontation.

Two explanations can be offered for this development. First, by 1961 the greater complexity of international relations and the increasing diversity in the international communist movement and of Soviet society and politics almost inevitably had led to inconsistencies and contradictions in the various elements of Soviet theory and practice. Congruence of left/right priorities and commitments had become a thing of the past. Second, in 1948 Soviet doctrine still clung to leftism not only in the form of the "two camps" theory but also the Leninist thesis on the "fatal inevitability of war." This thesis, as I have argued, was a dangerous thing for crisis diplomacy, and it is not surprising that it was first "clarified" and then modified by Stalin and finally abandoned by Khrushchev.[20] By 1961 it had become standard Soviet practice to try to combine a rightist ideological approach of the "carrot" toward the West with that of a military and political "big stick."

The discussion of ideology as a factor shaping Soviet behavior in the two Berlin crises underlines the fact that it is difficult to uphold the distinction between "Marxist–Leninist ideology" and "the Soviet national interest." Even authors who subscribe to the validity of such a dichotomy for analytical purposes hasten to add the reservation that this is a "crude antithesis."[21] This is true not only because Soviet ideology is a complex phenomenon but also because "the Soviet national interest" (like any national interest) is a highly subjective and ambiguous concept, capable of manipulation and almost limitless reinterpretation, so that in reality political leaders are faced with a complex tangle of interests (in the plural), always changing according to specific social, economic, military, political, *and* ideological conditions, both of an international and domestic dimension, and making it necessary every time to distinguish between costs, benefits, and risks of a long-term or short-term nature.

Despite these complexities one must be wary of worrying about a tautological trap that in reality does not exist. It could be argued that "national interests," vital or peripheral, can be defined only *ex post facto*: more specifically, that the relative importance of particular interests can be measured only in retrospect by the degree of commitment made by a particular state on their behalf. However, this argument resembles recent criticisms of Darwin's theory of natural selection. By defining fitness as "differential reproductive success" (that is, by considering evolution as a change in numbers, not as a change in quality), a vacuous tautology results because natural selection is no more than "the survival of those who survive." However, certain morphological, physiological, and behavioral traits can be considered *a priori* superior as designs for living in new environments. Certain traits "confer fitness by an engineer's criterion of good design, not by the empirical fact of their survival and spread."[22]

Similarly, in international relations political leaders and analysts are able to make their own *a priori* judgments as to the degree to which a particular state's interests are involved, whether they are of primary or secondary importance, and whether the design to safeguard the various interests is adequate, effective, legitimate, and the like. The mutually perceived balance of interests thus comes to be of crucial importance for the origin, course, and outcome of international crises. For an actor to succeed in conveying the idea that vital interests are at stake for himself, and only secondary interests for the adversary, confers to him tremendous advantages in the bargaining process.

NOTES

1. See Hannes Adomeit, *Soviet Risk-Taking and Crisis Behavior: A Theoretical and Empirical Analysis* (London: Allen and Unwin, 1984), pp. 56–58.

2. The image also often implies that the more "pragmatic" the Soviet Union becomes, the easier it will be to deal with it, and the greater the tendency for the Soviet Union to become a status quo–oriented power.

3. This is a point made by Alfred G. Meyer, "The Functions of Ideology in the Soviet Political System," *Soviet Studies* 17, no. 3 (January 1966), p. 273.

4. Ibid.

5. See Adomeit, *Soviet Risk-Taking*, p. 57.

6. Meyer, "Functions of Ideology," p. 273. Meyer also included the official history of the CPSU and pronouncements made by the party concerning the interpretation of current affairs and the setting of goals and priorities.

7.   The first four of the five functions named above conform roughly to distinctions made by Marshall Shulman. Similar distinctions have appeared in print, e.g., William Zimmerman, *Soviet Perspectives on International Relations* (Princeton, NJ: Princeton University Press, 1969), pp. 282–83.

8.   Alexander George, "The 'Operational Code': A Neglected Approach to the Study of Political Leaders and Decisionmaking," in *The Conduct of Soviet Foreign Policy*, 2nd ed., Erik Hoffmann and Frederic Fleron, eds. (Hawthorne, NY: Aldine 1980), pp. 165–90.

9.   V. I. Lenin, *"Left Wing" Communism, and Infantile Disorder: A Popular Essay in Marxist Strategy and Tactics* [written in 1920] (New York: International Publishers, 1969), p. 59.

10.   *Ibid.*, p. 53.

11.   This is a point made long ago by Zbigniew Brzezinski and Samuel Huntington, *Political Power* (New York: Viking, 1964), p. 66, but it is still right.

12.   Leo Labedz, "Ideology and Soviet Policies in Europe," paper delivered at the Twentieth Annual Conference of the International Institute for Strategic Studies (IISS), September 7–10, 1978, p. 3. See also my paper, "Ideology in the Soviet View of International Affairs," delivered at the same conference, which very much agrees with Labedz's approach and conclusions. Both papers are published in *Prospects of Soviet Power in the 1980s*, Christoph Bertram, ed. (London: Macmillan, 1980).

13.   Labedz, "Ideology and Soviet Policies in Europe," p. 6.

14.   *Ibid.*, p. 3.

15.   Robert G. Wesson, "Soviet Ideology: The Necessity of Marxism," *Soviet Studies* 21, no. 1 (July 1969), p. 69.

16.   *Ibid.*

17.   See Adomeit, *Soviet Risk-Taking and Crisis Behavior*, pp. 36, 190.

18.   Vernon V. Aspaturian, "Ideology and National Interest in Soviet Foreign Policy," in *Process and Power in Soviet Foreign Policy* (Boston: Little Brown, 1971), p. 331.

19.   The West Germans, and politically indifferent "East Germans," have always referred to "East Germany" as *Mitteldeutschland* (Central Germany). If the SED rejected this label it was not because of its disagreement with the geographical distinction, but because what it wanted was to see the official political term of "German Democratic Republic" implanted in the consciousness of the Germans.

20.   See Adomeit, *Soviet Risk-Taking*, pp. 113–14, 177–80, 21–22.

21.   Robin Edmonds, *Soviet Foreign Policy* (London: Oxford University Press, 1975), pp. 153–54. The author also concedes that "Soviet historians and statesmen are guilty neither of dishonesty nor cynicism when they claim, in effect, that what is good for their country is good for world communism." To this can be added the view that "Soviet ideology itself defines 'national interest,' 'power,' and 'world revolution' in such a way as to make them virtually as indistinguishable as the three sides of an equilateral triangle" (Aspaturian, "Ideology and National Interest," p. 333). Finally, there should be little disagreement with the argument that "Depending on the perceptions of fact and value among these people [Soviet leaders], Soviet national interest may be served by the aggressive pursuit of power by Communist Parties in all countries. Or, Soviet national interest may not be served by such a course at all. The national interest is a *conclusion*, derived logically from premises of fact and value, some of which may have been drawn from, or conditioned by, the precepts of Marxism–Leninism" [Jan Triska and David Finely, *Soviet Foreign Policy* (New York: Macmillan, 1968), p. 114].

22.   Stephen Jay Gould, "Darwin's Untimely Burial," *Natural History* 85, no. 8 (October 1976), p. 26. To demonstrate the point the author adds that "it got colder before the mammoth evolved his shaggy coat."

11
Truth, Reality, and Power:
The World through Soviet Eyes*

Raymond F. Smith

> It is the Russian attitude to Truth that is, of all
> things, the most baffling. For the Russians, this
> attitude to Truth is at once a source of strength
> and an inspiration: for us it usually seems mere
> confusion.
>
> —Geoffrey Gorer and John Rickman,
> *The People of Great Russia*

If, as we have previously suggested, Soviet culture is much further toward the high-context end of the scale than is American, it becomes all the more important for U.S. negotiators not only to be expert in the particular substantive issue at hand, but also to be sufficiently sensitized to pick up the contextual clues to Soviet positions. Such clues will not be explicitly stated but are nevertheless likely to be far more important for understanding the Soviet approach and goals in the negotiation at hand than equivalent information about the lower-context U.S. approach.

Soviet expectations of negotiations derive from their view of the world, a view that passes through two distinctively important filters—Marxist-Leninist ideology and Russian political culture. Knowing something about the salient characteristics of these filters is the starting point for understanding Soviet negotiating behavior.[1] We also need to try to develop some sense of which aspects of these filters operate as ''front of the mind'' concepts and which generally operate at a deeper, unconscious level. The distinction can be important, since the likely success of a particular negotiating approach—in general terms, for example,

*Reprinted by permission of the author and Indiana University Press from Raymond F. Smith, *Negotiating with the Soviets*, Chapter 4. Copyright © 1989 by the Institute for the Study of Diplomacy, Georgetown University.

intellectual argument versus emotional appeal—may well depend on whether it corresponds to the type of belief system held by the other side. Moreover, the susceptibility of a belief system to change will vary. Those aspects that are accepted intellectually are likely to be much more susceptible to change through acquiring new knowledge and awareness of changed circumstances than those held at a more fundamental level. Corresponding attributes of negotiating behavior would also be more or less susceptible to ease and rapidity of change.[2]

IDEOLOGY

The role that Marxism-Leninism plays in Soviet international conduct has been endlessly debated, often with more heat than light shed on the subject. Are the Soviets godless communists with a blueprint for taking over the world? Or are they modern-day Russian nationalists, essentially status quo in orientation and with the historic Russian fear of attack from abroad? The persistence of the debate reflects the durability of our own ideological stereotypes and the need to transcend them. A widely held view that attempts to bridge these differences is that the most important thing to understand about Marxism-Leninism is the function it performs, which is the perpetuation in power of the Communist Party of the Soviet Union, or more specifically of its ruling component, the *nomenklatura*.[3] The operative parts of the ideology, then, are those that contribute to *nomenklatura* rule.

Unfortunately, this concept does not help us to understand what Soviet negotiators believe, since it is compatible with the view that they are complete cynics, using the ideology to perpetuate themselves in power, or that they believe it, partly because it perpetuates them in power. The first formulation suggests, in effect, that ideology does not matter in negotiations with the Soviets—it is necessary and sufficient to understand their behavior in pure self-interest terms. It is only the function of the ideology that matters, not the particular form it has taken. But it seems to me that R. N. Carew Hunt had a good point in telling us that we should hesitate before concluding that the Soviet leadership cannot possibly believe in the myths it propounds: "we should remind ourselves that no class or party ever finds it difficult to persuade itself of the soundness of the principles on which it bases its claim to rule."[4]

During the three years that I spent at the American embassy in Moscow, I sensed a general consensus among my colleagues that ideology does matter in Soviet behavior, but a difficulty in articulating exactly how it comes into play. Adam B. Ulam's distinction between the prescriptive, the analytical, and the symbolic, or quasi-religious, functions of ideology captures some of this sense. I share Ulam's view that the prescriptive, or blueprint, element of Marxism-Leninism no longer plays a significant role in foreign policy, but that the analytical (an approach to understanding both domestic and international politics) and the symbolic (the sense that the adherents are moving forward with the forces of history and that the success of their state is predicated upon the truth of the doctrine) remain important for understanding Soviet international behavior.[5] Two concepts that I have come to believe are important to understanding Soviet negotiating behavior are the dialectical nature of reality and the correlation of forces. The first, it seems to me, while having both analytic and symbolic components, operates at the level of basic, unquestioned belief, while the second is a consciously applied tool.[6]

Dialectics, Reality, and Truth

Wrapping the American mind around the Soviet "isms"—Marxism-Leninism and dialectical materialism—was no easy task for those of us at the U.S. embassy in Moscow, and we were living there with some claim either to being or to becoming Soviet specialists. Little wonder, then, that the "isms" are impenetrable to most Americans. But they do not necessarily come easy to Soviet citizens either, as the following Moscow anecdote illustrates.

A Russian peasant once went to the priest and asked him for a definition of dialectics. Said the priest: "If two men come to your house, one with dirty hands, one with clean hands, and you have only enough water for one of them to wash, to whom would you give the water?" To which the peasant replied: "To the one with the dirty hands!" "No," said the priest, "you'd give it to the man who cares most about his cleanliness. Now the next day, if the same two come to you and you have enough water for only one, would you give it to the man with the clean hands or the man with the dirty hands?" The peasant replied confidently, "To the one with clean hands." "No," said the priest, "you would give it to the one with the dirty hands because his hands are dirty. Do you understand?" "No," said the peasant, thoroughly confused. "Well," said the priest, "that's dialectics."[7]

Viewing the world through a dialectical or a Marxist-Leninist framework does not come easily to most Americans. In fact, it is so alien that there is a tendency, in a kind of realpolitik offshoot of the "they are humans just like us" school to consider the use of Marxist-Leninist terminology in the international arena simply a politically useful cover for an approach to world politics that boils down to simple, traditional pursuit of national interest. Raymond L. Garthoff, who believes that approach misses some essential factors, says:

We have not even begun to analyze critically the underlying postulates of either the American or the Soviet conceptions. For example, consider the Soviet proposition that "the class struggle" and "national liberation struggle" are not and cannot be affected by detente. . . . Most Americans see that proposition as communist mumbo-jumbo being used as a transparently self-serving argument to excuse pursuit of Soviet interests. In fact, a Soviet leader considers that proposition to be a self-evident truth: detente is a policy, while the class struggle is an objective phenomenon in the historical process that cannot be abolished by policy decision, even if the Soviet leaders wanted to do so.[8]

Americans generally find it easier to view Soviet leaders and officials as cynics, spouting nonsensical doctrine while pursuing personal aggrandizement because, while we may condemn the behavior, we find it comprehensible. It is easier for us to understand cynics than true believers, except for those among us inclined toward the latter themselves. But we have a responsibility to dig more deeply, a responsibility that comes with superpower status in the nuclear era. As Garthoff puts it: "The consistent failure of each side to sense and recognize the different perspectives and perceptions of the other has been strongly detrimental to the development of their relations, compounding their real differences. . . . Rather than recognize a different perception, judging it to be a valid alternative perception or misperception, both sides typically ascribe a different and usually malevolent purpose to each other."[9]

Alfred G. Meyer sees ideology functioning as the frame of reference for individuals in a society, their set of concepts for perceiving the world and its problems, hence their means of orienting themselves in the universe.[10] Ideology, then, has to do with what we perceive as reality, as truth. It also has to do with the process of reasoning or thought by which we apprehend reality. there is considerable reason to believe that this process operates differently in the Russian mind than in the American mind.

Hegelianism, which produced minimal impact on the American intellect, by most accounts exercised enormous influence in nineteenth-century Russia. James H. Billington considers that Hegel, more than any other single man, changed the course of Russian intellectual history during the remarkable decade from 1838 to 1848.[11] What was there about Hegelianism to which the Russian mind responded with such enthusiasm? Philosophy, Billington argues, as understood in the Russia of the time was closer to the occult idea of "divine wisdom" than to the understanding of philosophy of rational and analytical investigation in the manner of Descartes, Hume, or Kant.[12] Its objective was to discover and reveal Truth rather than to consider man's capability for doing so. Consider in this context Gorer and Rickman's description of the Russian apprehension of Truth.

> Although Truth is a coherent system it is not consistent according to the usual standards of Occidental logic. Truth embraces contradictions both in space and time; the fact that the truth revealed to-day, or the application of the truth demanded to-day, is not the same as the truth (or application) of yesterday, does not mean that one or the other ceases to be part of Truth. Truth is so great that it contains all contradictions; Russians do not reject these contradictions, nor is it certain that they perceive them as contradictions, in the way non-Russians would do. . . . It is this conviction that they live in the Truth and pursue it as do the people of no other nation which gives the mystical overtones to the phrase "Holy Russia" and the newer form "Soviet Motherland."[13]

Hegel presented an all-encompassing world vision, an interpretation of the whole of history and an intellectual tool for comprehending it—the dialectic. The dialectic both described the process of historical movement and provided a means of understanding it. Most educated Americans, when confronted with the term "dialectic," say to themselves "oh yes, thesis-antithesis-synthesis" and promptly forget about it. We approach problem-solving differently, and it is difficult for us to conceive of an approach to problem-solving that differs radically from our own. But suppose, as Garthoff argues, there is more to it. How can we get a handle on it, and how would it affect Soviet negotiating behavior?

Khrushchev's October 26, 1962 letter to President Kennedy during the height of the Cuban missile crisis is one of the most well-known documents of modern-day international politics, despite the fact that only small excerpts from it have been published. It is, by the accounts of those who have seen it, a remarkable document to have been written by one chief of state to another. Robert Kennedy described it as long and emotional, but not incoherent, marked chiefly by Khrushchev's horror of the effects of nuclear war.[14] Khrushchev attempted to assure President Kennedy that the missiles were in Cuba strictly for defensive purposes and would never be used to attack the United States. "You can be calm in this regard," he wrote, "that we are of sound mind and understand perfectly well that if we attack you, you will respond the same way. But you too will receive the same that you hurl against us. And I think that you also understand this. . . . This indicates that we are normal people, *that we correctly understand and correctly evaluate the situation.*"[15]

What, in this highly dangerous and emotional situation, did Khrushchev mean when he referred to "normal people" who "correctly understand and correctly evaluate the situation"? Evidently, on the surface he meant that both leaders comprehended the catastrophe that nuclear war would bring. But I believe that Khrushchev's use of this particular terminology reveals more than that. An essential component of the claim to legitimacy of the Soviet Communist Party, and of its leaders, is that their understanding of the forces of history and their ability to act in accordance with them give them the right to rule. The self-serving aspects of this claim are obvious, but there is more to it than that. The Soviet ruling class is taught from a very early age both a philosophy of history and a way of understanding reality that differ dramatically from ours. If we are to understand them, we must develop some ability to see the world through their eyes.

Russian intellectual history has proved infertile ground for any philosophy arguing skepticism or mankind's limited ability to comprehend reality fully. In religion, orthodoxy dominated thought. Major pre–nineteenth-century move-ments of resistance to authority came not from modernizers, but from believers who considered any change in religious practice or social mores a deviation from God's ordained order. The nineteenth-century Russian intellectual, exposed to Western thought, could easily be brought to reject Russian Orthodoxy as a hopelessly retrogressive religion. But their rejection was of a particular creed, not of the underlying belief that an all-encompassing understanding of the meaning of life or the nature of reality was possible. They had a "penchant for translating every practical problem into an abstract point of doctrine, for raising specific concrete issues to the level of universal laws [and] compounded a lovable, unselfish impracticality with a rigidly doctrinaire and uncritical approach to questions of dogma."[16]

Hegel's sweeping philosophy of history provided an intellectually and emotionally congenial substitute for the rejected faith of Orthodoxy. As Nicholas Berdyaev puts it, the religious make-up of the Russian people contributes to an inclination in Russian thinking "towards totalitarian doctrines and a totalitarian way of looking at life as a whole."[17] Later generations of Russian intellectuals found in Marx's materialist dialectic the same assurance that the course of history could be known and that they could gauge the rightness of their behavior accordingly. The Russian Marxist could thereby "live in Truth." It was not only the manifest injustices of tsardom that cried out for revolution; history demanded it.

Dialectical materialism performs for educated Soviets what Meyer sees as one of the fundamental functions of an ideology: it provides their set of concepts for perceiving the world and its problems, their means of orienting themselves in the universe. The foundation for this understanding is dialectical materialism's theory of knowledge.[18] It is important to reiterate that we are not making any claim here that the principles of this theory of knowledge operate on the conscious level, or even that most Soviets could, if asked, easily describe or interpret them. Neither do most Americans consciously adduce, for example, the "scientific method" when they engage in problem solving. And, if asked to describe it, they could probably give only the most general description. Nevertheless, their approach to problem solving is not random. The system they use may be unconscious and non-verbalized, but it is a system. Each culture has its own rules for learning; if we are to understand a different culture, we must be prepared to set aside the learning models handed down in our culture.[19]

There are three fundamental components to dialectical materialism's theory of knowledge. The first asserts that reality exists independently of the observer's perception of it. There is a real, material world out there that exists whether or not we can see it, or understand it, or even believe in it. In Lenin's words:

> The sole "property" of matter with whose recognition philosophical materialism is bound up is the property of being an objective reality, of existing outside our mind. . . . Dialectical materialism insists on the approximate, relative character of every scientific theory of the structure of matter and its properties . . . nature is infinite, but it infinitely exists. And it is this sole categorical, this sole unconditional recognition of nature's existence outside the mind and perceptions of man that distinguishes dialectal materialism from relativist agnosticism and idealism.[20]

We do not intend here to try to place dialectical materialism in the context of Western philosophy, a job that in any case, Thomas J. Blakeley, among others, has done very nicely.[21] But perhaps a couple of roadmarks may be of help. The materialist affirmation of the primacy of matter differs in essence from the idealist philosopher's assertion of the primacy of soul, idea, consciousness, the subjective. Plato, for example, insists that the material world as we perceive it with our senses differs from the unchanging world of Forms, which is in principle intellectually knowable. The quality of redness exists for Plato independently of our perception of the color red, which may change over time.[22] Reality consists in these (paradoxically) ideal Forms, not in our imperfect perception of them. With wisdom, with intellectual understanding, could come a fuller comprehension of this "real," nonmaterial world. At an even further remove from a materialist conception of reality is, for example, Berkeley's assertion that the material world exists only by virtue of our perception, or, in the absence of any human being's perception, as ideas in the mind of God.[23]

The second assertion of dialectical materialism's theory of knowledge is that reality operates in accordance with the laws of the dialectic. Thus, absent some understanding of dialectical processes, our ability to comprehend reality is inevitably limited. All the more so since, according to the third component, thought is a reflection of reality. Kant, on the other hand, does not fully accept the theory of reflection. While conceding that things may exist "out there" independently of our knowledge of them, he contends that the world that we can know is inevitably limited by the categories we impose on it. The world that we know is not only a material one, but also one we have partly created, and we cannot stand outside it.

Dialectical materialism's theory of knowledge asserts the ultimate knowability of the real world. Thought undertaken in conscious knowledge of the laws of the dialectic is naturally capable of being a considerably more accurate reflection of reality than thought that is ignorant of it. There is both a subjective dialectic and an objective dialectic. Our knowledge of reality is the subjective dialectic. Reality itself is the objective dialectic. It is dynamic, never at rest, always changing. It follows, then, that the subjective dialectic must also be in continual movement if it is to attain, and retain, correspondence with reality, the objective dialectic. In fact, Absolute Truth is the full correspondence of the subjective to the objective dialectic, of our thoughts to reality. "For us, Marxists, truth is that which corresponds to reality."[24] It is both a state of being and a process, a description of the state of correspondence, but a dynamic also, since reality is always changing, and unchanging Truth would be a contradiction in terms. Relative truth is knowledge that is a basically true reflection of reality, but is limited and valid only under certain conditions and relations.

The problem in making decisions, in acting, is to ensure that the reality one perceives is a true reflection of objective reality. This is accomplished by successfully making the leap from sense-knowledge (immediate, practical contact with the objective dialectic) to intellectual knowledge (an abstract and schematic reflection of the objective dialectic). The key to making the leap successfully is practice. In Lenin's words, "From living perception to abstract thought, and from this to practice, such is the dialectical path of the cognition of truth."[25] Employing your knowledge of history, of the dialectic, you act in the world. The outcome of your action is the criterion for judging how well you understood reality, and helps you to understand it more fully. "Life itself," the Soviets say repeatedly, "teaches." We lose touch with reality either by refusing to learn from life, from practice, or by lacking the intellectual tools to do so because we are incapable of thinking with either spontaneous or conscious awareness of the objective dialectic.

Any educated Soviet, particularly any Soviet leader, must approach problems with an understanding of the dialectic or be unfit for leadership. A major foreign policy reversal, or for that matter a major domestic failure, has in the Soviet system been taken to mean either that the person in charge has incorrectly applied Marxism-Leninism to the situation at hand, or, particularly under Stalin, that he deliberately acted treasonously.[26] Thus, when Khrushchev, in an evidently emotional state, wrote to Kennedy that "we are normal people" who "correctly understand and correctly evaluate the situation," he was saying far more than that the situation was dangerous. The Soviet leader had, in fact, made a profound mistake in his understanding and evaluation of the situation. He was in the process of agonizing reappraisal necessitated by the intractability of reality, by the fact that events had shown his analysis of the situation to have been fundamentally flawed.

The key point to be kept in mind in this context is that, if the Soviet leadership had made a fundamentally incorrect analysis of the situation, its primary responsibility was to bring its actions back into closer accord with reality. This responsibility devolved on them not only as Soviet leaders, or as communists, but also as human beings. Responsible people, acting in knowledge of the historical dialectic, would not take actions that would start a nuclear war. Madmen might, or persons out of touch with reality (and therefore unfit to rule), but not "normal people" who "correctly understand and correctly evaluate the situation." Moreover, considerations of face are decidedly secondary in this kind of situation. You may put the best face you can on a change in course, but it is less important how your change in direction looks to the outside world than that you bring your policy into closer correspondence with reality.

It is quite possible for Soviet decision-makers to be cynical about some aspects of Marxism-Leninism, perhaps particularly of its use as a means of justifying their own positions, and at the same time employ, not even at a conscious level, the analytical tools we have been discussing as a means of solving problems. Peter Reddaway suggests that middle rank Party officials probably accept the Party ideology more fully than any other, since they have little information to interfere with their ability to rationalize. He believes the top leadership may be more cynical. Uri Ra'anan, however, argues that this cynicism has its limits:

> Whatever cynicism vis-à-vis the tenets of its revolutionary creed the Soviet elite may display . . . there remains a residual ideological factor, unmatched by any phenomenon of the tsarist period, that plays a crucial role both in the Soviet analysis of the international situation and in the imperatives that motivate Soviet actions. The reference, of course, is to the dialectic.[27]

There is considerable evidence that force-feeding dialectical materialism to adults has little, or perhaps even negative, impact. Required classes in the subject at the university level are, by all accounts, attended only if there is no way out and marked by polite indifference at best, often by unconcealed inattention. Steven White has found that more than two-thirds of those who attended Party education classes in Rostov-on-Don admitted that they rarely made use of the Marxist-Leninist classics, and a further 15 percent confessed that they made no use of them at all. In Uzbekistan, as many as 61 percent made minimal or no preparation at all for their Party education classes.[28]

No one who has spent time in the Soviet Union would argue that there is not profound cynicism in the society as a whole. The ubiquitous posters proclaiming the triumph of one or another aspect of socialism/communism, glorifying the Party, or calling on the people for still greater achievements are remarkable both for the extent to which newly arrived Westerners see them and the extent to which Soviets fail to. The preoccupation of the Soviet people with material possessions as a symbol of status is as profound as that of any other people in the world. Many, perhaps most, of those who join the Party do so to get ahead in the world—to get a better job, to improve their chances of getting into the university of their choice, to get better housing. The leadership certainly manipulates ideological symbols as a tool for maintaining power. As we have previously seen, this has led some Westerners to argue that in contemporary Soviet society ideology is no more than an instrument for maintaining the dominance of the ruling class. Daniel Bell, for example, argues that "while dogma such as dialectical materialism, historical materialism, the superiority of collective property, and the nature of scientific communism remain on a formal level, the doctrinal core, the central fact is not any specific theoretical formulation, but the basic demand for belief in the Party itself."[29] It is, however, a long step from saying that the Party uses ideology to perpetuate itself in power to saying that the Party has no ideology other than the perpetuation of its power. The perpetuation of its rule is an interest of the Party, or of the ruling class, not an ideology.

Just as class interest must be distinguished from ideology, so also must Party doctrine. The same debate about whether the ideology is believed or simply used as a tool for perpetuating the position of the ruling class exists about doctrine. The fact that the Party leadership has at different times espoused contradictory doctrinal tenets (the inevitably of war versus peaceful coexistence, for example) has been taken to demonstrate that doctrine is used for *post hoc* rationalizations of policy decisions taken on strictly practical grounds rather than believed. But this is not as clear as it may seem. Doctrine has to do not with Absolute Truth, but with partial truth. It is taken to be a basically correct reflection of reality, but one that may be bounded by time and circumstance. As reality changes, doctrine will have to as well. Thus, two contradictory tenets of doctrine may both be accurate reflections of a reality that over time has undergone qualitative change. It is not cynical for someone whose view of reality has been filtered through dialectical materialism to espouse seemingly contradictory positions at different points in time. If reality has changed, so must doctrine.

Nevertheless, if we take doctrine to refer to pronouncements that are verifiable, but unverified (such as peaceful coexistence), and ideology to comprise both doctrine and the unverifiable concepts from which it is derived (the dialectical nature of reality, for example), it appears that the more empirical nature of doctrine, the fact that it is more "front of the mind," renders it more susceptible to conscious manipulation. We could, then, define doctrine as that set of intellectual constructs that the Party uses to legitimize the advancement of its interests. The Party leadership no doubt does consciously manipulate some of the ideological symbols that justify and legitimize its rule. Can we consider that the set of such symbols constitutes the doctrine of the Party—ideas to which public obeisance must be paid, which most likely play little or no role in actual decision-making, but against which all decisions must be capable of justification? Soviet leaders may understand Party doctrine only dimly, or may even be completely cynical about it, but because it is a primary instrument of rule they will never consider it unimportant. The role of keeper of the doctrine is critical and is treated as such. It has been held in the Politburo in recent years by Suslov, Andropov, Chernenko, and Gorbachev—all either king-makers or future kings or both. But is there a remainder? Is some of it believed and not simply manipulated? The point here, after all, is not how we define doctrine, but what Soviets think of it. I suspect that after self-interest and deliberate manipulation are removed, an element of belief remains, at least among some Soviets some of the time, but the rampant cynicism that Soviet emigrés attribute to their former leaders suggests that the component of actual belief in elements of the doctrine may be small.

In any case, Party doctrine generally plays little explicit role in international negotiations. Even if they believed it whole-heartedly, contemporary Soviet negotiators would not expect it to make any impression on representatives of the West. The language of Soviet negotiators may, therefore, be remarkably free of the cant that pervades the Soviet media. It would be a mistake, however, to conclude from the absence of recitations of doctrinal cant that Soviet negotiators do not bring with them to the table a set of ideological expectations and predispositions. Ideology is more subtle, more deep-seated, and more difficult to summarize in a few words than doctrine, but it is also a more important determinant of Soviet negotiating behavior. Adomeit's study of the 1948 and 1961 Berlin crises led him to conclude that ideology "furnished important portions of the analytical and perceptual framework, operational principles and legitimation of Soviet behavior in both crises."[30]

At some level, educated Soviets must absorb a system of understanding and interpreting the world around them, just as Americans learn something we call "the scientific method." Seweryn Bialer believes that ideology is best "understood as a part of culture, a slowly changing combination of doctrinal inputs and the historical experience and predispositions that run parallel to doctrine. This ideology, these beliefs, are operational for Soviet foreign policy-making." In this sense, "the study of Soviet ideology provides a key to understanding the changing Soviet definition of its national interest."[31]

The rote study of dialectical materialism may be no more interesting to a young Soviet than the memorization of catechism questions to a young American Catholic,[32] but basic concepts and outlooks may nevertheless be internalized. A Soviet official told his son some years ago that the Americans had put a man on the moon. His son refused to believe it, saying that it was not possible, the Americans were not communists and therefore could not have done such a thing.[33] Dialectics is a fundamental concept in Soviet schooling, introduced at a very early stage in a simplified form. Does it become a part of people's thought processes? A Soviet emigré puts it this way:

> Dialectics is incorporated everywhere, even in science courses, as a way of solving problems. People do acquire a dialectical way of thinking. You may not see it when you are talking about something like building a dacha, but whenever you see two people arguing you will see them using the dialectical method. They are using things such as the context, the need to understand circumstances. Even people who are not well educated will use dialectics. It becomes part of the back of the mind. In the camps, I have seen prisoners with very simple education using dialectics. Everything is permeated with it—the radio, etc.—so people learn it as a way of thinking.[34]

A Soviet negotiator who has internalized a dialectical approach to understanding reality is likely to differ in some important respects in his approach to negotiations from someone who has not. For one thing, he will not see things in either/or categories. Reality encompasses both conflict and cooperation.[35] The Soviet will see negotiations as a process, not as an event. Emigré Vladimir Bukovsky comments, "To a Soviet negotiator, negotiations are all process. Dialectics gives them another dimension which others lack. It is a strategy, even if it is not conceived in concrete terms by a negotiator in a particular negotiation."[36]

There is a tendency among American negotiators to view negotiations as an exercise in problem-solving. If a problem exists, you sit down at the table, hammer out an agreed solution, presumably with each side compromising from its original position, then you shake hands and part. That problem has been solved, bring on the next. A Soviet negotiator, on the other hand, will not view the signing of an agreement as the end of a negotiation, but as a stage in the process. Jonathan Dean describes the difference in the following way:

> Americans tend to consider that an agreement, once achieved, marks the end of the problem under discussion, and that the solution will administer itself. With a more accurate view of the ongoing character of East-West relations, the Soviets see implementation of an agreement as a continuing negotiation.[37]

This suggests that Soviet negotiators simply have a more accurate sense of *realpolitik* than do Americans. The almost innate sense of negotiations as a process stems, however, not from a *realpolitik* appreciation of East-West relations, but from a fundamentally different conception of reality. Someone who has been raised with a dialectical understanding of reality *knows* that as long as the issue about which a negotiation is concerned continues to exist, the negotiation will continue. It may be useful at various points in the negotiation to give current understandings between the parties concrete form in a written agreement. A carefully negotiated agreement will have validity because it will correspond to reality. But reality changes. The dialectic continues. Any agreement, because cast in concrete form, in writing, and therefore static, must over time bear less and less correspondence to reality. At some point, in order to bring it back into closer correspondence with reality, it will have to be either reinterpreted or renegotiated.

The preference of Soviet negotiators for agreements that use generalized wording has often been remarked, generally to the accompaniment of warnings to U.S. negotiators to beware of this, since the Soviets will interpret any ambiguity in their favor. We discussed this as an aspect of Soviet negotiating tactics. The point to be made here is that one of the explanations for Soviet preference for broadly worded agreements may well involve dialectics. A dialectical negotiator is likely to have a preference in most situations for a broadly worded agreement, since it will lend itself to reinterpretation, rather than requiring the generally more difficult process of renegotiation.

To take a hypothetical example, suppose during the early stages of World War II the United States and Great Britain had negotiated with the Soviet Union an understanding on the post-war political framework for Eastern Europe. Suppose further that this agreement precluded a Soviet military presence in the countries concerned and required genuinely free elections to determine their form of government. Would the Soviet Union have adhered to this agreement? Not likely. It might be sufficient to explain its violation to point to the fact that Stalin was personally treacherous, or that communists are inherently perfidious, or that overriding national interests were at stake. Any of these is possible, and any of them may be relevant to a particular situation, but I suggest that it adds a dimension to our understanding to consider that for someone who sees negotiations as part of a dialectical process, changes in objective reality would have been so overwhelming that the earlier agreement could no longer be considered valid. It would have been so totally out of correspondence with reality that a Soviet leader who adhered to it would have been in fundamental error. The agreement would have to be changed to reflect reality.

To an American, this is likely to be indistinguishable from sheer treachery. What about the principle of adhering to the agreements you have signed? There is no such thing as an abstract principle to a dialectical materialist. Nothing exists "out there" except reality. Correct behavior is that which corresponds to reality. This is different from saying that dialectical materialists have no principles. In fact, "principled positions" figure prominently in the Soviet negotiating lexicon. A principled position, if it is genuinely based on principle and not being floated as a negotiating ploy, accords with the historical dialectic and therefore partakes of historical truth. Abandoning a principled position, therefore, requires

a Soviet negotiator to commit an untruth: "To the Soviet negotiator a compromise is not a practical adjustment of principles by partial concession,
since principles are inviolable. Furthermore, there is only one 'right' way to proceed."[38] It may also be impossible if it requires him to deny the historical
dialectic, since that operates independently of the wishes of men. Of course,
one's understanding of the historical dialectic can always be clarified, or improved. It is constantly changing, and the principled positions of one set of
circumstances may be the negotiating concessions of another. In the hands of a
cynic, the possibilities for manipulation of such an outlook are inevitably vast,
but we should not assume that those who hold such an outlook are inevitably
cynics. Sophistry has antecedents, both philosophical and historical, which long
predate Marxism, or the Soviet government.

It may be objected that this begs the question of whether it is pointless to try to
negotiate with the Soviets. Whether cynics or believers, if the Soviet authorities
consider their international obligations subject to reinterpretation at times and
places of their own choosing, what reliance can be placed on them? In fact, this
question poses the alternatives more starkly than is generally the case in the real
world, as we understand it. In the first place, they will adhere to agreements that
bear a reasonable correspondence to reality as they understand it. And reality is
sufficiently intractable that despite all our differences we and they are not likely
in most situations to have greatly variant interpretations of one another's immediate interests. In the second, they are aware that others believe in abstract principles—and those beliefs are a part of reality. Therefore, a reputation for living up
to agreements may be in their interest.

Lenin commented on the relevance of "petit bourgeois" notions of morality in
his typically pungent fashion.

> The "legal and moral consciousness" of the broad masses of philistines will
> condemn, let us say, a blow struck at a blackleg [scab], when it was struck in the
> heat of defending a strike called for an increase of a starvation wage. We shall not
> advocate violence in such cases because it is inexpedient from the point of view of
> our struggle. But we shall not "respect" this philistine "consciousness."[39]

Adomeit's analysis of Soviet risk-taking behavior led him to conclude that
Lenin's dictum remains relevant. The Soviet leadership is guided by the belief
that it should "never lose sight of the political objectives to be achieved, and in
pursuing them [should not] be diverted by false notions of bourgeois morality."
This does not, in Adomeit's view, mean that "Soviet leaders are insensitive to
moral issues but their morality is different from ours."[40]

It should, moreover, be recognized that we, too, recognize the motive force of
changed circumstances and rarely enter an agreement affecting important national interests without providing mechanisms for withdrawal. But it will always be
difficult for a person operating from this framework to sacrifice a tangible,
immediate gain in favor of an intangible such as reputation, or world opinion.
The direction of influence runs primarily from the material world to the world of

ideas, rather than the reverse. Stalin expressed this outlook with characteristic bluntness when he asked how many tanks the Pope had. Another implication of this outlook is, as one perceptive observer of Soviet negotiating behavior noted, you cannot bank good will with them.[41] Nor, it should be added, do they expect to be able to bank it with you.

This is the theory. Does it, in fact, correspond to reality? A British Foreign Office expert, who has for years been a chief interpreter at top-level meetings, considers that ideological conditioning gives the Soviet leadership a dynamic view of world relations. They tend to see negotiation and agreements not as final or self-contained settlements of problems. A negotiation is a snapshot of a point in time; an agreement is an arrangement codifying the momentary relationship of forces or the relative positions of the parties at a particular moment. Since these relationships represent not static but ever-changing reality, an agreement has no intrinsic moral binding force. Life itself changes the outcome.[42] Malcolm McIntosh, who recently retired from the British Cabinet Office after forty years of working on Soviet affairs, believes the Soviets see a relationship as a non-stop trade. From time to time, events occur that make it essential to sit down across the table, or at the summit, to design a stepping stone for the process; then the process goes on.[43]

After years of high-level negotiations with the Soviets, Ambassador Max Kampelman is convinced that dialectics is an integral part of their thought system. He admits that he expected to find "a more pragmatic view, maybe a more cynical view."[44] An American diplomat, who has served at our embassy in Moscow and been involved in negotiating with the Soviets in both the CSCE and START contexts, believes that dialectics may get at a fundamental difference between us and them, particularly as concerns the implementation phase of an agreement. While the Soviets, he argues, do not usually commit outright violations of their agreements, they do try to take every possible advantage of any loopholes or vagueness of wording or interpretation.[45]

If there is a single leitmotif of advice to Americans in dealing with Soviet negotiators that has come down through the years, it is to be wary of imprecise agreements. Sloss and Davis call the "general formulation" approach "an integral part of their negotiating strategy, primarily designed to give the Soviets ample latitude for interpreting an agreement later." "This penchant for liberally interpreting treaty language," they continue, "has, throughout the history of U.S.-Soviet diplomacy, raised major questions about the credibility of Soviet compliance."[46]

The Soviet preference for general formulations in agreements and their penchant for interpreting them liberally derive from their dialectical understanding of the nature of negotiations. Wedge and Muromcew found in analyzing the SALT I talks that "the subordination of detail to principle appears to represent the reasoning pattern of Soviet negotiators quite genuinely; they are as puzzled by the West's procedures as the West is by theirs, and as suspicious. This contrast of epistemological principles is a serious impediment to understanding, but does not appear to be dictated by any wish to avoid agreement."[47] For Soviets to see negotiations as a process that continues beyond the signing of an agreement is as "natural" as for an American to view an agreement as a contract. The importance of this has once again been demonstrated in the INF Treaty implementation process. Implementing discussions, originally viewed by the U.S. side as purely technical, began with the Soviets several months after the treaty was signed. The Soviets, predictably, used them to see whether in the implementation phase they might through interpretation of treaty language walk back some of their late concessions. I took part in those talks and doubt that the Soviets expected their efforts either to succeed in any major way or to cause a major fuss. But they failed to understand the probable American reaction, particularly during the ratification period. Word of the problems soon leaked to the press, the Senate ratification process came to an abrupt halt, and the "technical" issues quickly became political ones, requiring an additional agreement between Secretary of State Shultz and Foreign Minister Shevardnadze to resolve. Could these issues have been resolved at the technical level? Probably, if either the Americans who went public had understood the Soviet negotiating process better or the Soviets had understood the American political process better.

We are not talking about right or wrong here. We are talking about understanding and effectiveness. Understanding negotiation as a process and alertness to the necessity for implementation have been commended to Americans as useful negotiating tools even within their own society.[48] They are crucial in negotiating with Soviets. Conscious of the fact that his Soviet counterpart approaches negotiations from a different perspective, the American negotiator can develop a strategy that maximizes his chances of achieving a favorable outcome.

The Correlation of Forces

Dialectics may, as Vladimir Bukovsky suggests, be a "back of the mind" concept, an analytic tool used routinely for interpreting the world, but rarely itself examined analytically. The correlation of forces appears, by contrast, to be decidedly front of the mind. A correct analysis of the correlation of forces in any situation is essential if the Party is to act correctly. The Party's right to rule rests on its assertion that its understanding of the forces of history permits it to do what is best not only for the Soviet Union but for all of mankind. In a world of unceasing conflict and change, the concept of the correlation of forces provides both a rock of stability and a compass of direction.

The discussion below is based primarily on Julian Lider's full-length study of the concept.[49] In keeping with dialectical materialism's theory of knowledge, the correlation of forces is a concept that purports to describe objectively existing reality. It exists "out there" independently of man's perception or interpretation of it. As an element of the real world, it is subject to the same dialectical laws as all other reality. The operation of these laws can be summarized in the following way. Any phenomenon that exists in the world is composed of both "old" and "new" parts, which exist simultaneously within it and which are in permanent conflict, or contradiction, with one another. The quantitative strength of the "new" increases gradually, as the strength of the "old" decreases. At some point, these changes lead to qualitative changes in the correlation of their forces and, through the clashes between them, to "radical changes in the essence of the phenomenon in question. . . . The final and most radical change consists in a revolutionary replacement (called 'negation') of the old essence of the phenomenon by a new essence, which means a transformation of this phenomenon into another one. In turn, the 'new' gradually becomes 'old' and weak and it is doomed to give way to yet another new phenomenon ('negation of the negation')."[50] The shape of the struggle between "old" and "new" is determined by the correlation of forces between them, a dynamic and constantly changing factor.

Policy must correctly reflect this objectively existing reality. When, for example, the struggle between the socialist and capitalist forces leads to a qualitative shift in the correlation of forces between them, policy must be changed to correspond to this new situation. The change from the doctrine of the inevitability of war to that of peaceful coexistence, to which we have previously referred, was required by a changed correlation of forces. The doctrine of the inevitability of war between the socialist and capitalist camps correctly reflected reality during an era when the socialist camp was encircled and fascism was the most dynamic force in the capitalist camp. The end of capitalist encirclement following World War II, the defeat of fascism, the growing strength of the socialist forces, and the advent of nuclear weapons produced a qualitative shift in the correlation of forces in favor of socialism. War, therefore, was no longer inevitable. The policy that corresponded to this new reality was peaceful coexistence. Robert V. Daniels cites the change under Khrushchev to the doctrine of peaceful coexistence as evidence for his view that doctrine is purely instrumental in the foreign policy area, that the objective of the Soviet leadership is "to retain a free hand for any opportune move, unrestricted by possible theoretical inhibitions."[51] This view assumes that underneath all of the ideological trappings the Soviet leadership's conceptual approach to international politics is essentially identical to ours, a view with which it is hopefully clear by now I am in considerable disagreement. Naturally Khrushchev perceived opportunities for himself and the Soviet Union under the new doctrine. A correct analysis of any situation always reveals opportunities. But the opportunities one perceives flow from one's intellectual constructs for understanding and interpreting reality. Those constructs are not identical to ours.

Your average Soviet negotiator is, of course, not likely to be thinking at this level of abstraction. But if we consider the phenomenon in question to be social forces, or social classes, we come quickly to a more concrete application of the concept. In analyzing the correlation of social forces, the analyst must include both their material and nonmaterial components. The former include economic assets, means of coercion, access to the mass media, and other means of information and ideological influence. The principal nonmaterial components are class consciousness, organization, and a rational and proper combat strategy.[52] The material components determine what the possibilities for struggle are. You must correctly assess them, but you cannot directly affect them. They exist independently of you. Strategy, on the other hand, is your responsibility. As Lider puts it, "the proper choice of the strategy and means used permits a successful exploitation of the [material] correlation of forces. Moreover, an appropriate strategy may lead to further advantageous changes in the correlation of forces," leading to even greater possibilities for action in the future. And in the final analysis, of course, one can only determine the accuracy of one's understanding of the correlation of forces by acting. Knowledge is by necessity incomplete; action increases knowledge. Wrote Lenin, "You cannot learn to swim unless you go into the water. There can be no contest in which all the chances are known beforehand."[53]

Turning to the international arena, Lider continues:

> The determining Marxist-Leninist category, which permeates the analysis of all three levels of international political relations . . . is the correlation of the two forces of the two socio-economic systems. This correlation cannot be reduced to a comparison of the parameters of military power. . . . It is a broad and complex class sociopolitical category. It should be viewed as a correlation of the class, social, economic, political, ideological, military, ethical and other forces in the two socio-economic systems of our times.[54]

Like the correlation of social forces, the correlation of international forces reflects objectively existing conditions in the international sphere and objective historical tendencies. But just as a proper strategy can affect the evolution of the correlation, so the actions of states affect the development of the correlation of international forces. In the current international system, Soviet theorists claim, the "impact of the military component of the correlation has diminished, while the importance of the economic, sociopolitical and moral-ideological components has increased."[55] Since the forces of history are on the side of the socialist camp, the greater influence of the nonmilitary components is yet another of that camp's assets.

One may question whether Soviet leaders or negotiators really believe this in light of abundant evidence that they, in fact, give inordinate attention to the military component of the correlation. This appears to be an area in which deep-seated elements of the political culture—to be discussed in the following section—clash with contemporary theory. As Lider notes, when we turn "from general concepts to the actual assessment, we see another picture. In both approaches the superpowers and their military power continue to be the main protagonists and the main items in the correlation."[56] In their behavior on the world scene, Soviet leaders appear often to rely heavily on those aspects of the correlation that concern military forces. " 'Forces' mean here both what a given protagonist possesses and what he is prepared to do in the non-material sense; the latter includes the will to act, the organizational abilities and, as mentioned above, the strategy prepared."[57] Lider's description of the importance of the nonmaterial components of the correlation during a war appears equally applicable to nonwar situations.

> It is considered than an active policy may profoundly affect the correlation of forces during a war. The outcome of war depends not only on the correlation of the military might of the countries or coalitions of countries, but also on a protagonist's ability to change the international situation to his own advantage and to create a military superiority at a given place and take advantage of it. Here the political strategy is closely linked to the military one.[58]

We must presume that the Soviets, like us, precede any negotiation with a policy review which produces guidelines for the conduct of the negotiations. An American foreign policy review will focus on U.S. interests: What are they? How can we advance/defend them? The equivalent Soviet policy review will use the correlation of forces as its organizing concept. But the questions that flow from it are likely to differ somewhat from those an American would ask. American interests are generally considered to be stable and consistent. If they change, it is only slowly and over an extended period of time. Thus, any analysis of the current situation will be presented against a background of constant U.S. interests. The Soviet, it is true, will also want to correctly analyze the current situation, the existing correlation of forces. But since the correlation is in constant movement, he will want to analyze very specifically the nature of the dynamic, the forces at play producing change and the direction of change. He will recommend a strategy or a course of action that will shift the correlation in favor of the Soviet Union, or create conditions favorable to such a shift. The organizing concept of his analysis requires such recommendations. An American asks: How can we defend U.S. interests? A Soviet asks: How can we shift the correlation in our favor? Even an unfavorable correlation can be made less unfavorable; losses can be minimized. And any agreement reached must be defendable in similar terms. As Thomas Wolfe put it, in reflecting on the SALT experience: "SALT and detente, as well as Soviet military power itself, are all seen as instruments of policy useful in one way or another to keep the United States from trying to arrest what, from the Soviet viewpoint, constitutes an inevitable, though admittedly uneven, process of transition to a new 'correlation of forces' in the world favorable to the Soviet Union and other 'fraternal' countries."[59]

American understanding both of the concept of the correlation of forces and how it is brought to bear on negotiations in which we are involved remains limited. Paul Nitze believes that it is an area to which we should be paying much greater attention in our strategic arms talks with the Soviets. Major Soviet foreign policy moves are preceded by a policy review, presumably reduced at some point to written form and given Politburo approval. A better understanding of how their perception of the correlation of forces affects the policy review—not just the military, but also the political, economic, and moral aspects—might, in Nitze's view, help us to get a better sense of where their policy review is going to come out and, thereby, to plan our own strategy more effectively.[60]

POLITICAL CULTURE

Behind the ubiquitous Communist Party slogans lies the other face of the Soviet Union, the older, more Russian face. It shows itself most visibly in the churches—Moscow, the city of a thousand churches, the Third Rome, now the capital of world atheism. The churches that remain open, many fewer than dot the skyline, are crowded. True, the attendees are mostly elderly women. But so have they reportedly been throughout the history of the Soviet regime, one generation after another taking its place before the iconostasis to celebrate the resurrection of Christ and the triumph of Christianity. They are, in effect, witnessing not only their faith, but also the stubbornness with which old Russia lives on despite a Soviet regime that has shown itself to be utterly ruthless in its efforts to impose its will upon the country. This is not to say that the present regime finds all aspects of old Russia uncongenial. To the contrary, as we shall see, it has drawn, both consciously and unconsciously, on Russian political culture for elements of support.

Much ink has been spilled in the perennial debate over the relative influence of Marxist-Leninist ideology and Russian political culture on Soviet foreign policy. Are the Soviets impelled by ideology or guided by traditional Russian national interests? It is hard to disagree with Teresa Rakowska-Harmstone's observation that the Soviet Union is neither Communist nor Russian; it is both.[61] The October Revolution did not abolish Russia, but neither has Russia been left unchanged by the Soviet regime. E. H. Carr nicely caught the dynamics of the process, while suggesting that ultimately old patterns exert more influence on new than the reverse.

> Revolutions do not, however, resolve the tension between change and continuity, but rather heighten it; . . . thus in the development of the revolution, the elements of change and continuity fight side by side, now conflicting and now coalescing, until a new and stable synthesis is established. The process may be a matter of a few years or a few generations. But, broadly speaking, the greater the distance in time from the initial impact of the revolution, the more decisively does the principle of continuity reassert itself against the principle of change.[62]

But what does this mean for Soviet negotiating behavior? We have already suggested that ideology enters the picture via thought processes deeply imbued with a dialectical approach to understanding reality and an analytical concept—the correlation of forces—that expects conflict and emphasizes the dynamic aspects of the negotiation process. What, then, of Russian political culture? How does it manifest itself in contemporary Soviet life and, more relevantly for our purposes, in Soviet negotiating behavior?

It is beyond the scope of this study to attempt a detailed analysis of Russian history and culture, a subject on which volumes have already been written. But we can at least make an effort to understand the principal shaping influences. While there may be no unanimity among scholars on what those influences were, there is considerable overlap. James Billington writes that three forces in particular, "the natural surroundings, the Christian heritage, and the Western contacts of Russia hover bigger than life" over the history of Russian culture. Steven White sees the "equation between belief, nationality and citizenship—expressed in the celebrated formula autocracy, orthodoxy, nationality"—as the "most distinctive contribution of the old regime to the political culture of the Soviet regime which succeeded it."[63] In his uniquely insightful way, E. H. Carr traced the lasting impact of geographic imperatives:

> The great distances over which authority had to be organized made state-building in Russia an unusually slow and cumbrous process; and, in the unpropitious environment of the Russian steppe, forms of production and the social relations arising from them lagged far behind those of the more favoured west. And this time-lag, continuing throughout Russian history, created disparities which colored and determined all Russian relations with the west. . . . This historical pattern of the development of the Russian State had three important consequences. In the first place, it produced that chronically ambivalent attitude to Western Europe which ran through all subsequent Russian thought and policy. It was indispensable to imitate and "catch up with" the west as a means of self-defence against the west; the west was admired and envied as a model, as well as feared and hated as the potential enemy. Secondly, the pattern of development rested on the conception of "revolution from above." . . . Reform . . . came through pressure of external crisis, resulting in a belated demand within the ruling group for an efficient authority and for a strong leader to exercise it. Hence reform meant in Russia a strengthening concentration of [State] power. Thirdly, the pattern imposed by these conditions was one, not of orderly progress, but of spasmodic advance by fits and starts—a pattern not of evolution but of intermittent revolution.[64]

Authoritarian political structures have dominated the landscape of Russian history. Many observers, both Russian and Western, have traced their strength and durability to the more than two centuries of Russian subjection to Tatar rule. Tucker sees Stalinism as at least in part a throwback to a revolutionary process seen earlier in Russian history, when the princes and tsars of Muscovy sought to resist Mongol domination by building a strong military-national state, which required one or another form of compulsory service from all classes. Tibor Szamuely treats the subject in more detail and is fairly representative in his stress upon the absolute, unlimited power of the Khan and the gradual acceptance by the emerging state of Muscovy of the basic Mongol principles of unqualified submission to the State and universal, compulsory, and permanent state service of all individuals and classes of society. Szamuely adds, however, that these principles were reinforced and fixed by three additional centuries of unremitting struggle against Tatar raiders from the south, seeking slaves and plunder. "The closing of the southern frontier and the establishment of security from Tatar incursion became, and remained until the end of the eighteenth century, the all-important, overriding object of the Russian State. This task demanded a total, unremitting and ruthless concentration of all national resources, both human and material, that for scope and intensity is probably unparalleled, over a comparable period of time, by any other nation." George Vernadsky traced in some detail the evolution in Muscovy of the authoritarian institutions imposed by the Mongols, while contrasting them with the freedom he sees as characteristic of the Kievan period of Russian history.[65] In a recent book, Charles J. Halperin argues against this view, asserting that Byzantium had bequeathed to Russia even before the arrival of the Mongols not only its form of Christianity, but also its political authoritarianism. Edward Keenan, however, considers that evidence is lacking for the assertion that Muscovite political culture was significantly influenced by either the form or the practice of Byzantine political culture or ideology.[66]

We will leave to others the resolution of these differences. The essential fact for our purposes is that authoritarian politics in Russia has deep roots and great durability. Over the past half millennium, while concepts of individual rights and limitations on political authority were slowly and painfully gaining a place in Western politics, authoritarianism remained deeply entrenched in Russia. It can be argued, in fact, as we look back from our current vantage point, that if there has been a trend in Russian history it has been toward increasing concentration of power in the State, and at least equally arbitrary use of that power. Tsars might be more or less capricious in their exercise of power. They might be reactionary or reformist. But all were dedicated to maintaining their hold on power, on the right to rule as they saw fit. Their Soviet successors fit comfortably into this tradition. The effect of this essential political fact on the Soviet style of negotiating has been vast.

In a significant article on Muscovite political folkways, Edward Keenan distinguishes between court, bureaucratic, and peasant political cultures and traces their development and ultimate melding in this century into a single Soviet political culture. The article defies easy summarization, but some attempt must be made to trace its main lines. Keenan suggests that in peasant society the imperatives of simple survival—against slave raiders, disease, and a harsh climate—made the village unit the most significant autonomous actor in peasant life. The village was far more important than the individual or even the family unit, neither of which had sufficiently assured viability in this environment. The village itself was so vulnerable that minimization of risk was the primary objective of collective decisions. Individual interests were subordinated to group viability and individual activity seen as potentially destructive of the group. Such destructive activity was to be avoided, not by the internalization of taboos, as in much of northern Europe, but by greater reliance on institutionalized subordination of the individual to the group. Within the household, its head was an autocrat, but both his power and that of the household were constrained by the larger interests of the village. This peasant political culture changed little before the advent of the twentieth century.

Court culture revolved around the tsar, who acted as a kind of referee in court politics, which essentially concerned clan maneuvering to arrange desirable marriages. Decision-making was collegial and the process was informal. Within the court, the tsar was not all-powerful, although that might be the impression conveyed to outsiders. Individuals were expected to adhere to group decisions and their interests were subordinated to those of the group. There were many similarities between court and bureaucratic cultures, but also some significant differences. While family connections were important, as in court society, there were no bureaucratic clans, and upward mobility, within this stratum, was not limited by heredity or family. Decision-making was not collegial, but vertical, via an institutionalized chain of command.

Keenan finds common features among the three cultures that he sees as the basic attributes of the Russian political culture.

1. Political status and social function were determined by a combination of birth, personal affiliation and the balance of interests of the other players, rather than by the rules of a political structure.
2. Membership in these closed and informal systems conferred significant rewards and an assured role in collective decision-making, but also required acquiescence in the decisions of the system's governing mechanism. Excessively aggressive attempts to increase individual power or status were seen as potentially threatening to the system and ran the risk of severe group sanctions.
3. Policy in all three cultures tended to opt for stability and risk-avoidance over change or "progress."
4. The systems were reluctant to allow nonparticipants access to the generalized principles of their operation, either by promulgating laws or articulating ideologies. In other words, participants followed the rule of neglasnost, not telling outsiders how the system really works.[67]

In discussing the effect of ideology on the Soviet outlook, we tried to point out that the Russian dissident tradition shared some important basic elements of the Russian outlook on the world with the system it sought to replace. Keenan reinforces this point. The dissident counter-culture, like the dominant Russian political culture, was not particularly interested in systematic political theory, in juridical or constitutional structures that would impact on the forms and limits of power. Rather, it sought to ensure the just and moral use of power. Power and the institutions of the state should be used, not to insure the rights of the individual, but his perfection.[68] Yet Russia's dissidents, particularly as the country moved through the nineteenth century, were also profoundly alienated from the numerically dominant, but politically quiescent, peasant society. They arose from the upper classes, the merged court and bureaucratic cultures, which looked to the West for intellectual stimulus. This ambivalence had a profound impact on the Russian revolutionary movement, and on the Soviet state which developed out of the ultimate merger of the peasant and upper class political cultures. We will turn to this shortly, as we consider Lenin and the Bolshevik party which he founded and led to victory in 1917.

First, however, we need to consider the effect of this tradition on the Soviet view of the world. The Soviet rulers, like their Russian predecessors, face the West with, as Carr put it, a mixture of admiration, envy, and fear. Russia's ruling class has always looked to the West for models, albeit sometimes models to be emulated, other times models to be despised. This chronic ambivalence also lies deep in Russian history. As Halperin puts it:

> During the Mongol period, Medieval Russia chanced to be at the interface of two vast and irreconcilable worlds. Considered from the West, Russia lay at the distant rim of European Christendom, on the most remote reaches of the frontier. Contemplated from the East, Russia was the westernmost of the huge Mongol dominions stretching all the way from the China Sea. It is part of the conundrum of medieval Russia that it was part and yet not a part of both realms. Tied culturally to Byzantium and the West, politically to the pagan and later Muslim East, Russia under the Golden Horde was from either perspective an anomaly.[69]

And so it has remained, its combination of European and Oriental traits and traditions a source of mystery to outsiders and confusion to its own inhabitants. As described by Seweryn Bialer: "Geographically, and to some extent culturally, Russia is both a European and Asian country. This geographic circumstance, however, instead of being a source of strength, led instead to its alienation from both Europe and Asia."[70]

But as the Soviet Union looks out on the world, its reaction to the view to the West differs greatly from its reaction to the view to the East. Its basic view of the West, I believe, is as technologically advanced, corrupt, and threatening. Its view of the East is as powerful, capricious, and threatening. The traditional, much-discussed Russian sense of insecurity is a component of both views, but manifests itself quite differently. During three years in the Soviet Union, I sensed a visceral component to the Soviet fear of China that is largely missing from its reaction to the United States. Sovietologist Bialer has written about his own similar impressions:

> Anyone who has traveled in the Soviet Union and has talked about China with Soviet citizens is struck by both the primitiveness and the intensity of their views. Such conversations leave the inescapable impression that in the Russian popular mind, China looms as a danger of overwhelming proportions. The citizen will give some lip service to the danger from the 'Western imperialists.' . . . But when it comes to the Chinese, his deepest feelings are unconcealed fear, distrust, aversion, even hatred. . . . There is a clear association between China and Genghis Khan and the Russian suffering under the Tatar-Mongol yoke.[71]

Age-old memories of the "Tatar yoke" may indeed play a part in this, but Russian history since the end of Tatar domination has reinforced those memories. In coping with military threats from the West, Russia has traditionally compensated for its technological inferiority with patience and numbers. It might take huge losses and surrender vast territories, but much more often than not it eventually prevails, regaining what it has lost and then some. The Soviet Union's posture toward the West today is that traditional one. For that reason, I believe, it is known and relatively comfortable. But as it looks East, Moscow faces a neighbor that not only stirs ancient fears, but is also in a military position analogous to Moscow's vis-à-vis the West. Clearly inferior technologically, China has vast reserves of manpower, a sense of time and history, and appears to have the will to use both effectively. Thus, the theme that dominates the Soviet Union's relations with the West is inferiority; the theme that dominates its relations with China is insecurity.

The Russian political culture cannot be understood without reference to orthodoxy. The Church early became subservient to, and a pillar of support for, the State. But the influence of religious orthodoxy goes far beyond that. Keenan is only one among a number of students of Russian history who have argued that following the era of Peter the Great, there were really two Russian histories—a history of the small, sophisticated urban upper classes, and that of the immense rural mass which essentially dropped into a historical backwater and did not emerge again until the time of the revolution, or perhaps of the emancipation of the serfs.[72] The upper classes, alternately repelled by and attracted to the West, gave birth to a remarkable cultural flowering in the nineteenth century. For the Slavophiles among them, Russia was the Third Rome, a repository of values long lost in a Western world that could corrupt, but not teach. Even the Westernizers considered that Russia had a mission, or a Word; it could bring something to the West, as well as learn from it. In their own thought processes, the Westernizers belonged to the classic Russian tradition. They might reject Orthodoxy, but they accepted Hegel or Marx with the same fervor and with the same expectation that herein lay the answer, herein lay the Truth which they could follow and live by.

None of this, however, found any resonance among the great masses of the population, "among whom the old religious beliefs and hopes were still preserved. The Western influences which led on to the remarkable Russian culture of the nineteenth century found no welcome among the bulk of the people."[73] The Russian people of the Petrine era, and their descendants, showed themselves to be both deeply and traditionally religious. As Billington puts it: "For the historian of culture, however, the real drama of the seventeenth century follows from the determination of many Russians to remain—through all the changes and challenges of the age—blagochestivye: ardently loyal to a sacred past."[74] This determination led, on the one hand, to the passive resistance of the Old Believers and, on the other, to peasant insurrections. These rebellions "were animated by one recurring political ideal: belief in a 'true tsar'," who would "come to their aid if only the intervening wall of administrators and bureaucrats could be torn down."[75] Tsardom was not in question, only the identity of the ruler.

Against this background we need to consider the impact of Lenin on the Soviet Union, of Russia on Lenin, and of the Bolshevik synthesis of Marxism and Russian political culture.

THE RUSSIAN PAST, THE SOVIET PRESENT

Writing as X in *Foreign Affairs* forty years ago, George Kennan posed the difficulties of understanding Soviet behavior in classic terms:

> The political personality of Soviet power as we know it today is the product of ideology and circumstances: ideology inherited by the present Soviet leaders from the movement in which they had their political origin, and circumstances of the power which they now have exercised for nearly three decades in Russia. There can be few tasks of psychological analysis more difficult than to try to trace the interaction of these two forces and the relative role of each in the determination of official Soviet conduct. Yet the attempt must be made if that conduct is to be understood and effectively countered.[76]

An additional four decades of knowledge and experience have only emphasized the difficulty of the task.

Tracing the interaction of these forces must begin with Lenin. Over the years, Lenin has taken on the attributes of a combination of Jesus Christ, George Washington, and Abraham Lincoln in Soviet eyes. With the disgrace of Trotsky, the ambivalent status of Stalin, and the nonperson status of most of the other purged and murdered heroes of the Revolution, Lenin stands not simply as *primus inter pares*, but alone in the pantheon of the Soviet Union's leaders. Viewed from the Soviet context, this status is not undeserved. By dint of single-minded determination and intellectual and political genius, Lenin brought a small group of exiles and outcasts with a history of ineffectuality and infighting to the leadership of the largest country on earth. His genius was in the adaptation of Marxism to the Russian political culture.[77] His single-mindedness was in the pursuit of power.

Lenin is a complex and contradictory figure. Descended from one Kalmuk and two German grandparents, he remained quintessentially Russian while in constant revolt against both his country's socioeconomic and political system and the pernicious effects of that system on the ideals and morals of his countrymen. Berdyaev saw Lenin as combining in himself two traditions: "the tradition of the Russian revolutionary intelligentsia in its most maximalist tendency, and the tradition of the Russian government in its most despotic aspect." Billington, on the other hand, stresses how Lenin differed from almost all of his intellectual predecessors in nineteenth-century Russia: "It was his profound alienation from the dominant intellectual trends of the late imperial period which enabled him to appear as the bearer of a genuinely new order of things. . . . Lenin focused his attention on one all-consuming objective that had not traditionally been uppermost in the thinking of the intelligentsia: the attainment of power." J. N. Bochenski believed that it is not possible to understand dialectical materialism correctly without knowing Lenin's character. "He was," wrote Bochenski, "a man of outstanding ability, and an engineer on a vast scale—a technician of power and of revolution."[78]

For Lenin, the quintessential political question was *"kto kovo,"* who rules whom, or who has power over whom. He did not consider power divisible, nor did he consider that it could be shared in any but the very short term. In any situation of power-sharing, one side or the other would sooner or later, and probably sooner, rule. In his own political struggles, Lenin showed himself ready to sacrifice size, whether of adherents or of geography, in return for retaining full control over his organization. In "On the Eve of October 1917," Lenin wrote: "At the conference, we must immediately consolidate the Bolshevik faction without worrying about numbers, without being afraid about leaving the vacillators in the camp of the vacillating: they are more useful to the cause of the revolution there than in the stronghold of the resolute and courageous fighters."[79] He insisted upon rigid control of the trade unions by the party elite, even at the price of some narrowing of the labor movement.[80] The Bolshevik/Menshevik split at the 1903 Party congress concerned both power and doctrine about it. Again, Lenin showed himself prepared to split the Party rather than share power or compromise on Party organization. The issue began with a division over whether the party should stick to its Western model or adapt itself to specifically Russian conditions and quickly broadened into fundamental questions of Marxist doctrine. The Mensheviks, Carr argues, were unconsciously from the very first, Westernizers and the Bolsheviks the Easterners.[81] Lenin was determined to have a party that corresponded with his sense of political reality, a very home-grown, Russian sense. "Classes," he said in 1918, "are led by parties and parties are led by individuals who are called leaders. . . . What is necessary is individual rule, the recognition of the dictatorial powers of one man. All phrases about equal rights are nonsense."[82] For Lenin, the Treaty of Brest-Litovsk was about keeping power. The Germans might acquire some territory, but the Bolsheviks would remain in power. History would show whether Germany could keep control of the territory it had gained.

Nathan Leites's ambitious and controversial *A Study of Bolshevism*[83] attempts, by drawing primarily though not exclusively on the work of Lenin, to show how the ideas of Marx and Engels were transmuted into a code of Bolshevik behavior for acquiring and maintaining power. At the psychological level, Leites sees the Bolsheviks as driven by a reaction against the perceived weaknesses in the Russian character, by a conviction that all relations between people turn on the question of who controls whom (another variant of Lenin's *kto-kovo*), and by a deep-seated fear of being controlled by an outside force. In fact, of course, at the same time the Bolsheviks were at one level reacting against some elements of the Russian tradition, they were at another level embracing other aspects of it. Lenin's success was not simply a matter of having burned away from his own character the impurities of the Russian outlook. It was, as discussed above, at least equally a matter of having embodied within himself an acute awareness of what Russia needed and would permit in a revolutionary movement.

"Russian" traits that Bolshevism opposes include carelessness in making decisions, procrastination, lack of mental alertness, vagueness, a tendency to be divorced from reality.[84] Leites drew together the axioms of behavior that he believed Bolsheviks developed to counter these and other undesirable Russian characteristics into what he termed an "operational code." The implications in this terminology of an ideological blueprint for behavior have led many, who see such an approach as simplistic, simply to dismiss Leites's effort, even to view it as bizarre. Without explicitly mentioning Leites, though presumably having him, as well as others, in mind, Samuel L. Sharp called it "dubious scholarship to collect quotations . . . from Lenin and Stalin without regard to the time, place, circumstances, composition of the audience, and, whenever ascertainable, immediate purposes of such utterances." Robert Jervis suggests that several aspects of the operational code are not unique to Bolshevism, but rather are commonly held by a state that believes that it is confronted by an implacably hostile adversary.[85] (But if two men exhibit the symptoms of paranoia, is it irrelevant that one really is being pursued by an implacably hostile adversary and one is not? The path toward eliminating the symptoms, or at least dealing effectively with the person exhibiting them, would seem to be considerably different in the two cases. Why does the Soviet Union see itself as confronted by an implacably hostile adversary? Because it is? Because its view of the world convinces it that it is? If the latter, what are the respective roles of ideology and political culture in producing that world view? And what are the implications for negotiating with it?)

In fact, though Leites's work must be handled with care, it is as full of insights about Soviet negotiating behavior as it is provocative. Alex George has drawn on it for a convincing analysis of Soviet "optimizing" behavior in the international arena, which he contrasts with a Western tendency toward "satisficing." George likens the beliefs and premises Leites discussed to a prism that influences perceptions of political events and estimates of particular situations. They also provide standards and guidelines that influence the choice of strategy and tactics, the structuring and weighing of alternative courses of action. They are an important, but not the only, variable in decision-making.[86]

The Bolshevik outlook on political action rejects strategies that confine goals to those that are highly feasible. It argues instead for attempting to maximize the gains sought in a particular situation, reasoning that: (a) action must often be taken on the basis of incomplete knowledge; only action itself can increase knowledge; (b) what can be achieved cannot be predicted in advance—it can only become known in the process of struggle, by attempting to get the most out of a situation; (c) in choosing goals in a particular situation, one should, therefore, limit them only by assessing what is objectively possible in the situation—that is, not impossible to achieve by intelligent use of resources at one's disposal.[87] In a particular situation, a person espousing this outlook will have not a single objective, but a set of graduated objectives, how many of which can be achieved will be determined in the course of the struggle.

Hannes Adomeit, who contrasts his inductive approach to understanding Soviet behavior with the deductive approach used by Leites and George, con-

cludes that the approaches coincide in their finding that operational principles
and recurring patterns of behavior exist that are specifically Soviet. He believes
they must be explained in significant part by Soviet ideology.[88]

Lenin's bequest to Russia was not only the approach to the analysis of political
action we have been discussing, but also an organization, the Communist Party
of the Soviet Union, which has shown itself to be an exceptionally adept
instrument for the maintenance of political power. Like Lenin himself, the Party
is rooted deeply in Russian culture and has over the decades adapted itself to
Russian realities. While it can be argued with some justice that it has expressed
those realities in forms so perverted as to be virtually unrecognizable, it is far
closer to the truth to see the durability of Communist Party rule in the Soviet
Union as reflective of its adaptation to Russian realities than to see it solely as an
alien influence imposed by force on an innocent and unwilling Russian people.
The Bolshevik Party, Lenin's carefully forged instrument of revolution, whose
creed of centralism, elitism, and conspirational rule was most compatible with
traditional patterns, became, of all the "organizations and trends that had
competed for hegemony in the revolutionary period . . . the principal agent and
beneficiary of the reestablishment of political stability."[89]

Those who study political culture find it useful to distinguish between official,
dominant, and elite political cultures. Archie Brown defines dominant political
culture as "subjective perceptions of history and politics, fundamental political
beliefs and values, foci of identification and loyalty, and political knowledge and
expectations."[90] Ideology, in Bialer's understanding of it as "a part of culture, a
slowly changing combination of doctrinal inputs and the historical experience
and predispositions that run parallel to doctrine,"[91] forms a part of the dominant
political culture of the Soviet Union. Marxist-Leninist doctrine, on the other
hand, is its official political culture.

The Soviet Union of today differs from tsarist Russia less in the contrast
between its dominant and its official cultures than in the fact that the great gap in
Russia between the elite and dominant political cultures has been considerably
narrowed in Soviet society. The Bolshevik revolution was a product of the
dissident strain of Russia's elite political culture, intellectually influenced by the
West, but fundamentally more deeply attached to older Russian values than its
members themselves knew. So deeply, in fact, that the Revolution itself can be
seen as essentially a revitalization and restoration of long dominant patterns of
the political culture rather than as a break with them. But the intelligentsia that
led this Revolution had yet to come to terms with Russia's peasant culture and
were, in fact, alienated from it.[92]

During the first several decades of Soviet rule, the Communist Party was a
vehicle of social mobility. Lenin and his cohorts may have been form the Russian
intelligentsia, but their successors were not. It has been argued, in fact, that
Stalin's accession to power initiated a revolution within the revolution, the
second at least as significant for Russian history as the first. The murder of

massive numbers of the intelligentsia, combined with the education and accession to positions of influence of former peasants at last brought to a substantial end the centuries-old split in Russia between the urban upper classes and the rural masses. Vakar sees in this the triumph in Soviet society of the peasant point of view, which instead of yielding to "Marxist enlightenment," supplanted it, or at least forced an amalgam owing more to the traditions of the village than to the writings of Marx. The immediate historical background of Soviet society, in his view, is the Muscovite state up to the time of Peter the Great, when the split in Russian society occurred. Billington also sees the Stalin era as having some of its deepest roots in pre-Petrine Moscow. Stalin, in his view, "was able to succeed Lenin as supreme dictator not only because he was a deft intriguer and organizer but also because he was closer than his rivals to the crude mentality of the average Russian. Unlike most other Bolshevik leaders—many of whom were of Jewish, Polish, or Baltic origin—Stalin had been deeply schooled in the catechistic theology of Orthodoxy."[93]

Tucker considers that the Stalinist period resurrected some patterns of thought, values, and institutional forms characteristic of tsarism at certain times. Bialer's view is similar:

> Another factor promoting stability is the predominantly lower-class origin of the upper political strata in the Soviet Union. Since the working class and the political elite share the same tradition and come from similar socioeconomic backgrounds, there results a symmetry of cultural attitudes and tastes cutting across the rulers and the working classes. This is reflected in the official culture and language of the society. The Soviet Union is one of the few societies where the cultures of the mass and the elite are almost inseparable. . . . The institutional framework that emerged in the Stalin era fitted rather well with the antecedent political culture of Tsarist Russia at the most critical points, and to all appearances the contemporary Soviet political culture still "fits" this relatively unchanged institutional pattern quite well.[94]

This "fit" between contemporary Soviet political culture and its Russian antecedents is critical to an understanding of the Soviet negotiating style. The stable political culture that began to emerge toward the end of the Stalin era was characterized by: the establishment of a new political elite, drawn predominantly from the peasant class, but increasingly self-perpetuating; the reestablishment of extreme centralization; loss of military, bureaucratic, and party autonomy, except in the innermost party circles; the replacement of ideological revolutionism by the traditional combination of pragmatism and distrust of innovation; reassertion of old patterns of caution and risk-avoidance.[95] Areas in which contemporary ideology reinforces traditional institutional patterns and outlooks of political culture should be particularly important drivers of Soviet negotiating style and behavior. Conversely, in areas where the traditions are in conflict, we should expect far greater ambivalence, uncertainty, and mixed signals in how the Soviets negotiate.

Lenin's authoritarianism was securely rooted in the Russian political culture. The Party he bequeathed to Soviet society institutionalized that authoritarianism.

But Lenin and, although perhaps to a somewhat lesser extent, most of his fellow Bolsheviks were revolutionaries, risk-takers on a grand scale. Their influence dwindled and was eventually lost in Stalin's Soviet Union, as they were murdered and replaced by leaders with peasant roots, who brought with them the Russian peasant's traditional risk-aversion. The murderous excesses of the Stalin era only reinforced this risk-aversion until, under Brezhnev, it became the dominant leitmotif of an era. Cohen sees this social and political conservatism expressing itself "daily in all areas of life as a preference for tradition and order and a fear of innovation and disorder."[96]

But Stalin also brought something qualitatively new to the political culture of his country. His crucial operative aim was *control*, and the system he left behind was an "elaborate, completely centralized bureaucratic mechanism for the command and control of society."[97] Lenin's authoritarian party was transformed into a mechanism for a degree of social control of unprecedented scope. From what we know of Stalin, control was probably in large part an end in itself. But there was another objective, perhaps partly rationalization, but also partly real. The Party was to be the instrument for achieving progress, for transforming the material basis of Soviet society. And by exercising an unprecedented degree of control over Soviet society, it could achieve progress, while avoiding risk. Thus, Stalin's "new Soviet man" could incorporate within himself traditional Russian authoritarianism and risk-aversion, while persuading himself that the control mechanisms in place were instruments of progress.

Before summarizing the elements of ideology and political culture that affect Soviet negotiating behavior, a couple of general points should be made about the present impact of long-established patterns in Russian society. The first concerns the relationship between power and status. The Soviet Union has throughout its history been a society of scarcity, both of material items and of the other things people find desirable. Obtaining them has not been a function of wealth, as in Western society, but rather of access. Power, or position, or access to persons with one or the other, is the key to getting things done, or getting what you want. Wealth, in the United States, provides access to power. In Soviet society, power produces access to wealth, or to whatever other good—influence, status, etc.—is desired. The Soviet Union and tsarist Russia are more alike than different in this regard. Bialer puts the relationship in the following way:

> Two traditional Russian characteristics are noteworthy for their imprint on the Soviet mind-set. First, there is the relationship between status, class, and political power in Russian history: traditionally, political power has been more of a source of high status or class than vice versa. Second, there is the lack of status and class autonomy vis-à-vis the state. Accordingly, even the highest status has always required services to the state and is reaffirmed by that service. The Soviet theory and practice of politics, wherein relations to the Party-state serve as the wellspring of class and social status, falls well within the Russian tradition.[98]

Soviet negotiators are enormously privileged members of their society. While they are not well paid in monetary terms, they have access to housing and other material goods which enable a life-style about which most of their countrymen can only dream. And they have access to the rarest good of all in Soviet society: the opportunity to travel abroad. All of this depends entirely upon the positions they hold. It is a rare Soviet negotiator who has an important Party position or any other source of power that would provide a basis for independent maneuvering. The positions they hold give them access; loss of the position carries with it many more implications than loss of an equivalent position in the United States. The age of mass communications has produced a loss of independence for diplomats the world over, but perhaps no negotiators feel more constrained by their instructions, or more compelled to play to the home audience, than the Soviets. This can be frustrating for American negotiators, but it can also provide opportunities.

Finally, as students of Lenin and as individuals acculturated in their own society, Soviet negotiators will be keenly attuned to power relationships, both as they affect the negotiations at hand generally and as they operate on the other side of the table. The American negotiator who, anxious to put his Soviet counterpart into an understandable frame of reference, identifies this focus on power as essentially the same as a Western negotiator's pursuit of his country's interests makes an oversimplification that in the long run will hurt his effectiveness.

Russian political culture, then, manifests itself in Soviet negotiating behavior via: (a) authoritarian political traditions; (b) ambivalence toward the West— insecurity tinged with inferiority, but also accompanied by a sense of moral superiority; (c) a cast of mind that welcomes the traditional rather than the new, but that at the same time seeks to understand life in its entirety; and (d) aversion to risk-taking. The impact of ideology on these traits is mixed. Marxism-Leninism is fully compatible with Russia's authoritarian political traditions. It reinforces the old Russian sense of mission or destiny. The West is corrupt and doomed, but also dangerous; the Soviet Union is history's handmaiden and must remain pure in order to fulfill her destiny. Reality, truth can be understood, and men can act in accordance with it. Excessive risk, or adventurism, must be avoided, but one must push to the limits of the achievable. This can be accomplished by exercising firm and complete control over one's own behavior and over the process in which one is involved. What we observe of Soviet negotiating behavior—its style and tactics—has its origins in these deeply engrained traits of ideology and political culture.

NOTES

1.   This view has much in common with that of Wedge and Muromcew, who based their research on Soviet negotiating behavior during the SALT talks on the "thesis that the Soviet government views the world in terms of assumptions which are generally shared within its own social framework. Soviet representatives must interpret the negotiations in terms of the reality world of the Soviet government; this is the only world they know.''

Bryant Wedge and Cyril Muromcew, "Psychological Factors in Soviet Disarmament Negotiations," *Journal of Conflict Resolution* 9, no. 1 (March 1965), pp. 18–19.

2. One distinction which has been proposed is between cognitive standards, appreciative standards, knowledge, and power. The first, which has to do with criteria for establishing the validity of information and is not itself subject to ultimate verification, should be far less susceptible to change than the last, which has to do with an individual's perception of his capacity to affect his environment. Rita M. Kelley and Frederic J. Fleron, Jr., "Personality, Behavior, and Communist Ideology," in *The Conduct of Soviet Foreign Policy*, ed. by Erik Hoffmann and Frederic J. Fleron, Jr. (New York: Aldine, 1980), pp. 195–96.

3. *The Conduct of Soviet Foreign Policy* reprints a classic debate between scholars holding the ideological and the national interest views of Soviet foreign policy. On the functions of ideology, see in that text John A. Armstrong, "The Domestic Roots of Soviet Foreign Policy," esp. pp. 93–95, and Richard Lowenthal, "The Logic of One-Party Rule," p. 119. See also Alexander Dallin, "The Domestic Sources of Soviet Foreign Policy," in *The Domestic Context of Soviet Foreign Policy*, ed. by Seweryn Bialer (Boulder, CO: Westview Press, 1981), p. 335; and Hannes Adomeit, *Soviet Risk-Taking and Crisis Behavior: A Theoretical and Empirical Analysis* (London: George Allen & Unwin, 1982), p. 330.

4. R. N. Carew Hunt, "Ideology and Power Politics: A Symposium," in Hoffmann and Fleron, *The Conduct of Soviet Foreign Policy*, p. 103.

5. Adam B. Ulam, "Soviet Ideology and Soviet Foreign Policy," in Hoffmann and Fleron, p. 141.

6. John A. Armstrong's essay, "The Domestic Roots of Soviet Foreign Policy," points out the various distinctions scholars have made between ideology, doctrine, dogma, and various other permutations of what the Soviet leaders think versus what they say. I like the distinction between unverifiable beliefs (grand ideology) and verifiable but unverified beliefs (petty ideology or dogma). Grand ideology includes the concepts we will be discussing below about the nature of reality. Doctrine, or petty ideology, comprises propositions such as the inevitability of war, or peaceful coexistence.

7. Ronald Hingley, "That's No Lie, Comrade," *Problems of Communism* 11, no. 2 (March/April 1962), p. 54.

8. Raymond L. Garthoff, "American-Soviet Relations in Perspective," *Political Science Quarterly* 100, no. 4 (Winter 1985–86), p. 546.

9. Ibid., pp. 550–51.

10. Alfred G. Meyer, "The Functions of Ideology in the Soviet Political System," *Soviet Studies* 17, no. 3 (January 1966), p. 276.

11. James H. Billington, *The Icon and the Axe: An Interpretive History of Russian Culture* (New York: Alfred A. Knopf, 1966), p. 324.

12. Ibid., p. 266. Mead and Metraux make essentially the same point: "Empirical ways of thinking, which stress the detailed steps through which something happens and the detailed clues by which it is found out, have had less time to take hold in Russia than in the West. The ideal of knowledge remains much more an immediate and complete revelation of the core of events, of the soul of another person." Margaret Mead and Rhoda Metraux, eds., *The Study of Culture at a Distance* (Chicago: University of Chicago Press, 1953), pp. 439–40.

13. Geoffrey Gorer and John Rickman, *The People of Great Russia* (New York: Chanticleer Press, 1950), pp. 186–88.

14. Robert Kennedy, *Thirteen Days* (New York: W. W. Norton & Co., 1969), p. 64.

15. Ibid., p. 65, emphasis added.

16. Tibor Szamuely, *The Russian Tradition* (New York: McGraw-Hill, 1974), p. 157.

17. Nicholas Berdyaev, *The Russian Idea* (New York: Macmillan, 1948), p. 31.

18. The following discussion draws substantially on Thomas J. Blakeley's excellent *The Soviet Theory of Knowledge* (Dordrecht, Holland: Reidel, 1964).

19. Edward T. Hall, *Beyond Culture* (Garden City, NJ: Anchor Press/Doubleday, 1976), pp. 114–15.

20. Lenin, "Materialism and Imperio-Criticism," in *Selected Works* (New York: International Publishers, 1943), pp. 317–19.

21. Blakeley, *The Soviet Theory of Knowledge*, pp. 95–99, 114–21.

22. A. J. Ayer, *The Central Questions of Philosophy* (London: Weidenfeld and Nicolson, 1973), p. 8.

23. Ibid., p. 60.

24. Lenin's widow, Krupskaya, speaking at the 14th Party Congress in 1925, quoted in Margaret Mead, *Soviet Attitudes toward Authority* (New York: McGraw-Hill, 1951), p. 15.

25. Lenin, *Conspectus of Hegel's Book "The Science of Logic,"* in *Collected Works*, from the Russian 4th ed. (London: Lawrence and Wishart, 1961), vol. 38, p. 171.

26. Ulam, "Soviet Ideology and Soviet Foreign Policy," p. 140.

27. Peter B. Reddaway, "Aspects of Ideological Belief in the Soviet Union; Comments on Professor Meyer's Essay," *Soviet Studies* 17, no. 4 (April 1966), pp. 482–83. Uri Ra'anan, "Soviet Decision-making and International Relations," *Problems of Communism* 29 (November/December 1980), p. 41.

28. Steven White, "The USSR: Patterns of Autocracy and Industrialism," in *Political Culture and Political Change in Communist States*, ed. by Archie Brown and Jack Gray (London: Macmillan, 1977), p. 47.

29. Daniel Bell, "Ideology and Soviet Politics," *Slavic Review* 24, no. 4 (December 1965), pp. 591–603.

30. Adomeit, *Soviet Risk-Taking and Crisis Behavior*, p. 333.

31. Bialer, *The Domestic Context of Soviet Foreign Policy*, pp. 263–65.

32. On this, the author speaks from experience.

33. The Soviet official told this anecdote to his State Department counterpart, who related it to me during a background interview in December 1986.

34. Conversation with Vladimir Bukovsky, Cambridge, England, January 1987.

35. Tucker notes that Soviet theorists point out this difference between their "dialectical" approach to coexistence and the "metaphysical" approach of "bourgeois ideologues." Robert Tucker, *The Soviet Political Mind: Studies in Stalinism and Post-Stalinist Change* (New York: W. W. Norton and Co., 1971), pp. 246–47.

36. Conversation with Vladimir Bukovsky, Cambridge, England, January 1987.

37. Jonathan Dean, "East-West Arms Control Negotiations: The Multilateral Dimension," in *A Game for High Stakes*, ed. by Leon Sloss and M. Scott Davis (Cambridge, MA: Ballinger, 1986), p. 86.

38. Wedge and Muromcew, "Psychological Factors in Soviet Disarmament Negotiations," p. 33.

39. Lenin, in *Proletarskaya Pravda*, 7 December 1913; reproduced in *Collected Works* (London: Lawrence and Wishart, 1963), vol. 19, p. 523.

40. Adomeit, *Soviet Risk-Taking, and Crisis Behavior*, p. 324.

41. John R. Deane, *The Strange Alliance* (New York: Viking Press, 1947), p. 297.

42. Tony Bishop, *A Guide to Negotiating with the Soviets*, unpublished paper. Conversation with author in September 1986.

43. Conversation at British Cabinet Office, January 1987.

44. Max Kampelman, "Madrid Conference: How to Negotiate with the Soviets," American Bar Association, *Law and National Security Intelligence Report*, vol. 7, no. 2. Ambassador Kampelman made the comment on dialectics during a meeting with the author in December 1986.

45. Conversation in January 1987.

46.   Leon Sloss and M. Scott Davis, "The Soviet Union: The Pursuit of Power and Influence through Negotiation," in *National Negotiating Styles*, ed. by Hans Binnendijk (Washington, DC: Center for the Study of Foreign Affairs, Foreign Service Institute, U.S. Department of State, 1987), p. 29.

47.   Wedge and Muromcew, "Psychological Factors in Soviet Disarmament Negotiations," p. 33.

48.   On negotiation as process, see the popular work by Herb Cohen, *You Can Negotiate Anything* (New York: Bantam Books, 1982), p. 102.

49.   Julian Lider, *Correlation of Forces: An Analysis of Marxist-Leninist Concepts* (New York: St. Martin's Press, 1986).

50.   Ibid., p. 10.

51.   Robert V. Daniels, "Doctrine and Foreign Policy," in Hoffmann and Fleron, eds., *The Conduct of Soviet Foreign Policy*, p. 164.

52.   Lider, pp. 67–68.

53.   Lenin, "A Poor Defense of a Liberal Labour Policy," *Zvezda*, April 1, 1912; as reproduced in *Collected Works* (Moscow: Foreign Languages Publishing House, 1963), vol. 17, p. 560.

54.   Lider, p. 124.

55.   Ibid., pp. 145–46.

56.   Ibid., p. 217. Lider's reference to "both approaches" is a comparison of Western balance of power theory with the Soviet correlation of forces.

57.   Ibid., p. 233.

58.   Ibid., p. 261.

59.   Thomas W. Wolfe, "Concluding Reflections on the SALT Experience," in Hoffmann and Fleron, *The Conduct of Soviet Foreign Policy*, p. 413.

60.   Conversation with Paul Nitze in Washington, D.C., February 1987.

61.   Comments at American Political Science Association annual meeting. September 1986, Washington, D.C.

62.   Edward Hallet Carr, *Socialism in One Country, 1924–1926* (London: Macmillan & Co., 1958), p. 4. Brzezinski shares Carr's view that over time, the more enduring patterns of Russian political culture have begun to exert greater influence. Zbigniew Brzezinski, "Soviet Politics: From the Future to the Past?" in *The Dynamics of Soviet Politics*, ed. by Paul Cocks, Robert V. Daniels, and Nancy Whittier Heer (Cambridge, MA: Harvard University Press, 1976), p. 337.

63.   Billington, *The Icon and the Axe* p. ix. Stephen White, "The USSR: Patterns of Autocracy and Industrialism," in Brown and Gray, *Political Culture and Communist Studies*, p. 34.

64.   Carr, *Socialism in One Country, 1924–1926*, pp. 9–10.

65.   Robert C. Tucker, *Political Culture and Leadership in Soviet Russia: From Lenin to Gorbachev* (New York: W. W. Norton, 1987), pp. 88–89. Szamuely, *The Russian Tradition*, pp. 15, 19–20, 24–25. George Vernadsky, *The Mongols and Russia* (New Haven, CT: Yale University Press, 1953), esp. pp. 335–49. Another who has stressed the impact of Mongol/Tatar rule on Russia's authoritarian political traditions is Ronald Hingley, *The Russian Mind* (New York: Charles Scribner's Sons, 1977), p. 197. For a dissenting view, see Charles J. Halperin, *Russia and the Golden Horde: The Mongol Impact on Medieval Russian History* (Bloomington: Indiana University Press, 1986). Brzezinski also considers that the central reality of Russian politics has been its predominantly autocratic character (p. 337).

66.   Halperin, *Russia and the Golden Horde*, pp. 102–3. Edward L. Keenan, "Muscovite Political Folkways," *The Russian Review* 45 (April 1986), pp. 115–81, esp. p. 118.

67.   Keenan, "Muscovite Political Folkways," pp. 155–57.

68.   Ibid. For more on the subordination of the interests of the individual to those of society in the Russian dissident tradition, see Szamuely, *The Russian Tradition*, pp. 170–71.

69.   Halperin, *Russia and the Golden Horde*, p. 126.

70.   Seweryn Bialer, *The Soviet Paradox: External Expansion, Internal Decline* (New York: Alfred A. Knopf, 1986), p. 200.

71.   Ibid., p. 240.

72.   See, for example, Nicholas Vakar's *The Taproot of Soviet Society* (New York: Harper & Brothers, 1961), p. 17. Keenan's view is essentially the same, although he distinguishes two elements of the early upper classes—court and bureaucratic—which over time melded (Keenan, "Muscovite Political Folkways").

73.   Berdyaev, *The Russian Idea*, p. 16.

74.   Billington, *The Icon and the Axe*, p. 123.

75.   Ibid., p. 198. See also Szamuely, *The Russian Tradition*, p. 72.

76.   George Kennan, "The Sources of Soviet Conduct," *Foreign Affairs* 65, no. 4 (Spring 1987), p. 852; (a reprint of the 1947 "X" article).

77.   Lenin, of course, stood on the shoulders of others. He acknowledged his debt to Plekhanov, the father of Russian Marxism. And many of his organizational principles had antecedents in the principles of *Narodnaya volya*, a debt that he also acknowledged. See the discussion in Szamuely, *The Russian Tradition*, pp. 354–69.

78.   Nikolai Aleksandrovich Berdyaev, "The Origin of Russian Communism," in *The Mind of Modern Russia*, ed. by Hans Kohn (Rutgers, NJ: Rutgers University Press, 1955), p. 254. Billington, *The Icon and the Axe*, p. 254. J. M. Bochenski, *Soviet Russian Dialectical Materialism* (Dordrecht, Holland: Reidel, 1963), p. 28.

79.   Quoted in Kohn, *The Mind of Modern Russia*, p. 244.

80.   Thomas T. Hammond, "Lenninist Authoritarianism before the Revolution," in *Continuity and Change in Russian and Soviet Thought*, ed. by Ernest J. Simmons (Cambridge, MA: Harvard University Press, 1955), p. 154.

81.   Carr, *Socialism in One Country 1924–1926*, p. 16. For further on Lenin's view of party organization and its influence on communism, see Robert C. Tucker "Lenin's Bolshevism as a Culture in the Making," in *Bolshevik Culture: Experiment and Order in the Russian Revolution*, ed. by Abbott Gleason, Peter Kenez, and Richard Stites (Bloomington, Indiana University Press, 1985).

82.   Lenin, "On the Eve of October, 1917," in Kohn, *The Mind of Modern Russia*, p. 235.

83.   Nathan Leites, *A Study of Bolshevism* (Glencoe, IL: The Free Press, 1953).

84.   Ibid., pp. 148, 152, 155, 162.

85.   John A. Armstrong, who is sympathetic to Leites's work, at least insofar as he considers the study of psychological processes relevant to international affairs, concedes the approach fell into disrepute following the appearance of *A Study of Bolshevism* ("The Domestic Roots of Soviet Foreign Policy," in Hoffmann and Fleron, *The Conduct of Soviet Foreign Policy*, p. 96) Samuel L. Sharp, "National Interest: Key to Soviet Politics," in Hoffmann and Fleron, *The Conduct of Soviet Foreign Policy*, p. 110. Robert Jervis, *Perception and Misperception in International Politics* (Princeton, NJ: Princeton University Press, 1976), p. 103, note 88.

86.   Alexander L. George, " 'The Operational Code': A Neglected Approach to the Study of Political Leaders and Decision-Making," in Hoffmann and Fleron, *The Conduct of Soviet Foreign Policy*, p. 166.

87.   Ibid., p. 178.

88.   Adomeit, *Soviet Risk-Taking and Crisis Behavior*, p. 328.

89.   Keenan, "Muscovite Political Folkways," p. 168.

90.   Archie Brown, ed., *Political Culture and Communist Studies* (New York: M. E. Sharpe, 1985), p. 156.

91. Bialer, *The Soviet Paradox*, pp. 263–65.

92. On the Revolution as a movement of restoration, see Brzezinski, p. 340. *Bolshevik Culture*, Gleason et al., discuss the interaction of the intellectual and peasant cultures.

93. Vakar, *The Taproot of Soviet Society*, pp. 8, 17–18. Billington, *The Icon and the Axe*, pp. 534, 539.

94. Tucker, *The Soviet Political Mind*, p. ix. Bialer, *The Soviet Paradox*, pp. 24, 31.

95. Keenan, "Muscovite Political Folkways," p. 168. Joyce also stresses the central role risk-avoidance plays in the Soviet political culture [John Michael Joyce, "The Old Russian Legacy," *Foreign Policy*, no. 55 (Summer 1984), pp. 132–53].

96. Stephen F. Cohen, *Rethinking the Soviet Experience: Politics and History Since 1917* (New York: Oxford University Press, 1985), p. 146.

97. Tucker, *The Soviet Political Mind*, pp. 175, 229.

98. Bialer, *The Soviet Paradox*, pp. 161–62.

IV

Prospect and Retrospect

12

The Sources of Soviet Conduct*

George F. Kennan (X)

The political personality of Soviet power as we know it today is the product of ideology and circumstances: ideology inherited by the present Soviet leaders from the movement in which they had their political origin, and circumstances of the power which they now have exercised for nearly three decades in Russia. There can be few tasks of psychological analysis more difficult than to try to trace the interaction of these two forces and the relative rôle of each in the determination of official Soviet conduct. Yet the attempt must be made if that conduct is to be understood and effectively countered.

It is difficult to summarize the set of ideological concepts with which the Soviet leaders came into power. Marxian ideology, in its Russian-Communist projection, has always been in process of subtle evolution. The materials on which it bases itself are extensive and complex. But the outstanding features of Communist thought as it existed in 1916 may perhaps be summarized as follows: (a) that the central factor in the life of man, the factor which determines the character of public life and the "physiognomy of society," is the system by which material goods are produced and exchanged; (b) that the capitalist system of production is a nefarious one which inevitably leads to the exploitation of the working class by the capital-owning class and is incapable of developing adequately the economic resources of society or of distributing fairly the material goods produced by human labor; (c) that capitalism contains the seeds of its own destruction and must, in view of the inability of the capital-owning class to adjust itself to economic change, result eventually and inescapably in a revolutionary transfer of power to the working class; and (d) that imperialism, the final phase of capitalism, leads directly to war and revolution.

The rest may be outlined in Lenin's own words: "Unevenness of economic and political development is the inflexible law of capitalism. It follows from this that the victory of Socialism may come originally in a few capitalist countries or even in a single capitalist country. The victorious proletariat of that country,

*Reprinted by permission of the author and publisher from *Foreign Affairs*, (July 1947). copyright© 1947 by the Council on Foriegn Relations, Inc., New York.

having expropriated the capitalists and having organized Socialist production at home, would rise against the remaining capitalist world, drawing to itself in the process the oppressed classes of other countries."[1] It must be noted that there was no assumption that capitalism would perish without proletarian revolution. A final push was needed from a revolutionary proletariat movement in order to tip over the tottering structure. But it was regarded as inevitable that sooner or later that push be given.

For 50 years prior to the outbreak of the Revolution, this pattern of thought had exercised great fascination for the members of the Russian revolutionary movement. Frustrated, discontented, hopeless of finding self-expression—or too impatient to seek it—in the confining limits of the Tsarist political system, yet lacking wide popular support for their choice of bloody revolution as a means of social betterment, these revolutionists found in Marxist theory a highly convenient rationalization for their own instinctive desires. It afforded pseudo-scientific justification for their impatience, for their categoric denial of all value in the Tsarist system, for their yearning for power and revenge and for their inclination to cut corners in the pursuit of it. It is therefore no wonder that they had come to believe implicitly in the truth and soundness of the Marxian-Leninist teachings, so congenial to their own impulses and emotions. Their sincerity need not be impugned. This is a phenomenon as old as human nature itself. It has never been more aptly described than by Edward Gibbon who wrote in "The Decline and Fall of the Roman Empire": "From enthusiasm to imposture the step is perilous and slippery; the demon of Socrates affords a memorable instance how a wise man may deceive himself, how a good man may deceive others, how the conscience may slumber in a mixed and middle state between self-illusion and voluntary fraud." And it was with this set of conceptions that the members of the Bolshevik Party entered into power.

Now it must be noted that through all the years of preparation for revolution, the attention of these men, as indeed of Marx himself, had been centered less on the future form which Socialism[2] would take than on the necessary overthrow of rival power which, in their view, had to precede the introduction of Socialism. Their views, therefore, on the positive program to be put into effect, once power was attained, were for the most part nebulous, visionary and impractical. Beyond the nationalization of industry and the expropriation of large private capital holdings there was no agreed program. The treatment of the peasantry, which according to the Marxist formulation was not of the proletariat, had always been a vague spot in the pattern of Communist thought; and it remained an object of controversy and vacillation for the first ten years of Communist power.

The circumstances of the immediate post-revolution period—the existence in Russia of civil war and foreign intervention, together with the obvious fact that the Communists represented only a tiny minority of the Russian people—made the establishment of dictatorial power a necessity. The experiment with "war Communism" and the abrupt attempt to eliminate private production and trade had unfortunate economic consequences and caused further bitterness against the new revolutionary régime. While the temporary relaxation of the effort to communize Russia, represented by the New Economic Policy, alleviated some of this economic distress and thereby served its purpose, it also made it evident that the "capitalistic sector of society" was still prepared to profit at once from any relaxation of governmental pressure, and would, if permitted to continue to exist, always constitute a powerful opposing element to the Soviet régime and a serious rival for influence in the country. Somewhat the same situation prevailed with respect to the individual peasant who, in his own small way, was also a private producer.

Lenin, had he lived, might have proved a great enough man to reconcile these conflicting forces to the ultimate benefit of Russian society, though this is questionable. But be that as it may, Stalin, and those whom he led in the struggle for succession to Lenin's position of leadership, were not the men to tolerate rival political forces in the sphere of power which they coveted. Their sense of insecurity was too great. Their particular brand of fanaticism, unmodified by any of the Anglo-Saxon traditions of compromise, was too fierce and too jealous to envisage any permanent sharing of power. From the Russian-Asiatic world out of which they had emerged they carried with them a skepticism as to the possibilities of permanent and peaceful coexistence of rival forces. Easily persuaded of their own doctrinaire "rightness," they insisted on the submission or destruction of all competing power. Outside of the Communist party, Russian society was to have no rigidity. There were to be no forms of collective human activity or association which would not be dominated by the Party. No other force in Russian society was to be permitted to achieve vitality or integrity. Only the Party was to have structure. All else was to be an amorphous mass.

And within the Party the same principle was to apply. The mass of Party members might go through the motions of election, deliberation, decision and action; but in these motions they were to be animated not by their own individual wills but by the awesome breath of the Party leadership and the overbrooding presence of "the word."

Let it be stressed again that subjectively these men probably did not seek absolutism for its own sake. They doubtless believed—and found it easy to believe—that they alone knew what was good for society and that they would accomplish that good once their power was secure and unchallengeable. But in seeking that security of their own rule they were prepared to recognize no restrictions, either of God or man, on the character of their methods. And until such time as that security might be achieved, they placed far down on their scale of operational priorities the comforts and happiness of the peoples entrusted to their care.

Now the outstanding circumstance concerning the Soviet régime is that down to the present day this process of political consolidation has never been completed and the men in the Kremlin have continued to be predominantly absorbed with the struggle to secure and make absolute the power which they seized in November 1917. They have endeavored to secure it primarily against forces at home, within Soviet society itself. But they have also endeavored to secure it against the outside world. For ideology, as we have seen, taught them that the outside world was hostile and that it was their duty eventually to overthrow the political forces beyond their borders. The powerful hands of Russian history and tradition reached up to sustain them in this feeling. Finally, their own aggressive intransigence with respect to the outside world began to find its own reaction; and they were soon forced, to use another Gibbonesque phrase, "to chastise the contumacy" which they themselves had provoked. It is an undeniable privilege of every man to prove himself right in the thesis that the world is his enemy; for if he reiterates it frequently enough and makes it the background of his conduct he is bound eventually to be right.

Now it lies in the nature of the mental world of the Soviet leaders, as well as in the character of their ideology, that no opposition to them can be officially recognized as having any merit or justification whatsoever. Such opposition can flow, in theory, only from the hostile and incorrigible forces of dying capitalism. As long as remnants of capitalism were officially recognized as existing in Russia, it was possible to place on them, as an internal element, part of the blame for the maintenance of a dictatorial form of society. But as these remnants were liquidated, little by little, this justification fell away; and when it was indicated officially that they had been finally destroyed, it disappeared altogether. And this fact created one of the most basic of the compulsions which came to act upon the Soviet régime: since capitalism no longer existed in Russia and since it could not be admitted that there could be serious or widespread opposition to the Kremlin springing spontaneously from the liberated masses under its authority, it became necessary to justify the retention of the dictatorship by stressing the menace of capitalism abroad.

This began at an early date. In 1924 Stalin specifically defended the retention of the "organs of suppression," meaning, among others, the army and the secret police, on the ground that "as long as there is a capitalist encirclement there will be danger of intervention with all the consequences that flow from that danger." In accordance with that theory, and from that time on, all internal opposition forces in Russia have consistently been portrayed as the agents of foreign forces of reaction antagonistic to Soviet power.

By the same token, tremendous emphasis has been placed on the original Communist thesis of a basic antagonism between the capitalist and Socialist worlds. It is clear, from many indications, that this emphasis is not founded in reality. The real facts concerning it have been confused by the existence abroad of genuine resentment provoked by Soviet philosophy and tactics and occasionally by the existence of great centers of military power, notably the Nazi régime in Germany and the Japanese Government of the late 1930's, which did indeed have aggressive designs against the Soviet Union. But there is ample evidence that the stress laid in Moscow on the menace confronting Soviet society from the world outside its borders is founded not in the realities of foreign antagonism but in the necessity of explaining away the maintenance of dictatorial authority at home.

Now the maintenance of this pattern of Soviet power, namely, the pursuit of unlimited authority domestically, accompanied by the cultivation of the semi-myth of implacable foreign hostility, has gone far to shape the actual machinery of Soviet power as we know it today. Internal organs of administration which did not serve this purpose withered on the vine. Organs which did serve this purpose became vastly swollen. The security of Soviet power came to rest on the iron discipline of the Party, on the severity and ubiquity of the secret police, and on the uncompromising economic monopolism of the state. The "organs of suppression," in which the Soviet leaders had sought security from rival forces, became in large measure the masters of those whom they were designed to serve. Today the major part of the structure of Soviet power is committed to the perfection of the dictatorship and to the maintenance of the concept of Russia as in a state of siege, with the enemy lowering beyond the walls. And the millions of human beings who form that part of the structure of power must defend at all costs this concept of Russia's position, for without it they are themselves superfluous.

As things stand today, the rulers can no longer dream of parting with these organs of suppression. The quest for absolute power, pursued now for nearly three decades with a ruthlessness unparalleled (in scope at least) in modern times, has again produced internally, as it did externally, its own reaction. The excesses of the police apparatus have fanned the potential opposition to the régime into something far greater and more dangerous than it could have been before those excesses began.

But least of all can the rulers dispense with the fiction by which the maintenance of dictatorial power has been defended. For this fiction has been canonized in Soviet philosophy by the excesses already committed in its name; and it is now anchored in the Soviet structure of thought by bonds far greater than those of mere ideology.

II

So much for the historical background. What does it spell in terms of the political personality of Soviet power as we know it today?

Of the original ideology, nothing has been officially junked. Belief is maintained in the basic badness of capitalism, in the inevitability of its destruction, in the obligation of the proletariat to assist in that destruction and to take power into its own hands. But stress has come to be laid primarily on those concepts which relate most specifically to the Soviet régime itself: to its position as the sole truly Socialist régime in a dark and misguided world, and to the relationships of power within it.

The first of these concepts is that of the innate antagonism between capitalism and Socialism. We have seen how deeply that concept has become embedded in foundations of Soviet power. It has profound implications for Russia's conduct as a member of international society. It means that there can never be on

Moscow's side any sincere assumption of a community of aims between the Soviet Union and powers which are regarded as capitalist. It must invariably be assumed in Moscow that the aims of the capitalist world are antagonistic to the Soviet régime, and therefore to the interests of the peoples it controls. If the Soviet Government occasionally sets its signature to documents which would indicate the contrary, this is to be regarded as a tactical manœuver permissible in dealing with the enemy (who is without honor) and should be taken in the spirit of *caveat emptor*. Basically, the antagonism remains. It is postulated. And from it flow many of the phenomena which we find disturbing in the Kremlin's conduct of foreign policy: the secretiveness, the lack of frankness, the duplicity, the wary suspiciousness, and the basic unfriendliness of purpose. These phenomena are there to stay, for the foreseeable future. There can be variations of degree and of emphasis. When there is something the Russians want from us, one or the other of these features of their policy may be thrust temporarily into the background; and when that happens there will always be Americans who will leap forward with gleeful announcements that "the Russians have changed," and some who will even try to take credit for having brought about such "changes." But we should not me misled by tactical manœuvers. These characteristics of Soviet policy, like the postulate from which they flow, are basic to the internal nature of Soviet power, and will be with us, whether in the foreground or the background, until the internal nature of Soviet power is changed.

This means that we are going to continue for a long time to find the Russians difficult to deal with. It does not mean that they should be considered as embarked upon a do-or-die program to overthrow our society by a given date. The theory of the inevitability of the eventual fall of capitalism has the fortunate connotation that there is no hurry about it. The forces of progress can take their time in preparing the final *coup de grâce*. Meanwhile, what is vital is that the "Socialist fatherland"—that oasis of power which has been already won for Socialism in the person of the Soviet Union—should be cherished and defended by all good Communists at home and abroad, its fortunes promoted, its enemies badgered and confounded. The promotion of premature, "adventuristic" revolutionary projects abroad which might embarrass Soviet power in any way would be an inexcusable, even a counter-revolutionary act. The cause of Socialism is the support and promotion of Soviet power, as defined in Moscow.

This brings us to the second of the concepts important to contemporary Soviet outlook. That is the infallibility of the Kremlin. The Soviet concept of power, which permits no focal points of organization outside the Party itself, requires that the Party leadership remain in the theory the sole repository of truth. For if truth were to be found elsewhere, there would be justification for its expression in organized activity. But it is precisely that which the Kremlin cannot and will not permit.

The leadership of the Communist Party is therefore always right, and has been always right ever since in 1929 Stalin formalized his personal power by announcing that decisions of the Politburo were being taken unanimously.

On the principle of infallibility there rests the iron discipline of the Communist

Party. In fact, the two concepts are mutually self-supporting. Perfect discipline requires recognition of infallibility. Infallibility requires the observance of discipline. And the two together go far to determine the behaviorism of the entire Soviet apparatus of power. But their effect cannot be understood unless a third factor be taken into account: namely, the fact that the leadership is at liberty to put forward for tactical purposes any particular thesis which it finds useful to the cause at any particular moment and to require the faithful and unquestioning acceptance of that thesis by the members of the movement as a whole. This means that truth is not a constant but is actually created, for all intents and purposes, by the Soviet leaders themselves. It may vary from week to week, from month to month. It is nothing absolute and immutable—nothing which flows from objective reality. It is only the most recent manifestation of the wisdom of those in whom the ultimate wisdom is supposed to reside, because they represent the logic of history.

The accumulative effect of these factors is to give to the whole subordinate apparatus of Soviet power an unshakeable stubbornness and steadfastness in its orientation. This orientation can be changed at will by the Kremlin but by no other power. Once a given party line has been laid down on a given issue of current policy, the whole Soviet governmental machine, including the mechanism of diplomacy, moves inexorably along the prescribed path, like a persistent toy automobile wound up and headed in a given direction, stopping only when it meets with some unanswerable force. The individuals who are the components of this machine are unamenable to argument or reason which comes to them from outside sources. Their whole training has taught them to mistrust and discount the glib persuasiveness of the outside world. Like the white dog before the phonograph, they hear only the "master's voice." And if they are to be called off from the purposes last dictated to them, it is the master who must call them off. Thus the foreign representative cannot hope that his words will make any impression on them. The most that he can hope is that they will be transmitted to those at the top, who are capable of changing the party line. But even those are not likely to be swayed by any normal logic in the words of the bourgeois representative. Since there can be no appeal to common purposes, there can be no appeal to common mental approaches. For this reason, facts speak louder than words to the ears of the Kremlin; and words carry the greatest weight when they have the ring of reflecting, or being backed up by, facts of unchallengeable validity.

But we have seen that the Kremlin is under no ideological compulsion to accomplish its purposes in a hurry. Like the Church, it is dealing in ideological concepts which are of long-term validity, and it can afford to be patient. It has no right to risk the existing achievements of the revolution for the sake of vain baubles of the future. The very teachings of Lenin himself require great caution and flexibility in the pursuit of Communist purposes. Again, these precepts are fortified by the lessons of Russian history: of centuries of obscure battles between nomadic forces over the stretches of a vast unfortified plain. Here caution, circumspection, flexibility and deception are the valuable qualities; and their value finds natural appreciation in the Russian or the oriental mind. Thus the Kremlin has no compunction about retreating in the face of superior force. And being under the compulsion of no timetable, it does not get panicky under the necessity for such retreat. Its political action is a fluid stream which moves constantly, wherever it is permitted to move, toward a given goal. Its main concern is to make sure that it has filled every nook and cranny available to it in the basin of world power. But if it finds unassailable barriers in its path, it accepts these philosophically and accommodates itself to them. The main thing is that there should always be pressure, unceasing constant pressure, toward the desired goal. There is no trace of any feeling in Soviet psychology that that goal must be reached at any given time.

These considerations make Soviet diplomacy at once easier and more difficult to deal with than the diplomacy of individual aggressive leaders like Napoleon and Hitler. On the one hand it is more sensitive to contrary force, more ready to yield on individual sectors of the diplomatic front when that force is felt to be too strong, and thus more rational in the logic and rhetoric of power. On the other hand it cannot be easily defeated or discouraged by a single victory on the part of its opponents. And the patient persistence by which it is animated means that it can be effectively countered not by sporadic acts which represent the momentary whims of democratic opinion but only the intelligent long-range policies on the part of Russia's adversaries—policies no less steady in their purpose, and no less variegated and resourceful in their application, than those of the Soviet Union itself.

In these circumstances it is clear that the main element of any United States policy toward the Soviet Union must be that of a long-term, patient but firm and vigilant containment of Russian expansive tendencies. It is important to note, however, that such a policy has nothing to do with outward histrionics: with threats or blustering or superfluous gestures of outward "toughness." While the Kremlin is basically flexible in its reaction to political realities, it is by no means unamenable to considerations of prestige. Like almost any other government, it can be placed by tactless and threatening gestures in a position where it cannot afford to yield even though this might be dictated by its sense of realism. The Russian leaders are keen judges of human psychology, and as such they are highly conscious that loss of temper and of self-control is never a source of strength in political affairs. They are quick to exploit such evidences of weakness. For these reasons, it is a *sine qua non* of successful dealing with Russia that the foreign government in question should remain at all times cool and collected and that its demands on Russian policy should be put forward in such a manner as to leave the way open for a compliance not too detrimental to Russian prestige.

III

In the light of the above, it will be clearly seen that the Soviet pressure against the free institutions of the western world is something that can be contained by the adroit and vigilant application of counter-force at a series of constantly shifting geographical and political points, corresponding to the shifts and maneuvers of Soviet policy, but which cannot be charmed or talked out of existence. The Russians look forward to a duel of infinite duration, and they see that already they have scored great successes. It must be borne in mind that there was a time when the Communist Party represented far more of a minority in the sphere of Russian national life than Soviet power today represents in the world community.

But if ideology convinces the rulers of Russia that truth is on their side and that they can therefore afford to wait, those of us on whom that ideology has no claim are free to examine objectively the validity of that premise. The Soviet thesis not only implies complete lack of control by the west over its own economic destiny, it likewise assumes Russian unity, discipline and patience over an infinite period. Let us bring this apocalyptic vision down to earth, and suppose that the western world finds the strength and resourcefulness to contain Soviet power over a period of ten to fifteen years. What does that spell for Russia itself?

The Soviet leaders, taking advantage of the contributions of modern technique to the arts of despotism, have solved the question of obedience within the confines of their power. Few challenge their authority; and even those who do are unable to make that challenge valid as against the organs of suppression of the state.

The Kremlin has also proved able to accomplish its purpose of building up in Russia, regardless of the interests of the inhabitants, an industrial foundation of heavy metallurgy, which is, to be sure, not yet complete but which is nevertheless continuing to grow and is approaching those of the other major industrial countries. All of this, however, both the maintenance of internal political security and the building of heavy industry, has been carried out at a terrible cost in human life and in human hopes and energies. It has necessitated the use of forced labor on a scale unprecedented in modern times under conditions of peace. It has involved the neglect or abuse of other phases of Soviet economic life, particularly agriculture, consumers' goods production, housing and transportation.

To all that, the war has added its tremendous toll of destruction, death and human exhaustion. In consequence of this, we have in Russia today a population which is physically and spiritually tired. The mass of the people are disillusioned, skeptical and no longer as accessible as they once were to the magical attraction which Soviet power still radiates to its followers abroad. The avidity with which people seized upon the slight respite accorded to the Church for tactical reasons during the war was eloquent testimony to the fact that their capacity for faith and devotion found little expression in the purposes of the régime.

In these circumstances, there are limits to the physical and nervous strength of people themselves. These limits are absolute ones, and are binding even for the cruelest dictatorship, because beyond them people cannot be driven. The forced labor camps and the other agencies of constraint provide temporary means of compelling people to work longer hours than their own volition of mere economic pressure would dictate; but if people survive them at all they become old before their time and must be considered as human casualties to the demands of dictatorship. In either case their best powers are no longer available to society and can no longer be enlisted in the service of the state.

Here only the younger generation can help. The younger generation, despite all vicissitudes and sufferings, is numerous and vigorous; and the Russians are a talented people. But it still remains to be seen what will be the effects on mature performance of the abnormal emotional strains of childhood which Soviet dictatorship created and which were enormously increased by the war. Such things as normal security and placidity of home environment have practically ceased to exist in the Soviet Union outside of the most remote farms and villages. And observers are not yet sure whether that is not going to leave its mark on the overall capacity of the generation now coming into maturity.

In addition to this, we have the fact that Soviet economic development, while it can list certain formidable achievements, has been precariously spotty and uneven. Russian Communists who speak of the "uneven development of capitalism" should blush at the contemplation of their own national economy. Here certain branches of economic life, such as the metallurgical and machine industries, have been pushed out of all proportion to other sectors of economy. Here is a nation striving to become in a short period one of the great industrial nations of the world while it still has no highway network worthy of the name and only a relatively primitive network of railways. Much has been done to increase efficiency of labor and to teach primitive peasants something about the operation of machines. But maintenance is still a crying deficiency of all Soviet economy. Construction is hasty and poor in quality. Depreciation must be enormous. And in vast sectors of economic life it has not yet been possible to instill into labor anything like that general culture of production and technical self-respect which characterizes the skilled worker of the west.

It is difficult to see how these deficiencies can be corrected at an early date by a tired and dispirited population working largely under the shadow of fear and compulsion. And as long as they are not overcome, Russia will remain economically a vulnerable, and in a certain sense an impotent, nation, capable of exporting its enthusiasms and of radiating the strange charm of its primitive political vitality but unable to back up those articles of export by the real evidence of material power and prosperity.

Meanwhile, a great uncertainty hangs over the political life of the Soviet Union. That is the uncertainty involved in the transfer of power from one individual or group of individuals to others.

This is, of course, outstandingly the problem of the personal position of Stalin. We must remember that his succession to Lenin's pinnacle of preëminence in the Communist movement was the only such transfer of individual authority which the Soviet Union has experienced. That transfer took 12 years to consolidate. It cost the lives of millions of people and shook the state to its foundations. The attendant tremors were felt all through the international revolutionary movement, to the disadvantage of the Kremlin itself.

It is always possible that another transfer of preëminent power may take place quietly and inconspicuously, with no repercussions anywhere. But again, it is possible that the questions involved may unleash, to use some of Lenin's words, one of those "incredibly swift transitions" from "delicate deceit" to "wild violence" which characterize Russian history, and may shake Soviet power to its foundations.

But this is not only a question of Stalin himself. There has been, since 1938, a dangerous congealment of political life in the higher circles of Soviet power. The All-Union Party Congress, in theory the supreme body of the Party, is supposed to meet not less often than once in three years. It will soon be eight full years since its last meeting. During this period membership in the Party has numerically doubled. Party mortality during the war was enormous; and today well over half of the Party members are persons who have entered since the last Party congress was held. Meanwhile, the same small group of men has carried on at the top through an amazing series of national vicissitudes. Surely there is some reason why the experiences of the war brought basic political changes to every one of the great governments of the west. Surely the causes of that phenomenon are basic enough to be present somewhere in the obscurity of Soviet political life, as well. And yet no recognition has been given to these causes in Russia.

It must be surmised from this that even within so highly disciplined an organization as the Communist Party there must be a growing divergence in age, outlook and interest between the great mass of Party members, only so recently recruited into the movement, and the little self-perpetuating clique of men at the top, whom most of these Party members have never met, with whom they have never conversed, and with whom they can have no political intimacy.

Who can say whether, in these circumstances, the eventual rejuvenation of the higher spheres of authority (which can only be a matter of time) can take place smoothly and peacefully, or whether rivals in the quest for higher power will not eventually reach down into these politically immature and inexperienced masses in order to find support for their respective claims? If this were ever to happen, strange consequences could flow for the Communist Party: for the membership at large has been exercised only in the practices of iron discipline and obedience and not in the arts of compromise and accommodation. And if disunity were ever to seize and paralyze the Party, the chaos and weakness of Russian society would be revealed in forms beyond description. For we have seen that Soviet power is only a crust concealing an amorphous mass of human beings among whom no independent organizational structure is tolerated. In Russia there is not even such a thing as local government. The present generation of Russians have never known spontaneity of collective action. If, consequently, anything were ever to occur to disrupt the unity and efficacy of the Party as a political instrument, Soviet Russia might be changed overnight form one of the strongest to one of the weakest and most pitiable of national societies.

Thus the future of Soviet power may not be by any means as secure as Russian capacity for self-delusion would make it appear to the men in the Kremlin. That they can keep power themselves, they have demonstrated. That they can quietly and easily turn it over to others remains to be proved. Meanwhile, the hardships of their rule and the vicissitudes of international life have taken a heavy toll of the strength and hopes of the great people on whom their power rests. It is curious to note that the ideological power of Soviet authority is strongest today in areas beyond the frontiers of Russia, beyond the reach of its police power. This phenomenon brings to mind a comparison used by Thomas Mann in his great novel "Buddenbrooks." Observing that human institutions often show the greatest outward brilliance at a moment when inner decay is in reality farthest advanced, he compared the Buddenbrook family, in the days of its greatest glamour, to one of those stars whose light shines most brightly on this world when in reality it has long since ceased to exist. And who can say with assurance that the strong light still cast by the Kremlin on the dissatisfied peoples of the western world is not the powerful afterglow of a constellation which is in actuality on the wane? This cannot be proved. And it cannot be disproved. But the possibility remains (and in the opinion of this writer is a strong one) that Soviet power, like the capitalist world of its conception, bears within it the seeds of its own decay, and that the sprouting of these seeds is well advanced.

IV

It is clear that the United States cannot expect in the foreseeable future to enjoy political intimacy with the Soviet régime. It must continue to regard the Soviet Union as a rival, not a partner, in the political arena. It must continue to expect that Soviet policies will reflect no abstract love of peace and stability, no real faith in the possibility of a permanent happy coexistence of the Socialist and capitalist worlds, but rather a cautious, persistent pressure toward the disruption and weakening of all rival influence and rival power.

Balanced against this are the facts that Russia, as opposed to the western world in general, is still by far the weaker party, that Soviet policy is highly flexible, and that Soviet society may well contain deficiencies which will eventually weaken its own total potential. This would of itself warrant the United States entering with reasonable confidence upon a policy of firm containment, designed to confront the Russians with unalterable counter-force at every point where they show signs of encroaching upon the interests of a peaceful and stable world.

But in actuality the possibilities for American policy are by no means limited to holding the line and hoping for the best. It is entirely possible for the United States to influence by its actions the internal developments, both within Russia and throughout the international Communist movement, by which Russian policy is largely determined. This is not only a question of the modest measure of informational activity which this government can conduct in the Soviet Union and elsewhere, although that, too, is important. It is rather a question of the degree to which the United States can create among the peoples of the world generally the impression of a country which knows what it wants, which is coping successfully with the problems of its internal life and with the responsibilities of a World Power, and which has a spiritual vitality capable of holding its own among the major ideological currents of the time. To the extent that such an impression can be created and maintained, the aims of Russian Communism must appear sterile and quixotic, the hopes and enthusiasm of Moscow's supporters must wane, and added strain must be imposed on the Kremlin's foreign policies. For the palsied decrepitude of the capitalist world is the keystone of Communist philosophy. Even the failure of the United States to experience the early economic depression which the ravens of the Red Square have been predicting with such complacent confidence since hostilities ceased would have deep and important repercussions throughout the Communist world.

By the same token, exhibitions of indecision, disunity and internal disintegration within this county have an exhilarating effect on the whole Communist movement. At each evidence of these tendencies, a thrill of hope and excitement goes through the Communist world; a new jauntiness can be noted in the Moscow tread; new groups of foreign supporters climb on to what they can only view as the band wagon of international politics; and Russian pressure increases all along the line in international affairs.

It would be an exaggeration to say that American behavior unassisted and alone could exercise a power of life and death over the Communist movement and bring about the early fall of Soviet power in Russia. But the United States has it in its power to increase enormously the strains under which Soviet policy must operate, to force upon the Kremlin a far greater degree of moderation and circumspection than it has had to observe in recent years, and in this way to promote tendencies which must eventually find their outlet in either the break-up or the gradual mellowing of Soviet power. For no mystical, Messianic movement—and particularly not that of the Kremlin—can face frustration indefinitely without eventually adjusting itself in one way or another to the logic of that state of affairs.

Thus the decision will really fall in large measure in this country itself. The issue of Soviet-American relations is in essence a test of the over-all worth of the United States as a nation among nations. To avoid destruction the United States need only measure up to its own best traditions and prove itself worthy of preservation as a great nation.

Surely, there was never a fairer test of national quality than this. In the light of these circumstances, the thoughtful observer of Russian-American relations will find no cause for complaint in the Kremlin's challenge to American society. He will rather experience a certain gratitude to a Providence which, by providing the American people with this implacable challenge, has made their entire security as a nation dependent on their pulling themselves together and accepting the responsibilities of moral and political leadership that history plainly intended them to bear.

NOTES

1. "Concerning the Slogans of the United States of Europe," August 1915. Official Soviet edition of Lenin's works.

2. Here and elsewhere in this paper "Socialism" refers to Marxist or Leninist Communism, not to liberal Socialism of the Second International variety.

13

Sources of Soviet Foreign Conduct*

William Taubman

Edward N. Luttwak. *The Grand Strategy of the Soviet Union.* New York, St. Martin's Press, 1983.

Richard Pipes. *Survival Is Not Enough: Soviet Realities and America's Future.* New York, Simon and Schuster, 1984.

Zbigniew Brzezinski. *Game Plan: How to Conduct the U.S.-Soviet Contest.* Boston, MA,

Atlantic Monthly Press, 1986.

Seweryn Bialer. *The Soviet Paradox: External Expansion, Internal Decline.* New York, Knopf, 1986.

Leon Sloss and M. Scott Davis, Eds. *A Game for High Stakes: Lessons Learned in Negotiating with the Soviet Union.* Cambridge, MA, Ballinger, 1986.

The ironic combination of external expansion and internal decline has been the most striking feature of Soviet politics in recent years. Seweryn Bialer calls this situation "the Soviet paradox." These two trends have produced an unusual degree of agreement among usually differing US observers of the Soviet Union. All but the most complacent of them admit that in the 1970's the USSR had achieved a massive military buildup and had also made vigorous expansionist efforts, especially in the Third World. At the same time, even those most alarmed by Soviet expansionism concede that the Soviet system has suffered a series of debilitating economic, social, and political setbacks at home. But if the five books under review here (written by some of the leading American Sovietologists) are any indication, there is still plenty of disagreement about the meaning of the two trends, and especially about the connection between them. Why, how, and with what success has the Soviet Union been expanding? How serious are its domestic problems? Are internal troubles likely to constrain external expansion or provoke it? Might Soviet domestic troubles be turned to the West's advantage?

*Reprinted by permission of the author from *Problems of Communism* XXXV, 5 (September–October 1986).

Edward Luttwak, Richard Pipes, and Zbigniew Brzezinski are alarmed about Moscow's expansionism and call for Western resistance that goes not only beyond the late and (by them) unlamented détente but beyond containment as well. Brzezinski probably speaks for all three when he urges that the United States seek to "prevail historically" over the Soviet Union (p. 239). Seweryn Bialer, on the other hand, is more willing to meet Moscow halfway in arms control and other negotiations, and more resigned to an endless process of "competitive coexistence" (p. 369). The fifth book, *A Game for High Stakes*, is a collection of short essays by Americans who have negotiated with the Soviets on issues ranging from arms control to trade. Although these essayists take no overall position on the meaning of the Soviet paradox, their experiences do bear on the debate.

Luttwak, Pipes, and Brzezinski find different roots of the current danger from the Soviet Union and offer different prescriptions for how to cope with it. Bialer is less pessimistic about that danger, but also less optimistic than they about finding any enduring solution, because he believes that "winning" is as unlikely as a settlement of US differences with Moscow. This contrast is especially ironic because Pipes and Brzezinski revel in an unblinking realism that rejects as utopian any hope for an early end to the East–West conflict. Brzezinski insists on "the historical depth of the American-Soviet antagonism, the degree of conflict between the geopolitical interests of the two powers, and the intensity of regional turbulence that by itself generates conflicting superpower responses" (p. 246). The central proposition of his book, Brzezinski writes, is that "the American-Soviet contest is not some temporary aberration but an historical rivalry that will long endure" (p. xiii). Pipes would not disagree. And yet, each recommends in the end a plan for "prevailing" over the Soviet Union that seems highly unrealistic to this reviewer, who tends to share Bialer's perspective. At the same time, although certain key conclusions of Luttwak, Pipes, and Brzezinski strike me as questionable, many of their arguments are all too convincing.

Let us begin a more detailed consideration of the Soviet paradox with a closer look at its expansionist aspect. All four authors agree that Russia always was, and the Soviet Union still is, an expansionist power. Thus, they stress the indigenous roots of recent Soviet expansionism. Luttwak and Pipes are particularly keen to trace the Russian roots of Soviet imperialism. In previous works, Pipes has stressed the resemblance between Tsarist and Soviet police-states, thus bringing down on himself the wrath of Russophiles like Aleksandr Solzhenitsyn.[1] *Survival Is Not Enough* further debunks Russia's allegedly golden age, pointing out, for example, that "between the middle of the sixteenth century and the end of the seventeenth, [Russia] acquired every year the territorial equivalent of modern Holland for 150 years running" (p. 37). Besides insisting on the Tsarist-Soviet continuity, Pipes helpfully suggests how it came to be: "The violence of 1917–1920 resulted in the wholesale destruction of the upper and middle classes, which happened to have been the principal Westernized groups in Russia . . . it

permitted the unregenerate Muscovite Russia, which had survived intact underneath the veneer of European influences, to float to the surface''(p. 23).

Along with traditional Russian factors, Marxist-Leninist ideology was usually
seen in the West as a key determinant of Soviet foreign policy. Yet, increasingly
in recent years, that ideology has been perceived as eroding in the USSR. A sign
of that perception is that none of the four authors emphasizes the ideological
roots of Soviet expansionism. Indeed, Pipes claims that "the Soviet official is a
cynic who ascribes to human beings only the basest of motives. He views people
as driven exclusively by self-interest. Any other motive he dismisses as hum-
bug'' (p. 45). Bialer is more willing to credit Marxism-Leninism (not so much its
fine points of doctrine, as its broad analytical categories) with motivating Soviet
leaders, because "if they were simply cynics they could be bought off by their
wealthier adversaries" (p. 349).

A third "internal" source of Soviet expansionism is seen in the nature of the
Soviet system itself. Drawing on the writings of Michael Voslensky,[2] a former
Soviet official now living in emigration, Pipes zeros in on the link between
repression and expansion. Expansion, he argues, legitimizes the regime in
general and its political leaders in particular. The absence of democratic participation both requires Soviet leaders to seek such legitimation and allows them to
do so free from domestic constraints. The converse of these two propositions—
that a more open and pluralistic society would have less need to expand and less
ability to do so—is the key to Pipe's recommendation that the West encourage
reform in the Soviet system as a way of altering Soviet international behavior.

Soviet fear of threats from the West—a favorite explanation of more dovish
Western analysts— is conspicuously missing from the sources of Soviet aggressiveness noted by Luttwak, Pipes, and Brzezinski. At an abstract level, all three
authors recognize this phenomenon. All would agree, I think, with Hudson
Institute analyst Max Singer, whom Brzezinski quotes as calling the Soviets
"insatiably defensive," that is, so wedded to the notion that the best defense is a
good offense that, as Brzezinski puts it, "the defensive and offensive elements of
the strategy are thus inseparable" (p. 65). But when it comes to concrete East-
West interactions, Luttwak, Pipes, and Brzezinski have trouble pinpointing any
US action that might have given Moscow legitimate cause for alarm. Pipes goes
farthest, insisting not only that "the contingency plans of NATO have always
been defensive," but also that "whatever they say in public . . . the Soviets are
well aware of these facts" (p. 225). Luttwak contends not just that the Soviets
are now clearly and unambiguously the world's number one military power, but
that they see themselves as superior to the Americans (p. 55). Brzezinski's
depiction of the nuclear balance as "a situation of ambiguous strategic equivalence" is more balanced and judicious. But only Bialer can really imagine how
Moscow can still consider itself the world's second military power, partly
because in many ways it still is "number two." It also falls to Bialer to issue the
warning that "it is wrong to . . . demonize the Soviet leaders, denying any
validity to their fear of war, their legitimate security concerns, and their recogni-

tion of the imperative need to create some sort of *modus vivendi* with the other nuclear powers'' (p. 352–53).

If the above are among the motives for Soviet external expansion, what are Moscow's long-term goals and shorter-term strategy and tactics? Regarding aims, Pipes writes: "As concerns the objective, no one familiar with Communist theory can entertain much doubt. It is the elimination, worldwide, of private ownership of the means of production and the 'bourgeois' order which rests upon it, and its replacement with what Lenin called a worldwide republic of soviets" (p. 49). Pipes accuses those who dismiss these terms as mere rhetoric of misconceiving the kind of world domination the Soviets seek. Not physical control of the world, but global hegemony is Moscow's goal, he insists, adding that the goal is all too likely to be achieved. "In a world from which the United States has been eliminated as a power of the first rank, the Soviet Union would enjoy such overwhelming economic and military preponderance that opposition to its wishes on the part of any other 'socialist republic'—which is all that would remain—would be inconceivable" (p. 50).

But is not such a Soviet-dominated globe itself inconceivable? How could a country with so many domestic problems lord it over the whole world? Brzezinski's geopolitical analysis warns how the worst could happen. According to him, the United States and the Soviet Union are engaged in a duel over Eurasia, even though the United States does not always seem to be aware of this. For its part, Moscow is intent on evicting Washington from its positions on the eastern, western and southern fringes of that immense territory. In Brzezinski's geostrategic universe, if the Soviet Union captured "the peripheries of this landmass . . . it would not only win control of the vast human, economic, and military resources, but also gain access to the geostrategic approaches to the Western Hemisphere—the Atlantic and Pacific oceans." From this it follows that "the United States must view its transoceanic positions as the forward lines of defense that spare it from having to mount a defense of North America" (p. 23). By the end of the century, if things go badly in Central America, "it is quite possible," according to Brzezinski, "that a fourth central strategic front may be opening up on the Rio Grande" (p. 98). To avoid being kept on the "geopolitical defensive," Washington must succeed in projects such as "protectively sealing off the Persian Gulf and the Middle East from a contiguous Soviet military-political presence" (p. 53).

Brzezinski's book is replete with terms like "earth control," "political and military leakout," and "linchpin states," and with maps illustrating such concepts. But even such a formidable theoretical apparatus may leave the reader unconvinced. For example, what exactly would it mean for the USSR to achieve "domination" over fiercely anti-Soviet Iran? How likely is such an eventuality, even if the United States does not adopt the countervailing strategy that Brzezinski recommends?

Bialer is more skeptical about Soviet plans for world domination. He writes that although the Soviet elites expect an ultimate victory of communism, "the goal of worldwide communization has not been the operating principle of Soviet foreign policy'' even in Stalin's time, and that Soviet ''formulation of short-and middle-range foreign policy is not so different form that of any nation-state'' (p. 348), including, presumably, the United States itself.

Turning from goals to strategy and tactics, Luttwak, Brzezinski, and Pipes agree that Moscow pursues a ''grand strategy'' combining military intimidation, the sowing of political divisions in the West, and vigorous attempts to subvert and destabilize the Third World. Bialer sees the Soviets more as opportunities than grand strategists, but he too emphasizes the crucial importance to them in their long-sought, hard-earned, military power. All four authors contend convincingly that although the United States was first with the atomic bomb, and has led the way in many strategic technologies, nuclear weapons have taken on a special value for the Soviet Union. Bialer puts it as follows: ''Nuclear weaponry acts as a great equalizer of the actual, conventional military potential of the Western and Soviet alliances and therefore as a guarantor of the security of the Soviet Union'' (p. 272). Pipes points out how the old Soviet technique of mixing war scares with peace campaigns has been raised to new heights in the nuclear era, and how, free from democratic political constraints, Moscow is able to play on the nuclear nerves of the Western democracies.

In contrast to its growing military power, the economic and ideological appeal of the USSR has diminished in recent years. Whereas in the 1950's, Nikita Khrushchev counted on the example of Soviet-style socialism to win converts around the world, his successors have turned to more Machiavellian means. According to Brzezinski, who was President Jimmy Carter's National Security Adviser, and to Pipes, who served as Soviet specialist on President Ronald Reagan's National Security Council Staff, the Soviets have encouraged terrorism as a means of destabilizing both Western Europe and the Third World. The evidence cited, including Soviet training camps for terrorists, is disquieting. But one can ask whether it is adequate to justify Brzezinski's conclusion—after listing groups as diverse as the Italian Red Brigades, the West German Red Army Faction, the Basque separatists, the Irish Republican Army Provisionals, and others—that ''the Soviet objective in all this is the attrition of the global order. It is essentially a long-term diversionary strategy designed to promote erosion on the flanks, while Soviet military-political pressure is applied on the central front'' (p. 140).

The other side of the Soviet paradox is the economic, social, and political deterioration that deepened in the later Brezhnev years and now has become the target of Mikhail Gorbachëv's reform efforts. The broad outlines of the problem are widely known in the West; equally widespread is the Western view that its root cause is the Soviet system itself. There is, therefore, no disagreement among the four authors on what has gone wrong, and why, in the USSR. Instead, they in effect divide the labor of summarizing the symptoms and, more important, of estimating the foreign policy implications. Luttwak and Brzezinski stress socioeconomic stagnation. Pipes focuses on political disarray as well, particularly on the widespread corruption that has been draining the system of morale as well as money. Bialer's approach is more historical and wide-ranging. He traces both the deepening decline and the efforts and non-efforts to do something about it. Particularly incisive is his chapter on the politics of reform—including the powerful resistance to change observable at middle and lower levels of the Soviet party/state machine.

The rising costs of the Soviet empire is yet another point on which the four authors are in general agreement. Pipes cites Rand Corporation estimates that the annual cost to the Soviet Union of controlling its "colonies and dependencies" has grown from about US$18 billion in 1971 to $41 billion in 1980 (p. 187). Bialer spotlights seemingly unresolvable Soviet problems in Eastern Europe, especially in post-Solidarity Poland. For Luttwak, the clash between Russian and non-Russian nationalism within the USSR itself is the most threatening development facing the Soviet leaders. Brzezinski, who is refreshingly candid in viewing the United States, too, as an imperial power, offers some typically brilliant insights on the different characteristics of the two imperial domains.

Where the authors part company again is in gauging the linkage between Soviet internal decline and external expansion. On this issue, Luttwak's assessment is the most somber: rather than constraining Soviet expansion, Moscow's domestic problems may encourage it. In Luttwak's scenario, which he presents as a theoretical possibility rather than a geopolitical likelihood, Soviet pessimism about long-term domestic improvement combines with a temporary military superiority to tempt Moscow to use force. "It is not a question," Luttwak writes, "of using uncommitted divisions (and all that goes with them) to expand the empire further, but rather of employing a transient military advantage before it is too late, to gain a permanent enhancement in the security of the empire" (p. 82).

Most analysts of the Soviet Union, including the other authors under review, think it unlikely that the Russians would risk war when other less dangerous tactics promise favorable results. Furthermore, Luttwak's search for a spot in the world where the benefits of aggression would exceed its costs and dangers strains credibility. It leads him in the end to western China, to the notion of a limited Soviet attack designed to lop off sparsely populated sections of the Chinese provinces of Xinjiang and Qinghai. Nonetheless, if one sets aside Luttwak's specific scenario and focuses instead on his Schumpeterian conception of how empires grow, his conclusions are cause for concern. For the point is not, he insists, whether a particular act of aggression really makes sense, that is, whether it addresses some pressing external or internal need. The point, as Joseph Schumpeter pointed out in his classic study of imperialism,[3] is that once a military machine whose job it is to make war is established, it is only a matter of time until a war gets made. As Luttwak puts it: "But in truth all motives and all justifications are of small import: once the internal condition of society is in a state of disequilibrium, once its leaders acquire the physical capacity for conquest, once military institutions are created which have no sufficient role in self-defense strictly defined, all manner of reasons and all sorts of rationalizations will emerge to make expansion seem attractive and to make its costs and risks seem worthwhile'' (p. 74). Add to that, which Luttwak does not, that similar sorts of pressures are at work in the West and in volatile areas in the Third World, and there is reason for concern that goes far beyond the specter of a new "Turkestan People's Repulic" grafted by force onto the USSR.

Pipes and Brzezinski are less concerned than Luttwak about the danger of Soviet military aggression. Brzezinski, in particular, seems wedded to the assumption that nuclear weapons have prevented a Soviet-American war since 1945 and that they can deter war between the two superpowers into the indefinite future. For Pipes and Brzezinski, the main significance of Soviet internal decline is that it somewhat reduces the Soviet threat, at least for the time being, and, more important, that it offers the United States new leverage over the Soviet Union. Pipes and Brzezinski both call on the United States to match the Kremlin militarily, to resist it politically, and to take advantage of Moscow's troubles to influence it internally.

Brzezinski, in keeping with is geostrategic orientation, emphasizes the military and political aspects of Soviet-American relations. Militarily, he recommends a mix of offensive and defensive forces that would provide "greater flexibility in war-fighting options." Specifically, he would build counterforce weapons of the sort that could be used in a first strike, but deploy them "in numbers deliberately contrived not to pose a threat of a disarming first strike to Soviet strategic forces." He would also move toward deployment of a "limited strategic defense," not in order to achieve President Reagan's dream of a strategic shield for the nation, but rather to "inject a degree of randomness into any Soviet planning of a first-strike nuclear attack" (p. 261). Undergirding these recommendations is an odd sort of confidence in the Soviet Union. As little as Brzezinski trusts the Russians, he trusts them not to adopt a "worst case" view of the American deployments he recommends; he trusts them not to conclude, in other words, that such US deployments are but steps toward an American capacity if not to attack the Soviet Union without risking retaliation, then at least to blackmail it as Washington tried to do in an earlier era of US strategic superiority. The fact that the United States itself has reached just such worst-case conclusions about the Soviet Union on the basis of equally ambiguous Soviet deployments does not give one confidence that this aspect of Brzezinski's "game plan" will work out as intended.

Brzezinski's strategic recommendations also rest on a conception of nuclear war that merits more reflection than is offered in his book. Brzezinski claims partial credit for injecting the notion into Carter Administration thinking that "a nuclear war might not be simply a short, spasmodic apocalypse that could best be deterred by a posture relying on the doctrine of MAD [mutual assured destruction], but that it might entail engagements at varying levels of intensity and over an extended period of time. It followed that to wage such a conflict effectively and, more important, to deter it, the United States needed a mix of offensive and *defensive* capabilities" (p. 161, emphasis in original). What is missing from this passage is an acknowledgment that the notion of waging a nuclear war "effectively" has been powerfully challenged in recent years both as a possibility in itself, and as an approach to deterrence. One hardly expects Brzezinski to embrace Jonathan Schell's apocalyptic vision of the fate of the earth, or even the US Conference of Catholic Bishops' injunction against any except the most narrow conception of deterrence.[4] But Brzezinski's failure even to note such views bespeaks a too easy confidence that ever-new generations of nuclear weapons can be deployed without increasing the risk of a nuclear war.

Politically, Brzezinski's most controversial proposal (a version of which Pipes also endorses) is that Washington encourage West European self-reliance by gradually redeploying troops from Europe "to meet other geopolitical priorities and to prompt European leaders to address the issue of their own defense" (p. 263). The danger in this is that European leaders will address no such thing, but will instead scale back, or even abandon, their efforts to stand up to the Soviets. Why European governments should do more, not less, to defend themselves if the Americans begin to pull out is no clearer than why Europeans should respond to a no-first-use of nuclear weapons declaration by the United States by building up European conventional weapons. Yet, Brzezinski, who points convincingly to that flow in no-first-use, sees no such inconsistency in "gradual redeployment." Nor does he make clear how the United States could effectively "reinforce the anti-Soviet resilience" of a militantly anti-American Iran, or how a "renewed push to advance the Arab-Israeli peace process" can be expected to be any more successful than previous efforts to foster that obviously desirable but infernally elusive goal (pp. 222, 227).

In addition to military might, European self-reliance, and containment of Soviet power to the south of Soviet borders, Brzezinski's game plan also includes Chinese-Japanese-American solidarity. Moreover, Brzezinski calls for an effort "to transform the essence of Eastern Europe's relationship with Moscow without necessarily disrupting its formal framework" (p. 232), and for mobilizing within the Soviet Union "the forces for genuine political participation, for greater national codetermination, for the dispersal of central power, and for the termination of heavy-handed central domination that breeds the expansionist impulse" (pp. 236–37). Just how the last feat is to be accomplished is not clear. Brzezinski's main concrete suggestion—that the United States "take the initiative by an intensified program of multilanguage radio broadcasts, the inflow of audiovisual cassettes, and an effort to provide technical support for independent domestic political literature" (p. 237)—seems puny when compared to the purpose it is supposed to promote.

In *Survival Is Not Enough*, the means Pipes recommends for "prevailing" (a term the author implies but does not, himself, use) seem more proportionate to the end, but no more likely to achieve it. Pipes begins from the premise (shared by all the other authors) that the Soviet system badly needs greater legality, wider scope for private enterprise, and administrative decentralization. He also assumes that such reforms will restrain Soviet expansion by allowing citizens preoccupied with domestic concerns to increase their influence over foreign policy. (Brzezinski, by the way, fears that economic reforms, without reforms in other areas, might "enhance the Soviet capacity to compete with the United States.") Pipes admits that, left to its own devices and short of the most painful kind of crisis, the Soviet Communist Party establishment will resist radical changes. Hence the task of the West is to aggravate the Soviet situation by denying Moscow badly needed goods and credits. The purpose of such economic restrictions, Pipes emphasizes, should not be to bring down the Soviet system but rather to stop propping it up, to force it to face a day of reckoning that is primarily of its own making. But as in the case of Brzezinski's strategic nuclear prescriptions, this distinction may be lost on the suspicious Soviets. Moreover, apart from Soviet perceptions of American intentions, the further issue is whether the medicine is likely to produce the desired cure.

The central thesis of Pipes's book is that "the Soviet regime will become less aggressive only as a result of failures and worries about its ability to govern effectively and not from a sense of enhanced security and confidence" (p. 140). This premise is anathema to liberal observers of the Soviet Union who believe the exact opposite. But the more sobering possibility is that neither Pipes nor his liberal critics are right, that neither enhanced security and confidence nor more failures and worries (especially of the sort the United States is in a position to create) are likely to alter the general direction of Soviet foreign policy. It is precisely this important truth that Bialer's book emphasizes and reinforces. His central theme is that the USSR faces not a "crisis of survival" but only a "crisis of effectiveness." Whether we like it or not, the Soviet system has a reservoir of what the Kremlin calls "reserves," that is, of strength and support that equip it to ride out the efforts at economic embargo that the West (invariably divided on the issue of economic sanctions) is likely to be able to mount. Not the least of these reserves is an authoritarian political culture, of which Pipes himself makes a great deal in another context,[5] which disposes so many Soviet citizens to deem their regime legitimate even though it denies them genuine political participation.

Bialer's proposals for American foreign policy are more modest and conventional than those of the other authors reviewed here. Unlike Pipes and Brzezinski, who regard arms control as a weak reed at best, Bialer has retained faith in such negotiations. His is not the naive hope that arms control agreements can transform US-Soviet relations and remove the threat of war from the world. Bialer's point is merely that such negotiations, combined with continued efforts to contain Soviet power and even with occasional confrontations when they are warranted, constitute the best way to hold the world together during the long, dangerous years that lie ahead.

No one who reads the first-hand accounts of negotiations with the Soviets in *A Game for High Stakes* can be under any illusion that such talks will be easily or quickly successful. Rather, negotiations will be plagued in the future, as they have been in the past, by differences in approach and technique, by persistent misperceptions rooted in the two sides' divergent political cultures, and by deep-seated political and ideological antagonisms. Nonetheless, ambitious grand strategies designed to "prevail" over the USSR may end up delivering less than may more modest attempts to coexist with the Soviets. This ironic prospect should perhaps be called "the Soviet-American paradox."

NOTES

1. See Aleksandr Solzhenitsyn, *The Mortal Danger: How Misconceptions about Russia Imperil America* (New York: Harper and Row, 1980).

2. Michael Voslensky, *Nomenklatura: The Soviet Ruling Class* (New York: Doubleday, 1984).

3. See Joseph A. Schumpeter, *Imperialism and Social Classes: Two Essays* (New York: Meridian Books. 1955), pp. 64–65.

4. See Jonathan Schell, *The Fate of the Earth* (New York: Knopf, 1982).

5. Richard Pipes, *Russia under the Old Regime* (New York: Scribner, 1975).

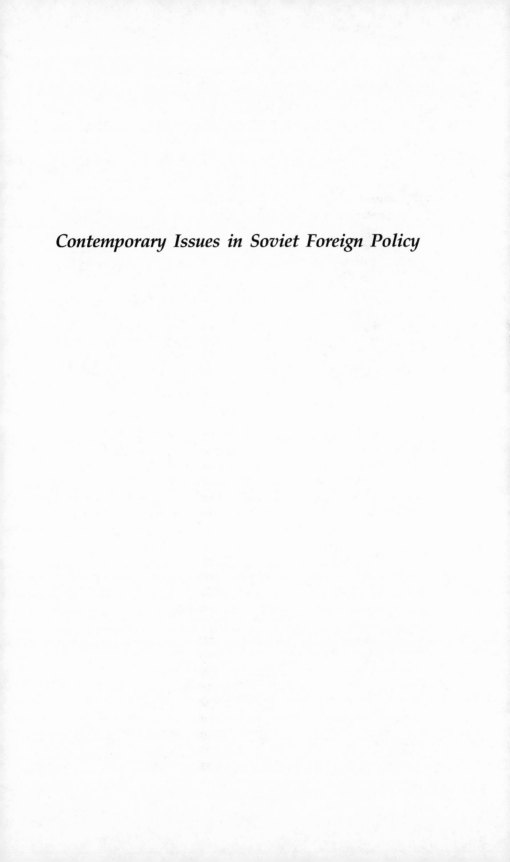

Contemporary Issues in Soviet Foreign Policy

Introduction

Erik P. Hoffmann

The purpose of this second half of the anthology is to deepen Western understanding of the sources, substance, and significance of Soviet foreign policy since the mid-1980s. This half is designed primarily for students of Soviet politics, comparative foreign policies, and international relations. Also, it is structured to help government, business, legal, and media professionals and other citizens assess the USSR's contemporary international aims, activities, and accomplishments. The present work complements our anthologies *Contemporary Issues in Soviet Domestic Politics* and *Classic Issues in Soviet Domestic Politics* (both Hawthorne, NY: Aldine de Gruyter, 1992). Together, these volumes provide a comprehensive survey of notable Western writings about Soviet external and internal behavior and their interrelationships. They are successors to our previous lengthy anthologies (also published by Aldine de Gruyter): *The Conduct of Soviet Foreign Policy*, 2nd ed. (1980), *Soviet Foreign Policy in a Changing World* (1986), and *The Soviet Polity in the Modern Era* (1984).

Contributions to this collection come from academic specialists on Soviet foreign policy, present and past government officials, and full-time researchers in organizations that counsel government leaders. These contributions address many key topics and are among the most insightful and knowledgeable in the field. Also, they express the competing viewpoints of Americans, West Europeans, and Japanese inside and outside their governments. By juxtaposing different viewpoints we hope to raise the level of international and intranational debate and to stimulate informed and independent-minded analysis of Soviet foreign policy and its implications for the West. In a word, the present anthology is of policy and practical relevance as well as of academic and general interest. It is written by and for Western policymakers and their advisors as well as the university community and the international professions.

We intend to supplement, not supplant, the preeminent histories of Soviet international behavior: Adam B. Ulam's *Expansion and Coexistence: The Histo-*

ry of Soviet Foreign Policy, 1917–73, 2nd ed. (New York: Praeger, 1974), and *Dangerous Relations: The Soviet Union in World Politics, 1970–1982* (New York: Oxford University Press, 1983). Likewise, our volume complements succinct texts such as Jonathan R. Adelman and Deborah Anne Palmieri, *The Dynamics of Soviet Foreign Policy* (New York: Harper & Row, 1989); Joseph L. Nogee and Robert H. Donaldson, *Soviet Foreign Policy since World War II*, 3rd ed. (Elmsford, NY: Pergamon, 1988); Alvin Z. Rubinstein, *Soviet Foreign Policy since World War II: Imperial and Global*, 3rd ed. (Glenview, IL: Scott, Foresman, 1989); and Richard F. Staar, *Foreign Policies of the Soviet Union* (Stanford, CA: Hoover Institution Press, 1991). In addition, our anthology complements collections of carefully selected and translated Soviet writings such as Fred Schulze, ed., *Soviet Foreign Policy Today: Reports and Commentaries from the Soviet Press*, 4th ed. (Columbus, OH: Current Digest of the Soviet Press, 1990).

This half of the book is divided into three broad parts: perspectives and policymaking, policy and performance, and retrospect and prospect. Part V begins with Robert Legvold's essay, which contends that Mikhail Gorbachev revolutionized Soviet thinking about international politics and Soviet international behavior. Legvold affirms that Gorbachev dramatically changed both the strategy and tactics of Soviet foreign policy. This is precisely the argument questioned by John W. Coffey, who insists that Gorbachev's innovations in declaratory policy far outstripped his innovations in actual policy. He concludes that the "new thinking" functions primarily as post facto justification rather than as a guide to action and consists primarily of new tactics to pursue traditional strategies. Allen Lynch, like Legvold, maintains that many of Gorbachev's ideas were in currency but of little policy relevance during the Nikita Khrushchev and Leonid Brezhnev periods. Lynch details the revolutionary and evolutionary changes in the most fundamental elements of official Soviet thinking—for example, the concepts of "peaceful coexistence," "détente," and "security." Stephen Sestanovich focuses on novel Soviet interpretations of the USSR's "national interest." He argues that the Gorbachev leadership "de-ideologized" the concept by stressing its elastic and subjective nature and by inviting debate about more feasible and prudent aims in the increasingly complex and competitive international arena.

Alex Pravda investigates the linkages between domestic and foreign policy and among their political, military, and economic components. He documents that there was a much greater congruence between Soviet internal and external priorities and much more open debate about these priorities under Gorbachev than under Brezhnev. Mark Kramer's is the first of three chapters focusing on the institutions that formulate and implement Soviet foreign policy. He traces the changing responsibilities of the Communist Party's International Department and of the USSR Government's Ministry of Foreign Affairs, especially in the broadly defined field of national security. Amy W. Knight elucidates the extensive covert activities of the KGB (Committee on State Security) in the international arena.

She makes us ponder the issue of continuity and change, because Gorbachev was the protege of the long-time KGB chief Yuri Andropov and because the KGB continues to work closely with the party's International Department. Condoleezza Rice evaluates the relative influence of political and military institutions in the formulation of foreign and defense policy. She underscores the growing involvement of civilian researchers in debates about defense issues and the growing involvement of military officers in debates about foreign affairs.

Part VI begins with William E. Odom's comprehensive survey of the Soviet military's composition, capabilities, and challenges in the rapidly changing domestic and international environments of the early 1990s. Discussing the sovereignty claims of the USSR's republics, he raises the most basic questions about civil-military relations and about the aims, content, and impact of defense and foreign policies. Susan L. Clark elaborates on the innovative aspects of Soviet military thinking and on the practical implications of alternative schools of thought. She pays close attention to the ideas of professional military officials as well as civilian analysts in international affairs institutes. Akio Kawato highlights the difficulties of marketizing the Soviet economy and integrating it into the world economy. He addresses a wide variety of short- and long-term problems and opportunities such as joint ventures, currency convertibility, free-trade zones, and participation in international economic organizations.

Stephen Sestanovich surveys Soviet policies in all parts of the world, with emphasis on the interaction between East-West relations and Soviet activities in the Middle East, Asia, Africa, and Latin America. He argues that the USSR's declining capabilities to influence events in Third World countries has stemmed largely from internal decay and that external policy has therefore become increasingly defensive. Charles H. Fairbanks, Jr., agrees that the Soviet Union is facing daunting domestic challenges, but he contends that Gorbachev's abrupt and unintended abandonment of the East European empire has been accompanied by a sustained and deliberate commitment to most Third World client states. Fairbanks maintains that the Gorbachev leadership is finding diverse ways to reduce the risks and costs of influencing many of the foreign policies, if not the social systems, of the Third World's key socialist and nonsocialist countries. Pierre Hassner assesses Gorbachev's differentiated policies toward the United States and the major democracies of Western Europe as well as their differentiated responses to the Soviet Union. Hassner stresses Gorbachev's pursuit of political and economic advantages rather than military parity as well as the shifting mix of conflict and cooperation in the East-West rivalry.

Arnold L. Horelick focuses on Soviet-American relations in the late 1980s. He explores diplomatic, military, and commercial aims and accomplishments, especially the increasing cooperation that led to the end of the Cold War and also the mounting domestic problems that reduced the influence of both superpowers vis-à-vis their chief allies and other countries. F. Stephen Larrabee examines Gorbachev's security policies toward Western and Eastern Europe as well as the political and economic relations among Western and Eastern European countries

before and after the disintegration of the Soviet bloc in 1989. Paying special
attention to the reunification of Germany, Larrabee evaluates Soviet initiatives
and responses during Western Europe's drive for economic integration in 1992
and during Eastern Europe's struggle to establish legitimate and effective post-
Communist governments. Donald S. Zagoria details our attention to the increasing Soviet initiatives in East Asia, reminding us that the Soviet Union is both a
European and an Asian power and that several Pacific rim countries as well as
Australia and New Zealand are prosperous contributors to the world economy.
He attributes special importance to Soviet relations with China, Japan, and South
Korea because of their geostrategic and economic significance as well as their
complex and shifting relationships with one another and with the United States.

Alvin Z. Rubinstein and David E. Albright offer comprehensive and complementary analyses of Soviet policies toward the Third World. Both note Gorbachev's predisposition and ability to establish good relations with existing
governments of all political persuasions. But Albright stresses the diversity of
Soviet views about the Third World and the differentiation of Soviet policies,
which include significant reduction of commitment and diminishing expectations. Rubinstein concentrates on the USSR's general strategy toward major
Third World regions and on the policy implications for the West. Albright's
interpretation is more akin to Sestanovich's, Rubinstein's to Fairbank's. Thomas
G. Weiss and Meryl A. Kessler examine the USSR's increasingly constructive
involvement in the work of the United Nations, especially peacekeeping efforts
in regional trouble spots. They contend that the Gorbachev administration actively pursued innovative policies in the Third World but often chose to do so
through the United Nations for both idealistic and pragmatic reasons.

Part VII includes historically grounded essays on the basic characteristics of
Soviet foreign policy. Detailed discussions of continuity and change yield dramatically different conclusions. Jack Snyder maintains that Soviet expansionism
declined precipitously under Gorbachev. Colin S. Gray affirms that the Soviet
Union still poses a security threat to the West and Third World. Snyder sees
policy emerging from the competition among conservative, centrist, and reformist bureaucratic elites. Gray sees policy emerging from a much more cohesive top
leadership. Stanley Kober argues that an idealist rather than a realist approach
best explains the Gorbachev administration's international behavior. Kober emphasizes the importance of Soviet "new thinking" and the linkages between
internal and external politics. Also, he anticipates that Soviet domestic and
foreign policy will continue to contribute to and benefit from the democratization
of Europe and the entire world.

Similar hopes are expressed by James A. Baker III, who on behalf of the U. S.
Government identifies the spheres in which Soviet-American cooperation is most
needed. Crucial spheres are arms reduction and economic partnership as well as
the creation of an integrated and free Europe, the resolution of regional conflicts
in the Third World, and the guarantee of human rights in all countries. Robert
Legvold presents an important case study: Soviet behavior in the Persian Gulf

crisis of 1990–91. He emphasizes that the prior "revolutionary" thinking and behavior of the Gorbachev administration, especially its retrenchment in the Third World and its affirmation of support for the United Nations, paved the way for the unprecedented Soviet-American cooperation after Iraq's occupation of Kuwait. To conclude, Robbin F. Laird assesses the aims and accomplishments of Gorbachev and his predecessors and reflects on the historical, cultural, and geostrategic factors that have shaped and will shape Soviet foreign policy. Focusing on East-West relations, he underscores the transformations taking place in the structure and functioning of the Soviet and international political systems and their interrelationships.

Part V of our anthology presents different Western views on the world outlooks and motivations of present-day Soviet leaders, the formulation and implementation of Soviet foreign policy, and the relationships between the USSR's domestic and international priorities. Westerners will continue to argue about these key substantive issues because the presuppositions of Sovietology are still debatable and the problems of studying Soviet politics are still formidable. Most analysts agree that fresh theories and methodologies are needed to elucidate current developments in the USSR, but few analysts concur about the merits of old and new analytical approaches and research techniques.

How does one ascertain whether the Gorbachev leadership's evolving perspectives on the United States, Western Europe, and Japan comprise a new international strategy? We use the term *perspective* in the broadest sense to include images as well as perceptions, expectations, motivations, goals, and priorities. Images are created verbally and in writing, but perceptions, expectations, motivations, goals, and priorities must be inferred from words and deeds. From the content of Soviet public and private declarations one must infer the propaganda strategy and tactics, and from the propaganda strategy and tactics one must infer the operational strategy and tactics. Also, one must infer the linkages between the leaders' unverifiable motives and beliefs and the country's verifiable political, economic, military, and geographical capabilities and performance. Only then can one distinguish between Soviet declaratory and actual policies and begin to explain the purposes and effects of these policies and their changing relationships. Finally, one can assess the congruence of Soviet public pronouncements and international behavior with particular theories—for example, the theories that Gorbachev's Politburo and Presidency have pursued a recklessly expansionist, opportunistically assertive, or prudently defensive strategy in all or most geographical and issue areas and historical periods.

Even in highly stable political systems it is difficult to confirm generalizations about propaganda strategy and tactics (declaratory policy) and operational strategy and tactics (actual policy). It was especially challenging to identify and order these variables in the first years of the Gorbachev administration, because leading foreign-policy personnel were being rapidly replaced and vital institutions and institutional relationships were being substantially altered. Also, Gorbachev and other top officials affirmed that they were espousing "new political thinking," "breaking away from stereotypes and prejudices," and "gradually learning a lot" and that "international relations are too complex [and] have too many layers and too many facets for us to be able to settle in advance on any one method of doing business."[1]

Gorbachev, in a 1986 meeting with a group of Soviet writers, is reported to have said: "Our enemy has figured us out. They are not frightened of our nuclear might. They are not going to start a war. They are worried about one thing: if democracy develops under us, then we will win. Therefore, they have started a campaign against our leadership, using all available means, right up to terror. They write about the apparatus that did in Khrushchev and that will now do in the new leadership."[2] Also, a Soviet deputy foreign minister responded to an Austrian journalist's question as follows: "Yes, we have discovered Western Europe as an independent power—and we are facing it more actively, dynamically, and openly. More contacts, more talks, more ideas. But very often we encounter a Western Europe that says: 'Better talk with America.' Obviously you are still too much ashamed of your own interests.[3] And the head of the Soviet delegation to the Conference on Security and Cooperation in Europe declared: "we do not want to drive a wedge between the allies, [because] it is much easier to deal with a sensible, united will of the West instead of different, even opposite opinions."[4]

Such pronouncements can reveal information about the USSR's actual policies, policymaking procedures, and policy alternatives under consideration. But what kind of information? One's ability to answer this question in particular cases is increased by a knowledge of empirically verifiable patterns of Soviet declaratory and actual policies and their interrelationships. Western analysts had good reason to be cautious about Gorbachev's initial pronouncements, because his intentions were problematical and so were his capabilities to induce other Soviet leaders and bureaucrats to accept and implement his policy preferences. However, there emerged an increasing congruence between declaratory and actual policy under the Gorbachev leadership. It revealed through public debate and private communications, many of the priorities, calculations, and data behind Soviet foreign policy. Gorbachev and his international affairs spokespersons were remarkably forthcoming about domestic and international linkages, the strategic and tactical presuppositions of policies, and even their emotional reactions to the consequences of previous and current initiatives.

Some Soviet leaders and analysts, including Gorbachev, made a concerted effort to understand Western perspectives on international politics. They considered misperceptions of one's adversaries to be a mutual problem and implied that accurate perceptions were necessary but not sufficient to produce greater trust or cooperation. Also, Soviet and Western political, military, economic, and scientific leaders exchanged privileged information through unprecedented on-site visits to one another's facilities. To be sure, the worldviews of Gorbachev and other Soviet leaders contained various logical inconsistencies, factual distortions, and lacunae. But reasoned argumentation and documented assertions became commonplace in negotiations between socialist and capitalist leaders, who perceived each other as "enemies." And personal ties grounded on respect, trust, and friendship developed between some ranking Soviet and Western officials. Briefly stated, Soviet foreign affairs professionals cautiously but unmistakably applied the policy of *glasnost* (openness or candor), which was initially limited to domestic politics, to more and more levels of international relations.

Did Gorbachev initiate a shift in the USSR's international strategy and actual behavior or merely in its tactics and propagandistic declarations? Did his efforts to restructure the Soviet polity, economy, and society motivate arms control initiatives, foreign trade reform and closer political ties with noncommunist governments? Did Soviet foreign policies and foreign policymaking institutions adapt to Western diplomacy and to scientific-technological, socioeconomic, environmental-ecological, medical-nutritional, and ideological-cultural developments abroad?

The Soviet concept of *perestroika* (restructuring or reformation) and the Western concept of modernization have much in common. If the Soviet Union is to modernize, it will have to do so in at least seven key ways:

1. participate broadly and deeply in worldwide scientific and technological progress;
2. tailor Soviet economic reform to practices and developments in the international economy;
3. heighten industrial and agricultural productivity as well as growth;
4. heed the recommendations of scientists, technicians, and ordinary citizens in policymaking as well as policy implementation;
5. mediate increasingly diverse and conflicting interests;
6. meet consumer needs and wants more expeditiously;
7. and facilitate the freer flow of all kinds of information.

Although Soviet reformers had voiced all of these ideas from inside and outside the Khrushchev and Brezhnev administrations, Gorbachev persuaded the Communist Party's Politburo and Central Committee to translate them into official ideology. Especially important were the following Gorbachevian presuppositions: the Soviet Union must contribute to and benefit from the global "scientific-technological revolution," especially the "information explosion" since the late 1970s; systemic political, economic, technological, environmental, and cultural problems stem from the party-state's unwillingness and inability to resist debilitating forces at home and mounting pressures from abroad; and internal dilemmas and external disadvantages have reached "crisis" proportions and will soon bring "tragic consequences" if the Soviet people do not de-Stalinize their political values and institutions and create a democratic and human *socialist* society.

Gorbachev, with seminal contributions from Aleksandr Yakovlev, produced a distinctive ideology whose key tenet was that the Soviet Union could become a freer and more prosperous society only if certain preconditions were expeditiously met. *Glasnost* was a precondition for democratization; democratization for *perestroika; perestroika* for radical economic reform and social justice; and radical economic reform and social justice for an exemplary material and spiritual culture. And all of this domestic progress could be achieved only in a more harmonious and cooperative international environment, which the Soviet Union could help to create by espousing "panhuman" (global) rather than "class" (Marxist-Leninist-Stalinist) values and by pursuing "mutual" rather than "unilateral" interests.

Here is a list of the core concepts underlying reformist perspectives in the Gorbachev administration. There are at least thirteen each from the increasingly interconnected and indistinguishable domestic "ideology of renewal" and international "new political thinking."

The *domestic politics* concepts are *glasnost, perestroika,* democratization, scientific-technological revolution, radical economic reform, social justice, law-governed state, civil society, human rights, socialist pluralism, power to the soviets, federalism, and separation of powers. (Notable deletions from such a list for the Khrushchev and Brezhnev periods are communism, developed socialism, the leading role of the party, the scientific management of society, the merging of nationality groups, the state of the whole people, and the new Soviet man.)

The *international politics* concepts are the unthinkability of nuclear war, a correlation of forces unfavorable to socialism, peaceful coexistence without class struggle, multipolarity, interdependence, mutual security (defined in political, economic, and military terms), military sufficiency (not parity), military détente (including unilateral arms reduction), conversion from military to civilian economies, decentralized foreign economic decision-making, non-Soviet ownership of joint ventures, different roads to and away from socialism, and panhuman values and interests. (Notable deletions from such a list for the Khrushchev and Brezhnev periods are world revolution, the intensifying crisis of capitalism, peaceful coexistence with class struggle, strategic and conventional arms race, wars of national liberation, proletarian internationalism, and military support for endangered and disintegrating Communist regimes.)

But Soviet politicians and commentators disputed the content of these concepts, to say nothing of their practical ramifications. Candid debates about internal and external issues (e.g., economic reform, defense spending, and environmental protection) and mounting difficulties (e.g., ethnic rivalries, lack of commercial competitiveness, and the disintegration of the Soviet bloc) were frequently published in the Soviet press and were increasingly aired on television and radio. One could easily distinguish among "reformist," "centrist," and "conservative" orientations. Also, "secessionist" and "confederative" sentiments became quite vocal as more and more republics proclaimed their intention to break away from the USSR and conducted their own foreign policies. Hence, public and private communications yielded abundant information about the diverse perspectives of leading Communist party and nonparty officials and their military and civilian advisors.

Linking particular Soviet views to political organizations and coalitions and to the struggle over power and policy continued to be problematical. But competing parties, party factions, governmental bodies, and informal groups participated much more openly in policy formulation and implementation. For example, Gorbachev had separate staffs of advisors for his dual positions as president and general secretary. Former foreign minister Eduard Shevardnadze promised not to commit Soviet armed forces to the Persian Gulf without authorization from the Supreme Soviet. Several republics appointed their own ministers of foreign affairs and foreign economic relations. And grass-roots environmental groups blocked prospective joint ventures and forced the shut-down of over 1000 factories. In short, Gorbachev's "new thinking" launched dramatic changes in political and administrative relationships and stimulated unprecedented regional and local involvement in international relations.

Gorbachev greatly expanded diplomatic, economic, cultural, and scientific-technological ties with Western, Communist, post-Communist, and Third World countries. For example, he participated actively in arms control negotiations with the United States. Also, Soviet and American military leaders candidly divulged some of their intentions and strategy, and their aides made on-site inspections of each other's weapons production and weapons destruction facilities. Soviet and American participants in the Cuban missile crisis of 1962 shared information and insights more than a quarter-century later. Soviet and American diplomats cooperated in major Third World trouble spots (e.g., Nicaragua and the Persian Gulf). Soviet and West and East German leaders negotiated the reunification of Germany. And Soviet factory executives established more and more direct links with American, West European, and Japanese businessmen, including over 200 operational joint ventures in the USSR by early 1991. Hence, Western observers—because of much more extensive contact with Soviet officials and much more open disagreements among Soviet foreign policy professionals— have gained additional insights about Soviet policymaking and administration and can make better informed assessments of Soviet motivations and capabilities.

Part VI focuses on the goals and priorities of Soviet foreign policy and assesses its successes and failures. The ramifications of Soviet international behavior for the Western democracies are also addressed. Although the essays in this section offer different conclusions and prescriptions, they generally confirm our judgment that East-West relations and Soviet economic weakness became increasingly important elements of the Gorbachev administration's foreign policy, and North-South relations and Soviet military strength became decreasingly important elements. But first let us place these developments in historical context.

Soviet leaders since Lenin have stressed that the USSR's goals and policies must be tailored to the current period, which has distinctive characteristics shaped by the relative power and ambitions of competing socioeconomic systems. For an important example, the weapons buildup under Khrushchev and especially Brezhnev led to the attainment of nuclear parity with the United States about 1970. This hard-won achievement was an integral part of the policies of "peaceful coexistence" and "détente" before Gorbachev. Also, the gradual weakening of the Soviet economy, the winding down of the Vietnam War, the eagerness of the German social democratic leadership to improve relations with the USSR and East Germany, and the efforts of President Richard Nixon to negotiate simultaneously with the USSR and archrival China considerably influenced Soviet foreign policy. They induced Brezhnev to pursue East-West economic and nuclear arms control accords while not decentralizing and marketizing the domestic economy, not diminishing research, development, and manufacturing of weapons, and not precluding the use of conventional forces to advance the USSR's interests in Eastern Europe and the Third World.

During the 1970s, top Communist party officials believed that the USSR could simultaneously support "national liberation movements," modernize and stockpile strategic and conventional weapons, *and* participate more fully in the East-West and North-South division of labor. On the one hand, Angola was the first in a series of Soviet and Soviet-supported adventures in the Third World, which culminated in the invasion of Afghanistan in December 1979. On the other hand, nuclear arms limitation agreements and expanded US/USSR economic and scientific-technological cooperation were actively pursued and still seemed within reach in the late 1970s. Many Soviet leaders emphasized the importance of commercial and diplomatic ties with Western Europe and Japan as well as the pitfalls of Soviet-American trade and arms control talks. Indeed, some Soviet commentators concluded that vigorous pursuit of the two chief elements of détente-selected East-West *cooperation* in economic relations and strategic arms reduction and selected East-West *confrontation* in the Third World—had the added advantage of weakening the Atlantic alliance.

The USSR called for collaboration and mutual restraint in East-West relations within Europe as a means of continuing—even accelerating—the rivalry with the West in the Third World. The United States advocated East-West cooperation and restraint within Europe as a means of reducing international tensions and of stabilizing the multifaceted Soviet-American competition. The Jimmy Carter and Ronald Reagan administrations' responses to the Soviet occupation of Afghanistan from 1979 to 1989 made very clear the American rejection of this Soviet interpretation of détente. However, American political, military, and economic power was unable to deter the Brezhnev leadership from acting on its own conception of détente, especially vis-à-vis selected African and Asian countries in the 1970s and major West European democracies in the 1970s and 1980s.

Unlike the United States, Western Europe maintained a détente relationship with the USSR throughout the 1970s and 1980s. This relationship was based on political, economic, and scientific-technological ties that both sides perceived to be mutually advantageous. Had the Soviet–West European bonds created in the early 1970s failed to constrain the USSR from dispatching additional Red Army troops into Poland in the early 1980s, West European governments and citizens would have been much more inclined to accept President Reagan's initial sharp criticism of Soviet motivations and behavior. But, because the USSR did not directly intervene in Poland, the West Europeans' support for commercial and diplomatic collaboration increased.

Western observers often overlooked or minimized the diverse *Soviet* interpretations of détente in the Brezhnev administration. Soviet leaders and analysts perceived East-West relations as a dynamic mix of conflict and cooperation and of centrifugal and centripetal tendencies. But conservatives emphasized East-West conflict and West-West cooperation; modernizers emphasized East-West cooperation and West-West conflict; and there were numerous centrist positions.

Soviet modernizers underscored the opportunities for improving the USSR's economic growth and productivity through mutually beneficial interdependencies with the formidable industrialized Western powers. Soviet conservatives underscored the opportunities for exacerbating "the general crisis of capitalism" and for shielding the socialist and Third World states from the alienating and exploitative capitalist systems. The first orientation stressed the cooperative elements of détente and the vulnerabilities generated by East-West confrontation. The second orientation stressed the adversarial elements of détente and the vulnerabilities generated by East-West collaboration. Some centrists favored closer East-West ties to avoid domestic economic reforms, whereas others favored closer East-West ties to spur domestic economic reforms. And some centrists preferred ties with the United States, whereas others preferred ties with Western Europe and/or Japan.

Gorbachev was a modernizer from the mid-1980s at the very latest. He recognized that military capabilities had made the USSR a superpower after World War II and that the increasing stagnation of the Soviet polity, economy, and society were diminishing its appeal abroad. But he failed to create a multifaceted superpower and greatly weakened the USSR as a military superpower. Indeed, he unleashed forces that seriously jeopardized his own authority, the legitimacy of the political system, and the territorial integrity of the nation.

Gorbachev understood the importance of the political, economic, and social components of national security as well as the military component. He viewed economic problems as more urgent than military problems, and the Politburo's numerous arms control concessions were spurred more by industrial and agricultural decline in the USSR than by a security threat from the West. The General Secretary and his fellow reformers perceived the heightened East-West tensions of the early and mid-1980s, especially the U. S.-initiated Strategic Defense Initiative (SDI) and Intermediate Nuclear Force (INF) deployment, to be economic challenges as much as security challenges. Soviet research and development had long concentrated on defense industries, and spin-offs from the military to the civilian sector of the economy had been few. These trends would continue or even accelerate if the Warsaw Pact countries had to counter the seemingly enhanced first-strike nuclear capability and advanced information technologies of the North Atlantic Treaty Alliance (NATO). The West's sophisticated computers and telecommunications would jeopardize the Soviet bloc's economic competitiveness and might have destabilizing military applications in outer space as well as in strategic and conventional forces.

Gorbachev and his colleagues experimented with diverse methods to reduce the West's cohesiveness and to cooperate with a unified Western alliance. The exacerbation of "interimperialist contradictions" was the cornerstone of the USSR's anticoalition strategy from Lenin to Brezhnev, but Gorbachev used this tactic selectively. Trying to sow discord among the Western allies was not an end in itself and, until Soviet-American summitry had fulfilled or exhausted its potential, was no longer the chief means of achieving larger ends. Rather, overt and covert efforts to undermine Western unity, bilateral negotiations with large and small West European countries, and direct talks between East and West European multinational institutions such as the Warsaw Pact and NATO (North Atlantic Treaty Organization), the CEMA (Council on Mutual Economic Assistance) and EC (European Community), and the Soviet Congress of Peoples' Deputies and European Parliament were among the diverse instruments that Gorbachev simultaneously and serially used in the pursuit of military, economic, and political détente. With the rapid progress in nuclear and conventional arms reduction, the legislation enabling Soviet enterprises to trade directly with foreign firms and governments, the increasing political and economic assertiveness of many Soviet republics, and the virtual disintegration of the Warsaw Pact and CEMA after 1989, the Soviet Union's state-to-state and subnational foreign commercial ties became more important.

The Gorbachev leadership wanted neither a strong United States presence in Western Europe nor a powerful and independent Western Europe that was united militarily, economically, and politically. Gorbachev and his reformist colleagues probably sought to keep the United States in Western Europe but in a weakened condition. Soviet observers considered fissures in NATO and the EC to be enduring components of West-West relations, because West Europeans resented or merely tolerated American political, military, economic, and cultural influences on the European continent. Moreover, Soviet analysts thought that widening splits in the Western alliance would help the USSR establish and strengthen ties with large and small West European countries. Furthermore, Gorbachev had considerable confidence in the short-term efficacy of his conciliatory image among the leaders and citizens of the West. He had confidence as well in the long-term benefits of supporting Western "realists" and expanding their numbers rather than confronting or capitulating to "conservatives," "neoconservatives," and "reactionaries." Gorbachev's diplomacy focused on foreign elites and organized counterelites, but he and his colleagues successfully appealed to world opinion through the Soviet and Western media. Hence, the Gorbachev administration directly and indirectly influenced the policies of conservative Western governments and helped bring into power governments less conservative in their policies toward the USSR.

Gorbachev was much more concerned than Brezhnev about the impact of North-South relations on East-West relations. Although Gorbachev did not want Soviet-American rivalry in the Third World to undermine superpower cooperation, these two components of "peaceful coexistence" were difficult to balance. The general secretary tried to expand the USSR's influence in the Third World but not at a high risk or cost. Gorbachev's Politburo understood that the occupation of Afghanistan had shattered Soviet-American détente, had angered Muslims in the USSR and throughout the world, and had accelerated the strategic and conventional arms race. The Red Army had been mired in a demoralizing war against divided guerrilla groups, which received increasingly effective weapons from the United States and other nations. Also, Gorbachev recognized that preponderant support for either Iran or Iraq in their protracted war could threaten vital Western oil supplies from the Persian Gulf and prompt a hostile Western response in this or another geographic or issue area. And, in unprecedented international and binational cooperation in the Middle East, the USSR firmly supported United Nations resolutions to oust Saddam Hussein's forces from Kuwait and quietly strengthened ties with Israel.

The Gorbachev administration consolidated prior commitments in Third World countries such as India, Syria, and Peru, and it initially increased military and economic support to client states such as Cuba, Mongolia, and Vietnam. Gorbachev and his colleagues eventually reduced material assistance to Marxist as well as non-Marxist regimes, as Yuri Andropov had advocated immediately following Brezhnev's death in 1982. But Soviet lending to the Third World dramatically increased after the sharp drop in world oil prices in 1986. *PlanEcon Report* calculated that the USSR dispensed nearly four times as much money annually during 1986–89 than 1980–82 ($8.5 versus $2.2 billion), which greatly augmented the Soviet budget deficit in a period of declining domestic economic growth and productivity. "The really bad news is that the Soviets may at best be able to collect one-third of what they lent to the 'socialist' bloc and between one-third and one-half of what was lent to the Third World."[5]

Soviet leaders have cautiously weighed the international and national implications of current commitments in the Third World and may have foresworn new obligations and aggressive initiatives for the foreseeable future. Since the early 1980s the Soviet Communist Party has supplied weapons and technical assistance to the Philippines Communist Party, for example. But large-scale Soviet military support for an incipient revolutionary regime is highly unlikely unless the two parties' geostrategic, economic, and political interests and capabilities are congruent and Western displeasure is minimal. Far more likely are well-planned Soviet diplomatic and commercial ventures in the Third World's most prosperous and stable non-Marxist countries and measured Soviet disengagement from the most impoverished and unstable countries. Although Gorbachev took some economic risks to support the client states he inherited, he took much greater risks for strategic and conventional arms reduction, the construction of a "common home" with capitalist Europe, the liberation of socialist Eastern Europe, the creation of a Soviet multiparty system that accelerated centrifugal forces at the national and subnational levels, and the establishment of a modified federal order that sought to avoid the breakup of the USSR.

Gorbachev's domestic and international objectives were closely intertwined. He viewed arms reduction and diplomatic, commercial, and cultural ties between East and West as prerequisites for his country's economic and social transformation. But the purpose of these changes was not to convert the USSR into a Western-style democracy and market economy, nor was it to preserve with modern technologies a highly centralized and self-sufficient Soviet political and economic system. Rather, Gorbachev tried to enhance his country's participation in the rapid internationalization of scientific, technological, economic, and arms limitation initiatives. Only two months after becoming General Secretary he told the party's Central Committee that "the development of microelectronics, computer equipment, instrument building, and the whole information industry is the catalyst of present-day scientific and technical progress" and that "a new stage of the scientific-technological revolution, ensuring a manifold increase in labor productivity, huge savings of resources, and improvements in the quality of output, is beginning." He declared that "it is essential to improve substantially the whole system of incentives for enterprises to produce goods for the export market." And he promised to "continue to apply maximum effort to end the arms race and move toward mutual disarmament and reduced military spending."[6]

The key element of Gorbachev's "new thinking" was his revised conceptualization of national and international security. He recognized that the USSR's attainment of nuclear parity had made his country and the world *less* secure. He rejected Brezhnev's emphasis on military capabilities, because it had damaged the Soviet civilian economy, had emboldened the aging party leadership to employ proxy forces in the Third World, and had precipitated the Reagan administration's military buildup, which featured SDI and INF. Instead, Gorbachev underscored the importance of nonmilitary scientific-technological, socioeconomic, political-administrative, and cultural-humanitarian capabilities. Also, he stressed the importance of international cooperation and global concerns. For example, he insisted that international politics is a multiple-sum game, not a zero-sum game, and that "peaceful coexistence" is a permanent strategy of international cooperation, not a temporary tactic of class struggle.

The Gorbachev administration's mounting emphasis on the economic dimensions of power and security and on the interconnections between domestic and foreign policy was striking. Then Foreign Minister Shevardnadze made the following observations in a speech to top officials of the Ministry of Foreign Affairs in 1987:

> If the idea that foreign policy is an extension of domestic policy is true—and it undoubtedly is true—and if the thesis that the goal of diplomacy is to form an external environment that is favorable for internal development is correct—and it

undoubtedly is correct, then we are compelled to recognize that the backwardness of our power and its steady loss of status is partially our fault too.[7]

The time has come to "introduce economics" into Soviet foreign policy for, until it merges completely with economics, it will not be able to assist in restructuring the Soviet internal economy and society in general and as a whole, which otherwise will not be able to participate on equal terms in the competitive political struggle for making its social and political model of development attractive.[8]

Gorbachev and his closest colleagues thought multifaceted foreign economic ties were essential to the modernization of the Soviet economy. They were deeply dissatisfied with Soviet economic growth and productivity and wanted to increase significantly the quality and quantity of Soviet manufactured goods for domestic consumption and for export. Also, the Gorbachev leadership understood that a reduction in East-West tensions would make it possible to transfer scientists and engineers from military to civilian research and development and to convert existing factories from military to civilian production (e.g., in the aircraft, shipping, nuclear energy, and agricultural machinery industries). Even without substantial technology imports or with poor use of these imports, détente could further economic progress. Maximally, Gorbachev wanted greatly expanded international economic ties and, minimally, a more tranquil international political system to provide "breathing space" for domestic socioeconomic reforms.

In short, the Gorbachev administration's creative thinking about domestic and international change was the driving force behind efforts to democratize or at least liberalize a moribund authoritarian system and to make it in fact or at least in appearance a respected member of the global community. By 1990 the extraordinary innovations in the core concepts of the Soviet leadership had helped to transform most core elements of the Soviet policymaking process and especially Soviet foreign policy. Together with failures and fumblings in internal economic, nationalities, and ecological policies, Gorbachev launched a dramatic restructuring of the Soviet policy and its linkages with the rest of the world. His willingness to liberate Eastern Europe and his pursuit of significant arms reductions earned him the Nobel Peace Prize in 1990.

But Gorbachev gradually lost control over many of his domestic policymaking and policy reforms, which had spurred nationwide ethnic assertiveness and economic decline, thereby jeopardizing the territorial integrity of the Soviet Union and its continuation as a socialist state and military superpower. Gorbachev's response diminished his status as a Nobel laureate at home and abroad. By early 1991, the Soviet army and KGB had forcibly repressed independence movements in many republics, and the likely implications for Soviet foreign policy included curtailed East-West conventional arms agreements and delayed Soviet troops withdrawals from Eastern Europe. A wide range of new institutional relationships and priorities was possible, but the preservation of the status quo or a return to the internal and external conditions before Gorbachev was highly unlikely.

Part VII draws upon historical experience to peer into the future and to envision desirable East-West relations in rapidly changing domestic and international contexts. The results of Gorbachev's initiatives cannot be fairly assessed for years or even decades, but the magnitude and portentousness of his efforts were abundantly clear by 1990. His ideological and policy innovations were intended to produce new political, ethical, and work cultures at home and abroad. He envisioned an enlightened Soviet political leadership joining forces with an increasingly well-educated population to combat the corruption, parochialism, incompetence, waste, and inertia in the major bureaucracies (e.g., the central and regional party apparatuses, foreign affairs and foreign trade ministries, and armed forces and security police). He envisioned an international order where real and perceived security threats and physical and spiritual deprivation were greatly reduced by cooperative problem-solving. To the Soviet people he vowed that the USSR would "stop hopelessly lagging behind world scientific, technical, and social progress" and would seize "missed opportunities."[9] And to the people of all other countries he vowed that the USSR would contribute significantly to the amelioration of global problems such as nuclear proliferation, regional conflicts, environmental pollution, terrorism, hunger, and AIDS.

But Soviet citizens increasingly questioned Gorbachev's sincerity, judgment, decisiveness, administrative skills, and democratic proclivities. Even if the crackdown of 1991 were stopped, democracy and prosperity in the Soviet Union and its former East European allies are by no means inevitable and are almost certain to take decades in coming. The failure to democratize the USSR's disintegrating internal empire and its discarded East European empire could generate much more disruptive and deviant behavior within and among these countries. The stronger national and regional governments might be tempted to conduct assertive foreign policies in selected geographic and issue areas. Segments of populations and newly created countries might vent their frustrations by exacerbating international tensions or by trying to mobilize support from world public opinion. And subsequent editions of this volume might have to be entitled "*Russian* Foreign Policy," "Soviet Foreign *Policies*," or "*Post-Soviet* International Behavior."

Thus, there are very different Soviet views about international politics as well as very different Western views. Although the sources of these differences are numerous, the governments and citizens of the Soviet Union and Western democracies can influence one another's outlooks and policies at the margins and sometime closer to the core. For example, if post-Communist countries become democratic, they could create political, economic, and military benefits for capitalist countries, traditional alliances, and huge regional trading blocs. East-West and North-South accords in the 1990s cannot guarantee a more stable and prosperous global order, but they can help to conceptualize and lay the foundations for such an order.

International relations are being shaped more and more by the interdependencies stemming from unprecedented scientific-technological, socioeconomic, ecological-environmental, and medical-nutritional changes.

Foremost among these changes is the capacity of nuclear weapons or nuclear accidents to destroy the human species. Soviet "new thinking" and unilateral weapons and troop reductions notwithstanding, the USSR or its Russian republic will remain a military superpower. The reversal of the East-West strategic and conventional arms race notwithstanding, nuclear and chemical terrorism and accidents will pose grave threats to regional, world, and outer-space security. And the persistence of ethnic and religious conflicts notwithstanding, national borders will become increasingly porous because of satellite photography, global telecommunications, international manufacturing and trade, educational and cultural exchanges, and reduced emigration and travel restrictions.

All of these international developments underscore the benefits of fast and accurate communication, agreed-upon methods of conflict resolution, and mutually advantageous resolving of problems and seizing of opportunities. The 35-nation Helsinki human rights agreement, the Soviet-American strategic, conventional, and chemical weapons treaties, and the United Nations condemnation of Iraq's annexation of Kuwait may be harbingers of much greater multilateral and bilateral collaboration in the post–Cold War era. But the government officials and citizens of the United States, Western Europe, and Japan must continuously reassess Soviet perspectives, pursuits, and performance. Internal tensions and the possible disintegration of the USSR pose critically important military, economic, and ideological challenges to its current republics and to many other countries. It is imperative that Westerners better understand these challenges if we are to compete effectively and judiciously with the USSR or its successor countries, and if we are to create a new world order by progressing from East-West *détente* to East-West *entente*.

NOTES

1.   All quoted statements by Soviet officials, unless otherwise noted, are from primary source materials translated and dated in *Daily Report: Soviet Union,* Foreign Broadcast Information Service (hereafter FBIS), Washington, DC. For example, these statements are by Mikhail Gorbachev, 15 October 1986, pp. DD9–DD10; Georgii Arbatov, 14 November 1986, p. AA9; and Valentin Falin, 28 August 1986, p. AA8.

2.   Quoted in *Radio Liberty Research Bulletin,* No. 399/86, New York, p. 4. Also in FBIS, 9 October 1986, pp. R1–R3.

3.   FBIS, 25 July 1986, p. R7.

4.   FBIS, 12 November 1986, p. CC3.

5.   "Analysis of Soviet Foreign Trade Lending," *PlanEcon Report* Vol. 6, Nos. 11–12 (21 March 1990), pp. 24–25 ff.

6.   FBIS, 12 June 1985, pp. R4, R9, R15.

7.   FBIS, 27 October 1987, p. 52.

8.   FBIS, 30 October 1987, pp. 50–53; also *Summary of World Broadcasts: USSR,* 9 September 1987, British Broadcasting Co., London, pp. A1/3–A1/4.

9.   FBIS, 16 November 1989, pp. 66–67, 71–73.

V
Perspectives and Policymaking

14

The Revolution in Soviet Foreign Policy*

Robert Legvold

A revolution is under way in Soviet foreign policy greater than any in the postwar period, indeed greater than any since Lenin in the early years of his regime accepted the failure of the pan-European revolution and allowed the Soviet Union to join the game of nations. The current upheaval is on a scale with the other dramatic foreign policy reorientation of the last half-century; comparable to the 1940s when U.S. foreign policy moved from isolation to global engagement; greater, in fact, than the 1950s when French policy passed from the modest aims of the Fourth Republic to the grand enterprises of deGaulle's Fifth Republic; and greater, too, than the 1960s in Chinese policy, a ten-year transition from a troubled alignment with the Soviet camp to an emerging realignment with the West.

Steadily but chaotically, with a lurching, creative energy, the transformation has cut wider and deeper into the rudiments of Soviet foreign policy. For three and a half years, changes have accumulated, spreading from one sphere to the next, altering not merely the workaday calculations that trapped Mikhail Gorbachev's predecessors in their Afghan imbroglio and in their leaden approach to the Euromissile challenge, but altering the assumptions by which the Soviets explain the functioning of international politics and from which they derive the concepts underlying the deeper pattern of their actions. Revolutions of this kind do not make states into saints nor do they remove them as preoccupations in the policies of other nations, but they do leave a vastly different challenge. Once understood by the outside world, such revolutions create new imperatives and often new opportunities.

Why now? Why, when only a few years ago Soviet policy seemed so menacing in its rigidity? A part of the answer lies in the fact that radical circumstances often stirs radical change, and the Soviet circumstance these days is surely radical. Rarely, if ever, has a leadership under the duress of a basic failure of its system attempted so much. It would be difficult to do what

*Reprinted by permission of the author and publisher from *Foreign Affairs* 68, 1 (1988/89). Copyright© 1988 by the Council of Foreign Relations, Inc.

Gorbachev wants to do to the Soviet economic and political order and not also affect the foreign policy order, to focus on massive problems in one sphere and ignore those in another, to turn society upside down but leave the external stakes of the country untouched, or to reexamine the entire Stalinist experience but give no thought to the lessons of the last twenty years in foreign affairs.

When a foreign policy has diminished national welfare and weakened the state's ability to influence or control external change, as so many Soviet spokesmen now freely admit has been true of Soviet policy, the price of not responding mounts. Moreover, no country, least of all a superpower such as the Soviet Union, can disregard the constraints and requirements of a changing international environment, one less and less amenable to old formulas and presumptions. In the Soviet case, intellectuals and various parts of the foreign policy establishment have known this for some time, and over the last decade they have slowly created the foundation of a substantially different Soviet approach to international politics. When all these influences converge, especially in the presence of a leader like Gorbachev, great, even revolutionary, departures come more naturally.

Revolution is not a word to be used lightly. To qualify, change must be of historic proportions. It would not be enough for the Soviet leadership to alter its actions in this or that respect, even if some of those shifts represented important breaks with the past. Even far-reaching modifications in strategy would be insufficient.

What must change is thinking. Real revolutions are, ultimately, conceptual. Unless the national leadership's understanding of the realities of the world undergoes a modification, no initiative, no matter how surprising, carries sufficient depth or conviction. Therefore, to assume that only deeds, and not words, count, as cautious Western audiences have so often done in reacting to Gorbachev, ignores what deeds owe to words, when words represent the concepts by which leaders come to terms with reality. Before behavorial revolutions come conceptual revolutions.

II

Since Gorbachev came to power in March 1985, Soviet ideas about international politics and how the Soviet Union should perform as a superpower have been in constant flux. No aspect of policy, no dimension of the intellectual underpinning of policy, remains untouched. In the process the tumult has slowly engulfed the whole of policy, from the mechanisms of its formulation to the core assumption on which it rests. Indeed, the sheer sweep of the drama is what should have first caught our eye.

There is, however, a good deal more. What gives such power to the conceptual revolution currently under way is its appearance on three different and critically linked levels. Change at any one level would be important enough. Take, for example, change in what might be called *basic concepts,* or the key notions by which the Soviet leaders and foreign policy elites make sense of the opportunities and problems posed for them by the world outside. These have not been so thoroughly reconsidered for more than sixty years—not since the wrenching adaptations to the Treaty of Brest Litovsk, the civil war and the Rapallo accords. Literally every dimension of Soviet policy is being touched.

First, Gorbachev has radically altered the Soviet concept of national security, or, at least, the framework within which it is discussed. He has raised the most fundamental questions: What constitutes national security in these waning years of the twentieth century? How is a superpower like the Soviet Union to pursue it without becoming its own worst enemy? His answer, boiled down to its two essential parts, stresses, as the answer of no Soviet leader has before, (1) the insufficiency of military power as the way to national security, and (2) the link between national and mutual security.

As early as the 27th Party Congress in February 1986, Gorbachev began to convey an unusually complex appreciation of what constitutes national security. The military dimension, he has since said over an over, is but one aspect of the problem—almost certainly not the main one. It is not merely, to use his words form the party congress, that "the character of contemporary weapons leaves no country with any hope of safeguarding itself solely with military and technical means, for example by building up a defense system, even the most powerful one." More to the point, in the present era, according to Gorbachev, most threats to national well-being are not military but economic and political—and the possession of military power, let alone its use, provides little or no solution to these threats.

The second theme emerged in the fall and winter of 1985. After that year's Geneva summit Gorbachev went out of his way to emphasize his "deep conviction" that, were the United States to possess less security than the Soviet Union, only bad could come of it, because inevitably only mistrust and greater instability would follow. No nation's security, he has repeated often since, can be achieved at the expense of another country. Thus national security cannot be divorced from mutual security. "To think otherwise," he said in August 1986, "is to live in a world of illusions, in a world of self-deception."

Of still greater significance, Gorbachev has also helped to reorder a second basic concept. From Lenin's day it has been an article of Soviet faith that the struggle between two social systems, capitalism and socialism, creates the core dynamic of international politics. The notion is not simply hollow cant. What the Soviets have thought about the possibilities of East-West relations and what they have felt obliged to do for Third World revolutions derive from it.

No longer, say Gorbachev and the many who take their cue from him. Not the struggle between classes but the common plight of man forms the central imperative. Not a Manichaean contest between good and evil, but the entangling effect of interdependence, holds the upper hand. Aleksandr Yakovlev, Gorbachev's alter ego in the Politburo, spoke last August of a "planet compressed to an unprecedentedly small size," a world whose history can end with "the touch of a button,'' a world in which ''any event becomes the property of five billion people within hours,'' a world needing not the primacy of ''individual countries or classes, people, or social groups,'' but ways of countering ''the forces of separation, of opposition, of confrontation, and of war, which have already delayed the development of civilization by whole centuries.''[1] The Soviet foreign minister, Eduard Shevardnadze, third among the most powerful Soviet foreign policy figures, views as ''anti-Leninist'' the Khrushchev-Brezhnev thesis of peaceful coexistence as a specific form of class struggle.

The third change concerns the place of the Third World in international politics, and of the superpowers in the Third World. Soviet thinking in this respect no longer resembles what prevailed in the pre-Gorbachev era. Hardly anyone pretends any longer that the woes and turmoil in Asia, Africa, the Middle East and Latin America are part of some grand, heroic ''national liberation struggle,'' once the excuse for Soviet commitments and intrusions. Instead, Third World conflicts are portrayed more as a vast drain on the pitiful resources of developing countries and a ''catalyst to local and international tensions.''[2] Or, as Gorbachev proclaimed in his speech before the U.N. General Assembly this past December: ''The bell of every regional conflict tolls for all of us.'' There is a corollary: not so long ago Soviet leaders and elites treated their own country's role in the Third World imperiously (beyond reproach and none of the United States' business); now they agree that any future agenda of détente with the Americans must set limits to superpower intervention.

Finally, the concepts by which Soviet leaders order their relations within the world of socialism—with Eastern Europe, China and nonruling communist parties—are no less in flux. Considering the importance and scope of the conceptual categories already discussed, to add this fourth one is to say that no piece of the foundation of Soviet foreign policy remains unaffected.

From the late 1940s, when Stalin made over Eastern Europe in his own image, according to the Soviet catechism, the socialist world has been a universe unto itself: Soviet leaders have refused to admit that within it relations could be anything other than harmonious, built as they were on the ''general laws'' (or imperatives) of socialist development, laws validated first and foremost by the Soviet model. Assuming a natural, even preordained, unity, Soviet leaders and their proconsuls in Eastern Europe presumed not merely a need, but a right to discipline any serious deviation from it.

Under Gorbachev, the catechism has changed. Those who reflect deeply on the power of the Soviet Union in its relations with Eastern Europe (and, in the long run, in Sino-Soviet relations), including Gorbachev, Yakovlev and Shevardnadze, now acknowledge that socialist international relations are no different form those of any other type of polity. They are as prone to conflicts, including armed engagements arising from self-interest and ambition, as are relations among and with other systems. In light of this, Soviet leaders now ask: Why pretend, let alone demand, that a ''single truth,'' a single shared wisdom, should prevail within what until recently was called the socialist commonwealth?

III

The revolution in Soviet foreign policy is occurring on yet another level, where notions more directly inform practical choice, the level of *policy concepts*. The change is stunning and portentous. If Soviet leaders are rethinking the very notion of national security, they are also revising the concepts that guide their defense decisions and their negotiating posture in arms control settings. Three new ideas form the core of this transformation.

The first is the notion of "reasonable sufficiency," an idea Gorbachev himself first introduced at the 27th Party Congress in 1986. By these words, he and other nonmilitary commentators mean something less than parity, not to mention superiority. In simple terms, they are advocating that the Soviet Union cope with, rather than keep up with, the Joneses. Rather than imitate every new U.S. program, such as the Strategic Defense Initiative, it would be better, in their view, if the Soviet Union were to take the cheaper and simpler route of developing means of foiling the weapons the Americans field. And rather than match the capabilities of each and every country whose arms could threaten the Soviet Union, they would ask of Soviet defenses only that they meet threats that might be plausibly imagined.

Gorbachev has not provided specifics, doubtless because he does not yet have them in mind. But others, beginning with his foreign minister, are filling in the blanks, and their thoughts have far-reaching implications for the Soviet approach to the military competition with the West.[3] In the strategic nuclear realm "reasonable sufficiency" would end the quest for a Soviet arsenal designed to overmatch the United States at every rung up the ladder of nuclear escalation— including, in the end, a force designed to devastate the nuclear arms of the other side—and replace it with a secure retaliatory force capable of ensuring some essential but minimal level of deterrence. In conventional arms the concept would leave the Soviet Union with forces capable of defending against a surprise attack but not of launching one or, more important, of conducting a large-scale, extended offensive. As for Soviet military power usable at great remove, according to the new doctrine there should be enough to help discourage outside interference in local crises, but not to make revolutions or save clients too feeble to defend themselves.

The other two ideas are strategic stability and defensive defense, the latter with its corollary of asymmetrical arms reductions. Strategic stability incorporates the technical, and narrower, American notion of crisis stability (namely, a structured nuclear balance that reduces the temptation for hair-trigger response in crisis situations) but goes much further. For more than a year, Soviet experts working on the problem have struggled to imagine a more stable nuclear regime at drastically reduced levels of armament, one that takes into account not merely the characteristics of weapons systems, but also the effects of strategic doctrine and even of political context.

Defensive defense embodies the simple idea that in no sphere of military power, conventional or nuclear, should either side be able to launch and maintain a vast frontal offensive. The idea is simple; figuring out how to achieve it is another matter. Gorbachev, however, in summer 1986 did introduce a new, albeit vague, guideline for proceeding, one that has since become a standard Soviet formula: let the side with an edge be the one to sacrifice more in order to create a more stable balance at lower levels.

The knowledgeable reader is no doubt protesting: "But these notions have not been embraced by much of the soviet professional military—and is that not a complication of some consequence?" Indeed it is, yet not one to be overestimated. First, to say that the military by and large does not use the same concepts is not to say they have consciously chosen against them. Second, where their preferences are clearly in conflict with the new ideas, that is not to say they will fight to have their way. And third, in those instances where they do choose to fight, this is not to say that they will win, given their current comparative political disadvantage.

Other new policy concepts parallel Gorbachev's reformulated insight into the basic dynamic of contemporary international politics, an insight that exalts interdependence and devalues class struggle. Reduced to their essence, these concepts stress multilateralism in place of great-power unilateralism and substitute responsibility of the many for the arrogated duty of the two superpowers. This in turn means strengthening international institutions, such as the United Nations, to give them a larger role with all manner of tasks, from facilitating communication during crises to providing aid in environmental emergencies, from managing regional violence to policing the fragile settlements by which such violence is ended. However, it also means altering Soviet institutions and practices that make the U.S.S.R. an unfit participant in other international institutions, such as the General Agreement on Tariffs, and Trade (GATT) and the International Monetary Fund.

The Soviet leadership has not been as successful at developing policy concepts to go along with shifts in its thinking about the place of the Third World in international politics. Since late summer 1987 Soviet speakers have begun favoring political over military settlements and suggesting the notion of "national reconciliation" as the way out of the chaos in places like Afghanistan, Angola and Cambodia—and this might be taken as a new policy concept. But it may only represent a recoiling from the ardors of these particular entanglements, rather than a more durable new approach to regional instability as such. In the last year or so, however, Soviet academics have urged that the United States, the Soviet Union and other great powers begin designing an explicit code of conduct regulating their intrusions into he Third World. The outlines of such a code remain foggy and, at times, distinctly prejudicial to the far–flung basing of U.S. military power.

Of the transformations in basic concepts, the gravest and most traumatic is the process of rethinking Soviet relations within the socialist world, particularly with Eastern Europe. Not surprisingly, therefore, Soviet leaders are not having an easy time generating concrete concepts to guide policy in this area. Two departures, however, have enormous implications. First, the old notion of "socialist internationalism," for decades a euphemism for Soviet tutelage, has been replaced by something far closer to laissez-faire. East European regimes are to be left essentially alone to solve their own problems and make their own mistakes. Second, the Brezhnev Doctrine, while not actually lifted, no longer sets the same limits to change. Put differently, doubtless there are still circumstances in which the Soviet Union would intervene with force, but they would probably not include those of 1968 and 1981.

In sum, we are witnessing significant changes in basic concepts and operational policy. What makes all of these changes on the two levels still more momentous, however, is the passage occurring on a third level.

To a degree particularly difficult for Americans to understand, *fundamental assumptions,* on which the entire edifice of Soviet foreign policy beliefs ultimately rests, are at stake. Never, not even in the 1940s or as a result of the Vietnam War, have Americans been forced to reexamine the basic premises of their worldview. In the Soviet Union, today, people are engaging in such a reexamination. No two matters are more fundamental to the Soviet mind than revolution and capitalism, and the view of each has come to a remarkable pass.

Twice before, the Soviet conception of revolution has undergone profound change. The first time was in the years following 1917, when Lenin's rationalization of the Russian Revolution as the "spark" for a European revolution died, and Soviet leaders were left to fend for themselves. The second time was in the 1950s, when the advent of the nuclear era forced them to rethink the relationship between war and revolution, and, therefore, accept the argument for peaceful coexistence.

Now comes a third transformation: the end of revolutionary faith. Its last repository had been the Third World, but nothing any longer convinces most Soviet observers that revolution is the probable fate of most developing countries (not, at least, the kind of revolution that they would wish to see); more likely their fate is either political vagrancy or, for those that escape into the ranks of the newly industrializing countries, something more akin to capitalism.

Capitalism, too, is coming to represent something vastly different for Gorbachev and his supporters. They are more attentive to the durability of capitalism, as the twentieth century draws to a close, than to its predicted doom. More of their sensitivity is concentrated on its dynamism than on its crises, a dynamism that some openly, others by implication, acknowledge has shamed socialism. For capitalism has successfully made the transition form the industrial to the technical-information age, while socialism has yet to prove that it can—an admission that one finds in Soviet journals these days. (Hence, not so incidentally, the "crisis" of communist parties in the West, to put it as Soviet commentators now do.) And the discovery that certain ills, such as militarism, are not in fact intrinsic to capitalism engages more attention now than do the features which the Soviets continue to regard as capitalism's flaws.

When Gorbachev can come to New York and deliver a speech in praise of tolerance and diversity and "the universal human idea," raise the revolution of 1789 to equality with that of 1917 as a source of "a most precious spiritual heritage," identify "freedom of choice" as "a universal principle that should allow for no exception," reject force or the threat of its use as an instrument of policy, and call for a more open international order, he may risk being "a little too romantic—and Gorbachev has acknowledged that some of his own people think he is. But his words should not be regarded as mere bluster. Not when values, assumptions and prescriptions are being recast at every turn, at every level, in every dimension of policy.

IV

Is the revolution in Soviet foreign policy really so radical? What evidence might be offered to the skeptic? The evidence is threefold: first, the nature of the process Gorbachev has set in motion; second, the opposition to it; and, third, the actions accompanying the process.

First, what is the nature of the process? It seems reasonable to suspect that something so comprehensive cannot be easily scripted by one oligarch—or even by a score. When literally every dimension of policy is affected, an invisible, not a human, hand is at work. What is more important, the process has been from the start unsystematic in its essence, far to much so to be simply a cleaver contrivance. In a less natural process, the progression would be more logical: first, the affectation of shift in fundamental assumptions, then the supposed adjustment of basic concepts, and from these an appropriately modified array of policy concepts.

But that is not at all what has been happening. On the contrary, change has come piecemeal and out of any logical order. It has tumbled forth on all levels at once. The process has been like some great random sewing machine, stitching back and forth, slowly exposing the pattern. Gorbachev starts by acknowledging, at last, the interconnection of national and mutual security, or maybe simply by coming forward with a new negotiating position in the Strategic Arms Reduction Talks (START), or maybe by vaguely suggesting a new standard for defense, which he calls reasonable sufficiency, all of which did happen between October 1985 and February 1986. Others then seize the opening and push the argument forward, taking a notion like reasonable sufficiency and spelling it out, adding as well other logically related new ideas, such as strategic stability or defensive defense. Within months these accumulating notions make their way back into the next Gorbachev or Shevardnadze pronouncement.

Meanwhile, each part of the establishment—the policy leaders in a vague and sweeping fashion, the policy intellectuals in a more elaborate and specific fashion—attacks one issue, only to find itself led to another still more fundamental conclusion. Thus, someone sets out to elaborate an idea, say the notion of "reasonable sufficiency." He then begins to question the role of military power in Soviet policy and finally to admit, as did Americanologist Georgi Arbatov, that "in the past we did not realize, as we realize now, the limited possibilities of the use of military power"; as a result "our national security policy over-emphasized military means."[4] Such questioning of the place of military power in Soviet foreign policy prompts others to challenge the whole Soviet concept of what threatens the U.S.S.R., a question tat began to emerge in academic articles by early 1988 and now threads its way through leadership speeches.

We were wrong, these Soviet policy makers say, to conceive of the threat in thoroughly military terms, to represent the military threat as one of war, and to imagine the war would likely break out in central Europe. In fact, they argue, the real threat has increasingly become the deformation of the Soviet economy produced by a preoccupation with military power, a debilitating order of priorities consciously imposed on the Soviet Union by a richer West. Indeed, they ask, how is it that Soviet military power grew throughout the 1970s, while Soviet national security, when thought of in terms of the country's economic, social and political stability, shrank?

The process continues. It is not enough to stop with a rethinking of the nature of the threat, a growing number of Soviet leaders contend; the need is to grapple with the larger question of where Soviet national interests lie. Shevardnadze referred explicitly to this problem in an important address to a foreign ministry conference last July, and since then a number of writers have offered bold responses.[5] Their common theme is that the mindless willingness to make commitments in the past, the reflexive jockeying for international position and the struggle for spheres of influence scarcely corresponded to the nation's real national interests. They urge instead that foreign policy be corralled and made to serve the interests of society, not a disembodied "bureaucratic international-ism," as one of them puts it.

Although paradoxical, a second reason to take the process seriously is the opposition to it, or at least to certain aspects of it. (Of course, opposition is also a reason to fear for the future of the process.) When Yegor Ligachev, thought to be the second-ranking member of the Soviet Politburo until recently, argues on behalf of a class-based view of international politics and defends the notion of class struggle, as he did last summer, it is a reasonable deduction that he regards the new ideas as more than an artifice.

But, if the misgivings of more traditional minds give us further reason to believe something real is afoot, are they not also reason to avoid overrating its chances of success? If there is indeed a struggle under way, who is to say the architects of the new concepts will prevail? In the abstract this is a perfectly prudent concern. In reality, it gravely miscalculates the current state of affairs.

Gorbachev, Yakovlev and the others are *not* locked in a furious battle with critics of their foreign policy program. Ligachev obviously worries about the potential loss of self-identity and ballast when old and familiar ideological frameworks are abandoned. But to compare the 28 lines in one of his speeches with a virtual avalanche of pent-up new ideas seems less than judicious. Conservative skepticism over what is being said and done by Gorbachev in foreign policy certainly must exist but, to keep matters in proportion, one has to look long and hard to find traces of it in the public record, quite unlike the case with criticism of his domestic reforms. Moreover, with the important exception of the military, when we consider the ranks of those who make or influence Soviet foreign policy—whether the dominant figures in the foreign ministry or the international apparat of the party, the personal advisers to key Politburo members, senior figures in the media or the most powerful personalities within the Academy of Sciences—an overwhelming proportion are part of the revolution, not a threat to it.

Finally, Soviet actions over the last three years, particularly in the last year and a half, suggest that the churning in Soviet minds is genuine. Some of the evidence lies in a wide range of what might be called symptomatic behavior. Releasing Andrei Sakharov from internal exile in Gorky in December 1986 was an early illustration. Paying long-owed obligations for U. N. peacekeeping operations in May 1988 was another. Handling the hijacking of a Soviet cargo aircraft in November 1988 as Washington itself might have was a third. This behavior is symptomatic because, while none of these actions is crucial, taken together they represent something qualitatively different from the Soviet Union's past demeanor.

By now the list is long: the end to the jamming of foreign broadcasting; the bid for observer status in GATT, the Asian Development Bank and the Pacific Economic Cooperation Council; collaboration with British law-enforcement agencies against drug trafficking; cooperation with the International Atomic Energy Agency investigating the Chernobyl disaster; the vote in favor of keeping Israel and South Africa in that agency; the creation of a commission to examine the so-called blank spots in Polish-Soviet history—and so the list swells. It is already too long and too diverse to be only a nondescript series of random occurrences.

The same can be said of Soviet actions in areas that truly count. For a long time after Gorbachev came to power, skeptics had a point when they reminded audiences that the deeds of the Soviets were less inspiring than their words. But this case is harder and harder to make. The agreement to eliminate intermediate-range nuclear forces (INF), largely on NATO's terms, could be explained as a hard-headed, albeit courageous, corrective to a politically and materially expensive mistake. So could the decision to withdraw from Afghanistan. One realizes, however, that even these decisions carry more profound implications. Leaving an agony like Afghanistan by cutting and running, as others like the French and Americans know too well, sets limits to future interventions. Making a deal with the West on INF involving the destruction of a whole generation of modern weapons (without the destruction of the threat for which they were designed) and allowing the most intrusive forms of verification is an impingement on defense decision-making such as has not been allowed under any Soviet leader since Khrushchev.

From the start, there have also been other actions that broke more clearly with the past. One such action was the decision in October 1985 to offer 50-percent reductions in strategic nuclear forces, including subceilings that could greatly lessen the Soviet threat to U. S. fixed land-based missiles (at one time the essence of the American fear of a "window of vulnerability"). The acceptance of on-site verification in the INF agreement is another. A third is the effort to address China's three "obstacles" to better Sino-Soviet relations by initiative rather than rhetoric, including since later 1987 the active cajoling of Vietnam to pull its troops out of Cambodia.

In December 1988 in New York came a fourth break—one which almost no one was prepared to pass over. A unilateral decision to cut Soviet active military forces by 500,000 troops, or almost 15 percent, and to withdraw more than 40 percent of Soviet tank divisions from Eastern Europe, together with 50 percent of Soviet tanks, is a giant shift in the Soviet approach. Only some very basic adjustment of Soviet thinking can explain it. If, in fact, a less-publicized but more significant pledge in the Gorbachev speech comes about, a very real revolution in behavior will have occurred. "All Soviet divisions remaining, for the time being, on the territory of our allies are being reorganized," he said. "Their structure will be different from what it is now; after a major cutback of their tanks it will become clearly defensive."

V

What is the West to do? How are we to cope with one of the great foreign policy reorientations of our times?

The answer, in most capitals is "cautiously." The reason, even for those who take Gorbachev at his word, has ultimately to do with another kind of uncertainty. What if it all ends tomorrow? What if Gorbachev disappears—or, if he survives, what if the pressure of circumstances causes him to retreat? Most counsel: "Take hope from the change, but don't lower your guard, don't overestimate the new, and don't count on the future."

This time, however, caution is the enemy of the sensible. The problem arises from a misreading of the sources of the transformation taking place in Soviet foreign policy. Most take it for granted that what is happening is owed entirely or largely to the Soviet crisis at home or, at a minimum, to the way Gorbachev sees the crisis. It follows that, should the Soviet predicament worsen (or, less likely, ease) or should Gorbachev be replaced by someone who takes a different view of it, the same impulse to change will no longer exist.

Unquestionably the Soviet leadership's domestic preoccupations are a major factor. Gorbachev says so in every foreign policy speech. At the April 1985 Central Committee plenum and often since, he has made it plain that his domestic agenda dictates everything else and that foreign policy will comply with its needs. Those at the forefront of the new thinking freely admit that, but for the domestic drama, the changes they care about would not be coming so rapidly and dramatically. Almost certainly there is another connection: when Gorbachev and the others engage in soaring thoughts about change within the Soviet Union, presumably they find it easier and more natural to entertain great conceptual leaps in the foreign policy realm as well.

Important though the domestic factor is, however, it does not alone, or perhaps even primarily, account for the revolution under way in this other context. The requirements of the international setting also play a role. The truth is that virtually every dimension of the change has antecedents in the period before Gorbachev, because the realities of international politics have for more than a decade been forcing Soviet foreign policy elites to rethink many of their assumptions. Quite apart from the trouble at home, they understand the need to reconsider the problems of managing alliances, of using force, of achieving influence and of making commitments. It is the world outside, not the mess inside, that has led them to think through the character and weaknesses of their power abroad, the hazards of interventionism, the causes of insecurity, the significance of interdependence and the costs of autarky. Whatever happens to Gorbachev or to his effort at perestroika, the same pressures will be there. He has most assuredly accelerated and deepened the process of adjusting, and his passing would slow its momentum—but not end it. The conceptual revolution I have been describing can be undone only by leaders who plan to disregard powerful and unforgiving realities (and the failures of past policy).

No one should conclude from all this that the Soviet Union will soon cease to be a concern of U. S. policy. Talk of what it will do to the United States and the Western alliance to lose the Soviet Union as an enemy is wildly premature. Nothing in what I have laid out implies that the Soviet Union will soon embrace Western ways, forswear great ambitions abroad or cease to be a military superpower. Nothing guarantees that Soviet leaders will never again offend the West by the use of force at home or in Eastern Europe, or worry it by their involvements far from their own borders.

But a historic opportunity now presents itself to the United States and its allies, and neither timidity nor old ways of framing the issue are the right response. It is fashionable these days to say the cold war is over and the West has won. What many people do not realize is that we in the West are in danger of ending it on Soviet terms. For it would end on Soviet terms if Moscow finally established itself in the eyes of the world, including those of our own people, as the leadership with the greater vision and the more compelling foreign policy values, as the leadership more willing to run risks for a safer and less militarized international order, as the leadership more committed to strong and effective international institutions, and as the leadership more ready to free us from the contests of the past.

Thus, when NATO, after a great deal of debate, puts forward a proposal by which the Soviet Union does all the cutting of conventional forces while we only watch, a proposal in which the objective is to relieve Western concerns and defer Eastern concerns, and when the first instinct of prominent Western public figures faced with Gorbachev's pledge of unilateral arms reductions is hand-wringing over the impediments it will put on efforts to modernize NATO's tactical nuclear weapons, then the West is doubly foolish: first, for not understanding the opportunity now open to it; and second, for casting itself in the eyes of the rest of the world as the hidebound.

Not so many years ago many commentators located the root of the Soviet challenge in the Russian quest for absolute security. Maybe it is now the West that is more in danger of calculating excessively the margin of security, not daring to run risks in the uncertain hope of creating far greater stability and safety.

The West makes some of the same mistakes when it underestimates or, worse, dismisses Gorbachev's new emphasis on multilateralism. If by his statement and the accompanying array of proposals he is telling the West of his country's readiness to diminish the role of both superpowers in supervising international politics and to transfer to others many of the rights and duties seized by these two over the last forty years, it is not in the West's interest to turn a blind eye. What gain is there for the United States and other Western powers to be seen as cynical toward the United Nations and other international institutions with a political contribution to make, while the Soviet Union moves in the other direction?

As the new Soviet leadership has begun to stir interest in the West, the closest thing we have had to statesmanship is the urging that we "test" Gorbachev, by which is meant that we take him seriously and probe to see how far he is willing to alter Soviet policy. It seems increasingly irrelevant advice, as Gorbachev meets more and more tests we have not yet collected ourselves to pose. Increasingly the test is for the West: Do we have the imagination, creativity and courage to respond to the very revolution in Soviet foreign policy for which we have waited half a century?

NOTES

1.   From *Service Vremya* broadcast. 12 August, 1988, as reported in *Foreign Broadcast Information* 16 August, p. 52.
2.   A. Kislov, in the journal *Mirovaya ekonomiks i mezhadunarodnye otnosheniya* (August 1986). p. 39.
3.   A particularly compelling example is Aleksei Arbatov, "Parity and Reasonable Sufficiency," International Affairs (October 1988), pp. 75–87.
4.   "Perestroika, Glasnost and Foreign Policy," unpublished paper, 1988.
5.   For one of the boldest, see Igor Malashenko, "Ideals and Interests," *New Times* (November 1988), pp. 26–28.

15

New Thinking or New Tactics in Soviet Foreign Policy?*

John W. Coffey

For the last three years Soviet leader Mikhail Gorbachev has waged a vigorous peace offensive, persuading some Westerners that radically "new thinking" about world politics is brewing in the Kremlin. Gorbachev's public relations flair, however, may conceal both less and more than meet the eye.

In a September 1987 *Pravda* article, Gorbachev reiterated his concept of a "comprehensive system of international security" broached at the 1986 27th Party Congress.[1] This new system would operate within an enlarged U.N. framework. Among other things, Gorbachev called for: strict observance of the U.N. Charter; non-interference in nations' internal affairs (except for the struggle against apartheid); a multilateral center to reduce the danger of war and verify compliance with international agreements; a guarantee of regional security by U.N. Security Council permanent members; a global information network to erase stereotypes and the "energy image" of peoples; and a consultative council of the world's intellectual elite. He urged progress toward a "new world economic order" to ensure security for all states and a global environmental protection program. Asserting that human rights are incompatible with placing "the chandeliers of exotic weapons" in space, Gorbachev affirmed the human (particularly economic) rights of all peoples.

Describing nuclear weapons as "the greatest evil," Gorbachev advocated their abolition along with all other means of mass destruction. Peace must be maintained, he said, with drastically reduced and balanced levels of conventional arms. Gorbachev stressed the new Soviet doctrine of "military sufficiency," that is, a level of forces adequate to repel aggression but unable to conduct offensive operations. He proposed moving toward a new security regime by withdrawing nuclear and other offensive weapons from borders and creating demilitarized zones; eventually military blocs would dissolve, and all troops stationed abroad

Reprinted by permission of the author and publisher from *Global Affairs*, IV, 1 (Winter 1989). Copyright © 1989 by the International Security Council.

would return home. Gorbachev claimed his system of international security would herald a "new organization of life in our common planetary home."

The next month, in a regional application of his new security regime, Gorbachev gave a speech in Murmansk calling for an Arctic peace zone.[2] Invoking his familiar image of "our common European home," Gorbachev set forth a six-point program: a nuclear-free zone in northern Europe, including Soviet territory; restriction of air and naval activities in adjacent seas and creation of confidence-building measures; cooperation in natural resource extraction, scientific study, and environmental protection; and access for foreign shipping to the Arctic sea route to Asia.

Gorbachev's themes of a new international security system, "defense sufficiency," and the denuclerization and demilitarization of international relations were reflected in the Warsaw Pact military doctrine announced at an East Berlin conference in May 1987.[3] The pact communique endorsed the following goals: a test ban leading to nuclear disarmament and prevention of a space arms race; abolition of chemical and other mass destruction weapons; reduction of conventional arms in Europe to preclude sudden attack or offensive operations; creation of nuclear- and chemical-free zones; strict verification measures, including on-site inspection; and elimination of force asymmetries paving the way to the dissolution of NATO and the Warsaw Pact. Stating that the nuclear age makes war and power politics too dangerous, the pact document professed a purely defensive posture and recommended consultations with NATO on their respective doctrines.

These ideas were reaffirmed in a speech by Defense Minister Dimitri Yazov in July 1987.[4] Yazov defined "defense sufficiency" as a level of nuclear forces able to inflict unacceptable retaliation and a level of conventional forces to ensure defense only. Yazov proposed a number of arms control measures, including a reduction of forces to a minimum level where NATO and the Warsaw Pact meet, a withdrawal of offensive arms from this zone, and creation of a 300-kilometer nuclear-free zone along with unspecified chemical-free zones. In a world that admits no alternative to "peaceful coexistence," Yazov added, nations must extend reciprocal consideration of their security interests.

Gorbachev's scheme contains less than meets the eye, for it merely carries to utopian lengths the obligations and structure of collective security already embodied in the U.N. Charter. International security would be immeasurably enhanced if the Soviets would only live up to their U.N. and other (such as Yalta, Helsinki, and arms control) obligations. At Potsdam in 1986, Gorbachev praised the agreements made there and at Yalta by Allied leaders a generation ago for having created "the possibility of a development of free and democratic states in Europe" as well as forty years of peace.[5] But the fact is that the promises of Yalta were betrayed, and the continued division of Europe with its Eastern half under Soviet occupation remains the principal threat to peace and security on that continent. That is why President Reagan has stated, "The reason Yalta remains important is that the freedom of Europe is unfinished business."[6]

Similarly, over the last several years five administration reports and a study by an independent presidential advisory committee have extensively documented the Soviet record of non-compliance with arms control treaties. Beyond an array of breaches of SALT and non-SALT treaties, the gravest violations stand as an indictment of the centerpiece of arms control, the 1972 ABM Treaty. The large, phased-array radar at Krasnoyarsk, in addition to a number of other ABM-related activities, suggest that the USSR may be preparing an ABM defense of its national territory. These developments, if unanswered by the United States, hold dire implications for the strategic balance and international security. We do not, then, need new systems and agreements like Gorbachev's grandiose scheme, only compliance with old ones.

Furthermore, if Gorbachev is serious about the political resolution of disputes, non-interference, and human rights, he could withdraw his own and his proxy forces from an extended, decrepit empire. To take a few examples,[7] while the U.S. Congress haggled over whether to send token military support or Band-Aids (or nothing) to the Nicaraguan Contras, in 1986 Managua received $500 million in economic aid from the East bloc and $600 million in military equipment, over five times the amount for all of 1985. Since 1960, Cuba has received about $9 billion in military aid, and during the 1980s the USSR gave Cuba over $4 billion per year in economic aid and subsidies. In return for use of the largest naval base outside the USSR at Cam Ranh Bay, since 1978 Hanoi has received almost $9 billion in military and $8 billion in economic assistance. In 1986 the Marxist-government of Angola received $1 billion in military aid, marking a 50 percent increase over the previous year and bringing total Soviet military assistance to $4 billion in the past decade. UNITA's 63,000 troops face 140,000 government troops backed by 36,000 Cuban military surrogates together with Soviet and East bloc advisers. By contrast, in 1986 UNITA received $15 million in U.S. military aid. In sub-Saharan Africa, over $4 billion in military hardware along with substantial logistics support and 1,700 Soviet military advisers have given Ethiopia the largest army in the region. Over the last ten years, Soviet aid to Ethiopia has been ten times greater than that provided by the United States to the neighboring nations of Kenya, Sudan, Somalia and Djibouti.

As of this writing, due in large measure to U.S. support for the *mujahideen,* Moscow has begun to withdraw its troops from Afghanistan, but in view of the fact that the United States spends less than $1 billion a year in support for all anti-communist resistance movements, for a modestly enhanced investment the United States could encourage Gorbachev to follow suit elsewhere. A low-cost, low-risk strategy for the West could assist Gorbachev in divesting the USSR of its imperial burden in other places such as Angola, Ethiopia, Mozambique, South Yemen, Kampuchea, Laos, and Nicaragua. Gorbachev could also demonstrate his "new thinking" by abolishing the Soviet forced labor system and releasing his Helsinki and psychiatric watch groups from prison and psychiatric hospitals, allowing Solidarity to organize in Poland, and freeing his captive East European population. But if Gorbachev's utopian plan to attain mankind's "immortality" through lasting peace on earth is implausible, we must take its strategic aims seriously.

Several critical objectives propel Gorbachev's propaganda campaign. First, Gorbachev needs a respite from Western military competition in order to "restructure" the USSR's stagnant, backward economy. His goal of strengthening, not dismantling, a Leninist regime will not promote international security and peace, but the breathing space required for the Soviet Union to remain a superpower in the twenty-first century can only be obtained by sapping Western vigilance and resolve.

Gorbachev's charm offensive has achieved remarkable success in disarming Western leaders. At a Kremlin banquet for French President Francois Mitterrand during a four-day visit in July 1986, Gorbachev said that Europe should not allow itself to be treated as a "theater of operations," but should set an example of "peaceful coexistence."[8] The general secretary exhorted Europe to pursue its own interests and upheld the Gaullist vision of a Europe stretching "from the Atlantic to the Urals" that would rid itself of "the explosive burden of armaments."[9] Gorbachev presented his version of a European third force:

> Everybody sees that Europeans are tired of nerve-wracking confrontations and tension . . . They need the air of détente. Europe's economic and political potential is large enough for it to speak more definitely and confidently on its own behalf, to press for progress at all the ongoing talks.[10]

Mitterrand avoided criticizing the Soviet Union as he did in his June 1984 visit, when he defended Andrei Sakharov at a Kremlin reception. "Europe," he agreed with Gorbachev, "must again become the master of its own destiny."[11] Mitterrand observed that Franco-Russian relations extended back ten centuries and described their futures as "complementary." Courted and cajoled as a major world leader, Mitterrand later told aides he was "overtaken" by his host in enthusiasm for Europe and praised Gorbachev as a "man of his time" with whom the West could do business.[12]

Within two weeks after the signing of the INF Treaty at the December 1987 Washington summit, Christian Social Union leader Franz-Josef Strauss flew to Moscow for talks with Gorbachev and returned proclaiming, "We have nothing to fear from the Soviet Union. The postwar period is over. A new era has started."[13] In February 1988, Lothar Spaeth, deputy chairman of Chancellor Helmut Kohl's Christian Democratic Party, traveled to Moscow to plan closer trade relations. Spaeth assured Gorbachev "that the government and political forces of West Germany support this intensification and long for it,"[14] and he criticized restraints on the export of Western technology to the USSR, vowing that such restrictions would not impede German-Soviet cooperation.

The amiable Gorbachev even seems to have charmed the "Iron Lady" of Great Britain, Prime Minister Margaret Thatcher. During his journey to Britain in late 1984, before Gorbachev became general secretary, Thatcher called him a man "we can do business with," and she now lauds his reforms as benefiting not only the Soviet Union, but the world. In an interview before the May 1988 Moscow summit, Thatcher expressed a desire to help Gorbachev usher in a "new era" by supporting his reforms: "I think you need to think very much, 'Now, how can we reciprocate?' because bearing in mind always that the reason which I have welcomed these things so much is that I do see a new era opening up if they succeed."[15]

Greeting crowds of Soviet citizens during the Moscow summit, a euphoric President Reagan hailed changes in the Soviet Union as "this Moscow spring" and credited Gorbachev's reform program as leading to "a new world of reconciliation, friendship and peace."[16] In an emotional farewell where he declared the Cold War over, the president stated that he and his "friend" Gorbachev "slayed a few dragons" as allies in the common struggle against "threats to peace and to liberty."[17] Gorbachev concurred that the four summits had "dealt a blow to the foundations of the Cold War."[18] In a speech at the Royal Institute of International Affairs in London on his way home, the president recommended Western assistance to Gorbachev in bringing about an age of "lasting change in the Soviet Union." Reflecting on Soviet strides toward democratic reform and his stroll with Gorbachev on Red Square, the president thought "all of this is cause for shaking the head in wonder."[19]

The second strategic objective of Gorbachev's "new thinking" is to obtain the Western and Japanese trade, credit, and technology without which he cannot accomplish his "restructuring" (perestroika). Gorbachev's ambitious reform program cannot succeed within the limits of socialism and of a people lacking historical experience with limited government, individual rights and personal initiative indispensable to economic progress. To acquire capitalist assistance, therefore, Gorbachev must attempt to dispel the "enemy image" of the USSR. During the Washington and Moscow summits, Gorbachev assiduously solicited American economic support. In Washington he spoke to a group of seventy top business executives, urging them to pressure their government to repeal trade restrictions and grant the Soviet Union most-favored-nation status. "You can't," he asserted, "conduct a political dialogue without strengthening economic ties."[20] American industrialist Armand Hammer termed the summit "a great beginning" and predicted that the INF Treaty "sets the stage for improvements in economic relations to come."[21] At the Moscow meeting, the Tass news agency cited Gorbachev as criticizing the president and Congress for erecting "logjams in the way of healthy economic cooperation" and reminding readers that Reagan had agreed to seek improvement in this area as well." Closer economic ties, he claimed, would establish "greater dependence" between the two countries and promote "predictability in politics."[22] During a post-summit news conference, Gorbachev condemned "intimidation" of American "business circles . . . in favor of cooperation" and denounced the Jackson-Vanik amendment as the dead hanging on "our coattails." He insisted that the amendment, passed in a totally different world, was out of touch with "present-day realities."[23]

It appears that Gorbachev's campaign has begun to bear fruit. In November 1987 Hammer's Occidental Petroleum Corporation announced a joint venture with Soviet oil producers and Japanese and Italian firms to build a chemical complex to produce sulfur, polypropylene, and polyethylene from oil and gas fields in the Caspian Sea. The $6 billion enterprise represents the largest Western/Soviet joint venture on record. During the summit in Washington the following month a delegation from the National Academy of Sciences met with Soviet officials and scientists, promising to furnish advice on how to install more than one million computers in Soviet classrooms by the early 1990s and to explore other projects with the Soviets.

Also during the summit Commerce Secretary C. William Verity, formerly chairman of Armco, Inc., met privately at the Soviet Embassy with Gorbachev and other Soviet officials and businessmen and at the Commerce Department with Yuri Kamentsev, deputy chairman of the Soviet Council of Ministers in charge of banking and joint ventures. Details of these meetings to discuss joint venture possibilities were never revealed. Present as well at the embassy were James H. Giffen, chairman of the U.S.-U.S.S.R. Trade and Economic Council, and co-chairman Dwayne Andreas. A declassified State Department report recently identified at least one-third of the Soviet members of the council as known or suspected KGB agents. Giffen informed NBC's "Today" show that he had a "very good conversation" with Gorbachev about the future of U.S.-Soviet trade; asked if the United States wanted the Soviet Union to become an economic superpower, he replied, "Yes, we do."[24] Verity, a friend of Hammer and co-chairman of the council from 1977–1984, told reporters that he believes in "building bridges" to the Soviet Union through trade. As he put it "It's the old Yankee clipper ship all over again."[25]

Along with increased trade, Gorbachev hoped to obtain expanded access to U.S. technology and bank loans and to cultivate cordial relations with Western financial institutions—the International Monetary Fund (IMF), World Bank, and General Agreement on Trade and Tariffs (GATT)—that the Soviets would like to join. From 1984–86, Moscow's debt to the West rose from $21 to $38 billion, and the Eastern bloc as a whole owes the West about $127 billion, up 55 percent since 1985. Approximately 80 percent of Western loans are "untied," that is, not limited to a specific trade transaction or project and hence available to use as the borrower wishes. At least ten American banks, including First Chicago, Citibank, Morgan Guaranty, and Manufacturers' Hanover Bank of America, supply untied loans to the Soviet bloc.

In April 1988, prior to the Moscow summit, Verity led a U.S. delegation of five hundred business executives to Moscow for the tenth meeting of the U.S.-U.S.S.R. Commercial Commission, an organization established in 1972 during the first era of détente. The contingent went to Moscow to form high-level working groups to expand exchanges in five areas—food processing, energy, construction equipment, medical products, and the services sector. By 1987, the volume of U.S.-Soviet trade had fallen to $2 billion from a level of $4.5 billion in 1979, and Verity would like to enlarge that amount to $5 to $10 billion annually. Under the chairmanship of Giffen, seven major U.S. corporations (Archer Daniels Midland, Chevron, Eastman Kodak, Johnson & Johnson, Ford, Mercator Corp., and R. J. R. Nabisco) formed the American Trade Consortium to promote a series of joint ventures. Said Giffen, "This is not aid, this is trade . . . What we're after is profit."[26] Hammer unveiled a plan to build two plastics factories in the Ukraine in a $200 million joint venture. Earlier, Honeywell, Inc. announced a project to supply automated production controls for Soviet fertilizer factories, and Combustion Engineering, Inc. proposed a project to develop automated control systems for Soviet oil refining and petrochemical plants.

The Commerce Department professed an interest only in nonstrategic trade, but one aim of the trip was to offer American help to the Soviet oil and gas industry. In a May 6, 1988, letter to Robert E. Howson, president of McDermott International in Louisiana, Verity acknowledged that a purpose of the trip was to eliminate obstacles to trade in the oil and gas industry. In the letter Verity said that he interceded with Soviet Premier Nikolai Ryzhkov to approve a McDermott proposal for a joint venture to drill for oil and natural gas off the coast of the Soviet-controlled island of Sakhalin near the four northern Japanese islands annexed by the Soviets as the close of World War II. This deal would run counter to established U.S. policy of discouraging Japanese participation in joint ventures with Moscow to develop the Sakhalin oil and gas fields. The Verity deal contradicting U.S. policy and undercutting Japan was reportedly not cleared in advance with the Departments of State, Defense, or Energy.[27]

The allies have eagerly followed the example of the Reagan administration in inaugurating a second era of détente. At their June economic summit in Toronto the leaders of the seven major industrial democracies acclaimed Soviet reforms and welcomed expanded East/West commerce. The previous year they had avoided explicit mention of increased trade in deference to Reagan, but they now took "positive note" of the Kremlin's desire to end its economic isolation and proclaimed that expanded economic relations can "serve our common interests."[28] West German Chancellor Kohl was delighted at the prospect of new openings to the East, and Assistant Secretary of State Rozanne Ridgway said a "new atmosphere" provides opportunities for American commercial interests.[29]

Following the Toronto meeting, the twelve-nation European Community (EC) and the East European economic organization COMECON (Council for Mutual Economic Assistance) ended thirty-one years of hostility with a declaration of mutual recognition unlocking the door to new East/West trade agreements. "We have embarked on a new chapter in the history of postwar Europe,"[30] affirmed West German Foreign Minister Hans-Dietrich Genscher upon signing the declaration in Luxembourg. In the wake of the agreement, Soviet bloc countries rushed to negotiate trade compacts with the EC to obtain Western technology and establish joint ventures. Czechoslovakia and Romania negotiated or extended agreements, and talks began with Poland and Bulgaria. An April U.N. report revealed that new joint ventures with the East bloc rose from 75 to 91 in 1986–87 for a total of 166 and that the total of pledged foreign investment stood at $500 million. West German companies led with 36 joint ventures, followed by Austria with 30 and the United States with 17. Finally, in August, spurred by the farm vote in the autumn election as well as by the spirit of détente, the Reagan administration announced completion of a new grain accord with the Soviet Union extending the existing agreement that expired September 30 another five years and raising Soviet purchases beyond the annual minimum of nine million metric tons in the former pact.

When Gorbachev wined and dined Verity's business entourage at a lavish Kremlin dinner last April, he declared that a "window of hope" in U.S.-Soviet relations had opened, and he lobbied his audience for expanded trade, especially in high technology. Doubtless recalling Lenin's prediction that the bourgeoisie would supply the rope with which to hang itself, Gorbachev entreated his guests, "New thinking should at long last enter the sphere of economic relations."[31] The Free World, however, has no interest in building a more powerful and efficient Leninist regime; if we wish to see genuine change in the Soviet Union, we will let Moscow confront its own internal problems. To the extent that Western economic assistance relieves the Kremlin's domestic crisis, it allows Soviet rulers to divert resources to the military sector and to escape the economic and political changes that would foster openness and pluralism.

A third strategic aim behind Gorbachev's "new thinking" derives from the Kremlin's long-standing arms control objective of denuclearizing the West and its overriding post-1945 goal of disengaging the United States from Europe. The abiding Soviet goal of global hegemony can be achieved by uncoupling the Atlantic alliance and outflanking the United States in the Third World; without its trans-Atlantic mooring Europe would inevitably fall under Moscow's sway, and Japan and China would then soon come to terms with the new correlation of forces. Gorbachev realizes that Leonid Brezhnev's tactics in the 1970s, nuclear intimidation and military adventurism, finally alarmed the West and provoked it to react. Gorbachev, therefore, has replaced crude coercion with a more subtle tactic of seduction.

To its traditional military muscle in Asia, Moscow has added diplomatic and economic initiatives, although it has not abandoned the instrument of military force. Moscow's fifty-five divisions deployed in the Far East double the number of forces it had there twenty years ago. Its airpower has quadrupled since 1978, and today one-third of its naval aviation is located in the region. The largest of its four fleets, the Soviet Pacific fleet, has grown 80 percent in size since the mid-1960s and today possesses a modern submarine force of 120 submarines in the Pacific. The ratio of Soviet to U.S. forces in the region is 20 to 1 in ground forces, 1.5 to 1 in air forces, 2 to 1 in submarines, and 4 to 1 in total naval forces. The U.S. commander in the Pacific, Adm. Ronald Hays, has stated that the Soviets are building a four-million-gallon fuel storage facility at Cam Ranh Bay in Vietnam to support naval and air forces operating out of that base, and the completion of a seventh pier at the installation increases dock space by 20 percent.[32] A continuing Soviet military buildup, therefore, has not been replaced but rather supplemented by politico-economic overtures.

Affirming that "the Soviet Union is also an Asian and Pacific country," Gorbachev launched his "new Asian policy" in a speech at Vladivostok in July 1986, advocating closer political and economic ties with Pacific-Asian countries, particularly Japan and China.[33] Since Vladivostok, Moscow has sought improved relations with both nations together with Thailand, Indonesia, and Australia and would like to gain membership in the Asian Development Bank. Last March the newly created Soviet National Committee for Asia-Pacific Economic Cooperation was placed under the leadership of Yevgeniy Primakov, director of the Institute of World Economics and International Affairs at the USSR Academy of Sciences.

Gorbachev amplified his "new Asian policy" in a September 1988 speech in the Siberian city of Krasnoyarsk.[34] In addition to offering to place the Krasnoyarsk radar complex under international control for space exploration, he proposed: a withdrawal of Soviet naval forces from Cam Ranh Bay in exchange for U.S. relinquishment of its Philippine bases; establishment of a regional security forum and multilateral talks to reduce tensions; normalization of relations with Japan; development of economic relations with South Korea; negotiations to limit naval activities in the Pacific and a "zone of peace" in the Indian Ocean; and a freeze on the number of Soviet nuclear weapons in the region. The general secretary reiterated his bid for a Sino-Soviet summit, saying Moscow stood ready to begin preparation for a meeting "without delay."

Thus far Gorbachev's rapprochement with China and Japan has proceeded slowly. The Chinese remain skeptical of any basic change in Moscow's Asian policy and are disturbed over the growing Soviet military threat; relations have thawed somewhat, but the Sino-Soviet rivalry will most likely intensify in the long run as China grows stronger. Nevertheless, over the past two years the Soviets and Chinese have made perceptible progress toward removing China's "three obstacles" to normal relations: Sino-Soviet border disputes, the Soviet presence in Afghanistan, and the Vietnamese occupation of Cambodia. In the spring 1987, the Soviet new agency Tass announced the departure of a Soviet motorized division from Mongolia, and Soviet forces have begun to withdraw from Afghanistan. Before the Moscow summit Soviet Deputy Foreign Minister Igor Rogachev commended Vietnam's plan to withdraw 50,000 troops from Cambodia as the first step toward evacuation of all troops by 1990. In August Rogachev and senior Soviet and Chinese officials met in Beijing to hasten a resolution of the Cambodian issue. On the occasion of his Krasnoyarsk speech Gorbachev addressed the third "obstacle," Cambodia, encouraging direct talks on the issue between Hanoi and Beijing. The previous week Chinese Premier Li Peng acknowledged that a Sino-Soviet summit, which has not been held since 1959, could occur if the two sides reached a consensus on Cambodia, and he stated that China "would like very much to normalize relations"[35] with Moscow.

On the other hand, Chinese leaders take a sober view of the Soviet threat, warning Philippine President Corazon Aquino on a visit to Beijing last spring of the Soviet menace to Southeast Asia. The Aquino government, until recently at an impasse with the United States over its Philippine bases, prefers to dismiss a Soviet threat. However, the Chinese Foreign Ministry presented her with an assessment of the Soviet buildup at Cam Ranh Bay prepared by the Shanghai Institute of International Studies. The paper concluded that "this unprovoked military escalation radically altered the region's strategic balance," and it went on to caution that "Moscow is increasingly conducting espionage and other activities in the region."[36]

Without Soviet concession on the Northern Islands it seized at the end of World War II, relations with Japan are unlikely to change appreciably. The Japanese Foreign Ministry responded coolly to Gorbachev's Asian peace plan at Krasnoyarsk, labeling it "basically a repetition" of earlier proposals. Recently, the Soviets, through an unofficial third party in Paris, reportedly sounded out Japan on the Northern Islands dispute, suggesting a leasing arrangement for the four islands plus part of Sakhalin to which Japan does not lay territorial claim. The Soviets may have hoped to prepare the groundwork for a visit by Foreign Minister Eduard Shevardnadze to Japan later in the year, but a Japanese Foreign Ministry spokesman repudiated the offer as "totally unacceptable. It doesn't show any change in their position that these four islands belong to them."[37]

Like Beijing, Tokyo is wary of Soviet intentions. Before he left office Prime Minister Yasuhiro Nakasone lifted the ceiling limiting Japanese defense spending to 1 percent of GNP, and in March 1988 Prime Minister Noboru Takeshita told graduating military cadets at the National Defense Academy that Japan's military power should match its economic strength. At the same time Tsutomu Kawara, director general of Japan's Defense Agency, testified to a Diet committee considering defense legislation that the Soviet Union had increased its military power in the Pacific. His agency issued a report documenting the increase in Soviet naval, ground, and air forces in the region, and Kawara pointed out: "The latent threat to Japan has increased owing to the remarkable buildup of Soviet forces in the Far East in terms of both quality and quantity and the intensification of related activities."[38]

In view of China's and Japan's skepticism about Gorbachev's designs, Moscow is more apt to make greater inroads among the small island-states of the Pacific where economic instability, residual anti-colonialism, and anti-nuclear sentiment offer targets for exploitation. Among these states, Soviet aid and trade overtures are intended to deny the United States access to ports and airports, that is, to neutralize the "ANZUS lake."

Trade bids have been made to Fiji, and in 1986 Moscow offered aid to Papua New Guinea and several other states; personal contacts and exchanges have increased throughout the region. In 1986 the Soviets signed the South Pacific Nuclear Free Zone Treaty (SPNFZ), and in early 1988 Shevardnadze visited Fiji,

Australia, and New Zealand, stressing his country's desire for trade and a nuclear-free South Pacific. A 1985 fishing pact with Kiribati was replaced by a 1987 agreement with Vanuatu, an island close to French New Caledonia and Australia, giving the Soviets fishing rights along with the use of three ports and shore facilities. As Australian Foreign Minister Bill Hayden has noted, there is "evidence that when they get on the ground they engage in other activities that are unrelated to commercial matters."[39]

Elsewhere in the Third World Gorbachev has courted major, non-socialist nations instead of fomenting new national liberation movements. The Soviets have not acquired costly, new dependencies lately, but as the figures cited earlier attest, they have not cut support to former clients. This continuity of policy is further illustrated in the Middle East, where Moscow has sent new weapons to Libya and Syria, including SA-5 missiles and MiG-25 fighters. The new diplomatic tack, however, can be seen in Latin America, where Moscow has endeavored to broaden commercial and diplomatic relations. In Peru the Soviets have offered to buy fishing and commercial vessels along with personal computers. Cultural and economic accords have been signed with Brazil and Uruguay, and in 1986 the USSR concluded its first major fishing agreement with Argentina. Moscow has offered to sell Brazil a launching vehicle to boost a Brazilian satellite into space and has agreed to a joint venture to produce ferromanganese along with cooperation in other areas such as energy and fishing. The Soviets have also negotiated to buy optical fibers from Brazil and have shown keen interest in computers and computer software.

In the West, Gorbachev has conducted a charm offensive and has manipulated arms control to use anti-nuclear and neutralist sentiment to drive a wedge in the Western alliance. It would be folly to believe, however, that Gorbachev intends to forfeit Soviet military, especially nuclear, might, which alone makes the USSR a superpower; without that power the level of its economy and society would place the Soviet Union in the ranks of Third World countries. Gorbachev has put to effective use Lenin's advice to Foreign Minister Chicherin before the 1922 Genoa Conference: "Both you and I have fought against pacifism as a program for a revolutionary proletarian party. This is obvious. But where, when and who denied utilization of pacifists by this party in order to demoralize the enemy, the bourgeoisie?"[40]

Finally, but far from least, Gorbachev's "new thinking" about international security is designed to fuel pressure against the American program he most fears, SDI. Gorbachev does not lose a wink of sleep over being hit by what he calls "space-strike weapons;" rather, he is alarmed by the prospect of losing his nuclear leverage and by the immense potential that SDI research and development hold for conventional military applications as well as for scientific and economic advances. Gorbachev worries about being left in the dust technologically. That is why his interest in economic reform serves Soviet military interests.

According to a CIA/DIA report delivered to Congress in April 1988, *per-*

estroika badly foundered in 1987, registering less than 1 percent growth in GNP and showing no increase at all in the machine-building sector, the key to Gorbachev's modernization drive. Output in that sector was supposed to rise 43 percent between 1986 and 1990, with even higher targets in the area of high-technology equipment. Defense procurement grew 3 percent in 1987, but Gorbachev has increasingly importuned the military to support his modernization program. Defense spending still accounts for 15–17 percent of the GNP and consumes an inordinately large share of the machine-building sector and the highest quality materials. Defense industrial participation in civilian modernization would not curtail production in the short term, due to extensive military modernization in the 1970s, but after the early 1990s defense planners will need to invest in the next generation of weapons. The report observed, therefore, that "one way to shift resources from the defense sector and head off criticism would be to reach arms control accords that would slow the pace of US weapons programs, especially SDI."[41] Through the arms control process Gorbachev hopes to avoid new military expenditures, constrain Western force modernization, accelerate Soviet industrial modernization, and "expand commercial ties with the West." In his modernization effort, the report concluded, Gorbachev will seek relief from East Europe and above all the West, whose products will become indispensable, "if this year's economic performance repeats last year's."[42]

It is small wonder, then, that Gorbachev heartily endorses "new thinking" in East-West trade relations, primarily in the transfer of high technology. The importation of Western high technology and the development of modern information technology constitute the critical element of Gorbachev's economic reform program. The link between advanced information technology and the effectiveness of all weapons, particularly strategic defense, was noted by Soviet General Staff spokesman Yuri Lebedev in July 1987:

> At the present stage of the military-technological revolution, the progress in information technology . . . begins to play a decisive role and increases by many times the combat effectiveness of all weapons. There is a direct interconnection between space militarization and the "informatization" of the arms race.[43]

In October 1986, former Chief of the General Staff Nikolai Ogarkov, a leading proponent of the protracted conventional war option that has figured prominently in Soviet military thought since Brezhnev's 1977 speech in Tula, wrote an article published by Novosti news service, stressing the importance of more technically sophisticated conventional weapons. The chief factor in the combat readiness of the arms forces, he maintained, "lies in the high level of their technical equipment." Ogarkov's conventional emphasis coincides with Gorbachev's anti-nuclear campaign and points to the convergence of economic and military modernization. "The level of the socialist economy's development reached at the present," he argued, "allows for the successful solution of the most complicated technical defense tasks."[44]

Shortly afterwards in the *New Times,* Deputy Minister of Defense for Armaments Vitaly Shabanov wrote that qualitative improvements in conventional weapons have given them "the level of effectiveness of tactical nuclear arms" and that due to the West's military buildup the Soviet Union and its allies must "develop and manufacture the necessary quantities of all modern types of conventional weapons."[45] In an August 1987 article in the *Military Herald* Doctor of Technical Sciences Col. B. Makarenko again discussed the need for technologically advanced weapons and observed that, in perfecting the means of command and control, the solution depends on the "automation of command and control of troops on the basis of modern computer technology and communications equipment."[46] Finally, in a November 1986 article in *Communist of the Armed Forces,* Col. V. Bondarenko underscored Ogarkov's focus on the military applications of advanced technology and illustrated how Soviet military interests are congruent with *perestroika,* which he supported for bringing scientific-technical innovation into industrial production. Scientific-technical progress, Bondarenko wrote, marked the "decisive" factor in military affairs, thus making technological innovation in industry a prerequisite for military power. The next stage in military technology involves "the perfecting of conventional weapons" whose enhanced automation and precision can make them comparable to nuclear missiles.[47]

As an avowed Leninist, Gorbachev understands that politics in a continuation of war by other means, and not since Lenin has the West faced such an adroit practitioner of strategic maneuver and tacking. Gorbachev's widely touted "new thinking" about world politics attempts to achieve certain long-standing Soviet goals as well as to address current domestic exigencies. At the 1986 27th Party Congress he candidly acknowledged the need for the tactical dexterity he has so skillfully demonstrated in international affairs. "Continuity in foreign policy," he explained, "has nothing in common with the simple repetition of the past, especially as far as approaches to accumulated problems are concerned . . . What is required is firmness in defending principles and positions coupled with tactical flexibility."[48] Western citizens should not mistake his objectives or underestimate the man who, Andrei Gromyko said, has "steel teeth." At this point it remains an open question whether Western avarice and wishfulness will come to the rescue of a regime bankrupt at its Leninist foundation.

NOTES

1. Mikhail S. Gorbachev, "The Reality and Guarantees of a Secure World," *FBIS Daily Report: Soviet Union* (September 17, 1987), pp. 23–28.
2. *FBIS, Daily Report: Soviet Union* (October 2, 1987), pp. 27–42.

3. "On the Military Doctrine of the Warsaw Pact Member States," cited in *Strategic Review* 15 (Summer 1987), pp. 90–92.

4. Gen. D. T. Yazov. "The Military Doctrine of the Warsaw Pact Is the Doctrine of the Defense of Peace and Socialism." FBIS Daily Report: Soviet Union (July 27, 1987). pp. BB1–BB7.

5. *Washington Post*, April 21, 1986, p. A19.

6. Statement by the President, February 5, 1985 (White House: Office of the Press Secretary).

7. See *Soviet Military Power* (Washington, D.C.: U.S. Government Printing Office, 1987). pp. 134–143.

8. *New York Times*, July 8, 1986, p. A9.

9. *Ibid.*

10. *Ibid.*

11. *Washington Post*, July 8, 1986, p.A9.

12. *Washington Post*, July 14, 1986, p. A13.

13. *Washington Times*, May 11, 1988, p. 9.

14. *Ibid.*

15. *Washington Post*, May 26, 1988, p. A16.

16. *Washington Post*, June 1, 1988, p. A1.

17. *Washington Post*, June 3, 1988, p. A1.

18. *Ibid.*, p. A26.

19. *Washington Post*, June 4, 1988, p. A18.

20. *Washington Post*, December 11, 1987, p. A31.

21. *Ibid.*

22. *Washington Times*, June 1, 1988, p. B5.

23. *Washington Post*, June 2, 1988, p. A27.

24. *Washington Times*, December 22, 1987, p. 3.

25. *Ibid.*

26. *Washington Post*, April 14, 1988, p. A26.

27. *National Security Record*, Heritage Foundation (June, 1988), p. 5.

28. *Washington Post*, June 21, 1988, p. A1.

29. *Ibid*, p. A14.

30. *Washington Post*, June 16, 1988, p. A22.

31. *Washington Post*, April 14, 1988, p. A26.

32. See *Omaha World-Herald*, September 18, 1987, p. 5; *Soviet Military Power*, p. 137.

33. *FBIS Daily Report: Soviet Union* (July 29, 1986), pp. R1–R20.

34. *FBIS Daily Report: Soviet Union* (September 20, 1988), pp. 29–41.

35. *Wall Street Journal*, September 19, 1988, p. 20.

36. *Washington Times*, April 15, 1988, p. 9.

37. *Wall Street Journal*, September 20, 1988, p. 32.

38. *Washington Times*, March 23, 1988, p. 18.

39. *Washington Times*, June 23, 1987, p. 18.

40. Quoted in *The Philosophical Heritage of V. I. Lenin and Problems of Contemporary War* (Washington, DC: U.S. Government Printing Office, 1972), vol. 5, *Soviet Military Thought*, p. 37.

41. "Gorbachev's Economic Program: Problems Emerge," A Report by the Central Intelligence Agency and the Defense Intelligence Agency, presented to the Subcommittee on National Security Economics of the Joint Economic Committee, April 13, 1988, pp. 33, 35.

42. *Ibid.*, p. 42.

43. Quoted in James M. McConnell, "SDI, the Soviet Investment Debate and Soviet Military Policy," *Strategic Review* 16 (Winter 1988), p. 50.

44. *Washington Post,* October 28, 1986, p. A21.
45. Quoted in *Strategic Review* 15 (Winter 1987), pp. 88, 89.
46. Quoted in *Strategic Review* 16 (Winter 1988), p. 87.
47. Quoted in *Strategic Review* 15 (Winter 1987), pp. 86–87.
48. Quoted in Dimitri K. Simes, "Gorbachev: A New Foreign Policy?" *Foreign Affairs* 65 (America and the World 1986), p. 491.

16

Changing Soviet Elite Views on the International System and Soviet Foreign Policy*

Allen Lynch

> It seems that I have left out a section of Lenin's fundamental thoughts to the program and they are worth recalling.
>
> —Aside by Mikhail Gorbachev in his political report to the twenty-seventh CPSU Party Congress, February 25, 1986

INTRODUCTION

The profound changes that the political leadership of Mikhail Gorbachev has introduced and induced, into the conduct of Soviet foreign relations, and by consequence in the entire fabric of East-West relations, has shaken the world and compelled its attention. Until the release of Eastern Europe from Communist rule in the summer and fall of 1989, however, many in the West held back from conceding the "revolution" in Soviet foreign policy that some had identified, arguing, as did the CIA's deputy director in October 1988 that "[i]n foreign policy, the new [Soviet] leadership has retained long-term objectives and strategies. . . . The Party leadership remains committed to the long-term objective of establishing the USSR as the dominant world power."[1] However, one could understandably see not merely the Soviet abandonment of its comrades in

*Copyright © 1991 by Allen Lynch

385

Eastern Europe but its remarkable acquiescence at the prospect of German unity, or West German and American terms, as a simple reflection of the political collapse of Russia in Europe. While the former thesis hardly seems credible any longer in light of the CPSU's renunciation of its assumed "leading role" in Soviet society in February 1990, the latter view bears more scrutiny. How to interpret Soviet foreign policy conduct depends in substantial measure on how Soviet observers—politicians and increasingly policy-oriented analysts and advisers—are thinking about the foundations and direction of Soviet foreign policy and its relationship to the international environment which inevitably shapes Soviet policy choices. If we are to understand adequately the reasons for Soviet foreign policy conduct, we need to address the analytical and conceptual foundations of that policy. This is particularly true if one is interested in the question of the range of choice and change in future Soviet foreign policy behavior. Our understanding of the direction of Soviet foreign policy, especially in the current exceptionally fluid period in Soviet domestic political life, depends critically on whether or not there is general support within important elite circles for the reevaluation of the USSR's international role that has taken place under Gorbachev. Understanding the cognitive world of the Soviet elite as applied to Soviet foreign policy should they occupy a prominent place in our studies of Soviet foreign relations. As Bertil Nygren, a Swedish Sovietologist, has written:

> If observable changes in Soviet foreign policy behave are *not* reflected in cognitive changes, then we should be more careful in our judgments about Gorbachev's policies, or more skeptical about his intentions: either he is not very serious, or he is alone. If on the other hand, important cognitive changes seem to be present, then we should be more prepared to accept observable policy changes as serious and permanent; then we might very well have some "Gorbachevism" or "new thinking" even with Gorbachev.
>
> Thus, the stronger the ideological foundation of the "New Thinking," the greater the probability that it will survive Gorbachev.[2]

One could adduce a variety of powerful political as well as analytical evidence that the foreign policy course that Gorbachev has mapped out is deeply rooted not only in Gorbachev's own political strategy but in the crisis of power and influence in which the USSR finds itself and that Gorbachev has made clear to the Soviet people through the medium of *glasnost'*. The purpose of this chapter, however, is to concentrate on the analytical and intellectual strands of contemporary Soviet foreign policy, as a way of clearing the ground for the broader discussion of Soviet policy and Soviet-American relations to which it stands as antecedent.

The analytical and conceptual context for Gorbachev's international policies cannot be reduced to a new or altered understanding of purely international phenomena, such as the distribution of global power, the impact of nuclear weapons, or the nature of international technological change and economic growth, as important as they have been in reshaping Soviet international perspectives. Clearly, there is an important internal dimension as well, as the possibilities of the Soviet economy constrain the ways in which the USSR interacts with the global environment. Alternatively, one's analysis of the international system is likely to be related in significant ways to one's attitude to the internal distribution of power and resources within the USSR. That is, someone favoring a major decentralization of power and demilitarization (or de-ideologization) of values at home has an interest in depicting, and influencing, a different sort of international political-military order, with a correspondingly different set of threat images, than one who is essentially satisfied with the traditional distribution of Soviet power and resources. Indeed, in the course of the Gorbachev period this relationship between the internal and international dimensions of reform has tended to become explicit, as the argument over domestic reform became couched in polemics over the nature of the external "imperialist" threat and thus of the permissible degree of internal reform. Yet in the pre-Gorbachev period, which for our purposes extends through the Brezhnev period to the later 1950s and which embraces the intellectual origins of the "new political thinking," this external:internal relationship of the foreign policy discussion, while undoubtedly present, was difficult for the outside observer to establish and in practice probably much weaker than at present. This had much to do with the fact, especially since the renewed repression of internal dissent following 1966 and the invasion of Czechoslovakia after 1968, that the Brezhnevian political order had to be taken essentially as a given by Soviet "liberal" elites.[3]

At the same time, Soviet foreign policy analysts were busily attempting to assimilate a series of remarkable international political-military trends that had been set in motion in the postwar world (such as the impact of nuclear weapons; the prosperity, stability, and cohesion of the West; and the emergence of a communist China as the chief foreign policy threat to the USSR) and which did not square easily with the traditional Leninist analysis of imperialism as the wellspring of global conflict.[4] By the mid-1970s foreign policy analysts who have now come to occupy important positions within the Gorbachev "administration," such as Fyodor Burlatsky and Gyorgy Shakhnazarov (one of Gorbachev's personal advisors), were arguing that the influence of "external" factors on socioeconomic systems, including communist ones, "is greater than ever before." By clear implication, the increasing influence of scientific-technological innovation in the military and economic fields on domestic social structures meant that states—including the USSR—must increasingly adapt to the universal demands of what in Soviet parlance was now called the "scientific-technological revolution." Soviet specialists on international relations emphasize the importance of the international milieu, or system, on world politics (as distinct from the Leninist projection of a state's internal system as the key explanatory factor in international relations) by speaking of the "reverse influence" of the system of international relations on, for example, Soviet-American relations.[5] The international-relations texts written in the late 1960s and 1970s reveal little of the substantive relationship to domestic preoccupations, which, judging from the current prominence of many of these authors in the Gorbachev reform effort, must certainly have been strong. The contemporary political visibility of such analysts of the 1970s as Evgenii Primakov (now a candidate member of the Politburo and member of the Presidential Council), Vitalii Zhurkin (director of the newly formed Institute of European Studies), Shakhnazarov, Vladimir Petrovskii (deputy foreign minister), and Burlatskii (prominent political commentator, editor of *Literaturnaya Gazeta* and head of the new semiofficial Human Rights Commission), among others, bears striking witness to the direct link between international analysis and internal reform characteristic of so many in the 1950s generation (the *piatidesiatniki*) who came of political age during the partial but heady and soon-to-be interrupted reforms of Nikita Khrushchev. Nevertheless, it is the absence of any such overt substantive link that characterizes the Soviet international relations literature of the Brezhnev period, which forms the essential context to interpreting Gorbachev's foreign policy course today.[6]

As a frame for the initial discussions of the evolution of Soviet elite views on international relations, and in anticipation of the fuller discussion of Gorbachev's foreign policy outlook to come, the essential elements of the "new political thinking" may be summarized as follows:

1. The near absolute priority of domestic economic and social policy over foreign policy and international commitments.
2. The maintenance of a favorable international environment through a sound and comprehensive political *modus vivendi* with the leading democratic industrial powers, above all the United States.
3. The strict subordination of military-technical and operational criteria to political ones in the formulation and execution of Soviet security policy; this affects both conventional and nuclear arms.
4. The subordination of class/ideological criteria to geopolitical and even internal political ones in the definition of Soviet external interests.
5. Recognition that Soviet interests can only be furthered by coming to terms with a multipolar and interdependent world; in this connection, Soviet security cannot be advanced at the expense of other leading powers, but rather only in collaboration with them.
6. A thoroughgoing reevaluation of Leninist orthodoxy on the wellsprings of international conflict, and thus of the propensity of the United States and other "imperialist" forces to threaten Soviet interests; this is leading to an entirely new concept of international relations and Soviet foreign policy captured under the rubric of the "new political thinking."

This new Soviet philosophy of international relations is associated with such dramatic initiatives as (1) the Soviet adoption of the NATO "zero-zero" position on intermediate-range nuclear missiles, with disproportionate Soviet reductions; (2) acceptance and faithful implementation of the principle of mandatory international on-site inspection in several arms control forums; (3) withdrawal of Soviet troops from Afghanistan; (4) a decided upgrading of Soviet support for UN peacekeeping activities; (5) the unilateral reduction of the Soviet armed forces by

500,000 men and associated offensive equipment, as well as agreement—again unilaterally—to withdraw all Soviet troops from Poland, Hungary, and Czechoslovakia; and (6) finally, acquiescence in the collapse of Communist authority throughout Eastern Europe, leading to the reunification of Germany on West German terms. One might interpret such moves as a remarkable set of tactical adjustments by the Gorbachev leadership in the face of a weak and deteriorating international and internal position, which are designed to come to terms with Soviet weakness yet at the same time attempt to transform through dramatic strokes the security problem facing the USSR. Certainly, there is much to such an interpretation. But the broader meaning of these moves, if they have one, can only properly be addressed in light of the conceptual schema that lies behind them. Understanding that schema requires an analysis of the political and analytical ancestry of the "new political thinking."

This "new political thinking" may be seen as a determined effort by the Gorbachev leadership to redefine conceptually, as well as through a process of political interaction, the nature of the international environment facing the USSR and the range of appropriate Soviet choices in foreign and security policy. This new definition of the international system reflects both a revised evaluation of long-term international political and military trends, which has its roots in the pre-Gorbachev era, and the pressing character of Soviet domestic needs, as Gorbachev searches for ways of limiting the scope of demands placed upon the Soviet system as it proceeds on the path of structural reform—economic and political—at home. At the same time, the "new thinking" is intended to help provide Soviet foreign policy with a more appropriate set of ends and means.

Gorbachev has forged the "new political thinking" by drawing upon the pioneering conceptual work done during the Brezhnev and Andropov periods and adapting it to the basic foreign-policy priorities as determined by the Soviet political leadership. It is important to keep in mind that the "new political thinking" itself is first of all a political rather than an intellectual or conceptual act. It reflects preestablished political priorities of the Gorbachev leadership, which in turn has assiduously coopted strains of thinking—some of it actually new, much of it developed quietly by specialists during the Brezhnev period— that suit its purposes and long-term goals. Partly, this is aimed at making more persuasive, to both foreign and domestic audiences, the new course that Gorbachev has set for himself in foreign affairs. Encouragement of debate is also intended to provoke discussion in normally reticent quarters, such as the military, and thus to raise issues and elicit information that the political leadership requires in making effective national decisions. Furthermore, it is now clear that Gorbachev and his closest colleagues find the world view offered by the new thinkers in many respects a more persuasive interpretation of reality than that bequeathed them by their predecessors. But most of all, the "new political thinking" represents a determined political effort by the Soviet leadership to recast the nature of the threat environment said to be facing (and actually facing) the USSR and thereby to monopolize domestic Soviet discussion of the future military, economic, and political agendas of the Soviet state.[7]

There is a direct link between the revision of fundamental Soviet foreign-policy concepts that took place on the specialist level throughout the Brezhnev period and much of the "new" thinking on international relations expounded by Gorbachev and his associates. Such "new" ideas as the rejection of nuclear war as a conceivable act of policy, the heightened significance attached to political factors in security policy, and increasing recognition of the multipolar and interdependent character of contemporary international relations all find lucid expression by currently influential Soviet policy analysts from the pre-Gorbachev era. Indeed, the emerging Soviet world view represents a synthesis of tendencies present in Soviet policy circles since the Twentieth CPSU Congress in 1956. Clearly, it has been changes in the international system as well as within the Soviet system that have triggered revisions in the formulation of Soviet foreign policy, first on the conceptual level and now in the actual making of policy itself. Since the source for many of these revisions arises from the USSR's external environment i.e., from factors beyond Soviet control, they cannot be interpreted as simple "tactical" adjustments, ready to be reversed at an expedient moment. Instead, they are part and parcel of an ongoing process of adjustment, between both East and West, and thus should be of particular concern to Western analysts and officials at an exceptionally fluid moment in Soviet relations with the outside world.

THE KHRUSHCHEV PERIOD

Most observers, both Soviet and Western, see the year 1956, the year of the Twentieth CPSU Congress and Khrushchev's secret speech denouncing Stalin's crimes against the Communist party, as the critical turning point in Soviet thinking on international relations.[8] Two ideological revisions—concerning the breaking of the "capitalist encirclement" by the Soviet Union and the non-inevitability of general war—were of special significance. They openly suggested, as had been implicit in Stalin's policy of socialism in one country, that henceforth the revolutionary transformation of the world would be effected through international relations, rather than through the class struggle as such.[9] States had now become the formally recognized protagonists in the class conflict. The increased importance that relations among nation-states were held to have for the future of socialism required going beyond the "rather mechanistic [Leninist] transplant of these regarding internal relations and laws of society to external, intersocietal relations."[10] From this date also ensues the proliferation of Soviet research institutes devoted to the systematic study of international relations, a consequence of the transformation of international relations into a legitimate area of inquiry below the apex of the Party-government apparatus.[11]

The key trends emerging from this post-Stalin analysis of international relations included: *first,* the view of international relations as an arena populated by a plurality of corporate actors, with states (as opposed to the two camps) as dominant; *second,* increasing attention paid to the role of political institutions as sources of foreign-policy conduct; third, recognition of the noninevitability of world war in the nuclear age, which tended to undermine the Soviet view of international relations as a closed system, i.e., comprehensible by a general theory that posits a predictable solution at every point. Too many critical elements are in the hands of others; the idea of general war as the handmaiden of revolution is thereby negated. *Finally,* there appeared to be a marked tendency for Soviet perspectives on international relations to converge with much American analysis on (1) the course of international relations as indeterminate; (2) the basic (state) structure of the modern international system; (3) recognition of the role of internal politics in American foreign policy; and (4) preoccupation with the political significance of technology (especially weapons technology) and the constraints thereby imposed on the behavior of states in the atomic age.[12]

BREZHNEV ERA ANALYSIS—THE NATURE OF THE INTERNATIONAL SYSTEM: THE DEIDEOLOGIZATION OF VISION

Soviet international analysis during the Brezhnev era continued these trends and went considerably beyond the "two-camp" concept in identifying the basic structural elements of the international system. The character of relations between and within "camps" of states changed significantly. Though the United States and the Soviet Union continue to occupy the central position on the world stage, each is challenged by forces emanating from other states and from the international system as a whole. These forces, often issuing from states of the same socioeconomic order (or alliance), result in a relative weakening of the position of both the United States and the Soviet Union within their own alliance systems. The economic recovery of Western Europe and Japan after World War II, together with the loosening of tensions between the Soviet and American blocs, had led to an assertion of national claims against American interests on the part of its allies.

Also, "difficulties" within the Soviet alliance system, traceable to the persistence of national interests and uneven levels of economic development, had diminished the coherence of the Soviet bloc and even threw into question some of the "achievements of socialism." This was brought out with particular clarity in the case of the Soviet-led invasion of Czechoslovakia in 1968. The "Brezhnev Doctrine," which asserted that "the entire [socialist] system was responsible for maintenance of socialism in particular countries," in effect acknowledged a structural deficiency in the socialist state system, which required armed Soviet intervention to ensure its survival. This meant an enhanced appreciation of the indeterminacy of the competition between socialism and capitalism and the concession that now socialism, like capitalism, relied on "subjective" political (as opposed to "objective" socioeconomic) forces for its survival. Similarly, the eruption of the Polish crisis in 1980–81 sent shudders throughout the Soviet leadership, as it witnessed the progressive disintegration of the authority of the

Polish Communist party in the face of the mass workers' movement represented by Solidarity. The message was clear for all to see: as Konstantin Chernenko himself observed, the Polish crisis presented an object lesson of what happens when a Communist party loses contact with the masses. Even the Soviet Union might no longer be able to avoid such instabilities, which would strike at the heart of the power and cohesion of the Soviet-style party-states.[13]

The supplanting of classes by states as the chief actors in world politics has consequently been accompanied by a serious erosion in the ability of the two most powerful states to maintain the cohesion of their alliances. The challenge to the American position, however, does not necessarily strengthen the Soviet one, according to many Soviet analysts. Indeed, to the degree that the same processes are at work on both countries, the international standing of the Soviet Union may be considerably weaker. As Evgenii Primakov wrote in the early 1970s, increased multipolarity in the international system enhances the significance of the "uncontrollable" factor in world politics, especially in crisis situations.[14]

What is most important in this emerging Soviet view, which holds despite the apparent resurgence of U.S. power in the Reagan years, is that American power is diminished by all of the salient processes in contemporary international politics. Nationalism, the economic recovery of Europe and Japan, the recovery of the Soviet Union itself and its vastly increased military potential—all permit a Soviet analyst to observe a qualitative transformation in the international position of the United States, which is to say, an important change in the international system itself. Aleksandr Yakovlev, member of the Politburo, chairman of the new Central Committee Commission on International Relations, and one of Gorbachev's most trusted associates, has spoken of the "relative decline" of the United States in world affairs, which he regards as a "normal development."[15] Whereas once, in the 1950s and early 1960, the United States, employing a diplomacy predicated on the swift and credible deployment of armed force, could be said to occupy a "hegemonic" position, this is no longer so. One Soviet historian cites the "widespread recognition" among American scholars that American "hegemony" in Western Europe, as an international relations as a whole, is a thing of the past. Its defeat in Vietnam served to catalyze a number of latent tendencies in the international system that tend to constrain the application of American power.[16] In its search for an end to the Vietnam debacle, the United States approached the Soviet Union and began a process that culminated in American recognition of Soviet strategic nuclear parity. The concomitant political détente signified to America's allies that relations with the Soviet bloc could be cultivated without incurring American displeasure, while their economic recovery gave them the means to move in that direction. Specifically national interests could be furthered, thus reinforcing the loosening of "imperialist" alliances, which to a certain extent had been both cause and consequence of détente.

The irony for the Soviets, and it seems to be well appreciated, is that in attempting to redress the balance of power in the wake of Vietnam, the United

States took measures, specifically the opening to China, which had the effect of creating further and quite serious obstacles to the achievement of Soviet goals. "The very departure of such a country as the People's Republic of China," two Soviet theorists declared, "from the forces of peace to positions relying on the forces of war has damaged the international correlation of forces on issues of war and peace."[17] Furthermore, the loosening of "imperialist" alliances took place within definite limits, so that antagonisms between the United States and its chief allies respected the fundamental distinction between what remained of the capitalist and socialist camps. From this point of view, the United States, though no longer a hegemon, still occupied a powerful, if not quite commanding position in world politics. This was so not because the United States can determine or influence the outcome of every conflict or dispute of importance to it, but rather because, as Kenneth Waltz has noted, the United States remains the only power that by itself can substantially alter the "rules" by which the other states "play the game."[18]

Whence, in the Soviet view, does this special position of the United States derive? It is to be found in the fact that the United States, uniquely, stands astride the two critical axes of world politics: the strategic-military axis, composed of the United States, the Soviet Union, and China; and the political-economic axis, composed of the United States, Western Europe, and Japan.[19] In this economic-military-political constellation, the United States disposes of formidable leverage: first, in its own right, as a great power with great mobility of power; second, as the leader of a great alliance system, which incidentally incorporates the two most powerful agglomerations of economic power in the world, after the United States and the Soviet Union; and third, as the privileged beneficiary of Sino-Soviet tension and the improvement of relations between itself and the People's Republic of China. Furthermore, the United States and its allies stand to profit more than the Soviet bloc from the application of the fruits of the increasingly important scientific-technological revolution.[20]

True, the course of the "national-liberation struggle" in the underdeveloped countries registered some marked successes for "progressive" and even pro-Soviet forces in the late 1970s (e.g., Vietnam, Angola, Ethiopia). Yet the very strength of the "imperialist" economy worldwide provides the capitalist alliance system with "a powerful economic potential" in its policies toward the underdeveloped countries. On the whole, victories for "progressive" forces in the Third World have tended against imperialism rather than directly in favor of the socialist bloc.[21] Indeed, for Soviet policy intellectuals of the late Brezhnev period there is a real question as to the continued validity of the Soviet model for the developing countries.[22] At best, those developing countries that have started on the road of "noncapitalist development" only find the prospects for socialism opening up before them, and they represent a minority still.[23] In short, "imperialism's" ability to influence events in the developing world, though certainly not what it once was, remains quite considerable.[24]

In this light, the CPSU 1986 program declared that multinational corporations,

greatly strengthened as a result of "the capitalist concentration and internationalization of production . . . undermine the sovereignty of young states."[25] This is a
world order from which the Soviet Union is essentially excluded, isolated in its
own ghetto of satellite states. When the Soviet Union does affect their order, it is
often a disturber of that order as a collaborator in it, and it is certainly not,
despite the rhetoric, the "determining" force in international relations. The
successes it has achieved are defensive ones, securing first its right to exist and
then recognition as a great power. At least, this is how it claims to see itself.
When it challenges the existing order it is as an outsider, as one who does not
contribute markedly to defining the rules and, as we have seen, deals from a
weak position in relation to the main axes of world politics. The vision, rooted in
views put forward in the late Brezhnev era, that was increasingly suggested by
Soviet analyses of international relations in the mid-1980s was that of a world
that, from the standpoint of Soviet interests, was beginning to get out of control.[26]
In an international system with Europe as the chief "arena," China as the chief
security challenge, and the United States—occupying a favorable position in
relation to both—as the chief global adversary, it is apparent that the Soviet
Union is faced, and perceives itself as being faced, with an international system
that both defies simple class analysis and is resistant to the easy extension of
Soviet influence.[27]

THE GORBACHEV SYNTHESIS

In many ways, the worldview that Gorbachev and his colleagues have been
formulating represents an explicit crystallization of tendencies that have been
present—albeit often in piecemeal form—in Soviet policy circles since Nikita
Khrushchev's anti-Stalin speech at the Twentieth CPSU Congress in 1956. The
resultant synthesis constitutes a distinctly "Gorbachevian" perspective, reflected most dramatically in the statements of the general secretary himself, which
seek to integrate foreign and domestic policy in a mutually reinforcing combination. This synthesis may be summarized as follows:
    1. The Soviet leadership has concluded, and repeatedly made explicit to both
foreign and domestic audiences, that the USSR's international relationships are
not to be a distraction from, and wherever possible are to be a positive induce-
ment to, the prime task of economic modernization at home. "The main thing,"
Soviet Foreign Minister Eduard Shevardnadze said in a speech to the Soviet
diplomatic community in June 1987, "is that our country not incur additional
expenses in conjunction with the need to maintain its defense capacity and
protect its legitimate foreign policy interests. This means that we must seek ways
to limit and reduce military rivalry, eliminate confrontational features in relations
with other states, and suppress conflict and crisis situations."[28] The logic of
Gorbachev's policy of domestic reform has induced the Soviet leader to search
for structures of stability in critical areas—in arms control most visibly, and now

international organizations as well—so as to provide a durable and predictable framework for the resource choices that must be made in the coming decade and beyond. The need for such stability assumes double importance for Gorbachev since instability in the USSR's foreign relations will affect not only the politics of resource allocation but the viability of Gorbachev's own political position, which assumes that far-reaching reform at home is consistent with the USSR's geopolitical influence abroad.

2. The Gorbachev leadership has come to the conclusion that a favorable international environment can only be created on a *political* basis with the leading industrial powers, and above all with the United States. With remarkable tenacity, Gorbachev has sought to strike a *modus vivendi* with the United States, which is the key toward establishing predictability in the USSR's foreign affairs and security requirements and would translate into a major victory for Gorbachev at home. The Soviet choice for détente thus represents more than a "tactical" adjustment to shifting circumstances, the "breathing spell" that some in the West have detected, and reflects a strategic and realistic reevaluation of the international environment—based on dealing with established governments in the advanced industrial world—and of the USSR's position in relation to that environment.

3. There has been a major reexamination of security issues, led by the official confirmation by Gorbachev *and* the Soviet military that a nuclear war cannot under any circumstances be won. "The time has come," Mikhail Gorbachev said in his Political Report to the Twenty-seventh CPSU Congress, "to realize thoroughly the harsh realities of our day: nuclear weapons harbor a hurricane which is capable of sweeping the human race from the face of the earth."[29] As a corollary, the leadership now argues, with implicit criticism of Soviet security policy under Brezhnev, that security cannot be obtained through military means alone. Security in the nuclear age is said to be mutual in character and, due to the destructive potential of modern weaponry, a common concern of all countries. Relatedly, Soviet policy analysts and Gorbachev himself reject nuclear weapons as a durable guarantor of peace. They claim that even nuclear parity, which they continue to regard as a major historical achievement of socialism, could cease to be a determining factor for stability in the face of an unregulated arms competition between East and West. Nuclear arms control thus assumes priority as a means of reducing the external threat, limiting resource requirements for the military, and establishing a framework of stability in East-West strategic relations. In Europe, Gorbachev has apparently come to the conclusion that, in principle, the USSR cannot secure a significant further diminution of NATO's nuclear presence on the continent without at the same time addressing the issue of its own conventional posture and operational doctrine. Toward this end, Gorbachev has admitted the need to reduce "asymmetries" in the conventional arms balance in Europe, thereby admitting the problem posed by Soviet superiority in forward-based tank forces for further arms control in Europe. Most dramatically, in December 1988 he announced a unilateral reduction of Soviet

forces by 500,000 men and the intention of making the remaining forces unmistakably defensive in orientation. Interestingly, in a series of journal articles published in the latter half of 1987, a number of political-military analysts developed the concept of "reasonable sufficiency," and applied it to the East-West arms relationship.[30] Parity, they write, is not a simple quantitative concept. What counts is the ability of the USSR to deliver a devastating counterblow, not the precise numerical balance or the parallel development of weapons systems on both sides. The realities of the nuclear balance are such that deterrence is very stable within a broad range of weapons balances. The criterion in Soviet nuclear weapons procurement should be the capacity to maintain a reliable retaliatory force, *not* what the Americans have *per se*. In the process, the authors are evidently seeking to lay down new criteria for Soviet military and arms control policy, which, by establishing *minimum* standards for credible deterrence, would help to demilitarize Soviet thinking about security and in the long run release considerable resources now tied up in defense for domestic economic and social development.

That these views are not merely voices in the wilderness is shown by the vigorous reaction by the Soviet military beginning in the second half of 1987 to much of the civilian discussion of nuclear weapons and policy, which by then had gone beyond the bounds of specialist discussion and had come to absorb the special attention of the highly visible Writers Union.[31] When the rhetoric is separated from the analysis, what appears to concern the military is not the specific interpretation of deterrence offered by the civilian specialists but rather its public articulation, which they fear will have the effect of discrediting their mission within the armed forces and ultimately undermine their ideological-educational role in Soviet society. It would now appear that this is exactly what Gorbachev, surveying the military stranglehold over much of Soviet culture, has in mind.

A related point, brought to the fore by the American SDI program, concerns the future stability of the superpower arms balance. If even the maintenance of parity may not ensure stable deterrence, due to the pace of military-technological development and the possible qualitative leaps in the balance, and if superiority is not an attainable objective, then more efforts must be devoted to restraining the military competition. A revised view of military sufficiency, as indicated above, would provide the USSR with greater flexibility in pursuing arms control options to institutionalize constraints on (primarily U.S.) military-technological development and its translation into operational weapons systems. The *Volte–face* in the Soviet position on the Intermediate Nuclear Force (INF) issue has thus proved to be only the first shot in a series of such efforts to provide a more predictable, less threatening, and ultimately less costly strategic environment. While the outcome is not entirely clear, an important debate with serious consequences for key institutional actors has been launched. In that process, concepts are evidently seen as deeds too.

4. The Soviet concept of peaceful coexistence is being revised. Key Soviet policy analysts and officials now interpret peaceful coexistence less as a form of

class struggle—the traditional Soviet viewpoint—and more as a long-lasting condition in which states will have to learn how to live with each other for the indefinite future.

As Primakov noted in a key article in *Pravda* in the summer of 1987, peaceful coexistence is no longer regarded "as a breathing space" by the Soviets. "Interstate relations," he emphasized, "cannot be in the sphere in which the outcome of the confrontation between world socialism and world capitalism is settled."[32] Such "active" coexistence is said to imply not simply the absence of war but instead an international order in which not military strength but relations of confidence and cooperation prevail, and "global problems"—the arms race, ecological problems, Third World development—can be resolved on a collaborative basis. Gorbachev has written that the Soviet leadership has "taken the steps necessary to rid our policy of ideological prejudice."[33] If this in fact leads to a more pragmatic understanding of peaceful coexistence, with "class interests" strictly subordinate to geopolitical criteria in the daily conduct of foreign policy, a central obstacle to more genuinely collaborative East-West relations would have been removed. Certainly, it would mean that the United States and the Soviet Union might actually agree on the operational significance of "normal" relations, which proved impossible during the détente of the early 1970s. "New rules of coexistence," as Gorbachev put it in a key article on September 17, 1987 (reported to have been drafted by Deputy Foreign Minister Petrovskii), might then be drawn up.[34] Soviet officials, both pro- and anti-Gorbachev, have themselves recognized the centrality of this point for the integrity of Gorbachev's foreign and domestic policy vision and program. Speaking to the Soviet diplomatic community after the June 1988 party conference, Foreign Minister Shevardnadze explicitly declared the secondary significance of ideological/class values in contemporary Soviet foreign policy. In the words of the TASS account of Shevardnadze's speech:

The new political thinking views peaceful coexistence in the realities of the nuclear century. We are fully justified in refusing to see in it a special form of class struggle. One must not identify coexistence . . . with class struggle. The struggle between two opposing systems is no longer a determining tendency of the present-day era.[35]

The implications of Shevardnadze's remarks were underscored with dramatic effect, when Yegor Ligachev, at the time the "second secretary" of the CPSU, joined the issue in early August in the first open challenge to Gorbachev's foreign policy vision. At the end of a speech on domestic affairs, in which he again cast scorn on market-oriented reforms, Ligachev suddenly turned to foreign policy and declared: "We proceed from the class nature of international relations. Any other formulation of the issue only introduces confusion into the thinking of the Soviet people and our friends abroad. Active involvement in the solution of general human problems by no means signifies any artificial 'braking' of the social and national liberation struggle."[36] Having earlier failed to curb the scope of Gorbachev's reforms on domestic grounds, Ligachev seems to have turned to foreign policy, where he may have hoped to find a more receptive audience. He evidently saw foreign policy as the "weak link" in Gorbachev's strategy: by attacking foreign policy reform, domestic reform might also be scaled down and vested party interests respected.

That the leadership is sensitive to the interdependence between foreign and domestic policy is shown by Gorbachev's Politburo ally Alexandr Yakovlev's quick and brisk defense of the new foreign-policy line several days later, when he reiterated the subordination of class interests to "all-human" interests such as survival in the nuclear age. At issue is the right to define the nature of the threat environment facing the USSR, and thus the nature and level of the Soviet political and military response to it. If "class" values remain paramount, then the threat from the class enemy remains high and the USSR cannot afford the relative diminution of Soviet military expenditures, the (again relative) demilitarization of Soviet foreign policy—especially in the Third World—and therefore the reorientation of political values implied by Gorbachev's domestic economic reform. In this way, a debate over arcana of ideology is really a struggle for the acceptable framework of choice in reform, in both foreign and domestic policy, and bears directly on the prospects for reform at home. It is thus not coincidental that on October 4, 1988, shortly after Gorbachev's "purge" of the top leadership, including the reassignment of Ligachev, the new party secretary for ideology, Vadim Medvedev, should issue a ringing defense of the Gorbachev line on this point.[37]

5. *Finally,* the Gorbachev leadership evidences increasing recognition of the multipolar and interdependent character of contemporary international relations. This view has been reflected in a Soviet tendency to deal with key regional actors, such as China and Japan in the Far East, Egypt and Israel in the Middle East, and Mexico in Central America. The West can expect increasingly sophisticated and pragmatic Soviet policies throughout the world, as Soviet diplomacy seeks both to reduce the isolation that the rigidity of the late Brezhnev era—with its "excessive devotion to ideology" and its near obsession with the United States—had at times forced upon the USSR and to multiply Soviet options.[38]

Gorbachev's November 2, 1987, speech commemorating the seventieth anniversary of the Bolshevik Revolution included a synthesis of many of the analytical and political tendencies discussed in this paper.[39] The development of nuclear weapons, Gorbachev said, by threatening "the very survival of the human race," has led to a redefinition of the Leninist concept of peaceful coexistence, which had originally been designed to buy time for the young Soviet state to build up its strength. But the global interdependence underlined in starkest form by nuclear weapons has caused a shift in the concept of peaceful coexistence from an instrument of the international class struggle to "a condition for the survival of the entire human race." Gorbachev directly links this conceptual shift to the idea of "reasonable sufficiency" as the criterion for NATO and Warsaw Pact military forces and to the strengthening and better utilization of the United

Nations to assist "a balance of interests of all countries and to discharge its peacemaking functions effectively."

Elsewhere in the speech, Gorbachev reaffirms the recent official Soviet recognition of the basic stability, and even dynamism, of the West. "The changes occurring within the technological and organizational infrastructure of the capitalist economy," he notes, "also helped to allay contradictions and to balance different interests." His discussion of intersocialist relations proceeds from the recognition of specific national interests under socialism and reflects some humility as regards the general applicability of the Soviet model of development, even to its Warsaw Pact neighbors. "Life has corrected our notions of the laws and rates of transition to socialism, our understanding of the role of socialism on the world scale." Interestingly, Gorbachev argued that "the practice of socialist internationalism rests on . . . a strict observance of the principles of peaceful coexistence by all." In retrospect, the application of the concept of peaceful coexistence—which has previously applied only to "class-antagonistic" states—to intrabloc affairs appears to have signified a move toward a more normal relationship between the Soviet Union and Eastern Europe, foreshadowing the revolutionary changes in Eastern Europe in 1989 much in the same way that such a formulation actually provided a basis for the normalization of Sino-Soviet state-to-state relations in the early 1980s.

The revised Soviet estimate of prospects for socialist change and Soviet influence in the Third World also found expression in Gorbachev's speech. Noting references to "the decline of the national liberation movement" (which he admitted was "certainly waning"), Gorbachev paints a complex and pessimistic picture. Factors making for progressive impulses in the Third World are "varied and far from simple" and should not "yield to pessimism," though it is clear from the whole tone of the analysis that prospects for quick Soviet influence are dim. Indeed, Gorbachev refers to a time span of fifty years, during which it is difficult to predict developments. As with the West and even Soviet allies, Gorbachev alludes to the frustration of earlier Soviet hopes for the applicability of the Soviet model: the Third World, he says, "is a world of its own."

Most remarkably, Gorbachev raises a series of questions in his speech that go to the heart of the traditional Leninist of international politics. These include:

- Is it possible to influence the (aggressive) nature of imperialism and block its more dangerous manifestations? (Gorbachev leaves the question unanswered.)
- Can capitalism get rid of militarism and function and develop in the economic sphere without it? (He suggests the answer is yes.)
- Can the capitalist system do without neocolonialism, which is currently one of the factors essential to its survival? (Here too he suggests that the answer is yes.)

- Will the awareness of the nuclear threat that "is making its way even into the higher echelons of the Western ruling elite . . . be translated into practical policies? (Unanswered.)

Simply to raise such ideologically charged questions, not to mention answering in the affirmative, implicitly challenges central Leninist tenets on the nature of imperialism and the well springs of conflict in world politics. The debate over the nature of imperialism, i.e., whether it can be restrained only by external (Soviet) power or by forces intrinsic to it ("bourgeois democracy"), has fundamental implications for the kind of external threat said to be facing the USSR. If imperialism can be contained by internal forces, then the requirements on Soviet security policy (and defense spending) are reduced accordingly. That Gorbachev has raised these questions in this way, and provided even partial answers, shows that new flexibility in Soviet rhetoric and policy reflects a fundamental reevaluation of the relationship between the Soviet Union and its external environment. Taken together, and in light of the analytical background with its roots in the Brezhnev and Khrushchev periods, one may even speak of the emergence of a new Soviet theory of international relations.

CONCLUSION

The remarkable innovations in both the concept and application of Soviet international policy reflect a shift in both the role and content of Soviet international ideology that is due especially to the intensity of the present relationship between Soviet internal and foreign policies. A change in the attributed capacity of the international system to threaten vital Soviet interests has become an important precondition for the character, scope, and pace of the economic, social, and political reform at home, with its attendant redistribution of political authority, reallocation of material values, and (relative) decentralization of the federal power that has always served as the vehicle for the expression of the raw power interests of those who have ruled the Russian nation.

In this change in both content and role of ideology in foreign policy, and so in the direction of foreign policy in general, both international and internal factors have played a role, although it has been the internal political and economic reform that has acted as the catalyst. The reevaluation of internal sources of power and legitimacy that constitute the essence of the Gorbachev reform had demanded, and also made possible, the assimilation of the new understanding of the international system that had been put forward by many now influential experts and officials well before the Gorbachev period. Taken together with the intrusion of a series of highly pragmatic political considerations—in particular those relating to events in East Central Europe and the absence of means by which the Soviet leadership could have exercised any restraining influence without at the same time jeopardizing the course of reform within the Soviet Union itself—these factors have led to a vigorous and progressive exclusion of *traditional* ideological considerations from the conduct of Soviet foreign policy. What, then, is the political foundation of this new ideology of Soviet external policy known as the "new political thinking?" In fact, it is far from clear, as much of both ideology and policy remain in a formative stage of flux. This has led some observers both in and out of the Soviet Union to argue for the essential vulnerability of the "new political thinking." They argue for the fragility of a political and philosophical reorientation that is based mainly on a nuclear threat, which is after all only one component of a whole matrix of interrelated problems and which could—if ironically the new Soviet security policy is maximally successful—be significantly diminished, thereby undermining the very foundation of the new approach.[40] Thus, precisely because this new Soviet ideology has not found its voice and has yet to take root throughout established political structures, its future is closely tied to the new structures of political-institutional authority and legitimacy, which are central to the Gorbachev reform enterprise but which today coexist uneasily alongside the old. Its fate is thus intimately connected with the further consolidation of Gorbachev's political base and the establishment of more effective decision-making mechanisms for addressing problems and issues of a national—as opposed to sectoral, institutional, or local—character.

Yet if the fate of the new foreign policy philosophy is closely found to Gorbachev's own set of policies and practices, it is much less certain that future Soviet foreign policy conduct can revert to past patterns of hegemonic influence, regardless of the ideological foundation of the political leadership. In this respect, the relatively narrow following of the new political thinking as an ideology loses much of its significance. The collapse of communism throughout East Central Europe and the unification of Germany within NATO have revolutionized the entire context of Soviet foreign and security interests in the heart of Europe, which remains for Soviet observers the central theater of world politics. The political, military, and economic means by which the Soviet Union asserted its superpower status throughout the postwar period have shriveled up. Any future Soviet leader, Gorbachev or not, will have to adapt to these profound constraints on Soviet international influence. Thus, while the character of the Soviet adaptation to its reduced circumstances will depend in important measure on the prevailing philosophy of international relations, the necessity to do so seems now a foregone conclusion. Indeed, what is remarkable about the collapse of the Soviet Union's international position is how little resistance has been voiced from a very broad range of the political spectrum. The very concept of superpower is broadly rejected by those from "left" to "right" in the Soviet political system who see such status, and the set of ambitions and commitments it engenders, as running counter to the primary need to resurrect the Soviet state and/or the Russian people. On the official level Marshal Sergei Akhromeev, Gorbachev's military adviser, has forcefully rejected the concept of "limited sovereignty" in future Soviet–East European diplomatic relations, arguing that the Soviet Union must adapt to the East European revolution of 1989. Correspondingly Ygor Ligachev has time and again reaffirmed the essential interest of the Soviet state in disarmament and reduced military budgets as the precondition for the comprehensive reforms required to save the Soviet system.[41] This general consensus on the near absolute priority of internal social, economic, and political development, combined with the impressive set of political and material limitations on Soviet external policies, should reinforce the foreign policy tendencies of the Gorbachev period. Indeed, the worldview presented by the new political thinking would appear to provide a convenient, if not convincing, rationale for making a virtue out of the painful necessity of accommodation.

In many respects events in East Central Europe and the Soviet response to them have constituted the acid test of change in Soviet foreign-policy thinking and conduct. Originally, Gorbachev's *laissez-faire* policy toward East Central Europe, aside from reflecting both the Soviet preoccupation with its own domestic affairs and the increasingly assertive political leaderships (both popular and governmental) throughout East Central Europe, was apparently based on two key assumptions: (1) that Communist parties would preserve a powerful say in government, and (2) that there would be no tampering with the Warsaw Pact. In the meantime the pace of events has forced Gorbachev's hand on the first point, as Solidarity's triumph in leading the Polish government with the effective neutralization of the communists, and the self-destruction of the Communists in Hungary, and now throughout the rest of Eastern Europe, including East Germany, show. On the second point—the Warsaw Pact—the issue is more complicated, but again Soviet policy is moving toward a very flexible position *vis-à-vis* its Western allies, and has essentially conceded the game by acquiescing in the reunification of Germany on West German terms.

It can no longer be disputed, as is also clear in the case of the non-Russian nations within the USSR itself, that Gorbachev vastly exaggerated the consensus on Soviet-type values within Eastern Europe, including within the respective communist establishments themselves. Yet to have intervened at any stage of the reform process in the region would have meant conceding the argument of Gorbachev's (to date ineffective) opponents: i.e., it is not possible to embark on the structural reform of the Communist party–state system without calling into question the privileged place of the Communists in the Soviet polity. Furthermore, there was clearly no way to intervene forcefully in East Central Europe without at the same time calling a halt to the reform process at home. The political dynamics of his own reform thus prohibited Gorbachev from making the effort to intervene—even politically, economically, or ideologically—in East Central European reforms and thereby divorced the future of socialism in the USSR from the fate of socialism abroad, i.e., removed the Marxist-Leninist "world historical process' as a desideratum, at any level, of Soviet foreign policy. Taken to its logical conclusion, and in light of the evolution of the Soviet worldview that we have just examined this means that in the formulation and execution of foreign policy it no longer makes a significant difference that the Soviet Union is also a Communist state.

NOTES

1. Robert Gates, "Recent Developments in the Soviet Union and Implications for U.S. Security Policy," speech delivered to the American Association for the Advancement of Science, October 14, 1988.

2. Bertil Nygren, "New and Old in Gorbachev's 'New Thinking'," *Nordic Journal of Soviet and East European Studies,* Volume 6:1 (1989), p. 5.

3. Cynthia Roberts and Elizabeth Wishnick correctly note the tendency, including in this author's work, to overlook the domestic aspect of the new Soviet international analysis. See their review article, "Ideology Is Dead. Long Live Ideology?" *Problems of Communism* (November/December 1989), p. 58.

4. Interestingly, criticism of China's Cultural Revolution was at times advanced as a veiled critique of the Stalinist heritage in Soviet politics. See Fyodor Burlatsky (now a key exponent of reform), *Mao Tszedun i ego nasledniki* (Moscow: Mezhdunarodnye Otnosheniya, 1979).

5. Fyodor Burlatskii and A. Galkin, *Sotsiologiya. Politika. Mezhdunarodnye Otnosheniya* (Moscow: Mezhdunarodnye Otnosheniya, 1974), pp. 235, 237–238; Gyorgy Shakhnazarow, "Politika skvoz' prizmu nauki," *Kommunist,* no. 17 (1976), pp. 111–12; Pavel T. Podlesny, "Vvedeniye," in Genrikh A. Trofimenko et al., eds., *Sovetsko-amerikanskiye otnosheniya v sovremennom mire* (Moscow: Nauka, 1987), p. 5.

6. For a representative list of their writings at the time, see the bibliography in Allen Lynch, *The Soviet Study of International Relations* (Cambridge: Cambridge University Press, 1987), pp. 174–95. Dusko Doder and Louise Branson bring to light a revealing story, which points to the political relevance of the dissenting establishment views of foreign policy in the pre-Gorbachev period. Upon meeting West German Chancellor Helmut Kohl after the funeral of Konstantin Chernenko, Gorbachev asked, "*Kuda driftuyet Federalnaya Respulika?*" Use of the American "drift" suggested to the West German deputy foreign minister present, a Soviet expert, that Gorbachev either was studying English or had accepted the jargon of Moscow think-tank experts. Dusko Doder and Louise Branson, *Gorbachev: Heretic in the Kremlin (New York: Viking, 1990). p. 67.*

7. For a similar viewpoint see Stephen M. Meyer, "The Sources and Prospect of Gorbachev's New Political Thinking on Security," *International Security* 13, no. 2 (Fall 1988), pp. 125, 128, 134, 137, 156.

8. William Zimmerman, *Soviet Perspectives on International Relations, 1956–1967* (Princeton, NJ: Princeton University Press, 1971), p. 275 and *passim;* Dimitrii Tomashevskii, *On the Peaceful Coexistence of States* (Moscow: Novosti, 1973), p. 34.

9. V. Kubalkova and A. Cruikshank, *Marxism-Leninism and the Theory of International Relations* (London: Routledge and Kegan Paul, 1980), p. 107.

10. Silviu Brucan, *The Dissolution of Power: A Sociology of International Relations and Politics* (New York: Alfred A. Knopf, 1971), pp. 48–49.

11. Oded Eran, *The "Mezhdunarodniki": An Assessment of Professional Expertise in the Making of Soviet Foreign Policy* (Tel Aviv: Turtle Dove Press, 1979); Zimmerman, *Soviet Perspectives,* p. 275.

12. Zimmerman, *Soviet Perspectives,* pp. 275–279, 282.

13. For an example of high-level Soviet concern over the place of Poland in the Soviet alliance system, see Diplomaticheskaia Akademiia M.I.D. SSSR, *Vneshnyaya politika i diplomatiya sotsialisticheskikh stran* (Moscow: Mezhdunarodnye Otnosheniya, 1981), p. 93. See also Elizabeth Teague, "Perestroika: The Polish Influence," *Survey* 30, no. 3 (October 1988), pp. 39–58.

14. Vitalii Zhurkin and Yevgenii Primakov, *mezhdunarodnye konflikty* (Moscow: Mezhdunarodnye Otnosheniya, 1972), p. 15. Zhurkin is the director of the New Institute of Europe, which began operations in 1988. Primakov is now a candidate member of the Politburo.

15. Interview with Aleksandr Yakovlev, *La Repubblica* (Rome), May 21, 1985, p. 7, in *FBIS Daily Report: Soviet Union*, May 24, 1986, pp. CC1–CC2.

16. S. I. Appatov, *S. Sh.A. i Yevropa: obshchiye problemy amerikanskoi kontinental'noi politiki* (Moscow: Mysl', 1979), p. 202. Along these lines, one political-military analyst, with ties to the General Staff, argued recently that there is a secular tendency, when compared to the 1950s, for a progressively diminishing U.S. reliance on "political-military actions" in support of its foreign policy, "in spite of the subjective efforts of the most aggressive circles of imperialism to increase the role of military force in their country's foreign policy objectives." I. Mochalov and A. Podberyozkin, "V. I. Vernadskii: antimilitarism XX veka" [V. I. Vernadsky and Twentieth-Century Anti-Militarism], *Politicheskoye Samoobrazovaniye* (Spring 1988).

17. N. M. Nikol'skiy and A. V. Grishin, *Nauchno-tekhnicheskiy progess i mezhdunarodnye otnosheniya* (Moscow: Mezhdunarodnye Otnosheniya, 1978), p. 55. See also Andrey A. Kokoshin (now deputy director of the Institute of U.S. and Canada Studies), *S.Sh.A.: za fasadom global'noi politiki* (Moscow: Izdatel'stvo Politicheskoy Literatury, 1981), pp. 24–25.

18. Kenneth Waltz, *Theory of International Politics* (Reading, MA: Addison-Wesley, 1979).

19. D. M. Proyektor (a retired colonel in the Soviet armed forces, now at the IMEMO think tank), *Puti Yevropi* (Moscow: Znaniie, 1978), pp. 126–27; N. I. Doronina, *Mezhunarodnyy konflikt. O burzhuaznykh teoriyakh konflikta. Kriticheskiy analiz metodologii issledovaniy* (Moscow: Mezhdunarodnye Otnosheniya, 1981), p. 10; I. G. Usachev, *Mezhdunarodnaya razryadka i S.Sh.A.* (Moscow: Mysl', 1980), pp. 138, 150, 167.

20. Proyektor, *Puti Yevropi*, pp. 128, 159; V. I. Antyukhina-Moskovchenko, A. A. Zlobin, and M. A. Khrustalev, *Osnovy teorii mezhdunarodnykh otnosheniy. Uchebnoye posobiye* (Moscow: Moskovskiy Gosudarstvennyy Institut Mezhdunarodnykh Otnosheniy, 1980), p. 79.

21. N. N. Inozemtsev *et al.*, eds., *Leninskaia teoriia imperializma* (Moscow: Mysl', 1977), p. 212.

22. O. B. Borisov, Yu. V. Dubinin, I. N. Zemskov, *et al*, *Sovremennaya diplomatiya burzhuaznykh gosudarstv* (Moscow: Izdatel'stvo Politcheskoy Literatury, 1981), p. 49. Dubinin is the former Soviet Ambassador to the United States, now posted to Paris.

23. N. N. Inozemtsev *et al.*, *Leninskaya teoriya imperialzma*, p. 215.

24. Lebedev *et al*, eds., *Mezhdunarodnye Otnosheniya i bor'ba idei* (Moscow: Izdatel'stvo Politicheskoy Literatury, 1981), p. 8. This observation was made by V. V. Zagladin, candidate member of the Central Committee since 1976, deputy head of the International Department of the Central Committee from 1967 to 1988. See also Evgenii Primakov, "Leninist Analysis of Imperialism and Contemporaneity," *Kommunist* no. 9 (June 1986), as translated in Joint Publications Research Service, UKO-88-016, October 21, 1986, pp. 127–28; Elizabeth Kridl Valkenier, "New Soviet Thinking About the Third World," *World Policy Journal* 4, no. 4 (Fall 1987), pp. 651–74; and Viktor Yasmann, "The New Soviet Thinking and Regional Conflicts: Ideology and Politics," *Radio Liberty Research*, RD 493/87, December 3, 1987.

25. *Pravda*, March 7, 1986, as translated in *FBIS Daily Report: Soviet Union (Supplement)*, March 10, 1986, p. 5.

26. See V. V. Zagladin, "Predisloviye" in Lebedev *et al.*, *Mezhdunarodnye Otnosheniya*, pp. 3–18.

27. Kokoshin, *S.Sh.A.*, pp. 14–15, 20; Appatov, *S.Sh.A. i Yevrop*, p. 5; Proyektor, *Puti Yevropi*, pp.109–110, 112.

28. See Shevardnadze's candid speech to the Soviet foreign-policy community in *Vestnik Ministerstva Inostrannykh Del SSSR*, no. 2 (1987), pp. 30–34, in which Shevardnadze clearly sets forth the priority of internal economic development in all of the USSR's foreign relationships.

29. Mikhail S. Gorbachev, *Political Report of the CPSU Central Committee to the 27th Party Congress* (Moscow: Novosti, 1986), p. 78.

30. In addition to Zhurkin and Pimakov, *Mezhdunarodnye konflikty*, see Vitalii Zhurkin, "O razumnoy dostatochnosti," *S.Sh.A.*, no. 12 (December 1987), pp. 11–21; Igor Malashenko, "Parity Reassessed," *New Times*, no. 47 (1987), pp. 9–10, and "Reasonable Sufficiency and Illusory Superiority," *New Times*, no. 24 (1987), pp. 18–20.

31. See Thomas Nichols, "Intellectural Pacifists Criticized by Military Officer," *Radio Liberty Research*, RL 308-987, July 28, 1987, and "The Military and 'The New Political Thinking': Lizichev on Leninism and Defense," *Radio Liberty Research*, RL 80/87, February 26, 1987; Eugene Rumer, "Soviet Writers Clash Over Morality of Nuclear Deterrence," *Radio Liberty Research*, RL 299/87, July 13, 1987; Dominique Dhombres, "Le general et les pacifistes vegetariens," *Le Monde*, May 10–11, 1987, p. 5; and D. Volkogonov, "The Most Just War," *Kommunist*, no. 9 (June 1986), pp. 114–123 (JPRS translation UKO-86-016, October 21, 1986, pp. 130–40). For background see F. Stephen Larrabee, "Gorbachev and the Soviet Military," *Foreign Affairs* (Summer 1988), pp. 1002–26.

32. "Novaya filosofiya vneshnei politiki," *Pravda*, July 10, 1987, p. 4. See also Yevgenii Primakov, "Leninist Analysis," p. 128.

33. Mikhail S. Gorbachev, *Perestroika: New Thinking for Our Country and the World* (New York: Harper & Row, 1987), p. 250.

34. For Gorbachev's article, entitled "The Reality and Guarantees of a Secure World," see *Pravda*, September 17, 1987, pp. 1–2, translated in *FBIS Daily Report: Soviet Union*, FBIS-SOV-87-180, September 17, 1987, pp. 23–28.

35. *Pravda*, July 26, 1988, p. 4, as translated in *FBIS Daily Report: Soviet Union*, July 26, 1988, p. 30.

36. *Pravda*, August 6, 1988, p. 2, as translated in *FBIS Daily Report: Soviet Union*, August 8, 1988, p. 39.

37. Central Television, August 12, 1988, as cited in Elizabeth Teague, "Kremlin Leaders at Loggerheads," *Radio Liberty Research*, August 16, 1988, p. 5. For Medvedev's remarks see *Pravda*, October 5, 1988, p.5.

38. See the *Pravda* interview with Soviet diplomat Aleksandr Belonogov, in which Belonogov, the Soviet permanent representative at the UN, criticized the conduct of Soviet foreign policy during Gromyko's tenure as foreign minister. *Pravda*, October 3, 1988.

39. The following quotes from Gorbachev's speech comes from the TASS English translation provided by the Soviet Embassy to the United States, "October and Perestroika: The Revolution Continues," pp. 39–55.

40. As discussed in Sylvia Woodby, *Gorbachev and the Decline of Ideology in Soviet Foreign Policy* (Boulder, CO: Westview Press, 1989), pp. 58–59.

41. Akhromeev has stated in this respect, "Limited sovereignty must not exist and ideology must no longer find a place in interstate relations" (*La Repubblica*, November 22, 1989, as translated in *FBIS Daily Report: Soviet Union*, FBIS-SOV-89-229, November 30, 1989, p. 106. For Ligachev's most recent statement, see the Associated Press, June 8, 1990. For a particularly student *cri de coeur* against the loss of Eastern Europe, see the statement of Soviet Army Gen. Albert Makachev, at the founding conference of the Russian Communist Party on June 19, 1990, as summarized in *Le Monde*, June 21, 1190, p. 4. It is interesting to note, however, that the criticisms of Gorbachev at the twenty-eighth CPSU Congress in July 1990 did not dwell on the collapse of communism in Eastern Europe. Based on the Harriman Institute's review of Soviet television throughout the Party Congress and *The New York Times*, July 5, 1990, p. A10.

17
Inventing the Soviet National Interest*

Stephen Sestanovich

At the end of July 1988, Eduard Shevardnadze called together the staff of the Soviet Foreign Ministry to consider the results of the just-concluded 19th Party Conference. There was much to digest: at the conference Mikhail Gorbachev had unveiled his plan to create a new legislature, thereby beginning the redistribution of institutional power that continues to this day. In addressing his colleagues, Shevardnadze himself introduced an important innovation: Soviet policy would now be guided by a new concept, which he grandly described as "a *massif* of vitally important categories stand[ing] here before us in its full height." That concept was "the national interest."[1]

The oddly dramatic unveiling of this everyday Western term was an effort to back out of two separate dead ends of Soviet diplomacy—one practical, the other theoretical. The more familiar of these was the failed foreign policy of the Brezhnev era, which, in the new leadership's view, had wasted resources and brought the world's leading states together in a solid anti-Soviet coalition. A clear verdict was possible: the "national interest" had not been well served.

By mid-1988, denunciations of past policy had become a staple of Soviet rhetoric, and what made Shevardnadze's speech significant was not that it repeated the criticism yet again. Of far greater moment was the attempt to alter the terms by which policy, past and future, was to be exhausted. The leadership apparently wanted a new political vocabulary for weighing—and justifying— changes in the Soviet Union's international role. In beginning to talk about "the national interest," Shevardnadze inaugurated what has since become a full-blown discussion of the principles and purposes that should guide the world's most formidably armed post-imperial, non-ideological medium power.

PRECURSORS

The work of devising a terminology to criticize the Brezhnev record began with (and in some respects even before) Gorbachev's accession to power in 1985. That terminology quickly became known as "new thinking," and its slogans had

*Reprinted by permission of the author and publisher from *The National Interest* no. 20 (Summer 1990). Copyright© 1990 by *The National Interest*, Washington, DC.

an airy, often irritating piety. According to Aleksandr Bessmertnykh, the new ambassador to Washington, what was involved was nothing less than a shift from "egoism" to "altruism." The Soviet Union proclaimed its conversion to "common human values"—a set of objectives said to include avoiding a nuclear holocaust, staving off environmental catastrophe, promoting economic betterment among the world's poor, and so forth. Such laudable sentiments were perhaps not totally meaningless (and did help to downgrade Marxism-Leninism), but the high level of generality at which they were propounded made it hard to believe that they could be a practical guide for policy-makers. Moreover, Western efforts to get behind the Spaceship-Earth rhetoric were usually futile. Soviet diplomats seemed to have instructions to say that we are all, metaphorically speaking, in the same boat, but no brief to explain what that metaphor meant.[2]

The main substantive problem with the Soviet emphasis on common human values was that it failed to address those values that are *not* common. It provided, as a result, little evidence as to how the Soviet Union would view future clashes of interest between itself and other states. This was a more serious difficulty than whether Gorbachev was sincere about "new thinking," or whether the leadership as a whole shared his outlook. The vapidity of the outlook made sincerity easy. No conservative member of the Soviet national security establishment had to worry much that, at least in its early version, "new thinking" would put him out of business. Undoubtedly, the military was a little uncomfortable with the idea of "mutual security," but they did not need to (and did not) quarrel with it too openly. After all, some interests, such as preventing nuclear war, *are* mutual and cannot be secured for one side at the other's expense. But to admit this does not mean that other, narrower interests can or should be handled in the same way. Should the Kuriles be part of Japan or the Soviet Union? Should Germany be part of NATO or the Warsaw Pact? Such matters are unavoidably the stuff of zero-sum competition.

Until the internal Soviet debate took up the difficult job of distinguishing among interests, adjustments of policy were likely to be made on a case-by-case basis, with little cumulative effect. As one member of the Central Committee suggested recently, the genius of "new thinking" was that nobody could disagree with it—but this also blunted its impact. "Common human values" provided a picture of a new international order in which states would begin to act cooperatively. The new values did not describe how the Soviet Union should conduct itself in the meantime.

The language of "interest," by contrast, provided a framework in which unilateral Soviet actions—even unilateral concessions—might make sense. For a leadership seeking to reshape foreign policy, this was a major advantage. As it happens, we know that such steps were under review in the months immediately after Shevardnadze's speech. The troop cuts that Gorbachev announced at the UN in December 1988 were presented to the world as an expression of "common human values," but in the high councils of the Soviet state they were surely considered from the standpoint of interest.

In broaching the idea of a "national interest," Shevardnadze introduced a term that for decades had had almost no place in Soviet parlance. When Soviet leaders did use it, it was to refer to other countries, rather than their own, and then usually to disparage them. For example, Andrei Gromyko often complained in his annual address at the opening of the UN General Assembly about the American propensity to identify even small matters as "vital national interests." This, he said, was arbitrary, arrogant, insufferable, indefensible, etc. Nikita Khrushchev used the expression in issuing warnings to governments that cooperated with the U.S. or allowed American bases on their territory. In the event of war, he said (and here he conjured scenes of unlimited carnage), the result would not be, shall we say, in their "interest."

One surprising past use of the term was by the now little-lamented Leonid Brezhnev, who in addressing the 24th Party Congress in 1971 declared that the Soviet Union would never abandon its national interests. This peculiar remark was intended as a rejoinder to the taunts of Mao and other Chinese leaders that Moscow had abandoned its commitment to world revolution. His current reputation as an "old thinker" notwithstanding, Brezhnev adopted a modern position: ideology could not be allowed to push policy in directions that damaged the interests of the Soviet state.

The same counterpoint between ideology and interest was also implied by Gorbachev, who used the term before Shevardnadze's 1988 speech. Gorbachev has often quoted Palmerston's dictum that a state can have neither permanent friends nor permanent enemies, only permanent interests—meaning, of course, that Soviet interests are not really different from those of any normal state. They have been "de-ideologized." Yet he has had little to say, beyond this recurrent refrain, about exactly what Soviet interests are. Gorbachev frequently insists that disputes are to be resolved through a "balance of interests"—a principle that enshrines compromise as a rule of Soviet policy, but does not define the interests among which a balance should be struck.

Shevardnadze's approach has been more radical. Far from treating the national interest as something permanent, he described it to the Foreign Ministry as "a very mobile category, dynamic, *constantly changing*." In doing so, he was not (as one might have thought) simply dodging the difficult task of definition. He was acknowledging that the meaning of the term is politically up for grabs, subject to the same debate that glasnost has brought to other facets of Soviet life.

Such has been the purpose of the ensuing debate about the national interest— in defining it, to change it.[3] Three principal changes stand out: first, a repudiation of past policy in favor of more minimal goals; second, an opening up of the process by which foreign and defense policies are formulated; and third, a readiness to defer to international opinion. The first of these—minimalism—has narrowed the scope of Soviet interests. The second and third—domestic pluralism and sensitivity to outside views—have broadened the ranks of those with a say in defining legitimate and viable Soviet purposes.

MINIMALISM

In contemporary Soviet analyses, the national interest *is* constantly changing, just as Shevardnadze suggested—and the revisions are all in one direction: downward. Having asked themselves what the country's real interests are, Soviet leaders have consistently answered, much less than we used to think.

The answer began with a re-evaluation of the environment in which the Soviet Union finds itself—a re-evaluation, that is, of the nature of capitalism. Because past Soviet policy was so often justified by the need to prevent "encirclement," a more relaxed view of capitalist drives could be the starting point for a full overhaul of strategy. Khrushchev and Brezhnev, of course, established long ago that the growing power of the Soviet Union and its allies made nuclear war avoidable. The doctrinal change that Gorbachev has proposed is, however, much more thorough. In his February 1988 speech to the Central Committee, Gorbachev made clear that for him, the internal dynamics of capitalism cannot be said to lead automatically to imperialism. Western corporations have learned that they can do business profitably around the world without the support of aggressive foreign policies. Most of them do not depend on ever-higher military budgets for their profits, and in any event the democratic institutions of the West impose a strong check on any potential "war party."

This new assessment was not, it should be said, a sudden awakening from decades of nightmarish insecurity. What it did was undercut the public rationale that supported Soviet military power and an ambitious foreign policy. Soviet strength ceased to be the key to peace because capitalism, it could be last be seen, *checks itself.*

The impact of the "discovery" was plain in countless ways, including the somewhat light-hearted new tone of Soviet spokesmen on security issues. Viktor Karpov, the deputy foreign minister in charge of arms control, has advocated "a new psychological approach to international relations," whose wholesome lesson is that "no one should have an enemy as such." In a television discussion last year, *Izvestia* columnist Aleksandr Bovin stumped his fellow commentators by challenging them to specify what, if any, foreign dangers the Soviet Union faced.

In this safe new world, guidelines for the size of Soviet armed forces have steadily narrowed. Shevardnadze announced in 1988 that the effort to be as strong as all potential adversaries combined had harmed the national interest. This formulation (which did, strictly speaking, leave open the possibility that the Soviet Union should be the strongest *single* power) has since given way to others that retreat further, and retreat above all from claims of equality with the United States. Soviet officials are now busy correcting what N.N. Spassky, a Foreign Ministry specialist on the U.S., calls "deformations in our understanding of parity." The Soviet Union, he argued in a July 1989 article in the ministry's journal, *Mezhdunarodnaya Zhizn,* must get over the idea that "now that we are equal, that means everything they can do, we too have to be able to do."

"New thinking" has become, among other things, a case for unilateral Soviet withdrawal from the arms race. Obviously the deterioration of the Soviet economy and the domestic preoccupations of the leadership put a large premium on arguments explaining that nothing important will be lost by cutting back. Many Soviet analyses put the case more strongly: great damage would be done by *not* cutting back. In a landmark article (recommended to U.S. officials by Soviet diplomats and said to have been praised by Shevardnadze), the director of the Foreign Ministry's international organizations division, Andrei Kozyrev, described the harm done to international confidence when a state's military capabilities are out of proportion to its national interest.[4] Moreover, he suggested, what the Soviet national interest requires is less than that of other powers. Border forces can provide for Soviet security; the U.S. and Japan, by contrast, depend on secure access to foreign energy supplies, and more generally on maritime superiority. This acknowledgement of special Western needs was unusual in itself; more significant was the fact that it justified an American world role but dismissed one for the Soviet Union. The bottom line was simple and startling: "Our country has no interests justifying the use of military resources outside the borders of the socialist community."

Kozyrev also criticized past Soviet policy in the Third World, arguing that reflexive support for anyone quarreling with the West had only aroused distrust of Soviet motives. Underlying such support, he said, was a basic misunderstanding of conflicts between the West and the developing world. For Kozyrev, the latter's problems have to do with too little capitalism, not too much. Seen in this light, U.S. policy toward them can hardly be considered oppressive. To the contrary, conflicts between the United States and Third World states should be resolved "in a way that takes both sides' interests into account." Above all, the Soviet Union should stay out. What Moscow has too long refused to recognize is that Western interests in the Third World are "immeasurably broader and deeper" than those of the Soviet Union.

Other Soviet officials have taken aim at the world role of which Brezhnev and Gromyko boasted when they claimed that no major issue of international relations could be resolved without Soviet participation. This boast, it should be said, did not reflect a particularly ideological ambition, and at the time many in the west actually treated it as proof of the domestication of Soviet diplomacy. What Moscow wanted—so the argument went—was the respect and access symbolized by a place at the negotiating table. In the Soviet Union, by contrast, this *tous azimuts* diplomacy is today considered mindless aping of the West. In the September 1989 issue of *Kommunist*, Igor Malashenko, a member of the International Department of the Central Committee, advised against trying "to be equal in everything."

> Today, it seems, we can quite painlessly "exclude ourselves" from the struggle that has been forced on us for "spheres of influence" in regions that have no real meaning for our security. Our interests will not suffer even in the event that the American leadership lacks the political vision and realism to take analogous steps. How they waste their national resources—that is their business.

Such analyses do not shy away from stating their baldest conclusion: the Soviet Union cannot really expect to be a superpower and is harmed by the effort to be one. Andrei Kortunov, author of a number of influential articles on defense policy, has insisted that the quest for superpower status has kept the Soviet Union from behaving like a great power with national goals that go beyond mere equality with its rival. Futile competition with the U.S. lures Moscow into alliances that serve no perceptible interest other than a superficial diplomatic parity. Why, for example, pursue close ties with North Korea, when South Korea has so much more to offer? (Kortunov also faults Gorbachev for his sloganeering use of common human values: these have become a new "dogma" and prevent more substantive discussion of national interests.)

Accepting a larger American role in the Third World was one thing; accepting it in Eastern Europe, another. Western analysts rightly wondered whether the reassessment of Soviet interests could possibly extend to the Warsaw Pact. After all, even the most radical revisions of Soviet interests—such as Kozyrev's argument abut interests justifying the use of force—made exceptions for "the socialist community."

Nevertheless, as the governments of the old Soviet bloc fell in late 1989, Soviet officials stepped forward to explain that their collapse was, in Shevardnadze's words, 'unambiguously and unreservedly" good for the Soviet Union. Last February he told the Canadian parliament:

> I would like to say straight out that this is not an attempt to put a good face on things. It is in our national interest, our historical, and even our daily interest to ensure that the states that are our neighbors are stable and prosperous. We can only gain from this.

Having once taken precedence over the interest of neighbors, Soviet interests had now become *derivative* of them—of other states' prosperity and well-being. A month later, Shevardnadze went so far as to say that the Soviet Union shared the concern, often voiced in the West, that communist setbacks in Eastern Europe might be only temporary. It is therefore essential, he told a Soviet interviewer, that the changes in the region "gain momentum and become irreversible. . . . As to Soviet interests, a democratic East Europe will best protect them. That is my deep conviction."

These warm endorsements were, of course, accompanied by efforts to salvage something from what seemed an increasingly one-sided resolution of the Cold War. In particular, the issue of German membership in NATO became the crux of East-West maneuvering over the shape of the new order. Yet here too many Soviet statements signalled a lack of conviction. As the vice rector of the Foreign Ministry's Diplomatic Academy told the *New York Times* in November 1989:

> If the Governments of Eastern Europe want it, we must withdraw our troops from their territory. We can do this *even unilaterally*. As for American troops—I would leave that up to the Western European Governments. I know that some circles in Western Europe feel their security is greater with American troops. It's an understandable position. Let them have it.

While Soviet policy experimented with successive proposals for a "European security order" to supplant the two alliances, many commentators insisted that preserving a balance of military power made no sense as a Soviet goal. Vyacheslav Dashichev, now perhaps the best-known Soviet diplomatic historian, explained to *Die Welt* in March that the very idea of such a balance was a vestige of the Cold War. The Soviet Union no longer had any expansionist goals, and "as for the threat from the west, nobody believes in the aggressive intentions of that side." In any case, hoping to keep Germany out of NATO was "unrealistic."

Other writers have also dismissed the idea of a German military danger, and even Ambassador Bessmertnykh (then first deputy foreign minister) reassured a Soviet TV audience that Western self-restraint would protect Soviet interests.

> The U.S. Administration understands that in its activities in the East European region it must have an awareness of the boundary which it ought not to cross. What is this boundary and what is it determined by? It is primarily determined by the interests of these states themselves, and these states must also manifest due vigilance and common sense in their relations with all other states. It is determined by the Soviet Union's interests and the interests of other neighboring states and the interests of stability in Europe.

Putting their confidence in the good sense of others, Soviet spokesmen steadily narrowed their definition of what they require in a German settlement. The increasing reference to the constraints of public opinion—in a *Pravda* interview, Gorbachev appealed to the Germans to "respect not only the interests but also the *feelings* of other peoples"—may have won some sympathy among poll conscious Western leaders. At the same time, the suggestion that what Moscow needed was a formula to save face at home clearly weakened its bargaining position.

The Soviet desire to withdraw from military and diplomatic competition is so pronounced that one has to wonder whether the country will stand aloof from competition of all kinds. When Khrushchev said (not quite sincerely) that peaceful coexistence should be considered an ideological contest about which system is better, he certainly meant that the Soviet Union should conduct it vigorously. There are residues of his view in today's debate. Shevardnadze, for example, told the Foreign ministry in 1988 that "our main national interest" is to show that socialism, by stimulating the highest labor productivity, "provides man more than any other socio-political system." With the usual quotes from Lenin on his side, he actually insisted that Soviet national security be viewed "solely in this connection." The Soviet Union's goal, he said, is to seek "primacy in the intellectual and cultural area, to put our society in the position of world leader in formulating innovative ideas."

Such harmless-sounding sentiments barely seem to qualify as foreign policy objectives, and if they have any practical meaning at all, it is probably to strengthen the case for political and military retrenchment—by identifying a safer, less divisive form of East/West competition. Yet the mood of the contemporary Soviet debate can be measured by the fact that other spokesmen adopt an *even more minimalist* line. For them, if the Soviet Union is going to forswear competition, there should be no escape clauses of any kind. According to Kozyrev, "objectives of economic, ideological or cultural superiority" are known to encourage military adventures, and as such they "undermine confidence." "The entire range of policy and practice" must therefore be scrutinized to make sure it contains absolutely nothing that could be considered provocative. In the same spirit, Malashenko has deflated overly bold official talk about the Soviet Union becoming a real force in the world economy. It will be a long time, he has written, before the Soviet Union is "ready for full-fledged cooperation with the most developed capitalist countries."

The across-the-board minimalism in Soviet thinking about foreign policy was perhaps best captured in an off-hand remark by Aleksandr Yakovlev, Gorbachev's closest ally on the Politburo. "It is beyond my comprehension," he told *Der Spiegel* in January 1989, "why one power should want to be more important than another." Even if somewhat disingenuous, this was a telling aside. In both tone and content, it recalled Henry Kissinger's famous outburst, "What, in the name of God, is strategic superiority?" Both men, trying to find a more sustainable (that is, lesser) national role in the world, threw up their hands in frustration with those who did not understand the evident good sense of their approach, who continued to argue for more ambitious, competitive policies despite their obvious costs and risks.

PLURALISM

The chance to talk openly about the national interest has revealed the Soviet elite's disenchantment not just with past foreign policy but with foreign policy as such. Yet, however radical the discussion, it can hardly be said to have produced a precise new definition of Soviet interests. No matter how many speeches, articles, communiques, and reports one reads, the object of the quest remains elusive.

There are doubtless many reasons for the inconclusiveness of the debate. A full enumeration of national interests is always intellectually difficult and, for that matter, often politically counterproductive. The more precise the definition, the more objections there will be to this or that specific goal. Most important, a fundamental redirection of national policy is not primarily a matter of winning arguments but of winning power. Even if they defeat the old concepts, reformers also have to defeat the old institutions that embody them.

Not surprisingly, then, the search for a Soviet national interest has gone beyond the question of defining it to the question of *who* defines it. In this way, the Soviet experience neatly reenacts the struggle over America's world role that took place during and after the Vietnam War. The lasting impact of that debate was less conceptual than political: it redistributed power over policy between the executive and legislative branches of government, and between the government and pressure groups outside it. Since then, strategic concepts have come and gone, but the diffusion of power within the American system lingers on.

Those who want to institutionalize a more modest set of Soviet external goals know what success depends on. As Malashenko put it in *Kommunist:*

> We will hardly succeed in creating an effective mechanism for protecting our national interests as long as the public does not have a real chance to judge the state of affairs in this area and to participate in open democratic discussion of questions of foreign and military policy.

The national interest, it seems, is what emerges from democratic decision-making. There is a suggestion of the change in Shevardnadze's proposal to "merge science and diplomacy." In the past such a statement would have meant putting Marxist-Leninist theory into practice. Now it means listening to think-tank researchers, op-ed writers, pollsters, and consultants.

The crucial event in the reform of Soviet policy-making was Gorbachev's decision to beef up the powers of the legislature and—even more—to choose its members in elections. Although his report to the 1988 Party Conference, which presented these reforms in detail, hardly mentioned their intended impact on foreign policy, Shevardnadze's subsequent speech to the Foreign Ministry left no doubt that he expected the military to be their principal victim. With obvious relish, he (and his deputy ministers as well) forecast the growth of legislative control over military doctrines, budgets, plans, operations, etc. Past mistakes were ascribed to the secrecy in which decisions, especially military decisions, were made; this would at last be broken.

To judge by public rhetoric alone, the effort has been an astounding success. The onset of electoral politics has given life and legitimacy to anti-military sentiments that had no outlet in earlier phases of glasnost. On the Soviet campaign trail last year, there was no surer applause line than a promise to cut the military budget, and many candidates committed themselves to seek legislation (plainly modeled on the U.S. War Powers Resolution) requiring a congressional vote before troops were sent abroad. This new atmosphere has put military spokesmen at a distinct disadvantage: in presenting the 1990 budget, the deputy defense minister acknowledged that military prestige had reached a low point in Soviet history.

The Ministries of Foreign Affairs and Foreign Trade may have viewed this spectacle with a certain delight, but they too have been subjected to demands for openness and accountability. A typical proposal of the campaign for the new Congress of People's Deputies was that of Genrikh Borovik, chairman of the officially-sponsored Committee for the Defense of Peace, who called for mandatory television coverage of all important decisions—"major diplomatic steps, foreign trade policy, the amount of our aid to other countries, and so on." The

closed-door bureaucratic pluralism that had evolved under Gorbachev's predecessors was insufficient, he told a *Nedelya* interviewer in February 1989. It only
fostered

> collective irresponsibility and collective indifference. We must get away from
> anonymity! Precisely because the author of some rash step would know that his
> name would be associated with that step.

Hustings rhetoric, however, is not the same thing as a working system of checks
and balances, and many of the great expectations with which the new legislature
was launched have clearly been disappointed. Writing in the liberal magazine
Ogonek, Georgii Arbatov, the Soviet Union's best-known Americanist and
himself a member of the People's Congress, recently complained that the
military remains impervious to outside control, including the oversight role of
the Supreme Soviet Committee on Defense and State Security.[5] The committee's
chairman has echoed this judgment, admitting that he and his colleagues cannot
get the ministries to give them the basic information they need.

Even if these problems persist, however, there are other signs of political
change. In his March 15 "inaugural address," for example, Gorbachev pledged
that he would never send troops abroad without prior legislative authority. His
statement was surely designed to keep the "War Powers" bill bottled up in
committee and prevent any statutory encroachment on his restyled presidential
powers, but the mere need to position himself in this way implied that power is
not yet clearly demarcated.

On the issue of foreign aid, there was a similar hint of a political tug of war in
Shevardnadze's state-of-the-world report to the Supreme Soviet last October. He
described the report itself—intended to be a yearly event—as a sign of growing
cooperation between the ministry and the legislature. Yet, in a break with his
usual reformist tone, the foreign minister also delivered a stern little lecture to the
deputies about the importance of honoring past commitments to friends and
allies. Were Moscow abruptly to cut off foreign aid, he said, Soviet credibility
would be severely weakened.

These remarks could almost have been lifted from the congressional testimony
of an American cabinet secretary worried about possible cuts in his budget and
determined to prevent further damage. They were all the more striking because
Shevardnadze has been the most enthusiastic supporter of creating checks and
balances in foreign policy-making. That he has now begun to protest the consequences may suggest that they are taking effect. Certainly the official 1990
foreign aid budget showed a substantial drop, from 12 billion rubles to 9.7
billion; and although questions can be raised about what these figures mean, the
fact remains that the Soviet leadership chose to advertise a cut two-and-a-half
times larger in percentage terms than was made in the military budget— and that
the foreign minister publicly complained. Since then, moreover, legislative
attention to this issue has not subsided. In March, the Finance Ministry—in
response to a legislative request—published the first ever country-by-country

breakdown of Third World debts to the Soviet Union, with the admission that many would never be collected. Steady publicity and criticism, it is clear, are robbing foreign aid of its legitimacy.

REPUTATION AND SELF-RESPECT

In attempting to rethink the national interest, Soviet officials and reformers have loudly proclaimed their readiness to defer to foreign opinion. As Shevardnadze told his staff two years ago,

> We cannot simply pretend that the norms and ideas of what is proper, of what is called civilized conduct in the world community, do not concern us. If you want to be accepted in it, you have to observe them.

The circle of those entitled to a role in identifying interests has, in effect, been widened yet again. It now includes not only those inside the Soviet Union who did not have a real say in the past, but the institutions, individuals, and mores of the outside world.

The new importance of external authority is the flip side of what is often described as the Soviet campaign to "deprive the West of its enemy." Unquestionably, a negative image of the Soviet Union helped to sustain Western policy during the Cold War. But overcoming that image does more than constrain the West; it constrains the Soviet Union too. For Shevardnadze, reputation is "a component of state interests and national security." And if a nation's reputation counts, its freedom of action narrows.

Not everyone agrees about exactly *why* international respectability matters. For some writers and officials, reputation has a largely instrumental value: it makes Soviet diplomacy more effective. In this spirit Vyacheslav Dashichev and other scholars have argued that the purges of the 1930s so "blackened" the Soviet Union's image that an alliance with the West against Hitler was out of the question. The Foreign Ministry's Andrei Kozyrev has linked "trust" with the attempt to strike a workable "balance of interests": a government that enjoys the confidence of other states will be able to persuade them to moderate their own goals and to resolve disputes by compromise.

By strengthening respect for foreign opinion, Soviet reformers also expect to simplify their work at home. Anatoly Adamishin, one of Shevardnadze's deputy ministers, wrote in a recent issue of *Moscow News* that the ability to draw on the West's legal tradition is "an essential part of our domestic reform process."

> It means we do not have to invent things. More often than not we can simply borrow existing legal norms and, if necessary, adjust them to our reality. These norms have been elaborated in the West with the utmost care and thoroughness.

The Foreign Ministry's 1989 report to the Supreme Soviet showed what it means for external commitments to become a factor in domestic politics. The report

report grumbled that the new legislature had not yet carried out Gorbachev's year-old promise to the UN of new laws on religion and freedom of the press. It also presented a list of internationally-recognized rights not yet codified in Soviet legislation, and complained about the failure to live up to commitments to improve environmental policy and psychiatric practices. In this document and elsewhere, appeals to outside standards are routinely put forward to sway internal debate. When the Supreme Soviet considered the new emigration law this spring, the argument of the bill's floor manager, Fedor Burlatsky, was that final passage would increase the Soviet Union's "prestige."

Beyond making diplomacy more effective or speeding reform at home, a final element of the new Soviet readiness to accept the judgments of the world community is the most revealing of all. In the course of his 1988 speech to the Foreign Ministry, Shevardnadze paused to acknowledge that some people felt too much attention was being paid to what foreigners said about the Soviet Union. In the light of Soviet traditions, his reply was astonishing: "our self-respect," he said, depends on it.

Western scholars and diplomats have long spoken of a Soviet inferiority complex—rooted in the country's miserable living standards, in the peasant origins of many officials, in shame at the brutality of Stalinism, and in embarrassment at the preposterous rituals of an ideologized society. The analysis, if vague, had a certain plausibility, and yet anyone weighing it also had to deal with Soviet claims to have created a completely new culture and a superior morality. If the self-respect of "New Soviet Man" depended on the approval of foreigners, he certainly never admitted it. And when Soviet propaganda spoke, as it did ceaselessly, of the Soviet Union's "immense prestige" throughout the world, the boast was far from an acknowledgment that Moscow had to measure up to outside standards. The very assertion of Soviet "prestige" (often followed by a phrase like "in the eyes of peace-loving peoples everywhere") was meant as a rebuke to the West.

Now this psychological autarky has collapsed. The rhetoric of "common human values" may cushion the blow a bit, by offering a new—and for some, inspiring—universalism in place of the old one. This is why talk of "Western values" is so irritating to Gorbachev, and why he reportedly spent so much time at the Malta summit trying to convince President Bush that such ideas are not Western at all, but the birthright of all mankind.

Yet, such protests aside, the deference to outside opinion parallels the broader Soviet rethinking of the national interest. The idea that the Soviet Union can live by its own moral standards has about as much support as the idea that it can remain a military superpower. According to Andrei Kortunov, "the theme of repentance" must acquire a place in Soviet foreign policy. "We must see ourselves," as Nikolai Popov wrote in *Literaturnaya Gazeta* last year, "through the eyes of others."

This effort is in its way humiliating, but its advocates accentuate the positive. No one is more upbeat than Shevardnadze, whose UN speech last fall again described the progress of Soviet policy in the language of self-esteem. "The

Soviet Union," he declared, "feels more comfortable in the international arena than ever before."

GORBACHEV'S GAULLIST ALTERNATIVE

The search for a Soviet national interest has so far been conducted largely by process of elimination. Whatever costs too much, whatever is too risky or confrontational, whatever is decided in secret, whatever weakens Soviet prestige, whatever gets in the way of perestroika—whatever falls into these categories is *not* in the national interest. A Soviet citizen might be forgiven for asking whether the leaders of his country have stumbled upon the idea of the national interest only to discover that they do not have one.

The term has, of course, been used as a principle of exclusion in other countries as well. Despite an affinity with *realpolitik*, "national interest" is often the rallying cry of a skeptical near-isolationism that asks of events elsewhere, what concern are they of mine? Many who employ the term in American debate do so precisely to restrain what they see as over-reaching.[6]

Yet the fact that a bare-minimum foreign policy has its advocates in both the U.S. and the USSR does not make it equally palatable in both countries. Americans are now considering a scaled-back world role, but without the sting of defeat. The record of Soviet foreign policy in the past several years, by contrast, makes discussion of the national interest look like a feeble attempt to paper over poor results.

This suspicion had its most famous expression in the speech of the Soviet ambassador to Poland (a former *apparatchik* serving in diplomatic exile) at the February 1990 plenum of the Central Committee:

> Our country, our mother, has been reduced to a poor condition and has been turned from a power admired in the world into a state with a mistaken past, a joyless present, and an uncertain future. . . . Yet we are trying to present all this as a dizzying success for perestroika and new thinking in international affairs.

Ambassador Brovikov's outburst should not be over-interpreted. He was not, it seems, acting as the spokesman of an organized challenge to Gorbachev's foreign policy (and has since lost his job). Yet he clearly did not speak for himself alone. Similar complaints have been heard from representatives of most other institutions of the Soviet system. The senior military leadership, in particular, has continued to warn of the external military threat facing the Soviet Union. In *Literaturnaya Rossiya*, one widely-read pro-military writer, Aleksandr Prokhanov, describes the impact of "new thinking" as "neglect of the interests of the socialist state and satisfaction of the ambitions of imperialist oligarchies." In the Third World, he writes, the effect is especially severe:

> The Soviet Union, weak and displaced from the regions of the world, can no longer serve as a restraining factor to the expansion of bourgeois empires. A multitude of

small countries and peoples who have derived advantage from the recent stand-off are obediently running to Washington's call like mice after the Pied Piper.

Creating support for a national interest in retreat is hard enough. The problem is compounded by liberal reformers' extreme deference to foreign views; hence the complaints, also voiced at the February plenum, about truckling to traditional adversaries like Pope John Paul II. Many who worry about such developments— and they are not limited to the Communist old guard—focus on the internal impact of the Soviet Union's falling status. A manifesto drawn up last year by a Russian nationalist faction in the Congress of People's Deputies lamented the "decline of superpower patriotism among our youth."[7]

Even the increased pluralism that Gorbachev has brought to the making of foreign policy creates problems. In two regions that looms especially large in Soviet calculations—the Middle East and Central Europe—public opinion and the openness of debate often seem to narrow Soviet flexibility rather than widen it. Soviet-Israeli rapprochement has been complicated by the hostility to Israel (which they are now quite free to express) of both Russian nationalists and Islamic fundamentalists. In similar fashion, Moscow's credibility on the German question has been eroded by self-described "advisers to Gorbachev" who confidently tell Western journalists that tough Soviet positions on the future of Germany are only for show.[8]

Witnessing all this, many in the West have begun to doubt the staying power of a Soviet conception of the national interest that is so closely associated with failure. The very term "national interest" has been a minor rhetorical fraud, pressed into service by Gorbachev and Shevardnadze to give a hard nationalist edge to what is in reality the soft accommodationist agenda of Soviet reformers. In the West their program would be called liberal internationalist: an anti-imperial, anti-military drive that puts trade above politics and threatens to submerge individual states in supranational structures. Because this program is unpopular wherever nationalism is strong—and because the Soviet Union will benefit only slowly from trying to integrate itself into such a world order—there is every reason to speculate about a coming Soviet backlash. If Gorbachev is playing the role of Carter, won't someone eventually play Reagan? If we are now dealing with Weimar Russia, how long will it be before National Bolshevism bursts on the scene?

The problem with these analogies—America in the 1980s, Germany in the 1930s—is that they presume a revival of national strength that is extremely hard to credit in the Soviet case. In 1930, despite massive unemployment, the Weimar Republic had the largest economy in Europe; post-Vietnam America, despite inflation and energy dependence, had the largest in the world. In each case, nationalist leaders who wanted to pursue a more ambitious, less compromising policy toward the outside world had a great deal to work with.

The Soviet Union, by contrast, faces a long stretch of hard times. It therefore makes little sense to ask whether its leaders will not be tempted to throw off the constraints that have marked Gorbachev's foreign policy—as though their problems could be solved by wishing them away. They cannot be, and this fact is understood across the entire Soviet political spectrum. The opening up of the system has revealed extremism of many kinds, but—and this is very important—*no Soviet irredentism.* (By contrast, in Weimar, everyone was irredentist. The foreign Policy debate was about how, not whether, to overturn the Versailles settlement.)

In the Soviet Union, the Soviet national interest will almost certainly continue to be defined as a search for relief from burdens, and for ways of buffering the transition to a diminished world role. Liberal accommodationism, which has to date dominated discussion of the Soviet national interest, is one version of this search. Are there alternatives that could, without requiring resources that are needed elsewhere, claim a better fit with the needs of a post-imperial medium power? History suggests one: Gaullism. For France in the 1950s and 1960s it was an attempt to slow the rapid loss of international influence, to insulate diplomacy from the confusions of domestic politics, and to make national pride a support for sovereignty. These themes have an obvious relevance to the Soviet Union's scaled-down national interest—to the minimalism that leaves Moscow seemingly without a role, to the pluralism that makes policy appear incoherent and confused, and to a dependence on the approval of outsiders that many find distasteful. To address these shortcomings, the Soviet Union may move toward what Fritz Stern a decade ago called "Gaullism by default . . . an improvised, depressed adaptation to unfavorable circumstances."[9]

There are already signs, for example, of Soviet second thoughts about one of the most sacred themes of "new thinking": abolishing nuclear weapons. One influential Soviet analyst, Sergei Karaganov, has written in *Moscow News* of "a definite temporary increase of psychological—certainly not military—reliance on the nuclear factor in our security." Others have echoed him, and while no one is prepared for an open challenge to the idea of a nuclear-free world, the mere expression of doubt is significant. It suggests an attempt to think through the break-up of the Soviet military position in Central Europe. Liberal reformers and military planners seem to be coming to the same conclusion. For liberals, nuclear weapons can be the key to reducing the size of the army—and its internal political influence. For the military, nuclear weapons ease the loss of conventional advantages over the West. They provide the *force de frappe* that every retreating medium power needs.

Gaullist diplomacy suggests other patterns that the Soviet Union may follow. French capabilities permitted no more than a relatively weak challenge to the East-West alliance system, but de Gaulle did achieve a kind of diplomatic reinsurance by building special relationships with Bonn and Moscow. And although withdrawal from Algeria meant abandoning the empire for good, French leaders nevertheless protected a residual role in the Third World, especially in Francophone Africa.

Soviet Gaullism would mean a like-minded attempt to find political advantage at the margin, despite tight limits on what Moscow can hope to accomplish. A special understanding with Germany has no real prospect of supplanting the much more important German connection with the U.S., but it would supplement the weak security guarantees likely to issue from the all-European negotiations that Soviet officials say they want. In the same way, a much reduced presence in the Third World would have very little strategic rationale, but it would symbolize the generic ideological commitment that Gorbachev, with some defensiveness, expressed in his inaugural address:

> The policy of new thinking by no means signifies a cooling of our interest in the developing countries, as some people try to present it, both inside our country and beyond its borders. Our solidarity with those who are fighting for equal rights, for social progress, democracy and a life that is worthy of man is immutable.

De Gaulle's partners found him exasperating. Gorbachev's find him captivating, but a little self-regarding Gaullist amoralism could change that. The current Soviet enthusiasm for multilateral problem-solving—UN peacekeeping forces, negotiated limits on arms exports, and the like—may encounter some of the same temptations that led France to assist Israel's nuclear weapons program. Cash-strapped and cutting back on defense, the Soviet Union will have good Gaullist reasons to keep increasing hard currency military sales to the Third World.

French Gaullism had as much to do with the making of policy as with its actual content. To a political system foundering in multi-party confusion, the advent of de Gaulle meant presidential leadership. Now that Gorbachev has created the same office for himself (justified by frequent references to the French model), he will begin to show whether he really intends to open up the institutions responsible for foreign and defense policy. Many Western analysts have concluded that the political influence of the military is growing; this ought to mean that, as president, Gorbachev will avoid confrontation with his generals and shield them from anti-military sentiment in the media and legislature. Yet the evidence of his inaugural address is different. Its strong statement that the time had come for "profound military reform" suggested that he is preparing another challenge to the military leadership. (De Gaulle, it might be remembered, ruled for a time with emergency powers—to put down a military coup and cope with its aftermath.)

Of the many strands of Gaullism, the one that may carry the most perplexing message for Gorbachev is the reassertion of national pride. The Soviet effort to win international respectability has been hugely successful, but at home it appears to be the least popular theme of foreign policy. Perhaps as a result, there are now the first signs of an attempt to give Soviet policy a more credible nationalist appearance—primarily by co-opting figures who are popular in the Russian nationalist movement into the new Presidential Council.

Whether or not this effort continues, linking patriotism and foreign policy will surely be the hardest part of creating a workable Soviet Gaullism. The multinational make-up of the Soviet state does not by itself mean that a coherent national interest is impossible, but it will make it extremely difficult to bolster the defense of that interest with appeals to national pride. If so, Gorbachev may have to settle for (again quoting Fritz Stern) Gaullism "without grandeur"—a formula that is, in any case, much truer to the revolution he has made in Soviet politics. He has sought to overcome a hated, fearful past, not evoke a grand one; and to deny, rather than assert, a special calling in world affairs.

Everyone knows that Churchill said: "I cannot forecast to you the action of Russia. It is a riddle wrapped in a mystery inside an enigma." Hardly anyone recalls that he continued: "But perhaps there is a key. That key is Russian national interest."

For Churchill, as for many others, the "national interest" provided a fixed point by which statesmen could steer. Its origins lay in a given nation's geography and history and in the competitiveness of the international system. Its dictates were moderation (because overcommitment to ideological or personal goals can put the nation at risk) and self-assertion (because any slackening can jeopardize its security). As a forecast of Soviet conduct, this meant that Moscow would probably take no extreme risks for the sake of world revolution, but also that there was no serious prospect of an end to the rivalry between East and West. The imperatives of empire were much too great.

In the hands of new Soviet leaders, the "national interest" has lost its objective character, its seeming permanence. What Gorbachev, Shevardnadze, and their colleagues have found under the rubble of Leninism is not some Palmerstonian mandate to protect the Soviet Union's global position at all costs. They have discovered that the reconsideration of their external strategy can be just as radical as the reform of their internal order and is indeed inseparable from it. "National interest" may be the key, but it is a key they make—and now, remake—themselves."

NOTES

1. *Vestnik Ministerstva Inostrannykh Del SSSR*, August 15, 1988.

2. Central Committee official Vadim Zagladin, for example, offered the intriguing thought that common human values are "dialectically" linked with all other interests and values. In other words, they are in some respects the same, in other respects the opposite, and in the end will be supplanted by something new.

3. This enterprise, it should be said, is not mere sport for maverick Soviet academics making the most of glasnost. The participants include Politburo members and Foreign Ministry officials as well as the more familiar "policy intellectuals."

4. "Trust and the Balance of Interests," *Mezhdunarodnaya Zhizn*, October 1988.

5. "The Country for the Army—or the Army for the Country?" *Ogonek*, no. 5 (February 1990).

6. Charles William Maynes uses the term this way in his Spring 1990 *Foreign Policy* article, "America without the Cold War." For him, a policy based on "strict national interest"—not his preference—would sharply reduce U.S. engagement in most of the world.

7. Bill Keller, "Russian Nationalists: Yearning for an Iron Hand," *New York Times Magazine,* January 28, 1990, p. 50.

8. Seeing the effect on Soviet bargaining strength, the Foreign Ministry in April took the unusual step of announcing that one of the most provocative Soviet commentators on Germany, Vyacheslav Dashichev, had no role in preparing policy.

9. See "Germany in a Semi-Gaullist Europe," *Foreign Affairs* 58 (Spring 1980), p. 873. Stern was referring to Western Europe's drift away from U.S. leadership in the Carter years. It could be argued that his description applies even to de Gaulle's own Gaullism.

18

Linkages between Soviet Domestic and Foreign Policy under Gorbachev*

Alex Pravda

Domestic and foreign policy are more closely connected under perestroika than at any previous stage in Soviet development. Gorbachev has himself highlighted the unprecedented priority of internal factors: 'Our foreign policy today stems directly from our domestic policy to a greater extent than ever before.'[1] Soviet leaders have, of course, always placed domestic needs first, yet the weight accorded them in the last four years is certainly greater than at any time since the early Khrushchev period. Arguably, domestic considerations have figured more prominently under perestroika than in any peacetime period since the years immediately following the Revolution. Indeed, Soviet observers have drawn parallels between the domestic priorities under Gorbachev and those that led to the Treaty of Brest-Litovsk and later the New Economic Policy (NEP).[2]

If the Gorbachev years stand out in the salience of domestic factors in foreign policy, they are even more remarkable for congruence between the thrust of change on internal and external policy fronts. In previous periods of major change in Russian and Soviet history, domestic and foreign policies have been inconsistent and even divergent. Even those periods which at first glance appear to be similar in congruence to perestroika, prove on closer consideration to have been less congruent. Take NEP for instance: moves towards greater involvement in the international system in the early twenties corresponded to domestic economic reform but were at odds with political centralization. This partial incongruity helped to weaken what was anyhow a temporary rather than permanent strategy of development.

*This chapter draws in part on my paper 'Linkages between domestic and foreign policy in the Soviet Union', in A. Clesse and T. C. Schelling (eds), *The Western Community and the Gorbachev Challenge* (Baden Baden: Nomos, 1989), pp. 92–107.

*Reprinted by permission of the author and the Royal Institute of International Affairs from *Perestroika: Soviet Domestic and Foreign Policies*, T. Hasegawa and A. Pravda (eds.), pp. 1–24. Copyright © 1990 by the Royal Institute of International Affairs. Published by Sage Publications for the Royal Institute of International Affairs, London.

Any serious assessment of the correlation between domestic and foreign policy strategies at different stages in Soviet development would require the elaboration of a complex set of criteria.[3] For our present purposes we can use the rather crude, though helpful, criteria of tendencies towards 'open' or 'closed' policy strategies at home and abroad. 'Closed' policies in the domestic setting are associated, self-evidently, with conservation of the concentration of economic and political power within few institutions; 'open' strategies strive to introduce economic decentralization and wider political participation and accountability. On the security and foreign policy front, the terms are self-explanatory, denoting on the 'closed' side tendencies towards isolationism and autarky and on the 'open' side efforts towards greater economic and political interaction with the Western world. Using these rough yardsticks, policy in the Stalin period tended to consistency at the 'closed' end of the spectrum (with obvious exceptions in foreign policy in the mid to late 1930s and in both contexts during the war). Under Khrushchev the picture is predominantly one of striving towards greater 'openness' on both fronts, notably in the first de-Stalinization period (1953–7), which laid the basis for many of the reforms which perestroika has taken far further. It was only the last years of Khrushchev's rule that saw retreat from reform on both fronts. Inconsistency between domestic and foreign policy became the hallmark of the Brezhnev era, in which strategies appeared to diverge. A 'closing' of political and economic reform went hand in hand with a foreign policy of detente which opened up contacts with the West. In fact the disquieting influences involved in the detente policy probably reinforced the natural inclination of a conservative and cautious regime to maintain tough controls over political developments, particularly dissidence. Incongruity and tension between the two sets of policies reflected and deepened the general incoherence in policy which Neil Malcolm sees as characterizing the end of the Brezhnev period.[4] Fear of change paralysed movement on both domestic and foreign policy fronts from the late 1970s (except for the short Andropov interregnum) to Gorbachev's accession. Reluctance to tackle mounting problems at home and abroad associated with 'stagnation' *(zastoi)* compounded the tensions within and between domestic and foreign polices in the late 1970s and early 1980s.

Since assuming office and assessing the legacy of *zastoi* in terms of systemic crisis, Gorbachev has pursued a comprehensive, radical and highly activist policy of 'opening up' on both domestic and international fronts—the strategy of perestroika. Gorbachev is the first Soviet leader to see the salvation of the Soviet Union in a strongly Westernizing strategy rather than temporary tactic. He is the first to consider the USSR to be in systemic crisis sufficiently grave to warrant revolutionary change and at the same time the first to have sufficient confidence to attempt this by exposing the Soviet Union to outside influences and involvement. The Gorbachev years have thus seen a stronger and, most notably, more dynamic and proactive congruence of movement towards 'open' domestic and international policies than at any time in the Soviet period. Domestic and foreign policy perestroika form integral and interactive parts of an ambitious strategy of modernizing the Soviet Union, bringing the system into the twenty-first century, through opening up politics to the population and the Soviet Union to the developed world.

Gorbachev's references to the 'organic unity' of perestroika should thus not be seen merely as an effort to create the image of policy consistency.[5] They reflect what amounts to a general strategic concept of perestroika, one developed in the process of practical change yet one that from the outset has stressed the close connections between internal and external reform.[6] As the process of perestroika has developed in ever more radical directions, so the links between its domestic and external components have thickened. Domestic perestroika has broadened from economic to political reform (and reform on both those fronts has become progressively more radical), while foreign policy has gone from efforts to re-establish detente to the determined pursuit of entente and a qualitatively new involvement in the international system. All this does not mean that there is any *absolute* correlation between progress of perestroika at home and abroad (Marie Mendras rightly rejects any 'automatic' synchronization).[7] Yet the processes of internal and external perestroika are symbiotically connected both in terms of policy impetus and policy momentum. The interconnections are complex, and influence flows in both directions. On the one hand, declining international standing certainly contributed to the initial decision to undertake radical domestic change, which in turn required a neo-detentist policy in order to obtain international tranquility. On the other hand, democratizing reforms with the Soviet Union have contributed substantially to the creation of a non-threatening and more acceptable image abroad which remains essential to the successful pursuit of Gorbachev's more cooperative foreign policy strategy. To complete the internal–external policy circle, as it were, a successful international strategy of this kind is in turn the key to creating a climate favourable to economic interaction with the West that can provide the Soviet Union with both the short-term material aid and longer-term cooperation which many see as important to the success of perestroika.

This chapter seeks to map some of the contours of the linkages between major domestic and foreign policy areas under *perestroika*. To do this we discuss linkages under three broad headings: resources, policy thinking and domestic politics.[8]

RESOURCES

Resource-based linkages provide the most direct and palpable connection between domestic and foreign policy since they self-evidently involve basic questions of allocation of priorities between guns and butter, or more accurately between developing different dimensions of security and economic capabilities. Two sets of resource linkages have proved particularly critical under perestroika. The first may be labelled 'harnessing the military', and has involved efforts to reduce the security burden and make more effective use of military resources for domestic economic development. The second may be summarized as greater interaction with the world economy, and relates to maximizing the domestic benefits of external economic ties. Whereas foreign policy considerations have played an important part in resource allocation decisions, particularly in the first area, domestic priorities have largely driven policy change.

HARNESSING THE MILITARY

A close policy connection between security demands and domestic economic development has long figured prominently in the Soviet Union. For the most part leaders, notably Stalin, have invoked security imperatives in order to justify domestic privation. An awareness of the need to reduce the military burden emerged, however, under Khrushchev, who attempted to cut back—ultimately unsuccessfully—on military size and expenditure. Although this policy was reversed through the late 1960s and 1970s, debates around this issue resurfaced in the late Brezhnev period which saw a slowdown in military spending. While the Brezhnev leadership undoubtedly regarded the attainment of military parity with the United States as a major achievement, some realized the costs of such sustained defence priorities for civilian economic development in general and consumption in particular.[9]

Under Gorbachev, concern about the costs of established policy with its high military priority has stemmed from anxiety both about military performance as well as about the development of the economy in general. Many in the defence establishment have from the late 1970s realized that Soviet technological capabilities would not easily be able in future to compete with Western weapons development, notably in the area of emerging technologies. The threat of the United States racing ahead in this field was intensified by the appearance of the SDI programme. Hence Gorbachev's early emphasis on using vigorous arms control policy to try and slow down the pace and scope of American military technological development. The emphasis on the ABM treaty, and Soviet willingness to consider deep cuts in strategic arsenals, as well as the unsuccessful effort to bring about a test moratorium through unilateral moves, all underscored the policy urgency of constraining the technological arms race and taking pressure off the Soviet defence industry. As well as contributing to the reinvigoration of its arms control policy, the problem of keeping technological military pace with the West has reinforced the case for radical economic reform in the Soviet Union. Even in the late Brezhnev years the military began to realize that they needed a more dynamic and innovative economy in order to generate the advanced technologies vital to maintain parity with the United States in a qualitative rather than the traditional quantitative sense. Gorbachev has taken account and also possibly full political advantage of this realization and used the qualitative-based technology security argument to strengthen the case for a more efficient and integrated economy, one that eliminates what he has dubbed the 'internal Cocom' which confines the development of key technologies largely to the defence sector.[10] The perestroika leadership have shown keen appreciation of the crucial importance to national security of the economic and technological capability to innovate. 'Today what is instrumental to the security of a country', Shevardnadze told a foreign ministry meeting in July 1988, 'is not so much its stockpiles as its capacity to develop and produce new things.'[11] The case for radical economic reform is thus strengthened by a wider security argument which depicts such change as the only way to prevent the Soviet Union from sliding further down the international league table and losing its standing as a superpower or even a great power. As Japan and West Germany show, the path to world status and influence lies increasingly through developing economic and civilian technology rather than military strength.

To some extent, therefore, the rationale of perestroika serves mid-term security purposes. On the other hand, perestroika also involves a reduced emphasis on the overall importance of defence priorities in overall Soviet development. The main thrust of this emphasis is for a reduction in the defence burden and a reallocation of scarce resources to the civilian sector. Ryzhkov and others have stressed the enormous burden imposed upon the economy by the yoke of military expenditure, a burden both in financial, and perhaps more importantly, in general resource terms—scarce materials and skills.[12] Indeed a major case for the pursuit of radical disarmament policies—aside from the much vaunted danger of nuclear conflict—is couched in terms of releasing Soviet economic development from the narrow confines of the arms race and allowing it to evolve in more diverse and profitable civilian directions, thus improving living standards and raising the economic and general standing of the USSR in the world.[13] That domestic economic pressures have themselves played a key role in driving the policy to reduce military expenditure (and press for disarmament) is suggested by the growing emphasis placed on defence cuts since 1987 as the economic situation has worsened. Public admission of a deficit of over 100 billion roubles, slowing growth rates and deteriorating supplies, was the background for the announcement in December 1988 of unilateral troop cuts and in January 1989 of a 14.2 per cent cut in military expenditure[14] which is now officially estimated at approximately 80 billion roubles per year.[15] Deeper cuts of up to 50 per cent in defence expenditure are planned by 1995[16] as long as progress is maintained towards ambitious objectives in conventional arms reductions.

The onslaught on the defence burden has several external and domestic policy ramifications. On the foreign policy front it obviously increases the credibility of Soviet disarmament intentions. It also clearly provides the main driving force to pursue further arms cuts, particularly in conventional forces. The INF treaty, while a major political and psychological breakthrough, involves considerable verification costs and relatively small direct savings. A START agreement would save on future expenditure but only far-reaching conventional cuts can make a really useful contribution in the economic sense. It is perhaps the general thrust of disarmament policy rather than its specific components that matters, for it creates a political climate that facilitates a downgrading of military priorities. On the domestic front targeting military expenditure for cuts may well help to show that the leadership is doing something to try and improve the general economic situation, something that is politically useful at a time when other economic reform measures seem to be making little if any impact on living standards. In fact a direct connection is frequently made between reductions in defence and benefits in the civilian sector—witness the support of the Minister of Health for lower military spending.[17] More importantly, subordinating military to civilian priorities has helped substantially to shift resources towards the civilian sector. Julian Cooper has examined the moves made since 1988 to convert more military production facilities to civilian use, to transfer light industrial enterprises to military management and expose the defence industry to economic reform.[18] As he argues, these moves represent not merely a tactic to ease economic pressures and build up technological strength but also a 'historic and long-term shift of priorities from military to civilian purposes'. This shift stems from the twin imperatives of maintaining technological parity and modernizing the domestic economy, both of which require demilitarization of security and of the domestic economic system. The complex of interconnected security and domestic factors involved in harnessing the military thus constitutes a very strong resource linkage between internal and external policy under perestroika.

INTERACTION WITH THE WORLD ECONOMY

A less dramatic yet in the long term arguably a more important resource linkage involves Soviet external economic relations. If one part of the perestroika argument is that Soviet development has been diverted and handicapped by excessive military contest with the United States, another is that the USSR has been weakened by insufficient contact and economic competition with the advanced industrial world. Awareness of the decline of the Soviet Union by world economic standards undoubtedly helped to increase the sense of impending crisis that informed the decision to embark on perestroika. For not only had the Soviet Union slipped in its share of world product, it also occupies a lowly (fiftieth to sixtieth) position in world per capita consumption and compared badly in some basic respects even with tsarist Russia.[19] Such international comparisons continue to be used to point up the urgency of persisting with economic reform. Awareness of international decline might not have resulted in perestroika had it not been coupled with a conviction that isolation is partly responsible for Soviet backwardness and that the only way to close the widening gap and modernize the economy lay in closer long-term economic interaction with an increasingly interdependent global economy. As Shevardnadze told a Ministry of Foreign Affairs audience in July 1987, 'we have to become a more organic part of the world economic system'.[20] This conviction lies at the heart of the 'open' strategy that distinguishes perestroika from many previous Soviet attempts at reform, and, if anything, its centrality has become more apparent since 1987. 'Our restructuring', Gorbachev told the Supreme Soviet in August 1989, 'is inseparable from a policy of full-blooded participation in the international distribution of labour.'[21]

At present participation is far from being full-blooded. The Soviet Union has a meagre 4 per cent share in world trade. As Akio Kawato makes clear (Chapter 24 of this anthology), the structure of that trade makes USSR a very weak player of the world economic stage. The composition of trade is reminiscent of a Third World country, with energy accounting for over 60 percent of exports. Despite the evident difficulties of increasing economic involvement, more rigorous interaction is seen as an important aid to domestic economic perestroika in at least three respects. Most clearly the improvement of foreign trade performance is the only way to repay existing hard currency debts, which in 1989 stood at around 34 billion roubles. More importantly, it is essential for purchase of technology necessary for modernization. Even if the leadership is anxious to avoid the mistakes of the 1970s, when too much emphasis was placed on importing capital goods, it sees Western technology as a vital component of effective modernization. Export earnings are also important for purchases of foodstuffs and perhaps increasingly of manufactured consumer goods economically and politically necessary in the short term at least to buoy up perestroika.

The most important function of increased economic involvement with the advanced world lies in stimulating and promoting radical reform and efficiency within the Soviet economy.[22] Unlike Brezhnev, who used foreign trade as a kind of substitute for domestic reform, Gorbachev seeks to help shake up and modernize the economy by exposing the Soviet Union to world involvement. The decentralization of the foreign trade system is intended to help break down ministerial and departmental power and foster a sense of independence and initiative as well as to boost export capabilities and educate Soviet managers. 'Know how' has made its way into the Russian language yet has still not penetrated Soviet economic and managerial culture. To try and remedy this Moscow has signed training agreements with major Western states including Britain, France, the United States and West Germany. Inculcation of Western managerial techniques is also one of the objectives behind the policy of joint ventures with capitalist partners. From a slow start in 1987 this policy had resulted by mid-1989 in 685 agreements on joint ventures with the West.[23] Although joint ventures and other production cooperation schemes are unlikely to make a major economic impact on Soviet performance, they could act as catalysts of wider domestic economic modernization both by means of incentives and competitive pressures.

Neither joint ventures nor the foreign trade system can make much headway, however, unless domestic economic reforms make real progress, allowing the new decentralized trade system to operate effectively and steps to be taken towards currency convertibility which remains essential to any substantial growth in inward investment and trade. As Philip Hanson and Akio Kawato argue,[24] the obstacles and problems remain formidable and there is only a slim chance of the Soviet Union becoming anything like internationally competitive before the early years of the next century. Most Soviet economists would concur with this assessment; even Gorbachev has become increasingly sober since 1988 about overcoming the knot of linked domestic and international economic problems. As he told the new Soviet parliament in summer 1989: 'Whereas at the start it appeared as if change in human rights and arms control would be difficult to implement and economic relations looked relatively simple, it now seems to be the other way round.'[25]

Despite, or perhaps because of, the fact that the problems appear more formidable, economic objectives have come to figure increasingly importantly in Soviet foreign policy. Shevardnadze has called on Soviet diplomats to 'economize' Soviet foreign policy[26] and Soviet relations with all major Western states have placed economic agreements high on the agenda. Interest has also been expressed in joining international economic organizations such as GATT, and Gorbachev has made clear, most directly in his message to the G7 meeting in Paris in July 1989, that the Soviet Union wishes to be more fully involved in international economic affairs. This policy is driven by a mixture of motives. On the one hand Soviet interest flows from a concern to use economic channels to become more involved in the established international system and stabilize relations with its key actors. 'Doing business' rather than competing militarily with the rest of the world, Gorbachev seems convinced, is an important way of getting the Soviet Union accepted as a 'normal' member of the international community. Economic motives are equally or more important. Doing business, Soviet leaders hope, may help them in modernizing the Soviet economy; as realists they understand that future Soviet standing and international influence will depend increasingly on how the country performs economically by world standards. This element, and, indeed, the entire nexus of resource issues, thus provide an ever more important and complex linkage connecting the domestic and international dimensions of perestroika.

POLICY THINKING

The scope and depth of the connection between the domestic and international dimensions of perestroika emerges more clearly when we turn to the area of policy thinking. We are concerned here with policy approaches and frameworks of analysis as well as policy values, common norms and perspectives shaping strategy and tactics. The perspectives and prescriptions associated with Soviet foreign policy under perestroika go under the official label of 'new thinking'. Possibly more coherent a body of policy principles than its domestic equivalent, 'new thinking' intersects to a remarkable degree with innovative thinking on domestic affairs. Both share a pool of central ideas, beliefs, principles and perspectives that bestride the domestic and foreign policy spheres. Gorbachev has described 'new thinking' as 'in essence the ideology and theory of restructuring as a whole and not only in foreign policy.'[27] This common pool of ideas may for the sake of convenience be called 'perestroika thinking'. Its sources and major elements are sketched in the following section.

One of the reasons for the emergence of perestroika thinking has been the rise to influence of a number of policy specialists who advise and write on both domestic and international issues. These 'dual policy influentials' include people such as Bovin, Burlatsky, Butenko, Frolov, Primakov, Shmelev and Shakhanazarov. Academics, journalists and commentators who have often spent time in official academy and party think-tanks, these 'dual specialists' share key formative political experiences with many of their reformist colleagues in either the international or the domestic operating policy fields. These experiences have given them an antipathy towards Stalinism and a favourable memory of Khrushchev's efforts at de-Stalinization, coupled with a vivid experience of the negative aspects of the Brezhnev period as well as of the more positive specialist discussions of the 1970s that produced and reinforced many of the ideas that now form the basis of perestroika thinking.[28] These 'dual specialists' share with one another the additional experience of living abroad (in the West or Eastern Europe) or at least enjoying extensive international contacts which have often informed and radicalized the ideas they derived from domestic sources. To some extent, therefore, they have injected Western, as well as East European and Chinese, perspectives into perestroika thinking (their colleagues specializing solely in international affairs are often more strongly Westernized) and stand in contrast to the more closed, Russian-centred commentators and theorists who typically take a more conservative line.

The overlap found among 'dual specialists' is paralleled and reinforced by the dual domestic/foreign policy orientation among progressive members of the top leadership. Foreign Minister Shevardnadze retains a strong interest in domestic policy as he spent his entire previous career in that area, and continues to play an important role at home (as in the aftermath of the Tbilisi clashes of spring 1989). Medvedev, now in charge of ideology, for a time oversaw relations with socialist states. His predecessor as Secretary for Ideology, Yakovlev, plays a key role in internal and external affairs, both being one of Gorbachev's closest associates in the general area of ideology and head of the new International Affairs Commission of the Central Committee, thus effectively in charge of coordinating foreign policy strategy. Gorbachev himself started with little or no international experience (though he had visited Canada and Eastern Europe), but since becoming General Secretary has of course devoted a remarkable amount of time and energy to foreign affairs.

To do justice to the connections between policy thinking in the domestic and international field would require a comprehensive analysis of recent theoretical innovations in both areas as well as their interplay. The aim of this paper is simply to sketch some of the main traits of 'perestroika thinking'. Most of these traits amount to perspectives and tendencies of analysis rather than specific recommendations, even if some do suggest and are closely associated with clear policy strategies and tactics.

The first trait is analytical eclecticism, a strong tendency away from circumscribed Marxist-Leninist approaches to analysing policy problems to one employing wide-ranging social science theories and methods. As realistic and pragmatic politicians, out to modernize the entire Soviet system, Gorbachev, Yakovlev and Shevardnadze have called for innovative approaches in the analysis of international as well as domestic developments. Rather than asking social scientists in traditional style to spin new variations on ideological themes, they now urge them to use any kind of analysis that will produce penetrating assessments of key policy problems.[29] After all, in many instances, Western literature is of infinitely more use than the works of Marx or Lenin for dealing with critical domestic problems, such as bureaucratic inefficiency, or foreign policy ones like regional conflicts or arms control. The fact that the political leadership now apply criteria of effectiveness in problem solving rather than doctrinal orthodoxy has cleared the way for a whole spectrum of new policy ideas and concepts derived from Western specialist literature. In the security policy area these include the action–reaction process of the arms race, the role of enemy images, non-provocative defence, reasonable sufficiency, mutual security and interdependence. In the domestic context, as Archie Brown details,[30] many of the concepts once rejected as bourgeois have now been given authoritative endorsement. He also notes how some Western states, including Switzerland, have recently come to qualify as models for socialist development. And indeed many of the key reform policies have drawn heavily on the experience of both socialist and capitalist states. As economic perestroika has become more radical, so the focus of 'learning' has shifted—differently in various policy spheres—from the GDR and China, to Hungary, Japan and Sweden.[31]

The approach to analysis promoted by policy specialists and encouraged by the reform leadership effectively involves the de-ideologization or at least the de-dogmatization of policy thinking. Even if Gorbachev may wish ideally to build a new Marxist-Leninist framework to explain and legitimate perestroika policies, his priority as a pragmatic politician is to encourage innovative thinking which produces policies that will work rather than be doctrinally acceptable. Such pragmatic realism has strongly come to the fore on the domestic and foreign policy fronts. Gorbachev has, for instance, defined socialist quality *(sotsialistichnost)* in terms of effectiveness, while Shevardnadze in similar vein has made 'profitability' the key yardstick of foreign policy.

This eclectic problem-solving approach has raised to prominence two analytical perspectives that figure importantly in perestroika thinking: recognition of the legitimacy of diverse interests and of the need to reconcile these for the general rather than class good. The lifting of doctrinal constraints has made possible shifts in policy views of the nature of interests both within Soviet policy and in the world at large. Rather than trying to fit domestic and international interest into the Procrustean bed of class analysis, perestroika thinking acknowledges that the situation is far more complex and that interests have deep historical, national, psychological roots which are as, or possibly more important than, their traditional class dimensions.

The same approach sheds doubts on traditional assumptions about ineluctable historical tendencies either within Soviet society or the international community. To assume inexorable progress towards 'new Soviet man', a predominant Soviet identity for ethnic groups in the USSR or towards the socialist commonwealth of nations and an international communist movement is now seen as an unrealistic base for the conduct of domestic and foreign policy. Given the failure of past Soviet efforts to mould opinion at home and impose frameworks of development on other countries, it is hardly surprising that the present leadership has far less confidence in domestic or international 'social' engineering. Pluralism as diversity and complexity is accepted as a normal and almost natural feature of domestic and international life.

At the same time pluralism does not mean irreconcilable conflict. Emphasis on diversity of interests as normal goes hand in hand with stress on interdependence. Gorbachev and others have emphasized the harm of thinking in old zero-sum terms of *kto kogo* (who overcomes whom). Rather than focusing on the essential conflictual class nature of differences, 'perestroika thinking' highlights the overarching importance of common 'all human' interests and values that link all members of domestic and international communities.[32] The primacy of such 'all human' values and interests over those of class means that policy must be directed not towards emerging victorious in a struggle but towards bringing about agreement and reconciliation. In the domestic context this has meant greater efforts to recognize rather than confront minority interests—whether in the case of the Baltic republics or the miners. Internationally it has involved seeking to reconcile what were previously considered antagonistic forces, whether in Afghanistan or, as Yutaka Akino notes, in Kampuchea. In the East–West context this reconciliation approach is evident in Moscow playing down military, political and ideological conflict and pointing up the need to go beyond peaceful coexistence towards co-development.[33]

This de-ideologized approach to interests involves important shifts in policy tactics and methods towards accommodation, compromise and more political and legalistic means of managing domestic and international problems. Rather than being seen as a sign of weakness, concessions made to secure agreement are now lauded as a mark of political maturity: Gorbachev takes every opportunity to stress the virtues of 'sensible compromise' (partly, of course, in order to defend himself against criticism).[34] The use of force, on the other hand, is seen as a last resort in both the domestic and international arena. At home vigorous criticism of Stalinism has spilled over into the questioning of more recent uses of coercion to deal with dissent. As Tsuyoshi Hasegawa notes,[35] the rehabilitation of Bukharin is symptomatic of support for a more peaceful way of building socialism. Recent steps to regularize emigration procedures, ease restrictions on religious practices, and release the vast majority of prisoners of conscience all indicate serious movement away from traditional coercive methods. Although the enormous coercive machine remains intact, the Gorbachev leadership has taken a far more permissive view of protest and a more sophisticated political stance towards its management. Traditional coercive responses have been the exception rather than the rule under perestroika, and have attracted official regret and widespread condemnation, as in the case of the Tbilisi clashes of spring 1989. Generally, the regime has exhibited remarkable restraint in the face of movements such as the Baltic protests and the miners' strikes of summer 1989, which would in the past have elicited violent repression. Instead, Gorbachev has preferred political means of accommodation, something he has commended to Chinese leaders in connection with the crushing of protests in Beijing.[36]

Similar shifts have taken place in international policy. One of the major lessons drawn from critical discussion of international politics in general and Soviet foreign policy in particular is the declining utility of military force. Its use is now seen as rarely yielding gains but often exacerbating problems (for example, in Afghanistan) and a strengthening cohesion among adversaries (such as SS-20 deployment).

Complementing this shift away from coercive means is a more tentative yet equally significant move towards legal frameworks and instruments to manage conflict both at home and abroad. Gorbachev's declared aim to elevate law and create a law-based state *(pravovoe gosudarstvo)* parallels his stress on the importance of the international law and international regulatory agencies. The new level and quality of commitment to law under perestroika could still be seen as a largely declaratory one. Yet steps taken to codify and clarify domestic laws, strengthen judicial process and introduce mechanisms of checks and balances and constitutional review all point to a serious intent to create a legal culture.[37] Moves in a similar direction on the international front include acceptance of the mandatory jurisdiction of the International Court in The Hague and of the principle that all Soviet legislation, especially that relating to civil and human rights, must be brought into line with international covenants.[38] A new commitment to the role of international law and associated organizations is reflected in the substantial increase in Soviet financial as well as political support for the United Nations.[39]

Trends in thinking about the management of domestic and international policy problems thus run along remarkably similar lines. This of course does not mean that they necessarily produce identical prescriptions in every case. General approval of pluralism, for instance, translates into greater latitude for autonomous action for groups the further they are located from Moscow. Acceptance of socialist pluralism has hardly dented the principle of democratic centralism within the party and made limited inroads into the party's leading role while it has extended radically the leeway for informal political activity. 'Freedom of choice' as a principle of 'new thinking' is understandably applied in more qualified fashion to the republics of the USSR than to the states of Eastern Europe, let alone the Third World. But however differentiated according to context, what remains remarkable is the distance travelled by 'perestroika think-ing' towards greater democracy and openness within the USSR *and* in relations between the Soviet Union and the world.

Advances in thinking in both spheres have interacted to generate overall forward movement. Whereas the 'new thinking' on foreign policy issues clearly owes its ascendancy to the change in domestic climate, influence has flowed predominantly from the international to the internal sphere. This is due to the fact that new thinking was easier to formulate and deploy successfully than reform ideas on the less tractable domestic front. Success has given 'new thinking' and associated policies considerable impact on domestic developments. The with-drawal from Afghanistan and endorsement of movement towards greater autono-my in Hungary has, for instance, encouraged nationalist leaders in the Baltic to pursue national independence.[40] Although this is one example of the unintended stimulation of domestic change by foreign policy innovation, Gorbachev has on occasion deliberately sought to use the international success of 'new thinking' to boost the domestic fortunes of perestroika.[41] The need to build on improved ties with the West is invoked to promote domestic reforms (mostly in the area of civil and human rights) that flow from international undertakings or policy commit-ments. The notion of a Common European House performs a useful function not just in policy towards Western Europe;[42] it also acts as a vehicle for advancing 'European' democratic values in the domestic political arena. Efforts of this kind to reinforce the linkage between international and domestic policy thinking contribute to the general thickening of connections between international issues and domestic politics, to which we now turn.

DOMESTIC POLITICS

The remarkable changes on the Soviet domestic political scene, coupled with the radical shifts in foreign policy, have exposed international issues to more probing debate, greater controversy and wider involvement. As a result, foreign and security policy has become more politicized under perestroika.

Glasnost has helped to create a freer discussion on foreign policy, though, as Marie Mendras notes,[43] criticism came later and more hesitantly to the interna-tional than to the domestic policy field. Only since 1988 have critical discussions focused on foreign policy issues. Many such discussions have taken the form of reassessments of historical questions, such as Stalin's conduct of the war, Katyn, and the Molotov–Ribbentrop pact, the issue with the greatest domestic ramifica-tions. Criticism has also extended to more recent episodes in Soviet foreign policy, notably the deployment of the SS-20s and the decision to intervene in Afghanistan. Glasnost has also helped to lift a corner of the heavy veil of secrecy that has traditionally hung over all security and military affairs.

Discussion of previously taboo foreign and security issues has heightened pop-ular awareness and interest in this area. Yet, given natural preoccupation with debates surrounding domestic changes, it would be surprising if the *relative* salience of international affairs had not diminished under perestroika. Gorbachev himself has expressed concern about the relative neglect of foreign policy issues.[44] One obvious motive the President might have for urging that greater attention be paid to international issues is that his foreign policy offers a source of much-needed popularity. There is little doubt that Gorbachev has profited considerably at home from his success in reducing East–West military tensions and withdrawing Soviet troops from Afghanistan. Popular feelings also played a part in the politics of the decision. Before Gorbachev came to power, a growing majority of the population were eager to see an end to the war which was beginning to affect families throughout Soviet society. The ground-swell of complaint, amplified by glasnost, probably figured importantly in the leadership's decision, both as a reason to withdraw and as a hedge against criticism.

Soviet public opinion may well increasingly play a role of this kind in other issues that straddle the areas of domestic and foreign policy. For instance, measures to reduce defence expenditure seem to evince strong feeling and command public support. In a June 1989 poll, large majorities of respondents in major cities endorsed the 14 per cent cut announced and many wanted to see larger reductions.[45]

The political importance of such public attitudes is enhanced by the apparent tendency of many of the newly elected parliamentary deputies to share these views, not just on defence but on the entire thrust of security and foreign policy. Deputies signalled their support for the new departures in foreign policy by giving Shevardnadze a smooth passage through the reappointment process. In one poll deputies gave Shevardnadze a far higher approval rate than any other minister.[46] Whereas even two years ago the opinions of Supreme Soviet deputies might have been dismissed as politically unimportant, this is no longer the case as the new parliament looks set to play a significant role in foreign policy as in other areas.[47] It is not simply that Shevardnadze and others have called for a more open and democratic foreign policy process; the deputies themselves have shown an ability to submit ministers to probing questions on sensitive issues, such as to Yazov on the military, and to refuse on occasion to sanction reappointment (as in the case of Kamentsev, the minister in charge of external economic relations). The parliament, and especially its committees, are likely to exercise important scrutiny and some influence over foreign and security policy. Even at this early stage, domestic political reform has begun to affect the way in which foreign policy is presented and alternatives are formulated.

Major decisions will of course continue to be made within the leadership where foreign policy changes and their domestic ramifications have stirred considerable controversy, albeit less than the radical nature of those changes might have led one to expect. This is largely because conservative leaders and elites have been preoccupied with fighting rearguard actions on domestic issues. At the same time, while critics of perestroika do not align exactly on domestic and international issues, their leaders do make a point of linking radical internal reforms with those in foreign policy. The notorious Andreeva letter, published in March 1988 as a major broadside against perestroika, attacked the whole notion of opening up the country to nefarious foreign influences. Ligachev, in his Gorkii speech in the summer of 1988, pointedly criticized both domestic moves to a socialist market and the de-ideologization of international relations, thus linking these as planks of a single political platform. Gorbachev has further tightened this policy linkage by identifying such critics with hard-line Western opponents of perestroika.[48]

A closely related aspect of the politicization of external issues under perestroika is the extent to which power configurations within the leadership have affected foreign and security policy.[49] Although we have little hard evidence by which to assess this, some analysts have linked hesitation and even temporary retreat in foreign and security policy with shifts in leadership alignments.[50] There does appear to be some correlation between improvements in Gorbachev's position within the leadership and vigorous pursuit of foreign and security policy initiatives, as for instance in the autumn of 1986 and 1988.

Differences on foreign and security policy within the leadership, and indeed within the public debate generally, have centered around three areas: the acceptance of universal (Western) values; the demilitarization of security; and closer economic interaction with the capitalist world. All these issue areas have attracted controversy because they question basic traditions and affect a large number of interests. In doing so they have furthered the politicization of security and foreign policy by deepening the political debates surrounding it and enlarging the constituencies concerned with international issues.

The first issue area revolves around the elevation of all-human values and interests above those of class. This fundamental innovation of perestroika thinking seems to be supported by a majority of specialists working in the international relations field. Few of these apparently believe that ideology has an important role in relations with the United States or should play a key role in Soviet foreign policy objectives.[51] However, the demotion of class goals and norms does worry many conservatives. Marie Mendras has traced the public exchanges between Ligachev on the one hand and Shevardnadze and Yakovlev on the other about the official reformist declaration that peaceful coexistence is no longer to be considered a form of class struggle.[52] It is hardly surprising that Ligachev concentrated his critical fire on this new foreign policy principle since it symbolizes and legitimizes the whole strategy of more 'open' cooperation with capitalist states, and implies a corresponding weakening of commitment to socialism throughout the world, a general acceptance of international (Western) standards and an opening of the Soviet Union to Western influence. Conservatives see the principle as intimately linked with excessively permissive attitudes towards undesirable forces at home.[53]

Although such conservative views attract very little support from specialists and probably only minority sympathy from the population, policy opinion is more evenly divided on the second area of controversy and politicization—the demilitarization of security. Even many specialists apparently find it difficult to accept the new stress on the economic rather than military nature of the Western threat which is one of the rationales for far lower levels of Soviet capabilities. As Naomi Koizumi has shown, opinions differ within the military establishment on the reforms in security policy Gorbachev and his civilian advisers advocate.[54] Whereas some in the armed forces may agree that traditional Soviet policy tended towards military 'over-insurance', others feel uneasy about the notion of 'reasonable sufficiency' now central to security policy. Even key Gorbachev appointees, such as Defence Minister Yazov, tend also to use the term 'reliable' sufficiency and lay stress on more traditional concepts like equal and identical security.[55] If the military leadership generally seem to accept the principle of a more defensive military doctrine, they remain chary of civilian proposals on technical issues relating to restructuring forces in non-offensive postures. Not only do many in the military resent this as unwarranted interference in areas traditionally their professional preserve. They also tend to feel strongly that the Soviet armed forces must retain the capacity to launch counter-offensive operations.

Policy differences over these issues overlap with those over arms control and disarmament. Although Gorbachev's overall strategy here has encountered little if any direct opposition, its speed and asymmetry have aroused concern, particularly within military circles. The Soviet unilateral moratorium on nuclear testing, the unfavourable asymmetries of the INF treaty, acceptance of intrusive verification and greater transparency and the unilateral cut in conventional forces all stand out as politically controversial moves.[56]

The fact that many of the innovations in military doctrine and arms control made under perestroika have aroused controversy and scepticism among the military does not mean that the military as a whole have responded negatively. The younger and more forward-looking members of the military establishment probably appreciate the role which disarmament can play in freeing resources for technological modernization which in turn holds the key to the qualitative cutting edge of military capabilities. Still, important groups in the military elite, perhaps especially its older contingent, view with apprehension the mounting chorus of deprecation, from politicians, journalists and writers alike, of the utility of military force and the performance of the armed forces. It is in the context of what many generals see as a wider erosion of the military's traditional, almost sacred unassailability that they find the prospect of deep cuts in forces and budgets particularly worrying. The larger these cuts and the greater the economic transfers from military to civilian production, the more will security become enmeshed in domestic politics. Given the very large reductions in armed forces and expenditure scheduled for the first half of the 1990s, the next few years are likely to see a continued growth in the politicization of security policy.

Closer economic interaction with the capitalist world is the third issue area attracting controversy and acting as an avenue for the politicization of external policy change. External economic policy has long attracted heated debate in the

Soviet Union—witness the sharp differences voiced in the early 1920s over the dangers of exploitation and dependency involved in the NEP policy of opening up towards the West.[57] Persistent concern with the problems of dependency inherent in taking larger Western credits is reflected in the critical stance that Gorbachev and Ryzhkov have adopted on this issue.[58] Even though most of the additional consumer goods imported under the pressure of labour unrest in summer 1989 came from socialist states, imports from the West have risen and arguments to take on larger debts to reduce popular dissatisfaction may well grow. Any moves to take on more debt are likely further to increase the criticism voiced by a wide spectrum of opinion over the dangers of expanding and intensifying economic exchange and involvement with capitalist states. Critics of joint ventures (and mooted special economic zones) question the material benefits they are likely to bring and raise the spectre of capitalist exploitation.[59] By extension, similar arguments can be applied to other forms of interaction with the West, such as cooperation on environmental problems.

However one assesses such critical views of more openness, the issue evokes widespread controversy. And as the new foreign economic policy makes progress, so the greater penetration of the Soviet economy by foreign commercial interests will make these issues the subject of growing controversy. Progress will also politicize this area by bringing a much larger number of questions related to foreign economic policy onto the domestic political agenda. And these will be of direct interest to a far greater number of actors. For the development of joint ventures and direct, decentralized trade links will mean a dramatic extension of the range of groups with vested interests in Soviet economic relations in particular and Soviet foreign policy in general. Apart from the approximately 5,000 units (ministries, departments, local authorities, enterprises and cooperatives) involved in foreign trade activity in mid-1989, the decision to introduce by 1991 part-payment in hard currency for farmers whose production makes possible savings on food imports[60] means a further extension of the range of groups with stakes in developments in foreign economic policy.

This multiplication of constituencies with international policy concerns is likely to alter the environment for Soviet foreign policy makers. For the first time since NEP they will have to deal with a wide array of preferences and even pressures from outside the traditional range of institutions. And they will have to do this within the framework of a changing political system which imposes greater constraints and affords far greater opportunities for group lobbying activity. Powerful potential lobbyists include associations of foreign traders, economic regions (and special economic and enterprise zones if these are established in any numbers) and, most importantly, republics. Union republics have been encouraged to pursue their own economic strategies and develop autonomous external economic links. As far as future republican roles in foreign policy are concerned, Baltic developments suggest that we may see the increasing pursuit of distinctive external economic policy which in turn will affect the republics' general foreign relations with key commercial partners. All this, when added to the domestic social and political repercussions of direct foreign trade links and joint ventures, promises to make the running of Soviet foreign policy a far more complex political exercise. Opening up the Soviet Union to global economic influences will inevitably expand the role of 'low politics' in the foreign policy process. In this sense perestroika is likely to change the web of connections between domestic and foreign policy into something more akin to that found in Western states. A broader, more complex, variegated and ultimately thicker web does not of course necessarily mean a shift of Soviet foreign policy in any predetermined direction. None the less, it makes likely a more open foreign policy debate and process involving larger numbers of constituencies and participants who will bring to bear a wider range of domestic considerations and interests. Greater interdependence between East and West may thus bring closer links between domestic and foreign policy within the Soviet Union.

NOTES

1. Speech at dinner for Mrs. Thatcher, *Pravda,* 1 April 1987, p. 2.
2. For example, L. Lyubimov, "Novoe myshlenie i sovetsko-amerikanskie otnosheniya," *Mirovaya ekonomika i mezhdunarodnye otnosheniya* 10 (1987), pp. 3–14.
3. Alex Dallin perhaps has discussed this problem most thoroughly; see "The Domestic Sources of Soviet Foreign Policy" in S. Bialer (ed.), *The Domestic Context of Soviet Foreign Policy* (Boulder, CO/London: Westview Press/Croom Helm, 1981), pp. 335–408. Also see M. Schwartz, *The Foreign Policy of the USSR: Domestic Factors* (Encino, CA: Dickenson, 1975); J. N. Rosenau, "Towards Single-country Theories of Foreign Policy: The Case of the USSR," in C. F. Hermann, C. W. Kegly, and J. N. Rosenau (eds.), *New Directions in the Study of Foreign Policy* (London: Allen & Unwin, 1987), pp. 53–76; and for one general treatment of these issues, J. N. Rosenau, *The Domestic Sources of Foreign Policy* (Princeton, NJ: Princeton University Press, 1965).
4. Neil Malcolm, "De-Stalinization and Soviet Foreign Policy: The Roots of 'New Thinking,' " in T. Hasegawa and A. Pravda (eds.), *Perestroika: Soviet Domestic and Foreign Policies* (London: Royal Institute of International Affairs, 1990), Chapter 9.
5. Gorbachev speech to CPSU Central Committee, *Pravda,* 19 February 1988, p. 2.
6. Gorbachev, speech in the British Parliament, 18 December 1984, appendix 8 of House of Commons, Foreign Affairs Committee, Second Report, 1985–86 session, *UK-Soviet Relations,* vol. II (London: HMSO, 1986), p. 333.
7. Marie Mendras, "Soviet Foreign Policy: In Search of Critical Thinking," in Hasegawa and Pravda (eds.), *Perestroika: Soviet Domestic and Foreign Policies,* Chapter 10.
8. Cf. S. Bialer, "Soviet Foreign Policy: Sources, Perceptions, Trends," in *The Domestic Context of Soviet Foreign Policy,* pp. 409–41; Bialer organizes his discussion under the headings Capabilities, Politics, and Beliefs.
9. See, for instance, M. McCain, "Allocation Politics and the Arms Race: A Soviet Constituency for Arms Control," in T. F. Remington (ed.), *Essays in Honour of F. C. Barghoorn* (London: Macmillan), pp. 125–30.
10. Gorbachev at meeting with members of the Trilateral Commission, see *Pravda,* 19 January 1989, p. 2.
11. Shevardnadze report on 25 July 1988 to the Ministry of Foreign Affairs post-nineteenth Party Conference meeting, *International Affairs,* 10 (1988), p. 8.

12. Ryzhkov, *Izvestiya*, 8 June 1989, p. 2.
13. For instance, see M. S. Gorbachev, *Perestroika: New Thinking for our Country and the World* (London: Collins, 1987), p. 219.
14. Gorbachev at meeting with members of the Trilateral Commission: see *Pravda*, 19 January 1989, p. 2.
15. The official Soviet figures given by Ryzhkov on 7 June 1989 were 77.3 billion roubles for the military and 3.9 billion roubles for space developments with military applications; see *Izvestiya*, 8 June 1989, p. 3. This is well below the range of CIA estimates of 120 to 137 billion roubles but not far below those of SIPRI of 100 billion roubles; see World Armament Capitals and Disarmament, *SIPRI Year Book 1989* (Oxford: Oxford University Press), pp. 150–53.
16. Ryzhkov, *Izvestiya*, 8 June 1989, p. 3.
17. Chazov, *Pravda*, 30 June 1988.
18. Julian Cooper, ''Soviet Resource Options: Civil and Military Priorities,'' in Hasegawa and Pravda (eds.), *Perestroika: Soviet Domestic and Foreign Policies*, Chapter 7.
19. Meat consumption in urban areas in 1913 exceeded that in the USSR in 1985; see A. S. Zaichenko, ''O novom myshlenii v sovetsko-amerikanskom ekonomicheskom sotrudnichestve,'' *SShA. Ekonomika, Politika, Ideologiya* 12 (1988), p. 16. For Gorbachev's emphasis on general decline, see *Perestroika*, pp. 18–20.
20. Shevardnadze, ''Bezuslovnoe trebovanie- povernut'sya litsom k ekonomike,'' speech on 4 July 1987 at a meeting of the *aktiv* of the Ministry of Foreign Affairs, *Vestnik Ministerstva inostrannykh del SSSR* 3 (1987), p. 4.
21. *Izvestiya*, 2 August 1989, p. 2.
22. For a review of the current stage of reform, see Philip Hanson, ''Gorbachev's Economic Policies after Four Years,'' in Hasegawa and Pravda (eds.), *Perestroika: Soviet Domestic and Foreign Policies*, Chapter 5.
23. Joint ventures numbers in first half-year report for 1989. Tass in English, 19 July 1989, in BBC, *Summary of World Broadcasts*, SU/WOO87 A/3, 28 July 1989.
24. See Chapters 5 and 6 in Hasegawa and Pravda (eds.), *Perestroika: Soviet Domestic and Foreign Policies*.
25. *Izvestiya*, 2 August 1989, p. 2.
26. Shevardnadze, 4 July 1987.
27. Speech to the Supreme Soviet, Moscow radio home service, 1 August 1989, BBC, *Summary of World Broadcasts*, SU/0525, p. C/7.
28. See Chapters 4 and 9 in Hasegawa and Pravda (eds.), *Perestroika: Soviet Domestic and Foreign Policies*. In Chapter 4 Nobuo Shimotomai discusses the role of specialists in perestroika, while in Chapter 9 Neil Malcolm examines the evolution of the ideas in 'new thinking'.
29. See in particular the vigorous comments in Shevardnadze's important report to the post-19th party conference meeting of the Ministry of Foreign Affairs, *International Affairs*, 10 (1988), pp. 25–26.
30. Archie Brown, ''Perestroika and the Political System,'' in Hasegawa and Pravda (eds.), *Perestroika: Soviet Domestic and Foreign Policies*, Chapter 3.
31. See, for instance, Abalkin, *Spiegel*, 6 July 1987, translated in *Foreign Broadcast Information Service, Soviet Union Daily Report*, 10 July 1987, p. 51.
32. See Marie Mendras, ''Soviet Foreign Policy: In Search of Critical Thinking.''
33. See Gorbachev's speech to the UN, Soviet television, 7 December 1988, BBC, *Summary of World Broadcasts* SU/0330, C1/2.
34. *Izvestiya*, 2 August 1989, p. 1.
35. Tsuyoshi Hasegawa, ''Perestroika in Historical Perspective,'' in Hasegawa and Pravda (eds.), *Perestroika: Soviet Domestic and Foreign Policies*, Chapter 2.
36. Ibid., p. 2.
37. See Archie Brown, ''Perestroika and the Political System.''

38. For instance, see V. S. Vershchetin and P. A. Myullerson, "Novoe myshlenie i mezhdunarodnoe pravo," *Sovetskoe gosudarstvo i pravo* 3 (1988), pp. 3–9.

39. For an early major statement on the UN, see M. S. Gorbachev, "Realnost' i garantii bezopasnosti mira," *Pravda*, 17 September 1987, pp. 1–2

40. See an interview with T. Velliste, a prominent Estonian nationalist, in *Kodumaa*, 22 March 1989, translated in BBC, *Summary of World Broadcasts*, Soviet Union 0426, pp. B1–4.

41. See, for instance, his speech to the Supreme Soviet, *Izvestiya*, 2 August 1989, p. 2.

42. See Hannes Adomeit, "The Impact of Perestroika on Soviet European Policy," in Hasegawa and Pravda (eds.), *Perestroika: Soviet Domestic and Foreign Policies*, Chapter 12.

43. See Marie Mendras, "Soviet Foreign Policy: In Search of Critical Thinking."

44. Ibid.

45. *Izvestiya*, 4 June 1989, p. 1. Support for the officially announced 14 percent cut ranged from 10 percent in Tbilisi to 45 percent in Alma Ata. Between a quarter (Alma Ata) and two-thirds (Tallin) wanted deeper cuts.

46. *Literaturnaya gazeta*, 21 June 1989, p. 11.

47. See Archie Brown, "Perestroika and the Political System."

48. Gorbachev, 29 March 1989.

49. See Marie Mendras, "Soviet Foreign Policy: In Search of Critical Thinking."

50. See, for instance, B. Parrott, "Soviet National Security under Gorbachev," *Problems of Communism* 37, no. 6 (Nov.–Dec. 1988), p. 23.

51. Only one in fifteen of the 120 specialists (including military and diplomats as well as academics (thought that spreading the socialist system on a global scale should be the main objective of Soviet foreign policy; see A. Iu. Mel'vil' and A. I. Nikitin, "Sovetskie eksperty o mirovoi politike," *SSha. Ekonomika, Politika, Ideologiya* 6 (1989), p. 15.

52. Ibid.

53. See, for instance, Chebrikov, *Pravda*, 11 September 1987.

54. Naomi Koizumi, "Perestroika in the Soviet Military," in Hasegawa and Pravda (eds.), *Perestroika: Soviet Domestic and Foreign Policies*, Chapter 8.

55. For a thorough analysis of the debate on security issues, see R. L. Garthoff, "New Thinking in Soviet Military Doctrine," *The Washington Quarterly* 11, no. 3 (Summer 1988), pp. 131–58.

56. For one survey, see H. Gelman, *The Soviet Military Leadership and the Question of Soviet Deployment Retreats*, Rand Report R-3664-AF, November 1988.

57. See L. Geron, "Soviet Foreign Economic Policy under NEP and Perestroika: A Comparative Analysis." Ph.D. thesis, Oxford University, 1989, pp. 78–104.

58. For instance, Gorbachev, *Pravda* 24 January 1989; and Ryzhkov in Supreme Soviet debate, Soviet television, 30 June 1989, *Foreign Broadcast Information Service, Soviet Union. Daily Report*, 89–126, p. 60.

59. For instance, see M. Antonov, "Idti svoim putem," *Molodaya gvardiya* 1 (1988), p. 197, cited in Geron, "Soviet Foreign Economic Policy," p. 246, 239–63.

60. See the *Financial Times*, 11 August 1989.

19

The Role of the CPSU International Department in Soviet Foreign Relations and National Security Policy*

Mark Kramer

Since March 1985, when Mikhail Gorbachev became General Secretary of the CPSU, the party and state organisations responsible for shaping Soviet foreign policy have undergone many important changes. This article will highlight some of those changes by examining the role of the CPSU International Department and its relationship with the Soviet Foreign Ministry.

The first part of the article, which briefly discusses the evolution of the International Department (ID) before Gorbachev came to power, will provide a basis for appreciating the significance of recent shifts in the ID's role. The second part of the article will look at the period from 1985 to early 1990, with particular emphasis on the sweeping 'restructuring' of the Soviet foreign policy bureaucracy that occurred during the two-and-a-half years that Anatolii Dobrynin served as head of the International Department, from March 1986 to September 1988. This section will also consider how the ID's functions, including its new role in arms control and national security affairs, were affected by the formation of a CPSU Commission on International Policy in the autumn of 1988. The third and final section will summarise recent trends in the International Department's role and offer a few concluding thoughts about the future.

EVOLUTION OF THE INTERNATIONAL DEPARTMENT
BEFORE GORBACHEV

Ultimately, the top Soviet leader and his closest aides decide the course of Soviet foreign policy.[1] Before key decisions reach the highest level, however, a number of party and state organisations have crucial roles in gathering information,

*Reprinted by permission of the author and publisher from *Soviet Studies*, 42, 3 (July 1990). Copyright © 1990 by the University of Glasgow, U.K.

framing the terms of debate, influencing top officials, and running day-to-day affairs. The most important state organisations with a say in foreign policy are the Ministry of Foreign Affairs (MFA) and, on certain matters, the Ministry of Defence; the most important party organisation, until the autumn of 1988, was the International Department of the Central Committee. Since late 1988 the International Department has been working under the supervision of a new Commission on International Policy, which is now supposed to be the leading party body responsible for Soviet foreign relations. The ID, however, has retained a key role in day-to-day matters and even in longer-term policy formulation, and its functions within the CPSU have, if anything, expanded.

The International Department was founded in 1943 at roughly the same time that the Comintern was abolished.[2] The specific duties of the ID during the first several years of its existence are unknown. Most probably, the department, which until 1948 was headed by Andrei Zhdanov, was supposed to take over the Comintern's responsibilities for binding together the world's Communist parties under Soviet leadership. This task, however, was apparently too much for the fledgling department, as became evident in 1947 when the Cominform was created for a similar purpose. Not until the collapse of the Cominform in late 1948 (the Cominform officially existed until 1956 but effectively ceased to function after the rift with Yugoslavia in 1948) did the International Department gain a clear-cut mandate to oversee Soviet relations with all foreign Communist parties. The ID retained that function through the rest of the Stalin period and for another few years after Stalin's death.[3] But the situation changed abruptly in the aftermath of the events of late 1956 in Poland and Hungary, which led, in the spring of 1957, to the formation of a separate Central Committee department (the Department for Liaison with Communist and Workers' Parties of Socialist Countries) that was to handle relations with ruling Communist parties.[4] The International Department, though shorn of part of its mandate, remained in charge of relations with all Communist parties (and, later, socialist parties) in the capitalist world and in developing countries. This basic division of labour—with one department handling relations with ruling Communist parties and the other handling relations with non-ruling parties—lasted for the next 31 years.

Starting in the late 1950s, the International Department came into its own under the auspices of Boris Ponomarev and his patron, Mikhail Suslov. Although Suslov did not occupy any formal post within the ID, he exercised broad influence over foreign policy for nearly 35 years in his capacity as a Central Committee Secretary (1947–82) and Politbureau member (1952–53 and 1955–82). With Suslov's backing, Ponomarev became head of the International Department in 1955 and the next year rose to full membership of the Central Committee. Although Ponomarev experienced a temporary setback in early 1957, when foreign policy responsibilities were bifurcated and the Department for Liaison with Communist and Workers' Parties was established, both he and Suslov benefited politically from their support of Khrushchev against the 'Anti-Party Group' in June 1957.[5] Soon afterwards, Ponomarev's career resumed its upward climb. In 1961 Ponomarev was accorded membership in the Central Committee Secretariat, and in 1972 he also became a candidate member of the Politbureau. Ponomarev remained in all his high-level party positions, including his job as head of the International Department, until the XXVII Congress in 1986.

Under Ponomarev's leadership, the International Department became especially prominent in dealing with radical movements in Third World countries, in sponsoring front organisations throughout the non-Communist world, and in promoting close ties with powerful Communist and socialist parties in Western Europe (e.g., in France, Greece, and Italy). Although the ID had some wider foreign policy responsibilities as well, its sphere of jurisdiction was confined primarily to these key tasks of administering front organisations and maintaining liaison with non-ruling Communists and other revolutionary groups. The role of the ID in the Third World gained particular importance from the late 1950s on, when the Soviet Union began to seek greater political and military influence among the developing countries and began offering active support to national liberation movements. Much of the economic and military aid that the Soviet Union provided to Third World clients, especially the money transferred to local Communist parties, passed directly through the International Department.[6] Throughout the 1970s, the ID was consistently the most vigorous bureaucratic advocate of a forceful Soviet presence in the Third World, a theme espoused with particular vehemence by Ponomarev and his top deputy, Rostislav Ul'yanovsky.[7]

During most of the time that Ponomarev was in office the International Department's relationship with the Ministry of Foreign Affairs was relatively stable. Initially, the ID's activities in the Third World encountered resistance among some Foreign Ministry officials, who were reluctant to extend large-scale aid to non-Communist radical movements.[8] Following the defeat of the Anti-Party Group, however, Andrei Gromyko assumed the post of foreign minister, and the relationship between the ID and the MFA was placed on a more solid footing. Nevertheless, even under these improved arrangements, it was only natural for conflict and disagreement to surface from time to time between the International Department and the Foreign Ministry. A top Soviet official, Valentin Falin, has acknowledged that there were 'attempts on the part of the International Department to interfere in the [MFA's] activities' and that 'no good came of them'.[9] Likewise, the former Soviet diplomat Arkadii Shevchenko has indicated that acute 'tensions [did] sometimes arise from overlapping each other's turf'.[10] Although Ponomarev and Gromyko 'more often than not [would] try to compromise their differences rather than let them break into open conflict that [would have to] be arbitrated by the Politbureau', attempts at conciliation were not always successful. Gromyko disliked Ponomarev 'intensely' and on at least one occasion emphasised 'with considerable heat that there should not be two centres for handling foreign policy'.[11] Ponomarev, for his part, was tenacious in sticking to his ideological principles, knowing that he could ultimately rely on Suslov's authority to overcome most bureaucratic obstacles.

Yet, as heated as some of the disagreements between the International Department and the Foreign Ministry became, they usually were not of lasting consequence.[12] Except on questions relating to the Third World, where Ponomarev's aggressive support for radical movements continued to provoke tension with MFA officials who wanted to improve ties with existing governments, conflicts between the two organisations could be kept in check. For one thing, Suslov had such an important say in key foreign policy decisions until his death in 1982 that both the ID and the Foreign Ministry would at times recast or tailor their policies according to his wishes. Furthermore, on many issues the International Department had relatively little role to play. In policy towards the United States, for example, the ID's responsibilities consisted largely of maintaining ties with the small US Communist party. Although Ponomarev did meet US officials from time to time and his first deputy, Vadim Zagladin, occasionally served as a spokesman on arms control, responsibility for nearly all dealings with the US government fell to the Foreign Ministry and Defence Ministry, while the ID and other Central Committee departments generally refrained from interfering.[13] The same applied to Soviet relations with most other NATO countries. Only in the Third World did the functions and activities of the International Department and Foreign Ministry overlap enough to raise the prospect of serious jurisdictional disputes.

Even in these areas of potential conflict, the ID and the Foreign Ministry normally had an incentive to avoid a direct clash or, better still, to cooperate. Each organisation had certain strengths that tended to complement and reinforce the strengths of the other. The Foreign Ministry, for example, was a much larger organisation and it had an extensive, independent network of foreign intelligence gathering by virtue of its influence over the Soviet diplomatic service and the staffing of Soviet embassies.[14] The International Department, with a staff in Moscow of only around 150, had to make do with a much smaller network abroad consisting mainly of contacts with foreign Communist officials and radical Third World leaders, plus a handful of personnel who were assigned to Soviet embassies in most non-Communist countries (generally one ID representative per embassy).[15] The International Department was able to make up for this deficiency by maintaining access to top CPSU policy-making bodies. On certain issues, especially those pertaining to the Third World, the International Department was responsible for sifting through information gathered from KGB intelligence sources, from the Foreign and Defence Ministries, and from other pertinent agencies, and then preparing background papers, speeches, and policy recommendations for the Central Committee and the staff of the General Secretary. These materials, which were put together by the ID's small group of 'consultants' under Zagladin's direct supervision, were used in helping to set the agenda for meetings of the Secretariat and of the Politbureau.[16]

In formal bureaucratic terms, the Foreign Ministry had no comparable access on a regular basis to top party bodies, and thus MFA officials had an incentive to work together with the ID in preparing recommendations for policy towards the

Third World. Informally, of course, the ID's and Ministry's combined access to top party leaders were facilitated by the political clout of Gromyko and Ponomarev, the former of whom became a full Politbureau member in 1973 and the latter of whom was both a member of the Secretariat and a candidate member of the Politbureau. Although Ponomarev never attained full Politbureau status, he 'wielded greater practical policy influence', according to Soviet officials, 'than some full Politbureau members from outside Moscow'.[17] Gromyko, for his part, had become a dominant figure in Soviet foreign policy from the early 1970s onward.

Thus, by the time Gorbachev took power in Moscow in 1985, the relationship between the International Department and the Foreign Ministry, though at times discordant, was largely free of serious conflict. The ID, as a leading party organ, clearly had *formal* precedence over the Foreign Ministry, but Gromyko's personal status and the Foreign Ministry's wide range of expertise ensured that it had at least as prominent a voice in top decision-making bodies. Furthermore, most of the ID's chief responsibilities—for liaison with Communist and socialist parties in Western Europe, for the sponsorship of front organisations, and for limited state-to-state dealings—did not entail any inherent conflict with the Foreign Ministry's own goals; and even in the Third World, disputes between the two organisations arose in only a relatively small number of countries.[18] Much of the time, in fact, the ID and MFA had an incentive to work together (or at least not at cross purposes) on behalf of common objectives.

The narrower scope of the International Department's main activities allowed the Foreign Ministry to enjoy greater latitude in certain areas, and Gromyko used that latitude to good effect. But neither the MFA nor the ID had the expertise or inclination to delve into military affairs. Questions relating to weapons development, force posture and military strategy remained, up till the mid-1980s, under the strict control of the General Staff and the Defence Ministry, subject to approval by the Politbureau and Defence Council. Only after Gorbachev came to power did the jurisdiction of the International Department and the Foreign Ministry spread into the military arena.

CHANGES UNDER GORBACHEV

Since March 1985 the Soviet foreign policy bureaucracy has been in almost constant flux. Sweeping replacements of personnel and extensive organisational restructuring have greatly altered the process of foreign policy making. This section will concentrate on the way these changes have affected the International Department, both in its relationship with the Foreign Ministry and in its influence on Soviet foreign policy. Of particular interest will be the new responsibilities that the ID and MFA have acquired in national security affairs.

Personnel Changes

Major changes of personnel in the foreign policy apparatus began soon after Gorbachev became General Secretary. In July 1985 Andrei Gromyko, who had been foreign minister for 28 years, relinquished that post to become chairman of the Presidium of the Supreme Soviet, a nominal promotion. His successor at the Foreign Ministry, Eduard Shevardnadze, had been accorded full membership of the Politbureau and the day before Gromyko's transfer. Shevardnadze and Gorbachev had been friends for 30 years, dating back to the time when both were members of the Komsomol (Communist Youth League).[19] Although Shevardnadze had virtually no background in foreign affairs, he was obviously viewed by Gorbachev as a reliable and dynamic official who could inject new vigour into a ministry that Gromyko had come to rule with an iron hand.[20] More important, by bringing in an outsider like Shevardnadze who had worked his way up through the Georgian party and KGB, Gorbachev paved the way for an assault on the fiefdoms and power bases of officials who had served their whole careers in the Foreign Ministry with Gromyko.[21] Shevardnadze's lack of experience, in any case, did not seem to hinder his ability to learn quickly on the job, as he demonstrated in November 1985 by providing valuable support for Gorbachev at the US–Soviet summit meeting in Geneva.

Significant though the changes were in the Soviet foreign policy establishment in 1985, the process sharply accelerated the following year, especially in the wake of the XXVII Congress. Among the shifts of high-level personnel approved at the Congress was the appointment of Anatolii Dobrynin, the long-time ambassador to the United States, to replace Ponomarev as head of the International Department. Dobrynin also replaced Ponomarev a few months later as Chairman of the Foreign Affairs Committee of the Supreme Soviet's Council of Nationalities.[22] Although Dobrynin was already 66 years old at the time of his appointment, he was some 15 years younger than the ageing Ponomarev. Dobrynin could offer experience, broad knowledge and bureaucratic finesse, yet still be able to bring a fresh perspective to the ID that would complement the less experienced Shevardnadze at the Foreign Ministry. Gorbachev undoubtedly intended Dobrynin to serve long enough to provide needed advice (especially about US–Soviet relations) and maintain stronger party control over foreign policy while enabling Shevardnadze to gain greater experience and establish a solid presence as foreign minister.

The personnel changes at the top of the International Department and the Foreign Ministry were soon followed by a series of key appointments at the tiers just below.[23] In April 1986 Georgii Kornienko, who had been a first deputy foreign minister since 1977, was moved over to the ID to join Vadim Zagladin as one of Dobrynin's two first deputies. (Kornienko had worked in the early 1960s for Dobrynin in Washington and, like Zagladin, was knowledgeable about arms control.) Over the next several months Dobrynin also appointed two new deputies, Andrei Urnov and Yurii Zuev; and in April 1988 he appointed a third new deputy, Mikhail Smirnovsky. Replacements at lower levels of the ID, including sector heads and deputy sector heads, continued apace as well.[24]

The turnover of personnel at the Foreign Ministry was even more sweeping. In May 1986 Shevardnadze appointed two new first deputy ministers, Anatolii Kovalev and Yulii Vorontsov, who together took over the position vacated by Kornienko. They were joined by seven new deputies (out of nine in total) whom Shevardnadze designated between December 1985 and August 1986.[25] Most of the Ministry's department chiefs were also replaced at around this time. Along with these removals of high-level officials came wholesale changes in the Soviet diplomatic corps; in just the first two years Gorbachev was in power, Soviet ambassadors were replaced in 60% (74 of 124) of the countries maintaining full diplomatic relations with the USSR, including nine of the 16 members of NATO.[26] Ambassadorial replacements continued at a breakneck pace during Gorbachev's next two years in office; as a result, only 15% (19 of 128) of the pre-1985 ambassadors remained in their posts by March 1989, including just two in NATO countries.[27] The rate of turnover among Soviet ambassadors had become so high by mid-1988 that it even led to concern among top-level MFA officials about 'the virtual exhaustion of the supply of reserve diplomats'.[28]

For the International Department in 1986 and early 1987 the significance of the personnel changes, both in the department itself and in the Foreign Ministry, was immense. The transfer of Kornienko provided Dobrynin with a long-time associate who knew (perhaps even better than Dobrynin) precisely what needed to be done in the Foreign Ministry to assert firmer party control, improve the style and substance of Soviet foreign policy, and enable Shevardnadze to avoid being overwhelmed by entrenched officials. It was with Dobrynin's and Kornienko's assistance, apparently, that many of the personnel changes were carried out in the ministry, especially the replacements of ambassadors.[29] Dobrynin's role in this process was buttressed in part by the supervision he maintained over Stepan Chervonenko, the head of the Cadres Abroad Department.[30] In the past, the Cadres Abroad Department's main responsibility was to work with the MFA and the KGB in screening and monitoring candidates for diplomatic assignments; but under Chervonenko (who, in turn, reported to Dobrynin) the Cadres Abroad Department evidently acquired greater say and leeway in replacements of MFA personnel.[31]

Dobrynin's potential influence in the Foreign Ministry was further augmented by the appointment of the new first deputy foreign minister, Yulii Vorontsov, who had been one of Dobrynin's closest aides in Washington for 11 years in the 1960s and 1970s. Three of the new deputy ministers—Aleksandr Bessmertnykh (who was appointed a first deputy minister in October 1988), Vadim Loginov and Igor Rogachev—also had close ties to Dobrynin from earlier stints in Washington.[32] Bessmertnykh, in particular, had worked under Dobrynin for some 13 years, and it was thus fitting that Bessmertnykh's new position included general responsibility for Soviet relations with the United States. The International Department appears to have been strengthened still further by the appointment of Anatolii Chernyaev, who had been deputy head of the ID, to be a special foreign policy assistant to Gorbachev.[33] That post had been held for the previous 22 years by a Foreign Ministry official, Andrei Aleksandrov-Agentov (and for a time by another MFA official, Anatolii Blatov), who was transferred to an unspecified diplomatic assignment in December 1986.

Thus, the changes of personnel in both the International Department and the Foreign Ministry, though not based strictly on 'patron–client' relationships, tended to give the ID new authority and strengthen the party's control over the foreign policy apparatus. Dobrynin's position in the bureaucracy was solidified by an interlocking network of high-level officials in the International Department and the Foreign Ministry, as well as by his newly gained influence vis-à-vis the diplomatic corps. In relative terms, then, power was shifting somewhat in 1986 from the Foreign Ministry to the International Department, as Shevardnadze himself acknowledged later on:

> . . . we [in the Ministry] must first of all improve our own efforts. However, we also need the help of our colleagues. The country's foreign policy is not simply that of the Ministry of Foreign Affairs. *All of its practical achievements in recent years have been the fruit of concerted, well-coordinated action by several foreign policy departments working under the supervision of the party.* . . . Such coordination has been especially important in the national security sphere.[34]

Nevertheless, it would be wrong to suggest—as some Western observers initially did—that Gorbachev went along with all the personnel changes simply to enervate the Foreign Ministry and build up the policy-making role of the International Department at the Foreign Ministry's expense. Instead, what seems to have happened is that Gorbachev needed Dobrynin to assist Shevardnadze both in the restructuring of the Foreign Ministry and in the transition to Shevardnadze's new role as foreign minister. Stricter party control was not merely a desirable objective in itself; it was also a crucial means of enabling Gorbachev's appointee to acclimatise himself to the office and gradually assert his authority over the country's foreign policy agenda.[35] The more forceful presence that Shevardnadze displayed in 1987 and 1988 confirmed that the partial eclipse of the Foreign Ministry in 1986 was merely a transitory phenomenon, not a lasting trend. By 1989 the ministry had gained a dominant role in almost all areas of foreign policy.

ORGANISATIONAL RESTRUCTURING

The campaign to restructure the whole Soviet foreign policy bureaucracy has taken the form not only of sweeping personnel changes but also of an organisational shake-up of both the International Department and the Foreign Ministry. The reorganisation of the Foreign Ministry came first, starting soon after Shevardnadze took office; and although it has not been as radical as the shake-up of the Central Committee departments, it has come to affect virtually the entire allocation of responsibilities within the MFA. The alignment of the ministry's regional offices, for example, which had been carried over largely intact from the old tsarist system, was drastically altered in 1986 to conform with the political geography of the late 20th century.[36] As part of this realignment, new offices were created to oversee relations with Communist countries in Europe and in Asia and with non-Communist countries in the Middle East and North Africa, in sub-Saharan Africa, in North America, and in Southeast Asia and the Pacific.

Several other new agencies were established within the MFA to carry out specific functional duties: a Directorate for Humanitarian and Cultural Ties, an International Economic Relations Directorate, a Directorate for Liaison with Soviet Embassies, a Non-Aligned Movement Department, a Directorate for Information, and an Arms Control and Disarmament Directorate. In addition, a separate Research Coordinating Council was set up to facilitate greater collaboration with outside 'think-tanks' and institutes, and a Directorate for International Scientific and Technological Cooperation was established to deal with technical security matters. More recently, two special MFA departments were created, one of which handles legislative affairs and contacts with the Supreme Soviet, and the other of which deals with nationality problems and their effect on foreign policy.[37] The main purpose of establishing all these bodies, according to Shevardnadze, was to promote 'democratic discussion and collective decision making' within the Ministry, thus ensuring the full 'participation of competent experts' and others who 'can think keenly and unconventionally'.[38]

Although organisational changes in the ID and other Central Committee departments did not begin until after the realignment of the Foreign Ministry, they ultimately proved to be more sweeping. Under the restructuring of the central party apparatus that took effect in the autumn of 1988, most of the 22 Central Committee departments were abolished, and six new CPSU Commissions were created to supervise key domestic and foreign matters.[39] The nine departments that survived were subordinated to one or more of the six Commissions, and these in turn were made directly accountable to the Politbureau, as explained in the resolution approving their formation:

> The Commissions of the CPSU Central Committee are to study the problems in their areas of responsibility and draft proposals for the CPSU Central Committee. . . . According to the results of their studies, the Commissions are to present draft documents and analytical materials to the Politbureau.[40]

As one of the surviving departments, the ID was subordinated to the Commission on International Policy, which was given broad oversight of foreign affairs and placed under the control of a senior Politbureau member, Aleksandr Yakovlev. In keeping with this reorganisation, the three top officials in the old ID— Dobrynin, Zagladin, and Kornienko—all stepped down. (Dobrynin and Zagladin have been retained as personal advisers to Gorbachev, however.) Under the new leadership of Valentin Falin (who, unlike his two predecessors, was not elevated to the Secretariat), the ID was supposed to serve as a working organ for the Commission on International Policy, overseeing the day-to-day affairs, providing expertise when needed, and helping to draft materials for higher party bodies.[41]

In that sense, the restructuring of the central party apparatus resulted in a significant downgrading of the ID's role. Other aspects of the restructuring, however, tended to strengthen the International Department. Most notably, the ID gained a wider sphere of jurisdiction as it took over the duties of two other Central Committee departments that ceased to exist: the Cadres Abroad Department and the Department for Liaison with Communist and Workers' Parties of Socialist Countries. Thus, for the first time since 1957, the International Department was again responsible for Communist as well as non-Communist countries. In addition, the ID formally took charge of the diplomatic clearing procedures that the Cadres Abroad Department had overseen in the past. By acquiring these added responsibilities, the International Department at least partly made up for the prestige and status that it lost through its subordination to the Commission on International Policy.

Furthermore, some of the ID's long-standing functions—in particular, its sponsorship of international front organisations and its role in Soviet 'active measures' (covert disinformation campaigns)—were unaffected by the restructuring of the central party apparatus.[42] The importance of these activities has been growing throughout the Gorbachev period, despite the advent of 'new political thinking'. For this reason, if for no other, the International Department (or an equivalent body under a different name) is bound to remain a prominent organ of Soviet foreign policy in the years ahead.

Finally, it is worth noting that although the Commission on International Policy was given the task of overseeing the ID's activities, the exact powers and supervisory functions of the Commission were unclear. For one thing, the new head of the ID, Valentin Falin, was also a member of the Commission, and he was therefore well situated to influence the 'oversight' of his department. Moreover, the Commission was never meant to be a permanent body; it was required to meet only once every three months, and it did not convene at all until March 1989, some six months after it was created.[43] Even when the Commission did meet, it consisted of only 24 members, all of whom had full-time jobs elsewhere.[44] Although most of the members had impressive foreign policy credentials, the time they could devote to the Commission was obviously limited. As a result, meetings of the Commission in 1989 tended to cover only a limited range of topics.[45]

Hence the International Department continued, of necessity, to play a vital role for the CPSU not only in day-to-day matters but also in longer-term policy formulation, under Yakovlev's personal supervision. It is true, of course, that, as part of the cutbacks in the Central Committee apparatus, the size of the International Department was reduced by at least one-third compared to the staffing levels of the three abolished departments whose duties it came to perform.[46] It is also true that some positions in the ID went unfilled for a considerable time.[47]

Nevertheless, most of the personnel changes in the International Department after the reorganisation of 1988, especially the appointments of Karen Brutents and Rafail Fedorov as first deputies, were clearly intended to bolster the department's expertise on both Communist and non-Communist countries. Although the ID was increasingly overshadowed by the Foreign Ministry from 1988 onward, that was largely a consequence of Gorbachev's desire to transfer power from the party to the state. Within the CPSU itself the International Department remained, and should remain, a key organ.

The New Roles of the ID and MFA in Military Affairs

One of the most notable features of the organisational restructuring was the creation of an Arms Control and Disarmament Directorate in the Foreign Ministry in June 1986. The new agency was placed under the supervision of Viktor Karpov, the chief Soviet arms control negotiator, who had earlier worked for Dobrynin in Washington.[48] Karpov received a broad mandate to consolidate and oversee all of the Foreign Ministry's arms control negotiating efforts on such diverse issues as strategic nuclear weapons, ballistic-missile defence, military uses of space, nuclear testing, chemical weapons, confidence- and security-building measures, conventional arms reductions, and multilateral proposals in the Conference on Disarmament.[49] These efforts had previously been dispersed among several different ministerial offices.[50] Karpov's agency was also placed in charge of the Soviet Union's Nuclear Risk Reduction Centre (set up under a US–Soviet agreement in 1987), although the NRRC itself is located in the Ministry of Defence.[51] More recently, the Arms Control and Disarmament Directorate has assumed responsibility for all Soviet on-site inspections of foreign military facilities as permitted under the Intermediate-Range Nuclear Forces (INF) Treaty.[52] The importance of the new agency in all these areas was underlined in November 1988 when Karpov was promoted to deputy foreign minister.

The formation of the Arms Control and Disarmament Directorate in the Foreign Ministry was paralleled by the establishment in July 1986 of a special arms control sector in the International Department. In the past, as noted above, the ID had never been responsible for national security matters. Military affairs and arms control policy since Khrushchev's ouster had always been left to the professional military, and any necessary political input had come from the Foreign Ministry.[53] Thus the new sector in the ID was a striking innovation, especially since the appointment of Lieut.-General Viktor Starodubov as head of the sector was a clear indication that it was to be a genuine source of military and technical expertise, and not merely a bureaucratic figurehead. Starodubov had been the principal military adviser on the Soviet delegation to the Strategic Arms Reduction Talks (START) and since 1979 had been the chief Soviet representative on the Standing Consultative Commission (SCC); he had also served in the 1970s on the Soviet delegation to the Strategic Arms Limitation Talks (SALT). Starodubov enjoyed a reputation as 'an adept and highly accomplished negotiator' among US officials who dealt with him at the SCC.[54] Moreover, he had worked closely with Karpov, both during the strategic arms control talks and during Starodubov's first few months at the SCC, when Karpov was finishing up as the deputy Soviet commissioner. Karpov, as the chief START negotiator, had regularly counted on Starodubov to sort out technical military matters and, on at least one occasion, had even permitted Starodubov to correct him in front of the American delegation.[55] Hence, not only were Starodubov and Karpov ideally qualified to provide advice on all aspects of arms control; they were also well-suited to work comfortably together and reinforce one another's efforts.

The creation of the two arms control units was not intended, of course, to shut the professional military out of the decision-making process. Soviet officials have remained—and will remain—heavily dependent on the General Staff and other parts of the Defence Ministry for military and technical advice. Indeed, Gorbachev has engaged a prominent officer, Marshal Sergei Akhromeev, the former chief of the General Staff, as a personal adviser on arms control and military affairs. Moreover, the new 'civilian' agencies themselves have relied, in part, on senior military officers, most notably Starodubov, whose new post enabled him to try to exert a restraining influence on Soviet arms control efforts. Likewise, Karpov's first deputy is Lieut.-General Konstantin Mikhailov, an arms control expert who had earlier been assigned to the General Staff; and the MFA's Research Coordinating Council includes yet another former high-ranking General Staff officer, Admiral Nikolai Amel'ko.[56] These military officials, particularly Starodubov and Akhromeev, have not been hesitant about expressing hard-line views that presumably reflect dominant sentiments within the senior officer corps.[57] Thus, even in the narrowest sense, the military has by no means been excluded from key policy decisions.

Nevertheless, the formation of arms control sections within the ID and the Foreign Ministry, as well as the greater prominence enjoyed by civilian research institutes connected with the Academy of Sciences, does seem to reflect a desire on Gorbachev's part to ensure that the military will no longer enjoy an un-challenged monopoly on defence expertise and that there will be a regular mechanism outside the General Staff to provide input into arms control decisions (and therefore into other military decisions as well). Unlike in the past, when military officers were the only ones deemed competent to offer advice on national security matters, Gorbachev and his closest aides apparently believe that civilian analysts must eventually develop expertise sufficient to permit their recommendations on key matters to be accorded a weight equal (or nearly equal) to those of the military. As one high-level Foreign Ministry official recently explained:

The mentality [in the past] was that national security matters were so classified and so sensitive that the fewer people who dealt with them the better. . . . Now the role of expert analysis in the Ministry has increased considerably. . . . We are also collaborating much more closely with Soviet academe, with both institutes and individual scholars. During the years of stagnation, little was heard from them. Now, however, they too have received 'freedom of speech' and the opportunity to prove themselves and their abilities.[58]

Again, it must be stressed that Gorbachev's aim is not to *displace* the military as a source of national security advice; rather, he simply wants to have non-military alternatives available in the Central Committee apparatus, the Foreign Ministry, and the Academy of Sciences' research institutes. As Shevardnadze put it, the aim is to develop 'a smoothly operating mechanism that can produce realistic, complex assessments of the threats to our national security, a mechanism that is free of strong external pressure from anybody'.[59]

The rationale for cultivating these alternative sources of expertise is presumably connected with the Soviet Union's domestic priorities.[60] The prospects for Gorbachev's success in revitalising the Soviet economy—especially the prospects for his ambitious programme of industrial modernisation—will depend in part on his ability to set a limit on the resources that will have to be committed to the Soviet armed forces over the next two to three decades. The problem is not so much that the *current* military budget has to be reduced (although that would be desirable) as that *future* resource commitments have to be constrained and predictable, starting with the 13th Five-Year Plan in 1991. If all the best resources, both human and material, continue to go to military industries at the expense of the non-military industrial base, Soviet economic restructuring and technical prowess will be jeopardised.[61] Thus Gorbachev and his aides have clearly been seeking to reduce the domestic pressures for a future military build-up, and they apparently concluded some time ago that the only way to do so was to bring into the national security process non-military voices who can move away from the traditional Soviet style of threat assessment and force planning.[62]

Viewed in that light, the new role of the International Department, MFA, and civilian 'think-tanks' in Soviet national security policy seems more important yet also more precarious. In the near term, of course, the expanded role of these non-military organs is probably not in danger. Although many professional officers have already expressed strong resentment at the 'intrusions' of civilian analysts into what had formerly been the military's exclusive preserve, Gorbachev's approach has generally been accepted—if only grudgingly—in the upper levels of the armed forces.[63] One high-ranking officer, in fact, has called for 'greater purposeful cooperation between scholars from the leading civilian institutes and scholars from the military academies in studying the problems of . . . war and peace'.[64]

Nevertheless, it remains to be seen whether senior military commanders will continue to acquiesce in these changes if the non-military analysts strive for a further institutionalisation of their role and seek greater access to classified military data. Recent complaints by high-level MFA officials about the Defence Ministry's 'excessive secrecy unwarranted by security needs' and about the 'absurd difficulty that civilian specialists have in obtaining information on the Soviet armed forces' may portend the sort of problem that will arise with increasing frequency in the future.[65] It also remains to be seen whether Gorbachev himself will continue to listen to the non-military analysts if their advice does not yield prompt and tangible benefits or if things somehow go awry.

At least for now, though, the Central Committee personnel who are handling arms control issues, and their counterparts in the Foreign Ministry and research institutes, do appear to have taken full advantage of their opportunity to influence national security policy. Several of Gorbachev's arms control initiatives—particularly has unilateral nuclear test moratorium, his acceptance of disproportionately large Soviet cuts in the INF Treaty, and his decision to reduce Soviet conventional forces unilaterally by 1991—clearly seem to have been inspired by civilian advisers, most likely to the discomfort of the military. Moreover, assessments of a wide range of topics, including military doctrine and military intervention abroad as well as arms control, have poured forth from non-military commentators.

For the International Department, according to the former first deputy Zagladin, this expanded role meant an 'incredibly large workload' and 'a need for constantly growing activity, initiative taking and path seeking'.[66] No doubt the workload is even greater for the Arms Control and Disarmament Directorate at the Foreign Ministry, whose supervision of verification and on-site inspections is an enormous undertaking in itself, one that previously would have been left exclusively to the military and KGB. Shevardnadze has emphasised that 'without the Arms Control and Disarmament Directorate we could hardly have coped with the volume of work required of us in this crucial area'.[67] But if the advice Gorbachev is receiving from analysts outside the General Staff is to remain timely and incisive, the arms control sections in the International Department and, even more, the Foreign Ministry may have to be enlarged.[68]

CONCLUSION

The roles and functions of the International Department changed more during Gorbachev's first four years in office than they did during the previous four decades. Although the ID under Ponomarev had an important role as a conduit of foreign policy advice for the Secretariat, the department's main responsibilities were limited to sponsoring international front organisations, maintaining close ties with non-ruling Communist parties and other radical groups, and supporting revolutionary movements in the Third World. High-ranking ID officials such as Zagladin were occasionally selected to announce Soviet positions on arms control and related security matters (for example, the 1983 Korean airliner incident), but the department clearly did not have a set role in national security policy making. Moreover, the authority and expertise that Gromyko wielded at the Foreign Ministry in the 1970s and early 1980s tended to diminish the influence that the ID derived from its access to top party organs.

Soon after Gorbachev came to power, virtually all of these conditions changed. The International Department remained in charge of front organisations and liaison with non-ruling Communists, but its duties temporarily expanded far beyond what they had been previously, compensating for the change of guard at the Ministry of Foreign Affairs. Following Gromyko's removal as foreign minister, his successor, Shevardnadze, needed time to stake out a role for himself and restructure the Ministry from top to bottom. The International Department, under Dobrynin's leadership after the XXVII Congress, was enlisted to help Shevardnadze in his house-cleaning tasks and to take on added responsibilities in the meantime that would normally be left to the Ministry. Once Shevardnadze began to assert himself in foreign policy, as he did from early 1987 on, the Foreign Ministry no longer had to depend on the ID, and the shift in power (or, at least, temporary devolution of responsibility) ceased. Since then, the Shevardnadze's role has been steadily increasing in all aspects of foreign affairs and national defence, and the Foreign Ministry has gained clear preeminence over the International Department.

Once the overhaul of the Foreign Ministry was essentially complete, the International Department itself was subjected to a thorough restructuring. The subordination of the ID to a new Commission on International Policy, and the retirement of Dobrynin, Kornienko, and Zagladin, seemed initially to portend a sharp contraction of the department's role. From late 1988 on, however, the ID continued to carry out most of its traditional duties plus other tasks that it was recently assigned. The department's new responsibilities included some functions that it once performed long ago (for example, liaison with ruling Communist parties), but they also included activities that the ID had never been authorised to pursue in the past. This latter category applied most notably to the new role in arms control and national security policy that the International Department acquired from mid-1986 on.

The expansion of the ID's jurisdiction into military affairs stemmed from Gorbachev's desire to develop a coterie of experts on national security who would be independent of the General Staff. That goal required the extension of broad leeway for analysts in the International Department, the Foreign Ministry, and other organisations to offer judgments about sensitive matters that had long been reserved for the sole discretion of military officers. The formation of special arms control sections in both the ID and the MFA, and the appointment of two such eminently knowledgeable figures as Starodubov and Karpov to head the new sections, indicated that Gorbachev was serious about developing alternatives to the General Staff. Although advice from the professional military will remain crucial to Soviet national security decision making, the role of analysts outside the military continued, and indeed grew, under the expanded ID and the new Commission on International Policy.

In the long run, however, if the ID sector is retained, its influence in the national security process—and the influence of other civilian advisory bodies—may still fade, especially if the non-military analysts fail to produce the kinds of results that Gorbachev is seeking. Moreover, the role of the ID will be declining, in any event, as the CPSU loses its predominant grip on power. Nevertheless, at least for the next year or two, the International Department and its governing Commission will probably have nearly as extensive a role in Soviet national security policy as the department occupied under Dobrynin between 1986 and 1988. If things go well, an even wider role for the ID's new arms control sector, as well as for other deference experts outside the military, may be in the offing.

NOTES

1. Until March 1990, the highest foreign policymaking organ was the Defence Council, which consisted of leading political, military, and military–industrial officials. Although the Defence Council was always nominally a state organ, it functioned for many years as little more than a sub-group of the CPSU Politbureau. All General Secretaries—from Brezhnev to Gorbachev—were identified as heading the Defence Council, regardless of the state positions they held. Under the constitutional changes of 1988, however, the Chairman of the Supreme Soviet rather than the General Secretary, was explicitly designated as head of the Defence Council. This shift reflected Gorbachev's desire to consolidate a separate base of power for himself by transferring functions from the party to the state and by downgrading (and perhaps eventually eliminating) the office of the General Secretary. At the very least, the constitutional changes effectively ensured that the top Soviet leader would automatically be head of state, something Gorbachev did not attain until October 1988, long after he had been identified as head of the Defence Council. The creation of a Presidency and Presidential Council in March 1990, which largely supplanted the Defence Council, further weakened the CPSU and strengthened Gorbachev.

2. Elizabeth Teague, "The Foreign Departments of the Central Committee of the CPSU," Supplement to *Radio Liberty Research Bulletin,* 27 October 1980, pp. 6–7; Robert W. Kitrinos, "International Department of the CPSU," *Problems of Communism* 34, no. 5 (September–October 1984), pp. 48–49; Jerry F. Hough, "Soviet Policymaking toward Foreign Communists," *Studies in Comparative Communism* 15, no. 3 (Autumn 1982), pp. 168–69; and Leonard Schapiro, "The International Department of the CPSU: Key to Soviet Policy," *International Journal* 32, no. 1 (Winter 1976–77), p. 42.

3. Between 1948 and 1955 the ID underwent several name changes, but for the sake of simplicity it will be referred to here as simply the International Department.

4. Kitrinos, "International Department," pp. 49–50; Vladimir Petrov, "Formation of Soviet Foreign Policy," *Orbis* 17, no. 3 (Fall 1973), pp. 824–27; and Hough, "Soviet Policymaking," pp. 171–72.

5. Teague, "The Foreign Departments," pp. 15–16.

6. Ibid., pp. 14–15.

7. See Sally W. Stoecker, *R. A. Ulianovsky's Writings on Soviet Third World Policies, 1960–1985,* P-7177 (Santa Monica, CA: RAND Corporation, February 1986); and Harry Gelman, *The Brezhnev Politburo and the Decline of Detente* (Ithaca, NY: Cornell University Press, 1984), pp. 48, 60.

8. Kitrinos, "International Department," p. 50.

9. "V. Falin: 'Kriticheski otnosit'sya k sebe,' " *Argumenty i fakty,* no. 9 (4–10 March 1989), p. 4.

10. Arkady N. Shevchenko, *Breaking with Moscow* (New York: Alfred Knopf, 1985), p. 189.

11. Ibid.

12. See Kenneth A. Myers and Dimitri Simes, *Soviet Decision Making, Strategic Policy, and SALT* (Washington, DC: Georgetown Center for Strategic and International Studies, December 1974), p. 23.

13. Dimitri K. Simes, "The Domestic Environment of Soviet Policy Making," in Arnold L. Horelick, ed., *U.S.–Soviet Relations: The Next Phase* (Ithaca, NY: Cornell University Press, 1986), p. 162.

14. Until 1986 the Foreign Ministry shared control of the diplomatic service with the Cadres Abroad Department, not with the International Department; the Cadres Abroad Department's chief task was to get clearance from the KGB. See Teague, "The Foreign Departments," p. 6. The situation changed somewhat when Anatolii Dobrynin was made head of the ID, as discussed below. The situation changed even more once the Cadres Abroad Department's functions were absorbed by the International Department.

15. Shevchenko, *Breaking with Moscow*, pp. 189–90, and interview by the author with Evgenii Novikov, former staff member of the ID stationed in Prague, in Washington, D.C., 19 October 1988.

16. See Shevchenko, *Breaking with Moscow*, p. 190, and the comments of a senior CPSU Central Committee official, Valentin Falin (who, coincidentally, was Dobrynin's successor as head of the ID), in Henry Brandon, "How Decisions Are Made in the Highest Soviet Circles," *The Washington Star*, 15 July 1979, p. A9. Also see Gelman, *The Brezhnev Politburo and the Decline of Detente*, pp. 48, 61–62; and Archie Brown, "The Foreign Policy-Making Process," in Curtis Keeble, ed., *The Soviet State: The Domestic Roots of Soviet Foreign Policy* (Boulder, CO: Westview Press, 1985), p. 205.

17. Cited in Ned Temko, "Soviet Insiders: How Power Flows in Moscow," in Erik P. Hoffmann and Robbin F. Laird, eds. *The Soviet Policy in the Modern Era* (New York: Aldine de Gruyter, 1984), p. 181.

18. In the 1950s and 1960s this would have included countries like Egypt and Indonesia; in the 1970s and 1980s it would have included countries like Iran and Argentina.

19. Thomas L. Friedman, "Shevardnadze and Baker: Two Southerners Who Could Deal," *The New York Times*, 5 March 1989, p. E-3.

20. Shevardnadze implied as much in two key speeches in mid-1987, the first at the Foreign Ministry's conference in May and the second before the diplomatic academy *aktiv* in June. See "Doklad E. A. Shevardnadze na soveshchanii v MID SSSR 3 maya 1987 g.," *Vestnik Ministerstva inostrannykh del SSSR*, no. 1 (5 August 1987), pp. 17–22; and "Vystuplenie E. A. Shevardnadze na sobranii aktiva diplomaticheskoi akademii, Instituta mezhdunarodnykh otnoshenii i tsentral'-nogo apparata MID SSSR," *Vestnik Ministerstva inostrannykh del SSSR*, no. 2 (26 August 1987), pp. 30–4.

21. See the interview with Soviet deputy foreign minister Vladimir Petrovsky in *La Repubblica* (Rome), 17 June 1986, p. 4.

22. "Informatsionnoe soobshchenie o zasedaniyakh Verkhovnogo Soveta SSSR," *Izvestiya*, 20 June 1986, p. 4.

23. Dates for most of the appointments mentioned here can be found in US Central Intelligence Agency, *Directory of Soviet Officials: National Organizations*, LDA87-12090, June 1987; and US Central Intelligence Agency, *Directory of USSR Ministry of Foreign Affairs Officials*, LDA 87-12484, July 1987.

24. See Wallace Spaulding, "Shifts in CPSU ID," *Problems of Communism* 36, no. 4 (July–August 1986), pp. 80–86.

25. The seven new deputy ministers, in order of appointment were Vadim Loginov, Valentin Nikiforov, Aleksandr Bessmertnykh, Boris Chaplin, Anatolii Adamishin, Vladimir Petrovsky, and Igor Rogachev. Bessmertnykh was subsequently (in October 1988) promoted to first deputy minister, joining Kovalev and Vorontsov. His replacement as deputy minister was Viktor Karpov, whose role is discussed below.

26. CIA, *Directory of Soviet Officials*, pp. 79–86; and CIA, *Directory of USSR Ministry of Foreign Affairs Officials*, pp. 21–37. For a useful but preliminary summary, see Alexander Rahr, "Winds of Change Hit Foreign Ministry," *Radio Liberty Research*, RL 274/86, 16 July 1986, esp. pp. 2–3.

27. US Central Intelligence Agency, *Directory of Soviet Officials: National Organizations Update 3*, March 1989, pp. 70–93.

28. Valentin Nikiforov, "O kadrovoi politike," *Mezhdunarodnaya zhizn'*, no. 9 (September 1988), p. 53.

29. Interview with the Soviet ambassador to the United Nations, Aleksandr Belonogov, 25 May 1988, in Cambridge, Massachusetts. Also see Rahr, "Winds of Change," p. 4.

30. James P. Nichol, *Perestroika of the Soviet Ministry of Foreign Affairs During the Gorbachev Period*, Program in Soviet and East European Studies Occasional Paper Series No. 16 (Amherst, MA: University of Massachusetts International Area Studies Program, 1988), p. 31.

31. Evidence for this assertion includes, first, Chervonenko's participation in all major Foreign Ministry conferences between 1986 and 1988; and, second, the content of the statements he presented at these conferences. See, for example, "Kadrovuyu politiku—na sluzhbu perestroike," *Mezhdunarodnaya zhizn'*, no. 10 (October 1988), pp. 53–59.

32. Another deputy foreign minister, Viktor Komplektov, who was appointed in 1982, had also worked for several years (1963–69) in the Washington embassy under Dobrynin.

33. Alexander Rahr, "Gorbachev's Personal Staff," *Radio Liberty Research*, RL 216/88, 30 May 1988, pp. 2–4.

34. "Doklad E. A. Shevardnadze," *Vestnik Ministerstva inostrannykh del SSSR*, no. 15 (15 August 1988), p. 36 (emphasis added).

35. It is interesting to note that Dobrynin and the heads of other Central Committee departments responsible for foreign affairs were all present at the May 1986 conference on the restructuring of the Foreign Ministry. See "Soveshchanie vneshnepoliticheskikh rabotnikov," *Pravda*, 24 May 1986, p. 1.

36. For a useful overview, see Nichol, *Perestroika*, pp. 16–25.

37. M. Yusin, "Respubliki vykhodyat na mezhdunarodnuyu arenu," *Izvestiya*, 20 November 1989, p. 3.

38. "Doklad E. A. Shevardnadze," pp. 43–44; and interview with Shevardnadze in *Izvestiya*, 22 March 1989, p. 3.

39. "Postanovlenie Plenuma TsK KPSS: O Komissiyakh Tsentral'nogo Komiteta KPSS," *Pravda*, 29 November 1988, pp. 1–2.

40. Ibid., p. 1.

41. For an official view of the ID's new role, see the interview with Falin in "V. Falin: 'Kriticheski otnosit'sya k sebe,' " pp. 4–5.

42. See British Foreign and Commonwealth Office, *The Soviet Communist Party's External Propaganda Activities* (Background Brief), July 1989, esp. pp. 3–6. Also see "V. Falin: 'Kriticheski otnosit'sya k sebe,' " p. 4. For an earlier assessment of the ID's role in "active measures" during the Gorbachev period, see US Department of State, *Soviet Influence Activities: A Report on Active Measures and Propaganda, 1986–87*, Department of State Publication No. 9627, October 1987.

43. For the communiqué of this meeting, see "Zasedanie Komissii TsK KPSS po voprosam mezhdunarodnoi politiki," *Pravda*, 15 March 1989, p. 2.

44. The 24 original members, as listed in the initial resolution, were Aleksandr Yakovlev, Georgii Arbatov, Suren Arutyunyan, Sergei Akhromeev, Boris Batsanov, Abdul-Rakhman Vezirov, Evgenii Velikhov, Vaino Vyalyas, Vladimir Kamentsev, Anatolii Kovalev, Vladimir Kryuchkov, Ivan Laptev, Petr Luchinsky, Yurii Manaenkov, A. S. Maselsky, Valentin Nikiforov, Rafik Nishanov, Genrikh Novozhilov, Evgenii Primakov, Grigorii Revenko, Valentina Tereshkova, Gennadii Ulanov, Valentin Falin, and Anatolii Chernyaev. Vezirov was removed in January 1990 in the wake of violent unrest in Azerbaijan.

45. See, for example, the notes from the Commission's July 1989 session, "O novom opyte sotrudnichestva s zarubezhnymi stranami, priobretennom v protsesse perestroiki vneshneekonomicheskikh svyazyei," *Izvestiya TsK KPSS*, no. 8 (August 1989), pp. 40–45.

46. "V. Falin: 'Kriticheski otnosit'sya k sebe,' " p. 4.

47. Karen Dawisha, "Perestroika, Glasnost, and Soviet Foreign Policy," *The Harriman Institute Forum* 3, no. 1 (January 1990), p. 2.

48. Agence France Presse, 17 June 1986.

49. "Doklad E. A. Shevardnadze," p. 44, See also US Central Intelligence Agency, *The USSR Foreign Ministry: Organizational Structure*, LDA 89-10850, March 1989, p. 1; and Charles Glickham, "New Directions for Soviet Foreign Policy," *Radio Liberty Research*, Supplement 2/86, 6 September 1986, p. 11.

50. See Rose E. Gottemoeller, "Decision Making for Arms Limitation in the Soviet Union," in Robbin F. Laird and Erik P. Hoffmann, eds., *Soviet Foreign Policy in a Changing World* (Hawthorne, NY: Aldine de Gruyter, 1987), pp. 167–68.

51. Interview by the author with Aleksandr Bessmertnykh, Soviet First Deputy Foreign Minister, in Moscow, 29 March 1989.

52. "Doklad E. A. Shevardnadze," p. 44.

53. Igor S. Glagolev, "The Soviet Decision-Making Process in Arms-Control Negotiations," *Orbis* 21, no. 4 (Winter 1978), p. 771; Thomas W. Wolfe, *The SALT Experience* (Cambridge, MA: Ballinger, 1979), pp. 60–61; and Gottemoeller, "Decision Making," p. 166.

54. Sidney N. Graybeal and Michael Krepon, Making Better Use of the Standing Consultative Commission," *International Security* 10, 2 (Fall 1985), p. 186. Graybeal is a former US commissioner on the SCC.

55. Strobe Talbott, *The Master of the Game: Paul Nitze and the Nuclear Peace* (New York: Alfred Knopf, 1988), p. 259.

56. On Mikhailov, see CIA, *Directory of Soviet Officials*, p. 67, *USSR Foreign Ministry*, p. 1; also see F. Stephen Larrabee, "Gorbachev and the Soviet Military," *Foreign Affairs* 67, no. 3 (Summer 1988), p. 1011. Information about Amel'ko comes from an interview by the author with Ambassador Vladimir Shustov, head of the Research Coordinating Council, in Moscow, 27 March 1989.

57. For recent examples of Starodubov's views, both before and after the September 1988 Central Committee session, see "Strategicheskoe ravnovesie: o neobkhodimosti peregovorov po voenno-morskim silam," *Izvestiya*, 8 January 1990, p. 9; "SOI khoronit' rano," *Krasnaya zvezda*, 24 October 1989, p. 3; "Somnitel'nye eksperimenty," *Pravda*, 21 May 1989, p. 4; "Staroe v voennoi politike," *Pravda*, 27 January 1989, p. 4; "O disbalansakh i asimmetriyakh: esche raz o sootnoshenii vooruzhennykh sil OVD i NATO," *Izvestiya*, 20 September 1988, p. 5; and "Mezhdunarodnye zametki: chto budet s Dogovorom po PRO?" *Krasnaya zvezda*, 10 September 1988, p. 3. For a typical example of Akhromeev's views, see "Napadki na Vooruzhenye sily SSSR: Pochemu?" *Krasnaya zvezda*, 8 April 1990, p. 2.

58. Lev Mendelevich, "Sorok let v diplomaticheskoi sluzhbe," *Mezhdunarodnaya zhizn'*, no. 5 (May 1989), p. 69.

59. "Doklad E. A. Shevardnadze," p. 29.

60. See Stephen M. Meyer, "The Sources and Prospects of Gorbachev's New Political Thinking on Security," *International Security* 13, no. 2 (Fall 1988), esp. pp. 127–32.

61. See four reports prepared jointly by US Central Intelligence Agency and US Defense Intelligence Agency: "The Soviet Economy under a New Leader," 19 March 1986, reprinted in US Congress, Joint Economic Committee, Subcommittee on Economic Resources, Competitiveness, and Security Economics, *Allocation of Resources in the Soviet Union and China—1985*, Part 11, 99th Cong., 2nd Sess., 19 March 1986;

"Gorbachev's Modernization Program: A Status Report," 19 March 1987, reprinted in US Congress, Joint Economic Committee, Subcommittee on National Security Economics, *Allocation of Resources in the Soviet Union and China—1986*, Part 12, 100th Cong., 1st Sess., 19 March and 3 August 1987, esp. pp. 28–31; "Gorbachev's Economic Program: Problems Emerge," 13 April 1988, reprinted in US Congress, Joint Economic Committee, Subcommittee on National Security Economics, *Allocation of Resources in the Soviet Union and China—1987*, Part 13, 100th Cong., 2nd Sess., 13 April 1988, esp. pp. 21–27; and "The Soviet Economy in 1988: Gorbachev Changes Course," 14 April 1989, pp. 14–27, reprinted in David R. Jones, ed., *Soviet Armed Forces Review Annual*, Vol. 11: 1987–88 (Gulf Breeze, FL: Academic International Press, 1989), pp. 426–47.

62. Meyer, "Sources," p. 128.

63. For examples of military officers' dismay over the new role of the civilian analysts, see Maj.-Gen. Yu. Lyubimov, "O dostatochnosti oborony i nedostatke kompetentnosti," *Kommunist vooruzhennykh sil*, no. 16 (August 1989), pp. 21–26; Col. Vladimir Dvorkin and Col. Valerii Torbin, "O real'noi dostatochnosti oborny," *Moskovskie novosti*, no. 26 (25 June 1989), p. 6; Lt.-Gen. E. Volkov, "Ne raz'yasnyaet, a zatumanivaet," *Krasnaya zvezda*, 28 September 1989, p. 3; Maj.-Gen. Yu. Lebedev and Aleksandr Podberezkin, "Voennye doktriny i mezhdunarodnaya bezopasnost," *Kommunist*, no. 13 (September 1988), pp. 110–19; Cap. S. Ishchenko, "Armiya Zashchishchaet nas, a kto Zashchitit armiyu?" *Molodaya gvardiya*, no. 11 (November 1989), pp. 220–225; and Maj.-Gen. G. Kirilenko, "Legko i byt' oborone dostatochnoi?" *Krasnaya zvezda*, 21 March 1990, p. 2.

64. Lt.-Gen. V. Serebryannikov, "S uchetom real'nostei yadernogo veka," *Kommunist vooruzhennykh sil*, no. 3 (1987), p. 16.

65. See, for example, the comments of Yulii Vorontsov and Vladimir Petrovsky in *Mezhdunarodnaya zhizn'*, No. 9, September 1988, pp. 39 and 49, respectively.

66. Hungarian Television, 8 January 1987, transcribed in US Foreign Broadcast Information Service, *Daily Report: Soviet Union*, FBIS-SOV-87-6, 9 January 1987, pp. CC-4.

67. "Doklad E. A. Shevardnadze," p. 44.

68. In this regard, the deputy foreign minister Valentin Nikiforov recently stated that: "we have reason to presume that in the years ahead the demand for experts in disarmament and security problems will steadily grow. We will have to draw up a special curriculum for the training of disarmament experts at the Moscow State Institute for International Relations and the Diplomatic Academy and to give jobs at the Foreign Ministry to graduates of military academies and staff members of research centres of the USSR Academy of Sciences" ("O kadrovoi politike," pp. 53–54).

20

The KGB and Soviet Foreign Policy*

Amy W. Knight

Although this study is concerned primarily with the KGB's role in Soviet domestic politics and society, this role cannot be properly understood without taking into consideration the KGB's involvement in foreign affairs. Domestic and foreign issues are closely intertwined in the Soviet policy process, and developments in both areas have a significant impact on each other. The state of East-West relations, for example, appears to be a crucial factor in the determination of Soviet policy toward dissent. The close connection between domestic and foreign policy is exemplified by the fact that the KGB itself combines both internal security and foreign intelligence functions in one organization. In this respect Soviet practice differs from that of most Western governments, where these functions are usually assigned to separate agencies. Such a dual role stems from the ideological preconceptions of the Soviet regime, in particular its tendency to blur the distinction between internal and external security threats. The foreign and domestic functions of the KGB are, of course, executed by separate directorates whose personnel tend, with some exceptions, to follow career tracks that are distinct from one another. At the top level of the KGB hierarchy, however, these roles are combined in the person of the KGB chairman, who, in his current capacity as a full member of the Politburo, participates in the policy process as a coordinator of the KGB's domestic and foreign operations.

The KGB's multifarious foreign operations have drawn wide attention in the Western press and have been the subject of numerous Western studies. Yet few, if any, attempts have been made to assess the KGB's influence on the foreign policy process. Is the KGB simply an instrument of the party leadership in implementing its objectives, or does it have a significant role in decision making? Does the KGB as an institution take a stand on various foreign policy issues that it brings to bear on policymaking? This chapter presents a general overview of the KGB's foreign activities and will then consider how these activities, taken

*Reprinted by permission of the author and publisher from Amy W. Knight, *The KGB: Police and Politics in the Soviet Union*, Chapter 9. Copyright © 1988 by Harper Collins Academic (formerly Unwin Hyman).

together with the KGB's domestic role, affect the KGB's institutional perceptions and its ability to influence policy.

ORGANIZATION OF FOREIGN OPERATIONS

The organizational structure for the foreign operations of the political police has changed relatively little over the years. Although the Cheka engaged in limited espionage operations from its inception, it had no formal agency for operations abroad until December 1920, when a foreign department (*Inostrannyi otdel*, or INO) was first established under its auspices. The chief of the INO from 1921 to 1929 was M. A. Trilisser, who from 1926 onward was simultaneously second deputy chairman of the OGPU. The INO's functions during this time were straightforward: collecting political, military, and economic intelligence on foreign states; monitoring emigré groups abroad; and conducting surveillance of Soviet officials posted abroad. Cheka intelligence officers served under legal cover as members of Soviet diplomatic and commercial missions, often as second secretaries or attachés. Later, when operations of the INO expanded under the OGPU, illegal agents were sent abroad, functioning under deep cover with false identity papers.[1]

After the NKVD was formed in 1934 the INO, as a department of the Main Administration of State Security (GUGB), continued to expand its foreign network, devoting particular attention to operations against the different political groups and organizations of Russian emigrés abroad. The INO (which later became the INU, or foreign administration) was not the only organization responsible for espionage and covert foreign activities. Rather, it was part of a network of contiguous agencies that operated abroad and whose work was coordinated at the center by the Politburo.[2] Shortly before World War II these agencies included three additional departments of the GUGB: the Economic Department, responsible for counterespionage in the Soviet industry and agriculture as well as for military and technical espionage abroad; the Secret Political Department (SPO), responsible for political surveillance of the Communist party, intelligentsia, religious, and other groups; and the Counterintelligence Department (KRO), charged with detecting foreign agents within the Soviet Union. The latter two departments were active abroad only insofar as the ramifications of a case they were working on led them outside the country.

Among the other agencies executing foreign tasks for the Politburo were the Military Intelligence Administration of the General Staff, the All-Union Council of Trade Unions, the People's Commissariat of Foreign Affairs, the People's Commissariat of Foreign Trade, various other cultural and trade societies, and the Executive Committee of the COMINTERN. These agencies carried out their work separately, but all had the common purpose of furthering the Kremlin's foreign policy designs. As far as the specific tasks of the INU were concerned, they involved, broadly speaking, active counterintelligence (infiltration of foreign intelligence organizations); universal espionage—all-around detailed study of important free-world countries; covert propaganda and political work directed toward the establishment of a political situation favorable to the development of communism (including disinformation, forgeries, provoking internal conflicts, fomenting political discontent, etc.); and surveillance of Soviet citizens abroad.[3]

There were some changes in the postwar organization of security police foreign operations. According to some sources, INU operations were coordinated with those of military intelligence (GRU) in a so-called Committee of Information (KI), established in 1947–1948 and headed by a series of foreign ministry officials. But the GRU reverted to the control of the Ministry of Defense in 1948 and the KI was later dissolved.[4] Despite these changes, the tasks of the INU remained essentially the same during the war and postwar years and throughout the period of its transformation into the First Chief Directorate after the USSR KGB was created in 1954.

The First Chief Directorate of the USSR KGB is responsible for KGB operations abroad. According to John Barron, the First CD is composed of three separate directorates: Directorate S, which oversees illegal agents (those under deep cover) throughout the world; Directorate T, responsible for the collection of scientific and technological intelligence; and Directorate K, which carries out infiltration of foreign intelligence and security services and exercises surveillance over Soviet citizens abroad. In addition, the First CD has three important services: Service I, which analyzes and distributes intelligence collected by KGB foreign intelligence officers and agents, publishes a daily current events summary for the Politburo, and makes forecasts of future world developments; Service A, which is responsible for planning and implementing so-called active measures; and Service R, which evaluates KGB operations abroad. The operational core of the First CD lies in its eleven geographical departments, which supervise KGB employees assigned to residencies abroad. These officers or *"rezidents,"* operating under legal cover, engage in intelligence collection, espionage, and active measures.[5] The head of the First CD is Col. Gen. V. A. Kriuchkov, who served under Andropov in the Soviet Embassy in Hungary and later was a leading official in the CC Department for Liaison with Ruling Communist Parties, again serving under Andropov. He followed Andropov to the KGB in 1967.[6]

While the overall tasks of the First CD are similar to those of its predecessors, its role has expanded considerably since Stalin died and particularly since the early 1970s. This is partly a result of the fact that the dimensions of Soviet foreign policy in general have expanded, with greater involvement in the Third World, foreign trade, arms control, and so on. Furthermore the Kremlin has placed increased emphasis on covert operations and intelligence gathering as a means of implementing Soviet foreign policy objectives. As greater manpower and resources have been devoted to this type of activity, the techniques and methods have become more sophisticated and effective.

Before turning to the KGB's operations abroad it should be noted that the Second CD plays an important support role in the regime's intelligence operations. First, it recruits agents for intelligence purposes from among foreigners stationed within the USSR—diplomats, journalists, businessmen, students, and tourists. Second, it engages in counterintelligence by uncovering attempts on the part of foreign intelligence services to recruit Soviet citizens.[7]

INTELLIGENCE, COUNTERINTELLIGENCE, AND ACTIVE MEASURES

The KGB's foreign activities can be divided roughly into two categories. The first involves intelligence collection, espionage, and so-called offensive counterintelligence and the second involves "active measures" (disinformation, propaganda, sabotage, etc.). Not surprisingly, there are no precise open-source estimates on the number of agents whom the First CD employs abroad, but most experts seem to agree that the KGB operates the world's largest and most far-reaching foreign intelligence apparatus. There was a marked increase in KGB intelligence gathering in the West after the era of détente began in 1972. Détente permitted a vast influx of Soviet and Eastern European diplomatic, cultural, and commercial officials into the United States and other Western countries. According to former FBI Director Clarence Kelly, between 1972 and 1977 the number of Communist bloc officials in the United States rose by 50 percent.[8] KGB officers and their Eastern European counterparts operate under various guises— diplomats, trade officials, journalists, scientists, and so on. The proportion of Soviet officials abroad who are engaged in intelligence gathering has been estimated to range from 30 to 40 percent in the United States to over 50 percent in some Third World countries. In addition, many Soviet representatives who are not intelligence officers are nevertheless given some sort of assignment by the KGB.[9]

Apparently the First CD has little trouble recruiting personnel for its foreign operations. The high salaries, military rank, access to foreign currency, and opportunity to live abroad offer attractive enticements to young people choosing a career. There is also the power and prestige associated with working for the KGB. According to the Soviet defector and former UN diplomat Arkady Shevchenko, KGB Chairman Andropov elevated KGB *rezidents* (who used to occupy junior or mid-level diplomatic rank as a cover) to more important administrative positions, with a corresponding increase in authority.[10] The First CD recruits are said to represent the "cream of the crop" among those setting out on a career. They are usually graduates of one of the more prestigious higher educational institutes and have knowledge of one or more foreign languages. The KGB has a two-year postgraduate training course for these recruits at its Higher Intelligence School located near Moscow. The curriculum includes the use of ciphers, arms, and sabotage training, Communist party and Marxist history, economics, law, and foreign languages.[11]

A former Czechoslovak intelligence officer, Ladislav Bittman, described the typical KGB foreign officers of the post-Stalin era:

> Chosen for their loyalty, appearance and family connections with party and agency officials, the new breed of KGB candidates includes graduates of Soviet universities and institutes, particularly the prestigious Institute for International Studies in Moscow. In addition to courses dealing with Marxist-Leninist doctrine, they study foreign history, culture, languages, and official diplomatic techniques. After joining the KGB, they are subjected to intensive schooling in methods and techniques employed by the intelligence service. When a KGB officer completes training in foreign policy and clandestine techniques and begins to operate in a foreign area, he radiates more self-confidence and personality than a diplomat without the KGB connection. The mundane and boring Russian diplomats are not usually KGB members. A KGB official dresses more elegantly, entertains more freely and shows more individuality even in discussing sensitive foreign policy issues and Soviet politics.[12]

This impression is confirmed by the accounts of a former employee of the Soviet Ministry of Foreign Affairs, Nicolas Polianski, who described the KGB *rezident* in Berne, Switzerland: "He was amiable, very courteous, whether feigned or not, he was well-dressed. He knew how to control himself without losing his vigor, he exuded a tranquil forcefulness, measured and confident."[13] Polianski also refers to the high salaries and numerous privileges enjoyed by KGB foreign intelligence officers.[14]

The KGB is the primary agency responsible for supplying the Kremlin with political intelligence. According to Shevchenko, Moscow cables out questions on a daily basis to KGB *rezidents* abroad to guide them in their tasks. Shevchenko's view of the quality of such KGB intelligence in the 1970s was not very high. He claims that too much emphasis was placed on producing large quantities of information rather than on quality: "It enabled the KGB to overwhelm the relatively smaller amount of data supplied by the Foreign Ministry and by military intelligence operations."[15] As noted earlier, raw intelligence is reportedly analyzed and disseminated to the Soviet leadership by KGB Service I. (In cases of especially important agent reports the Politburo is said to receive them in raw form.) Apparently Service I lacks the manpower to process the large amount of intelligence it receives, despite the fact that it expanded considerably during the 1970s. Nevertheless according to former KGB officer Stanislav Levchenko, Service I makes a well-informed and conscientious effort to provide an accurate and objective picture of the Politburo and other clients.[16]

In addition to political intelligence, KGB officers have concentrated increasingly on efforts to acquire advanced Western technology. A 1985 U.S. government publication on this subject reported that "the magnitude of the Soviets' collection effort and their ability to assimilate collected equipment and technology are far greater than was previously believed."[17] According to this report, the

KGB acts as a collector of militarily significant Western technology (in the form of documents and hardware) on behalf of the Military Industrial Commission (VPK) of the Presidium of the Council of Ministers. This commission coordinates the development of all Soviet weapons systems along with the program to acquire Western technology. The VPK levies requirements among the KGB, the GRU, and several other agencies, including those of Eastern European intelligence services. This collection program is judged in the West to be highly successful, lightening the burden on Soviet research and improving the technical performance of Soviet military equipment and weapons systems.

The VPK expands its collection requirements by approximately 15 percent annually. According to this U.S. government report, KGB Directorate T, which is responsible for technological collection, employs about 1000 officers, including 300 abroad. Most of these officers are professionally trained scientific specialists occupying cover posts as science attachés in Soviet embassies or as officials in Soviet trade missions. Interestingly the GRU, which has about 1500 officers abroad engaged in scientific collection, is judged to be more successful than the KGB in terms of fulfilling requirements: "The GRU probably is more successful because of its overall scientific orientation, its bolder operational style, its increased collection opportunities that reflect a wider variety of technology-related cover positions overseas and its clearer understanding of collection objectives."[18] Nevertheless the KGB collects slightly more of the acquisitions judged to be most significant for purposes of military research by the Soviets. Both the KGB and the GRU increased their technical collection efforts considerably in the early 1980s, when the average number of requirements levied on them by the VPK increased by about 50 percent.

It might be added that the Andropov era in the KGB saw a greater orientation toward electronic espionage—communications interception and satellites—to supplement intelligence gathered by agents. According to Robert Campbell, the USSR now deploys at least three satellites for intelligence collection.[19] Some of this intelligence may be strictly military and therefore collected by the GRU, but the KGB probably also makes use of these satellites. The relative weight of this type of intelligence may well increase in the future.

The increase in the use of so-called active measures as an element of Soviet foreign policy has attracted considerable attention—and alarm—in the West in recent years. This type of activity has long been employed by the Soviets abroad, but it has become more widespread and more effective since the late 1960s. A great deal of information has appeared in the West documenting the extensive use of active measures by the Soviets, so there is no need to present a detailed account here.[20] Active measures are clandestine operations the purpose of which is to further Soviet foreign policy goals and to extend Soviet influence throughout the world. Among these covert techniques is disinformation: leaking of false information and rumors to the foreign media or the planting of forgeries in order to deceive the public or the political elite in a given country or countries.

A KGB training manual defines disinformation as follows:

> Strategic disinformation assists in the execution of state tasks and is directed at misleading the enemy concerning the basic questions of state policy, the military-economic status and the scientific-technical achievements of the Soviet Union; the policy of certain imperialist states with respect to each other and to other countries; and the specific counterintelligence tasks of the organs of state security. Tactical disinformation makes it possible to carry out the individual task of strategic disinformation and, in fact, comprises the principal disinformation work of the organs of state security.[21]

The United States is the prime target of disinformation, in particular forgery operations, which are designed to damage U.S. foreign and defense policies in a variety of ways. From 1976 to 1980 forgeries of U.S. government documents and communiqués were estimated to have appeared at a rate of four to five per year.[22]

The use of international front organizations and foreign Communist parties to expand the USSR's political influence and further its propaganda campaigns is another form of active measures. Front organizations such as the World Peace Council and World Federation of Trade Unions profess noncommunist goals but are funded and manipulated behind the scenes by the Soviets. The programs advocated by front organizations mirror Soviet programs and echo Soviet media themes. Together with the International Department of the Central Committee, the KGB funnels money to these organizations and recruits Soviet agents to serve on their administrative bodies. The KGB also assists the International Department in the use of foreign Communist parties to further Soviet aims by smuggling financial aid to these parties and by maintaining liaison with them.[23]

On the darker side of active measures are those involving support for terrorists and insurgents. Although there is no direct open-source evidence that the Soviets plan or orchestrate terrorist acts by groups from Western Europe or the Middle East, there is much indirect evidence to show that the Soviet Union does indeed support international terrorism. The Soviets maintain close relationships with a number of governments and organizations that are direct supporters of terrorist groups. Moscow sells large quantities of arms to Libya and Syria, for example, and also maintains a close alliance with the PLO, providing it with arms, monetary assistance, and paramilitary training. Moscow's surrogate, Cuba, plays a central role in Latin American terrorism by providing groups with training, arms, and sanctuary, and Moscow's European satellite states often serve as middlemen or subcontractors for channeling aid to terrorist groups. Although the KGB, not surprisingly, avoids direct involvement with terrorist operations, it plays an important role in diverting aid to these groups and providing the Soviet leadership with intelligence reports on their activities.[24]

The KGB also has been heavily involved in the support of "national wars of liberation" in the Third World. Together with satellite intelligence services, the KGB helps to organize military training and political indoctrination of leftist guerrillas, as well as the provision of arms and advisers. The manipulation of national wars of liberation enables the Soviets to influence the political future of the country in question and to make its new government more responsive to Soviet objectives. The Soviets concentrated mainly on African countries until the late 1970s but then extended their support for "national liberation movements" to Central America, where they have regularly employed the services of the Cubans.[25] There are indications that the Kremlin has recently been reassessing its Third World policy and may devote more resources to its own economy than to new revolutionary movements in economically backward countries. Nevertheless as one Western analyst has stressed, this does not mean an end to Soviet intervention in the Third World; rather, the Kremlin might be more selective in providing support to radical movements.[26]

The KGB relies heavily on the intelligence services of Soviet satellite countries in carrying out both its active measures and espionage operations. The East German, Czechoslovak, Polish, Hungarian, Bulgarian, and Cuban services, which have reportedly made great improvements in their operations in recent years, form an important adjunct to the KGB. While formally subordinated to their own governments, these satellite services are, according to most Western experts, heavily influenced by the KGB. As a former official in the Czechoslovak intelligence service states, "Soviet intelligence is informed about every major aspect of their activities, and Russian advisors (called liaison officers) participate in planning major operations and assessing the results."[27] As far back as the 1960s the KGB introduced a new element of coordination with the satellite services through the creation of departments for disinformation in East German, Czechoslovak and Hungarian services and the establishment of direct lines of communication from these departments to the KGB. These changes augmented the KGB's covert operational capability considerably.[28]

According to Barron, the Eleventh Department of the KGB's First CD is responsible for liaison with satellite intelligence services, each of which performs a variety of tasks for the KGB. The Bulgarians, for example, engage in the direction of terrorist groups and the smuggling of drugs and arms; the East Germans conduct broad espionage efforts against West Germany; and the Cubans assist KGB operations in both the United States and the Third World.[29] Chebrikov himself made reference to the close working arrangements between the KGB and satellite intelligence services in his 1985 *Kommunist* article: "Soviet Chekists carry out their work against enemy subversive activities in close contact with security organs in other countries of the socialist community. . . . On the basis of corresponding agreements, ties among the state security organs of our fraternal countries are becoming stronger and the forms of their cooperation in the struggle against the class enemy are being improved."[30] The fact that Chebrikov makes frequent, publicized trips to satellite countries reinforces the impression of close ties between the KGB and satellite services.[31]

It is important to stress that Soviet active measures involve not only the KGB and satellite intelligence services but also several other Soviet agencies, which all participate in a coordinated effort to further Soviet policy objectives. In this sense the Kremlin has a distinct advantage over democratic regimes because the Communist party's monopoly over the political process enables it to control all Soviet organizations and agencies abroad and to employ their services for any given program of action. Aside from the KGB, the Central Committee's International Department (ID) takes a leading role in directing and implementing active measures. The ID, which is responsible for liaison with nonruling Communist parties, international front organizations, and national liberation movements, as well as for the operation of a number of clandestine radio stations, is one of the most important foreign policy bodies in the Soviet system. It is responsible for coordinating and reviewing information on foreign policy from a variety of sources and briefs the Politburo on key foreign policy issues.[32]

The chief of the ID and a CC secretary is Anatolii Dobrynin, former ambassador to Washington. Dobrynin, who replaced the long-time ID chief Boris Ponomarev in early 1986, is widely regarded as a skillful and experienced diplomat with extensive knowledge of foreign policy. His appointment signifies the importance of the ID to the Soviets.

Another key agency was the International Information Department (IID), created in 1978 to improve the effectiveness of Soviet foreign propaganda by coordinating the efforts of the USSR's major propaganda channels.[33] Its formation reflected the leadership's desire to make the foreign propaganda network more responsive to the needs of policy makers, but sometime in late spring 1986 this department was abolished, apparently because it was not achieving this goal. Its chief, Leonid Zamiatin, was made ambassador to Great Britain.

The Soviet campaign against NATO's INF deployment offers one of the clearest examples of a coordinated active measures effort by Moscow. The campaign, which began in late 1979, mobilized the entire Soviet arsenal of active measures resources, as well as diplomatic efforts. As one Western analyst pointed out, Moscow's tactics involved a dual-track approach: a "campaign from above" to influence NATO's decision makers and a "campaign from below" to create mass opposition to the INF deployment by exploiting popular fears of nuclear weapons.[34] The campaign from above attempted to drive a wedge between the United States and its NATO allies by portraying the United States as an aggressive, villainous power that endangered the security interests of Western Europe. At the same time, the Soviet Union was presented as a benign, well-meaning neighbor anxious to reach a compromise and to achieve a security balance with the West. In the campaign from below the Soviets exploited the growing political disaffection and disillusionment in Western Europe arising from European government policies, as well as the distinct rise in anti-Americanism, particularly among the younger generation.

While making broad use of its vast foreign propaganda apparatus, the Kremlin enlisted the KGB to carry out numerous disinformation activities that enhanced the overt propaganda campaign. In addition, the KGB, the ID, and the IID worked with the various international front organizations and European Communist parties, which organized mass demonstrations, marches, and petitions to protest NATO's plans. The Soviet campaign did not succeed in blocking the INF deployment, but it did not fail completely. The campaign did much to promote the cause of the peace movement in Europe and to erode popular support for NATO's security objectives. As one Western scholar observed,

> Moscow's ability to mount a propaganda and "active measures" campaign of the magnitude of the "campaign from below" is quite impressive. It also demonstrates the effective work and coordination of the various Soviet fronts, whose important role in Soviet foreign political activities is often underestimated or even dismissed. The anti-INF campaign illustrated the parallel activities of and coordination among the different elements that make up the means and instrumentalities of Soviet foreign political pursuits.[35]

THE KGB AND FOREIGN POLICY DECISION MAKING

The discussion thus far has illustrated the KGB's key role in implementing the Kremlin's foreign policy objectives, a role that appears to have grown in importance since the early 1970s. This brings us to the question raised at the beginning of the chapter. Is the KGB merely an executor of the Kremlin's directives or does it actually influence policy formulation in some significant way? In order to address this question effectively we must first consider the framework of the Soviet foreign policy process.

Western scholars have developed several different approaches to understanding this process. For example, Jiri Valenta, in his study of the Soviet invasion of Czechoslovakia, employs the bureaucratic politics model to conceptualize Soviet decision making.[36] This model postulates that Soviet foreign policy stems not from a single actor but rather from the political interaction of several actors who represent different bureaucratic elites. Valenta portrays Soviet foreign policy decision making as a process fraught with political maneuvering and conflicting interests. No single leader possesses sufficient power to decide all issues, so decisions are reached collectively only after considerable political bargaining and arduous debate:

> Despite the shared images of national security, senior Soviet decisionmakers differ on how various issues should be approached and resolved. As in Western societies, the Soviet decisionmaking process is political, not scientific. The decisionmakers are not necessarily cast in the same mold. Often their backgrounds and areas of bureaucratic experience contrast sharply and often they assume different administrative duties and bureaucratic responsibilities and have different domestic and personal interests.[37]

A rather different approach is taken by Hannes Adomeit, who sees a broad consensus among Soviet leaders about operational principles in foreign policy, particularly in international crises: "Soviet decisionmaking in international crises will typically demonstrate a 'rallying around the flag,' the concentration of decisions in the hands of a select executive committee, the restoration of important elements of centralization and a return to traditional reflexes and responses.''[38] While Adomeit allows that some conflict affects foreign policy decision making, he sees this conflict as occurring within a relatively narrow framework.

What about the inclusion in 1973 of the chiefs of the KGB, the Foreign Ministry, and the Defense Ministry on the key policymaking body, the Politburo? This could be seen as strengthening the tendency toward bureaucratic coalition politics, or, as Adomeit suggests, it could be viewed as part of "a trend towards further integration of various interests into a broad consensus and hence a dilution of conflict.''[39]

Although the consensus model does not deny the KGB's influence on decision making, it is probably more useful to examine how the KGB affects foreign policymaking by employing the bureaucratic politics paradigm. Valenta, for example, has offered insights into how the KGB, as a defender of its institutional interests, may have influenced Soviet behavior in the Czechoslovak crisis of 1968. Nevertheless neither the bureaucratic nor the consensus model distinguishes clearly between different levels of participation in the decision-making process, which in the case of the KGB is important in understanding its influence. The KGB participates in the foreign policy decision-making process at the highest level, the Politburo, where its chief, Chebrikov, is a member of the collective leadership. At the same time, it influences the formulation of foreign policy at a lower level as an executor of that policy, a provider of information, and a generator of ideas, solutions, and alternatives. It may well be that the consensus model accurately describes decision making at the highest level, while the bureaucratic model is better suited to understanding lower-level KGB influence.

It is also important to consider whether or not the KGB represents a united voice in the decision-making process. If we are looking at the Politburo, we can assume that Chebrikov has consolidated the various views and opinions of his staff and therefore presents a single KGB stance. Below that level, however, it is quite possible that a monolithic KGB viewpoint does not exist. Officials responsible for domestic security and those who work in foreign operations may well feel very differently on certain issues. Thus, for example, Brezhnev's policy of détente inaugurated in 1972 was probably welcomed by officials in the First Chief Directorate because it offered opportunities for the assignment of increased numbers of KGB officers to Western countries under legal cover. Yet for those in charge of internal security détente meant an increase in the number of foreigners visiting the USSR, widening of communications with the West, and relaxation of the crackdown on dissent—all of which made the KGB's job inside the USSR more difficult. Thus when we examine the KGB's influence on foreign policy and its probable stance on certain issues, we must look at both the domestic and foreign concerns of the KGB as well as the level of its policy input.

Evidence of KGB influence on foreign policy decisions, as a participant in high-level decision making, a provider of information, and an implementer of policy, is best considered on a case-by-case basis. The KGB's relatively low political status in the Khrushchev years meant that it was not represented as an institution on the key decision-making body, the Presidium (as the Politburo was then called). Indeed from 1961 to 1964 the KGB chairman did not even have full membership on the Central Committee. Furthermore before Andropov's 1967 appointment, KGB chairmen had little experience in foreign policy. Serov had served abroad as a police official in the Soviet Army, but this was primarily a security function. Both Shelepin and Semichastnyi had been involved entirely in the Komsomol and party apparatus before their appointments to the KGB.

Nonetheless these KGB chairmen presided over their organization's foreign operations and no doubt developed their own views on foreign policy. Judging from their public statements, both Shelepin and Semichastnyi were hard-liners who did not favor rapprochement with the West. Robert Slusser has offered considerable evidence to show that both men opposed Khrushchev's efforts in this direction. Shelepin, for example, found nothing positive to say about the West in his speech to the Twenty-Second Party Congress in 1961, preferring to discuss only the threat posed to the USSR by Western military and intelligence agencies. Semichastnyi revealed his intense hostility toward the United States (as well as his very negative assessment of Yugoslav revisionism) on several occasions.[40]

Without direct access to the Presidium, the KGB leadership apparently embarked on a few autonomous police initiatives to impede Khrushchev's efforts at limited détente, such as the arrest in 1963 of Yale Professor Frederick Barghoorn on trumped-up charges of spying. This deliberate KGB provocation, which ended when President Kennedy managed to obtain Barghoorn's release, was highly embarrassing to Khrushchev.[41] Even more detrimental to Khrushchev was a KGB mustard gas attack on a West German technician, Horst Schwirkmann, at precisely the time that Khrushchev was making an effort to conclude a major trade agreement with West Germany. The incident, which occurred in September 1964, shortly before Khrushchev's ouster, outraged Bonn and destroyed all possibilities for a trade agreement.[42] The KGB leadership, aware of the impending coup, probably realized that such an act could be committed with impunity.

By late 1965 the influence of the so-called Shelepintsy (the faction surrounding Aleksandr Shelepin and including Semichastnyi; former KGB deputy V. S. Tikunov; Dmitrii Goriunov, head of Tass; and N. G. Egorychev, first secretary of the Moscow *Gorkom*) had risen considerably. Shelepin himself, who continued to oversee police matters, had been a full Politburo member since 1964. His group apparently advocated greater Soviet involvement abroad and in 1967 urged a policy of belligerence toward Egypt, at the time a Soviet ally.[43] As far back as December 1964 Shelepin had travelled to Cairo to promise Soviet assistance in the struggle against imperialism, after which several diplomatic posts in the

Middle East were gradually filled by Shelepintsy from the KGB. In spring 1967 Shelepin's protégé Egorychev also visited the Middle East. In addition to circulating false reports about Israeli plans to attack Syria, the KGB (and the GRU) seriously underestimated Israel's military potential, and their reports persuaded Nasser that the Arabs could defeat Israel. The Shelepintsy paid for their adventurist policies, however. Following a June 1967 CC plenum, Egorychev lost his post as head of the Moscow *Gorkom* and Shelepin was removed from the Secretariat (Semichastnyi has already been dismissed from his post as KGB chief in May 1967).[44]

According to Galia Golan, the KGB remained in the background during decision making over the October 1973 Yom Kippur War. The only evidence of high-level KGB involvement was a statement made by Sadat to the effect that Andropov, as a close friend of Egypt's former intelligence chief Ahmad Ismail, had voiced his willingness to intervene on Egypt's behalf. Andropov did participate in some meetings with the Egyptians, but, although he was by now a full member of the Politburo, there were no other signs of his influence. According to Golan, Andropov even "put off with feeble excuses an invitation from Sadat to go to Egypt."[45]

The KGB's role in providing intelligence during the Yom Kippur War was highly important, however. In contrast to their earlier intelligence failures, the KGB and the GRU were well informed about Arab plans. According to one source, "not only were the Russians aware of Egyptian-Syrian intentions at least ten days in advance, thanks to their antennae in Damascus, but having learned from their former disappointments, they decided to furnish Sadat with all the material assistance necessary for the realization of his objectives."[46] The same source adds that a KGB report presented at a meeting of the Politburo in 1974 was responsible for the Kremlin's decision to change its Middle East policy. The report is said to have recommended greater support for extremist and terrorist groups and concentration on penetrating the regions of the Persian Gulf and the Horn of Africa.[47]

The Soviet decision to invade Czechoslovakia in August 1968 offers a good illustration of the involvement of the KGB as an institution in foreign policy decision making. At this time KGB Chairman Andropov was only a candidate (nonvoting) member of the Politburo, but, having presided over the Soviet invasion of Hungary in 1956 and having served for over ten years as chief of the CC Department for Liaison with Ruling Communist Parties, he was a leading expert on Eastern Europe and was no doubt consulted extensively during the crisis. Andropov had accompanied Brezhnev on several "discipline trips" to Eastern European countries in 1966–1967, intended mainly to prevent their establishment of diplomatic relations with West Germany.[48]

Valenta has suggested that although the collective leadership decides the most important policy questions, not all leaders participate on a day-to-day basis, and most issues are decided upon by experts in the specific area of concern. Thus "players prominent in foreign affairs appear to be heavily represented in deciding issues where national security interests are at stake."[49] In the specific case of Czechoslovakia, Valenta found that the decision-making circle was broadened to include CC bureaucrats and party officials responsible for domestic affairs, presumably because the problem directly affected internal Soviet interests. Valenta also suggested that the decision-making circle is broadened whenever there is disagreement within the Politburo, which there appears to have been in the case of Czechoslovakia.[50] Given these circumstances, it is likely that Andropov, with both foreign and domestic responsibilities and a direct line of intelligence from Czechoslovakia, probably had a significant impact on the decision-making process.[51]

What were Andropov's views on the Czechoslovak problem? Judging from the few public remarks Andropov made in reference to Czechoslovakia, it appears that his views coincided with those of the interventionists. In December 1967 he warned of the dangers posed by foreign intelligence services that tried to "weaken the might of the socialist countries and shake their unity and cohesion with the forces of the workers' and national liberation movement."[52] After the invasion Andropov made the following comments in a speech to KGB Komsomol members:

> Today the correlation of forces has shifted in favor of socialism. Such a powerful factor as the community of socialist nations is standing in opposition to hostile intrigues. . . . The enemy gives direct and indirect support to counterrevolutionary elements, engages in ideological sabotage, establishes all sorts of antisocialist, anti-Soviet and other hostile organizations and seeks to fan the flames of nationalism. Graphic confirmation of this is offered by the events in Czechoslovakia, where that country's working people, supported by the fraternal international assistance of the peoples of the nations of the socialist community, resolutely nipped in the bud an attempt by counterrevolutionaries to turn Czechoslovakia off the socialist path.[53]

Not surprisingly, statements made by other leading KGB officials indicate that Andropov's views reflected those of the KGB as a whole. USSR KGB Deputy Chairman A. N. Malygin voiced strong approval for the invasion in an early 1969 article in a Komsomol journal. He noted that the intervention in Czechoslovakia had successfully thwarted "imperialist" plans to weaken the socialist structure there.[54] V. V. Fedorchuk, at the time an official in the KGB's Third Directorate, also appeared to concur on the necessity for the invasion when he referred afterward to the grave threats that had been posed to Czechoslovakia by "imperialist" counterrevolutionary strategies.[55]

Valenta offers two strong reasons why the KGB, including those responsible for both domestic and foreign operations, probably favored the invasion. First was the threat posed to the USSR's internal stability by a possible spillover of unrest into the USSR. This anxiety was shared by Soviet bureaucrats in charge of ideological supervision and by republic party leaders such as Shelest in the Ukraine. Second was the effect of Prague reformism on the Czechoslovak intelligence service. In spring 1968 a new reformist minister of interior, Gen. Josef Pavel, was appointed in Prague. Pavel attempted to reorganize the state

security apparatus and purge it of pro-Soviet Stalinists, on whom the KGB relied
for cooperation. Furthermore when the investigation of Jan Masaryk's death was
reopened in May 1968, it had potentially serious ramifications for the Czechoslovak security police. All of this jeopardized the operations of the KGB in
Czechoslovakia.[56]

Although Andropov himself did not participate directly in the high-level
negotiations with Czechoslovak leaders that took place in the months preceding
the invasion, he was, as noted earlier, probably consulted frequently. Furthermore the KGB, as the main provider of intelligence estimates to the leadership,
was in a position to influence decision making by screening and interpreting the
information. Considerable evidence shows that the KGB, in order to bolster the
prointerventionist position, used intelligence and covert action to produce proof
of counterrevolution in Czechoslovakia. Ladislav Bittman, who was serving in
the Czechoslovak intelligence service at the time, observed:

> The active role of the Soviet intelligence service in the events of 1968 and 1969 in
> Czechoslovakia, centered on the systematic implementation of political provoca-
> tion, disinformation and propaganda campaigns aimed at influencing Czechoslovak
> public opinion, terrorizing a selected group of liberals and creating supportive
> arguments for the legitimation of the Soviet invasion.[57]

As Valenta points out, the invasion of Czechoslovakia enabled the KGB to
restore its mission and intelligence capabilities there and also removed a potential
threat to KGB officials responsible for Soviet political security at home. The
organizational interests of the KGB made themselves felt and no doubt influenced the Kremlin's decision to invade.[58] In this case the KGB probably exerted
its main influence by virtue of its role as executor of policy and provider of
information. However, as Andropov's personal authority grew, particularly after
he gained full membership in the Politburo in 1973, the KGB's involvement in
leadership decision making increased.

Much has been made in the West of Andropov's so-called liberalism.[59] While
it is difficult to reconcile such an image with Andropov's advocacy of the
Czechoslovak invasion and with KGB treatment of political dissenters under his
leadership, public statements made by Andropov in the 1970s revealed strong
support for Brezhnev's policy of détente. In a speech delivered in late 1973
Andropov noted enthusiastically: "Never before has the foreign policy of the
Soviet Union been so effective or produced such splendid results within so short
a time. . . . The entire foreign policy of our party has led to the fact that the
international situation is now being shaped to a great extent under the influence
of the peace initiative of the Soviet Union."[60] Andropov continued to hail détente
and the relaxation of international tensions throughout the 1970s. His enthusiasm
for this trend and his optimism about the future of East-West relations contrasted
noticeably with the views expressed by certain Politburo colleagues such as
Minister of Defense Ustinov and Ukrainian Party Chief Shcherbitskii.[61]

Andropov's views on détente also appeared to differ from those expressed by other KGB officials, in particular First Deputy Chairman Semen Tsvigun. Judging from his statements, Tsvigun took a dim view of the Kremlin's efforts to improve relations with the West. In 1972, the year in which these efforts began, Tsvigun was still writing about the lessons to be learned from Czechoslovakia: "The events of 1968 in Czechoslovakia unequivocally confirm that the aim of imperialist politics of 'building bridges' was in fact a preparation for the restoration of capitalism in socialist countries.'"[62] Tsvigun had nothing positive to say about the West throughout the 1970s and continued to warn about the evil intentions of the "imperialists." In a 1977 article on Dzerzhinskii, Tsvigun took the opportunity to note that despite Brezhnev's policy of détente, "the confrontation of the two socioeconomic systems remains the leading trend in the development of the world." Indeed, according to Tsvigun, détente was providing imperialists with new opportunities for subversion against the Soviet Union.[63]

It may seem peculiar that Tsvigun did not always agree with the policies of his mentor and close relative, Brezhnev, but his distaste for détente and his hard-line attitude are understandable in view of his overall responsibility for the KGB's domestic security functions. Détente made the job of Tsvigun and other KGB officials working on the domestic side more difficult. By stressing the dangers of détente and discussing the increased budgets of Western intelligence services, Tsvigun was probably also lobbying for more money and resources for the KGB.

Andropov, by contrast, took a broader view, incorporating both domestic and foreign policy concerns. While supporting such policies as the invasion of Czechoslovakia, he did not necessarily advocate a hardline stance toward the West, particularly if it was accompanied by military interventionism and a stepped-up arms race. Not only does increased defense spending enhance the domestic influence of the Soviet military, it also places greater strains on the economy, draining more resources from the already weak consumer sector. Food shortages and other failures to meet consumer needs could eventually create political unrest, just as they did in Poland. It might be added that Andropov was one of the first to question the Soviet policy of open-ended military and economic assistance to Third World clients, presumably because of the deleterious effects on East-West relations and the growing economic burden it placed on the Soviet Union.[64]

Nonmilitary solutions are no doubt seen as preferable by those implementing KGB operations abroad, particularly where there are opportunities for exploiting social and political factors to the benefit of the Soviet Union. This gives the KGB greater influence over Soviet global strategy. An aggressive Soviet military posture makes the ideological struggle more difficult, as it is not easy for the KGB to exploit social and political tensions in the West and influence the course of "liberation movements" when the Soviet Union has the image of an aggressor.

The Soviet invasion of Afghanistan, for example, created obstacles for the KGB in implementing the campaign against NATO's INF deployment. Indeed Andropov's remarks in his 1980 RSFSR Supreme Soviet election speech indicate that he may have disagreed with the Soviet decision to send a large-scale military force into Afghanistan, or at least that he was not happy about the result. He was the only Politburo member to express pessimism over the world situation after the invasion, noting that "it must be said frankly that there are real grounds for anxiety about the future and the destiny of détente and peace."[65] By contrast, Ustinov stated positively that "imperialism's opportunities for disposing of people's destinies as it sees fit have shrunk considerably. . . . The relaxation of tension has become the dominant trend of world development."[66]

Other members of the KGB leadership may have viewed the Afghanistan invasion in a different light. In the opinion of most Western analysts there was little immediate threat to the USSR's internal stability from Muslim insurgency in Afghanistan in 1979.[67] Unlike the case of Czechoslovakia, where the spirit of reform threatened to spill over into the Ukraine and other Soviet republics, the likelihood of repercussions for Soviet Central Asia or the Caucasus from Muslim fundamentalism or Amin's nationalism was small. Nevertheless KGB officials on the domestic side, particularly those serving in areas near Afghanistan, may have favored the invasion because they worried about the long-term effects of the Muslim movement. Writing in the press a year later, Azerbaidzhan KGB Chief Iusif-Zade expressed such concern: "In view of the situation in Iran and Afghanistan, the U.S. special services are trying to exploit the Islamic religion, especially in areas where the Muslim population lives, as one factor influencing the political situation in our country."[68]

It is difficult to speculate on how KGB officials viewed the Polish crisis of 1980–1981. Andropov himself spoke very little on the problem. Presumably although they were gravely concerned about the possible political ramifications of events in Poland, they did not want to see the USSR resort to military intervention. Again, from the point of view of those dealing with KGB foreign operations, such intervention would have had negative consequences. In particular the USSR's international image would have declined precisely when the KGB, the International Department, and the International Information Department were working hard, by means of a vast propaganda and active measures campaign, to mobilize Western European public opinion against NATO's INF plans. Furthermore an invasion of Poland would have signified Soviet inability to curb political unrest there by peaceful means and thus would have enhanced the Soviet military's role in solving foreign policy problems.

As an expert on Eastern Europe, the head of the agency responsible for providing political intelligence on events in Poland, and a full member of the Politburo, Andropov no doubt greatly influenced the decision to refrain from military intervention in Poland—a decision that may even have run up against opposition from some of the Brezhnev's marshals and generals.[69] The strategy of quelling disturbances in Poland by using internal Polish forces instead of Soviet troops and meant an important role for the KGB in coordinating these efforts. The success of this strategy can, in part at least, be attributed to Andropov, whose political star began to rise in the Kremlin at this time.

While the internal political system has been in continuous flux since Brezhnev's death, Andropov's KGB successors have not faced foreign policy crises like those discussed earlier. This is fortuitous because neither Fedorchuk nor Chebrikov had foreign policy expertise when each took up his post. After twelve years of suppressing dissent in the Ukraine before assuming the KGB chairmanship, Fedorchuk was especially virulent in his criticisms of the West and evinced no favorable inclinations toward the idea of détente. Not surprisingly, when he served as KGB chairman in the Ukraine Fedorchuk had expressed grave concern about events in Poland and had been a strong advocate of the suppression of Solidarity. In 1981 he declared: "Today the enemies of peace and socialism are linking their insidious designs with growing political and economic pressure on the socialist community; this can be clearly seen from the example of Poland." Fedorchuk went on to point out how events in Poland proved that "any kind of belittling of Marxist and Communist ideology, any mistake, shortcoming or violations of the economic laws of socialism and relaxation of ideological and political education of the masses backfires."[70] Such a highly orthodox and rigid approach no doubt made Fedorchuk an effective KGB chief in the Ukraine but hardly suited the demands of the job of chairman of the KGB.

Chebrikov's admission into the Politburo as a full member in April 1985 gave him a voice in foreign policy at the highest level. In addition, most Western experts believe that the KGB chairman serves on the Defense Council, an important collegial decision-making body that provides top-level coordination for defense-related activities of the Soviet government.[71] Given that he has served in the KGB for almost twenty years, it might be assumed that Chebrikov, like Andropov, represents the institutional interests of the KGB in this decision-making capacity. Although Chebrikov lacks Andropov's foreign policy expertise, his numerous trips to Eastern Europe since he became head of the KGB indicate that he is now very much involved in KGB operations beyond Soviet borders and is encouraging cooperative efforts with satellite intelligence agencies. Furthermore his forceful advocacy of Soviet "counterpropaganda" efforts abroad implies a commitment to a strong foreign policy role for the KGB.

Chebrikov made few public statements before he became chairman of the KGB in December 1982. In one article, which appeared in a Komsomol journal in 1981, Chebrikov expressed his concern about the Polish situation by mentioning the dangers of nationalist and separatist tendencies, as well as "revisionism," but in general was much less alarmist than Fedorchuk.[72] In his speeches and articles since taking over the KGB Chebrikov expressed concern about the internal political effects of the "communications revolution" and such Western technological innovations as videos and computers. His continual warnings about "ideological sabotage" suggest that he is not a strong advocate of expanding ties with the West. Furthermore, if we assume that Chebrikov's views influenced the handling of the Daniloff affair and the Mathias Rust case, which were under the investigative purview of the KGB, then it seems clear that he considers security concerns to be more important than smooth relations with the West.[73]

Chebrikov voiced considerable optimism about prospects for the 1985 Geneva summit between Reagan and Gorbachev. In his speech to commemorate the October Revolution in autumn 1985, Chebrikov noted,

> As is known, the Soviet-U.S. summit meeting in Geneva is due to be held very soon. The CPSU Central Committee and the government of the USSR attach great importance to it and are doing everything to ensure that it yields tangible results. We believe that if political courage is manifested and if we meet each other halfway it will still be possible to put a lot of things right.[74]

His more recent comments, however, have been more negative. In particular, his speech on 11 September 1987 suggested that he is opposed to Gorbachev's arms control initiatives.[75]

Chebrikov and his colleagues may welcome the arms control process as a means of curbing military spending, but they may be uneasy about the thorny problem of verification of arms control agreements. Considering that the KGB is responsible for protecting nuclear secrets, its officials probably do not welcome the idea of allowing Western representatives access to Soviet defense installations. In a speech delivered in 1984, for example, Chebrikov accused the United States of making an artificial issue out of verification as a means of dragging out negotiations.[76]

What will be the future impact of the KGB on foreign policy? Given the Kremlin's apparent inclination to avoid high-risk military intervention as a means of furthering its international objectives, a greater emphasis has been placed on diplomacy and active measures in recent years. This trend, which has resulted in a significant expansion of KGB operations abroad, is likely to continue even if the Soviet Union reduces support for new radical movements in the Third World. There is every indication that the Gorbachev leadership, while curtailing the more repressive internal functions of the KGB, will depend heavily on the foreign activities of this institution.

The conduct of foreign policy under Gorbachev has revealed more tactical flexibility and pragmatism than that of the Brezhnev era. Gorbachev has assembled a forward-looking national security team that places strong emphasis on public relations and dynamic approaches to international problems.[77] Despite the apparent discrepancies between the views of Chebrikov and Gorbachev, the KGB's foreign intelligence officers, who represent a sophisticated, well-educated elite, should fit well into this mold and provide useful expertise to further Soviet objectives abroad. Indeed, for a long time KGB officials have worked closely with the International Department and "think tanks" such as the Institute on the United States and Canada, which are said to be taking a greater role in foreign policy decision making. Andropov himself was reportedly on close terms with officials such as Georgii Arbatov and Aleksandr Bovin, who have emerged as influential figures in the foreign policy realm. We can probably assume that Andropov's protégés who remain in the KGB, V. A. Kriuchkov in particular, have retained this connection. Thus whatever the personal authority of the KGB chairman at any given time, as a provider of information and an executor of policy the KGB will continue to have a strong impact on foreign policy.

NOTES

1. George Leggett, *The Cheka: Lenin's Political Police* (Oxford: Clarendon Press, 1981), pp. 231–32, 298–99; *Soviet Intelligence and Counterintelligence* (Washington, DC: Foreign Documents Branch, Central Intelligence Group, no. 84, 31 July 1947; declassified 6/10/83), pp. 1–10.

2. *Espionage Activities of the USSR* (Ms. No. P-137, Historical Division, Headquarters U.S. Army Europe, 1952).

3. Ibid.; Simon Wolin and Robert Slusser, eds., *The Soviet Secret Police* (New York: Praeger, 1957), pp. 138–42.

4. Wolin and Slusser, *Soviet Secret Police*, pp. 25–26; Robert Conquest, *The Soviet Police System* (New York: Praeger, 1968), p. 91.

5. John Barron, *KGB Today: The Hidden Hand* (New York: Readers Digest Press, 1983), pp. 444–49. Also see Cord Meyer, *Facing Reality: From World Federalism to the C.I.A.* (New York: Harper & Row, 1980), pp. 315–29.

6. For further details on Kriuchkov see chapter 4, pp. 122–23.

7. John Barron, *The KGB: Secret Work of Soviet Secret Agents* (New York: Bantam Books, 1974), pp. 113–17.

8. As cited in Ladislav Bittman, *The KGB and Soviet Disinformation: An Insider's View* (Washington, NY: Pergamon-Brassey's, 1985), p. 25.

9. Ibid., pp. 25–27; *The Washington Post*, 25 April 1983, p. 20.

10. Arkady N. Shevchenko, *Breaking with Moscow* (New York: Ballantine, 1985), p. 315. Apparently it was not so easy for the KGB to recruit well-educated personnel for its foreign operations in the late 1950s. First, there was a dearth of graduates with foreign language training, and second, the disclosures about the security police after Stalin's death did significant damage to its image. Later, however, the number of students at Moscow's foreign language and area studies programs expanded and more students from worker and peasant families were admitted, which alleviated the KGB's recruitment problem. In addition, the KGB's professional image began to improve significantly. See a paper prepared by a Soviet foreign language graduate and Intourist guide who defected in 1974: "KGB Procedures and Problems in Recruiting Foreign Language Personnel," *Radio Liberty Background Report*, no. 1-75, 20 January 1975.

11. See Rose E. Gottemoeller and Paul F. Langer, *Foreign Area Studies in the USSR: Training and Employment of Specialists* (Santa Monica, CA: Rand Corp., 1983), pp. 47, 98–101.

12. Bittman, *The KGB and Soviet Disinformation*, p. 15.

13. Nicolas Polianski, *M.I.D. 12 ans dans les services diplomatiques du Kremlin* (Paris: Pierre Belfond, 1984), p. 106. This impression is not universally held, however. Shevchenko characterized the KGB *rezident* in New York during the 1970s, Boris Solomatin, as "cynical, boorish, and a drunk." Shevchenko, *Breaking with Moscow*, p. 57.

14. According to Polianski, for example, KGB officers receive salaries that are one and a half to two times higher than those for corresponding ranks in other ministries. *M.I.D.*, p. 308.

15. Shevchenko, *Breaking with Moscow*, pp. 325–26.

16.   Barron, *KGB Today*, pp. 446–447. In his earlier book (*KGB: Secret Work*, pp. 107–9) Barron stated that Service I distributed raw intelligence to party leaders but provided no analysis. Presumably on the basis of new information such as the testimony of Stanislav Levchenko, Barron's more recent book states that Service I does in fact analyze and interpret the intelligence and only sends the occasional report in raw form to the Politburo.

17.   *Soviet Acquisition of Militarily Significant Western Technology: An Update* (Washington, DC, September 1985), p. 1.

18.   Ibid., p. 16. Also see Philip Hanson, "Soviet Industrial Espionage," *Bulletin of the Atomic Scientists* 43 (April 1987), pp. 25–29.

19.   Robert W. Campbell, "Satellite Communications in the USSR," *Soviet Economy* 1, no. 4 (October–December 1985), p. 330.

20.   Among the Western open-source publications on this subject are U.S. Congress, House Permanent Select Committee on Intelligence, *Soviet Covert Action (The Forgery Offensive)* (Washington, DC: U.S. Government Printing Office, 1980), *Soviet Active Measures* (Washington, DC: U.S. Government Printing Office, 1982); U.S. State Department Special Report No. 110, *Soviet Active Measures* (September 1983); Richard H. Shultz and Roy Godson, *Dezinformatsia. Active Measures in Soviet Strategy* (Washington, NY: Pergamon-Brassey's, 1984); Bittman, *The KGB and Soviet Disinformation;* and Brian D. Dailey and Patrick J. Parker, eds., *Soviet Strategic Deception* (Stanford, CA: Hoover Institution Press, 1987).

21.   U.S. Congress, *Soviet Covert Action*, p. 63.

22.   Ibid., p. 66.

23.   Ibid., pp. 79–81; U.S. Department of State, "The World Peace Council's Peace Assemblies," *Foreign Affairs Note*, May 1983; U.S. Department of State, "World Federation of Trade Unions: Soviet Foreign Policy Tool," *Foreign Affairs Note*, August 1983.

24.   See U.S. Senate Committee on the Judiciary, Subcommittee on Security and Terrorism, *Terrorism: The Role of Moscow and Its Subcontractors* (Washington, DC: U.S. Government Printing Office, 1982); "Patterns of International Terrorism: 1980" (CIA Research Paper, June 1981); U.S. Department of State, "Patterns of Global Terrorism: 1984," November 1985.

25.   Bittman, *The KGB and Soviet Disinformation*, pp. 140–43; U.S. Congress, *Soviet Covert Action*, pp. 85–86.

26.   See Francis Fukuyama, "Gorbachev and the Third World," *Foreign Affairs* (Spring 1986), pp. 715–31. As Fukuyama points out, it was Andropov who first began questioning the expediency of extensive Soviet activities in the Third World. See the discussion later in this chapter.

27.   Bittman, *The KGB and Soviet Disinformation*, p. 29.

28.   Ladislav Bittman, *The Deception Game: Czechoslovak Intelligence in Soviet Political Warfare* (Syracuse, NY: Syracuse University Research Corp., 1972), pp. 16–17. For a general discussion of the satellite intelligence services see Jeffrey T. Richelson, *Sword and Shield: Soviet Intelligence and Security Apparatus* (Cambridge, MA: Ballinger, 1986), pp. 205–8.

29.   Barron, *KGB Today*, p. 449.

30.   V. M. Chebrikov, "Sverias s Leninym, rukovodstvuias trebovaniem partii," *Kommunist*, no. 9 (June 1985), pp. 52–53.

31.   In May 1983 it was reported that Chebrikov flew to Bulgaria, which naturally aroused further speculation about the KGB connection with the assassination attempt on the pope (see *Pravda*, 19 May 1983, p. 4). He was reported as visiting Warsaw in late November 1983 (*Izvestiia*, 26 November 1983, p. 4), and in May 1984 his visit to East Germany was announced (*Pravda*, 23 May 1984, p. 4). More recently he visited Hungary

in April 1986, Yugoslavia in December 1986, and Cuba in April 1987. See *FBIS Daily Report, Soviet Union* 3, no. 078 (23 April 1986), p. F3; *Izvestiia,* 6 December 1986, p. 4; and *Pravda,* 5 April 1987, p. 4.

32.   See Leonard Schapiro, "The International Department of the CPSU: Key to Soviet Policy," *International Journal* 32 (Winter 1976–77), pp. 41–55; Robert W. Kitrinos, "International Department of the CPSU," *POC* 33 (September–October 1984), pp. 59–69; and Lilita Dzirkals, Thane Gustafson, and A. Ross Johnson, *The Media and the Intra-Elite Communication in the USSR* (Santa Monica, CA: Rand Corp., 1982), pp. 20–23.

33.   See Shultz and Godson, *Dezinformatsia,* pp. 21–31; Dzirkals et al., *The Media and Intra-Elite Communication,* p. 23.

34.   Alex R. Alexiev, "The Soviet Campaign against INF: Strategy, Tactics and Means," *ORBIS* 29, no. 2 (Summer 1985), pp. 319–50. Also see Wynfred Joshua, "Soviet Manipulation of the European Peace Movement," *Strategic Review* 11, no. 1 (Winter 1983), pp. 9–18; and U.S. Congress, *Soviet Covert Action,* pp. 70–75.

35.   Alexiev, "Soviet Campaign," pp. 348–49.

36.   Jiri Valenta, *Soviet Intervention in Czechoslovakia, 1968: Anatomy of a Decision* (Baltimore and London: Johns Hopkins University Press, 1979).

37.   Ibid., p. 5.

38.   Hannes Adomeit, "Consensus versus Conflict: The Dimension of Foreign Policy," in *The Domestic Context of Soviet Foreign Policy,* Seweryn Bialer, ed. (Boulder, CO: Westview Press, 1981), pp. 49–86 (quotation, p. 49). Also see Hannes Adomeit, *Soviet Risk-Taking and Crisis Behavior: A Theoretical and Empirical Analysis* (London: Allen & Unwin, 1982).

39.   Adomeit, "Consensus versus Conflict," p. 72.

40.   See Slusser's articles on Shelepin and Semichastnyi in George W. Simmonds, ed., *Soviet Leaders* (New York: Thomas Y. Crowell, 1967); and Robert Slusser, "America, China and the Hydra-Headed Opposition," in *Soviet Policy-Making: Studies of Communism in Transition,* Peter H. Juviler and Henry W. Morton, eds. (London: Pall Mall Press, 1967).

41.   For a firsthand account of this incident see Frederick C. Barghoorn, "The Soviet Security Police," in *Interest Groups in Soviet Politics,* H. Gordon Skilling and Franklyn Griffiths, eds. (Princeton, NJ: Princeton University Press, 1971).

42.   Barron, *KGB: Secret Work,* pp. 10–11; Slusser, "America, China and the Hydra-Headed Opposition," p. 259.

43.   Alexander Dallin placed Shelepin in the camp of the "action-oriented, know nothing, anti-Western, anti-intellectual elements." See Alexander Dallin, "The Domestic Sources of Soviet Foreign Policy," in Bialer, *The Domestic Context of Soviet Foreign Policy,* pp. 335–408.

44.   See *Der Spiegel,* 4 December 1967, pp. 162–64; Jacques Derogy and Hesi Carmel, *The Untold History of Israel* (New York: Grove Press, 1979), pp. 208–20; and Barron, *KGB: Secret Work,* pp. 11–12.

45.   Galia Golan, "Soviet Decisionmaking in the Yom Kippur War," in *Soviet Decisionmaking for National Security,* Jiri Valenta and William C. Potter, eds. (London: Allen & Unwin, 1984), pp. 185–217 (quotation, p. 194).

46.   Derogy and Carmel, *Untold History of Israel,* pp. 294–95.

47.   Ibid., pp. 10–11, 296–97.

48.   See Jiri Valenta, "Soviet Decisionmaking and the Czechoslovak Crisis of 1968," *Studies in Comparative Communism* 8, nos. 1–2 (Spring–Summer 1975), pp. 155–56.

49.   Valenta, *Soviet Intervention in Czechoslovakia,* p. 10.

50.   Ibid., pp. 10–11, 58–63.

51. Karen Dawisha, in her study entitled *The Kremlin and the Prague Spring* (Berkeley, Los Angeles, London: University of California Press, 1984), concluded that because Andropov was silent in public about Czechoslovakia and absent from negotiations, the KGB had little influence over the decision to invade (pp. 361–62), but the evidence discussed below counters this impression.

52. *Pravda*, 21 December 1967, p. 3.

53. See his 23 October 1968 speech, reprinted in Iv. V. Andropov, *Izbrannye rechi i stat'ei* (Moscow: Politizdat, 1983), pp. 120–25 (quotation, p. 121).

54. A. Malygin, "V bitve idei net kompromisov," *Molodoi Kommunist*, no. 1 (1969), pp. 49–62.

55. V. V. Fedorchuk and S. A. Stepanov, "Otravlennoe oruzhie imperialistov," *Vestnik protivovozdushnoi oborony*, no. 2 (1969), pp. 86–89.

56. Valenta, *Soviet Intervention in Czechoslovakia*, p. 23; Bittman, *The Deception Game*, pp. 186–90; Josef Frolik, *The Frolik Defection* (London: Leo Cooper, 1975), pp. 147–52; and Dawisha, *Kremlin and the Prague Spring*, pp. 52–54.

57. Bittman, *The Deception Game*, pp. 187–96.

58. Valenta, *Social Intervention in Czechoslovakia*, p. 107.

59. The first suggestion that Andropov was a "liberal" came from a former CC adviser and member of the USSR Academy of Sciences, Boris Rabbot. See *New York Times Magazine*, 6 November 1977, p. 3.

60. From an Estonian Radio broadcast on 27 December 1973, translated in *FBIS Daily Report, Soviet Union* 3 (2 January 1974), p. R6.

61. See, for example, Andropov, *Izbrannye rechi i stat'ei*, pp. 119–34, 135–49. Also see A. Knight, "The Powers of the Soviet KGB," *Survey* 25, no. 3 (112) (Summer 1980), pp. 150–51.

62. S. Tsvigun, "Ideologicheskaia diversiia orudie imperialisticheskoi reactsii," *Kommunist*, no. 5 (March 1972), p. 110.

63. S. Tsvigun, "Nash Feliks," *Znamia*, no. 12 (1977), pp. 199–211 (quotation, p. 210).

64. On this point see Fukuyama, "Gorbachev and the Third World." Fukuyama notes that "Andropov was the first senior political leader to revive the dictum of Lenin and Khrushchev that the Soviet Union's chief influence in the world revolutionary movement comes about less through direct economic assistance than as a result of the force of its example as a socialist society" (p. 719).

65. *Pravda*, 12 February 1980, p. 2.

66. *Pravda*, 14 February 1980, p. 2.

67. See, for example, Jiri Valenta, "Decisionmaking in Afghanistan, 1979," in Valenta and Potter, *Soviet Decisionmaking*, pp. 218–36.

68. *Bakiinskii rabochii*, 19 December 1980, p. 3.

69. On the role of the Soviet high command in the Polish crisis and their efforts to push for military intervention, see Richard D. Anderson, Jr., "Soviet Decision-making and Poland," *POC* 31, no. 2 (March–April 1982), pp. 22–36.

70. From an article in the Ukrainian journal *Pid praporom leninizmu*, no. 19 (October 1981), pp. 10–17. As quoted in Roman Solchanyk, "Ukrainian KGB Chief Warns of Ideological Sabotage," *RLRB*, RL 422/81, 22 October 1981.

71. On the defense council see Ellen Jones, *Red Army and Society: A Sociology of the Soviet Military* (Winchester, MA: Allen & Unwin, 1985), pp. 6–10; and Jan Sejna and Joseph D. Douglass, Jr., *Decision-making in Communist Countries: An Inside View* (Cambridge, MA, and Washington, DC: Institution for Foreign Policy Analysis, 1986), pp. 30–39.

72. V. M. Chebrikov, "Vigilance—A Well-Tried Weapon," *Molodoi Kommunist*, no. 4 (April 1981), pp. 28–34. Translated in *FBIS Daily Report, Soviet Union* 3 (11 June

1981), USSR Annex. Sidney Ploss, in his study of the Polish crisis, concludes from statements such as those by Fedorchuk and Chebrikov that the KGB as an institution favored military intervention. See Sidney I. Ploss, *Moscow and the Polish Crisis: An Interpretation of Soviet Policies and Intentions* (Boulder, CO, and London: Westview Press, 1986), pp. 94–95. There is no indication, however, that Andropov, as KGB chief, advocated military intervention.

73. Rust was tried in Moscow in early September 1987 and received a sentence of four years in a general regime labor camp under Articles 83 (unlawful entry into the Soviet Union), 84 (violation of rules of international flights), and 206 (hooliganism) of the RSFSR Criminal Code.

74. *Pravda,* 7 November 1985, p. 2.

75. *Pravda,* 11 September 1987, p. 3. Chebrikov made a pointed reference to the opposition of Dzerzhinskii, the first Soviet security chief, to the treaty of Brest-Litovsk in 1918, and later noted that many of Dzerzhinskii's assessments "sound topical today." Furthermore, he went out of his way to stress that the West was attempting to use democratization in the Soviet Union for its own subversive goals.

76. See his speech delivered in honor of the fortieth anniversary of the "liberation" of Estonia, printed in *Sovetskaia estoniia,* 23 September 1984, pp. 2–3.

77. For a good overview of Gorbachev's foreign policy see Roderic Lyne, "Making Waves: Mr. Gorbachev's Public Diplomacy, 1985–6," *International Affairs* 63, no. 2 (Spring 1987), pp. 205–24.

21

*Is Gorbachev Changing the Rules of Defense Decision-Making?**

Condoleezza Rice

The Gorbachev revolution has touched every aspect of Soviet life, and defense policy is no exception. It is not hard to see that the Soviets have tried to deemphasize the role of military power in international politics, both in their rhetoric and, to a certain extent, in their behavior. Gorbachev himself has said that military power has limited utility in the nuclear age.[1] With extraordinary economic problems at home, the Soviet Union cannot afford to participate in another round of the arms race, whatever the utility of military power. The Soviets have left Afghanistan, and they have made an effort to signal their apparently benign intentions through restrictions on exercises at sea and along the border with China.[2] At home, military parades and demonstrations of hardware have been scaled back. And criticism, even ridicule, is directed at the Soviet military in an uncharacteristically public fashion. The new foreign policy clearly relies on building a different image of the Soviet Union than the one that Leonid Brezhnev, adorned in World War II medals, nurtured.

Yet, in spite of these trends and statements, elements of old and new coexist in Soviet military policy as *perestroika* in this sector proceeds cautiously. Flexibility at the arms control table has been coupled with continued modernization of Soviet weaponry. Whatever the long-term future of military power in the international system, the Soviet Union intends to have its share.

The political-military picture in the Soviet Union is thus very complex. Gorbachev is clearly determined to put his imprimatur on the nature and exercise of Soviet military power. Some of the unfolding changes are unparalleled in Soviet history but others are not. The shifting of personnel, the attacks on corruption in the military and the downgrading of the military's presence in public life are important but not at all unprecedented or even unusual in party-military relations.[3] In this regard, the weeding out of several of the aging leaders

*Reprinted by permission of the author and publisher from *Journal of International Affairs*, 42, 2, (Spring 1989). Copyright © 1989 by the Trustees of Columbia University in the City of New York.

from the Brezhnev period—such as former Minister of Defense Sergei Sokolov, who was removed on the heels of the Rust affair, the late Admiral Sergei N. Gorshkov and the former chief of the Main Political Administration, General Alexei Yepishev, all septuagenarians—is understandable without reference to policy preferences of the Gorbachev leadership. After all, these officers must have seemed the personification of stagnation.

On the other hand, the decision to keep, for a while, Chief of the General Staff Sergei Akhromeev and the commander-in-chief of the Warsaw Pact, Viktor Kulikov, suggests that competence was also an important issue. Moreover, some changes initially thought to be promotions of new thinkers have given platforms to extremely conservative officers, like General Ivan Tretiak, sent to head the Main Inspectorate and later the Air Defense Forces. Akhromeev has finally retired and Kulikov's replacement followed not far behind. One suspects that Tretiak's days are also numbered.

Clearly, the general secretary is determined to have officers in the top echelons who are energetic and who support his programs. Thus, the decision to pluck from the military the colorless Dmitri Yazov for minister of defense is in line with many such appointments historically. For instance, while Marshal A. A. Grechko, a World War II hero and traditional ground forces man, qualified as a powerful representative of the professional officer corps, Brezhnev also appointed his crony, the civilian-in-uniform Dmitri Ustinov, for minister of defense in 1976. And the ascendance of S. L. Sokolov in 1984 was hardly a victory for articulate advocacy of military views. This is a thoroughly civilian-controlled military. Chiefs of the General Staff and ministers of defense are fired regularly in the Soviet Union for insubordination. After all, at the height of stagnation in 1984, Nikolai Ogarkov, one of the most forceful Chiefs of the General Staff in Soviet history, was dumped without a whimper from the military.

However, the attack on corruption and bureaucratic stagnation in the military is more virulent than at almost any other time in Soviet history. Boris Yeltsin's now famous statement, uttered at the time of the Rust affair, that the air defense leadership was characterized by "bureaucratism, nepotism . . . and cliquishness," sounded the alarm, and it has been followed by significant criticism of the military for those vices.[4] The new chief of the Main Political Administration, General Alexei Lizichev, has been vocal in calling for increased party vigilance to control corruption, including the abuse of soldiers by officers and the weeding out of incompetents.[5] It should also be noted that similar criticisms have been levelled at the military from within. But the military is not a unitary institution, and while one faction loses in an anticorruption campaign, another always wins. There is no reason to believe that all military officers resent the outcome of the process, even if they are not enthralled by the process itself.

The problem for the analyst, then, is to separate those elements of military reform that are natural in a change of leadership, personnel shifts for instance, from innovations with wider implications for the role of military power in Soviet foreign policy. As we try to assess the potential for a reversal in Soviet policy, the major changes for which we should search are not in the number of officers on reviewing stands or articles about corruption in the Soviet military. Rather, the key is to look for evidence that Gorbachev's vision of the role of military power is penetrating downward into military planning. The most powerful potential changes in this regard involve attempts to actually restructure the institutions of defense.

In general, Gorbachev has devoted more attention to institutional restructuring in the economy and the political system than any leaders since Stalin, who constructed the current party apparatus in the 1930s. The evidence is accumulating that Gorbachev also wishes to restructure the institutions of defense decision-making. The goal appears to be the creation of a more effective system for advice and option generation; one that is more capable of linking political and military goals effectively. If these decision-making institutions can be made to respond to the imperatives of the new foreign policy. Gorbachev's view of the world will have a lasting impact on Soviet defense policy.

A number of Western scholars have noted that important shifts appear to be taking place in the institutional structure of decision-making. Stephen Larabee has argued that Gorbachev has restructured the Soviet military in order to force new thinking on the ossified structures of the Soviet defense establishment.[6] Others, among them Robert Legvold, have noted that discussions of Soviet military strategy and force posture appear regularly in journals of the civilian institutes of the Academy of Sciences.[7] The most persuasive case is made by Stephen Meyer, who argues that the very character of defense decisions under Gorbachev signals a shift in their institutional locus; that it is unlikely that the unilateral moratorium on nuclear testing or the global double-zero for intermediate- and medium-range nuclear forces originated with the General Staff.[8]

That there have been changes recently in the traditional patterns of Soviet defense decision-making seems clear. While most of the examples come from Soviet arms control policy, which has never been the exclusive preserve of the professional military, many of the questions that Soviet civilians are now asking impinge upon the core jurisdiction of the General Staff: strategy, force posture and organization. Obviously, the long-term significance of these changes, as well as their durability, is unclear at this time. But it is important to ask critical questions about even the short-term impact of these shifts, and to examine the institutional implications of what the Soviet leadership is trying to do.

This paper explores several elements of *perestroika* in defense decision-making. First, it revisits briefly the character of the institutional structure that Gorbachev inherited. Only then can we understand better the critique of those structures and implications for the creation of new ones. The paper tries to sort out the elements of the critique because, in the argument for new institutional arrangements, not all of the criticisms of the Soviet military are of equal weight.

Second, the paper looks for clues to the character of those institutional arrangements that might be more in accordance with the goals of the leadership. In general, the trend is toward greater debate of defense issues and broadening the concept of security to take more account of political concerns, even in the consideration of narrowly defined military problems. This would argue, at least in theory, for a greater role for civilian analysts in the process. Some within the Soviet Union are promoting "multiple advocacy" in the defense debate. Multiple advocacy is a term coined by Alexander George to describe a decision-making system in which there are numerous advocates within the policy-making system who cover a range of viewpoints and policy options on a given issue.[9] Should this trend develop, it would be a major departure for a system that has traditionally operated on the principle of closely held "scientific planning from the top down.

The difficulty of changing traditional patterns should not be underestimated. The only way to ensure multiple advocacy is to create competing structures for option generation, and that will encounter inertia and resistance. This is not the first time that Soviet leaders with radical ideas have tried to break the stranglehold of the military bureaucracy on security policy. The failure of Nikita Khrushchev's reforms to endure holds useful lessons for Gorbachev 30 years later. Therefore, this paper will also examine the counter-critique that has emerged in recent months from conservatives both in and out of uniform.

THE CRITIQUE OF SOVIET DEFENSE DECISION-MAKING

Why is there a perception in the Soviet Union that defense decision-making structures need to be recast? A short answer is that everything is being restructured in the Soviet union these days. In the current environment, the attack on stagnation was bound to engulf one of the areas to which Brezhnev was most attentive, namely, defense policy. In fact, the emerging criticism of the structure of decision-making is less a blast at the military institution itself than, as are many of the other critiques, a broadside attack on Brezhnev and his abdication of authority to the bureaucracy. Nonetheless, the implications of this critique have real ramifications, though not yet realized, for the position of the professional military in defense decision-making.

Several aspects of the critique are less profound than others. The Brezhnev leadership is accused of having made Soviet security policy in a cliquish and secretive manner; without debate and thus subject to "groupthink" and egregious policy mistakes. (This, of course, begs the question of why secrecy continues to surround Soviet foreign and defense policy decisions today.) This, in and of itself, does not argue for widening the range of institutions involved in the details of defense decision-making. Of the military, presumably only Dmitri Ustinov, the civilian-in-uniform who was minister of defense, was a part of the inner circle. Furthermore, it can be argued that he was included as much by virtue of his close association with Brezhnev as by his position. Thus, the invasion of Afghanistan, for instance, is said to have been decided by a very small circle of leaders and, while there are apparently some who argue that the military "caused Afghanistan," this policy decision is placed largely in the lap of the political leadership."

The more profound criticism portrays the Brezhnev leadership as the captive of a decision-making structure that generated limited options, narrowly military in perspective. This suggests that the very structure of decision-making in the Soviet Union was ineffective. The argument is not that the military overstepped its authority or the boundaries of its competence. Rather, the concern is that the very drawing of a boundary between the military-technical and political aspects of security policy is dangerous. In making decisions well within its jurisdiction but with myopic attention to preparing for war, the military has made the job of foreign policy and avoidance of conflict more difficult.

This criticism reflects an important shift in Soviet thinking about institutional relationships. The Soviets are finally coming to grips with the limitations of a system that is "loosely coupled;" that is, one in which decision authority rests with the party leadership while the responsibility for the formation of options resides with the professional military.[11] Historically, Soviet decision-making has been structured so that the party leadership, through the Defense Council at the top of the decision-making hierarchy, sets the broad direction of security policy. In modern Soviet parlance, this is called the socio-political side of military policy. It includes issues such as the character of international politics and the assessment of the immediacy of the threat to the Soviet Union and its allies. Issues of why, when, where and against whom to go to war, and the magnitude of economic resources devoted to defense, have always been for the party to decide. The party maintains this authority primarily through its control of the major defense appointments. Chiefs of the General Staff and ministers of defense have not lasted long when they disagreed with the party leadership on major issues of defense policy.

On the other hand, the details of military policy, usually described as the military-technical aspect of defense policy, are left largely to the professional military; this means effective control of a narrow but extremely important segment of security policy, including military strategy, construction of force posture and organization. In other words, the issues of how to fight and with what forces are within the jurisdiction of the professional military.

This division of labor has amounted to an institutional split between civilian authority and military management. The Defense Council is almost completely civilian while the General Staff—charged with the leadership of the armed forces and effectively the Defense Council's staff—is completely military. Options generated within the General Staff are presented formally along with an assessment of the variants. Though it is the party leadership that decides among options or rejects requests, such as the creation of commands or large scale weapons programs, the attractiveness of options can be fundamentally shaped by the General Staff. Moreover, since policy concerns can be brought unsolicited to the attention of the political leadership, the Soviet military has traditionally had a large say in setting the course of defense policy.

Obviously, the socio-political and military-technical aspects of security policy must meet at some juncture. The question is when and how to harmonize the guidelines and the details in the decision-making process. The Soviet Union has never had an institutional layer between the professional military and the civilian Defense Council to perform this function. (The Main Political Administration, the party's arm within the military, did not develop as an alternative institution for the generation of options for defense policy. Rather, it has been the party's means to ensure control of professional military personnel and a vehicle for indoctrination.) In a closed and hierarchical system, it is not surprising that the authority and expertise to debate certain policy questions are held by a small set of actors. In the Soviet Union, most of that expertise and authority, with regard to defense, rests with the General Staff.

THE LEGACY OF LOOSE COUPLING

The structural division of labor goes back to the very beginning of the evolution of Soviet institutions of military decision-making. The military staff was always theoretically responsible for the details of military strategy, force posture and organization, and was always kept at arm's length in matters of foreign policy and the economics of defense. This was not problematic since the system accommodated both military expertise and political authority. In fact, the one proposal in 1924 to create a civilian staff for the Council for Labor and Defense, the predecessor to the Defense Council, was abandoned for fear of duplicating the responsibility of the Main Military Staff in the proposed institution.[12] For most of its history, the Soviet Union has been surrounded by economically and technologically superior enemies and therefore has not been able to afford the inefficiencies of overlapping authority and responsibility. The most efficient system was one that could move coherently from the development of strategy to the structuring of forces and all the way through to the training of troops.

The actual functioning of this loosely coupled system has been highly dependent on the attitude of the general secretary toward military expertise. Josef Stalin left the structure intact but interposed himself and a few favorite cronies, such as Kliment Voroshilov and the hated Main Political Administration officer Lev Mekhlis, into the details of defense policy. They made such a mess, however, that by the midpoint of World War II, Stalin was more receptive to the options generated by his General Staff. Stalin forced a coupling between his guidelines and the details of military policy by sowing abject fear of his personal reprisals in the professional military. Josef Stalin did not need institutional reform to bridge the gap between military and political policy.

Nikita Khrushchev, on the other hand, needed institutional reform but never managed to bring it about. No Soviet leader, including Gorbachev, has affected the major restructuring of the military that Nikita Khrushchev temporarily, at least, achieved. In doing so, Khrushchev brought the collective hatred of the military upon him and armed his opponents with yet another round of ammunition against his "subjectivist" schemes in policy. Khrushchev's radical policies stemmed from his own understanding of the character of international politics in the nuclear age. While he initially drew on work prepared by the General Staff on the character of nuclear warfare—work that supported the notion of spasm warfare in which the battle would end in hours—Khrushchev pushed those arguments, in the view of the military professionals, far beyond their proper limits. He pushed through a reorganization of the Soviet military: He created a new service, the Strategic Rocket Forces, for control of strategic nuclear weapons; abolished the ground forces command and slashed budgets and manpower.

Khrushchev failed, however, to institutionalize alternative mechanisms for the generation of options. He seemed to be flying blind most of the time, without a proper staff to carry through the ideas that he proposed. This led, for instance, to a sudden and tremendous glut of personnel after his reduction of forces. There is no evidence that anyone had thought through the implications of the presence of 1.5 million discharged soldiers.[13] His nuclear diplomacy, which led to a number of foreign policy embarrassments including the Cuban missile crisis, made him an easy target for those who argued that his failure to heed expert advice led to bad policy.

In fact, his failure to find institutional mechanisms to ensure the adoption of his policies also meant that many of Khrushchev's reforms failed to survive him. The Strategic Rocket Forces were created upon the recommendation of both the General Staff and Khrushchev, and for a time they survived and prospered. Three years after Khrushchev's dismissal, however, there was a return to an emphasis on large conventional forces and the recreation of the Ground Forces command, suggesting that his ideas about military power were resisted and ultimately defeated.

Leonid Brezhnev was far more tolerant of loose coupling and a division of labor than were his predecessors. As part of the general trend toward rationalization and bureaucratization of planning. Brezhnev allowed the military broad authority to generate options and pursue the details of defense policy. In fact, Brezhnev's respect for military expertise was a reaction to Khrushchev's failure to heed it.[14] However, it is worth restating that the General Staff's authority existed within the limited spheres of strategy, force posture and organization.

Furthermore, there were really two Brezhnev periods. In the first, the military had not only free reign in developing options for defense policy, but extraordinary resources with which to carry out those recommendations. It is estimated that the Soviet Union spent 15 to 18 percent of its GNP for defense between 1967 and 1976. In the latter half of the Brezhnev years, however, growth in procurement slowed and a number of analysts have argued persuasively that civil-military tensions over resource allocation rose considerably. The accumulating evidence indicates that the Soviet military had been informed that the days of free spending were over almost 10 years before Gorbachev, and even under Brezhnev and his geriatric successors, it was unable to stay the change.[15]

In some sense, this system has functioned very well. The Soviet Union has enough military power to deserve the title of superpower (used prematurely in the Khrushchev era), to dominate its allies and extend its reach in the Third World. However, this was achieved at perhaps an excessive economic cost, which is one of the criticisms of the Brezhnev period.

The Soviets are beginning to realize, though, that the economic burden of the defense buildup was only one cost. The real irony is that the Brezhnev buildup also produced political and foreign policy problems. This critique of a narrowly defined military view of military-technical policy is a potentially powerful argument for restructuring defense institutions. Brezhnev is accused, rightly or wrongly, of allowing loose coupling to become no coupling at all. Military policy, pursued myopically, collided with foreign policy. Political means are said to have been undervalued.[16] The Soviets themselves have noted that this was the case with the decision to deploy the SS-20 missiles, which taken for arguably sound military reasons—the modernization of the aging SS-4 and SS-5 force—led to an international perception of an enhanced threat to Europe. That, in turn, created support for the NATO deployment of ground-launched cruise missiles and the Pershing II, which with its prompt, hard-target kill capability actually qualitatively increased the threat to the Soviet Union.[17]

There is a tension, however, between preparing for war against other states and improving relations with them. The old guard is accused of having seen only the positive side of military power, failing to understand the political implication of the threat that is posed to Soviet foes. But even the sternest critic of Brezhnev would recognize that the structure of Soviet decision-making, when taken to its extreme, would create precisely this problem. The Soviet military was charged with preparing for war and the political leadership was charged with preventing it. With little or no staff permanently concerned with the connection between the two, the divorce between military-technical and political policy spheres was bound to occur.

THE DEBATE OVER INSTITUTIONAL REFORM

Those who wish to reform the system focus their attention on several elements of defense decision-making. First, there is an argument that more open debate would serve Soviet defense policy better. Although few have argued that public debate should be encouraged, the primary concern of key actors in the system (such as Anatoly Dobryinin) is the presentation of competing options by alternative institutions within the government. A. A. Primakov, director of the Institute of World Economy and International Relations, voiced the same concern when he said that "alternative variants were poorly presented in the adoption of decisions."[18]

Defense Minister Yazov has responded defensively but self-critically to such charges by noting that military thought is "fettered by passivity, stereotyped thinking, and a lack of competition between ideas and opinions. . . . Creativity, initiative, bold questing, reasonable risk—these represent oxygen for real science."[19] Yazov has even tried to turn the critique into an argument for the allocation of more resources to a reorganized military research establishment.

But this response does not really answer the criticisms of Primakov and others. Implicit in their argument for alternative inputs is a belief that the professional military, because of its limited vision, training and parochial interests, cannot be expected to see beyond the boundaries of military policy. The problem, as they see it, is that decisions in the military realm affect policies beyond these boundaries. For instance, while the party's authority to decide resource allocation has never been questioned, there is a perception among the reformers that the leaders have viewed the requirements for defense through a lens provided by the professional military's view of the threat. Militaries are assumed to know only one way to meet a threat, and that is head on. If an alternative is available, such as restructuring the threat through diplomacy, it is an option that is not likely to be generated by the military. In a period of even greater resource constraint than Brezhnev faced, alternative methods for meeting security threats are welcome.

There is thus an argument that the military-technical details can no longer be left exclusively to the professional military. The assault on the division of labor began two years ago when Anatoly Dobrynin, newly appointed to head the Central Committee's International Department, argued that matters of war and peace were too important to be left to technical experts. There is inherent in this a recognition that the line between foreign policy and "purely" military issues, like that between strategy and force posture, is somewhat artificial. This is considered especially dangerous in the nuclear age when avoiding war takes on even greater importance. The importance of political means has been trumpeted by officials at all levels.

The argument about the importance of political means is producing interesting counter-arguments. The issue is whether the most recent defense buildup, which the Soviets still defend as a reaction to Western militarism, went too far. Would it have been possible to use political means, for instance a "peace offensive," instead of participating the arms race? Marshal Akhromeev argues that this position is not wholly correct. Admitting that the Soviet "response to the American arms buildup might have been shortsighted," he says that political means were not ignored but that "more specific steps that would have been understood by the world's publics to demonstrate the dangers of the arms race were underemployed."[20]

More conservative commentators argue that the luxury to critique defense policy in this way may be, in part, a result of the Soviet military's success in constructing potent forces. Thus while expressing enthusiasm for political solutions they vociferously argue that the defense buildup was not misdirected and that without it, the "new foreign policy" would have been unthinkable.[21]

This is not an idle debate about the mistakes of the past. The basic issue is how to respond to the continuing pressures of the arms race. Peace through strength still has many advocates in this debate. Indeed, the threats to the Soviet Union are no longer chiefly military. No state is likely to try to roll back the rule of the Soviet Communist party by military force: The Soviet Union is a recognized and viable military superpower and one that can wield considerable influence. However, Gorbachev faces a different political-military environment than his predecessors. There are now threats to Soviet power from economic malaise, some of which are traceable to the defense buildup and the Soviet Union's inability to use the more nuanced instruments of diplomacy to build better relations with critical states. Military professionals are the wrong analysts to understand how to address such concerns.

RESTRUCTURING INSTITUTIONS: A VERY LONG-TERM PROPOSITION

All of this argues for the restructuring of defense decision-making. But what is it that is being restructured? It is more important than ever for Western analysts to think about institutional relationships in the Soviet Union in terms of the level and type of decision, and to differentiate between the license to debate issues, participation in option generation, authority to make policy decisions and the responsibility for implementation.

The philosopher Alfred North Whitehead has said that education has three stages: "romance," in which interest is aroused; "discipline," in which concepts, methods and expertise are acquired; and "fruition," in which methods and concepts are applied so that the structure and function may be understood and improved. This progression captures nicely the problem of restructuring institutional relationships.

The creation of counter-institutions, or even the alteration of traditional patterns, will be a long-term process. The Soviet Union is currently in the romance phase in which a number of institutions outside of the General Staff have become interested in the military-technical aspects of defense policy. Greater attention is being given to defense policy in several quarters: the civilian institutes of the Academy of Sciences, the Foreign Ministry and, most importantly, the Central Committee. The problem is to take the next two steps and create real, permanent expertise, and, finally, mechanisms for follow-through so that the structure of Soviet defense decision-making can be significantly improved.

Currently, many of these new actors are operating in the realm of debate, raising interesting questions about the character and purpose of armed forces. This is not unimportant, but it is a long way from controlling the agenda or even affecting the decision-making process through option generation. General ideas in debate do not translate into policy options. If the Soviets wish to take the next step and restructure executive decision-making, creating a basis for the advocation of different options within the government, they will need institutions that they do not have at this time. (The other possibility is to create incentives for the General Staff to produce more broadly gauged options, but it is inherently difficult for institutions to move beyond their fairly limited vision.)

The creation of counter-institutions will be no easy matter. Institutions have four characteristics that make them difficult to change: jurisdiction, expertise, norms and traditions. Jurisdiction is an institution's legitimate realm of authority. A claim to expertise and competence is the basis on which jurisdiction is maintained. Norms are the principles that guide, control and regulate acceptable behavior within an institution. Both the right to dominance in deciding a set of issues and the legitimacy of one group or another to ask and answer a given set of questions stem from a set of societally or politically generated norms. Though these norms may be legally based, they often reflect traditional patterns and expectations. These traditions reinforce the sense of jurisdictional boundaries for both the institution and the polity at large. Breaking through such existing boundaries is very difficult.

It is sometimes difficult for Americans to grasp the concept of jurisdictional boundaries because overlapping authority and parallel mechanisms of debate and decision are commonplace in our political system. In the Soviet Union, however, decision authority is tightly and hierarchically held, even in the current environment. The proliferation of structures for debate of defense policy would be a real departure.

The norms of the Gorbachev era support some pluralization of debate; issues that were previously within the jurisdiction of bureaucrats are now being debated more broadly. In the military sphere, this is reflected in the widening of institutions that debate issues previously confined to the pages of military journals. But what jurisdictional boundaries have actually been crossed, and by whom?

NUCLEAR STRATEGY AND ARMS CONTROL

The civilian institutes have acquired a license to debate matters of military strategy. The most significant inroads have been in matters of nuclear strategy.[22] While there has long been discussion of nuclear matters in the Soviet academic press, the current period is producing more analytic and more neutral (though not completely neutral) analyses of the strategic balance. In particular, this work adopts the Western concept of strategic stability, a linchpin of American arms-control theology. Until recently, this concept was also an anathema to the Soviet military, which is sensitive to the fact that the primary weapon in the Soviet arsenal, land-based ballistic missiles, was considered by American specialists to be the most destabilizing of strategic weapons.[23]

The boundaries around nuclear strategy have been permeable to civilian input for a long time, however. No one has ever fought a nuclear war and an engineer or a physicist is as well-qualified, perhaps better qualified, as an operations officer to discuss the effects of nuclear weapons. The Soviet Union has many veterans of arms control negotiations who have expertise in nuclear issues. The boundaries around nuclear strategy were permeable even under Brezhnev. Many analysts argue that Brezhnev understood that nuclear weapons were qualitatively different. His renunciation of military superiority as a goal enabled the Soviet Union to agree to a bilateral cap, albeit a very high one, with the United States on nuclear forces.[24]

It has been argued that the General Staff came to accept the concept of sufficiency in nuclear weapons in the late 1970s. The argument cannot be explored in detail here, but Ogarkov's quote, "you do not need to be a military man to see that stockpiling of nuclear weapons is senseless," is taken as a statement of sufficiency from the Soviet Union's then chief of the General Staff.[25]

With rough parity established through ceilings, and now, in a more detailed way, in the Strategic Arms Reduction Talks (START), there are hard and fast criteria for equating and structuring "sufficient" forces. The Soviet military would argue, though, that parity is a dynamic concept and that it must be aggressively maintained. In this way, the military makes an effective argument for continued modernization of Soviet military forces.[26] But acceptance of sufficiency should not be equated with minimum deterrence. It means only that the nuclear balance is stable enough to ensure that an attack could be answered, as they say, under any conditions. A persuasive case can be made that the General Staff's primary preoccupation since the mid-1970s has been the creation of a conventional option for war in Europe: one in which Soviet political leaders would never be confronted with the decision of nuclear use.[27]

Much of Soviet nuclear arms control policy is consistent with a view of sufficiency in nuclear weapons. But who makes certain that Soviet forces are structured in accordance with principles of sufficiency and stability? The Central Committee has created a new military department within the International Department that may play an important role in this process. And although the October 1988 reorganization apparently abolished the International Department and put in its place a Commission on International Affairs headed by Yakovlev, presumably the military department was transferred to that new body. Two senior military officers, General V. M. Staradubov and General V. F. Batenin, form the core of an increasingly important military staff for the Secretariat.

But with all of the diversification of institutions and actors discussing nuclear strategy, it was the chief of the General Staff Akhromeev who was the Soviet Union's principal negotiator on arms control at Reykjavik, Washington and Moscow. Akhromeev was the counterpart to Paul Nitze, who represented the State Department. This suggests that the union of military strategy and arms control is still an important consideration for Gorbachev. Akhromeev's departure as chief of the General Staff may change this situation though he is said to hold a post as an advisor on arms control. The emergence of Akhromeev and several officers, like General N. V. Chervov of the Legal and Treaty Department of the General Staff as key actors in negotiations was an interesting adjustment by that institution to the demands of more radical arms control initiatives.

One conservative civilian spokesman has made the case that the military must play a dominant role in arms control policy. The arms race, he says, is complex and cannot be reversed by "peace marches alone. . . . While it is indeed true that the beginning phase of disarmament is directed by political leaders, this is done with the direct participation of military experts. And, naturally, generals will sit down next to politicians . . . because only they, who have created this megastructure are able to neutralize and slowly dismantle it so that it does not come crashing down on our heads."[28]

CONVENTIONAL STRATEGY AND DOCTRINE

The more difficult institutional issues are raised by the prospect of pluralizing the debate on conventional force posture and strategy. The emerging debate about defensive doctrine and reasonable sufficiency in conventional forces thus represents a real break with tradition. Here it is important to pay attention to the role that civilians are actually playing in this debate. That civilians are trying to participate in the reevaluation of defensive doctrine is clear, but the obstacles they would face in trying to affect the generation of options for operational strategy, troop training or force deployments are formidable. The General Staff has everything going for it as the primary voice for restructuring Soviet conventional force, and the outcome turns on how tightly constrained the General Staff will be in interpreting the meaning of defense.

Understanding the debate about defensive doctrine is made more difficult by the confusing manner in which offense and defense interact in Soviet military thought. The Soviet Union has always claimed that its political doctrine (on the socio-political level) is defensive in nature and that the Soviet Union would use military force only in response to outright aggression or in expectation of imminent attack. (Indeed one does not have to attribute benign intentions to the Soviets to admit that the number of political contingencies that would warrant a full scale conventional attack against Western Europe are few. The threat of escalation to nuclear war reinforces Soviet caution.) Furthermore, socio-political doctrine has always stated that prevention of war is the most important task. At the military-technical level, however, Soviet strategy prepared the forces for offensive war if the attempt at prevention failed. In short, the rapid offensive in Europe has been the Soviets' preferred strategy in the unlikely event of war in Europe.

If ever the effects of loose coupling were felt, it has been in the divergence between Soviet force posture and their political line in Europe. The problem has been a divorce between an offensive, even preemptive, military strategy and political intent. The Soviets now say that they are bridging the gap between the two and are constructing a defensive military strategy whose chief aim is also the prevention of war. This implies that the exigencies of preparation are to be subordinate to those of prevention. The key question remains whether in the pursuit of these goals defensive operations will replace, complement or remain the handmaiden of the offensive, should war come.

Well before Gorbachev came to power, the Soviet military began to reexamine the role of defensive operations in military strategy. Important articles appeared in the theoretical/historical journal *Voenno-istoricheskii zhurnal* in 1984. Even earlier, in 1982, the Ground Forces journal *Voennyi vestnik* published several articles on defensive combat.[29] The military, however, has talked primarily about defensive operations within the structure of a traditional military strategy that might seek ultimately to move to the offensive. The emphasis on defense in this historical context was driven by growing pessimism about the chances for success of the conventional offensive, particularly since it was dependent on an early decision to go to war. Changes in NATO's strategy that threatened the ability of the Soviet Union to reinforce the first echelon of forces and the continuing threat of nuclear escalation made it difficult for the proponents of a preemptive and rapid conventional offensive to defend their position.

What has changed since Gorbachev came to power is the emphasis on defense: it is now afforded the status of being the primary operational form. But the Soviet military continues to argue that after an active defensive phase, it would be necessary to go over to the counteroffensive.[30] Active defense contrasts with positional or static defense, which amounts to trench warfare and has been categorically rejected by Soviet military men. The difference is not insignificant for stability on the Central Front. Soviet forces, though still dependent on armor, could presumably be thinned out and redeployed under the new doctrine. Confidence-building measures to prevent rapid mobilization without notification could be added. In this way, the potential for surprise attack would be lower, even though the Soviets would still possess significant offensive capability.

The debate that has opened up in the Soviet Union about a defensive doctrine clearly highlights another problem: Civilians face several barriers when attempting to discuss conventional forces that they do not face with nuclear forces. While no one has ever fought a nuclear war, military men train for and have experienced conventional combat. Operational factors such s battle conditions, the impact of mobilization and transport timelines, troop response, and command and control are not easily understood without exposure to the rigors of battlefield training. While civilian analysts argue that modern conventional war is fundamentally different, given the destructive potential of new, highly accurate weaponry, the military would seem to have retained a natural advantage due to its jurisdiction over conventional strategy.

Interestingly, one of the most active civilians in this debate has chosen the path of finding allies within military institutes to make the case for defensive doctrine. Andrei Kokoshin, deputy director of the USA and Canada Institute, has looked both to military history and to a retired officer who is now a professor at the

General Staff Academy, V. V. Larionov, to strengthen the legitimacy of the proposal for defensive doctrine. The historical case that they chose, however, the Battle of Kursk, and both a defensive phase and a massive counteroffensive. Further, Kursk was the site of the largest tank battle of World War II—hardly supporting an argument for major cuts in Soviet armor.[31]

Soviet civilians are also attempting to utilize the Soviet military's own 1930s debate about defensive doctrine to support the case that there is nothing militarily stupid about a defensive strategy. Thus the name A. A. Svechin, a military theoretician from that period, has been resurrected in a number of articles. Svechin, a former tsarist officer who served in the Red Army, argued for positional defense and preparation for a war of attrition. His primary antagonist was Mikhail Tukhachevsky, chief of the General Staff and a proponent of the rapid offensive and large heavy armored forces.[32] In fact, Svechin's theories were so unpopular in the Soviet military that an entire volume was devoted to refuting them.

It should be noted, too, that some of the more serious civilian thinkers on this matter have warned an increasingly vocal Soviet pacifist community that unilateral disarmament is not on the horizon. Some extreme positions of unnamed people in the peace movements and in the Writer's Union have been scored by a number of critics.[33] As interesting as the debates on defensive doctrine are, the real battleground will be what this means for Soviet forces: Given a shift to defensive doctrine, what level of forces would be sufficient?

CONVENTIONAL FORCE POSTURES

"Reasonable sufficiency," the formulation preferred by civilian analysts, is apparently an argument for an internally driven calculation of "how much is enough?" "Defensive sufficiency," the military's preferred formulation, is dependent on negotiated levels.[34]

The concept of sufficiency for conventional forces was first raised by Gorbachev during a visit to France and then elaborated in his Party Congress speech in January 1986. Civilian analysts in the institutes were then apparently given a chance to give definition to that vague idea. Two of the Academy institutes created new departments for general purpose forces and began to bring more retired officers into their ranks to improve their expertise in the area. These analysts implicitly reject the view that sufficiency only has meaning in a bilateral context by arguing that the Soviet Union must not, as it did in the 1970s, try to respond to the West in kind and number. Even with conventional forces, they say, there is a threshold of deterrence at much lower levels than the two sides now have. To date, however, they have been unable to articulate a formula for calculating sufficiency unilaterally.

The military, on the other hand, has been vocal against unilateral cuts. Negotiated levels, the preferred means to sufficiency from the military's point of view, may be more difficult to define than parity was for nuclear forces. This is not encouraging, considering the laborious process of establishing essential equivalence in SALT and later in START.

Indeed, it is difficult to imagine the conventional equivalent of the nuclear concept of minimum deterrence. The calculus for conventional war is so complicated and the interaction between forces so important that it is almost impossible to develop a unilateral measure of what number of forces would inflict unacceptable damage. Thus, the Soviet military's view that only negotiated levels can determine sufficiency is hard to refute and portends a protracted and difficult course for conventional arms control. Gorbachev's decision, announced in the speech to the United Nations on 7 December 1988, is therefore extremely interesting. The decision to undertake a unilateral cut must be seen as a significant defeat for Soviet military officers who were so publicly against unilateral moves. Akhromeev's retirement on the morning of the speech may not have represented disagreement with a policy of troop reductions per se. But since he had been such an outspoken opponent of unilateral cuts, he may have been unwilling to remain chief of the General Staff once the decision was taken. On this particular issue, the advice of the professional military was apparently rejected.

Nevertheless, the actual restructuring of Soviet forces and any further troop reductions are likely to bear the imprimatur of the General Staff. Because of the importance of operational factors, the military will play a large role in devising a reasonable plan for the redeployment of Soviet forces.

Whether the Central Committee staff could develop real expertise to move from the realm of debate to option generation for conventional force restructuring, and thus speed up the process of negotiation, remains to be seen. Information and access could be granted to the Central Committee, though, generally, bureaucratic institutions are very good at controlling the flow of information to other groups. The General Staff is very established, and so much depends on how information flows are managed. For instance, are raw data actually handed over to the Central Committee or does it receive informational inputs in which assumptions about the character of the war are as crucial as are the data presented?

Expertise is also an important issue, and the continued reliance on military officers that are assigned to the Central Committee to provide expertise begs the question of where the departure in gestalt necessary for thinking about radical changes in force posture will come from. A nagging question is whether military men leave their uniforms and their loyalties behind when they move to civilian institutions. Arms control negotiations may be, as they were in the nuclear area, as important a forum for putting new ideas into the Soviet system as they have ever been.

Gorbachev's new approach to security has sanctioned a role for civilian analysts outside of government and in institutions other than the General Staff to raise new ideas concerning Soviet strategy and force posture. So far, though, the institutes are largely involved in an exercise in debate and in the stimulation of new ideas. Unfortunately, less is known about the activities of Central Committee personnel. One could posit that some of the ideas underlying Soviet arms control proposals come from this source, and that its institutional expertise appears to be growing as officers from the General Staff continue to be assigned to the Central Committee.

There are two ways that the Central Committee staff could broaden and deepen its impact on Soviet military policy, particularly with regard to conventional forces. First, arms control negotiations could provide a stimulus for assessment of Western proposals and from there options could be structured that challenge the professional military's views of sufficiency. This would be one form of at least dual advocacy. A second, less difficult task for this small staff would be to pose questions and scenarios for the professional military and monitor and assess the options that the General Staff generates. A staff that could question underlying assumptions and intelligence estimates, and thus critically review options, would be an improvement in giving the general secretary another view of the political and military balance. The Soviets might even try to encourage competition within the General Staff itself. Over 50 years ago, the then chief of the General Staff, Tukhachevsky, created a predecessor to what is now called the Military Sciences Directorate. Its job was to think broadly and radically about the demands of the modern battlefield. This was an attempt to institutionalize innovative thinking within a military staff that Tukhachevsky thought was often given to stereotypical thinking. These two latter variants would modify the formal options structure that Brezhnev used, but would fall short of true multiple advocacy in which competing institutions have relatively equal resources for the generation of options.

What is really at issue is finding a more effective institutional structure for generating advice at the highest levels. Gorbachev clearly believes in debate. That is obvious from almost all aspects of his policy. He wants new ideas and the General Staff was probably not the place to get broadly gauged views of security.

Yet it is worth noting that the general secretary's own positions on conventional forces track closely with those of the professional military. For instance, in the early stages of proposal-making, Gorbachev admitted that asymmetries in Europe existed and that the stronger side might have to reduce more. The assumption in the West was that this augured an acceptance of disproportionate cuts in Soviet armor. But it was not long before the view that asymmetries in Soviet armor were offset by NATO's air power (and now naval forces), first voiced by Akhromeev in Stockholm in 1985, crept into Gorbachev's own formulation. Similarly, the position, again Akhromeev's, that symmetries on the Southern Flank of Europe that favor NATO must be accommodated, has also been adopted by the general secretary. Furthermore, in his speech to the 19th Party Conference Gorbachev used the military's preferred formulation for sufficiency: sufficiency for defense.

This is not to say that Gorbachev is captive of his General Staff, as Brezhnev was said to be. It does mean that neither is he captive of the civilian *institutchiki*. On conventional force posture, the early evidence is that the General Staff has been very effective in structuring the debate and ensuring that any shift in strategy, force posture and organization will bear its imprimatur.

CONCLUSION

The Soviet Union is trying to structure a national security layer between the purely political and the purely military. In order to do that, military and political expertise must be merged. Afghanistan may have helped to convince them that military strategy divorced from political reality is impotent. Political problems in Europe (and in Asia) brought on by myopic attention to military concerns had a similar impact. Arms control, now moving into the conventional realm, is part military policy and part politics. This is in line with Gorbachev's general strengthening of the Secretariat as a stronger policy arm. It is unlike Brezhnev's perhaps extreme reliance on the bureaucracy for ideas.

Nevertheless, the pluralization of the debate and the creation of a small staff in the Central Committee should not yet be taken as a fundamental shift in the character of defense decision-making in the Soviet Union. In fact, instead of the confrontational approach that Khrushchev took with the General Staff—firing its chief and slashing its size—Gorbachev has apparently worked to achieve a consensus and, in the process, increased the visibility of his chief of the General Staff and many officers from its arms control directorate.[35]

There would seem to be many advantages and few dangers connected with broadening the institutional basis of debate in the Soviet Union. There are issues, however, that a shift in policy-making norms raises for a Soviet system that has operated very differently throughout its history. One potential problem in the so-called democratization of the defense debate is that Gorbachev could find himself having cultivated an environment that encourages detractors to his own policies. Gorbachev has the difficult job of trying to build a consensus on the tenets of the new foreign and defense policy. As valuable as alternative views can be, their propagation runs counter to coherence in policy.[36] Democratic centralism is a principle that assumes that debate will be cut off when the party leadership reaches a final decision. But in order to have an effective system of multiple or even dual advocacy, policy actors must feel free to make their views known and to question existing policy, at least privately. In a one-party system, there is no institutionalized opposition to promote the continuous examination of options. As the tenets of the new foreign policy become fixed and are identified with Gorbachev, it will be interesting to see whether he himself wishes to tolerate continuing criticism of his policies.

A more interesting issue is raised by the attempt to blend political and military expertise in a way that is relatively new in the Soviet system: Soviet military men, too, are broadening their jurisdiction. Indeed, the General Staff is being encouraged to think more broadly about political questions, and military officers who are still on active duty are being brought into the ranks of the Central Committee's International Department. Soviet military officers once scoffed at the Western notion of grand strategy, saying proudly that the Soviet military considered its realm to be narrowly military. Now the Gorbachev leadership has signalled that it considers the boundaries between military and foreign policy to be quite weak.

An interesting turf battle may be emerging between the Foreign and Defense Ministries. The growth of the political activity of officers of the Legal and Treaty Department like Chervov and the wide-ranging activities of Akhromeev, part politician and part military man, suggest an acquaintance with issues that were once considered the exclusive purview of the Foreign Ministry. Foreign Minister Eduard Shevardnadze has suggested that the plans of the Defense Ministry should be subject to review by the Foreign Ministry to insure harmony between foreign policy and military goals.[37] While this suggestion may be extreme, it is revealing: One major goal of this restructuring is to improve the coordination between all agencies involved in national security.

On the other hand, there has recently been criticism of the Foreign Ministry as well for shutting out other opinions on foreign policy. The Foreign Ministry representative's answer was instructive: He noted that the Defense Ministry is almost as closely involved as foreign policy as in military policy and that the ministry was not guilty of isolation.[38]

For a country that has worked so hard to keep the military at arms length, granting only narrow jurisdiction and insisting on apoliticism in broader issues, this is a curious turn of events. The politicization of the Soviet General Staff's horizons may be one of the most interesting and unpredictable developments of this current trend.

NOTES

1. See his speech to the Party Conference, 30 June 1988.

2. Based on conversations during a recent trip to China and the Soviet Far East with officials in Harbin, China, 29 June 1988.

3. The deputy defense minister for personnel, D. V. Sukhorukov, has argued that Soviet personnel policy has hindered "rejuvenation" and produced an age hump throughout the ranks, preventing the promotion of younger officers. "But there is a sensible limit to changes," he notes, "youth is not everything." *Krasnaia zvezda*, 23 January 1988.

4. "Po zakonam vysokoi otvetstvennosti," *Krasnaia zvezda*, 17 June 1987. The military has also taken pains to point out that these trends were pervasive in society. "The army is the country—but dressed in a different uniform," according to one observer. Radio program interview with Colonel Viktor Ivanovich Filatov of the editorial board of *Krasnaia zvezda* on Moscow Domestic Service, 17 June 1988. Reported in *FBIS*, 18 June 1988.

5. See the interview with Lizichev in *Izvestiia*, 29 May 1988. In fact, Lizichev has often sounded more conservative than the professional elite, arguing, for instance, against disregarding "the militarist danger inherent in the nature of imperialism."

6. F. Stephen Larrabee, "Gorbachev and the Military," *Foreign Affairs* 66, no. 5 (Summer 1988), pp. 1002–26.

7. Robert Legvold, "Gorbachev's New Approach to Conventional Arms Control," *The Harriman Institute Forum* 1, no. 1 (January 1988), pp. 1–8.

8. See Stephen Meyer's forthcoming article in *International Security* and also his testimony, "The Impact of Gorbachev's New Political Thinking on Soviet Military Programs and Operations," before the Defense Policy Panel of the House Armed Services Committee, 14 July 1988.

9. Alexander George, *Presidential Decisionmaking in Foreign Policy: The Effective Use of Information and Advice* (Boulder, CO: Westview, 1980).

10. There have been veiled criticisms of the military's conduct of the war and spirited defenses of the tactics and strategies employed there in *Krasnaia zvezda*. See, for instance, the letters to the editor on 17 June 1988.

11. See Condoleezza Rice, "The Party, the Military and Decision Authority in the Soviet Union," *World Politics* 40 (October 1987), pp. 51–81.

12. Cited in M. A. Gareev, *Frunze: voennyi teoretik* (Moscow: Voenizdat, 1985).

13. On the long-term effects of Khrushchev's personnel policies see the interview with General Ivan Tretiak in *Moscow News*, 20 February 1988, and the comments of Deputy Defense Minister for Personnel Sukhorukov, *Krasnaia zvezda*, 23 January 1988. There are many such examples. Khrushchev's precipitous decision to close down aircraft production in Poland led to enormous dislocation there. The critique is discussed in Roy Medvedev, *Khrushchev* (Oxford: Basil Blackwell, 1982), pp. 243–44.

14. The most cogent critique is that of the then chief of the General Staff who was fired by Khrushchev and then reinstated. M. V. Zakharov, *Krasnaia zvezda*, 4 February 1965.

15. See Abraham Becker's excellent account of defense allocation debates in *Ogarkov's Complaint and Gorbachev's Dilemma: The Soviet Defense Budget and Party-Military Conflict* (Santa Monica, CA: RAND, 1987). Some would argue that Ogarkov was calling for greater integration of the military view into economic planning. Dale Herspring, "Nikolai Ogarkov and the Scientific-Technical Revolution in Soviet Military Affairs," *Comparative Strategy* 6, no. 1 (1987), pp. 29–59.

16. Gorbachev in his speech to the Party Conference reported in *Pravda*, 30 June 1988.

17. One of the most interesting discussions of the shortcomings of Brezhnev's foreign policy comes from a roundtable sponsored by and reported in *Literaturnaia gazeta*, 29 June 1988.

18. Reported from Moscow Television Service, 25 June 1988, in *FBIS*, 27 June 1988.

19. Dmitri Yazov in *Krasnaia zvezda*, 9 August 1988.

20. Akhromeev's comment during the *Literaturnaia gazeta* roundtable, 29 June 1988.

21. Deputy Chief of the General Staff Lobov in *Bratislava Pravda*, *FBIS*, 27 July 1988, and Aleksandr Prokhanov in *Literaturnaia Rossiia*, 29 June 1988.

22. It should also be noted that a few civilian analysts, notably Alexei Arbatov and Andrei Kokoshin, are said to have consulting relationships with governmental institutions and may therefore have more direct input than do the research staffs of the institutes.

23. The work of Alexei Arbatov is especially interesting in this regard since it equates "destabilizing" American systems like the MX missile and those of the USSR like the SS-18. See, for instance, IMEMO's *Disarmament and Security Yearbook: 1987* (Moscow: Novosti, 1988), of which Arbatov is the head author.

24.   Brezhnev's Tula speech in 1977 is generally noted as the point of departure from
the belief in military superiority. Four years later Brezhnev stated that a nuclear war
would have no winners. *Pravda,* 21 October 1988, p. 7.

25.   Ogarkov in an interview, *Krasnaia zvezda,* 9 May 1984.

26.   One of the best statements of the criteria for sufficiency can be found in a reply to
a reader in *Krasnaia zvezda,* 26 February 1988.

27.   This view is put forth obliquely in Gareev, *Frunze: voennyi teoretik.* Stephen
Meyer has described this evolution in his Adelphi Paper, *Soviet Theater Nuclear Forces*
(1983).

28.   See Aleksandr Prokhanov, "Defense Consciousness and New Thinking," *Literaturnaia rossiia,* 6 May 1988.

29.   Steve Meyer's research suggests that there were already General Staff Academy
conferences on defensive operations in the late 1970s. Ted Warner has also written an
excellent essay on the growth in the importance of defense.

30.   The need for an active defense is usually illustrated by examples from World War
II. See, for example, A. N. Bazhenov, "Puti povysheniia ustoichivosti operativnoi
oborony," *Voenno-istoricheskii zhurnal* (May 1987). This view was also expressed by
General N. V. Chervov in conversations in Moscow, April 1988.

31.   A. A. Kokoshin and V. V. Larionov. "Kurskaia bitva v svete sovremennoi
oboronitel'noi doktriny," *MEMO,* no. 8 (1987). The most recent article by a military
specialist on the battle of Kursk emphasizes the importance both of defense and counteroffensive. S. I. Postnikov, "The Development of Soviet Military Art in the Battle of
Kursk," *Voennoistoricheskii zhurnal* 7 (July 1988).

32.   *Protiv reaktsionnykh teorii na voenno-nauchnom fronte: Kritika strategicheskikh
i voennoistoricheskikh vzgliadov Professora Svechina* (Moscow: Gosudarstvennoe voen-
noe izdatel'stvo, 1931).

33.   Arbatov, *Disarmament and Security Yearbook.*

34.   Based on conversations in Moscow with analysts at the Institute for USA and
Canada and General Nikolai Chervov of the General Staff's Legal and Treaty Department.

35.   Dale Herspring has called this an attempt to put together a national security team
committed to the general secretary and his ideas. See an unpublished paper, "The High
Command Looks at Gorbachev" (1988).

36.   I would like to thank George Breslauer for a comment that called this to my
attention.

37.   From a speech reported in *Vestnik Ministerstva Inostrannykh del SSSR,* 26
August 1987.

38.   L. Mendelevich, chief of the Foreign Ministry's Evaluation Administration,
reported in *Literaturnaia gazeta,* 29 June 1988.

VI
Policy and Performance

22

The Soviet Military in Transition*

William E. Odom

Surprising changes are occurring in Soviet military policy, developments that raise fundamental questions about the nature of the Soviet political system as well as about the Soviet military threat. Interpreting this upheaval in Soviet military affairs is therefore not simply an academic matter. How well the appraisal is done has important implications for Western security calculations.

The military policy of any country is a complex and intricate matter for analysis, and the danger of getting lost among its many aspects is great. So as to see the forest despite the many trees, it is helpful to have a taxonomy of military policy categories. The six categories presented here have the virtue of being comprehensive and providing a proper context for analyzing Soviet military policy. Any aspect of Soviet military policy falls into at least one of these categories, and some may fall into several.

The first category is foreign policy, which military policy reflects and supports. What is the present character of Soviet foreign policy? Does it reflect a status-quo outlook, or is it expansionist, seeking to alter the balance of power in the world? The answer to this fundamental question creates the foundation for most aspects of military policy.

Second, there is military strategy, which relates to the ways in which military power is used to attain specific objectives. While military strategy concerns the use of military forces in wartime, it is also about the use and political utility of military power in peacetime. In the Soviet view, strategy encompasses arms races and how the USSR competes in them, as well as how it conducts arms control negotiations. Foreign policy and military strategy are sometimes merged into a single category by some analysts and called "grand strategy."

Closely related to military strategy is military doctrine. Doctrine, in the Soviet view, is the official state policy on both the socio-political and the military aspects of military affairs in a particular state. It links military structure to the political goals of the state. Although doctrine is based on the findings of military

*Reprinted by permission of the author from *Problems of Communism*, XXXIX, 3 (May–June 1990).

science, which hold for all countries, it is also particularized for the geographical, social, political, and economic character of a given state. It dictates the general guidelines for organization, tactics, operations, and strategy.

A fourth category is military manpower policy. It concerns who will serve, who will lead, who will follow, and what the education, training, and ethnic mix of the armed forces will be. It affects a large portion of the population and has deep political ramifications for the relationship between the military and society.

Military industry is the fifth category. It includes research and development, weapons and equipment procurement, how these activities are financed, what proportion of the national income is devoted to military industry, how weapons and equipment are modernized, and the relationship of military industry to the rest of the economy.

The last category comprises all aspects of military organization, from the highest command levels and their relation to the political authorities, down to small-unit tables of organization and equipment. It includes the command-and-control structure and how it works, as well as the "rear," i.e., the full depth of the homeland and how it will be mobilized and protected.

This article looks at current developments in each of these six areas. Where appropriate, it provides some historical perspective to highlight the significance of the current changes. It is far from the complete story of the tumultuous unfolding events, but it does reveal their major contours and many of the forces influencing Soviet military policy. A seventh section turns to the nexus of party-military relations, both for what it tells us about the prospects for further change in the various areas of military policy and for what it suggests about the evolving nature of the entire Soviet polity. The conclusion ventures a tentative prognosis of the future course of military policy and of the ways in which recent domestic developments may impede changes not only in this sector but throughout the Soviet system.

FOREIGN POLICY

The changes that have occurred in Soviet foreign policy since Mikhail Gorbachev came to power in 1985 need not detain us long. Suffice it to highlight here several key points that shape the basic orientation of contemporary Soviet military policy.

Gorbachev's first and perhaps most critical step in foreign policy was to revise the official ideology and thereby create a basis for a new definition of "peaceful coexistence."[1] Peaceful coexistence as a policy has its roots in Lenin's abrupt reversal of direction in 1921, both at home and abroad.[2] Since communist revolutions were not occurring in the advanced industrial states of Europe as the Bolsheviks had anticipated, they had to decide how to hold on to power and preserve revolutionary gains in an isolated Russia. The policy formula with respect to foreign relations was found in the separation of "state-to-state" relations from "party-to-party" relations, and the pursuit of different policies along these two dimensions. Unable to provoke successful revolutions in the capitalist states of the West, Lenin sought to normalize relations with them, to give them the impression that Bolshevik Russia was not a threat, and to develop as much economic interaction with them as possible in order to advance Soviet industrialization. At the same time, he by no means intended to surrender the pursuit of international revolution in the name of the working class. Through the Comintern, an organization formed in 1919 to direct policies of communist parties allied with Moscow, the Bolsheviks would continue to promote working-class revolutionary consciousness throughout the world.[3]

This formula, in one variation or another, has been the Soviet official line ever since, except in the period when Stalin allied first with Germany, then with the Western democracies, and finally with Sovietized Eastern Europe after World War II. Nikita Khrushchev returned to the old Leninist formula, naming it "peaceful coexistence"—Lenin never actually used the term, but occasionally spoke of "cohabitation" *(sozhitel'stvo)*—and gave it a new twist to accommodate the dangerous new realities introduced by nuclear weapons.

As a policy, peaceful coexistence did not mean renunciation of competition with capitalism. Rather, it was defined as "a specific form of the international class struggle," one that temporarily avoided war. Unlike Lenin, who believed that a final showdown in war with the West was inevitable. Khrushchev conceived of peaceful coexistence as a strategy for defeating the West through internal revolutions without having to resort to global war or the use of nuclear weapons.

However, peaceful coexistence did not mean that the Soviet Union had renounced war. It seems fairly clear from recent Soviet statements that the Soviet political and military leadership expected that the competition between systems might lead to a nuclear war. Guided by a fundamentally offensive military doctrine, the Soviet leadership built its forces not simply for "deterrence" in the Western understanding of the concept but rather for making the best of the situation were a war to occur.[4]

The fundamental ideological assumptions underlying peaceful coexistence, then, dictated both an expansionist foreign policy and a military policy striving for military pre-eminence. In this light, the large Soviet military buildup over the past three decades is not an aberration; it is quite logical. The seriousness of the policy was evident in the great economic sacrifices forced on the population in order to pay for the military buildup.

When Gorbachev came to power, the Soviet Union was facing a major crisis in policy, both domestic and foreign. A new revolution in military affairs was demanding forces and weapons that the Soviet scientific-technological and industrial bases could not provide. The United States was winning the qualitative arms race. Soviet foreign policy, with its inherently expansionist character, was provoking a Western reaction that the Soviet economy and political system could not counter successfully.

As Gorbachev's supporters have argued, the large military component in the Soviet Union's past foreign policy has caused the West to arm more vigorously. In effect, massive military power has not translated into the political influence that Soviet leaders had expected. The implications of this view for military doctrine and force structure have been dramatic.

Gorbachev's approach to dealing with the crisis was not to tinker with the symptoms but rather to launch a fundamental attack on the disease itself. This meant radical changes in domestic policy that, in turn, required a different foreign policy orientation toward the world. Such shifts in course had been seen earlier in the repeated Soviet peace offensives, but those had been largely tactical in nature. The present shift is strategic, that is, it is meant to endure for a long time. It involves not merely a pause for obtaining Western technology to improve defense industries, but appears to include a basic restructuring of the entire economic and political system.[5]

It is against this background that Gorbachev's ideological revisions must be seen. He went right to the assumptions of Marxism-Leninism that had grounded all previous Soviet military doctrine: class interest and class struggle. In his book *Perestroika: New Thinking for Our Country and the World*, he declared that in the present age new interests have emerged—"humankind interests"—that transcend class interests. Nuclear weapons make the avoidance of war a "humankind interest." Saving the global environment is another such interest. These humankind interests, in Gorbachev's exegesis, take precedence over class struggle and require cooperative efforts with imperialist states. Moreover, they render irrelevant the view that war is but the continuation of political relations by other means. Thus, Gorbachev insists, Carl von Clausewitz must be put back on the shelf and forgotten. Given Lenin's admiration for Clausewitz's views on war, this is quite a reversal.[6]

Gorbachev did not stop here. He removed from the definition of peaceful coexistence the notion that it was a "specific form of the class struggle." The 27th Congress of the Communist Party of the Soviet Union (CPSU) gave peaceful coexistence a new and much longer definition, one that made no mention of class struggle and put the emphasis on proper and peaceful interstate relations with all foreign countries, regardless of their politico-economic system. While Gorbachev still holds that class analyses and class struggle are relevant in states where class antagonisms persist, he views the issue as of low priority in the larger context of East-West relations, where cooperative interstate dealings are to be the order of the day.

The foreign policy component of this policy change has the task of presenting the Soviet Union as a status-quo power, one committed to nonintervention even in Eastern Europe, where Moscow has abided by the policy even in the face of unprecedented challenges to the socialist systems there.

Given these extraordinary ideological revisions, Gorbachev's new prescription for military doctrine was quite logical: it must be "defensive." No other justification for military capabilities would do. Of course, the old formula for

Soviet military doctrine had included its "defensive character," but this had been socio-political and had not extended to its military-technical component. Gorbachev now insists that the military-technical side of doctrine must also emphasize the defense, not offense. The strategic aim in the new policy is the "prevention," not the "waging" of war.

We cannot know with confidence the long-term "intent" of Soviet foreign policy. The goal might be expansionist. We can, however, infer with confidence that Gorbachev has made the Soviet Union a status-quo power for the present. Moreover, centrifugal political forces in the union republics even raise questions whether the present Soviet territorial composition and political structure can be maintained intact. The extraordinary direction that Soviet foreign policy has taken under Gorbachev clearly requires major adjustments in all aspects of Soviet military policy.

MILITARY STRATEGY

What do the foreign policy changes mean for contemporary Soviet military strategy? As understood by the Soviet Union, military strategy is a subcategory of "strategy" writ large—which includes ideology, foreign policy, military strategy and policy, and economic policy. The military leadership has a special responsibility for the internal logic of military strategy, but the political leadership has always held authority over where military strategy fits into the overall Soviet strategy in the international class struggle and foreign and economic policy. Thus, while military strategy as a subcategory has an internal logic of its own, this logic is not pursued independently. Arms control, conducted as diplomacy, naturally has a fundamental impact on military strategy as it relates to weapons development and force-building. Accordingly, the military leadership has been called upon to coordinate the various military factors that bear on arms control negotiations.

Gorbachev's "new thinking" has triggered an unusually sharp debate over Soviet military strategy. The debate encompasses a wider group of participants than any such discussion since the early 1920's. The Foreign Ministry has asserted itself in an uncharacteristic fashion, not only in the formal policy process but also by allowing its publications, particularly its *Vestnik,* to be used by civilian critics to enter the debate. And of course, the institutes of the USSR Academy of Sciences concerned with foreign, economic, and security policy have been vocal participants.

As noted above in the discussion of Soviet foreign policy, Gorbachev and his reformers have already recast the basic framework in which military strategy must operate. They have done this primarily through ideological revisions that relegated "class struggle" to a secondary place and, as a consequence, heightened Soviet engagement with the West and China.

Consequently, the role of military strategy in the larger external strategy—

what is often called "grand strategy"—has been markedly reduced. Civilian critics have argued with great force that the mix of military, ideological, political, and economic means in Soviet strategy has not been too heavily weighted toward the military. They insist that enormous military power has not translated into increased political effectiveness vis-à-vis the West. Rather, it has provided cohesion to NATO and served to justify the large military buildup in the United States over the past decade. Moreover, these critics point to the period 1955–58, when Khrushchev effected a 37-percent reduction of forces without reducing Soviet security, since the reductions were accompanied by a major peace offensive against the West.[7]

As evidenced by his decisions to reduce forces unilaterally and to reduce defense spending, Gorbachev has clearly been persuaded by these arguments. In fact, almost all of the developments in Soviet military policy over the past three years make sense only in the context of a new strategy in which the role of military power is greatly reduced.

Gorbachev can point to considerable successes for his new strategy. The Soviet Union is being seen in the West as much less threatening, and the Western military establishments are beginning their own responses in the form of reductions of spending and forces. Even in Afghanistan, the withdrawal of Soviet forces has not yet meant the collapse of the client government.

In Germany and Eastern Europe, however, the record looks mixed in the eyes of some of Gorbachev's critics, not least, the military. Obviously Gorbachev intended a withdrawal of some Soviet forces from the Warsaw Pact states, but it is doubtful that he anticipated the rapid collapse of communist regimes there, particularly in East Germany. Soviet spokesmen had been telling Westerners for some time that Soviet forces would be out of Eastern Europe by the year 2000, but as political developments have spun out of the Kremlin's control, the date will have to be considerably advanced. The reformers supporting Gorbachev may not see this as a misfortune but rather as an opportunity for reducing further the role of the military in the mix of instruments for Soviet strategy.

Arms control negotiations have been de-emphasized somewhat as a component of Soviet strategy if only because events in Eastern Europe and Western military reductions have tended to move ahead of what diplomats can achieve at the negotiating table. This is particularly true for conventional arms control. However, when it comes to nuclear weapons—particularly strategic weapons—arms control negotiations are likely to retain an important place. Gorbachev may well achieve something close to his aim of denuclearizing Europe—except for the British and French forces. Large reductions of nuclear arms appear to be coming, but the rhetoric of a nuclear-free world is likely to remain just that: rhetoric.

Although the military component of the current Soviet strategy is necessarily small, placing an emphasis on the primacy of defense, the overall strategy remains very much geared to the offense. This point was emphasized by Colonel-General V. N. Lobov, then first deputy chief of the General Staff, in a television interview: "Now, in order to avert war, an active policy must be pursued; an active economic policy and an active diplomatic struggle must be waged."[8]

Not only is the role of military strategy in Soviet strategy being reduced, the very orientation of military strategy is apparently also being revised. This is perhaps best detected by examining changes in the closely related area of Soviet military doctrine (doctrine being the play book on which the strategic game plan draws).

MILITARY DOCTRINE

The latest revolution in military technology and Moscow's new foreign policy and military-strategic orientation have seriously undermined the "offensive" bias that has informed the military-technical aspects of Soviet military doctrine since the early 1920's. The first revolution in Soviet military affairs, which began the emphasis on the offense in Soviet military doctrine, stemmed jointly from Bolshevik ideology and from the new technologies of aviation, motorization, and chemical weapons that emerged in World War I. The advent of nuclear weapons brought about a second revolution in the Soviet military, one that reinforced the focus on the offense in Soviet military thinking and force development.[9]

In the 1970s, the advent of new technologies, particularly micro-electronics and directed-energy applications in non-nuclear weapons and military equipment, heralded a third revolution in military affairs. The initial response of the Soviet military was to place even greater emphasis on the offense, on higher-speed theater operations, on operations on a larger scale with "strategic" importance. Marshal Nikolay Ogarkov's term for this development was the "theater strategic operation," which envisioned the capture of most of Western Europe in about one month, or less than half the time assumed necessary for the task in the 1960's and 1970's.[10]

However, as the unfolding military revolution precipitated unprecedented difficulties for the USSR, the focus of military doctrine took a sharp turn. In his report to the 27th CPSU Congress in early 1986, Gorbachev unveiled the idea of "reasonable sufficiency" in national defense.[11] In subsequent months, he explained that this doctrine required a structure of Soviet military forces sufficient for repelling aggression but insufficient for concluding offensive actions. The ambiguity inherent in this definition generated a Soviet debate over what levels of nuclear and conventional forces are required for "reasonable sufficiency."

Civilian analysts of military affairs, most of whom work in institutes of the USSR Academy of Sciences, have called for the most dramatic changes in the military-technical aspect of doctrine. They have borrowed heavily on American concepts from the 1960's concerning nuclear weapons, and they go so far as to argue that far from protecting the USSR, Soviet military programs have been the major stimulus to the arms race and the source of an increased Western threat to the Soviet Union.[12]

Senior military spokesmen have fought a delaying action against this onslaught by civilian critics. They agree with the civilians to the extent of fixing on Gorbachev's notion that the purpose of Soviet military might must be to "prevent war," not to wage it, as the old definition of military doctrine specified.[13] Minister of Defense Yazov has produced what he calls a "new model" for Soviet security, one that accommodates the "defense" rhetoric and some cuts in Soviet forces, but avoids the explicit criteria for defensive posture that the civilian critics advocate.[14]

The focal point in this struggle in late 1989 and early 1990 was the USSR Supreme Soviet's effort to draft a "law on defense." Clearly, the civilian critics of existing policies have their main leverage in this legislative process. In the new Committee on Defense and State Security, where the law is under discussion, the conflict has become quite volatile. It is here that a few field-grade officers even joined the effort to push through a radical change.[15] While it is too early to know how this struggle will turn out, Gorbachev told the senior military in the context of the May 9, 1990, Victory Day celebration that they must prepare for considerably more *"perestroyka"* in the military.[16] Yazov reported the main outlines of the Ministry of Defense version of military reform in the June 5, 1990, issue of *Krasnaya Zvezda*. While it makes minor concessions toward eventual professionalization of the armed forces and reflects several force structure changes in progress, it probably appears too conservative to the radical reformers in the Supreme Soviet.

Regarding nuclear forces, the debate involves at least three issues. The first is whether "military-strategic" (nuclear) parity with the West should continue to be maintained on a "quantitative" basis or be redefined on a "qualitative" basis. The former relies on parity in numbers of strategic nuclear delivery vehicles and warheads, while the latter relies on parity in ensuring the infliction of an unacceptably damaging second strike. A second but closely related issue involves whether counter-force or counter-value targeting should define future military requirements. The final issue involves whether the precise level of "reasonable sufficiency" should be maintained unilaterally or continue to be determined by the perceived level of external threat.

In this debate, the civilian analysts have introduced such Western terms as "deterrence," "counter-force," "counter-value," and "second strike," whereas the military spokesmen have eschewed such language and have insisted that these Western doctrinal concepts, particularly "deterrence," are wholly outdated and irrelevant to the Soviet debate.[17] In the absence of an official and uniform statement of guidelines, we have little clue as to the precise form the new doctrine will take.

There also remain numerous ambiguities at the conventional level. According to Marshal Sergey Akhromeyev, the Soviet Defense Council deliberated for two years before having the Warsaw Pact announce a new "defensive" doctrine in

May 1987.[18] The official rhetoric insists that Warsaw Pact forces are strictly defensive and are being restructured to prevent a surprise attack—a process whose completion is conditional on a similar restructuring of NATO forces. However, the concept of a "counteroffensive" is very much in the center of discussions in the Soviet press—the issue being whether a counterattack by forces of the Warsaw Treaty Organization should be at the tactical level only or also at the operational and strategic levels. Among others, Marshal Akhromeyev argues that a "strategic-level" counteroffensive capability is compatible with the new doctrine.[19]

Again, as in the case of strategic nuclear forces, it is not yet clear precisely how the new policy of "reasonable sufficiency" will affect conventional force structure. In casting its future modernization efforts, the Soviet military has begun to focus on "advanced conventional munitions" (ACM's). Yet, the work of Soviet military science in this connection raises real questions about how defensive Soviet military doctrine really is. The new weapons, according to Soviet theorists, make even more ambiguous the distinction between offense and defense. Moreover, ACM's are seen as equaling nuclear weapons in their effect on the nature of future war. In most regards, ACM's will displace nuclear weapons because they permit more effective achievement of intercontinental targeting for military purposes than nuclear weapons afford.[20]

Whatever the tactical and operational doctrine, the trend is to put the emphasis on quality of weapons and forces, not—as in the past—on quantity or both. It might be noted that in the past revolutions in Soviet military affairs, too, the emphasis was initially on quality—on obtaining new weapons and equipment and mastering them—and only later was there expansion of the overall size of the forces. Given the state of the Soviet economy and the broad nature of Gorbachev's economic reforms, a return to quantity of forces is not to be expected in the next few years, perhaps not even in a decade or two.

Naturally the implementation of the changes in doctrine is bound to have a large impact on all other categories of military policy—manpower, military industry, and military organization.

MILITARY MANPOWER POLICY

The present Soviet manpower system was developed to meet the requirements of military doctrine spelled out by Marshall V. D. Sokolovskiy's volume *Soviet Military Strategy*.[21] Accepting the possibility of nuclear war at the tactical, operational, and strategic levels, the Soviet General Staff believed that manpower needs would be greater than for any previous war. The technical-cultural level of the troops and officers would also have to be higher.

A new military service law, promulgated in 1967, was supposed to meet the new realities. It retained the principle of universal military service, and it shortened the term of service from three to two years for most soldiers, and from

four to three years for the navy and technical branches.[22] The growing urbaniza-
tion of the population and the greater number of conscripts with a secondary
education were expected to provide a qualitative improvement in manpower. The
new system had the advantage of bringing a larger portion of each annual cohort
of draft-age youths to active duty, which, in turn, served to build a very large
pool of reserves in the event of general mobilization. Those youths who did not
serve in the armed forces received elementary military training in secondary
school and in DOSAAF, a mass voluntary society dedicated to teaching military
specialities. Everyone, therefore, was being trained in military skills on a basic
level.

The manpower system inherited by Gorbachev had two other features that
deserve mention. The first was the principle of "extraterritoriality," or "service
in a distant place," which assigns soldiers to units far from their home region.[23]
Although it has never been officially admitted, this principle appears to have a
political motivation. It ensures that troops in any garrison will have no close
personal ties with families and friends in the surrounding civilian society. If
troops must be used to maintain order, it is best to use troops whose sympathies
for the local populace are unlikely to be strong.

Second, there are no "national" units, i.e., units based on a single ethnic
group or using a language other than Russian.[24] All units have a mix of nationalities. In the construction forces and some others, ethnic minorities bulk large,
and in the combat units and technical branches, Slavs tend to predominate. In
spite of these ethnically biased manning policies, the general principle of mixing
nationalities is maintained. Not surprisingly, language is a problem. The official
policy line, however, is that mixed units perform a positive social function by
bringing members of different nationalities together so that they get to know and
respect each other. Military service is said to perform the role of "Sovietizing"
the population and diminishing separatist feelings. It is supposed to foster a
common Soviet culture based on the Russian language. Realities, of course, have
been somewhat different.

Three major developments in manpower policy have been initiated during
Gorbachev's rule. The first concerns the senior command cadres. The second
concerns a unilateral force reduction. And the third involves a broad debate about
the current system of universal military service.

Purge of Senior Military Cadres

In the aftermath of the Cessna flight to Moscow's Red Square by the West
German youth Mathias Rust, Gorbachev started a sweeping purge of senior
officers.[25] Marshal Sergey Sokolov, the incumbent minister of defense, and
Marshal Aleksandr Koldunov, deputy minister for Air Defense Forces, were
promptly relieved of their duties. This was followed by the relief of several
generals and many lower-ranking officers in the Air Defense Forces. As the
months passed, reasons were found to remove several deputy ministers of
defense, and Marshal Viktor Kulikov departed from his post as commander of
the Warsaw Pact forces.

Potentially the most significant change was Marshal Akhromeyev's retirement from the post of chief of the General Staff not long after Gorbachev announced to the United Nations General Assembly in December 1988 his plans for a unilateral reduction of half a million in Soviet military personnel. It is not certain, however, that this retirement reflected Akhromeyev's disapproval of the reduction, as has been suggested.[26] After all, Akhromeyev had been in the United States trying to persuade Americans of the genuineness of the Soviet Union's new defensive military doctrine. Moreover, he seems to be highly trusted by Gorbachev and, in retirement, has become a member of Gorbachev's personal staff of experts.

Akhromeyev's departure nonetheless marked the removal from active duty of the last of the marshals of the Soviet Union. Ogarkov was retired from his post as commander of the Western High Command, and several others departed their posts for "heaven," the nickname of the inspectorate General in the Ministry of Defense where retired senior officers are assigned. This clean sweep of the most prestigious and strong personalities among the senior military elite was a major step by Gorbachev, but one hardly noticed in the West.

No less important were the choices Gorbachev made to lead the military. General of the Army Dmitriy Yazov, who replaced Sokolov as minister of defense, had only recently been brought by Gorbachev from the Far Eastern Military District command to serve as deputy minister of defense for personnel. Yazov was a surprising choice in light of the past criteria for such a post. He was an obscure officer with little to distinguish him, either in command-and-staff experience or in demonstrated intellectual qualities as a military theorist. Compared to Marshals Akhromeyev, Kulikov, Ogarkov, and many others, including several lesser-ranking colonel-generals, Yazov was remarkably unimpressive. That may be the very factor that prompted Gorbachev to choose him. Gorbachev does not need as minister of defense a strong figure who might challenge his policies. He needs someone dependent on him and loyal in carrying through military reforms. In the course of 1989 and 1990, Yazov has, it is true, taken some strong stands against more radical proposals for change, and he was directly involved in curbing unrest among the national minorities, visibly so in the cases of Georgia, Azerbaijan, and the Baltic republics (in the last case, it is not clear whether his actions betoken independence from, or compliance with, Gorbachev's will). By and large, though, he has proven a responsive subordinate.

Gorbachev's selection of then Colonel-General Mikhail Moiseyev as the new chief of the General Staff seemed to reflect similar calculations. An equally undistinguished officer with no experience on the General Staff, and only a 1982 graduate of the General Staff Academy, Moiseyev must have struck most of the general officers as an insult to the tradition of the post. Former incumbents have been highly distinguished as military intellectuals as well as strong leaders. In Moiseyev, neither characteristic is evident to date.

The change of personnel in the senior ranks has not been confined to these few key figures.[27] A look at all of the deputy ministers of defense, the first deputy chiefs of the General Staff, the commander and chief of staff of the Warsaw Pact forces, all the commanders of Soviet groups of forces and fleets, and all military district commanders reveals only two incumbents with a tenure predating Gorbachev's becoming general secretary: Aleksandr Yefimov, deputy minister of defense for Aviation since 1984, and Vitaliy Shabanov, deputy minister of defense for Armaments since 1978. Some of the new incumbents, to be sure, have been promoted or moved from other high-level posts, i.e., all the faces are not new. This turnover in leadership rivals that resulting from Stalin's bloody purge of the Red Army in 1937. Clearly, Gorbachev has attempted to break bureaucratic lethargy and passive resistance in the military leadership by the traditional revitalization of cadres.

Manpower Reduction

The second development in manpower policy is Gorbachev's unilateral reduction of Soviet military forces by 500,000 personnel. All the senior military had been insisting in public that there should be no unilateral reductions, only negotiated ones. Moreover, there are rumors that Gorbachev actually intended to announce a 1-million man reduction but met such strong disapproval that he compromised on half a million.[28]

Reductions in the enlisted ranks can be effected by normal attrition and the lowering of the number of conscripts. Reduction in the number of officers is more troublesome. The General Staff has apparently been in turmoil over the method of selecting officers to be released from active duty. Many voices have cried out that high-quality officers should be retained and the weaker ones released, but the administrative means for realizing such a selection process apparently do not exist. According to American visitors who discussed this issue with military officials in the Soviet Ministry of Defense, a number of ad hoc measures have been devised to try to save the best officers. The officer efficiency report system, however, does not make this easy, and the tendency is to make the choice at the local level. Officers of the General Staff were fearful that all kinds of non-meritocratic criteria would be used and yield some very undesirable results. Moreover, able officers tend to be more confident about finding a civilian career and are more likely to try to leave, while weak officers will try to stay on active duty.

Concerned with overall officer morale, the General Staff has apparently tried to find civilian housing and jobs for released officers, treating each case separately.[29] The task has proven enormous and is likely to continue throughout 1990.[30]

Conscription and Universal Service

It is the questioning of the conscription and universal service system that has upset the military leadership the most. The matter surfaced in the fall of 1988, when Moscow TV called for a public discussion of the present system. A short time later a free-ranging round-table discussion was held in Moscow, and its deliberations were published.[31] At the round table, seven officers and six civilians vigorously debated a number of shockingly radical arguments. Predictably, follow-on articles, reporting, letters to the editor, and debate have deluged the popular press. Moreover, the issue has come up on the Supreme Soviet.

A number of critical questions have been raised concerning the existing system of military service in the Soviet Union. In the first place, the public sees the external threat to Soviet security as declining or even as nonexistent. Some see such threat as there is to be emanating not from the West but rather from Islamic southwest Asia. The main point here is that Gorbachev's new directions in foreign policy have begun to have a profound effect on the public consciousness and traditional views of "How much defense is enough?" The public answer on manpower is that the diminishing threat justifies "a lot less" than in the past.

Then there is the strong feeling that the military lives in a closed and privileged world, separated from and hostile to society. The number of voices making this charge is quite large. In some garrison cities, political officers have tried to dispel this attitude by opening up the barracks to visits by the local population, but the results have not been good, if press reporting is a valid indication. To reformers, a large military presence also has the unsettling potential for bolstering the internal threat from domestic conservative forces who might try to turn back *perestroyka*. "On whose side will the army be?" in that event, one commentator in the round-table debate asked.

The distance between the society and the military is evident in resentment against the relatively privileged life of the officer corps, who are seen as living far above the societal norm, as receiving special access to consumer products, and as enjoying better housing. At the lower ranks and in remote garrisons, the charge of great privilege is simply not valid, but in the case of the general-officer ranks and in some of the field-grade ranks and posts it is accurate.

Also, the war in Afghanistan has had a deeply demoralizing effect on the public, undercutting the icon-like image enjoyed by the Soviet Armed Forces since victory in World War II. Returning veterans have carried their stories home, painting the Soviet military in a very bad light. Numerous rumors abound regarding the total number of soldiers killed in Afghanistan.[32] Veterans are forming support groups and trying to help one another adjust to their lives as civilians as they deal with the psychological impact of the war.[33]

Then there is the issue of *dedovshchina*—the hazing of first-year soldiers by second-year soldiers (the latter known as "granddads," or *"dedy"*). Such hazing has sometimes been quite vicious, leading to deaths from suicides and beatings. Although Western analysts have been aware of *dedovshchina* for some time, it has only been during the past year of its open discussion that we have learned how widespread the public's knowledge and condemnation of it is. Parents of youths who will soon become conscripts have been particularly vocal. The issue has ethnic overtones, with charges increasing that Slavic soldiers single out soldiers of other ethnic groups for hazing.[34]

There is also concern regarding the trade-offs between the needs of the society at large and those of the military for educated and skilled young people. The system of universal military service has been accused of disadvantaging Soviet higher education by forcing the best university prospects to delay their education for several years while they serve in the military. Promising students, because they are the best candidates for the technical services, frequently end up in branches requiring three years of active service. The 1967 service law was amended in the summer of 1989 to permit greater latitude for deferment of such youths, and a considerable number were released early from service later in the summer.[35] The impact of this move on the military has been sharp. According to accounts by some US visitors to Soviet military units, especially at naval installations, the loss of these young men has hurt combat readiness quite seriously.

The problem of assuring that servicemen have adequate educational and technical-cultural skills to operate modern weapons is becoming more acute, notwithstanding the relatively great strides the Soviet military has made in upgrading officer training and in recruiting more urban youth with a better familiarity with modern industrial life. Even under the existing system, the demands of high-technology weapons and equipment in general are said by some critics to exceed the skill levels of the conscripts even after they have been on active duty their entire term. These critics insist that a voluntary system with five-year tours of duty is essential to train adequately an enlisted manpower base. As one observer put it: "In two years, our soldiers only learn how to break modern weapons, not how to use them. That requires at least five years."[36] The military, particularly the Navy, has tried to deal with this problem by having a very large complement of warrant officers and junior officers performing what would be the jobs of privates and junior noncommissioned officers in a Western army.

Finally, growing ethnic awareness and self-assertion in the Soviet Union are affecting the military service system. The principle of "extraterritoriality" for place of service is under heavy attack. In the Baltic republics and in Georgia, the local legislatures have tried to pass laws requiring that local youths perform military service near their homes, or at least in their union republics.[37] The Ministry of Defense has been under strong public pressure on this issue, and unless Moscow is prepared to crack down on the nationalities in general, it is likely to be forced to yield ground on this matter. In fact, the center has already granted informal concessions to Georgia and the Baltic republics, allowing one-fifth of the conscripts from those republics to serve near their homes.[38]

Nationality concerns have surfaced in other ways, particularly in criticism of hazing. Moreover, the popular fronts in the Baltic republics have actively encouraged conscripts not to serve in the Soviet army. They have picketed military installations and carried banners demanding that Soviet forces go home. The political officers have tried to dampen some of this local national activity, but press accounts indicate that they have had little or no success.

A few small measures have been taken to respond to some of these pressures. As mentioned, more deferments of university-bound youth are being authorized. In addition, a new post of "legal officer" has been created in parallel with the political officers,[39] with an eye to dealing with *dedovshchina* and other abuses of soldiers. Where a large cadre of trained legal officers will come from, however, is far from clear.

A variety of concrete proposals regarding the system of military service have been put forward, but essentially there are three positions.[40] First, some call for a wholly voluntary force, with sufficiently high pay to attract enough skilled manpower. This proposal envisions a greatly reduced force structure, far below anything discussed in official circles. A second proposal harks back to the mixed system of a regular "cadre" army and a much larger territorial militia that was devised by Mikhail Frunze and existed from the early 1920's until about 1936. Finally, some advocate no change.

The "no-change" position is primarily held by the senior military leaders, although Fleet Admiral Vladimir Chernavin, chief of the Navy, has shown sympathy for a professional enlisted force.[41] Figures like Yazov, Moiseyev, and Aleksey Lizichev (Chief of the Main Political Directorate of the Soviet Army and Navy) have been scathing in their criticism of the "incompetence" of the reform advocates.[42] In defending the status quo, the senior military elite has not always used the best arguments. Moiseyev declared that a professional army based on voluntary recruitment would cost "five to eight times as much" as the present system. Several weeks after a civilian critic had chided him sharply for such an imprecise cost estimate, the Chief of the General Staff lowered his estimate to "three to four times," but the precision obviously had not improved very much.[43]

The only other proponents of "no change" are members of the "Council of Socialist Movements," a pro-Russian "informal" organization set up to oppose the popular fronts in the Baltic republics and elsewhere.[44] One of the three major points in its political program is maintenance of the present strong military posture of the Soviet Union. CPSU Politburo member Yegor Ligachev has endorsed similar views in talks to meetings of "workers' fronts."[45]

A surprisingly large number of lower-ranking officers and ordinary soldiers have joined the critics of the current system in the open press.[46] Surprisingly, many of these are political officers, i.e., part of the system of political commissars through which the party has traditionally sought to guard the "redness" of the troops. Some are retired. What political weight they carry is far from clear. Some have formed a military union, which seeks higher pay, opposes the activities of the CPSU in the military, and objects to hazing.[47]

The Ministry of Defense has made a number of efforts to deal with this gap opening up between the junior and senior ranks of the officer corps. The most conspicuous has been the convocation of an "All-Army Officers' Assembly" in December 1989,[48] a move evocative of the "officer assemblies" of tsarist times, which also were dedicated to improving the morale of junior officers.

Civilian critics have been the strongest proponents of change to a smaller, professionally competent manpower base. A few of them have offered bitter diatribes against the present military policies, and have even taken Gorbachev to task for some of his figures on spending and the imprecision or inadequacy of promised cuts in military budgets. Finally, the chairman of the Supreme Soviet Committee on Defense and State Security has come out publicly in favor of changing the military manpower system, although he added that the costs must be closely examined before the present system is altered.[49]

Some signs of compromise on the issue have appeared recently. In June 1990 report on military reform,[50] Marshal Yazov noted that in 1991, a form of "contract service" will be tried out in the Navy. Conscripts will choose whether to serve for a fixed term of two years (previously three years), or under contract for three years at a pay rate of 150 rubles a month (the regular conscript pay is about 5 rubles a month). If this test program works, it may be expanded later. In the larger context, this is a very minor concession by Yazov.

How are we to interpret this public debate? How did it get started? Perhaps it was wholly spontaneous, a fortuitous coincidence of a number of criticisms that sparked a wider discussion. However, given Gorbachev's unilateral reduction of 500,000 military personnel and the resistance he met in pushing it through, it may be that he and his liberal supporters orchestrated the discussion in order to create the proper public climate for even larger reductions of active-duty manpower. The way in which the debate began—with TV discussions and a huge number of articles in the press—favors the second view.

If the debate was indeed instigated by Gorbachev, he took a rather large risk in exploiting anti-military sentiments, not just among the public at large but also among the national minorities. He has also risked undercutting the moral foundations of the Soviet military by letting it be knocked off the iconostasis of the church of Soviet patriotism and subjected to widespread and sharp public criticism. Indeed, Gorbachev has begun to back-pedal on making the military put up with public abuse. For example, he recently stated in a talk to Komsomol congress delegates that a volunteer army is precluded for the present because of the large costs it would entail.[51] After the army met public resistance to call-ups for units used in repressing the Popular Front in Azerbaijan in January 1990, his language toward the military has become more conciliatory (and he even promoted Yazov to Marshal of the Soviet Union on May Day 1990).

Resistance to conscription increased sharply in the course of 1989 and 1990. Various figures for the number of resisters have been published. Chief of the General Staff, General Moiseyev, mentioned 7,500 in the USSR,[52] but other reports mentioned 5,000 in Lithuania alone.[53] Although rumors of a postponement of the May call-up proved unfounded, the semiannual call-ups are becoming tests of Soviet authority in the union republics, and are causing a crisis for the military in particular and the Soviet regime in general. Thus, military manpower policy now stands at the very center of the national secessionist struggle, particularly in the Baltic republics and the Transcaucasus.

Whither Soviet military manpower policy in general? It is too early to say, but the context is being created for rather dramatic additional changes. The purges of the senior ranks, the unilateral cut of 500,000, and the growing resentment against the present conscription system suggest that more than minor changes could occur. We should not be surprised at additional large reductions in active-duty manpower and perhaps the adoption of a new military service law that would create a much smaller regular force and extend the length of service. The more technical services—the Navy, the Air Force, and the Strategic Rocket Forces—may well shift to a de facto professional force.

At the same time, some factors are working against this outcome. The problems in the union republics are probably frightening some of those who earlier were willing to support major changes. It is difficult to believe that they want to see national minority military units, but abandonment of the principle of "extraterritoriality" would lead, de facto if not de jure, to such a consequence. It might well prove impossible to maintain Russian as the language of command and training in units dominated by one ethnic group. Finally, conservative voices, such as those in the senior military and party circles, are bound to raise objections to the deleterious impact that public criticism is having on the image of the military and on patriotic sentiment.

The policy could go either way, toward more radical changes or toward retreat and maintenance of the present system. Clearly the pro-Gorbachev reformers will push for more radical changes.

MILITARY INDUSTRY AND PROCUREMENT

The present poor state of the Soviet economy has been perhaps the major catalyst for the turn in Soviet military policies. This highlights the long-term symbiosis of economic policies and military considerations in the Soviet Union. A brief historical review of the relationship between the military and industry can help bring into sharper focus what is new and what remains unchanged in today's situation.

As the young Soviet regime developed a strategy for economic development in the mid-1920's, the impact of aviation, motor transport, and chemical weapons on warfare was articulated repeatedly by the military leaders, and not without effect. The profile of leading sectors of industrialization in the first Five-Year Plan reflected the party's deep concern with military-industrial potential. It can be argued that military factors were the dominant criteria in the structure of the plan and the determination to accelerate the pace of industrialization in 1927.[54]

As a result, during World War II, Soviet weapons and the capacity of domestic industry to produce them were quite remarkable, given the backward state of the Soviet economy two decades earlier. The wartime experience reinforced the propensity in elite party and military circles to let military-technological considerations drive industrial priorities. After the war, a new "revolution in military affairs"—the advent of nuclear weapons, rocketry, cybernetics, computers, and guidance systems—had a serious impact on economic reconstruction and development. Military industries were given priority, particularly in the post-reconstruction period beginning in the late 1950's. Notwithstanding the vicissitudes introduced by Khrushchev's somewhat erratic military policies, the military-industrial base expanded steadily throughout the next two decades.

The Military-Industrial Commission (VPK), headed by a deputy chairman of the Council of Ministers and linking all economic ministries with a role in military production and research and development, held a firm grip on the economy.[55] The State Planning Commission (Gosplan), whose deputy chairman for a long time was a colonel-general, ensured that overall economic planning supported the military sector adequately. The State Committee for Material-Technical Supply (Gossnab, the agency controlling allocation of producer goods) gave first priority to military industries in both quantity and quality of material supplies. Finally, the network of "military representatives" inside military-industrial firms enabled the Ministry of Defense to control quality and reject projects that did not meet its standards.

Tasks of research and development (R&D) were managed in a number of places. The design bureaus in the Armaments Directorate of the Ministry of Defense have traditionally played the leading role in this regard, but the more complex character of newer weapons shifted the center of gravity for military R&D to the design bureaus in the Ministry of Defense Industry. By the 1970's, however, the various bureaus were proving inadequate to the task. More and more often, they were forced to contract research work with institutes in the Academy of Sciences. "Big science," as it was called, required a coordinated effort transcending the resources of design bureaus. The State Committee on Science and Technology (GKNT) played this coordinating role and also worked with the KGB in the acquisition and utilization of foreign technologies.

But by the mid-1970's, it was becoming clear to Soviet military leaders that they were facing a third wave of new military technologies.[56] The developments in micro-electronics, the semiconductor revolution and its impact on computers, distributed processing, and digital communications were affecting many aspects of military equipment and weaponry. Lasers, or directed-energy systems, were having a similar impact. Yet another family of technologies, genetic engineering, seemed to have potential for biological and chemical weapons. The Soviet Academy of Sciences and the military have invested heavily to stay abreast in this last area of technological change.

During this tenure as chief of the General Staff, Marshal Ogarkov aggressively pursued the practical inferences of these new technologies for weapons and doctrine.[57] He was explicit in calling their impact yet another revolution in military affairs, rivaling the change generated by nuclear weapons. Although doctrine and military planning moved quite far in adjusting to the potential of "advanced conventional munitions," as they are called, the large bureaucratic Soviet military-industrial complex was proving unable to hold up its end. As observed earlier, it was here that a crisis was developing, not only for the economy at large but also for the military.

The sense of crisis was compounded by the realization that in dealing with the new challenge, the Soviet economy would be less able than previously to exploit what economists have called "the advantages of backwardness," i.e., the possibility of borrowing technology from advanced industrial states and thereby avoiding the costs of development. In the first two revolutions in military affairs, this approach had yielded satisfactory results. However, in the "information age"—in the application of the new technologies concerned with microelectronics, computers, and lasers—it is not so clear that borrowing in the traditional fashion will work effectively. The Soviet society and economy had been remarkably resistant to the far-reaching educational and cultural changes required to exploit the potential of these technologies. To Soviet planners, therefore, it probably appears that they have come to an economic and R&D dead end. To get out of it requires more than adaptations. Fundamental reforms are imperative.

Minister of Defense Yazov and Chief of the General Staff Moiseyev have themselves both acknowledged that the US military buildup of the last decade has led the Soviet Union into a "qualitative" arms competition that is exhausting the Soviet economy.[58] Capable of winning the "quantitative" competition—i.e., the building of more weapons—Soviet military industry has lost the competition to exploit technology for qualitatively superior weapons. Moreover, the strains induced by both military competitions have contributed to a crisis of the economy as a whole. To escape from the latest arms competition is thus essential for the Soviet economy in general and for the military in particular.

The current crisis is so severe that Gorbachev has apparently decided to focus on the overall health of the economy at the expense of the military-industrial complex, relying on "new thinking" in foreign policy and doctrine to diminish the threat from abroad while the economy gets back on its feet. The Soviet effort to deal with the crisis has involved a number of sometimes disconnected and not terribly effective policies. However, these measures may, in the aggregate, have a dramatic impact on the old entrenched military-industrial structure and procedures.

First, reform economists have pushed for price reform and the introduction of market forces in industry in general, including in the military sector. They clearly appreciate that the present command economic system and existing investment priorities are biased in favor of the military sector. A fundamental objective of economic reform, they argue, must be to break the priority enjoyed by the military industries. But this is no easy task. Although the military establishment may be willing to surrender on some fronts, it has invoked the Gorbachev-approved slogan of quality over quantity to claim priority in most R&D allocations and to justify major industrial endeavors.

Had Gorbachev been able to introduce a market system in the distribution of production inputs, something he apparently intended to do with the new economic law on enterprises promulgated in July 1987, the market might have drawn resources away from the military sector. But, the new law, as approved, was a compromise with the central planning bureaucracy, and there has been only marginal growth in the activity of the factors market.

Third, in the last two years, there has been much discussion of a program for "conversion of defense industries."[59] It envisions the shift of many military-industrial firms to the production of consumer goods. The Academy of Sciences has created a new "National Commission for Assistance to Conversion of War Industries to Civilian Production," and a number of other organizational moves to support conversion have been taken. But, to date, the promise has been much greater than the delivery.

A number of things make conversion difficult. Although military-industrial firms have traditionally had two lines of production—one military and one civilian (the latter existing in order to make full use of plant capacity when there are slowdowns in military output)—the kinds of goods these plants produce for civilian consumption are not the ones that the population most needs at present. For example, a radar plant may produce television sets. That does not address present shortages of clothing, soap, and food. Nor is it the kind of product needed for restructuring civilian industrial plants to make them more effective in their production.

To convert the civilian output of defense industry to the proper mix of new goods, a large investment in new plant equipment and tools is required. The conversion process, instead of providing easy relief by shifting neatly from "guns to butter," is thus placing a new demand for investment on an economy that is already woefully short of investment capital. What is worse, lacking market-determined scarcity prices, there is no basis for judging where investments will yield the greatest efficiency in new production.

Nevertheless, the current leadership appears to place great hope in conversion.[60] The goal is to have 60 percent, as opposed to the current 40 percent, of the output of the military-industrial sector be civilian products by 1995.[61]

There are some who question the real aims of the defense conversion program and ask who is really swallowing whom. Although the restructuring is supposed to push 420 military firms toward the civilian sector, there are cases where civilian plants are being moved under the control of the Military Industrial Commission. In the view of one critic, Premier Nikolay Ryzhkov's recent call for an additional 9 billion rubles to convert military industries looks more like a measure of further militarization than of "demilitarization."[62]

Of greater importance of military industry is the 14.2 percent cut in defense spending for 1990 announced by Gorbachev. Until recently, it was not clear of what sum that figure represented a percentage. The official calculation of the all-Union defense budget is in flux. Gorbachev admitted that the 1989 figure was 77.3 billion rubles, far above the originally stated 20-plus billion rubles, which apparently included only operations and maintenance for the military but not procurement costs. The projection for 1990 was originally announced as 82.9 billion rubles, and it is from this sum that the 14.2 percent reduction is apparently to be taken. Thus, in a report to the Supreme Soviet, Finance Minister Valentin Pavlov gave a revised projection of 70.9 billion rubles for 1990 Soviet defense expenditures. According to Pavlov, this included a drop in the operations and maintenance budget from 20.2 billion to 19.0 billion rubles, a 15 percent decline in military construction, and a 19.5 percent decrease in procurement.[63]

These reductions will have a significant impact on the defense sector, but they will certainly not destroy the dominant position of military industries in the command economic system. The prices designated by Gosplan for purchase of military goods have always been notoriously low, or so many Western estimates have inferred. The costs of production are not covered fully by the monies earned from sales to the state. The gap has been taken up by credits extended by the State Bank. Thus the true costs of defense, even in state-fixed prices, have been hidden.

To deal with this, reformers are trying to force into the open the true extent of military production costs. According to an article in the party journal *Kommunist,* all defense industries were put on the system of *khozraschet,* or cost accounting, in January 1989. No additional state monies were to be provided, and firms were to cover their production costs entirely from what they recover by sales of products. According to the article, existing state prices are too low to cover costs, and thus most defense firms are experiencing deficits. To prevent chaos and deterioration in military-industrial firms, the commentator proposed that the state negotiate new prices with the firms, treating them as "cooperatives"—i.e., leasing them plant and equipment and letting their managers develop real costs for products. The newly negotiated prices would have to cover the production costs and related expenditures, such as research and development.[64] Were such a reform of the prices of military products to be carried out, the overall procurement budget for the military would rise dramatically, or, alternatively, the state would be forced to purchase fewer weapons. Without one or the other step, the firms face bankruptcy or will require a financial bailout by the state.

Whether or not such drastic steps will be taken, the issue of military procurement will be brought into the open as never before and make it harder for both the military and the central planning bureaucracy to suppress debate over its high costs. It remains to be seen whether Gorbachev and the reformers will prevail in imposing *khozraschet* or be forced to rescue ailing military firms with state credits.

There are signs that procurement of weapons is being curtailed. Marshal Akhromeyev, in his appearance before the US House of Representatives Armed Services Committee in July 1989, promised that Soviet tank production would be decreased by 50 percent in the near future.[65] If this and the proposed decrease of 19.5 percent in the 1990 defense procurement budget are an index of general trends, then quite large reductions are to be expected. If they do not occur, then it will be a sign that the economic reformers are losing their struggle for a basic restructuring of the economy.

A change in military-industrial policy, any way one looks at it, is a key factor in the overall Gorbachev reform program, and it will be one of the weather vanes for his progress. By themselves, however, cuts in military industry and conversions to civilian production will not deal with the basic problem of the Soviet economy. Until market forces are allowed to determine prices and production, the inefficient bureaucratic features will prevail.

REORGANIZATION OF THE MILITARY

Gorbachev's restructuring efforts have already affected virtually all levels of military organization and promise to go on. They have been quite sweeping in the aggregate, including changes at the top in command and control and extending downward into force structure. Although restructuring is still incomplete in many cases, it is possible to describe the general outlines of the reorganization and give some impressions of the direction, rationale, and implications of Gorbachev's changes.

Political Command

To begin at the top, Gorbachev has revitalized the Defense Council and expanded its membership. He blurted out a few details on this development during Yazov's confirmation appearance before the Supreme Soviet. The General Secretary acknowledged that the Defense Council had been at work for a long time dealing with his proposed reforms, that the marshals were resistant, and that the Council membership was being expanded to allow better civilian representation. Belated efforts to censor this part of the open record of the Supreme Soviet proceedings suggest that these changes were not meant to be made public. We cannot, therefore, expect to learn a great deal more about the details, but those that Gorbachev provided are interesting.[66]

The present membership, as he outlined it, includes Gorbachev himself (in his capacity as president of the Supreme Soviet), the minister of defense, the chairman of the Council of Ministers, the foreign minister, officials who supervise defense industries (probably the chairman of the VPK, the head of Gosplan, the minister of the Defense Industry, and maybe the Central Committee secretary in charge of defense industries), and some of the "principal command staff," i.e., senior military personnel (probably the chief of the General Staff and some of the deputy ministers of defense). A surprising omission in Gorbachev's enumeration of the present membership were the two traditional members, the chairman of the KGB and the minister of internal affairs, both of whom control significant numbers of armed forces.

Gorbachev complained that the Defense Council had become dormant under Brezhnev and that its actions were merely "formal." From his remarks, Gorbachev seemed intent on making the Defense Council the focal point for all military policy at the highest level. Lev Zaykov, a Politburo member, has been made deputy chairman and relieved of his duties as Moscow party chief, thus allowing a high-level figure with defense industry experience to devote full time to the Defense Council. Presumably Marshal Akhromeyev, as Gorbachev's military adviser, is also a key figure. Such appointments tend to make the Defense Council less dependent on the Central Committee apparatus for staffing. This offers one more piece of evidence of Gorbachev's scheme for moving real political power into the Supreme Soviet at the expense of the party.

After all this buildup, however, the Defense Council has recently suffered an eclipse. With the creation of a new position of President of the Supreme Soviet as head of state, there was also created a new Presidential Council. Its functions include "elaborating measures to ensure state defense" and providing guidelines for both foreign and security policy. It cannot issue decrees or instructions, but merely serves as an advisory body for the President, who has enormous powers in these areas. To all appearances, the old role of the Defense Council seems to have been subsumed under the Presidential Council, which includes most of the members of the Defense Council, in addition to numerous other persons with little background or authority in defense matters.[67]

The military leadership was clearly upset with the new arrangements. General Moiseyev, for one, found the new law creating the Presidency and the Presidential Council seriously flawed. It omitted, he said, any role for the Defense Council, and therefore the new body's functions with regard to military affairs required clarification. The Chief of the General Staff noted the law's failure to provide adequate specificity regarding important powers of the President, including "the right personally to make the decision and issue authority to use nuclear weapons as a retaliatory measure."[68] Apparently, nuclear command authority is ambiguous in the new Soviet state structure!

The Defense Council's political troubles are not only with the Presidential Council. According to some Soviet officials working with the Supreme Soviet's Committee for Defense and State Security, the committee has challenged the role of the Defense Council.[69] In seeking to learn the precise functions spelled out by law for the Council, the Supreme Soviet committee discovered there were none, beyond vague references to defense policy. The committee has tried, without notable success, to absorb some of the functions that would otherwise belong to the Defense Council.

The Committee on Defense and State Security is truly a new kind of player in Soviet military policy-making. The Ministry of Defense sees it as a source of problems and has tried to pack its membership with officials from the military-industrial sector. The committee has struggled, with little success, to get information about defense spending and other matters. Drafting the new law on defense has given it only limited leverage over the Ministry of Defense. The liberal reformers on the committee realize that they do not yet control the power of the purse.[70] Realization of this aim will remain remote as long as instruments of the command economy, especially Gosplan and Gossnab, remain in control of resources, priorities, prices, and budgets.

At present, the highest-level defense policy organs are in a state of confusion about which has what functions. The outcome is unpredictable. The Presidential Council could develop a subgroup effectively replacing the Defense Council. Or the Defense Council could reemerge with legally specified functions. It is not clear how strong Zaykov's position is after his removal from the Moscow City party organization. The Supreme Soviet's Committee on Defense and State Security has proven a rather feckless newcomer to military policymaking. If it can push through new laws, it might become significant in the policy arena, especially if those laws affect the levels of resource allocations for the military in a significant fashion.

Military Command

Moving to the military proper, the General Staff has also undergone changes, but again few details are available. According to one report, its size has been reduced by one-fifth.[71] Whether the cut represents only a personnel reduction or includes structural changes as well is not clear, but in light of other changes in the General Staff, structural changes would seem to be indicated. While the General Staff apparently continues to be the working organ, the executive body for the supreme military and civilian leadership, its dominant role—one it has built since the 1960's—is being trimmed back.

This is evident from a recent change in military organization. Since the fall of 1989, the Border Troops, the Ministry of Internal Affairs (MVD) forces, KGB formations, and the Railroad Troops are no longer a part of the Armed Forces of the Soviet Union.[72] The meaning of this reorganization for the General Staff is not immediately clear, but it can be inferred from a review of the General Staff's history. The General Staff only dates back to 1935.[73] The previous General Staff of the Red Army had operational control only over ground forces, and not over the Navy, the People's Commissariat of Internal Affairs (NKVD), the Border Troops, and other formations. Although the General Staff assumed control over many more military units during World War II, after the war, its powers were restricted again, and the Navy's relation to it became ambiguous at best. By the late 1960's, however, the General Staff had clearly regained a dominant position in the military structure, asserting operational control over all aspects of military activities and not just over the activities of the forces under the Ministry of Defense.

In practice, this meant that operational control for an episode such as the use of military forces in Georgia to deal with public demonstrations was exercised by the General Staff. The new status of the KGB, Border Troops, MVD forces, and Railroad Troops means that they are not under the operational direction of the General Staff, and are now apparently subordinated directly to the Defense Council. Thus, Gorbachev has a more immediate role in their use and direction.

Another small change related to the internal security forces is the creation of "special-purpose detachments" in several cities to control crowds and demonstrations. They are recruited mainly from former paratroopers and *Spetsnaz* soldiers with an average age above 30. Press reports declare that they are receiving extensive training in putting down disorderly crowds with as little physical abuse of individuals as possible.[74]

So far there have been no announced cutbacks in the "high commands"— combining several groups of forces (fronts in wartime) and military districts (also fronts in wartime)—which marked the major structural development of the 1980's in the Soviet armed forces. However, at the next level, reductions have already been made. The old system of 16 military districts covering the entire Soviet Union has been reduced by two, as the Central Asian Military District and the Ural Military District have been merged into neighboring military districts.[75]

A similar kind of consolidation also has apparently occurred in the Soviet forces in Eastern Europe. It has been reported that the former Group of Soviet Forces Germany (GSFG) has been renamed the Western Group of Forces.[76] Given the small size of the Northern, Central, and Southern Groups of Forces in Poland, Czechoslovakia, and Hungary respectively, the renaming of the GSFG suggests (although there has been no public evidence for the inference) that these other groups may have been merged under the new Western Group of Forces command.

There have also been changes in the force complement of the so-called "border districts."[77] Henceforth, they are to have as their primary force structure machine gun–artillery divisions, units that have a purely defensive mission. Where and in what number such units will be deployed is not clear.

Dropping down to the divisional level of organization, Gorbachev asserted to the Supreme Soviet during General Yazov's confirmation hearings that 101 divisions had already been demobilized.[78] They were, he said, found only to be "feeding troughs" for officers. The validity of this figure was called into question when a delegation from the US House Armed Services Committee tried to confirm it during its visit to the Soviet Union in late 1989. The Soviet respondent said Gorbachev meant 101 "units," not "divisions," although some of the units were divisions. Given the Soviet practice of keeping a large number of divisions manned at 10 to 15 percent of full strength, it could be that this reduction involves a cut of 101 such divisions. More recently, in reporting on military reform, Marshal Yazov specified a cut of 21 divisions, two combined-arms armies, two army corps, and a number of formations *(ob'yedineniya)* and units *(chasti)* of other branches of services.[79]

An additional feature of the restructuring of divisions is the removal of 20 percent of the tanks from Soviet tank divisions and 40 percent of the tanks from Soviet motorized rifle divisions in Eastern Europe.[80] Precisely what the new composition of the divisions will be is not yet clear. Nor is it clear whether the change applies only to divisions in Eastern Europe or will be instituted more widely throughout the Soviet military.

A number of other structural changes are resulting from Gorbachev's unilateral force reductions. In addition to the removal of six Soviet tank divisions from Eastern Europe, the USSR has announced and begun an overall reduction of 10,000 tanks (5,300 from Eastern Europe), 8,500 artillery pieces, and 800 combat aircraft (260 from Eastern Europe), and the withdrawal of some air-assault units and assault-bridging equipment from Eastern Europe as well.[81] In line with the new emphasis on defense, increases in air defense, anti-tank, and obstacle capabilities are planned. The concept of "fortified regions" has also emerged in the discussion of these efforts to strengthen the defensive capabilities of Soviet and Warsaw Pact forces.[82]

This rundown of the general outlines of organizational change reveals a number of trends and implications. First, the proposed changes are not small ones; if carried through, they will be far more than cosmetic. At the top, they have thus far introduced a great deal of confusion about defense policy responsibilities. The greatest potential for significant change lies with the Supreme Soviet Committee on Defense and State Security. Were it to acquire a genuine "power of the purse," that would be a dramatic shift. Such a development seems unlikely, however, barring a fundamental dismantling of the whole command economy bureaucracy.

Second, while the changes consolidate the military command structure, creating savings in personnel and headquarters, they do not reverse the major command-and-control developments that Ogarkov's General Staff sponsored in the late 1970's and early 1980's. The new "high commands" remain in place, and the General Staff appears to retain the dominant control over all Ministry of Defense forces, although it has lost operational authority over the Border Troops, the MVD troops, and the Railroad Troops.

Third, the organizational changes do seem to negate the capability for a faster and larger-scale theater strategic operation that Ogarkov labored to create. The unilateral force reductions in Eastern Europe, at least on first reflection, eliminate the Western High Command's capability to take the offensive quickly. More mobilization time will be needed, and some of the restructured units may not have the capability to participate in deep offensive thrusts.

Fourth, while much force structure is being cut, nothing has occurred to prevent a new approach based on "quality versus quantity" in modernizing Soviet forces. Whether that modernization will be aimed at creating a force with little or no offensive potential remains a wide-open issue, and we are not likely to know the answer for some time. What we do know is that much of the recent literature on doctrine for the present revolution in military technology raises questions regarding the new primacy accorded defense over offense by asserting that the distinction between these two forms of warfare is declining.

On the whole, Gorbachev has shown a remarkable capacity to force *perestroyka* on Soviet military institutions. But whether the reform has passed the point of no return remains unclear. He appears to have the momentum, and the final results could include far more dramatic changes than those discussed here.

PARTY-MILITARY RELATIONS

The critical question is: can Gorbachev continue his military *perestroyka* without creating a crisis in party-military relations? Many in the West have thought not, and as rumors of military coups abounded, Western observers have predicted that sooner or later the General Secretary will be a casualty of a coup directed against him. Yet, the fusion in the party-military relationship that occurred in the first decade of the Soviet regime has remained unbroken thus far.

Western analysts have long argued about the degree to which Soviet party-military relations are inherently conflict-ridden.[83] In the 1960's, Roman Kolkowicz predicted increasing military autonomy and a tendency toward the emergence of institutional pluralism in Soviet policies at the expense of party control. Had that analysis been valid, today we should be seeing a quite different military, one that would never have let Gorbachev go so far in changing military policy.

Another view, held by Timothy Colton, judged the relationship as much less conflict-ridden; however, he also saw the potential for conflict and serious control problems for the party—it was just that in the 1970's, the military was getting everything it asked for. If this analysis were valid, we should be seeing today a Soviet military that is very active in politics, refusing to accept unilateral cuts and budget reductions, and stretching the limits of party control.

Yet a third view, held by this author, insisted that there exists in the Soviet Union a basic congruence of party and military values and ideology and that the military is essentially a sub-unit within the party—its military component. Disputes over issues of military policy are normal, but they cut across the military-civilian boundary to become intraparty disputes. In this analysis, marshals and generals are party executants. Moreover, the network of party and police controls within the military virtually ensure subservient military behavior. The remarkably obedient behavior of the military leadership in the face of the traumatic changes Gorbachev has forced on the Ministry of Defense since 1985 seems to vindicate this last interpretation of the party-military relationship.

True, military leaders are beginning to show overt public resistance to Gorbachev and appear quite angry at *glasnost* and *perestroyka*, not only as it applies to the military but in application to the society at large. (Ironically—for those Western observers who see the party's ideology as alien to the military—some of the strongest apologists for ideological orthodoxy are military spokesmen!) The military is speaking up, but only belatedly, and it is still following orders. On the whole, the view that the party-military tie is one of ideological congruence and institutional solidarity, reinforced by police and party ties, seems to hold up even in the turbulent times of *perestroyka* when the relations are under more than a little strain. And it should be noted that bureaucrats in the economic agencies and the party apparatus have been no less vocal in opposing *perestroyka*, and in the case of the economic apparatus, much less compliant than the military.

Does this mean that the party-military connection is solid and that the congruence of interests will endure? Not necessarily. To be sure, *glasnost'* and *perestroyka* have much in common with past efforts at political and economic revitalization. Lenin, Stalin, and Khrushchev all believed that party purges and economic reorganization were periodically necessary to overcome stagnation within the system. One of the most spectacular achievements of *perestroyka* to date has been the purge of the party officialdom, including the senior military. But unlike previous purges, this one is not strengthening the party. It is demoralizing and weakening it. At the same time, the reorganization schemes within the Secretariat of the CPSU Central Committee and within the state structure— e.g., the creation of the elective Congress of People's Deputies, the Supreme Soviet, and in new Presidency—are introducing enormous confusion and uncertainty about where power resides, whose authority holds, and who has which duties.

These developments raise fundamental questions about the continuing effectiveness of the old fusion of the party and the military. The KGB counterintelligence departments still exist in the military although they have been compromised and corrupted in many units.[84] The apparatus of party-military administration within the Armed Forces still exists, but it is demoralized, undergoing reform, and apparently yielding ground to new institutions like "officers' assemblies" and "legal officers."

Somewhat more precarious for the party is the emergence of discontent among junior members of the officer corps. A serious bifurcation may be occurring between the senior ranks, on the one hand, and company- and field-grade officers, on the other. The latter show alienation not just from the party but also from the senior military leadership. And they are willing to support civilian radical reformers on military policy.

Our old concepts of civil-military relations will have to be modified to take into account the wide range of changes now in progress. Even if there is a reassertion of authoritarian power at the expense of *glasnost'* and *perestroyka,* some of the changes have gone too far to let us be confident that the old analytic conceptions are still entirely valid.

CONCLUSIONS

We are witnessing a profound transformation in the Soviet military—perhaps even greater than the one in the 1920's that created the basic outlines of the present military, military-political, and military-economic structures. Precisely where it will go, and how far, are questions we cannot now answer. The changes, however, are far deeper and broader than the popular image created by Gorbachev's unilateral reductions and enthusiasm for arms control suggests. It affects not only the military but also society at large and the command economic system. Indeed, success in a number of other major areas of reform will depend on carrying through the military reforms.

If it were only that simple, one might be optimistic about the overall prospects for Gorbachev's *perestroyka*. But Gorbachev's broader reform agenda is having paradoxical consequences for military reform. The very strategy of *glasnost'* and *perestroyka* that in foreign policy has removed the rationale for a large standing military has stimulated internal political developments—in particular, secessionist sentiment and ethnic strife in a number of republics—that increase the rationale for maintaining large, politically reliable standing forces. Moreover, *glasnost'* and *perestroyka* tend to undercut the political reliability of those forces. That was dramatically visible during the intervention of January 1990 in Baku. The mothers of Russian and Ukrainian soldiers did not want their sons called up for such an operation and said so publicly.[85] The impact on the Soviet Army was also apparent this spring when a commander in Tajikistan refused to direct his division to help restore order in Dushanbe for fear of being blamed for the violence, as happened to the commander in Georgia after the Tbilisi affair. Senior military leaders are speaking out bitterly about this problem, not sparing even Gorbachev in their expressions of rage.[86]

Carrying the military changes to this point has contributed to major domestic problems, most notably public outrage at the military, resistance to conscription, and an exacerbation of the nationality issue. In many regards, the paradoxes arising from trying to liberalize a multinational empire in an age of nationalism and attempting to reform the command economy are the very same paradoxes that occur in the restructuring of the Soviet military.

Looking back, it may be that the early part of 1990 represented a major turning point. Until then, the reformers had the initiative, and they were dismantling much of the old structure of the Soviet system, including the military. Yet the social forces unleashed during the debate on military service and the increasing resistance by the union republics to Soviet rule seemed to have intersected in a way that has forced Gorbachev to make a major withdrawal. Sending the army into Baku to arrest the Popular Front of Azerbaijan was an unprecedented step for him. Sending the army to keep order was not new, but this time, the army was sent to destroy a local political movement. Military power is being applied more subtly toward the same end in Lithuania. This is a basic reversal of policy, a serious drawing back from *glasnost'* and *perestroyka* as it was coming to be understood.

The change may be temporary and might be reversed. It has, nonetheless, forced Gorbachev into retreat on some aspects of *perestroyka* in the military, in particular the reform of the military service system. That in turn probably means less dramatic economic reforms in the near term. The requirements for political stability have risen, and given the weakened state of the party, the military is the only fallback for dealing with large-scale resistance and disorders. The KGB and the MVD are too small. The inherent growing dependency on the military for internal political purposes threatens to halt or reverse the radical attempts at military *perestroyka* so vigorously pursued under Gorbachev, especially since 1987.

In this regard, the transformation of the military is a good indicator of how the overall reform process—economic, social, and political—is going.

NOTES

1. See his *Perestroika: New Thinking for Our Country and the World* (New York: Harper & Row, 1987), for his most comprehensive statement on his matter.

2. See Adam Ulam, *Expansion and Coexistence: The History of Soviet Foreign Policy 1917–67* (New York: Praeger, 1968), for an interpretive account.

3. Franz Borkenau, *World Communism* (New York: Norton, 1939).

4. For example, see Marshal of the Soviet Union Sergey Akhromeyev's unpublished speech to the Council of Foreign Relations in New York, June 1987; and Vadim Zagladin, "On the Course of Reason and Humanism," *Pravda* (Moscow), June 13, 1988.

Western analysts have long debated the Soviet stand on the question of the inevitability of war in the nuclear age. For an overview, see William E. Odom, "The Soviet Approach to Nuclear Weapons: A Historical Review," *American Academy of Political and Social Science. Annals* (Beverly Hills, CA) (September 1983), pp. 117–35.

5. See Gorbachev's speech to the All-Union Student Forum, *Pravda,* Nov. 16, 1989, for a review of his vision for transforming the Soviet Union.

6. Ibid., pp. 143–48.

7. V. V. Zhurkin, S. A. Karaganov, and A. V. Kortunov, "On Reasonable Sufficiency," *SShA—Ekonomika, Politika, Ideologiya* (Moscow), no. 12 (1987), pp. 14–20; S. Blagovolin, "Geopolitical Aspects of Defensive Sufficiency," *Kommunist* (Moscow), no 4 (March 1990), pp. 114–23; and A. Kireyev, "Conversion in the Soviet Dimension," *Mezhdunarodnaya Zhizn'* (Moscow), no. 4 (1990), pp. 99–110.

8. Moscow Television Service in Russian, Oct. 15, 1988, translated in Joint Publication Research Service, *USSR: Military Affairs* (Washington, DC—hereafter, *JPRS-UMA),* no. 88–025 (Oct. 21, 1988), p. 6.

9. William E. Odom, "Soviet-Force Posture: Dilemmas and Directions," *Problems of Communism* (Washington, DC) (July–August 1985), pp. 1–13.

10. Ibid.

11. M. S. Gorbachev, *Politicheskiy doklad XXVII s'yezdu Kommunisticheskoy Partii Sovetskogo Soyuza* [Political Report to the 27th Congress of the Communist Party of the Soviet Union] (Moscow, Politizdat, 1986), p. 95.

12. For example, see A. Arbatov, "How Much Defense Is Sufficient?" *International Affairs* (Moscow), no. 4 (1989), pp. 31–44; "A Conversation to the Point Is More Useful," *Kommunist Vooruzhennykh Sil* (Moscow), no. 22 (1989), pp. 17–21; G. Arbatov, Speech at the Congress of People's Deputies, Moscow Television Service in Russian, Dec. 16, 1989, trans. in Foreign Broadcast Information Service, *Daily Report: Soviet Union* (Washington, DC—hereafter, *FBIS-SOV)* (Dec. 18, 1989), pp. 68–70; S. Blagovolin, "The How and Why of Military Power," *Mirovaya Ekonomika i Mezhdunarodnyye Otnosheniya* (Moscow—hereafter, *MEiMO),* no. 8 (1989), pp. 5–19; Blagovolin, "Geopolitical Aspects of Defensive Sufficiency," V. Zhurkin, S. Karaganov, and A. Kortunov, "Old and New Challenges to Security," *Kommunist,* no 1 (January 1988), pp. 42–50; and G. Kunadze, "On the Defensive Sufficiency of the USSR Military Potential," *MEiMO,* no. 10 (1989), pp. 68–83.

13. See General of the Army D. T. Yazov, "The Military Doctrine of the Warsaw Pact, a Doctrine of Defending Peace and Socialism," *Pravda,* July 27, 1987; "On the Basis of the New Thinking," *Krasnaya Zvezda* (Moscow), Apr. 13, 1989; General of the Army M. A. Moiseyev, "Soviet Military Doctrine: Realization of Its Defensive Thrust," *Pravda, Mar.* 13, 1989; and Marshal S. F. Akhromeyev, "The Doctrine of Preventing

War, Defending Peace and Socialism," *Problemy Mira i Sotsializma* (Prague), no. 12 (1987), pp. 23–28.

14. D. T. Yazov, "New Model for Security and the Armed Forces," *Kommunist,* no. 18 (December 1989), pp. 61–72.

15. See Stephen Foye, "The Radical Military Reforms and the 'Young Turks'," Radio Free Europe-Radio Liberty, *Report on the USSR* (Munich) (Apr. 13, 1990), pp. 8–10; also, "Pressure on Officers Drafting Reform Reputed," *Komsomolskaya Pravda* (Moscow), Apr. 8, 1990, trans. in *FBIS-SOV,* Apr. 10, 1990, p. 66, for details of the programs pushed by the Supreme Soviet committee.

16. See M. S. Gorbachev, "Lessons of the War and Victory," *Pravda,* May 9, 1990.

17. See V. Dmitriyev and V. Strebkov, "Outdated Concept," *Krasnaya Zvezda,* Apr. 10, 1990.

18. Unpublished speech to the Council on Foreign Relations in New York, June 1987.

19. The author heard Akhromeyev make this argument twice during his visit to the United States in 1987.

20. See Mary C. FitzGerald, "Advanced Conventional Munitions and Moscow's Defensive Force Posture," *Defense Analysis* (Elmsford, England) (May 1990).

21. V. D. Sokolovskiy, *Voyennaya strategiya* [Military Strategy], (Moscow: Voyenizdat, 1962). The volume was published in English translation under the editorship of Harriet Fast Scott as *Soviet Military Strategy* (New York: Crane, Russak, and Company, 1975).

22. Ellen Jones, *Red Army and Society* (Boston: Allen and Unwin, 1985), pp. 37ff, 52ff.

23. Ibid., p. 185.

24. Ibid.

25. *Krasnaya Zvezda,* June 17, 1987.

26. For example, see Bernard Trainor, "Soviet Split Seen on Military Cuts," *The New York Times,* Dec. 8, 1988.

27. Linda S. Brewer, "The Soviet Military Elite under Gorbachev," unpublished paper by the Air Force Intelligence Agency, Aug. 22, 1989.

28. For example, see *Moskovskiye Novosti* (Moscow), Feb. 21, 1988, trans. in *FBIS-SOV,* Feb. 24, 1988, p. 73.

29. *Kraznaya Zvezda,* Mar. 30, 1989; and *Sovetskaya Rossiya* (Moscow), Mar. 8, 1989, trans. in *FBIS-SOV,* Mar. 10, 1989, p. 101.

30. *The Washington Post* of May 26, 1990, carried a report from East Berlin that the Soviet Union was blaming a massive housing shortage at home for delays in the withdrawal of some 36,000 troops from East Germany.

31. "Army and Society," *XX Century and Peace* (Moscow), no. 9 (1988), pp. 18–28.

32. Radio Free Europe-Radio Liberty, *Daily Report* (Munich—hereafter, *RFE-RL Daily Report),* no. 211, Nov. 6, 1989.

33. Ibid., no. 204, Oct. 26, 1989.

34. Suzanne Crowe, "Soviet Conscripts Fall Victim to Ethnic Violence," *Report on the USSR,* Oct. 13, 1989, pp. 8–9.

35. *Izvestiya* (Moscow), Apr. 12, 1989; and Radio Free Europe-Radio Liberty, *Radio Research* (Munich), RAD Background Report/200, Oct. 30, 1989.

36. "Army and Society."

37. Crowe, "Soviet Conscripts."

38. See Elizabeth Fuller, "Georgians Win Concession on Military Service," *Report on the USSR,* July 7, 1989.

39. *RFE-RL Daily Report,* no. 124, July 3, 1989.

40. See A. Savinkin, "What Kind of Armed Forces Do We Need?" *Moscow News,* Nov. 6, 1988, p. 6.

41. See Mikhail Tsypkin, "Will the Soviet Navy Become a Volunteer Force?" *Report on the USSR*, Feb. 2, 1990, pp. 5–7.

42. See D. T. Yazov, *Krasnaya Zvezda*, Apr. 13, 1989. For others, see discussion in Robert Arnett and Mary C. FitzGerald, "Restructuring the Armed Forces: The Current Soviet Debate," *Journal of Soviet Military Studies* (London) (June 1990).

43. Moscow TASS International Service in Russian, May 3, 1989, trans. in *FBIS-SOV*, May 3, 1989, p. 88.

44. *Krasnaya Zvezda*, July 19, 1989.

45. *RFE-RL Daily Report*, no. 138, July 24, 1989.

46. See, for example, ibid., no. 21, Jan. 29, 1990.

47. For example, see A. Davydov, " 'Shield' Will Protest from Injustice," *Izvestiya*, Oct. 25, 1989.

48. See *RFE-RL Daily Report*, no. 233, Dec. 8, 1989.

49. *Izvestiya*, June 26, 1989.

50. *Krasnaya Zvezda*, June 6, 1990.

51. *Pravda*, Apr. 12, 1990.

52. *RFE-RL Daily Report*, no. 243, Dec. 22, 1989.

53. Ibid., no. 35, Feb. 19, 1990.

54. Odom, "Soviet Force Posture."

55. David Holloway, "Innovation in the Defense Sector," in Ronald Amann and Julian Cooper, eds., *Industrial Innovation in the USSR* (New Haven, CT: Yale University Press, 1982), pp. 303–11.

56. Odom, "Soviet Force Posture."

57. Ibid.

58. D. Yazov, *Krasnaya Zvezda*, Feb. 9, 1989; and M. Moiseyev, ibid., Feb. 10, 1989.

59. John Tedstrom, "Conversion and Problems of Industrial Science," *Report on the USSR*, Aug. 25, 1988, pp. 19–20.

60. In outlining the targets for the 1991–96 economic plan, Premier Nikolay Ryzhkov noted that 176 military-industrial firms are now producing for the agro-industrial complex. See *RFE-RL Daily Report*, no. 196, Oct. 16, 1989.

61. *RFE-RL Daily Report*, no. 234, Dec. 11, 1989.

62. See Kireyev, "Conversion," for the best explanation of the competing aims of the conversion program.

63. Ibid.; *RFE-RL Daily Report*, no. 183, Sept. 26, 1989.

64. Aleksandr Isayev, "Reform of the Defense Sector," *Kommunist*, no. 5 (March 1989), pp. 24–30.

65. Statement of MSU S. F. Akhromeyev to the US Congress on July 21, 1989; see report in *The New York Times*, July 22, 1989.

66. Alexander Rahr, "Gorbachev Discloses Details of the Defense Council," *Report on the USSR*, Sept. 15, 1989, pp. 10–12.

67. See *The New York Times*, Mar. 25, 1990.

68. See his interview in *Krasnaya Zvezda*, Mar. 16, 1990.

69. From conversations the author had with Soviet officials.

70. From conversations the author had with Soviet officials connected with the Supreme Soviet and research institutes.

71. *RFE-RL Daily Report*, no. 212, Nov. 7, 1989.

72. Article 86. On the Removal from the Composition of the USSR Armed Forces of the Border, Internal, and Railroad Troops," *Vedomosti Verkhovnogo Soveta Soyuza Sovetskykh Sotsialisticheskykh Respublik* (Moscow), Mar. 22, 1989, p. 136, trans. in *JPRS-UMA*, no. 89–016, June 27, 1989, p. 34.

73. M. A. Gareyev, *M. V. Frunze: voyennyy teoretik* [M. V. Frunze: Military Theoretician] (Moscow: Voyenizdat, 1985), p. 171.

74. *RFE-RL Daily Report,* no. 125, July 6, 1989.
75. *Izvestiya,* June 3, 1989; and *RFE-RL Daily Report,* no. 169, Sept. 6, 1989.
76. Moscow TASS in Russian, June 29, 1989, trans. in *FBIS-SOV,* June 30, 1989, p. 70.
77. D. T. Yazov, "In the Interests of Universal Security and Peace," *Izvestiya,* Feb. 28, 1989.
78. Aleksei Pakin, "Army for the People or for Generals?" *Moscow News,* July 23, 1989, p. 13; and Moscow Domestic Service in Russian, July 3, 1989, trans. in *FBIS-SOV,* July 5, 1979, p. 49.
79. *Krasnaya Zvezda,* June 5, 1990.
80. D. T. Yazov, *Izvestiya,* Feb. 28, 1989.
81. Ibid.
82. See Colonel A. G. Khor'kov, "Fortified Regions on the Western Borders of the USSR," *Voyenno-Istoricheskiy Zhumal* (Moscow), No. 12, 1989, pp. 47–54; and V. I. Levykin, *Fortifikatsiya: proshloye i sovremennost'* [Fortification: Past and Present] (Moscow: Voyenizdat, 1987), pp. 150–59.
83. The three positions presented below were debated in Dale R. Herspring and Ivan Volgyes, eds., *Civil-Military Relations in Communist Systems* (Boulder, CO: Westview, 1978).
84. Moscow TASS in Russian, Oct. 4, 1989, trans. in *FBIS-SOV,* Oct. 4, 1989, p. 106.
85. *RFE-RL Daily Report,* no. 209, Nov. 2, 1989.
86. For examples, see Army General D. T. Yazov's interview in *Pravda,* Nov. 13, 1989, Colonel-General V. F. Yermakov, *Leningradskaya Pravda* (Leningrad), Nov. 24, 1989; and Colonel-General V. Lobov, *Sovetskaya Rossiya,* Oct. 18, 1989.

23
New Thinking on Security Issues*

Susan L. Clark

The vast changes that have occurred in the Soviet Union since Mikhail Gorbachev became its leader in March 1985 have unleashed a revolution in the Eastern bloc and fundamentally altered Soviet–East European relations and East-West relations. In particular, the changes that have unfolded in Eastern Europe since the fall of 1989 have important implications for Western security policy. As a result of the revolutionary political changes in Europe, foremost among them the unification of Germany, it is clear that NATO and the Warsaw Pact are altering their basic orientations and reordering priorities they have pursued for the last four decades.

Nuclear weapons have obviously been a cornerstone of security policy in the postwar age, providing the West with a credible deterrent in the face of Warsaw Pact conventional superiority in numerous areas and granting legitimacy to Soviet claims of superpower status. But as the conventional forces become balanced at lower levels and as the Soviet empire crumbles, what does the future hold for nuclear weapons? This essay examines the evolution of Soviet thinking about military policy and the role of nuclear weapons. It is divided into two basic sections: an overview of what Soviet literature has said about these issues, followed by a section that speculates on the possible implications of future changes in the international environment for Soviet thinking about security policy, including the utility of nuclear forces. Thus, the second section concentrates on the world as it has taken shape since the events of November 1989, whereas the first focuses on the Gorbachev period to that point.

ELEMENTS OF SOVIET POLICY

When examining Soviet writings today, one must understand the historical difference between Soviet and Western publications. Until the advent of *glasnost*, the range and scope of debate evident in the official Soviet press was markedly constrained and narrow. Moreover, these debates were well controlled by the party apparatus. Today, however, numerous and wide-ranging points of view are freely expressed, making it increasingly difficult to determine who may be considered "authoritative" and who is on the fringes.

This section first outlines key changes in military doctrine over the last several years. Next, it treats the subject of parity, delineating three broad schools of thought that could be called parity via arms control, reasonable sufficiency, and minimum deterrence. A review of the extensive discussions in the Soviet press about sufficiency follows. The section then focuses on the dramatic changes in Soviet thinking—first with respect to the role of arms control in the strategic debate and then with respect to the use of nuclear weapons and nuclear deterrence.

Military Doctrine

Gorbachev has distinguished his leadership from that of previous Soviet leaders by allowing military doctrine—as well as all other elements of Soviet life—to become subject to debate. Gorbachev has, in fact, sought to place military power *within* the corpus of Soviet foreign policy rather than allowing it to dominate the foreign policy process. In this connection, new players have begun contributing to security policy analysis, thereby broadening the scope of the debate. Historically, only the Soviet military has had a role in debates about security policy, doctrine, and military-technical issues. While military officers still far outnumber the civilians in these discussions, the expertise among civilian analysts is growing. Indeed, civilian input into security debates has had a considerable impact, as evidenced by certain political decisions and by some readjustments of the military's own thinking.

It is also important to realize that until the events of 1989, the terms "Warsaw Pact doctrine" and "Soviet doctrine" were essentially synonymous. As Soviet domination of the Pact has begun to wither, these terms can no longer be interchanged automatically. Today, Soviet military doctrine has become a *part* of the debate rather than dictating the entire framework. The numerous recent changes in Eastern Europe indicate that Moscow's Eastern bloc allies are interested in exploring the creation of their own national military doctrines. Before Gorbachev's rise to power any discussions along these lines would have been viewed as heresy, and treated as such. An entirely new framework is emerging, as the Warsaw Pact member states try to decide the future orientation of this organization.

Before examining the doctrinal debate in greater detail, it is first important to understand that Warsaw Pact military doctrine consists of two components: the political and the military-technical. Western military doctrine does not follow this pattern; we would view the political component more as policy statements and propaganda. What we consider military doctrine is seen by the Soviets to be only a part of doctrine—the military-technical aspect. Today the Soviets emphasize that, although the military-technical component remains important, the political element is becoming more significant.

The most authoritative statement about the "new" Warsaw Pact doctrine is found in the communique issued by the Political Consultative Committee of the Warsaw Pact in May 1987. It asserts that the bloc's doctrine is purely defensive and that this now applies not only to the political component of their military doctrine, but also to the military-technical element, a claim that has sparked considerable debate in the West. The foundation for this defensive doctrine lies in two tasks: *preventing* war (a new aim) and searching for an economically viable strategy (given the serious economic problems of the USSR and its allies).

In addition, the May 1987 statement unveiled new terns such as reasonable sufficiency and defensive defense. While these concepts have been discussed extensively in the Soviet literature, no one has yet precisely defined them. Nevertheless, the Soviets have entered these concepts into the East-West security debate, in part to define them through further interaction with the West. Because these terms have not yet been clarified, the West has an unprecedented opportunity to help shape and influence Soviet thinking on its security policy.

Strategic Parity and Stability—Three Schools of Thought

The concept of strategic parity and the related concept of stability have received considerable attention in the Soviet literature over the past few years. Clearly, an impetus for rethinking parity at the strategic nuclear level came from the imperative of the Nineteenth Party Conference to develop the Soviet armed forces according to "qualitative parameters." Thus, emphasis is to be placed more on quality than on quantity when assessing parity.

Yet while discussions and debates about parity have abounded, in truth, much of the discussion remains confusing and contradictory, and the outcome is far from resolved. All involved in the current debate probably would accept the following assumptions: achieving parity with the United States in the early 1970s was an important milestone; this parity has been vital in maintaining world security and stability to date; parity at ever higher levels of nuclear weapons is more unstable; and, as a result, the future holds considerably more uncertainty. Beyond these working assumptions, the paths of the debate diverge.

Broadly speaking, three general schools of thought could be said to represent significant points on the emerging continuum of Soviet thinking on this issue. This is not to say that these are the only schools of thought; rather, they demonstrate the wide range of thinking and debate currently underway in the Soviet Union. The first group links strategic parity with arms control, the second school identifies itself with the reasonable sufficiency concept, and the third group consists of those advocating a minimum deterrence posture.

1. Parity Via Arms Control. The first school of thought believes that strategic parity is defined by negotiated, quantitative limits. Supporters of this thinking see utility in adhering to current arms control approaches in order to effect a negotiated reduction of military forces, thereby maintaining parity but at lower levels. The emphasis is on the continued centrality of the bilateral U.S.-Soviet relationship, the continued importance of quantitative indices, and the rejection of any further unilateral Soviet force cuts. This school represents a conservative way of thinking—most frequently espoused by certain military officers and some civilian analysts—which essentially adheres to the status quo but recognizes the need for at least moderate reductions in current force levels.

For this first school of thought, the focus of attention clearly remains on the U.S.-Soviet relationship. Therefore, the arms control process would continue along its current lines (particularly with respect to nuclear weapons); that is, it would concentrate on bilateral negotiations between the two superpowers, with little attention paid to the other nuclear powers in Europe. Should this way of thinking dominate the decision-making process, a future Soviet force structure would remain much the same as the current one, but at lower levels. Namely, it would probably maintain the approximate 70:30 split in nuclear land-based and sea-based forces, respectively.

2. Reasonable Sufficiency. The concept most frequently identified with the second school of thought is "reasonable sufficiency." This school believes that the political and military situation should determine what a reasonably sufficient force level is. In this context, it is seeking to redefine the role of nuclear weapons in the new military equation that is evolving. The rejection of the traditional quantitative parameters of parity (which cost too much and did not guarantee stability or security) has made it possible to argue that the USSR no longer needs the same number of strategic weapons as the United States. Thus, nuclear weapons are still seen to be valuable components of a nation's strength, but the reasonable sufficiency school has not yet determined what their value and role is. This line of thinking falls between the other two schools, rejecting the conservative approach of the first, but also rejecting the idea that absolute, minimum levels of nuclear weapons can be determined and that reductions to these levels can be made unilaterally, as the third school believes. Proponents of reasonable sufficiency advocate using both arms control negotiations and political statements (public diplomacy) as vehicles for helping to shape perceptions and altering current military force postures.

If the reasonable sufficiency school comes to dominate the decision-making process, several important results will be evident. First, Soviet forces will be reduced significantly both to alleviate the defense burden on the Soviet economy and to perpetuate the favorable image of the USSR that has developed in the West. The combination of arms control negotiations and public diplomacy efforts will also afford the Soviets considerable flexibility in dealing with the West on a multiplicity of issues. Finally, in terms of the forces themselves, the intention would be to make them look less threatening than the current force posture, while still maintaining a credible range of options.

Some officers argue that an imbalance in nuclear weapons would give the U.S. opportunities for blackmail; still, it should not be assumed that all members of the military ranks are opposed to thinking along the lines of reasonable sufficiency. As Dale Herspring shows in his book, *The Soviet High Command, 1967–*

1989, even members of the Soviet high command appear to be leaning more toward this school of thinking than the first. While there are some differences of opinion between military and civilian analysts about the reasonable sufficiency concept, such differences are considerably greater with respect to the third school of thought.

3. *Minimum Deterrence.* One of the most interesting and spirited debates of the past year has been that surrounding the concept of minimum deterrence. Espoused by a small group of civilian analysts—and ridiculed by the military— this third school of thought goes beyond what the second school advocates, essentially arguing that the Soviet Union should learn to live with nuclear inferiority. While at its extreme, this is not a serious alternative in the current thinking about redefining parity, the minimum-deterrence discussions do represent a critical input to the overall debate.

For the civilians who have embraced the concept of minimum deterrence, the first and most important assumption is that the West presents no real threat of war as an aggressor; rather, today's vast arsenals of weapons increase the likelihood that war may occur accidentally. Therefore, the first step in seeking greater stability and security is to reduce the force posture drastically—to a minimum-deterrent posture. Moreover, this school believes that an absolute number of nuclear weapons can be identified that will be able to deter any aggression. In terms of implementation, the minimalists have questioned whether it would not be best to scrap arms control negotiations completely; thus, they would be much more likely than the other schools to focus on additional unilateral force reductions. This potential shift away from resolution through negotiations is arguably as significant as the minimalists' identification of absolute weapons levels. Finally, because of the drastic cuts involved, the role of the other nuclear powers (namely, Britain and France) is increasingly important in the strategic equation.

The current debate about minimum deterrence began in June 1989 with a *Moscow News* article by Radomir Bogdanov and Andrei Kortunov. The authors argue that the USSR should unilaterally adopt a minimum-deterrence posture consisting of 500 warheads deployed on SS-25 mobile land-based single-warhead missiles and Delta-4 submarines. The first step in this process is unilaterally to implement the proposed 50 percent reduction in strategic weapons. The goal is to retain a force posture capable of inflicting "unacceptable damage" on the United States, which the authors believe can ultimately be accomplished with as few as five large warheads detonated over the East or West Coast.

In the final analysis, the minimum-deterrent arguments will continue to be seriously undermined until the notion of unacceptable damage can be adequately defined and its validity as a criterion for determining sufficiency widely accepted. Moreover, notwithstanding philosophical differences over what constitutes unacceptable damage and the force posture required to inflict it, the Soviet military would reject unilateral adoption of a minimum-deterrent posture because such a posture would, in their view, provide no credible guarantee against "nuclear blackmail" by the United States, as Colonels Dvorkin and Torbin argue in their scathing rebuttal to the Bogdanov-Kortunov article also published in *Moscow News*. Certain civilian analysts, such as Igor Malashenko writing in *New Times* in 1989, refute the nuclear blackmail thesis by arguing that the value of nuclear weapons lies in statesmen's perceptions about the role and benefits of nuclear weapons: "militarily meaningless weapons are significant politically only if political leaders believe them to be important."

Assuming that steps were taken to move toward a minimum-deterrent posture, the nuclear capabilities of the other European powers—Britain and France—would obviously be of increased significance and concern, particularly as these two countries modernize their existing nuclear forces. At the same time, the Soviets' previous declarations that they needed nuclear forces equivalent to the nuclear forces of all other nuclear powers combined have been increasingly challenged, not only by the minimalists but also by those supporting relative sufficiency. In fairness, it should be recognized that the Soviets have not steadfastly adhered to the goal of equaling all nuclear adversaries combined, as seen in the signing of the SALT agreements, which were made on a bilateral U.S.-Soviet basis.

A related problem raised by adherence to minimum deterrence is that of nuclear proliferation. Equally convincing arguments can be made for the idea that minimum deterrence will invite proliferation or that it will reduce the pressures that would drive it. On the one hand, some countries might perceive the Soviet Union's nuclear capacity to be so diminished that they would fear no serious reprisals if they started their own nuclear programs. On the other hand, others might feel less threatened and therefore less in need of their own capability if the Soviet Union no longer maintained large numbers of nuclear weapons.

In terms of the force structure per se, the minimalists would seek to eliminate MIRVs since MIRVs would concentrate so much of the remaining force's capability in only one weapon. As Bogdanov and Kortunov explain, sea-based forces would be preferred because they would be more survivable and flexible. On the other hand, because of the minimum numbers available, the forces may need to appear more threatening (versus the relative-sufficiency school, which makes them look less threatening) in order to provide an effective, credible deterrent.

In conclusion, it is useful to note Gorbachev's own perceptions of minimal deterrence. During his speech to the Council of Europe in Strasbourg on 6 July 1989, the Soviet leader discussed bridging the gap between Eastern and Western views on nuclear weapons, arguing that the gap can be reduced "with the USSR remaining true to nuclear-free ideals, and the West to the concept of minimal deterrence." He then asked: "What stands behind the concept of minimal [deterrence]? And where, here, is the limit beyond which the potential for nuclear retribution is converted into the potential for an attack?" Thus, Gorbachev himself has raised the issue of trying to determine just what the absolute numbers are.

The Concept of Sufficiency.

Mikhail Gorbachev first set forth the idea of reasonable sufficiency during his first visit abroad as General Secretary to France in October 1985. He has defined the concept in the following way: "that the states would not possess military forces and armaments above the level which is indispensable for an effective defense, and also . . . that their military forces have such a structure which would provide all necessary means needed for repulsing potential aggression but at the same time would not permit [them] to be used for the unfolding of the offensive missions." Put simply, the purpose is to have enough military capability to guarantee one's own security, but not enough to threaten others. The problem, of course, lies in defining what is "enough."

Soviet analysts have recognized that there are different stages of sufficiency, depending on the types of forces existing. For example, Lev Semeiko—writing in 1987 in *Izvestiya* and *XX Century and Peace,* respectively—has explained that in today's world, it is necessary to have a guaranteed nuclear retaliation capability as well as conventional forces sufficient for collective defense. In the future, however, Semeiko sees the possibility of a different kind of reasonable sufficiency; it would adopt a truly defensive conventional-force posture, limit both sides' military potential to equal security levels, and (eventually) even eliminate weapons of mass destruction entirely.

The evolution of the sufficiency concept has produced a great deal of debate and has raised fundamental questions about the Soviet military and its doctrine. Most important, the notion of sufficiency has focused attention of redefining the role of nuclear weapons in the new military equation. While nuclear weapons are still valued, the debate has yet to resolve exactly what that value is and how to use them.

The sufficiency debate has also brought military power and the priority the military has enjoyed within the Soviet system under greater scrutiny. No longer is it automatically accepted that the military must have priority access to virtually all goods and services at the expense of the general public. True, the system is still mired in a hopeless bureaucracy, but greater emphasis is being placed on consumer goods production. Concomitantly, the military must now justify what it does expect to receive. Thus, it must more accurately determine the source(s) and level of possible security threats and identify what equipment and force structure(s) are needed to counter these challenges. This is not to imply that the scope of the sufficiency debate has been confined to some theoretical framework; major structural changes already have occurred within the Soviet armed forces, and more are sure to follow.

One of the greatest debates surrounding reasonable sufficiency is whether absolute levels of sufficiency can be identified. Many military officials have stressed that defining any such levels can be done only in the context of maintaining a balance of forces, with reductions on both sides. The minimalists believe it is possible to establish some absolute number for sufficiency. Somewhere between these two extremes lies Soviet mainstream thinking, which advances the notion of reasonable sufficiency. In other words, the Soviet Union must strive to have armed forces that are sufficient relative to the military and political situations it faces. But this raises the questions of what forces the Soviet military must be relative to, and how much is enough. In any case, there is no doubt that the chosen force level will be lower than it is now.

Arms Control

The role of arms control in the strategic debate has changed dramatically over the past two decades. Before Marshal Nikolai Ogarkov became Chief of the General Staff, officers in the General Staff (as well as civilian analysts) were not generally conversant in arms control issues. Ogarkov sought to develop a new model whereby arms control became a key factor in the development and maintenance of nuclear forces. For his part, Marshal Sergei Akhromeev continued this approach during his tenure as Chief of the General Staff. Under Gorbachev, the trend initiated by Ogarkov has made the subject of arms control central to the strategic discourse rather than peripheral, as it was previously, and it has come increasingly to involve civilian analysts as well as military officers.

Soviet assessments focus on arms control to validate nuclear weapons. Within this context, a number of difficulties and problems have been identified in Soviet analyses of how a post-START world might be configured. First, it is uncertain how and when third countries will participate in strategic arms control. Especially as France and Britain modernize their nuclear forces, and if the United States and USSR reduce their own forces, the issue becomes, When will these third countries be brought into the negotiations? For his part, Andrei Kokoshin, Deputy Director of ISKAN, wrote in February 1988 in *SShA*, that when the stage of 75 percent reductions in strategic nuclear forces is reached, other countries must be included in the process. Sergei Vybornov and others argued in *International Affairs* in March 1988, that East-West strategic nuclear parity could be divided, at least initially, into two components: the USSR–United States and the USSR–Western Europe. To accomplish this, the authors propose that all countries maintain only their nuclear-missile submarines and that each country be assigned a particular geographic area in which to operate.

At the same time, the Soviets apparently see a variety of advantages in engaging in the arms control process. In addition to genuine military incentives, there are potential political implications of substantial nuclear force reductions that are important to consider. On the military-political level, if the Soviets could push the United States to a low enough level of nuclear weapons, they would likely succeed in undermining U.S. and Western support for maintaining and/or modernizing the theater nuclear weapons associated with extended deterrence commitments. In truth, the dramatic changes taking place in Eastern Europe, especially the unification of Germany, have effectively derailed Western efforts to modernize the Lance tactical missile. But the possibility still remains that a European-made missile (conceivably of joint British-French manufacture) could fill this gap in the future.

A major political advantage has been the enormous positive impact that the disarmament process has had on the Western publics. Gorbachev's considerable diplomatic skills have clearly contributed to Soviet successes in this realm. Put bluntly, the Soviet leadership believes that the access its nation can gain to the West through diplomatic efforts far outweighs the importance of a few thousand nuclear warheads. Moreover, the Soviets can influence public opinion to undermine the ability of the Western governments to maintain their own force levels.

Deep nuclear reductions would also benefit the Soviets politically in that the United States is perceived to rely on nuclear weapons to hold its alliances together, whereas the Soviet Union does not. To validate its commitment to its European allies, it is critical for the United States to maintain a credible nuclear deterrent, that is, one that can be used. Therefore, if the arms control process reduced parity to such a low level of forces that the threat of using nuclear weapons no longer seemed credible, U.S. alliances might well dissolve. Nevertheless, the West still holds some cards in this game, of which the Soviets are well aware. Their concern is that the European nuclear powers might opt to fill this gap themselves, creating their own Eurostrategic force, one that would actually combine British and French capabilities (in contrast to these countries' current emphasis on the national independence of their forces). Such an outcome could prove even more troublesome to the Soviet leaders than the current allied system, so they must play this hand carefully.

A third consideration in negotiating nuclear reductions lies in the belief that a superabundance of nuclear weapons in a time of alliance disintegration can actually increase the level of danger and threat to peace, best articulated by the minimum-deterrence advocates. Indeed, it may be possible to witness a convergence of Soviet and U.S. perceptions of the danger related to countries having too many nuclear weapons.

The Use of Nuclear Weapons

For several decades the Soviet Union has sought to undermine the Western consensus on nuclear weapons and nuclear deterrence. Its leadership has advocated the creation of nuclear-free zones in many regions of Europe and its adjacent waters, declared a policy of no first use of nuclear weapons, and proposed the elimination of all nuclear weapons by the end of this century. Laying aside the political and diplomatic incentives the Soviets might have in making such initiatives, it does appear that concrete changes are taking place in the parameters of the debate about nuclear weapons.

A key aspect of this debate remains to be discussed, that is, how nuclear weapons might be used. There are increasing signs that Soviet analysts are subscribing more firmly and in greater numbers to the belief that nuclear weapons only deter nuclear weapons. The Soviet leadership's current policy is that nuclear deterrence has become obsolete. The alternative to the concept of nuclear deterrence is (ultimately) the compete elimination of nuclear weapons, according to Soviet statements.

What must be understood in analyzing the debate is the fact that the Soviet Union has rarely, if ever, defined its nuclear requirements in the same way that the United States has. While the Soviet leadership is aware of the value of flexible response and extended deterrence to the United States, because of the USSR's geostrategic location and the nature of its alliance system, it has not required such political guarantees from its nuclear forces. In other words, while the United States has found nuclear weapons to be the most effective guarantee of its commitment to its allies across the Atlantic, the Soviet Union is not bound by these same considerations.

To the Soviet leadership, the political and military requirement of nuclear weapons are quite similar. In essence, these forces must be capable of destroying U.S. nuclear forces. If they can accomplish this military objective, this may be sufficient for their political objectives as well. In contrast, the U.S. forces must be able to carry out this military objective, but they must also satisfy the political task of guaranteeing U.S. coupling to Western Europe.

IMPLICATIONS OF THE CHANGING INTERNATIONAL ENVIRONMENT

The preceding section has identified some of the key elements of Soviet security policy, including the role of nuclear weapons. This section seeks to move beyond these elements as it speculates about many of the fundamental changes taking place in Europe today. November 1989, with the fall of the Berlin Wall and the rapid movement toward democratization throughout Eastern Europe, can be viewed as the turning point. At that time, the Soviets must have begun to develop new approaches to many of the elements of the European security equation, but in doing so, the dynamics had clearly changed; the Soviet leadership found its policies being essentially shaped *by* events rather than shaping them. To assess these changes, this section details differences in Soviet views of the overall political architecture of the European security system between the pre- and post-November 1989 worlds. It must be underscored here that this section contemplates emerging trends in the new Europe and is therefore necessarily speculative.

Table 1 outlines the parameters of the security environment and how Soviet views of these dimensions have changed since the Revolution of 1989. Each of these dimensions is then addressed in individual subsections.

European Security System

The broadest issue to be addressed is that of the European security system. From the end of World War II until recently, this system was dominated by the U.S. Soviet relationship. The two superpowers shaped the agenda and were the determining forces in the state of East-West relations. While the East and West Europeans could certainly make a contribution to the trends within the system,

Table 1.   Political Architecture

	Old approach	New approach
European security system	Superpower dominance	European pluralism
Eastern European factor	Soviets defined interests	Emerging partnerships
	Protection of ruling	Democratization process
	communist parties	
German factor	Divided	Unification
	Bulwarks of the two	Key actors redefining the
	alliances	European security
		order
Arms control focus	U.S.-centric	Enhanced role for
		European nuclear
		powers
Basic nuclear role in the	Key element in the	Subordinate (but still
political architecture	transatlantic	relevant) element in
	relationship	the building of the
		new Europe

they were not the central players. Even before Gorbachev came to power, Soviet analysts were beginning to recognize that the U.S.-Soviet relationship would be rivaled by Soviet–West European relations as the latter countries emerged to form a new "power center" in the world. Specifically, they saw West European efforts to unify militarily under a revitalized Western European Union, and economically under the European Community, as significant steps in the evolution of a European power center. In effect, the days of a world dominated by the bipolar superpower relationship were on the wane, a fact that the events of 1989 have underscored as never before. Thus, while the United States and the Soviet Union will certainly have a role to play in the new European security order, their role will be a less pivotal one as the age of European pluralism comes to the fore. The clear concern for all is that the two Germanies not acquire full control over this process.

B. Eastern European Factor

Certainly nothing has changed so dramatically since 1989 as have the role of Eastern Europe in international affairs and Soviet relations with these former satellite countries. Until recently, the Soviet Union dominated the decision-making process in this alliance of states, especially with respect to Warsaw Pact military issues. Thus, while some of the East European members might occasionally make recommendations, it was clear that their proposals had actually been defined by the Soviets, with the framework and details all worked out in advance. In the postwar era, a key purpose of the Warsaw Pact has been to ensure the survivability of the ruling Communist parties in Eastern Europe, for example, the Pact's military actions in Hungary in 1956 and Czechoslovakia in 1968. In addition, the Pact was established and maintained for the purpose of conducting a "coalition strategy"; recent events call into question the viability of this purpose as well.

In the new world taking shape in Europe, the USSR's relations with its former satellites are being radically transformed as the democratization process unfolds in these countries. Today's situation can best be characterized as one of "emerging partnerships" as the Soviets seek to redefine their relations with now-independent allies. And while the Warsaw Pact may still have some function in serving as a counter to the NATO alliance, several fundamental reasons for its existence—including the protection of ruling Communist parties and the maintenance of a coalition strategy—have been or are being eroded. In effect, the Warsaw Pact is now dead; what will replace it still remains to be seen, but it is likely that any security system that might emerge would seek a broader framework incorporating neutrals and other European nations, probably similar to the membership composition of the Conference on Security and Cooperation in Europe (CSCE).

Whatever security system eventually does emerge, the question of Soviet relations with its allies must be addressed on several counts. First, as the democratization process continues, new elites will emerge within the East European countries, elites that will not share the opinions of the old guard. For one thing, these people will certainly place greater emphasis on the representation of national interests. Thus, the trend toward greater assertiveness among the West European countries not to have their soil become a nuclear battlefield may well be mirrored in Eastern Europe.

Yet greater assertiveness on the part of these countries does not necessarily mean that they would reject the utility of nuclear weapons out of hand. In fact, an argument can be made that the only security guarantee the East Europeans may desire from the Soviet Union is to be included under a Soviet nuclear umbrella. First, such a guarantee would be useful in assuaging Eastern European fears about becoming a battlefield—conventional or nuclear—in the new Europe. Moreover, particularly in light of German unification and continuing concerns about future challenges to the postwar border agreements, the East European countries would want an extension of a nuclear guarantee to their countries to counter possible threats emanating from Germany.

Finally, it is also important to consider the possibility of long-term instability in some of these countries. Faced with such prospects, the question then becomes: What will the Soviet Union do and what types of forces might it need to deal with the situation? What would be the relationship between the remaining Soviet forces in this region and nuclear weapons? Here it is necessary to consider how secure nuclear weapons are on Eastern European soil. On the one hand, if the Soviets cannot guarantee secure protection of their nuclear weapons, they will want to redeploy them on Soviet territory, which could raise problems of its own given persistent domestic turbulence within the USSR. On the other hand, the Soviets could conclude that keeping nuclear weapons stationed in Eastern Europe would deter challenges to their remaining forces there.

German Factor

Reform within the USSR virtually invited parallel efforts elsewhere. Of all the changes that have unfolded in Eastern Europe, the most dramatic and most important (certainly from a security perspective) have been those in the German Democratic Republic (GDR). When the East European Communist parties first began to fall, many assumed that the Soviet Union might allow reform among some of its satellites, but that the GDR would not be permitted to experience the same degree of freedom and change. The Soviets might even have to intervene militarily, it was speculated, in order to protect the East German communist system. In the postwar order, it was commonly accepted that the Germanies would remain divided. Both East and West came to see the two countries as the bulwarks of their respective alliances. Changes in the level of security commitment might be tolerable in the case of other countries, but the two Germanies represented the very core of the alliance systems, located as they were in the center of the potential future battlefield.

Since the fall of the Berlin Wall—another event that many thought would never happen without Soviet military intervention—and the subsequent rush toward unification, East and West Germans find themselves the key actors in redefining the European security order. Chancellor Helmut Kohl has perhaps summarized this change in the Germanies' role best, pointing out that previously they were the objects of their respective alliance structures, whereas now they are the subjects for creating the new European structure. The question of Germany's relationship to NATO and the Warsaw Pact—still in the process of being elaborated—will have its own impact on Soviet security policy and thinking about nuclear weapons.

Arms Control Focus

The fourth element to be considered in the political architecture of European security is that of arms control. Throughout the long and tortuous process of arms control negotiations, from SALT to MBFR to INF to START, the Soviet focus has been on the United States. This orientation is understandable since the entire European security system was seen to be dominated by the superpowers, and legitimately so in the case of nuclear capabilities. In general, the stagnation that characterized East-West relations during this time was mirrored in the arms control arena. But over the last several years, this trend has begun to reverse itself. Assuming progress continues toward a START accord, and given the dynamics of the new European security environment, the degree of Soviet attention focused on British and French nuclear weapons is bound to increase, particularly as their modernization efforts proceed.

For their part, the Conventional Forces in Europe (CFE) talks clearly hold much greater promise of an agreement than did the preceding MBFR talks. Indeed, it is now widely accepted that a conventional agreement will be obtained in the near future and a CFE-2 process begun almost immediately. The impetus behind much of this rapid progress appears largely due to the cuts already being planned in many of the countries. If a CFE agreement is reached, the West will find itself without the primary rationale that has until now made the retention of (and reliance on) nuclear weapons politically tolerable. The West has long argued that it has been forced to counter the Warsaw Pact's conventional superiority in certain areas with nuclear weapons; without such superiority, the West's current rationale is undermined.

At the same time, in this new world, the Soviet leadership will find itself faced with a fundamentally different military equation: one of conventional parity, which could alter the Soviet's own thinking about nuclear weapons. Logically, Soviet analysts and policymakers would see the need for greater dependence on nuclear weapons in a post-CFE world, now that they could no longer rely on conventional advantages to overwhelm the enemy. Thus, while the West may feel greater pressure to justify its reliance on nuclear weapons, the East may reluctantly come to recognize that its own need for nuclear forces has increased. Another alternative is that the Soviets will continue to see conventional high-technology developments as the key to future security requirements.

Nuclear Weapons in the Political Architecture

Finally, within the political architecture of East-West relations, it is necessary to define the basic role of nuclear weapons. Until recently, the Soviets saw nuclear weapons as the key element in the transatlantic relationship. These forces were, in fact, designed to provide the vital guarantee to the West Europeans that the United States' security was inextricably linked with their own. In other words, nuclear forces provided the means to couple the transatlantic partners. This link was particularly apparent in the U.S.–West German relationship. Today, the while nuclear weapons remain an important element of the transatlantic dynamic, the focus has shifted away from the U.S.–West European relationship. Given the new focus of attention—that of building a new Europe—nuclear weapons are now a subordinate element in this new scheme. This is not to say that they are unimportant, but rather that their relative importance has declined because of the change in emphasis in East-West relations.

CONCLUSIONS

The future of Soviet security policy will be determined by numerous considerations. In addition to the traditional determinants, there are several new factors to be considered as well. First, policymakers must take into account the new landscape emerging in Europe as the traditional East-West divide disappears. Equally important (if not more so) are future developments *within* the Soviet Union. The future will look very different depending on whether Gorbachev remains in power or if he should be replaced by a conservative or by a radical reformer. Additionally, the various movements calling for sovereignty of individual Soviet republics can have serious implications for decision-making processes on security issues: Will the central government be able to retain control of these processes or will each republic establish its own security policies and priorities?

Rarely have so many fundamental security elements been in flux at one time. The task of developing and maintaining a coherent security policy, especially regarding the future role of nuclear weapons in the new international environment, will present President Gorbachev with yet another serious challenge as he tries to hold the Soviet empire together.

24

The Soviet Union: A Player in the World Economy?*

Akio Kawato

The economy of the Western world is undergoing possibly one of the most profound transformations experienced since World War II. The United States no longer dominates international economics: its declining productivity, together with an inclination to over-consumption, has exposed the dollar to speculation in international currency markets. Consequently, to prevent any major economic disruption, coordination of economic policy among the industrialized nations of the West is now indispensable. Furthermore, increasing divergence of productivity rates among industrialized countries has encouraged some of them to form economic blocs, thereby accelerating the disintegration of the established order. As a result of these recent developments the international economy now finds itself at a crossroads.

However, this is not to say that the capitalist economic system as a whole has lost its vitality: technological innovation is advancing ever more rapidly, and in the Pacific area new markets are expanding. In most Western countries, high levels of both consumption and investment continue and, in spite of high unemployment rates in some West European countries, there is no serious threat of social unrest. In the capitalist economic system, the trend towards economic deregulation, together with the modernization of telecommunications, has diminished the significance of borders between states; the 'borderless economy' is gradually emerging in the shape of free capital flows, international cooperation among large enterprises and international mergers and acquisitions.

In the West, wars fought to win new markets are a thing of the past; the balance of power is no longer determined by military force but by economic strength. In such an economic environment, the Soviet Union is in an awkward position since the source of its power has traditionally been military rather than

*Reprinted by permission of the author and the Royal Institute of International Affairs from *Perestroika: Social Domestic and Foreign Policies*, T. Hasegawa and A. Pravda (eds.), pp. 122–140. Copyright © 1990 by the Royal Institute of International Affairs. Published by Sage Publications for the Royal Institute of International Affairs, London.

economic strength. Its stagnating economy no longer has many admirers abroad; it has, on the contrary, discredited socialism.

President Gorbachev has embarked on a sweeping overhaul of the economic system, even proclaiming that the global economy is being 'unified' and that the Soviet Union should take a more active part in this process. If he succeeds in his endeavor, his reforms will achieve the greatest revolution ever seen in the history of the Soviet economy.

Discussion in the West is now focused on how to deal with this fresh wind from Moscow. Supporters of perestroika argue that it is high time to 'incorporate' the Soviet Union into the global economy: by so doing, we could transform this formidable military power into a docile mercantile partner and thus achieve permanent stability in the world. Indeed, some even speak of the necessity of 'helping perestroika'. However, encouraging as the developments in the USSR may be, the West should not embark upon any hasty, unconsidered course of action. Little evidence of real change in the Soviet economy has been seen so far and the prospects of success are uncertain; indeed, the kind of incomplete reforms witnessed thus far could eventually be counter-productive. The Soviets are in serious trouble and are appealing for international economic cooperation, but in reality their economy is ill-prepared for this kind of ambitious step: it is neither flexible nor open enough and, furthermore, has little to offer the West. Soviet exhortations to international economic cooperation are therefore little more than a cry for help. Without unnecessarily antagonizing the Soviet Union, it must be acknowledged that the West cannot afford to help the Soviets out of trouble. Its needs are limitless and its economic system cannot exploit foreign assistance effectively. What is more, its dreadful military machine is, by and large, still intact. The purpose of this article is to evaluate the opportunities which exist to incorporate the Soviet Union into the global economy and the obstacles standing in the way of this.

WILL THE SOVIET ECONOMY RECOVER?

The Soviet Union's desire to play a more active role in the world economy seems to be genuine, and such a development will be welcomed in the West if the necessary improvements in its economy are brought about in a fair manner. But how far the Soviets can succeed will depend upon their own economic strength; in other words, how well the Soviets manage to revitalize and reform their own economy will determine the degree to which they can be integrated into the global economy. The outlook is not reassuring. The Soviet economy suffers from many scarcities and bottlenecks in the supply of materials and labour, problems which are aggravated by a lack of technological innovation and of efficiency in general. The path to economic reform is dogged by deadly political pitfalls, such as inflation, unemployment and widening income differentials, not to speak of the considerable and still widespread resistance to opening up the Soviet economy; it would be hard to imagine, for instance, a merger between the Soviet automobile manufacturers Volga and Volkswagen or Toyota.

Obstacles to Economic Development

By paying too much attention to the Soviet economic mechanism, we tend to overlook the fact that the economy itself suffers from many shortages and bottlenecks. The USSR has openly acknowledged a deficit, which runs at 7 per cent of its total budget. In addition, capital resources for investment have always been tight, due mainly to the rising cost of energy.

The shortage of capital, however, could be easily overcome: it is widely known that the ill-managed lending practices of Soviet banks have flooded the economy with money. Furthermore, the Soviet Union has a large, untapped reserve of monetary resources—almost one-third of personal savings is not deposited in banks. These 'hidden' savings could be mobilized by issuing government bonds or liberalizing the stock exchange.

'Money can always be found, but not materials'—this is the most frequent complaint made by directors of Soviet businesses. The principal problem facing the Soviet economy is not shortage of money but of goods. Despite the fact that existing deposits of oil, coal and iron ore are being exhausted and their productivity is rapidly declining, conservation of energy and materials has not yet become a priority for Soviet entrepreneurs, as the failure to meet annual conservation targets demonstrates. For one unit of production, Soviet industry consumes 1.75 times more iron and 1.53 times more energy than the Western average.[1] Shortage of electricity is also a perennial problem in the USSR; voltage fluctuates between 240 and 200 volts, and frequently sometimes drops to 49 kHz, which can damage electronic devices and disrupts their normal functioning.[2] Chernobyl has exacerbated the problem by delaying the construction of nuclear plants. Another problem is the shortage of labour: fresh influxes of labour have decreased from 11 million during 1976–80 to 3 million during 1981–5 (of whom 2.5 million came from Azerbaijan and Soviet Central Asia).[3] Poor transport and communications networks constitute yet another hindrance to economic development. The Soviet Union is proud of its brilliant tradition in science, but the fact remains that the fruits of these labours are seldom utilized in civilian production. The non-military economy is also burdened with Soviet directors' preference for meeting quantitative targets as opposed to improving product quality by introducing technological innovation: indeed, sometimes they are physically incapable of introducing new technology because Soviet machines are not designed to carry out delicate processes and because they lack the necessary high-quality materials. There are now signs that the Soviets are even beginning to lag behind in basic research, an area in which they have traditionally excelled. This is due to lack of sufficient computers in terms of both quantity and quality. Obsolete machinery is therefore a serious problem in the Soviet economy: almost half of its plants are more than twenty years old.[4]

Gorbachev is trying to overcome this handicap by accelerating the renovation of equipment and pumping more resources into the machine-building sector but, ironically, this comprehensive wave of renovation has itself incurred a shortage of machinery. Furthermore, most 'new' machines are not much more efficient than their predecessors.

Is a Market Economy Possible in the Soviet Union?

The key problem in the Soviet economy is the shortage of raw materials (*defitsit*): this shortage necessitates the central distribution of materials, hampers competition and, accordingly, does not provide incentives to improve quality or introduce new technology. The *defitsit* has been produced by the protectionist nature of the Soviet economy: in the Soviet Union, unprofitable business (about 13 percent of the total)[5] and internationally uncompetitive sectors are maintained by government subsidy—which means, in part, by the profits of successful businesses. Another consequence of the absence of competition is waste of materials, which of course exacerbates the *defitsit* problem. Central distribution has deprived Soviet enterprises of incentive to show initiative and innovation. Businesses are run not according to the principles of entrepreneurship but of bureaucratism. They avoid responsibility and risk, and react not to the demand of the consumer but to the demands of central bureaucracy.

Marketization of the economy and the introduction of competition can only be effected where there is flexibility on the supply side: if the supply of materials is tight or centralized, firms will not be able to react quickly to a shift in the market, or conversely, to expand production of competitive goods. But creation of such flexibility would be a difficult task for the Soviet economy. The Soviets contend that current reforms will force firms to conserve materials because most of the profits are no longer required to be turned over to the state but are left to businesses to dispose of at their discretion. However, this claim has yet to be verified: since industries collect more bonuses by fulfilling production quotas than by conserving materials, conservation targets have consistently not been met. One benefit of disarmament has been that some resources are now being diverted from the military to the civil economy. But this redistribution of resources will not prove to be a panacea for the Soviet economy because the military will most probably try to keep the better scientists, along with high-quality materials and machine tools. It is an established tradition in the Soviet Union that the consumer-goods sector of the economy is allotted second-class resources.

The best way to overcome this *defitsit* would be to reduce or liquidate uncompetitive sectors and businesses. However, this would involve immense social sacrifice and is fraught with political risk: the authorities would be faced with the gigantic task of economic restructuring, complicated by the severe social problems arising from mass unemployment and bankruptcies on a hitherto unprecedented scale. Since prices in socialist economies are severely distorted by all manner of subsidies, all major economic reforms should be preceded by drastic price reform. As a result of frequently arbitrary pricing, some prices guarantee unjustifiably large profit margins while others do not even cover production costs. Under the present system, it is impossible to judge which enterprises are unprofitable and which sectors are internationally uncompetitive; to correct this, state subsidies should be reduced and market prices introduced. These measures will inevitably incur inflation, as was the case in Poland and Hungary, but this is an inescapable stage on the way to economic reform.

As we have seen, the transition from a protectionist, centralized economy is accompanied by almost unendurable sacrifice and considerable political risk. The Gorbachev administration has embarked on a very bold reform course; the centralized system is to be liberalized and private economic activity encouraged. In the agricultural sector the rent *(arenda)* system is being introduced, which is tantamount to individual land ownership. In this eagerness to reform, however, Gorbachev has put the cart before the horse: he has granted independence to businesses without first introducing price reform and liberalizing the distribution of raw materials, inadvertently unleasing monopolistic tendencies in the economy. Firms now produce fewer goods with low profit margins and arbitrarily raise prices under the pretext of providing new products. Consequently, some household goods have become unobtainable and inflation is beginning to bite. As stated above, businesses are now accorded more jurisdiction over the disposal of their profits, but consumers are disappointed at the lack of goods to spend their money on.

Private economic activity is growing, but is hampered by heavy taxation, harassment by local officials and shortage of necessary materials. The 'co-operative restaurants', much applauded by the Western media when they opened, have turned out to be luxuries which only the rich can afford and now excite only resentment among the general population, especially as they tend to buy up much of the scarce supplies of meat and vegetables in the state wholesale shops. The problem is that most of the Soviet people have lost whatever skills in private economic activity they still possessed at the time of the New Economic Policy (NEP). The *arenda* system is unpopular among the peasants because it would result only in harder work and unstable incomes; a secure existence on the collective farms have not yet acquired the skills needed to succeed at private farming.

Having realized the error of granting more autonomy to the business sector before reforming the price system and materials distribution, Gorbachev is now trying to correct his mistake by declaring that the supply system should be liberalized by 1990 and price reforms completed by 1991. Measures are being taken to close unprofitable enterprises or rent them to cooperatives. The future of the Soviet economy will depend on whether these aspirations can be translated into reality. So far, the prospects are not encouraging. Liquidation of unprofitable businesses is proceeding but on a limited scale and only small firms are affected. Ministries resist the closure of 'their' enterprises because of fear of disgrace, and also it makes the task of meeting production quotas more difficult. The difficulty of enforcing the liquidation of unprofitable businesses is underlined by the fact that even in Hungary, where the leadership is committed to rigorous reforms, the process of liquidation has tended to lose momentum. The renting of unprofitable enterprises to cooperatives has not always been a complete success either; workers sometimes resent it because it makes labour more intensive. Merging unprofitable businesses into larger ones is another solution, but is at best only a makeshift policy, not a long-term strategy.

In sum, then, there does not appear to be much hope of alleviating the shortages of goods. There will continue to be insufficient competition in the Soviet economy, with the result that the improvement of product quality and the introduction of technological innovation will take place slowly. In such circumstances, three scenarios can be proposed: (1) most of the reform efforts will be sabotaged and the old system will survive; (2) the authorities will succeed in enforcing economic reform, at least superficially, but this will ultimately bring about economic chaos; (3) the administration will slow down the tempo of reform in order to avoid economic disruption. In none of these scenarios does the Soviet economy become either liberalized or revitalized enough to be able to participate seriously in the global economy.

THE SOVIET UNION: A PLAYER IN THE WORLD ECONOMY?

Changing Ideology

Faced with such gloomy prospects for the economy, Gorbachev has directed his attention outward and revised the traditional approach to the world economy. In this regard Soviet ideology has undergone a thorough revision. The world, once clearly divided between socialists and capitalists, has suddenly become united, and interdependence is now the key word. The Soviet Union has even become a quasi-member of OPEC, declaring in March 1989 that it would reduce oil exports by 5 per cent. At the party plenum in January 1987, Gorbachev stated that ''the world today forms a single entity. All nations are interrelated and interdependent in spite of all their fundamental differences. The globalization of economic activities, the revolutions in science and technology and the dramatic new role of telecommunications have all contributed to this phenomenon.' Gorbachev considers foreign trade to be an integral part of the Soviet economy, and not merely, as used to be the case, a means of compensating for domestic shortages. He now says openly that active participation in foreign trade will introduce competitive thinking into the Soviet economy.

The objectives of the 'internationalization' of the Soviet economy are as follows: (1) the Soviet Union needs advanced Western technology, otherwise it will be left behind in the contest for technological superiority now being fought in the West. Technical research and development is very costly but international cooperation and the division of labour thus effected could reduce costs substantially for the Soviet economy. (2) The Soviet administration is trying to restructure exports, stressing above all the need to export more manufactured goods.

This would be much more lucrative than simply exporting energy resources and would force Soviet businesses to become more competitive. When the fall in oil prices reduced foreign currency income by $8 billion, thus aggravating the budget deficit (I estimate that at least 10 per cent of Soviet revenue comes from oil exports), Soviet leaders could not help but appreciate how deeply their economy is affected by developments at the international level.

However, there is still a long way to go before the Soviet Union can become a major player in the world economy: trade with the West is still marginal (about $50 million) given the size of the economy, amounting to only 2.5 per cent of GNP, and exports to capitalist countries, as a proportion of total exports, have declined from 32.6 per cent in 1980 to 20.2 per cent in 1988. This was due mainly to the fall in oil prices. The Eastern bloc's share in trade with the West has decreased from 2.37 per cent in 1980 to 1.95 per cent in 1987.[6] A further difficulty is the fact that the Soviet domestic market is still largely closed to outside trade, due to the inconvertibility of the rouble and the lack of foreign currency.

(a) Increasing Exports of Manufactured Goods. In order to become an economic force to be reckoned with at the international level, the Soviet Union must increase its exports of manufactured goods. Its present export structure is heavily dependent on the export of raw materials; it is inefficient and fails to provide a good enough basis for closer integration into the global economy. The percentage of manufactured goods as a proportion of total Soviet exports has declined from 21.6 per cent in 1980 to 20.9 per cent in 1986; in both 1986 and 1987 exports of machinery and equipment fell by 1 per cent in 1985 prices.[7] Furthermore, there is a structural imbalance in Soviet manufactured goods exports, making them vulnerable. Exports of consumer goods are very small, less than 3 per cent of total exports, while the bulk of manufactured exports is machinery and equipment. About 70 per cent of exports of manufactures to the West is made up of four groups of commodities: motor cars, power plant, technical instruments and laboratory equipment, and railway rolling-stock, with motor cars making up 46 per cent of this figure.[8] However, since 1987 there have been some hopeful signs. The proportion of manufactured goods in Soviet exports rose to 21.5 per cent in 1987. Soviet exports to industrialized capitalist countries have grown by 5 per cent, as opposed to only 0.1 per cent for total exports.[9] But further analysis is necessary to determine whether this indicates a substantial new trend, since some increases may be due to such unfair trade practices as dumping or counter purchase.

(b) Direct Trade with the West. Trading procedure in the Soviet Union has been liberalized to provide a more stimulating business environment and to get rid of bureaucratic interventionism. From 1987 onwards, twenty ministries and seventy enterprises have been authorized to conduct foreign trade without the intervention of the Foreign Trade Ministry, and from April 1989 this right was extended to all internationally competitive businesses.[10] As of 1987, 19.5 per

cent of all trade was done according to this new formula.[11] This certainly represents liberalization, but liberalization is not without its own problems, as we shall see below. Foreign businessmen are now forced to travel vast distances in order to negotiate with their Soviet counterparts, and many Soviet businessmen suffer from a permanent shortage of skilled personnel who are experienced in foreign trade.

Thus far liberalization has been incomplete. For instance, firms are not allowed to dispose of all their foreign income as they see fit: only one-quarter of the car manufacturer Volga's foreign currency income is left at the firm's own disposal, and even then permission from the Foreign Trade Ministry is required (now the Foreign Economic Relations Ministry).[12] Such conditions are hardly conducive to increasing exports. There are limits also to what Soviet industry can cope with; for example, if an export becomes popular abroad, businesses cannot respond appropriately to the increased demand because of scarcities of materials. Conversely, the drive to increase exports occurs sometimes at the expense of domestic consumption. Muscovites now complain that it has become more difficult to purchase a car under perestroika, since more are now exported. Exports of passenger vehicles increased sharply from 20 per cent of total exports in 1985 to 23 per cent in 1986.

(c) Joint Ventures. The adoption of the Law on Joint Ventures in January 1987 caused a sensation in the West. Until then it had been inconceivable that a Soviet administration firmly committed to public ownership of the means of production should permit joint ventures with Western capitalists. Even now, the Soviet constitution does not provide for such forms of property, making the concept of a joint venture actually unconstitutional. The aim of joint ventures is to attract foreign capital without incurring more debt and to acquire new technology and Western management skills. But this is not a new idea; even in the Brezhnev era, the Soviets insisted on 'industrial cooperation', which went far beyond simple trade and required foreign enterprises to become closely involved in management and technological research and development.

The Soviet Union's active encouragement of joint ventures recalls the 'concessions' offered to foreign firms during Lenin's NEP. Like Gorbachev, Lenin then attempted to rescue the Soviet economy by injecting foreign capital and technology, but his efforts to persuade conservative colleagues of the merits of this scheme did not pay off and only few foreign industrialists took up his offer.

Now, as then, the number of joint ventures in the Soviet economy is low: at the beginning of 1989 they numbered 164, but Western investment in them comes to only about $500 million.[13] The reasons for this are many. Most foreign firms are concerned about possible restrictions on repatriation of profits, while poor infrastructure and unreliable supplies of materials are further drawbacks. Yet another barrier is the Soviet authorities' preference for export-oriented joint ventures, whereas Western businessmen tend to be more interested in the domestic market.

In order to remedy these deficiencies, the authorities adopted a new strategy in

December 1988. From that point onwards, the foreign partner in a joint venture could hold up to 99 per cent of the capital, and foreigners could also become directors of joint ventures. Joint ventures for domestic production were also sanctioned by the new measures. But in spite of these improvements, conditions are still not favourable for the establishment of joint ventures. Frequent changes in the economic legislation and the instability of the rouble deter would-be investors. Therefore, the impact of joint ventures on the economy is likely to be limited.

(d) Free Trade Zones. Although successful experiments with free trade zones in China have made these fashionable among Eastern bloc countries, governments will discourage Western investors interested in such free trade zones would be faced with problems similar to those associated with joint ventures: investments could be jeopardized by poor social infrastructure, unreliable supply of materials or arbitrary interventions by local officials. In establishing free trade area, Eastern bloc countries would have to compete with one another to provide as favourable conditions for investment as possible. This is especially true today, given the emergence of such attractive locations for investments as Spain, Portugal or the Newly Industrialized Economies countries. All in all, it appears unlikely that free trade zones will become feasible in Eastern Europe. So far the Soviet Union has failed to establish even one such area, and where there are possible candidates, they lack the proper qualifications. The countries of the Soviet Far East have no proper infrastructure and labour is in short supply, while the resurgence of nationalism in the Baltic states has made the area unstable and therefore unattractive to investors.

(e) Accession to International Economic Organizations. The Soviet Union's expressed desire to join organizations such as GATT also caused rather a sensation in the West: it was felt that the Soviets, who had participated in the founding of the IMF but later withdrew because of the cold war, had finally offered proof of their willingness to join a Western 'club'. However, this is no romantic pipe dream on the part of the Soviet Union: they have concrete objectives in applying for membership of GATT, among which are the expansion of manufactured goods exports and the acquisition of Most Favoured Nation status which membership would bestow, and which would make its exports less vulnerable to arbitrary import restrictions. The difficulty here is that the Soviet economy is not 'compatible' with GATT. GATT is a network of concrete obligations and mutual concessions, which means that, in order to join, the Soviet Union would have to abolish its complicated multiple exchange rates, lift quantitative restrictions and suspend government subsidies. The accession of some of the Eastern European countries to GATT did not cause much disruption as their economies are small, but the accession of an economy the size of that of the Soviet Union could cripple GATT. Another impediment to its accession is that GATT is now preoccupied with major issues such as the Uruguay Round and the accession of China. At present, GATT has not much capacity to discuss the

USSR's accession, which is neither urgent nor of advantage to the organization. Unless the Soviet economy becomes strong enough to become truly open to international business, its accession to GATT would benefit only the Soviets themselves. The West should therefore carefully weigh hoped-for political gains against the likely economic burdens before admitting the Soviet Union to GATT. Fortunately for the West, the Soviets are in no hurry to join GATT. They are fully aware that their economy could not yet absorb such a move, which would have to be preceded by modification of their price and tariff system.

As for the IMF, they have yet to express any interest in joining. The Soviet Union is indeed adapting its foreign trade system, albeit slowly. As mentioned above, direct trade is now allowed, and reforms have been announced for the tariff system: by 1990 new tariff rates will be enforced, and regulations concerning non-tariff barriers will be elaborated from 1989 onwards.[14] Multiple exchange rates are to be abolished and the rouble devalued. However, whether these reforms will succeed remains to be seen.

(f) Relations with the EC. The CMEA Secretariat and the EC Commission adopted a Joint Declaration in June 1988. The Soviet Union now has an ambassador to the EC and is about to conclude a trade agreement with the Community it once regarded as an enemy. Will these developments provide a solid basis for closer economic ties with the West? It must be said that the likelihood of this happening is not great, mainly because the Joint Declaration is a purely formal document and involves neither rights nor obligations on either side. It has, rather, a propaganda character. The EC Commission, however, instead of being taken in by such propaganda, has won Soviet consent to pursue a bilateral strategy in concluding trade agreements with Warsaw Pact countries, which means that it can adopt a differentiated attitude to each Eastern bloc country, depending upon how far their reform measures have advanced. This is a victory for the economic strength of the West. The EC's trade agreement with Hungary is the most generous so far, including, as it does, the extensive abolition of quantitative restrictions. However, the EC will not lift all restrictions, even for Hungary, since the Community could not absorb a flood of imports from Eastern Europe. Since the Soviet Union is incapable of increasing its exports to the West as much as it would like, due to the lack of competitive goods, the enhanced integration of the EC in 1992 will not necessarily strengthen economic ties between the EC and Comecon, but it might exert psychological pressure on Soviet bloc countries to reform their economic systems.

(g) Borrowing from the West. As the measures described above have yet to bear any fruit, the Soviet Union has resorted to increased borrowing in the financial markets of the West. Western banks are responding positively to Soviet approaches—for them, the Soviet Union is one of the few countries to which they can lend money safely. In 1988 the Soviet Union achieved a debt service ratio of 21, much lower than the average of 42 for the other East European countries. Not surprisingly, therefore, Soviet indebtedness to the West is grow-

ing. At the end of 1988 its estimated net debt in convertible currencies stood at about $23 billion; in 1984 it was $11 billion, the lowest figure for the last ten years. The Soviet Union has even begun to issue bonds in Western markets, breaking a tradition which has survived since the Revolution: in 1988 they issued bonds for 100 million Swiss francs and 500 million Deutschmarks.[15]

This new trend in foreign borrowing will not increase unchecked: it will not reach pre-revolutionary levels, when foreign funds financed almost 40 per cent of total Soviet investments. The Soviet press is already reporting popular concern about the rapid increase in foreign borrowing, and the administration itself is showing restraint. The much-advertised lending by Western banks in 1988 (the credit extended was reported to amount to about $9 billion) has been disbursed only slowly, with some contracts not even being concluded. At current levels, foreign borrowing will not be able to do much to revitalize the Soviet economy to any great degree: the Soviet Union's annual investments total $300 billion and the potential need for finance to improve infrastructure is immense.

What is more, funds from foreign borrowing are not used efficiently: imported goods are often embezzled or wasted through careless transportation and imported plants are not operated efficiently. *Pravda* reported that in one imported chemical plant 3.5 times as many engineers and workers were working compared to its Western equivalent.[16] Furthermore, secrecy and lack of precision instruments and high-quality materials prevent the diffusion of high technology. The Soviet administration is now compelled to use foreign currency to import consumer goods in order to avert a popular backlash against perestroika, which means that foreign money will not be used to prevent an economic crisis but merely to afford a brief breathing space.

(h) The Asian Dimension. The Soviet Union has recently become more interested in the Pan-Pacific basin area than heretofore. Gorbachev stated his interest in this area in major speeches in Vladivostok in July 1986 and Krasnoyarsk in September 1988. What attracts the Soviets to this area is its potential for economic development. In this rapidly growing region, it is anxious to gain more political as well as economic influence, as can be seen by its current eagerness to join the PECC (Pacific Economic Cooperation Conference) and the Asian Development Bank. However, it is not at all certain that the Soviet Union can become a major partner in this region. The population of the Soviet Far East makes up only 2.5 per cent of the Soviet Union's total population. Soviet trade with its four major partners in this area (Japan, China, Vietnam and North Korea) amounts only to 5.9 per cent of total trade and is only 2 per cent of the total turnover of the Pan-Pacific region.[17] So far, the Soviet Union is a negligible partner in this region.

In August 1987 the Soviets adopted a programme, grandiosely entitled 'The Long-Term State Programme for Complex Development of Production Capability in the Far East Area until 2000'. It foresees 200 billion roubles' investment for the coming fifteen years (twice as much as for the period between 1970 and 1985). According to its projection, production of machinery will also increase by

3.9 times, petroleum by 3.1–3.8 times, electricity by 2.6 times, and foreign exports will triple. If the goals of this programme are fulfilled, this would certainly provide a solid basis for serious Soviet participation in the Pan-Pacific economy. However, in an interview with *Izvestiya* on 4 September 1988, the main author of this programme, Dr Minakir, vice-director of the Economic Research Institute of the Far East Branch of the Soviet Academy of Sciences, disclosed with the utmost frankness the impracticability of this programme. He complained that it was merely an uncoordinated summing up of ideas presented by the ministries concerned. The goal of this programme, the improvement of infrastructure by 100 per cent in fifteen years, is completely beyond the Soviet Union's means. Instead, he contended that while machinery will be produced in large quantity, there will not be enough foreign customers, apart from the socialist countries, and the Soviet Far East will not be opened to tourism because of the reluctance of local officials, since many areas are 'militarily sensitive'.

The outlook for rapid economic development of the Soviet Far East is there-fore not good: it is generally short of labour and production infrastructure, and the Soviets themselves are not ready to pour resources into the region—at least for another ten years. Their main concern now is the modernization of production equipment and the improvement of the infrastructure of the western half of the Soviet Union, where serious problems have to be tackled: supply of raw mate-rials from mines is guaranteed until 2000, and the much advertised BAM Railway is not yet in operation, having already been criticized as a colossal waste of resources. The capitalist economies in the Pacific basin have no urgent interest in undertaking projects in Siberia. The Japanese demand for raw materials will be satisfied for years to come by long-term contracts with other countries; they therefore see no need to spend astronomical amounts of money in Siberia. Furthermore, as long as the territorial dispute over the Kurile Islands remains unresolved, the Japanese government will hardly feel inclined to support Sibe-rian projects.

The Soviet Union is now trying to force Japan into economic cooperation by playing the 'Korean card'. South Korean enterprises are showing increasing interest in trade with the Soviet Union to compensate for shrinking US markets. While generally endorsing such a move, the Korean government has adopted a rather cautious attitude to joint projects with the Soviet Union in Siberia. The chief obstacle to increased economic cooperation is political: as long as the Soviet Union does not officially recognize South Korea, the South Koreans are not likely to embark upon large-scale economic cooperation in Siberia. Soviet military assistance to the North is another impediment to economic cooperation between the two. In spite of all the sensational estimates, Soviet-Korean trade is only one-tenth of the trade between South Korea and China. Economic con-straints also inhibit the rapid growth of Soviet-Korean trade: South Korea has only limited financial resources, and its markets could not absorb the vast quantities of raw materials which Siberia would wish to export.

Other NIEs do not hold out much prospect of successful economic cooperation with the Soviet Union either. Taiwan has as yet not even allowed direct trade with the Soviet Union, and trade with the ASEAN countries has always been marginal, since the Soviets do not have much to offer in the way of suitable exports. In its current economic state, the Soviet Union is not yet qualified to join the Pacific club. If the Soviets are allowed to 'slip in', they will benefit at our expense, both politically and economically.

(i) Convertibility of the Rouble. The culmination of all economic reforms would be the convertibility of the rouble: only with full convertibility will the Soviet Union be able to embark seriously on the internationalization and revitalization of its economy. However, convertibility will only be achieved with a sound economy and free trade, and progress towards this goal will necessarily be slow. First of all, Soviet prices will have to be brought into line with international market prices. Furthermore, subsidies to certain commodities will have to be suspended and the prices amended to reflect exact marginal production costs.

The exchange rate must also be corrected, which will entail devaluing the rouble by perhaps ten times its present value, otherwise the Soviet economy would not survive the onslaught of a torrent of foreign imports and an astronomical trade deficit would inevitably accumulate. The difficulties involved in moving to full convertibility of the rouble are underlined by the case of South Korea, which, despite its flourishing economy, has only recently begun to make progress towards the convertibility of the won. The Soviet Union is gradually implementing measures to bring about convertibility of its currency: in December 1988, a decision was taken to devalue the rouble by 200 per cent, starting in 1990, and to introduce a new rate in 1991.[18] In 1989, an open auction of foreign currencies was allowed. All this constitutes nothing other than an official admission of the black market rate.

(j) Cooperation within the Council for Mutual Economic Assistance (CMEA). In conjunction with its commitment to becoming more deeply involved in the Western economy, the Soviet Union is simultaneously trying to improve the efficiency of the CMEA, obviously with regard to the possible economic benefits which might accrue to itself. Since 60 per cent of Soviet trade is with Comecon countries, this concern is understandable. The main prescriptions for reinforcing the CMEA are intensification of cooperation in science and technology; the establishment of joint ventures and so-called 'direct links' between CMEA enterprises; joint exploitation of energy sources and convertibility of the 'transferable rouble'.

The Soviet Union is also anxious that other CMEA members provide consumer goods of better quality than heretofore. However, most other Comecon countries are more eager to expand their trade with the West since only from the West can they acquire the advanced machinery and technology they desperately need. They comply with Soviet pressure to improve cooperation within the CMEA, but unwillingly, out of political obligation rather than for their own economic benefit. The 'Complex Programme for the Development of Science and Technology up to the year 2000', adopted in June 1984, has achieved little, and the number of 'direct links' among CMEA countries has increased only on paper.

Relations among the CMEA countries are hampered by red tape and lack of advanced telecommunications equipment. Uncoordinated price systems are an obstacle to convertibility of their currencies. In October 1987 they agreed on the introduction of partial convertibility of the transferable rouble, limited to convertibility in transactions among joint ventures and 'direct links', but without the participation of Romania and the GDR. Romania has maintained its traditional reservation toward any attempt to strengthen CMEA integration, and the DGR is afraid that her commodities will be bought up by poorer colleagues, without proper counter-offers. Along with the failure to improve cooperation within the CMEA, the turnover of trade among CMEA members has been declining, due mainly to the fall in the price of Soviet oil. After constant growth up to 1986, Soviet trade with Comecon countries showed a 0.5 per cent decline in 1987. In contrast to the first half of the 1980s the Soviets now have trade deficits with some CMEA members. At the forty-fourth plenum of the CMEA in July 1988, the establishment of an 'integrated market' was agreed as a goal: this would mean free movement of goods, services, capital and labour.[19] But only the future will reveal exactly when this integrated market might actually come about.

CONCLUSION

All in all, the outlook for the Soviet economy is rather grim. Only in its very initial stages, economic reform has already caused disruption, and further liberalization could lead to chaos. But if fear of social unrest causes perestroika to falter now, then the Soviet economy would regress to its state under Brezhnev, or worse. The Soviet people, more sophisticated and conscious of their rights than under Stalin, would not tolerate such a set-back; an increase in social friction appears increasingly likely. Such is the dilemma now facing the Soviet authorities. Importing Western technology can offer only slight relief, and even this option is constrained by limited foreign currency reserves as well as the COCOM regulations restricting technology transfer. In such circumstances, serious involvement of the Soviet economy in the international system is inconceivable. If it were a result of the Soviet Union's own efforts and at her own cost, such involvement would be welcomed, but as things stand now, there is no reason to 'help' perestroika, at great cost to ourselves, by extending subsidized credits or allowing Soviet products to be dumped on our markets. The Soviet economy has to a certain extent become incorporated into the international economy this already has been achieved without the type of aid described above. Furthermore, the Soviet Union is already compelled to moderate its activities abroad in order to preserve good relations with the West.

We should therefore interpret Gorbachev's conciliatory attitude as an appeal for help and not as an expression of generosity towards the West; the Soviets are in the weaker position. However, this does not mean that we should exploit this opportunity to 'corner' the Soviet Union: on the contrary, we should make progress in disarmament so that the balance of power can be maintained at as low a level as possible. Equally, economic relations should be dealt with on a basis of mutual benefit and costly forms of assistance avoided in favour of practical and relatively inexpensive measures such as the transfer of capitalist management methods.

East–West relations now seem to be moving towards stabilization and *rapprochement*. However, this superficial phenomenon is being fuelled by the erosion of the (bipolar) political system we have had since 1945. One of the two pillars of this system, the Soviet Union, is threatened by economic chaos and nationalist unrest, either of which could some day become serious enough to jeopardize the economic and political stability of the whole world. If this were to happen, the West might find itself faced with the immediate problem of deciding whether or not to help the Soviets out of trouble. Even in this type of 'worst case', Western aid to the Soviet Union should involve certain conditions; for instance, the Soviet Union would first have to relinquish some of the unfair advantages (territorial gains) it has enjoyed since World War II. Otherwise, Western aid would merely result in reviving a superpower which occupies the northern half of the Eurasian land mass. Relations with the Soviet Union must always take geopolitical as well as ideological considerations into account. A strategy of crisis management to cope with the instability which could result from the decline of the Soviet economy must now be on the agenda for the West.

NOTES

1. *Sotsialisticheskaya industriya,* 22 March 1983; Slyunkov's speech at the Party Central Committee Meeting on 6 June 1987.
2. *Izvestiya,* 21 Sept. 1986.
3. *Trud,* 28 Aug. 1984.
4. *Pravda,* 8 March 1987.
5. *Izvestiya,* 12 Oct. 1986.
6. United Nations Material. UN TD/B/1195/Add. 1, 89.2.20.
7. *Izvestiya,* 18 Dec. 1987.
8. *Vneshnyaya torgovlya* 11 (1988).
9. *Vneshnyaya torgovlya* 3 (1988).
10. *Ekonomicheskaya gazeta* 51 (1988).
11. *Vneshnyaya torgovlya* 3 (1988).
12. *Pravda* 10 March 1986.
13. *Vedomosti Pravitel'stva* SSSR 1 (1989).
14. *Ekonomicheskaya gazeta* 51 (1988).
15. *Nihon keizan sinbun* 24 Nov. 1988.
16. *Pravda,* 8 March 1987.
17. 1985 figures. Tatsuo Kaneda, *Soviet New Economic Policy and the Asian Economy* (1988).
18. *Ekonomicheskaya gazeta* 51 (1988).
19. *TASS,* 18 July 1988.

25
Gorbachev's Foreign Policy: A Diplomacy of Decline*

Stephen Sestanovich

Mikhail Gorbachev practices the diplomacy of the unexpected. His international maneuvering and high-pressure negotiating style put him in a long tradition of leaders who have pursued innovative foreign policies. Although, for example, Gorbachev would not ordinarily be compared with Egyptian President Anwar al-Sadat, there are striking similarities between the two:

> [Sadat's method was] to cut through trivia to the essential, to make major, even breathtaking, tactical concessions in return for an irreversible psychological momentum. . . . [T]he improvement he might have achieved by haggling would have been cosmetic or a bow to vanity. Wise statesmen know they will be measured by the historical process they set in motion, not by the debating points they score.[1]

Sadat's ploys seemed exceptionally skillful in their time, and the adulation he enjoyed in the West is very similar to the Gorbachev phenomenon today. Sadat was seen as a decisive statesman able—at a stroke—to change the terms of diplomatic debate, to push negotiating partners toward agreement, and to overcome old and fruitless animosities.

In retrospect, however, Sadat's achievements look a little different. What stands out most is not his ability to produce victory but to orchestrate retreat. The results of his diplomacy were politically sustainable at home primarily because, after more than two decades of overly ambitious, extremely costly, and largely failed foreign policy undertakings. Egyptian opinion was ready for a more modest international and even regional role.

Egypt, in other words, was in decline, and Sadat's policy was both a recognition of and a response to this reality. He seemed so successful in large part because he wanted so much less. There were, to be sure, concessions that he could not make: in sacrificing long-standing Egyptian goals, he had to be careful

Reprinted by permission of the author from *Problems of Communism*, XXXVII, 1, January 1988. An earlier version of this article was presented at the Aspen Institute's conference on US-Soviet relations, January 12–16, 1988.

not to inflame domestic controversy or tempt foreign adversaries to exploit his interest in accommodation. In principle, these constraints were real. In practice, however, they did not materially slow Sadat's drive for retrenchment. Nor did they oblige his successor to restore the earlier activism and futile ambition of Egyptian foreign policy.[2]

Other leaders have taken a similar route, even when adapting to much more transient downturns in national fortunes. Certainly, Richard Nixon's and Henry Kissinger's policies—withdrawal from Vietnam, plus détente with both China and the Soviet Union—followed roughly the same strategic outline. Their aim was to make diplomatic maneuvering carry more of the weight of American strategy, because domestic support for other instruments of foreign policy (above all, military force and covert action) was waning. On balance, Nixon and Kissinger were less successful than Sadat had been, both in preserving a consensus at home and in discouraging others from trying to take advantage of US weakness.[3]

Is Gorbachev also practicing a diplomacy of decline? It may seem odd even to ask this question about a leader who has evoked such worldwide acclaim and whose manipulative gifts (whether in public or in private) are hardly open to doubt. Yet decline is not the same thing as collapse, nor does it have to mean one sharp setback after another. And, as the example of Sadat suggests, it is not inconsistent with major policy innovations. The pace of decline can be slow and irregular, and clever policies can do a great deal to conceal its extent—from adversaries, from allies and clients, and from domestic audiences alike. Beneath the best camouflage tactics, however, the features of decline will be visible: a deterioration in the elements of national strength, diminished effectiveness in applying that strength to the pursuit of national goals, a recasting of those goals to make them more modest and attainable, and a careful reinterpretation of the international environment to make it appear less threatening.[4]

SOVIET CRITICISMS OF PAST POLICY

There is considerable evidence that Gorbachev views his own predicament in these terms—as a search for ways of dealing with decline. His foreign policy has been decisively shaped by the fact that he inherited both an extremely daunting domestic agenda and a record of recent diplomatic reverses. It was the combination of the two that mattered: neither half of this inheritance would by itself have required the same kind of policy review.

Gorbachev is not alone in his reading of the Soviet Union's situation; it appears to be shared by the entire group of leaders that came to power with the passing of the Brezhnev generation. The members of this group have given unprecedented public expression to the pessimistic frame of mind in which they approach their foreign policy dilemmas. In a pair of speeches in mid-1987, for example, Foreign Minister Eduard Shevardnadze told officials of his own ministry: *"Beyond the borders of the Soviet Union, you and I represent a great country that in the last 15 years has more and more been losing its position as one of the leading industrially developed nations.*"[5] Unless the decay of its power base is reversed, he observed, the Soviet Union will be *"unable to participate on equal terms in the competitive political struggle over the attractiveness of our social-economic model of development."*[6] The Politburo's "second secretary," Yegor Ligachev, has sometimes tried to rein in his colleagues' criticisms of past internal policies, but in the realm of foreign policy, he too has acknowledged that under Leonid Brezhnev "the USSR's international prestige declined."[7]

What Shevardnadze called "the backwardness of our power and gradual loss of position" has not been ascribed by him or other members of the leadership exclusively to the weakness of the Soviet domestic economy. He has in fact made precisely the opposite connection as well: the wasteful use of scarce resources in foreign policy undertakings has become a burden at home. *"[W]e frequently cooperated in and at times even provoked enormous material investments in hopeless foreign policy projects and tacitly encouraged actions that in a direct and indirect sense have cost the people dearly even to this day."*[8] Shevardnadze's most scathing charge has been that Soviet foreign policy was conducted "out of touch with the fundamental vital interests of the country."[9] Similarly, in his November 2, 1987, speech on the 70th anniversary of the Bolshevik Revolution, Gorbachev himself (while clearly tilting in Ligachev's direction on many domestic questions) spoke of Soviet foreign policy "errors," of failures "to make use of opportunities that were opening up", of reactions to Western policy that were "not always adequate."[10]

These complaints were admittedly very general. Lower-ranking officials have zeroed in on specific instances of poor policy. Among military and diplomatic issues, some have implied that the decision to deploy SS-20 missiles against Western Europe was counterproductive; others, that the subsequent Soviet "war-scare" campaign to prevent NATO missile deployments was a mistake; still others, that past Soviet policy toward Japan and China was unnecessarily rigid.[11] Similar errors have been identified in international economic policy—in particular, the failure to increase exports of items other than raw materials. One high-level official has recently complained about the Soviet Union's standing in the global economy at the start of the 1980's: *"We were in no way able to exceed 4 percent of world trade. That is to say, we had become a great industrial power and accounted for 20 percent of world output, and yet in this sphere, we have been unable to become a big foreign trade power."*[12]

Such statements by members of the new leadership show that they came to office with a very critical appraisal of the Soviet Union's recent international record. Optimism—or even complacency—had no strong advocates within the Politburo. Yet a negative assessment did not by itself require immediate or radical adjustments in Soviet policy. Nor was it self-evident that adjustments, if made, would involve any narrowing of Soviet horizons. A new leadership might instead have been expected to fight decline through the infusion of additional resources, through better planning and coordination, through the reaffirmation of traditional goals, or even through mindless self-assertion. (This last possibility, in particular, was the forecast of those Western analysts who speculated that a "wounded Soviet bear" might lash out in the face of repeated failures.)[13]

Trying harder, making more efficient use of one's strengths—this is one way of reacting to the threat of decline; and some Soviet initiatives, in foreign and domestic policy alike, can be read as efforts of this kind. Wholesale changes of personnel, for example, may have been made in the belief that better management could ease Soviet difficulties.[14] Similarly, in trying to exploit diplomatic openings that were either ignored or bungled by Brezhnev and his foreign minister, Andrey Gromyko, Gorbachev may have believed that the Soviet Union's situation could be improved by merely reversing certain obviously mistaken decisions.

Such approaches represent the foreign policy analogues to the internal program often associated with Brezhnev's immediate successor, Yuriy Andropov: install new people, impose greater discipline, exploit underutilized "reserves." In individual instances, such measures can yield good results. As a broad response to crisis, however, they are likely to be inadequate. In coping with both domestic and foreign policy difficulties, the Soviet leadership confronts this dilemma: experimenting with halfway measures may only prolong decline. Averting deeper problems in the long term may be possible only by accepting setbacks in the short. The domestic version of this dilemma is familiar enough from Western—and Soviet—analyses of economic reforms: *perestroyka*'s success depends on taking steps whose initial results will be worse economic performance. An overhaul of enterprise management, introduction of up-to-date technology, reduction of the labor force—all these are likely to mean widespread confusion and poor results at the outset. To an economist, in fact, the absence of such turmoil would mean that serious changes were not really under way.[15]

Applied to relations with the outside world, this analogy suggests a choice between policy changes that minimize immediate disruptions and those that accept short-term setbacks. As will be argued below, this choice—and sometimes the inability to make it—is evident in both the conceptual and practical adjustments that Gorbachev has made in Soviet foreign policy.

PESSIMISM ABOUT THE FUTURE

The negative reading of the Soviet Union's position shared by Gorbachev and his colleagues is most vividly demonstrated by the extreme conceptual conclusions they have drawn from it. The "new thinking" that ostensibly guides today's policy does not openly call for a smaller Soviet role in the world, but it does incorporate the core elements of a strategy of retrenchment as it might be pursued by almost any great power. These include: a devaluation of ideological precepts, a more complacent assessment of outside threats, a re-examination of national interests and a heavier stress on global "common" interests, a cap on resource commitments, a search for less expensive policy instruments, a more flexible and less demanding stance in negotiations, an arms-length attitude toward friends in need and an insistence that they do more to help themselves, avoidance of actions that adversaries can treat as provocations, and so forth.

For Gorbachev, these elements of "new thinking" doubtless have several different purposes apart from coping with decline. They have served the new general secretary's need to put a personal stamp on policy; they have also increased his freedom of action in dealing with particular matters under international negotiation.[16] And, not least, they have had undeniable propaganda value in projecting a new face to the West. Yet none of these motives is as important as the broad substantive meaning of the themes of "new thinking" as described above: together, they rationalize lower expectations. They announce an "era of limits."

Perhaps the most significant part of the new leadership's efforts to impose such limits has been to question the principles on which past policy has been based. For example, Shevardnadze has said: "*We are people of ideas, but their power should not be put above considerations of common sense. Otherwise, in being completely subordinate to them, you lose many things, among them the ability to improve the economic condition of your own country and, in that manner, to increase the degree of its policial influence in the world.*"[17] To do better, in short, means freeing Soviet policy from ideological preconceptions and constraints.

The most pointed reshaping of dogma has been the move to revise the official view of capitalism, a shift that Gorbachev himself authorized in his speech observing the 70th anniversary of the revolution and then repeated in remarks to the Central Committee plenum on February 18, 1988. He posed the following "fundamental question": "*Is it possible at the present stage, given the interdependence and unity of the world at the end of the 20th century, to exert the kind of influence on the nature of imperialism that would block its most dangerous manifestations?*"[18]

In a bow to ideological orthodoxy, Gorbachev granted that capitalism could not "become 'good'," but he nevertheless made it clear that he envisioned the checks on imperialist policies as coming from within. By suggesting that imperialism was not incorrigibly aggressive, he implied that the Soviet Union might be able to devote less effort to the East-West competition. (To paraphrase another leader who wanted to cut the costs of competing, Gorbachev appeared to mean that the Soviet Union can safely consider putting aside its "inordinate fear of capitalism.")[19] One important adviser, Yevgeniy Primakov, has put this same point slightly differently:

Comparatively recently we considered peaceful coexistence a respite that would be cut short by those who again would try to strangle the first country of victorious socialism. This situation also insistently dictated the requirement for an increase in military effectiveness, once again as virtually the only means of ensuring the country's security. . . . Today such assessments and interpretations are clearly insufficient and inaccurate.[20]

This conclusion, like Gorbachev's, nicely served the main practical goal of the "new thinking" as stated by Shevardnadze: belt-tightening to limit the burden of achieving Soviet external goals. "The main thing," the foreign minister announced last year, "is that the country not bear additional expenses in connection with the need to maintain its defense capability and protect its legitimate foreign policy interests."[21] To announce budget austerity is one thing; to enforce it on an unenthusiastic bureaucracy, quite another. Doing so is obviously far easier if these "legitimate foreign policy interests" are themselves subjected to closer scrutiny, and Soviet statements have begun to suggest such a re-examination. (American analysts of what Samuel Huntington has called the "Lippmann gap" have launched a similar effort.)[22] The now-familiar phrase that Gorbachev has put forward to describe how nations should deal with each other—by seeking a "balance of interests"—connotes more than just being, as he puts it, "ready for compromise."[23] Beyond new bargaining tactics and a less rigid style, setting a "balance of interests" as a goal raises the more fundamental possibility that some traditional Soviet interests can be sacrificed. In discussing the need to make concessions, for example, Aleksandr Bovin has claimed that even the most vital international interests are essentially arbitrary:

> Compromise is the air without which constructive policy will choke. . . . Of course, each partner has a limit for concessions determined by the supreme interests of state security and commitments to allies. But to a significant extent *this limit is subjective*. It is determined not by interest "in itself," but by precisely how a given interest is understood and formulated.[24]

Viewed in this way, "state security and commitments to allies" lose their status as near-absolutes. Other, more authoritative, statements than Bovin's have suggested that these objectives are to be treated more flexibly in the future. Soviet doctrinal discussions aimed at limiting, among other things, military costs have been well studied by Western analysts.[25] The same pattern can be seen in Soviet discussions of the needs of allies, whose claims to assistance are for the most part judged quite harshly—even by once-sympathetic writers.[26] Statements by members of the top party leadership do not formulate dissatisfaction with imperial burdens quite so bluntly. Nevertheless, while expressing support for Third World regimes under pressure, Gorbachev has chosen to do so in a thoroughly conservative phrase—what he calls the right to the "social status quo."[27]

Certain Soviet officials have pushed "new thinking" outlandishly far. One should keep in mind that in the age of *glasnost'*, many statements, even by those in high positions, are probably not authoritative. Embellishing the idea that competing national interests can be reconciled, for example, Georgiy Shakhnazarov (since 1986, first deputy chief of the Central Committee department for bloc relations) has written about the possibility of "world government"[28] But in this he has gone only slightly farther than his superiors. At the United Nations General Assembly session last September, Shevardnadze himself made the extraordinary statement that the Soviet Union sought a world in which peace was ensured "exclusively" by the UN and its Security Council.[29]

It is hard to take seriously formulations that announce the virtual "demobilization" of Soviet foreign policy. But to dismiss them is to miss their deeper function: the "new thinking" explains the reverses and costs incurred in the course of innovation and experimentation. It provides evidence, moreover, that in foreign policy as in domestic, Gorbachev believes that the only way to improve long-term Soviet prospects is to weather reverses in the short term. Of course, radical adjustments are only a part of the story. In implementing them, Soviet policy-makers may be continually tempted to try to minimize the practical costs of a full break with past policy.[30] As with economic reform, the reluctance to make such a break is one among many reasons why performance may simply continue to decline. A review of Gorbachev's innovations in the most important areas of policy—relations with the United States, with US friends and allies, with Soviet Third World clients—reveals the difficulties he faces in trying to put Soviet foreign policy on a sounder long-term footing.

AFGHANISTAN

The Soviet war effort in Afghanistan has emerged as the outstanding example of failure and retreat under Gorbachev. At the February 1988 Central Committee plenum, he declared that the leadership had in April 1985, at the very outset of his tenure, conducted a review of the problem and put policy on a new course.[31] Despite this claim of a slowly unfolding strategy, the available evidence suggests something different. The policies that followed this alleged review indicate that the Politburo really wanted to explore whether better results could be obtained by more sophisticated and active management. The leadership appeared, in particular, to hope for three kinds of improvement: first, that new figures at the top would invigorate the Afghan communist party and increase its popular appeal; second, that better military tactics would obviate the need to deploy more Soviet combat troops; and third, that internal pressures in Pakistan and divisions among Pakistan, the United States, and the Afghan resistance would permit a negotiated solution on terms advantageous to the Soviet Union.[32]

Like other Soviet efforts to squeeze better results from previously unused "reserves," Gorbachev's attempt to do so in Afghanistan failed. The replacement of Babrak Karmal by Najibullah in May 1986 only increased the number of factions vying to control the People's Democratic Party of Afghanistan (PDPA); it did little to "broaden the base" of the regime. Greater emphasis on small-unit military operations could not match the effect of increased Western aid to the resistance. Soviet forces began to do worse, not better, and it became harder than ever to envision a military turnaround. Finally, the underlying unity of purpose between the United States and Pakistan was preserved despite occasional public differences over how to respond to Soviet overtures.

Against this background of failed halfway measures, Gorbachev's declaration of February 8, 1988, in which he announced Soviet willingness to begin troop withdrawals on May 15, was an ingenious attempt to seize the diplomatic initiative.[33] It showed obvious parallels to his handling of the INF negotiations in 1987: in both instances, a rapid pace was designed to carry the other parties along despite hesitations. His move succeeded briefly in casting Pakistan as an obstacle to a political solution, and won an official US acknowledgment (from Secretary of State George Shultz) that Gorbachev sincerely wanted to end the war.[34]

These were fleeting advantages, however. Soviet pressure tactics did not succeed in changing the underlying bargaining situation. Neither the US or Pakistani governments, nor the resistance appeared to believe that the February 8th statement represented Moscow's final offer. In fact, all were so confident of Soviet weakness that over the next two months they raised rather than lowered their demands.[35] When, on April 6, 1988, Gorbachev traveled to Tashkent to meet with Najibullah, it was to announce withdrawal of Soviet troops without the proviso that the flow of American military materiel to the Afghan resistance be stemmed—a demand that Soviet spokesmen had for years identified as the essential precondition for withdrawal.

RESTORING DÉTENTE WITH THE US

It is not surprising that Gorbachev has sought to limit the damage from the retreat in Afghanistan by creating a broad improvement in East-West relations. Since the beginning of the cold war, periods of high East-West tension (and of policy failure by one side or the other) have invariably been followed by a decompression in political and military relations. The Berlin blockade, the formation of NATO, and the Korean War were followed in the mid-1950's by a renewal of Big Four summitry, agreement on the partition of Vietnam, the neutralization of Austria, and the first significant arms control negotiations. Another period of tension over Berlin and then over Cuba was followed by the conclusion of the Limited Test Ban Treaty in 1963 and Khrushchev's pursuit (before his ouster) of a bargain on Germany. With the winding down of the Vietnam war came the détente of the early 1970's, which yielded the SALT I agreements and a partial stabilization of the Central European order (as reflected in the Berlin agreement of 1971, recognition of the two German states, and the Helsinki Final Act of 1975).

These precedents suggest that Gorbachev, coming to power against the very difficult background of NATO's INF deployments and the war in Afghanistan, was highly likely to pursue a détente with the United States. The real issue was less whether he would do so, than how and on what terms. How would he seek to

create a calmer environment without provoking an escalation of Western demands, particularly as the Soviets' estimate of their own weakness (and their
domestic preoccupations), became clear?

Two factors simplified Gorbachev's task: the snarling style of Brezhnev,
Andropov, and Gromyko in the early 1980's made him seem less menacing
abroad, and crucial Soviet policy decisions—to call off the "war-scare" propaganda campaign and to end the boycott of arms talks with the United States—had
been made before he even took office.[36] But if the Soviet leadership had decided
under Konstantin Chernenko to resume negotiations, it fell to Gorbachev to
decide *how* to negotiate. In doing so, he elaborated two different approaches,
which might be called the "Reykjavik" and "Geneva" styles. He experimented
with diplomatic brinkmanship—the pattern made famous at Reykjavik—in
which the Soviet side pushes to the edge of a dramatic deal, either to extract
American concessions that would otherwise be unthinkable or to cast the United
States as the obstacle to arms control. At other times, however, Gorbachev put
into practice a more conciliatory, business-as-usual style, in which differences
between the two sides are fudged and big disagreements are put to one side for
the sake of incremental progress.[37]

Reykjavik-style brinkmanship frames a large, stark choice—forcing the United States to choose either a big breakthrough or a tense stalemate; the Geneva
style nurtures the diplomatic momentum that can put a deal over the top. Soviet
alternation between the two approaches reflects the inadequacies of each. The
Reykjavik style has sometimes left Soviet positions looking extortionist and
unreasonable; as such it risks a return to Brezhnev-era isolation. The Geneva
style runs a different risk: its steady backtracking conveys an impression of
exploitable weakness.

Given these limitations, the most striking feature of recent Soviet policy has
been the near-total dominance of the Geneva style. This was clearest in the
stream of Soviet concessions of INF during the first half of 1987, and after that in
the steady weakening of demands for restrictions on US strategic defense programs.[38] The Geneva style was also evident in Soviet handling of lesser arms
control issues. In early 1987 Gorbachev called off his long, futile nuclear-testing
moratorium (a Reykjavik-style ploy that Western governments had more or less
ignored), and accepted an American formula to discuss verification measures
that would permit ratification of the treaties on a threshold test ban and on
peaceful nuclear explosions that had been negotiated in the 1970's. Gorbachev
also made incrementalism his watchword on issues other than arms control. The
Washington summit of December 1987 was preceded by a new round of releases
of political prisoners and refuseniks, by increased Jewish emigration, and by
small concessions on Afghanistan—steps designed to soften Gorbachev's reception in the United States by showing steady movement on issues where Soviet
policy was most damagingly on the defensive.

This innovative and flexible style was part of a broader effort to change the
Soviet Union's image and standing in world affairs. Gorbachev has frequently

said that he aims to erase the Western image of a "Soviet threat," which he claims has sustained the entire repertoire of anti-soviet policies since the days of the cold war.[39] Successfully casting the Soviet Union as a "normal" participant in international politics would certainly reduce demands made on the Soviet Union by other states, and the Soviets themselves now treat progress toward this goal as a mark of the practical success of "new thinking." In this spirit, Primakov has written: *"The situation today is far from what it was two or three years ago. It is becoming more and more difficult for anti-Sovieteers in the West to maintain their artificially created image of the USSR as a bellicose, undemocratic state that threatens the West and thinks about nothing but expansion."*[40]

The practical meaning of this change, however, remains in doubt. While the old image of the Soviet Union softens, what has come to be called the "agenda" of US-Soviet relations is essentially unaltered: it is a list of American demands for change in Soviet policies and conduct across the board.[41] The constant repetition of these demands on two issues in particular—human rights and Afghanistan—was one of the hallmarks of Gorbachev's meetings with representatives of the American elite.[42] Moreover, in responding to US demands, Soviet officials have betrayed some anxiety about the impression left by their conciliatory approach as a whole. For this reason they have tried to deflect attention from their concessions and even to deny that they made any in the first place. Yuliy Vorontsov, the first deputy foreign minister, insisted, for example, that letting Americans observers visit the Krasnoyarsk radar site was nothing more than a "concession to reason and logic."[43] When Gorbachev changed the Soviet position by cutting Soviet INF missiles in Asia to zero, Georgiy Arbatov declared: "We did not give in to the United States—we gave in to common sense."[44] Shevardnadze himself, after his quickly scheduled October trip to Washington, in which he had to undo Gorbachev's refusal to hold a summit, claimed that "everybody has won."[45] And at the signing of the INF treaty, Gorbachev repeated that Soviet concessions had been made only to "reason."[46] These protestations suggest that Soviet officials feel their reputation for bargaining toughness has suffered.[47]

Gorbachev has successfully created the détente that his own negative assessment of the Soviet Union's situation clearly required. This more tranquil relationship, however, continues to be built around a set of American demands for Soviet concessions. In this sense, Gorbachev has not yet managed to "restructure" US-Soviet relations.

OPENINGS TO US ALLIES: EUROPE

The principal benefits to the Soviet Union of détente with the United States may, of course, be reaped elsewhere in the world rather than in relations between the superpowers themselves. It has been a long-standing Soviet objective to weaken the American presence in Europe and Asia, and the writings of Gorbachev's advisers (in particular those of Aleksandr Yakovlev) express strong interest in exploiting what they see as latent conflicts between the United States and its allies over political, economic, and military issues. Gorbachev's own statements suggest that he subscribes to this view—with the crucial stipulation that such fissures can best be widened in an atmosphere of low US-Soviet tensions. He has paid particular rhetorical attention to the theme of a European "common home"—a formula that inevitably casts the United States as an outsider in European affairs.[48] Similarly, his July 1986 speech in Vladivostok portrayed the Soviet Union as an Asian power sharing many interests in economic development with its neighbors in the Far East.[49]

One Central Committee foreign policy specialist recently looked back on 1987 as the "Year of Europe" in Soviet diplomacy.[50] The label makes some sense, given the prominence of the INF issue in the last year. The debate over this treaty—together with the aftershocks of the Reykjavik summit—led to a debate about the reliability and desirability of Western Europe's American connection. Successive Soviet proposals sought to follow this first step of nuclear reduction with others intended to lead to the complete "denuclearization" of Europe—in other words, to the removal of the weapons that are at the heart of the US guarantee of West European security.[51]

It was unquestionably a large Soviet achievement to place this issue on the agenda, but doing so had the simultaneous effect of reintroducing new difficulties into relations with those West European states that feel Gorbachev's program is aimed against them. Britain and France (admittedly, each with a distinctive emphasis and not always in agreement with each other) have now aligned themselves as the likely opposition to Soviet initiatives. It was Mrs. Thatcher who said during Gorbachev's stopover on his way to the Washington summit that "there is no scope for further [nuclear] reductions in Europe" until Western concerns about the existing imbalances in conventional and chemical weapons are addressed; President Reagan repeated the same formula a week later after the conclusion of the summit.[52] British Foreign Secretary Sir Geoffrey Howe followed up with an unusualy blunt (and doubtless somewhat ill-received) message during his visits to Moscow in February 1988. "It is easy to see," he said to his hosts, "why you should want *perestroyka* to succeed. It is not so obvious why the West should want it to work."[53] Small wonder, then, that Great Britain has been described in *Pravda* as "the pacesetter in a buildup of tensions."[54]

The cost for Soviet policy in this trend is not the discomfort of a frank toast at a Kremlin dinner. It is the reassertion of a diplomatic pattern in which the West sets stiff preconditions for better relations—preconditions that can only be met by continuing Soviet concessions. The potential exception to this pattern is, of course, the Federal Republic of Germany. After several years in which Soviet relations with the FRG were worse than with any major Western power, the second half of 1987 brought many signs of improvement between Bonn and Moscow. The long-deferred homecoming visit by Erich Honecker, head of the East German party, was held at last; a West German credit of one billion deutsche mark for the Soviet Union was announced; Chancellor Kohl offered a key INF concession (on dismantlement of Pershing IA's), for which the Soviets effusively expressed their thanks; visits to Moscow by Franz-Josef Strauss (Chancellor Kohl's most formidable conservative critic) and Lothar Spaeth (a possible successor) provided firm approval from the right for a bilateral rapprochement; and, finally, Shevardnadze visited Bonn in January 1988, and left the expectation that Gorbachev would not be far behind.

Soviet attention to West Germany, which aims to kindle neutralism in the most important European member of NATO, clearly has hope of paying real dividends. In the foreseeble future the Federal Republic will not, like Britain and France, put itself to the right of the United States on East-West security issues. During Shevardnadze's visit, Foreign Minister Hans-Dietrich Genscher expressed an apparent national consensus in saying that he hoped to "turn a new page in Soviet–West German relations and fill it with a qualitatively new content."[55]

Yet the hope of putting distance between Germany and the United States remains far from realized.[56] And one element in the new détente as it has taken shape with the Federal Republic is plainly undesirable from Moscow's point of view. The new open and accommodating Soviet style seems to encourage Western governments to make demands of Moscow that at an earlier time would have seemed pointlessly farfetched. In West Germany, for example, there is increased attention to the underlying and unresolved division of Europe, an issue that the 1970's détente was supposed to have made less contentious (and certainly less salient). In today's improved atmosphere, the issue of the division of Europe has received more prominence than it has in many years. As one sign of this, both Kohl and Reagan made the Berlin Wall a significant rhetorical theme in 1987. And even Genscher, while greeting the visiting Shevardnadze with hopes for better relations, referred to the division of Europe: "*We must not look at the partition of Europe as an immutable fact but must overcome it. . . . [The common European home] must be a home in which doors do not bar but open up the way to each other.*"[57] It would have been easy to embrace this sentiment, but Shevardnadze did not do so. His reply showed that the détente sought by the Soviet Union is one that supports the status quo, not one that transforms it. "Everything," he said, "can and should stay as it is."[58] Whether a European détente can be constructed on these terms remains open to question.

OPENINGS TO US FRIENDS: EAST ASIA

In East Asia, a more flexible and experimental approach to Japan would appear to be one of the most obvious innovations to be explored by a bold new Soviet leadership. Instead, Soviet policy toward Japan has remained in extremely old grooves. A much-rumored Gorbachev visit to Tokyo in 1987 was postponed, no progress was made in finding a way around the issue of the disputed "Northern Territories," Japanese reservations continued to obstruct major investment in

Siberian development (an area of special interest to the Soviet leadership, as Gorbachev had underscored at Vladivostok), and although imports from Japan dropped by over 20 percent, the Soviet bilaterial trade deficit remained (along with the imbalance in trade with the US) the largest deficit with any country of the West.[59] For now, Gorbachev's strategy is based on a hope that if Japan sees a broad East-West détente taking shape, it wil drop its most extreme demands for Soviet concessions. This hope has so far proven unfounded and, as a policy position, it is hardly innovative. It is the same approach taken (unsuccessfully) by Gorbachev's predecessors.

By contrast, Soviet officials have begun to depict policy toward China as a major success. Certainly, there have been more superficial signs of change in Sino-Soviet relations than in relations with Japan. Trade has increased—reportedly tenfold since the early 1980's—and an agreement has been signed to refurbish some of the plants and equipment provided to China by the Soviet Union in the 1950's. On political issues, border talks have been spurred forward by a key Soviet concession in 1986; and technical teams have been meeting in 1988 to develop a common map of the border. The Soviets also showed their responsiveness to Chinese security concerns by making a small reduction in their forces stationed in Mongolia. Soviet statements about China now manifest exceptional respect, emphasizing how much the world's future depends on the two giants of socialism. And Gorbachev has repeatedly expressed a personal desire for a Sino-Soviet summit meeting, presumably intended as vivid proof that the great schism is over.[60]

Soviet policy toward China is perhaps the supreme example of the incremental Geneva style. What is not clear is how much progress can be made without addressing the core issues of Sino-Soviet discord, and whether Gorbachev and his colleagues will be willing to extend the accommodating Geneva approach to questions like Cambodia. After political consultations in Beijing in October 1987, Soviet spokesmen acknowledged that there had been sharp disagreement on this issue.[61] They claim, moreover, that what the Chinese call "obstacles" to normal relations need not block progress in other areas. Gorbachev, for example, argued in his *Liaowang* interview against setting preconditions for a summit; some problems, he said, can only be solved at a summit, not before.[62]

The same Soviet official who spoke of the "Year of Europe" has boldly forecast that 1988 will be in effect the "Year of Asia."[63] Nevertheless, on neither continent can one see major breakthroughs as a result of Gorbachev's diplomacy. His focus on China, as on Germany, means a pursuit of benefits within the confines of the Geneva style, and an evasion of the more substantive demands that these governments continue to press upon him.

THE THIRD WORLD

It is now a familiar claim, for which there is no shortage of evidence, that the Soviet Union has reassessed the diplomatic and political opportunities available to it in the Third World.[64] Even before the advent of "new thinking," the leadership appeared dissatisfied with both the risks to be run and the resources to be committed in the name of preserving the client network acquired in the late 1970's, the heyday of Soviet Third-World activism. Accordingly, Soviet clients have been assigned a lower ideological status; Soviet complaints about the clients' use of aid have become routine; and Soviet diplomats are more aware that exploiting every possible opening in the Third World means paying a price in East-West relations.

As in other areas of policy, a negative diagnosis hardly means Soviet passivity in the Third World. Aid to most radical clients has remained at high levels; and to Leninist regimes under acute insurgent pressure, it has increased steadily. While trying to protect clients from being overthrown, the Soviets have also opened a second front in the Third World: closer relations have been actively pursued with many states once written off as American lackeys.

One sign of this new interest was Gorbachev's praise in his 70th anniversary speech of regional organizations like ASEAN and even of the Islamic Conference—groupings that have not been notably friendly to the Soviet Union and that in Marxist terms could best be described as "bourgeois" and "feudal" respectively.[65] (The reference in Gorbachev's speech was especially striking in light of his failure to make any mention at all of "socialist" allies in the Third World). This courtship goes beyond mere talk. The Soviets have, for example, used small but well-timed trade deals to make a political point, offering to make commodity purchases at above-market prices from states whose access to the US market has been cut (rice from Thailand, sugar from Costa Rica and the Dominican Republic).[66] With Thailand, there is also talk of possible "military cooperation."[67]

Most significant, the Soviet Union has experimented with developing good ties to both sides of certain Third-World regional conflicts—potentially a very formidable innovation in Soviet diplomacy, which has generally been limited to cooperative relations with one side only. Moscow has launched diplomatic probes of Israeli and Iranian interest in putting aside past hostility. With both states, diplomatic channels have been activated. Although the nominal agenda has usually been narrow (with Israel, emigration and other "consular" matters; with Iran, trade), the Soviet role as the largest military backer of their respective enemies has given the exchanges added importance. Soviet success in blocking a UN Security Council call for an arms embargo of Iran has been a further source of potential influence.

Despite such experimentation, however, crucial difficulties have continued to dog Soviet Third World policy. First, being on both sides of conflicts has so far produced more new problems than new leverage. In the Middle East and Persian Gulf, Arab governments protested that the Soviet Union had abandoned their cause in favor of Zionism and Iranian fundamentalism.[68] And both Israel and Iran have recently delivered rebuffs to Soviet overtures: Israel, by scuttling plans for an international peace conference; Iran, by besieging Soviet diplomatic establishments.[69] In Southeast Asia, even while exploring new formulas for talks on

Cambodia, the governments that make up ASEAN have maintained a strong common position against Vietnam and have reined in members that stray from it.

Second, although the United States has applied the "Reagan Doctrine" very unevenly, a few Soviet clients face severe and growing military troubles. Apart from Afghanistan (discussed above), both the Vietnamese and Angolan regimes also appear unable to achieve military victories over the insurgencies they face. One Soviet diplomat has been quoted as saying that Vietnam's burden in Cambodia is "simply intolerable."[70] As for Angola, a large and costly offensive by the Soviet-backed Luanda government in the fall of 1987 again failed to break through UNITA positions.[71]

Soviet Third-World policy has also become stalled in the economic area. Despite pressures from Moscow to use aid more efficiently, both Cuba and Vietnam remain a large drain on Soviet resources. Soviet policy-makers may have hoped that expanded trade with more successful developing economies might somehow counter this drain, but the results have been very meager.[72] Soviet commercial relations with Third World states are likely to add little or nothing to the success of Gorbachev's economic reforms. Indeed, the link between these two may be exactly opposite: trade wil not expand by much until the Soviets have more to sell abroad—that is, until economic reform succeeds at home.

Soviet policy in the Third World is obviously becoming more diversified, but as yet not more successful. Moreover, in contrast to the 1970's, these efforts seem unlikely to contribute very much toward improving the Soviet position in the East-West balance of power.

DEFEAT OR DECLINE?

The same analysis made here of difficulties in Soviet policy toward the West, China, and the Third World could be extended to other areas. The Soviet position in the international economy, for example, has steadily deteriorated in recent years; energy prices fell during the mid-1980's, and imports from the West contracted.[73] In the process, an important Soviet policy tool—not only for economic reconstruction at home but also for the pursuit of more "normal" relations with both Western and Third World states—was blunted.

Relations with the bloc states of Eastern Europe have also become more difficult. Gorbachev and his colleagues are in the odd position of urging perestroyka-style reforms on bloc governments, while at the same time proclaiming the right of all socialist states to make their own choices. The latter message has to date helped Eastern European leaderships to defy Gorbachev.[74] In time, however, the former message may encourage the peoples of Eastern Europe to defy their leaderships, with less fear of Soviet intervention.[75] In any event, Moscow's control over political developments within its own bloc will have been eroded.

In these, as in the other areas of policy that have been examined here, the extent of decline obviously depends on the goals against which Soviet policy is to be measured. The more it is measured against the goals that guided it in the 1970's and early 1980's, the more easily one can say that it has fallen short of the mark. Pursuit of military encirclement of China, for example, has done little to make Beijing—or other governments of East Asia—more responsive to Soviet preferences or open to specific Soviet initiatives. And the cost of sticking to old policies may actually be increasing. In the case of China, the goal of military encirclement probably argues for protecting the Soviet relationship with Vietnam at almost any cost; yet, doing so stunts relations with the new Chinese leadership at the very moment when its policies are most open to re-examination. By the same token, trying to continue business-as-usual in Eastern Europe may defer a real restructuring of East-West relations in an area—NATO's Central Front—where competing is most expensive for the USSR.

Only in relation to new goals does Soviet policy seem likely to do better, and it is for this reason that Gorbachev—like Sadat—has experimented with innovative approaches. Yet, asserting different goals hardly averts all the problems of decline, for the transition to new policies involves heavy costs, and in some instances even major defeats. Serious setbacks, and the turmoil that goes with them, are inherent in truly changing Soviet relations with the outside world. "New thinking" tries to make these setbacks more bearable; it cannot wish them out of existence.

If the Soviet leadership has to choose between defeats and decline, many of its members will be reluctant to make the choice cleanly, or soon. They will almost certainly seek to blur it, and will be able to adduce seemingly good reasons for doing so. They will doubtless acknowledge the need to correct the worst errors of the past, while trying to minimize the negative impact of a new course on Soviet standing in the world. They will argue—correctly—that Soviet flexibility has simply encouraged some adversaries to make more demands.

If this line of thought prevails within the Soviet leadership over the next several years, it will often be extremely difficult to say with confidence where Soviet policy is heading. Yet Gorbachev has demonstrated a preference for clean breaks so often that a more radical foreign policy line—one that accepts the heavy costs of a new course—can hardly be ruled out. In defending such a line, Gorbachev will presumably argue that much of the weakness of Soviet diplomacy stems from the desire to have it both ways and that only the retrenchment he advocates can mark out a path to future success. Once a new course is fully implemented, however, his position will be different—and more exposed. Gorbachev will then have to show that the "new thinking" and the diplomacy he has practiced with such skill do not merely point the way to continuing decline.

NOTES

1. Henry Kissinger, *Years of Upheaval* (Boston: Little, Brown, 1982), pp. 642–43. Admittedly Gorbachev's recent performances (especially with the Western media) show him eager to score debating points too.

2. It was widely argued after Sadat's assassination in 1981 that he had enjoyed little real popular support. His foreign policy, however, obviously had strong roots and remains largely in place under Hosni Mubarak—even though Mubarak shuns the global showmanship that served as an additional prop for Sadat's diplomacy.

3. I have elaborated the comparison between Gorbachev's and Nixon's strategies more fully in "What Gorbachev Wants," *The New Republic* (Washington, DC), May 25, 1987.

4. The theme of great-power "decline" has been made especially current by Paul Kennedy's new work, *The Rise and Fall of the Great Powers: Economic Change and Military Conflict from 1500 to 2000* (New York: Random House, 1987). Kennedy, who treats American policy in far greater depth than Soviet policy, measures decline in somewhat narrower terms than are used in this essay. He focuses on military power and its economic base, giving less attention to the nature of a state's diplomatic goals and to the overall effectiveness of its policy in attaining them.

5. "At the Ministry of Foreign Affairs of the USSR: Speech by E.A. Shevardnadze, June 27, 1987," in *Vestnik Ministerstva Inostrannykh Del SSSR* (Moscow—hereafter, *VMID*), no. 2 (Aug. 26, 1987), p. 31.

6. "An Unconditioned Requirement—Turn to Face the Economy," Shevardnadze speech of July 4, 1987, in *VMID*, no. 3 (Sept. 10, 1987).

7. *Uchitel'skaya Gazeta* (Moscow), Aug. 27, 1987, in Foreign Broadcast Information Service, *Daily Report: Soviet Union* (Washington, DC—hereafter, *FBIS-SOV*), Aug. 28, 1987, p. 23. In the same passage, Ligachev also quoted a remark by Lenin that Gorbachev has frequently used, that in the past revolutionary parties have perished because they were afraid to confront their weaknesses. Unwillingness to do so, said Ligachev, meant that "danger loomed over" the CPSU.

8. *VMID*, no. 2 (1987), p. 31.

9. Ibid.

10. *Pravda* (Moscow), Nov. 2, 1987, p. 2.

11. For the views of Deputy Foreign Minister Aleksandr Bessmertnykh, see *New Times* (Moscow), no. 46, Nov. 23, 1987; also "Moscow Aide Doubts SS-20 Decision," *The Washington Post*, Nov. 21, 1987. For comments by Valentin Falin, head of Novosti press agency, see *FBIS-SOV*, Dec. 22, 1987, p. 11. See also the comments by arms control negotiator V. Karpov and *Izvestiya* political observer A. Bovin in *FBIS-SOV*, Apr. 12, 1988, pp. 6–13.

12. Comment by Chairman of the State Economic Commission Ivan Ivanov during a Moscow Television roundtable program on Feb. 10, 1988, in *FBISO-SOV*, Feb. 18, 1988, p. 82. Ivanov may have put the case too positively. Paul Kennedy, while pointing out the obstacles to precise measurement, records the Soviet 1980 share of Gross World Product as 11.4 percent (down from 12.4 percent a decade earlier). See Kennedy, *Rise and Fall*, p. 436. For other comparisons, see Herbert Stein's analysis, "America Is Rich Enough to Be Strong," *The AEI Economist* (Washington, DC) (February 1988), pp. 2–3.

Some Soviet analysts seem to believe that economic noncompetitiveness puts Soviet great power status at stake. One economist, for example, has argued as follows: "Now that a military strategic equilibrium exists between East and West and encouraging progress has taken shape in disarmament, economic and technological forces will increasingly determine world status, the degree of influence of any country or region of the world on the development of international relations. The socialist countries, and first and foremost the Soviet Union, canot stand aloof from the objective process of the international division of labor, whether within or outside the framework of the socialist community." See "Not by Oil Alone" *Literaturnaya Gazeta* (Moscow), Feb. 10, 1988, in FBIS-SOV, Feb. 12, 1988, p. 70.

13. See, for example, Edward Luttwak: "[W]hen leaders are pessimistic about the long-term future of their regimes and at the same time have high confidence in the strength

and ability of their armed forces, then all that they know and all that they fear will conspire to induce them to use their military power while it still retains its presumed superiority." *The Grand Strategy of the Soviet Union* (New York: St. Martin's Press, 1983), p. 40.

14. To a new leadership team, the conduct of Soviet foreign policy (again, like domestic) perhaps appeared so unproductive that the mere shift to coherent, conscientious stewardship would yield better results. In exploring this possibility, Gorbachev and those who had risen to the top with him—all of whom had had little foreign policy experience— apparently believed that it would be a very large task to reorient the institutions of Soviet foreign and defense policy. It is hard to see any other explanation for the fact that, since 1985, outsiders of one sort or another have been appointed to head four of the five principal institutions that handle relations with the outside world: the ministries of foreign affairs, defense, and foreign trade; the Central Committee's International Department; and the KGB. This pattern contrasts with Gorbachev's restaffing of state institutions that handle domestic affairs, where he has usually promoted from within. [See Thane Gustafson and Dawn Mann, "Gorbachev's Next Gamble," *Problems of Communism* (Washington, DC) (July–August 1987), p. 18] In putting the foreign ministry under Eduard Shevardnadze's control, Gorbachev turned not to a diplomatic specialist but to a party official from outside Moscow, with a police background and a strong anti-corruption reputation. Ten of 12 deputy foreign ministers, more or less equivalent to American assistant secretaries of state, have also been replaced since 1985. Only one of these new appointees is an outsider like Shevardnadze, but he occupies the key post of deputy minister for personnel. In assigning Anatoliy Dobrynin to head the Central Committee's International Department, Gorbachev put the party's ideologues and Third World activists under a professional diplomat who does not possess the usual credentials in Marxism-Leninism. The top defense ministry posts went to relatively junior generals who are still outranked by many of their subordinates; and the foreign trade apparatus went to a party official. [See Dale Herspring "Gorbachev, Yazov, and the Military." *Problems of Communism* (July–August 1987), Philip Hanson, "Foreign Trade: The Restructuring of the Restructuring," *Radio Liberty Research Bulletin* (Munich), RL 58/88, Feb. 9, 1988.] Interestingly, only the KGB has retained control over its own personnel. Its top officials continue to come from within, and it has apparently prevented a change in oversight by the party apparatus: the only Central Committee department head not replaced under Gorbachev is Nikolay Savinkin, who, as head of the Administrative Organs department, has overseen military and police personnel since 1968. (I am indebted to Myron Rush for pointing this out as a measure of KGB autonomy).

15. For analyses along these lines, see Ed. A. Hewett, *Reforming the Soviet Economy: Equality versus Efficiency* (Washington, DC: Brookings Institution, 1988), also Jan Vanous, "Why Gorbachev Isn't Producing," *The Washington Post*, Apr. 3, 1988; and Richard E. Ericson, "The State Enterprise Law," *Harriman Institute Forum* (New York, Columbia University) 1, no. 2 (February 1988).

16. Gorbachev seems to approach politics a little pedantically—for him, solving a problem means identifying the one or two key concepts that are the root of the trouble and need to be changed. Once this is done, a program of practical measures can more easily be put in place. With regard to the Soviet economic downturn, for example, Gorbachev worked slowly to bring his colleagues to a common analysis of the problem's scope. Before joining the battle over the details of governmental decrees on questions like price reform, he first pushed the Central Committee to embrace the broad principles on which reform would be based.

Interestingly, in one of his speeches to the foreign ministry, Shevardnadze indicated that *glasnost'* was meant to have a similar effect in easing the shift to a new foreign policy. He complained that, in contrast to the bold exploration of Soviet domestic failures the media had not paid enough attention to past foreign policy mistakes. See *VMID*, no. 2 (1987), p. 33.

17. *VMID*, no 3 (1987), p. 4. The traditional claim that Soviet policies derive from "scientific analysis" meant that Marxist-Lennist ideology provided a way of avoiding mistakes; by contrasting it with common sense, Shevardnadze implied that ideology leads to mistakes.

18. *Pravda*, Feb. 19, 1988, p. 3.

19. *Public Papers of the Presidents of the United States: Jimmy Carter, 1977* (Washington, DC: US Government Printing Office, 1977), Vol. 1, p. 956.

20. *Pravda*, July 10, 1987. This claim was not much different, of course, from Khrushchev's assertion that nuclear war in not inevitable. Primakov virtually conceded that Gorbachev is trying to resell the same goods. In explaining why "new thinking" appeared only when Gorbachev became general secretary, he acknowledged that the East-West nuclear balance could not really explain its timing. The real explanation for its emergence was this: "Over the decade (1976–85) preceding the April plenary session, the gap in national income between the USSR and the USA not only did not decrease, it increased." In other words, the discovery that the Soviet Union was less likely to be attacked followed a period of growing American strength relative to the USSR. Earlier Soviet theoreticians, it seems safe to say, would have derided this idea.

Jack Snyder has made the interesting point that Gorbachev does not rely on the idea that a changing "correlation of forces" imposes restraint on capitalism ["The Gorbachev Revolution: A Waning of Soviet Expansionism?" *International Security* (Cambridge, MA) (Winter 1987–88), p. 1207. Primakov's analysis suggests that the "correlation" is still relevant—but that it is seen to be turning against the Soviet Union.

21. *VMID*, no. 2 (1987), p. 31.

22. See Samuel P. Huntington, "Coping with the Lippmann Gap," *Foreign Affairs—America and the World 1987/88* (New York) 66, no. 3 (1988); also James Chace, "A New Grand Strategy," *Foreign Policy* (Washington, DC) (Spring 1988).

23. Gorbachev and others have spoken frequently about the need to reconcile class interests with universal "human" interests, such as avoiding nuclear war and ecological disaster. (See, for example, the Feb. 25, 1988, *Pravda* editorial, "Hope Reborn.") By suggesting the subordination of proletarian goals, this theme may indicate the continuing downgrading of ideology. Such a process is not unimportant, but Gorbachev's formulation dodges (probably intentionally) the more pointed political issue: the other interests that the Soviets must come to terms with are not in fact those of all humanity but those of other nations. The phrase "balance of interests" comes closer to recognizing this fact, and therefore has more practical significance for Soviet policy than the theme of common "human" interests.

24. A. Bovin, "From the Art of War to the Art of Negotiations," *Izvestiya* (Moscow), June 4, 1987, p. 5. Emphasis added.

25. See Robert Legvold, "Gorbachev's New Approach to Conventional Arms Control," *Harriman Institute Forum* 1, no. 1 (January 1988); also Andrew C. Goldberg "The Present Turbulence in Soviet Military Doctrine," and Raymond L. Garthoff, "New Thinking in Soviet Military Doctrine," *Washington Quarterly* (Summer 1988).

26. Two widely noticed examples are Aleksandr Prokhanov, "A Writer's Opinion: Afghan Questions" *Literaturnaya Gazeta*, Feb. 17, 1988; and Boris Asoyan, "Africa: Not so Far Away," ibid., Oct. 7, 1987, p. 14. Both articles derided Soviet radical clients and past Soviet indulgence of them. The Prokhanov piece was especially significant, not only because it addressed the immediate and very sensitive Afghanistan policy issue, but because it (1) specified the Soviet groups and institutions responsible for the mistaken decision to invade, (2) said the Afghan communists themselves have abandoned their goals, thus freeing the Soviet Union from any obligation to help them, and (3) warned of a bitter public debate on the matter in the future.

27. Realities and Guarantees of a Secure World," *Pravda*, Sept. 17, 1987. Admit-

tedly, the Brezhnev Doctrine had a similar meaning, but it did not announce a general right to the status quo shared by non-socialist and socialist nations alike.

29. See TASS International Service in Russian, Sept. 23, 1987, in *FBIS-SOV*, Sept. 24, 1987, p. 8.

30. Shevardnadze has said, for example, that "the transitional period will abound in difficulties." Citing Gorbachev, he added that the goal must be to get through this period "as fast as possible and with the fewest losses." *VMID*, no. 3 (1987), p. 4.

31. *Pravda*, Feb. 19, 1988, in *FBIS-SOV*, Feb. 19, 1988, p. 56.

32. The evolution of Soviet diplomatic and military policies is surveyed by Don Oberdorfer, "Afghanistan: The Soviet Decision to Pull Out," *The Washington Post*, Apr. 17, 1988, p. A30.

33. *Pravda*, Feb. 9, 1988.

34. *The New York Times*, Feb. 24, 1988, p. A14.

35. For a discussion of Soviet efforts to limit the broader repercussions of withdrawal from Afghanistan, see "Kabul Crunch: Can Gorbachev Survive Defeat?" *The New Republic*, Apr. 18, 1988.

36. The United States and the Soviet Union agreed in January 1985 to resume negotiations on reductions in strategic and intermediate-range nuclear forces and on stragegic defense. The return to a more businesslike tone with the United States reflected Moscow's failure not only to prevent the INF deployments, but to derail US defense policies by inciting public pressure against them—rather than by negotiating. Soviet policy in the first half of the 1980's relied heavily on the Western peace movements as a potential substitute for real bargaining. The propaganda and pressure campaign against INF in 1983 was followed, for example, by a similar 1984 drive against testing anti-satellite weapons—and, more generally, against "the militarization of space." In the end, Moscow gained almost nothing from this approach.

37. This was the animating idea of the 1985 Geneva summit communiqué. In it, after having previously claimed that the Stragegic Defense Initiatve (SDI) was an obstacle to other agreements, Gorbachev waived insistence on linkage between separate arms control issues, and agreed to push forward in those areas where the two sides had already established "common ground."

38. Michael Gordon, "INF: A Hollow Victory?" *Foreign Policy* (Fall 1987), pp. 159–79.

39. Mikhail Gorbachev, *Perestroika: New Thinking for Our Country and the World* (New York: Harper & Row, 1987), pp. 148–49.

40. *Pravda*, July 10, 1987.

41. Soviet officials have increasingly sought to leave the impression that they have their own "agenda" of demands, but the effort has been somewhat unconvincing. A recent example is Shevardnadze's statement after his Moscow meeting with Shultz in late February 1988, in which he claimed that he had raised not only the familiar issues of homelessness and treatment of Indians but also the problem of wage discimination: "In particular we spoke about the fact that men and women are not paid the same for their work when they do identical jobs, and we cited statistics." *FBIS-SOV*, Feb. 24, 1988, p. 10.

42. Michael Mandelbaum analyzed this issue after the summit as follows: the general secretary's "angry response to a human-rights question during a meeting with American publishers, a response he later characterized as 'perhaps overemotional,' indicates that he is tired of hearing about it from Americans. But the summit should have made clear to him that, like it or not, he will continue to hear about human rights, and will need to make some concessions if he wants to make headway in his new dealings with the United States," *U.S. News & World Report* (Washington, DC), Dec. 21, 1987, p. 24.

43. See *FBIS-SOV*, Oct. 27, 1987, p. 31.

44. Interview on Tokyo Television (NHK), Sept. 18, 1987, in *FBIS-SOV*, Sept. 21, 1987, p. 1.

45. *Pravda*, Nov. 1, 1987.

46. *Pravda*, Dec. 9, 1987, p. 4.

47. When Gorbachev (in a brief outburst of the Reykjavik style) refused to set a summit date during his meeting with Secretary Shultz on October 23, 1987, the only question on the minds of American officials was reportedly how quickly the Soviets would back down.

48. The Soviets disclaim any thought of excluding the United States, and when it comes to European political-military negotiations, this would clearly be futile. Yet Gorbachev's rhetoric does aim to isolate the US by casting it at least as an alien cultural force in European affairs. "Sometimes," he writes, "one has the impression that the independent policies of West European nations have been abducted, that they are being carried off across the ocean; that national security interests are farmed out under the pretense of protecting security. A serious threat is hovering over European culture, too. The treat emanates from an onslaught of 'mass culture' from across the Atlantic. We understnad pretty well the concern of West European intellectuals. Indeed, one can only wonder that a deep, profoundly intelligent and inherently European culture is retreating to the background before the primitive revelry of violence and pronography and the flood of cheap feelings and low thoughts." *Perestroika: New Thinking for Our Country and the World*, p. 208.

49. *Speech by Mikhail Gorbachev in Vladivostok, July 28, 1986*, (Moscow: Novosti Press Agency Publishing House, 1986).

50. The speaker was Nikolay Shishin. See *FBIS-SOV*, Oct. 16, 1987, p. 20. Apparently no reference to Henry Kissinger's own failed "Year of Europe" was intended.

51. The Soviet campaign for "denuclearization" represents the application of the Reykjavik style to Europe. Yet Gorbachev appears to have miscalculated about European reactions to this style in the past. Having most likely assumed that West Europeans would condemn the US for rejecting his package of proposals at Reykjavik, Gorbachev found that instead they condemned President Reagan for considering it at all. The West Europeans prefer the Geneva style—incremental Soviet backtracking—and that is what conditional Western endorsements of his "denuclearization" proposals amount to: a demand for his other style.

52. Mrs. Thatcher's comments are reported in *The Washington Post*, Dec. 8, 1987; the President's speech at the Center for Strategic and International Studies, in *The New York Times*, Dec. 15, 1987.

53. *FBIS-SOV*, Feb. 16, 1988, p. 56.

54. *Pravda*, Feb. 19, 1988, p. 7.

55. *FBIS-SOV*, Jan. 19, 1988, p. 41.

56. Viewed from Moscow, the portents must seem evenly balanced: on the one hand, Genscher's support for further nuclear cuts in Central Europe; on the other, the unprecedented election of a West German hard-liner, Manfred Wörner, as Secretary General of NATO.

57. *FBIS-SOV*. Jan. 19, 1988, p. 44.

58. Ibid.

59. See *PlanEcon Report* (Washington, DC) IV, nos. 1–2 (Jan. 15, 1988), p. 6. The Soviet claim is that this trade drop is only "temporary." *Pravda*, Jan. 28, 1988, p. 5.

60. E.g., see *Liaowang* interview, published in *Pravda*, Jan. 11, 1988, p. 1.

61. *FBIS-SOV*, Oct. 16, 1987, p. 30.

62. *Pravda*, Jan. 11, 1988, p. 1.

63. *FBIS-SOV*, Oct. 16, 1987, p. 20.

64. This change is put in historical context by Francis Fukuyama in "Patterns of Soviet Third World Policy, *Problems of Communism* (September–October 1987).

65.   Gorbachev has attracted a stream of visiting leaders, some of whom would never have thought to visit the Soviet Union—or, in some cases, been invited—under his predecessors.

66.   Such Soviet purchases are, of course, far from unprecedented. In 1954, the Soviet Union bought Burma's rice crop when it found no buyers in the West; in 1960, when Cuba's sugar import quota was cut by the US, the Soviets quickly offered to buy the crop. See J. M. Mackintosh, *Strategy and Tactics of Soviet Foreign Policy*, (Oxford University Press, 1962), p. 303.

67.   *FBIS-SOV*, Mar. 3, 1988, p. 16.

68.   Foreign Minister Shevardnadze was obliged to describe claims of Soviet betrayal of the Arabs as "utterly fictitious," at a Washington press conference (*Pravda*, Oct. 25, 1987). Other Soviet officials are incessantly questioned on this subject. [See, for example, the interview given by Karen Brutents, one of Anatoliy Dobrynin's deputies, in *Al-Majallah* (London), Jan. 27–Feb. 2, 1988, in *FBIS-SOV*, Feb. 5, 1988, p. 25]. Questioning of Soviet reliability will only increase as a result of a recent claim by an Afghan resistance leader that the Soviets made an offer to Iran to reduce Soviet aid to Iraq in return for Iranian concessions on the Afghan issue (see *The Washington Post*, Mar. 23, 1987).

69.   In this light, the Soviets are no better positioned than in the past to put together a "double-Tashkent" formula in which they would be at the center of regional diplomacy. For a contrary view, see Robert Neumann, "Moscow's New Role as Mideast Broker," *The Washington Post, Outlook*, Oct. 25, 1987.

70.   Agence France Presse report by Pierre-Antoine Donnet in *FBIS-SOV*, Feb. 18, 1988, p. 30.

71.   See Bernard E. Trainor, "Angola Drive on the Rebels is Said to Fail," *The New York Times*, Nov. 22, 1987. Elsewhere in the region, officials of the African National Congress have reportedly complained of the steady negative advice they receive from Soviet officials. See Michael Parks, "Soviets Urging ANC to Seek South Africa Political Accord," *Los Angeles Times*, Feb. 5, 1988.

72.   Shevardnadze has said that "a certain portion of our foreign economic activity will be, so to speak, 'subsidized,' but only a certain portion" (*VMID*, No. 3, 1987, p. 5). As evidence that this portion may in fact be falling, Cuban documents reportedly show a slight drop in Soviet exports to Cuba in 1987 (*The New York Times*, Mar. 16, 1988, p. A13). It is not clear, however, that the Soviets will be able to build up their trade elsewhere in the Third World. Despite heavy promotion, trade with ASEAN has fallen; with Latin America, it has almost collapsed—from 3.2 billion rubles in 1985 to 920 million rubles in 1986. See analyses by Paul Wolfowitz and Ilya Prizel in *The National Interest* (Washington, DC) (Summer 1988).

73.   See *PlanEcon Report* III. nos. 39–40 (Oct. 1, 1987), pp. 21–22. Soviet economists show a heightened awareness of the price paid by what they now frequently call a "colonial" position in the world economy. Gorbachev has made it a high priority to improve Soviet trade relations, and this represents innovation. Yet as policy in other areas has shown, innovation can lead to turmoil and even to worse results in the short term. Reform of the institutions that conduct trade has been one source of trouble: the ministry of trade first gave way to a state committee for foreign economic relations, then to a new ministry of foreign economic relations (as part of this reform, Vneshtorgbank was abolished). Changes in bureaucratic structure may prove less disruptive than the transfer of authority for trading decisions to enterprises. See Terence Roth, "Soviet Union's Bureaucrats, Secret Police Slow Gorbachev's Drive to Expand Trade," *The Wall Street Journal*, Mar. 9, 1988, p. 23.

74.   Erich Honecker has been especially firm in insisting that East Germany has no need to emulate Soviet reforms. There is also some reason to think that Miloš Jakeš was not Moscow's first choice to replace Gustáv Husák as leader of the Czechoslovak party.

75.   If this happens, the declaration issued by Gorbachev and the Yugoslav government during his visit to Yugoslavia in March 1988 (widely interpreted as a repudiation of the "Brezhnev Doctrine") will very likely be seen to have played a part in emboldening popular opposition. For the joint communiqué, see *Pravda*, Mar. 19, 1988, p. 1.

26

Gorbachev's Global Doughnut: The Empire with a Hole in the Middle*

Charles H. Fairbanks, Jr.

The abandonment of the Eastern European communist regimes by the USSR has astonished everyone. Less spectacular, but equally unexpected, has been the substantial continuity of the Soviet commitment to its many Third World communist clients: Afghanistan, Cambodia, Ethiopia, Angola, Cuba, Nicaragua, the Salvadoran guerrillas.

With the striking exception of the Salvadoran guerillas, it is true that Soviet policy has changed in each of the conflicts in which these clients are engaged, and in a direction more acceptable to the West. In Afghanistan, Cambodia, and Angola, as earlier in Ethiopia, the foreign troops that supported weak communist regimes have been or are being withdrawn. In Angola, Ethiopia, and Nicaragua, regional or internal negotiations have taken place that may hold out the promise of ending civil wars. While internal and U.S. domestic factors have played a role in some of these developments, their appearance in sequence is clearly linked to a shift of Soviet policy.

But the overall picture of Soviet policy in these "regional conflicts" shows a continuing commitment to shoring up the threatened communist regimes. According to U.S. government officials, Soviet security assistance to the Third World in general has been going down—but apparently not to Afghanistan, Cuba, Angola, Cambodia, Vietnam, and the FMLN in El Salvador. Soviet military assistance to the communist government in Afghanistan was increased to $200-$400 million a month, after U.S. aid to the *mujaheddin* was drastically cut. In Cambodia, the first nine months of 1989 saw an approximate doubling of Soviet arms deliveries over 1988 levels—an all-time record. Soviet assistance to Vietnam itself has remained the same or even increased. In Central America, Soviet-bloc military assistance to Nicaragua decreased only about 20 percent from the 1988 level, despite the fact that U.S. military support for the *contras* went down to nothing. A larger share of these munitions was evidently passed

*Reprinted by permission of the author and publisher from the *The National Interest* no. 19 (Spring 1990). Copyright © 1990 by The National Interest, Washington, D.C.

through to the FMLN in El Salvador—including the previously withheld SA-7 surface-to-air missiles—enabling them to mount a Tet-style offensive against the capital in late 1989.

The willingness to increase support for some Third World clients raises important questions in its own right. But the combination of this willingness and the withdrawal of support from the Eastern European communists presents an intriguing paradox. Gorbachev has abandoned his country's old servitors, the Honeckers and Husaks, at the same time that he continues to nurture communist client states in the Third World. This has overthrown all our expectations. Ever since the consolidation of the Soviet Empire in Eastern Europe after World War II, the predominant American view has been that Eastern Europe, and above all East Germany and Poland, constitutes a "vital interest" of the Soviet Union that could never be relinquished and, therefore, should never be threatened by the United States. This feeling underlay the inaction of the United States during the various crises in Eastern Europe. But at the same time we generally assumed that Soviet gains in the Third World could be reversed by some combination of American policy and local nationalism, and that the Soviet side would accept setbacks, including expulsion.

The opposite has turned out to be the case. Gorbachev has hastened the loss of his "vital" interests in Eastern Europe while clinging tenaciously to his vexing burdens in the Third World. Of course, this contradiction may turn out to be temporary. In a period when every week brings something that we never expected to see in our lifetimes, we could see Gorbachev renouncing his Third World outposts as well. But, as of now, the divergence in stance toward the two groups of clients represents a clear paradox, one worth thinking through.

THE LOGIC OF IDEOLOGICAL EMPIRES

This paradox is not unprecedented in history. It has been the pattern of many ideological empires to rot at the core but remain vital at the periphery.

To give one example: During the long "ideological" struggle between the Fatimid (Shi'ite) Caliphate of Cairo and the Abbasid (Sunni) Caliphate of Baghdad from the tenth to the twelfth century, the Fatimid Caliphate collapsed at the center from the dead weight of arbitrary rule, but the Fatimids continued to make gains beyond the caliphate's frontiers, in what are now Iraq, Iran, Yemen, India, and Afghanistan. When, in 1059, Baghdad and the rest of Iraq was finally seized by local Shi'ites, the Fatimid Caliphate had lost all authority in its own capital, Cairo, disordered by famine, cannibalism, and civil war between rival army groups. The path of the Isma'ili Shi'i revolutionry movement through the Islamic world was thus from the west, from its original hearth in Algeria, toward the east, with its old centers abandoned or demoralized as new areas were converted or conquered. That is, its movement was like a fire, which burns outward leaving ashes in the center. If not for the existence of the Mediterranean and the Sahara, which channeled the shift of Fatimid zeal in a west-east direction, it would have assumed the shape of a ring or, better still, a doughnut. The doughnut shape is the one now being assumed by the Soviet bloc: it is falling in at the center, still fairly vigorous at the periphery in the Third World.

This shape is not altogether surprising. Revolutionary movements are given their early impetus by hatred of the existing reality, by the hope for an improvement that is rapid and decisive, by the desire to implement abstract formulae never tested against reality, and by personal desires to transform the world and one's position in it. All of these motives are most vivid at the beginning and in the presence of the enemy; but they are attenuated by having to run an established political order and by the passage of time. In addition, where they were victorious, both the Fatimid Caliphate and the Bolsheviks established repressive regimes, ones in which most of the people, while nominally co-participants in the loftiest of human undertakings, were actually excluded from any responsibility for governing themselves. As Tacitus was the first to argue, despotic power kills energy and ambition in the citizens; it nourishes apathy. Meanwhile the shining dreams that had originally motivated attachment to the new political order are stifled by the contrast with the prosaic reality, and by the artificiality with which they are propagandized.

The human costs of centralized power also affected Soviet foreign policy. Because all human activity in the USSR and in Eastern Europe was so tightly controlled, the Soviet Union was deprived of the influence exerted abroad on behalf of the West by independent business and journalism, and by the independent foreign policy activity of America's allies. (The activities of France in Africa and the Middle East and of Britain in the Persian Gulf are cases in point.)

The tendency of ideological empires to gradually assume a ring-like form has, in the postwar era, been increased by certain characteristics of the international system. In any period of history, conflicts that are likely to be very costly or risky for the participants are less likely simply to disappear than to be "displaced" to other areas where the stakes are not as high. In the nineteenth century, for example, the conflict between Britain and France that began in 1882 over Egypt was "fought out" not in Egypt but in confrontations in West Africa (Borgu, 1895–98), in the Southern Sudan (Fashoda, 1898), and even in Thailand (1893). The incentives for such "displacement" have been vastly increased by the arrival of nuclear weapons. Because nuclear war cannot be regarded as a way of resolving contested issues, and the specter of nuclear war discourages recourse to force in Europe, conflicts have been pushed into the Third World, where the risk of escalation is lower. This accounts in large part for the fact that, despite the acute tensions that have characterized the era of the Cold War, it has been simultaneously a time of almost unprecedented peace between the major powers, and one of continual terrorism, guerilla struggles, proxy war, and superpower confrontations over Third World issues.

THE IMPORTANCE OF EASTERN EUROPE

In the postwar era, the Soviet client states in Eastern Europe and in the Third World were useful to the USSR in very different ways. The acquisition of Eastern Europe after World War II powerfully reinforced the central myth of communism, that it represented the future. Our failure to anticipate that communism could be displaced in Eastern Europe shows how successfully this myth was propagated even among noncommunists and anticommunists. Keeping the myth alive was the first useful function Eastern Europe served for the USSR.

The second was the military advantage conferred by geography. Eastern Europe, by providing strategic depth, assured that another war, to the extent it was a conventional one, would not be fought on Soviet soil. But Eastern Europe also created offensive superiority that had immense political weight. Stalin created the greatest concentration of military power in Europe since the time of Charlemagne. But the Soviet Union of the 1930s, which already had more soldiers, tanks, and aircraft than any nation in the world, was not a superpower; it was the location of vast military power in the very heart of Europe, in Germany, after 1945 that first made it one. Militarily, the blitzkrieg strategy taken over from the Nazis depended on a short war, on the ability to reach the English Channel quickly—that is, on a combination of military power and geography. Politically, it was the presence of military power (and of client states) in the center of Europe that settled the recurring issue of whether Russia is a European power (as under Alexander I and Nicholas II) or an Asiatic power essentially outside Europe (as under Nicholas I and between the world wars). By being a preponderant factor *in Europe* the USSR became a superpower.

The occupation of part of Germany and Austria was particularly crucial to the Soviet Union's security and political status. By splitting Germany, the USSR prevented a revival of the dangers it faced in 1917–18 and again in 1941–42. Because the German Question was left undecided, and could not be decided without the USSR, the USSR became not only a military but a diplomatic factor in Europe.

But these advantages of holding Eastern Europe did not come without major liabilities. To hold Eastern Europe against the will of the inhabitants required erecting an Iron Curtain. This prevented Eastern Europe governments and people from being active on behalf of the Soviet Union on a wider scale. The Iron Curtain was ambiguous: it was simultaneously the wall of a fortress and the wall of a prison. While Western culture and business freely ranged the globe, the Iron Curtain tended to keep its own architects cooped up in the center of Eurasia.

A second liability was that Eastern Europe was hard to hold. Yugoslavia and Albania broke away completely, Romania broke away diplomatically—events almost entirely overlooked by Western opinion in judging that Eastern Europe was a vital Soviet interest which could and would be held in spite of everything. As terror lifted and civil society revived in Eastern Europe, it became a more and more open fact that communism was unpopular there: part of the center of the

Soviet empire had begun to weaken, and a more ring-like physiognomy was emerging in the empire. When rebellions were suppressed, it was at the cost of weakening communism's legitimacy both within Eastern Europe and interna-tionally.

As time went on Eastern Europe became a small but persistent drain on Soviet resources, a drain that became more nagging as the Soviet economy began failing in the 1970s. The military and political advantages of holding a political base in the center of Europe were slowly depreciated by the emergence of strategic nuclear forces, which reduced the significance of geography. Détente made the Soviet empire in Eastern Europe less threatened politically, but more exposed to different threats, arising out of increased economic, cultural, and political con-tact with the West. As it became clearer that there was to be no revival of the German military threat, the value of a geographical position to cope with it diminished. Finally, the passage of time and the blurring of human memory worked their inevitable decay. Only new acquisitions, not old ones, could continue feeding the myth of communist momentum. The advantages conferred by the Eastern European client states were obvious to Stalin because they had been missing earlier. As time went on, the advantages of Eastern Europe began to be taken for granted by Soviet leaders, while it was the disadvantages that had novelty.

THE DISCOVERY OF THE THIRD WORLD

As the Soviet Union became increasingly aware of Eastern Europe's limited usefulness for an activist foreign policy, the dismantling of Western empires offered growing temptations to increase Soviet global influence by an "indirect approach" through the Third World. The Soviet Union began to acquire non-Western clients, both states and insurgent movements. As instruments of Soviet foreign policy, these had uses and liabilities very different from those of the Eastern European clients.

One important difference was that the policies of the new Third World clients were usually less fully controlled by the USSR. We have tended to assume that Soviet clients are useful to the USSR to the extent that their activity is controlled or coordinated by Moscow, with the Eastern European satellites being the model. This assumption is plausible but wrong.

The policies pursued by the Soviet Union and its clients have frequently not coincided. To take only a few examples, the Soviet Union has guided Ethiopian efforts to crush the Eritrean insurgency, but Cuba, conscious of its old links to the Ethiopian efforts to crush the Eritrean insurgency, but Cuba, conscious of its old links to the Eritreans, has abstained even while it has protected the Ethiopian regime. In Grenada, there is evidence that the Soviet Union supported the conspiracy against Maurice Bishop, while Castro wrote to the New Jewel Movement that "Everything which happened was for us a surprise, and disagreeable.'' In North Yemen, the Soviet Union has armed the government generously, while the People's Democratic Republic of Yemen (PDRY) has conducted the insurgency against the government. In the Iran-Iraq War the Soviet Union armed mainly Iraq, while North Korea gave huge quantities of military aid to Iran.

The partial independence of Soviet clients' activity enhances rather than diminishes their usefulness to the USSR, in several ways. When the Soviet Union and one or more of its clients are active in a country, it creates multiple channels of influence. It is also an insurance policy, a safeguard against the sudden expulsion of the Soviet presence, as happened earlier in Egypt and Ghana. In the Iran-Iraq War the Soviet Union would be connected with whichever side won, or with both if the war ended in a stalemate. In Yemen, whoever wins the internal struggle, the outcome will probably not be the ouster of Soviet bloc influence. This would not be the case if the client had been rigidly guided by the Soviet Union in its policy. Ethiopia—where the channels of Soviet-bloc influence included Cuban troops, Soviet arms (and arms debt), and the Communist party organization formed at Soviet insistence—provides another example. Independent but parallel activities by different pro-Soviet actors reinforce and support one another.

In addition to this, many clients have channels the Soviet Union and its Eastern European clients would never have. Libya and Syria have access to the Arab world because they are Arab and Moslem states, Cuba has access to Latin America because it is Spanish-speaking. Thus the existence of client states widely distributed around the globe and with varying cultural and religious backgrounds, increases the political resources available to the Soviets.

A third crucial fact which makes Soviet Third World clients more effective is that they are not understood to be Soviet clients by a large part of international opinion. Even Cuba has been able to head the Non-Aligned Movement, and a number of clients are seen as less implicated than Cuba in Soviet designs. Grenada provides a striking case. The cooperation of the New Jewel Movement with Cuba and the Soviet Union was extremely close across a great range of foreign policy issues, yet most interested international observers labeled Grenada as a Third World socialist country rather than communist. The somewhat disguised character that many Third World clients of the USSR have springs partly from the absence of tight control already mentioned, but also from the international climate of opinion about the Third World.

Because many client states are not understood to be acting on behalf of the Soviet Union, they can carry out actions against the United States and its friends that the Soviet Union itself could never attempt. It is difficult to imagine that there could be tens of thousands of Soviet troops in Angola and Ethiopia without provoking a strong reaction in the West and among other African countries. Yet the presence of such a number of Cuban troops in these countries did not have that impact. Again, Libya was able to bomb the capital of the Sudan during the decline of Nimeiri's authority without provoking any retaliation. The event would have been far more dramatic, and would have drawn a much more hostile reaction, if a Soviet airplane had bombed Khartoum.

We can draw the following general conclusion: *Third World clients have increased the reach of Soviet world power and reduced the risks of Soviet action.* They have enabled the Soviet Union to damage or threaten Western interests in ways that would not otherwise have been possible. This was not true of the clients in Eastern Europe. Indeed, at the very time that the uses of Third World clints were becoming clearer, the usefulness of the Eastern European clients was being diminished by time and changing circumstances.

One important consequence of the political independence of Third World clients is that they may engage in local initiatives drawing the USSR into attacks on Western interests which it would not otherwise undertake. As with other countries, the relationship between Soviet goals and Soviet instruments is a dynamic one: What the Soviet Union cannot find a way of doing, it ultimately gives up; what it finds itself able to do, it is tempted to undertake. If client initiatives develop in a successful way, opportunities may impel the Soviet Union to follow. Thus the existence of Third World clients with special interests, superior access, and greater immunity from international criticism tends to make the Soviet Union more activist, more adventurous.

This is not a merely theoretical conclusion. In Central America, the support of the Sandinistas was originally a Cuban initiative, which accorded with the historic Cuban preference for armed struggle in Latin America. Not until the Sandinistas overthrew Somoza in 1979 was the Soviet Union converted to a strategy of armed struggle. Those concerned about Soviet power have been accustomed to speak of "Soviet subversion" in places such as Nicaragua, Angola, Ethiopia, and Grenada. This is misleading in that it assumes one-way traffic. Perhaps we need also to speak, coining a deliberate paradox, of Cuban and Nicaraguan subversion in Moscow. Because of its greater vitality and zeal, the periphery of the Soviet empire has sometimes led the flagging center: again, a growing emergence of the ring-like structure latent in ideological empires.

GLOBAL CLIENTS

The Eastern European clients of the Soviet Union were among the countries most shut off from the rest of the world. But two of the new Third World clients—Cuba and Libya—were (together with the superpowers, China, and France) among the six countries most active in the widest range of places around the globe.

Cuba was regarded by most Americans in 1959 as an obscure "banana republic," unimportant in the Latin America context and negligible in the world balance. Since then, Cuba has become a major problem for the United States; not merely a local problem, but a worldwide one. Cuba is playing a larger role in world politics than any Latin American country has played since 1492. To appreciate the magnitude of this transformation, consider the reception that would be given today to a prediction that, over the next two decades, Ecuador (a country with a population and GNP roughly similar to Cuba) is destined to become a significant global actor—that it will have stronger armed forces than any Latin American country other than Brazil; that it will be coordinating and supplying guerrilla movements throughout Latin America; that it will have over 60,000 troops on another continent as well as a significant presence in half a dozen other parts of the world. Such a prediction would simply be dismissed as mad. Yet this is precisely what has occurred in the case of Cuba over the last quarter century.

A similar transformation has occurred in the case of Libya, which (to give only a partial list) has been active against American interests in Tunisia, Egypt, Sudan, Somalia, Lebanon, Iran, the Philippines, Western Sahara, Upper Volta, Mali, Chad, Central African Republic, Burundi, Uganda, Grenada, Nicaragua, St. Lucia, and Antigua.

The *global* roles of Cuba and Libya have made them quite different international actors from equally powerful countries that pursue merely regional roles. This global reach presents Soviet foreign policy with special opportunities and risks, and makes the problem they set for American foreign policy quite different. Some other Soviet clients show a tendency to emulate Cuba or Libya by becoming active on a global scale. Vietnam and Ethiopia still pursue predominantly local interests, but the Vietnamese have sent arms to the Salvadoran guerrillas and Ethiopia has been active in destabilizing the southern Sudan, an area traditionally outside Ethiopian imperial ambitions.

We have usually been more worried by the kind of local activity characteristic of Nicaragua and the PDRY in North Yemen than by the Cuban and Libyan type, fearing subversion in our "backyard" and a "domino effect" on nearby countries. This is probably an error, for there is a reason why the "domino effect" usually does not go very far. Local activity by Soviet clients tends to be self-limiting in that it creates and stiffens local opposition and causes the threatened states to seek stronger ties with the U.S. or some other protector. The Sandinista threat caused the United States to establish a quasi-institutionalized military presence in Central America. PDRY subversion deepened the intervention of Saudi Arabia in Yemeni affairs, and brought Iran into Oman. To avoid such developments, Soviet clients have an interest in showing restraint and not using all the power available to them. Nicaragua has reasons not to antagonize Costa Rica, Honduras, and El Salvador. Ethiopia, thanks to massive Soviet military aid, has unquestioned military dominance in the Horn of Africa, but the knowledge that a more aggressive use of that power against Somalia would antagonize and activate other neighboring countries, such as Kenya and Saudi Arabia, has caused it to be utilized moderately. Thus the domino effect is countered by an intrinsic tendency back toward equilibrium in local conflicts. Brushfires have a tendency to put themselves out.

This local tendency toward equilibrium, however, does not operate against *global* client activity. Honduras can act effectively against Nicaragua, but not in the same way against Cuba. Somalia and the Sudan have cards to play against Ethiopia—weak ones, to be sure—but none against Cuba. The global activity of Cuba and Libya is a very powerful weapon in the hands of a revisionist power.

By the time that Gorbachev was named general secretary in 1985, Cuba had shown itself to be an instrument many times more powerful on the Soviet side than any Eastern European country.

THE ARRIVAL OF GORBACHEV

These were the ways in which the two groups of Soviet clients had evolved when Mikhail Gorbachev became leader of the Politburo. As a member of the Communist party apparatus, Gorbachev was a member of a very specialized subculture, like the old Jesuit order or the clergy in Iran. Unlike Western politicians, the members of the nomenklatura spent their entire lives in this career, lived in different apartment buildings from other people, went to different stores and resorts. They were unusually *isolated* from the people they ruled. This group possessed a distinctive world view, comprising a distinctive idea of leaership and distinctive political tactics. The concept of leadership in the CPSU has not been one of managing problems but transforming society, as Lenin and Stalin did. The view of tactics, or "operational code," comprises a complex and sophisticated doctrine that can be summarized only briefly here.[1]

Politics, both domestic and foreign, is, in the traditional communist view, *always* a struggle. The outcome of this struggle depends on the correlation of forces, and success depends on the realistic estimation of that correlation. Because that correlation varies, success ebbs and flows. Consequently, as Lenin said in 1921, "Our strength will always be a capacity to take account of the real relationships and not to fear them, however disagreeable they may be."[2] Sometimes it is necessary to retreat even when pride rebels against it. Stalin elaborated: "there are moments when one must . . . begin a planned retreat and give up, without fighting, whole cities and areas for the sake of winning time and collecting forces for new decisive battles in the future."[3] The classic example, taught to every Soviet schoolchild, is the 1918 Brest-Litovsk Treaty with Germany in which the Bolsheviks surrendered vast tracts of territory to survive. Lenin sometimes spoke of the possibility of retreating to the Urals, or even to Vladivostok.

In the traditional communist operational code, skill in attacking and skill in retreating are regarded as equally important. To determine the appropriate moment for maneuvering and for giving in is a key part of the Bolshevik's political training. In phases of retreat it is necessary to be flexible and to accept noncommunist allies such as the Left Social Revolutionaries, the NEP traders, and the Social Democrats in the Popular Fronts of the 1930s. Leninist tactics include a complex array of means by which temporary allies can be manipulated, as some peace movements, front organizations, and the Eastern European Popular Fronts of 1945–48 were manipulated. But retreat does not mean giving up. An important part of Gorbachev's training included mastering tactics for turning a forced retreat into an advance by different means.

Gorbachev, as I have argued elsewhere,[4] was given his political direction by the crisis of the communist system, by his own ambition which was stimulated by the magnitude of the challenge, and by the ingrained habits of the Bolshevik operational code. He felt increasingly pressed by a need to make drastic changes in the society, changes blocked by a divided Politburo and a bureaucracy that resisted change and eluded control. Thus consolidating his personal power was essential, even disregarding his own ambition. Gorbachev sought to do this by discrediting earlier rulers and institutions (through glasnost); by forcing structural changes in governing institutions in order to give himself a power base independent of the party apparatus; and above all by mobilizing forces outside normal politics (as Mao Zedong did in his Cultural Revolution).

One might consider this strategy cynical if it did not dovetail so neatly with the transformation of society Gorbachev wanted. Gorbachev felt that the Soviet public had become apolitical, bored with communism, apathetic, and lazy. By mobilizing the public, he hoped both to involve them in a new revolutionary struggle under the banner of communism and to reinvigorate the party by forcing it once again to compete for the people's allegiance. This was a project of noble daring, but not of prudence: it rested on large and untested assumptions about the motives of the Russians and their subject peoples. Gorbachev proclaimed that "perestroika is a revolution": he wanted to re-live the revolution within a civil order settled and petrified for seventy years. Such a possibility was inherent in the communist project, but by its very nature it threatened to shatter the existing order, the communist regime. During 1989, Gorbachev's cultural revolution went out of control. The popular forces mobilized by Gorbachev turned against the regime with demands for national self-determination and political freedom. Eastern Europe was the first part of the Soviet Empire to be shattered by the explosion Gorbachev had ignited.

THE LOSS OF EASTERN EUROPE

In the first years of Gorbachev's reign, the news from Eastern Europe was such as to allow a certain overconfidence. Nowhere were there moves away from old political patterns that were not sponsored or regulated by the ruling Communist parties. The Eastern European countries remained isolated from each other and from the USSR. Their limited international usefulness made it easier to neglect them.

In Poland and in Hungary the ruling parties felt the need, in the tradition of Brest-Litovsk, to retreat in the face of looming economic disaster. In Hungary, Imre Poszgay tried, like Gorbachev, to bring noncommunist forces into politics and manipulate them. In Poland, such a strategy had been explicitly sketched by Jerzy Urban as early as 1981[5] and it guided the roundtable negotiations with Solidarity and the June elections. The Polish Communists, with Soviet assent, bungled the elections and the negotiations before and after, so that these two events led to the wholly unexpected result of a Solidarity-led government.

During these early Gorbachev years Soviet officials wrestled with the issue of redefining their attitudes toward the Brezhnev Doctrine for a largely different audience. Gorbachev finally unambiguously disavowed the doctrine in a July 6, 1989 speech at Strasbourg to the parliamentary assembly of the Council of Europe. The communique of the Warsaw Pact immediately afterward was much vaguer, showing a continued nervousness about pulling out the ultimate prop of the Eastern European regimes. But of course, Gorbachev's words, uttered before there was an acute general crisis in Eastern Europe, could not easily be recalled. They conditioned everything that happened shortly afterwards.

The conflagration was triggered by the concatenation of events as small as the removal of the border wire between Hungary and Austria (May 2) and the Hungarian willingness to allow East Germans to leave through that border (August 22). From this point a chain reaction started, spread to enough countries to create a "critical mass," and then rapidly consumed the entire Warsaw Pact. The unpredictable nature of the process and Gorbachev's shocked reaction to the likelihood of German reunification after early November strongly suggest that he intended none of this. The military and psychological keystone of the Warsaw Pact was the German Democratic Republic. Once it had fallen, the other Eastern European peoples knew that the Soviets would not avert the fall of their own masters. The decisive event occurred at the beginning of October. In the conditions created by Gorbachev's July 6 repudiation of Soviet intervention, Honecker suddenly halted emigration again, goading the public to fury. At this perfect moment Gorbachev arrived on his scheduled visit, repeating the slogans about the need for change designed to achieve a different result in different circumstances. It was Gorbachev who precipitated the avalanche.

From the communist point of view, Gorbachev is a jinx, a hoodoo, a Jonah. His arrival anywhere presages disaster. Like Jaruzelski and Poszgay, he did not undersand the people's deep weariness of communism, nor could he sense the people's mood at a particular crux. Perhaps Gorbachev's soaring ambition, his splendid vision of the future, and his courage are spoiled by his lifetime as a member of an isolated priestly caste, whose pride was its ability to manipulate people.

Gorbachev sensed, with Bolshevik lack of sentimentality, that the decomposition of the East German regime signalled the end. In this crisis he seems to have reverted to the ingrained example of Brest-Litovsk. He retreated to the next defensible position: the boundary of the USSR. The communists of Eastern Europe were simply abandoned, an act made easier by their diminished usefulness. The new strategy combined an attempt to contain by diplomacy the movement toward German reunification and an attempt to put himself at the head of the process, urging the Czech party not to use the iron fist and arranging a coup in Bulgaria (November 6–10). These efforts did not change the reality of a forced retreat. What Stalin and his successors had built up over decades with unceasing effort and the expenditure of vast resources, Gorbachev had lost in three months.

THE FATE OF THE PERIPHERY

After giving up Eastern Europe, the Communist party of the Soviet Union is faced with the possibility of annihilation as a political entity. Most of the factors that produced the collapse in Eastern Europe are present, to a lesser degree, in the Soviet Union itself: the combination of rage against the rulers; new expectations; a demoralized and divided party apparatus; and Gorbachev's overconfidence in his ability to persuade people to do what he wants rather than what they want. As it is subsiding and partly falling in, the Soviet empire is more and more assuming the doughnut form latent in ideological empires. As Radio Free Europe's Vladimir Kusin has argued, exaggerating only somewhat, "the geographical focus of communist rule thus shifted from Europe to the Third World."[6]

The seeming paradox of abandoning the Eastern European communists while continuing to shore up the Third World regimes emerged from the interaction between specific policy choices and the divergent paths of development experienced by the two groups of clients. The winter of 1989–90 displayed a vivid contrast in morale: in El Salvador, guerrillas spent their lives for communism in suicidal attacks; in Berlin and Prague, the leaders would not defend communism even to save themselves. The historical development had both sapped the vitality and reduced the usefulness of Eastern Europe in an active foreign policy strategy, while making the Third World the arena of active international conflict and the point of the West's greatest vulnerability.

The very differnet practical benefits offered by the two sets of clients may very well have been decisive in Gorbachev's mind when he made the specific policy choices to retreat in one place and not in the other. Certainly, as some Soviet clients in the Third World—Afghanistan, Ethiopia in 1989—have been under pressure as acute as the Eastern European clients were under in the fall of 1989, it is impossible to explain the different Soviet policies as a mere adaptation to circumstances.

The tactics suggested by the communist operational code may also have affected the different outcomes. In the Eastern European case the code held out the hope that communist leaders could manipulate public opinion during a retreat so as to avoid giving up the position altogether. This hope was a fatal delusion. Gorbachev is not tempted in the same way in the Third World: he will not go to the Panjsher Valley, as he did to East Berlin and to Lithuania, to try to persuade people to like what they don't like. The methods by which the Third World outposts are held are simpler—fighting, security assistance, diplomacy—and at this point the Soviet Union probably knows how to employ them more successfully.

We cannot predict Soviet conduct toward the periphery of its empire; we do not even know whether, in five years, the government framing policy will be communist, democratic, or fascist. We can only specify the conditions that will shape Soviet conduct. At the center of the empire, these will be a declining interest in foreign policy, and, to some extent, a concern to save money.

Subsidies to Third World clients may be reduced, but these clients are not particularly expensive. They are in fact so cheap compared to the staggering outlay on Soviet military forces that they are not the first place from which funds are likely to be taken to shore up the economy, if a communist oligarchy survives in Russia. On the other hand, a system in which public opinion and elected deputies shaped policy more significantly would be much less attracted to the defense of Third World clients; they are unpopular with the Soviet public.

On the outer periphery of the ring, in the third World, communism will have continued vitality and appeal, as Peru and the Philippines currently demonstrate. It was an important insight of the Western Left that people in the Third World are not attracted to communism and to the Soviet Union for Soviet reasons, but for their own, local reasons. The crisis of faith in the center is therefore likely to affect the periphery only slowly.

Third World clients will hold a continuing interest as long as the USSR wants to show the continuing vitality of its foreign policy. Beyond the usefulness they displayed in earlier years, they hold out some opportunities specific to the present moment. Because many Soviet clients are clients in disguise, they are compatible with the "New Thinking" in foreign policy. At the Malta summit, Gorbachev could deny Nicaraguan arms were his arms. The New Thinking, while fundamentally of Western origin, is close to the Third World's conceptual framework, as displayed in the international organizations in recent decades. If it fails to satisfy expectations as a general basis for Soviet foreign policy—as is very likely—Soviet clients will provide a bridge to the Third World as an arena of future Soviet leadership. The Soviet clients can, for example, help the USSR to refocus American foreign policy. As the Cold War appears to many to be over, the tendency is already evident to push the United States out of Europe. This has been a long-standing objective of Soviet policy and, after an interval during which the USSR may need the United States to create an appearance of stability, will probably be so again. To the extent that the United States faces concrete, difficult, and divisive problems in the Third World—like El Salvador—a pull is added to this push out of Europe.

Another motive for supporting Third World clients stems from the loss of Eastern Europe itself. The sense of the Soviet Union as a superpower rested heavily on the presence of vast armies on the Elbe, in the heart of Europe, with a firm base behind them. If the Soviet Union wants to retain the sense of being a powerful player in world politics in the absence of such a presence, its Third World outposts will be increasingly important as its image suffers and its status-anxieties increase.

Soviet commitment to Third World clients is likely to continue above all because, as argued above, the Soviet-client relationship is not one-way: the Soviet Union becomes active in response to invitations from friendly states and forces, as well as in pursuit of its own agenda. Once an opportunity is offered to the Soviet Union, the inherent advantages of working through clients make it difficult to refuse. This may become even more true when the Soviets want to stop their global retreat without endangering détente, for Third World clients provide them with an opportunity to stay in the game of world politics without having to take full responsibility for conflict, and thus without attracting too much hostility.

DIRECTIONS FOR WESTERN POLICY

Today the periphery of the Soviet empire is more of a problem for us than the center. But the damage done by the periphery is now limited by the quiet emanating from the center. Will this situation continue? It is probably best to think of the future in terms of two very different periods. In the present one we have a breathing space (perhaps a year, perhaps several years). In this phase there are enormous opportunities—if we have the imagination to seize them—to strengthen the Western position in both Eastern Europe and the Third World.

In the second phase we will be hit by the consequences of the instabilities now being created every day. The terminal crises of empires are *dangerous*. The collapse of the Old Regime in France led quickly to the conquest of Europe by revolutionary armies. The long decline of Austria-Hungary was marked by civil war, regional wars, the emergence of new ideological solutions (Hitler was a product of Linz and Vienna), and finally by the abrupt decision to attempt to check the growing threats to the system's existence through the ultimatum to Serbia in July 1914.

Various factions and ideologies will struggle to inherit the former Soviet empire, and the host of historic problems artificially "frozen" by communist order will come alive: Moldavia, Transylvania, the Dobruja, Macedonia, Turks in Bulgaria, Russian settlers and Muslim natives in Kirgizia and Kazakhstan, the relationship between Soviet and Iranian Azerbaijan—this list is long. In this very complex, rapidly changing, and charged atmosphere, saturated with newly-awakened fears and hopes, the vast military power accumulated by Soviet rulers during the rigid and unchanging era of bipolarity will be available—to someone. It is unlikely that it will go unused.

In making this point one frequently encounters the cynical admission that there will, of course, be massacres right and left, but how will they affect us? This is a valid question, but one should not assume an answer that justifies complacency. A situation in which 25,000 nuclear warheads are up for grabs and a secular faith faces annihilation is intrinsically a dangerous one, even if we cannot foresee (as we could not in the 1920s) in what exact form the dangers may arrive.

Of course, these dangers will not simply be a continuation of those we face today. The Soviet capability to wage a general war without long mobilization is ebbing; financial stringencies and the withdrawal of Soviet forces from Eastern Europe will accelerate this process. Any projection of the dangers we are likely to face in the second phase is hazardous; nevertheless, we need to begin thinking about them now. Low-intensity conflict (e.g., terrorism) is likely to become more important; it requires few resources, is deniable, and can be used to shape Western public attitudes on political issues. The Third World, of course, has been the basic arena of low-intensity conflict.

A second source of danger will be civil wars and other domestic conflicts that, together with irredentist ambitions, lead to military clashes. The likely source of many of these problems will be the periphery of the Soviet empire, but some of them will be "displaced" to the Third World, where the stakes are lower.

Iranian militants have already crossed into Azerbaijan, and Turkish public opinion is increasingly called to take sides in the bloody struggles unfolding across the border. The last struggles, in 1918, were decided when the Turkish army marched to Baku. The most readily available and the least risky way for the Soviet Union to prevent Turkish and Iranian involvement is through terrorism and the use of its client states—Syria, Afghanistan, to some extent Iraq—to make it clear to the Turks and Iranians that intervention would involve serious costs. More generally, we should anticipate that during the time of troubles in which it has now entered, the Soviet Union will attempt to use its Third World clients to create diversionary measures intended to keep the West preoccupied.

While the exact nature of these diversions is beyond our vision, we need to get ready for them. We need to do two things above all. The first is to maintain our military forces (although we can and should restructure them). The second is to change the nonmilitary correlation of forces in the world, to take advantage of the benign first phase of the current evolution, the breathing space, in order to strengthen the West's position in the coming era of instability.

If the reasoning above about the potential of Third World clients as instruments of Soviet strategy is even approximately correct, forcing Soviet client regimes from power—the objective of the Reagan doctrine—must be an important element in the needed shift in the nonmilitary correlation of forces. To displace Soviet clients is easier because they are not acknowledged to be such, and because of Gorbachev's peace offensive; such actions need not rupture our better relations with the USSR itself. They serve the purpose of denying the bridge to the Third World provided by Soviet clients; of depriving the Soviet Union of positions that may be used to put pressure on us in the next phase; and of controlling beforehand the tendency of radical Third World regimes to lead the Soviet Union into adventures it would not otherwise undertake.

While accumulated American blunders have made the Sandinistas largely immune for the time being, the repressive regimes in Afghanistan, Ethiopia, and Angola are as vulnerable as those in East Germany and Czechoslovakia. The fall of communism in Eastern Europe has suggested that regimes such as Cuba's may already be more fragile than we had thought. It would be hard for anyone to deny that a world without communist rule in Afghanistan, in the Horn of Africa, in Southern Africa, and, if possible, in Central America and the Caribbean would be a better world for the people who live in those parts. It would also be a safer world for us.

Because of the breathing space we have in this phase, it is now easier and less risky for us to take the necessary measures; and because we are moving almost inexorably toward a more dangerous second phase, it is more urgent that we take them. Recent events in Eastern Europe have shown that communism will retreat under pressure, but only under pressure, as the communist operational code has always recommended. If that is true at the core, why don't we find out whether it also applies at the rim?

NOTES

1. The description of the "operational code" that follows is drawn particularly from the work of the late Nathan Leites, beginning with *The Operational Code of the Politburo* (New York: McGraw-Hill, 1951) and *A Study of Bolshevism* (Glencoe, IL: Free Press, 1953).

2. *Sochineniya*, 3d ed. (Moscow: Gospolitizdat', 1928–1937), vol. 27, p. 126.

3. *Sochineniya* (Moscow: Gospolitizdat', 1948), vol. 5, pp. 167–68.

4. See "La revolution culturelle de Gorbatchev," Part I, *Commentaire* (Paris), no. 48 (Winter 1989–90); Part II forthcoming in no. 49. Originally published (in shorter form) as "Gorbachev's Cultural Revolution," *Commentary* (August 1989).

5. Jerzy Urban, letter to the Polish first secretary, translated in the journal *Uncaptive Minds* (November–December 1988), pp. 2–7.

6. Summarized in RFE/RL *Soviet/East European Report* VII, no. 13, p. 1.

27

Gorbachev and the West*

Pierre Hassner

In his remarkable *World Communism: The Disintegration of a Secular Faith*,[1] Richard Löwenthal began with a citation of Max Weber stating that historical materialism is not a vehicle one can exit at will. His purpose was to underscore how the dialectic of interaction could lead people's actions to consequences completely opposite to their initial intentions—in this case Khrushchev's twin campaigns of foreign expansionism and domestic deStalinization and their import in terms of the Sino-Soviet conflict.

In the case of General Secretary Mikhail Gorbachev, this dialectical approach is once again the only way to avoid the pitfalls in choosing between interpretations that are either deterministic or voluntaristic, systemic or individualistic. Gorbachev is neither an anonymous product of an unchanging system nor a heroic reformer secretly won over by liberal values. Above all, he ought to be seen as "the grand co-opter," concurrently the agent and the instrument of a dialectic mixing both adaptation and manipulation.

Every government has a twin mission: relations with its own people and relations with other states. In the case of a totalitarian regime, particularly if it is communist, there is a structural conflict between the dynamics of the system and both the demands of civil society and those of the international order. Moreover, given that Gorbachev neither wants nor is able to establish impenetrable barriers between these two missions, the interior and the exterior of his regime are themselves constantly interacting, sometimes positively, sometimes negatively. The result is a genuinely triangular relationship between the Soviet government, Soviet domestic factors, and the external world.

Gorbachev strives simultaneously to control and manipulate this relationship and he succeeds in giving the impression of constantly holding the initiative in the face of divided or paralyzed adversaries. However, analysis of the actual content of his policies and reforms reveals a conclusion surprising to many—they are essentially reactive in character. Many are borrowed from the conceptual arsenals of others, be they of Soviet dissidents, reformers in Eastern Europe, or

* Reprinted by permission of the author and publisher from *Revere Pouvoirs*, no. 45, P.U.F., Copyright © 1988, Paris.

Western liberals, pacifists, ecologists, and even capitalists. Thus, one might well ask: is Gorbachev truly looking for a real compromise with societies of the East and West? Does he acknowledge their aspirations in order to adjust to certain fixed realities? Or does he acknowledge them in order to conquer them and to reestablish control and the totalitarian initiative?

An answer seems nearly impossible to discern. If it is the latter, how does one account for the new tolerance for those voices critical of the Soviet establishment, including those who deride the official ideology and *glasnost* itself, or for foreign voices, including those of émigrés and of Western radio? If in fact we are witnessing an authentic conversion to domestic and international pluralism, how does one explain the contrast between bold rhetoric and diplomatic audacity and hesitation with structural economic, political, and military reform?

Useful insight into this dilemma is offered in Adam Michnik's theory of counterreform, in which he argued that a counterreform includes a portion of the reform program in order to nip it in the bud more effectively.[2] Perhaps Gorbachev's originality consists in taking a solid cue from the great achievement of Western societies, that of co-opting or integrating their rebels, which contrasts with the traditional rigidity of communist systems, which knew of no other response than repression. Even ascribing to this theory, however, Gorbachev risks finding himself finishing as the co-opted co-opter, or the manipulated manipulator. Intellectuals and informal groups, national minorities, and satellite societies are all striving to rush into any open gaps and render the changes irreversible.

Who will win at this game of sorcerer's apprentice? Or will it finish with a return to the classic dynamics of revolt and repression in the interior of the empire and of crisis and hardening in the exterior? Will the result be the same on the domestic and international scenes? We do not claim to answer these questions, but we do claim that they constitute a frame of reference more enlightening than the eternal "Is Gorbachev a good guy or a bad buy?" into which most discussions of this topic in the West seem to fall.

GORBACHEV AND WESTERN OPINION

Until now Gorbachev has had the paradoxical effect in the West of putting an apparent end to the conflicts that raged over détente and disarmament while sowing the seeds of a deeper, more structural fragmentation than seen heretofore. At present in the West, the favorable assessment of Gorbachev is virtually unanimous and seems to have silenced the old debates between Americans and Europeans, hawks and doves, proponents and opponents of Euromissiles and of technology transfers to the East. Naturally, almost all are quick to caution against the rash conclusion that the adversarial nature of the ideological and geopolitical relationship of the two alliances has disappeared. However, one after the other, the conservative critics of the "evil empire" and of the illusions of détente find the way of Damas in succumbing to the personal seduction of the Soviet leader. Thatcher, Mitterrand, Reagan, and Strauss have all in turn rendered him homage while assuring their constituents of the pacific intentions of the Soviet Union. The discreet unease of the military and the frenetic denunciations by lingering hard-core anti-Soviets already are considered anachronistic.

However, the stress put on one or the other side of the balanced formulations accepted by the new consensus contains the risk of new misunderstandings that will lead to new cleavages. To begin with, the meaning of the generally accepted distinction between the man and the system is far from clear. The image of Gorbachev, ubiquitously positive, is much more favorable than that of the Soviet Union, which remains essentially negative. However, even in France where the public opinion gap between the two is the biggest, Gorbachev's popularity is moderating impressions of the USSR to the point where today the two super-powers are credited equally with wanting peace (notably, the USSR has by far the advantage elsewhere in Europe). Moves toward the elimination of U.S. and Soviet nuclear arms in Europe are considered positively. These all indicate a reversal of opinion—to the credit of Gorbachev.[3]

Of course, even Gorbachev's most enthusiastic admirers admit that he will either be paralyzed, digested, or reversed by the system. These people tend to present everything coming from Gorbachev as good for the West as well as for the peoples of the Soviet empire; any negative factors are attributed to the resistance of his conservative rivals, the bureaucracy, or the constraints of the communist system. This analysis is almost entirely correct for the short run, but it may have to be reversed. Gorbachev's intentions may well be to render his system more viable and seductive for the long run, hence more dangerous to the West. But efforts to energize the system or to make it acceptable to domestic and international public opinion may in fact make it more vulnerable by sharpening its inconsistencies, perhaps ultimately requiring of Gorbachev or his successors that they in fact practice what they currently only preach in order to avoid catastrophe. Alternatively, in shaking up Soviet society in order to get the economy moving, he might encourage rebellions in the former without disturbing the inertia of the latter.

This leads to a second distinction—between words and deeds. The phrase of Hans-Dietrich Genscher in his February 1987 Davos speech (also currently used by Franz Josef Strauss), "We should take Gorbachev at his word," and the reply of former French foreign minister Jean Bernard Raimond, "We should judge him by what he does," have become paradigmatic. Of course, the contrast is smaller than it seems. Genscher meant not simply to count on Gorbachev's word but rather to put his word to the test. Raimond intended not simply that we wait passively for Soviet actions without exerting any influence; rather, Raimond recommended a "double vigilance"—remaining alert for signs of real change specifically in order to respond favorably while not making premature unilateral concessions before being certain that the changes are real.

The difference concerns the importance of words. In this era of mass communications and in a regime that one can qualify as "logocratic" more than any other, words are acts and are alrady established as facts. As the wooden language opens itself a bit to a discourse more Western in style and as artists are sent abroad from Moscow who proclaim the bankruptcy of Marxism-Leninism and of the Soviet regime in their declarations and published works (provided that they pay their verbal tribute to the new wooden language of peace and disarmament), this may indeed mean a genuine step away from totalitarianism and at the same time be part of a strategy furthering the moral disarmament of the West. Gorbachev's expressions are of Western origin, such as "the security community," "the common house of Europe," "the new way of thinking," and "the elimination of hostile stereotypes." If the West, following Genscher, accepts them back from Gorbachev, this is both legitimate and dangerous. As Humpty-Dumpty said, "When I use a word, it means exactly what I want it to mean. It all depends on who has the power." Notwithstanding the historic origins and abstract significance of the concepts employed by Gorbachev, to accept and applaud the operation by which he uproots and inserts them into a political context of his choosing is to appoint him master of the rules of the game and of the tests to which Westerners pretend to submit him. To take Gorbachev at his word certainly should mean not leaving him a verbal monopoly but also not leaving him an interpretive one. It should mean waging a political battle in order to force Gorbachev to react to Western conceptions of Europe and its security, of law, and of peace.

Clearly, the East-West dialogue is inscribed in the interior-exterior dialectic and in the important differences between short-term actions and long-term evolutions. The danger of Western euphoria is to accord immediate and irreversible advantages to the Soviet Union in exchange for spectacular but revocable gestures or, on the contrary, in exchange for a justifiable but fragile hope for the long-term evolution of the Soviet regime. However, the danger of permanent mistrust is to be immobilized to respond to change, denying the West the means to encourage the regime when the change is real and to denounce it when it is feigned. Westerners will avoid these pitfalls if they strive to discern more exactly the variable and complex factors shaping Soviet behavior and Gorbachev's policies.

DIMENSIONS AND CONTRADICTIONS

The central challenge in understanding the complex factors shaping Soviet behavior is in distinguishing between the interior and exterior facets of Soviet policies, and to discern the varying import of cultural, economic, military, and political factors. Conceptually, it is impossible to fully separate each dimension; nevertheless, they are not necessarily convergent.

Examples abound. Stalin and Mao had defensive foreign policies during the times of their worst internal excesses (the Great Purge and the Cultural Revolution); however, the negative image generated by these excesses necessarily had an impact on their relations with other countries, who perceived a general aggressiveness of a tyrant toward his people. In contrast, Khrushchev combined an adventurist foreign policy with internal reform, and his example shows that liberalization itself can lead to repression, as in Hungary. Although such activities have decreased the attraction of the Soviet model for the outside world, they have also served its international designs—though they may have harmed détente for the short term, the imposition of the Berlin Wall and the invasion of Czechoslovakia have convinced the West to accept at least provisionally the status quo—i.e., Soviet domination of Eastern Europe.

The relationship between internal and external factors in Soviet behavior was similarly complex during the Brezhnev years. In the absence of internal reforms, doors were opened to Western trade and technology as a way to resolve the crisis of the Soviet economy and society—along with compensation in the form of an unprecedented military buildup. In hindsight, this policy endangered détente and access to the Western technological manna (which, moreover, seemed less and less like a miracle cure) and further aggravated internal stagnation until it became intolerable. Hence, Gorbachev.

With Gorbachev, the relationship between internal reform and external détente seems simple: he pursues them simultaneously and they must mutually support each another. But at least in the Soviet discourse, one sees a clear shift of priorities: the military priority seems to be declining in importance relative to economic modernization and the ideological-diplomatic offensive. However, for the moment, this rhetorical offensive is sufficiently ambiguous to warrant further questions and complex interpretations of its causes, objectives, and consequences.

WHAT IS THE NEW THINKING?

In relations with the West, Gorbachev's policies appear to be based on a simultaneous manipulation of *glasnost* and the new thinking. Gorbachev seems to make a deliberate and impressive use of two themes for Western consumption. The first is that of internal change. This includes of course *glasnost*, the priority of economic reform, and, last but not least, the acknowledgment of the weaknesses of the USSR (including Chernobyl and the escapade of the young Mathias Rust). It would be absurd to claim that all that is nothing but a show *à la Potemkin*. But it remains true that these changes, genuine as they are, are systematically advertized and occasionally exaggerated in order to convince the West that the Soviet Union is no longer a threat, at least not militarily. The second theme is the impressive adoption of all the West's fashionable themes. Gorbachev has picked up those of the United States in the 1970s (stability, reasonable sufficiency, the disutility of force, interdependence, the fate of the planet), those of the European left (particularly the West German alternatives and left-wing social democrats) in the 1980s (the security community, non-offensive defense, the structural inability to attack), and some French themes of the Gaullist years (Europe from the Atlantic to the Urals, the Common European house). Like Woody Allen's Zelig, Gorbachev seems to adopt the traits of his interlocutor, whoever he may be.

One cannot help being struck by the difficulty in separating real changes from their manipulative exploitation. It is interesting to note that despite Gorbachev's greater freedom of action and activism abroad than at home (where institutional and social constraints are known by all), his most important innovations are made at home in the new dialogue with society evidenced by *glasnost*, particularly in cultural matters. In foreign affairs, one still has to wonder if a new realism and skill in public relations have not been put in service of a global role that remains essentially unchanged. As this author observed in another context,[4] one has the impression that, at least in matters concerning European security, that which is new is not very credible (the idea of a non-nuclear, nonviolent world in which all wars and weapons are banned) and that which is credible is not very new (the idea of a denuclearized Europe and a European system of security replacing the two alliances). Compared with Brezhnev's, is Gorbachev's arms-control policy different in content or in propagandistic skill? However, Gorbachev's proposals can be seen both as a tactical response to Ronald Reagan's SDI proposal and antinuclear themes and as a return to the ban-the-bomb campaigns of the time of the Stockholm appeal in the 1950s. With the Intermediate-range Nuclear Forces Treaty, he succeeded in extremis where the support for the pacifist movements failed, i.e., in avoiding the deployment of the U.S. intermediate-range missiles in Europe.

To date, real and irreversible changes in Soviet foreign policy are still too few and tentative to erase completely the impression that behind the changed outward appearances are traditional Soviet international policies and goals. Gorbachev has, however, broken with traditional positions in a number of important areas. He appears inclined to renounce, strictly speaking, certain military advantages in order to obtain certain economic and political advantages. (How else to interpret the renunciation of not only the SS-20s but also shorter-range systems where Soviet superiority is considerable as well as the acceptance of on-site verification?) Even more, in order to promote economic modernization and ideological competition, Gorbachev wishes to modify the priorities of his predecessors and to avoid military adventures and the acceleration of the arms race—for the moment at least. The views of Gorbachev's closest counselor, Alexander Yakovlev, are instructive in this regard: he has written that military competition in the area of technology was a snare destined to exhaust the USSR, that competition in the economic domain was similarly unfavorable to the USSR, and that, instead, the Soviet Union should focus on the ideological, social, and political competition.[5] His views undoubtedly indicate a real shift in emphasis.

But uncertainty remains about the significance of this shift. Is it caused above all by the internal stagnation, even crisis, of Soviet society? Milan Simecka, the best analyst of Czech normalization, forcefully made this case in a recent text.[6] One can also trace the influence of Western ideas, in particular those of the liberal and university establishments in the United States, on Soviet research institutes, whose leaders seem to be attaining a new measure of influence under Gorbachev.[7] Whatever the structural causes or the degree of penetration of Western ideas may be, it is difficult to believe that international circumstances do not figure into the Gorbachev watershed.

Ironically, it may have taken the Reagan administration to convince the Soviets to adopt the thinking, or at least the rhetoric, of the Carter administration, which they had rejected 10 years ago as a crude trap. Another important factor—by the Soviets' own admission—is their fear of the U.S. ability to exploit its technological superiority, particularly as a stimulant of Soviet interest in arms control and in computers as compared to rockets and tanks. Similarly, the devaluation of the Third World in Soviet strategic thinking is no doubt linked to a variety of factors including local disappointments and limited Soviet resources, but also the risks of reaction by the Reagan administration. Finally, if the USSR regrets its involvement in Afghanistan, it is surely because of the obstinate resistance of the Afghans and the increased U.S. aid.

If multiple causes exist, how should one choose between interpretations that emphasize Soviet economic problems and those that emphasize their role as alibis for Soviet political plans? Once again, the two are reconcilable if observers differentiate between long-term objectives and necessary short-term measures. From the Soviet point of view, current economic and military considerations seem to converge: the Soviets would prefer a return to détente (which would decelerate the U.S. defense effort and encourage East-West technology transfer) and an emphasis on the new civilian and military technologies.

Westerners should appreciate the primacy of Soviet economic difficulties while also understanding that the Soviet Union and particularly its current leader excel at taking advantage of the system's own weaknesses and at extending Soviet influence via measures taken to counter unfavorable trends. Whether Gorbachev's intentions are defensive or offensive, the USSR certainly has an interest in blocking new strategies for NATO as well as European military cooperation so as to emerge as the dominant power on a denuclearized continent.

The outward incoherence of Soviet European policy—which seems to oscillate between the primacy of the United States and of Europe, of France and of West Germany, of the Right and of the Left—also can be seen to have a certain consistency if one distinguishes between its various time dimensions. At the moment, the USSR desires contacts with all the European governments, especially the conservative ones, for at least three reasons. First, it wants to extract technological and commercial advantages; second, it wants the Europeans to use their influence in Washington on its behalf; and, third, it wants to enhance differences of opinion among the allies. In all three respects, the Federal Republic of Germany, after having been kept in the dog house, recently has been the object of seduction and France the object of sarcasm. This may change again if President Mitterrand seems to become more interested in détente. However, concurrently, the Soviets give priority to agreement with the United States on disarmament, economic exchanges, and, perhaps, the joint management of regional conflicts. Europe is not forgotten and remains the principal stake in the competition—dialogue with the European left is still inspired by the long-term prospect of a denuclearized Europe, a marginalized United States, and a dominant USSR resting on its superior local military power. There is thus a return to the primacy of political goals after what may be described as the militaristic deviation of the Brezhnev era. However, the idea of the indirect route to military dominance by way of economic modernization instead of armaments has had some illustrious precursors, from Witte[8] to Deng Xiaoping—to say nothing of Stalin.[9]

For the short run the possibility of limited compromise which can benefit both East and West should be noted and encouraged. One can only hope that the long-term process Gorbachev has set in motion will result in a rival not only more efficient but also more civilized, less expansionist, and less hostile. But these justified hopes for the short run and the long run should not blind us to some equally justified fears for the strategically crucial middle run. The West may be deprived of some important military options, such as its intermediate-range nuclear weapons, tactical nuclear arms, long-range conventional weapons, a counteroffensive strategy in Europe, and antimissile defense, while the USSR would use a 10- or 20-year respite to make itself more powerful, even militarily.

This last dynamic is just one more reason for the West to practice a strategy of double vigilance with the goal of encouraging the USSR to choose the path of structural transformation by not allowing it to succeed with rhetoric or cunning.

CRITERIA FOR THE WEST

The years to come will put these ideas to the test and will reveal whether Gorbachev's words are harbingers of or substitutes for authentic changes. On myriad international problems, the language of the Soviet Union has changed drastically. Two issues stand out because of their explosive significance: Afghanistan and conventional disarmament in Europe. In both, Gorbachev's speeches herald sensational reverses: a total withdrawal of Soviet troops in one case and a defensive restructuring in the other. It was reasonable to suspect a propaganda trick in both cases with the goal of blocking, respectively, U.S. aid to the Afghan resistance and NATO strategy. But a desire for authentic change cannot be dismissed categorically despite its weak a priori plausibility; such change would bring significant advantages for the Soviet economy and for its foreign relations as well as notable risks for the control of its empire. The West should not fall into the trap of being satisfied with words and paying for them with acts of commission or ommission; should the USSR choose a fundamental change in its military posture, the West should not act so that the USSR loses face or fears for its own security. In the first of the two major test cases, that of Afghanistan, a real withdrawal does look more and more plausible. But it is too early to tell if it will encourage the consolidation of Gorbachev's rule or begin the unraveling of the Soviet empire.

The day of reckoning also approaches in Soviet domestic affairs. By the early 1990s the inadequate and contradictory nature of Gorbachev's economic reforms will have resulted in either their failure or, at best, their very limited and insufficient success. The Soviets will then confront the choice between regression and a qualitative leap forward and the political risks it entails. Progress in the area of human rights will also be easier to gauge because the Soviets will face a choice between beginning to institutionalize greater respect for those rights; more independent justice, and a pluralism of opinions or suppressing those forces and revealing the current concessions as a temporary tactic. The same issue of institutionalization and regularity will occur in East-West communications, where current progress regarding verification, information, and emigration will have to be cast in permanent agreements.

A more stable coexistence with a more open and less aggressive Soviet Union will be possible only if the West remains firm in gauging change in the USSR and offers compromises of its own only when concrete actions follow Soviet promises and when structural changes follow gestures or good graces. The dangers will always exist—principally an explosion in Eastern Europe, an erosion in Western unity and firmness. However, a Soviet Union inclined to seduce rather than intimidate, to focus on social rather than intimidate, to focus on social rather than military factors, would make a turn, which, in spite of all its dangers, could only be looked on favorably by the West. In any case, the West would betray itself if it chose a policy of "the worse, the better" and if, in order to avoid encouraging the illusions of détente, it preferred the continuation of Afghan genocide and of the gulag. The West must ensure that the years ahead will be a period of socialization (in the sociological sense) of the USSR by the international system, rather than one of socialization (in the ideological sense) of the international system by the USSR. Both risks and opportunities are greater than in the previous era, and the outcome is more unpredictable. As a French socialist said when the Left took over in 1936, "At last the difficulties commence!"

NOTES

1. Richard Löwenthal, *World Communism: The Disintegration of a Secular Faith* (New York: Oxford University Press, 1964).
2. "Gorbatchev vu de Varsovie," *La Nouvelle Alternative*, December 8, 1987.
3. Compare "Les Français, le désarmement et l'union Soviétique," Chronique Alain Duhamel, *SOFRES*, July 1987; "Fidarsi da Gorbaciov," *L'Espresso*, July 19, 1987 (opinion poll of nine countries); "Le Match Reagan-Gorbatchev," *Sondage BVA–Paris Match*, January 15, 1988.

4. Compare "L'offensive Gorbatchev," *L'Autre Europe*, no. 14 (1987).

5. *Vestnik Academii Nauk SSSR*, no. 6 (1987).

6. "From Class Obsessions to Dialogue," January 1988 (Report at the conference on the new détente organized by the University of the United Nations, Amsterdam, January 9–10, 1988).

7. Compare S. Shenfield, *The Nuclear Predicament, Exploration in Soviet Ideology* (London: Royal Institute of International Affairs, Chatham House Paper no. 37, 1987).

8. Compare J. Sapir, *Le système militaire soviétique* (Paris: La Découverte, 1987), pp. 226–228.

9. Compare Christopher Donnelly, "The Military Dimension," in *Gorbachev, Economics and Defense* (Sandhurst: The Royal Military Academy, Soviet Studies Research Centre, 1988), pp. 133–134.

28
U.S.-Soviet Relations: Threshold of a New Era*

Arnold L. Horelick

As the decade of the 1980s closed, the United States and the Soviet Union appeared finally to have mastered their forty-year-old conflict. At the Malta summit between Presidents George Bush and Mikhail Gorbachev, the convergence of American and Soviet positions on most agenda items was unprecedented. Their relationship seemed likely to develop with minimum tension, low risk and, prospectively, at greatly reduced cost.

But precisely at the moment when they seem to have perfected their methods for managing the conflicts of the cold war era, that era has abruptly ended. The finely honed instruments of conflict management face early obsolescence. Instead, policymakers in both capitals face a new international politics in which their bipolar competition will no longer provide the dominant framework for ordering the system and disciplining the behavior of states. For the United States the adjustment will surely be difficult, but incomparably less so than for the Soviet Union.

II

By every measure of conventional postwar scorekeeping, 1989 was the year in which the West won the cold war. During the fall and winter, communist rule was toppled or irretrievably compromised in the three key northern-tier states of the Warsaw Pact—Poland, the German Democratic Republic and Czechoslovakia. The Communist Party itself, not to speak of its "leading role," was extinguished in a fourth country, Hungary, and was on the slippery slope of multiparty reform even in Bulgaria. Only in Romania did the communist leader Ceauşescu attempt to hold the line by force, but by year's end he had been executed and his entire Politburo placed under arrest.

*Reprinted by permission of the author and publisher from *Foreign Affairs*, 69, 1, (1989/90). Copyright © 1989 by The Council on Foreign Relations, Inc.

Moscow, moreover, seemed helpless or unwilling to prevent the sudden deterioration of its most sensitive geopolitical position. The Soviet Union was immersed in a profound domestic crisis that threatened both the political stability and the territorial integrity of the state. The Soviet economy was in a shambles. Discontent and pessimism were endemic. In Moscow, supporters and critics competed in making estimates of how many months Gorbachev still had left in which to deliver on perestroika's promise before a "revolution from below," a military coup or a hard-line conservative backlast swept both him and his program away, or compelled him to suspend *demokratizatsia* and glasnost.

In foreign policy, according to the old calculus, Gorbachev may have gained some breathing space for the beleaguered Soviet Union, but only at a high cost: surrendering the "socialist gains" in Eastern Europe, abandoning Third World friends and clients to U.S.-supported counterrevolution, and making an uninterrupted series of grossly asymmetrical arms control concessions, which after five years still had not been seriously reciprocated by the West. Thus, when he arrived at Malta for his first meeting with the new American president, Gorbachev held the weakest geopolitical hand any Soviet leader has had to play in a summit meeting. To a Soviet "old thinker," Bush's praise of Gorbachev and his suspension of a few minor discriminatory economic restrictions were merely the cosmetic part of "rollback with a human face."

There was evidence at year's end of direct criticism of Gorbachev's foreign policy from within the Central Committee. The Western world, however, was lavish in its praise of his statesmanship and diplomacy and not at all inclined to gloat over the crumbling of the Soviet empire or to take satisfaction from the U.S.S.R.'s domestic crisis. In this view, Gorbachev had not lost the cold war for the Soviet Union; he simply had stopped playing the game according to the old rules. His performance was therefore to be judged by a set of new, distinctly different non-zero-sum rules that gave the highest grades for self-restraint and unilateral arms reductions.

Never mind that Gorbachev's capacity to play the game by the old rules had been crippled by the failure of the Soviet economy and the crumbling of communist rule in Eastern Europe; never mind that even the greatest strategic gain of the cold war years—the achievement of nuclear parity with the United States—had failed to yield military or political benefits remotely commensurate with its enormous costs. Having boldly concluded the game was not worth the candle, Gorbachev cut his losses—in some cases brilliantly making a virtue of the hardest necessity and redefining the rules so that what might have counted as defeats and retreats became bold initiatives and daring challenges to old-thinking partners. Indeed, since according to the now virtually universally accepted view that Gorbachev's survival is key to sustaining the more benign global trends, inflicting defeats on him could hardly any longer be the object of Western policy.

In the Soviet Union, however, it was a year that saw the steady erosion of Gorbachev's popularity as perestroika continued to founder, straining the patience of an increasingly assertive and critical public. Paradoxically, Gorbachev's personal power position in Kremlin politics not only failed to be adversely affected, but was appreciably strengthened. Fearing that any wave of discontent strong enough to topple Gorbachev would wash them away as well, conservatives in the party elite had little alternative but to give him grudging support, even as he systematically removed their most prominent spokesmen from the Politburo or demoted them. For radicals and liberals, Gorbachev also remained, as the late Andrei Sakharov described him, "the only realistic alternative leader."

At year's end Gorbachev was nevertheless beleaguered, playing for time and fighting fires, delaying implementation of the most critical parts of perestroika, which were bound to be painful and unpopular. Without such changes in the economic incentive system, however, there could be no breakthroughs and no self-sustaining growth. Even more precariously, he also was walking a tightrope in dealing with the rebellious nationalities, employing all of his persuasive powers to slow down, if not to turn back, a swelling secessionist tide in Lithuania. Following the example of the Baltic states, militant popular fronts were emerging all along the periphery of the Soviet Union. Moldavia was in the throes of anti-Russian ethnic self-assertion, bound to be exacerbated by the fall of Ceauşescu in the Romanian homeland. Most menacing from Moscow's perspective, a popular front was growing in the Ukraine as well. In other republics there were repeated instances of inter-ethnic violence, unchecked in the Caucasus and festering in Central Asia.

Even Gorbachev's most positive domestic achievement of the year, the election of a Congress of People's Deputies and the formation of a new Supreme Soviet, was a mixed blessing for him. Gorbachev clearly sought to create for himself and his programs a broad parliamentary base of political support that he could employ to whip the still indispensable party into line. But the March elections, even though partially rigged, revealed a disaffection from the Communist Party so deep and so widespread that its effectiveness as an instrument of rule was called seriously into question. Moreover, the new forum became a genuine cockpit for debate and conflict that, on the whole, did not enhance Gorbachev's authority or prestige in the country. At the end of the year, Gorbachev found himself defending the constitutionally mandated and symbolically crucial "leading role of the party" against surprisingly strong opposition in the Congress. In comparison to the "socialist countries" of Eastern Europe, which lagged far behind the Soviet Union in political reform at the beginning of 1989, by the year's end only in the U.S.S.R. was the Communist Party still clinging doggedly to its political monopoly.

Ironically, viewed against the background of Gorbachev's forthcoming and welcome departures in foreign policy, his troubles at home helped him abroad. They encouraged the evolution of the Bush Administration's policy from skeptical, watchful waiting to broad engagement with the Soviet Union. The president finally endorsed both Gorbachev and his policies. Amid mounting evidence that perestroika might be failing, Bush claimed to be second to none in supporting it.

III

During the waning years of President Reagan's second term, the running battle over how to deal with Gorbachev's Soviet Union was finally resolved. There were those centered in the office of the secretary of defense who had been the "squeezers." They opposed any relaxation of competitive pressure on the Soviet Union, which they saw as the key to forcing the Kremlin into global retreat and compelling it to choose between outright abandonment of communism or collapse. There was another group, in the State Department, the "dealers," who saw the shifting global correlation of forces and Gorbachev's preoccupation with internal reform as an opportunity to reach arms control and regional agreements on unprecedentedly favorable terms. As Soviet reforms deepened, the "dealers" even grew prepared for such agreements to help Gorbachev as well. By the end of the Reagan Administration, the president's own growing confidence in Gorbachev and Secretary of State George Shultz's persistent efforts to overcome right-wing attachment to the militantly anti-Soviet stance of Reagan's first term had prevailed. "Squeezing" Gorbachev had effectively dropped out of the operative spectrum.

By the time George Bush took office in January, virtually the entire American foreign policy establishment, including its most prominent conservative members, were "dealers" of one kind or another. There were, however, stil important differences. Many observers outside the new administration were prepared to deal quickly with Moscow, and for larger stakes. They were not only ready but eager to help Gorbachev in the bargain. Others, including most of the senior policy figures in the new administration, wanted to move much more cautiously.

At first President Bush and the experienced, pragmatic foreign-policy team around him still had doubts about Gorbachev's intentions. There was a deep skepticism about his chances for survival, not to speak of his chances for succeeding with perestroika, and a gnawing anxiety that his diplomacy was loosening the cohesion and resolution of the Western alliance. In general, the new administration seemed to place a higher priority on preventing the premature dismantling of tried-and-true security structures that had held a hostile Soviet Union at bay for forty years than on risking new initiatives with Gorbachev. For example, in a television interview just prior to Bush's inauguration, Brent Scowcroft, the new national security adviser, questioned whether Gorbachev's real intention was not to weaken the Western alliance and drive a wedge between the United States and its allies.

Initially, no major policy pronouncements on the Soviet Union were made, pending completion of a "comprehensive" national security policy review. The review, however, dragged on for months and reportedly ended up endorsing the unexciting goal of "status quo plus." Administration policymakers seemed preoccuped with the arcane alliance politics of short-range nuclear missile modernization and arms control negotiations, in which Soviet diplomacy was still perceived as a threat to be parried, rather than an opportunity to be explored. This attitude provoked a growing domestic criticism of the administration's slowness and timidity in dealing with the bigger picture. Some European allies also were urging Washington to respond more effectively to Gorbachev's initiatives, if only because they were attracting wide public support in Europe.

In the spring, the president dealt with East-West relations in a series of five speeches that grew progressively more positive in tone. In a speech in May in New London, Connecticut, Bush previewed his administration's new watchword, declaring it was time to "move beyond containment" and to integrate the Soviet Union into the "community of nations." These new slogans in fact turned out to foreshadow a policy shift that was already under way. But the new policy was so entwined with conditions and reservations that it made relatively little impression at the time. More attention was paid to the president's speech in April in Hamtramck, Michigan, where he unveiled a modest program of aid to Poland and Hungary that was widely criticized as insufficient.

Meanwhile, the trials and tribulations of perestroika were making Gorbachev all the more impatient for achievements in foreign policy and arms control that would permit larger and faster transfers of resources from the swollen military sector to the sputtering civilian economy. In Moscow, some Soviet officials were expressing nostalgia for the good old days of Reagan and Shultz.

A major milestone in the evolution of the Bush Administration's policy was Secretary of State James A. Baker's first meeting with Soviet Foreign Minister Eduard Shevardnadze in Moscow in early May. During that visit Gorbachev presented Baker with specific numbers for several categories of weapons to be reduced in the new Conventional Forces in Europe (CFE) negotiations. The numbers were so close to NATO's figures as to convince administration officials that the Soviets were serious about concluding an agreement on terms highly favorable to NATO.

In response to this initiative, President Bush, at a NATO summit in Brussels at the end of May, laid out his own conventional arms reductions proposals. He called for deep Soviet reductions and a break in the logjam that had developed in Vienna over whether to include aircraft and stationed-troop levels in the negotiations.

A second Baker-Shevardnadze meeting, in Wyoming in September, was marked by unusual cordiality, and further accelerated the movement of U.S. policy toward the Soviet Union. The meeting produced new Soviet concessions on a key stalemated issue in the Geneva negotiations on strategic arms reductions: Moscow offered to "de-link" a final agreement in the Strategic Arms Reduction Talks from resolution of the deadlocked defense and space issues. This seemed to remove a major obstacle to the conclusion of a new START agreement by the late spring or early summer of 1990, and cleared the way for an agreement to hold a full-fledged Bush-Gorbachev summit during that period. In fact, private exchanges between Bush and Gorbachev had already begun on the holding of the "informal" summit at Malta.

Those secret exchanges must have been greatly influenced by developments in Eastern Europe. In announcing the scheduling of the Malta meeting, President Bush acknowledged that during his July visit to Eastern Europe, Solidarity leaders in Poland and reformers in Hungary had linked their prospects to Gorbachev's survival; they had urged the president to meet sooner rather than later with the Soviet leader. Six weeks after Bush's visit, Tadeusz Mazowiecki, a Catholic intellectual, was confirmed as prime minister in Warsaw to head a Solidarity-dominated coalition government. A month later, thousands of East Germans were pouring out of their country through Hungary and Czechoslovakia into the Federal Republic of Germany, and pro-democracy demonstrations were breaking out in major cities of the German Democratic Republic. Against this dramatic background Secretary Baker gave two speeches in mid-October, spelling out a U.S. policy of engagement with the Soviet Union. Not only would the United States support perestroika, but the administration had concluded that Gorbachev's success was itself in America's fundamental interest, and was prepared to provide Moscow with advice and technical assistance to help restructure the Soviet economy.

What was new and decidedly different about Baker's October speeches was his treatment of what had become the most hotly debated issue of U.S. policy toward the Soviet Union: how to deal with uncertainties about Gorbachev's survival and the ultimate fate of perestroika. Secretary of Defense Dick Cheney and Deputy National Security Adviser Robert Gates in particular had publicly rated the prospects for both Gorbachev and perestroika as poor, in contexts suggesting that such uncertainty was a strong reason for the administration to proceed with the greatest caution. Secretary Baker stood that position on its head. He asserted that uncertainty about the fate of Gorbachev's reform program should provide "all the more reason, not less, for us to seize the present opportunity" to make agreements to cut back superpower military arsenals and reduce the Soviet threat. This reflected the administration's recognition that it was in the West's interest to move expeditiously toward concluding the arms control agreements now under negotiation, regardless of the uncertainty about the future of Gorbachev and perestroika. If Gorbachev survived and perestroika prospered, the groundwork would be laid for moving further toward institutionalizing a much more stable and less confrontational military relationship. Once the Soviet Union had destroyed nuclear weapons and withdrew or dismantled conventional forces as required by the agreements, it would be difficult, costly and time-consuming for any future Soviet leadership, even one more hostile or assertive, to reverse the process. The stage thus was set for Malta; the Bush Administration had made its choice.

The collapse of communist domination of Eastern Europe had made a crucial difference. It provided dramatic, tangible evidence of a change both in the policies and geopolitical position of the U.S.S.R. that could not possibly be explained away as a ruse or a temporary tactical retreat which might leave the Soviet Union free to resume the old struggle after a respite. The crisis in Eastern Europe reinforced a Western perception that real strategic opportunities lay ahead, not only in arms control but in political arrangements that could fundamentally improve European security—the principal area of competition and the heart of the cold war. It suddenly became critical for the West to see Eastern

Europe through a period of free elections and in the process to reassure Moscow that its security would not be threatened.

IV

It was not surprising that at Malta both Bush and Gorbachev used almost identical language in proclaiming that their two countries were ''at the threshold of a new era.'' But Malta was not the place, and the first week in December was too soon, for the two leaders to exchange architectural plans for a new European political order. The Berlin Wall had been breached only three weeks before, and the outcome in East Germany was still very much in question. Chancellor Helmut Kohl had placed the reunification of Germany on the active political agenda only a few days before Malta; there had not yet been face-to-face meetings between the president and other alliance leaders, and the United States was determined to avoid even the slightest hint of another Yalta.

Going into Malta, the Soviet and American leaders had slogans, not visions, and much less blueprints, for a new European order. While Gorbachev had surrounded his long-standing call for a ''Common European Home'' with thousands of words, there was not much more substance to his theme than to President Bush's more recent call for a ''Europe Whole and Free.'' Moreover, if there was more to Gorbachev's thinking about the design of a ''Common European Home'' than he had revealed before Malta, the sudden changes in Eastern Europe almost certainly would have required a searching reexamination.

Gorbachev himself had inspired the change in Eastern Europe, which he subsequently acknowledged as inevitable. What he clearly had hoped for was to spread perestroika to Eastern Europe, where a wave of reform would be instituted by rejuvenated and restructured Communist parties that would ''renew socialism.'' His vision was a voluntary community of Eastern States pursuing common socialist agendas and led by like-minded reformers. Those states would still be linked, but far more loosely than in the past. For enduring geopolitical and economic reasons, the alliance with the Soviet Union would continue, but in a less militarized and more politicized grouping that would occupy the Eastern wing of the European ''common home.''

This vision had already been upset by the transfer of power to Solidarity in Poland, and had been completely overtaken by events in East Germany and Czechoslovakia. Gorbachev acknowledged that the Communists had ''lost'' the confidence of the people. The hope that some vague common commitment might still emerge to a democratized version of socialism may not have been entirely abandoned in Moscow, but the prospects were poor, and fading. Moscow had to look more and more to a geopolitical rationale persuasive and acceptable to its allies. To do that Gorbachev had to rely on the West's shared concern about stability and enlist Western support for a ''calm and peaceful'' transition in Eastern Europe.

At some point, Gorbachev may have had a game plan for meshing the interrelated processes of demilitarization in the West and reform in the East. The revolt of Eastern Europe, however, destroyed whatever balance Gorbachev had hoped to maintain between these two aims. Gorbachev must surely have understood that his unmistakeable support for reform in Eastern Europe, together with his unilateral force reductions and proposed CFE cuts, would produce more independent allies and weaken Soviet control of the Warsaw Pact—a trend confirmed by the evolution of events in Poland and Hungary.

But earlier, in December 1988 when he announced the decision to cut troops unilaterally, Gorbachev probably hoped—not implausibly—that rapid changes in the West's perception of a Soviet threat would stimulate a comparable weakening of NATO's military efforts and cohesion. By the summer and fall of 1989 changes in Eastern Europe were completely outstripping the more careful arms reduction process on which Gorbachev may have been relying. Moreover, by November it was clear that the issue of German reunification would have to be faced not at the end of a gradual process of change but at a much earlier stage, and under conditions in which the security structures of the East were disintegrating while NATO remained wholly intact. Once the issue of German reunification was raised, it became even more crucial for Gorbachev to emphasize to the uneasy Western allies of the F.R.G. their common interest with Moscow in maintaining stability in Europe during the transition, and to encourage a multilateral approach to the German question such that Moscow would not be obliged to be the sole naysayer.

V

The emergence of the German question must have caused second thoughts in Moscow about continuing the Soviet campaign to dissolve the opposing alliances and to seek the withdrawal of foreign forces from Europe. In such a reappraisal, Gorbachev was no doubt encouraged by reassuring evidence that the United States and its allies were not seeking to undercut Moscow during its time of troubles in Eastern Europe, and that they too preferred a stable orderly transition, rather than a precipitous upheaval, to end the division of Europe. In the West as well as in the East there was a clear preference for stability: "This is not the time," Gorbachev told the French foreign minister, "to destroy the established international political institutions."

While the superpowers did in fact have certain common interests in a stable process, their objectives were a mix of overlapping interests and potential new conflicts.

For the West the approach to a new European security order is likely to be to preserve and strengthen Western institutions that have proved so effective during the cold war, and to ensure that the democratic Eastern countries that may emerge have an opportunity for broader and deeper relations with the West. The

Western design will probably be to ensure that a reunified Germany would remain strongly anchored in the West.

In stressing gradualism, emphasizing stability and calling for the adaptation and transformation of existing institutions, the West's approach is not incompatible with the Soviet desire to play for time. For the Soviet Union there can only be the hope that, by slowing down the process of change in the East and buying time, Moscow can still keep open the option for developing some kind of community of interests between a vaguely socialist Eastern Europe and a reconstructed Soviet Union. On this basis, the Soviet Union as well as the East Europeans could begin to share in the economic and technological benefits of closer ties with the West. Being left out altogether is Moscow's nightmare.

Thus far Moscow and the West have demonstrated a common interest in peaceful and gradual change in Eastern Europe. That the West should wish change in Eastern Europe to be peaceful is hardly surprising, but the implication that to be peaceful it must also be gradual reflects a Western sensitivity, which Moscow obviously shares, to the potential for a destabilizing crisis. This concern was dramatically demonstrated by Secretary Baker's quick visit in mid-December to East Berlin, where he expressed support for the reformist policies of the shaky new Communist prime minister, Hans Modrow. Baker reportedly made the visit on the strength of the advice of the U.S. ambassador to the G.D.R. that chances for a peaceful transition to democracy in East Germany would be better if the Modrow government survived.

A second area of common interests is likely to be an orderly deliberate process to reduce military forces in Europe, to be negotiated and implemented through CFE by existing alliance groupings.

For the Soviet Union, the CFE process provides a vehicle for securing at least some reciprocal returns from the West for reductions in swollen Soviet forces. Moscow wishes desperately to make substantial force reductions for its own reasons, but a second round of deep unilateral cuts might be politically impossible for Gorbachev. Moreover, the process of negotiating, implementing and verifying a CFE agreement provides the Warsaw Pact with a raison d'être that serves what is perhaps the only remaining common interest in the Eastern alliance. The CFE process can also estblish a pace for Soviet withdrawals as a result of negotiations with the West, rather than of potentially explosive bilateral negotiations between Moscow and East European capitals.

The United States wil seek to lock in an overwhelmingly favorable reductions agreement by substantially eliminating Soviet conventional advantages through asymmetrical reductions that only marginally affect NATO force levels. Moreover, such an agreement would help forestall premature dismantling of NATO, dampen pressures for much larger withdrawals of U.S. forces and buy insurance against reversals and new instabilities in the East.

Thus arms control, if given time to unfold, would tend to perpetuate the two alliances in Europe; any movement toward German reunification would be contained within this framework. Gorbachev has explicitly argued for retaining existing institutions in formulations that do not distinguish between NATO and the Warsaw Pact. Officially, the United States has taken no position on the desirability of the Warsaw Pact's survival. Nevertheless, the CFE process that the United States and NATO have continued to endorse serves to stabilize the Warsaw Pact and give it a rationale that democratic governments in Eastern Europe might also be able to accept and use to defend against nationalist anti-Soviet electoral pressures at home.

On the other hand, both Moscow and Washington have talked, in strikingly similar language, about the transformation of their alliances from military organizations to more "political" ones. For both this is a means of giving their alliances, and their leading roles in them, a new dispensation in a world in which the alliances' primary military functions are waning in importance.

But prospects for a political NATO and a political Warsaw Pact are quite different. NATO is necessarily a political alliance. While there may be some resistance, especially from the French, to permitting Atlanticist NATO to intrude on the political prerogatives of the European Community, the transformation of NATO into an alliance with growing political functions faces no profound obstacles.

To transform the Warsaw Pact into a more "political" organ is a much more dubious proposition. As Soviet European specialists have acknowledged, the political infrastructure of the Warsaw Treaty Organization is poorly developed. It lacks a permanent political staff headquarters; its highest political organs meet only rarely and for largely ceremonial purposes; and its most important political decisions in the past were made in party, not state, channels—a practice that has been overtaken by the collapse of ruling Communist parties in Eastern Europe.

VI

On the question of German reunification, the official objectives of the United States and the Soviet Union are widely divergent, if not directly contradictory. The United States, along with all of the Western allies, has long been committed to supporting the goal of German unity so long as it is the result of the "free self-determination of the German people." Gorbachev and Shevardnadze now also have endorsed the principle of "self-determination of peoples and states" and "freedom of choice" in Eastern Europe. But Moscow clearly hopes that the East Germans, exercising their right of free choice, will choose to remain a separate German state. For the time being the Soviet Union refuses to deal concretely with the contingency of a different choice. Gorbachev emphasizes the "existing realities" of the two German states and prefers to leave it to "history" to decide, implying that history is to be measured in large increments of time. For now, according to Moscow, the issue of German reunification is not on the agenda.

Moreover, just prior to the Malta summit the Bush administration added several other conditions, including that German reunification "should occur in the context of Germany's continued alignment with NATO." That was new; in the past, the emphasis had been almost exclusively on the democratic political organization of a unified German state. By attaching continued alignment with NATO to its formulation, the United States has laid out a resolution of the German question that is diametrically opposed to the official Soviet position. For the Soviets, reunification—if it is to occur at all—can only be envisioned in the context of a larger process of "overcoming the division of Europe," including the simultaneous dissolution of both NATO and the Warsaw Pact.

Yet while Moscow responded harshly to Chancellor Kohl's 10-point outline for reunification—which conspicuously failed to specify that a reunified Germany would remain aligned with NATO—the Soviets have not been visibly perturbed by the new American position. Indeed, it seems clear that, on the whole, Moscow welcomed the prompt intervention of the United States to slow down the momentum imparted to German reunification by the surprise unilateral Kohl initiative. The U.S. call for a unified Germany to remain in NATO is embedded in a set of other conditions, which, taken together, underline that the German question should not be decided by German states alone, and that other parties whose interests must be considered include, in addition to West Germany's NATO allies, the U.S.S.R. The U.S. formulation of conditions for German reunification, as Secretary Baker has suggested, may not be "a distasteful one to the Soviet Union."

Thus, the U.S. position states that the achievement of German unity must be "peaceful and gradual, and part of a step-by-step process," It must be in accord with the 1975 Helsinki agreements, which stipulated that the postwar boundaries of Europe are fixed and can be changed only by "peaceful negotiation." In his remarks on the future of Europe at the post-Malta NATO summit in Brussels, President Bush added another principle that had not been included in the list announced by Secretary Baker before Malta, namely that reunification should occur "with due regard for the legal role and responsibilities of the Allied Powers." While perhaps intended in the first instance to be responsive to the expressed interests of the British and French, that statement was the clearest U.S. endorsement yet of a legitimate Soviet role in resolving the question of German reunification. It was given symbolic expression soon after by the first formal meeting in 18 years of the U.S., Soviet, British and French ambassadors in Berlin, called on Soviet initiative ostensibly to discuss a two-year-old American proposal to improve air traffic safety and other Berlin issues.

Immediately after the fall of Honecker and the breaching of the Berlin Wall, there was concern in some Western capitals that Gorbachev might respond with a characteristic preemptive diplomatic strike. If he foresaw that East Germany would soon cease to be a viable state and that events might reach a point where reunification could only be prevented by force, Gorbachev might offer to withdraw Soviet troops entirely from the G.D.R. and accept the reunification of Germany in return for neutralization.

A proposal to trade German unity for neutralization has of course been in Moscow's portfolio since Stalin's "peace note" of March 1952. In the radically altered circumstances of late 1989, however, it loomed as a very risky and even less promising gambit for the Soviet Union. The collapse of communism in East Germany had gravely weakened Moscow's bargaining position. Playing the German card in these circumstances would have threatened to damage, fatally, those residual political forces in the G.D.R. that were prepared to hold out for a separate East German state.

Moreover, it was hard for the Soviets to know how such a preemptive offer might have played out in West German public opinion. The Bonn government would have either rejected it outright or redefined its terms to preserve German security ties to the West. Gorbachev knew that such a ploy would severely antagonize the United States and its NATO allies, who would regard it as an act of political warfare; it might perhaps have disrupted the entire pattern of European diplomacy so painstakingly constructed by Gorbachev and Shevardnadze. Finally, it was highly uncertain that the U.S.S.R. would be satisfied with the "success" that playing the German card might produce. With West Germany in such a powerful position and still so firmly anchored economically and politically to the West, even formal neutralization could not ensure a benign balance for Soviet interests.

Thus far Soviet intentions point in a rather different direction. Within days of the opening of crossing points in the Berlin Wall, Moscow began to put out strong signals that it was preparing not a preemptive diplomatic ploy but a political holding action. In meeting with the French, Italian and other West European diplomats and journalists, the Soviets sought to make common cause with those in the West alarmed by the sudden prospect of German reunification. Reunification, Moscow insisted, was not on the agenda. The existence of two German states was a "reality" that had to be accepted; "history," in some fashion, would decide.

The surprise unveiling of Kohl's reunification "outline," however, directly challenged Soviet efforts to keep the issue off the agenda. Had Gorbachev chosen to pursue it, Moscow might have explored the opening provided by Kohl's failure to call explicitly for keeping a unified Germany in NATO. Instead, the Soviet Union attacked Kohl frontally for preempting the German question, seeking to destabilize the G.D.R., and ignoring the interests of other European powers. The Soviets vowed "to defend the G.D.R." against efforts from the outside to interfere with its right to choose a separate sovereign existence. Shevardnadze, during his visit to NATO headquarters, was even more emphatic in his opposition. Whether this position can be held after the May elections in East Germany remains a critical question for Gorbachev.

VII

In sum, the two powers have reaffirmed the CFE arms control process, endorsed the Helsinki framework, urged gradualism on the democratic governments of Eastern Europe and endorsed a role for the wartime Allied Powers in resolution of the German question.

Inevitably the question arises: Is the United States throwing Moscow a life preserver to keep the Warsaw Pact afloat in stormy waters in which it would otherwise soon drown? In other words, does a U.S. decision to use the CFE arms control forum and the two alliances as the instruments for managing the transition help to perpetuate and legitimize an Eastern alliance that is imploding? Would a better course be to seek to end the Warsaw Pact quickly while keeping NATO as insurance? This approach would argue, if not for dropping CFE altogether, then for concluding it quickly and stopping there, forgoing CFE II, and letting events take their course. This approach would also call for resisting any Soviet effort to draw the U.S. into a dialogue on management of the transition, discussion of a European settlement or, especially, joint four-power responsibilities for a peace treaty with Germany—all based on the two blocs.

There are clear dangers to such a course. On the one hand, withdrawal of Soviet military forces from the territories of most, and possibly all, of its Warsaw Pact allies is surely conceivable, as is the transformation or even dissolution of the Warsaw Pact. Soviet forces in Hungary and those introduced into Czechoslovakia since the 1968 invasion may well be withdrawn by agreement between the Soviet Union and the "host" countries even in advance of a CFE agreement. Such a withdrawal might be treated as a "down payment" against the reductions that will be required to bring Soviet force levels down to an agreed-upon ceiling. In the same way, through bilaterial agreement with Warsaw, Soviet forces in Poland also may be reduced to minimal levels required to maintain lines of communication to East Germany.

On the other hand, to count on the Soviet Union to comply sheepishly with a demand by an East German government of any political persuasion to sever alliance ties and withdraw the Soviet army from the G.D.R., absent agreement on reciprocal (even if not entirely symmetrical) changes in American forces in West Germany, stretches even the most generous interpretation of the new thinking to the breaking point. Gorbachev has accepted as inevitable the dramatic upheavals that have convulsed Eastern Europe and has refrained from using force to save dying communist regimes, but it would be a mistake to assume he would be willing to see the perimeter of Soviet security interests, like the zone of communist political dominance, moved back from the Elbe to the Soviet border.

Nevertheless, the retraction of Soviet military power from Eastern Europe, and especially from East Germany, is and has been an abiding Western interest. Exploration of ways to roll back Soviet military power by negotiation and agreement is well under way. CFE should be regarded as but the first installment of such a negotiation. Moreover, agreements need not necessarily produce perfectly symmetrical outcomes. For example, given constraints and guarantees that East German territory could not be used for hostile military purposes, it is even conceivable that ultimately the Soviet Union would agree to accept a residual U.S. military presence in West Germany, even if all Soviet forces are withdrawn from the G.D.R. Such an arrangement would be compatible with "confederal structures" linking the two German states politically and economically to each other, to the European Community, and to whatever all-European institutions may evolve out of the Helsinki process. But such a benign outcome seems plausible only as the end-point of a process in which the Soviet Union has clearly participated along with the East Europeans.

As democratic governments are formed in Eastern Europe, choices affecting the pace and character of that process will be largely in the hands of the people of Eastern Europe and their freely elected governments. They could throw over restraints, leave the Warsaw Pact, and demand immediate withdrawal of all Soviet forces well before some new security structure has been put in its place. It would then be for the Soviet Union to decide whether to acquiesce or to accept the costs and risks of confrontation. One cannot preclude that the Soviets would yield in the end, but it is not a gamble the West should invite.

Of crucial importance is getting through the short run. The present, initial stage of the liberation of Eastern Europe is the most dangerous and sensitive one (as Romania demonstrated). The Bush Administration has rightly put the main priority on helping East European reformers and opposition through this delicate period and making the loss of the Soviet empire seem as nonthreatening a prospect as possible for Moscow.

In return, the West must insist, as a minimum and indispensable condition, that the Soviets continue scrupulously to observe a policy of noninterference in domestic political processes in Eastern Europe. If Soviet military forces are not directly challenged, it is hard to see why the Soviets at this late date might choose to use force to save local Communist parties. The last good chance has long since been missed, and the costs would be astronomical.

As long as there is no such interference, continued existence of the Warsaw Pact should not be objectionable to the West on military grounds during this transition process. It is already an empty shell and no longer a useful adjunct to a Soviet offensive strategy. Indeed, its existence may be some additional insurance against surprise, serving as an early warning system for the West.

It is true that arms control and other arrangements preserving the two alliances might somehow legitimize efforts of the Soviets to maintain a military presence in Eastern Europe longer. But the spontaneous evaporation of the Soviet Union is not the most plausible alternative.

VIII

Neither Moscow nor Washington can yet see what will replace the cold-war system. The 1990s are likely to be a transitional period for relations between the two superpowers. In the multipolar world now emerging, they are likely to have more parallel and convergent interests than before. The Soviet Union, however, will find itself in radically altered circumstances that are still evolving and that could change even more radically. It now prefers gradualism and preserving existing institutions, but desperation could lead to more risky strategies. As for the United States, it needs to consult with its allies to work out a Western position before further engaging the Soviet Union on a new "architecture" for Europe.

It is misleading to conclude, however, that these new circumstances will place the superpowers on the sidelines because they no longer control events and no longer dominate their alliances. So long as large Soviet forces remain in Eastern Europe, there can be no definitive end to the confrontation with the West and no complete solution to the German question. Some significant potential for reversing policy in Eastern Europe, by a different Soviet regime, will persist.

In this light, it is the United States alone among all NATO members that is capable of leading the Western effort to negotiate the Soviet Union out of Europe as a military presence. Reciprocal military moves to compensate Moscow will have to come chiefly from Washington. The nuclear dimension is still almost exclusively a U.S.-Soviet issue to negotiate. Finally, the United States is best positioned to broker a Western consensus on the German question and to lead in negotiating it with the Soviets.

As the United States and the Soviet Union reach the threshold of a new era in their relations, their roles in shaping the post-cold war world will be different from those they played in managing the East-West conflict, but no less crucial. Both will have to adapt their policies and behavior to environments in which they will have substantially diminished control and influence. In making this adjustment, the United States can draw on its own democratic institutions and traditions and on its long experience in heading an alliance of free and often contentious partners. For the Soviet Union, this will be an entirely new experience for which the history of its foreign relations and its domestic political traditions have poorly prepared it. In the long run, its success in adjusting to a new and constructive international role will depend on its success in transforming the Soviet system itself. It is in this sense above all that the success of perestroika is in the fundamental interest of the Western world as well as of the peoples of the Soviet Union.

29

The New Soviet Approach to Europe*

F. Stephen Larrabee

Under Mikhail S. Gorbachev, Soviet policy toward Europe has undergone the most dramatic changes since the end of World War II. Soon after coming to power, Gorbachev embarked on a policy designed to strengthen ties with Western Europe and exploit transatlantic differences. At the same time, he tried to redefine relations with Eastern Europe, putting greater emphasis on "freedom of choice" and economic efficiency.

Gorbachev's policy was predicated on a gradual evolution of the bipolar security system in Europe and the continued existence of two German states. His initiatives, however, unleashed forces that took on a dynamic of their own and resulted in the collapse of communism in Eastern Europe and the destruction of the bipolar security order based on the division of Europe into two opposing political-ideological blocs. As a result, the Soviet leadership is now faced with the need to construct a new policy not only toward Eastern Europe but toward Europe as a whole. Moreover, it must do so at a time when the Soviet Union faces major internal difficulties that could severely limit its capacity to pursue a vigorous and coherent European policy.

BREZHNEV'S LEGACY

Soviet policy in Europe under Gorbachev must be seen against the background of the policy that he inherited from his predecessors, especially Leonid I. Brezhnev. Brezhnev's policy during his latter years was characterized by two principal features. The first was the USSR's isolation in Western Europe. Brezhnev's military buildup, especially the development of the SS-20 medium-range missile, proved to be a major strategic blunder and had a negative impact on Soviet relations with Western Europe. Rather than weakening Western cohesion and

*Reprinted by permission of the author and publisher from *The New Europe: Revolution in East-West Relations*, Nils Wessell (ed.), pp. 1-25. Copyright © 1991 by The Academy of Political Science, New York.

providing the USSR with important military advantages—as was its apparent intention—the buildup had the opposite effect, strengthening the cohesion of the North Atlantic Treaty Organization (NATO) and leading to a counterdeployment of United States missiles on European soil.

This miscalculation was compounded by a serious tactical error: the decision to walk out of the intermediate-range nuclear forces (INF) talks in Geneva in November 1983. This walkout made the Soviet Union appear to be the main obstacle to arms control, further tarnishing its image in Western Europe. As a result, by the time Gorbachev assumed power in March 1985 the Soviet Union had become seriously isolated.

The second feature of Brezhnev's policy was a visible erosion of Soviet hegemony in Eastern Europe. On the economic side, progress toward integration within the Council for Mutual Economic Assistance (CMEA) had virtually ground to a halt. On the political side, the Soviet effort to freeze East-West relations after the collapse of the INF talks upset the USSR's East European allies and accentuated differences within the Warsaw Pact, particularly with Hungary and East Germany, both of which had developed a strong vested stake in East-West détente. These problems were compounded by the impact of the succession issue, which increasingly preoccupied the Soviet leadership, deflecting attention away from pressing international problems, including those in Eastern Europe. As a result, Soviet policy toward Eastern Europe was increasingly characterized by drift and stagnation.

In short, by the mid-1980s the Soviet empire, as Charles Gati aptly put it, was "alive but not well."[1] The once monolithic bloc had become not only more diverse but also more fragmented. Stability had been bought at the price of stagnation, and ideological corrosion had replaced ideological cohesion as the hallmark of Soviet policy toward Eastern Europe.

NEW THINKING AND WESTERN EUROPE

When Gorbachev assumed power in March 1985, he inherited a European policy in deep crisis. In Western Europe, the Soviet Union was isolated, its policy stalled as a result of the INF debacle. In Eastern Europe, the USSR found itself at odds with its allies, many of which increasingly sought to exploit the Soviet preoccupation with internal problems—particularly the succession issue—to expand their room for maneuver. At the same time, Gorbachev was confronted with a mounting economic crisis that threatened to undermine the Soviet Union's ability to remain a major military and political power.

These developments required changes in Soviet policy toward Europe. Moreover, they coincided with a shift in Soviet perspectives on Western Europe and NATO. In the 1950s and 1960s the Soviet Union had seen Western Europe (with the exception of France) largely as a pliant tool in the United States global strategy. While the Soviets realized that West European interests were not always identical with those of the United States, they thought that American economic and military power ensured that American interests would largely prevail.

In the 1970s and 1980s, however, there was a growing recognition of the importance of Western Europe as an independent "power center" within the capitalist world. As Alexander Yakovlev, one of Gorbachev's closest advisers, noted in 1985: "The distancing of Western Europe, Japan, and other capitalist countries from U.S. strategic military plans in the near future is neither an excessively rash fantasy nor a nebulous prospect. It is dictated by objective factors having to do with the rational guarantee of all of their political and economic interests, including security."[2]

Gorbachev's report to the Twenty-seventh Party Congress reflected some of these insights. He noted that the economic, financial, and technological superiority that the United States had exercised in the past had been "put to a serious test" and that Western Europe and Japan were challenging the United States even in areas where it had traditionally exerted undisputed hegemony, such as high technology. Many sectors of West European public opinion, he claimed, "had begun to openly discuss whether US policy coincides with Western Europe's notions about its own security and whether the US was going too far in its claims to leadership." While admitting that the economic, political, military, and other common interests of the three centers of power (the United States, Japan, and Western Europe) could not be expected to break up in the near future, he warned that the United States "should not expect unquestioning obedience of its allies" and predicted that "contradictions" within the capitalist camp were likely to increase as a result of the emergence of new centers of power.[3]

Gorbachev's early statements clearly suggested that he intended to take a more differentiated approach to relations with the West, according greater importance to Western Europe. Soon after coming to power, for instance, he acknowledged the importance of relations with the United States but noted: "We do not view the world solely through the prism of these relationships. We understand the importance of other countries."[4] In effect, this represented an upgrading of the role of other areas, especially Western Europe, in Soviet policy.

There were other signs that the USSR was according Western Europe greater priority. One of the most important was the creation in late 1987 of the Institute on Europe, headed by a highly respected academic, Vitali Zhurkin, former deputy director of the Institute of USA and Canada. The establishment of the new institute reflected the Kremlin's growing appreciation of the importance and autonomy of Western Europe. At the same time, it provided the Soviet leadership with an important additional source of information and informed analyses on current developments in Europe.

This is not to argue, as some observers have, that Gorbachev has adopted a "Europe first" strategy.[5] Indeed, one of the striking features of Gorbachev's first years in power was his high priority on obtaining an accommodation with the

United States. Relations with Western Europe, though accorded a higher priority than in the past, were still regarded as secondary to the improvement of relations with the United States.

Some Soviet officials, in fact, openly complained that this preoccupation with the United States had blinded the USSR to trends toward greater political and military self-assertion on the part of Western Europe:

US monopoly on engaging in dialogue with the USSR consolidates American leadership in the West, leaving Western Europe a secondary role in world politics. In our view, we largely facilitated this ourselves. Bewitched by the industrial and military might of the United States, we failed to notice, or—to be more precise— did not take fully into account, the fact that Pax Americana was shaking and had begun to crumble, while other imperialist centres, including Western Europe, were becoming more active in world affairs.[6]

Soviet policy, they charged, had failed to pay sufficient attention to these changes. They pointed in particular to the intensification of European military integration, which "had picked up speed since Reykjavik," warning that "passivity" and attempts to ignore the creation of a European defense "will inescapably lead to a situation where this defense will be fashioned according to American formulas, to the prejudice of the USSR." As a result, the Soviet Union would be forced to deal with a joint NATO position, in this case a United States position, just as it was increasingly forced to deal with a joint European position of the European Community (EC). These officials called for "new approaches" that would take due account of the European desire for greater independence in security matters.

These remarks, though hardly typical, reflected a growing debate about the implications of European defense. On this issue, as on others, there was no consensus. One school of thought saw the prospects for serious cooperation as largely ephemeral; a second, taking the trend more seriously, argued that the intensification of economic integration was providing the basis for much closer security and military cooperation.

The key issue, in Moscow's view, was the impact of these developments on East-West relations. Were they an effort to develop Western Europe into a truly independent power center or simply an attempt to strengthen the European pillar of NATO and influence Western Europe's voice in the shaping of NATO military policy? Again, there were different views. However, the dominant one—at least within the Soviet Foreign Ministry—tended to regard the trend toward closer military cooperation as a potential threat to East-West détente and an effort to strengthen the European pillar of NATO. Writing in *International Affairs*, the journal of the Soviet Foreign Ministry, V. Stupishin, a high-ranking Foreign Ministry official, concluded:

The growth of military integration in Western Europe and creation of some new organizational forms of a "European buttress" of NATO may provide Western Europe with yet another instrument for influencing the USA. But a far more essential and really negative result of this will be that the split of Europe into opposed blocs will be consolidated and new obstacles will be put up in the general European process and the construction of a common European home will be impeded, to the detriment of our interests as well. That is why we are so concerned over the military-integration tendencies in Western Europe.[7]

The debate over European defense reflected a broader shift in Soviet attitudes in the late 1980s regarding developments in Western Europe. In the 1970s and early 1980s the greater self-confidence and assertiveness of Western Europe had generally been welcomed and seen as undermining United States influence within NATO. Gorbachev's remarks at the Twenty-seventh Party Congress had largely reflected this perspective. By the late 1980s, however, Soviet officials and analysts were beginning to take a more differentiated view of these developments. The critical West European reaction to the Reykjavik summit and the fears of "denuclearization" prompted by the INF treaty, especially in France and Great Britain, contributed to a growing recognition that his new West European self-assertiveness might not always work to Soviet advantage.

These growing doubts were also visible in the shift in Soviet attitudes and policy toward France. When Gorbachev came to power in 1985 he tried to make France the centerpiece of his West European policy. This effort, however, produced few positive results. Soviet commentary on France after 1986 reflected growing disappointment with the course of French policy. France's adherence to nuclear deterence and its plans to modernize its strategic nuclear arsenal caused particular concern. France was also seen as the spearhead behind the intensification of military and security cooperation in Western Europe, which, Soviet officials charged, was designed to justify France's adherence to nuclear deterrence: "The revival of the military articles of the 1963 Elysée Treaty with the FRG [Federal Republic of Germany] the stepped-up military cooperation with Britain, Italy and Spain, the reanimation of Western European Union, the Platform for European Security Interests adopted in the Hague—all these and other integrational processes in Western Europe have been inspired and organized mainly by Paris, which clearly is looking for a 'European' political justification of its policy of perpetuating 'nuclear deterrence.' "[8]

The intensification of French military ties with West Germany also provoked concern. "What and whom are these ties directed against?" asked Soviet officials.[9] Such questions reflected the USSR's fear that French-German military cooperation might provide the basis for broader West European cooperation in the military area and possibly even help West Germany acquire nuclear weapons through the back door. Thus, after 1986, Soviet enthusiasm for France's "Europeanism" was largely overshadowed by a concern that the emerging military cooperation with West Germany would strengthen NATO and tip the military balance in Europe against the Soviet Union.

THE EUROPEAN COMMUNITY

Concern with the implications of West European military integration has been one aspect of the broader Soviet concern with the process of West European integration generally. For many years the USSR regarded the EC as little more than an instrument to strengthen the European pillar of NATO. Soviet attitudes toward the EC, however, have undergone a significant evolution under Gorbachev. Since the mid-1980s, Soviet analysts have shown an increasing appreciation of the growing role of the EC as an economic and political actor in international affairs. In particular, analysts have pointed to a marked evolution toward formulating common EC positions on foreign policy.[10]

Soviet analysts see the EC decision to create a single internal market by 1992 as "a qualitatively new stage" in the integration process, which will have major implications for East-West relations.[11] This, they argue, will accelerate integration—including foreign policy and military—and encourage closer cooperation in other areas. In the 1990s the United States (and, by implication, the Soviet Union) will have to deal with a Western Europe that is economically and technologically stronger as well as politically and militarily more cohesive.

The emergence of the EC as a new power center has required the Soviet Union to adopt a new approach toward the organization. This new approach began to manifest itself soon after Gorbachev assumed power. During Italian Prime Minister Bettino Craxi's visit to Moscow in May 1985, the new Soviet leader announced the USSR's willingness to recognize the EC as a "political entity" and to resume negotiations regulating relations between the EC and the CMEA, which had been broken off in the spring of 1980.[12] These negotiations led to the signing of a "Common Declaration" between the EC and the CMEA on 25 June 1988, which provided the framework for the establishment of diplomatic relations and the conclusion of trade agreements between the EC and individual members of the CMEA.

The 1988 Common Declaration was primarily motivated by economic concerns, particularly the USSR's desire for access to West European trade and technology. But it also reflected the Soviet leadership's growing appreciation of the important political role that the EC had begun to play in East-West relations. Soviet officials and analysts have increasingly pointed to the long-term political implications of accelerated integration, which is seen as laying the groundwork for closer cooperation in other areas, including foreign policy and the military.

From the Soviet Union's perspective, the main danger is that West European integration will solidify the division of Europe into blocs, erecting new barriers to East-West trade, and deepening the economic and technological gap between the two parts of Europe. Gorbachev's emphasis on the "common European home" has thus partly been aimed at preventing the creation of new impediments to Soviet access to West European research and development programs and ensuring that the USSR will benefit from new technology as West European integration intensifies.

EASTERN EUROPE

Gorbachev does not appear to have had a "grand design" for Eastern Europe. Rather, his policy emerged gradually as a result of incremental changes and adjustments. The cumulative effect of these changes, however, has been seriously to erode Soviet influence in Eastern Europe.

Initially, Gorbachev's policy differed little from that of his predecessors. Its emphasis was on increasing political, economic, and military integration—albeit on a more consultative basis. In effect, Gorbachev tried to strike a balance between the legitimization of "national interests" and the promotion of "international obligations" and between the demands of diversity and the desire for unity. The greater weight, however, was clearly on the side of closer unity.

Gorbachev's statements during 1986 and 1987 continued to reflect this uneasy balance between the demands of diversity and the desire for unity. The sense of continuity in Soviet policy in this period was reinforced by the appearance of authoritative articles by top Soviet officials in the Soviet press stressing the importance of "proletarian internationalism" (a code word for Soviet hegemony) and attacking market-oriented policies and other steps that violated "general laws of socialist construction."[13] Such articles were counterbalanced, however, by others representing a more open and flexible policy, suggesting the lack of a firm line on Soviet policy toward Eastern Europe.[14]

During late 1987 and early 1988, however, the outlines of a new policy toward Eastern Europe—a "Gorbachev doctrine" began to emerge. In essence, this doctrine represented an effort to extend the principles of perestroika and "new thinking" to relations with the USSR's East European allies. It was designed to eliminate "distortions" that had inhibited socioeconomic development of the bloc countries in the past—many of them rooted in the Stalinist system imposed on these countries in the late 1940s and early 1950s—and to create a more balanced relationship based on true partnership and mutual respect for national differences.

In the political arena, Gorbachev showed a willingness to grant East European leaders greater flexibility and freedom to decide their own affairs—as long as their efforts did not directly contradict or undercut Soviet interests. Allies were allowed greater initiative, especially in disarmament matters and relations with Western Europe. Consultation between the Soviet Union and its allies became more regularized and more genuine. While the Soviet Union continued to set the agenda for bloc relations, especially on military matters, the views of the East European allies were more frequently solicited.

There was also greater recognition—and tolerance—of diversity within the bloc. As Gorbachev stressed in a speech in Prague in April 1987: "We are far from calling on anyone to copy us. Every socialist country has its specific features, and the fraternal parties determine their political line with a view to the national conditions. . . . No one has the right to claim a special status in the socialist world. The independence of every party, its responsibility to its people, and its right to resolve problems of the country's development in a sovereign way—these are indisputable principles for us.''[15] He reiterated this point in his speech commemorating the seventieth anniversary of the Bolshevik Revolution on 2 November 1987, noting: "Unity does not mean identity or uniformity.''[16] In short, the Soviet Union no longer claimed that there was a single path to socialism or that only one model is universally valid. Each national party had the right to decide how socialism should best be developed in its own country, taking into account its own circumstances as well as its obligations to the socialist community as a whole.

The most important shift, however, was Gorbachev's willingness to repudiate the Brezhnev doctrine. Initially, Gorbachev showed a reluctance to face the issue squarely, in part because he did not want to destabilize the Gustáv Husák/Milos Jakes regime in Prague, which was closely associated with the period of "normalization" following the Soviet-led invasion in 1968. Soviet domestic considerations—above all, resistance from the conservatives within the Communist Party of the Soviet Union (CPSU)—also probably played a role.

Beginning in 1988, however, Gorbachev began step by step to move closer to repudiating the doctrine. The communiqué issued at the end of the Gorbachev trip to Yugoslavia in March 1988, for example, expressed "respect for different paths to socialism and stressed the right of all countries to unimpeded independence and equal rights" regardless of their sociopolitical system.[17] In his speech to the Council of Europe in Strasbourg in July 1989 Gorbachev was even more explicit, stating that "any interference in internal affairs, any attempts to limit the sovereignty of states—both friends and allies or anyone else—is inadmissible.''[18]

Finally, during his visit to Finland in October 1989, Gorbachev openly repudiated the Brezhnev doctrine. The doctrine, Soviet Foreign Ministry spokesman Gennadi Gerasimov stressed, was "dead." It had been replaced by what he termed the "Sinatra doctrine," referring to Frank Sinatra's popular song entitled "My Way." This implied, as Gerasimov put it, that each East European country was free to carry out political and social changes "their way" without interference from the USSR. At the Warsaw Pact meeting in Moscow in December 1989 the 1968 invasion of Czechoslovakia was formally condemned as "illegal," and the member states committed themselves to following a policy of strict noninterference in each other's internal affairs.

These measures were accompanied by a strong emphasis on the need for economic reform. While Gorbachev did not force the Soviet model of reform on his East European allies, he made it clear that the East European economies had to be restructured to make them more efficient and competitive. On the one hand, he stepped up the pressure on his East European allies to increase the quality of their manufactured goods exported to the Soviet Union; on the other, he indicated that the USSR was no longer willing to provide Eastern Europe with raw materials and energy at previous levels.

Rather than creating greater cohesion within the bloc, however, Gorbachev's emphasis on reform accentuated the divisions among the Soviet Union's East European allies. Within Hungary and Poland, his calls for reform legitimized the reformers' calls for more radical, more rapid change. At the same time, these calls indirectly increased the pressure on the remaining bloc members to embrace reform more seriously.

By 1988 the bloc had in effect split into two camps. On one side was a reformist group composed of the USSR, Hungary, and Poland. On the other was a "rejectionist front" consisting of Czechoslovakia, East Germany, and Romania, which either rejected reforms outright or were less than enthusiastic about implementing them. Bulgaria was somewhere in between: General Secretary Todor Zhivkov paid lip service to reform, but he dragged his feet in actually implementing them.

To be sure, Gorbachev did not directly demand that his allies adopt the Soviet model of reform. However, by way of example and word he indirectly increased the pressure on the orthodox members of the bloc to embrace reform more seriously. Perhaps most important, he increased popular expectations and pressures for change from below. In many East European countries, such as East Germany and Bulgaria, Gorbachev became a symbol of reform and a rallying point for discontent, especially among intellectuals.

In several instances, moreover, Gorbachev directly intervened to accelerate the process of change. In Poland, for example, Mieczyslaw Rakowski, the party leader, reportedly agreed to the creation of a Solidarity-led government in August 1989 after a telephone call from Gorbachev. In Bulgaria, Foreign Minister Petar Mladenov apparently received a green light to oust Zhivkov during a stopover in Moscow just before the critical Central Committee meeting that led to Zhivkov's removal on 10 November 1989. And, in Czechoslovakia, Soviet officials reportedly worked behind the scenes in November 1989 to undermine the Jakes government.

Gorbachev's role in initiating the transition in East Germany was also critical. He did not stop Hungary from opening its borders and allowing the East German refugees camped in Budapest to emigrate to West Germany—the move that touched off the crisis in East Germany—and he intervened to press the East German leadership to allow the East German refugees in the West German embassy in Prague to emigrate to the Federal Republic. Moreover, in the crucial period in August and September 1989 the Soviets appear to have encouraged the efforts by Egon Krenz and some of his close associates to depose Erich Honecker.[19]

Finally, during his visit to East Berlin in early October 1989, Gorbachev made it clear to the East German leadership that in case of any turmoil the Soviet troops in East Germany would stay in their barracks. Thus, effectively withdrawing his support of Honecker, Gorbachev accelerated the crisis in East Germany (and indirectly the entire bloc). In the past the East German leaders had assumed that in case of major unrest they could count on Soviet "fraternal assistance." Gorbachev's remarks, however, made it clear that the East German leaders could no longer count on Moscow to intervene to save them if things got out of hand.

The unrest in East Germany had an important "demonstration effect" throughout Eastern Europe: it provided concrete proof that the Brezhnev doctrine was really dead. Once this became clear, the other regimes fell in rapid succession. Bulgarian leader Todor Zhivkov was ousted on 10 November 1989; Czechoslovak leader Milos Jakes stepped down in early December; and Nicolae Ceausescu was forced to flee on 22 December and was executed a few days later. By Christmas the spasm of revolt was over and the transition process had begun in all the former Communist countries of the Soviet bloc.

This is not to argue that Gorbachev consciously sought to introduce Western-style democracy in Eastern Europe. Clearly, he did not. What he hoped for was to replace orthodox Communists with more reform-minded ones. However, the legitimacy of the Communist parties in Eastern Europe was so weak that the process of change, once initiated, was impossible to control from above. Even in Hungary, where the party had begun the transition and carefully sought to stage-manage the process, the changes soon took on a momentum of their own, eroding support for the party and eventually sweeping it from power in the March 1990 elections.

THE GERMAN QUESTION

Soviet policy toward West Germany—and the German Question—also underwent a major, far-reaching shift under Gorbachev. Gorbachev's German policy, however, was not animated by any sort of grand design to resolve the German Question. Rather, it emerged incrementally, largely in reaction to events that Gorbachev unleashed but then proved powerless to control.

Gorbachev did not set out to unify Germany. On the contrary, he initially saw its division as a key element of a new European security order. However, he recognized the need for a new policy and saw that Andrey Gromyko's effort to isolate and "punish" West Germany after the collapse of the INF talks had largely back-fired, resulting instead in the Soviet Union's self-isolation. Soon after coming to power, therefore, Gorbachev gradually began to abandon the policy of isolation and to cultivate more cordial and cooperative relations with West Germany.

This shift in policy did not manifest itself immediately. During the first year and a half after Gorbachev assumed power, West Germany continued to be the subject of constant vituperation for its "revanchist" policy. Gorbachev made highly visible visits to Paris and London in 1985 and 1986 but bypassed Bonn. Indeed, Gorbachev's policy during this period bears striking similarities to Soviet West-politik in the late 1960s, when the Soviet Union sought to make France the centerpiece of its détente efforts and at the same time tried to isolate West Germany.

By 1986, however, the Soviet attitude showed signs of softening. The campaign against German "revanchism" initiated in the spring of 1984 gradually began to abate. During Foreign Minister Hans-Dietrich Genscher's visit to

Moscow in July 1986, Gorbachev offered to open a "new page" in relations; a number of important bilateral agreements were initiated or signed, including a long-delayed framework agreement on scientific and technological cooperation.

Genscher's visit was followed by other small but important signs that the Soviet attitude toward West Germany was softening: a visible increase in the number of high-level visits, an increase in the number of ethnic Germans allowed to emigrate to West Germany, and a more cooperative attitude toward Berlin. These changes contributed to an improvement in relations and paved the way for Chancellor Helmut Kohl's visit to Moscow in October 1988.

Kohl's visit was a watershed in relations. The visit essentially ended the quarantine that had been imposed on West Germany in the aftermath of the Soviet walkout from INF talks. During the visit, six new governmental agreements were signed in areas ranging from environmental protection to nuclear and maritime safety. In addition, more than thirty new contracts with West German firms were signed, including a major deal for the sale of a high-temperature nuclear reactor.

The Kohl visit was the culmination of the shift in Soviet policy that had begun soon after Gorbachev assumed power. In effect, it represented the Soviet Union's effort to bring its policy toward West Germany into harmony with its policy toward the rest of Western Europe. Given West Germany's key role in Europe and within the Western alliance, any détente policy that excluded it had little chance of success.

The reassessment of policy toward West Germany also reflected a disappointment with French policy. Initially, Gorbachev seemed to have had hopes of reviving the Soviet Union's special relationship with France and making France the centerpiece of Soviet policy toward Western Europe. The progressive hardening of French policy during President François Mitterrand's first term, however, and France's reserved attitude toward arms control—especially the INF agreement—dashed whatever hopes Gorbachev may have had in this regard and made rapprochement with West Germany more attractive. At the same time, West Germany's favorable attitude toward perestroika and arms control, embodied particularly in Foreign Minsiter Genscher's Davos speech in February 1989, undoubtedly encouraged Gorbachev to seek closer ties to West Germany.[20]

Economic factors also played an imortant role. West Germany was the Soviet Union's largest trading partner in the West. If Gorbachev's policy of perestroika were to succeed, the USSR would require financial assistance from the West. Since West Germany was the most likely source of both credits and technology, the Soviets had an additional incentive to improve their ties.

This rapprochement, however, did not imply a shift in the Soviet approach to German unification or Berlin. During Kohl's visit, Gorbachev emphasized that Germany's division was the result of a specific historical development. Any attempt to change the situation or pursue "unrealistic policies," he said, would be "an unpredictable and even dangerous business."[21] Similarly, he warned that efforts to seek improvements in the status of West Berlin contradicted the 1971

Four Power Agreement on Berlin as well as the Helsinki Accord. In other words, limited "reassociation" between the two German states was one thing, unification quite another.

Gorbachev's remarks during Kohl's 1988 visit, however, were made within the context of a relatively stable Eastern bloc. This situation changed dramatically in the latter half of 1989, after the Hungarian government allowed East German refugees camped in Budapest to emigrate to West Germany. This move precipitated a mass exodus of refugees from East Germany and contributed to Honecker's fall and to the collapse of the German Democratic Republic (GDR).

In sanctioning—or at least not stopping—the opening of the Hungarian borders, Gorbachev clearly did not intend to precipitate the collapse of the GDR. Rather, he apparently hoped to encourage the removal of Honecker and the installation of a more reform-oriented leader who would be more flexible but could still be counted on to maintain firm control of the reform process. Wittingly or not, however, Gorbachev's actions did contribute to the collapse of the GDR and the growth of pressure for unification. Once it was clear that the Soviets would not intervene militarily, the demands for reform took on a momentum of their own, sweeping first Honecker, then his successor Egon Krenz, and finally the whole Socialist Unity Party (SED) from power.

Gorbachev seems to have been caught off balance by the dynamism and rapidity of events in East Germany. From the onset of the crisis and throughout the spring of 1990, Soviet policy towards East Germany was largely reactive, and Gorbachev was more a prisoner of events than their master. Once the Berlin Wall fell, events took on a momentum of their own and Gorbachev was largely forced to react to fast-changing developments that neither he nor the Western allies proved capable of controlling. While he expressed a willingness to allow German unification during Chancellor Kohl's visit to Moscow in February 1990, he insisted that a united Germany could not be a member of NATO. Indeed, Soviet policy during the first months of 1990 was remarkably rigid and inflexible.

The reasons for this have both psychological and political roots. The division of Germany was regarded as the main prize of World War II. For many Soviets, especially those in the top ranks of the military and the party, it was inconceivable that a united Germany would be allowed to enter NATO, which they regarded as an "anti-Soviet" alliance. In their minds, this would suggest that World War II had been fought in vain.

Moreover, many of these officials failed to grasp how significantly Soviet political influence in Eastern Europe had eroded as a result of the collapse of communism in the area. They continued to act as if the Soviet Union still had more political leverage than it actually had. In addition, few Soviet officials had foreseen that pressures for unification would emerge so rapidly or so soon. Moscow thus had no contingency plans on which it could draw. As a result, the Soviet leadership was ill-prepared to deal with the growing pressure for unification and its policy had an ad hoc and inconsistent character.

Domestic factors also influenced Soviet policy calculations. Indeed, they may have been decisive. Before the Twenty-eighth Party Congress in July 1990, Gorbachev faced mounting criticism of his policies on a wide variety of issues. At a time when perestroika was under fire for having shown few concrete results and he was being attacked for having "sold out" Eastern Europe, Gorbachev could ill-afford to give his domestic critics another weapon to use against him. The military in particular was strongly opposed to a united Germany's membership in NATO. But it was not alone. Party conservatives also warned of a "new German danger."

As a consequence, Gorbachev put forward a variety of schemes designed to forestall or prevent the integration of a united Germany in NATO: neutrality, a continuation of four-power rights for an extended duration after unification, the integration of Germany into both alliances, a pan-European security system based on the Conference on Security and Cooperation in Europe (CSCE), and finally a "French" solution in which Germany would be a member of the alliance but not of its military command. None of these proposals, however, were acceptable to West Germany or the other Western powers. Moreover, the USSR found itself isolated within its own alliance: the majority of the East European members of the Warsaw Pact, including Poland, favored a united Germany integrated into NATO.

By the time of the Washington summit with President George Bush in June 1990 there were signs that Gorbachev was looking for a face-saving mechanism that would allow him to accept a united Germany's incorporation into NATO but which could be portrayed in such a way that it did not look like a Soviet defeat and capitulation to a Western ultimatum. The main elements of such a package were contained in the nine-point plan that Bush presented at the Washington summit. The package was designed to make German membership in NATO more palatable and involved, inter alia, a gradual and phased withdrawal of Soviet troops, no forward deployment of NATO troops on East German territory, and economic assistance and compensation to the Soviet Union.

For domestic reasons, however, Gorbachev was unwilling to agree to final terms until after the Twenty-eighth Party Congress. As noted earlier, he apparently feared that his critics would use any concession on the German issue against him. The defeat of Egor K. Ligachev and the conservative faction at the congress, however, removed this danger. At the same time, the shift in NATO strategy announced at the NATO summit in London in early July 1990, together with promises by West German Chancellor Helmut Kohl of economic assistance and a reduction of the united Germany's armed forces to 370,000 men made it easier for Gorbachev to argue that Germany's entry into NATO would benefit the Soviet Union.

West Germany's agreement to reduce the size of its army was particularly important. This demonstrated that West Germany was willing to make a concrete contribution to military détente and paved the way for Gorbachev's formal agreement to the membership of a united Germany in NATO, which was announced at a joint press conference during Chancellor Kohl's visit to the Soviet Union in mid-July. In order to provide Moscow with further assurance, this commitment to reduce the size of the armed forces of a united Germany to 370,000 men was explicitly incorporated in article 3 of the "Final Settlement" of the "two plus four talks" regulating the external aspects of German unification, signed in Moscow on 12 September 1990.

In addition, in September, West Germany and the USSR signed a separate treaty of Good-neighborliness, Partnership and Cooperation, designed to expand and update the Renunciation of Force Agreement signed by the two countries in August 1970. Like the 1970 treaty, the new agreement emphasizes that the two sides will refrain from using force to resolve their differences. However, it goes considerably further than the 1970 treaty and contains a controversial nonaggression pledge (article 3). Although the new treaty specifically states that it does not infringe on rights and obligations arising from other bilateral and multilateral agreements signed by the two parties (article 19), the nonaggression clause has raised concerns in some Western capitals that it could lead to a weakening of Germany's commitments to Western defense.

As part of the overall settlement of German unification, Bonn also agreed to provide a 12 billion DM (about $8 billion) package to help underwrite the cost of the housing and withdrawal of the 380,000 Soviet troops stationed in East Germany. This package also included a 3 billion DM interest-free credit to aid the ailing Soviet economy.

Despite these "sweeteners," the unification of Germany, particularly a united Germany's membership in NATO, is a bitter pill for the Soviets to swallow. It effectively means the Soviet Union's military expulsion from Europe and a dramatic shift in the balance of power in favor of the West. More fundamentally, it represents the collapse of the USSR's postwar strategy toward Europe, which at least since 1955 has been aimed at maintaining two separate German states. Thus the USSR is now faced with the need to construct a new policy not just toward Germany but toward Europe as a whole.

ARMS CONTROL

In contrast to his predecessors, especially Leonid I. Brezhnev, Gorbachev has seen arms control as the primary means of enhancing Soviet security and reducing East-West confrontation. Moreover, he has been willing to adopt more flexible positions than his predecessors, especially regarding verification, in order to obtain agreements. He has also shown a much greater appreciation of the political impact of such agreements.

This change is well illustrated by Gorbachev's approach to limitations on intermediate-range nuclear forces (INF). Leonid I. Brezhnev and Yuri V. Andropov had consistently rejected President Ronald Reagan's proposal to eliminate all INF systems (the "zero option"). Instead, they tried to maintain Soviet superiority in this category of weapons, arguing that they wanted only "equal security," which in reality meant that the USSR should be allowed to maintain intermediate-range weapons equal to all those possessed by the United States and its European allies. This refusal led to the breakup of the negotiations and the American counter deployment of American cruise and Pershing II missiles in late 1983.

In contrast to Brezhnev and Andropov, however, Gorbachev—after some hesitation—agreed to the total elimination of all Soviet medium-range missiles, including those based in Asia. Moreover, during United States Secretary of State George Schultz's visit to Moscow in April 1987, Gorbachev proposed eliminating not only all intermediate-range missiles but also all shorter-range missiles (with ranges from 500 km to 1,000 km)—the "double zero" option. This proposal caused considerable consternation within NATO, especially in West Germany, because it meant that the West would be left with only short-range missiles and nuclear artillery with ranges below 500 km for defense against a Soviet conventional attack. Many Europeans thought the proposal was a dangerous step toward the "denuclearization" of Europe. Once the United States had signaled its willingness to accept the offer, however, the West European countries, especially West Germany, had little choice but to accept the decision and put the best face on it.

Gorbachev's willingness to agree to eliminate all intermediate- and shorter-range missiles appears to have had several motives. First, in contrast to his predecessors, Gorbachev thought that Soviet security could be better ensured by "political means"—i.e., arms control—than through a continued military build-up. Second, Gorbachev needed to break the general deadlock in arms control in the wake of the collapse of the Reykjavik summit in October 1988. The West saw the INF issue as the main obstacle to improved East-West relations. Thus, Gorbachev apparently hoped that the INF agreement would have a positive impact on East-West relations and break the logjam in other areas, especially the Strategic Arms Reduction Talks (START).

Third, there were sound military reasons for agreeing to the zero option. While the accord required the Soviet Union to scrap its entire SS-20 force as well as its remaining SS-4s and SS-5s, it eliminated an important nuclear threat to Soviet territory—particularly from the Pershing II, which has a short flight time of twelve to fourteen minutes. Moreover, the Soviet Union could still cover many of the same targets in Europe by redirecting some of its strategic forces—a fact that may well have helped convince the Soviet military to go along with the decision.

Finally, the agreement threatened further to erode the credibility of the American nuclear deterrent and to increase fissures within NATO. As Western analysts and officials pointed out, the elimination of all INF and shorter-range nuclear missiles in Europe would make the strategy of flexible response much more difficult and probably require some changes in Western strategy. The pressure for further reductions was bound to increase, especially from West Germany, where most of the remaining short-range nuclear systems were deployed. Thus the long-term political benefits may have seemed worth the short-term military costs.

The INF accord also had imortant advantages for the West. First, it eliminated an important military threat to Western Europe. Second, it required the Soviet Union to make large asymmetrical reductions and set an important precedent for other negotiations, especially those related to conventional arms. Third, the agreement contained stringent verification provisions, including on-site inspection. This represented a significant shift in the Soviet position and set another important precedent for other negotiations.

In the field of conventional arms control, however, Gorbachev has shown the greatest inclination to depart from past Soviet policy. Gorbachev's predecessors, especially Brezhnev, showed little inclination to take conventional arms control seriously. Brezhnev gave top priority to strategic nuclear arms control. Moreover, he feared the consequences of any large-scale withdrawal of Soviet forces on the political stability within the bloc.

Gorbachev, by contrast, seems to believe that Soviet political and military objectives can be furthered by progress in conventional arms control. His interest in conventional arms control has probably been influenced by several factors. First, on the broadest political level, it had become increasingly clear that a major improvement in Soviet relations with Western Europe was impossible without seriously addressing West European concerns about Soviet conventional preponderance. This was the main source of West European insecurity and the main rationale for NATO's existence and its reliance on nuclear weapons for defense. Second, a major reduction of conventional forces promised substantial economic savings over the long run. Third, on the military level, there was increasing concern that Western advances in high-tech conventional weapons, especially precision-guided missiles, would erode traditional Soviet advantages in tanks and manpower.

Gorbachev's "new thinking" provided an imortant framework for the shift in the Soviet approach to conventional arms control. The concept of "reasonable sufficiency" was applied not only to strategic weapons but also to conventional arms. This meant, in effect, that the USSR could afford to reduce some conventional forces, since it only needed enough forces to repel an aggressor rather than to conduct an offensive on his territory.

Similarly, the shift in Soviet doctrine toward an increasing emphasis on defense and war prevention pointed in the same direction.[22] In the past, Soviet conventional forces had been configured and trained to conduct a rapid offensive designed to seize and hold Western territory if a conflict in Europe broke out. This required large-scale conventional superiority in order to overrun Western defenses. Under the new doctrine, however, Soviet forces were to be trained to fight defensively in the initial period of a conflict and then to reestablish the status quo ante rather than seek to carry the war immediately over the Western territory.

This new doctrine permitted a gradual reduction and restructuring of Soviet conventional forces in a less offensive and threatening posture. Under the new doctrine the Soviet Union no longer needed great numerical superiority in tanks and manpower. Nor did it need large quantities of offensively oriented materials, such as bridge-building equipment, which was primarily designed to enhance its capacity to conduct large-scale offensives. Long-range offensive aircraft could also be reduced.

Gorbachev's approach to conventional arms control reflected these new realities. Beginning in 1986 the Soviet Union began to adopt a more flexible approach to conventional arms control. The most important shifts in the Soviet position included: Gorbachev's willingness to extend the negotiating zone to admit Soviet territory up to the Ural Mountains, a long-standing Western demand; his open acknowledgment that asymmetries existed—which his predecessors had implicitly denied—and his commitment to eliminate them; the adoption of a more flexible position on verification, especially on-site inspection; a more forthcoming attitude toward the release of data; and a shift, noted above, in Soviet doctrine, putting greater emphasis on defense.

The latter shift was codified in a new Warsaw Pact Doctrine, announced at the meeting of the Warsaw Treaty Organization (WTO) Political Consultative Committee in East Berlin at the end of May 1987. The communiqué issued at the end of the meeting specifically stated that the doctrine of the WTO was defensive.[23] In addition, it asserted that the goals of the Vienna negotiations on Conventional Forces in Europe (CFE) should be guided by the principle of "reasonable sufficiency" and that the negotiations should seek to eliminate the capability for surprise attack and large-scale offensive action. These goals had long been espoused by the West, and the public commitment to them by the Warsaw Pact implied a significant rapprochement between the two alliances.

The most important indication of Gorbachev's seriousness about conventional arms control, however, came in his speech to the United Nations General Assembly in December 1988. Gorbachev promised unilaterally to withdraw 50,000 Soviet troops and 5,000 soviet tanks from Hungary, Czechoslovakia, and East Germany; reduce the Soviet armed forces by 500,000 men by 1990; withdraw from Eastern Europe assault-landing troops and other offensively oriented accessories, such as bridge-crossing equipment; cut Soviet forces in the Atlantic-to-the-Urals area by 10,000 tanks, 8,500 artillery systems, and 800 combat aircraft; and restructure Soviet forces in Eastern Europe along "clearly defensive" lines. Although the initiative still left the Soviet Union with substantial advantages in a number of important areas, it significantly undercut the Soviet capability to launch a short-warning attack—a long-standing Western concern.

Few Western officials or analysts had expected Gorbachev to make such a dramatic gesture. Moreover, in taking the initiative, Gorbachev seems to have over-ridden objections by the military, including those of the chief of the General Staff, Marshal Sergei Akhromeyev, whose removal was announced the same day. Indeed, the initiative was evidently the result of a prolonged debate between those favoring unilateral measures (located primarily in several Soviet think-tanks and in key positions in Foreign Ministry) and those opposed (located mostly in the Ministry of Defense and General Staff).[24] In the end, Gorbachev was apparently persuaded that a dramatic political gesture was needed to convince the West of his seriousness and to give new momentum to the conventional arms control talks in Vienna due to begin a few months hence. Gorbachev may have also hoped that the unilateral cuts would have a favorable impact on Western public opinion and stimulate pressure in the West to make a reciprocal gesture.

While the West did not respond with a reciprocal reduction, the initiative did have an important political impact on the general climate surrounding the opening of the CFE negotiations in Vienna in March 1989. In fact, by the time that negotiations opened, the Western and Soviet approaches were relatively close. The Soviet proposal presented at the opening round of the talks on 6 March by Foreign Minister Eduard A. Shevardnadze provided for a three-stage process:

- Both NATO and the WTO would reduce their armed forces and conventional armaments 10 to 15 percent below their current levels.
- Troop levels and armaments would be reduced by 25 percent.
- Each side's armed forces would be reduced in all categories of arms, including naval forces.

Shevardnadze also called for strict verification provisions and the immediate initiation of separate negotiations on short-range nuclear systems.

The Soviet proposal was in broad accord with NATO's proposal on several important points: equal limits on important weapons systems; the general magnitude of reductions (the WTO proposed cuts 10 to 15 percent below current levels, the West 5 to 10 percent), and the need for extensive verification measures. Moreover, both sides agreed that the overall goal of the talks should be to eliminate the capacity for surprise attack and large-scale offensive action.

Important differences, however, remained on whether to include aircraft and troops—the United States wanted to focus solely on tanks and offensive armor—and on short-range nuclear weapons. These differences were narrowed by the USSR's proposal at the end of May, which suggested geographic ceilings on weapons and essentially accepted the basic Western framework for cutting tanks, artillery, and armored troop carriers. The differences were further reduced by President George Bush's proposals at the NATO summit a few days later. The president agreed to include combat aircraft and attack helicopters in the negotiations. He also proposed that each side reduce its armed forces to 275,000 soldiers—a move that would require the United States to withdraw 30,000 and the Soviets 350,000 soldiers. Finally, he agreed that talks on short-range nuclear forces (SNF) could be initiated once the CFE negotiations had been concluded. Bush insisted, however, that the SNF talks should be designed to lead to a "partial reduction" of SNF, not their total elimination. And in deference to West German concerns, a decision regarding the modernization of 88 Lance short-range missiles (FOTL) was postponed.[25]

These two moves significantly reduced the gap between the two sides and contributed to rapid progress in the talks. The negotiations were given new impetus in March by the agreement in Ottawa to limit each side to 195,000 soldiers in the central zone. The United States, however, was allowed to maintain 225,000 overall in Europe. The latter agreement marked an important compromise by Gorbachev in that it codified unequal ceilings—a major American goal.[26] The Soviets, by contrast, were given no right to deploy troops outside the central zone.

However, Soviet interest in a rapid conclusion of the talks waned visibly in the spring of 1989, slowing their momentum. The deadlock appears to have been related to Soviet concerns about the process of German unification. The Soviet Union was apparently unwilling to move forward in Vienna to reduce its own forces substantially until there was greater clarity about the size and configuration of the military forces of a united Germany, as well as the future nature of NATO strategy. The changes in NATO nuclear strategy announced at the NATO summit in July, together with Chancellor Helmut Kohl's public assurances shortly thereafter that the forces of a united Germany would be reduced to around 370,000 men (less than half the current total of the two armies combined), appear to have allayed the most important Soviet concerns. Thereafter, rapid progress was made in resolving the remaining major outstanding issues—limits on weapon holdings by individual nations (the "sufficiency rule"), limitations on naval aircraft, and limitations on weapons in specific subzones. In early October the two sides agreed in principle on the outlines of a draft treaty. The final breakthrough in the negotiations was the result of an important Soviet concession: Moscow agreed to include land-based naval aircraft in the final agreement—a long-standing United States goal—without insisting that the same apply to carrier-based aircraft, which the United States wanted excluded. This concession removed the last major obstacle to an agreement.

The CFE treaty, which was officially signed at the thirty-four-nation CSCE Summit in Paris in November 1990, is the most important arms-control treaty signed in the postwar period. The treaty codifies a fundamental change in the balance of power in Europe by establishing equal ceilings on major categories of equipment, including tanks, artillery, and personnel carriers, thereby eliminating major Soviet advantages in these weapons systems. As a result of the treaty, the Warsaw Pact will have to destroy about 19,000 tanks, while NATO will have to destroy only about 4,000 tanks. The treaty will require no substantial cuts in NATO's armored troop carriers and no cuts in its artillery or combat aircraft. The Warsaw Pact, by contrast, will have to destroy thousands of these weapons.

The signing of the CFE treaty is likely to be followed by a new set of negotiations (CFE-IB) designed to establish national ceilings on the forces of individual countries. In these talks the Soviet Union's main goal will probably be low ceilings on the military forces of a united Germany. It is also likely to try to obtain treaty-related restrictions on NATO and German forces stationed in the former territory of East Germany.

The conclusion of a CFE I agreement will also open the way for negotiations on short-range nuclear forces (SNF). Such talks have long been a Soviet goal, but there has been a visible shift in the Soviet position on SNF negotiations since mid-1989. Originally, the Soviets seemed intent on pressing for total elimination of all short-range systems (the "third zero"). However, Gorbachev spoke of the creation of a "minimum nuclear deterrent" in his speech in Strasbourg in July 1989.[27] Similarly, during a visit to NATO headquarters in Brussels, Soviet Foreign Minister Shevardnadze suggested a two-stage process for SNF negotiations. In the first stage, SNF would be reduced to low common ceilings, and in the second stage they would be eliminated entirely. Leading Soviet analysts have also referred to such a two-stage process.[28]

The shift in the Soviet position appears to have several motivations. First, the Soviet Union seems to recognize that there is strong resistance in Western Europe, especially in France and Britain, to the total denuclearization of Western Europe and that pressing for such a goal at this point would be counterproductive, stiffening Western resistance to reductions and possibly inhibiting further progress in conventional arms control. Second, with the loss of Soviet conventional superiority, which will be codified in a CFE I agreement, the Soviets may feel a greater need to retain some nuclear weapons as a hedge against NATO's technological superiority. Finally, eliminating all tactical nuclear weapons could precipitate a withdrawal of American troops from Western Europe, thereby increasing instability during the transition period.

Thus, unless the West European countries, particularly Germany, press for a total elimination of short-range systems, the USSR is likely to accept the continued presence of some nuclear weapons on West European soil at least for an interim period. The first phase of the SNF negotiations will probably be directed at establishing equal but lower ceilings on land-based nuclear systems. Nevertheless, despite what appears to be an emerging consensus on the basic goals of the negotiations, substantial technical problems remain. There is no agreement, for instance, on the "unit of account"—warheads, launchers, or delivery vehicles—or the geographic scope of the negotiations. Moreover, the verification problems are formidable. Finally, the question of whether to include French and British nuclear systems remains unresolved.

The political evolution in Europe, however, may make the resolution of some of these problems easier. It is increasingly likely that the United States will unilaterally withdraw most, if not all, ground-based tactical nuclear weapons from Europe, leaving air- and sea-based nuclear weapons as the backbone of its deterrent strategy. Moreover, from the Soviets' perspective, the change in NATO strategy announced at the NATO summit in London in July 1990— whereby nuclear weapons will only be used as a "last resort"—diminishes the threat posed by the remaining weapons on European soil. At the same time, the withdrawal of Soviet troops and military equipment from Eastern Europe will significantly reduce the Soviet short-range nuclear threat to Western Europe. These developments have somewhat diminished the importance of the SNF negotiations. Nevertheless, since such weapons can be easily moved back into the negotiating zone, it will be useful to have agreed, verifiable constraints on them. For political reasons, moreover, the Soviet Union is likely to press for the rapid commencement of negotiations. They strengthen the impression, both at home and in Europe, that Europe is entering a new era of reduced confrontation, thereby legitimizing the Soviet push for a greater reliance of pan-European security structures. In addition, negotiations offer an important means to try to block the modernization of NATO's air-based component, particularly plans to develop a new tactical air-to-surface missile (TASM). Thus, in future talks, the Soviets are likely to press for deep cuts in nuclear-capable aircraft as well as restrictive provisions on air-to-surface missiles. Initially, the USSR may also try to link the negotiations to the question of tactical nuclear weapons at sea, though it seems likely that this issue will be dealt with in separate talks on naval arms control.

THE USSR AND THE FUTURE EUROPEAN SECURITY ORDER

The collapse of communism and the unification of Germany have shattered the foundations of the USSR's postwar policy toward Europe. This policy was based on three pillars: (1) Soviet hegemony in Eastern Europe; (2) the division of Germany; and (3) the bipolar political division of Europe. All three pillars are now destroyed beyond repair. The USSR is thus faced with the task of constructing a new policy not only toward Eastern Europe but toward Europe as a whole.

Originally, Gorbachev appears to have envisaged a gradual process of change in Europe during which both alliances would continue to exist but would lose their predominantly military character and take on increasingly political functions. The alliances, including the Warsaw Pact, were seen as stabilizing mechanisms. Soviet analysts argued, for instance, that the Warsaw Pact could play a useful role as an instrument for the "controlled and orderly transition" of the two blocs to a lower level of military confrontation and as a means for conducting arms-control negotiations.[29] Others argued that the pact should be maintained, but that it should be transformed into a "mature political partnership" in which all parties enjoyed equal rights.[30] They suggested that the East European role be expanded and that a permanent secretariat be set up in one of the East European countries.

The idea of a prolonged transition based on the continued existence of the two alliances, however, seems increasingly unrealistic. As a result of the rapid changes in Eastern Europe, the Warsaw Pact has become a hollow shell. It may continue to exist for several more years but as an effective military alliance it is clinically dead. The unification of Germany deprives the pact of its most important military asset. At the same time, the withdrawal of Soviet forces from Hungary and Czechoslovakia—scheduled to be completed by the end of 1991—severely weakens the USSR's ability to conduct coalitional warfare. Hungary, moreover, has announced that it will formally withdraw from the pact in 1991, which could lead to the formal disbanding of the Warsaw Pact.

As the pact has disintegrated, the Soviet Union has begun to push more forcefully for strengthening pan-European structures as an alternative to the two alliances. Some Soviet analysts, for instance, have suggested a two-phase approach. The first phase (1990–91) would begin with the creation of all-European centers for the prevention of crisis and arms-control verification. This phase would be followed by a second stage in which a permanent secretariat and agencies on ecology, migration, and economic cooperation would be set up.[31] Soviet analysts have also suggested that the Council of Europe could be expanded to take on a pan-European character.

There have also been hints that the USSR may favor setting up a two-tier security structure with a permanent council, composed of the USSR, the United States, France, Britain, and Germany, which would become the core of a new security system and report back to the 35. Such ideas, moreover, dovetail closely with those put forward by Moscow's former East European allies. The foreign minister of Czechoslovakia, Jiri Dienstbier, for example, has proposed that a European Security Commission be formed with headquarters in Prague. This commission would act as an executive organ of a pan-European system of collective security.

In the future the Soviets can be expected to push such pan-European schemes more vigorously. They are one of the few ways that the USSR can be assured of exerting influence in Europe. In addition, such schemes could contain the growth of instability and nationalism in Eastern Europe, which many Soviet analysts see as a growing threat to European security. To counteract this danger, some Soviet analysts have called for the intensification of ties to Western countries and the "accelerated construction of a new security system, particularly the creation of permanent institutions for all-European control of political processes."[32] Such a system is also seen as providing a "corset" to ensure that German unification evolves peacefully and does not pose a threat to the general trend toward increased East-West cooperation.

The Soviets recognize, of course, that NATO is unlikely to fade away immediately, but they hope that the general political climate of East-West détente will make it increasingly less relevant and that its military functions will gradually atrophy. Thus they can be expected to put intensified emphasis on disarmament proposals that will weaken NATO's military potential, especially its nuclear capability. As noted earlier, one of the USSR's prime goals will probably be eliminating land-based missiles and nuclear artillery and preventing any modernization of NATO's air-delivered nuclear component. Soviet negotiators are also likely to press for significant reductions of United States combat aircraft and troop levels in any follow-on negotiation to CFE.

This does not mean, however, that the Soviet Union wishes to see the United States withdraw from Europe. The USSR recognizes that it will take some time to create a new security order in Europe and that the transition period could be destabilizing. Thus, it has come to see the presence of American troops—albeit at significantly reduced levels—as a factor of stability, at least for the short to medium term.[33] In addition, it seems willing temporarily to accept some stationing of American nuclear weapons on European soil.

This shift has been part of a general evolution of the Soviet attitude toward the American role in the construction of the "common European home." Initially, the concept had a strongly anti–United States edge and Soviet officials were ambiguous about the American role. Recently, however, Soviet officials and analysts have stressed that the United States has an important place in the European home. In his speech before the Council of Europe in Strasbourg, for instance, Gorbachev noted that the United States and the Soviet Union were a "natural part of the European international-political structure" and that their participation was "not only justified but historically qualified."[34] Soviet analysts, echoing this line, have argued that without the participation of the United States, construction of the common European home would be more difficult.

The process of German unification, moreover, is likely to reinforce the Soviets' predisposition to keep the United States involved in Europe. Although Gorbachev has accepted German unification as well as German membership in NATO, the USSR cannot be sure about the long-term direction of political developments in Germany. The United States remains an important constraint on German freedom of action, especially regarding nuclear weapons. A total withdrawal of American forces might reopen the nuclear question in Germany— something the Soviet Union strongly wishes to avoid. This concern gives the USSR an added incentive to keep the United States engaged in Europe rather than to encourage its total withdrawal.

At the same time, Germany's importance in the Soviet Union's European policy is likely to increase. Germany is the USSR's largest Western trading partner and its main source of technology and credits, which will be important for the modernization of the Soviet economy. Moreover, Germany will be the most important political actor in Europe. Thus, if the Soviet Union wishes to pursue an active policy toward Europe, it will have little choice but to strengthen its ties with Germany. Indeed, Gorbachev's invitation to Kohl to visit his hometown of Stavropol during the chancellor's visit to the USSR in July 1990— an honor accorded no other Western leader to date—seemed designed to initiate a new era of more cooperative relations with a united Germany.

The unification of Germany, moreover, is likely to give a new push to the process of European unification. Over the long term, unification may lead to a weakening of Atlanticism and United States influence in Western Europe, but it will also pose serious dilemmas for the USSR. For one thing, it will increase the attractiveness of the EC to the countries of Eastern Europe, making any efforts by the Soviet Union to transform the CMEA or keep it alive more difficult. For another, it will make the export of Soviet industrial products and other commercial transactions to Western Europe more difficult.

On the political level, the process of integration is likely to foster a more cohesive foreign policy on the part of Western Europe, allowing EC members to speak more forcefully with one voice on international issues. Internally, moreover, it will accelerate a shift in the locus of decision-making power on many issues from national capitals to Brussels and Strasbourg. Thus, if the Soviet Union wishes to pursue an active European policy, it will have to develop stronger ties to the EC and its associated institutions rather than simply concentrating on expanding ties to individual West European countries.

The CMEA, however, is not likely to disappear, at least not immediately. The countries of Eastern Europe conduct 40 to 80 percent of their trade within the CMEA. If it were to be disbanded, they would have to redirect their trade toward new markets. Replacing the Soviet market quickly would be difficult—and costly—since many East European goods are not internationally competitive. Thus the CMEA will probably continue to exist in some form for the next few years, at least as a mean of facilitating bilateral trade. It is likely, however, to become much more of an "information gathering agency" like the Organization for Economic Cooperation and Development (OECD) in Paris than a mechanism for promoting close economic cooperation between the Soviet Union and its former East-European allies. Moreover, given the Soviet Union's own growing economic difficulties, the USSR is likely to reduce its delivery of energy and raw materials to Eastern Europe. This will exacerbate these countries' economic problems as they attempt to transform their economies along market lines.

CONCLUSION

The Soviet Union will face a substantially changed security environment in Europe in the 1990s. In order to adapt to this environment, major adjustments in Soviet policy will be necessary. These adjustments will have to be made at a time when the Soviet Union is undergoing profound change. How this process evolves will have a major influence on the Soviet Union's role in Europe in the coming decade.

Indeed, the disintegration of the Soviet internal empire is likely to be one of the most important factors affecting the future of Europe in the 1990s. It is highly questionable whether the Soviet Union will remain an integral multinational state. As centrifugal pressures increase, some of the republics, such as the Russian Federation and the Ukraine, are likely to seek greather autonomy—even independence—and may begin to pursue their own "European" policies, especially in the economic area. The growing political fragmentation of the USSR could be a major source of instability in Europe and make the integration of the Soviet Union—or major remnants of it—into a broader European framework more difficult.

It would be short-sighted, however, for the West to exploit this period of convulsion and weakness to exclude the Soviet Union from Europe. That would only strengthen the more radical nationalist and exclusionist forces in Soviet society. Rather, Western policy should encourage a gradual evolution toward greater internal democracy, a greater reform of the Soviet economy, and its integration into the world economy. A less inward-looking, more democratic Soviet Union integrated into a broader European security order in which it has a strong but not dominant voice is more likely to guarantee peace and stability than a frustrated but still militarily powerful empire that feels isolated and excluded from Europe.

NOTES

1. Charles Gati, "Soviet Empire: Alive But Not Well," *Problems of Communism* (March–April 1985), pp. 73–86.
2. Interview in *La Repubblica*, 21 May 1985 (reprinted in Foreign Broadcast Information Service, *Daily Report: Soviet Union*, 24 May 1985, CCI).
3. *Pravda*, 26 Feb. 1986.
4. Ibid., 8 Apr. 1985.
5. Jerry Hough, "Gorbachev's Strategy," *Foreign Affairs* 63 (Fall 1985), pp. 33–55.
6. S. Vybornov, A. Gusenkov, and V. Leontiev, "Nothing Is Simple in Europe," *International Affairs*, no. 3 (March 1988), p. 35.
7. V. Stupishin, "Indeed, Nothing in Europe Is Simple," *International Affairs*, no. 5 (May 1988), p. 73. This article was essentially a reply to the Vybornov, Gusenkov, and Leontief article cited in note 6.
8. Ibid., p. 72.
9. Nikolai Afanasyevsky, Eduard Tarasinkevich, and Andrei Shvedov, "Between Yesterday and Today," *International Affairs*, no. 5 (May 1988), p. 27.
10. See the report on the EC prepared by the Institute of World Economy and International Relations (IMEMO), in Moscow, "Europeiskoe soobshchestvo segodnia. Tezisy Instituty mirovoi ekonomiki i mezhdunarodnykh otnoshenii AN SSSR," *Mirovaia ekonomika i mezhdunarodnye otnosheniia*, no. 12 (April 1988), pp. 8–9.
11. See the material prepared by the West European Research Department of IMEMO on the implications of the formation of the internal market of the EC, "Posledstviia formiro-vaniia edinogo rynka Evropeiskogo soobshchestva material podgotovien otdelom zapadnoevropeiskikh issledovanii IMEMO," *Mirovaia ekonomika i mezhdunarodnye otnosheniia*, no. 4 (April 1989), p. 40.
12. On the background to the Gorbachev Initiative and the development of relations between the EC and the CMEA before 1985, see Christian Meier, "Die Gorbachev-Initiative vom 29 Mai 1985—vor neuen Verhandlungen zwischen RGW und EG," *Aktuelle Analysen*, Bundesinstitut fuer ostwissenschaftliche und internationale Studien, 20 Aug. 1985; and Bernhard May. "Normalizierung der Beziehungen zwischen der EG und den RGW," *Aus Politik und Zeitgeschichte* B 3/89, 13 Jan. 1989, 44–54.
13. See in particular O. Vladimirov, "Vedushchii faktor mirovogo revolyutsionnogo protsessa," *Pravda*, 21 June 1985. The article was reportedly written by Oleg Rakhmanin, the hard-line deputy chief of the Department for the Liaison with Socialist Countries within the International Department of the Central Committee. In the fall of 1986, Rakhmanin was replaced by Georgi Shakhnazarov, a prominent supporter of

reform. Rakhmanin's removal and Shakhnazarov's ascendancy were important signs that the reformist line was beginning to gain ground.

14. See in particular Oleg T. Bogomolov, "Soglasovanie ekonomicheskikh interesovi i politiki pri sotsialisme," *Kommunist*, no. 10 (July 1985), pp. 82–95.

15. *Pravda*, 11 Apr. 1987.

16. Ibid., 3 Nov. 1987.

17. Ibid., 19 Mar. 1988.

18. Ibid., 7 July 1989.

19. David B. Ottoway, *Washington Post*, 11 Nov. 1989.

20. "Nehmen wir Gorbatschow's 'Neue Politik' beim Wort" (Bonn: Auswaertiges Amt und Presse und Informationsamt der Bundesregierung, March 1987).

21. *Izvestiia*, 26 Oct. 1988. See also Gorbachev's assessment in his book *Perestroika: New Thinking for Our Country and the World* (New York: Harper and Row, 1987), p. 200, where he notes the "reality" of the German states with different political systems and asserts that "what there will be in 100 years is for history to decide." This became the standard Soviet line regarding unification up until the fall of the Berlin Wall in November 1989.

22. For a detailed discussion of the shift in Soviet doctrine, see William Odom, "Soviet Military Doctrine," *Foreign Affairs* 67 (Fall 1988), pp. 114–34; and Edward L. Warner III, "Soviet Military Doctrine: New Thinking and Old Realities in Soviet Defense Policy," *Survival* 30 (January-February 1989), pp. 13–33.

23. See *Pravda*, 30 May 1987.

24. See Roy Allison, "Gorbachev's New Program for Conventional Arms Control in Europe," in *Gorbachev's Agenda Changes in Domestic and Foreign Policy*, Susan L. Clark, ed. (Boulder, CO: Westview Press, 1989), pp. 5–13.

25. In May 1990 the Bush administration quietly shelved the idea of Lance modernization altogether after it became apparent that there was no support for the program in Europe. For a good discussion of the Lance modernization issue, see Hans Binnendijk, "NATO's Nuclear Modernization Dilemma," *Survival* 30 (March–April 1989), pp. 137–55.

26. The United States was eager to avoid equating American troops in Europe with Soviet troops. Hence, it pressed for unequal ceilings in order to avoid the appearance of parity. See R. Jeffrey Smith, "U.S., Soviets Reach Troops Cut Accord," *Washington Post*, 14 Feb. 1990.

27. *Pravda*, 7 July 1989.

28. See Paval Bayev et al., *Tactical Nuclear Weapons in Europe* (Moscow: Novosti Press Agency Publishing House, 1990), pp. 14, 40–46.

29. Andrei Kokoshin, "Konturi peremen," *SShA: Ekonomika, Politika, Ideologiya*, no. 2 (February 1990), pp. 31–33.

30. Mikhail Bezrukov and Andrei Kortunov, "What Kind of an Alliance Do We Need?," *New Times*, no. 41, 10–16 Oct. 1989, pp. 7–9; and idem, "Nuzhna Reforma OVD," ibid., no. 3 (March 1990), pp. 30–35.

31. Sergei Karaganov, "Architecture for Europe to Ensure the Transition Periods Safely," *Moscow News*, 21–27 May 1990, p. 12.

32. Sergei Karaganov, "Problemi evropeiskoy politiki SSSR," *Mezhdunarodnaya Zhizn* (July 1990), p. 93, features, the US military presence is a major stabilizing element in relations among Western nations, and to some degree, in the entire system of East-West relations," p. 12.

34. *Pravda*, 7 July 1989.

30

The Changing Role of the
Soviet Union in the Pacific*

Donald S. Zagoria

Since Mikhail Gorbachev became general secretary of the Soviet Communist party in March 1985, the Soviet Union has greatly increased its efforts to improve relations with all the countries of East Asia—particularly China but also Japan and South Korea—and with Southeast Asia, Australia, and New Zealand. There have been a new diplomatic flexibility, frequent visits, a drive for better trade links, an effort to join regional economic organizations such as the Asian Development Bank and the Pacific Economic Cooperation Council (PECC), a variety of arms control proposals, efforts to help solve regional tensions, and a determined effort to change the poor image of the Soviet Union in the region.

In a number of speeches, especially those in Vladivostok in July 1986 and Krasnoyarsk in September 1988, Gorbachev has said he wants to lower the level of military activity in the Pacific, to improve Moscow's bilateral relations with all the countries in the region, to advance multilateral cooperation, particularly economic cooperation, and generally to create a "healthier" situation.[1]

As an earnest of his peaceful intentions, Gorbachev has made a number of concessions to China, withdrawn Soviet troops from Afghanistan, put pressure on the Vietnamese to withdraw from Cambodia, agreed to remove all of Moscow's SS-20 intermediate range missiles from Siberia, indicated his intention to cut 200,000 Soviet troops from the "eastern" portions of the USSR, and, most recently, in September 1990, extended diplomatic recognition to South Korea.[2]

There is no euphoria about Gorbachev in Asia, but his initiatives have had an impact. Moscow has succeeded in normalizing relations with China. Trade and cultural exchanges are growing; both Beijing and Moscow are cutting back forces along the border, while border trade is increasing; and mutual threat perceptions are being substantially reduced. Also, it seems likely that the Soviet Union and Japan will reach some sort of modus vivendi when Gorbachev visits Tokyo in April 1991. The Russians understand that they must improve relations

---

*This is a revised version of an essay prepared for the fourth Asia-Pacific Report, published by the East-West Center in Honolulu, Hawaii. Copyright © 1991 by Donald S. Zagoria.

with Tokyo if they are to be recognized as a legitimate player in the Pacific, and the Japanese will not want to be left out of the global détente with Moscow. Meanwhile Moscow and Seoul have exchanged diplomatic personnel. Both sides are anxious to expand economic ties, and Seoul wants Moscow's help in improving relations with North Korea. Meanwhile, the Soviets are also improving their image in Southeast Asia. Most of the Association of Southeast Asian Nations (ASEAN) leaders have either visited Moscow or are planning to do so in the near future.

In sum, the Soviet Union may well succeed in normalizing relations with China and the non-Communist nations of East Asia during the next few years.

In this essay, I want to explore the sources of change in Soviet policy; the degree of continuity and change; the impact of changing Soviet policy on the nations of the region; and, finally, the implications of changing Soviet policy for the United States.

II

The two most important sources of change in Soviet policy in Asia are the failures of the past and the weaknesses of the present. The failures of the past are largely attributable to the rigid, overmilitarized policy of Gorbachev's predecessor, Leonid Brezhnev. When Gorbachev came to power in 1985, the Soviet Union was facing a number of adverse trends in the Pacific. Although Asia was the most economically dynamic region in the world, the Soviet Union was not participating in or benefiting from this dynamism. Because of Brezhnev's "guns over growth" policies, Siberia and the Soviet Far East had been turned into an armed camp, but these territories remained sparsely populated, economically underdeveloped, and sealed off from the rest of the Pacific. Indeed, Siberia was the most economically underdeveloped "country" in the entire Pacific region. As a result, Soviet economic relations with the dynamic market economies of the Pacific were minimal.

Meanwhile, the United States and Japan, two of Moscow's formidable rivals in the region, were substantially increasing their economic relations with each other and with the other Pacific countries, and there was growing talk of a new Pacific Basin economic community from which the Soviet Union was excluded. Even China, another long-range Soviet rival, was gradually being integrated into the Pacific economy. China's foreign trade grew from about $20 billion to some $115 billion in the 1980s, and three-fourths of that trade is with the Pacific market economies.

From a Soviet point of view, the strategic legacy in the Pacific that Gorbachev inherited from Brezhnev was even worse. The United States was recovering from its Vietnam trauma and pursuing a more activist policy. It was increasing its already powerful navy, adding several new carrier task forces, beginning to deploy Tomahawk cruise missiles and more powerful Trident submarines, increasing military cooperation with Japan, and developing a low-level but significant strategic relationship with China.

Just as worrisome, Japan—which had now overtaken the Soviet Union as the second largest economic power in the world—was being integrated into the Western alliance system and increasing a defense cooperation with the United States. Japan was staking out a thousand-mile zone to protect its sea lanes of communication, participating in Strategic Defense Initiative (SDI) research with the United States, and substantially modernizing its air and sea defense. Equally disturbing, China, after a long period of internal stagnation and class warfare under Mao Tse-tung, was beginning to modernize its economy with the help of the United States and Japan. And in Southeast Asia, the ASEAN states, especially Thailand, were determined to resist the Soviet-supported Vietnamese occupation of Cambodia and blaming Moscow for Hanoi's intransigence.

Meanwhile, the Soviet Union was bogged down in a stalemated war in Afghanistan, unrest was stirring in Soviet Central Asia, and the Soviet Union was facing a major economic crisis at home.

In sum, when Gorbachev came to power in 1985, the Soviet Union was presiding over a failed policy in the Pacific. Moscow was facing a prospect of encirclement by its three major adversaries—the United States, Japan, and China. Its stagnant Far East was irrelevant to the Pacific market economies. And its few allies and client states in the region were all poor, increasingly burdensome, and without much influence. Moreover, Moscow's enormous military buildup of ground, air, nuclear, and naval forces had not succeeded in intimidating other nations. On the contrary, it had succeeded in driving them closer together. In no other region of the world was there such a gap between Soviet military power and Soviet political influence.

If the failures of the past are one major source of change in Soviet policy in Asia, the economic weaknesses of the present are still another. The Soviet Union is badly overextended. It simply can no longer afford the imperial policy it has been conducting over the last few decades. The economic crisis at home has many dimensions. There is a huge budget deficit amounting to some 11 percent of total GNP, or four times larger than the budget deficit in the United States. The supply system has broken down, and there are shortages of food and the most basic consumer goods. The agricultural system is incapable of feeding the population. The health system is abysmal. The technological gap with the West is widening.

The mounting economic crisis at home is forcing Gorbachev to make substantial cuts in the Soviet military budget, to contemplate even greater cuts, and to reconsider the large and expensive commitments that Moscow is making to its vast empire. In a recent article in a widely read Soviet foreign affairs journal, two Soviet commentators, Aleksei Izyumov and Andrei Kortunov, both researchers at the Academy of Sciences' Institute on the U.S.A. and Canada, call for an orderly retreat from high-cost, low-yield positions abroad and a return to what they call "truly defensible" positions.

In sum, the Soviet empire is facing a crisis of solvency. Gorbachev must bring his commitments more into line with his limited resources. The key point to bear in mind in this connection is that the immensity of the Soviet economic crisis will almost certainly force Gorbachev to make even greater cuts in Soviet military spending than he has so far announced. And in order to justify those cuts to his colleagues, Gorbachev needs a substantial reduction in global tensions.

III

Turning now to the question of continuity and change in Soviet policy in Asia, there are five elements in Gorbachev's policy in East Asia that distinguish his policy from that of his predecessors: First, while Brezhnev and former Soviet Foreign Minister Andrey Gromyko treated most of the East Asian countries as pawns of the United States and paid little attention to them, Gorbachev recognizes that these countries have views and interests of their own and that, while they are generally friendly to the United States, they are far from being American puppets. Moreover, Gorbachev understands that rising nationalism in Asia and growing trade frictions between the Pacific nations and Washington provide the USSR with fertile grounds for fishing in troubled waters. Gorbachev thus sees an opportunity to woo the non-Communist nations of the Pacific in order to expand Soviet influence in the region. Thus, while Gromyko almost never visited Japan, former foreign minister Eduard Shevardnadze made frequent visits, and Gorbachev will visit in April 1991. And while Brezhnev and Gromyko denounced the ASEAN organization as an "imperialist" plot, Gorbachev and Shevardnadze carefully sought to cultivate it. Similarly, while Brezhnev and Gromyko had nothing to do with South Korea, Gorbachev has extended diplomatic recognition to Seoul.

A second area of change in Soviet policy in the region is Gorbachev's efforts to integrate the stagnant Soviet economy into the Pacific division of labor through increased trade, joint ventures, new investment laws, special economic zones, etc. Under Brezhnev and Gromyko, Moscow displayed little interest in economics and sought instead to build up a military capability in the Far East that was equal to any combination of potential adversaries. One result of this over-militarized policy was that Vladivostok, Moscow's main port in the Pacific, became a closed city and was sealed off to outsiders. This obsessive concern with secrecy and security defined exclusively in military terms contributed to the paranoid atmosphere in which the Soviets in 1984 shot down an unarmed South Korean civilian airliner that accidentally violated Soviet air space. The Soviets have now announced they intend to turn Vladivostok into an open city and to transform it into a center for conducting business and trade.

A third area of change in Gorbachev's policy in Asia is the willingness to make some military reductions in order to gain political advantage. Unlike Brezhnev, who consistently built up Soviet military power in Asia, Gorbachev was promised to cut some 200,000 Soviet troops in the "eastern" regions of the USSR. Although the details of these cuts have so far not been made public, it appears that most of them will come from forces deployed along the Sino-Soviet border and in Mongolia.

A fourth very important new element in Soviet policy in Asia is the changing attitude towards the U.S.-Japan alliance and the American military presence in Asia. Some Soviet diplomats and academics now speak of the U.S. military presence in Asia as a stabilizing factor. This stance contrasts sharply with the older approach that regarded the U.S. military presence in Asia as the principal source of tension.

A fifth new element in Soviet policy in Asia is the fact that Moscow is increasingly seeking to help the United States resolve outstanding regional conflicts. The most dramatic example of this, of course, is the Soviet decision to join with the United States and other members of the United Nations Security Council in seeking a peaceful settlement of the Persian Gulf crisis initiated by Iraq's invasion of Kuwait. In this instance, Moscow has sided with the U.S. against its former client state and imposed military and economic sanctions against it. In addition, Moscow has also joined with other members of the UN Security Council in developing a plan for a UN-sponsored peace settlement in Cambodia, and it has begun to play a more active role in pressuring North Korea to come to terms with Seoul.

These are all new and hopeful signs that Moscow is abandoning its old policy of global competition with the United States in an effort to develop a more constructive relationship with the West that will facilitate its economic and political reforms at home.

IV

Although there are a number of new elements in Soviet policy in East Asia under Gorbachev, there are still some elements of continuity with the past and some ambivalence about abandoning past policies. First, despite the announced reduction of ground forces on the Chinese border, Moscow continues to build up and to modernize its air and naval power directed against the United States and Japan. And despite the removal of SS-20 intermediate range nuclear missiles from Asia, the deployment of the longer range, mobile SS-25s ensures that Soviet nuclear power in the region is not diminished. Moreover, even after Moscow makes the announced reductions in its forces on the Chinese border, the Sino-Soviet military balance will remain heavily in the Soviet favor because Moscow continues to make qualitative improvements in its ground and air power directed against China. Also, the Soviets are not disbanding all of the units they are removing from the Chinese border. Rather, they are simply moving them to other locations further away from the border. In sum, the announced reductions in Soviet military power in Asia do not substantially change the existing military balances.

Second, while Moscow may be under great pressure to cut back on its economic and military assistance to its Asian client states, as of 1990 it was not yet doing so. In 1990, the USSR doubled its military assistance to the Najibullah government in Afghanistan and to the Heng Samrin government in Cambodia while continuing to provide substantial military aid to Vietnam, Mongolia, and North Korea. There are, however, likely to be substantial cuts in Soviet aid to all of these states beginning in 1991.

A third element of continuity is reflected in Moscow's one-sided arms control proposals, which so far seem largely designed to constrain U.S. naval activity in the Pacific. For example, the Soviets propose to establish "nuclear free zones" in Korea and Southeast Asia, where American forces are located, but not on the Kamchatka Peninsula and in the Sea of Okhotsk, where Soviet nuclear forces are located.

Fourth, as of December 1990, Moscow still refused to return the four islands north of Hokkaido that it seized from Japan at the end of World War II. Without a settlement of this territorial issue, it will be difficult, if not impossible, for Moscow to make any substantial headway toward rapprochement with Japan. It seems likely that Gorbachev will make some compromise proposal to resolve this issue when he visits Japan in 1991.

In sum, while there have been a number of significant and welcome changes in Soviet policy in Asia under Gorbachev, not all aspects of Soviet policy have changed. And, even where policies have changed, the extent of change still remains unclear. Moreover, there are many uncertainties about the future. The Soviet Union is mired in a deep domestic crisis, and its future political stability is in doubt. The possibility that a more repressive regime may yet come to power cannot be ruled out. In late 1990, there were open calls by conservative Soviet leaders for Gorbachev to suspend elected legislatures in the Soviet republics and, in effect, to impose martial law. If such a development were to occur, Soviet relations with the West would suffer a severe setback.

Thus, the new Soviet pragmatism offers both challenges and opportunities for the United States. The challenges arise from the fact that there are many uncertainties about the future of Soviet domestic and foreign policy. The opportunities lie in taking advantage of the new Soviet moderation to reduce the U.S. security burden and to ease global and regional tensions.

V

What have been the major payoffs so far from Gorbachev's new policy of engagement in the Pacific? And what are likely to be the major limitations on Moscow's ability to win friends in the region?

The major Soviet success in Asia so far has unquestionably been the new rapprochement with China. The deep freeze in Sino-Soviet relations has ended, and a new stage in Sino-Soviet relations is beginning. Both Beijing and Moscow have powerful reasons for wanting to continue improving relations with each other. Each believes that its most urgent priority for the next decade or more is to modernize its economy; this requires a peaceful international climate, reduced defense spending, and calm along the 4,600-mile border.

Also, since the June 4 Tiananmen Square massacres and the purge of the radical reform leader Zhao Ziyang, the new, more conservative Chinese leadership is beginning to cut back on its Open Door policy towards the West because of its fear of "spiritual pollution." And, as a result of political instability in China, Western investors are beginning to have second thoughts about the wisdom of large-scale involvement. Thus, the Chinese leadership may seek to increase trade and cultural exchanges with the Soviet Union and other socialist countries in order to compensate in part for these losses.

Still, there are substantial limits to any Sino-Soviet rapprochement. For years to come, China's two major concerns will be security and development, and in each category China has much more to gain from the West than from the Soviet Union. In the strategic realm, as long as the Soviet Union has the most powerful army on the Eurasian continent, keeps one-third of its nuclear weapons in the Far East, maintains a huge fleet off China's coast, and supplies arms to two of China's long-range adversaries, Vietnam and India, the Chinese will want to maintain stable relations with the West in order to balance Soviet power. One high-ranking Chinese military official has said recently that there are three new "obstacles" to any substantial improvement of Sino-Soviet relations: Moscow's military modernization; Moscow's arms supplies to Vietnam; and Moscow's arms supplies to New Delhi.

In the economic sphere, China's relations with the Pacific market economies are almost certainly going to be much more important than its economic relations with the Soviets. China conducts less that 5 percent of its trade with the Russians, while its trade with Japan, the United States, and other Pacific market economies constitutes about two-thirds of its total trade.

Finally, there has still been no final resolution of the Sino-Soviet border dispute.[3]

The Russians will face an even more severe challenge in their efforts to improve relations with Japan. Gorbachev wants technological assistance from Japan in order to jump-start the Soviet economy, and he needs Japan's support if the Soviet Union hopes to join the various Pacific economic organizations such as PECC and the Asian Development Bank, organizations in which the Japanese play a large role. But the Japanese are insisting on Soviet concessions on the territorial dispute before they make any substantial moves toward increasing economic relations.

Both Moscow and Tokyo have strong incentives to compromise. Moscow is keen to gain entrance into the Asian Development Bank and to achieve success to Japanese technology. For its part, Tokyo will not want to be left out of the worldwide rapproachment with the Soviet Union. Moreover, if European and American businessmen step up trade with Moscow, the Japanese private sector will want to do the same.

But even if Gorbachev is able to reach a modus vivendi of sorts with Tokyo, there will be significant limits to any Soviet-Japanese rapprochement. The first major constraint on Soviet-Japanese relations is Japan's firm alliance with the United States. Although the U.S.-Japanese marriage is now troubled by trade disputes, a divorce between the two countries is unthinkable. The United States and Japan have interests in common to a degree that is probably unparalleled in world history. The United States needs Japanese capital to finance its own industrial renovation; the United States also needs Japan to provide financial and economic assistance to a variety of geopolitically important but unstable Third World countries in which the West as a whole has important strategic stakes; and the United States needs Japanese assistance to maintain a stable and open international system.

Japan, for its part, needs American security protection for its homeland and its sea lanes of communication; it needs continuing access to the world's largest market and, through cooperation with America, secure access to a stable and expanding world market; and Japan needs continuing entry into America's vast research establishment, which is central to Japan's own technological innovation.[4]

Second, the limitations of the Soviet economy combined with recent structural changes in the Japanese economy make it unlikely that economic relations between the two countries will improve rapidly. In the 1970s, Japan was one of the top three capitalist countries in trade with the Soviet Union. But by 1981, Japan had fallen to fifth among the capitalist nations trading with Moscow. Most Japanese enthusiasm for getting involved in large Siberian development projects has evaporated. Since the 1970s, Japan has established a more fuel-efficient production method for its industries and greatly diversified its sources of oil supply. At a time of plentiful oil and relatively low energy prices, the Japanese have lost much of the appetite they once had for exploring Siberian coal and gas reserves. The Persian Gulf crisis may lead to a change in this situation. But of several hundred joint ventures the Soviets have signed recently, Japan's share is only a meager five—a good indication that Siberia is no longer so alluring to Japan's business sector.

Perhaps most important, there is a historically rooted legacy of mistrust between the two countries that is bound to inhibit any substantial warming of relations. The two countries have been at odds for most of the twentieth century, and they have yet to sign a peace treaty ending World War II. They fought four times in this century, the last time in 1945, when the Red Army entered Manchuria in the final weeks of the war. The Japanese still regard this as a "stab in the back," which violated the Soviet-Japanese treaty of neutrality of 1941. Moreover, the Soviets kept over half a million Japanese prisoners in the Soviet "gulag," and many of them never returned home. As a result of this history, Japanese public opinion polls regularly show that the Soviet Union is the least liked and most distrusted of all foreign countries.

Within the Japanese elite, and particularly among those of Japan's professional diplomats who are Soviet specialists, dislike of the Soviet Union is deeply rooted. It stems in part from the crude and condescending behavior that the Russians displayed towards Japan during the Gromyko era. As a result, perhaps more than any other country in the Western alliance, Japan is extremely skeptical and cautious about the changes taking place in the Soviet Union under Gorbachev.[5]

In Korea, the Soviets are playing a new game designed to have the best of both worlds. They are increasing their strategic relations with North Korea while extending diplomatic relations to South Korea. Since Kim Il-sung's visit to Moscow in 1984, there have been exchanges of naval port calls between the Soviet and North Korean navies, and the Soviet Union has gained overflight rights over North Korean territory. Soviet and North Korean negotiators have met to discuss the extension of broad-gauge railroad tracks from the USSR to the North Korean ports of Najin and Chongjin in order to facilitate the delivery of military equipment. More recently, the Soviets have supplied Pyongyang with new military hardware, including SU-25 ground-attack aircraft, the most effective of the Soviet Union's attack planes; MIG-29 Fulcrum aircraft, one of the most sophisticated planes in the Soviet arsenal; and SA-5 Gammon surface-to-air missiles together with the advanced Tin Shield early warning radar network, the first deployment of the Tin Shield system outside the Soviet Union. All of this contrasts with Moscow's reluctance in the 1970s to supply the volatile North Korean dictator with advanced weapons.

Meanwhile, Moscow is holding out olive branches to the Republic of Korea. The Soviets attended the Seoul Olympics in 1988 despite Pyongyang's boycott, and in his speech at Krasnoyarsk in October, Gorbachev signaled his intention to expand economic relations with South Korea. Recently, the Soviets have gone so far as to recognize South Korea, over Pyongyang's objections. In sum, the Soviets are pursuing a de facto "two Koreas" policy.

Seoul is responding favorably to Soviet overtures. It wants to reduce its excessive trade dependence on the United States and to prod North Korea into negotiation. President Roh Tae Woo has authorized the visit to Moscow by some of his top business leaders to scout the possibilities for trade, investment, and joint ventures. And Roh has formally proposed a six-power conference including the Soviet Union to help resolve the Korean issue.

In Southeast Asia, the Soviets are also trying to have it both ways by seeking to court ASEAN without completely alienating Vietnam. In sharp contrast to their behavior during the Brezhnev era, when Moscow denounced ASEAN as an imperialist bloc, former Soviet Foreign Minister Shevardnadze toured Indonesia and Thailand in 1987, the first such visit by a Soviet foreign minister in 20 years. The prime ministers of Malaysia, Australia, and Thailand have all visited Moscow with their foreign ministers and the presidents of the Philippines and Indonesia are expected. Moscow is also seeking to become a "dialogue partner" of ASEAN along with the United States, Japan, and the European Economic Community.

But although a more positive image of the Soviet Union is beginning to emerge among the ASEAN countries, acceptance of the Russians is still conditional and not uniform. Indonesia and Malaysia are the most positively disposed; Thailand and the Philippines are becoming more open to relations with Moscow; and Singapore and Brunei are most cautious.

Throughout the region, there is an historically rooted deep fear of communism. Most of the ruling parties in these countries fought Communist insurgencies for decades, and Communist parties are still illegal in all the ASEAN countries. The Philippines is still engaged in a struggle with a substantial Communist rebel force.

Moreover, there is a continuing concern throughout the region about Soviet espionage. Recently, the Thais arrested two Europeans allegedly spying for the Soviet Union, and the Thai National Security Council stated that approximately 50 percent of the 87 Soviet officials in Thailand are disguised intelligence officials whose main tasks are to recruit Thai nationals and to monitor American and Chinese activities in Thailand.

Fear of subversion and infiltration is even more acute in Indonesia. On one recent occasion, a Soviet ballet company was refused permission to enter Indonesia because of restrictions imposed by the Indonesian security agencies.

VI

What, finally, are the implications of changing Soviet policy in the Pacific for the United States? Despite a few caveats I have mentioned earlier, there has been a substantial change in Soviet policy in Asia. The United States should welcome this new moderation and engage the Soviets in a step-by-step policy of engagement designed to reduce tensions and achieve greater regional stability.

In order for a stable post–Cold War world to be brought into being in Asia it will be necessary to realize that the situation in Asia is quite different from what it is in Europe and that the patterns of accommodation in Europe cannot be mechanically transplanted to the Pacific. Whereas in Europe there are two multilateral alliance systems, NATO and the Warsaw Pact, in the Pacific there are no such multilateral security arrangements. Whereas in Europe regional economic integration is far advanced via the European Economic Community and other organizations, in Asia the forces of regional integrations are still rather weak. Whereas in Europe it is possible to make arms control tradeoffs because of the symmetries in NATO and Warsaw Pact force structures, both of which are largely ground forces, in Asia the asymmetries in the force structures of the United States and the Soviet Union make arms control much more difficult.

To reduce East-West tension in the Pacific, a formula quite different from the one applied in Europe will need to be employed. Several conditions must be met. First, the United States and the Soviet Union will need a realistic sense of strategic direction that takes into account the peculiar political, cultural, and geopolitical circumstances of the region. Second, there needs to be continuing improvement in the bilateral relations between the major powers whose interests intersect in the region—the United States, the Soviet Union, China, and Japan. Third, there must be a radical breakthrough towards a political resolution of the outstanding regional conflicts in Korea and Cambodia and of the territorial dispute between the Soviet Union and Japan. Fourth, there needs to be continuing progress towards regional cooperation, including the establishment of viable regional institutions. Fifth, there must be continued movement toward political and social pluralism throughout the region. Finally, there should be a variety of efforts to reduce the military confrontation in the region between the superpowers, between China and Vietnam, between North and South Korea, and between the Soviet Union and China.

As far as the superpowers' strategic direction is concerned, it should be recognized that the traditional Soviet approach to Asian security—which envisages the creation of a broad, comprehensive security dialogue modeled on the Helsinki Conference in Europe—is premature. Few countries in Asia have been attracted to Moscow's pan-Asian security proposals either in their Brezhnevian or Gorbachevian forms. Economic, political, and cultural differences in the region are simply too great to allow for the creation of a broad collective security system at this time.

A second important reality that must be taken into account is that the U.S. bilateral alliance system in the Pacific and the U.S. system of forward deployment that supports these alliances have helped preserve the peace and to stabilize the military, political, and economic environments. Without the stability brought about by the American presence, it is doubtful that the region would have achieved such extraordinary economic and political success in recent decades. Moreover, all of non-Communist Asia, and China as well, continues to look to America naval power as a necessary counterweight to the land-based military potential of the Soviet Union and to the military power of other countries in the region. None of America's allies and friends in Asia are calling for a reduction of the American military presence in the Pacific.[6]

Yet a third crucial reality is that the existing military and political status quo in the region strongly favors the United States and is therefore more acceptable to Washington than to Moscow. Unlike the situation in Europe, the United States is under little pressure from allies in Asia to respond to Gorbachev's various initiatives.

The Soviet Union's unsatisfactory position in Asia is largely attributable to its general economic weakness, which inhibits economic interaction with the dynamic market economies of the region, and to the underdevelopment of Siberia. Any change in this situation will take decades.

The single most important way to begin laying the foundations for a more stable system of international relations in the Pacific is not through premature calls for pan-Asian security schemes, but rather by improving bilateral relations among the major powers. There are already many encouraging signs of progress in this direction.

The United States and the Soviet Union are making progress on a new START agreement and on conventional and chemical weapons agreements, and they are discussing a variety of other ways to improve their bilateral relations. As discussed earlier, Soviet relations with China have been normalized, and Soviet-Japanese relations are also improving. Chinese-Indian relations are improving as well. Rajiv Gandhi, the former Indian Prime Minister, visited China in 1988: he was the first Indian leader to visit China since Nehru went to Peking in 1954.

This improvement in relations among the major powers has been accompanied by a variety of measures to increase transparency and mutual confidence. Soviet and American military leaders are beginning to exchange data and to visit each other's military installations. The Soviet Union has announced its intention to remove some 12 divisions from the Chinese border and to withdraw the majority of its forces in Mongolia, while China has already demobilized a million men from its armed forces. A joint Sino-Soviet military-political commission is now considering how to implement mutual force reductions along the border.

In addition to improving relations among the major powers, a second condition for a more stable Pacific is the need to achieve a breakthrough in resolving the outstanding regional conflicts in Korea and Cambodia. The stark facts of life on the Korean peninsula are that more than a million armed men face each other across the narrow waist of the thirty-eight parallel, and, despite recent North-South talks, there has been very little genuine progress in moving toward a North-South Korean détente. The principal obstacle to peace in Korea is the unreconstructed Stalinist regime in Pyongyang, which refuses to accept the legitimacy of the government in the south and which continues to try to reunify Korea on its own terms. North Korea remains one of the most highly militarized, secretive, and isolated countries in the world, and it is led by a dictator who may not be in touch with the realities of the modern world.

Until and unless North Korea moves toward its own version of glasnost and perestroika, it seems unlikely that there will be any substantial diminution in tension on the peninsula. Recent developments in Eastern Europe, where Communist regimes have been overthrown, must be strengthening the North Korean dictator's resolve to take a harder line.

Still, the great powers must do what they can to encourage and pressure North Korea to come to an accommodation with Seoul. The immediate objective should be a new dialogue between the Koreas, which leads to a substantial drawdown of forces along the thirty-eighth parallel, family reunification, the beginning of trade, and a variety of contacts between Seoul and Pyongyang. A later goal is a peace treaty between the Koreas and the entry of both of them into the United Nations. In Korea, as in Central Europe, mutual security can be improved by the opposing sides restructuring their armed forces into a mode of "defensive defense." This would be an appropriate form of mutual threat reduction for the Korean peninsula.

In Cambodia, the great powers should increase their efforts to arrange a political settlement among the four contending Cambodian factions. There are encouraging developments. The five permanent members of the UN Security

Council (the United States, the Soviet Union, China, Great Britain, and France), meeting in Paris, have already agreed on a plan to bring peace and free elections to Cambodia. The core of the plan is an enhanced role for the United Nations in Cambodia. It would require that the existing Vietnamese-backed Hun Sen government surrender the top posts in the administration to UN officials. A cease-fire, to be policed by the United Nations, would then come into effect between the Hun Sen regime and the three-party opposition coalition headed by Prince Norodom Sihanouk but militarily dominated by the Khmer Rouge, which has been fighting it. The United Nations would run the country for a year or so, during which time it would organize and oversee elections. It would then withdraw, leaving the elected government to rebuild Cambodia.

Such a UN operation would be expensive, but Japan has already promised to underwrite much of the cost. A more serious question is whether China, the principal external supporter of the Khmer Rouge, will be able and willing to rein in the Khmer Rouge's ability to wage war. If the Khmer Rouge go on fighting, the big powers and the United Nations will be forced to muster a real peacekeeping force in Cambodia, not just an election-watching operation similar to the one just carried out in Namibia.

A third condition for moving towards a more stable Pacific is to foster the development of regional and economic organizations such as ASEAN, PECC, the Asian Development Bank, and the newly created Asia Pacific Regional Cooperation (APEC), which brings together most of the market economies in the region.

Once there is a political settlement in Cambodia, Vietnam may be invited to sign the Bali Treaty, which led to the creation of ASEAN. Following this, there could be an increase of political and economic relations between Vietnam and the non-Communist countries of Southeast Asia. The prime minister of Thailand has already outlined a plan for turning all of Indochina into a marketplace, and there is a considerable potential for the development of economic relations between Vietnam and the ASEAN countries and between Vietnam and the other market economies of the Pacific rim.

For some time to come, the Pacific economic organizations will be largely confined to the market economies. But the Soviet Union has already become an observer at PECC and Asian Development Bank meetings, and over time, as the Soviet Union and other socialist countries in the Pacific move towards market reforms, these ties to regional economic organizations can be expanded.

Any stable security structure in the Pacific will also require continuing progress in the region towards political and social pluralism as a political principle respected within each country. The attempts by the new hard-line leadership in China to turn the clock back on reform, and the continuation in Pyongyang of an anachronistic Stalinist regime are incompatible with any genuine progress towards regional security and stability. By the same token, much will depend on the continuation of political and economic reform in the Soviet Union.

Finally, there need to be some efforts to reduce the military confrontation in the region between the United States and the Soviet Union. Some reduction of Soviet and U.S. military forces in the Pacific is almost certainly going to be brought about by defense budget constraints on both sides. The U.S. has already announced a 10 percent cut in its forces in the Pacific. Some of the existing "confidence-building" forums, such as the incidents-at-sea talks between the Soviet Union and the United States (which have been among the most successful of the various Soviet-American dialogues), could be expanded to include China and Japan. All four of the major powers could begin to exchange data on their respective defense budgets and defense plans. High-ranking naval officials from all four countries could enter into regular exchanges to discuss their respective naval doctrines and their future force projections. Military exercises could be reduced and made less provocative, and there could be prenotification of all naval exercises over a certain size.

In addition, since it is the common interest of all of the major powers to discourage nuclear proliferation and the spread of ballistic missiles and other advanced military technologies in the region, talks might begin on this subject.

Moreover, in the longer run, it will be necessary for both the United States and the Soviet Union to reassess their military strategies and their military deployments in the Pacific. On the Soviet side, there needs to be a substantial reduction in land-based aircraft, which now number more than 2,400, and in submarines, which now total about 140.

As far as the American side is concerned, if there is a conventional arms treaty that substantially reduces Soviet forces in Western Europe, and if the Eastern European countries continue to move in the direction of political pluralism, the danger of a Soviet attack on Western Europe will be greatly diminished. As a result, the current U.S. strategy of deterring a Soviet attack in Europe by posing a threat of "horizontal escalation" in the Pacific will lose much of it credibility.

The United States will therefore need to develop a strategy in the Pacific that focuses less on the threat from the Soviet Union and more on the multiple threats from other sources that can be expected to continue in the 1990s—threats to secure oil supplies from the Persian Gulf, threats of maritime interdiction, and, above all, threats from several flashpoints that could involve the United States in conflict at lower levels.

Any U.S. strategic reassessment in the Pacific should, however, take into account that for some time to come there will be a need for a substantial U.S. presence in the Pacific not just to shore up or protect threatened allies but also to underpin U.S. political/economic policy.

In sum, security and stability for the two superpowers in the Pacific, as well as for other nations in the region, could be considerably enhanced if these nations progress along six paths: (1) The superpowers in particular need to take realistic account of the particular political, cultural, and geopolitical circumstances of the region. (2) Further improvement is needed in all the bilateral relations involved, and especially in U.S.-Chinese and Soviet-Japanese relations. (3) Resolutions must be found to the serious confrontations in Korea and Cambodia. (4) Progress towards economic and other cooperation within the region needs to continue. (5) So must progress towards political and social pluralism. (6) And finally, efforts are needed to reduce the military confrontations in the region, especially the U.S.-Soviet confrontation. Progress in all these directions is certainly possible in the years to come. If that progress is made, there are real grounds for hope that all the nations in the region will be able to enjoy greater security.

NOTES

1. For a translation of the Vladivostok speech of July 1986, see Foreign Broadcast Information Service, *Daily Report: Soviet Union* (Washington, DC, hereinafter *FBIS-SOV*), July 29, 1986, pp. R/1–20. The foreign policy portion of the Krasnoyarsk speech appears in *News and Views from the USSR* (Washington, DC: Soviet Embassy Information Department, September 19, 1988), pp. 1–11.

2. For recent reviews of Gorbachev's initiatives in East Asia, see Donald S. Zagoria, "Soviet Policy in East Asia: A New Beginning," *Foreign Affairs, America and the World* (1988/89); Rajan Menon, "New Thinking and Northeast Asian Security," *Problems of Communism* (March–June 1989); and *Gorbachev's Asian Policy*, a Joint Report of the United Nations Association of the USA and the Asia Pacific Association of Japan (New York: United Nations Association, March 1989).

3. The major obstacle to a border settlement is the status of Heixiazi, a 330-square kilometer island at the confluence of the Amur and Ussuri rivers. The island is claimed by the Chinese but controlled by the USSR. Because Heixiazi overlooks Khabarovsk as well as the point where the Trans-Siberian Railway crosses the Amur River, the Soviets are reluctant to give it up.

4. See Zbigniew Brzezinski, "America's New Geostrategy," *Foreign Affairs* (Spring 1988).

5. On recent Soviet-Japanese relations, see the prolific writings of Peggy Falkenheim, Hiroski Kimura, and Tsuyoshi Hasegawa.

6. As Charles Krauthammer has pointed out: "No country [in East Asia] from South Korea to China to Thailand to Australia—not even Vietnam—fears the deployment of American troops. What they do fear is American withdrawal. Not that they expect immediate Japanese rearmament. But in the absence of Pax Americana there would be enough nervousness about ultimate Japanese intentions and capabilities to spark a local arms race and create instability and tension of a kind that has not been seen in Asia for decades." ["Universal Dominion: Toward a Unipolar World," *The National Interest* (Winter 1989/90), p. 48.]

31
Moscow's Third World Strategy*

Alvin Z. Rubinstein

The past several years have seen a fundamental transformation in Moscow's approach to Eastern and Central Europe and a shift in its relations with the United States, China, and the United Nations. Gorbachev's "new thinking" has also introduced far-reaching changes in Soviet policy toward the Third World: in Afghanistan; in movement toward political solutions to regional conflicts; in hesitant but nonetheless detectable signaling to major clients that military instruments will not be uncritically provided for the pursuit of national ambitions (as in Moscow's recent dealings with Syria and the Palestine Liberation Organization); in the demonstrated readiness to work more closely with the United States to curb and even end long-festering regional conflicts, thus far, in Angola, Kampuchea, and the Persian Gulf; and in renewed interest in upgrading the peacekeeping functions of the United Nations. We are not sure of the reasons that prompted Gorbachev to make these policy changes and we may disagree on their significance, but they are too extensive and potentially important in what they portend for Soviet foreign policy and the future of U.S.-Soviet rivalry to be relegated reflexively to the realm of "tactics."

Much of Soviet policy is still in flux. The persistence of old patterns amidst new trends results in a kind of uncertainty as to the dominant direction of Gorbachev's Third World policy. In his record to date, there are emergent tendencies that merit comment and comparison with those of his predecessors. Evaluating them may help us assess the impact of his "new thinking" on the USSR's Third World policy and what this implies for the future of Soviet relations with the United States.

For analytical purposes, the distinguishing aspects of Gorbachev's policy may be categorized as follows:

- De-emphasis on the military instruments;
- Acceptance of linkage in U.S.-Soviet relations;
- Encouragement of negotiated solutions to regional conflicts;
- Movement toward reducing the costs of maintaining an imperial policy;
- Glasnost in foreign policy evaluations.

*Reprinted by permission of the author and publisher from Alvin Z. Rubinstein, *Moscow's Third World Strategy*, Epilogue, pp. 295–312. Copyright © 1989 By Princeton University Press.

On the other hand, certain elements that have characterized Soviet foreign policy since the mid-1950s continue to be evident in Gorbachev's course:

- Regime maintenance;
- Comprehensive activism;
- Salience of arms transfers as an instrument of policy;
- Competitive rivalry;
- Limited insights provided for the basis of decisions.

Let us first turn to the differences under Gorbachev.

DE-EMPHASIS ON THE MILITARY INSTRUMENT

The shift away from heavy reliance on fostering the military instrument as a means of achieving political goals is the most significant difference between Gorbachev's Third World policy and that of his predecessors. Afghanistan was undoubtedly the watershed. As he said on February 8, 1988, "any armed conflict, including an internal one, can poison the atmosphere in an entire region and create a situation of anxiety and alarm for a country's neighbors . . . That is why we are against any armed conflicts." It was clear to him that Afghanistan could not be pacified short of massive new commitments, which were precluded by the need to concentrate on internal reforms and usher in an era of diminished international tensions. Moreover, the unending drain on resources in Angola, Ethiopia, Kampuchea, and Syria, to mention a few prominent cases, must also have forced Soviet leaders to face the unsustainability of seeking strategic advantage by essentially military means.

In Afghanistan, where Soviet forces were directly involved, Moscow manipulated the client regime at will, but still faced innumerable difficulties. Elsewhere in the Third World, where it exercised lesser degrees of control, the environment proved not only costly but intractable. As Melvin Goodman has observed, even when dependent on Soviet military aid, "Third World states have their own goals, capabilities, and independently determined priorities. When interests coincide, Moscow and a Third World leader cooperate; when interests differ frictions ensue. Continuing strains in Soviet relations with such close clients as Cuba, Syria, and Vietnam illustrate the perplexing difficulty of translating military power into political influence over clients."[1]

The downgrading of military means in the Third World is consonant with Gorbachev's call for the "demilitarization of international relations," a theme he sounded in his speech before the United Nations General Assembly on December 8, 1988. That "force and the threat of force neither can or should be instruments of foreign policy" was a principle that he held applicable not just to nuclear arsenals but to all aspects of international relations. This suggests Gorbachev's realization that the USSR's role in the militarization of regional politics in the Third World had not brought achievements commensurate with the costs, especially in light of tensions with the United States. Such being the case, we would expect to see some restraint in Moscow's policy of supplying arms to a regime merely because it is anti-imperialist, meaning anti-American. Its arms policy would manifest to clients that it was not about to make war a feasible option. This may be illustrated by the Soviet-Syrian relationship. While not distancing himself from Syrian President Hafez Assad, who is still Moscow's most important link to the Arab world, Gorbachev has put him on notice of changes in Soviet policy. During Assad's visit to Moscow in April 1987, Gorbachev said that the absence of diplomatic relations between the Soviet Union and Israel "cannot be considered normal."[2] Though Soviet arms continue to flow into Syria, and Moscow has upgraded Syria's "defense" capability, the message from Moscow is that Assad should not expect to be strengthened to the level of "strategic parity" with Israel; and disagreements with Damascus are permitted to become public in a way that marks a sharp departure from past Soviet practice.

One such expression of dissonance occurred on September 18, 1989. At a press briefing held in Moscow by the Ministry of Foreign Affairs, Alexander Zotov, the Soviet ambassador to Syria, said Soviet economic needs and reforms would inevitably affect relations with Syria. He suggested that in the future, Moscow might have to reconsider its level of economic and military assistance. Noting that Syria's requests for aid over the next five years were being reviewed, Zotov said, "I can tell you that they are being scrutinized critically and if there are any changes they will be in favor of reductions—all the more because the Syrian government's ability to pay is not unlimited."[3] If actually implemented, such relations would constitute a major shift in Moscow's attitude toward the arming of a prime client.

During Gorbachev's tenure, no opportunity in the Third World has yet appeared that might tempt him to undertake significant new military commitments, so the testing of the proposition that he is de-emphasizing the military instrument must await the future.

ACCEPTANCE OF LINKAGE IN U.S.-SOVIET RELATIONS

Unlike previous Soviet leaders, Gorbachev acknowledged that there is indeed a contradiction between the USSR's projection of military power in the Third World and its attempts to improve relations with the United States. Though Soviet writers were slow to face this dilemma directly, their allusions to it increasingly appeared in the months prior to Gorbachev's speech of February 8, 1988, announcing the withdrawal from Afghanistan and expressing the hope that this would serve as a model for solving other regional conflicts and removing them as barriers to better U.S.-Soviet relations.[4]

The most direct ascription of culpability to Moscow for the collapse of détente in the 1970s and early 1980s appeared in *Literaturnaya gazeta* in May 1988.[5]

Dashichev's article was a landmark in *glasnost*. Relying on balance of power rather than "class analysis" as an analytical tool, Dashichev denounced Stalin for his "hegemonist, great-power ambitions" which "repeatedly jeopardized political equilibrium between states," and blamed him for the "conflicts and frictions [that] developed with other socialist countries." Without mincing words, he went on to say that the failure of détente to take hold in the 1970s and the resulting severe exacerbation of East-West tensions were "caused chiefly by the miscalculations and incompetent approach of the Brezhnev leadership" in its expansion of Soviet power in the Third World, the critical limits of which were reached "in the West's eyes with the introduction of Soviet troops into Afghanistan." His criticism of Moscow's mistakes went far beyond any previous public Soviet assessment of the issue:

> We were wrong in assessing the global situation in the world and the correlation of forces, and no serious efforts were made to settle the fundamental political contradictions with the West. *Though we were politically, militarily (via weapons, supplies and advisers) and diplomatically involved in regional conflicts, we disregarded their influence on the relaxation of tension between the USSR and the West and on their entire system of relationships.*
>
> There were no clear ideas of the Soviet Union's true national state interests. These interests lay by no means in chasing petty and essentially formal gains associated with leadership coups in certain developing countries . . . The uncreative nature of the decisions resulted in our foreign policy becoming exceptionally costly. (Italics added.)

Dashichev's explicit linking of the deterioration of détente in the past to Soviet behavior is still the exception in Soviet writings on the Third World. Since then, most analysts who discuss the problems in U.S.-Soviet relations arising out of their competing interests in the Third World may admit that the Soviet approach has some shortcomings, but their critiques are general, unfocused, and quick to attribute principal responsibility to the United States.[6] Linkages on this subject are more apt to be found in the periodic discussions published in Soviet journals and held on Moscow radio and television programs than in serious academic writings. Scholars such as Viktor Kremenyuk of the USSR Academy of Sciences' Institute of the USA and Canada, and Alexei Vasilyev of the USSR Academy of Sciences' Institute of Africa are of the few who have forthrightly admitted that problems with the United States developed because of Moscow's failure to take into consideration a "balance of interests" and because of an excessive funneling of arms to clients in the belief "that the more arms you pour into a country the greater the influence, including political influence, you win there."[7] The growing recognition of the importance of linkage may also be seen in Moscow's repeated calls for U.S.-Soviet cooperation to solve regional conflicts and problems in the wide-ranging and continuous discussions taking place between American and Soviet officials. The implication is that if the superpowers cooperate in the Third World, not only will they be able to end or sharply limit the cycle of ever more costly and dangerous regional conflicts, but their own relationship will not suffer as it did in the past.

ENCOURAGEMENT OF NEGOTIATED SOLUTIONS TO REGIONAL CONFLICTS

Under Gorbachev the Soviet Union has, in the interest of fostering negotiated settlements, sought to establish contacts with all sides to regional disputes. The most striking example to date is the resumption of diplomatic contacts (though not formal ties) with Israel. Many Soviet scholars acknowledge that Moscow made a mistake in breaking off diplomatic ties with Israel in June 1967 at which time it saw a chance to heighten U.S. isolation from the Arab world by demonstrating its solidarity with the Arab cause in contrast to Washington's support for Israel's position. By 1989, Moscow had agreed to exchange de facto consular missions (though the Israeli mission in Moscow is still not authorized to issue visas); to permit a sharp increase in Soviet Jewish emigration; to meet frequently with Israeli officials to explore ways of generating movement on the Israeli-Palestinian issue; and to expand cultural and commercial contacts. Moreover, the decision of Hungary in September 1989 and Czechoslovakia and Poland in February 1990 to reestablish full diplomatic ties suggest that Moscow is prepared to follow suit, once it can do so without jeopardizing relations with the Arab states.

Wanting to be part of the Arab-Israeli peace process, Moscow advocates an international conference. However, it is demonstrating flexibility in giving guarded approval to Israeli Prime Minister Shamir's far more limited proposal that elections be held for Palestinians residing in the West Bank and Gaza strip. Its credibility was enhanced also by helping to persuade PLO Chairman Yasser Arafat to state publicly, as he did in Geneva in December 1988, his acknowledgment of Israel's right to exist, acceptance of UN Security Council Resolutions 242 and 338, and renunciation of terrorism. Gorbachev's policy has been to move this protracted conflict from armed struggle to political negotiation.

In southern Africa, Moscow played a constructive behind-the-scenes role in helping to fashion the Namibia-Angola settlement concluded at the end of 1988. Having recognized that "their Angolan strong-hold, acquired on the cheap 14 years ago, ultimately proved to be a political and strategic quagmire, costing more to maintain than to acquire," the Soviets and Cubans accepted the need for a political settlement.[8] Moscow has also had contacts with the government of South Africa, thus hinting its desire to see diplomatic normalization pushed. According to Chester Crocker, "The Soviet Union and Cuba have given Pretoria a stake in regional peace-making by their decision to join with South Africa in the work of the Namibia-Angola Joint Commission, whose first challenge— getting SWAPO back under control after its April [1989] incursions into northern Namibia, in violation of the accords—was met."[9]

In the Gulf, Moscow joined with permanent members of the UN Security Council in passing Resolution 598, which served as the basis for the cease-fire that was eventually arranged in August 1988, ending the fighting between Iraq and Iran. In this instance, however, its policy was not as clear-cut as in Angola, possessing a competitive as well as a cooperative aspect: "Playing a complicated double game of trying to improve relations with both sides of the conflict, the Soviets sought to weaken American efforts to build a consensus against Iran, while positioning themselves to pose as mediators to end the war."[10]

Moscow tried its hand in Lebanon. In August 1989, it sent a special envoy, Gennadi P. Tarasov, to Beirut in an effort to arrange a cease-fire between the Christian commander, General Michel Aoun, and Syrian-backed Muslim forces. Lebanon, wracked by civil war since 1976, has become a surrogate battlefield for rival Baathist regimes in Syria and Iraq. Moscow's initiative may have been prompted by fear of a Syrian-Iraqi clash if the local balance of power were suddenly upset—if, for example, Syria's Hafex Assad were to overrun the Christian enclave of General Aoun, for whom Iraq has been the principal arms supplier. Iraq's Saddam Hussein, eager to avenge himself on Assad for siding with Iran in the Iran-Iraq War, has found in Lebanon's communal and ethnic feuds a cost-effective way of draining Syria's resources and undermining its pretensions and prestige. In this setting Moscow had little to lose in undertaking the series of diplomatic discussions with the various parties to the dispute, from which it hoped to gain prestige and leverage in being perceived as a concerned yet neutral outside mediator.

In Nicaragua, Gorbachev urged the Sandinista leadership to accept the Central American Peace Plan proposed in August 1987 by the region's five presidents and seek a political solution to the insurgency generated by the U.S.-backed "Contras." The implementation of the Arias Plan (named after Costa Rica's President Oscar Arias) resulted in the electoral defeat of the Sandinistas on February 25, 1990. Taking his cue from the kind of political pluralism that Gorbachev had introduced in Eastern Europe in 1989, Daniel Ortega agreed to the first orderly transfer of power in Nicaraguan history and, with it, the advent of an era of contested elections and competing political parties. A successful solution through elections and "national reconciliation" in Nicaragua may lead Gorbachev to expect some kind of reciprocal moves by the United States to help bring an end to the Mujahideen insurgency in Afghanistan.

In at least two other areas, Moscow has been active in the search for a diminution of regional tensions. Its pressure was undoubtedly a key consideration behind Vietnam's decision to withdraw its forces from Kampuchea, effective September 20, 1989. And it has also apparently been trying to use its good offices to bring about the release of the kidnapped Americans held prisoner by terrorist groups in Lebanon."[11]

At a conference on foreign policy and diplomacy held for his staff on July 25, 1988, and devoted to examining key shortcomings and requirements of Soviet diplomacy in the era of *perestroika,* Soviet Foreign Minister Eduard Shev-ardnadze noted that given "the overriding task of diplomacy—to seek friends for the country or at least not acquire enemies" one priority was "to conduct energetic dialogue and talks *with all countries without exception* on the main areas of world politics." (Italics added.)[12] Moscow's continued emphasis on this principle, as in its talking to Israelis and South Africans, counselling moderation to the PLO, courting countries with which it had strained relations in the past (Iran, Egypt, Sudan), and stressing the inappropriateness of military means for the realization of diplomatic ends, is part of the Soviet policy to convey to client and competitor alike its serious interest in a peaceful resolution of regional conflicts. To the extent that future Soviet behavior bears out this assessment, Gorbachev will have significantly modified the policy of his predecessors.

MOVEMENT TOWARD REDUCING THE COSTS
OF MAINTAINING AN IMPERIAL POLICY

Underlying Gorbachev's policy of *perestroika* is the conviction that resources must be redirected from unproductive military-political purposes to the regenerative economic and social development of Soviet society. If he is to succeed, significant cuts must be made at home in the military sector and abroad in subsidies to prime clients like Cuba and Vietnam, which receive more than two-thirds of Moscow's outlay.

A recent study by the Congressional Research Service of the Library of Congress reported that "The Soviet Union registered a substantial decrease in its share of the Third World arms transfer agreements, falling from 50.3% in 1987 to 33.4% in 1988. The total value of the Soviet Union's agreements also fell dramatically in 1988—from $19.4 billion in 1987 to $9.9 billion."[13] We cannot yet tell whether this represents the beginning of a redirection of Soviet resources away from arms production to civilian production or is merely a fluctuation in the highly variable cycle of arms sales and subsidies—the data are hard to measure on a year-by-year basis.

Gorbachev's "new thinking" seeks to reduce wasteful expenditures in the Third World, but thus far has has not made any drastic cutbacks in commitments, economic or military. Cuba, Vietnam, Afghanistan, Syria, and Ethiopia continue to draw the lion's share of the unproductive (and unremunerated) assistance that Moscow extends to client regimes. However, Mengistu's war against his Tigrean and Eritrean ethnic minorities has become an embarrassment, and there are reports that Soviet Deputy Foreign Minister Yuli Vorontsov told him in late October 1989 that Moscow did not intend to renew the Soviet-Ethiopian friendship treaty when it expires in 1991.[14] Elsewhere, though still limited in scope, the USSR's withdrawal of some air and naval units from Cam Ranh Bay,[15] and its repositioning of naval units from the South Indian Ocean (off Africa's southeast coast) to the North Indian Ocean, may be symptomatic of a broader initiative to curb military costs in Third World areas.

Gorbachev is groping for ways of retrenching militarily without jeopardizing political relationships or strategic advantages. Soviet diplomacy has been active in trying to drum up trade and investment, but there is little to show for the intensified round of visits to Latin America, Southeast Asia, and the Middle East. Moscow is short on the surplus needed to extend credit to attract new customers, and it lacks the goods and services that paying customers seek.

Meanwhile, though speaking as if he wants to make generous concessions, Gorbachev acts in a businesslike fashion. In the UN General Assembly on December 8, 1988, he spoke of the truly serious economic problems that faced Third World countries, particularly that of foreign debt. He said that the Soviet Union was ready "to establish a long-term—up to one hundred years—moratorium on the repayment of this debt by the least developed countries, and to write it off completely in a number of cases." However, during a visit to Cuba four months later, he showed no inclination to forgive or significantly reschedule Cuba's debt, estimated to at 10 to 15 billion dollars, or perhaps higher, even though this would have been "a relatively painless gesture since Cuba is too poor to pay back its loans in the foreseeable future."[16] According to Fidel Castro, the issue had been discussed but nothing was decided: "We are in favor of abolishing our debt to the Soviet Union. We have been wanting to abolish this debt for over 30 years now. But during these 3 decades we have been continuing to receive credits from the USSR. For the time being, debates are taking place on problems of the foreign debt."[17] Gorbachev is using the carrot and stick with Castro. On the one hand, he did sign the treaty of friendship that Moscow had resisted for more than 20 years; on the other hand, he made no financial concessions, prompting Castro to state bitterly three months later that he could no longer expect "with certainty that supplies that have been coming to our country will continue to arrive with the usual clocklike punctuality and as previously guaranteed."[18] All of this may be part of Gorbachev's plan to use economic levers to extract political concessions from Castro regarding the withdrawal of Cuban forces form Angola and the diminution of Cuban arms to Nicaragua.[19]

On occasion, Shevardnadze has indicated that "only a certain portion" of Soviet economic activity in the Third World "will be, so to speak, 'subsidized.' "[20] But in the main it has been the leading Soviet economic reformers, like Oleg Bogomolov and Nikolai Shmelov, who have hammered at the necessity of bringing economic criteria to the forefront in aid-giving, of reducing uneconomic assistance and being more selective in the investments made and more businesslike in dealing with local elites. In his speech as an elected deputy to the first Congress of People's Deputies in June 1989, Shmelov proposed balancing the Soviet budget by, among other things, cutting aid to Cuba and Nicaragua: "Have you ever thought about how much our interest in Latin America costs? According to professional American calculation, it is around six billion to eight billion dollars a year. This source alone would suffice to maintain the balance of the consumer market for the years which we need to deal with our immediate problems, and step with both feet onto the road of reforms.''[21] In late December, Yurii Maslyukov, chairman of Gosplan (State Planning Committee), indicated that the government was considering a decrease in its aid to Third World countries, but he offered no specifics.[22]

Though his cost-reduction efforts have so far been suggestive rather than substantive, Gorbachev may be preparing to take some big steps in this direction, as regional conflicts increasingly wind down.

GLASNOST IN FOREIGN POLICY EVALUATIONS

Gorbachev's decision to fill in the "blank areas" of Soviet history is slowly coming to terms with critical developments in past Soviet foreign policy. An official admission—long known in the West and among informed circles in the Soviet Union itself—was made on August 18 1989, by Gorbachev's confidante, Politburo member Alexander N. Yakovlev, who acknowledged that Stalin had indeed signed a secret agreement with Hitler dividing Eastern Europe into spheres of influence on the eve of World War II. While there remains much to revise in the official account of Soviet-Polish relations since 1989, Moscow has given signs of accepting Stalin's responsibility for the massacre of thousands of Polish officers in the Katyn Forest in the fall of 1940. Khrushchev's Cuban policy in 1962 has been discussed critically by former officials. There has also been mention of Brezhnev's foreign policy mistakes—Afghanistan, the rupture of diplomatic relations with Israel, the invasion of Czechoslovakia in August 1968, and the deployment of intermediate-range missiles (SS-20s) in Europe in the late 1970s. The full story has yet to be told of any of these politically pivotal events. Official archives dealing with foreign policymaking during the Soviet period are still closed.

Still, these are signal steps. They may herald a process of providing authoritative information on how key decisions were made affecting Soviet foreign policy in general, and policy toward the Third World, in particular. Shevardnadze's call for "an influx of fresh ideas" and "a scientific analysis of past experience and a study of 'blank' and 'obscure' areas,''[23] differs significantly from the secretiveness of the Soviet foreign ministry under Andrei Gromyko.

Taken together, these tendencies in Gorbachev's policy denote an ongoing reassessment of Soviet behavior that could reduce the confrontational aspects of the superpower rivalry in the Third World. They are the logical expression of a policy in transition increasingly shaped by new thinking.

Concomitantly, there are certain characteristics of Soviet Third World policy that persist from the Khrushchev-Andropov-Chernenko periods. The following continuities sometimes reinforce, but also sometimes clash with, the direction of Gorbachev's changes.

REGIME MAINTENANCE

Gorbachev is not abandoning the Third World. Thus far his expenditures on Third World clients have contravened Western anticipations of sharp reductions in order to redirect resources to internal transformation. Through a skillful mix of diplomacy and assistance, he seems as committed as his predecessors to keeping friendly regimes in power and helping them resist inroads by anti-Marxist or American-backed local/regional rivals. In Afghanistan, which was regarded as a barometer of his intentions, Gorbachev's withdrawal showed that he was no longer willing to commit Soviet ground forces to retain political control. However, his willingness to pour in enormous military and economic resources to back a beleaguered client at a time of deteriorating Soviet domestic conditions has been a surprise. Soviet arms shipments alone, at current estimates, will have exceeded $2 billion for the year of 1989.[24] Gorbachev's determination to support the pro-Soviet communist PDPA regime as long as it is able to survive without Soviet troops perplexes U.S. officials and has somewhat dissipated the goodwill that accompanied his withdrawal of forces in February 1989, in accordance with the provisions of the UN-negotiated agreement of April-May 1988. Why is Moscow continuing to supply Najibullah's regime? According to one U.S. official, Soviet Foreign Minister Shevardnadze gave Secretary of State James Baker a direct answer, when they met in Paris in July 1989: "Because Afghanistan is next door."[25] Shevardnadze compared Moscow's concern to Washington's with Central America. In, in fact, he was implying that Afghanistan and Nicaragua are politically equivalent contexts. Gorbachev's intention to secure Afghanistan may be far more deep-rooted than a mere interest than a mere interest in a "decent interval" before finally disengaging. Najibullah's ability to maintain control in Kabul, the fratricidal fighting among the rival Mujahidin groups, Iran's interest in rapprochement with the USSR, and Pakistan's ambivalence about continuing the war lend support to the view that Gorbachev may see a chance for political advantage from the current situation—and with it some kind of justification for Soviet sacrifices and the Soviet army's having fulfilled its "international duty." Perhaps he hopes a show of resolve and toughness in Afghanistan will strengthen his bargaining position in negotiating other settlements with the United States.

In Central America (as in Kampuchea, Angola, and elsewhere), Moscow continues to provide the assistance necessary for the survival of key clients. At the Malta summit meeting between Presidents Bush and Gorbachev on December 2, 1989, Castro's Cuba and Ortega's Nicaragua were discussed, but apparently nothing was settled concerning the flow of Soviet aid: Cuba is to receive modern aircraft (the MiG-29); and Nicaragua, military and economic aid (about $500 million per year).[26] We must wait to see if the Sandinista defeat in the February 1990 elections will occasion a sharp cutback in Soviet military and economic assistance. Gorbachev has yet to disengage from costly undertakings. Strategic considerations continue to override economic constraints.

COMPREHENSIVE ACTIVISM

Like his predecessors, Gorbachev is trying to develop comprehensive relations with virtually all Third World countries, irrespective of ideological or political differences. Careful not to arouse expectations, he keeps aid packages modest (like the credits extended to Egypt in May 1989 for power projects in Sinai) and counsels the need for a political approach to regional problems. He is working hard to repair Soviet fortunes in Egypt, Indonesia, and Iran; allay concerns about alleged Soviet subversion in the conservative regimes of the Gulf (in the process establishing diplomatic ties with Oman and the United Arab Emirates in 1985 and with Qatar in 1988) and Southeast Asia (Malaysia and Thailand); and deepen ties to Mexico, Brazil, and Argentina. As was true of previous Soviet leaders, his approach is essentially reactive and consists of being receptive to regimes who, for a variety of reasons, seek to improve relations with the Soviet Union.

The courtship of moderate states is not new'[27] but the opportunities for diplomatic normalization provided by regional actors, whose interests and outlooks have changed in response to altered circumstances both at home and abroad—these are new. Like the superpowers, whom they try to use for the advancement of their own national interests, these Third World regimes are manifesting their own brand of "new thinking": in a period of U.S.-Soviet accommodations, they see no reason for not improving relations with Moscow, in the hope that a Soviet connection will bring added leverage in dealing with the United States. As long as the Third World remains a competitive, albeit less conflictual, arena for the two superpowers, such an adaptation makes sense. It motivates Moscow to expand its diplomatic relationships, which are intended to improve the strategic context within which the USSR seeks the accretion of advantages and the curbing of U.S. influence.

Commitments in the form of credits and subsidies are being made by Gorbachev for the same mix of reasons that determined those of his predecessors. One does not detect in his behavior an avoidance of new outlays or a curbing of the costs of operating in the Third World. Though he would like the USSR to become an integral part of the international economic system dominated by the Western powers and Japan, attract foreign investment, and adopt more capitalistic criteria in dealing with clients and customers, his policies toward Cuba, Afghanistan, Kampuchea, Syria, and India do not indicate that economic considerations have yet taken command in the Soviet approach.

Recall that in the middle and late 1960s, as now, leading Soviet analysts were urging retrenchment, a rationalization of commitments, and a lower profile in the Third World, and there were Western counterparts who believed the Kremlin could not indefinitely afford "the costs of empire." These Soviet voices are more influential today, the position they argue is seemingly that of the Gorbachev leadership; and Western assumptions of inevitable cutbacks in commitments are even more convincing. Still, the lines of argument do not fully mirror what is actually happening. There has been no diminished commitment to the forward policy of Khrushchev and Brezhnev—only Gorbachev's search for a more effective, less militarily threatening, and hopefully more cost-efficient ways of sustaining pro-Soviet regimes in the Third World.

SALIENCE OF ARMS TRANSFERS AS AN INSTRUMENT OF POLICY

When a superpower is involved, arms transfers inevitably acquire a significance far beyond commerce alone. Ever since Khrushchev used them for quick entrée into Afghanistan, Egypt, and Indonesia, successive Soviet leaders have been interested in arms, primarily because they are the most reliable instrument for strengthening Soviet relations with key regional actors. Judging by the available data, no supplicant has been turned away. For example, in early 1989 advanced Sukhoi 24-D bombers were delivered to Libya, presumably for the hard currency that Moscow sorely needs. The case of Syria is more complex. Moscow knows that Assad has serious economic problems; that he is diplomatically isolated in the Arab world, his policy in Lebanon opposed by most Arab governments; that he is militarily dependent on the USSR for high-performance weapons, because he lacks the currency to contemplate an alternative supplier; and that he disapproves of the USSR's efforts to encourage the Israeli-Palestinian peace process and moderation of PLO policy toward Israel. To underscore his view that Soviet relations with Israel must be normalized, Gorbachev sent Alexander Zotov, the aide who is said to have drafted his admonition to Assad in April 1987, to serve as ambassador in Damascus. Yet, despite the difficult Soviet-Syrian relations, despite the outstanding $15 billion debt for arms purchases with no prospects of payment, Soviet weapons pour in, not as much as Assad would like, but in substantial numbers—MiG-29s, tanks, air defense systems, and so on. Thousands of Soviet military advisers are in influential positions at all levels of the Syrian army and in air command and control centers; combined Soviet-Syrian maneuvers do not, according to Israeli intelligence sources, reflect a merely defensive strategy and the number of Soviet naval port visits and their duration is on the rise.[28] Gorbachev's support for Assad continues mainly for the same geostrategic reasons that attracted Moscow to him in the past.

Arms transfers still maintain the security of prominent clients. They prevented Iraq from succumbing to Iranian offensives in the 1982–1987 period of the Iran-Iraq War; and they enable the communist PDPA regime to hang on in Afghanistan, and pro-Moscow Marxist-Leninist regimes in Angola and Ethiopia to survive.

As a major source of hard currency, arms sales have assumed even greater importance in Gorbachev's calculations. Libya, Iraq, Kuwait, Algeria, and Iran can pay for their weapons, and in the highly competitive international market, the Soviet Union wants to retain a significant share for itself against the United States, France, West Germany, and China.

Finally, Moscow continues to use arms in exchange for "overflight and landing rights, port facilities, bases, and prepositioning of equipment," in countries such as Somalia (until 1977), Ethiopia, the PDRY, Syria, and Benin.[29]

COMPETITIVE RIVALRY

Like Khrushchev and Brezhnev before him, Gorbachev wants to deny strategic advantage to the United States, but without jeopardizing the improvement in Soviet-American relations of the past few years. After all, not even Brezhnev, whose actions went the farthest in exploiting Third World opportunities to undermine U.S. interests, willfully set out to destroy détente; what he did was misjudge the extent to which he could seek strategic advantage and still expect a passive Washington.

Gorbachev has been more prudent and averse to risk taking. But risk-avoidance does not mean that he intends to stop competing with the United States in the Third World or that superpower cooperation in regional conflict-containment will take hold. In the past, great powers have had interests in which were embedded the seeds of future tensions. A period of testing is going on now, to see whether Gorbachev can calibrate Soviet ambitions in such a way as to avoid the missteps of the past. In Afghanistan, he withdrew Soviet troops, but continues to supply the Kabul regime; in the Gulf, Moscow played a wary hand, wanting to see the Iran-Iraq War end but not on terms that would benefit the United States or jeopardize the prospects for improved Soviet-Iranian ties; and in mid-May 1989, Gorbachev wrote Bush that no *Soviet* military assistance was any longer going to Nicaragua,[30] but U.S. intelligence sources reported a continued flow of military hardware and related goods from *Warsaw Pact countries and Cuba*.[31] Gorbachev's position may be technically correct, but if he quibbles over the source of weapons while upgrading the Sandinista capability, he will likely find the same kinds of barriers to long-term improvement in U.S.-Soviet relations that bedeviled his predecessors. Similarly, though denying any responsibility for the continued supply of Soviet weapons to the FMLN (Farabundo Marti' Front for National Liberation) insurgents in El Salvador, Moscow has been apprised of Washington's concern that the insurrection is being sustained by Soviet weapons.[32] Finally, in the fighting that has torn Lebanon apart, all the warring factions—political, communal, religious, ethnic—are armed with Soviet and Soviet-bloc weapons.[33]

In all, it is too early to know how seriously Gorbachev's speech to the UN General Assembly in December 1988 favoring expanded use of UN peacekeeping forces is meant to be taken.

LIMITED INSIGHTS PROVIDED FOR THE BASIS OF DECISIONS

Glasnost has given us glimpses behind the Kremlin curtain, but we still know little of how Soviet foreign policy decisions are made, how priorities are determined, and why commitments are sustained. The tidbits of information coming out, as on the Kremlin's decision to intervene in Afghanistan, are not terribly illuminating. The willingness of scholars such as Oleg Bogomolov (Director of the USSR Academy of Sciences' Institute of the Economy of the World Socialist System), Yuri Gangovsky (Head of the USSR Institute of Oriental Studies Department of Afghanistan, Pakistan, and India), and A. Prokhanov, a journalist, to criticize past policy is welcome; but they do not discuss the motives for the current policy of liberally sending arms to Afghanistan (in early October 1989, the Bush administration declared that Soviet military personnel are operating SCUD missiles for the Kabul regime). Not even Foreign Minister Shevardnadze's admission to the Supreme Soviet on October 23, 1989, that, in invading Afghanistan in 1979, "We had placed ourselves in opposition to the world community, had violated norms of behavior, and gone against common human interests," was accompanied by any new insights into Soviet decision making.[34]

Most Soviet writing on Soviet foreign policy until very recently was pap, and though Soviet publications no longer write about the "liberating mission" of the Soviet Union in the Third World, we have yet to see works that illumine current policy in the Middle East, Southern Asia, Africa, or Central America: there is no probing into objectives, no weighing of costs and benefits, no discussions of constraints on existing policy. The searching criticism of the 1939 Nazi-Soviet pact and Stalin's postwar policy, and the broad-brush swipes at Brezhnev's shortcomings in foreign affairs, may well foreshadow what is coming in the foreseeable future, but in the meantime we must continue to evaluate Soviet policy by its actions rather than by its words.

CONCLUDING OBSERVATIONS

Under Gorbachev the Soviet leadership has restructured its approach to the Third World. Implicit in the de-emphasis of the military instrument as a means of influence building, in the nurturing of solutions to regional conflicts, and in the consideration of normalizing diplomatic ties with all parties, irrespective of alignment or outlook, is the USSR's apparent realization that it must avoid again putting at risk its relations with the United States over their competition for influence in the Third World. Frequent discussions between Moscow and Washington are designed to prevent threats to détente and to encourage regional antagonists away from the battlefield and toward the conference table. Soviet officials write, albeit in general terms, of the need for cooperation to reduce and eliminate the danger of proliferation of nuclear and chemical weapons, the dissemination of ballistic missile delivery systems, and the spread of terrorism.[35]

Gorbachev has begun the defusing of the Third World as a threat to the future of U.S.-Soviet relations. In our attempts to monitor the course of this policy, we might keep in mind several indicators of cooperation:

- Efforts to resolve existing regional conflicts;
- Restraint on arms transfers to clients perpetuating past policies;
- Retrenchment of commitments, especially to clients who cannot manage on their own;
- Avoidance of new commitments in areas peripheral to Soviet security;
- Manifestation of the "new political thinking" in concrete analysis of the USSR's policies in the Third World.

The full implications of these modifications will become clearer in the years ahead, but by changing the Soviet approach to the Third World, Gorbachev has opened the way for a new era in U.S.-Soviet relations.

NOTES

1. Melvin A. Goodman, "The Soviet Union and the Third World: The Military Dimension," in Andrzej Korbonski and Francis Fukuyama, eds, *The Soviet Union and the Third World: The Last Three Decades* (Ithaca, N.Y.: Cornell University Press, 1987), p. 56.

2. *FBIS/International Affairs,* April 28, 1987, H7.

3. Reuter's, September 18, 1989. The TASS and Syrian versions of the press conference did not include Zotov's comments about aid possibly being reduced: See FBIS/SOV, September 21, 1989, p. 20, and FBIS/SOV, September 19, 1989, p. 25, respectively.

4. Viktor Yasmann, "The New Soviet Thinking in Regional Conflicts; Ideology and Politics," *Radio Liberty Research,* December 3, 1987, p. 3. *Moscow News,* November 8, 1987.

5. As translated in FBIS/SOV, May 20, 1988, pp. 4–8.

6. For example, Vsevolod Ovchinnikov. *Pravda,* August 23, 1988. A. Kolosovskii, "Regional'nye konflikti i global'naya bezopasnost," *Mirovaya ekonomiki i mezhdunarodnye otnosheniya,* no. 6 (June 1988), p. 32. A. Kislov, "Nove politicheskoe myshleniye i regionalnye konflikty," ibid., no. 8 (August 1988), pp. 40–42.

7. See "The USSR and the Third World," *International Affairs,* no. 12 (December 1988). pp. 137–41.

8. Chester A. Crocker, "Southern Africa: Eight Years Later," *Foreign Affairs* 68, no. 4 (Fall 1989), p. 151. As Assistant Secretary of State for African Affairs in the Reagan administration, Mr. Crocker was instrumental in pursuing the patient, imaginative diplomacy that came to fruition in December 1988.

9. Ibid., p. 153. He notes also that Soviet officials speak of the African National Congress's need to move from armed struggle toward a political solution. Such a position is helping to transform the diplomatic environment and enhancing the prospects for political dialogue between "mainstream black opposition leaders" and the government of South Africa.

10. Francis Fukuyama, *Gorbachev and the New Soviet Agenda in the Third World,* RAND Report R-3634-A (Santa Monica, CA.: The RAND Corporation, June 1989), pp. 42–43.

11. According to a member of the Bush administration, "The Soviet response has been constructive, helpful and forthcoming. It's less than we would like them to do, but more than they would have done in the past." *The New York Times,* August 12, 1989.

12. "The 19th All-Union CPSU Conference: Foreign Policy and Diplomacy," *International Affairs,* no. 10 (October 1988), p. 21.

13. Richard F. Grimmett, *Trends in Conventional Arms Transfers to the Third World by Major Supplier, 1981–1988* (Washington, DC: Congressional Research Service: The Library of Congress, July 31, 1989), p. 3.

14. *The New York Times,* January 17, 1990.

15. *Washington Post,* January 19, 1990.

16. Bill Keller, *The New York Times,* April 4, 1989.

17. FBIS/SOV, April 6, 1989, p. 26.

18. Joseph B. Treaster, *The New York Times,* July 28, 1989.

19. *The New York Times,* October 5, 1989.

20. Quoted in Stephen Sestanovich, "Gorbachev's Foreign Policy: A Diplomacy of Decline," *Problems of Communism* 37, no. 1 (January–February 1988), p. 13.

21. *The New York Times,* June 9, 1989. In the future, the debates in the Congress of People's Deputies, the new legislative structure created by Gorbachev, may be a source of criticism of official foreign policy positions.

22. Michael Dobbs, *Washington Post,* December 14, 1989.

23. "The 19th All-Union CPSU Conference," *International Affairs,* p. 27.

24. David B. Ottaway, *Washington Post,* September 10, 1989; *Washington Post,* September 2, 1989.

25. Author's interview, September 1989.

26. Soviet Foreign Ministry spokesman Gennadi Gerasimov said that the MiG-29s to be supplied to Cuba would be "used for air-defense purposes" and as such accorded with the 1962 Kennedy-Khrushchev understanding ending the Cuban missile crisis. *FBIS/SOV,* November 20, 1989, p.3.

27. For a contrary view, see for example, Fukuyama, *Gorbachev and the New Soviet Agenda,* pp. 21–22.

28. For example, there has been an upgrading of the logistical and docking facilities available to the Soviet Navy at Tartus on the Syrian coast. Simon Elliott, "Syrian Base Boosts Soviet Power," *Jane's Defence Weekly* (July 29, 1989), p. 154.

29. Mark N. Kramer, "Soviet Arms Transfers to the Third World," *Problems of Communism.* 36, no. 5 (September–October 1987), p. 59. He mentions the rivalry with China and the opportunity for intelligence-gathering as other reasons for Moscow's arms transfers.

30. *The New York Times,* May 17, 1989.

31. *Washington Times,* September 18, 1989; *Washington Post,* September 19, 1989.

32. FBIS/SOV, November 28, 1989, p. 4; *The New York Times,* December 11, 1989.

33. *The New York Times,* June 13, 1989.

34. FBIS/SOV, October 24, 1989, p. 45.

35. For example, Andrei Kolosovsky, "Risk Zones in the Third World," *International Affairs,* no. 8 (August 1989), pp. 39–49. Mr. Kolosovsky is Assistant Deputy Minister of Foreign Affairs. Yevgeny Primakov, "USSR Policy on Regional Conflicts," *International Affairs,* no. 6 (June 1988), pp. 3–9, declares that "war and the use of force in general should be ruled out from interstate relations"; however, he affirms that this does not imply "non-recognition of the possibilities of national and social liberation forces for making use of every means at their disposal to ensure their legitimate rights."

32
*The USSR and the Third World in the 1980's**

David E. Albright[†]

Virtually all Western analysts today agree that Soviet policy toward the Third World has changed during the 1980's, but they differ widely in their assessments of the extent and meaning of the policy shifts. One group argues that although Moscow's policy has undergone some modification, the Soviet approach to the Third World remains fundamentally the same as before. However, members of this group disagree as to which factors explain this perceived continuity. Some trace it back to tsarist policies that have been reinforced in the Soviet era.[1] Others view it as the product of lingering ideological commitments on the part of the Soviet elite.[2] Still others see it in terms of recurrent patterns of Soviet behavior toward developing areas.[3]

A second group asserts that the alterations in Soviet policy reflect a basic change in the Soviet approach to the Third World, yet there is also no unanimity within this group about the reasons for the shift. Some maintain that it has resulted from the declining impact of ideology on Soviet perceptions of the Third World.[4] Others contend that it has stemmed essentially from domestic considerations—particularly the need to improve the performance of the USSRs economy.[5]

In addressing these issues, however, analysts tend to ignore some major new developments. In the last decade, the number of distinct Soviet schools of thought about what policy the USSR should pursue toward the Third World has multiplied significantly. The top Soviet leadership, in contrast with earlier periods, has not endorsed a single school of thought exclusively. Finally, the USSR's behavior in the Third World has combined elements of the policy prescriptions of all of the contending schools of persuasion, and the mix has varied substantially from region to region. Each of these developments, it should be stressed, antedates Mikhail Gorbachev's advent to power.

*Reprinted by permission of the author from *Problems of Communism*, XXXVIII, 2-3 (March-June 1989).

†The views expressed in this article are those of the author and do not necessarily reflect those of the US Air Force or the US Government.

These changes have important implications. Moreover, these implications relate not just to the nature of policy but to the nature of policy formulation as well. The present article will examine these changes and their likely bearing on future Soviet Third World policy.

CONTENDING POLICY VIEWPOINTS

Controversy in the USSR over policy toward the Third World is nothing new. It has prevailed almost constantly within the Soviet hierarchy since the early 1960's, as a result of differing assessments of circumstances in the Third World. However, prior to the early 1980's, the debate had never involved more than two perspectives on the issue at any given juncture. From about 1962 through the mid-1960's, for example, arguments over policy had focused on the merits of two alternative approaches to trying to expand the USSR's presence and role in the Third World.[6]

Proponents of the first approach held that at least some "bourgeois-nationalist" leaders in the Third World were undergoing radicalization. Not only did these leaders exhibit increased interest in Marxism-Leninism, according to the assessment, but they were also carrying out significant "progressive" reforms in their countries. Therefore, the USSR should enter into close alliances with the states under the rule of such leaders and serve as these leaders' revolutionary mentor. That is, it should help them deepen their understanding of "true" socialism and the measures required to achieve it.

Supporters of the second approach maintained that these leaders, despite their "progressive" attributes, would probably never preside over "real" socialist transformations of their countries. Consequently, the USSR should, while taking advantage of the openings that such leaders offered for enhancing its position in the Third World, pursue a policy of both "alliance" and "struggle" with them and their governments. Specifically, it should cooperate with the leaders to the extent possible in foreign affairs, but it should encourage leftist elements in the countries under the control of these leaders to try to increase their own influence in state affairs and bring about further radicalization of local situations.

By the early 1980's, however, the number of contending Soviet visions of what policy the USSR should follow with respect to the Third World had expanded to four, and the ensuing years have witnessed no reduction in that total. These visions have entailed often conflicting judgments about what entities should be the USSR's primary targets of interest, what sort of relationships Moscow should attempt to establish with these entities, what means it should employ to forge such links, and what posture it should strike toward the West in the Third World. As in the preceding years, the views have flowed from contrasting perceptions of conditions in the Third World.

To refer to these policy outlooks, it is useful to have short-hand designations. Thus, the analysis here will label them the "revolutionary-democratic" school, the "pro-military" school, the "national-capitalism" school, and the "economic-interdependence" school.

The "Revolutionary-Democractic" School

Adherents of this perspective insist that a gradual process of radicalization is taking place in Third World areas: these areas, despite some zigs and zags, are bypassing capitalism and advancing directly toward socialism. In the eyes of these individuals, not only have the ranks of Third World "socialist-oriented" states—and particularly the most radical of them, the "revolutionary democracies"—grown over time, but in some "revolutionary democracies" such as the People's Democratic Republic of Yemen, Angola, Mozambique, and Ethiopia, ruling parties of a "new" or "vanguard" type have emerged. As the revolutionary process in the Third World deepens, the estimate goes, the number of "revolutionary democracies" will continue to increase, the circle of "vanguard" parties will expand, and at least some of these parties will transform themselves into full-fledged communist parties.

Partisans of this line do admit that even existing "revolutionary-democratic" regimes with "vanguard" parties have severe faults, and they acknowledge that it is impossible to rule out a reversal of course in all cases. Nonetheless, they still maintain that the Third World is marching inexorably toward socialism and will avoid capitalism. Therefore, they hold that "socialist-oriented," and especially "revolutionary-democratic," goverments—however deficient—are the wave of the future and the best available allies for the USSR in the Third World at present.

In keeping with the stress on ties with "revolutionary-democratic" regimes, this school of persuasion urges that the USSR try to build long-term structural relationships with the states that these regimes run. Here proponents of the outlook have in mind joint collaboration in constructing institutions that will enable these regimes to entrench themselves in power. This includes cooperation in building a party apparatus, in establishing or strengthening intelligence and security services, in training military personnel, and the like.

As for instruments, advocates of this viewpoint lean toward reliance on nonmilitary tools. They do not, to be sure, reject military means. Indeed, they have approved Soviet use of military force to ensure the survival of "revolutionary-democratic" governments run by "vanguard" parties, and they have recognized the role of military assistance in the development of close Soviet ties with such regimes. Yet their specific vision of a long-term structural relationship with these governments implicitly pushes them toward stress on nonmilitary instruments, especially political ones.

With respect to posture toward the West in the Third World, backers of this perspective have on occasion evinced readiness to risk confrontation with the West where ruling "revolutionary-democratic" parties of a "vanguard" type have been concerned, but that willingness has declined noticeably over the course of the 1980's. Furthermore, adherents of the school have always discouraged military confrontation with the West in the Third World. Nevertheless, the group has appeared to foresee that Soviet relations with the West in the Third World will inevitably be contentious in nature.

Among those who have publicly subscribed to this policy line since it originated in the 1970's have been several eminent political figures, although the influence of many of them has diminished in the latter half of the 1980's. Grigoriy Romanov, a member of the Politburo of the Communist Party of the Soviet Union (CPSU) and Mikhail Gorbachev's chief rival to succeed Konstantin Chernenko as party general secretary, associated himself with the outlook before his ouster in July 1985. So did Boris Ponomarev, until February 1986 director of the CPSU International Department and an alternate member of the Politburo.[7] Rostislav Ul'yanovskiy vocally endorsed the approach prior to his retirement as a deputy head of the International Department in late 1986, and he has persisted in doing so since then as a consultant to the African Institute of the USSR Academy of Sciences. Anatoliy Gromyko, director of that institute and son of Andrey Gromyko (formerly A CPSU Politburo member, USSR foreign minister, and chairman of the Presidium of the USSR Supreme Soviet), has strongly supported such policy prescriptions since the 1970's.[8]

The "Pro-military" School

Exponents of this viewpoint emphasize the high percentage of Third World states under military rule, or at least dominated by military elements, and they contend that a substantial number of these military governments evince a resolve to effect major social transformations in the countries that they run and a willingness to enter into close relations with the USSR. In light of such factors, the group concludes that the USSR should devote its energies principally to military-controlled states—especially those with "progressive" regimes.

These Soviet observers do concede that, in the abstract, a "vanguard" party might constitute a more satisfactory vehicle for carrying out social change and a more reliable ally for the USSR than military leaderships do, but they point out that "vanguard" parties have not yet taken shape in most Third World countries under military domination. Nor does this situation appear to them likely to change in the years immediately ahead, for many militaries in power in the Third World see "vanguard" parties as potential competitors for political authority. Even where militaries have tolerated the formation of "vanguard" parties, the champions of this perspective assert, the armed forces remain the key institutions shaping the destinies of their countries. If they decide to act in opposition to local "vanguard" parties or to do away with such parties altogether, these parties do not have the mass base and the access to instruments of violence required to meet such challenges effectively. Hence, those committed to this outlook submit that ties with Third World militaries, and particularly radical militaries, afford the USSR the best openings available to advance the revolutionary process in the Third World and improve the Soviet position there.

Support for creating long-term structural relations with states in which militaries, and especially radical militaries, are preeminent flows naturally form these Soviet observers' rationale for focusing on such countries, but the structural links that the group advocates differ from those that the "revolutionary-democratic" enthusiasts favor. The "pro-military school" presses for cooperation that will render the countries at issue dependent on the USSR in a military sense.

Proposals to woo military-based regimes and to make these regimes highly dependent on the USSR militarily imply an inclination on the part of endorsers of this policy perspective to rely heavily on military means. They also tend to indicate that the group is willing to see the USSR engaged in the Third World in ways that could lead to military clashes with the West; however, since the mid-1980's, backers of the perspective have explicitly sought to expunge any impression that they advocate Soviet involvement in the Third World's military conflicts.

Public articulation of this school of thought has stemmed essentially from military quarters in the 1980's. The school came into being in the mid-1970's, and although it received open endorsement from at least some lower-level civilians at that time, it enjoyed support largely in military circles even then. During the late 1970's, moreover, all overt civilian backing disappeared. In fact, the outlook itself appeared to vanish entirely from the Soviet scene for a few years.[9] When it resurfaced in 1982, it failed to regain any public civilian endorsement. Among defenders of this viewpoint in the 1980's have been Colonel Ye. Rybkin, long a prominent figure in the shaping of Soviet military doctrine and strategy, and Major General Ye. Dolgopolov.[10]

The "National-Capitalism" School

According to adherents of this school, the vast majority of Third World states have now chosen the path of development that they intend to pursue, and the bulk of them have opted for a capitalist, or at least a nonsocialist, path. Thus, the analysis goes, most Third World countries will probably pass through a capitalist or nonsocialist phase of development before embarking on a socialist course. This prospect means that "socialist-oriented" countries will in all likelihood remain in the minority in the Third World for the indefinite future.

Furthermore, the group argues, the states that have adopted a "socialist orientation" have disturbing faults. Even the most "progressive" of these states—the "revolutionary democracies" with "vanguard" parties—have displayed a less than steadfast desire to implement far-reaching social transformations internally and have vacillated in their foreign policies. As a result, they have substantial deficiencies as Soviet allies.

Under such circumstances, proponents of this outlook assert, the USSR needs to diversify its relationships in the Third World. Diversification of ties is not only imperative but also possible, they suggest. The objective bases for it lie in "contradictions" between Third World "capitalist-oriented" states and the West that the USSR can exploit. Perhaps the most important of these "contradictions" have economic roots. In the opinion of subscribers to this viewpoint, the rulers of many "capitalist-oriented" Third World countries want to develop a "nationalist" type of capitalism in their domains, while the "imperialist" Western powers strive to foster a "dependent" form of capitalism there. But "contradictions" of a strictly political and ideological nature exist as well. For example, from the standpoint of the group, commitment to Islam coupled with resistance to Westernization can produce tensions between a "capitalist-oriented" Third World state and the Western powers.

Advocates of this perspective believe that the USSR has little chance of constructing long-term structural links with the great bulk of the states that they consider the prime targets for courtship. And these Soviet analysts accept the probability that over time there will be divergences of interests between the USSR and many of the countries that they pinpoint for attention. Nevertheless, as they see things, eclecticism in defining potential allies will tend to offset this difficulty, for profitable relations with a large and varied circle of states will reduce the impact that a setback in any one of these states can have on overall Soviet fortunes in the Third World. The sheer volume of ties, in short, will help to insulate Moscow's Third World position.

Although expounders of this vision of policy give no sign of eschewing military tools in forging links with the diverse states upon which they concentrate, the type of opportunities that they discern for building these ties prompts them to emphasize other instruments. Economic means play a prominent role in their calculations. Yet, because the economic capabilities of the USSR are limited at present, the group places greatest stress on political tools.

Besides downplaying military instruments, this school of persuasion appears to want to avoid confrontation with the West in the Third World. Nevertheless, it still seems to favor a highly conflictual approach toward the West there. The bases upon which it intends to construct relations with a wide range of Third World countries are varied types of anti-Western sentiment, and it anticipates fashioning and/or strengthening ties by fanning such sentiments.

The front ranks of the formulaters and champions of this policy outlook have long included Karen Brutents, formerly a deputy director and now a first deputy director of the CPSU International Department, and Yevgeniy Primakov, until the mid-1980's the director of the Institute of Oriental Studies of the USSR Academy of Sciences and since then head of the Academy's Institute of World Economics and International Relations.[11] In recent years, the perspective has acquired other supporters of consequence within the Soviet elite as well. Perhaps the outstanding illustration is Aleksandr Yakovlev, a full member of the CPSU Politburo, a key secretary of the CPSU Central Committee, and the supervisor of the Central Committee's new International Policy Commission.[12]

The "Economic-Interdependence" School

Partisans of this viewpoint note that most countries in the Third World, whether they be "capitalist-oriented" or "socialist-oriented," have to date chalked up poor records of economic performance. Not only have they been slipping farther and farther behind the advanced industrial powers, but they have also failed to achieve significant economic growth in absolute terms. Even those states that have done reasonably well economically have encountered difficulties of one sort or another—soaring debts, depressed demand for exports, and so on. Thus, according to this group's assessment, leaders of these diverse countries are seeking ways to improve their local economic situations.

This search, backers of the perspective contend, opens up new opportunities for the USSR to broaden its relations in the Third World, for even the top economic performers among "capitalist-oriented" states are prepared to intensify their dealings with the USSR substantially to further economic development. Moreover, endorsers of the line insist, the USSR has the wherewithal to take advantage of these opportunities. To be sure, the USSR has economic troubles of its own, and it does not possess the resources to solve the economic problems of Third World countries. But these deficiencies do not really matter. The only way of overcoming Third World economic woes anyway is through the working out of a coherent world system of economic interdependence. Within such a system, these Soviet observers maintain, the USSR could play a key part that would enable it to build up ties with a broad spectrum of states.

The system that the proponents of this outlook foresee has several features. First, the industrialized countries of the West would turn out goods of high technological sophistication for sale to the USSR and other members of the Soviet bloc. The USSR and its allies, for their part, would manufacture items of a lower level of technological sophistication for export to Third World states. This last category of countries would devote its energies, at least at the outset, to producing minerals and raw materials for sale to both the Western powers and the Soviet bloc. By specializing in such output, they would develop the necessary skills and surpluses to diversify their economies, beginning with labor-intensive food and processing industries. This projected system, it should be emphasized, entails no meaningful distinctions between "capitalist-oriented" and "socialist-oriented" states in the Third World.

Promoters of this policy outlook urge the creation of a long-term structural relationship with Third World countries that they deem to be worthwhile objects for wooing, but their vision of the relationship differs considerably from those put forth by other schools of thought. Advocates of this particular viewpoint focus on the fashioning of enduring economic links with Third World countries within a multilateral framework. That is, they anticipate that economic ties will flourish in a broader setting in which other actors also have major roles to perform.

Analysts of this persuasion do not dismiss out of hand the use of military instruments, but the character of the opportunities that they discern in the Third World dictates a heavy stress on economic tools. Even political means become decidedly secondary in such a light.

As for the stance toward the West in the Third World, exponents of this policy approach favor a less conflictual posture than do adherents of any of the other schools of thought. The group appears to assume that competition between the USSR and the Western powers will continue in the Third World, but it does not foresee that this competition will inevitably result in military clashes or even political strife. On the contrary, it entertains the possibility of Soviet-Western cooperation in certain situations. For instance, it sanctions close Soviet trade relations with the West, and it contemplates that both the West and the USSR will purchase the minerals and raw materials that Third World states will have to sell as these states attempt to develop economically.

Although no eminent political figures appear to have had a key hand in shaping this basic outlook, several have openly associated themselves with it. Among these have been Vadim Zagladin, until 1986 the sole first deputy chief of the CPSU International Department, then one of the two first deputy heads of the department, and since October 1988 a personal adviser to Gorbachev in his new capacity as president of the USSR Supreme Soviet; N. N. Inozemtsev, until his death in 1982 the director of the Institute of the World Economy and International Relations as well as a member of the CPSU Central Committee; Georgiy Arbatov, director of the Institute of the United States and Canada of the USSR Academy of Sciences and also a member of the Central Committee; and, most recently, Eduard Shevardnadze, a full member of the CPSU Politburo and USSR foreign minister since 1985.[13]

STANCE OF THE TOP LEADERSHIP

Up to the early 1980's, the top Soviet leadership had invariably singled out for broad official endorsement one of the positions articulated during periods of controversy over the USSR's Third World policy. During the last half of the 1970's, for instance, the leadership unequivocally lent the weight of its authority to the prescriptions of the "revolutionary-democratic" school, which had emerged in the mid-1970's. Speaking to the 25th CPSU Congress in February 1976, CPSU General Secretary Leonid Brezhnev contended that "the class struggle is building up" in "many liberated countries." As a result, he said, "Arab, African, and Asian states having a socialist orientation" were undergoing "new progressive changes" in their "economic and political life." These "important changes," he asserted, "facilitated" the "strengthening" of the USSR's cooperation with such countries. Moreover, in discussing Soviet relations with specific Third World states, he dwelt almost exclusively on those which Soviet commentators classified as "revolutionary democracies."[14]

The following year, Brezhnev dispatched Andrey Kirilenko, a full member of the CPSU Politburo and a key secretary of the CPSU Central Committee, to Angola as the Soviet representative to the congress of the ruling Popular Movement for the Liberation of Angola (MPLA) that proclaimed that party to be Marxist-Leninist. Kirilenko made clear that he viewed the emergence of this new "vanguard" party as a sign that the African revolutionary process was deepening, and as a harbinger of things to come in other "socialist-oriented" countries on the continent.[15]

Although Premier Alexey Kosygin's economic report to the 25th CPSU Congress mentioned the USSR's general desire to have "its cooperation with the developing countries take the form of a stable and mutually advantageous division of labor," Brezhnev's political report left no doubt that the General Secretary envisioned long-term structural ties that went well beyond economic relations in the cases of "revolutionary democracies" like Angola. He attested that the world's "progressive forces" had aided "Angola's struggle to defend its independence" in 1975–76, and he declared that "our party supports and will continue to support peoples who are fighting for their freedom."[16] At the 1977 MPLA Congress, Kirilenko highlighted the persisting internal and external opposition that the new Angolan regime faced and restated Brezhnev's pledge to help that regime survive.[17]

But by the early 1980's, the top Soviet leadership had ceased to uphold any single school of persuasion as official Third World policy. General Secretary Brezhnev's political report to the 26th CPSU Congress in February 1981 was indicative. It contained features that reflected aspects of at least three of the perspectives detailed above.[18]

In keeping with the "revolutionary-democratic" viewpoint, Brezhnev pointed out that the number of countries with a "socialist orientation" had risen in recent years, and he referred briefly to Soviet cooperation with seven "revolutionary democracies"—Angola, Ethiopia, Mozambique, the People's Democratic Republic of Yemen (PDRY), Syria, Algeria, and Guinea—and somewhat more extensively to Soviet collaboration with "revolutionary-democratic" Afghanistan. He also affirmed that the USSR was helping "to strengthen the defense capability of liberated states if they ask that we do so." As illustrations, Brezhnev cited aid to Angola, Ethiopia, and Afghanistan.

Other parts of the report, however, mirrored the perceptions and preferences of the "national-capitalism" and "economic-interdependence" schools of thought. For example, Brezhnev observed that "for all practical purposes," the 1970's had seen "the liquidation of the colonial empires," but he acknowledged that the countries "that have been liberated from colonial oppression" differed widely among themselves. Some had "taken a revolutionary-democratic path," while others had not merely opted for "capitalist orientation" but had "established capitalist relations."

Furthermore, the General Secretary paid far more attention to states that were not "socialist-oriented" than to those that were. He talked at some length about Iran. In the course of this discussion, he depicted the revolution there—despite "its complex and contradictory nature" and despite the attempts of "domestic and foreign reaction" to alter its character—as "basically an anti-imperialist revolution," and he indicated that the USSR was "prepared to develop good relations" with Iran. He underscored this willingness by failing to take "revolutionary-democratic" Iraq's side in the war that had broken out between Iran and Iraq five months earlier. On this issue, he merely urged the two battling countries to "draw the proper conclusions" from the "highly advantageous" situation that the war had created for "imperialism." Brezhnev also noted the "important place" that India occupied in the USSR's "relations with liberated countries," and he promised that "interaction with peace-loving, independent India" would remain "an important area of Soviet foreign policy." In addition, he maintained that "no obstacles" existed to "good cooperation with Indonesia" or with other members of the Association of Southeast Asia Nations (ASEAN). He even stressed that in the preceding five years, 10 states in Africa, the Caribbean, and Oceania had gained independence, and the USSR had recognized all of them "at once."

Last but not least, Brezhnev emphasized that the USSR was developing with the "liberated" countries "wide-ranging economic and scientific-technical cooperation" that was advantageous "to both sides."

In the short periods that Yuriy Andropov and Konstantin Chernenko served as CPSU general secretary, they said little in public about the Third World, and failed to associate themselves with any particular school of thought on the subject in the comments that they did make. Indeed, Andropov gave strong indications that he rejected some of the fundamental premises of the "revolutionary-democratic" outlook. Addressing a CPSU Central Committee plenum on June 15, 1983, he did depict states of "socialist orientation" as "the most close to us," yet he underscored their deficiencies as well. "It is one thing to proclaim socialism as one's aim," he argued, "and quite another to build it." Moreover, even though he pledged Soviet assistance to such countries "in the sphere of politics and culture" and in "the strengthening of their defense," Andropov insisted that "on the whole" their economic development could "only be the result of the work of their peoples and of a correct policy of their leadership."[19]

Gorbachev's elevation to CPSU general secretary has brought proliferating evidence that no school of thought about Third World policy can claim exclusive top-level support. Gorbachev's discussion of the Third World in his book *Perestroika: New Thinking for Our Country and the World*—comments that represent his most extensive and personal public statement about the Third World to date—is especially revealing in this regard.[20]

In this discussion, the General Secretary shied away from broad references to "socialist-oriented" states, to "revolutionary democracies," and to "revolutionary-democratic" parties of a "vanguard" sort, but he wrote at fair length about a number of the entities that normally show up on the lists set forth by partisans of the "revolutionary-democratic" line. For instance, he declared that "we fully appreciate the formidable tasks facing progressive regimes in Africa." Through "economic and financial means" and even "by resorting to arms," imperialism "is out to retain" the positions that it acquired in African countries during the colonial era. However, he stated, the "progressive" regimes there "are determined to pursue a course toward consolidating gains." For "these effort and these policies" he expressed firm Soviet backing, and he went on to underscore that "our country has always acted, and will continue to act, in support of the national liberation struggle of African nations."

With regard to Nicaragua, he charged the United States with pursuing "an undeclared war against a small country whose only 'fault' is that it wants to live its own way, without interference from the outside." In addition, he contended that the Nicaraguan revolution had come about in the first place because of "unbearable conditions" there that the United States had created by treating all of Central America as its "backyard." The USSR, he concluded, "sympathized" with "the liberation movements of peoples fighting for social justice," and it believed that "if the United States left Nicaragua in peace, this would be better for the US itself, for the Latin Americans, and for the rest of the world."

Consistent with the "economic-interdependence" perspective, Gorbachev pointed to "the growing tendency towards interdependence of the states of the world community." This tendency, he asserted, produces "global issues" which "become vital to the destinies of civilization" and require solutions "in the framework of the world community." Among the specific issues that he cited was the economic development of Third World states.

Such development, the General Secretary emphasized, did not threaten "traditional links between the United States and Western Europe, on the one hand, and developing countries on the other." He acknowledged "how important the Middle East, Asia, Latin America, other Third World regions, and also South Africa are for American and West European economies, in particular as raw material sources," and stated that "to cut these links is the last thing we want to do, and we have no desire to provoke ruptures in historically formed, mutual economic interests."

In consonance with the "national-capitalism" viewpoint, Gorbachev sought to portray the USSR as a champion of Third World "capitalist-oriented" states trying to shake off the vestiges of Western domination. He began by holding that "economic, political, and ideological competition between capitalist and socialist countries is inevitable," although, "it can and must be kept within a framework of peaceful competition." Then he proceeded to demonstrate his commitment to such competition by arguing that every Third World state" is entitled to choose its own way of development, to dispose of its fate, its territory, and its human and natural resources." Significantly, he did not confine his defense of this right simply to countries that opted for "socialist orientation," but extended it to states on their way to becoming modern industrialized countries of a capitalist type. According to him, even those in this category that were "growing into great powers" confronted "uneven and painful" economic growth, for the "rich Western states" continued "to collect neo-colonialist 'tribute'." He wound up, therefore, calling upon Western leaders to "set aside the psychology and notions of colonial times" and stop treating "capitalist-oriented" as well as other kinds of Third World countries as the West's "sphere of influence."

The General Secretary's ensuing remarks about specific Third World states testified to the importance that he assigned to "capitalist-oriented" ones. He indicated that the USSR was "ready to develop [its]relations with each of the ASEAN nations individually and with ASEAN as a whole." He depicted the

USSR's relations with India as "an example for others to emulate," and he saw in these relations "a budding world order in which peaceful coexistence and mutually beneficial cooperation based on goodwill will be universal norms." He avowed Soviet sympathy "with the Latin American countries in their efforts to consolidate their independence in every sphere and to cast off all neo-colonialist fetters," and praised the "energetic foreign policies" and the "responsible stances on disarmament and international security" of Mexico and Argentina, the "peace-making efforts of the Contadora Group. . . ."

Indirect yet striking confirmation of the absence of top-level endorsement of a sole school of persuasion about Third World policy emerged at a major conference of the Ministry of Foreign Affairs in late July 1988. It came from Karen Brutents, at the time a deputy director of the CPSU International Department and a key expounder of the "national-capitalism" viewpoint. He told the gathering: "It is . . . only fair to say that the problems of developing countries have yet to be worked out in accordance with the concept of new thinking."[21]

SOVIET BEHAVIOR

Before the early 1980's, Soviet conduct in the Third World at any given juncture had traditionally followed the recommendation of whichever policy outlook enjoyed official blessing. During the latter half of the 1970's, for instance, it conformed to the prescriptions of the "revolutionary-democratic" line. The USSR directed toward "revolutionary democracies" most of the energy and resources that it devoted to the Third World in these years. Moscow signed new treaties of friendship and cooperation with five Third World states, and from the Soviet standpoint, all of these fell into the category of "revolutionary democracies." The CPSU also developed strong ties with six ruling "revolutionary-democratic" parties of a "vanguard" kind (in Angola, Mozambique, Benin, Congo, the PDRY, and Afghanistan) and with one commission established to create such a party (in Ethiopia).

Between 1975 and 1979, the USSR delivered an estimated US$23.2 billion of weapons and equipment to 30 Third World countries, and of this total $19 billion went to 17 "revolutionary democracies."[22] In 1976, of the 9,080 Soviet and East European military technicians posted in Third World states, 5,975 were in eight "revolutionary democracies"; by 1979, 11 "revolutionary democracies" accounted for 14,800 of the 15,865 such technicians assigned to the Third World.[23]

During 1975–79, Moscow offered economic credits to 33 countries of the developing world, of which 17 met Soviet criteria for "revolutionary democracies." These 17 states, to be sure, received only an estimated $3.1 billion of the $10.8 billion that the USSR extended to the developing world over the period, but large commitments to three non–"socialist-oriented" countries introduced substantial distortions into the picture—Moscow proffered $2 billion to Morocco, $1.85 billion to Turkey, and $1.2 billion to Nigeria.[24] In 1977, Soviet and East European economic technicians in the Third World numbered 58,730, of which 36,540 were located in 12 "revolutionary democracies." By 1979, 63,275 of the 80,820 such economic technicians were to be found in 14 "revolutionary democracies."[25]

Throughout the second half of the 1970's, Moscow labored mightily to help Third World "revolutionary-democratic" regimes, particularly those with "vanguard" parties, to create and/or strengthen their instruments of control. Although it employed a variety of means to this end, it relied heavily on political tools.

As noted above, the CPSU fashioned close ties with the ruling "vanguard" parties in Angola, Mozambique, Benin, Congo, the PDRY, and Afghanistan and with the commission formed to set up such a party in Ethiopia. These links included providing advice on ideological and organizational matters.[26]

The USSR also assumed key military roles in five of the seven states. To Angola, Mozambique, and Ethiopia, it provided military advisers to assist with the development and training of local armed forces, and it became the principal supplier of weapons and equipment for the three countries. In the cases of Angola and Ethiopia, it even furnished the logistical support for large contingents of Cuban troops that stayed in these countries after, respectively, the 1975–76 Angolan civil war and the 1977–78 war between Ethiopia and Somalia in the Ogaden. As for the PDRY and Afghanistan, Moscow had served as the chief source of weapons and equipment for the two and had furnished military technicians to both prior to the mid-1970's, but it greatly expanded the amount of arms and number of military technicians that it sent to them after they established "vanguard" parties in 1978.[27] In all instances, the aid that Moscow gave was designed to improve the performance of local militaries against rebellious domestic elements and threatening neighboring countries.

Only in Afghanistan did the USSR involve itself directly in assisting a "revolutionary-democratic" regime to shape or reshape its intelligence and security services. However, the USSR's staunchest East European ally, the German Democratic Republic (GDR), played a prominent part in setting up the intelligence and security services of the governments of Angola, Mozambique, Ethiopia, and the PDRY.[28]

Finally, the USSR adopted a fairly provocative stance toward the West in the Third World. Not only did Moscow insist that there was no linkage between détente with the West and Soviet actions in the Third World,[29] but it even risked confrontation with the United States by indirect involvement in military conflicts in Angola and the Horn of Africa and direct intervention in Afghanistan. All of these undertakings were in behalf of "revolutionary-democratic" regimes.

In the early 1980's, however, a new diversity crept into Soviet activities in the Third World, and this diversity has persisted throughout the remainder of the decade. The USSR's behavior has reflected a mix of elements drawn from all four of the existing schools of thought about desirable policy toward the Third World, although it has had a dominant thrust along "national-capitalism" lines. Moreover, the precise amalgamation of elements has varied on a regional basis.[30]

Targets of Interest

The USSR has continued, as the "revolutionary-democratic" enthusiasts have preferred, to channel toward the "revolutionary democracies" the bulk of the actual resources that it has allocated to the Third World. During 1982–86, Moscow shipped an estimated $59.7 billion worth of arms to 32 Third World states, and 17 "revolutionary democracies" received about $46.3 billion of that sum.[31] Of the 18,205 Soviet and East European military technicians in the Third World in 1981, 13,225 were assigned to 11 "revolutionary democracies." By 1984, 18,775 of 21,335 such technicians were posted in 14 "revolutionary democracies;" in 1986, 16,375 of 17,995 were active in the same 14 countries.[32]

During 1982–86, the USSR also extended an estimated $13.6 billion in economic credits to 43 Third World states, and $8.3 billion of this amount went to 16 "revolutionary democracies."[33] Of 95,685 Soviet and East European economic technicians in the Third World in 1981, 74,650 were assigned to 15 "revolutionary democracies." By 1984, 101,195 of the 125,960 such technicians in the Third World were to be found in 13 "revolutionary democracies." As of the end of 1986, 17 "revolutionary democracies" had 73,695 of the 96,455 such technicians in the Third World.[34]

A similar distribution of resources has prevailed in all of the major regions where "revolutionary democracies" exist—North Africa, Sub-Saharan Africa, the Middle East, South Asia, and Central America and the Caribbean. For example, the Middle East's three "revolutionary democracies" (Iraq, the PDRY, and Syria) got more than $3.5 billion of the nearly $4 billion in economic commitments and $26.7 billion of the roughly $29.6 billion in arms deliveries that Middle Eastern countries obtained from the USSR during 1982–86.[35] In 1981, they accounted for 19,100 of the 27,150 Soviet and East European economic technicians and 4,900 of the 5,929 Soviet and East European military technicians in the Middle East. These figures stood at 23,025 of 33,100 and 7,700 of 8,310, respectively, in 1984; they were 21,485 of 30,005 and 5,100 of 5,700 in 1986.[36]

Since Gorbachev's advent to power in early 1985, to be sure, the percentage of Soviet resources going to "revolutionary democracies" has declined somewhat. For instance, the economic credits that Moscow offered to 16 "revolutionary democracies" during the period 1982–86 amounted to only a little more than half of the total that it extended to the whole of the Third World in these years, while the same number of "revolutionary democracies" had received a substantially larger share of Soviet commitments to the Third World during 1980–84 ($7.6 billion of $9.7 billion).[37] Still, the basic pattern of investment of Soviet resources has not altered under Gorbachev.

In accordance with the recommendations of advocates of the "pro-military" perspective, the USSR has assiduously courted "progressive" military regimes in the Middle East, North Africa, and Sub-Saharan Africa. To a considerable degree, of course, Moscow has ensured major Soviet attention to states with military governments in these three regions by devoting to "revolutionary democracies" the bulk of the concrete resources that it has expended there, for most of the "revolutionary democracies" in these regions have either been headed by or dominated by the military. There has, however, been less ambiguous evidence as well that Moscow has singled out at least some of the military-controlled countries in the three regions for special wooing.

For example, the USSR has gone to unusual lengths to cultivate Ghana and the Yemen Arab Republic (YAR). Neither of these states claims to be even "socialist-oriented." Yet the government of Ghana under Flight Lieutenant Jerry Rawlings has demonstrated populist tendencies, and the YAR has toyed with the notion of uniting with the PDRY, although its enthusiasm about the idea has risen and fallen over the years.

Since Rawlings took power for the second time in Ghana in March 1982, the USSR has greatly stepped up its interaction with that African country. Delegation traffic between the two states has reached levels not attained since Kwame Nkrumah's downfall in 1966, collaboration between them has blossomed in various spheres, and Moscow has agreed to furnish technical assistance and funding for a number of economic construction and repair projects in Ghana.[38] In accordance with the last commitment, the USSR had by the close of 1986 extended more than $15 million in economic credits to Ghana.[39] Moscow has even resumed delivery of arms to Accra for the first time since Nkrumah's political demise, and by the end of 1986, the cumulative value of these arms had climbed to an estimated $20 million.[40]

Although the USSR had had fairly close relations with the YAR in the 1960's, these ties had deteriorated by the early 1970's and remained at low ebb for most of the 1970's.[41] Only in late 1979 did they begin to revive, when Moscow reversed a long-standing policy and consented to supply arms to the Sanaa government to help it combat opposition forces backed by the PDRY. Ensuing years brought a burgeoning of ties. In 1981, the USSR proffered economic credits of $55 million to the YAR, the largest single offer that Moscow had ever made to a government in Sanaa since North Yemen became a republic.[42] An increase in Soviet and East European economic technicians assigned to the country followed this commitment, with the number mounting from 175 in 1981 to 565 in 1986.[43] In addition, the USSR has sent major quantities of arms to the YAR in the 1980's. During 1982–86 alone, Soviet arms deliveries amounted to an estimated $1.3 billion.[44] Although the total of Soviet and East European military advisers in the state peaked at 700 in 1981, it still stood at 350 in 1986.[45]

As proponents of the "national-capitalism" viewpoint have urged, the USSR has vastly increased the heed that it pays to "capitalist-oriented" countries. This shift has had two distinct dimensions.

First, Moscow has greatly expanded its contacts with two major regions that lack "revolutionary democracies" and have virtually no "socialist-oriented" states—South America and Southeast Asia. The heightened political interaction has been particularly striking. Soviet activity in Southeast Asia is illustrative.[46] During the first half of the 1980's, there was a modest rise in the number of delegations exchanged between the USSR and ASEAN countries, although most of the individuals involved were relatively low-ranking officials. Then the flow swelled dramatically and came to include many high-level figures. In March 1987, USSR Foreign Minister Shevardnadze toured Southeast Asia and stopped in both Thailand and Indonesia. His visit to Indonesia was the first by a major Soviet leader since Sukarno's ouster in 1965. Soon after Shevardnadze's trip, Soviet officials in Moscow welcomed the foreign ministers of Thailand and Malaysia for talks. Then in July 1987, Malaysian Prime Minister Mahathir Mohamad spent several days in Moscow at Soviet invitation. Indonesian Foreign Minister Mochtar Kusumaatmadja journeyed to the USSR for conversations with Soviet leaders in February 1988. Later in the year, the Soviet hierarchy entertained Prime Minister Prem Tinsulanon of Thailand in Moscow, and Shevardnadze went to the Philippines for discussions with leaders there. Second, even in regions where there are "revolutionary democracies," the USSR has wooed than 50 yearmany "capitalist-oriented" states with which it had had few links at the outset of the 1980's. These have included some with especially revealing attributes.

Thus, Moscow has determinedly courted countries which, in its eyes, are guilty of having abandoned a "socialist orientation" in the recent past. Egypt is a good example. In the wake of President Anwar al-Sadat's assassination in October 1981, the USSR strove to reconstruct the economic, cultural, scientific, and trade union ties with Egypt that he had broken during the final years of his rule. In July 1984, the USSR and Egypt finally agreed to resume full diplomatic relations and exchange ambassadors, and exchanges of delegations between the two states increased rapidly thereafter. Soviet officials in March 1987 addressed the last remaining source of friction between the USSR and Egypt by working out a rescheduling of Egypt's outstanding debt to Moscow on terms favorable to Cairo.[47]

The USSR has also resolutely cultivated states that it has long regarded as important "capitalist-oriented" countries but that had, at best, displayed coolness toward it in the last half of the 1970's. Examples are Zaire, Jordan, and Saudi Arabia.

Some details of the USSR's efforts with respect to Saudi Arabia should suffice to indicate the intensity of Soviet undertakings in these cases.[48] Soviet leaders had their first talks in Moscow with a Saudi foreign minister in December 1982, when they received Prince Saud al-Faysal as a member of an Arab League delegation. There followed some lower-level contacts over the next few years, and then in early 1987, Soviet officials welcomed Saudi oil minister Hisham Nazir to Moscow for conversations about cooperation between the USSR and members of the Organization of Petroleum Exporting Countries (OPEC). In January 1988, the Soviet hierarchy played host to Foreign Minister Saud again, who ostensibly headed a group representing the Gulf Cooperation Council but brought only Saudi officials with him. The following month, Gorbachev dispatched a special envoy, Vladimir Polyakov, to Saudi Arabia. Polyakov was the first Soviet representative to pay an official call there in more than 50 years.

Consistent with the wishes of the champions of the "economic-interdependence" outlook, the USSR has expanded its economic relations with Third World states without regard to political orientation. This approach has meant that its economic links with "capitalist-oriented" countries have multiplied significantly. The USSR's trade turnover with Third World states rose from roughly $4.8 billion a year on the average in 1975–79 to an annual average of more than $10.8 billion in 1982–86, and most of the increase came with "capitalist-oriented" countries. A major share of the growth, for instance, came in trade with South America and Southeast Asia, where, as already mentioned, there are virtually no "socialist-oriented" states. Soviet trade turnover with South America climbed from an average annual figure of only a little more than $800 million in 1975–79 to more than $2.1 billion a year on the average during 1982–86. Similarly, the USSR's annual trade turnover with non-communist countries in Southeast Asia averaged nearly $1.1 billion in 1982–86 as compared with an average yearly figure of about $460 million in 1975–79.[49]

Moscow has striven especially to enhance its economic ties with the best economic performers among developing countries, and these have been almost exclusively "capitalist-oriented" states. Examples are India, Brazil, Singapore, Thailand, Turkey, Tunisia, Sri Lanka, and Malaysia. In 1982–86, the USSR's trade turnover with India reached an average of $2.9 billion a year, whereas in 1975–79 it had amounted only to an average of $1.2 billion a year. The total for Brazil rose from about $320 million in 1975–79 to more than $630 million in 1982–86; for Singapore, from a little in excess of $115 million to almost $290 million; for Thailand, from roughly $22 million to more than $115 million; for Turkey, from $170 million to nearly $375 million; for Tunisia, from $17 million to $34 million; for Sri Lanks from $30 million to more than $46 million; for Malaysia, from about $170 million to more than $250 million.[50]

Relationships Sought

In the cases of "revolutionary democracies" and especially those with "vanguard" parties, the USSR has persisted in pursuing the sort of ties that adherents of the "revolutionary-democratic" perspective have touted. That is, it has tried to fashion long-term, structural links with these states by assisting the existing regimes in their efforts to solidify their rule.

For instance, Moscow has encouraged "revolutionary-democratic" regimes still without "vanguard" parties to form such parties, and it has endeavored to help strengthen existing "vanguard" parties. The leading example of Soviet efforts of the former type has to do with Ethiopia. For example, Soviet officials prodded Ethiopia's Mengistu Haile-Mariam to carry out his avowed intention to set up a "vanguard" party, and when he was preparing for the official launching of the Workers' Party of Ethiopia in September 1984, the USSR played a major part in the undertakings. This role included educating Ethiopians about the operations of a Marxist-Leninist party. No less than 12 important Ethiopian delegations visited the Soviet Union in 1983 alone to observe CPSU activities, and some of these groups comprised 30 or more persons.

As for Soviet bolstering of "vanguard" parties already in existence, the PDRY offers a good illustration. In January 1986, a coup there ousted President Ali Nasir Muhammad and resulted in the death of a large segment of the state's political elite. Subsequently, the USSR assumed a key role in reconstituting a government and rebuilding a viable party in the country.[51]

The USSR and its allies have also retained or taken over major functions with respect to the intelligence and security services of a number of "revolutionary democracies." Principal among these countries have been Angola, Mozambique, Ethiopia, the PDRY, Nicaragua, and (at least until early 1989) Afghanistan.[52]

Finally, the USSR has worked closely with several "revolutionary democracies" to enhance their capacity to deal with domestic and/or foreign military challenges. For example, it has furnished military advisers to Angola, Ethiopia, Mozambique, the PDRY, Nicaragua, and Afghanistan (until early 1989) to assist in the training of local military forces and to offer counsel on military strategy. In addition, it has constituted the primary source of the large amounts of arms that all six states have acquired during the decade. It even deployed a large contingent of its own troops in Afghanistan until early 1989, and it has furnished logistical support for the stationing of substantial numbers of Cuban troops in Angola and Ethiopia.[53]

It should be acknowledged, however, that the late 1980's have witnessed a growing Soviet leeriness about involvement in attempts to bolster "revolutionary democracies" militarily when these undertakings entail high costs for the USSR or antagonize the Western powers. Not only did Soviet troops leave Afghanistan in February 1989 in line with a decision that Gorbachev had announced in 1988, but Moscow also actively promoted the accords that Angola, Cuba, and South Africa concluded in December 1988. These call for the departure of all Cuban forces form Angola by July 1991 in return for South Africa's acceptance of Namibia's independence, although they do not affect the status of Soviet military advisers in Angola.[54]

In approaching military-rule countries in the Middle East, North Africa, and Sub-Saharan Africa, the USSR appears to have sought to create the kind of long-term structural relations of a military nature favored by the expounders of the "pro-military" school. For instance, it shipped arms to 16 military-controlled states in the three regions during 1982–86; furthermore, it served as the sole or primary source of arms for 11 of these states.[55]

As proponents of the "national-capitalism" viewpoint have counseled, the USSR seems to have eschewed attempts to establish lasting structural links with *most* "capitalist-oriented" countries—at least over the short term. Indeed, the great diversity of such states that Moscow has been wooing in the 1980's suggests that it has been hedging against possible setbacks here and there in its relations with them.

Moscow has been courting not only the more important "capitalist-oriented" countries but many fairly minor ones as well. For example, in 1984 alone, each of the African mini-states of Gambia, Togo, Niger, Mauritania, and Rwanda received at least one significant Soviet overture.[56] After extensive diplomatic preparations, the USSR opened up official ties with both Oman and the United Arab Emirates in October 1985. In February 1987, Moscow sent its ambassador in Costa Rica to Guatemala to explore the chances for resumption of Soviet-Guatemalan diplomatic relations.[57] No formal links had existed between the two countries since the unseating of the left-wing Arbenz government in Guatemala in the mid-1950's

In keeping with the prescriptions of the "economic-interdependence" school, however, the USSR has tried to foster long-term, structural ties in a multilateral frame work with *some* "capitalist-oriented" states and particularly with the best economic performers in the Third World. It has done this basically by pressing for increased purchases of Soviet goods, especially machinery. But the items that Moscow has been promoting have gone well beyond those that would improve the capabilities of these Third World countries to produce for the Soviet market; they have included any type of machine goods that would ensure "mutually advantageous" exchanges. Thus, the trade flows that the USSR has encouraged are intended to create linkages whose ultimate importance will derive from their connection to the global economic system instead of in a purely bilateral context.[58]

Instruments

The USSR has employed all of the diverse means at its disposal in its handling of the Third World as a whole, but it has emphasized different tools in addressing different targets there. In dealing with "revolutionary democracies" with "vanguard" parties, Moscow has heeded the recommendations of adherents of the "revolutionary-democratic" viewpoint. It has resorted primarily to a mix of political and military instruments, with a stress on the former. The means whereby the USSR has sought to help the existing regimes in Angola, Mozambique, Ethiopia, and the PDRY put down firm roots afford excellent illustrations. As already noted, Moscow has assisted these regimes with arms and training for local military forces to try to strengthen the capacities of the regimes to meet internal and foreign military threats; however, it has relied principally on undertakings designed to improve the control capabilities of these regimes' nonmilitary institutions.

In the cases of military-run states in the Middle East, North Africa, and Sub-Saharan Africa, as well as many "revolutionary democracies" lacking "vanguard" parties, the USSR has followed the desires of the exponents of the "promilitary" school. That is, it has used chiefly military tools. Political instruments, it is true, have played a not inconsequential role in Soviet wooing of these countries, particularly the "revolutionary democracies." Yet the absence of "vanguard" parties in all of these states has imposed limits on the effectiveness with which the USSR can employ political means. Of the other types of tools available, Moscow has clearly judged military ones to be of greater value and viability than economic ones. During 1982–86, for instance, 18 military-ruled countries in the Middle East, North Africa, and Sub-Saharan Africa received arms deliveries and/or economic credits from the USSR, and 15 of these state got more supplies of arms than economic commitments—usually by a large margin.[59]

As for most "capitalist-oriented" countries, the USSR has carried out its courtship largely through political means, as partisans of the "national-capitalism" outlook have counseled. For the most part, Moscow has found the economic and military "contradictions'" between these states and the West too costly to try to exploit, given Soviet resource constraints. Political "contradictions" are not as problematic. Thus, Soviet efforts to make common political cause with these states have proliferated and have covered a broad range of topics. For example, the USSR has supported the endeavors of the "capitalist-oriented" states of the South Pacific to declare their region a nuclear-free zone—a step opposed especially by the United States and France—and it has endorsed the calls by the "capitalist-oriented" countries of Latin America for the West to adopt a more flexible attitude toward their debts.

With respect to a few "capitalist-oriented" states, however, the USSR has followed the exhortations of those of an "economic-interdependence" persuasion by concentrating on economic means. The best illustrations are countries with which it has managed to establish a "mutually advantageous" economic relationship. Morocco, Turkey, and Egypt fall into this group. During 1981–86, Soviet exports to Morocco averaged about $151 million a year, while Soviet imports amounted to an annual average of almost $74 million. The figures for Turkey were, respectively, $211 million and roughly $161 million; for Egypt, more than $211 million and nearly $189 million.[60] All of these state, it should be underscored, qualify for listing among the developing world's better economic performers.[61]

Posture Towards the West

To a large extent, the USSR has adopted the stance toward the West endorsed by proponents of the "national-capitalism" perspective—that is, competition without confrontation. A few diverse examples will suffice for purposes of illustration. When Thailand and the Dominican Republic in the early 1980's found themselves deprived of quotas for sale of rice and sugar respectively in the US market, Moscow agreed to purchase substantial amounts of these commodities from them. Thus, Soviet trade turnover with Thailand jumped from $22.2 million a year on the average in 1975–79 to an annual average of $115.6 million in 1982–86; that with the Dominican Republic rose from nothing in 1975–79 to an average yearly figure of $36.4 million in 1982–86.[62]

In the early 1980's, the USSR contracted to supply weapons and equipment to Jordan for the first time after King Hussein had failed to get what he wanted from the United States or other Western powers. Over the 1982–86 period alone, Soviet arms deliveries to this Middle Eastern state totaled an estimated $1.1 billion.[63]

Although Moscow has throughout the 1980's encouraged Mu'ammar al-Qadhafi's antipathy toward the West and has attempted to exploit it to forge strong links with Libya, the USSR has carefully dissociated itself from Qadhafi's more provocative actions toward the West. For instance, Soviet media studiously avoided mention of Libya's likely role in the mining of the Red Sea in the summer of 1984, and the USSR quietly helped with the mine-clearing operations in the Bab el-Mandeb area.[64] Furthermore, Moscow did not respond in a direct military way to the US bombing of Libya in April 1986, which Washington characterized as retaliation for Qadhafi's fostering of international terrorism. The USSR merely offered Qadhafi some new, more sophisticated military hardware—especially SA-5 missiles.[65]

In line with the inclinations of the backers of both the "revolutionary-democratic" and "pro-military" schools of thought, however, the USSR maintained a limited confrontational attitude toward the West by supporting some "revolutionary democracies" until the mid-1980's. Among these were three states in which it had taken on fairly heavy military responsibilities in the latter part of the 1970's—namely, Angola, Ethiopia, and Afghanistan—but the group also included other countries such as Nicaragua. To the governments of these states, all of which faced serious domestic and/or external military challenges, Moscow provided large quantities of arms and, often in conjunction with its allies, significant numbers of military advisers.[66] Moreover, it did so despite the fact that the Western powers, and particularly the United States, were either seeking to end the conflicts or aiding the opponents of the existing regimes in the countries concerned.

But since early 1986, the USSR has gradually abandoned most of the confrontational aspects of its posture even in these cases. In March 1986, for instance, Gorbachev indicated explicitly that the USSR was prepared to help find political solutions to the conflicts engulfing Angola.[67] Although for nearly two years Moscow played a fairly minimal part in diplomatic efforts to such an end, in late 1987 it did begin to push actively for the agreements that Angola, Cuba, and South Africa signed in December 1988.[68] In October 1986, the USSR consented to normalize its relations with Somalia, one of the Ethiopian government's main antagonists.[69] Thereafter, Moscow pressed for a rapprochement between Ethiopia and Somalia. And finally, there is Afghanistan, where in May 1986, the USSR engineered a change in the leadership of the ruling party in Afghanistan that brought to power Najibullah, a man who appeared to be more amenable to some sort of "national reconciliation" in the country than his predecessor had been. Two months later, in a major speech in Vladivostok, Gorbachev announced the withdrawal of a number of Soviet regiments from Afghanistan.[70] By early 1988, Moscow had decided to pull all of its troops out, and it concluded a formal accord to this effect in April 1988.[71] In keeping with that document, the last Soviet troops left the country in February 1989.

Only with respect to Nicaragua have some elements of confrontation remained. To be sure, the USSR has endorsed peace initiatives such as the "Arias plan," set forth by the presidents of Central America in August 1987, and it has applauded conciliatory gestures by the Sandinista regime to its internal opposition. Yet Moscow has declined to involve itself in the Central American peace process. Moreover, it has promised to increase its military aid to the Managua government, although Gorbachev did indicate in early April 1989 that he was prepared to cut off this flow of arms if the United States ceased all of its shipments of arms to Central America.[72]

Since the mid-1980's, the USSR also has occasionally assumed the selectively cooperative stance toward the West that the champions of the "economic-interdependence" outlook favor. The manifestations of such a posture have come largely, though not exclusively, in connection with Third World conflict situations. The outstanding example is the negotiations that resulted in the pledge by Angola and Cuba to remove Cuban troops from Angolan soil in return for South Africa's acceptance of Namibian independence. Soviet and American officials worked closely together to facilitate this settlement.[73] The United States and Soviet Union also collaborated during the severe famine that hit Ethiopia in 1985. The USSR had little in the way of food to offer Addis Ababa, but Moscow furnished many of the trucks and airplanes required to get the relief supplies—provided by the West, especially the US—to affected areas of the country.[74]

IMPLICATIONS

What, then, do these shifts suggest about the USSR's policy toward the Third World? Two points stand out. First, from a substantive viewpoint, increased complexity has become the key feature of Soviet policy. Specifically, the policy now reflects several different, often clashing visions of what the Soviet approach to the Third World ought to be. It is true that, as the evidence laid out in the preceding pages attests, a good case can be made that today change outweighs continuity in the content of Soviet policy. Yet elements of continuity persist. More critical, even if these elements of continuity were to disappear, the heightened complexity of policy would still prevail as long as multiple schools of persuasion about desirable policy existed and the USSR's top leadership embraced no one of them exclusively.

The significance of this new complexity in Soviet policy toward the Third World arises from its impact on the predictability of that policy. In any concrete set of circumstances, it is hard to anticipate precisely what mix of the various policy perspectives will shape Soviet behavior. Thus, foreseeing the USSR's response to these circumstances is highly problematic.

From Moscow's standpoint, of course, this development is not necessarily a drawback. Nor is the greater flexibility that the added complexity permits in Soviet handling of the Third World. The absence of a firm official line, for example, gives Moscow more room to adjust its conduct in light of the conditions it may see as relevant in each individual situation.

Second, in terms of process, the formulation of the USSR's policy toward the Third World has also turned into a highly complicated affair. Policy now emerges from competition among a number of groups with diverse policy outlooks in the Soviet hierarchy.

Many signs do point to an evolution in the nature of this competition during the 1980's. In the final years of the Brezhnev era, during the brief tenures of Andropov and Chernenko as CPSU general secretary, and even in the initial stage of Gorbachev's rule, the competition resembled a free-for-all wrestling match. Advocates of the various policy lines picked concrete circumstances in which they believed that they could influence the USSR's behavior, and then they sought to exert this leverage.

Several factors contributed to this situation. Brezhnev, Andropov, and Chernenko were elderly and suffered from serious illnesses and/or infirmities during much or all of the periods that they were in office; thus, they did not function in an activist fashion. Moreover, they faced so many pressing problems that the Third World did not rank high on their lists of priorities. As a consequence, even though they refused to lend the weight of their authority to the "revolutionary-democratic" viewpoint that had enjoyed official sanction in the late 1970's, neither did they set forth a coherent alternative to it.

Gorbachev's rise to power brought a young, dynamic individual to the top leadership post, but he lacked experience in foreign affairs and had virtually no experience in dealing with the Third World. Perhaps more important, his immediate concerns were domestic in nature, and his need to solidify his political control reinforced this preoccupation. Hence, he devoted little attention to the Third World at the outset.[75]

In addition, until roughly 1987, officials with diverse prescriptions for the USSR's Third World policy were entrenched in those Soviet institutions that had a major hand in shaping the Soviet approach toward the Third World. The CPSU International Department, for example, included among its directing elements representatives of three of the four Soviet schools of thought about Third World policy.[76] Without firm policy guidelines from above, these and other strategically-placed individuals were in a position to affect Soviet conduct at least within their own spheres of responsibility.

Since about 1987, however, the competition has taken on a more structured form, as advocates of each policy line battle to influence the content of the "new thinking." An item published in a leading Soviet academic journal in mid-1988 affords a graphic illustration. Under the headline "Socialist Orientation and New Political Thinking," two prominent specialists on the Third World with long-standing, conflicting outlooks on Soviet Third World policy engaged in a dialogue on "socialist orientation." One expounded a "revolutionary-democratic" viewpoint; the other, a "national-capitalism" viewpoint. Yet both claimed that their arguments accorded with "new political thinking."[77]

The previously cited observation by Brutents at the Ministry of Foreign Affairs conference in July 1988 offers equally revealing evidence. In saying that "the problems of developing countries have yet to be worked out" in light of "the concept of new thinking," he implied that "new thinking" required further refinement. Given his long-term commitment to a "national-capitalism" perspective, there can be little doubt what sort of refinement he had in mind.

This shift in the nature of the competition has come about for a combination of reasons. Over the years, Gorbachev has greatly enhanced his power by engineering a variety of personnel and institutional changes in the USSR, although he still appears to confront strong opposition in some quarters.

The General Secretary has also begun to evince a fair degree of interest in the Third World, and he has even set forth some general principles for Soviet policy toward it. These flow essentially out of his larger political and foreign policy concerns. That is particularly true of the two primary principles. As Gorbachev sees things, Soviet involvements in the Third World must not impede the restructuring of the Soviet economy, and the USSR's behavior there must not undermine Soviet attempts to improve relations with the West in general and the United States in particular.[78]

Aside from insisting on adherence to a few governing principles, however, Gorbachev has shown a willingness to listen to expert advice on how to deal with the Third World. This willingness has legitimized efforts by representatives of all policy persuasions to make inputs on the subject, and despite Gorbachev's shakeup of the personnel and institutions handling Third World matters, diversity of outlook persists among the well-placed experts. Indeed, even Gorbachev's two top-ranking lieutenants in the realm of foreign policy—Yakovlev and Shevardnadze—seem to hold clashing views on desirable Soviet Third World policy.

PROSPECTS

None of the developments highlighted in this article, it should be recognized, is necessarily permanent. Therefore, an assessment of their likely future relevance requires answers to two basic questions. First, will debate continue over what the Soviet Union's policy toward the Third World should be, and especially will there be several schools of thought on the subject? Second, will the top Soviet leadership persist in avoiding an embrace of any single school of thought as an official line? Let us address each of these issues in turn.

Although the visions of desirable Soviet policy toward the Third World advanced by Soviet observers have totaled four since the early 1980's, there is nothing magical about that number, and it could alter in the years immediately ahead. The underpinnings of the "revolutionary-democratic" and "pro-military" outlooks, for example, have eroded substantially. Indeed, criticism of even the most radical forces in power in the Third World has come from supporters of the "revolutionary-democratic" and "pro-military" perspectives, as well as from partisans of other viewpoints.[80] Unhappiness with these forces could reach the point where the "revolutionary-democratic" and/or the "pro-military" schools of thought would disappear entirely.

By the same token, indications have cropped up since mid-1988 that a fifth vision of policy may be emerging, although these hints still remain scanty enough to leave questions about whether it has enough backing to quality as a full-fledged school of thought. This perspective accepts a basic premise of the "national-capitalism" outlook—that at least most Third World states will pass through a capitalist or nonsocialist phase of development before arriving at socialism. Yet it sees far less possibility of advance toward socialism under present circumstances than even the "national-capitalism" line does. Not only is this viewpoint skeptical that "capitalist-oriented" countries in the Third World will try to assert their independence vis-à-vis the Western "imperialist" powers in economic and other spheres by expanding their contacts with the USSR, but it is pessimistic about even modest steps toward socialism on the part of "socialist-oriented" states. Worst of all from its standpoint, even the most consistent of the USSR's Third World allies are seeking to broaden their political and economic ties with the West, and the USSR lacks the resources to reverse this situation. In fact, Moscow is even having troubles increasing these resources, for it bears heavy military burdens in the Third World and other areas. As a result, the socialist path of development is losing its appeal in the Third World.

Thus, according to advocates of this possible new school of thought, the USSR must reduce its involvements in the Third World so as to focus on restructuring its own economy and making the socialist path more attractive. In doing so, it should not use political orientation as a basis for retaining close relations; rather, it should adopt pragmatic criteria based on its political interests and goals in each region. Nor should it attempt to maintain or develop links with Third World countries that entail heavy commitments of resources, especially those of an economic character. In addition, it should rely chiefly on political means, instead of more costly military and economic instruments, in pursuing its ends. Finally, it should adopt a nonprovocative posture toward the West; otherwise, it might find itself embroiled in Third World conflicts that would drain off its resources.

So far, we have not been able to identify any high-level individual who has publicly associated himself with this line of argument.[81] Nevertheless, some (unnamed) senior members of the Ministry of Foreign Affairs, including ambassadors and high-ranking staff members of the ministry, did openly call at the ministry's July 1988 conference for a hard-headed reassessment of Soviet undertakings in the Third World. They urged that the USSR develop relations with Third World states "on realistic lines, with due regard to the peculiarities of each particular country and, first and foremost, to our actual possibilities."[82]

What appears beyond doubt is that controversy over Third World policy will continue in the USSR for the foreseeable future. Moreover, it seems highly probable that multiple schools of persuasion on the subject will remain in existence as well. The "revolutionary-democratic" perspective in particular has roots too deep in Soviet policy-making for one to anticipate that it will soon vanish completely.

Were the number of visions of policy to drop to two, of course, the complexity of current policy would inevitably diminish—especially if the two happened to be the "national-capitalism" and "economic-interdependence" viewpoints, which have elements of commonality in their prescriptions. Yet complexity would not vanish entirely if the top Soviet leadership still failed to extend its official sanction to one or the other. This point brings us to the second issue.

The top Soviet leadership's position on the merits of embracing as an official line one of the extant schools of thought about policy could undergo change in two ways. Someone amenable to the notion of sanctioning one of the schools could replace Gorbachev as general secretary, or Gorbachev himself could alter his attitude on the issue.

With regard to the possibility of Gorbachev's replacement, his hold on power will ultimately depend on how well his programs work, and that question remains unresolved. For the moment, however, he seems not only to have enhanced his dominance of the political system but to have prevented a coalescence of different groups of malcontents, as well as to have denied them a prominent figure around whom to rally. Consequently, no succession appears to loom on the near horizon. Even were one to take place, there is no guarantee that a new general secretary would abandon Gorbachev's stance on the matter at issue here.

As for the potential for a shift in Gorbachev's attitude, such a development seems most unlikely, although not utterly impossible. Gorbachev appears to welcome the flexibility that his decision not to endorse exclusively any school of thought about policy toward the Third World has afforded the USSR. Moreover, this increased ability to adjust policy to local conditions has to date served the USSR fairly well in its dealings with the Third World. Thus, it would probably take a major setback for the USSR in the Third World to persuade Gorbachev to reverse himself.

All in all, then, both Soviet policy toward the Third World and the process whereby that policy is formulated will probably continue to evince a high degree of complexity in the years immediately ahead. This judgment, it should be stressed, does not preclude change, but it does mean that change is likely to be at the margins.

NOTES

1. See, for example, Alvin Z. Rubinstein, *Moscow's Third World Strategy* (Princeton, NJ: Princeton University Press, 1988).

2. A typical illustration is Daniel S. Papp, *Soviet Perceptions of the Developing World in the 1980's: The Ideological Basis* (Lexington, MA: Lexington Books, 1985).

3. See, for instance, the writings of Francis Fukuyama—especially, *Moscow's Post-Brezhnev Reassessment of the Third World*, R-3337-USDP (Santa Monica, CA: RAND Corporation, February 1986); "Gorbachev and the Third World," *Foreign Affairs* (New York) (Spring 1986), pp. 715–31; "Patterns of Soviet Third World Policy," *Problems of Communism* (Washington, DC) (September–October 1987), pp. 1–13.

4. Both Jerry Hough and Elizabeth Valkenier fall into this category. See Hough, *The Struggle for the Third World: Soviet Debates and American Options*, (Washington DC: The Brookings Institution, 1986); Valkenier, *The Soviet Union and the Third World: An Economic Bind*, (New York: Praeger, 1983; "Revolutionary Change in the Third World: Recent Soviet Assessments," *World Politics* (Princeton, NJ) (April 1986), pp. 415–34; and "New Soviet Thinking About the Third World," *World Policy Journal* (New York) (Fall 1987), pp. 651–74.

5. Jack Snyder, "The Gorbachev Revolution: A Waning of Soviet Expansionism?" *International Security* (Cambridge, MA) (Winter 1987–88), pp. 93–131, affords a typical example.

6. For detailed discussion of this particular controversy, see especially Uri Ra'anan, "Moscow and the Third World," *Problems of Communism* (January–February 1965), pp. 22–31.

7. See, for example, Romanov's speech of September 7, 1984, at the founding congress of the Workers' Party of Ethiopia, as published in *Pravda* (Moscow), Sept. 9, 1984; and Ponomarev's "Real Socialism: The Liberated Countries," *Slovo Lektora* (Moscow) (March 1984), pp. 13–19.

8. Regarding Ul-yanovskiy, see his *Sovremennyye problemy Azii i Afriki* (The Contemporary Problems of Asia and Africa) (Moscow: Nauka, 1978); "On the Countries of Socialist Orientation," *Kommunist* (Moscow), no. 11 (July 1979), pp. 114–23; "The Twentieth Century and the National Liberation Movement," *Narody Azii i Afriki* (Moscow), no. 2 (1980), pp. 2–9; "Robbery under the Guise of 'Interdependence'," *Kommunist*, no. 16 (November 1981), pp. 76–87; "On National and Revolutionary Democracy: Paths of Evolution," *Narody Azii i Afriki*, no. 2 (1984), pp. 9–18; *Pobedy i trudnosti natsional'no-osvoboditel'noy bor'by* (The Triumphs and Difficulties of the National Liberation Struggle) (Moscow: Politizdat, 1985); "Pressing Problems of the National Liberation Movement and of Socialist Orientation," *Narody Azii i Afriki*, no. 6, (1986), pp. 3–13; and "Toward a Characterization of Contemporary Neo-Colonialism," ibid., no. 4, (1987), pp. 83–92.

With respect to Gromyko, see his "Pressing Problems of the Most Recent History of the Developing Countries," *Kommunist*, no. 4 (March 1979), pp. 117–24; "Socialist Orientation in Africa," *International Affairs* (Moscow) (September 1979), pp. 95–104; "Pressing Problems of Contemporary Africa," *Kommunist*, no. 2 (1980); "The Imperialist Threat to Africa," *International Affairs* (July 1981), pp. 47–53; "The Experience and Prospects in Research on Africa's Problems," *Narody Azii i Afriki*, no. 1 (1985), pp. 1–12; "The Revolution That Awakened Africa," *International Affairs* (December 1987), pp. 31–37; and "Africa: The Awakening," *The October Revolution and the World*," Special Supplement to *New Times* (Moscow) (1987), pp. 24–27.

9. For more detailed discussion of the emergence and fate of this vision of policy in the 1970's, see Mark Katz, *The Third World in Soviet Military Thought* (Baltimore, MD: Johns Hopkins University Press, 1982), pp. 81–83, 104–5.

10. On Rybkin, see, for instance, his "The Army in the Political System of Developed Socialism," *Voyenno-Istoricheskiy Zhurnal* (Moscow) (August 1982), pp. 3–12, and "Fundamentals of the Study of War and the Army."

With respect to Dolgopolov, see his "On Principles of Equality," *Soviet Military Review* (Moscow) (January 1984), pp. 49–50; *Sotsial'no-politicheskaya rol' armiy osvobodivshikhsya stran* (The Socio-Political Role of the Armies of the Liberated Countries) (Moscow: Voyennoye izdatel'stvo, 1986); and "Working for Independence," *Soviet Military Review* (July 1987), pp. 50–51.

722   David E. Albright

11. For representative commentaries by Brutents, see his *Osvobodivshiyesiya strany v 70-e gody* (The Liberated Countries in the 1970's) (Moscow: Politicheskaya literatura, 1979); article in *Pravda*, Feb. 2, 1982; "The Liberated Countries at the Beginning of the 1980's," *Kommunist*, no. 3 (February 1984), pp. 102–13; article in *Pravda*, Jan. 1, 1985; observations on a "Studio 9" program, Moscow Television Service in Russian, Feb. 27, 1988, as translated in Foreign Broadcast Information Service, *Daily Report: Soviet Union* (Washington, DC—hereafter, *FBIS-SOV*), Feb. 29, 1988, pp. 6–16.

With respect to Primakov, see his "Some Problems of the Developing Countries," *Kommunist*, no. 11 (July 1978), pp. 81–91; "The Liberated Countries: Community Problems," *Narody Azii i Afriki*, no. 5 (1980), pp. 15–28; "The Law of the Unevenness of Development and the Historical Fates of the Liberated Countries," *Mirovaya Ekonomika i Mezhdunarodnyye Otnosheniya* (Moscow—hereafter, *MEiMO*), pp. 28–47; *Vostok posle krakha kolonial'noy sistemy* (The East after the Collapse of the Colonial System) (Moscow: Nauka, 1982); "Leninist Analysis of Imperialism and the Current Scene," *Kommunist*, no. 9 (June 1986), pp 103–13.

12. See Yakovlev's "Inter-Imperialist Contradictions—The Current Context," *Kommunist*, no. 17 (November 1986), esp. p. 9.

13. On Zagladin, see his joint volume with I. T. Frolov, *Global'nyye problemy sovremennosti: nauchnyye i sotsial'nyye aspekty* (Contemporary Global Problems: Scientific and Social Aspects) (Moscow: Mezhdunarodnyye otnosheniya, 1981); his joint article with I. Frolov, "Global Problems and the Fate of Civilization," *Oktyabr'* (Moscow), no. 5 (1984); "Socialism and Contemporary Global Problems," *Politicheskoye Samoobrazovaniye* (Moscow) (September 1986), pp. 13–22; "The Present and the Future: Two Strategies for the 21st Century," *MEiMO* (September 1986), pp. 3–14; and "An Arduous but Necessary Path," *International Affairs*, (September 1988), pp. 28–37.

With regard to the other three, see Inozemtsev's edited volume, *Global'nyye problemy sovremennosti* (Contemporary Global Problems) (Moscow: Mysl', 1981); Arbatov's address to the 26th annual convention of the International Studies Association in Washington, DC, on March 6, 1985, as published in *International Studies Newsletter* (Columbia, SC) (May 1985), pp. 1–5; Shevardnadze's report of July 25, 1988, to a conference of the USSR Ministry of Foreign Affairs, *International Affairs* (October 1988), particularly pp. 14–15 and 23, and his closing speech of July 27, 1988, to the same gathering, ibid., especially pp. 61–62.

14. *Pravda*, Feb. 25, 1976.

15. Ibid., Dec. 6, 1977.

16. Cf. the reports of Kosygin (ibid., Mar. 2, 1976) and Brezhnev (loc. cit.).

17. Ibid., Dec. 6, 1977.

18. Ibid., Feb. 24, 1981.

19. Ibid., June 16, 1983.

20. See specifically Chs. 3 ("How We See the World of Today") and 5 ("The Third World in the International Community") in Mikhail Gorbachev, *Perestroika: New Thinking for Our Country and the World* (New York: Harper and Row, 1987). Other key items providing insight into Gorbachev's position include the new CPSU Program published in draft in October 1985 and approved in slightly revised form at the 27th CPSU Congress in early 1986, and the General Secretary's political report to the 27th CPSU Congress. The draft of the former may be found in *Pravda*, Oct. 26, 1985, while the final version appeared in *Moscow News*, no. 12, Mar. 30–Apr. 6, 1986, Supplement. Gorbachev's report to the 27th CPSU Congress was carried in *Pravda*, Feb. 25, 1986.

21. "Cooperation and Dialogue with Political Parties and Movements," *International Affairs*, (November 1988), pp. 38–39.

22. This analysis is based on data in US Arms Control and Disarmament Agency, *World Military Expenditures and Arms Transfers, 1970–1979*, (Washington, DC, 1982).

23. US Central Intelligence Agency (hereafter, CIA), *Communist Aid to the Less Developed Countries of the Free World, 1976* (hereafter, *Communist Aid, 1976*), ER

77-10296, (Washington, DC, August 1977), p. 4; and *Communist Aid Activities in Non-Communist Less Developed Countries, 1979 and 1954–79* (hereafter, *Communist Aid, 1954–79*), ER 80-10318U (Washington, DC, October 1980), p. 15.

24.   These figures were arrived at by the author from information in *Communist Aid, 1976;* CIA, *Communist Aid to Less Developed Countries of the Free World, 1977* (hereafter, *Communist Aid, 1977*), ER 78-10478U (Washington, DC, November 1978); *Communist Aid Activities in Non-Communist Less Developed Countries, 1978* (hereafter, *Communist Aid, 1978*), ER 79-10412U (Washington, DC, September 1979); and *Communist Aid, 1954–79;* plus Carol Fogarty and Kevin Tritle, "Moscow's Economic Aid Programs in Less-Developed Countries: A Perspective on the 1980's," in *Gorbachev's Economic Plans,* Study Paper Submitted to the Joint Economic Committee, US Congress (Washington, DC: US Government Printing Office, 1987), Vol 2, pp. 537–38.

25.   *Communist Aid, 1977,* p. 7, and *Communist Aid, 1954–79,* p. 21.

26.   See, for example, Brutents, *Osvobodivshiyesya strany v 70-e gody,* pp. 142–43; C. P. Nemanov, "Parties of the Vanguard Type in African Countries of Socialist Orientation," *Narody Azii i Afriki,* no. 2 (1979), p. 27; B. Ponomarev, "The Joint Struggle of the Workers' and National Liberation Movements against Imperialism, for Social Progress," *Kommunist,* no. 16 (November 1980), pp. 42–43; William F. Robinson, "Eastern Europe's Presence in Black Africa," in Radio-Free Europe-Radio Liberty, *Radio Free Europe Research* (Munich), Background Report no. 142 (June 21, 1979), p. 4; Henry S. Bradsher, *Afghanistan and the Soviet Union,* (Durham, NC: Duke University Press, 1983), pp. 96, 102–04; Norman Cigar, "South Yemen and the USSR: Prospects for the Relationship," *The Middle East Journal* (Washington, DC) (Autumn 1985), pp. 780–81.

27.   On these various activities, see, for instance, Morris Rothenberg, *The USSR and Africa: New Dimensions of Soviet Global Power* (Washington, DC: Advanced International Studies Institute, 1980), pp. 137–47; William M. LeoGrande, *Cuba's Policy in Africa, 1959–1980)* (Berkeley, University of California Press, 1980), pp. 37–45; J. B. Kelly, "The Kremlin and the Gulf," *Encounter* (London) (April 1980), pp. 87–88; Bradsher, *Afghanistan,* Chs. 5–6; *Communist Aid, 1977,* p. 3; *Communist Aid, 1954–79,* pp. 15, 35, 40; *World Military Expenditures and Arms Transfers, 1970–1979,* p. 127.

28.   Melvin Croan, "A New Afrika Korps?" *The Washington Quarterly* (Washington, DC) (Winter 1980), pp. 30–31; Mark Katz, *Russia and Arabia: Soviet Foreign Policy toward the Arabian Peninsula,* (Baltimore, MD: Johns Hopkins University Press, 1986), p. 85; Bradsher, *Afghanistan,* p. 123; Kelly, "The Kremlin," p. 87.

29.   See, for example, General Secretary Brezhnev's report to the 25th CPSU Congress, *Pravda,* Feb. 25, 1976.

30.   To explore in depth the regional differences in the nature of Soviet undertakings, compare the analyses in two works by the present author: *Soviet Policy toward Africa Revisited,* Significant Issues Series, Vol. IX, No. 6, (Washington, DC: Center for Strategic and International Studies, 1987); and "Latin America in Soviet Third World Strategy: The Political Dimension," in Eusebio Mujal-Leon, ed., *The USSR and Latin America: A Developing Relationship* (Winchester, MA: Unwin-Hyman, 1989), pp. 3–64.

31.   These statistics were put together by the author from data in US Arms Control and Disarmament Agency, *World Military Expenditures and Arms Transfers, 1987,* (Washington, DC, March 1988).

32.   This analysis derives from information in three publications of the US Department of State: *Soviet and East European Aid to the Third World, 1981* (Washington, DC, February 1983), p. 14; *Warsaw Pact Economic Aid to Non-Communist LDC's, 1984* (Washington, DC, May 1986), p. 20; *Warsaw Pact Economic Aid Programs in Non-Communist LDC's: Holding Their Own in 1986,*(Washington, DC, August 1988), p. 16.

33.   Calculated from data in *Warsaw Pact Economic Aid Programs in Non-Communist LDC's: Holding Their Own in 1986, pp. 8–9.*

724   David E. Albright

34. Based on Soviet and East European Aid to the Third World, 1981, pp. 20–21;
Warsaw Pact Economic Aid to Non-Communist LDC's, 1984, p. 16; Warsaw Pact
Economic Aid Programs In Non-Communist LDC's: Holding Their Own in 1986, p.12.

35. These figures were arrived at by the author from information in Warsaw Pact
Economic Aid Programs in Non-Communist LDC's: Holding Their Own in 1986, pp. 8–9;
World Military Expenditures and Arms Transfers, 1987.

36. See the references cited in notes 32 and 34.

37. For the data upon which the 1980–84 analysis is based, see Fogarty and Tritle,
"Moscow's Economic Aid," pp. 537–38.

38. For more detailed discussion, see Albright, Soviet Policy toward Africa Revisited, pp. 38–40.

39. Warsaw Pact Economic Aid Programs in Non-Communist LDC's: Holding Their
Own in 1986, p. 8.

40. World Military Expenditures and Arms Transfers, 1987, p. 127.

41. See, for instance, Katz, Russia and Arabia, Ch. 1.

42. Fogarty and Tritle, "Moscow's Economic Aid," p. 538; Communist Aid, 1976,
p. 13; Communist Aid, 1978, p. 10; and Katz, Russia and Arabia, Ch. 1.

43. Soviet and East European Aid to the Third World, 1981, p. 21; and Warsaw Pact
Economic Aid Programs in Non-Communist LDC's: Holding Their Own in 1986, p. 12.

44. World Military Expenditures and Arms Transfers, 1987, p. 130.

45. Communist Aid, 1954–79, p. 15; Soviet and East European Aid to the Third
World, 1981, p. 14; and Warsaw Pact Economic Aid Programs in Non-Communist
LDC's: Holding Their Own in 1986, pp. 8–9.

46. Details with respect to South America may be found in Albright, "Latin America
in Soviet Third World Strategy.

47. For more extended treatment of these various developments, see Albright, Soviet
Policy toward Africa Revisited, pp. 29–30.

48. On Zaire and Jordan, see ibid., pp. 31–32; and Melvin A. Goodman and Carolyn
McGiffert Ekedahl, "Gorbachev's 'New Directions' in the Middle East," The Middle
East Journal (Autumn 1988), pp. 571–86.

49. The statistics on trade turnover here were calculated by the author in light of
information in International Monetary Fund, Direction of Trade Statistics Yearbook for
1981, pp. 387–88, and for 1988, pp. 399–400.

50. Data on the economic performances of Third World states, as measured by the
growth of gross national product (GNP) per capita during 1975–85, appear in World
Military Expenditures and Arms Transfers, 1987. The figures on commercial exchanges
were arrived at by the author on the basis of information in Direction of Trade Statistics
Yearbook for 1981, pp. 387–88, and for 1988, pp. 399–400.

51. See the chapters by David E. Albright on the USSR and Africa in the annual
volumes of Colin Legum, ed., Africa Contemporary Record (London, Holmes and
Meier), for 1981–85; and David Pollock, "Moscow and Aden: Coping with a Coup,"
Problems of Communism (May–June 1986), pp. 50–70.

52. See the entries for Angola, Ethiopia, and Mozambique in the yearly editions for
the 1980's of The Military Balance (London: International Institute for Strategic Studies);
on the PDRY, see Pollock, "Moscow and Aden," p. 52; on Nicaragua, US Department
of State and Department of Defense, The Soviet-Cuban Connection in Central America
and the Caribbean (Washington, DC, March 1985), pp. 25–27; and on Afghanistan,
Zalmay Khalilzad, "Moscow's Afghan War," Problems of Communism (January–
February 1986), pp. 7–8.

53. On these various activities, see The Military Balance, 1987–1988, pp. 120, 123,
126, 129, 133; Warsaw Pact Economic Aid Programs in Non-Communist LDC's: Holding
Their Own in 1986, p. 16; The Soviet-Cuban Connection in Central America and the
Caribbean, p. 25; Khalilzad, "Moscow's Agfhan War," p. 2; and World Military
Expenditures and Arms Transfers, 1987.

54. See the texts of the agreements in *The New York Times,* Dec. 23, 1988.

55. This analysis is based on information in *World Military Expenditures and Arms Transfers, 1987,* pp. 127–30.

56. For details, see David E. Albright, "The USSR and Africa in 1984: Trials of an Aspiring Global Power," in Legum, ed., *Africa Contemporary Record 1984–85,* pp. 253–57.

57. Guatemala City Radio-Television in Spanish, Feb. 27, 1987, in Foreign Broadcast Information Service, *Daily Report: Latin America* (Washington, DC—hereafter, *FBIS-LAT*), Mar. 2, 1987, pp. P/2–3.

58. For more extensive treatment of this subject in a specific regional setting, see Elizabeth Valkenier, "Soviet Economic Strategy in Latin America," in Mujal-Leon, *USSR and Latin America,* pp. 65–89.

59. *World Military Expenditures and Arms Transfers, 1987,* pp. 127–30; *Warsaw Pact Economic Aid Programs in Non-Communist LDC's: Holding Their Own in 1986,* pp. 8–9.

60. These statistics were derived by the author from information in *Direction of Trade Statistics Yearbook 1988,* pp. 399–400.

61. *World Military Expenditures and Arms Transfer, 1987,* pp. 57, 70, 80.

62. Derived from data in *Direction of Trade Statistics Yearbook* for 1981, p. 388, and for 1988, pp. 399–400.

63. *World Military Expenditures and Arms Transfers, 1987,* p. 129.

64. Middle East News Agency (Cairo) in Arabic, Aug. 23, 1984, trans. in Foreign Broadcast Information Service, *Daily Report: Middle East and Africa* (Washington, DC), Aug. 24, 1984, p. D/1.

65. *Al-lttihad* (Abu Dhabi), May 31, 1986, pp. 1, 9.

66. See, for example, *World Military Expenditures and Arms Transfers, 1987,* pp. 127–30; *Soviet and East European Aid to the Third World, 1981,* p.14; *Warsaw Pact Economic Aid to Non-Communist LDC's, 1984,* p. 20; and *Warsaw Pact Economic Aid Programs in Non-Communist LDC's: Holding Their Own in 1986,* p.16.

67. Speech at a dinner in Moscow for President Samora Machel of Mozambique, as reported by TASS over Radio Moscow in English, Mar. 31, 1986, in *FBIS-SOV,* Apr. 1, 1986, pp. J/3–6.

68. ON the USSR's role in the undertakings after late 1987, see, for instance, *The New York Times,* June 6, 1988.

69. This step took place at a meeting of a Somali official and USSR Foreign Minister Shevardnadze in the Yemen Arab Republic. See *Indian Ocean Newsletter* (Paris), Oct. 18, 1986.

70. The text is in *Pravda,* July 29, 1986.

71. For the agreement, see *The New York Times,* Apr. 15, 1988.

72. See the press conference of the newly arrived Soviet ambassador to Nicaragua, as reported by Radio Belgrade, TANJUG in English, Nov. 5, 1988, in *FBIS-SOV,* Nov. 8, 1988, p. 35; Gorbachev's speech to the National Assembly in Havana, Cuba, on Apr. 4, 1989, as carried by Havana Domestic Radio and Television Services on Apr. 4, 1989, trans. in *FBIS-LAT,* Apr. 6, 1989, pp. 7–13, esp. p. 12.

73. For typical discussion of this cooperation, see *The New York Times,* June 6, 1988, and Jan. 28, 1989.

74. A revealing account of Soviet activities may be found in Z. Kadymbekov's dispatch in *Izvestiya* (Moscow), Sept. 6, 1985.

75. For more extended treatment of these points, see Roderic Lyne, "Making Waves: Gorbachev's Public Diplomacy, 1985–86," in Robbin F. Laird ed., *Soviet Foreign Policy,* New York, Academy of Political Science, 1987, pp. 235–53.

76. As already noted, Ponomarev, the head of the department, and Ul'yanovskiy, a deputy chief, subscribed to the "revolutionary-democratic" outlook; Brutents, a deputy director, to the "national-capitalism" viewpoint; and Zagladin, the first deputy chief, to

the "economic-interdependence" perspective. For elaboration, see David E. Albright, "The CPSU International Department and the Third World in the Gorbachev Era," in Donald Graves, ed., *The CPSU International Department and Soviet Foreign Policy*, Washington, DC, Center for Foreign Policy Development, forthcoming.

77. Vladmir Lee and Georgy Mirsky, "Socialist Orientation and New Political Thinking," *Asia and Africa Today* (Moscow), July-August 1988, pp. 64–70.

78. See his speech to the staff of the Ministry of Foreign Affairs in *Vestnik Ministerstva Inostrannykh Del, SSSR* (Moscow), Aug. 5, 1987, and his *Perestroika: New Thinking for Our Country and the World*, pp. 139–40. 174, 177–78, 188–89.

79. As pointed out previously, Yakovlev, Politburo member and head of the CPSU International Policy Commission, adheres to the "national-capitalism" school, while Shevardnadze, a Politburo member and minister of foreign affairs, identifies with the "economic-interdependence" school.

80. The writings of Ul'yanovskiy, one of the prime architects of the "revolutionary-democratic" viewpoint, are indicative. Before the appearance of his article "On National and Revolutionary Democracy: Paths of Evolution" in 1984, he had never attacked "revolutionary democrats" in any severe fashion, but in this article he took them to task for a variety of failings, even though he continued to insist that the Third World was going through a protracted process of by-passing capitalism. All of his subsequent publications have been in the same vein.

81. The most expansive statement to date of this vision of policy may be found in Alexey Izyumov and Andrei Kortunov, "The Soviet Union in the Changing World," *International Affairs*, August 1988, esp. pp. 51–56.

82. See the account by Deputy Foreign Minister Leonid Il'ichev of the deliberations of a section on "Policy Toward Developing Countries and Regional Conflicts" at this conference, in ibid., October 1988, pp. 49–50.

33
Moscow's U.N. Policy*

Thomas G. Weiss and Meryl A. Kessler

At the height of the Vietnam War, some disillusioned Americans called for a greater United Nations role in Indochina and in the management of conflicts elsewhere. Hubert Humphrey, during his 1968 presidential campaign, attempted to build upon this mood. He called for a more activist U.N., promising that under his presidency the United States would utilize the U.N. more fully as a tool for managing conflicts. Thus, out of despair over the failure of American unilateralism emerged a desire for a more multilateral approach to foreign policy.

If history repeats itself, it does so with a sense of irony. Two decades later, the U.N. is again being invoked as a remedy for the ills of unilateralism. This time, however, the sentiment emanates not from a dissatisfied American electorate, but rather from a frustrated Soviet leadership. Much as did the American experience in Vietnam, Moscow's counterinsurgency in Afghanistan revealed the pitfalls of unilateral superpower intervention. The Soviet Union has learned firsthand the dangers of military overextension, particularly because of serious economic crises at home and in Eastern Europe. As a result, the Kremlin has become perhaps the most active and vocal advocate for a more dynamic United Nations.

This new Soviet attitude departs radically from previous Soviet positions. From the 1960s until the mid-1980s, Moscow viewed the world body as little more than a convenient platform from which to take rhetorical shots at American and Western policy, thereby forging a convenient solidarity with the Third World. In contrast, the Soviets are now treating the U.N. as a workable and desirable mechanism for combating difficult global problems. Recent Soviet public statements have proposed a wide array of measures to increase U.N. activities in international peace and security and also in the economic, social, and environmental spheres.

For Americans accustomed to a far less cooperative USSR, the problem has now become how to interpret this multilateral "new thinking." The question is

*Reprinted by permission of the authors and publisher from *Foreign Policy* 79 (Summer 1990). Copyright © 1990 by the Carnegie Endowment for International Peace.

whether Moscow's recent statements can be taken seriously, or whether they are simply empty slogans aimed at generating favorable world opinion. Even if one assumes a genuine Soviet commitment toward strengthening the U.N., other questions remain: What is the extent of that commitment? After so many years of emphasizing the sovereign rights of states, how much of its own sovereignty is the USSR actually prepared to cede to world organizations? To what extent does Moscow's new approach to the U.N. signal a retreat from unilateralism, and possibly even from the world political stage? Ultimately, how should Washington respond to Moscow's new love affair with the U.N.?

When Humphrey advocated a larger role for the United Nations two decades ago, he clearly did not believe that it should occur at the expense of U.S. power and prestige. A stronger and more active U.N. was not related to an American retreat from the world stage. Rather, Humphrey was suggesting that the United States would be able to extend its influence through a strengthened United Nations.

In much the same way, recent Soviet statements and actions indicate that while Moscow appears committed to reenergizing the U.N., it does not intend to relinquish power and retreat into isolationism. Rather, Moscow has sent clear signals that it hopes to remain an important force in international politics through its participation in a reinvigorated United Nations. For the Soviets today, as for Humphrey two decades ago, the U.N. is emerging as a less costly and more legitimate way to influence world events.

A central question for the West is whether Moscow's recent statements are credible. One way to distinguish a state's genuine policy goals from empty rhetoric is to compare what it says and what it actually does. A comparison of Soviet words and deeds at the United Nations during the 1960s, 1970s, and early 1980s reveals an enormous discrepancy. Although Soviet diplomats referred to themselves as "the leading force" or most "dynamic factor" at the U.N., they actually tended to resist most measures that would have given the organization any real independence or authority. While paying lip service to multinational ideals and lobbying regularly for disarmament and development, the Soviets attempted to limit the scope of the U.N.'s activities by advocating strict limits on the growth of its budget. Although the Soviets routinely scored rhetorical points against such international pariahs as Israel and South Africa, they conveniently refused to provide significant aid or trade benefits to developing countries through the U.N., arguing that socialist countries were not responsible for the aftermath of colonialism.

Moreover, Moscow's personnel policies discouraged Soviets from developing any sense of loyalty to the organization. According to most observers, including Arkady Shevchenko, who defected to the United States in 1978 while serving as U.N. undersecretary general for political and Security Council affairs, Soviets assigned to the U.N. Secretariat and other U.N. bodies during this period acted primarily as Moscow's agents, not as international civil servants. The Kremlin had always systematically rejected the principles of independence and objectivity developed for employees of the League of Nations and reincarnated in the U.N. Charter and personnel statutes. Soviets were not supposed to serve the international community, but rather to maintain close ties to both the Soviet Ministry of Foreign Affairs and the local Soviet mission. They mostly lived within Soviet compounds in U.N. cities and were obliged to sign over a hefty portion of the dollars from their U.N. paychecks to their government. For the most part, Soviet personnel were restricted to limited-term assignments within U.N. organizations before returning to the Soviet bureaucracy. In contrast to about two-thirds of U.N. employees generally, very few of the Soviets working within the U.N. system had permanent contracts. These policies were designed to prevent the development of any strong nonnational ties and to keep Soviet citizens on a short leash.

In addition to the highly questionable commitment of staff to the United Nations, the Soviet leadership was unwilling to participate in and endorse a wide variety of U.N. activities. Perhaps most notable was Moscow's almost systematic resistance to peacekeeping and its repeated refusal either to pay its obligatory assessments or to offer voluntary contributions. Although the Soviet Union's financial record was somewhat better in terms of the U.N.'s social and economic activities, most of its contributions were made in nonconvertible rubles. It is also worth noting that during this period the Soviets belonged to relatively few of the U.N.'s specialized agencies, which deal with scientific, technical, and economic issues. By the early 1980s Britain, France, the United States, and China belonged to all 15 of the U.N.'s specializes agencied; the Soviet Union belonged to only 9. Even compared to communist countries of Eastern Europe the Soviets belonged to few of these organizations: Only East Germany and Albania belonged to fewer.

NEW SOVIET RESPONSE

In contrast to the earlier discrepancies between Soviet words and deeds at the United Nations, the years since Mikhail Gorbachev's rise to power have witnessed a gradual but undeniable narrowing of the gap. Under the guidance of Deputy Foreign Minister Vladimir Petrovsky—who earlier served in the U.N. Secretariat and as head of the International Organization Department in the Ministry of Foreign Affairs—Moscow has supplemented many of its lofty platitudes about the U.N. with concrete action. Particularly over the past two years, this new approach to the U.N. has resulted in important changes in the Soviet government's stance on personnel policy, peacekeeping, economic activities, and a wide variety of other U.N.-related issues.

In terms of personnel policy, Moscow has taken significant steps to increase the independence of Soviets employed by the U.N. The first gesture in this direction occurred in 1987 when, for the first time, the Kremlin allowed large numbers of Soviet nationals in U.N. service to live in their own apartments outside the central Soviet diplomatic complex. Petrovsky announced the following year that Moscow would also allow Soviet nationals to sign long-term contracts with the U.N., thereby enabling them to function more effectively as international civil servants. This change in policy met at least one of the Reagan administration's prerequisites for resumption of U.S. funding for the U.N., which Washington began withholding in 1986 in an attempt to force organizational and budgetary changes.

While these alterations in Soviet personnel policy are important, they have been largely overshadowed by even more significant developments in Moscow's approach to U.N. peacekeeping. Since 1987 the Soviet leadership has both said and done a number of things to suggest that it is treating this issue with seriousness and commitment. The Soviets have put aside their earlier vague statements about a "comprehensive system of international security" and have instead put forward a number of specific proposals. Beginning with Gorbachev's highly publicized September 1987 *Pravda* article (reportedly drafted by Petrovsky), the Soviet leadership began to focus on peacekeeping as a worthwhile mechanism for "disengaging the troops of warring sides and observing cease fires and armistice agreements."

Starting with the 43d session of the U.N. General Assembly, the Soviets fleshed out this position, putting forward a wide range of proposals aimed at making the existing peacekeeping regime more solvent, more politically active, and geared toward preventive diplomacy. Moscow, for example, has expressed its willingness to consider a variety of financing schemes in order to rectify the U.N.'s chronic funding difficulties. The Soviets have been pressing vigorously for an expanded U.N. role in conflict resolution and mediation among belligerents. Finally, the Soviet delegation has put forward a number of proposals for both preventing and settling conflicts. Moscow has advocated some of these ideas in the past, such as the revival of the moribund Military Staff Committee and the establishment of a U.N. military reserve. But Soviet proposals also include some provocative new ones, including the establishment of U.N. observation posts in explosive areas, the deployment of a U.N. naval force to patrol the Persian Gulf, and the stationing of U.N. forces along the border of any country that seeks to protect itself from outside interference.

The Soviets have also taken significant steps to reinforce these words with deeds. In 1988–89 they actively supported the establishment of five new peacekeeping operations in various troubled regions, including U.N. military observers to oversee the withdrawal of the Red Army from Afghanistan and Cuban combat troops from Angola, U.N. truce monitors astride the Iran-Iraq border, and the military forces and civilians in both the U.N. Transition Assistance Group in Namibia and the U.N. Observer Group in Central America. In addition, Moscow has actively engaged in behind-the-scenes diplomacy in southern Africa and Southeast Asia. Vladillen Vasev, head of the East and southern Africa section of the Ministry of Foreign Affairs, played a critical role in preventing Angolan and Cuban walkouts during the 1988 negotiations. The Soviets persuaded Cambodia and Vietnam to move closer to the negotiating table and recently joined with other permanent Security Council members in a plan to end the 20-year Cambodian conflict by having the United Nations administer the country and supervise elections, while U.N. peacekeepers ensure security.

As an apparent sign of their goodwill and in an effort to appease Western skeptics, the Soviets have reduced, with scarce hard currency, their outstanding debts for ongoing peacekeeping operations from about $200 million to $125 million and have committed themselves to repaying the remainder over the next three years. These payments contrast with Moscow's earlier practice of using a narrow conception of Soviet interests to determine whether to fund such activities. As such, these payments are particularly noteworthy because they symbolize the Kremlin's recent across-the-board endorsement of peacekeeping.

As for the U.N.'s technical and economic activities, the last few years have also witnessed important changes in Moscow's behavior. Whereas Soviet officials previously referred to technical organizations of the U.N. system as "arenas of conflict," Soviets now appear to view them as useful means of international regulation and coordination. Not only has Moscow considerably toned down its anti-Western rhetoric within these organizations, it has also demonstrated a far more forthcoming attitude. In the wake of two international public relations disasters—the shooting down of Korean Airlines flight 007 and the fire in the Chernobyl reactor—the Soviets cooperated extensively with the International Civil Aviation Organization and the International Atomic Energy Agency. Also, in yet another policy reversal, Moscow has ratified and paid its assessment to support the Common Fund of the United Nations Conference on Trade and Development to help stabilize world commodity prices.

In sum, the Soviet Union appears to have passed this somewhat crude credibility test: Not only has Moscow recently seized the high ground at the U.N. with some very forward-looking and provocative statements, but it has also followed up with meaningful actions. The Soviets now appear willing to say and do much of what is necessary to enable the United Nations to address pressing global problems.

By reading recent Soviet literature and speeches on the United Nations, one could easily come away with the impression that Soviet leaders and their senior advisers have been converted to world federalism. For example, in March 1988 Gorbachev adviser Georgi Shakhnazarov wrote a striking article optimistically appraising the possibility of "world government." Gorbachev and Foreign Minister Eduard Shevardnadze themselves liberally pepper their speeches with references to "interdependence"—a prominent concept in Western social science since the 1970s but until only recently anathema in the Soviet Union. Rather than stressing inevitable clashes between systems, Moscow now emphasizes the "balance of interests." Along these same lines, both Gorbachev and Shevardnadze have called repeatedly for a larger role for "the rule of law" in international affairs as well as an expansion of the compulsory jurisdiction of the International Court of Justice.

Given the Kremlin's long-standing antipathy toward the concepts of international law, world government, and interdependence, such statements are certainly surprising. Although globalist tendencies were present in the writings of such dissidents as the late Andrei Sakharov and some members of the Soviet scientific and scholarly community as early as the 1970s, these recent statements represent the first time such ideas have emerged in official parlance. They seem to reflect a new preoccupation with global interests, perhaps even at the expense of national interests. Indeed, one wonders whether Soviet foreign policy is being increasingly crafted by individuals schooled in *globalistika*, Russian for the study of world problems.

Contrary to the impression created by such statements, however, Moscow's new-found support for the United Nations is not based solely on idealism. As the Soviets themselves have made clear, this new attitude has not been derived from vague principles, but rather from concrete lessons of the last several years. Indeed, the central motivation for rethinking the U.N.'s role in global affairs appears to be a reassessment of the USSR's own interests and capabilities in a world in which power is increasingly diffuse. It is no coincidence that the Soviet's enthusiasm for U.N. peacekeeping has coincided with their search for a dignified means of disengagement from regional conflicts—most notably for their own troops in Afghanistan, but also for Soviet allies in southern Africa and Southeast Asia. Moscow is faced, on the one hand, with serious economic stagnation at home and, on the other, with the enormous costs and doubtful benefits of counterinsurgency in and military assistance to the Third World. The Kremlin appears anxious to reduce foreign commitments without creating a power vacuum. While this retrenchment is unlikely to entail the wholesale abandonment of such allies as Cuba and Vietnam, it does signal a new Soviet desire to avoid unpredictable and costly future entanglements in other parts of the Third World.

Greater reliance on U.N. institutions appears calculated to achieve these aims. The Soviets are able to extricate themselves abroad and cut the costs of military assistance elsewhere while using multilateral diplomacy to prevent the United States from taking advantage of this retreat. The strategy has the added benefit of preventing injury to the Soviet Union's status. In fact, increased support for and participation in U.N. peacekeeping can ultimately enhance Moscow's role as a responsible member of the international community. Such legitimacy represents an important first step toward an increased diplomatic role in Central America and the Middle East, where the United States has traditionally prevented the Soviet Union from playing a role commensurate with its superpower status.

The USSR thus is not relinquishing its ability to influence events in the Third World and has no intention of being sidelined there. Rather, judging from the content of many recent proposals, the Soviets clearly intend to remain an important force in world politics through their role in and contributions to an improved and expanded peacekeeping regime. In a 1988 aide-mémoire, Petrovsky suggested that Moscow would be willing to provide logistic support and assistance in training U.N. peacekeepers as well as volunteering its own troops for operations. Given that the superpowers have been routinely excluded from contributing troops to U.N. missions, such measures would certainly provide Moscow with a far greater say in the scope and mission of peacekeeping operations.

Another indication of Moscow's intention to remain a key international player is the emphasis it has placed on expanding the Security Council's role in the prevention and containment of regional conflicts. Gorbachev, Shevardnadze, and Petrovsky all have touched on this theme in major policy statements. Although the Soviets also supported augmented roles for the General Assembly and the U.N. Secretariat, they have stressed the primacy of the Security Council. For example, during his appearance before the General Assembly in September 1988, Shevardnadze proposed that the five permanent council members hold periodic meetings to review conflicts and that the entire council (including its 10 rotating members) convene periodically for special meetings at the foreign-minister level and in "regions of tension." As a permanent member, the Soviet Union has a vested interest in such measures which, by enlarging the Security Council's authority, also ensure a larger Soviet voice in international conflict management.

In much the same way, the Soviets have also signaled their desire to play a larger role in the U.N.'s economic, social, and environmental spheres. One of the most striking aspects of Moscow's recent pronouncements is the repeated emphasis on joining the important U.N.-related economic and scientific organizations from which it is currently excluded. As Shevardnadze repeated in his opening address to the General Assembly in September 1989, and as Gorbachev reiterated to President George Bush at the Malta summit meeting, the Soviet Union is now interested in joining the General Agreement on Tariffs and Trade (GATT), the International Monetary Fund (IMF), and the World Bank. This marks an important departure from previous Soviet policy, which vociferously denounced these organizations—and in particular the Washington-based financial institutions—as nefarious capitalist instruments.

If on the security side the Soviets are now indicating that they want to help lead, on the economic and humanitarian side they are letting it be known that they at lest want to get into the game. As Shevardnadze noted in September 1989, "the Soviet Union has programs for speeding up the integration of its economy, on an equal and mutually beneficial basis, into the world economy." While waiting for this integration, however, the Soviets have been actively trying to shape the U.N.'s agenda. Both Gorbachev and Shevardnadze repeatedly made Third World debt central to their discussions of world economic problems and have been quick to propose such far-reaching solutions as debt moratoria and forgiveness. While these are safe proposals given the Soviet Union's insignificant role as a creditor, their implementation would nonetheless require the USSR to forgive its loans to clients like Cuba, whose indebtedness to the Soviet Union is estimated to be at least $10 billion.

At the same time, the USSR has taken the lead in advocating greater U.N. attention to environmental issues. Prodded by their own serious domestic problems (such as the fouling of Siberia's Lake Baikal) and by the Chernobyl catastrophe, Moscow has been actively underscoring the importance of what Gorbachev has called "ecological security." For instance, Gorbachev suggested last year that the United Nations establish an emergency ecological assistance center and made proposals for the creation of an international space laboratory devoted exclusively to monitoring the environment. Despite the vagueness of such suggestions, the main point is that the Soviets are now identified as leading proponents of multilateral environmental cooperation.

Clearly, the Soviet Union is carving out a niche as a leader in multilateral thinking, which contrasts sharply with the previous practice of slavishly following the Third World in an attempt to gain its favor. Although the Soviets still have not completely renounced this earlier tendency, and on certain issues continue to vote with the majority, Moscow has begun to identify itself more closely with the concerns of the industrialized world; in fact, it has taken the lead in shaping the U.N. agenda for the 1990s.

ISOLATED AMERICA

Ironically, during much of the period that Moscow was busy discovering the United Nations, Washington was abandoning it. During President Ronald Reagan's two terms, official American support for the U.N. reached an all-time low. Believing—at times correctly—that U.N. goals contradicted its own, the Reagan administration withdrew or threatened to withdraw from a number of U.N. agencies, stepped up the use of its veto in the Security Council, and refused to pay its dues. After more than three decades of legitimately reprimanding the USSR for its lack of cooperation and fiscal responsibility, the United States became the U.N.'s leading foot-dragger and debtor. Instead of paying at least 20 per cent of the regular budget and 30 per cent of the peacekeeping bills as it had previously, Washington has yet to make good on Reagan's promise to reimburse what now amounts to more than $500 million in back or overdue payments, more than half of the total arrears owed to the U.N.

During most of the Reagan years, Washington seldom endorsed multilateral approaches to security, and only when its supposedly served U.S. interests. It resisted U.N. involvement in regions considered to be part of the American sphere of influence and where it would conflict with U.S. goals. Therefore, the Reagan administration welcomed U.N. mediation of the Soviet embarrassment in Afghanistan, at the end of the Iran-Iraq conflict, and also in Namibia, where the process had been underway since 1978. But the United States systematically resisted greater U.N. involvement in Central America and in the Arab-Israeli conflict, except for peacekeeping operations in the latter. At the same time, Washington practiced aggressive unilateralism, intervening in Grenada and bombing Libya as well as financing insurgents in Afghanistan, Angola, Cambodia, and Nicaragua.

This highly selective approach contrasted sharply with growing Soviet acceptance of U.N. peacekeeping in Third World hot spots. While it was inconceivable that the United States would have asked the U.N. to help extricate U.S. forces from Vietnam, the USSR actively sought U.N. involvement in settling conflicts in Afghanistan and Angola and pressed its Vietnamese client to negotiate an end to the war in Cambodia. Such practices demonstrate the Soviet's willingness to allow the U.N. to play a major role in settling not only peripheral disputes but also those in which they and their allies are directly involved.

The new Soviet approach to the United Nations has posed an unexpected challenge to Washington. Having relinquished its leadership role, the United States must now come to terms with the Soviet Union's far-reaching initiatives. For the Bush administration, which views the U.N. in a more favorable light than did its predecessor, this challenge may actually represent a much-needed opportunity to examine its own approach to multilateralism.

As a first step, Washington should recognize that Moscow's desire for a leading role in an enhanced United Nations is not a threat; rather, it represents an opportunity to work together on difficult global problems. While the USSR is certainly seeking a more prominent role in the organization, evidence suggests that it does not wish to achieve this goal at the expense of the United States. In fact, many Soviet initiatives reflect a belated return to the original logic behind the U.N. Charter, namely great-power solidarity. By all indications, the new Soviet approach seems to be premised on the assumption that the U.N.'s machinery can be revitalized only if both superpowers throw their weight behind it—and Moscow's recent proposals are clearly designed to entice Washington to cooperate.

Some of Moscow's new ideas about peacekeeping, such as those concerning training and finance, bear a striking resemblance to earlier U.S. suggestions. Others, such as a proposal to enlarge the scope of the secretary-general's autonomy, clearly reflect constructive shifts in earlier Soviet positions. Such concilitary gestures—combined with the positive mediating role the Soviets have already played—should help convince the Bush administration that the Soviets are not embracing peacekeeping as a means to pursue unilateral advantages in the Third World. Rather the USSR seeks to contain and prevent conflicts there, to pare military expenditures, and to prevent a negative spill over of regional conflicts into the East-West relationship.

While recognizing the opportunity for Soviet collaboration on mutually shared problems, the Bush administration at the same time should base its response on a critical evaluation of the recent Soviet proposals as well as on the strengths and weaknesses of the U.N. itself. With the enthusiasm of a recent convert, Moscow has produced an enormous number of proposals for reviving the United Nations. While a good many of these—such as improving the financial mechanism for peacekeeping and creating an elite, reserve peacekeeping force—are worthy of

serious consideration, others reflect a certain political naiveté by seeming to
ignore some of the U.N.'s inherent limitations. The proposal to station peacekeeping teams on the border of any country that requests them, for example,
violates the principle of neutrality underlying peacekeeping by placing the "blue
helmets" in a position where they might be drawn into fighting. The immediate
task for the Bush administration is therefore to sort through the dizzying array of
Soviet proposals, identifying those areas in which Soviet-American collaboration
under the auspices of the U.N. would be both feasible and desirable.

Members of the Bush administration first have to overcome many of their
underlying prejudices about international organizations. As the first U.S. president with direct experience as U.N. ambassador (1971–73), Bush knows first-
hand about the organization's weaknesses. Secretary of State James Baker, from
his experience as Treasury secretary during the last administration, is also
familiar with the shortcomings of international economic institutions operating
under U.N. auspices. To what extent they will be able to put aside these
preconceptions and think creatively about the potential strengths of multilateralism in a dramatically altered East-West context remains to be seen.

Thus far, the administration's record, though better than its predecessor's, is
mixed. On the one hand, aside from some warm words about the U.N. from U.S.
Ambassador Thomas Pickering and a White House dinner invitation to U.N.
Secretary-General Javier Pérez de Cuéllar after the Bush inauguration, the
administration offered no substantive responses to the Soviets' U.N. initiatives in
its first 15 months. Significantly, the president missed a historic occasion in his
September 1989 keynote address to the General Assembly either to react to
Moscow's proposals or to put forward a vision of his own. And despite U.N.
compliance with Washington's request that it trim its bloated bureaucracy, the
administration also has been unsuccessful in persuading Congress to release
funds for repayment of outstanding debts owed to the organization. In fact, in
1989 the Senate voted to cut $123 million from the president's request for
funding repayment of these debts. In addition, the administration has opposed a
U.S. return to the United Nations Educational, Cultural and Scientific Organization, from which the Reagan administration withdrew.

On the other hand, as recent developments suggest, the administration seems
to have begun to recognize some of the opportunities for superpower cooperation
created by the Soviets' new thinking about the U.N. Reversing previous policy,
the United States joined the Soviet Union and all other members of the Security
Council in November 1989 in authorizing unarmed military observers for Central
America. Their initial mission was to monitor the commitment by Central
American governments to stop aiding insurgents, while civilians from the U.N.
and the Organization of American States (OAS) monitored February's
Nicaraguan elections. Violeta Chamorro's election victory over the Sandinistas
set the stage for the Security Council's March 1990 endorsement of the second
stage of the operation. Some 800 lightly armed U.N. soldiers are to collect the
weapons of the *contras* in Honduras or in enclaves inside Nicaragua, while

another U.N. and OAS civilian group supervises the eventual repatriation and relocation of the rebels. These first U.N. peacekeepers in the Western Hemisphere are a concrete illustration of how the superpower can work together in regional security matters.

These decisions were preceded by two other firsts in U.N. history. In November 1989, for the first time in 44 years, the superpowers cosponsored a General Assembly resolution aimed at reinforcing the work of the organization; then they held a joint press conference to introduce their text. This cooperation was consistent with the Soviet Union's growing openness to multilateralism and was a visible and encouraging indication of the Bush administration's realization of the U.N.'s role in global problem solving.

However, it is still too early to tell whether these latest developments are harbingers of a new era of superpower collaboration at the United Nations. As demonstrated by Washington's December 1989 threat to cut off future funding during the General Assembly dispute over the status of the Palestine Liberation Organization, U.S. domestic politics could still detail the administration from a more multilateral track. Moreover, "Operation Just Cause" in Panama indicated subsequently that Washington still sees unilateral armed intervention as a viable tool of U.S. foreign policy. Indeed, Washington's continued use of financial intimidation at the U.N. and of military force in Panama suggest that it still has not fully recognized the critical contributions international institutions can make as the Cold War ends and gives way to a more multipolar world.

A MULTILATERAL PEACE DIVIDEND

The waning of the Cold War provides an unparalleled opportunity for superpower cooperation at the U.N. During the U.N.'s first four decades, the stark differences between the superpowers closely circumscribed the scope of its action in regional conflicts and contributed to the invective that characterized many activities and discussions in the economic, social, and environmental fields. Many U.N. activities amounted to, in former U.N. Undersecretary General Sir Brian Urquhart's words, "tiptoeing around the Cold War." In contrast, the Cold War's thawing allows the superpowers to address common, pressing problems in a less-politicized atmosphere. Diminished tensions raise the possibility that the U.N. may be able to function more along the lines that its founders intended—a point that even some of the U.N.'s most trenchant critics have conceded. As former U.S. ambassador to the United Nations Jeane Kirkpatrick wrote in December 1988, "One peace dividend of the Cold War's end may be a more effective United Nations."

Now is the most propitious time since the end of World War II to expand multilateralism. Both international and domestic support for multilateral activities appears to be running high. The Nobel Committee's decision to award its 1988 Peace Prize to 40 years of peacekeeping efforts by some 500,000 U.N.

soldiers symbolizes the high regard of the international community. As for U.S. public opinion, recent surveys indicate that by a three-to-one margin Americans would prefer U.N. troops, not U.S. forces, to intervene in Third World conflicts; by a four-to-one margin they believe that all U.N. member states, including the United States, should provide more tax money for U.N. efforts to keep the peace.

But more than just providing an opportunity, the impending end of the Cold War provides a reason for Washington to consider more seriously joining with the Soviets to strengthen the U.N. As the postwar bipolar coalitions break down and the world moves toward greater multipolarity, the United States is likely to see its ability to control events unilaterally eroded substantially. At the same time, this diffusion of power is likely to stimulate the emergence of regional superpowers whose interests may differ from those of Washington. Accordingly, U.S. national interests now may be better served by giving up some prerogatives to act unilaterally in order to secure the commitment of emerging powers to participate in future multilateral approaches to international relations.

In this context, it is crucial for the Bush administration to build immediately upon the momentum from recent successes in the realm of what is usually labeled the "high politics" of international security (such as peacekeeping and peace-making) and then to proceed to work for similar success in the realm of "low politics" (such as development and the environment). During the Cold War, functionalists argued the contrary—namely, that in order to foster multilateral-ism it was better to avoid actions in the security area and concentrate on the U.N.'s relatively noncontroversial humanitarian and developmental activities. Now that bilateral superpower relations are improving and the U.N. is earning praise worldwide as a mechanism for mitigating violence, it is essential to consolidate and expand the peacekeeping regime so that this success can them spill into the economic, social, and environmental agencies.

Whether or not this happens depends in large part on Washington's response to Moscow's "new thinking" at the U.N. Although it is true that the United Nations cannot operate supported solely by an entente between the United States and the USSR, it is equally true that the U.N. cannot realize its potential, or even function effectively, without U.S.-Soviet cooperation. If Washington is to seize the full potential of this opportunity, it will have to overcome its traditional antipathy toward proposals originating from Moscow and begin to treat the Soviet Union as a real partner.

In the security realm, the Bush administration should think more carefully about possible areas in which coordinated superpower activities might help implement peacekeeping operations. For example, as noted earlier, the USSR is now prepared to assist in training peacekeepers. A U.S. offer to join in such activities would make a good deal of sense, particularly since Washington itself has stressed the necessity of improving the quality of U.N. soldiers. Superpower cooperation also would be both feasible and desirable in expanding the provision of logistics and intelligence to U.N. peacekeeping and accompanying humanitarian relief operations. While the superpowers' direct military involvement in such activities must for a time necessarily be curtailed, Soviets and Americans can nonetheless play an important supporting role, which would serve well their respective national interests. For the United States, a more visible supporting role would go a long way toward reversing the international community's perception of American antagonism toward the United Nations. For the Soviet Union, which has a limited capacity to contribute funds for U.N. activities, such efforts would afford an opportunity for contributions in kind.

The late U.N. Secretary-General Dag Hammarskjöld aptly described the invention of peacekeeping as "Chapter six-and-a-half." While described nowhere in the U.N. Charter, it falls between the chapters dealing with the peaceful settlement of disputes and with enforcement. Now, with a decrease in Cold War tensions, Washington could collaborate with Moscow in moving toward "Chapter six-and-three-quarters." Increased superpower cooperation would mean a more effective and dynamic U.N. presence in stopping and helping to resolve Third World disputes. It also could mean that at the turn of the century, the U.N. would be in a position to extend its activities to combating illicit drugs and terrorism, delivering humanitarian assistance in civil wars, and verifying more arms control agreements and domestic elections.

As for the economic realm, there is little hope for cooperation between the superpowers until the United States allows the Soviet Union to become a full-fledged actor in global economic affairs. Bush took a notable first step in this direction at the Malta summit when he agreed to support Soviet observer status in GATT. Another important development at Malta involved steps toward ending trade restrictions against the Soviet Union. Since the 1950s, the Soviet Union has been denied most-favored-nation status by the United States. And since 1974, the Jackson-Vanik amendment has linked Moscow's tariff status to the elimination of its restrictions on emigration. Washington now has offered to eliminate punitively high tariffs (up to 10 times the normal rates) after the Supreme Soviet adopts more liberal emigration laws. The United States should follow up by supporting immediate Soviet observer status in the IMF and the World Bank, leading toward full membership once the Soviets have undertaken necessary economic reforms.

At their joint November 1989 press conference, the U.S. and Soviet government representatives declared: "Perhaps the most important thing about this resolution is not its specific language but what it symbolizes as a new beginning at the United Nations." If a new era is really on its way, it can only arrive with the help of the United States. American interests and the credibility of the United States as a leader in world affairs would be enhanced by joining the Soviet Union in taking the lead at the United Nations.

VII
Retrospect and Prospect

34

The Gorbachev Revolution: A Waning of Soviet Expansionism?*

Jack Snyder

Many Americans have long believed that Soviet expansionism stems from pathological Soviet domestic institutions, and that the expansionist impulse will diminish only when those institutions undergo a fundamental change.[1] The Gorbachev revolution in Soviet domestic and foreign policy has raised the question of whether that time is close at hand. At home, Mikhail Gorbachev, General Secretary of the Communist Party of the Soviet Union, has attacked many of the old Stalinist institutions as obsolete and self-serving, while promoting greater freedom of expression, contested elections at local levels, and an increased role for market mechanisms in the Soviet economy.[2] Abroad, Gorbachev has made some substantial concessions from former Soviet positions, especially in accepting the Reagan Administration's "zero option" as the basis for an agreement on Intermediate-Range Nuclear Forces (INF). In a more fundamental departure, he has also proposed to restructure NATO and Warsaw Pact conventional force postures and operational doctrines along strictly defensive lines.[3]

In assessing these developments, I will address the following questions. First, how fundamental and permanent are Gorbachev's domestic changes, and why are they occurring? Second, how new and how permanent is the "new thinking" in Soviet foreign policy? Is it just a dressed-up version of former General Secretary Leonid Brezhnev's approach to détente, which America found so unsatisfactory? Is it simply a tactic to buy time until Russia can regain its competitive strength? Or is it a qualitatively new development, organically and permanently rooted in the new domestic order that Gorbachev is creating? Third, how should the United States react to Gorbachev's policies? What influence might American policy have on the depth and direction of the domestic reforms? What opportunities has the new Soviet thinking created for enhancing Western security, and how can the West take advantage of them?

*Reprinted by permission of the author and publisher from *International Security* 12, 3 (1987), pp. 93–132. Copyright © 1987 by the President and Fellows of Harvard College and of the Massachusetts Institute of Technology.

A definitive analysis of the Gorbachev revolution is hardly possible at this stage, since the process is still only beginning to unfold. Nonetheless, it is important to have working hypotheses about the causes and consequences of the reforms, since timely American policy choices may hinge in part on that analysis. In that spirit, I advance four main arguments.

First, historical Soviet expansionism and zero-sum thinking about international politics have largely been caused by the nature of Soviet Stalinist domestic institutions, especially the militant Communist Party and the centralized command economy geared toward autarkic military production. These institutions, their authoritarian methods, and their militant ideology were necessary for the tasks of "extensive economic development"—namely, mobilizing underutilized labor and material resources and overcoming bottlenecks—in conditions of imminent foreign threat.[4] After these tasks were accomplished, the Stalinist institutions hung on as atavisms, using the militant ideology and the exaggeration of the foreign threat to justify their self-serving policies.[5] The offensive form of détente practiced by First Secretary Nikita Khrushchev and by Brezhnev was an attempt to satisfy simultaneously these atavistic interests and also newly emerging, post-Stalinist groups, especially the cultural and technical intelligentsia. As recently as the period when Yuri Andropov was General Secretary, in Harry Gelman's view, "the entrenched influence of the military and the ideologues" suppressed the lessons that the reformist intelligentsia was learning about Soviet geopolitical overextension of the late 1970s.[6]

Second, Gorbachev is aiming for nothing less than smashing the power of the entrenched Stalinist interest groups. He realizes that the extensive model of development has run into a dead end, because fallow labor and material resources have run out. There are no more reserves to mobilize. Consequently, new institutions are needed to address the tasks of "intensive development" in a modern economy—namely, efficient allocation of already-mobilized resources and sensitivity to user needs. In the Soviet reformers' view, the old institutions and the ideas associated with them have become fetters on production, serving only their own vested interests. As Gorbachev told the January 1987 Central Committee plenum:

> theoretical notions about socialism in many ways remained on the level of the 1930s and 1940s, when society was tackling entirely different problems. . . . What took place was a kind of translation into absolutes of the forms of the organization of society that had developed in practice. Moreover, such notions, in point of fact, were equated with the essential characteristics of socialism, regarded an immutable and presented as dogmas leaving no room for objective scientific analysis.[7]

According to his diagnosis, atavistic institutions and ideas must yield to new methods that allow greater initiative and autonomy from below.[8]

Third, the requirements of intensive development and the interests of Gorbachev's principal constituency, the intelligentsia, propel new thinking in foreign policy and arms control. These include a more organic Soviet involvement in the capitalist world economy, a reduced defense burden, and the durable détente that this requires. This is more fundamental and far-reaching than a short-lived desire to buy time or digest geopolitical gains. The new conception of détente, moreover, explicitly eschews the Brezhnevian idea of one-way benefits flowing from an improved "correlation of forces," the loose index of political and military trends that the Soviets invoke when discussing the balance of power. As Gorbachev told a Soviet national television audience, "today one's own security cannot be ensured without taking into account the security of other states and peoples. There can be no genuine security unless it is equal for all and comprehensive. To think otherwise is to live in a world of illusions, in a world of self-deception.'"[9]

Fourth, to promote the favorable aspects of the new foreign policy, the United States should (1) avoid extremely aggressive competitive behavior that might push the reforms in a militarized direction, (2) reciprocate genuine Soviet concessions to avoid discrediting the conciliatory line, and (3) bargain hard for structural changes in Soviet foreign trade institutions and in offensive conventional military postures in Europe. These latter changes, toward which Gorbachev appears favorably inclined anyhow, would be good in themselves and would work to institutionalize the new foreign policy in Soviet domestic politics.

In presenting these arguments, I will first explain how Stalinist domestic institutions fostered Soviet expansionism, and second, trace the effects of Gorbachev's domestic innovations on Soviet foreign policy. In concluding, I will discuss policy implications for the West.

THE OLD INSTITUTIONS AND OLD IDEAS

The need for forced-draft industrialization in the face of intense threats from more advanced societies shaped the militant institutions and ideas of Stalin's revolution from above.[10] These institutions and ideas lived on for decades, dominating domestic political coalitions and driving foreign and security policies in a militant, expansionist direction. It is against these atavistic institutions and ideas that Gorbachev and the reformers must contend.

The Institutions and Ideas of Stalin's Revolution from Above

Stalinist institutions were marked by their origins in the attempts of an autocrat to whip his backward society to modernize in the face of foreign competition. In this process, international pressure provided both the motive and the opportunity to smash obsolete institutions and replace them with more efficient, centrally controlled ones.[11] "Old Russia . . . was ceaselessly beaten for her backwardness," Stalin warned at the height of the First Five-Year Plan. "We are fifty or a hundred years behind the advanced countries. We must make good this lag in ten years. Either we do it or they crush us."[12]

The tsars, too, had tried to spur revolutions from above for much the same reason but, as Stalin explained, "none of the old classes . . . could solve the problem of overcoming the backwardness of the country."[13] Instead, they were barriers to the need transformation. Then, between 1917 and 1921, all of these old urban and elite classes, including the old working class, were swept away by war, revolution, foreign intervention, and civil war. The Bolsheviks were not immediately strong enough to break the peasantry and mobilize the material and labor surpluses needed for rapid industrialization. During the 1920s, however, they were able to form a vanguard of social transformation from the ranks of the new working class, which was younger and less tainted with reformist trade-unionism than the old working class had been.[14]

This revolution had institutional and intellectual consequences. Institutionally, its implementation required a more militant mobilizing party, the strengthening of repressive police institutions, and a more centralized authoritarian economic structure to overcome bottlenecks and to assert the priority of military-related heavy industrial production. By the late 1930s, the revolution also drew upward from the new working class a politically dependent, hothouse technical elite— what Stalin called "a new Soviet intelligentsia, firmly linked with the people and ready en masse to give it true and faithful service."[15] This was the Brezhnev generation, for which the Great Purges cleared the way.

Intellectually, these institutions and personnel were motivated and tempered by an ideology of political combat and the exaggeration of internal and external threats. This mobilized energies when pecuniary rewards were lacking, justified repression, and legitimated the priority of resource allocations for the military-industrial complex. According to the definitive study of the enlistment of workers in the campaign to collectivize agriculture:

> The recruitment drive took place within the context of the First Five-Year Plan mobilization atmosphere. The Stalin leadership manipulated and played upon popular fear of military intervention and memories of civil war famine, rekindled by the 1927 war scare and the grain crisis of the late 1920s. The dominant motifs of the First Five-Year Plan revolution were military and the imagery was that of the Russian civil war. The working class was called upon to sacrifice for the good of the cause and the preservation of the nation. The state sought to deflect working class grievances away from systemic problems and toward the "external" and the "internal" enemies—that is, the "kulak," the "bourgeois" specialist, the NEP-men, and the political opposition [inside the Party] all said to be in league with the agents of international imperialism.[16]

Though this paranoid, pressure-cooker atmosphere was largely generated from above by Stalin and his allies, recent studies have stressed that it was readily internalized and exploited by the upwardly mobile militants that were Stalin's shock troops. During the collectivization campaign and the later purges, these young radicals exaggerated the threat of foreign subversion to push campaigns to extremes and to sweep away the older bureaucratic elite that was blocking their path to social advancement.[17]

Stalinist Atavisms and the Politics of Expansion

These institutions and ideas lived on as atavisms after the period of rapid social mobilization that had created them. As early as the late 1940s, the institutional instruments of mobilization were turning into tools for justifying the interests of these Stalinist institutions. The role of orthodox ideology in shaping society, the priority of allocation of resources to the military-industrial complex, and petty interference by party bureaucrats in day-to-day economic administration now functioned more to justify their own continuation than to serve the needs of development.

Foreign policy ideas played an important role in rationalizing and reconciling group interests. By the 1950s, four schools of thought in Soviet grand strategy had emerged: one supported by the military-industrial complex, a second by party militants, a third by the intelligentsia. The fourth, offensive détente, resulted from the efforts of political entrepreneurs like Khrushchev and Brezhnev to form coalitions among the other three. For the sake of analytical convenience, these outlooks can be divided along two dimensions: first, whether imperialism's hostility toward socialism is conditional or unconditional upon Soviet actions, and second, whether offense is the best defense in international politics. See Figure 1.

Molotov: Western Hostility Is Unconditional; the Defense Has the Advantage

Vyacheslav Molotov, one of Stalin's henchmen, argued that Soviet efforts to relax tensions with the West would not reduce the imperialists' hostility, but would only reduce vigilance within the socialist camp. However, he saw very few opportunities to exploit imperialist vulnerabilities through offensive action, for example arguing against Khrushchev that the Third World and Yugoslavia were inextricably tied to the opposing camp. Attempts to woo them by reforming Russia's Stalinist image would only lead to unrest in Eastern Europe, he accurately predicted. Consequently, the Soviet Union should adopt a hedgehog strategy of autarky, internal repression, and the forced-draft development of Russia's military-industrial base.[18]

The constituencies for this outlook were, first, the old Stalinist henchmen like Molotov himself, and second, the military-industrial complex. Stalinists like Molotov and Lazar Kaganovich, weaned on Stalin's strategy of "socialism in one country," saw a militant defense as the best way to secure the revolution. As

Figure 1.

	Defense has the advantage	Offense has the advantage
Western hostility is unconditional	Molotov	Zhdanov
Western hostility is conditional	Malenkov Gorbachev	Khrushchev Brezhnev

Stalin put it in 1923, "of course, the Fascists are not asleep. But it is to our advantage to let them attack first; that will rally the working class around the communists."[19] Since Molotov's prestige and legitimacy hinged on being Stalin's chief lieutenant, especially in foreign affairs, his interests as well as his habits were served by being the guardian of orthodoxy.

A more enduring constituency for this hedgehog strategy lay among the military-industrial interests. When Khrushchev moved to limit military spending and simultaneously to provoke foreign conflicts, for example, a powerful leader of the opposition was Frol Kozlov, whose political base was rooted in Leningrad's military-oriented economy.[20] In Kozlov's view, which became so prominent in the Brezhnev era, the methodical development of Soviet military strength was the prerequisite for successful dealings with the West.

Zhdanov: Western Hostility Is Unconditional; Offensive Has the Advantage

Party Secretary Andrei Zhdanov represented a different brand of militancy. Like Molotov, he believed that Soviet concessions would not diminish the aggressiveness of the West, but he was distinctive in arguing that a political offensive was the best defense against imperialism's hostile onslaught. As part of his militant Cominform strategy, for example, Zhdanov promoted the use of violent strikes by Western Communist parties as a means to prevent the implementation of the Marshall Plan, which Zhdanov saw as the groundwork for an American policy of rollback of Communism in Eastern Europe.[21]

The constituency for the Zhdanovite strategy was the party bureaucracy and its orthodox ideologues, who needed a strategic ideology to use as a weapon in struggles against a competing faction led by Malenkov. As early as 1941, Malenkov was attempting to promote the professional interests of the new technical elite against meddling party bureaucrats. He decried the "know-nothings" and "windbags" in the party bureaucracy who exercise "petty tutelage" over industrial experts, reject sound technical advice, and spout empty quotations about "putting the pressure on."[22] The war greatly increased the autonomy of technical experts, so by 1945 Stalin needed to redress the institutional balance of power and turned to Zhdanov to promote a "party revival."

Zhdanov used foreign policy ideas as a weapon in this domestic political struggle. He inflated the threat of ideological subversion from abroad in order to justify the priority of ideological orthodoxy at home. He argued for the thorough communization of Eastern Europe, including East Germany, relying heavily on the mobilizing skills of the party to carry it out.[23] And he emphasized the strategic value of Communist fifth columns in the West.

Upon Zhdanov's death in 1948, the heir to his strategy and position in the Central Committee Secretariat was Mikhail Suslov, who defended the Zhdanov line against Malenkov's criticism that it had served only to unify and militarize the West.[24] Until Suslov's own death in 1982, he served as the proponent of militant and ideologically orthodox means for promoting progressive change abroad and as the enforcer of the party's corporate interests in the domestic coalition-making process.[25]

Malenkov: Western Hostility is Conditional; The Defense Has the Advantage

Georgi Malenkov, chairman of the Council of Ministers, in contrast, believed that Western aggressiveness could be diminished by Soviet self-restraint, and that defensive advantages dominated the international system. Malenkov's view dovetailed with the arguments of Eugene Varga, who contended that institutional changes in the American state during World War II had made it a stronger but less aggressive international competitor, more able to control the heedlessly aggressive impulses of the monopoly capitalists.[26] Malenkov argued that the imperialists had become realistic and sane enough to be deterred by a minimum atomic force, so that defense budgets could be safely cut and the heavy-industry priority reversed.[27] Moreover, he argued, Soviet political concessions in Europe would split the West, defuse its aggressiveness, and revive the close Soviet-German relations that had existed in the 1920s. There is evidence that Malenkov warned on similar grounds against invading South Korea.[28]

Malenkov sought a constituency for these views among the urban middle class and the cultural and technical intelligentsia. The charges leveled by Zhdanovite inquisitors against Varga's book read like a sociological profile of Malenkov's would-be constituency: "technical" and "apolitical," suffering from "empiricism," "burgeois objectivism," and a "non-party" outlook.[29] Malenkov's conception that the foreign threat is manageable through concessions served the interests of the intelligentsia by removing the major justification for oppressive petty tutelage over them by party ideologues and bureaucrats, for the economic priorities that enriched the military at the expense of their living standard, and for a renewal of the purges.[30]

Malenkov's strategy failed, however, because the class that Malenkov hoped to recruit was subject to counter-pressures: many worked in the military-industrial complex, and many had benefited from Stalin's "Big Deal," receiving some of the minimal trappings of petty bourgeois status and life-style in exchange for absolute political loyalty to the orthodox regime.[31] Even a decade later, Kosygin still found that this stratum constituted an inadequate social base for a similar strategic ideology.[32]

Khrushchev and Brezhnev: Western Hostility is Conditional; Offense Has the Advantage (Offensive Détente)

Khrushchev and Brezhnev shared the Malenkov-Varga thesis that "realists" in the West made possible a relaxation of international tension, but they coupled this with a belief in offensive advantage in international politics. Imperialism could behave in a heedlessly aggressive manner, they believed, but prudent forces within the capitalist camp, especially the bourgeois state and public opinion, could restrain the most reckless of the monopoly capitalists. The influence of such realists could be strengthened by Soviet policy in two ways: first, Soviet efforts to shift the world correlation of forces, including the military balance, to the advantage of socialism, would cause Western realists increasingly to shun the dangers of direct confrontation; second, Soviet projection of an image of restraint in the methods by which it pursues its expansionist goals would lull the West. These two elements would reinforce each other, according to Khrushchev and Brezhnev. The increased strength of the socialist camp would leave imperialism little choice but to accept détente on terms favorable to socialism. Détente in turn would weaken imperialism by hindering its counter-revolutionary interventions in the Third World. The success of the strategy depends, in their view, on active measures to improve the Soviet position at the expense of the West, not simply the passive acceptance of a stalemate or bal-ance.[33] As Khrushchev put it: "Peace cannot be begged for. It can be safeguarded only by an active purposeful struggle."[34]

In promoting this conception, Khrushchev and Brezhnev were acting as political entrepreneurs, cementing a broad political coalition with a strategic ideology that promised something for everyone: progressive change for Suslov and the ideologues; military modernization and enhanced national security for the military-industrial constituencies; détente and increased foreign trade for the cultural and technical intelligentsia. The problem was that this political formula worked at home but not abroad. In practice, it led to over-committed, contradic-tory policies that provoked the hostility of the West, revealing (as Gorbachev put it) that its strategic vision was "a world of illusions."[35]

This process played itself out somewhat differently under the two leaders, reflecting the different political uses to which Khrushchev and Brezhnev put the strategy of offensive détente. To both Brezhnev and, in his early period, Khrushchev, offensive détente was a strategic ideology that served to legitimate the outcome of political logrolling. But in the period between 1958 and 1962, Khrushchev tried to use offensive détente as a tool to escape the contraints of his logrolled coalition, provoking the worst of the cold war crises as a consequence.

Khrushchev's version of the strategy of offensive détente relied on nuclear technology and especially on the inter-continental ballistic missile (ICBM), which was to serve as a cheap cure-all. Khrushchev believed it would change the correlation of forces and lead to détente with the West, a favorable political settlement in Europe, low cost security, and the freeing of resources for a rise in Soviet living standards.[36] Such arguments were an attractive element in Khrushchev's political platform during the succession struggle.[37] They had the further advantage that they could not fully be tested until the ICBM was actually produced. By 1958, Khrushchev had his ICBM and was eager to move on to the next phase of his domestic game plan, in which he would cap military expendi-tures and increase investment in chemicals and other sectors that would benefit agricultural and consumer production.[38] However, the West refused to play its part. Instead of becoming more "realistic," the Americans rejected pleas for a summit, refused to move toward recognition of the German Democratic Republic, and seemed headed toward the nuclearization of the Bundeswehr.[39]

Khrushchev sought to push on with his budgetary reversal of priorities despite this, but several Politburo members balked. "Until the aggressive circles of the imperialist powers reject the policy of the arms race and preparations for a new war, we must still further strengthen the defenses of our country," said Suslov. This had been "the general line of our party . . . in the period 1954–1957," and implicitly it had been Khrushchev's own personal pledge during the succession struggle. Thus, Suslov called on Khrushchev to "honestly fulfill [the Party's] duties and promises before the Soviet people."[40] The Berlin crisis offered Khrushchev a way out of this impasse. Using it as a lever to gain a summit, the recognition of the German Democratic Republic, and progress on the test ban, Khrushchev hoped to demonstrate that the correlation of forces had already changed enough to achieve détente on favorable terms, allowing radical cuts in conventional forces and a leveling off of nuclear expenditures.[41]

This attempt to use offensive détente to escape from the constraints of political promises helped put Khrushchev on the slippery slope that led to his replacement in 1964 by the team of Brezhnev and Kosygin. Brezhnev learned from this that offensive détente could not be used to escape the strictures of coalition politics, but he did not learn that offensive détente was an inherently self-defeating policy. Indeed, the story of his own coalition-building strategy suggests that he thought that the distribution of political power in the 1960s still made offensive détente an indispensable tool in domestic politics.[42]

At first, Brezhnev maneuvered to create a coalition on the moderate left. He attracted ideologues and the moderate military with a foreign policy stressing support for "progressive" Third World states, notably the Arabs, and a military policy that emphasized a huge conventional buildup, while opening the door to nuclear arms control. This isolated Kosygin and Podgorny on the right, who were vulnerable because of their insistence on reduced defense spending, and Shelepin on the extreme left, who apparently hoped to use a platform of even more reckless Third World adventures and flat-out nuclear arms racing to attract a heterogeneous coalition of the military, radical ideologues, and Great Russian chauvinists.[43] But soon a flaw appeared in Brezhnev's policy of moderate appeasement of the cartels of the left. The strategy was extremely expensive, making him vulnerable to Kosygin's charge that it was wrecking the economy and scuttling indispensable reforms.

To counter this charge, Brezhnev developed a revised version of the "correlation of forces" theory and the strategy of offensive détente. The improved military balance and the liberation of progressive forces in the Third World would encourage realism in the West, leading to détente, arms control, and technology transfers that would solve the Soviet Union's economic problems without Kosygin's structural reforms. The memoirs of defector Arkady Shevchenko show graphically how these pie-in-the-sky arguments were crafted to appeal to the delegates to the 1971 Party Congress, which ratified the strategy and for the first time gave Brezhnev a commanding political advantage over his rivals.[44]

Despite this political victory, Brezhnev was nonetheless stuck with a strategy that was overcommitted and expensive. Through the mid-1970s, he fought a running battle with Marshal Grechko and the military over the budgetary implications of détente in general and SALT in particular. Only after 1976, with Grechko's death and the installation of a civilian defense minister, did strategic force procurement flatten out and nuclear warfighting doctrines wane.[45] The battle revived, however, as a result of the Reagan defense buildup, with Chief of the General Staff Nikolai Ogarkov insisting that it would be a "serious error" not to increase military outlays. In the wake of the Polish crisis, however, the civilians were more worried about the danger of cutting social programs, and Ogarkov was fired.[46]

Signs of growing skepticism about backing radical Third World regimes also began to surface in 1976,[47] but could not proceed very far until Suslov's death in 1982. A year later, Andropov himself was stressing the need to limit the cost of Soviet counterinsurgency wars in support of pseudo-Marxist regimes, noting that "it is one thing to proclaim socialism, but another to build it."[48]

Thus, through the failure of Brezhnev's strategy of offensive détente, some of the intellectual and political precursors to Gorbachev's new thinking were already in place.

Backdrop to Gorbachev's Revolution

In sum, Soviet expansionist behavior and strategic concepts have had their roots in the institutional and intellectual legacy of Stalin's revolution from above. Atavistic interests with a stake in military-industrial budget priorities and militant promotion of "progressive change" abroad have exploited the ideological baggage of Stalinism to legitimate the continuation of their dominant social role. When Malenkov tried to change this, pushing forward new ideas and a new social constituency, Stalin was quoted to justify his removal from office: "In face of capitalist encirclement . . . 'to slacken the pace means to lag behind. And those who lag behind are beaten.' "[49] To gain power, an innovator like Khrushchev had to distort his policies to try to attract or outflank the atavistic interests and ideas, leading to contradictions and over-commitment at home and abroad.

Though foreign policy ideas tended to line up with the interests of groups and coalitions, this was not entirely the result of conscious manipulation. Sometimes conscious manipulation did occur, as in Stalin's trumped-up war scare of 1927. More often, it was probably semi-conscious, as in Brezhnev's packaging of the "correlation of forces" theory for the 1971 Congress. Sometimes it may have been the result of unconscious motivated bias.[50] Khrushchev reports spending several sleepless nights grappling with the implications of atomic weaponry, until it came to him that these fearful instruments would never be used, but could nonetheless be of great political significance.[51] The connection between ideas and interests was also sustained by the political selection process. Thus, Khrushchev and Brezhnev prevailed in the succession struggle in part because of their strategies of offensive détente, whether or not they adopted those strategies for consciously political reasons.

Though I have stressed the role of the domestic environment, I do not mean to argue that Soviet policy-making has been utterly oblivious to its international environment. Most episodes of Soviet belligerence or expansionism have had international triggers—like the Marshall Plan, the rearming of West Germany, the U-2 affair, the Jackson-Vanik Amendment and the post-Vietnam syndrome—that made the strategic arguments of some Soviet factions more plausible, some less plausible.[52]

Moreover, the Soviet Union has typically been able to learn from negative feedback from its counterproductive aggressive policies, leading to at least tactical retreats. For example, the failure of the Berlin blockade and the West's reaction to the invasion of South Korea strengthened the hand of Malenkov and other leaders who wanted to reverse the confrontational Soviet policy. This differentiates the Soviet Union from Imperial Germany and Japan, which were so enmeshed in institutionally rooted strategic ideologies that policy failures produced not learning, but ever more reckless attempts to break out of their own self-encirclement.[53] Though the Soviet Union pays more attention to the realities of its environment than they did, objective conditions are nonetheless an insufficient explanation for even the milder Soviet case of self-encirclement. As Churchill asked in 1949, "why have they deliberately acted for three long years so as to unite the free world against them?"[54] Insofar as the answer lies in the peculiar domestic institutional and intellectual inheritance from Stalin's revolution from above, a sharp break with that domestic order under Gorbachev should produce a radically different foreign policy.

EMERGENT INSTITUTIONS AND THINKING UNDER GORBACHEV

Just as the requirements of extensive development gave rise to the old institutions and ideas of the revolution from above, so too the requirements of intensive development are forcing their replacement by new institutions and ideas. Restructuring for intensive development in both the domestic and foreign areas is creating some new institutions and changing the relative power and interests of many old ones. The military-industrial complex, old-style ideologues, and autarkic industrial interests are in eclipse. Civilian defense intellectuals, reformist ideologues, and supporters of liberalized trade policies among the intelligentsia are gaining influence and trying to force changes that would institutionalize the policies they prefer. The emphasis on two-way security and the deepening of economic interdependence in Gorbachev's new foreign policy thinking grows directly from the new domestic institutions he is promoting and the political constituencies that he is relying on.

Forces for Change

Four factors are impelling the Gorbachev reforms: the objective requirements of the stage of intensive development, the discrediting of old institutions, the gradual strengthening of the constituency for change as a result of natural processes of modernization, and ironically, the Stalinist legacy of centralized institutions suited to the task of social transformation from above.

First, there is the objective need for restructuring for the tasks of intensive development. As Western experts have argued for a long time, the success of a mature post-industrial economy depends on efficient resource allocation and sensitivity to user demand. These require decentralized price formation, competition among suppliers, and profit-oriented success criteria.[55] Gorbachev's economic reforms, some of them already enacted into law, seem to be heading precisely in this direction, though how far they will go remains in doubt.[56]

Second, these objective needs have become increasingly and widely recognized, as the policy failures of the late Brezhnev period have discredited most of the key Stalinist institutions—the administrators of the centralized economy, the militant "combat party," and the military-industrial complex. Economic stagnation, in particular, has led to the widespread conviction that the old institutions and the ideas that legitimated them have become fetters on production, atavistic organs surviving only to their own benefit. *Pravda* commentators explain that "individual and group egoism" on the part of "bureaucratic and technocratic elements who were guided solely by their immediate interests" led to "stagnation" in the period after the "October 1964 plenum."[57] Likewise, Suslov-style ideologues are now called "Old Believers"—the term for proponents of an especially archaic version of Russian Orthodox Christianity—who promote a dogma that "smacks of romanticism. They carry on about dangers, they issue warnings, and they admonish against overdoing things [i.e., overdoing the reforms]. Essentially what they are defending is not even centralism, but centralism's vehicle—the bureaucratic administration apparatus," but they "could be easily swept aside by a mass movement of the working people based on the will of the Party leadership."[58]

This kind of criticism has also been extended into the realm of foreign and security policy. Many Soviet political leaders and scholars have implicitly criticized the Brezhnev era's overoptimism about new Marxist-Leninist regimes in the Third World.[59] Recently, a Soviet commentator has explicitly criticized the logical contradictions and willful optimism among the orthodox ideologues, like many of those coordinating Third World policy in Brezhnev's Central Committee International Department.[60] Similarly, in the foreign trade area, the president of the Soviet Academy of Sciences was fired after warning that an "import plague" was stifling the development of homegrown technology and thus jeopardizing national security, and his research institutes were charged with nepotism and failure to promote productive young scientists.[61]

In the wake of the German Cessna landing in Red Square, the military has come in for even more fundamental rebukes. Boris Yeltsin, candidate Politburo member and then Moscow party secretary, told officers of the Moscow Military District that they manifest a "bourgeois mentality," acting "as though they are apart from society." "Rudeness, boorishness, and intimidation," widespread within the officer corps, "give rise to toadies, boot-lickers, sycophants, and window-dressers. . . . An atmosphere of smugness, boasting, and complacency emerged everywhere. This atmosphere deprives active people of initiative and the ability to assert a correct viewpoint" and encourages a "style that blunts the cutting edge of the idea of the motherland's security."[62] In short, the prevailing diagnosis blames all of the encrusted Stalinist institutions, with the partial exception of the KGB:[63] the orthodox combat party, the "administrative-voluntarist methods" of the command economy,[64] the military-industrial complex, autarkic industry.

A third factor promoting the emergence of the reforms is the strengthening of the constituency that naturally favors it, the cultural and technical intelligentsia. These urban, middle-class professionals have two strong motives to support a campaign for domestic restructuring: first, it will increase their professional autonomy from arbitrary bureaucratic interference, and second, it will increase their relative income. Inside the cocoon of the old system, the intelligentsia has been steadily growing in size and independence as a natural result of the gradual modernization of the economy and social structure. Between 1959 and 1979, the number of people with full higher education tripled, as did the number with secondary educations.[65] Thus, there is now in place a precondition of restructuring for intensive development, much as the wartime destruction of the old urban classes and the rise of a new working class in the 1920s were preconditions of restructuring for extensive development.

To some extent, the intelligentsia may still be divided between those who want to keep the system that provides their sinecures and those who have professional and economic interests in changing the system so they can earn more and have more to buy. As a whole, however, the professional middle class is not only larger but also more politically alert than the Brezhnev generation, the cohort of Stalin's "Big Deal." For example, though some journalists have not succeeded in making the transition to *glasnost,* the many who have are sufficient for Gorbachev's purposes.

A fourth factor favoring the reforms is, ironically, a Stalinist legacy: the strong administrative powers available to the top leadership. This includes power over both personnel and the potent propaganda instruments of the Soviet system. Gorbachev can also call upon the traditional argument of the modernizing Russian autocrat—either we reform or we will be unable "to bring the motherland into the twenty-first century as a mighty, prospering power."[66] This "Russia-was-beaten" argument is one that Gorbachev has used very sparingly, however, perhaps to avoid some of the implications of its prior invocations. He does not want to play into the hands of those who might prefer a more traditional, authoritarian, militarized revolution from above, legitimated by trumpeting the foreign threat. He wants a reform that creates "workers who are computer literate, with a high degree of culture," free to show initiative.[67]

In summary, the forces favoring radical change in domestic institutions and ideas are objective economic needs plus the clout of a strengthened professional class and an already strong reforming leadership. One prominent reformer puts it this way:

> Who does want changes? It's the far-sighted political leaders and management personnel and the outstanding people in science and the cultural sphere. They understand that in the twenty-first century the present variant of development will be dangerous for the country. Further, it's the leading contingent of the working class and of collective farmers, engineers and technicians who are striving to improve their lives and who want to earn more, but to earn it by their own labor, without any finagling. And it is the segment of the intelligentsia that is interested in scientific and technical progress.[68]

Domestic Restructuring

Intensive development requires central authorities and the grass roots to gain in power, while mid-level bureaucrats must lose it. The power relationships in Soviet society must thus be re-shaped from an inverted pyramid into an hourglass configuration. These requirements in practice call for some marketization of the economy, democratization of decisionmaking at the local level, a less inhibited press, and a curtailment of the role of local party organs in economic administration. These changes are needed both to break resistance to reform and to improve economic efficiency once the reforms are underway.

In terms of the institutional structure of power, Gorbachev's problem is to devise a system that will make an end run around the recalcitrant mid-level "transmission belts" of the Stalinist system—the government ministries and the regional party prefects, so-called because their whole raison d'être is to pass along information and orders in a command economy. Transforming Stalin's pyramid of power into an hourglass configuration means that, at the bottom of the hourglass, increased responsibility devolves onto the local level, through partial marketization and democratization. At the top, the power of the central authorities to set overall policy is being strengthened.[69] Reformist economists like Abel Aganbegyan are taking over direction of the "commanding heights" of the economy from the old-style central planners. They rely increasingly on the manipulation of "economic levers" rather than on administrative directives.[70] Similarly, reforming ideologues like Aleksandr Yakovlev are using centralized agitation and propaganda institutions to mobilize and guide the newly empowered locals.[71]

Gorbachev is not trying to build his constituency by collecting a winning coalition from pieces that are already on the board, as Brezhnev did. This would be a losing game for Gorbachev, as most existing organized interests stand to lose from the changes. Instead, like Stalin, Gorbachev is trying to empower new constituencies, working through new institutions and transforming old ones. Thus, in the economic sphere, Gorbachev promotes private or cooperative entrepreneurial ventures, increases in the service sector of the economy at the expense of blue collar jobs, the closing of unprofitable factories, and increased wage differentials.[72] Within the party itself, Gorbachev and Yeltsin call for a prime party task to be the training of new cadres with a liberal education and big-picture outlook, instead of petty tutelage over the economy.[73] More broadly, by increasing press and artistic freedom, Gorbachev hands power to the intelligentsia, who can for the most part be counted on to use it against his opponents. Gorbachev's campaign for economic reform was getting nowhere until he unleashed the journalists to denounce the self-interested conservatism of his opponents and to expose their corruption. Thus, *glasnost* is desired as an end in itself by the creative intelligentsia, but for Gorbachev it is a sledgehammer to smash the opposition "by force of public pressure."[74]

Restructuring Foreign Policy

In foreign and security policy, the old institutions and ideas of extensive development favored military-industrial spending, autarky, tension with the West, and militant support for progressive change abroad. Intensive development, in contrast, favors a deeper participation in the international division of labor, less costly military and Third World policies, and consequently a policy line that avoids upsetting stable relations with the West. Oleg Bogomolov, the prominent director of the institute that studies the socialist bloc's economy, puts it this way:

> Previously we reasoned: the worse for the adversary, the better for us, and vice versa. But today this is no longer true; this cannot be a rule anymore. Now countries are so interdependent on each other for their development that we have quite a different image of the solution to international questions. The worsening of the situation in Europe will not at all help the development of the socialist part of Europe; on the contrary, the better things are going in the European world economy, the higher the stability and the better the prospects for our development.[75]

The changes in foreign policy are being caused both by the needs of a reformed economy and by the interests of Gorbachev's main political constituency, the intelligentsia.

In the international economic sphere, the reformers argue that the Soviet Union must make the transition from primary-product exports to a new pattern of "intensive foreign trade," featuring machine exports and schemes for joint production with foreign firms.[76] The reformers recognize that this will require greater independence for individual firms to conclude profitable deals on their own initiative. Preliminary reforms along these lines have already been implemented.[77]

Such reforms create the danger, however, that "the 'monopoly' of the Ministry of Foreign Trade could give way . . . to a 'monopoly' of many ministries which have gained the right to foreign economic activity."[78] Unless domestic prices are pegged to world levels, traders will have an incentive to extract rents by exploiting arbitrary price discrepancies, instead of making profits by creating real value. An even more radical solution to this problem, advocated by some prominent Soviet economists and intellectuals, would be convertibility of the ruble into hard currency at market rates. This would allow "more flexible involvement in trade on the world market" and would create "a yardstick with which to measure the effects of restructuring" of the domestic economy.[79] Thus, the push for more intensive international trade, which the West could encourage, may give added impetus to domestic structural changes that Gorbachev says he wants anyway.

In the military sphere, radical changes in Soviet nuclear and conventional postures are taking a place on Gorbachev's agenda, largely because the military is no longer the powerful political participant in the Soviet ruling coalition that it was under Brezhnev. Gorbachev has promoted minions, not independently powerful allies, to oversee the military, and has created a civilian defense think-tank to provide him with alternative strategic analysis.[80] This has allowed him to seek structural changes in Soviet military posture that would stabilize the military competition and reduce its economic burden in a permanent way. The most notable, which I will discuss in more detail later, is a change of Warsaw Pact conventional forces from an offensive to a defensive configuration. If institutionalized, this would of course be less easily reversible than a mere policy change.

The taming of the military creates the possibility for the change from conventional offense to defense, and Western responses could forward implementation of this change, but there is nothing in Gorbachev's reformed system that absolutely demands it. In the long run, the large-scale production of high-technology, offensive military forces would not necessarily be incompatible with the logic of intensive development.

The logic of the reform and its constituency is also affecting Third World policy, though here its effects may be weaker and mixed. On one hand, some of Gorbachev's key supporters are reform-minded ideologues, like Alexander Yakovlev, who are basically internationalist in outlook. They would be loath to relinquish the idea of a global role for the Bolshevik party. The desire to participate more deeply in the world economy also favors a continued Soviet drive for international influence. On the other hand, the reformers are clearly sensitive to the economic and political costs of futile military involvements in extremely backward societies. Given this particular mix of constraints, it is natural that ideologues like Yakovlev and Karen Brutents have hit upon the promotion of Soviet political and economic relationships with large, prospering Third World countries—the Mexicos and the Argentinas—as the new, relatively benign incarnation of Soviet progressive internationalism.[81]

Emerging Security Concepts and Implications for the Future

Gorbachev and his allies have propounded strategic concepts that facilitate their own domestic program, just as leaders of the old Stalinist institutions rationalized their interests in terms of images of the adversary and assumptions about the relative advantages of offense and defense. Because the military-industrial complex, the orthodox ideologues, and autarkic interests are in eclipse, images of unappeasable opponents and offensive advantage are also in eclipse. Because the power of the intelligentsia is increasing, its ideas are on the rise. Like Malenkov, the Gorbachev reformers see a world in which the defense has the advantage and aggressive opponents can be demobilized by Soviet conces- sions and self-restraint. This similarity in strategic ideology is rooted in the rough similarity of their domestic goals and their domestic political constituencies.

However, because some of the domestic incentives for Gorbachev's new thinking may be ephemeral, some aspects of the new thinking might not survive unless they are institutionalized, for example, in arms control agreements. Offense-oriented, as well as defense-oriented, lower-budget, higher-technology strategies would be consistent with economic reform. At present, attacking the old, offensive military policies may give Gorbachev added arguments to use against holdovers from Brezhnev's top brass, but this is a transitory incentive. In such conditions, where the domestic base for desirable new defense-oriented strategies ideas is tenuous, American diplomacy might play a role in institu- tionalizing such strategies and promoting their domestic base.

Image of the Adversary

Gorbachev and his circle see America as innately hostile, but they believe that America's aggressiveness can be defused through Soviet self-restraint and con- cessions. Initially, some western Sovietologists feared that Gorbachev's foreign policy would come to be dominated by the ideas of Alexander Yakovlev, whom they saw as an inveterate America-hater. The author of several monographs excoriating America's messianic imperialism, Yakovlev has portrayed America as aggressive, but declining, eventually to be abandoned by other capitalist powers more amenable to détente:

> The distancing of Western Europe, Japan, and other capitalist countries from U.S. strategic military plans in the near future is neither an excessively rash fantasy nor a nebulous prospect. It is dictated by objective factors having to do with the rational guaranteeing of all their political and economic interests, including security. . . . As time goes by, we will witness the establishment of new centers of strength [and potential Soviet trading partners] such as Brazil, Canada, and Australia, not to mention China.[82]

Yakovlev admits, however, that America is far from collapsing and that splitting NATO through a separate détente with Europe is not a feasible prospect in the short run.[83]

Others in Gorbachev's circle, like journalist Alexander Bovin, go much further in portraying a more united, but tamer imperialism. Bovin argues that in response to the economic crisis of the mid-1970s, the capitalist powers have agreed to regulate their economic competition internationally in much the same way that the bourgeois state regulates capitalism domestically. "A new transna- tional model of imperialism is being created before our eyes," says Bovin.[84] Thus, he extends Varga's analysis one step further, implying that a major engine of imperialist aggressiveness, the inability of the monopolies and capitalist states to act in their own long-run enlightened self-interest, is coming under rational control. This is the old Kautskyite heresy of cooperative "ultraimperialism," which Lenin railed against because he realized that it cut to the core of his theory of the sources of aggressive imperialist behavior.[85]

More important than the degree of imperialism's aggressiveness, however, is the question of how that aggressiveness can be reduced. Yakovlev believes that a crucial link in American aggressiveness is the ability of "the colossal, all-penetrating and all powerful propaganda machine" to whip up a "jingoistic fever" among the masses.[86] The way to counteract this, he argues, is through effective, substantive Soviet peace proposals, which constrain even the worst cold warriors to reciprocate in order to save face with their own public.[87] This way of looking at the problem not only gives pride of place to Yakovlev's personal skills as a propagandist, but it also reflects Yakovlev's previous experiences, battling jingoistic *Russian* nationalists for control of the press in the early 1970s.[88] In this way, Yakovlev has developed a view of imperialism that reconciles the interests and outlook of reformist ideologue-activists, like himself, with those of Gorbachev's broader constituency in the intelligentsia, exemplified by Bovin.

Gorbachev has adopted this strategy as his own, explaining it this way to *Time* magazine:

If all that we are doing is indeed viewed as mere propaganda, why not respond to it according to the principle of "an eye for an eye, a tooth for a tooth"? We have stopped nuclear explosions. Then you Americans could take revenge by doing likewise. You could deal us yet another propaganda blow, say, by suspending the development of one of your new strategic missiles. And we would respond with the same kind of "propaganda." And so on and so forth. Would anyone be harmed by competition in such "propaganda"? Of course, it could not be a substitute for a comprehensive arms-limitation agreement, but it would be a significant step leading to such an agreement.[89]

Complementing this notion that convincing arms control proposals demobilize Western aggressiveness is its converse: that Soviet geopolitical misbehavior provokes the West and plays into the hands of cold war propagandists. Thus, "some comrades," including some of Gorbachev's closest foreign policy advisers, have been brave enough to argue that "rash" Soviet actions in Afghanistan "provoked" the anti-Soviet turn in American foreign policy.[90]

Of course, even Khrushchev understood that superficial concessions could demobilize the West, buying time and preparing the ground for a strategy of offensive détente. But the articulation of the correlation of forces theory by Khrushchev and Brezhnev clearly signaled their intentions from the outset of their détente diplomacy. There is nothing analogous to the correlation of forces theory in Gorbachev's strategic arguments. On the contrary, he insists that this kind of one-way approach to security constitutes a "world of illusions."

Offense and Defense in Military Strategy

The most significant aspect of Gorbachev's new thinking is his explicit understanding of the security dilemma: that security must be mutual to be stable, and that offensive means to security undermine this goal.[91] Consistent with this, Gorbachev and his circle have spoken out against nuclear counterforce and conventional offense. Measures must be taken, he says, to "rule out the possibility of surprise attack. The most dangerous types of offensive arms must be removed from the zone of contact."[92] The elimination of the military from the Soviet ruling coalition was a prerequisite to this intellectual revolution.

At the nuclear level, Yakovlev and others have argued that America cannot succeed in overturning the deterrent stalemate, which is objectively quite stable.[93] Bovin agrees "theoretically" with an *Izvestiia* reader who writes that "the USSR can deter the United States with a considerably lower quantity of strategic weapons. Parity is not mandatory" for deterrence, so the Soviets should move for a propaganda coup by making unilateral cuts.[94] Likewise, Bovin notes that "the building and deployment of hundreds of new [SS-20] missiles must have cost a huge amount of money. And if we agree to destroy these missiles: Why then were they built?"[95]

Increasingly, Soviet civilian defense intellectuals are writing about the "destabilizing" nature of "counterforce concepts," which might "make easier, especially in a situation of sharp crisis, the taking of a suicidal decision to begin an aggression."[96] Perhaps one reason for their concern is that the Soviet military continues to think in terms that, at best, blur the distinctions between nuclear preemption, launch on warning, and retaliation. Invoking the kind of formula that has traditionally been a euphemism for preemption, Marshal Akhromeev says that "combat readiness of the Soviet Armed Forces is being constantly enhanced which allows [them] to prevent a possible enemy aggression at any time and in any conditions, and also to deliver a crushing retaliatory blow should war be unleashed by the enemy anyway."[97]

Some Western critics have pointed out, however, that Soviet "new thinking" in the nuclear area may not be to the advantage of the West. The agreement to scrap the INF (Intermediate Nuclear Force) capabilities of both sides, for example, still leaves Western Europe under the shadow of the Red Army's formidable conventional offensive force posture. But Gorbachev has made important overtures in that area as well. The official Warsaw Pact position is that both sides should "reduce their forces to equal and minimum levels that will exclude waging any offensive operations against each other, so that the reductions will bring about such forces on both sides that will be sufficient only for defense."[98] Civilian journals in the Soviet Union have endorsed West European proposals to eliminate "highly mobile tank units" and "strike aircraft" in order to achieve the "goal of reorganizing the armed forces of the sides, such that defensive actions would be guaranteed greater success than offensive operations.[99]

The new defense-oriented thinking on conventional strategy seems to be taking on an operational cast. For some time, articles discussing the advantages of large-scale defensive conventional operations have been appearing in military journals, though articles on conventional offense still predominate.[100] Colonel-General M. A. Gareev, deputy chief of the General Staff, has said that one of the "main tenets of the *military-technical* aspect of military doctrine" is its "profoundly defensive direction." This represents a distinct break from the traditional position, which held that, while the "socio-political" character of Soviet military doctrine was defensive, its military-technical aspect stressed the operational benefits of the offensive. Military officers warn, however that defensive operations must not be passive. Rather, they should lead to a vigorous counter-offensive. The Warsaw Pact Chief of Staff insists, consequently, that a defensive strategic stance requires no restructuring of Soviet forces. This, of course, is in direct contradiction to Gorbachev's call for changes in force posture.[101]

Such heel-dragging suggests that Gorbachev could not have proceeded as far as he has with the articulation of a non-offensive military doctrine without the curtailment of the military as a significant factor in the Soviet ruling coalition. Circumstantial evidence suggests that a major cause of the increased role of the conventional offensive in Soviet strategy in the 1960s and 1970s was the increased political clout of the military under Brezhnev. Now that political conditions have changed, the strategy can change also.

It has been suggested that the rise of the Soviet "conventional option" stemmed from a rational desire to prevent nuclear escalation should war occur, and that this made sense as a reaction to NATO's shift from massive retaliation to a strategy of flexible response.[102] In fact, the conventional option makes no sense as a strategy for preventing escalation or as reaction to flexible response, since the decisive conventional offensive that it envisions would create precisely the conditions that would trigger nuclear escalation by NATO. Oddly enough, Soviet doctrinal discussions of the mid-1960s, when the conventional option emerged, seem to recognize this. They portray flexible response largely as a cover for a nuclear warfighting strategy and anticipate that the collapse of NATO's front would almost surely trigger nuclear use.[103] The most that can be said is that the Soviets' offensive conventional option is, on a superficial level, less obviously mismatched with flexible response than with NATO's massive retaliation strategy, which had preceded it.

The rise of the offensive conventional option appears to have had more to do with military organizational interests and civil-military relations than with rational strategy. In the middle and late 1950s, the Soviet military justified large conventional forces as necessary to press home the victory after an initial nuclear exchange. Many troops would die, so many were needed if enough were to survive. Khrushchev, however, argued that nuclear weapons alone would be decisive, and that lean conventional forces were best suited for exploiting the effects of nuclear strikes. When Khrushchev renewed his pressure for even deeper troop cuts in 1963–64, the military needed a new, more attractive argument for sizeable conventional forces.[104]

Thus, although the conventional offense was weak on strategic logic, it was strong on political logic. It suited the military's needs, because carrying out the conventional offensive would be such a demanding task that huge expenditures would be required.[105] It was attractive to the political leadership, because it gave them the illusion of retaining civilian control over the escalation process. Finally, it provided common ground for Brezhnev's tacit deal with Marshal Grechko: Brezhnev would name Grechko, not the civilian Ustinov, to the vacant post of Defense Minister; Grechko would also get his conventional buildup and nuclear counterforce programs. In return, Grechko would endorse Brezhnev's claim to be the "supreme commander in chief" and cooperate with Brezhnev in heading off an expensive ABM (anti-ballistic missile) race. According to Sovietological reconstructions, an arrangement roughly along these lines jelled around the time of the December 1966 plenum and an extraordinary Defense Council meeting in April 1967.[106]

In short, now that domestic political conditions have changed, the civilians have no reason to remain bound to a costly and destabilizing conventional military strategy, which Ned Lebow has aptly labeled "the Schlieffen Plan revisited."[107] However, Colonel General N. F. Chervov, of the General Staff's arms control directorate, has warned that "one should not expect unilateral steps on the part of the Warsaw Pact. The NATO countries must take practical steps to meet the Warsaw Pact halfway."[108] Indeed, it is not entirely clear that the civilians care as much about actually implementing a new defensive conventional doctrine as they do about announcing it. Vladimir Petrovskii, the deputy minister of Foreign Affairs, may have revealed more than he intended in saying that "already the very fact of the proclamation of the doctrine is having a salutary effect on the climate and situation in the world."[109] Thus, the West should respond to the Soviet's call for an experts' conference on the restructuring of conventional doctrines as a way of institutionalizing a trend that otherwise might slip away.

Offense and Defense in Geopolitical Strategy

To some extent, the new thinking about offense and defense also appears in a geopolitical context. Gone are Suslov, Boris Ponomarev, and the other old-style ideologues who were associated over the years with the Comintern, the Cominform, and more recently the International Department of the Central Committee.[110] Gone, too, is the bandwagon imagery of their "correlation of forces" theory.[111] Progressive change in the Third World is now universally portrayed as slow, reversible, and problematic. Gorbachev is prone to admonish visiting dignitaries from backward client states that "no country is secure against the desire of its vanguard to skip over unavoidable stages."[112]

Military conquest, even of backward states, is seen as difficult. This new view seems to be held even by military officers, suggesting that it may simply reflect learning rather than institutional change. In Grechko's time, the military had been a major enthusiast for Third World- involvement and later reportedly favored the intervention in Afghanistan.[113] But this recent Yugoslav interview with Marshal Kulikov, the Warsaw Pact commander, demonstrates a new ambivalence about the use of force:[114]

Q: If a country lacks an operative army as big as, for instance, the Warsaw Pact or NATO, but possesses an armed people willing to fight and a wide concept of defense, can such a country be defeated?
 Kulikov: Which country?
 Q: Any country.
 Kulikov: A victory may be attained. Indeed only for a time, for it is something else to rule such a country. World public opinion, other factors, all that is present. It is very difficult to defeat a people determined to defend itself.

Asked specifically about Afghanistan, Kulikov remarks that it is difficult to generalize lessons from it: "I tell you that war in Afghanistan is very strange."

Other Soviet officials, however, have been more willing to generalize. Noting that the Soviet Union has backed whichever side was on the defensive in the Iran–Iraq war in order to prevent the conquest of either, a Soviet U.N. delegate went on to claim that on principle the Soviet Union "does not support materially or in any other form the party that is on the offensive, and I think this is of some importance."[115]

Some caveats should be mentioned about the geographical aspects of the new thinking. First, even under Brezhnev, the line was that Soviet military power was used to "defend the gains of socialism," as in Ethiopia and Afghanistan, not to export revolution through military offensives. For example, the Soviets refused to allow the Ethiopians to roll Soviet-supplied tanks across the border into Somalia. Second, a number of instances of increased aggressiveness of Soviet Third World behavior might be noted under Gorbachev.[116] Perhaps the most important is the stepped-up cross-border bombardment of Pakistan. Though Gorbachev may want very badly to extricate himself from the mistakes of his predecessors, considerations of prestige and domestic politics may make it hard to take the direct route out. Like Nixon in Vietnam, Gorbachev may feel compelled to adopt a "Christmas bombing" strategy of extrication through massive escalation of the war into Pakistan. Though this seems unlikely at present, it underscores the need to use diplomacy, and not just military pressure, to help Gorbachev find a way out of Afghanistan.[117]

Alternative Trajectories of Change

In the preceding sections I have been discussing logical developments of institutions, policies, and ideas, given the assumption that Gorbachev will enjoy a significant degree of success in implementing his domestic reforms. Structural changes have made this a possibility, and the decisions of the June 1987 plenum, which ratified an ambitious economic reform plan and promoted three Gorbachev allies to the Politburo, make it even more likely.[118] Nonetheless, other scenarios deserve mention, especially insofar as the international environment might have some effect on their likelihood.

One cause of concern stems from the character of some of Gorbachev's closest allies. Yakovlev is essentially an ideologue and a propagandist. Though he seems to have devised a stunning formula for modernizing those roles, there is still a danger that some of their traditional content will sneak back in—and if not for Yakovlev personally, then for his underlings or successors. Likewise, Lev Zaikov, the overseer of the defense industries, has his roots in Leningrad's high technology military sector.[119] His orientation toward technological modernization makes him an appropriate backer for Gorbachev's restructuring, but it is hard to forget the role played by previous Leningrad party chiefs—Frol Kozlov and Grigorii Romanov—in backing big defense budgets. It would not be difficult to imagine Zaikov aligning with modernizing elements in the military, like Marshal Ogarkov, who favor a more militarized version of the reforms. Some research suggests that there are circles in the military who favor economic restructuring, but not of the market-oriented kind. Instead, their notion may be to advance some of the more successful practices of the hierarchical defense sector as a model for the economy as a whole.[120]

Another source of danger lies at the periphery of the reform coalition. Yegor Ligachev, the second secretary of the party, has supported the general idea of reform, but has often voiced reservations about the pace and direction of change. In the arts, he calls for "vivid and profound images of Communists" to counterbalance what he sees as the excessively critical outpouring under *glasnost*.[121] In the foreign trade area, he warns about the excesses of the "imported purchases' craze."[122] Moreover, his arguments for détente and reform take on an offensive, Brezhnevian caste:

> The restructuring is unbreakably linked with the USSR's vigorous peaceloving policy. On the one hand, its scope depends on the reliability of peace, on the stability of the international situation. On the other hand, the renewal imparts still greater dynamism and intensity to the foreign policy activity of the CPSU and the Soviet state, strengthens the foundations for their struggle for peace.[123]

Thus, if Gorbachev's radical program runs into obstacles, Ligachev will be there to put his stamp on a scaled-down version that retains many of the features of the Soviet domestic order and foreign policy under Brezhnev.

A final possibility is at least likely but the most worrisome. It is possible that Gorbachev may fail spectacularly, but only after he has so stirred up the social and political system that returning to a Ligachev-type solution is impossible. In that case, a variety of nefarious actors might be able to enter the political process. For example, *glasnost* has allowed the extreme Great Russian nationalists to emerge from the shadows and go so far as to compare the current liberal trends in Soviet culture to the German invasion of June 1941.[124] In the past, Shelepin tried to tap this source of political energy, linking it to a heterogeneous would-be coalition that was to attract the KGB, the radical military, and Khrushchevite populists.[125] He had almost no success with this project, but in a more wide-open political environment, an analogous coalition might form around a militarized, xenophobic version of the reforms.

Two factors might make these adverse trajectories more likely. One would be the discrediting of Gorbachev's version of the domestic reforms through dramatically poor economic performance. The second, interacting with the first, would be a hostile international environment, in which SDI was being deployed,[126] Eastern Europe was asserting its autonomy, and Soviet clients were losing their counterinsurgency wars in Afghanistan, Angola, and Ethiopia. This would discredit the international assumptions and requirements of the Gorbachev-style reforms, and possibly promote a more militarized version.

ALTERNATE VIEWS OF GORBACHEV'S REFORMS

I have argued that Gorbachev appears to be aiming for a change in the Soviet Union's fundamental institutions. In the past, these institutions, many of them rooted in Stalin's revolution from above, supported militant expansionism and offensive, zero-sum approaches to security. They also promoted the offensive approach to détente taken by Khrushchev and Brezhnev. Gorbachev's new domestic coalition and institutional innovations are likely to call forth and sustain a new, less militant foreign policy. This is true both because the old institutions are being checked or swept away by reforms, and also because of the new system's inherent need for more stable relations with the advanced capitalist countries.

Making this argument in a brief article, I have not been able to address fully some important rival theories. One is that Gorbachev's new thinking in foreign policy is not rooted in domestic institutions, but simply reflects lessons drawn from the failures of Brezhnev's foreign and security policies. If so, those lessons, like previous swings of the right/left pendulum in Soviet history,[127] could be as easily unlearned as they were learned. The validity of this objection hinges in part on how closely I—and the sources I have cited—have established the links between particular strategic ideas and the groups and coalitions that support them. Some Sovietologists, arguing for cognitive or international explanations of Soviet foreign policy, have questioned these domestic political connections, pointing out that the top leader himself has often been the source of expansionist policies and concepts.[128] What this argument has missed, however, is the extent to which the General Secretaries' policies and concepts were a response to a variety of domestic political pressures, identical to none of them individually, but caused by the need to manage all of them simultaneously.

Proponents of a second theory would hold that I have placed too much emphasis on the particularities of Stalin's revolution from above, and not enough on earlier pathologies of Leninism or of Russian autocracy.[129] Here, I would argue that Stalin's system, with its hypercentralism, authoritarianism, xenophobia, and military orientation, was a kind of apotheosis of those earlier patterns. If Gorbachev has broken Stalin's pattern, he has broken his predecessors' as well.

Finally, there is the theory that all great powers behave aggressively because of the consequences of international anarchy or for other reasons. While this may be true, there has nonetheless been a significant range in the aggressiveness of great powers, a good deal of it due to variations in their domestic systems. The Soviet Union under Brezhnev was already less pathological than some of the great powers that have populated the twentieth century. Gorbachev's Russia as I have extrapolated it should be still less aggressive.

POLICY PRESCRIPTIONS FOR THE WEST

In order to make the most of the opportunities presented by the new thinking, American policy should follow three guidelines. First, the U.S. should avoid mounting intense geopolitical challenges, like a Strategic Defense Initiative deployment or rollback attempts on the Soviet periphery, that would force the reforms to move in a militarized direction. Military-oriented, authoritarian revolution from above is the normal pattern of Russian response to intense pressure from its environment. Moderate international pressure helps Gorbachev, because it makes reform seem necessary, but intense pressure is likely to hurt him, since it makes an Ogarkov-type reform seem more appropriate.

Second, the U.S. should continue to reciprocate meaningful Soviet concessions, like the Soviet INF offers, to avoid discrediting the new thinking, parts of which may be quite fragile. Malenkov's fate is instructive in this regard. On one hand, it is true that the West's vigorous military response to the invasion of South Korea undoubtedly helped proponents of a less assertive Soviet foreign policy in the Kremlin, by discrediting the former hard line. On the other hand, once that point was proved, further American intransigence hurt proponents of a relaxation of tension after they came to power. Herbert Dinerstein has shown Malenkov's political career foundered in part on America's unhelpful reactions to his strategic innovations.[130]

Gorbachev is much stronger politically, but the same rule applies. America's reaction to Afghanistan probably worked in his favor, by discrediting the expansionist, militarist aspects of the old Brezhnev line. Bur further Western intransigence certainly would not help him, since he has implicitly promised that his strategy of competitive peace "propaganda" will lead to a more stable superpower relationship.

Third, the United States should press hard for meaningful restructuring of the Soviet foreign trade system and of the Soviet Army's offensive conventional posture in Europe. The West should be firm in tying Soviet membership in the General Agreement on Tariffs and Trade (GATT) and the International Monetary Fund (IMF) to some restructuring of Soviet price-setting practices, which it can justify as insurance against Soviet dumping of goods at prices below their cost of production. The U.S. should also take up Soviet offers to discuss changes in conventional force postures from offense to defense.[131] These are measures that could have important side-effects on Soviet domestic structure, deepening the reform and strengthening its institutions. Gorbachev may want to take these steps anyway, but unless America takes an active role and offers to meet him half way, they may be hard for Gorbachev to push through.

Finally, let me reinforce the qualifications with which I opened the argument. Social science does not predict the future. At best, it generates expectations about future outcomes, assuming that certain causal conditions are present. Thus, I could be wrong either because my theory about the domestic sources of Soviet expansionism is flawed, or because Gorbachev's reforms will not make sufficient changes in the causal variables to affect the outcome.

All the evidence is not yet in on the Gorbachev revolution. Nonetheless, it is important to advance hypotheses as best we can, in part so that we can recognize the relevant evidence when it does come in, and in part because our own interim actions may affect the outcome. Some of the most positive aspects of Gorbachev's new thinking, especially his interest in defensive conventional strategies, may be short-lived if the West creates an environment that is inhospitable to their survival.

ACKNOWLEDGMENT

I would like to acknowledge helpful suggestions and criticisms from Seweryn Bialer, Douglas Blum, Hope Harrison, Ted Hopf, Robert Legvold, Michael McGwire, Mark Pekala, James Richter, Cynthia Roberts, Elizabeth Valkenier and several participants at a Rand Corporation seminar, and financial support from the National Council for Soviet and East European Research.

NOTES

1. Such views are cited and briefly summarized in Alexander Dallin and Gail Lapidus, "Reagan and the Russians: United States Policy toward the Soviet Union and Eastern Europe," in Kenneth Oye, ed., *Eagle Defiant* (Boston: Little, Brown, 1983), pp. 191–236, esp. 232–33.

2. For an overview and evaluation of these changes, see Seweryn Bialer, "The Progress of Mikhail Gorbachev," *Foreign Affairs* 66, no. 2 (Winter 1988), and Bialer, "Gorbachev's Move," *Foreign Policy*, no. 68 (September 1987), pp. 59–87.

3. A useful, analytical overview is Robert Legvold, "The Revolution in Soviet Foreign Policy," Ch. 14 above.

4. The theory underpinning this analysis is based on Alexander Gerschenkron, *Economic Backwardness in Historical Perspective* (Cambridge, MA: Belknap, 1962). Current Soviet analyses are similar. Note Gorbachev's *Unità* interview, *Pravda*, May 20, 1987 *(Foreign Broadcast Information Service, Soviet Union [FBIS]*, May 20, 1987) on the imprint socialism bears from the "grim" conditions in which it was built—intervention, civil war, economic blockade, "the military provocations and constant pressure from imperialism."

5. Following the usage of Joseph Schumpeter, *Imperialism and Social Classes* (London University Press, 1951; original edition, 1919), and also that of Gerschenkron, I use the term *atavism* to mean a group or institution that continues to carry out a task that, due to changing conditions, has become dysfunctional for society.

6.   Harry Gelman, *The Brezhnev Politburo and the Decline of Détente* (Ithaca, NY: Cornell University Press, 1984), p. 215.

7.   *Pravda*, January 28, 1987; *Current Digest of the Soviet Press [CDSP]* 39, no. 4, p. 1. These themes were reiterated in Gorbachev's speech on the anniversary of the Bolshevik revolution, *The New York Times*, November 3, 1987, pp. A11–13.

8.   See especially the economic reform program ratified by the June 1987 Central Committee plenum, *Pravda*, June 27, 1987; *FBIS*, June 30, 1987.

9.   *Izvestiia*, August 19, 1986, as cited by Legvold, "The Renovation in Soviet Foreign Policy."

10.   When I use the term *institution*, I mean not only bureaucratic organizations, but also established ways of organizing social relationships, such as the institution of central planning or of the market.

11.   For a state-building perspective on the Bolshevik revolution, see Gerschenkron, *Economic Backwardness*, and Theda Skocpol, *States and Social Revolutions* (Cambridge: Cambridge University Press, 1979).

12.   Quoted in Isaac Deutscher, *Stalin* (New York: Oxford University Press, 1949), p. 328.

13.   Ibid., p. 321.

14.   Sheila Fitzpatrick, "The Russian Revolution and Social Mobility," *Politics and Society* 13, no. 2 (1984), pp. 124–26.

15.   Speech to the March 1939 Party Congress, quoted in Sheila Fitzpatrick, "Stalin and the Making of a New Elite, 1928–1939," *Slavic Review* 38, no. 3 (1979), pp. 377–402.

16.   Lynne Viola, "The Campaign of the 25,000ers: A Study of the Collectivization of Soviet Agriculture, 1929–1931" (Princeton University dissertation in history, October 1984), p. 59, also available as *Best Sons of the Fatherland: Workers in the Vanguard of Collectivization* (New York: Oxford University Press, 1986). For Stalin speeches clearly showing the manipulation of the 1927 war scare for factional and mobilizational purposes, see Jane Degras, *Soviet Documents of Foreign Policy, II, 1925–1932* (London: Oxford University Press, 1952), pp. 233–37, 301–2. While Stalin was trumpeting the threat in public, a briefing to the Politburo from Foreign Minister Chicherin argued flatly that the idea of an imminent danger of war was utter nonsense. See Michal Reiman, *Die Geburt des Stalinismus* (Frankfurt: Europaische, 1979), p. 37.

17.   Viola "The Campaign of the 25,000ers," p. 29; J. Arch Getty, *Origins of the Great Purges* (Cambridge: Cambridge University Press, 1985). For a debate on the new social history of the Stalin period, see the essays by Fitzpatrick, Stephen Cohen, and other commentators in *Russia Review* 45, no. 4 (October 1986). Wolfgang Leonhard recounts that the new intelligentsia was so steeped in the militant ideology of the revolution from above that, when given access to the foreign press, "we could hardly summon up any interest" in viewpoints couched in "expressions which were so entirely meaningless to us." Only Trotskyite publications were dangerous, he explains, because they "wrote in our own language." *Child of the Revolution* (Chicago: Regnery, 1958), p. 235.

18.   David J. Dallin, *Soviet Foreign Policy after Stalin* (Philadelphia: Lippincott, 1961), esp. pp. 229, 332–33; Mohamed Heikal, *Sphinx and Commissar* (London: Collins, 1978), pp. 90–92; Uri Ra'anan, *The USSR Arms the Third World* (Cambridge, MA: MIT Press, 1969), chapter 4.

19.   E. H. Carr, *Twilight of the Comintern, 1930–1935* (New York: Pantheon, 1982), p. 27.

20.   On the political economy of Kozlov's Leningrad, see Blair Ruble, *Leningrad: Shaping the Face of a Soviet City* (Franklin K. Lane Studies in Regional Governance, 1988), p. 33 and passim. On the budgetary and foreign policy stance of Kozlov and other military-industrial figures in the late Khrushchev period, see Carl Linden, *Khrushchev and the Soviet Leadership* (Baltimore, MD: Johns Hopkins University Press, 1966), pp. 50–54 and passim; Sidney Ploss, *Conflict and Decision-Making in Soviet Russia* (Prince-

ton: Princeton University Press, 1965), pp. 216–34; Christer Jonsson, *Soviet Bargaining Behavior: The Nuclear Test Ban Case* (New York: Columbia, 1979), pp. 133–208; Michel Tatu, *Power in the Kremlin* (New York: Viking, 1970). Hannes Adomeit, *Soviet Risk-Taking and Crisis Behavior* (London: Allen and Unwin, 1982), p. 262, points out that Kozlov was apparently not a risk-taker.

21.   Gavriel Ra'anan, *International Policy Formation in the USSR: Factional "Debates" during the Zhdanovshchina* (Hamden, CT: Archon, 1983). Werner Hahn, *Postwar Soviet Politics* (Ithaca, NY: Cornell University Press, 1982), sees Zhdanov as relatively moderate, especially in comparison with the party militants that succeeded him, like Suslov. In fact, Zhdanov's constituencies did lead him to be "moderate" on some foreign and security issues at least some of the time—e.g., limits on defense spending (to undercut Malenkov's heavy-industrial base), opportunities for foreign trade (a Leningrad interest), communization of Eastern Europe by political (not police) methods. But the suggestion that Zhdanov was actually opposed to the Cominform policy that he implemented so vigorously is certainly at odds with the memoirs of the European Communists who lived through it. See Ruble, *Leningrad*, pp. 30–32; Jerry Hough, "Debates about the Postwar World," in Susan J. Linz, ed. *The Impact of World War II on the Soviet Union* (Totowa, NJ: Rowman and Allenhead, 1985), p. 275; Eugenio Reale, *Avec Jacques Duclos au Banc des Accusés* (Paris: Plon, n.d.), pp. 10–11 and passim. Zhdanov's Cominform speech is reprinted in Myron Rush, *The International Situation and Soviet Foreign Policy* (Columbus, Merrill, 1969).

22.   William McGagg, *Stalin Embattled* (Detroit: Wayne State University Press, 1978), p. 117 for this quotation; passim for the interpretation on which this paragraph is based.

23.   On this point see also Timothy Dunmore, *Soviet Politics, 1945–1953* (New York: St. Martin's, 1984), pp. 116–117, and Radomir Luza, "Czechoslovakia between Democracy and Communism, 1945–1948," In Charles S. Maier, ed. *The Origins of the Cold War and Contemporary Europe* (New York: New Viewpoints, 1978), pp. 73–106.

24.   Ronald Letteney, "Foreign Policy Factionalism under Stalin, 1949–1950" (Ph.D. dissertation, Johns Hopkins University, School of Advanced International Studies, 1971), passim but especially p. 197, quoting a Suslov speech in *Pravda*, November 29, 1949. See also Marshall Shulman, *Stalin's Foreign Policy Reappraised* (New York: Atheneum, 1969), pp. 118–20.

25.   On Suslov and the International Department ideologues, see Roy Medvedev, *All Stalin's Men* (Garden City, NY: Anchor, 1984), chapter 3; Arkady Shevchenko, *Breaking with Moscow* (New York: Knopf, 1985), pp. 180, 190–91, 220, 262; Bruce Parrott, *Politics and Technology in the Soviet Union* (Cambridge, MA: MIT Press, 1985), pp. 193–98; also, the works cited above by Gelman, Tatu, Linden, and Ploss.

26.   G. Ra'anan, *International Policy Formation*, pp. 64, 68–70; Hough in Linz, *Impact of World War II*, pp. 268–74; Shulman, *Stalin's Foreign Policy*, pp. 32–34, 111–17; Parrott, *Politics and Technology*, pp. 82–91; Letteney, "Foreign Policy Factionalism," pp. 61–62, 65.

27.   Herbert Dinerstein, *War and the Soviet Union* (New York: Praeger, 1959), chapter 4.

28.   Letteney, "Foreign Policy Factionalism," p. 330. Letteney also provides indirect but voluminous evidence that Malenkov and his allies criticized the 1948 Berlin policy as having justified the formation of NATO and the deployment of American nuclear forces within striking distance of the Soviet Union; pp. 56, 77, 82–83, quoting *Izvestiia*, February 12, 1949; March 19, 1949; July 22, 1949. Note also that Zhdanov appointees ran Soviet policy in Germany until the lifting of the blockade in 1949, when they were replaced by Malenkov-Beria men. See Ann Phillips, *Soviet Policy toward East Germany Reconsidered: The Postwar Decade* (Westport, CT: Greenwood, 1986), p. 34. Authors like Dunmore who portray Malenkov as a belligerent cold warrior during this

period present virtually no evidence to support their view. It is likely, however, that Malenkov supported the military buildup at this time, because it led to the return to power of his wartime heavy-industry cronies. See Jeremy Azrael, *Managerial Power and Soviet Politics* (Cambridge, MA: Harvard University Press, 1966), chapter 5. I am indebted to Dr. Azrael for a helpful discussion of these issues.

29. Franklyn Griffiths, "Images, Politics, and Learning in Soviet Behavior toward the United States" (Columbia University dissertation, 1972), pp. 40–41.

30. Ploss, *Conflict and Decision-Making*, p. 68; Boris Nicolaevsky, *Power and the Soviet Elite* (New York: Praeger, 1965), chapter 3, esp. p. 153; Roger Pethybridge, *A Key to Soviet Politics* (London: Allen and Unwin, 1962), pp. 30–36.

31. Vera Dunham, *In Stalin's Time: Middleclass Values in Soviet Fiction* (Cambridge: Cambridge University Press, 1976).

32. Parrott, *Politics and Technology*, pp. 182–86, 190, 197; Gelman, *The Brezhnev Politburo*, p. 85 and passim; Heikal, *Sphinx and Commissar*, p. 194.

33. Franklyn Griffiths, "The Sources of American Conduct: Soviet Perspectives and Their Policy Implications," *International Security* 9, no. 2 (Fall 1984), pp. 3–50; and Raymond Garthoff, *Détente and Confrontation* (Washington, DC: Brookings Institution, 1985), pp. 36–68, elaborate on and qualify these basic themes.

34. Quoted by Adomeit, *Soviet Risk-Taking*, p. 224.

35. My interpretation closely parallels that of James Richter, "Action and Reaction in Khrushchev's Foreign Policy: Leadership Politics and Soviet Responses to the International Environment" (Ph.D. dissertation, University of California at Berkeley, 1988). Richter's very important dissertation, based on exhaustive research in primary source material, is in some respects an application to foreign policy of George Breslauer's authority-building argument, which *inter alia* showed how the Soviet coalition-making process leads to overcommitted, "taut" policy platforms. George Breslauer, *Khrushchev and Brezhnev as Leaders* (London: Allen and Unwin, 1982), esp. p. 288.

36. Richter, adding nuances, develops a similar argument from an analysis of leadership speeches, which can be corroborated by a variety of other kinds of sources. See Arnold Horelick and Myron Rush, *Strategic Power and Soviet Foreign Policy* (Chicago: University of Chicago Press, 1966) on nuclear diplomacy; Parrott, *Politics and Technology*, pp. 131, 158–63, and 171–72 on the political role of nuclear and other high technology policies; ibid, p. 137, for Khrushchev's ideas about "the social significance of the ICBM"; Heikal, *Sphinx and Commissar*, pp. 97–98, 128–29, for an exposition to Nasser of Khrushchev's strategic theory.

37. As early as 1954, Khrushchev had used nuclear strategy as a successful political weapon against Malenkov and, in a passage from a speech that his colleagues excised from the *Pravda* version, Khrushchev bragged that "we were even quicker than the capitalist camp and invented the hydrogen bomb before they had it; we, the Party and the working class, we know the importance of this bomb." Wolfgang Leonhard, *The Kremlin without Stalin* (Westport, CT: Greenwood, 1975), p. 88. Richter, however, shows that the mature form of Khrushchev's strategic ideology, featuring optimistic reliance on the ICBM and popular forces promoting progressive political change, was not fully worked out until later.

38. For some minor qualifications, see Breslauer, *Khrushchev and Brezhnev as Leaders*, pp. 67–71.

39. Jack Schick, *The Berlin Crisis, 1958–1962* (Philadelphia: University of Pennsylvania Press, 1971).

40. *Pravda*, March 12, 1958. Richter alerted me to this speech.

41. Linden advanced the hypothesis that, in some general way, a victory in Berlin would give Khrushchev the prestige he needed to check his domestic opponents and push on with his economic program. Richter, however, is the first to clarify this argument conceptually and to show in convincing detail how it worked.

42. The following reconstruction draws on Gelman, *Brezhnev Politburo*, Parrott, *Politics and Technology*, and Richter, "Action and Reaction."

43. For Shelepin's probable stance, in addition to sources cited by Gelman and Parrott, see Joan Barth Urban, "Contemporary Soviet Perspectives on Revolution in the West," *Orbis* 19, no. 4 (1976), pp. 1359–1402, especially p. 1379.

44. Shevchenko, *Breaking with Moscow*, pp. 211–12.

45. Bruce Parrott, *The Soviet Union and Ballistic Missile Defense* (Boulder, CO: Westview, 1987), pp. 27–39, on resource allocation debates in the mid-1970s; Michael MccGwire, *Military Objectives in Soviet Foreign Policy* (Washington, DC: Brookings Institution, 1987), pp. 61–62, 108–112, and Richard F. Kaufman, "Causes of the Slowdown in Soviet Defense," *Soviet Economy* 1, no. 1 (January–March 1985), pp. 9–32, on military policy changes in 1976–77. See also Jeremy Azrael, *The Soviet Civilian Leadership and the Military High Command, 1976–1986* (Santa Monica, CA: Rand R-3521-AF, June 1987).

46. Parrott, *Ballistic Missile Defense*, pp. 46–47; see also Garthoff, *Détente and Confrontation*, p. 1018, fn. 21. Mark Pekala has discovered an Aesopian piece in *Kommunist vooruzhennykh sil* no. 24 (December 1984), which portrays an alleged attempt by Trotsky in 1923 to exploit a period of foreign threat and leadership transition and illness to militarize the party and the country at the expense of the party's program of economic reform and restoration, which required decreased military expenditures. Translated in JPRS-UMA-85-027, April 19, 1985, Cynthia Roberts notes that this piece is full of historical inaccuracies, further suggesting that it had a current policy motivation.

47. Elizabeth Valkenier, "Revolutionary Change in the Third World: Recent Soviet Assessments," *World Politics* 38, no. 3 (April 1986), pp. 415–34, esp. 426.

48. *Pravda*, June 16, 1983; *CDSP* 35, no. 25, p. 8.

49. *Pravda*, January 24, 1955; *CDSP* 6, no. 52, p. 6.

50. For applications of this branch of psychological theory to foreign policymaking, see Richard Ned Lebow, *Between Peace and War* (Baltimore, Johns Hopkins University Press, 1981), chapter 5.

51. Heikal, *Sphinx and Commissar*, pp. 96–97.

52. The clearest cases are perhaps the U-2 (Tatu, *Power in the Kremlin*, part one) and Jackson-Vanik (Gelman, *The Brezhnev Politburo*, p. 161; Urban, "Contemporary Soviet Perspectives," p. 1379).

53. For example, Woodruff Smith, *The Ideological Origins of Nazi Imperialism* (New York: Oxford University Press, 1986). This is another case where Gerschenkron's perspective is helpful.

54. Shulman, *Stalin's Foreign Policy Reappraised*, p. 13.

55. For a summary of and citations to this literature, see Bartlomeij Kaminski, "Pathologies of Central Planning," *Problems of Communism* 36, no. 2 (March–April 1987), pp. 81–95.

56. For a variety of perspectives, some quite skeptical, see *Soviet Economy* 2, no. 4 (October–December 1986).

57. G. Smirnov, the new head of the Institute of Marxism-Leninism, "The Revolutionary Essence of Renewal," *Pravda*, March 13, 1987; *CDSP* 39, no. 1, pp. 15–16.

58. Gavriil Popov, "Restructuring the Economy," *Pravda*, January 20 and 21, 1987; *CDSP* 39, no. 3, p. 4. Popov was one of the main speakers at a meeting on economic reform attended by most of the Politburo just before the June 1987 plenum. Philip Hanson and Elizabeth Teague, "Party Conference Prepares for Plenum," Radio Liberty Report #228/87, June 15, 1985.

59. Francis Fukuyama, *Moscow's Post-Brezhnev Reassessment of the Third World* (Santa Monica, CA: The RAND Corporation, Rand R-3337-AF, February 1986).

60. G. Mirskii, "K voprosy o vybore puti i orientatsii razvivaiushchikhsia stran," *Mirovaia ekonomika i mezhdunarodnye otnosheniia [MEiMO]* no. 5 (May 1987), pp. 70–81.

61. A. P. Aleksandrov, *Pravda*, February 27, 1986; *CDSP* 38, no. 9, p. 9; Yegor Ligachev's criticism of research institutes in *Pravda*, October 2, 1986; *CDSP* 40, no. 8, p. 9.

62. As reported in *Krasnaia zvezda*, June 17, 1987; *FBIS*, June 17, 1987, pp. V2–V4. See also unsigned essay, "Armiia i usloviiakh demokratizatsii," *Kommunist* 14 (Sept. 1987), pp. 117–19.

63. Alexander Rahr, "Restructuring in the KGB," Radio Liberty Report No. 226–87, June 15, 1987.

64. Anatolii Butenko, Moscow State University Professor and analyst at Oleg Bogomolov's institute on the bloc economy, *Moskovskaia Pravda*, May 7, 1987; *FBIS*, May 26, p. R5.

65. Ruble, *Leningrad*, p. 16, citing *Narodnoe khoziaistvo SSSR v 1980g: Statisticheskii ezhegodnik* (Moscow: Finansy i statistiki, 1981), p. 27, and previous volumes.

66. Gorbachev to the Twentieth Komsomol Congress, April 16, 1987; *FBIS*, April 17, 1987, R3.

67. Ibid., R10.

68. Popov, "Restructuring the Economy," p. 4.

69. This is directly reflected in the June plenum resolution on economic reform, *Pravda*, June 27, 1987; *FBIS*, June 30. See also Tat'iana Zaslavskaia, "The Novosibirsk Report," *Survey* 27, no. 1 (Spring 1984), pp. 83–109, and other works cited in George Weickhardt, "The Soviet Military-Industrial Complex and Economic Reform," *Soviet Economy* 2, no. 3 (July–September 1986), pp. 193–220, esp. 211, 220.

70. Philip Taubman, "Architect of Soviet Change," *The New York Times*, July 10, 1987, p. D3.

71. Says Central Committee Secretary Vadim Medvedev: "We have succeeded in literally stirring up the masses, even those who previously used to be far from politics, and have succeeded in making them active participants in the restructuring in the outlying areas. The truth expands and reinforces its social base." *Pravda*, May 17, 1987; *FBIS*, May 27.

72. *The New York Times*, July 4, 1987, pp. 1–2; *The Washington Post*, June 27, 1987, p. A24.

73. For Gorbachev, see *Pravda*, January 28, 1987, *CDSP* 39, no. 6, pp. 8, 13. Yeltsin told the Party Congress that the Party is so "enmeshed in economic affairs that they have sometimes begun to lose their position as agencies of political leadership. It's no accident that the structure of the Central Committee's departments has gradually become all but a copy of the ministries. Many people have simply forgotten what true party work is." *Pravda*, February 27, 1986; *CDSP* 38, no. 9, p. 5.

74. Gorbachev in Krasnodar, *Pravda*, September 20, 1986; *CDSP* 38, no. 38, p. 5.

75. Czech TV interview, *FBIS*, April 16, 1987, p. F2. Bogomolov, who exemplifies the importance of the connection between the domestic and international aspects of the economic reform, was also one of the speakers at the June pre-plenum conference. Hanson and Teague, "Party Conference." For one of many similar statements on global economic and security interdependence from Gorbachev, see his speech of February 16, 1987; *FBIS*, February 17, p. AA22.

76. V. Shastiko, *Pravda*, May 22, 1987; *FBIS*, June 23, p. S2.

77. Charles Mathias, Jr., "Red Square, Just Off Wall St.," *The New York Times*, July 20, 1987, p. 19.

78. V. Shastiko, *Pravda*, May 22, 1987; *FBIS*, June 23, p. S3.

79. Gennadi Lisichkin, of the Institute for the Study of the Socialist World Economy, quoted by Agence France Presse, June 29, 1987; *FBIS*, July 1, 1987. See also Bill Keller, "New Struggle in the Kremlin: How to Change the Economy," *The New York Times*, June 4, 1986, pp. 1, 6, citing Nikolai Shmelyov, "Avansi i dolgi," *Novyi Mir*, (June 1987), pp. 142–158, esp. 153.

80. *The New York Times*, May 31, 1987. The civilian think-tank is a section, headed by Alexei Arbatov, within the Institute for World Economy and International Relations (IMEMO). The central committee staff is also playing a more prominent role in arms control policy under Anatoly Dobrinin. Stressing the importance of military advice from civilian scientists like Roald Sagdeev, director of the Institute of Space Research, and Evgenii Velikhov, vice-president of the Soviet Academy of Sciences, is Matthew Evangelista, "The Domestic Politics of the Soviet Star-Wars Debate," In Harold Jacobson, William Zimmerman, and Deborah Yarsike, eds., *Adapting to SDI* (forthcoming). Robert Hutchinson, "Gorbachev Tightens Grip on Soviet High Command," *Jane's Defense Weekly* 23 (June 13, 1987), pp. 1192–94.

81. On this development, see Valkenier, "Revolutionary Change in the Third World," and the other works reviewed in George Breslauer, "Ideology and Learning in Soviet Third World Policy," *World Politics* 39, no. 3 (April 1987), pp. 429–48.

82. Interview in *La Repubblica*, May 21, 1985; *FBIS*, May 24, 1985, p. CC1.

83. See Yakovlev's "Mezhimperialisticheskie protivorechiia—sovremennyi kontekst," *Kommunist* no. 17 (November 1986), pp. 3–17.

84. *Izvestiia*, June 13, 1987; *FBIS*, June 19.

85. See Lenin's *Imperialism: The Highest Stage of Capitalism*, in James E. Connor, ed., *Lenin on Politics and Revolution* (New York: Pegasus, 1968), pp. 130–131.

86. Alexander Yakovlev, *On the Edge of the Abyss: From Truman to Reagan* (Moscow: Progress, 1985; Russian ed., Molodaia gvardiia, 1984), p. 13.

87. Alexander Yakovlev, "Istoki urgrozy i obshestvennoe mnenie," *MEiMO* 3 (1985), pp. 3–17, esp. 8–12.

88. Alexander Yanov, *The Russian New Right* (Berkeley: Institute of International Studies, Research Series #35, 1978).

89. *Time*, August 28, 1985.

90. Vadim Zagladin, "Sovremennyi mezhdunarodnyi krizis v svete leniskogo ucheniia," *MEiMO* no. 4 (April 1984), p. 4, criticizing such views. For this and other examples, see Douglas Blum, "Soviet Perceptions of American Foreign Policy after Afghanistan" (Columbia University), paper delivered at the annual meeting of the International Studies Association, April 1987, in Robert Jervis and Jack Snyder, eds. *Strategic Beliefs and Superpower Competition in the Asian Rimland*. Thomas Bjorkman and Thomas Zamostny, "Soviet Politics and Strategy toward the West," *World Politics* 34, no. 2 (January 1984), pp. 189–214, show that Bovin argued publicly that the invasion of Afghanistan had provoked such a reaction and that others who are now close to Gorbachev have expressed similar views.

91. For a theoretical discussion, see Robert Jervis, "Cooperation under the Security Dilemma," *World Politics* 32, no. 2 (January 1978), pp. 167–214.

92. *Pravda*, February 14, 1987; *CDSP* 39, no. 7, p. 23.

93. Yakovlev, *MEiMO* no. 3 (1985), pp. 10–11. See also Vitalii Zhurkin, "O strategicheskoi stabil'nosti," *S.Sh.A.* no. 1 (1986), p. 16. For similar thinking by Gorbachev and Dobrynin underpinning their resistance to matching SDI, Parrott, *Ballistic Missile Defense*, p. 75.

94. *Izvestiia*, April 16, 1987; *FBIS*, April 22, pp. CC8; see also R. Sagdayev and A. Kokoshin, "Strategic Stability under the Conditions of Radical Nuclear-Arms Reductions," (Moscow, April 1987).

95. E. Teague, "Polemics over 'Euromissiles' in the Soviet Press," Radio Liberty 113/87 (March 20, 1987), citing *Moscow News*, March 8, 1987. This query provoked a neuralgic and unconvincing rebuttal in the subsequent issue of the *Moscow News* by the general who had been in charge of INF policy in the General Staff.

96. Zhurkin, "O strategicheskoi stabil'nosti," p. 15.

97. Akhromeev, "Soviet Military Science and the Art of Warfare," *International Affairs* no. 5 (May 1985), p. 85. Akhromeev, appointed Chief of the General Staff upon

Ogarkov's removal in September 1984, had been Ogarkov's Deputy Chief, and thus is a holdover the hierarchy of the late Brezhnev period.

98. Viktor Karpov, BBC TV, May 18, 1987; *FBIS*, May 21, p. AA1.

99. V. Avakov and V. Baranovskii, "V interesakh sokhraneniia tsivilizatsii," *MEiMO* no. 4 (1987), p. 30. Even more explicit are A. Kokoshin and V. Larionov, "Kurskaia bitva v svete sovremennoi oboronitel'noi doktriny," *MEiMO* no. 8 (August 1987), pp. 32–40, and Lt. Gen. Mikhail Mil'shtein et al., roundtable discussion, "Of Reasonable Sufficiency, Precarious Parity, and International Security," *New Times* no. 27 (July 13, 1987), pp. 18–21; *FBIS*, July 16, 1987, pp. AA1.

100. For example, Col. P. A. Savushkin, "Evoliutsiia vzgliadov na oboronu v mezhvoennye gody," *Voenno-istoricheskii zhurnal* no. 1 (1987), pp. 37–42. See also Michael MccGwire, "Military Logic Changes Foreign Policy," *Newsday*, June 14, 1987, p. 4.

101. Moscow TV news conference with Gareev, June 22, 1987; *FBIS*, June 23, 1987, emphasis added. Interview with Army Gen. A. I. Gribkov, chief of the staff of the Warsaw Pact Joint Armed Forces, *Krasnaia zvezda*, Sept. 25, pp. 2–3, as translated in *FBIS*, September 30, 1987, pp. 5–8. Thanks to Stephen Meyer for this citation.

102. MccGwire, *Military Objectives*, pp. 29–35.

103. Marshal V. D. Sokolovskii and Gen. Maj. M. I. Cherednichenko, "On Contemporary Military Strategy," *Kommunist Vooruzhennykh Sil'* (April 1966), reprinted in William R. Kintner and Harriet Fast Scott, eds., *The Nuclear Revolution in Soviet Military Affairs* (Norman: University of Oklahoma, 1968), p. 264. Col. D. M. Samorukov, "Combat Operations Involving Conventional Means of Destruction," *Military Thought (Voennaia mysl'*, a restricted circulation journal), no. 8 (August 1967), reprinted in *Selected Readings from Soviet Military Thought*, Part I, p. 175. I am grateful to Mark Pekala for sharing his analysis on this and on the following point.

104. Linden, *Khrushchev*, pp. 191–92, and Thomas Wolfe, *Soviet Strategy at the Crossroads* (Cambridge, MA: Harvard University Press, 1965), pp. 149–52, offer analyses sensitive to domestic political and budgetary aspects of arguments about conventional strategy in this period. For evidence relating early conventional-option thinking to this budgetary setting, see Wolfe, pp. 121–23, 131.

105. For a theoretical statement explaining this and other reasons for professional militaries' preference for offensive strategies, see Barry Posen, *The Sources of Military Doctrine* (Ithaca, NY: Cornell, 1984), esp. p. 49.

106. Edward L. Warner, *The Military in Contemporary Soviet Politics* (New York: Praeger, 1977), pp. 94, 100, 165, on ABM changes and Grechko; MccGwire, *Military Objectives*, App. A, on conventional option and December plenum; Benjamin Lambeth, *The Soviet Strategic Challenge* (Princeton, NJ: Princeton University Press), ch. 4 on the Defense Ministership and the April meeting.

107. Richard Ned Lebow, "The Soviet Offensive in Europe: The Schlieffen Plan Revisited?" *International Security* 9, no. 4 (Spring 1985), pp. 44–78.

108. TASS, June 22, 1987; *FBIS*, June 23, AA3. Arguing for unilateral Soviet reductions, however, are three scholars from the United States and Canada Institute, Vitaly Zhurkin, Sergei Karaganov, and Andrei Kortunov, "Reasonable Sufficiency—Or How to Break the Vicious Circle," *New Times* 40 (Oct. 12, 1987), pp. 13–15; *FBIS*, Oct. 14, pp. 4–7.

109. Ibid., p. AA4.

110. On the interwining of these personal and institutional histories, see Elizabeth Teague, "The Foreign Departments of the Central Committee of the CPSU," *Radio Liberty Reports*, October 27, 1980; Leonard Schapiro, "The CPSU International Department," *International Journal* 32, no. 1 (Winter 1976–77), pp. 41–55.

111. Ted Hopf, "Soviet Inferences from Their Victories in the Periphery" (Columbia University) paper presented at the annual meeting of the International Studies Association, April 1987, in Jervis and Snyder, *Strategic Beliefs*.

112. *Pravda*, February 11, 1987; *CDSP* 39, no. 6, 19.

113. Francis Fukuyama, *Soviet Civil–Military Relations and the Power Projection Mission* (Santa Monica, CA: The RAND Corporation, Rand R-3504-AF, April 1987).

114. Zagreb *Danas*, April 14, 1987; *FBIS*, April 21, 1987, AA11.

115. *The New York Times*, January 12, 1987. For other evidence, Blum, "Soviet Perceptions," p. 36.

116. Harry Gelman, "The Soviet Union, East Asia and the West: The Kremlin's Calculation of Opportunities and Risks," in *East Asia, the West and International Security*, Adelphi Paper No. 217 (London: International Institute for Strategic Studies, Spring 1987), pp. 3–26.

117. For background on Soviet positions, see Bohdan Nahaylo, "Towards a Settlement of the Afghanistan Conflict: A Chronological Overview," Radio Liberty 16/87, January 11, 1987.

118. *The New York Times*, June 27, 1987.

119. Ruble, *Leningrad*, chapter 2.

120. Weickhardt, "Soviet Military-Industrial Complex," pp. 214–15, 225.

121. *Teatr*, No. 8 (August 1986); *CDSP* 38, no. 44, p. 1.

122. *Pravda*, October 2, 1986; *CDSP* 38, no. 40, pp. 8–9.

123. TASS, April 17, 1987, reporting on Ligachev's interview with visiting Congressman Jim Wright; *FBIS*, April 20.

124. *Literaturnaia Rosiia*, March 27, 1987.

125. On the chauvinist radical right, see John B. Dunlop, *The Faces of Contemporary Russian Nationalism* (Princeton, NJ: Princeton University Press, 1983), esp. pp. 217–27; Felicity Barringer, "Russian Nationalists Test Gorbachev," *The New York Times*, May 24, 1987, p. 10.

126. For this argument on SDI, see Parrott, *Ballistic Missile Defense*, chapter 5.

127. Putting these developments in this light is Francis Fukuyama, "Patterns of Soviet Third World Policy," *Problems of Communism*, xxxvi, 5 (1987), pp. 1–13.

128. Adomeit, *Soviet Risk-Taking*, pp. 188–93.

129. For example, Richard Pipes, "Militarism and the Soviet State," *Daedalus* 109 (Fall 1980), pp. 1–12.

130. Dinerstein, *War and the Soviet Union*, chapter 4.

131. I will discuss these changes in more detail in the next issue of *International Security*.

35
The Soviet Threat in the 1990s*

Colin S. Gray

The current Soviet time of troubles assuredly will pass, as someone moves to reassert a strong grip from Moscow, and—no less assuredly— professional prudence will triumph in the field of military doctrine. Whether perestroika *succeeds or fails, and whether or not a rather authoritarian presidential system of government succeeds the reign of the CPSU, Russian geography, history, culture, and armament renders it a permanent threat to the balance of power in Eurasia.*

Contrary to the tide of official and public opinion at the present time, it is the central contention of this article that there is more peril than promise in the contemporary course of Soviet–American relations. Mikhail Gorbachev is but the latest in a long succession of reforming czars. It is all but inconceivable that he could direct and oversee the transformation of the brutal, continental multinational empire that is the USSR into something so much kinder and gentler that a truly objective basis for a structural improvement in political–security relations would be the consequence.

This is not to say that the United States and the Soviet Union are locked into a permanent enmity. Imperial Russia and the United States were functional allies *vis-à-vis* possible dangers from Britain through most of the nineteenth century;[1] generically similar policy calculation could reproduce that objectively based

*Reprinted by permission of the author and publisher from *Global Affairs* (Spring 1990). Copyright © 1990 by the International Security Council.

friendliness sometime in the future. But there is little about Gorbachev's *perestroika* that carries a plausible promise for the drastic rewriting of the terms and conditions of Soviet–American relations. Lest there be any misunderstanding, the skepticism that pervades this essay does not extend to many of Gorbachev's motives. It is entirely probable that Gorbachev sincerely desires to modernize the USSR and no less sincerely desires a period of international political relaxation while perestroika struggles to secure some lasting domestic grip. However, there is no reason to believe that Gorbachev is any more, or less, sincere about his variant of peaceful coexistence and "new thinking for our country *and the world*[2] than was his forebear, Lenin. Gorbachev's novel reference to "humankind interest" with respect to the obvious perils of nuclear war are very likely as sincere as they are fully compatible with the preferences of the General Staff.

Gorbachev's policy motives probably are both wholly traditional and close to irrelevant. His leadership role plainly is uniquely important, but the changes under way in the Soviet empire are by no means solely the result of one man's commitment to change. Even if Gorbachev personally would like to transform the USSR from ugly continental predator to global good neighbor (by reasonable definition of the neighbors), it seems highly unlikely that Russian/Soviet political–strategic culture, the great institutions of the Soviet state, or plain objective conditions (bearing upon domestic political stability for the leading consideration) would permit him to succeed—whether or not the CPSU has been deprived of its "vanguard" role in favor of a rather authoritarian presidential system of government.

WHAT DRIVES SOVIET–AMERICAN RELATIONS?

Soviet–American relations should not be liable to radical restructuring in the face of the words of the latest reforming czar. The decades of variable hostility were not the product of words, of personalities, or of the ever-shifting fashion in beliefs, which so alters the tone of domestic politics in the West. Superpower relations in the miscalled Cold War, or "long peace,"[3] are explicable near totally with reference to the universal logic of the balance of power.[4]

The United States truly arrived as an essential player in the global balance of power in the winter of 1916–17, when its terms and conditions for the purchase of war materials by the allies became quite literally critical for the continued conduct of the war. It was not until 1943, however (in the context of policy planning for postwar Europe), and perhaps not even then, that the United States recognized that its statecraft would be a factor critical for the quality of international security in the postwar world.

Unfortunately, America's appearance as a self-aware superpower (certainly as a power noticeably greater relative to potential peers than great powers usually had been) coincided with both the emergence of the USSR as the latest hegemonic menace to the balance of power in Europe and Asia and the availability of (very few) atomic weapons. The novel mix of peacetime activism in balance-of-power statecraft, perception of Soviet menace, and nuclear peril has had the understandable effect of encouraging people to view the Soviet–American security relationship as something extraordinary—which it is, *for Americans*—rather than merely as the latest episode in anti-hegemonic conflict. Failure to appreciate the geostrategically rather ordinary character of their antagonism toward the USSR can spur in Americans the kind of thinking which looks to the rapid and benign transformation of Soviet–American relations.

This is not to deny the unique, or at least unusual, features in the post-1945 history of Soviet–American relations. But a good part of the imprudent optimism currently being projected for superpower relations flows from American inexperience in statecraft and from the absence of a mature tradition of prudent behavior in the maintenance of a balance of power. The baseline for normalcy in the American worldview is the baseline for a country that did not play an essential active role in the balance of power. The Cold War of such ill-renown is magnified in its alleged historical distinctiveness because, in the U.S. experience, it is contrasted not with international politics as typically conducted from the chancellories of Europe but rather with the international politics of an age remembered imperfectly as one of American innocence.

Soviet–American antagonism certainly has some ideological content, but that content is more of an overlay than essential fuel. The so-called Cold War, like the two world wars of this century, the Crimean War, and the great wars against revolutionary and Napoleonic France and—a century previously—against the France of Louis XIV, has been a balance-of-power conflict. Ideology is a weapon in contemporary international relations, certainly by contrast, say, with the international relations of the 1850s,[5] but it has little to do with what drives the strategic relations of mixed conflict and cooperation among states.

For reasons of ideology, the USSR's leaders have been rather less respectful of the ideas that other polities have legitimate interests and that the contemporary international order has value in and of itself than were the statesmen of imperial Russia. However, there is little of significance in Soviet statecraft that can be attributed uniquely to the ideology of the regime.[6] The Cold War has been about the balance of power in Eurasia. Rightly or wrongly, successive generations of American statesmen have come to believe that a single power or coalition should not be permitted to dominate Eurasia. With clear reference to the geopolitical theory of the British geographer Sir Halford Mackinder,[7] the U.S. government has stated that

> The first historical dimension of our strategy . . . is the conviction that the United States' most basic national security interests would be endangered if a hostile state or group of states were to dominate the Eurasian landmass—that area of the globe often referred to as the world's heartland.[8]

The Soviet polity is heir to the continentalist legacy bequeathed by the Russia of the Romanovs. The unique quality of Soviet threat discerned by Americans has not pointed to anything very extraordinary in Soviet statecraft but rather to the absence of adequate balancing elements within Europe and Asia and to the novel range and destructiveness of modern weapons. Personalities, policies, and ideological emphases will alter over time. But the USSR—or a Russian successor state—as an inherently insecure multinational empire,[9] can cease to pose a plausible threat to the balance of power only if other states rise to a new preeminence—as did imperial Germany after 1871—or if the country is paralyzed in its ability to act externally for reason of domestic fragilities (as was the case, for example, for several years after the 1905 revolution).

By virtue of location, size, and political–strategic culture, the Soviet Union/ Russia can hardly help posing a threat to the security of its neighbors. Whether or not Gorbachev succeeds with perestroika (whatever success would mean), the USSR is going to remain a very large military power that, on capability grounds alone, must breed anxiety abroad. The military professionals on the Soviet General Staff can go along with "new thinking" or "reasonable sufficiency," and even with paying renewed attention to defense.[10] Those ideas are entirely compatible with, indeed are helpful for, the needs of the Soviet armed forces for qualitative improvement and for an improved ability to protect against new Western strike assets. But the idea of a truly inoffensive defensive defense, as contrasted with a synergistic defense–offense, is an affront to common sense, to likely strategic conditions for the Soviet empire, and to Soviet military science.[11] Soviet military leaders do not need to be told that a thoroughly defensive mode of warfare is an invitation to defeat. "Defensive defense" would concede the initiative to an enemy who, in this case, enjoys a global agility bequeathed by maritime supremacy and a great superiority in defense mobilization potential.

It is close to ludicrous to postulate a Soviet military establishment capable only of functioning defensively at the operational level of war. The objective basis in actual Soviet military power for Western *net* assessment of threat is unlikely to alter dramatically. The idea of a USSR-scale Switzerland, literally incapable of pursuing an "active defense" to the Channel coast, is the realm of dreams.

PRESSURES FOR CHANGE

It may not much matter for international peace and security whether Gorbachev succeeds or fails. On the one hand, a Soviet Union revitalized by a healthy shot of perestroika and with its tacit social contract between rulers and ruled in good order would be a formidable competitor in those security stakes that still have zero-sum features. One may believe that the Soviet Union/Russia and its role in the world would be transformed radically for the better as a consequence of Gorbachev's institutionalizing his apparent—and certainly novel—recognition of the classic security dilemma.[12] On the other hand, a Russia whose domestic troubles notably did not yield to Gorbachev's medicine, although less formidable to other states as a long-term competitor, could probably function as a very dangerous, destabilizing factor in world politics. Hypothetically, Russian leaders witnessing the evident failure of perestroika to modernize the USSR might well conclude that the domestic path to the restructuring of the Soviet condition—and particularly the long-term security condition—was proven to be unavailable (or politically intolerable), that tacit acquiescence in the slow relative decline of the Soviet Union was unacceptable, and that intimidation and the limited use of armed force offer the superior route for Soviet national security policy as it enters the twenty-first century. These points are not predictions; they are not offered in blithe disregard of the distinctive dangers of the nuclear age, and neither are they dismissive of the grand-strategic difficulties of translating military pressure into political and economic benefit.

It is obviously true that the USSR is in crisis, is perceived by Soviet leaders to be in crisis, and that that perception of crisis is being exploited in order to advance reforms (as well as careers). However, it is well to remember that, as the old saying goes, "There is a great deal of ruin in a nation (or empire)." Notwithstanding allegations to the contrary from incautious foreigners, the USSR is not on the brink of collapse; the Soviet system, in the most important respects, works well enough for life to totter on. In some very particular respects, in areas that the state designates as highest priority, the Soviet system works much better than does the United States (for example, in lead times for designing, developing, testing, and procuring most military equipment). As noted already, imperial Russia, and even the USSR, has a history of periodic flurries of drastic reform activity. The Gorbachev era is new mainly in that it is new to most of the people in the West who think about Soviet matters and who have never laid much store by what they might learn from history books.

The pressures for modernization in the USSR today, including the possible abandonment of the USSR in favor of a move "back to the future" with some imperial Russian polity, would seem to be generically as near identical as makes little difference to the pressures that moved Peter the Great, Catherine the Great, Alexander II (in his reforming period), Lenin, and Stalin *(inter alia)* in their turns to direct radical change from above. Namely, Russia/the USSR could not compete for sufficient security with a modernizing and intrinsically menacing outside world unless it reshaped its domestic house. Gorbachev recognizes that the Soviet economy is in the process of losing technological touch with the leading economies of the West and the East.[13] That fact is anything but a novelty in the Russian and Soviet historical experience. Gorbachev's answer to the impending military, and actual civilian, technological backwardness of his country is necessarily twin-headed. Internally, and without success to date, he is endeavoring to find a path toward a more efficient economy. Externally, through the manipulation of greedy and ignorant foreigners, as well as through appeal to that which is worthy and noble in people, Gorbachev is seeking to persuade putative enemies both that there is little need to compete with the USSR militarily and that this country is a reliable partner for joint economic ventures of all kinds. Lenin would have smiled on all of this (save for the impending sidelining of the CPSU)—after all, imitation is the sincerest form of flattery.

Contrary to appearances, perhaps, it is not presumed here that Gorbachev is wholly insincere and cynical in his use of words and phrases that evoke a positive resonance when translated for Western ears. There can be little doubt that he is genuinely appalled by the prospects of nuclear war (as is his General Staff and, indeed, as are all sensible people); undoubtedly he is uninterested in undertaking military operations against NATO; he is sincere in wishing for improvement in the living standards of the Soviet peoples—and not only for considerations of political stability; and he would welcome a lengthy period of international relations sufficiently relaxed in dominant character as to allow him to reallocate scarce economic assets away from near-term military production in favor of medium-term civilian economic capital improvement and growth (and hence for the potential long-term benefit of the military establishment).

Amid all that is unknown, and notwithstanding his flamboyant personal style of leadership, there are some very important fixed features on the landscape of Soviet policy choices.

- Gorbachev will not preside purposefully over a process of change deemed likely to imperil the political stability of the USSR unless he has no practical alternatives (a situation that appears to be approaching rapidly).
- The Soviet Union is and will remain a super-centralized empire. The Great Russian empire to which Gorbachev is the current legatee was not forged by the voluntary accession of peoples. *No* Soviet leader has proved willing to experiment with any serious devolution of Moscow's authority upon regional bodies, let alone to risk appearing weak in face of local demands for a much greater measure of self-rule.
- Marxist–Leninist ideological baggage is irrelevant to the details and the course of governance, but—and this is a very large but—it is still *the* totemic bulwark proclaiming the legitimacy of the Soviet political system. Marxism–Leninism is not a manual for statecraft, but it does shape concepts and terms of reference. Autocratic, at least authoritarian, rule is as Russian as borscht. The reasons the Soviet Union is unlikely to evolve into the condition of a stable and popular pluralistic democracy are at least as much Russian as they are contemporary–ideological.[14] It remains to be seen just how democratic Gorbachev's post-CPSU Russia will be, *and how stable*.

It would be unwise to attempt crystal-ball gazing concerning ultimate purposes behind the current commitment to change from the highest level in Moscow. There is no way to know what policy ambitions may lurk in the deepest recesses of Gorbachev's mind, how long his tenure of office may prove to be, and how policy choice could alter with evolving opportunities. The words and actions undertaken thus far under the umbrella of perestroika by and large lend themselves to interpretation either as examples of exactly what they profess to be or as cases of very intelligent grand—strategic management of the inter-state competition as usual.

Soviet frontal opposition to NATO's INF deployment and to President Reagan's SDI proved counterproductive. Democracies have a way of finding tolerable coherence and sense of purpose when perceiving themselves to be under threat. However, a peace offensive is potentially devastating to the will to sustain defense effort. An enduring weakness of a democracy is its inability to discern apparently distant danger through the fog, or smoke screen, of pacific sentiments and friendly gestures. It is always possible that the next several years could witness a gradual, but cumulatively dramatic, change in Soviet political and strategic culture.[15] It is conceivable that whatever Gorbachev's policy motives, he is riding the tiger of a societal and political transformation that truly will produce a Soviet Union vastly different from the bureaucratic autocracy, not to mention the "evil empire," of recent decades. While being properly attentive to the deeply rooted cultural characteristics of a society and polity, one must beware of being captured by rigid "essentialisms."[16] It is always easy to show that "what is" "had to be." By way of contrast, some scholars believe that czarist Russia, without the fatal strains of the Great War, might have evolved into a constitutional monarchy. Of similar genus, some people believe that the development of the USSR was critically and idiosyncratically diverted into the most brutal and brutalizing path imaginable as a consequence of the distinctly noninevitable seizure of Lenin's inheritance by Stalin.[17] The implication of these speculations is that the future of the Soviet Union/Russia could include a course surprising to those who are disinclined to view history as an ever-dynamic set of possibilities.

THE MILITARY DIMENSION

NATO, the Delian League of modern history, was founded and developed to provide the political architecture necessary for the organization of Western security in the face of perceived military danger from the East. Unlike the Delian League, NATO has not become an instrument for empire. But, NATO is fairly strictly an instrument for the deterrence of Soviet military attack upon Western Europe. U.S. guardianship does not weigh down as heavily upon its foreign dependencies as did the Athenian hegemony-turned-empire, but still it can be irritating to local pride as well as potentially dangerous to vital local interests. Alliance with a very great power has always been a distinctly mixed blessing.[18] It seems improbable that continental Western Europe would choose to exchange even the somewhat ragged architecture and practices of NATO—which still amount to a security wardship under the United States—for Soviet (or, almost as likely, German) goodwill. But, the Western alliance as extant cannot function in its traditional mode in the absence of a perceived military threat from the East.

A central problem for NATO is that the political cohesion of the alliance is under both purposeful and incidental assault from Gorbachev's "new thinking," while the likelihood of Gorbachev's succeeding in his domestic reform endeavors becomes ever more problematic. The Soviet Union is the beneficiary of a

Western goodwill that may undermine the foundations of Western defense, even though the future course and outcome of perestroika are profoundly uncertain. Although there remains considerable inertia behind the NATO alliance, budgetary pressures in the United States, generational changes on both sides of the Atlantic, changes in the ethnic composition of the U.S. public, and trade competition—to cite but the more obvious factors making for alterations in policy—already have NATO appearing distinctly entropic and old-fashioned (and this ignores the structural problem posed by a reunified Germany). If Moscow psychologically can continue to disarm key segments of Western European opinion, then NATO's days truly are numbered. That is not to say that some residual political framework from the containment era would not remain.[19] But, NATO as developed in principle, in organization, and in terms of critical obligations between 1949 and 1954, the NATO still familiar today in formal purpose, in structure, and in strategy (with the U.S. extended nuclear deterrent as the instrument of the security guarantee) would vanish very rapidly indeed.[20] One should not, as it were reflexively, lament the passing of old political forms and yesterday's strategic arrangements. However, the issue here is whether the gold of good relations that appears to be very much on offer from Gorbachev's ailing Soviet empire is of the twenty-four carat or the fool's variety.

Two points merit particular notice at this juncture. First, the issue really is not Gorbachev's personal sincerity. So, the subject for investigation here is not framed in terms of a debate over whether the promised changes in Soviet military doctrine and posture are or are not intended as a snare and a delusion. Second, with some good reason it came to be fashionable in the 1980s to consider the USSR a "one-dimensional superpower."[21] That one dimension is, of course, the military. Bearing in mind the enormous uncertainty over the prospects for perestroika's success in restructuring the Soviet economy, non-trivial if not wholesale reduction in the (offensive) fighting power of the Soviet armed forces—however helpful for domestic resource reallocation—would deprive Moscow of much of its leverage in world affairs. Smiles will accomplish more than threats vis-à-vis Western Europe, but latent threats have their utility and certainly are critical for that quality of political respect or prestige that binds the ever-fissionable materials of empire tolerably well together. Furthermore, a Soviet Union/Russia shaken in the prestige it enjoys and damaged in its self-confidence by the unprecedented retreat from empire in Afghanistan, by the collapse of the structure of Communist Party rule throughout East–Central Europe, and by the crisis of legitimacy proclaimed via the formal demotion of the CPSU is unlikely to be knowingly willing to devalue the heavily military currency of its international standing.[22]

Before citing the grounds for skepticism over the medium-turn significance of the proclaimed changes in Soviet military thinking and posture, it is essential first to identify what appears to be occurring in Soviet thought and policy. In summary form:

- The Gorbachev reforms and future, rather traditional, Soviet military goals are by and large compatible. The emphasis upon replacing quantity with quality has been promoted by the Soviet military leadership since the late 1970s.
- The Soviet Union is very serious about all aspects of denuclearization— consistent with maintenance of an all-level nuclear counterdeterrence to possible Western nuclear initiatives.
- Gorbachev does favor arms reduction agreements. They diminish the Western will and limit the Western license in compete, while they provide excuses/reasons for near-term domestic reallocation of scarce resources away from defense research, development, and production.
- The Soviet General Staff is serious about a more defensive military posture, though only in the traditional context of defensive–counteroffensive (an offensive defense) military planning. A truly, indeed strictly, defensive defense would be an affront to strategic common sense, military science, and the lessons of history.[23] A rising level of Soviet interest in defense predated Gorbachev's accession in 1985 and can be attributed in good part to the notably more offensive cast to U.S. and NATO ideas, plans, and capabilities (AirLand Battle, Follow-on Forces Attack, the U.S. Navy's Maritime Strategy, Samuel P. Huntington's influential espousal of the notion of "conventional retaliation," and so on)[24] in the 1980s. Soviet defense professionals now are arguing that new generations of advanced conventional munitions (ACMs) are all but removing traditional distinctions between defensive and offensive weaponry.
- The elusive concept of reasonable sufficiency (for what?) has been embraced and promulgated at the highest level. Its precise meaning is open to debate. The deputy chief of the Soviet General Staff advises that *"all countries* should adopt and consistently implement the 'principle of defence sufficiency' at the minimum necessary level *and should completely renounce the strategy of nuclear deterrence* (emphasis added)."[25]
- Although the USSR long has denied the thesis that war between East and West is fatally inevitable, the current emphasis being laid upon the importance of the prevention of war suggests that war certainly is deemed to be possible. The Soviet military establishment may be somewhat confused over what is meant by a "defensive sufficiency," but it is unlikely to be confused over its inalienable duty to attempt to win any war that cannot be prevented.

Soviet leaders and spokespeople have been talking unusually systemically about national security, acknowledging unambiguously that one country cannot, or should not, seek security at the expense of the security of others. In short, there are ample grounds for optimism. Moscow is talking peace, is undertaking unilateral force reductions, and endorsing the idea of arms reduction regimes intended to express inoffensive purposes on the part of the High Contracting Parties (including highly unfavorably asymmetrical force reductions). Can it be that George Kennan's original containment hypothesis has been proven correct— as have the arguments of the Reagan conservatives of the early and mid-1980s who urged no compromise with an unrestructured evil empire? It should be recalled that Kennan wrote in 1947:

> But the United States has it in its power to increase enormously the strains under which Soviet policy must operate, to force upon the Kremlin a far greater degree of moderation and circumspection than it has had to observe in recent years, and in this way to promote tendencies which must eventually find their outlet in either the breakup or the gradual mellowing of Soviet power.[26]

It is not at all clear that Gorbachev's USSR is "mellowing" in systemic ways of structural significance for the organization of international security. The arms reduction treaty already signed, on INF, works militarily very much in the favor of the Soviet Union. Indeed, any arms control agreement that forwards the cause of denuclearization, diminishes available steps for nuclear escalation, and reinforces the "nuclear taboo" cannot help but harm uniquely the security of the coalition that persists in pretending that nuclear threats comprise the heart of its defense concept (that is, NATO). The pending START regime, though dramatic in the scale of its promised reductions (to approximately 50 percent of START-accountable central nuclear warheads) is as bereft of a solid strategic rationale for the West as was the INF Treaty. Unless one adheres to the witless proposition that the best strategic forces posture is the least strategic forces posture, the START possibility promises—as one should expect from the long, disappointing history of negotiated measures of arms control—to have modestly negative implications for a reasonable Western view of the stability of the central balance.

More interesting than either INF or START are the talks on Conventional Armed Forces in Europe (CFE). These talks address the relative capabilities of the Soviet military instrument of excellence—its landpower. CFE has to be approached in the context both of Soviet claims for a claimed shift to a defensive orientation in both the social—political and the military—scientific wings of their military doctrine—though since they have always asserted the defensiveness of their doctrine,[27] some skepticism is in order—and of recognition of the fact of lively debate in the dimension of military science. Optimists in the West may need to rediscover what their forebears in the 1930s learned through exhausting diplomatic experience. Namely, that there are offensive policies and strategies, but there are no inherently offensive weapons.[28] At the very least, the granting that offensive operational intentions should provide tell-tale logistic and deployment signatures, the distinction between offensive and defensive capability often is very blurred.

It is possible that Soviet military intentions in Europe are as advertised. Perhaps it is the Soviet purpose to transform their forward deployments—or such forward deployments as residual Pact "allies" fail to see ejected into garrisons objectively innocent of the ability to threaten to take ground in the West. One must remain agnostic on that important point at present. Furthermore, Christopher Donnelly notes that:

> The Soviet Army is so uniquely tailored for the offensive (believing it to be the only sensible means of defence in event of war) that to change this in any meaningful way would be the work of years. We cannot expect to see significant results in the short term.[29]

However, as Donnelly also observes, "[t]he Soviet Army faces the need for imminent reform and reorganization."[30] Some of those announced withdrawals of forces that the USSR is claiming as evidence of its novel rejection of offensive ideas and plans, and indeed Soviet proposals for mutual, if asymmetrical, force thinning through CFE, could be held to serve rather traditional Soviet military ideas. By diminishing force-to-space ratios—not to mention the cumulative impact on NATO's political cohesion of the aura of détente—the Soviet Union may well be hoping to provide itself with real running room for an armored non-nuclear *Blitzkrieg*.[31] It is by no means self-evident that this is the case, but the evidence to date could lend itself to this interpretation *(inter alia)*. Of course, the unexpectedly rapid political collapse of real Soviet authority in East–Central Europe in 1989 has to figure as an important, though not necessarily fatal, potential handicap to rather traditional Soviet campaign designs.

CONCLUSIONS: REASONS FOR SKEPTICISM

It is the broad conclusion of this article that there is probably a lot less to the apparent, announced, or discussed as possibly pending changes in the USSR than meets the eye. Further, it is concluded that such changes as have happened to date in the structure and behavior of the Soviet empire do not *yet* warrant any radical recasting on the Western part of established international security arrangements. This author is agnostic, though admittedly leaning toward very skeptical, over the prospects for the thoroughgoing benign transformation of Lenin's legacy into a gentler and kinder polity. Indeed, if there is a somewhat different Soviet Union/Russia waiting in the wings of history for its turn on stage, it is very likely a more overtly nationalistic and authoritarian Greater Russian/Soviet empire, rather than a democratic socialist union of Soviet peoples. In addition to those Russians who recall with a strange nostalgia—if only second hand—the Golden Age of truly firm government under Stalin, there are many ethnic Great Russians who discern in *glasnost,* perestroika, and "new thinking" a flabby liberalism that affronts their political culture. Great Russian chauvinism is alive and well in the Soviet empire and may yet recapture its ethnic patrimony if Gorbachev stumbles too badly. Behind the CPSU is a living tradition of Mother Russia that is ethnically intolerant, spiritually arrogant, and deeply respectful of autocratic rule. The *Pamyat'* (memory) movement is an expression of this patriotic Russian tradition.[32]

The broad conclusions just registered rest upon eight principal threads of argument. First, it is likely to be the case that the Soviet empire will be a source of menace to its neighbors (and to those distant lands whose balance-of-power policies support the Soviet empire's neighbors) whether or not Gorbachev's perestroika succeeds in modernizing the Soviet economy. A successfully modernized Soviet economy must mean a Soviet Union better able to bear the costs of military competition and even of distant empire.[33] A Soviet economy that could not be modernized by politically acceptable methods and policies might present Soviet leaders with the grim alternatives either of acquiescence in long-term decline from superstate standing or of an attempt to change the terms of the international security condition through near-term exploitation of favorable military balances. This author admits to being uncomfortable either with a much more powerful USSR or with a USSR deeply pessimistic about its future security.

Second, Gorbachev is attempting the strategically impossible, in that he does not seem willing or able properly to align means with ends. There is little room for doubt that the motivating factor behind perestroika, glasnost, and the "new thinking" on foreign policy is the need to revitalize the Soviet economy. Gorbachev requires a relaxed Western world that will extend credits and technological assistance and will slow down the pace of its high-technology military challenge. However, the Soviet problem is not in the system, rather it is *with* the system. Thoroughgoing economic reform almost certainly requires thoroughgoing, systemic, political reform. The dropping of Article 6 of the Soviet constitution on the leading role of the CPSU could lead to such reform, but in and of itself it is no panacea for the ailments of today. Then-Deputy Director of the CIA Robert M. Gates characterized the Soviet economic reform problem in the following graphic terms:

> Trying to reshape the entire Stalinist economic structure gradually while leaving key problems of price reform and the government monopoly over goods until last is like a phased change from driving on the right hand side of the road to the left. The results are likely to be similar.[34]

Third, Russian culture, geography, and the dynamics of imperial rule all militate against the radical transformation of the Soviet Union as a player in world politics. Of course, states have changed their roles quite dramatically in response to altered circumstances: for example, Portugal, Sweden, Spain, the Ottoman Empire, and more recently the erstwhile great powers of Western and Central Europe (France, Germany, and Britain). But, it is virtually inconceivable that a Soviet empire at the peak of its relative military prowess would choose quite voluntarily to attempt to settle permanently for a comfortably semi-retired status from the rough and tumble of world politics. In short, severe economic problems may well invite and require severe solutions. But, the Russian culture that is the product of a half-millennium of national experience is not going to be cast off and replaced at the policy convenience of a reforming czar.

Fourth, if the past is any guide, Gorbachev's reform campaign is likely to be yet another of history's potential turning points where history actually fails to turn.[35] The study of history should not breed cynicism, but a healthy skepticism over the significance of Gorbachev's perestroika must be encouraged by the realization that the past three hundred years have witnessed many past instances of perestroika (for example, in 1763, 1801, 1861, 1907, 1922, plus the no less short-lived Khrushchev and Kosygin reforms of the early and mid-1960s). Admittedly, *this time* it might be different. However, the historical record suggests that cycles of reform and repression are entirely Russian/Soviet.

Fifth, even if the most optimistic interpretation of Gorbachev and his evolving program is appropriate, he personally might be run over by the locomotive of history in the form of entrenched vested interests responding to clear and present danger. Whether or not perestroika and "new thinking" on security policy would survive the political demise of Gorbachev is sufficiently an open question as to encourage caution in the West.

Sixth, popular democracies are so prone to fits of enthusiasm for quite different assessments of foreign danger or opportunity that Western policymakers should risk erring on the side of being tardy in their reaction to Soviet policy changes. The Soviet Union could alter its main policy line in the course of an afternoon. But, the West would require months or years to repair the danger it could impose upon its collective security structures in a burst of enthusiasm for the apparent evidence that peace was breaking out. Moreover, if the Western alliance were to unravel itself in a more or less unplanned reaction to the apparent disappearance of the Soviet threat, one wonders how Soviet policymakers would define their responsibility to their country in such a new situation. European security should not repose upon Soviet goodwill.

Seventh, both optimistic and pessimistic judgments are compatible with current trends in Soviet foreign, military, and arms control policy. It is prudent for the West to assume that the Soviet Union is pursuing its traditional purposes, though with a rather different mix of, and weighting among, means. U.S. influence could not be expelled from Western Europe by threats, but the offering of olive branches bears the promise of yielding that geostrategic effect. One can always hope that the announced changes in Soviet military doctrine in favor of "defensive sufficiency" are as benign as Soviet spokespeople affirm. However, the close fit between Soviet strategic interests and the terms of the INF Treaty, their proffered terms for START, and the ground-forces slimdown all lend themselves to a less charitable interpretation. To date, nothing has been presented by way of verified changes in military posture that provides unmistakable evidence of a truly radical change of course in Soviet military policy and plans. Furthermore, even if Gorbachev means exactly what he has said and written about military matters, he may not fully appreciate just how truly ambivalent military capability tends to be as between offense and defense.

Eighth and finally, even at some risk of appearing to argue that miraculously he is right, even if he is wrong, this author believes that the West can best serve the Soviet peoples, as well as its own security, if it declines to ease Gorbachev's policy path—beyond the utterance of encouragement, that is. It is not in the interest of the West for Gorbachev to succeed in the economic revival either of the bloated Leninist policy that is still the Soviet Union or of an authoritarian Great Russian successor state. This is not to deny that there are dangers for the West associated with policy failure in Moscow. Policymakers in the West probably cannot exercise much influence over Moscow for good or harm. But, whatever influence they can wield should be in favor of obliging Gorbachev to proceed with thoroughgoing political reform.

NOTES

1. See John Lewis Gaddis, *Russia, the Soviet Union, and the United States: An Interpretive History* (New York: John Wiley and Sons, 1978), particularly Chapter 1, "A Heritage of Harmony: 1781–1867."
2. Emphasis added. The addition of "and the world" tends to pass notice in much Western commentary. Mikhail Gorbachev, *Perestroika: New Thinking for Our Country and the World* (New York: Harper and Row, 1987).
3. See the title essay in John Lewis Gaddis, *The Long Peace: Inquiries into the History of the Cold War* (New York: Oxford University Press, 1987), pp. 215–45.
4. See Colin S. Gray, *The Geopolitics of Super Power* (Lexington, KY: University Press of Kentucky, 1988).
5. It was very noticeable that neither side in the Crimean War sought to employ nationalist sentiments among the subject peoples of the other. See Hugh Seton-Watson, *The Russian Empire, 1801–1917* (Oxford: Clarendon Press, 1967), pp. 330–31.
6. Summarizing George F. Kennan's view in 1947, John Lewis Gaddis has written as follows: "Ideology, then, was not so much a guide to action as a justification for action already decided upon." Gaddis quotes Kennan's January 1947 opinion that "ideology is a product and not a determinant of social and political reality." *Strategies of Containment: A Critical Appraisal of Postwar American National Security Policy* (New York: Oxford University Press, 1982), p. 34.
7. See Halford J. Mackinder, *Democratic Ideals and Reality* (New York: W. W. Norton and Company, 1962; title essay first pub. 1919); W. H. Parker, *Mackinder: Geography as an Aid to Statecraft* (Oxford: Clarendon Press, 1982); and Brian W. Blouet, *Halford Mackinder: A Biography* (College Station, TX: Texas A&M University Press, 1987).
8. Ronald Reagan, *National Security Strategy of the United States* (Washington, DC: White House, January 1988), p. 1.
9. Multinational empire, particular in the modern era of nationalism, by its very nature has a structure problem of legitimacy.
10. To date, the military typically has insisted that the path to defensive sufficiency should not be taken by the USSR acting in isolation. "Unilateral implementation of defensive sufficiency is practically impossible. Sufficiency is determined by the nature of the military threat. Therefore, the implementation of the principle of sufficiency is a mutual, bilateral process." Col. Gen Nikolay Chervov, "On the Military Doctrines of East and West; In the Interest of Strategic Stability," *JPRS* UMA-88-014 (July 18, 1988), p. 3.
11. Gorbachev has written of "a change in the entire pattern of armed forces with a view to imparting an exclusively defensive character to them." *Perestroika*, p. 203.

12. "The new political outlook calls for the recognition of one more simple axiom: security is indivisible. It is either equal security for all or none at all." *Perestroika*, p. 142.

13. An outstanding Western study is Ed A. Hewett, *Reforming the Soviet Economy: Equality versus Efficiency* (Washington, DC: Brookings Institution, 1988).

14. See Richard Pipes, *Russia under the Old Regime* (New York: Charles Scribners Sons, 1974).

15. For differing perspectives, see Stephen White, *Political Culture and Soviet Politics* (London: Macmillan, 1979); and Robert C. Tucker, *Political Culture and Leadership in Soviet Russia: From Lenin to Gorbachev* (New York: W. W. Norton and Company, 1987). Cultural sensitivity is pervasive in Christopher Donnelly, *Red Banner: The Soviet Military System in Peace and War* (Coulsdon, Surrey [U.K.]: Jane's Information Group, 1988). Indeed, if anything Donnelly may overstate the thesis of cultural distinctiveness.

16. Discussing the historical fact that Soviet doctrine has changed, it was useful for David Holloway to warn "that one should not take an 'essentialist' view of Soviet policy, seeing it as springing from some innate characteristic of Russian culture or the Soviet system, impervious to phenomena in the real world." "Military Power and Political Purpose in Soviet Policy," *Daedelus*, 109, no. 4 (Fall 1980), p. 28. A similar warning is portentously conveyed, with this author allegedly as the guilty party, in Joseph S. Nye, Jr., "The Role of Strategic Nuclear Systems in Deterrence," *Washington Quarterly* 11, no. 2 (Spring 1988), p. 54. It is important, as Nye and Holloway warn, to beware of an essentialist view, which could well blind one to real changes in Soviet thought. But, it is also important to beware of the reverse error of unduly discounting that which is truly cultural in the U.S. or Soviet approach to security. William E. Odom has noted that "the two aspects [of military doctrine, social–political and military–technical] are viewed [in the Soviet Union] as highly interactive, *and are unique* for each state because the political, social, economic, cultural and geographical realities of no two states are precisely the same. While much of military science holds for all states, military doctrine must be designed for the realities of a single state. A shared U.S. and Soviet military doctrine, therefore, would strike a student of Soviet military thought as either absurd or a misunderstanding of the definition." "Soviet Military Doctrine," *Foreign Affairs* 67, no. 2 (Winter 1988/89), p. 117. Emphasis added.

17. Tucker frames the question thus: "was Stalin's transformative decade a resumption and culmination of the Bolshevik Revolution or in basic ways a negation of it?" *Political Culture and Leadership in Soviet Russia*, p. 52. Tucker favors his second opinion.

18. Understandably, if somewhat unrealistically, the United States' European allies have always wanted their superpower guardian to be prepared to subordinate its interests elsewhere in the world to the cause of peace and order in the European region. It may be recalled that in World War II the British government endeavored none too successfully to hold the United States to fairly strict adherence to the agreed grand-strategic principle of "Germany First." "The pull of the Pacific" was a fact of American political culture— obviously magnified by the events of the early morning of December 7, 1941—to which London was notably culturally unempathetic.

19. For a useful collection of reflective essays on the subject, see Terry L. Deibel and John Lewis Gaddis, *Containment: Concept and Policy* (Washington, DC: National Defense University Press, 1986).

20. Prominent among the better studies generically supportive of the NATO enterprise is Stanley R. Sloan, *NATO's Future: Toward a New Transatlantic Bargain* (Washington, DC: National Defense University Press, 1985). Variably radical views of NATO are well argued in Melvyn Krauss, *How NATO Weakens the West* (New York: Simon and Schuster, 1986); John Palmer, *Europe without America? The Crisis in Atlantic Relations*

(New York: Oxford University Press, 1988); and David P. Calleo, *Beyond American Hegemony: The Future of the Western Alliance* (New York: Basic Books, 1987).

21.   Caspar W. Weinberger, *Department of Defense Annual Report, Fiscal Year 1987* (Washington, DC: U.S. Government Printing Office, February 5, 1986), p. 29.

22.   Writing of the effects of the successive victories of the Greeks at Salamis (480 B.C.) and Plataea (479 B.C.), J. F. C. Fuller observed that "it was loss of prestige which not only checked the expansion, but undermined the foundations of the Persian Empire, and, like most empires before or since, led to its eventual ruin." *The Decisive Battles of the Western World and their Influence upon History,* Vol. 1 (London: Eyre and Spottiswoode, 1954), p. 51.

23.   For reasons definitely outlined in Carl von Clausewitz, *On War,* Michael Howard and Peter Paret, eds. (Princeton, NJ: Princeton University Press, 1976; first pub. 1832), Books 6 and 7.

24.   Samuel P. Huntington, "Conventional Deterrence and Conventional Retaliation in Europe," *International Security* 8, no. 3 (Winter 1983–84), pp. 32–56. Huntington has written one of the best early appreciations of U.S. strategy in the 1980s, in "U.S. Defense Strategy: The Strategic Innovations of the Reagan Years," in *American Defense Annual, 1987–1988,* Joseph Kruzel, ed., (Lexington, MA: Lexington Books, 1987), pp. 23–43. Huntington argues persuasively that prior to the Reagan years, U.S. and allied planning for the use of general purpose forces was overly defensive, while U.S. central strategic systems were greatly unbalanced in favor of the offense.

25.   Col. Gen. Makhmut Gareev, "Soviet Military Doctrine: Current and Future Developments," *RUSI Journal* 133, no. 4 (Winter 1988), p. 8. Gareev also emphasizes an alleged shift in doctrine from war-winning to war prevention. See also Army Gen. D. T. Yazov, "On Soviet Military Doctrine," *RUSI Journal* 134, no. 4 (Winter 1989), pp. 1–4. Particularly useful Western commentaries on the current ferment in Soviet military doctrine include C. N. Donnelly, "Gorbachev's Military Doctrine: Implications for Arms Control Negotiations," unpub. paper (October 1988); idem., *Red Banner;* Odom, "Soviet Military Doctrine;" and Harriet Fast Scott and William F. Scott, *Soviet Military Doctrine: Continuity, Formulation, and Dissemination* (Boulder, CO: Westview Press, 1988). Fairly sympathetic commentaries on Gorbachev's new thinking on the foreign and domestic contexts for changes in military doctrine include Jack Snyder, "The Gorbachev Revolution: A Waning of Soviet Expansionism?" *International Security* 12, no. 3 (Winter 1987/88), pp. 93–131; Seweryn Bialer, " 'New Thinking' and Soviet Foreign Policy," *Survival* 30, no. 4 (July/August 1988), pp. 291–309; and David Holloway, "Gorbachev's New Thinking," *Foreign Affairs* 68, no. 1 (1988/89), pp. 66–81.

26.   George F. Kennan (or Mr. X), "The Sources of Soviet Conduct," in *Containment: Documents on American Policy and Strategy, 1945–1950,* Thomas H. Etzold and John Lewis Gaddis, eds. (New York: Columbia University Press, 1978), p. 89.

27.   Gareev argues that "from the political angle Soviet military doctrine has always had a defensive orientation because the Soviet Union has never attacked anybody but has been forced to fight wars only of the kind which were forced upon it, and to do so with the exclusive aim of repelling aggression." "Soviet Military Doctrine," p. 7. Stalin no doubt acted preemptively in 1939 to forestall Polish and Finnish aggression. As recently as 1984, Gareev was asserting: "The experience of the war demonstrated that a combination of the offensive as the main type of military action and the defensive *is an objective pattern of warfare,* and like any pattern, *it operates with the strength of necessity* and it is very dangerous to disregard it." *M. V. Frunze, Military Theorist* (Washington, DC: Pergamon-Brassey's, 1988; first pub. 1984), p. 208. Emphasis added.

28.   See Marion William Boggs, *Attempts to Define and Limit "Aggressive" Armament in Diplomacy and Strategy,* The University of Missouri Studies, Vol. XVI, No. 1 (Columbia, MO: University of Missouri, 1941); and Jack S. Levy, "The Offensive/Defensive Balance of Military Technology: A Theoretical and Historical Analysis," *International Studies Quarterly* 28 (1984), pp. 219–38.

29. Donnelly, "Gorbachev's Military Doctrine," p. 8.

30. *Ibid.*, p. 7.

31. On the long-standing character of the Soviet interest in "deep operations," see Bruce W. Menning, "The Deep Strike in Russian and Soviet Military History," *The Journal of Soviet Military Studies* 1, no. 1 (April 1988), pp. 9–28. Also see Kerry L. Hines, "Competing Concepts of Deep Operations," pp. 54–80.

32. See Nicolai N. Petro, "Rediscovering Russia," *Orbis* 34, no. 1 (Winter 1990), pp. 33–49.

33. See Henry S. Rowen and Charles Wolf, Jr., eds., *The Future of the Soviet Empire* (New York: St. Martin's Press, 1987).

34. Robert M. Gates, "Recent Developments in the Soviet Union and Implications for U.S. Security Policy." Speech to the American Association for the Advancement of Science, Colloquium on Science, Arms Control and National Security, October 14, 1988, p. 8.

35. For example, see Edward Crankshaw, *The Shadow of the Winter Palace: The Drift to Revolution, 1825–1917* (New York: Viking Press, 1976), particularly Chapter 10, "Revolution from Above."

36
*Idealpolitik**

Stanley Kober

A revolution is sweeping the world—a revolution of democracy. The success of this democratic revolution has shaken Europe to its foundations and shattered the strategic guideposts used to chart American foreign policy for more than 40 years. Groping through this new landscape, foreign policy specialists are struggling to develop policies to encourage democratic change while safeguarding strategic stability.

The failure to anticipate these changes, however, has understandably introduced a note of caution into the American response. The events were unexpected but they should not have been if the policy framework had been correct. Throughout the postwar era, American foreign policy has been dominated by a philosophy of realism, which views international politics as a struggle for power in which the interests of the great powers must be in conflict. This was a natural vision of foreign policy during a time in which then Soviet Foreign Minister Andrei Gromyko declared that "the world outlook and the class goals of the two social systems are opposite and irreconcilable."

It is precisely this "realistic" approach to foreign policy that is now being challenged, however, as Soviet President Mikhail Gorbachev and his allies in the Soviet leadership explicitly repudiate Gromyko's position. "Coexistence" proclaimed Foreign Minister Eduard Shevardnadze in July 1988, "cannot be identified with the class struggle." Instead, it "should have universal interests as a common denominator." The realignment of the Soviet Union's foreign policy has been accompanied by an even more fundamental transformation of its domestic political structure. Indeed, Gorbachev himself has described *perestroika* (restructuring) not as economic reform but as "a legal revolution" designed to keep excessive power from being concentrated in the hands of a few people and to govern society according to the rule of law.

Until November 1989, debate in the West centered on the sincerity of these intentions. However, with the collapse of the Berlin Wall, attention is turning to the survivability of Gorbachev and his reforms, with the attendant question of

*Reprinted by permission of the author and publisher from *Foreign Policy* 79 (Summer 1990). Copyright © 1990 by the Carnegie Endowment for International Peace.

what the United States and its allies should do. This debate, in turn, is affected by another more fundamental issue: What makes nations adversaries? Are the United States and the Soviet Union doomed by geopolitics to remain enemies? Or does the prospective transformation of the Soviet Union into a parliamentary democracy herald an end to the danger of superpower conflict? The answers should be sought in the competing philosophies of American foreign policy: realism or idealism.

At the end of World War I, President Woodrow Wilson traveled to Europe to help develop a structure assuring that "the war to end wars" would be just that. Wilson's approach consisted of two main parts. First, the Central European empires were dismantled and new states based on the principle of national self-determination were established. Second, Wilson proposed the creation of the League of Nations to handle future threats to international security.

Wilson's ideas were immediately challenged by the great British geopolitician Sir Halford Mackinder. In *Democratic Ideals and Reality*, which was first published in 1919, Mackinder argued that Wilson's democratic idealism might be noble but failed to deal with world realities. "Idealists are the salt of the earth," he wrote condescendingly; but, he warned, "democracy is incompatible with the organization necessary for war against autocracies." Mackinder asserted that "political moralists" like Wilson "refused to reckon with the realities of geography and economics." Mackinder defined these realities in his famous formulation: "Who rules East Europe commands the Heartland: Who rules the Heartland commands the World-Island: Who rules the World-Island commands the World." Given the importance of Eastern Europe, the prevention of another world war would depend on the establishment of "a tier of independent states between Germany and Russia." The political structure of these states did not concern him; what interested him was the balance of power.

Mackinder challenged not only Wilson, but also another American, Alfred Thayer Mahan. It was Mahan who, in the late nineteenth century, attributed England's preeminence to its reliance on sea power. "The due use and control of the sea is but one link in the chain of exchange by which wealth accumulates," he wrote in 1890, "but it is the central link."

Mackinder replied that control of the sea was well and good, but extended naval power would require land bases. Yet this point of disagreement between the geopoliticians of land and sea obscures their more fundamental points of accord. In the first place, Mahan, like Mackinder, was contemptuous of the unmartial spirit of democracy. Second, both were hostile to free trade and the trading classes. Mahan may have praised the use of the sea trade as the source of England's wealth, but it was clearly the control of the sea that captivated him.

Mackinder also believed that economic wealth could not depend on free trade. For Mackinder the classical theories of the division of labor and comparative advantage were not only economically flawed but politically dangerous. Echoing, perhaps unwittingly, Leninist analysis, Mackinder saw the competitive struggle for markets as a major source of war.

To sum up the geopolitical view as defined by Mackinder and Mahan, the strongest country or alliance is the one with direct control over the greatest resources. The benefits of trade outside of one's own zone are illusory because they are bound to lead to vulnerability. The geopolitician is hostile toward business classes and democratic systems of government since they lack martial qualities. Rather, the geopolitician would prefer to have decisions made by people endowed with strategic vision and unaffected by any sectional interests.

POSTWAR REALISM

Mackinder's "realistic" critique of Wilson's idealism found an echo in U.S. policy in the late 1940s. Haunted by the failure of democracies to prevent World War II, American political leaders decided to assume the burden of world leadership they had abandoned in the interwar period. "Soviet pressure against the free institutions of the Western World," wrote George Kennan in his famous "X" article of 1947, "is something that can be contained by the adroit and vigilant application of counterforce at a series of constantly shifting geographical and political points, corresponding to the shifts and maneuvers of Soviet policy." This definition of containment was purely reactive, however. The United States not only had to respond to the "shifts and maneuvers of Soviet policy," it had to anticipate them. What mechanism could it use for understanding the Kremlin's designs?

According to the political realist, the answer was simple. "The main signpost that helps political realism to find its way through the landscape of international politics is the concept of interest defined in terms of power," wrote Hans Morgenthau, probably the foremost exponent of the realist school. Morgenthau's book, *Politics Among Nations: The Struggle for Power and Peace* (1948), helped provide the intellectual basis for America's engagement in power politics. "Politics, like society in general, is governed by objective laws that have their roots in human nature," observed Morgenthau. Since these laws are objective, they are necessarily universal, and consequently it is futile and deceptive to examine foreign policy exclusively by looking at the motives of government officials. Instead, it is assumed that "statesmen think and act in terms of interest defined as power." On this assumption, "we put ourselves in the position of a statesman who must meet a certain problem of foreign policy under certain circumstances, and we ask ourselves what the rational alternatives are from which a statesman may choose . . . and which of these rational alternatives this particular statesman, acting under these circumstances, is likely to choose."

Morgenthau placed little emphasis on appeals to ideals as a way of gaining influence in the world. It was only in the preface to his second edition, published in 1954, that he acknowledged, as a result of decolonization, "the struggle for the minds of men as a new dimension of international politics to be added to the traditional dimensions of diplomacy and war.'' Although Morgenthau acknowledged ''the attractiveness . . . of its political philosophy, political institutions, and political policies'' as one element of a state's power, in the final analysis ''the state has no right to let its moral disapprobation of the infringement of liberty get in the way of successful political action.'' Rather than viewing the clash of ideologies as basic to politics, the realist sees it as an unfortunate intrusion into his relatively stable world. ''This struggle for the minds of men,'' lamented Morgenthau,

> has dealt the final, fatal blow to that social system of international intercourse within which for almost three centuries nations lived together in constant rivalry, yet under the common roof of shared values and universal standards of action. . . . Beneath the ruins of that roof lies buried the mechanism that kept the walls of that house of nations standing: the balance of power.

By acknowledging that the effective functioning of international politics depends on the existence of ''shared values,'' Morgenthau admitted that the ''laws'' of power politics are not so objective after all. Yet if Morgenthau grieved for a world order that was no more, former Secretary of State Henry Kissinger insists that it still exists and is irreplaceable. ''To have stability,'' he wrote in a recent *Washington Post* article, ''an international system must have two components: a balance of power and a generally accepted principle of legitimacy.'' Like Morgenthau, Kissinger believes that the study of policy statements is misguided and bound to lead to error. He wrote in an essay in 1968:

> If we focus our policy discussions on Soviet purposes, we confuse the debate in two ways: Soviet trends are too ambiguous to offer a reliable guide—it is possible that not even Soviet leaders fully understand the dynamics of their system; it deflects us from articulating the purposes we should pursue, whatever Soviet intentions. . . . Confusing foreign policy with psychotherapy deprives us of criteria by which to judge the political foundations of international order.

Similarly, Kissinger shares Morgenthau's conviction that the realities of power politics compel the subordination of a nation's ideology to more basic interests. ''National security concerns should be in harmony with traditional American values,'' he explained in a 1986 article, but ''this ideal cannot always prevail, imposing the necessity to strike a balance.'' Underlying this view is Kissinger's assessment, expressed at a 1977 lecture at New York University, that ''the United States is now as vulnerable as any other nation.'' Not only is it subject to the danger of nuclear annihilation, but American ''prosperity is to some extent hostage to the decisions on raw materials, prices, and investment in distant countries whose purposes are not necessarily compatible with ours.'' Thus, although ''our morality and our power should not be antithetical,'' in the final analysis ''all serious foreign policy must begin with the need for survival.''

THE NEW IDEALISM

In contrast to geopolitics and realism, idealism has never had a distinct line of philosophical development. The German philosopher Immanuel Kant wrote that the rule of law would result in "perpetual peace," but he provided little guidance on how governments should behave until that day arrives. By contrast, the Manchester school in the nineteenth century, putting its trust in economic self-interest, believed that free trade would make war irrational. Yet the outbreak of World War I demonstrated that governments do not always behave rationally. It is not surprising, therefore, that historian E. H. Carr, in his 1939 volume *The Twenty Years' Crisis, 1919–1939*, described the alternative to realism as utopianism, which he characterized as "the primitive . . . stage of the political sciences."

Viewed in this manner, it is no wonder that the idealist alternative fell into disrepute. Unfortunately, idealism is still seen as a naive philosophy that fails to understand the realities of power politics. Because of the uncompromising moralism with which it is endowed by its opponents, idealism is viewed as leading either to withdrawal from an imperfect world or to unrestrained interventionism to right all the world's wrongs. It is time for a new, more rigorous idealist alternative to realism.

A proper understanding of idealism, therefore, begins with the recognition that ideologies matter, and that the foreign policy of a state is an outgrowth of the values embodied in its domestic institutions. In the idealist view, the structure of a government determines how aggressive it can be. Specifically, dictatorships will be more aggressive than parliamentary democracies, since dictators can undertake military actions on their own initiative without having to obtain prior consent from popularly elected legislatures.

In taking this position, idealists recognize that democracies have behaved aggressively in the past but add that they are also evolving institutions. Democracy embodies strict criteria for majority rule and minority rights. Majority rule means that all the people are entitled to vote, and that those elected are accountable to the voters at frequent and regular intervals. The idealist views a democracy in which women, minorities, or other groups are excluded as more likely to be aggressive, since those making the decisions for war or peace are not accountable to everyone affected. In order to be accountable, representatives must provide the voters with the information they need to exercise their authority properly, and the people must have some mechanism for obtaining this information if it is being improperly withheld.

Minority rights are widely regarded as contradictory to majority rule, but this view is misguided. As recent ethnic conflicts demonstrate, majorities can change over time, and majority rule in the absence of guaranteed minority rights is a prescription for catastrophe. More to the point, however, guarantees of minority rights, which can be enforced only by the voluntary consent of the majority, signify respect for the weak by the strong. This value system of respect for law rather than for power is the best assurance of order and stability, both domestically and internationally.

Thus, the idealist is an unabashed proponent of democracy, seeing democracy as the best guarantee of world peace. While admitting that there is little historical experience of democracies of the sort described, the idealist would point to the relationship between the United States and Canada as instructive. Although these two countries were at war with each other at the beginning of the nineteenth century, they now share the longest undefended border in the world. The idealist would attribute this outcome to their mutual development of democratic institutions and would challenge the realist to explain why, if the balance of power is so important, Canadians do not tremble in fear at the prospect of an American invasion. The realist might reply that although there is an imbalance of power between the United States and Canada, they share an accepted principle of legitimacy. This answer is incomplete, for what is the source of that accepted principle of legitimacy if it is not the democratic values and respect for law both countries share?

In short, if it is democratic values that bring peace, one should say so forthrightly and not pretend that one principle of legitimacy is as good as another so long as it is generally accepted. If the balance of power cannot explain the peaceful U.S.-Canadian relationship, neither can it explain the outbreak of World War II. No geopolitical arrangement achievable at the time could have deterred Adolf Hitler because he saw war as the glorious means for achieving his objective, the occupation and subjugation of lands to the east. "No one will ever again have the confidence of the whole German people as I have," Hitler observed in August 1939. "All these favorable circumstances will no longer prevail in two or three years' time. No one knows how much longer I shall live." Whereas normal people are afraid of war, Hitler was afraid he would die before he could start a war.

The cause of World War II, therefore, must be sought not in the geopolitics of Europe, but in the domestic politics of Germany. The question is not how Hitler could have been deterred, because it is impossible to deter an absolute ruler who is seeking war. Rather, the question is how Hitler could have led a reluctant German people into war. Although many factors contributed to the outbreak of World War II, one overlooked cause is the imperfection of the Weimar Constitution. Instead of the American concept of inalienable rights, the Weimar Assembly placed individual rights at the "service of the collectivity," as René Brunet wrote in his 1922 book *The New German Constitution*. "Individual liberties are no longer an end in themselves, nor do they constitute any longer an independent good," he explained. "They have no value and are not protected except in the measure that they serve for the accomplishment of this social duty."

Because of this fundamental constitutional defect, Hitler was able to destroy the Weimar democracy and create in its place an instrument of domestic terror and foreign aggression. A democracy that does not have ironclad guarantees of individual rights cannot endure. As Abraham Lincoln observed, "a majority, held in restraint by constitutional checks and limitations . . . is the only true sovereign of a free people. Whoever rejects it does, out of necessity, fly to anarchy or to despotism.'' Weimar, born of military defeat, had the additional misfortune of being subject to a worldwide economic depression beyond its control. Its political and legal institutions were too new, too fragile, too unprotected to resist Hitler's assault once he came to power.

The outbreak of World War II, therefore, cannot be explained by realism. Indeed, if anything, British Prime Minister Neville Chamberlain followed realist analysis too closely. A realist assumes that because of objective laws of human behavior, all rational people will solve a given problem of foreign policy alike. But this leaves two problems. First, what is the problem of foreign policy the statesman is trying to solve? By defining Hitler's objective as the national self-determination of the German people, Chamberlain and his supporters totally missed the enormity of Hitler's ambition.

Second, what is the definition of rationality? The realist might respond that Hitler was irrational and therefore outside the bounds of realist analysis, but that answer is too glib. Intent on starting a war of expansion, Hitler initiated a massive military buildup while using diplomacy to hide his true intentions. On the eve of war, he reached an agreement with the Soviet Union, his greatest enemy, thereby easing enormously the military challenge immediately confronting him. In other words, Hitler's purposes were certainly irrational, but the purposefulness with which he pursued his objectives cannot be so easily dismissed. And indeed, if Hitler falls outside realist analysis because of his irrationality, how useful is realism as an analytical tool?

Hitler demonstrates the folly of relying on objective laws of human behavior in determining foreign policy. Hitler's methods make perfect sense once one understands his objectives. But to understand those objectives, one would have to look not to his assurances to Chamberlain at Munich, but to statements he made elsewhere and especially to his destruction of Germany's democracy. To the realist such an investigation is meaningless; to the idealist it is of fundamental importance: Hitler's treatment of the Jews and others he disliked foreshadowed how he would behave in the international arena once he was strong enough. If the people of Europe and their leaders had been aware of idealist analysis, they would have readily understood the purpose behind Hitler's military buildup and therefore the danger confronting them.

Idealist analysis provides criteria for assessing whether a military buildup is the result of perceptions of insecurity or the product of a drive for military supremacy to achieve political objectives by the threat or use of arms. The difference is crucial in determining the proper response. If the former, policy should focus on alleviating the political causes of insecurity. In this case, arms control has its greatest effect by building confidence. In the latter case, however, political measures are of limited, if any, use since there is no insecurity to alleviate. On the contrary, policy here should focus on a countervailing arms buildup, both to safeguard one's own security and to convince the arming power that it cannot achieve its objective. Arms control in this case can play a modest role by directing the competition away from the most destabilizing weapons, but it cannot achieve its ultimate objective of building confidence.

Faced with the need to choose between these two causes of an arms race, realism is helpless, since either cause might be rational depending on the policy objectives of a country's leaders. Unwilling to trust policy statements and rejecting the connection between domestic and foreign policy, realists ultimately base their assessments on their own values biases with no independent test. The idealist, on the other hand, insists that policy statements, particularly those designed for domestic officials, are revealing. More to the point, the idealist believes that even if such statements are too ambiguous to be a guide for formulating a response, the values embodied in a country's domestic policy and institutions provide invaluable insight into its purposes in foreign policy.

It is incorrect, therefore, to say that idealism rejects the balance of power. In fact, idealism recognizes that in the face of a military threat, there is no alternative to maintaining a balance, or even a preponderance, of power. What idealism rejects is the idea that international peace is solely the product of a balance of power. For the idealist, a country can have friends as well as interests. The ultimate objective of idealism is to broaden the circle of friendship by fostering the spread of democratic values and institutions. In the meantime, recognizing the dangers of the world as it exists, idealism provides a mechanism for assessing the degree of threat posed by hostile regimes, in particular the threat posed by a military buildup.

But if idealism is more effective than realism in providing timely and accurate warning of military threats, it is also careful not to exaggerate them. For example, the idealist would disagree with Kissinger's assessment that the United States is as vulnerable as any other country. The only credible threat to America's national survival at this time comes from Soviet nuclear weapons; assuming the Kremlin is not suicidal, the United States has more than enough retaliatory power to deter such an attack. Conventional military threats to American interests do not threaten U.S. survival. Perhaps most important, the United States does not have to depend on any other country to assure its security.

Similarly, the idealist would question the idea that the United States is economically vulnerable. While recognizing America's dependence on imports, the idealist believes that so long as the sources of commodities are diversified and market forces are in operation, a cutoff of supplies from one country or a group of countries should be manageable. If further protection is needed, stockpiles of critical goods can be accumulated.

This is not to say that economic sanctions cannot have an effect against relatively small countries, for they ultimately did in Rhodesia and may now be having an effect in South Africa. But these are special cases rather than universal examples. When then President Jimmy Carter embargoed American grain exports to the Soviet Union following the invasion of Afghanistan, Moscow was easily able to find alternative suppliers. Similarly, when tin producers formed a cartel to duplicate the success of the Organization of Petroleum Exporting Countries in the 1970s, the effort collapsed.

In contrast to the realist, the idealist does not believe that U.S. imports of vital commodities pose a security risk so long as proper economic policies are followed. Idealists see American economic security in a vibrant economy producing goods that other people want, rather than in a government-directed policy of import substitution, let alone in military intervention.

This difference in the assessment of American economic vulnerability also extends to policy toward the Soviet Union; underlying the doctrine of containment is the assumption that Soviet expansionism will necessarily increase Soviet power. This assumption reflects the geopolitician's mistaken evaluation of the sources of economic wealth. As the British economic historian Eric Hobsbawm observed in *Industry and Empire* (1969), the imperial expansion that occurred in the late nineteenth century was for Britain "a step back. She exchanged the informal empire over most of the underdeveloped world for the formal empire of a quarter of it, plus the older satellite economies."

For the idealist it is free trade rather than empire that sustains economic growth. One's trade must be protected against attack, but that is different from developing an exclusive economic zone that does not depend upon the goodwill of others. Idealists believe that the wealth of a nation depends not on the extent or characteristics of the territory directly under its control, but as Adam Smith states, "first, [on] the skill, dexterity, and judgment with which its labour is generally applied; and, secondly, [on] the proportion between the number of those who are employed in useful labour, and that of those who are not so employed." Since prosperity "seems to depend more upon the former of those two circumstances than upon the latter," it is important that the labor force of the most advanced country constantly improve its skills so that it can continue to produce innovative goods and services with high added value. Otherwise, it will inevitably fall behind.

Continuing economic prosperity requires a flexible economic system. The problem with empires, as Carlo Cipolla notes in *The Economic Decline of Empires* (1970), is that "all empires seem eventually to develop an intractable resistance to the change needed for the required growth of production. . . . An empire is inevitably characterized by a large number of sclerotic institutions. They hinder change for their very existence." Hobsbawm, assessing the British condition at the time Mahan and Mackinder wrote, agrees with this judgment. "Britain had escaped from the Great Depression (1873–96) . . . not by modernizing her economy, but by exploiting the remaining possibilities of her traditional situation," he wrote. "When the last great receptacles of cotton goods developed their own textile industries—India, Japan, and China—the hour of Lancashire tolled. For not even political control could permanently keep India nonindustrial."

Hobsbawm's analysis points to the second fundamental reason why the geopolitical interpretation of the wealth of nations is flawed: Political control over people who resent that control is an unstable basis for continuing economic growth. It is not enough to assert that "who rules the Heartland commands the World-Island." The idealist, mindful of Machiavelli's warning that "princes . . . must first try not to be hated by the mass of the people," will immediately inquire whether that rule is by popular consent or in spite of it. If the latter, it must be a source of economic weakness rather than strength over the long run. Not only will a sullen people be relatively unproductive, but the effort to keep them under control will over time amount to a huge drain on the government's resources.

REVOLUTION IN THE '90s

Viewed in this manner, idealism provides a fundamental challenge to realism and geopolitics. It is no longer possible to dismiss idealists as utopian dreamers who do not understand the harsh reality of power. On the contrary, idealists can respond that it is realists and geopoliticians who have oversimplified the concept of power, and misunderstood the lessons of history. The debate between them is of critical importance in formulating policy to respond to the revolutionary changes now confronting the world.

Of all the momentous changes now occurring, the most dramatic is the transformation of the Soviet bloc. It is worth noting that the Soviets have always accepted some principles of idealism. Unlike realists, the Soviets have always stressed the importance of ideology and insisted that it is impossible to understand the foreign policy of a country without appreciating its domestic values and institutions. Similarly, like idealists, the Soviets professed to see the ultimate guarantee of world peace in the domestic structure of states. However, they saw that domestic structure in the communist principles of Karl Marx and V. I. Lenin, rather than in the democratic institutions of Thomas Jefferson and James Madison.

What is so revolutionary about the current changes in the Soviet Union is that they are based on the acknowledgement that the guarantee of world peace lies not in the spread of socialism, but in parliamentary control over war-making power. According to a January 1988 article in *Kommunist*, the theoretical journal of the Soviet Communist party, "there are no politically influential forces in either Western Europe or the U.S." that contemplate "military aggression against socialism." But even if there were, America's democratic institutions would make such large-scale aggression impossible. The article emphasizes that "bourgeois democracy serves as a definite barrier in the path of unleashing such a war. . . . The history of the American intervention in Indochina clearly demonstrated this. . . . The Pentagon now cannot fail to recognize the existence of limits placed on its actions by democratic institutions." By formulating the question of war and peace in this way, the authors posed, albeit implicitly, an extremely profound question: If it is democratic institutions like those in the

West that prevent war, then where is the threat to peace? Logically, it must come from those countries without such democratic institutions—countries like the Soviet Union. Astonishing as it may seem, this realization is one of the foundations on which *perestroika* is being built.

"The use of armed forces outside the country without sanction from the Supreme Soviet or the congress is ruled out categorically, once and for all," Gorbachev affirmed in assuming his new powers as president in March 1990. This statement reflects the fundamental nature of the changes taking place in the Soviet Union, which have little, if anything, to do with Marxism-Leninism. Indeed, as the former head of the Soviet Institute of State and Law, Vladimir Kudryavtsev, has forthrightly acknowledged, "Marxists criticized the 'separation of powers' theory which drew a clear dividing line between legislative and executive power." Now Soviets are recognizing their mistake and embracing the separation of powers and the rule of law. The philosophical basis for these changes can be found in the writings of Kant. "The philosophical foundation of the rule-of-law state was formulated by Kant," Kudryavtsev and Yelena Lukasheva, a doctor of juridical science, flatly stated in a *Kommunist* article following the June–July 1988 19th party conference, which established the rule of law as a major objective of *perestroika*. Soviet officials from Gorbachev on down now routinely refer to Kant, and Shevardnadze has specifically identified Kant's 1795 booklet *Perpetual Peace* as a work deserving special attention.

Perpetual Peace was a major contribution to idealist philosophy. An admirer of the principles behind the American Revolution, Kant saw perpetual peace as a product not of the balance of power, but of republican government. Similarly, he rejected economic mercantilism, which is the foundation of geopolitics, in favor of Adam Smith's promotion of free trade. These themes are now commonplace in the Soviet media.

Viewed from the realist perspective, Gorbachev's actions, particularly in Eastern Europe, are puzzling; viewed from an idealist position, however, they are easily explicable. Since it is commerce rather than control of resources that is the source of wealth, better to abandon the territory where people are resentful of occupation. Free trade will provide more economic benefits than occupation. Nor is there any security risk; Soviet security is, in the final analysis, assured not by the territorial glacis or even by the might of the Soviet armed forces, but by the institutions of Western democracy.

The point is so startling to realists, who emphasize the balance of power, that it deserves elaboration. The Soviets are not deideologizing policy, but rather *re*-ideologizing it on a new basis. The Soviets are not replacing the value-laden system of Marx and Lenin with the value-neutral system of the balance of power, but are instead turning to a new set of values, those of the Enlightenment and especially of Kant. As Gorbachev told the 19th party conference in words that anticipated the revolutionary changes in Eastern Europe: "A key factor in the new thinking is the concept of freedom of choice. . . . To oppose freedom of choice is to come out against the objective tide of history itself. That is why power politics in all their forms and manifestations are historically obsolescent."

Underlying this shift in the Soviet world view is a reassessment of its domestic value system. "The image of a state," Shevardnadze has proclaimed, "is its attitude to its own citizens, respect for their rights and freedoms and recognition of the sovereignty of the individual." By emphasizing the sovereignty of the individual, Shevardnadze is turning communist philosophy upside down. In addition, he is paying an extraordinary compliment to the principles of the American Revolution. The European tradition has been one of national self-determination. "The basis of all sovereignty lies, essentially, in the Nation," states the French Declaration of the Rights of Man and the Citizen. But the pursuit of national self-determination has proved to be a chimera. What, after all, is a nation? How can it be defined? And the most painful question, which the Soviet Union is now confronting: How can national self-determination be achieved in a multi-ethnic state?

The American principle, on the other hand, is *individual* self-determination, not national self-determination. Americans believe in *e pluribus unum*: one out of many. So long as rights are guaranteed on an individual basis, the concept of a nation is irrelevant. In a multi-ethnic state—and, one is tempted to say, in a multinational world—there can be no other basis for preserving peace.

The changes in Eastern Europe go to the heart of the debate between realism and idealism. Since realists maintain that it is power rather than ideology that matters, they view Gorbachev's changes with suspicion. Realists are concerned that if Gorbachev is successful, the result could be a stronger Soviet Union and thus an even greater threat to the United States. Realists do not see a necessary link between the Soviet Union's domestic changes and its foreign policy. "*Glasnost* [openness] and *perestroika* represent attempts to modernize the Soviet state," Kissinger wrote in a January 1988 article in the *Washington Post*. "That is an internal Soviet matter, relevant to the democracies only if accompanied by a change in Soviet foreign policy." Indeed, Kissinger worries "whether Americans can be brought to see foreign policy in terms of equilibrium rather than as a struggle between good and evil." In his view, this was the problem with former President Ronald Reagan's policy toward the Soviet Union, which in a few years went from denunciations of an evil empire to an embrace of Gorbachev. "Such an approach," Kissinger stressed in another *Washington Post* article in February 1989, "neglects the realities of power, ambition and national interest."

For the idealist, on the other hand, there are no immutable "realities of power, ambition and national interest." All these must be viewed through the prism of policy, which changes as people change. Policy will be affected by a society's values, which in turn are embodied in its domestic institutions. Thus, the idealist rejects the notion that there is no connection between *perestroika* and Soviet foreign policy. Whereas the realist is in perpetual pursuit of a stabilizing equilibrium—believing, in former President Richard Nixon's words, that "the only time in the history of the world that we have had any extended periods of peace is when there has been balance of power"—the idealist seeks the spread of freedom, which ultimately would eliminate the need for a balance of power.

The difference between the two approaches is manifest in the way their adherents assess current developments in Europe. According to President George Bush, "the enemy is instability." But although instability can be dangerous if it is a prelude to chaos, stability by itself cannot be the highest American value. "Those who won our independence by revolution . . . did not fear political change," Justice Louis Brandeis wrote in 1927. "They did not exalt order at the cost of liberty." Affirming this idealist view, President Vaclav Havel of Czechoslovakia told the American people in February 1990 that "the best guarantee against possible threat or aggressivity is democracy," and, accordingly, he told Congress that the United States should "help the Soviet Union on its irreversible but immensely complicated road to democracy."

Safeguarding and spreading democracy in Eastern Europe means, above all, fostering the demilitarization of the Soviet Union and accelerating the withdrawal of its armed forces from foreign territory. Arguments that Gorbachev's position is too uncertain to be a basis for security decisions are unconvincing because arms control agreements are one of the best ways to bolster Gorbachev's position against hardline rivals. The more the USSR disarms and the more troops it withdraws from Eastern Europe, the more difficult it will be for any regime that might overthrow Gorbachev to reconstitute a significant military threat. In such a situation, moreover, violations of agreements will provide warning of the change in Soviet intentions, thereby further protecting American security.

Thus the current negotiations should focus on ways to accelerate the withdrawal of Soviet forces from Eastern Europe, while two other measures would help demilitarize Soviet society. The first is a mutual East-West ban on conscription. Conscription is the foundation of militarism in the Soviet Union. Eliminating it would not only benefit Western security enormously, but would also represent a diplomatic triumph for Gorbachev because conscription is extremely unpopular in the USSR.

The second step should be assistance designed to foster economic conversion. In this regard, the United States should encourage equity investment by private firms, which has several advantages over loans. First, it would not involve any U.S. government funds, so it would not worsen the budget deficit. Second, there would be no requirement to pay dividends as there would be to pay debt, so the poor in the USSR would not bear the burden if investments should go bad. Third, it would promote change in the Soviet Union toward a free-market economy. Fourth, it would provide managerial assistance because the firms making investments would want to assure their success. Finally, it would promise further investment because owners would have a continuing interest in the success of their ventures.

Would the Soviets allow Western investment in areas that might still be sensitive? Recent developments suggest they would. For example, the Votkinsk missile plant, which used to produce SS-20 missiles, is now planning a joint venture with an American firm to produce civilian rockets.

Perhaps the most interesting piece of evidence in this regard is an August 1989 *Wall Street Journal* article by Soviet economist Andrei Kuteinikov stating that "as the most talented people desert the state sector, Soviet co-ops can offer Western partners a highly educated and low-wage labor force. . . . This could turn out to be an intriguing opportunity for many Western industrial companies and venture capitalists, as the most motivated and aggressive scientists leave state labs and factories to launch their own ventures." By providing capital to skilled workers presumably leaving the Soviet defense industry, Western firms would facilitate the process of economic conversion, thereby augmenting Western security while simultaneously providing a financial lift to the struggling Soviet economy.

Two hundred years ago, the Enlightenment produced one of the great eras of human civilization. Its spirit, the spirit of tolerance, was captured by Voltaire: "Every individual who persecutes a man, his brother, because he does not agree with him, is a monster. . . . We should tolerate each other because we are all weak, inconsistent, subject to mutability and to error." This spirit was one of the inspirations for the American form of government. In the words of George Washington, "the Citizens of the United States of America have a right to applaud themselves for having given to mankind examples of an enlarged and liberal policy: a policy worthy of imitation. All possess alike liberty of conscience and immunities of citizenship."

Today, Americans are witnessing the reaffirmation of these principles of the Enlightenment and the power of the American example. For too long Americans have compromised their principles in the name of geopolitics. By doing so, they gave rise to a perception of moral equivalence between the United States and the Soviet Union, which undermined American interests. More to the point, they betrayed their special heritage. "Let us be diverted by none of those sophistical contrivances wherewith we are so industriously plied and belabored." Lincoln urged the American people in 1860 on the eve of their greatest test. "Let us have faith that right makes might, and in that faith, let us, to the end, dare to do our duty as we understand it."

The ultimate objective of American foreign policy, therefore, should not be the establishment of an equilibrium but the spread of freedom. The best way for the United States to do this is by setting an example to the world of the benefits of democracy. Unfortunately, the U.S. obsession with its world role has led it to neglect its domestic problems. American democratic institutions are strong, but they face mounting social problems. With the pressures of the Cold War easing, the United States must turn its attention increasingly to domestic issues in order to strengthen its democracy.

Internationally, U.S. assistance should be guided by two criteria: whether those asking for help share American values and the degree to which they are willing to help themselves. American economic assistance should encourage the development of capitalist institutions as the only means of fostering economic progress. The use of military force needs to be subject to nationwide debate. The successful use of force in Grenada and Panama has obscured its failures in Vietnam and Lebanon. Moreover, the fears generated by the Cold War gave virtually unlimited discretion for the use of force to the president, which may have harmful consequences for democratic government. "Our [Constitutional] Convention," Lincoln once stated, "resolved to so frame the Constitution that no one man should hold the power of this oppression [of war] upon us." Although the world has changed dramatically since Lincoln wrote these words, the Constitution, on this point, has not.

Indeed, a general American debate on the role of the president, the Congress, and the people in foreign policy is long overdue. In recent years, especially, presidents have attempted to claim a virtually exclusive role in the formulation of foreign policy by virtue of their position as commander in chief, even though Alexander Hamilton, in the *Federalist* No. 69, defined the president's powers in this regard as inferior to those of the British monarch. Excessive secrecy, in particular, is bound to erode the foundations of democratic government; the people have a right to know what their government is doing in their name. Claims that matters of foreign policy are too sensitive to be discussed in public must be rejected as incompatible with the American ethos. In Jefferson's words: "It is error alone which needs the support of government. Truth can stand by itself."

The realist perspective has gone unchallenged long enough. Idealism is not naive utopianism but a rigorous approach to the conduct of foreign policy. Moreover, it is idealism that is the great American tradition. As Washington declared in his Farewell Address:

> Observe good faith and justice toward all nations. Cultivate peace and harmony with all. Religion and morality enjoin this conduct. And can it be that good policy does not equally enjoin it? It will be worthy of a free, enlightened, and at no distant period a great nation to give mankind the magnanimous and too novel example of a people always guided by an exalted justice and benevolence. Who can doubt that in the course of time and things the fruits of such a plan would richly repay any temporary advantages which might be lost by a steady adherence to it?

Americans should not fear that the spread of the democratic system created by the founders of their republic could present a threat to their security. They should instead follow Washington's advice and reject the realist's compromises as leading only to those "temporary advantages" of which he spoke. The long-term interests of the United States are fulfilled when it is true to its ideals, thus setting an example for the rest of the world. "We shall be as a City upon a Hill, the Eyes of all people are upon us," John Winthrop proclaimed in 1630. More than 350 years later, our revolutionary world demonstrates that it is the power of America's ideals, and not the might of its armies, that is the real source of U.S. influence in the world.

37

Points of Mutual Advantage: Perestroika and American Foreign Policy*

James A. Baker III, Secretary of State

Since the end of World War II, the United States and the Soviet Union have been engaged in constant struggle; a contest of superpower strength, but also a contest of values and vision. No relationship has been more difficult, or ultimately, more promising. Difficult because traditional Soviet ideology has used the same words as we do—democracy, human rights, freedom, peace, and justice—while in practice denying the values behind them. Promising because in the nuclear age, the imperative of avoiding disaster has compelled us both to search for common interests.

We are in a time of rising promise. Relations with the Soviet Union have improved considerably since 1985, when Mikhail Gorbachev launched what he called *perestroika*—a total restructuring of Soviet society, including Soviet foreign and defense policy. And this Administration has been building on what was achieved during the Reagan years so that improved American-Soviet relations will last. As President Bush has declared, "We will work together to move beyond containment of the Soviet Union."

We now have a historic opportunity with the Soviet Union. We have the chance to leave behind the postwar period with the ups and downs of the cold war. We can move beyond containment to make the change toward better superpower relations more secure and less reversible. Our task is to find enduring points of mutual advantage that serve the interests of both the United States and the Soviet Union.

There are two reasons why we think that the prospects for a lasting improvement in U.S.-Soviet relations are better than ever before. First, we in the West have demonstrated through our strength, unity, and fidelity to our values that

*This article is an address prepared by Secretary Baker for the Foreign Policy Association, New York City, October 16, 1989.

Published by the United States Department of State, Bureau of Public Affairs, Office of Public Communication, Editorial Division, Washington, D.C., October 1989. This material is in the public domain and may be reprinted without permission.

democracy and free market economies work, and work well together. Second, the alternative vision advocated by the Soviet Union has failed to produce either prosperity or an attractive society. Simply put—freedom works! Communism doesn't!

As a consequence of the failure of their system, the Soviets, led by Mikhail Gorbachev, have begun the process of reform and rebuilding called *perestroika*. And it is this process, combined with our own achievements, that offers promise for the future.

The President has said, and I have said, that we want *perestroika*—including the restructuring of Soviet-American relations—to succeed. We have reached this conclusion, not because it is our business to reform Soviet society or to keep a particular Soviet leader in power—we can really do neither—but because *perestroika* promises Soviet actions more advantageous to our interests. Our task is to search creatively for those points of mutual U.S.-Soviet advantage that may be possible—and many more may be possible because of *perestroika*. Ultimately, of course, even as we explore Soviet "new thinking," we must be prepared to protect our vital interests, come what may. We must maintain a defense budget commensurate with our security requirements, and we must be vigilant and push Moscow toward cooperative behavior across the full range of our relations.

Now, I want to explain this policy of ours in more detail—specifically, what we see in *perestroika*, why we want it to succeed, and what we are doing to find those points of mutual advantage that will benefit both American interests and *perestroika* itself.

PERESTROIKA AND SOVIET DOMESTIC POLICY

I think it is important to begin by understanding the origins of *perestroika*. First and foremost, it is a Soviet response to a rapidly changing world in which they see themselves increasingly hard pressed to compete economically, technologically, politically, and militarily. The exponents of *perestroika* see their country as rich in natural resources and human talent but stifled by the legacy of stagnation—a system incapable of producing the economic progress and political legitimacy which Soviet citizens have the right to expect. And, as both President Gorbachev and Foreign Minister Shevardnadze have emphasized in their conversations with me, the cause of this problem goes beyond just a question of material assets. It is rooted in the very psychology of Soviet society, reinforced by equally stagnant political and legal systems.

Thus, the very logic of *perestroika* requires that the Soviets themselves must solve their own problems in a comprehensive, organic way. Not only must the economic system be reformed but the political and legal systems, too. *Perestroika* is, therefore, different than earlier, failed attempts at reforming the state Lenin founded and Stalin built. Gross inputs such as the redistribution of rural labor to industry or sources of cheap raw materials are no longer available to "jump-start" the economy.

Nor are Soviet problems susceptible to rescue from abroad through abundant Western credits—the failed policy of Brezhnev's "era of stagnation." President Gorbachev bluntly expressed this point in his 1988 New Year's address when he said: "We must not think, comrades, that someone will resolve our problems for us, that everything around us will change at the wave of a magic wand as midnight strikes on New Year's Eve. No. We must create the future ourselves, help the restructuring by our actions." As Ed Hewett, a Western expert on the Soviet economy, has put it, "however strong Western feelings may be about the possible outcomes of this reform effort, Western policymakers should see that their 'influence' on this process can be no more than modest."

The self-reliant and radical nature of domestic *perestroika* has become even more crucial as the reforms have encountered increasing difficulties. Thus far, Mr. Gorbachev and his colleagues have been willing to place their bets on reform and to double them if necessary.

Perestroika may have reached a turning point where the bets will have to be redoubled again. Consumer shortages are not likely to be relieved nor productivity increased without the incentives of a stable currency, free and competitive markets, private property, and real prices. Elements of Marxist-Leninist ideology such as the dominant, exclusive role of the Communist Party appear to be incompatible with the decentralized political and economic system necessary to solve Moscow's ills. And new political arrangements will be necessary to alleviate the grievances and demands of Soviet ethnic minorities and republics.

Finally, the systemic, organic nature of *perestroika* takes it beyond the category of an exclusively domestic reform. President Gorbachev has repeatedly pointed to the links between domestic reform and the new thinking in foreign policy, saying just a few months ago, "there exists an indissoluble link between the new foreign policy and *perestroika* within the country."

And that is where we come in. Fascinating as domestic change in the Soviet Union may be, we are mainly affected by the way the Soviet Union approaches the rest of the world. Here, too, *perestroika* promises a radical reform.

PERESTROIKA IN SOVIET FOREIGN AND DEFENSE POLICY

Compare the kind of Soviet foreign policy we used to face with what we see today. Under Brezhnev, Soviet influence, primarily through armed proxies, expanded around the globe. Hand-in-hand with these adventures, the Soviets undertook an across-the-board defense buildup, well-expressed by former Secretary of Defense Harold Brown when he said, "When we build they build; when we stop, they build."

Yet for all the expansions of their military forces and their efforts to establish beach heads around the globe, the Soviets bought neither greater security nor lastir. ' success.

Indeed, the lessons of the 1970s learned by today's Soviet leadership appear to contradict, fundamentally, the rose-colored view of the Brezhnev era. Gorbachev and his group of "new thinkers" now speak of the following lessons:

- The Brezhnev military buildup brought greater insecurity instead of increasing security. Soviet actions—such as the deployment of SS–20s in Western Europe, for example—provoked Western responses, making the correlation of forces less favorable to Moscow, not more.
- The military buildup also bankrupted the economy. The military's across-the-board first call on more and more resources had to cease.
- Security could not be achieved unilaterally, only multilaterally.
- Military and political gains in the Third World were expensive, and the shallow successes were nearly always fleeting.
- Regional conflicts could escalate and produce undesired confrontations. Possible gains were not worth the risks inherent in such situations.

These are the lessons the Soviets speak of having learned from Brezhnev's failures, theoretical lessons that have shaped the new thinking and *perestroika*. But while in theory they have learned these lessons, they have not put them all into practice by any means.

In defense policy and arms control, the Soviets have shown greater understanding of the need to promote mutual security. In both conventional and nuclear arms control talks, the Soviets have shifted their positions to correspond more closely with long-held Western assumptions about preventing war and producing greater stability. President Gorbachev has promised cuts in the Soviet defense budget. He has promised to turn swords into plowshares by transforming tanks into tractors. Here we are still looking for concrete results.

In regional conflicts, the picture is very mixed. The Soviets have withdrawn from Afghanistan. And they fostered the settlement in Angola. But, overall, Moscow appears less willing to make hard choices on the regional questions than on arms control. We've seen a surge in Soviet arms shipments to Afghanistan and Ethiopia; in Cambodia, Soviet shipments this year are already twice as high as all of 1988; and Soviet-bloc arms continue to end up in Nicaragua. These disturbing actions, this seeming preference for military solutions, may work in the short run to keep a Najibullah or a Hun Sen or a Mengistu in power. In the long run, however, only political solutions based on national reconciliation can settle these conflicts. That's the true lesson of the 1970s.

PERESTROIKA AND AMERICAN POLICY

What explains this mixed record? Some analysts, invoking past disappointments, argue that the Soviets are engaged in a mere *peredyshka*—a breathing space until Leninism is strong enough to do battle once more with capitalism. Others, invoking future hope, argue that the new thinkers are so consumed by domestic concerns that old thinking still holds sway over certain aspects of foreign policy. But to me, it reveals something else. I find a certain parallel between the course of Soviet domestic *perestroika* and new thinking in Soviet foreign policy. Domestically, as Gorbachev has sought to turn theory into practice, his program has altered and evolved. And just as the Soviets have come face to face with domestic dilemmas that must now be resolved if progress is to be made, so they will come face-to-face with the need for further change in their foreign policy.

Domestically, we can have but small direct impact on how the Soviets resolve their dilemmas. But in foreign and defense policy, through a prudent search for points of mutual advantage, we can more readily shape and alter the calculus, so that the Soviets face up to the contradictions between the new thinking and old habits. In arms control, the Kremlin has made some politically difficult choices and in some areas selected the path of mutual progress. Now, we must also shape the Soviet calculus so that Moscow chooses the path of progress in regional conflicts.

In the course of our search for mutual advantage, we must not succumb to a false optimism that *perestroika* in Soviet foreign policy has gone far enough and that we can rely on the new thinking to take account of our interests.

It would be an equally great blunder to ignore the possibility that *perestroika* might go much further and to retreat instead into a suspicious stance of disengagement that would never put *perestroika*'s promise to the test. Either approach would sacrifice the great opportunity before us.

Thus, our mission must be to press the search for mutual advantage. Where we find Soviet agreement, we'll both be better off. Where we meet Soviet resistance, we'll know that we have to redouble our efforts so that Moscow practices, not just preaches, the new thinking. By acting realistically to engage Moscow in the search for mutual interests, we can seize the opportunities inherent in Gorbachev's revolution. By standing pat, we would gain nothing and lose this chance to revolutionize East-West relations.

In practice, our search to find mutual advantage has focused on resolving political conflicts—both in Europe and in the Third World—on reducing the risk of war through arms control, and on promoting internal Soviet change. Progress in these areas will serve Soviet and American interests in their broadest sense, both by relieving tensions and by releasing resources for the work of peace.

EUROPE WHOLE AND FREE

Our first search for mutual advantage must concern the most important and vital flash point of the cold war: the division of Europe. President Bush has stated our purpose to be a Europe that is whole and free, and our allies in NATO have agreed on a comprehensive program to attain that goal. Part of that program is an accelerated timetable for an agreement on conventional force reductions in

Europe that would correct existing asymmetries and reduce the risks of surprise attack. Such an agreement would make not only for a more secure deterrent but would also promote greater military openness, which will strengthen mutual confidence and reduce the chances of misunderstanding and miscalculation.

Even more importantly, an agreement on Conventional Armed Forces in Europe (CFE) could redraw the European security map, severely inhibiting Soviet military intimidation not only of Western Europe but of Eastern Europe, too. Soviet occupation forces in Eastern Europe would have to be cut to less than half the levels they had at the beginning of this year.

CFE would also help *perestroika* in the Soviet Union. Moscow can save billions on conventional forces by agreeing to a CFE agreement. If Gorbachev is serious about converting guns into butter, then CFE is the surest path to big savings. Above all, an agreement would demonstrate clearly to the world that East and West could dispel the political and military legacy of the cold war.

A whole and free Europe, however, is more than arms control or arms reduction. The Helsinki agreement provides for common measures on human rights to prevail in Europe.

Both we and the Soviet Union are challenged to deal with change in the countries behind the now-rusting Iron Curtain. Because they each followed the same ill-suited Stalinist models, each of them has been afflicted in varying degrees with the same ailments that provoked *perestroika* in the Soviet Union. These nations, however, cannot be treated as a single case. Some of them— notably Hungary and Poland—have begun to take bold steps away from the economic and even the political systems they have known.

In East Germany, the people themselves are taking bold steps. As I said last week, it is time for *perestroika* and *glasnost* to come to East Germany. The status quo is as unacceptable to the people of that nation as it is to the peoples of Poland and Hungary. The people of East Germany cannot be forever denied at home the better life they now seek by fleeing to the West. Of course, the United States and our NATO partners have long supported the reconciliation of the German people. Their legitimate rights must some day be met. But let me be clear: Reconciliation through self-determination can only be achieved in peace and freedom. Normalization must occur on the basis of Western values with the end result being a people integrated into the community of democratic European nations.

We have made clear our view that a Europe can never be whole or free if the so-called Brezhnev doctrine justifying Soviet military intervention against its Warsaw Pact allies continues to be a principle of Soviet foreign policy. Without explicitly renouncing that doctrine, President Gorbachev and [Foreign] Minister Shevardnadze have declared that the use of force to determine the political systems of other countries is impermissible. They have said that each state should be able to choose its own course. My only change in that formula would be to say that the people of each state should be able to choose their own course.

We have seen in Poland the election of a noncommunist prime minister to lead a coalition, including the Communist Party, as that country seeks a way out of its legacy of disastrous economic mismanagement. This is a remarkable development which gives us hope. Political institutions truly responsible to the people are the only guarantee of long-term stability. We hope this model of change will be followed elsewhere in the region.

We seek to encourage reform so that these countries may once again regain their rightful place as independent nations, working within a European framework to make social and economic progress. As with *perestroika* in the Soviet Union, the essential decisions must be taken by those nations themselves. Building upon these decisions, we and our allies in Western Europe can offer help at three stages. In the short term we can offer aid, especially food, that can help to alleviate the immediate crisis. Over the medium term, working through the IMF [International Monetary Fund] and other multilateral financial institutions, we can put together packages that combine monetary stabilization, structural reform, and effective debt management. Over the long term, we can encourage and stimulate the creation of a private sector and conditions to attract private capital for the reconstruction of these economies.

None of this will be easy. The margins for error after years of compounded blunders are very thin. That is why we dare not repeat our earlier mistakes of the 1970s. Our assistance must be carefully targeted, integrated with effective reforms by the countries themselves, and supported by the international community. That is why the President, after visiting Poland and Hungary this summer, asked for and received the cooperation of our European allies in devising such a program. Such a program is now taking shape in cooperation with our Western partners. The United States must continue to be the catalyst to make it work.

A final comment on political change in Eastern Europe. As I have noted, we favor a process that gives these countries their right to self-determination and freedom. President Bush has made clear that it is not our purpose to exploit the movement toward freedom in order to harm the security of the Soviet Union. No one—I repeat, no one—will benefit if the entire trend toward beneficial economic and political change is engulfed in violence.

But all will benefit if the reforms succeed in Eastern Europe. The people of Eastern Europe will benefit as their Stalinist shackles are lifted. West Europeans will benefit as their continent is made whole again. Gorbachev and the reformers will benefit as examples flourish in Eastern Europe of the power of reform. And we will benefit as we move beyond the cold war.

RESOLVING REGIONAL CONFLICTS

A second major point where we must search for mutual advantage with the Soviets concerns regional conflicts. Each of these bears, to some degree, the potential for becoming the scene of superpower rivalry and tension. With the spread of missiles and chemical weapons throughout volatile regions, conflicts in the Third World are likely to take on a more dangerous character. Regional conflicts are likely to be more difficult to contain, more likely to engulf more countries, and more susceptible to escalation.

Neither the United States nor a Soviet Union in the midst of *perestroika* has an interest in being drawn into such conflicts. As President Gorbachev said recently, "We now need, perhaps more than ever before, favorable external conditions so that we can cope with the revolutionary and broad task toward renewing Soviet society." Resolution of conflicts in Central America, Afghanistan, Cambodia, and Africa would surely spare the Soviets the billions they spend each year on supporting client states. This is an area where the Soviets can help themselves. And we have made it clear that we are ready and willing partners; partners who recognize that settling and defusing regional tensions can diminish the dangers we all face.

REDUCING THE RISKS OF WAR

Arms control is the third area where we are seeking points of mutual advantage with Moscow. In our various efforts, we can work with the Soviets to lower the risk of war and the cost of preventing it. Our arms control efforts have focused on reducing the risk of war by lowering the incentives for surprise attack, not arms reductions in and of themselves. To this end, we have focused in CFE on those weapons—tanks, artillery, and armored personnel carriers—most suited to launching and sustaining invasions. In START [strategic arms reduction talks], we've placed a premium on reducing weapons most suited to a first strike—such as the Soviet SS–18s—while encouraging those which are more stabilizing and less useful for striking first, for example, bombers. We've moved off our ban on mobile missiles, contingent on congressional funding, because mobile missiles, if effectively verified, increase survivability and enhance stability.

We've also attempted to foster greater openness between East and West to provide greater reassurances about intentions and capabilities and to reduce misperceptions. To that end, the President announced his "open skies" initiative, which has been received positively by the Soviets.

In pursuing these arms control objectives, this Administration has sought to learn from its predecessors. We have kept our eye firmly on the ball, working to bring home treaties which the Senate will ratify and which will verifiably lock in new U.S.-Soviet security relations. This emphasis on realistic, verifiable agreements was the impetus behind our verification and stability measures in START and our data exchange with the Soviets on chemical weapons—both of which the Soviets agreed to in Wyoming.

We also took realistic steps there to begin U.S.-Soviet cooperation geared toward controlling growing threats not just in the East-West arena but to global security as well. The chemical weapons initiative announced by the President at the United Nations will produce massive reductions in Soviet and U.S. stockpiles at an accelerated pace.

PROMOTING *PERESTROIKA* INTERNALLY

While our primary focus is on those points of mutual advantage that we can find in these three areas—Europe, regional conflicts, and arms control—we are also seeking a fourth area: the strengthening of *glasnost* and democratization. Through our exchanges, we are actively encouraging the growth of pluralistic institutions and practices in the Soviet Union. We believe the emphasis on the rule of law in the writings of the reformers is a positive step. We are encouraging the Soviets to make permanent in their legal code and practice the protection of individual rights to which they subscribed in the Helsinki accord. Through our transnational dialogue, we also hope to involve the Soviets on those global issues, especially the environment, where Soviet practice in the past has not lived up to international standards. Foreign Minister Shevardnadze showed great interest in Wyoming about these transnational problems, particularly global warming, and I believe greater U.S.-Soviet cooperation can pave the way for more effective international action.

Finally, we have begun to explore a fifth area of potential mutual advantage. This last area relates to *perestroika*'s internal aspects. We are prepared to provide technical assistance in certain areas of Soviet economic reform. The Soviets are entering uncharted waters, experimenting with markets, competitive enterprises, and realistic pricing, all of which we take for granted. In Wyoming, [Foreign] Minister Shevardnadze and I had extensive discussions on the kinds of steps that would facilitate price reform, a necessary step toward ruble convertibility. The Soviet leadership is clearly interested in our ideas about their economic reforms, and we will continue our discussions on these issues.

These areas offer fertile ground in which to find points of mutual advantage. *Perestroika*, after all, means, for the Soviet Union, a new way of conducting their political, economic, and legal affairs—a new set of standards, if you will.

We do neither of us any good if we relax our own standards in the name of helping reform. That is why we have told the Soviets to codify the changes we are seeing in their emigration practice so that we can waive [the] Jackson-Vanik [amendment] as we have promised. That is why today we see discussions about Soviet membership in GATT [General Agreement on Tariffs and Trade] or the other international financial institutions as premature. That is also why our approach to trade, based on previous experience both with the U.S.S.R. and other countries, must be on a commercial basis. Mutually beneficial, non-strategic commercial exchanges are the best way to expand Soviet participation in the international economy.

CONCLUSION

Let me sum it all up. We want *perestroika* to succeed at home and abroad because we believe that it will bring about a less aggressive Soviet Union, restrained in the use of force and less hostile to democracy. A *perestroika* that resulted simply in a more efficient and more capable Soviet state would, indeed, be a more formidable and dangerous competitor.

But I do not believe that *perestroika* can succeed without increasing measures of free markets, free speech, and institutions more accountable to the people—in short, without more freedom! And that means a more democratic society, more respectful of human rights and legal norms which could provide a lasting foundation for more constructive, less dangerous Soviet behavior abroad; a society that produces not subjects who are to be acted upon but citizens who participate in the policy process; and a society where citizens have a say in what their government does at home and abroad. In such a Soviet Union, the people and the government will agree that, as Foreign Minister Shevardnadze has said (and I quote), "A foreign policy that is not open and explained to the people and does not gain their support is impossible." That government is far more likely to establish as its measure of success internal progress, rather than external expansion.

That is why a prudent policy of searching for mutual advantages between the United States and the Soviet Union is worth our serious and substantial effort. It is the best way to find out whether the promise of *perestroika* in foreign policy can be fulfilled.

Let me conclude this review of *perestroika* and American foreign policy by reiterating my convictions that, indeed, we do have a historic opportunity to make lasting improvements in U.S.-Soviet relations. It is an opportunity produced by actions on both sides. And, as President Bush has stated, "Our aspiration is a real peace, a peace of shared optimism, not a peace of armed camps."

And what could that aspiration, that shared optimism, really mean? Nothing less than an end to the dangerous East-West stalemate, which has disfigured postwar international politics. It could mean a new U.S.-Soviet relationship, which replaces competition where possible with a creative and cooperative approach to international problems. A new relationship that would be sustained not by rhetoric or pious hope but by the reality of a Europe, free, whole, and at peace with itself. A new relationship where the reality of regional conflicts would be resolved at last, so that the promise of development can be fulfilled. A new relationship that would produce a sustainable arms control process that provided more security through enhanced stability and greater openness at lower cost. And a new relationship, above all else, that would lead to the fulfillment of those human rights which are the birthright of all mankind.

38

The Gulf Crisis and the Future of Gorbachev's Foreign Policy Revolution*

Robert Legvold

Few doubted history had tacked a new direction when with one voice the Americans and Soviets instantly and angrily condemned Saddam Hussein's invasion of Kuwait, and called for a world-wide arms embargo of his country. But even the most credulous individual would have had trouble imagining the partnership to follow, and the hopes of a new world that would spring from it. Vast changes, of course, had already occurred in Soviet foreign policy by the time Hussein moved against Kuwait, changes fundamentally altering the nature of the superpower relationship, changes that at their most stunning undid the Coldwar European order. But the Gulf crisis carried the revolution in Soviet foreign policy across another threshold—and, along the way, altered the Bush Administration's view of the Soviet Union more than almost anything that had come before.

Even without knowing how the drama will end, therefore, the Gulf crisis is already a moment of historic proportion. In an incredible and tumultuous age, it ranks with the most powerful and creative of events. More than a fascinating and revealing case study, its effects already represent a seminal lurch of history.

THE FIRST NINETY DAYS

On August 1, while Saddam Hussein's troops massed for the invasion, the American secretary of state happened to be in Irkutsk meeting with the Soviet foreign minister. Baker, alerted by U.S. intelligence of troubling signs that the Iraqis were poised for attack, warned Shevardnadze, and urged him to do something to prevent it, to do something to "restrain these guys."[1] Curiously Shevardnadze knew much less than his U.S. counterpart. (Either Soviet intelligence missed the signs, or failed to inform Shevardnadze, or, most likely, had

*Reprinted by permission of the author and publisher from the *Harriman Institute Forumn* Volume 3, no. 10 (October 1990). Copyright © 1990 by the Harriman Institute Forum.

been deceived by Hussein.) He told the Secretary of State—more than once, because by the next day a worried Baker had learned from Washington that the invasion was only hours away—not to worry. Saddam had assured his Soviet friends that Iraq had no intention of attacking, and Shevardnadze was confident the confrontation between Iraq and Kuwait had gone as far as it would, in fact, that it was "being defused."[2] A day later, with the invasion well-advanced and the UN Security Council in emergency session, Shevardnadze confessed his misjudgment.[3] Baker had been right, he said, but "I virtually ruled out any further aggravation. . . . I did not expect the Iraqis to commit such naked aggression against a defenseless and peace-loving country which did not pose a threat to anyone."

Secretary Baker and his entourage were the first to know how differently this time the Soviet Union would deal with a major regional crisis. In their private meetings, Shevardnadze had been visibly agitated by confirming news of the invasion. He made no effort to offer excuses for the Iraqis, notwithstanding a long Soviet-Iraq friendship, or to buy time while he and his colleagues sorted out where the balance of Soviet interests lay. He instead condemned the act, and offered to work together in thwarting Iraq's aggression. Before the day of the attack was out, Moscow and Washington led the way in securing a UN Security Council resolution censuring Baghdad and demanding its withdrawal from Kuwait. Twenty-four hours later, the two issued their joint statement, announcing to the world the full alignment of their positions. (When Arabists in the Soviet foreign ministry had supposedly resisted a tough declaration, including the call for a general arms embargo, Shevardnadze had quickly overridden them.[4])

From the start, however, there were important differences in accent between the two leaderships. The Soviet Union fully supported the U.S. Administration's uncompromising opposition to the conquest of Kuwait, including the fast-formed plans to impose comprehensive economic sanctions. But it also stressed the need to act under the auspices of the United Nations. Keeping the enterprise under UN aegis merged with another Soviet priority, namely, to avoid at nearly all costs war with Iraq, particularly one triggered by unilateral U.S. military actions.

When the Americans early the next week decided to send U.S. forces to Saudi Arabia as a deterrent to an Iraqi attack, and, rather than catch the Soviets unaware, first to inform them, Shevardnadze was distinctly unhappy over the news. Even Baker's invitation to join the United States with forces of his country's own—remarkable considering the tenacity with which American leaders through the years had fought to keep the Soviet military out of the region— did not do much to ease his concern. In the end, he grudgingly acceded, but, consistent with the Soviet stress on working through the United Nations, he first pushed the Americans to take seriously the Military Staff Committee of the Security Council, a neglected relic of the UN's founding when people dreamed the five permanent members would want to coordinate military actions designed to keep the peace. By the end of the crisis' second week, with U.S. forces flowing into the area, the Bush Administration seemed ready to turn economic sanctions into a formal blockade, enforced by U.S. naval power, with or without Security Council approval. Again, the Soviets demurred, this time with widespread sympathy among the other Security Council members, and, again, they insisted on the importance of mobilizing the UN and its machinery.

When over the weekend of August 18–19, the Americans decided to bend, rather than charge off without Security Council blessing, and a modestly chastened Baker telephoned Shevardnadze to confess that perhaps the United States "should have consulted more" and that his government did want Soviet help in enforcing the embargo, did want to act within the authorization of a Security Council resolution, the Soviet foreign minister repeated the Soviet determination to see the Military Staff Committee reinvigorated.[5] Washington, eager to secure passage of the U.S.-British resolution permitting forceful implementation of the sanctions, this time, as another country's diplomat put it, "threw the Soviets the bone they wanted."

The to and fro leading to a favorable vote on Resolution 665, the sanction for a formal blockade, revealed another contrast in the two countries' concerns. Moscow had never, even at the outset of the crisis, severed ties with Baghdad. Arms deliveries promptly stopped, but diplomatic contacts continued. Indeed, between August 2 and the third week in August, Moscow had become the cockpit of diplomacy among the Arab states and with Iraq. Prince Bandar Bin Sultan al-Saud, the special emissary of the Saudi royal family came to Moscow; so did Saddun Hammadi, Iraq's Deputy Prime Minister; and the Kuwaiti and Egyptian foreign ministers were on their way. The Soviet leadership may have rejected as firmly as the United States Iraqi aggression, but from the start they left the door open to diplomatic persuasion. Before they would vote for Resolution 665, they wanted to give Hussein one last chance. So, Gorbachev sent him a message: To comply with UN resolutions and withdraw from Kuwait territory, restore the government, and assure the safety of foreigners, or, failing that, the Security Council would be "compelled to adopt appropriate additional measures."[6] August 24, Alexander Belonogov, the Deputy Foreign Minister, summoned U.S. Ambassador Jack Matlock, and reported that "We've heard from the Iraqis and the answer is unsatisfactory."[7] At four in the morning the next day, the Soviets joined twelve other members of the Security Council in voting to call on states with naval forces in the area to act "as may be necessary" to "ensure strict implementation" of the embargo. The resolution did not provide for a UN flag or command, something Soviet representatives had wanted but on which they did not insist.

Thus, by August 25, three weeks into the crisis, all the elements in the Soviet approach, an approach utterly transformed, were in place. First, and at the most essential level, the Soviet Union had not merely condemned the deed of a Third-World ally, but sought with others to inflict on it a clear and full defeat. Second, Soviet leaders had made the United Nations, particularly the Security Council and its five permanent members, the focus of their cooperation. Denying success to Hussein, thus, was only one objective; ensuring that his defeat was accomplished through potent international institutions was the other. Third, they had sought to protect a diplomatic route out of the impasse, rather than entrust the entire enterprise to coercive means.

There were also lesser features of the policy. One was a determination to keep Soviet military involvement to a minimum (again, in sharp contrast with desiderata in the Brezhnev years). A second was to save the 8000 Soviet nationals in Iraq from the fate of other nation's citizens, whom the Iraqi leadership had turned into de facto hostages. A third was to nurture a consensus with China, and where possible to gain credit with a range of skeptical governments, such as the Japanese, Saudi, and South Korean. A fourth was to do the least damage possible to the long-term standing of the Soviet Union with the largest range of Arab regimes. Finally, by early September a fifth element emerged: Returning from Harbin, Tokyo, and Pyongyang, Shevardnadze gingerly probed the possibility of linking the crisis to the solution of the other two major conflicts in the region, within Lebanon and between Israel and its neighbors.

Three weeks into the crisis, the profound effect of the Soviet Union's metamorphosis on American attitudes was also apparent. From the beginning the Administration had taken the Soviet leadership into its confidence, and treated it like a partner in a common enterprise. Secretary of State Baker, who served as the direct channel of contact, spoke daily by telephone with Foreign Minister Shevardnadze. Word of American initiatives was conveyed in advance, assessments of developments in the region, shared, and strategy, talked over. When President Bush was asked early in the crisis how supportive the Soviets were being, he answered that he could not "ask for more favorable response" than Baker had received.[8]

Even when an issue arose over 198 Soviet military advisors still on the job in Iraq, the Administration went out of its way to minimize controversy, and the President continued to report "superb cooperation from the Soviets."[9] (In turn, when some of the Moscow policymaking community expressed doubts over ultimate U.S. intentions, including the suspicion that Washington meant to establish a permanent military presence in the region, Gorbachev cut short this line of commentary by noting in an August 31 press conference that the United States military was there at the invitation of the Saudis and in conformance with the UN Charter.)[10]

In early September the Administration hastily organized a summit with Gorbachev, an act that itself underscored the change taking place. The two leaders had only two months earlier met at the summit, and, while the Americans insisted this encounter was simply a natural follow on, in fact, for a U.S. president to seek an urgent meeting with the Soviet leader in order to coordinate policy in a crisis spoke volumes of just how differently the President now thought of his counterpart from their first meeting on Governors Island in fall 1988 or even from their first summit on Malta in December 1989. And he showed it. Slowly, over the Administration's first two years, the President had edged toward a more favorable view of Gorbachev's *perestroika*, and, in the process, had eased his originally openly negative view of Western economic assistance to the Soviet Union. At the Malta summit he sketched a series of supportive economic measures the Administration would seek from the Congress, provided the Soviet Union satisfied a number of conditions. His representatives in other settings had often talked of making aid contingent on its use to privatize the Soviet economy and promote democracy. Now, after their interchange at Helsinki and the events of August, Bush had come full circle. Asked at the summit press conference whether he felt more sympathetic to suggestions for Western aid to the Soviet Union, he confessed that "this remarkable cooperation . . . gets me inclined to recommend as close cooperation in the economic field as possible," and he promised to say so to the Congress on his return.[11] A few days later Commerce Secretary Robert Mosbacher led a group of corporate executives to Moscow to discuss, among other things, ways of revitalizing the Soviet Union's declining oil industry.

Another episode at the summit was even more revealing. At one point during the press conference Gorbachev playfully let the correspondents in on a "secret." In their talks, he said, the President had confessed that "there was a long time when our view was that the Soviet Union had nothing to do in the Middle East, . . . had no business being there," but that no longer seemed important.[12] The next day the *New York Times* filled in the rest of the story. Bush in fact had invited the Soviet Union to play a greater diplomatic role in the region, and had even raised the possibility of working together on problems like the Arab-Israeli conflict.[13]

In the second and third months of the crisis, Soviet policy continued to evolve, but within the pattern set at the beginning. Some observers were surprised when in late September the Soviet Union aggressively took the lead in pushing for an air embargo of Iraq and, for emphasis, urged the unusual step of a Security Council meeting of foreign ministers to pass the measure. Shevardnadze, on the occasion, delivered the strongest Soviet speech to date and one of the strongest given by any leader. Iraq, he said, had committed "unprovoked aggression," resorted to "unprecedented blackmail," and, more importantly, "dealt a blow to all that mankind has recently achieved" in creating a new international order.[14] If it continued, he warned, "war may break out . . . any day, any moment." "We should remind those who regard aggression as an acceptable form of behavior that the United Nations has the power to suppress acts of aggression," and that "there is ample evidence that this right can be exercised," and "will be, if the illegal occupation of Kuwait continues."

Observers were surprised, because until then, and most conspicuously at the Helsinki summit, the Soviets had gone out their way to avoid threats and to stress what a disaster anything other than a political solution would be. Gorbachev, in his meeting with Bush, had constantly dodged the issue of a Soviet military contribution to forces in the Gulf, putting great emphasis on avoiding the use of force. So clear was this theme that many saw a gulf growing between the two countries: The United States bearing the burden of the sword; the Soviet Union, the olive branch. Indeed, in one of the larger unremarked ironies of the unfolding crisis, a great many American commentators had begun to resent the Soviet Union for not being willing play a larger military role.

Shevardnadze's strong words, however, were not inconsistent with this earlier reluctance. On the contrary, if anything, they reflected a sudden, deep alarm that the momentum toward war had gathered speed, and that, unless Hussein could be turned around, events were marching toward the abyss. Predictably what followed, therefore, was not a firming up of the Soviet military commitment or new initiatives designed to squeeze the Iraqis harder, but a diplomatic offensive.

In early September, before the Helsinki summit, on the way back from China, Japan, and North Korea, Shevardnadze volunteered that he was "ready if necessary" to go to Iraq in pursuit of peace.[15] At the time, the offer startled outsiders, and set a number of people to wondering if the Soviet Union might have an idea of trying to mediate the conflict. Had the U.S. administration suspected that the Soviets hoped to turn themselves into an honest broker, the partnership would have fast disintegrated. That was not the case, but even diplomatic probing by a Soviet Union, however loyal it remained to the united front, stirred less than enthusiastic U.S. support. Bush at Helsinki treated the idea as something to be indulged rather than applauded.

But, when Shevardnadze took the lead in the Security Council in late September, the Soviet leadership was galvanized by a growing dread, and no longer merely exploring alleys that might lead somewhere. Within days, it dispatched one of its own (one with special knowledge of the Arab world) on a serious mission to the region. Evgeny Primakov, before advancing up the political ladder and into the ultimate leadership circle, had been the Soviet Union's most prominent academic specialist on the Middle East. He traveled to Baghdad with the growing weight of Soviet apprehension on his shoulders. He also went with an obvious determination to give direct diplomacy a vigorous go.

For the better part of October, he engaged in a shuttle diplomacy reminiscent of Henry Kissinger's mid-1970s Middle East efforts. From Iraq, after long conversations with Hussein, he headed for Washington, and then back to Cairo, Riyadh, and Baghdad. The reports of his progress hardly quickened hopes, but the effort itself was telling. First, it was evident that the Soviet Union had now decided to take matters into its own hands. No longer would it operate in the shadows of U.S. policy, dutifully marching in step, shunning any risk of getting too far out in front. When Baker and then Bush received Primakov the third week in October, it was as someone in the thick of things, someone who might even represent a crucial alternative way out. And, when Gorbachev sat down with Mitterrand in Paris the next week, he was leading a fully independent policy, albeit one still firmly part of the common front against the Iraqi aggression.

Second, it was also evident that Primakov was not shuttling among capitals as a passive rapporteur. He had come to twist arms, particularly the Iraqis'—to try out ideas, to test where there might be give, where common ground might be developed. In Washington, after his meeting with Bush, the word was that he had come "with no plans whatsoever."[16] It was a technically accurate description, but scarcely one that captured the flavor of the variety of angles he had pressed on Hussein a week before. The Americans were determined that no compromise would be struck "rewarding" Hussein in any way for his aggression, but by the latter half of October the air was thick with devices by which Hussein might save face and find it worthwhile to lift his boot off Kuwait. Primakov had tried them all.

Third, the more prominence the Primakov mission took on with Soviet policy, the more plain it became that the Soviet leadership—as many others—sensed war looming nearer. But on the Soviet side the apprehension seemed to rest on the growing perception that neither the American nor the Iraqi leadership really understood the other party, that a fatalistic acceptance of war was taking hold in the United States, and, worst of all, that the Americans appeared not to appreciate how disastrous a war might prove to be. If the political and economic situation at home were not so crushingly grave, Soviet diplomacy might have been energized even more than it was.

BACK TO BASICS

Wondrous policy changes do not materialize out of thin air, and this one had an extraordinary genesis. A revolution in the whole of Soviet foreign policy prepared the way. Without this larger, prior transformation, almost certainly the Soviet Union would have reacted differently in the Gulf crisis. And, in reverse, the fact that it reacted as it did greatly solidified the new foreign policy, although not without difficulties.

People who were surprised by the degree of Soviet cooperation with the other four permanent members of the Security Council and by the strong support given the UN in the course of the Gulf crisis had simply not been paying attention. For more than three years Gorbachev had been exhorting a greater, indeed, a decisive role for the United Nations and its key agencies.

In September 1987, *Pravda* published a major article by him appealing for a whole new approach to the problem of international security and to the role of the United Nations.[17] His argument was that an increasingly "complex, diverse, and interdependent" world needed "a mechanism" capable of addressing transcendent problems, a mechanism adequate to underpin an alternative "comprehensive system of international security" built around drastically lower levels of nuclear and conventional arms, and a mechanism able, in place of the superpowers, to keep or make peace in troubled regions. The United Nations must be that mechanism, he contended, and, for it to be, much would have to be done to strengthen the organization.

Beginning that fall and at each subsequent General Assembly session, the Soviet Union came with a varied and detailed program for accomplishing this goal. For the most part, others, including the United States, largely disregarded or even dismissed these initiatives. In December 1988 Gorbachev delivered the most important foreign policy address of his leadership. He spoke before the General Assembly on the eve of a new U.S. Administration, conveying his notion of a world at a crossroads, a world either that would find new enhanced forms of cooperation to deal with old forms of conflict and new threats and would enthrone "the supremacy of the common human idea over the countless multiplicity of centrifugal forces" or that would prolong the history of "ubiquitous wars, and sometimes desperate battles, leading to mutual destruction."[18] In what he called "this specific historical situation," states, he said, needed to "rethink" their "attitude to such a unique instrument as the United Nations Organization, without which world politics is no longer imaginable." Then, as part of a sweeping reformulation of Soviet foreign policy concepts on every matter from the meaning and character of national security to the "freedom of choice" for all states (including Eastern Europe), he presented a vastly upgraded set of tasks for the United Nations. These touched all spheres of its activity, beginning with the military-political and extending to the economic, the scientific and technical, the ecological, and the humanitarian.

Thus, long before Hussein set the world on edge, and gave the United Nations a new reason for being, Gorbachev had begun working for a stronger UN. He did this, to judge from his argument, not merely to enhance this institution, but as an integral part of an altered image of the role of the superpowers. He meant for international politics to be reformed, for many of the rights arrogated by the superpowers to be curtailed and transferred to collective institutions, for the policing of the peace to be done by the community, and for the United Nations to become a vehicle and symbol of a new international order. Thus, the sudden effectiveness of the Security Council in the Gulf crisis not only owed to Soviet cooperation, but conformed to Soviet concept.

There was another dimension of Gorbachev's foreign policy revolution equally vital to Soviet behavior in this crisis. Had the Soviet stake in much of the Third World not been thoroughly recast in the two or three preceding years, had the Soviet Union not radically shifted its approach to regional crises from Angola to Cambodia, and had it not, for that matter, reconceived the essence of its national security policy, the Soviets are not likely to have rejected their Iraqi allies so emphatically.

But, by the time Hussein moved his army, the Soviet leadership had already decided that regimes like his—even those where the Soviet investment was exceptionally high as in Afghanistan—held too little value to bleed or pay for them in large coin of any kind. When Gorbachev and his colleagues decided to cut their losses in Afghanistan, they were, it turned out, offering the first dramatic testimony to a profound reordering of their Third World priorities. The historic commitment to "national liberation," admittedly warped over the years by superpower aspirations and superpower rivalry, had gone by the boards. The gambles, toil, and sacrifices made in the name of this cause, like the sister burdens of competing with the Americans, the Chinese and all other comers for power and influence in these regions, had been reappraised and judged basically senseless.

From there, the stakes shifted to freeing the Soviet Union from the more onerous of these entanglements, and seeing to it that no new ones took their place. In most instances the way out was through the settlement of regional conflicts. By 1988 the Soviets featured a new theme everywhere that their progressive friends were locked in combat: Let matters be resolved by political rather than military settlements, and let governments of "national reconciliation" do the job rather than their progressive, but discredited friends. In subsequent months they not only sounded the theme, but lived by it in Angola, Cambodia, and Nicaragua. Saddam Hussein, if he counted on old Soviet affinities and priorities to prevent East and West from making common cause against him, failed to appreciate how much what counted for Soviet leaders had changed.

LIFE'S COMPLEXITIES

End product, of course, is what mattered to the United States and the rest of the outside world, but back home policy's political rear was far from calm and uncomplicated. There were not only the obvious constraints and distractions created by a deepening social, economic, political, and national crisis. There were also the direct controversies and demurs stirred by the policy itself.

The earliest and most obvious of these involved the military. Wrecking an elaborate, useful relationship with their Iraqi counterparts did not come easy. Senior figures within the military did not hide the regret they felt. Appearing in a joint press conference with a spokesman for the foreign ministry on August 22, Colonel Valentin Ogurtsov openly confessed how painful it was to see this longstanding relationship collapse. Not that they opposed the basic decision to side with the other permanent members of the Security Council, but they obviously preferred that ties with Iraq not be fully and peremptorily cut. They, along with the Middle East specialists in the foreign ministry, presumably disapproved of Gorbachev and Shevardnadze's original decision to stop all Soviet arms shipments forthwith, let alone, to announce it in a joint U.S.-Soviet statement.

As a sign of the times, however, discontent came not only from the right. Within a few weeks voices appeared attacking the leadership for not going far enough—for talking about a new morality and a new order, but then lacking the courage to run risks for it.[19] "We have interfered in the internal affairs of other countries so soften," Galina Sidorova wrote, "that today we are trying to draw a boundary between what is our business and what is not, and we are doing it not always right." "The young U.S. Marine hugging his little daughter" before shipping out to the Gulf, she said, is not defending only U.S. interests, but "our common home." Before long deputies on the Supreme Soviet's Foreign Affairs

Commission also challenged the decision to allow Soviet technicians to remain in Iraq, arguing that, if Soviet specialists were not withdrawn, the Soviet Union would soon be regarded by "world opinion as an accomplice to the aggressor."[20]

Nor, even when the policy was basically supported, did the support come unqualified. Early on Soviet commentators raised doubts about the Bush Administration's ultimate reasons for rushing troops into the region. Stanislaw Kondrashov, one of the country's most respected journalists, wrote scarcely ten days into the crisis that Washington had sent forces more to strengthen its influence in the area than to protect the kingdom from Iraqi attack. As he wryly put it, "Every cloud has a silver lining."[21] Later, Deputy Foreign Minister Belonogov seemed to echo these suspicions when he told a parliamentary committee that there were "no guarantees that the United States will leave Saudi Arabia after the crisis is over," and then added that the Soviet Union had never formally approved the dispatch of U.S. troops to the area.[22]

The military's stated doubts were blunter yet. General Vladimir Lobov, Chief of Staff of the Warsaw Treaty Organization, suggested that the United States might have in mind extending "its forces along the Soviet Union's southern flank, establishing a bridgehead from which to control Middle East oil flows and put pressure on Moscow."[23] With events leading the United States to scale back its forces in Europe, he said, "the current crisis over Iraq and Kuwait opens new possibilities" for Washington. When President Bush, at the Helsinki summit, responded to a reporter's question by saying that he had "made very clear to President Gorbachev . . . that we have no intention of keeping [U.S. forces there] a day longer than is required," Gorbachev had reason to be enthusiastic. One could see him stir visibly as he leaped upon the President's words to "do everything possible to ensure that the forces are withdrawn from the region," declaring that to be "a very important statement."[24]

As the crisis wore on, other angrier denunciations were heaped upon Gorbachev's policy. When Shevardnadze appeared before the Supreme Soviet in mid-October, he ran into a storm of censure from several of the hard-line deputies, most of them from the military. Led by Colonel Nikolai Petrushenko, co-chairman of the conservative group, Soyuz, they attacked the leadership for weakening the country generally, for abandoning the Iraqi alliance without consulting the parliament, and for taking "a casual approach to the possible use of military force" in the Gulf.[25] Evgeny Kogan, a conservative deputy from Estonia, warned that Soviet military involvement in the Gulf would provoke a backlash among millions of Soviet Muslims.[26] Acting under UN auspices, Petrushenko asserted, was no help. The Soviet Union's relations with Iraq would still be irreparably damaged, its standing among the Arab nations undermined, and the U.S. military position in the region strengthened.

Not to overstate the matter, extremist criticism of this sort did not represent a central challenge to policy. There is no indication that these views were widely shared, or that they existed where real power resided, including senior levels of the military command. But they did give a raucous edge to a far wider uneasiness over the direction events might take and the dangers these might pose for the country. To that more widespread misgiving the leadership was compelled to bend. Shevardnadze sought to pacify the parliamentarians by promising that no Soviet troops would ever be sent without their advance vote of approval. For good measure, he added, and "the Security Council is in a position to pass a decision like this only if the Soviet Union votes for it."[27]

THE FUTURE

What might then be expected of the Soviet Union, if it comes to a crunch in the Gulf? Ninety days into the crisis, Soviet reluctance to send Soviet soldiers could not be more evident, nor Soviet fear greater that events were gyrating toward a moment when the government would be faced with the choice. As Primakov told a Soviet television audience on his return from Baghdad, before a solution will be achieved through diplomacy, "we have a long journey ahead of us, and it might, I am very sorry to say, be interrupted by other events."[28]

But this nervousness, great as it was, should not obscure a more essential aspect of the Soviet position. Soviet leaders have constantly drummed on the need to stay on this side of war's threshold, but they have never ruled out Soviet participation should war come. At the Helsinki summit, when pressed on a Soviet military role in the region, Gorbachev implied that, if such were the decision of the Security Council, the Soviet Union would do its part. "We shall continue to act in cooperation within the Security Council," he said to the reporter, "in strict compliance with *all* of its decisions."[29]

In the end, the decisive impulse is likely to be what from the beginning has been the source of revolution in the Soviet approach: A deep desire to be a part of a community mobilized against aggression, mostly as a first fragile step toward a different international order. This larger enterprise, after all, goes to the heart of Gorbachev's foreign policy vision, and, if the Soviet Union flees its first test, the whole thing begins to crumble.

Any Soviet military role will have to be within the framework of the United Nations. Indeed, as Soviet Chief of Staff, Mikhail Moiseyev, made clear early in October, Soviet support for anybody's military role in the Gulf, including the United States, will depend on whether the Security Council approves.[30] Any Soviet role will also surely be very limited, more symbol than substance. Still, many on the Soviet side understand the importance of even a limited Soviet contribution, for, "even a limited involvement in primarily defensive actions could have great military and political significance." Alexei Arbatov, whose words these are, proposes, for example, the deployment in Saudi Arabia of "several anti-aircraft defense squadrons" or "anti-aircraft artillery units to protect the Syrian contingent."[31]

Arbatov knows that, "given the extremely difficult economic and political situation inside the Soviet Union" and the popular opposition to military involvement anywhere these days, doing even this much will not be easy. He, for example, argues that it can only be done if Soviet servicemen are sent on a voluntary basis. But the commitment must be made, he says, "because in the final analysis, the stakes in the Gulf crisis include more than the liberation of Kuwait and the security of its neighbors. The very future of a post-Coldwar world free of the Soviet-American global confrontation is at stake." "Can our state," he concludes, "as the pioneer of the new political thinking, stand aloof at the hour of trial, when words must be verified by deeds?"

The longer-run question, of course, concerns the future. How exceptional is Soviet behavior in this crisis? And, for that matter, the behavior of everyone else? Can the Soviet Union be counted on to exercise the same restraint in the next crisis, or lend the same level of support to the collective effort? Or is Hussein's act so egregious, the oil so important, and the Soviet Union's internal distractions so great that no future event will likely rally the international community in the same way and oblige the Soviet Union to cooperate to the same degree?

This is what makes the Gorbachev foreign policy revolution so important. If Soviet ideas about the world and the Soviet place in it had not been already utterly revised, and Soviet behavior, already so different in all other vital spheres, prudence would have favored no rush to judgment. The Iraq case *was* unusual. But, when the pilings and struts of an entire foreign policy are so thoroughly reconstructed, and, when this reconstruction, at every turn, argues against the Brezhnev approach to Third World violence, it is reasonable to expect, in most instances, a Soviet response generically similar to the present one. The Soviet Union and the United States may not see eye to eye on all aspects of the next crisis, for that rarely happens even among allies, but so long as the current Soviet leadership guides policy it seems unlikely that the Soviet Union would return to its competitive ways.

But what if the current Soviet leadership does not survive, or what if the Soviet Union does not survive? Then what is the meaning of value of Soviet cooperation in the Gulf crisis? Hazarding confident predictions for any part of the Soviet future, including its foreign policy, is fool's work. But there are a few signs. First, considering the apparent priorities of at least parts of the Soviet military in the Iraqi crisis, any future government beholden to the military or under its influence could not be counted on to jettison its special relationships with Third World militaries as readily as the Gorbachev leadership has in this case. But even the most conservative, authoritarian Soviet regime will not have the wherewithal to turn back the clock and engage again in Third World adventures.

On the other hand, and the more likely scenario, if Soviet policy comes under the increasing influence of the republics, particularly, the Russian Republic, those who presently lead are likely to push the Gorbachev policy even further and faster. Andrei Kozyrev is the new Russian foreign minister, and, when he was recently asked his view of Soviet involvement in the Third World, he responded: "Aid to developing countries will be rendered only after we have attained the level of highly advanced countries. As for military aid to such countries as Cuba, Libya, and Syria, such aid reflects neither their interests nor ours."[32]

What this surely all means, therefore, is that, as far as the Soviet Union is concerned, for the first time in this century, if the international community will give collective security another try, Moscow will do its part to make it work. By collective security, I mean the principle underlying the League of Nations and the United Nations: All nations banded together against the rogue aggressor state. Indeed, among the great powers, the Soviet Union may be the only one willing to entrust the general welfare to this principle. The only one willing to make this a rule of policy, rather than a recourse when convenient.

NOTES

1. From Margaret Garrard Warner, "The Moscow Connection: The Inside Story of Secret Diplomacy between the Superpowers," *Newsweek*, 17 September 1990, p. 24.
2. Ibid.
3. He spoke at a press conference at Vnukovo-2 Airport in Moscow, after Baker and he had completed work on the joint statement. See "Together against Aggression," *Vestnik*, September 1990, p. 15.
4. Warner, "The Moscow Connection," p. 25.
5. Elaine Sciolino and Eric Pace, "How the US Got UN Backing for Use of Force in the Gulf," *The New York Times*, 30 August 1990.
6. See the account by Bill Keller in *The New York Times*, 25 August 1990.
7. Sciolino and Pace, "How the US Got UN Backing."
8. See his press conference in *The New York Times*, 9 August 1990.
9. *The New York Times*, 23 August 1990.
10. *Pravda*, 2 September 1990.
11. The text of the press conference is in *The New York Times*, 10 September 1990.
12. Ibid.
13. See Andrew Rosenthal's report, "Bush, Reversing US Policy, Won't Oppose a Soviet Role in Middle East Peace Talks," *The New York Times*, 11 September 1990.
14. His speech to the General Assembly can be found in *Izvestiya*, 26 September 1990.
15. See David Remnick's report in the *Washington Post*, September 8, 1990.
16. Maureen Dowd's report in *The New York Times*, 20 October 1990.
17. "Realnost i garantii bezopasnogo mira," *Pravda*, 17 September 1987. Reportedly the article was a speech that he had intended to deliver before the General Assembly on a trip to the United States that never came off.
18. The speech is reprinted in *Pravda* and *Izvestiya*, 8 September 1988.
19. See, for example, Galina Sidorova, "The World Closes In: Why Do the Soviets Opt to Stay Out?" *New Times*, no. 36 (September 4–10, 1990), pp. 4–6. Sidorova is a *New Times* political observer and special correspondent.
20. Interview with Anatoly Ananyev, " 'We Shall Not Fight There' " *New Times*, no. 38 (September 18–24, 1990), p. 5. Ananyev is deputy chairman of the Commission.
21. *Izvestiya*, August 14, 1990, p. 4. His colleague, Melor Sturua, had written a few days earlier from Washington that American military interventions in the Middle East have not normally brought benefit to everyone. (See *Izvestiya*, August 10, 1990, p. 4.)
22. Bill Keller's report in *The New York Times*, August 31, 1990,
23. Ibid.

24. Text of the press conference, *The New York Times*, 10 September 1990.

25. See *RFE/RL Daily Report*, no. 197 (16 October 1990).

26. See Bill Keller's report in *The New York Times*, 16 October 1990.

27. Bill Keller, *The New York Times*, 10 October 1990.

28. Reuters in *The New York Times*, 1 November 1990.

29. Press conference, *The New York Times*, 10 September 1990, p. 9. My emphasis.

30. This was part of a joint interview that General Colin Powell and he gave to the editors of *The New York Times*, during his visit to the United States. See *The New York Times*, October 3, 1990.

31. Alexei Arbatov, "Arab Dilemma for Soviet Politics," *Moscow News*, no. 41 (21–28 October, 1990), p. 3.

32. Interview with Andrei Kozyrev, *Moscow News*, no. 43 (4–11 November 1990), p. 13.

39

The Evolution of Soviet Foreign Policy and the Future*

Robbin F. Laird

With the dramatic changes in Europe and the Soviet Union at the end of the 1980s and in the early 1990s, both the nature of Soviet foreign policy and the analytical questions necessary to understand that policy have changed as well. This chapter will examine the basic dynamics of change in the Soviet Union from the vantage point of early 1991 and will assess the implications of those dynamics for the study of Soviet foreign policy.

Soviet foreign policy has gone through a number of significant phases of development, and each phase has left its imprint on the evolving debate about the nature of that policy. First, there was the period of the Russian revolution and the civil war in which the basic ideological nature of Soviet foreign policy was established. The regime sought to protect the revolution from "counterrevolutionary" forces and inundation from the "backward" Russian masses at home.

The most notable feature to outside analysts in this period was the ideological cast of Soviet foreign policy. The goal of the Soviet Union was to build a revolutionary order, and traditional European geopolitics was to take a back seat to the new class character of Soviet foreign policy. The Soviets sought to accelerate the revolution at home by promoting revolution abroad. This phase of Soviet foreign policy left in its wake the issue of the role of ideology in the making of foreign policy. Was Soviet foreign policy different from other Euro-Asian states on ideological grounds? If so, how important was the ideological variable in the conduct of Soviet foreign policy?

Second, the ascendancy of Stalin as General Secretary of the Communist Party of the Soviet Union (CPSU) in the 1920s led to a new phase of Soviet foreign policy, which lasted until World War II. In this period, the party purges and the great terror closed off the Soviet Union from the outside world. The Russians became, as Churchill put it, a "riddle wrapped in a mystery inside an enigma." A "fortress USSR" was built to protect the Communist revolution of 1917, the

*Copyright © 1991 by Robbin F. Laird

state building and forced-draft industrialization and collectivization of the late 1920s and 1930s, and the personal rule by the general secretary of the CPSU. A new "tsar" and a new autocracy began to emerge triumphant in this period.

The Stalinist model of economic and political development altered Soviet foreign policy as well. A new model of domestic development required the subordination of foreign policy to this model. Autarky or the closing off of the USSR from outside influences became the order of the day. International revolution no longer was an operational goal, which required a revolutionary interaction with the outside world. Instead, "socialism in one country" required the protection of the dynamic new model from outside disturbances.

This period of Russian foreign policy underscored the tension between autarky and global influences. Did the Russians now possess a unique model of development? Could the Russians develop an autarkic model of development that would allow them to shape a new force in the global arena? (When I use the term *Russians*, I am referring to the Russian leadership of the Soviet Union.)

The third major period of Soviet foreign policy was that of the years of the "Great Patriotic War." The German invasion of the Soviet Union ended the debate about the preservation of "socialism in one country." Instead, the question became the preservation of the Russian nation. Stalin suddenly embraced pre-Communist symbols of Russian nationalism. Also, Stalin shifted dramatically from the foreign policy premises of the 1930s. Defense of the homeland required an alliance with the Western democracies. In short, Stalin shifted from autarkic modernization to a more classic authoritarian model, one that combined traditional nationalism and cooperation with major capitalist nation states.

This period introduced new questions, most of them associated with the failure of the wartime coalition to continue to cooperate in the postwar period. Had the Russians shifted from ideological goals to national ones? Could the Russians cooperate with capitalist countries in pursuing a classic Russian geopolitical strategy? As the Stalin leadership appeared to revive the national style of the tsars from the sixteenth to the nineteenth centuries, did nationalism matter more than communism? Had the operational ideology of the Soviet leadership undergone a dramatic transformation?

The fourth major period was the formation of the Cold War, bipolar international system. Stalin rapidly shifted from the interdependent authoritarianism embraced during the war to the autarkic totalitarianism of the pre–World War II period, especially since the blood purges of the mid-1930s. But now this system was to be imposed on the new "allies" of the Soviet Union, namely the people's democracies of Eastern Europe.

In retrospect, it is clear that the downfall of the classic Stalinist model began with the attempt to engulf Eastern Europe and to promote a "socialist model of development." The Stalinist system rested upon isolating Russia from the outside world, but the building of even a system of socialist "interdependence" undercut the classic autarkic model.

The great tragedy for the Soviet Union was the reimposition of the system of 1930s upon the Soviet Union of the late 1940s and early 1950s. Now the challenge was to preserve a socialist model built upon Russian nationalism by imposing that model upon Eastern Europe. Foreign policy shifted from defending "socialism in one country" to building socialism in Eastern Europe and forging a new "socialist community" in the East as a basis for competition with the West.

In the early 1950s the ideological confrontation took on new dimensions. Now the Soviets had a bridgehead in the West and military forces within that bridgehead to challenge the West. The "old" values of the bourgeois West were now challenged by the "new" values of the Soviet socialist order.

But the ingestion of Eastern Europe from the beginning was based on a contradiction. How could an autarkic model of development incorporate national entities with traditions and ties to an outside world that rejected isolation? How could one destroy the influence of hundreds of years of "alien" influence in Eastern Europe simply by Soviet occupation and by establishing surrogate "communist" regimes?

This period introduced a new set of questions for analysis. Was the Soviet Union inherently expansionist? Would "socialism in one country," become the model for "international socialism"? Was war with the West inevitable? Did the Russians believe that military victory over the West was the way to advance socialism, even in the nuclear age?

The fifth period was associated with Khrushchev and the reexamination of the Stalinist legacy. Khrushchev's secret speech in 1956 denouncing Stalin and Stalinism began a debate that continues today. To what extent is Stalinism the same as Communism? Is there a genuine socialist alternative for the Soviet Union devoid of Stalinism? Did Stalin represent the Russian national character, or were nonauthoritarian alternatives possible in a continent with no democratic experience?

But the times of Khrushchev were optimistic ones. The Soviet economy was growing; the Soviets were consolidating their control over Eastern Europe; and the Soviet leaders believed in their spiritual superiority over the West. In 1956, Soviet tanks repulsed the Hungarian revolution. In 1961, Khrushchev promised to "bury capitalism" by peaceful means, and the party program boasted that the USSR would surpass American economic growth before the end of the century.

The sixth period was initiated by the overthrow of Khrushchev and the installation of the collective leadership. The Brezhnev-Kosygin leadership of the mid-1960s promised to combine the "advantages of socialism with rapid scientific and technological advancement." These less impulsive new leaders claimed to be more "rational" and more responsive to the "objective laws" of historic development.

The foreign policy of collective leadership was to be less ideological and more pragmatic. While continuing to view the West as a competitor, Soviet leaders hoped to let the West participate in its own demise. Western cooperation with the USSR in economic and arms control accords was possible as long as the West's cultural influence was held at arms length.

But this hopeful beginning was dashed by the seventh period of Soviet foreign policy. This period was begun with the repression of the Czechoslovakian revolution in 1968 and ended with the ascendancy of Andropov as General Secretary in early 1982. In retrospect, the Czech reform movement in the mid-1960s was the last chance for Soviet socialism to become a force of global significance. The Russians along with their Warsaw Pact allies crushed a peaceful revolution within the confines of the Czech Communist party. Unlike the action against the Hungarians in 1956, the 1968 repression was against a ruling Communist party.

The so-called Brezhnev doctrine was articulated by the collective leadership in the wake of the events in Czechoslovakia. This doctrine allowed Russian intervention within Eastern Europe to eliminate antisocialist elements. Needless to say, the Russians would identify these elements. Never had a regime more boldly stated a naked power principle than did that of Brezhnev and his cohorts. It was also a clear statement of an empire in decline. It could tolerate only those changes it sanctioned itself.

The dynamic thrust of domestic change associated with the revolution and with Stalinism was waning. Economic problems became noticeable, and political sources of legitimacy began to be challenged. Attachment to the Party became less significant than personal aggrandizement. The moral crisis that would bring down the regime was beginning in earnest in the 1970s.

Soviet foreign policy became ever more traditionalistic in this period. It became increasingly geopolitical and global. In order to defend the Soviet empire in Eastern Europe and within the USSR, the Soviet leaders sought to promote socialism abroad. The Soviet leadership sought to preserve the legitimacy of their empire by showing its continued relevance to a dynamic global development. They could do this less by show of example or by dynamic economic growth than by military aid and intervention.

As the Soviet leadership aged, it followed an ever more myopic policy. Top politicians began to believe their own rhetoric about the collapse of capitalism and the salience of the Soviet Union to global development. They saw their economic and social problems as solvable by only modest changes within the existing order. They sought to enhance the "scientific management" of society and nurture "developed socialism," which was to evolve into a more advanced variant of the old system.

The foreign policy necessary for this leadership was that which would protect the Soviet Union from outside influence but promote pragmatic links with the West. Given Soviet leaders' confidence in their ability to compete globally, the USSR's competition with the West was pursued in areas of perceived Soviet advantage. But there could be no linkage between Soviet compromises with the West in arms control (and other technical issues) and the continued "political competition" with the West in Europe and beyond.

Critical issues for analysis that emerged in this period were how to understand the pragmatic aspects of Soviet foreign policy and their interconnections with broader Soviet foreign policy objectives. Did Soviet pragmatism mean an end to the classic Soviet definitions of East-West competition? Or did the policy of peaceful coexistence merely mean that the Soviets were continuing the international class struggle on another basis?

The eighth period of Soviet foreign policy was from the emergence of Andropov and the rise of Gorbachev to the revolution of 1989. The disintegration of the Soviet empire in Eastern Europe and the unification of Germany constituted a genuine revolution in European affairs; the consequences have not fully worked themselves out.

The new Soviet leadership saw the system in crisis. The Soviet Union was suffering a moral, cultural, and economic crisis. The main difference between Andropov and Gorbachev was that the latter promoted genuine political change in addition to dealing with the other crisis confronting the USSR.

The Soviet leaders became increasingly preoccupied with the process of change, or *perestroika* as it became known. The vigorous domestic debate and struggle over the future of the Soviet domestic model became closely tied to a new political style and approach in the USSR. Rather than emphasizing the most dangerous aspects of competition, the Soviet leaders began to embrace the possibilities of cooperation. But this cooperation was to occur between a reformed socialist Europe and USSR, on the one hand, and the United States on the other. A new synthesis of East and West would somehow aid the *perestroika* process.

Gorbachev's initial policy toward the West and Europe in particular represented a mutation in the basic Soviet approach. But major innovations occurred primarily in dealing with the Revolution of 1989 and its aftermath. What were the fundamental elements of Gorbachev's policies toward the West?

A. Direct Recognition of the Soviet Threat to Western Europe

Unlike previous Soviet leaders, Gorbachev and his advisors explicitly recognized the existence of a Soviet threat to Western Europe. In the past, Soviet analysts referred to the significant role the "myth" of the Soviet threat played in justifying Western defense efforts. Under Gorbachev a more open discussion of the threatening aspects of Soviet conventional forces was generated. The Soviets limited this discussion, but a fundamental understanding of the threat that a surprise attack scenario poses for the West underlay Gorbachev's unilateral arms reductions.

B. Explicit Recognition of a Common "European" Civilization

Gorbachev adopted the common "European home" theme to underscore the notion of a common European civilization cutting across the ideological divide of East and West. To Americans, the Soviets underscored that the common European home theme did not exclude Americans. But in private discussions with West Europeans the Gorbachev leadership underscored the common interests between Europe and the Soviet Union at the expense of the United States.

Gorbachev's speech in 1989 in Strasbourg before the Council of Europe provided the most explicit and wide-ranging presentation of the common European home theme. The basic notion was that the Europe of the blocs should be replaced by a cooperative security environment with no military alliances within Europe. What was new was the explicit recognition of the dynamics and legitimacy of Western European economic and political cooperation. In the past, Soviet analysts as well as policymakers were skeptical of the value and validity of the European integration process. Increasingly, Soviet analysts and leaders recognized the reality of these processes and the need to come to terms with West European political, economic, and security cooperation.

C. Coping with Europeanization

To deal with the Europeanization process, the Soviets argued that there was a good and bad form of Europeanization. The good form of Europeanization occurred in the economic domain. Economic integration and economic cooperation across the ideological divide were supported. The bad form of Europeanization was West European military integration. Soviet analysts were especially concerned that European military integration would allow the United States to remain in Europe but at a much lower cost. The military "confrontation" would continue, but with the dynamic of a European integrative process as its stimulant.

D. Pursuit of Differentiated Bilateralism via a "Softer" Touch

To deflect such Europeanization pressures, a softer touch was required. The policy of threat reduction would undercut European military integration efforts. The notion was that Western European elites and publics would be much more interested in military integration if there were a perception of a serious Soviet threat. If the Soviets altered threat perceptions, the Western European military integration process would be deflected.

Also, critical to deal with the Europeanization process was the continued pursuit of a policy of differentiated bilateralism. For example, the Soviet approach toward France played on French concerns vis-à-vis other West Europeans, notably the reunification challenge posed by Germany. The Soviets emphasized privately to French officials the idea of reviving the "old" alliance between them to deal with a resurgent Germany.

E. Nuclear Disarmament Pursued via Conventional Reductions

The Soviet campaign against nuclear weapons is as old as nuclear weapons themselves. Under Gorbachev, the Soviet leadership pursued this campaign with new vigor and energy. The Soviet leader introduced significant conventional reductions as a means to achieve the elimination of nuclear weapons from Europe.

F. *Conventional Restructuring via Defensive Defense*

Soviet leaders and security analysts also introduced discussions of alternatives to the extant structures of defense. They drew on the assessments of the European left in developing alternative defense concepts. Even the Soviet General Staff was drawn into discussions of alternative defense concepts with Europeans as well as Americans. The General Staff's concepts focused more on restructuring for maneuver warfare than on restructuring to eliminate an ability to attack.

The Revolution of 1989 challenged the Gorbachev mutation and, indeed, the Gorbachev revolution in the Soviet Union was an important precondition for that Revolution. Throughout his General Secretaryship of the CPSU, Gorbachev has nurtured "new thinking" in Soviet foreign policy. Most fundamentally, the theme of the Gorbachev administration has been the goal of overcoming the East-West divide. Gorbachev's book on *perestroika* (which sold millions of copies in the Western world) was simplistic and awkwardly written. Nonetheless, it contained one powerful and overriding theme: the Soviet Union was in the process of change and this process would lead to the end of the East-West confrontation in Europe. The Soviets were no longer the enemies of the West, and the West should be partners in the reconstruction of the Soviet Union.

The reform process in the Soviet Union is complicated and difficult. This process has been widely perceived in Western Europe as eliminating the Soviets as an immediate threat to the West. Already before Gorbachev, the Soviets had been perceived by West European publics to be a much less immediate threat than to the American public. After Gorbachev, this gap deepened and a new element was added. Increasingly, West European publics began to perceive the Soviets as a declining threat in the middle and long terms as well. The reform process has been perceived to be part of a long-term trend in Soviet policy whereby the Soviet Union is being transformed from an enemy into either a benign or incompetent source of competition to Western Europe.

These shifts in opinion occurred before the crumbling of the Communist regimes in Eastern Europe in 1989. The Soviet leadership debated among itself throughout the Gorbachev period how to handle the future of Eastern Europe. This debate led to wide swings in Soviet approaches to Eastern Europe in the Gorbachev period.

Nonetheless, by 1989 the Soviet leadership had reached the following conclusions:

1. Eastern Europe under Communist rule was more a liability than an asset in the reform process of the Soviet Union.
2. Reformist Communist parties would energize change in the Soviet Union.
3. The failure of reform communism would not prevent Eastern Europe from pursuing deeper reforms.

4. Noncommunist regimes would be acceptable to the Soviets as long as basic Soviet security interests were protected.
5. Soviet security interests in the region would be determined through interaction with West European regimes.
6. The Americans would be important interlocutors in the process of protecting Soviet interests.

As the Soviets began to let Eastern Europe reform, they shifted other elements of their policy as well. They embraced the concept of conventional parity. They began unilateral conventional arms reductions. They began to promote a concept of minimal nuclear deterrence. But above all, Gorbachev argued for the necessity of the Soviet Union becoming a key player in building the new Europe.

In the wake of the Revolution of 1989, the classic elements of Soviet foreign policy, which have been designed and implemented by the Communist Party and the Soviet state, were crumbling. What are those classic elements, how have they changed, and what new elements seem to be emerging for Soviet foreign policy?

In retrospect, the classic Soviet foreign policy paradigm consists of ten key elements: First, there is an ideological basis to Soviet foreign policy, whereby regimes embracing Soviet-style socialism are the core allies of the USSR. Allies are determined at least in part on the basis of ideological affinity with the Soviet model of socialism.

Second, policy is defined with regard to the interests of the leading force in Soviet society, the Communist Party of the Soviet Union. The CPSU embodies the general will of the Soviet people, and the party leadership frames current definitions of the national will.

Third, the goal of foreign policy is to aid the development of the Soviet model of socialism. It is necessary to protect this model from contamination by outside forces, but limited involvement with the outside world is necessary for reasons of global economic development and competition.

Fourth, ideological and party objectives are blended with geopolitical ones. Allies are determined in part according to the importance of states or political forces, not just on the basis of ideology alone. Any contradictions between ideological and geopolitical definitions of state interest are to be resolved by the party leadership. To a large extent, geopolitical considerations are considered temporary, whereas ideological ones are considered permanent factors dictating alliances.

Fifth, defense of the socialist commonwealth is critical to the vitality of the Soviet Union. The construction of an interdependent socialist system gradually supplanted socialism in one country.

Sixth, the defense of the empire in Eastern Europe was conjoined with defense of the empire at home. The Soviet Union was building a new Soviet people. Nationalism was becoming overcome in the creation of a new commonwealth of socialist nations. This experience at home was to be the basis of change in the Soviet-East European relationship.

Seventh, pragmatic compromises were possible with the West. Contradictions between the socialist and capitalist systems could be overcome by peaceful means, but it was necessary to have a substantial military capability to defend the interests of socialism against imperialist pressures.

Eighth, there was a centralized elite capable of making a coordinated national policy. Diplomatic, economic, political, and military instruments were combined through a highly centralized party-state system. Objectives could be set from above and enforced throughout the socialist community.

Ninth, the power of the Soviet Union was enhanced by the ability to have centralized control at home and the ability to split the class enemies abroad. By pursuing an anticoalition strategy against the West, the Soviet Union could compete effectively with a far more powerful Western system.

Above all, the classic approach of Soviet foreign policy rested upon a careful balance between competitiveness and cooperation with the West, especially at the end of the 1970s and early 1980s. The West provided a model of progress in the economic sphere, but not in the cultural, political, and military spheres. In other words, the West provided elements to emulate for economic, scientific, and technological progress, but challenges as well to the viability of the socialist system from a security and cultural standpoint.

Each of these elements of classic Soviet foreign policy is under challenge today. Most importantly, the viability of the Stalinist model of development became widely doubted within the Soviet Union and perhaps especially within the Soviet elite. The clear ideological guides of the past no longer seemed relevant: If the autarkic model was not relevant, then what was the point of a separate socialist commonwealth? What is the meaning of a Soviet socialist model today? Gradually, the belief in a unique Soviet socialist model gave way to a search for a new model.

Next, the party organization began to crumble. The old system whereby the CPSU and its leadership embodied the will of the proletariat gave way to fragmentation of the political system. The will of the people seemed to dissipate into tribal political warfare. With the collapse of belief in the superiority of the Soviet model, elites began searching for new alternatives. Such intellectual and political quests require interaction with the outside world rather than defensive reactiveness. Geopolitical objectives remain important for the new USSR, but they have been overshadowed by the necessity to transform the Soviet polity. There is a quest for partners in development of the USSR, and this quest has become more significant at the beginning of the 1990s than was the pursuit of the classic ideological or geopolitical objectives.

Not only have Soviet objectives shifted, but the old USSR is disappearing. With the pressures for disintegration within the USSR and the collapse of the Soviet empire within Eastern Europe, the socialist commonwealth is collapsing at home and abroad. New elites are emerging within the USSR at the union republic and subregional levels and they are participating in the interaction with the outside world. This interaction is helping to shape the new Soviet system.

The patterns of interaction between the emerging national and subnational elites in the USSR and their Western counterparts will become increasingly central to the definition of Soviet foreign policy itself.

Even though interaction with the outside world has been vastly expanded, the power instruments available to the Soviet elites to develop their country are not at all clear. Military power remains important. But how will the Soviet elites develop the economic power to participate in their own reconstruction within a global economic setting? How will the Soviets develop a culture compatible with twenty-first-century modernization?

The difficulty is that the Soviets remain a great power within Europe solely on military terms and are struggling to find other ways to become key actors in the global arena. But even in the military sphere the Soviets are important more in a negative than positive sense. The Soviet military challenge continues, but less as a threat and more as a factor of danger. The Russians maintain the largest army within Europe and its size may grow proportionally as the arms control process bogs down. If the Germans cap their forces at low levels, the French continue to reduce forces, and the Americans withdraw significant forces for budgetary reasons, these unilateral Western actions might fundamentally alter the military balance in the Russians' favor. Indeed, the Russians will justify large forces to deal with domestic difficulties.

In addition to the conventional weapons challenge, the nuclear challenge will continue. Even with reductions in forces, the Russians will deploy the largest nuclear arsenal by far within Europe. If the German connection with nuclear deterrence is decisively weakened, the Russians might be tempted to try nuclear blackmail in the years ahead. This would become more likely if the USSR were unable to participate effectively in the European construction process either by the fact or feeling of exclusion or by the structural inability to compete.

The tension between the centrifugal and centripetal forces within Russia and the Soviet empire will drive Russian definitions of security. Fear of outside pressures could return as a justification for isolation, which could lead to striking back at the Western world—a world the Russians admire but can never seem to emulate. The redefinition of the Russian character along lines that extol a Russian nationalism of discipline and spiritual superiority over the West could provide fertile grounds for remilitarization.

Trying to avoid the collapse of the Russians onto themselves is an important goal of the construction of the new collective security system in Europe. It is a central goal for the European consultation process of the 1990s.

Quite obviously there is no centralized elite coordinating the power instruments of the Russian state and thereby enhancing the capability of the Soviet Union to exercise influence on the world stage. One of the West's most important challenges will be to try to weaken further the Russian-Soviet legacy of a highly centralized elite maintaining the military predominance of Russia–Soviet Union in the world.

Can a new pluralism emerge in which diversity within the USSR sees a more flexible interaction with the outside world? Will this interaction lead to progress in European and Western development, or will it lead to nationalistic explosion within Europe? Will the difficulties of the new "sick man of Europe" reduce the ability of Western Europe to build a new integrated structure?

In short, the USSR remains central to the future of Europe and to the West as a whole. It no longer threatens the West by means of a cohesive national elite with awesome military might at its disposal and with the intention of crushing Western growth and development. It is primarily a challenge in terms of whether it can overcome its past and join the modernization process. Can it develop a new model of development that revitalizes all or parts of the Soviet Union? What will be the foreign policy dimensions of this effort? How will foreign policy-making change in the process? If the Soviets fail to find a peaceful transition to the future, the weight of the past will challenge the West once again. The dreams of building a new Europe and new world will be dashed by the inability of the Russians to leave their autocratic and autarkic past. This is the challenge the Soviet Union poses to itself and the rest of the world in the ast part of the twentieth and into the twenty-first century.

Index